ROGET'S THESAURUS

OF SYNONYMS AND ANTONYMS

BY

PETER MARK ROGET, M.D., F.R.S.

ENLARGED BY

JOHN LEWIS ROGET, M.A.

NEW EDITION REVISED AND ENLARGED BY

SAMUEL ROMILLY ROGET, M.A.

TOPHI BOOKS

Unit 5A, 202–208 New North Road, London N1 7BJ

PLAN OF CLASSIFICATION

TABULAR SYNOPSIS OF CATEGORIES

Class I. ABSTRACT RELATIONS

I. EXISTENCE

1°. ABSTRACT............	1. Existence.	2. Inexistence.
2°. CONCRETE..........	3. Substantiality.	4. Unsubstantiality.
3°. FORMAL............. {	*Internal.*	*External.*
	5. Intrinsicality.	6. Extrinsicality.
4°. MODAL............. {	*Absolute.*	*Relative.*
	7. State.	8. Circumstance.

II. RELATION

	9. Relation.	10. Irrelation.
	11. Consanguinity.	
1°. ABSOLUTE.......... {	12. Correlation.	
	13. Identity.	14. Contrariety.
	15. Difference.	
2°. CONTINUOUS........	16. Uniformity.	16a. Non-uniformity.
	17. Similarity.	18. Dissimilarity.
3°. PARTIAL............ {	19. Imitation.	20. Non-imitation.
	20a. Variation.	
	21. Copy.	22. Prototype.
4°. GENERAL...........	23. Agreement.	24. Disagreement.

III. QUANTITY

	Absolute.	*Relative.*
1°. SIMPLE.............	25. Quantity.	26. Degree.
	27. Equality.	28. Inequality.
	29. Mean.	
	30. Compensation.	
	By Comparison with a Standard.	
2°. COMPARATIVE....... {	31. Greatness.	32. Smallness.
	By Comparison with a similar Object.	
	33. Superiority.	34. Inferiority.
	Changes in Quantity.	
	35. Increase.	36. Decrease.
	37. Addition.	38. { Non-addition. / Subduction.
	39. Adjunct.	40. Remainder.
		40a. Decrement.
3°. CONJUNCTIVE....... {	41. Mixture.	42. Simpleness.
	43. Junction.	44. Disjunction.
	45. Vinculum.	
	46. Coherence.	47. Incoherence.
	48. Combination.	49. Decomposition.

SYNOPSIS OF CATEGORIES

SYNOPSIS OF CATEGORIES

CLASS III. MATTER

SYNOPSIS OF CATEGORIES

Class IV. INTELLECT

Division (I.). Formation of Ideas

SYNOPSIS OF CATEGORIES

Division (II.). COMMUNICATION OF IDEAS

Division (II.). Intersocial Volition

II. PERSONAL

1°. PASSIVE

827. Pleasure.		828. Pain.	
829. Pleasureableness.		830. Painfulness.	
831. Content.		832. Discontent.	
		833. Regret.	
834. Relief.		835. Aggravation.	
836. Cheerfulness.		837. Dejection.	
838. Rejoicing.		839. Lamentation.	
840. Amusement.		841. Weariness.	
842. Wit.		843. Dulness.	
844. Humorist.			

2°. DISCRIMINATIVE

845. Beauty.	846. Ugliness.
847. Ornament.	848. Blemish.
	849. Simplicity.
850. Taste.	851. Vulgarity.
852. Fashion.	
	853. Ridiculousness.
	854. Fop.
	855. Affection.
	856. Ridicule.
	857. Laughing-stock.

3°. PROSPECTIVE

858. Hope.	859. Hopelessness.
	860. Fear.
861. Courage.	862. Cowardice.
863. Rashness.	864. Caution.
865. Desire.	867. Dislike.

866. Indifference.

	868. Fastidiousness.
	869. Satiety.

4°. CONTEMPLATIVE

870. Wonder.	871. Expectance.
872. Prodigy.	
873. Repute.	874. Disrepute.
875. Nobility.	876. Commonalty.

5°. EXTRINSIC

877. Title.	
878. Pride.	879. Humility.
880. Vanity.	881. Modesty.
882. Ostentation.	
883. Celebration.	
884. Boasting.	
885. Insolence.	886. Servility.
887. Blusterer.	

III. SYMPATHETIC

1°. SOCIAL

888. Friendship.	889. Enmity.
890. Friend.	891. Enemy.
892. Sociality.	893. Seclusion.
894. Courtesy.	895. Discourtesy.
896. Congratulation.	
897. Love.	898. Hate.
899. Favorite.	
	900. Resentment.
	901. Irascibility.
	901a. Sullenness.
902. Endearment.	
903. Marriage.	904. Celibacy.
	905. Divorce.

	906. Benevolence.	907. Malevolence.
		908. Malediction.
2°. DIFFUSIVE.........		909. Threat.
	910. Philanthropy.	911. Misanthropy.
	912. Benefactor.	913. Evil doer.
3°. SPECIAL...........	914. Pity.	914a. Pitilessness.
	915. Condolence.	
	916. Gratitude.	917. Ingratitude.
4°. RETROSPECTIVE....	918. Forgiveness.	919. Revenge.
		920. Jealousy.
		921. Envy.

IV. MORAL

	922. Right.	923. Wrong.
	924. Dueness.	925. Unduedeness.
1°. OBLIGATIONS.......		927. Dereliction.
	926. Duty.	927a. Exemption.
	928. Respect.	929. Disrespect.
		930. Contempt.
	931. Approbation.	932. Disapprobation.
2°. SENTIMENTS........	933. Flattery.	934. Detraction.
	935. Flatterer.	936. Detractor.
	937. Vindication.	938. Accusation.
	939. Probity.	940. Improbity.
		941. Knave.
	942. Disinterestedness.	943. Selfishness.
3°. CONDITIONS........	944. Virtue.	945. Vice.
	946. Innocence.	947. Guilt.
	948. Good Man.	949. Bad Man.
	950. Penitence.	951. Impenitence.
	952. Atonement.	
	953. Temperance.	954. Intemperance.
		954a. Sensualist.
	955. Asceticism.	
4°. PRACTICE..........	956. Fasting.	957. Gluttony.
	958. Sobriety.	959. Drunkenness.
	960. Purity.	961. Impurity.
		962. Libertine.
	963. Legality.	964. Illegality.
	965. Jurisprudence.	
	966. Tribunal.	
	967. Judge.	
	968. Lawyer.	
5°. INSTITUTIONS......	969. Lawsuit.	
	970. Acquittal.	971. Condemnation.
		972. Punishment.
	973. Reward.	974. Penalty.
		975. Scourge.

V. RELIGIOUS

	976. Deity.	
1°. SUPERHUMAN BE-	977. Angel.	978. Satan:
INGS AND REGIONS..	979. Jupiter.	980. Demon.
	981. Heaven.	982. Hell.
	983. Theology.	
2°. DOCTRINES........	983a. Orthodoxy.	984. Heterodoxy.
	985. Revelation.	986. Pseudo-revelation.
3°. SENTIMENTS........	987. Piety.	988. Impiety.
		989. Irreligion.

SYNOPSIS OF CATEGORIES

ABBREVIATIONS, &c.

Adj.	*adj.*	Adjectives, Participles, and Words having the power of Adjectives.
Adv.	*adv.*	Adverbs and Adverbial Expressions.
Int.	*int.*	Interjections.
Phr.	*phr.*	Phrases.
V.	*v.*	Verbs.

The numbers are those of the headings, or Categories.

Words in italics within parentheses are not intended to explain the meanings of the words which precede them, but to indicate the nature of allied group of words under the numbers which follow them.

THESAURUS

OF

ENGLISH WORDS AND PHRASES

1. Existence.—N. existence, being, entity, *ens, esse,* subsistence, quiddity.

reality, realness, actuality; positiveness etc. *adj.*; fact, matter of fact, sober reality; truth etc. 494; actual existence.

presence etc. (*existence in space*) 186; coexistence etc. 120.

stubborn fact; not a -dream etc. 515; no joke.

substance, essence, prime constituent, hypostatis. [Science of existence], ontology.

V. exist, be; have -being etc. *n.*; subsist, live, breathe, stand, obtain, be the case; occur etc. (*event*) 151; have place, rank, prevail; find oneself, pass the time, vegetate.

consist in, lie in, reside in, inhere in.

come into -existence etc. *n.*; arise etc. (*begin*) 66; come forth etc. (*appear*) 446.

become etc. (*be converted*) 144; bring into existence etc. 161; coexist, preexist, endure etc. 141.

Adj. existing etc. *v.*; existent, subsistent, under the sun; in -existence etc. *n.*; extant; afloat, on foot, current, prevalent, rife, in force, -vogue; undestroyed.

real, actual, positive, absolute; true etc. 494; substan-tial, -tive; self-existing, -ent.

well-founded, -grounded; un-ideal, -imagined; not -potential etc. 2.

Adv. actually etc. *adj.*; in -fact, − point of fact, − reality; indeed; *de −, ipso-facto.*

2. Nonexistence.—N. nonexistence; inexistence, -subsistence; nonentity, *nil*; negativeness etc. *adj.*; nullity; nihil-ity, -ism; *tabula rasa,* blank; abeyance; absence etc. 187; no such thing etc. 4; nothingness, oblivion, *non esse.*

annihilation; extinction etc. (*destruction*) 162.

V. not -exist etc. 1; have no -existence etc. 1; be null and void; cease to -exist etc. 1; pass away, perish; be −, become-extinct etc. *adj.*; die out; disappear etc. 449; melt away, dissolve, leave not a rack behind, leave no trace; go, be no more; die etc. 360.

annihilate, render null, nullify; abrogate etc. 756; destroy etc. 162; take away; remove etc. (*displace*) 185.

Adj. inexistent, non-existent etc. 1; negative, blank, null and void; missing, omitted; absent etc. 187; visionary etc. 515.

unreal, potential, virtual; baseless, *in nubibus*; unsubstantial etc. 4; vain.

un-born, -created, -begotten, -conceived, produced, -made.

perished, annihilated etc. *v.*; extinct, exhausted, gone, lost, departed; defunct etc. (*dead*) 360;

fabulous, ideal etc. (*imaginary*) 515; supposititious etc. 514.

Adv. negatively, virtually, etc. *adj.*

3. Substantiality.—N. substantiality, *hypostasis*; person, thing, object, article; something, a being, an existence; creature, body, substance, flesh and blood, stuff, *substratum*; matter etc. 316; physical nature.

[Totality of existences], world etc. 318; *plenum.*

Adj. substan-tive, -tial, concrete; hypostatic; personal, bodily; tangible etc. (*material*) 316; real, corporeal, evident.

Adv. substantially etc. *adj.*; bodily, essentially.

4. Unsubstantiality.—N. un-, in-substantiality; nothingness, nihility.

nothing, naught, *nil*, nullity, zero, cipher, no one, nobody; never −, ne'er -a one; no such thing, none in the world; nothing -whatever, − at all, − on earth; not a -particle etc. (*smallness*) 32; all -talk, − moonshine, − stuff and nonsense, matter of no import.

thing of naught, man of straw, John Doe and Richard Roe; *nominis umbra,* nonentity, figurehead, lay figure; flash in the pan, *vox et praeterea nihil.*

shadow; phantasm, phantom etc. (*fallacy of vision*) 443; dream etc. (*imagination*) 515; *ignis fatuus* etc. (*luminary*) 423; 'such stuff as dreams are made of;' air, thin air; bubble etc. 353; 'baseless fabric of a vision;' mockery.

hollowness, blank; vacuity, void etc. (*absence*) 187.

inanity, fool's paradise, fatuity, stupidity, emptiness of mind.

V. vanish, evaporate, fade, sink, fly −, die −, melt- away, dissolve, disappear etc. 449; become extinct, become invisible.

Adj. unsubstantial; fleeting; base-, ground-less; ungrounded; without −, having no- foundation.

visionary etc. (*imaginary*) 515; immaterial etc. 317; spectral etc. 980; dreamy; shadowy; ethereal, airy, imponderable, tenuous, vague.

vacant, vacuous; empty etc. 187; eviscerated; blank, hollow; nominal; null; inane.

Phr. there's nothing in it.

1

5. Intrinsicality.—N. intrinsicality, inbeing, inherence, inhesion, immanence; subjectiveness; *ego*; essence; essentialness etc. *adj.*; essential part, essential stuff, substance, quintessence, incarnation, quiddity, gist, pith, core, kernel, marrow, sap, life-blood, backbone, heart, soul, life, flower; important part etc. (*importance*) 642.

principle, nature, constitution, character, ethos, type, quality, crasis, *diathesis*.

habit; temper, -ament; spirit, humor, grain, disposition, streak, tendency etc. 176.

endowment, capacity; capability etc. (*power*) 157; moods, declensions, features, aspects; peculiarities etc. (*specialty*) 79; idiosyncrasy; idiocrasy; diagnostics.

V. be −, run- in the blood; be born so; be -intrinsic etc. *adj.*

Adj. derived from within, subjective; idiocratic, idiosyncratic, intrin-sic, -sical; fundamental, cardinal, normal, inherent, essential, natural; in-nate, -born, -bred, -dwelling, -grained; -wrought; radical, incarnate, thoroughbred, hereditary, inherited, immanent; congen-itai, -ite; connate, running in the blood; coeval with birth, genetic, ingenerate, -genite; indigenous; in the -grain etc. *n.*; bred in the bone, instinctive; inward, internal etc. 221; to the manner born; virtual.

characteristic etc. (*special*) 79, (*indicative*) 550; invariable, incurable, ineradicable, fixed, settled, constant, unchanging.

Adv. intrinsically, etc. *adj.*; at bottom, in the main, in effect, essentially, practically, virtually, substantially, *au fond*; fairly.

6. Extrinsicality.—N. extrinsicality, objectiveness, *non ego*; extraneousness etc. 57; accident; letter of the law.

Adj. derived from without; objective; extrinsic, -sical; extraneous etc. (*foreign*) 57; modal, adventitious, additional, supervenient, fortuitous; a-, ad-scititious; incidental, casual, accidental, unessential, non-essential, accessory.

implanted, ingrafted; instilled, inculcated.

outward etc. (*external*) 220.

Adv. extrinsically etc. *adj.*

7. State.—N. state, condition, category, estate, lot, case, trim, mood, pickle, plight etc. 704; temper; aspect etc. (*appearance*) 448.

constitution, habitude, *diathesis;* frame, fabric etc. 329; stamp, set, fit, mold.

mode, modality, schesis; fettle; form etc. (*shape*) 240.

tone, tenor, turn; trim, guise, fashion, light, complexion, style, character.

V. be in −, possess −, enjoy −, labor under- a -state etc. *n.;* be on a footing, do, fare; come to pass.

Adj. conditional, modal, formal; structural, organic.

Adv. conditionally etc. *adj.;* as -the matter stands, − things are; such being the case etc. 8.

8. Circumstance.—N. circumstance, situation, phase, position, posture, attitude, place, point; terms; *régime;* footing, standing, status.

occasion, juncture, conjuncture; contingency etc. (*event*) 151.

predicament; emergen-ce, -cy; exigency, crisis, pinch, pass, push; turning point; crossroads.

bearings, how the land lies.

Adj. circumstantial; given, conditional, provisional; critical; ` modal; contingent, incidental; adventitious etc. (*extrinsic*) 6.

Adv. in the circumstances etc. *n.*, under the conditions etc. 7; thus, in such wise.

accordingly; that −, such- being the case; that being so, since, seeing that.

as matters stand; as -things, − times- go.

conditionally, provided, if, in case; if -so, − so be, − it be so; if it so -happen, − turn out; in the event of; in such a -contingency, − case, − event; provisionally, unless, without.

according to -circumstances, − the occasion; as it may -happen, − turn out, − be; as the -case may be, − wind blows; *pro re natâ.*

9. Relation.—N. relation, bearing, reference, connection, apposition, interconnection, concern, cognation; applicability, appositeness; correlation etc. 12; analogy; similarity etc. 17; affinity, intimacy, friendship; homology, alliance, homogeneity, association, rapport; approximation etc. (*nearness*) 197; filiation etc. (*consanguinity*) 11; interest; relevancy etc. 23; relationship, relative position; relativity; inter-relation etc. 12.

comparison etc. 464; ratio, proportion.

link, tie, bond, bond of union.

V. be-related etc. *adj.;* have a relation etc. *n.;* relate −, refer- to; bear upon, regard, concern, touch, affect, have to do with; pertain −, belong −, appertain- to; have respect to; answer to; interest.

bring -into relation with, − to bear upon; connect, associate, draw a parallel; link etc. 43.

Adj. relative; correlative etc. 12; cognate; relating to etc. *v.;* relative to, in relation with, referable *or* referrible to; belonging to etc. *v.;* appurtenant to, in common with.

related, connected; implicated, associated, affiliated, akin, allied to; collateral, cognate, congenial, kindred, affinitive, *en rapport,* in touch with.

approxima-tive, -ting; approaching; proportion-al, -ate, -able; allusive, comparable.

in the same -category etc. 75; like etc. 17; relevant etc. (*apt*) 23.

Adv. relatively etc. *adj.;* pertinently etc. 23.

thereof; as -to, − for, − respects, − re-gards; about; concerning etc. *v.;* anent; relating −, as relates- to; with -relation, − reference, − respect, − regard-to; in respect of; while speaking −, *à propos -*of; in connection with; by the -way, − by; whereas; for −, in -as much as; in point of, as far as; on the -part, − score- of; *quoad hoc; pro re natâ;* under the -head etc. (*class*) 75- of; in the matter of, *in re.*

Phr. 'thereby hangs a tale.'

10. Irrelation. [Want, or absence of relation.]—N. irrelation, dissociation; inapplicability; inconnection; multifariousness; disconnection etc. (*disjunction*) 44; inconsequence, independence; incommensurability; irreconcilableness etc. (*disagreement*) 24; heterogeneity;

unconformity etc. 83; irrelevancy, impertinence, *nihil ad rem;* intrusion etc. 24.

V. have no -relation etc. 9 to, — bearing upon, — concern etc. 9 with, — business with; not -concern etc. 9; have -nothing to do with, — no business there; intrude, etc. 24.

bring —, drag —, haul —, lug- in head and shoulders.

Adj. irrelative, irrespective, unrelated, irrelated; arbitrary; independent, unallied; un-, dis-connected; adrift, isolated, insular; extraneous, strange, alien, foreign, outlandish, exotic.

not comparable, incommensurable, heterogeneous; unconformable etc. 83.

irrelevant; rambling etc. 279; inapplicable; not -pertinent, — to the purpose; impertinent, inapposite, beside the mark, *à propos de bottes;* away from —, foreign to —, beside the -purpose, — question, — transaction, — point; misplaced etc. (*intrusive*) 24.

remote, far fetched, out of the way, forced, neither here nor there, quite another thing; detached, segregated, segregate.

multifarious; discordant etc. 24.

incidental, parenthetical, *obiter dictum,* episodic.

Adv. parenthetically etc. *adj.;* by the -way, — by; *en passant,* incidentally; irrespicitively etc. *adj.;* without reference, — regard- to; in the abstract etc. 87; *a se.*

11. Consanguinity. [Relations of kindred.]—N. consanguinity, relationship, kindred, blood; parentage etc. (*paternity*) 166; filiation, affiliation; lineage, agnation, connection, cognation, alliance; family -connection, — tie; ties of blood; blood relationship; nepotism.

kins-man, -folk; people; kith and kin; relation, -tive; connection; sib; next of kin; uncle, aunt, nephew, niece; cousin, -german; first —, second- cousin; cousin -once, — twice etc.- removed; near —, distant-relation; brother, sister, one's own flesh and blood.

family, patriarch, matriarch; fraternity; brother-, sister-, cousin-hood.

race, stock, generation; sept etc. 166 ; stirps, side; strain; breed, clan, tribe.

V. be -related etc. *adj.* — to; claim -relationship etc. *n.*- with.

Adj. related, akin, consanguineous, matrilinear, patrilineal, of the blood, family, allied, collateral; cog-, ag-, con-nate; kindred; affiliated, affine; fraternal, avuncular.

intimately —, nearly —, closely —, remotely —, distantly- related, — allied; german.

12. Correlation. [Double or reciprocal relation.]—N. reciprocalness etc. *adj.;* recipro-city, -cality, -cation; mutuality, correlation, correspondence, interdependence; interchange etc. 148; exchange, barter; interrelation, interconnection; alternation, see-saw.

V. reciprocate, alternate; interchange etc. 148; exchange; counterchange; interact, correspond, mutualize, give and take.

Adj. reciprocal, mutual, commutual, correlative; alternate; interchangeable; international; correspondent, complementary, analogous.

Adv. *mutatis mutandis; vice versâ;* each other; by turns etc. 148; reciprocally etc. *adj.;* to and fro etc. 314.

13. Identity.—N. identity, sameness, oneness, ditto, homogeneity; unity, coincidence, coalescence; convertibility; equality etc. 27; selfness, self, oneself; identification.

monotony, tautology etc. (*repetition*) 104.

synonym.

fac-simile etc. (*copy*) 21; *alter ego* etc. (*similar*) 17; *ipsissima verba* etc. (*exactness*) 494; same; self —, very —, one and the same; very —, actual-thing, no other.

V. be -identical etc. *adj.;* match, coincide, coalesce.

treat as —, render--the same , —identical; identify; recognize the identity of.

Adj. identical; self, ilk; the -same etc. *n.;* self same; synonymous; one and the same.

coincid-, coalesc-ent, -ing; indistinguishable; one; equivalent etc. (*equal*) 27; much -the same, — of a muchness; unaltered.

Adv. identically etc. *adj.:* on all fours; ibid-, -em.

14. Contrariety. [Non-coincidence.]—N. contrariety, contrast, foil, antithesis, oppositeness; counterpole; contradiction; antagonism etc. (*opposition*) 708; counteraction etc. 179.

inversion etc. 218; the -opposite, — reverse, — inverse, — converse, — antipodes, — other extreme etc. 237

antonym.

V. be -contrary etc. *adj.;* contrast with, oppose; differ *toto coelo.*

invert, reverse, turn the tables etc. 218.

contra-dict, -vene; antagonize etc. 708.

Adj. contrar-y, -ious, -iant; opposite, counter, dead against; ad-, con-, reverse; opposed, antithetical, contrasted, antipodean, antagonistic, opposing; conflicting, inconsistent, contradictory, at cross purposes; negative; hostile etc. 708.

differing *toto coelo;* diametrically opposite; as opposite as -black and white, — light and darkness, — fire and water, — the poles, as different as chalk from cheese; 'Hyperion to a satyr;' quite the -contrary, — reverse; no such thing, just the other way, *tout au contraire.*

Adv. contrarily etc. *adj.; contra,* contrariwise, *per contra,* on the contrary, nay rather; topsy-turvy; *vice versâ;* on the other hand etc. (*in compensation*) 30.

15. Difference.—N. difference, unlikeness; heterogeneity; vari-ance, -ation, -ety; diversity, dissimilarity etc. 18; disagreement etc. 24; disparity etc. (*inequality*) 28; distinction, contradistinction; distinctness; discrepancy, divergence, contrast etc. 18; nonconformity, incompatibility, antithesis.

discord etc. 713.

modification, moods and tenses.

nice —, fine —, delicate —, subtle- distinction; shade of difference, *nuance;* discrimination etc. 465; *differentia.*

different thing, something else, variant, apple

off another tree, horse of another color, another pair of shoes; this that or the other.

V. be -different etc. *adj.*, differ, vary, ablude, mismatch, contrast; diverge −, depart −, deviate- -from; divaricate; differ -*toto coelo*, − *longo intervallo*.

disagree etc. 713.

vary, modify etc. (*change*) 140.

discriminate etc. 465.

Adj. differing etc. *v.*; different, diverse, divided, heterogeneous; distinguishable; varied, modified; divergent, incongruous, diversified, various; discrepant, dissentient, differential; divers, all manner of; variform etc. 81; discordant etc. 713.

other, another, not the same; unequal etc. 28; unmatched; widely apart.

distinctive, characteristic; discriminative; distinghishing.

Adv. differently etc. *adj.*

Phr. *il y a fagots et fagots, tot nomines tot sententiae;* one man's meat is another man's poison.

16. Uniformity.—N. uniformity; homogeneity, -ousness; continuity, stability, consistency; connatural-ity, -ness; homology, accordance; conformity etc. 82; agreement etc. 23.

regularity, constancy, even tenor, routine; monotony, evenness, sameness, dead level; steadiness, equability, unity.

V. be -uniform etc. *adj.*; accord with etc. 23; run through.

become -uniform etc. *adj.*; conform to etc. 82.

render uniform etc. *adj.*; assimilate, level, smooth, dress.

Adj. uniform; homo-geneous, -logous; of a piece, consistent, steady; connatural; monotonous, changeless, dreary, even, invariable, equable, level, regular, stereotyped, unchanged, unvarying; methodical etc. 60; habitual etc. 613.

Adv. uniformly etc. *adj.*, uniformly with etc. (*conformably*) 82; in harmony with etc. (*agreeing*) 23; in a -rut, − groove.

always, ever etc. 112; invariably, without exception, never otherwise; by clock-work; endlessly etc. 112.

Phr. *ab uno disce omnes.*

16a. Non-uniformity. [Absence or want of uniformity.]−N. diversity, irregularity, unevenness; multiformity etc. 81; unconformity etc. 83; roughness etc. 256; heterogeneity, heteromorphism.

Adj. diversified, varied, irregular, uneven, rough etc. 256; multifarious; multiform etc. 81; of various kinds; all -manner, − sorts, − kinds-of.

Adv. in all manner of ways, here there and everywhere.

17. Similarity.—N. similarity, resemblance, likeness, similitude, semblance; affinity, approximation, parallelism; parity; agreement etc. 23; ana-logy, -logicalness; correspondence, equality etc.

connatural-ness, -ity; brotherhood, family likeness.

alliteration, rhyme, pun.

repetition etc. 104; sameness etc. (*identity*) 13; uniformity etc. 16.

analogue; the like; match, *pendant*, fellow, companion, pair, mate, twin, double, counterpart, brother, sister; one's second self, *alter ego*, chip of the old block, *par nobile fratrum, Arcades ambo*, birds of a feather, *et hoc genus omne*.

parallel; simile; type etc. (*metaphor*) 521; image etc. (*representation*) 554; photograph; close −, striking −, speaking −, faithful etc *adj.* − likeness, − resemblance.

V. be -similar etc. *adj.*, look like, resemble, bear resemblance, favor; savor −, smack- of; approximate; parallel, match, rhyme with; take after; imitate etc. 19; run in pairs.

Adj. similar; resembling etc. *v.*; like, alike; twin.

analog-ous, -ical; parallel, of a piece; such as, so.

connatural, congeneric, allied to; corresponding, cognate; akin to etc. (*consanguineous*) 11.

approximate, much the same, near, close, something like, such like; a show of; mock, *pseudo*, simulating, representing.

exact etc. (*true*) 494; lifelike, faithful, realistic; true to -nature, − the life; the -very image − pic ure- of; for all the world like, *comme deux gouttes d'eau;* as like as -two peas, − it can stare; *instar omnium*, case in the same mold, ridiculously like.

Adv. as if, so to speak; as −, as if- it were; *quasi*, just as, *veluti in speculum*.

18. Dissimilarity.—N. dissimil-arity, -itude; unlikeness, diversity, disparity, dissemblance; divergence, inequality, difference etc. 15; novelty; variation, variety, originality, disguise.

V. be -unlike etc. *adj.*; vary etc. (*differ*) 15; bear no resemblance to, differ *toto coelo*.

render -unlike etc. *adj.*; vary etc. (*diversify*) 140.

Adj. dissimilar, unlike, disparate; of a different kind etc. (*class*) 75; unmatched, unique; new, novel; unprecedented etc. 83; original.

nothing of the kind; no such −, quite anotherthing; far from it, other than, cast in a different mold, *tertium quid*, as like a dock as a daisy, 'very like a whale;' as different as -chalk from cheese, − Macedon and Monmouth; *lucus a non lucendo*.

diversified etc. 16a.

Adv. otherwise, *alias*.

19. Imitation.—N. imitation; copying etc, *v.*; transcription; repetition, mimeograph, mimeotype, duplication, reduplication; quotation; reproduction.

mockery, mimicry, mime, simulation, personation; representation etc. 554; semblance, pretence; copy etc. 21; assimilation.

paraphrase, parody etc. 21.

plagiarism; forgery etc. (*falsehood*) 544.

imitator; echo, cuckoo, parrot, ape, monkey, mocking-bird, mimic, impersonator, copyist.

V. imitate, copy, mirror, reflect, reproduce, repeat, borrow; do like, echo, re-echo, catch; transcribe; match, parallel.

mock, take off, mimic, ape, simulate, personate, impersonate; forge; act etc. (*drama*) 599; represent etc. 554; counterfeit, duplicate; portray, parody, travesty, caricature, burlesque.

follow −, tread- in the- -steps, − footsteps, − wake- of; pattern after, take pattern by; follow - suit, − the example of; walk in the shoes of, take a leaf out of another's book, strike in with; take −, model -after; emulate.

Adj. imitated etc. v.; mock, mimic; counterfeit, false, pseudo; modelled after, molded on, paraphrastic; literal; imitative, apish; second-hand; imitable; sham etc. 545.

Adv. literally, to the letter, strictly, precisely, *verbatim, literatim, sic, totidem verbis,* word for word, *mot à mot.*

Phr. like master like man.

20. Non-Imitation.—N. no imitation, enuineness, originality; creativeness.

Adj. unimitated, uncopied; unmatched, un-aralleled; inimitable etc. 33; *unique,* original, rimordial, primary, pristine, underived, first-and, archetypal, prototypal.

20a. Variation.—N. variation; alteration etc. *hange*) 140, modification, moods and tenses; nodulation.

divergency etc. 291; deviation etc. 279; aberration; innovation.

V. vary etc. (*change*) 140; deviate etc. 279; diverge etc. 291.

Adj. varied etc. v.; modified; dissimilar etc. 18; diversified etc. 16a.

21. Copy. [Result of imitation.]—**N.** copy, facsimile, counterpart, *effigies,* effigy, symbol, image, form, likeness, similitude, semblance, resemblance, cast, electrotype, stereotype, tracing, ectype; imitation etc. 19; model, representation, adumbration, study; counterfeit presentment, portrait etc. (*representment*) 554.

duplicate; transcript, -ion; reflex, -ion; shadow, echo; chip of the old block; reprint, reproduction, casting, engraving, replica; transfer; second edition etc. (*repetition*) 104; *réchauffé* apograph, fair copy; revise.

parody, caricature, cartoon, burlesque, travesty, paraphrase.

servile -copy, − imitation; counterfeit etc. (*deception*) 545; *pasticcio.*

Adj. faithful; lifelike etc. (*similar*) 17

22. Prototype. [Thing copied.]—**N.** prototype, original, model, pattern, founding, precedent, standard, scantling, type, arche-, anti-type; protoplast, copy-book, module, exemplar, example, ensample, specimen; paradigm; guide; templet; lay-figure.

text, copy, manuscript, MS., design; fugle-man, keynote.

die, mold; matrix, engraving, last, plasm; pro-, proto-plasm; mint; seal, punch, *intaglio,* negative, stamp.

V. be −, set- an example; set a copy; standardize.

23. Agreement.—N. agreement; ac-cord, -cordance; unison, harmony, concord etc. 714; concordance, concert, understanding, convention, *entente -cordiale, consortium,* consensus of opinion, pact, mutual understanding, unanimity.

conformity etc. 82; conformance; uniformity etc. 16; consonance, consentaneousness, consistency; congruity, -ence; keeping; congeniality; correspondence, concinnity, parallelism, apposition, union.

fitness, aptness etc. adj.; relevancy; pertinence, -cy; sortance; case in point; aptitude, propriety, applicability, admissibility, commensurability, compatibility, suitability; cognation etc (*relation*) 9.

adaptation, adjustment, arrangement, graduation, accommodation; reconcil-iation -ement; assimilation; attunement.

consent etc. (*assent*) 448; concurrence etc. 178; co-operation etc. 709.

right man in the right place, very thing; quite − just- the thing.

be -accordant etc. adj.; agree, accord, harmonize; correspond, tally, respond; meet, suit, fit, befit, do, adapt itself to; fall in −, chime in −, square −, quadrate −, consort −, comport- with; dovetail, assimilate; fit like a glove; fit to a -tittle, − T; match etc. 17; become one.

consent etc. (*assent*) 488.

render -accordant etc. adj.; fit, suit, adapt, accommodate; graduate; adjust etc. (*render equal*) 27; dress, regulate, readjust; accord, harmonize, reconcile; fadge, dovetail, square.

Adj. agreeing, suiting etc. v.; in accord, accordant, concordant, consonant, congruous, consentaneous, correspondent, corresponding, homologous, congenial; becoming; harmonious, reconcilable, conformable; in -accordance, − harminy, − keeping, − unison, etc. n.;-with; at one with, of one mind, of a piece; consistent, compatible, proportionate, answerable; commensurate; on all fours.

. apt, apposite, pertinent, pat; to the -point, --purpose; happy, felicitous, germane, *ad rem,* in point, bearing upon, applicable, relevant, admissible.

fit, adapted, *in loco, à propos,* appropriate, seasonable; sortable, suitable, idoneous, deft; meet etc. (*expedient*) 646.

at home, in one's proper element.

Adv. *à propos of;* pertinently etc. adj.; *pro rata.*

Phr. *rem acu tetigisti,* the cap fits.

24. Disagreement.—N. disagreement, discord, -cordance; disunion, dissonance, dissidence, discrepancy; unconformity etc. 83; incongru-ity, -ence; discongruity, *mésalliance, oxymoron;* jarring etc. v.; clash, collision, dissension etc. 713; conflict etc. (*opposition*) 708; controversy etc. 720; falling out, wrangle, argument.

disparity, mismatch, misfit, disproportion; disproportionateness etc. adj.; variance, divergence, repugnance.

unfitness etc. adj.; inaptitude, impropriety; inapplicability etc. adj., inconsistency, inconcinnity; irrelevancy etc. (*irrelation*) 10.

misjoin-ing, -der; syncretism, intrusion, interference; *concordia discors.*

fish out of water.

V. disagree; clash, quarrel, jar etc. (*discord*) 713; interfere, intrude, come amiss; not concern etc. 10; mismatch; *hymano capiti cervicem jungere equinam.*

Adj. disagreeing etc. *v.;* discordant, discrepant; at -variance, — war; hostile, antagonistic, repugnant, factious, contradictory, dissentious, incompatible, irreconcilable, inconsistent with; unconformable, exceptional etc. 83; intrusive, incongruous; disproportionate, -ed; unharmonious; unconsonant; divergent, repugnant to.

inapt, unapt, inappropriate, inept, infelicitous, improper; unsuit-ed, -able; inapplicable; un-fit, -fitting, -befitting; unbecoming; ill-timed, ill-adapted, unseasonable, *mal à propos,* inadmissible; inapposite etc. (*irrelevant*) 10.

uncongenial; ill-assorted, -sorted, -matched; mis-matched, -mated, -joined, -placed; unaccommodating, irreducible, uncommensurable, unsympathetic.

out of -character, — keeping, — proportion, — joint, — tune, — place, — season, — its element; at -odds, — variance with.

Adv. in -defiance, — contempt, — spite-of; discordantly etc. *adj.; à tort et à travers.*

25. Quantity. [Absolute quantity.]—N. quantity, magnitude; size etc. ((*dimensions*) 192; amplitude, mass, amount, *quantum,* measure, measurement, substance, strength.

[Science of quantity.] Mathematics, Mathesis. [Definite or finite quantity] arm-, hand-, mouth-, spoon-, thimble-, capful; stock, batch, lot, dose, ration, quotum, quota, pittance, driblet, part, portion etc. 51.

Adj. quantitative, some, any, more or less.

Adv. to the tune of.

26. Degree. [Relative quantity.]—N. degree, grade, extent, measure, proportion, amount, ratio, stint, standard, height, pitch; reach, amplitude, range, scope, size, caliber; gradation, shade; tenor, compass; sphere, station, rank, standing; rate, way, sort.

point, mark, step, stage etc. (*term*) 71; intensity, strength etc. (*greatness*) 31.

V. compare, graduate, calibrate, measure.

Adj. comparative; gradual, shading off, gradational; within the bounds etc. (*limit*), 233.

Adv. by degrees, gradually, inasmuch, *pro tanto*; how-ever, -soever; step by step, bit by bit, little by little, inch by inch, drop by drop, gradatim; by -inches, — slow degrees, — little and little; in some -degree, — measure; to some extent; just a bit.

27. Equality. [Sameness of quantity or degree.]—N. equality, parity, co-extension, symmetry, balance, poise; evenness, monotony, level.

equivalence; equi-pollence, -poise, -librium, -ponderance; par, quits; not a pin to choose; distinction without a difference, six of one and half a dozen of the other; identity etc. 13; similarity etc. 17; isotropism; coequality.

equalization, equation, equilibration, co-ordination, adjustment, readjustment.

drawn -game, -battle, draw, stalemate; neck and neck- race; tie, dead heat.

match, peer, compeer, equal, mate, fellow, brother; equivalent.

V. be -equal etc. *adj.;* equal, match, reach, keep pace with, run abreast; come —, amount —, come upto; be —, lie- on a level with; balance; cope with; come to the same thing; level off.

render -equal etc. *adj.;* equalize, level, dress, balance, equate, handicap, give points, trim, adjust, poise; fit, accommodate; adapt etc. (*render accordant*) 23; strike a balance; establish —, restore- equality, — equilibrium; readjust; stretch on the bed of Procrustes.

Adj. equal, even, level, monotonous, coequal, symmetrical, coordinate;-on a -par, — level, — footing- with; up to the mark; equiparent.

equivalent, tantamount; quits; homologous; synonymous etc. 522; resolvable into, convertible, much at one, as broad as long, neither more nor less; much the same —, the same thing —, as good- as; all -one, — the same; equi-pollent, -ponderant, -ponderous, -balanced; equalized etc. *v.;* drawn; half and half; isochronous; isoperimetrical.

Adv. equally etc. *adj.; pari passu, ad eundem, caeteris paribus; in equilibrio;* to all intents and purposes.

Phr. it -comes, -adds up, — amounts- to the same thing.

28. Inequality. [Difference of quantity or degree.]—N. inequality; dis-, im-parity; odds; difference etc. 15; ill-balanced; unevenness; inclination of the balance, partiality; shortcoming; casting —make- weight; superiority etc. 33; inferiority etc. 34.

V. be -unequal etc. *adj.;* countervail; have —, give- the advantage; turn the scale; kick the beam; topple, -over; over-match etc. 33; not come up to etc. 34.

Adj. unequal, uneven, disparate, partial; un-, over-balanced; top-heavy, lop-sided.

Adv. *haud passibus aequis.*

29. Mean.—N. mean, medium, intermedium, average, run of the mill, normal, balance; mediocrity, generality, rule, ordinary -run, -ruck; golden mean etc. (*mid-course*) 628; middle etc. 68; compromise etc. 774; neutrality; middle point, middle course.

V. split the difference; take the -average etc. *n.;* reduce to a -mean etc. *n.;* strike a balance, pair off.

Adj. mean, intermediate; medial; middle etc. 68; average, normal, standard, neutral; middling, moderate.

médiocre, middle-class; *bourgeois,* commonplace etc. (*unimportant*) 643.

Adv. on an average, in the long run; taking - one with another, — all things together, — it for all in all; *communibus annis,* in round numbers.

30. Compensation.—N. compensation, equation; commutation; indemnification; compromise etc. 774; neutralization, nullification; counteraction etc. 179; reaction; measure for measure; retaliation etc. 718; equalization etc. 27; redemption, recoupment, recompense.

set-off, offset; make- casting-weight; counterpoise, equipoise, ballast; indemnity, reparation etc. 790; equivalent, *quid pro quo;* bribe, hushmoney, tribute etc. 784; amends etc. (*atonement*) 952; counterclaim, counterbalance, equiponderance, countervail, cross demand.

V. make -amends, – compensation; compensate, -pense; indemnify; counter-act, -vail, - poise; equiponderate; balance; out-, over-, counterbalance; set off, offset, cancel; hedge, square, give and take; make up -for, – lee way; cover, fill up, neutralize, nullify; equalize etc. 27; make good; redeem etc. (*atone*) 952; recoup, pay etc. 973.

Adj. compensat-ing, -ory; amendatory, reparative, countervailing etc. *v.;* in the opposite scale; equivalent etc. (*equal*) 27.

Adv. in -return, – consideration; but, however, yet, still, notwithstanding; neverthe-, nathless; although, though; al-, how-beit; in spite of, despite; mauger; at -all events, – any rate; be that as it may, for all that, even so, on the other hand, at the same time, *quoad minus, quand même,* however that may be; after all, – is said and done; taking one thing with another etc. (*average*) 29.

31. Greatness.— N. greatness etc. *adj.;* magnitude; size etc. (*dimensions*) 192; multitude etc. (*number*) 102; immensity, enormity, infinity etc. 105; might; strength, intensity, fulness; importance etc. 642; fame etc. 873.

great quantity, quantity, deal, power, sight, pot, volume, world; mass, heap etc. (*assemblage*) 72; stock etc. (*store*) 636; peck, bushel, load, cargo; cart –, wagon –, car –, truck –, shipload; flood, spring tide; abundance etc. (*sufficiency*) 639.

principal –, chief –, main –, greater –, major –, best –, essential- part; bulk, mass etc. (*whole*) 50.

V. be -great etc. *adj.;* run high, soar, loom up, tower, bulk large, transcend; rise –, carry- to a great height; know no bounds; scale, overtop, ascend.

enlarge etc. (*increase*) 35, (*expand*) 194.

Adj. great; greater etc. 33; large, considerable, fair, above par; big, massive, huge etc. (*large in size*) 192; ample; abundant etc. (*enough*) 639; Herculean etc. 159; full, intense, strong, sound, passing, heavy, plenary, deep, high; signal, at its height, in the zenith.

world-wide, wide-spread, extensive; wholesale; many etc. 102.

goodly, noble, precious, mighty; sad, grave, serious; far gone, arrant, downright; utter, -most; crass, gross, arch, profound, intense, consummate; rank, unmitigated, red-hot, desperate; glaring, flagrant, stark staring; thorough-paced, - going; roaring, thumping, thundering, strapping, whacking; extraordinary; important etc. 642; unsurpassed etc. (*supreme*) 33; complete etc. 52.

vast, immense, enormous, extreme; inordinate, excessive, extravagant, exorbitant, outrageous, preposterous, unconscionable, swinging, monstrous, over-grown; towering, stupendous, prodigious, astonishing, incredible; terrific, frightful; marvelous etc. (*wonder*) 870; grand.

unlimited etc. (*infinite*) 105; unapproachable, unutterable, indescribable, ineffable, unspeakable, inexpressible, beyond expression, fabulous.

un-diminished, -abated, -reduced, -restricted.

absolute, positive, stark, decided, unequivocal, essential, perfect, finished.

remarkable, of mark, marked, pointed, veriest; noticeable, uncommon, noteworthy, eminent etc. 873.

Adv. [in a positive degree] truly etc. (*truth*) 494; decidedly, unequivocally, purely, absolutely, seriously, essentially, fundamentally, radically, downright, in all conscience; for the most part, in the main.

[in a complete degree] entirely etc. (*completely*) 52; abundantly, etc. (*sufficiently*) 639; widely, far and wide.

[in a great or high degree] greatly etc. *adj.;* much, muckle, well, indeed, very, very much, a deal, no end of, most not a little; pretty, – well; enough, in a great measure, passing richly; to a - large, – great, – gigantic- extent; on a large scale; so; never –, ever- so; ever so much; by wholesale; mightily, mighty, powerfully; with a witness, *ultra,* in the extreme, extremely, exceedingly, intensely, exquisitely, acutely, indefinitely, immeasurably; beyond -compare, – comparison, – measure, – all bounds; incalculably, infinitely.

[in a supreme degree] pre-eminently, superlatively etc. (*superiority*) 33.

[in a too great degree] immoderately, unduly, monstrously, grossly, preposterously, inordinately, exorbitantly, excessively, enormously, out of all proportion, with a vengeance.

[in a marked degree] particularly, remarkably, singularly, curiously, uncommonly, unusually, peculiarly, notably, signally, strikingly, pointedly, mainly, chiefly; famously, egregiously, prominently, glaringly, emphatically, strangely, wonderfully, amazingly, surprisingly, astonishingly, incredibly, marvelously, awfully, stupendously.

[in an exceptional degree] peculiarly etc. (*unconformity*) 83.

[in a violent degree] furiously etc. (*violence*) 173; severely, desperately, tremendously, extravagantly, confoundedly, deucedly, devilishly, with a vengeance; *à –, à toute- outrance.*

[in a painful degree] painfully, sadly, grossly, sorely, bitterly, piteously, grievously, miserably, cruelly, woefully, lamentably, shockingly, frightfully, dreadfully, fearfully, terribly, horribly, distressingly, balefully.

32. Smallness.—N. smallness etc. *adj.;* littleness etc. (*small size*) 193; tenuity; paucity; fewness etc. (*small number*) 103; meanness, insignificance etc. (*unimportance*) 643; mediocrity, moderation.

small quantity, *modicum, minimum;* vanishing point; material point, electron, atom, particle, molecule, corpuscle, point, dab, fleck, speck, dot, mote, jot, iota, ace; *minutiae,* details; look, thought, idea, *soupçon,* whit, tittle, shade, shadow; spark, *scintilla,* gleam; touch, cast; grain, scruple, granule, globule, minim, sup, sip, sop, spice, drop, droplet, sprinkling, dash, smack, tinge, tincture; inch, patch, scantling, dole; scrap, shred, tag, splinter, rag, tatter, cantlet, flitter, gobbet, mite, bit, morsel, crumb, seed, fritter, shive; snip, -pet; snick, snack, snatch, slip, scrag; chip, -ping; shiver, sliver, driblet, clipping, paring, shaving, hair.

nutshell; thimble-, spoon-, hand-, cap-, mouthful; fragment; fraction etc. (*part*)51; drop in the ocean, drop in the bucket.

animalcule etc. 193.

trifle etc. (*unimportant thing*) 643; mere —, next to- nothing; hardly anything; just enough to swear by; the shadow of a shade.

finiteness, finite quantity.

V. be -shall etc. *adj.;* lie in a nutshell.

diminish etc. (*decrease*) 36, (*contract*) 195.

Adj. small, little, tiny, weeny; diminutive etc. (*small in size*) 193; minute; minikin, fine, inconsiderable, dribbling, paltry etc. (*unimportant*) 643; faint etc. (*weak*) 160; slender, light, slight, scanty, scant, limited; meager etc. (*insufficient*) 640; sparing; few etc. 103; low, so-so, middling, tolerable, no great shakes; below —, under-par, — the mark; at a low ebb; half-way; moderate, modest; tender, subtle; petty, shallow, skin-deep.

inappreciable, evanescent, infinite-simal, homeopathic, very small, atomic, molecular, ultra-, -microscopic.

petty, shallow etc. 499.

mere, simple, sheer, stark, bare; near run.

Adv. [in a small degree] to a small extent, on a small scale; a -little, — wee, — tiny bit; slightly etc. *adj.;* imperceptibly; miserably, wretchedly; insufficiently etc. 640; imperfectly; faintly etc. 160; passably, pretty well, well enough.

[in a certain or limited degree] partially, in part; in —, to a certain degree; to a certain extent; comparatively; some, rather; in some -degree, -measure; some-thing, -what; simply, only, purely, merely; at —, at the- -least, — most; ever so little, as little as may be, *tant soit peu;* in ever so small a degree; thus far, *pro tanto;* within bounds, in a manner, after a fashion.

almost, nearly, well nigh, short of, not quite, all but; near —, close- upon; *peu s'en faut,* near the mark; within an -ace, — inch- of; on the brink of; scarcely, hardly, barely, only just, no more than.

[in an uncertain degree] about, therabouts, somewhere about, nearly, say; be the same -more, — little more- or less.

[in no degree] no- ways, — wise; not -at all, — in the least, — a bit, — a bit of it, — a whit, — a jot, — a shadow; in no -wise, — respect; by no -means, — manner of means; on no account, at no hand.

33. Superiority.

N. superiority, supremacy, majority; greatness etc. 31; advantage, odds, pull; preponderance, -ation; predominance, vantage ground, coign of vantage, prevalence, partiality; personal superiority; sovereignty etc. 737; nobility etc. (*rank*) 875; Triton among the minnows, *primus inter pares, nulli secundus,* superman; captain etc. 475.

supremacy, pre-eminence; primacy, lead, *maximum;* record; climax, crest, top; culmination etc. (*summit*) 210; transcendence; *ne plus ultra;* lion's share, Benjamin's mess; excess; bisque, surplus etc. (*remainder*) 40, (*redundance*) 641.

V. be -superior etc. *adj.;* exceed, excel, transcend; out-do, -balance, -weigh, -rival, -Herod, outrank, pass, surpass, surmount, get ahead of; over-top, -ride, -pass, -balance, -weigh, -match; top, o'er-top, cap, beat, win out, cut out; beat hollow; outstrip etc. 303; eclipse, throw into the shade, take the shine out of, put one's nose out of joint; have the -upper hand, — whip hand of, -advantage; turn the scale, play first fiddle etc. (*importance*) 642; preponderate, predominate, prevail; precede, take .precedence, come first; come to a head, culminate; beat etc. all others, bear the palm; break the record, take the cake.

become —, render- -larger, etc. (*increase*) 35, (*expand*) 194.

Adj. superior, greater, major, higher; exceeding etc. *v.;* great etc. 31; distinguished, *ultra;* vaulting; more than a match for.

supreme, greatest, maximal, maximum, utmost, paramount, pre-eminent, foremost, crowning; first-rate etc. (*important*) 642, (*excellent*) 648; unrivalled; peer-, match-less; none such, second to none, *sans pareil;* un-paragoned, -paralleled, -equalled, -approached, -surpassed; superlative, inimitable, *facile princeps,* incomparable, sovereign, without parallel, *nulli secundus, ne plus ultra;* beyond -compare, — comparison; culminating etc. (*topmost*) 210; transcendent, -ental; *plus royaliste que le Roi.*

increased etc. (*added to*) 35; enlarged etc. (*expanded*) 194.

Adv. beyond, more, over; over —, above- the mark; above par; upwards —, in advance- of; over and above; at the top of the scale, on the crest, at it height.

[in a superior or supreme degree] eminently, egregiously, pre-eminently, surpassing, prominently, superlatively, supremely, above all, of all things, the most, to crown all, *par excellence,* principally, especially, particularly, peculiarly, *a fortiori,* even, yea, still more.

Phr. 'we shall not look upon his like again.'

34. Inferiority.

N. inferiority, minority, subordinancy; shortcoming, deficiency; handicap; *minimum;* smallness etc. 32; imperfection, shabbiness.

[personal inferiority] commonalty etc. 876; subordinate, substitute, sub.

V. be -inferior etc. *adj.;* fall —, come- short of; not -pass, — come up to; want.

become —, render- smaller etc. (decrease) 36, (*contract*) 195; hide its diminished head, retire into the shade, yield the palm, play second fiddle, take a back seat; bow.

Adj. inferior, smaller; small etc. 32; minor, less, lesser, deficient, minus, lower, subordinate, secondary; second-rate etc. (*imperfect*) 651; sub, subaltern; thrown into the shade; weighed in the balance and found wanting; not fit to hold a candle to.

least, smallest etc. (*see* little, small etc. 193); lowest.

diminished etc. (*decreased*) 36; reduced etc. (*contracted*) 195; unimportant etc. 643.

Adv. less; under —, below- -the mark, — par; at -the bottom of the scale, — a low ebb, — a disadvantage; short of, under.

35. Increase.—N. increase; augmentation, addition, enlargement, extension; dilatation etc. (*expansion*) 194; multiplication; increment, accretion; accession etc. 37; production etc. 161; development, growth; aggrandizement, aggravation, intensification; rise; ascent etc. 305; anabasis; ex-aggeration, -acerbation; spread etc. (*dispersion*) 73; flood-, spring-, -tide; gain, produce, profit etc. 618; booty, plunder etc. 793.

V. increase, augment, add to, enlarge; dilate etc. (*expand*) 194; grow, wax, mount, swell, get ahead, gain strength; advance; run –, shoot- up; rise; ascend etc. 305; sprout etc. 194.

aggrandize; raise; exalt; deepen, heighten; lengthen; thicken; strengthen; intensify, enhance, inflate, magnify, double, redouble; multiply; aggravate, exaggerate; ex-asperate, -acerbate; add fuel to the flame, *oleum addere camino,* superadd etc. (*add*) 37; spread etc. (*disperse*) 73.

Adj. increased etc. v.; on the increase, undiminished, additional etc. (*added*) 37; increasing etc. v.; growing, crescent, intensive, cumulative.

Adv. *crescendo,* increasingly.

Phr. *vires acquirit eundo.*

36. Non-Increase. Decrease.—N. decrease, diminution, lessening etc. v.; subtraction etc. 38; reduction, abatement, declension; shrinkage etc. (*contraction*) 195; coarctation; abridgment etc. (*shortening*) 201; extenuation.

subsidence, catabasis, wane, ebb-, neap-tide, decline; descent etc. 306; decrement, reflux, depreciation; erosion, wear and tear, deterioration etc. 659; anticlimax; mitigation etc. (*moderation*) 174.

V. decrease, diminish, lessen; abridge etc. (*shorten*) 201; shrink etc. (*contract*) 195; drop –, fall –, tail- off; fall away, waste, wear, erode; wane, ebb, decline; descent etc. 306; subside; deliquesce, melt –, die -away; retire into the shade, hide its diminished head, fall to a low ebb, run low, languish, decay, crumble, consume away.

bate, abate, dequantitate; discount; depreciate; extenuate, lower, weaken, attenuate, fritter away; mitigate etc.(*moderate*) 174; belittle, minimize; dwarf, throw into the shade; keep down, reduce etc. 195; shorten etc. 201; subtract etc. 38.

Adj. unincreased etc. (*see* increase etc. 35); decreased etc. v.; decreasing etc. v.; on the -wane etc. n.; deliquescent.

Adv. *diminuendo, decrescendo,* decreasingly.

37. Addition.—N. addition, annexation, adjection; junction etc. 43; super-position, -addition, -junction, -fetation; accession, reinforcement; increase etc. 35; increment, supplement; accompaniment etc. 88; interposition etc. 228; insertion etc. 300; summation etc. 85; adjunct etc. 39.

V. add, annex, adject, affix, attach, superadd; subjoin, superpose; clap –, saddle- on; tack to, postfix, append, tag; ingraft; saddle with; sprinkle; introduce etc. (*interpose*) 228; insert etc. 300.

become added, accrue; ad-, supervene; add up etc. 85.

reinforce, strengthen, swell the ranks of; augment etc. 35.

Adj. added etc. v.; additional; supplement, -al, -ary; suppletory, subjunctive; adjec-, adsci-, ascititious; additive, extra, spare, further, fresh, more, new, ulterior, other, auxiliary, supernumerary, accessory.

Adv. in addition, more, plus, extra; and, also, likewise, too, furthermore, further, item; and -also, – eke; else, besides, to boot, *et cetera;* etc.; and so -on, – forth; into the bargain, *cum multis aliis,* over and above, moreover.

with, withal; including, inclusive, as well as, not to mention, let alone; together –, along –, coupled –, in conjunction- with; conjointly; jointly etc. 43.

38. Non-Addition. Subduction.—N. sub-traction, -duction; deduction, retrenchment; removal; ab-, sub-lation; abstraction etc. (*taking*) 789; garbling etc. v.; mutilation, detruncation; amputation, severance; abs-, ex-, re-cision; curtailment etc. 201; minuend, subtrahend; decrease etc. 36; abrasion.

V. sub-tract, -duct; rebate, de-duct, – duce; bate, retrench; remove, withdraw; take – from, – away; detract.

garble, mutilate, amputate, sever, detruncate; cut -off, – away, – out; expurgate; abscind, excise; pare, thin, prune, decimate; abrade, scrape, file; geld, castrate, emasculate, unman, spay, caponize; eliminate.

diminish etc. 36; curtail etc. (*shorten*) 201; deprive of etc. (*take*) 789; weaken.

Adj. subtracted etc. v.; subtractive.

tailless, acaudal.

Adv. in -deduction etc. n.; less; short of; minus, without, except, excepting, with the exception of, barring, bar, save, exclusive of, save and except, with a reservation.

39. Adjunct. [Thing added.]—N. adjunct, addit-ion, -ament; *additum,* affix, appendage, annex; augment, -ation; increment, reinforcement, supernumerary, accessory, item; garnish, sauce; accompaniment etc. 88; adjective, *addendum,* accession, complement, supplement; continuation; extension, subscript, tag, appendix, postscript, interlineation, interpolation, insertion.

rider, codicil, off-shoot, episode, side issue, corollary; piece; flap, lapel, label, tab, strip, fold, lappet, apron, skirt, embroidery, trappings, *cortège*; tail, suffix etc. (*sequel*) 65; wing.

Adj. additional etc. 37.

Adv. in addition etc. 37.

40. Remainder. [Thing remaining.]—N. remainder, residue; remains, *remanet,* remnant, rest, relic, relict; leavings, heel-tap, odds and ends, cheese-parings, candle ends, orts; *residuum;* dottle, dregs, etc. (*dirt*) 653; refuse etc. (*useless*) 645; stubble, result, educt; fag-end, stub; ruins, wreck, skeleton, stump; *alluvium.*

surplus, overplus, excess; balance, complement; superfluity etc. (*redundance*) 641; survival, -ance; afterglow.

V. remain; be -left etc. adj., exceed, survive; leave.

Adj. remaining, left; left -behind, – over;

residu-al, -ary; over, odd; unconsumed, sedimentary; surviving; net; exceeding, over and above; outlying, -standing; cast off etc. 782; superfluous etc. (*redundant*) 641.

V. remain; be -left; left -behind, − over; residual, -ary; over, odd; unconsumed, sedimentary; surviving; net; exceeding, over and above; outlying, -standing; cast off etc. 782; superfluous etc. (*redundant*) 641.

40a. Decrement. [Thing deducted.]—N. decrement, discount, rebate, defect, loss, deduction, eduction, tare; drawback; waste, wastage; reprise.

41. Mixture. [Forming a whole without coherence.]—N. mix-, admix-, commix-ture, -tion, mingling; commixion, immixture, interfusion, intermixture, alloyage, matrimony; junction etc. 43; combination etc. 48; entanglement, interlacing; miscegenation, interbreeding.

impregnation; in-, dif-, suf-, transfusion; infiltration; seasoning, sprinkling, interlarding; interpolation etc. 228; adulteration, sophistication.

[Thing mixed] tinge, tincture, touch, dash, smack, sprinkling, spice, seasoning, infusion, *soupçon.*

[Compound resulting from mixture] alloy, brass, bronze, pewter etc.; amalgam, *magma,* blend, half-and-half, *mélange, tertium, quid,* ·miscellany, *ambigu,* medley, mess, hash, hotchpotch, hodgepodge, *pasticcio,* patchwork, odds and ends, all sorts; jumble etc. (*disorder*) 59; salad, sauce, mash, *omnium gatherum,* gallimaufry, ragout, *olla podrida, olio,* salmagundi, *potpourri,* Noah's ark; texture, mingled yarn; mosaic etc. (*variegation*) 440.

half-blood, -caste, -breed, Eurasian; mulatto; terc-, quart-, quinteron etc.; quad-, octo-roon; *griffo, zambo;* cross, hybrid, mongrel etc. 83.

V. mix; join etc. 43; combine etc. 48; com-, im-, inter-mix; mix up with, mingle; com-, inter-, be-mingle; shuffle etc. (*derange*) 61; pound together; hash −, stir- up; knead, brew; impregnate with; interlard etc. (*interpolate*) 228; intertwine, -weave etc. 219; associate with, miscegenate, interbreed.

be mixed etc.; get among, be entangled with.

instil, imbue; in-, suf-, trans-fuse; infiltrate, dash, tinge, tincture, season, sprinkle, besprinkle, attemper, medicate, blend, cross; alloy, amalgamate, compound, adulterate, sophisticate, infect.

Adj. mixed etc. *v.;* implex, composite, half-and-half, linsey-wolsey, hybrid, mongrel, heterogeneous; motley etc. (*variegated*) 440; miscellaneous, promiscuous, indiscriminate; miscible.

Adv. among, amongst, amid, amidst, with; in the midst of, in the crowd.

42. Simpleness [Freedom from mixture.]—N. simpleness etc. *adj.;* purity, homogeneity.

elimination; sifting etc. *v.;* purification etc. (*cleanness*) 652.

V. render -simple etc. *adj.;* simplify.

sift, winnow, bolt, eliminate; narrow down; get rid of, exclude etc. 55; clear, purify etc. (*clean*) 652; disentangle etc. (*disjoin*) 44.

43. Junction.—N. junction; joining etc. *v.;* joinder, union; con-nection, -junction, -jugation, compendency, annex-ion, -ation, -ment; coalition; astriction, attachment, compagination, vincture, ligation, alligation; accouplement; marriage etc. (*wedlock*) 903; infibulation, inosculation, symphysis, anastomosis, confluence, communication, concatenation; concurrence, meeting, reunion; assemblage etc. 72.

copulation, coition, intercourse.

joint, joining, juncture, chiasma, pivot, hinge, articulation, commissure, seam, suture, gusset, stitch, splice; link etc. 45; miter, mortise.

closeness, tightness etc. *adj.;* coherence etc. 46; combination etc. 48.

V. join, unite; con-join, -nect; associate; put −, lay −, clap −, hang −, lump −, hold −, piece −, tack −, fix −, bind up- together; embody, re-embody; roll into one.

attach, fix, affix, saddle on, fasten, bind, secure, clinch, twist, make -fast etc. *adj.;* tie, pinion, string, strap, sew, lace, stitch, tack, paste, knit, button, buckle, hitch, lash, truss, bandage, braid, splice, swathe, gird, tether, moor, picket, harness, chain; fetter etc. (*restrain*) 751; lock, latch, belay, brace, hook, grapple, leash, couple, accouple, link, yoke, bracket; marry etc. (*wed*) 903; bridge over, span.

pin, nail, bolt, hasp, clasp, clamp, screw, rivet; impact, solder, braze, cement, set; weld −, fuse-together; wedge, rabbet, mortise, miter, jam, dovetail, enchase; graft, ingraft, inosculate; en-, in-twine; inter-link, -lace, -twine, -twist, -weave; entangle; twine round, belay; tighten; trice −, screw-up.

be -joined etc.; hang −, hold- together; cohere etc. 46.

Adj. joined etc. *v.;* joint; con-joint, -junct; corporate, compact; hand in hand.

firm, fast, close, tight, taut, taught, tense, secure, set, intervolved; in-separable, -dissoluble, -secable, -severable.

Adv. jointly etc. *adj.;* in conjunction with etc. (*in addition to*) 37; fast, firmly etc. *adj.;* intimately.

44. Disjunction.—N. dis-junction, -connection, -unity, -union, -association, -engagement, -sociation; discontinuity etc. 70; inconnection; abstraction, -edness; isolation; insul-arity, -ation; oasis; separateness etc. *adj.;* severalty; *disjecta membra;* dispersion etc. 73; apportionment etc. 786.

separation; parting etc. *v.;* detachment, segregation; divorce, sejunction, seposition; diduction, diremption, discerption; elision; *caesura,* division, subdivision, break, fracture, rupture; compartition; dis-memberment, -integration, -location; luxation; sever-, dis-sever-ance; scission; re-, ab-scission; circumcision;

lacer-, dilacer-ation; dis-, ab-ruption; avulsion, divulsion; section, resection, cleavage; fission; separability; separatism.

fissure, breach, rent, split, rift, crack, slit, slot, incision.

dissection, anatomy; decomposition etc. 49; cutting instrument etc. (*sharpness*) 253; saw.

V. be -disjoined etc.; come −, fall- -off, − to pieces; peel off; get loose.

dis-join, -connect, -engage, -unite, -sociate, - pair; divorce, part, dispart, detach, uncouple, separate, cut off, rescind, segregate; set −, keep- apart; insulate, isolate; throw out of gear; cut adrift; loose; un-loose, -do, -bind, -tie, -hitch, - chain, -lock etc. (*fix*) 43, -pack, -ravel; disen- tangle; set free etc. (*liberate*) 750.

sunder, divide, subdivide, sectionalize, sever, dissever, abscind; cut; segment; in-cide, -cise; circumcise; saw, snip, nib, nip, cleave, rive, rend, slit, split, splinter, chip, crack, snap, break, tear, burst; rend etc. -asunder, − in twain; wrench, rupture, shatter, shiver, cranch, crunch, craunch, chop; rip up; hack, hew, slash; whittle; haggle, hackle, discind, lacerate, scamble, mangle, gash, hash, slice.

cut up, carve, quarter, dissect, anatomize; take −, pull −, pick −, tear- to pieces; tear to tatters, − piecemeal; divellicate; skin etc. 226; dis-in- tegrate, -member, -branch, -band; disperse etc. 73; dis-locate, -joint; break up; mince; com- minute etc. (*pulverize*) 330; distribute, appor- tion etc. 786.

part, − company; separate, leave; alienate, estrange.

Adj. disjoined etc. *v.;* discontinuous etc. 70; bipartite, multipartite, abstract; digitate; dis- junctive; isolated etc. *v.;* insular, separate, dis- parate, discrete, apart, asunder, far between, loose, free; unattached -annexed, -associated, - connected; distinct; adrift; straggling; rift, reft, cleft, split.

[capable of being divided] scissile, partible, divisible, separable, severable, detachable.

Adv. separately etc. *adj.;* one by one, sever- ally, apart; adrift, asunder, in twain; in the abstract, abstractedly.

45. Vinculum. [Connecting medium.]—N. vinculum, link, *nexus;* connec-tive, -tion; junction etc. 43; bond of union, copula, intermedium, hyphen; bracket; bridge, stepping-stone, isthmus.

bond, tendon, tendril; fiber; cord, -age; riband, ribbon, rope, guy, cable, line, halser, hawser, paint- er, moorings, wire, chain; string etc. (*filament*) 205.

fastening, tie; liga-ment, -ture; strap; bowline, halliard, tackle, lanyard, rigging, shrouds; stand- ing −, running- rigging; traces, harness; yoke; band, -age; brace, roller, fillet; inkle; with, withe, withy; thong, braid; girder, tie-beam; girt, cinch, girth, girdle, cestus, garter, braces, suspenders; halter, noose, lasso, lariat, surcingle, knot, hitch, running knot, frog.

pin, corking pin, nail, brad, tack, skewer, staple, cleat, clamp; cramp, screw, button, buckle, clasp, hasp, hinge; hank, catch, latch, bolt, ring, latchet, pawl, tag; tooth; stud; hook, − and eye; morse, lock, holdfast, padlock, rivet; anchor, grappling-iron, drawbar, coupler, draw-

head, coupling, treenail, trennel, stake, pale, pile, post, bollard.

cement, glue, gum, paste, size, wafer, solder, lute, putty, bird-lime, mortar, stucco, plaster, grout.

shackle, rein etc. (*means of restraint*) 752; suspender etc. 214; prop etc. (*support*) 215.

V. bridge over, span; connect etc. 43; hang etc. 214.

46. Coherence.—N. co-, ad-herence, -hesion, - hesiveness; concretion, accretion; con-, ag- glutination, -glomeration; aggregation; con- solidation, set, cementation; sticking, soldering etc. *v.;* connection.

tenacity, toughness; stickiness etc. 352; insepara-bility, -bleness; bur, remora.

conglomerate, concrete etc. (*density*) 321.

V. cohere, adhere, stick, cling, cleave, hold, take hold of, hold fast, close with, embrace, clasp, hug; grow −, hang-together; twine round etc. (*join*) 43.

stick like -a leech, − wax; stick close; cling like -ivy, − a bur; adhere like -a remora, − Deja- nira's shirt.

glue; ag-, con-glutinate; cement, lute, paste, gum; solder, weld; cake, coagulate, consolidate etc. (*solidify*) 321; agglomerate.

Adj. co-, ad-hesive, -hering etc. *v.;* tenacious, tough; sticky etc. 352.

united, unseparated, sessile, inseparable, in- extricable, infrangible; compact etc. (*dense*) 321.

47. Incoherence. [Want of adhesion, non-ad- hesion, immiscibility.]—N. non-adhesion; im- miscibility; incoherence; looseness etc. *adj.;* lax- ity; relaxation; loosening etc. *v.;* freedom; dis- junction etc. 44; rope of sand.

V. make -loose etc. *adj.;* loosen, slacken, relax; un-glue etc. 46; detach etc. (*disjoin*) 44.

Adj. non-adhesive, immiscible; incoherent, detached, loose, slack, baggy, lax, relaxed, flap- ping, streaming; dishevelled; segregated, like grains of sand; un-consolidated etc. 321; -com- bined etc. 48; non-cohesive.

48. Combination.—N. combination; mixture etc. 41; alloy; junction etc. 43; union, unification, synthesis, incorporation, amalgamation, embodiment, coalescence, crasis, fusion, blend, blending, absorption, centralization, federation.

compound, amalgam, composition, *tertium quid;* resultant, impregnation.

V. combine, unite, incorporate, alloy, inter- twine etc. 41; amalgamate, embody, absorb, re- embody, blend, merge, fuse, melt into one, con- solidate, coalesce, centralize, impregnate; put −, lump- together; federate, associate; fraternize; cement a union, marry, wed, couple, pair, ally.

Adj. combined etc. *v.;* conjunctive, conjugate, conjoint, allied, confederate; impregnated with, ingrained, inoculated.

49. Decomposition.—N. decomposition, analysis, diaeresis dissection, resolution, catalysis, electrolysis, hydrolysis, photolysis, dis- solution; dispersion etc. 73; disjunction etc. 44;

putrescence, caries, necrosis, corruption etc. (*uncleanness*) 653.

V. decom-pose, -pound; analyze, disembody, dissolve; resolve −, separate- into its elements; electrolyze; dissect, decentralize, break up; disintegrate; disperse etc. 73; unravel etc. (*unroll*) 313; crumble into dust; decay etc. *n.;* deteriorate etc. 659.

Adj. decomposed etc. *v.;* catalytic, analytical.

50. Whole. [Principal part.]—**N.** whole, totality, integrity; totalness etc. *adj.;* entirety, *ensemble,* collectiveness; unity etc. 87; completeness etc. 52; indivisibility, indiscerptibility; integration, embodiment; integer, integral.

all, the whole, total, aggregate, one and all, gross amount, sum, sum-total, *tout ensemble,* length and breadth of, Alpha and Omega, 'be all and end all,' lock, stock and barrel.

bulk, mass, lump, tissue, staple, body, torso, *compages;* truck, bole, hull, hulk, skeleton; greater −, major −, best −, principal −, mainpart; essential part etc. (*importance*) 642; lion's share, Benjamin's mess; the long and the short; nearly −, almost- all.

V. form −, constitute- a whole; integrate, embody, amass; aggregate etc. (*assemble*) 72; amount to, come to.

Adj. whole, total, integral, entire; complete etc. 52; one, individual.

un-broken, -cut, -divided, -severed, -clipped, -cropped, -shorn; seamless; undiminished; undemolished, -dissolved, -destroyed, -bruised.

in-divisible, -dissoluble, -dissolvable, -discerptible.

wholesale, sweeping, comprehensive.

Adv. wholly, altogether; totally etc. (*completely*) 52; entirely, all, all in all, considering all things, in a body, collectively, all put together; in the -aggregate, − lump; − mass, − gross, − main, − long run; *en masse,* on the whole, as a whole, bodily, *en bloc, in extenso,* throughout, every inch; substantially.

51. Part.—**N.** part, portion; dose; item, particular; aught; any; division, ward; subdivision, section; chapter, verse; article, clause, count, paragraph, passage; phrase; number, volume, book, fascicule; sector, segment; fraction, fragment; cantle, -t; frustum; detachment, parcel, unit, class etc. 75.

piece, lump, bit; cut, -ting; chip, chunk, collop, slice, scale, shard; lamina etc. 204; moiety; small part; morsel, scrap, crumb; particle etc. (*smallness*) 32; instalment, dividend; share etc. (*allotment*) 786.

débris, odds and ends, oddments, *detritus; excerpta;* member, limb, lobe, lobule, arm, wing, scion, branch, bough, joint, link, offshoot, ramification, twig, stipule, tendril, bush, spray, sprig; runner; leaf, -let; stump; constituent, ingredient, component part etc. 56.

compartment; department etc. (*class*) 75; county etc. (*region*) 181.

V. part, divide, break etc. (*disjoin*) 44; partition etc. (*apportion*) 786.

Adj. fractional, fragmentary; sectional, aliquot; divided etc. *v.;* in compartments, multifid, incomplete, partial, divided etc. 44.

Adv. partly, in part, partially; piecemeal, part by part; by -instalments, − snatches, − inches, − driblets; bit by bit, inch by inch, foot by foot, drop by drop; in -detail, − lots.

52. Completeness.—**N.** completeness etc. *adj.;* completion etc. 729; integration; integrality.

entirety; universality; totality; perfection etc. 650; solid-ity, -arity; unity; all; *ne plus ultra,* ideal, limit.

complement, supplement, make-weight; filling up etc. *v.*

impletion; satur-ation, -ity; high water; high −, flood −, spring- tide; fill, load, bumper, belly-ful; brimmer; sufficiency etc. 639.

V. be -complete etc. *adj.;* come to a head.

render -complete etc. *adj.;* complete etc. (*accomplish*) 729; fill, charge, load, replenish; make-up, − good; piece −, eke- out; supply deficiencies; fill -up. − in, − to the brim, − the measure of; saturate etc. 869.

go the whole -hog, − length, go all lengths.

Adj. complete, entire; whole etc. 50; perfect etc. 650; full, good, absolute, thorough, plenary; solid, undivided; with all its parts.

exhaustive, radical, sweeping, thorough-going; dead.

regular, consummate, unmitigated, sheer, unqualified, unconditional, free; abundant etc. (*sufficient*) 639.

brimming; brim-, top-ful; chock −, choke-full; as full as- an egg is of meat, − a vetch, − a tick; saturated, crammed; replete etc. (*redundant*) 641; fraught, laden; full-laden, -fraught, -charged; heavy laden.

completing etc. *v.;* supplement-al, -ary; ascititious.

Adv. completely etc. *adj.;* altogether, outright, wholly, totally, *in toto,* quite; over head and ears; effectually, for good and all, nicely, fully, through thick and thin, head and shoulders; neck and -heel, − crop; all out; in all respects, − every respect; at all points, out and out, to all intents and purposes; *toto coelo;* utterly, clean, − as a whistle; to the -full, − utmost, − backbone; hollow, stark; heart and soul, root and branch; down to the ground.

to the top of one's bent, as far as possible *à outrance.*

throughout; from -first to last, − beginning to end, − end to end, − one end to the other, −Dan to Beersheba, − head to foot, − head to heels, − top to toe, − top to bottom; *de fond en comble; à fond, a capite ad calcem, ab ovo usque ad mala,* fore and aft; every -whit; − inch; *cap-à-pie,* to the end of the chapter; up to the -brim, − ears, − eyes; as ... as can be.

on all accounts; *sous tous les rapports;* with a -vengeance, − witness.

53. Incompleteness.—**N.** incompleteness etc. *adj.;* deficiency, short -measure, − wieght; shortcoming etc. 304; insufficiency etc. 640; imperfection etc. 651; immaturity etc. (*non-preparation*) 674; half measures.

[part wanting] defect, deficit, shortage, ullage, defalcation, omission, *caret;* interval etc. 198; break etc. (*discontinuity*) 70; non-completion etc. 730; missing link.

V. be -incomplete etc. *adj.;* fall short of etc. 304; lack etc. (*be insufficient*) 640; neglect etc. 460.

Adj. incomplete; imperfect etc. 651; unfinished; uncompleted etc. (*see* complete etc. 729); defective, deficient, wanting; failing; in -default, − arrear; short, − of; hollow, meagre, lame, half-and-half, perfunctory, sketchy; crude etc. (*unprepared*) 674.

mutilated, garbled, mangled, docked, lopped, truncated; bobtailed, cropped, bobbed, shingled.

in -progress, − hand; going on, proceeding.

Adv. incompletely etc. *adj.;* by halves.

Phr. *caetera desunt; caret.*

54. Composition.

—N. composition, constitution, crasis, synthesis; make-up; combination etc. 48; inclusion, admission, comprehension, reception; embodiment, formation, conformation, production.

compilation etc. 72. (*musical*) composition etc. 415; painting etc. 556; writing etc. 590; typography etc. 591.

V. be -composed, − made, − formed, − made up- of; consist of, be resolved into.

include etc. (*in a class*) 76; subsume; synthesize; contain, hold, comprehend, take in, admit, embrace, embody; involve; implicate, drag into.

compose, constitute, form, make; make −, fill −, build- up; weave, construct, fabricate; compile; write, draw; set up (*printing*); enter into the composition of etc. (*be a component*) 56.

Adj. containing, constituting etc. *v.*

55. Exclusion.

—N. exclusion, non-admission, omission, exception, rejection, repudiation; exile etc. (*seclusion*) 893; preclusion, lock out, ostracism, prohibition; disbarment, expulsion, ban.

separation, segregation, seposition, elimination, coffer-dam.

V. be excluded from etc.

exclude, bar, ban; leave −. shut −, thrust −, bar- out; reject, repudiate, spurn, blackball; ostracize, boycott; lay −, put −, set-apart, − aside; relegate, segregate; throw overboard; strike -off, − out; neglect etc. 460; banish etc. (*seclude*) 893; separate etc. (*disjoin*) 44.

pass over, omit; garble; eliminate, weed, winnow.

Adj. excluding etc. *v.;* exclusive.

excluded etc. *v.;* unrecounted, not included in; inadmissible; preventive, interdictive.

Adv. exclusive of, barring, except; with the exception of; save, bating.

56. Component.

—N. component; component −, integral −, integrant-part; element, constituent, ingredient, leaven; part and parcel; contents; appurtenance; feature; member etc. (*part*) 51; personnel.

V. enter into, − the composition of; be a -component etc. *n.;* be −, form- part of; merge −, be merged- in; be implicated in; share in etc. (*participate*) 778; belong −, appertain- to.

form, make, constitute, compose.

Adj. forming etc. *v.;* inclusive; inherent etc. 5.

57. Extraneousness.

—N. extraneousness etc. *adj.;* extrinsicality etc. 6; exteriority etc. 220; alienism.

foreign -body, − substance, − element; alien, stranger, intruder, interloper, foreigner, tramontane, *novus homo*, new comer, immi-, emi-grant; creole, Afrikander; outsider, outlander, tenderfoot.

Adj. extraneous, fore:gn, alien, ulterior; exterior, external, outside, outlandish; oversea; tra-ultra-montane.

excluded etc. 55; inadmissible; exceptional.

Adv. in foreign -parts, − lands; abroad, beyond seas, overseas.

58. Order.

—N. order, regularity etc. 80; uniformity, symmetry, *lucidus ordo;* harmony, music of the spheres.

gradation, progression; series etc. (*continuity*) 69.

subordination; course, even tenor, routine; method, disposition, arrangement, array, system, economy, discipline; orderliness etc. *adj.*

rank, place etc. (*term*) 71.

V. be −, become- in order etc. *adj.;* form, fall in, draw up; arrange −, range −, place- itself; adjust; fall into −, take- one's place, − rank; rally round; arrange etc. 60.

Adj. orderly, regular; in -order, − trim, − apple-pie order, according to Cocker, − its proper place, neat, neat as a pin, tidy, *en règle*, well regulated, correct, methodical, uniform, symmetrical, ship-shape, business-like, systematic; habitual; unconfused etc. (*see* confuse etc. 61) arranged etc. 60.

Adv. in order; methodically etc. *adj.;* in -turn, − its turn; step by step; by regular -steps, − gradations, − stages, − intervals; *seriatim*, systematically, by clockwork, *gradatim;* at stated periods etc. (*periodically*)138.

59. Disorder.

[Absence, or want of Order, etc.]—N. disorder; derangement etc. 61; irregularity; anomaly etc. (*unconformity*) 83; anar-chy, -chism; want of method; dishevelment, untidiness etc. *adj.;* disunion; discord etc. 24.

confusion; confusedness etc. *adj.;* disarray, jumble, mix-up, huddle, litter, lumber; *cahotage;* farrago; mess, muss, mash, muddle, hash; hotchpotch; *imbroglio*, chaos, *omnium gatherum*, medley; mere -mixture etc. 41; fortuitous concourse of atoms, *disjecta membra, rudis indigestaque moles.*

complexity; complexness etc. *adj.;* com-, implication; intri-cacy, -cation; perplexity; network, maze, labyrinth, wilderness, jungle; involution, ravelling, entanglement; coil etc. (*convolution*) 248; sleave, tangled skein, knot, Gordian know, kink, web; wheels within wheels.

turmoil; ferment, etc. (*agitation*) 315; to do, trouble, pudder, pother, row, disturbance, convulsion, tumult, pandemonium, uproar, riot, rumpus, stour, scramble, *fracas*, embroilment, *mêlée*, spill and pelt, rough and tumble; whirlwind etc. 349; bear garden, Babel, Saturnalia, Donnybrook Fair, confusion worse confounded, most admired disorder, *concordia discors;* Bedlam −, hell- broke loose; bull in a china shop;

all the fat in the fire, *diable à quatre*, Devil to pay; pretty kettle of fish; pretty piece of -work, — business.

slatte n, slut, sloven; draggle-tail.

V. be -disorderly etc. *adj.*; ferment, play at cross purposes.

put out of order; derange etc. 61; ravel etc. 219; ruffle, rumple; bungle, botch.

Adj. disorderly, orderless; out of -order; — place, — gear, — whack; irregular, desultory; anomalous etc. (*unconformable*) 83; acephalous, disorganized, straggling; un-, im-methodical; unsymmetric; unsystematic; untidy, slovenly, bedraggled, messy; dislocated; out of sorts; promiscuous, indiscriminate; chaotic, anarchical, lawless; unarranged etc. 60; confused, tumultuous, turbulent, tempestuous; deranged etc. 61; topsy turvy etc. (*inverted*) 218; shapeless etc. 241; disjointed, out of joint.

com-plex, -plexed; intricate, complicated, perplexed, involved, ravelled, entangled, knotted, tangled, inextricable; irreducible.

troublous; riotous etc. (*violent*) 173.

Adv. irregularly etc. *adj.*; by fits and -snatches, — starts; pell-mell; higgledy-piggledy; helterskelter, harum-scarum; in a ferment; at -sixes and sevens, — cross purposes; upside down etc. 218.

Phr. the cart before the horse, chaos is come again.

60. Arrangement. [Reduction to Order.]—N. arrangement; plan etc. 626; preparation etc. 673; dispos-al, -ition; col-, al-location; disbribution; sorting etc. *v.*; assortment, allotment; grouping; apportionment, *taxis*, taxonomy, *syn-taxis*, graduation, organization, grading; re-organization, rationalization.

analysis, classification, division, digestion; systematism.

[Result of arrangement] order, orderliness, form, array; digest, synopsis etc. (compendium) 596; *syntagma*, table, atlas; register etc. (*record*) 551; score etc. 415; cosmos, organism, architecture.

[Instrument for sorting] sieve etc. 260; file, card index.

V. reduce to - , bring into- order; introduce order into; rally.

arrange, dispose, place, form; put —, set —, place- in order; straighten up, tidy up; set out, collocate, allocate, pack, marshal, range, size, rank, array, group, parcel out, allot, space, distribute, deal; cast —, assign- the parts; dispose of, assign places to; assort, sort; sift, riddle; put —, set- -to rights, —, into shape, — in trim, — in array.

class, -ify; divide; file, string together, thread; register etc. (*record*) 551; list, catalogue, tabulate, index, alphabeticize, graduate, digest, grade, codify; orchestrate, score.

methodize, regulate, systematize, standardize, co-ordinate, organize, settle, fix.

unravel, disentangle, ravel, card; disembroil.

Adj. arranged etc. *v.*; embattled, in battle array; cut and dried; methodical, orderly, regular, systematic, tabular.

61. Derangement. [Subversion of Order; bringing into disorder.]—N. derangement etc. *v.*; dis-

order etc. 59; evection, discomposure, disturbance; dis-, de-organization; involvement; dislocation; perturbation, interruption; shuffling etc. *v.*; inversion etc. 218; corrugation etc. (*fold*) 258; insanity etc. 503.

V. derange; dis-, mis-arrange; dis-, mis-place; mislay, discompose, disorder, de-, dis-organize; embroil, unsettle, disturb, confuse, trouble, perturb, jumble, tumble; huddle, shuffle, muddle, toss, hustle, fumble, riot; bring -, put -, throwinto -disorder etc. 59; break the ranks, disconcert, convulse; break in upon.

unhinge, dislocate, put out of joint, throw out of gear.

turn topsy-turvy etc. (*invert*) 218; bedevil; complicate, involve, perplex, confound; im-, embrangle; tangle, en-tangle, ravel, tousle, dishevel, ruffle, rumple etc. (*fold*) 258; dement.

litter, scatter; mix etc. 41.

Adj. deranged etc. *v.*; syncre-tic, -tistic.

62. Precedence.—N. precedence; coming before etc. *v.*; the lead, *le pas*; superiority etc. 33; importance etc. 642; anteced-ence, -ency; anteriority etc. (*front*) 234; precursor etc. 64; priority etc. 116; precession etc. 280; anteposition, preference.

V. precede; come -before, — first; forerun, head, lead, take the lead; lead the -way, — dance; introduce, usher in; have the *pas*; set the fashion etc. (*influence*) 175; lead off, kick off, open the ball; take —, have- precedence; outrank; have the start etc. (*get before*) 280.

place before; prefix; premise, prelude, preface.

Adj. preceding etc. *v.*; pre-, antecedent; anterior, prior etc. 116; before; former, foregoing; before-, above-mentioned; aforesaid, said; precurs-ory, -ive; prevenient, preliminary, prefatory, introductory; prelus-ive, -ory; proemial, preparatory.

Adv. before; in advance etc. (*precession*) 280.

Phr. *seniores priores.*

63. Sequence.—N. sequence, coming after; going after etc. (*following*) 281; consecution, succession; posteriority etc. 117.

continuation; prolongation, order of succussion; successiveness; Elijah's mantle.

secondariness; subordinancy etc. (*inferiority*) 34.

V. succeed; come -after, — on, — next; follow, ensue, step into the shoes of; alternate.

place after, suffix, append.

Adj. succeeding etc. *v.*; sequent; sub-, consequent; sequacious, proximate, next; consecutive etc. (*continuity*) 69; alternate, amoebaean.

latter; posterior etc. 117.

Adv. after, subsequently; behind etc. (*rear*) 235.

64. Precursor.—N. precursor, antecedent, precedent, predecessor; forerunner, van-courier, *avant-coureur*, pioneer, prodrome, *pfodromos*, outrider; leader, bell-wether; herald, harbinger; dawn.

prelude, preamble, preface, prologue, foreword, *avant-propos*, *protasis*, prolusion, proem, *prolepsis*, *prolegomena*, prefix, introduction;

lead, heading, frontispiece, groundwork; preparation etc. 673; overture, voluntary, *exordium*, symphony, *ritornello;* premises.

prefigurement etc. 511; omen etc. 512.

Adj. precursory; prelu-sive, -sory, -dious; pro-emial, introductory, prefatory, prodromous, inaugural, preliminary; precedent etc. (*prior*) 116.

65. Sequel.—N. sequel, suffix, successor; tail, *queue*, train, wake, trail, rear; retinue, suite; appendix, postscript, subscript; epilogue; conclusion; peroration; codicil; continuation, *sequela;* appendage etc. 39; tail -, heel-piece; tag, more last words; *colophon.*

follower, after-glow, -growth, -crop, -taste, -math.

after-part, -piece, -course, -thought, -game; *arriere pensee,* second thoughts.

66. Beginning.—N. beginning, commencement, opening, outset, incipience, inception, inchoation; introduction etc. (*precursor*) 64; *alpha;* initial; foundation; inauguration, *debut, le premier pas,* embarcation, rising of the curtain; zero hour; exordium, curtain raiser; maiden speech; prelude; outbreak, onset, brunt; initiative, move, first move; gambit, narrow -, thin- end of the wedge; fresh start, new departure; forefront.

origin etc. (*cause*) 153; source, rise; bud, germ etc. 153; egg, rudiment; genesis, birth, nativity, cradle, infancy, incunabula; start, starting-point etc. 293; dawn etc. (*morning*) 125.

title-page; head, -ing, caption; van etc. (*front*) 234.

en-trance, -try; inlet, orifice, mouth, chops, lips, porch, portal, portico, *propylon,* door; gate, -way; postern, wicket, threshold, vestibule; skirts, border etc. (*edge*) 231; tee.

first -stage, - blush, — glance, — impression, - sight.

rudiments, elements, outlines, *principia,* grammar, *protasis;* alphabet, ABC.

V. begin, commence, inchoate. rise, arise, originate, institute, conceive, initiate, open, dawn, set in, take its rise, enter upon, start; enter; set out etc. (*depart*) 293; embark in.

usher in; lead -off, — the way; take the -lead, — initiative; inaugurate, head; stand -at the head, — first, — for; lay the foundations etc. (*prepare*) 673; found etc. (*cause*) 153; set -up, — on foot, — agoing, — abroach, — the ball in motion; apply the match to a train; launch, broach; open -up, — the door to; set -about, — to work; make a -beginning, — start; handsel; take the first step, lay the first stone, cut the first turf; break -ground, — the ice, — cover; pass —, cross- the Rubicon; open -fire, — the ball; ventilate, air; undertake etc. 676.

come into -existence, — the world; make one's *début,* take birth; burst forth, break out; spring —, crop- up.

begin -at the beginning, — *ab ovo,* — again, — *de novo;* start afresh, make a fresh start, shuffle the cards, resume, recommence.

Adj. beginning etc. *v.;* initi-al, -atory, -ative; inceptive, introductory, incipient; proemial, inaugural; incho-ate,. -ative; embryonic, rudimental; primogenial; primeval etc. (*old*) 124; rudimentary, aboriginal; natal, nascent.

first, foremost, front, leading, head; maiden.

begun etc. v.; just -begun etc. v.

Adv. at —, in- the beginning etc. *n.;* first, in the first place, *imprimis,* first and foremost; *in limine;* in -the bud, — embryo, - its infancy; from -the beginning, — its birth; *ab -initio, — ovo, — incunabilis,* primarily, originally.

67. End.—N. end, close, termination; desinence, conclusion, *finis, finale,* period, term, *terminus,* last, *omega;* extreme, -tremity; gable -, butt -, fagend; tip, nib, point; tail etc. (*rear*) 235; verge etc. (*edge*) 231; tag, epilogue, peroration; *bonne bouche,* bitter end, tail end; terminal; *apodosis;* appendix.

consummation, *dénouement;* finish etc. (*completion*) 729; fate; doom, -sday; crack of doom, day of Judgment, fall of the curtain, wind-up; goal, destination; limit, stoppage, end all, determination; expiration, expiry; death etc. 360; end of all things; finality; eschatology.

break up, *commencement de la fin,* last stage, turning point; *coup de grâce,* death-blow; knock-out.

V. end, close, finish, terminate, conclude, be all over; expire; die etc. 360; come —, draw- to a -close etc. *n.;* have run its course; run out, pass away.

bring to an -end etc. *n.;* put an end to, make an end of; determine; get through; achieve etc. (*complete*) 729; stop etc. (*make to cease*) 142; shut up shop.

Adj. ending etc. *v.;* final, terminal, definitive, conclusive; crowning etc. (*completing*) 729; last, ultimate; hindermost; rear etc. 235; caudal.

contermin-ate, -ous, -able.

ended etc. *v.;* at an end; settled, decided, over, played out, set at rest.

penultimate; last but -one, — two, etc.

unbegun, uncommenced; fresh.

Adv. finally etc. *adj.;* in fine; at the last; once for all.

68. Middle.—N. middle, midst, mediety; mean etc. 29; medium, middle term; center etc. 222; mid-course etc. 628; *mezzo termine; juste milieu* etc. 628; half-way house, nave, navel, omphalos; nucle-us, -olus.

equidistance, bisection, half-distance; equator, diaphragm, midriff; interjacence etc. 228.

Adj. middle, medial, mesial, mean, mid; middle-, mid-most; middling; mediate; intermediate etc. (*interjacent*) 228; equidistant; central etc. 222; mediterranean, equatorial.

Adv. in the middle; in the thick; mid-, halfway; midships, *in medias res.*

69. Continuity. [Uninterrupted sequence.]—N. continuity; consecu-tion,, -tiveness etc. *adj.;* succession, round, suite, progression, series, train, chain; cat-, concatenation; catena; scale; gradation, course, constant flow, perpetuity.

procession, column; retinue, *cortège,* cavalcade, rank and file, line of battle, array.

pedigree, genealogy, lineage, race etc. 166.

rank, file, line, row, range, tier, string, thread, team; suit; colonnade.

V. follow in —, form- a series etc. *n.;* fall in.

arrange in a -series etc. *n.;* string together, catenate, file, thread, graduate, tabulate.

Adj. continu-ous. -ed; consecutive; progressive, gradual; serial, successive; immediate, unbroken, entire; linear; in a -line, — row etc. *n.;* uninter-rupted, -mitting; unremitting; perennial, evergreen; constant.

Adv. continuously etc. *adj.; seriatim;* in a -line etc. *n.;* in -succession, — turn; running, gradually, step by step; *gradatim,* at a stretch; in -file, — column, — single file, — Indian file.

70. Discontinuity. [Interrupted sequence.]—**N.** discontinuity; disjunction etc. 44; anacoluthon; interruption, break, fracture, flaw, fault, split, crack, cut; gap etc. (*interval*) 198; solution of continuity, *caesura;* broken thread; parenthesis, episode; rhapsody, patchwork; intermission; alternation etc. (*periodicity*) 138; dropping fire.

V. be -discontinuous etc. *adj.;* alternate, intermit.

discontinue, pause, interrupt; intervene; break, — in upon; interpose etc. 228; break —, snap- the thread; disconnect etc. (*disjoin*) 44.

Adj. discontinuous, unsuccessive, broken, interrupted, *décousu;* dis-, un-connected, discrete, disjunctive; fitful etc. (*irregular*) 139; spasmodic, desultory, intermit-ting etc. *v.;* -tent; alternate; recurrent etc. (*periodic*) 138; few and far between.

Adv. at intervals; by -snatches, — jerks, — skips, — catches, — fits and starts; skippingly, *per saltum; longo intervallo.*

71. Term.—**N.** term, rank, station, stage, step; degree etc. 26; scale, remove, grade, link, peg, round —, rung- of the ladder, *status,* position, place, point, mark, *pas,* period, pitch; stand, -ing; footing, range.

V. hold —, occupy —, fall into- a place etc. *n.*

72. Assemblage.—**N.** assemblage; col-lection, location, -ligation; compilation, levy, gathering, ingathering, mobilization, meet, foregathering, muster, *attroupement;* con-course, -flux, -gregation, -tesseration, -vergence etc. 290; meeting, *levée, réunion,* drawing room, at home; conversazione etc. (*social gathering*) 892; assembly, congress, eisteddfod; conven-tion, -ticle; gemote; conclave, etc. (*council*) 696; posse, *posse comitatus;* Noah's ark.

miscellany, *collectanea,* symposium; museum, menagerie, etc. (*store*) 636.

crowd, throng, multitude; flood, rush, deluge; rout, rabble, mob, press, crush, *cohue,* jam, horde, body, tribe; crew, gang, knot, squad, band, party; swarm, shoal, school, covey, flock, herd, drove, kennel; array, bevy, galaxy; *corps,* company, troop, *troupe;* army, force, regiment, etc. (*combatants*) 726; host etc. (*multitude*) 102; populousness.

clan, brotherhood, association etc. (*party*) 712. volley, shower, storm, cloud.

group, cluster, Pleiades, clump, pencil; set, batch, lot, pack; budget, *dossier,* assortment, bunch; parcel; pack-et, -age; bundle, *fasciculus,* fascine, bale; ser-on, oon; faggot, wisp, truss,

tuft; shock, rick, fardel, stack, sheaf, swath, gavel, haycock, stook.

accumulation etc. (*store*) 636; congeries, heap, lump, pile, *rouleau,* tissue, mass, pyramid; drift; snow-ball, -drift; acervation, cumulation; amassment, glom-, agglom-eration; conglobation; conglomeration, -ate; coacervation, coagmentation, aggregation, concentration, congestion, *omnium gatherum, spicilegium,* black hole of Calcutta; quantity etc. (*greatness*) 31.

collector, gatherer; whip, -per in.

V. [be or come together] assemble, collect, muster; meet, unite, join, rejoin; cluster, flock, swarm, surge, stream, herd, crowd, throng, associate; con-gregate, -glomerate, -centrate; center round, *rendezvous,* resort; come —, flock —, get —, pig- together; forgather; huddle; reassemble.

[get or bring together] assemble, muster, mobilize; bring —, get —, put —, draw —, scrape —, lump- together; col-lect, -locate, -ligate; get —, whip- in; gather; hold a meeting; con-vene, -voke, -vocate; rake up, dredge; heap, mass, pile; pack, put up, truss, cram; acervate; ag-glomerate, -gregate; compile; group, aggroup, concentrate, unite; collect —, bring- into a focus; amass, accumulate etc. (*store*) 636; collect in a drag-net; heap Ossa upon Pelion.

Adj. assembled etc. *v.;* closely packed, dense, serried, crowded to suffocation, teeming, swarming, populous; as thick as hops; all of a heap, fasciculated; cumulative.

Phr. the plot thickens.

73. Non-assemblage. Dispersion.—**N.** dispersion; disjunction etc. 44; divergence etc. 291; scattering etc. *v.;* dissemination, broadcasting, diffusion, dissipation, distribution; apportionment etc. 786; spread, respersion, circumfusion, interspersion, spargefaction.

waifs and estrays, flotsam and jetsam, *disjecta membra.*

V. disperse, scatter, sow, disseminate, radiate, diffuse, shed, spread, ted, bestrew, overspread, dispense, disband, disembody, demobilize, dismember, distribute; apportion etc. 786; blow off, let out, dispel, cast forth, draught off; strew, straw, strow; spirtle, cast, sprinkle, shatter; issue, deal out, retail; utter; re-, inter-sperse; set abroach, circumfuse.

turn —, cast- adrift; scatter to the winds; sow broadcast.

spread like wildfire, disperse themselves.

Adj. unassembled etc. (*see* assemble etc. 72); dispersed etc. *v.;* sparse, dispread, broadcast, sporadic, widespread; far-flung; epidemic etc. (*general*) 78; adrift, stray; dishevelled, streaming.

Adv. *sparsim,* here and there, *passim.*

74. Focus. [Place of meeting.]—**N.** focus; point of- convergence etc. 290; corradiation; center etc. 222; gathering-place, resort; haunt; retreat; *venue, rendezvous;* rallying point, head-quarters, home, club; *dépôt* etc. (*store*) 636; tryst, trysting-place; place of -meeting, — resort, — assignation; *point de —, lieu de- réunion;* issue.

V. bring to- a point, — a focus, — an issue; focus.

75. Class.—N. class, category, *categorema*, head, order, section; division, subdivision; department, province, domain, sphere.

kind, sort, genus, .species, variety, branch, family, race, tribe, caste, sept, clan, breed; *clique, coterie*; type, kit, sect, set; assortment; feather, kidney; suit; range; gender, sex, kin.

manner, description, denomination, persuasion, connection, designation. character, stamp; predicament; conviction etc. 484.

similarity etc. 17.

76. Inclusion. [Comprehension under, or reference to a class.]—N. inclusion, admission, incorporation, comprehension, reception.

composition etc. (*inclusion in a compound*) 54.

V. be -included in etc.; come −, fall −, range- under; belong −, pertain- to; range with; merge in.

include, compromise, comprehend, contain, admit, embrace, receive; enclose etc. (*circumscribe*) 229; incorporate, cover, embody, encircle.

reckon −, enumerate −, number- among; refer to; place −, arrange-under, − with; take into account.

Adj. includ-ed; -ing etc. *v.;* inclusive; comprehensive, all-embracing; congen-er, -erous; of the same -class etc. 75.

Phr. *et hoc genus omne*, etc.; *et caetera*.

77. Exclusion.*—N. exclusion etc. 55.

* The same set of words is used to express *Exclusion from a class* and *Exclusion from a compound.* Reference is therefore made to the former at 55. This identity does not occur with regard to *Inclusion*, which therefore constitutes a separate category.

78. Generality.—N. general-ity, -ization; universality; catholic-ity, -ism; miscel-lany, -laneousness; drag-net.

every-one, -body; all hands, all the world and his wife; any body, N or M, all sorts; *tout le monde.*

prevalence, run.

V. be -general etc. *adj.;* prevail, obtain, be going about, stalk abroad.

render -general etc. *adj.;* generalize; spread, broadcast.

Adj. general, usual, current, generic, collective; broad, comprehensive, sweeping; encyclopedical, panoramic, widespread etc. (*dispersed*) 73.

universal; catho-lic, -lical; common, world-wide; e-cumenical; transcendental; prevalent, prevailing, rife, epidemic, besetting; all over, covered with.

every, all; indeterminate, indefinite, unspecified, impersonal.

customary etc. (*habitual*) 613.

Adv. what-ever, -soever; to a man, one and all, without exception.

generally etc. *adj.;* always, for better for worse; in general, generally speaking; speaking generally; for the most part; in the long run etc. (*on an average*) 29.

79. Speciality.—N. speciality, *spécialité;* individ-uality, -uity; particularity, peculairity;

idiocrasy etc. (*tendency*) 176; personality, characteristic, mannerism, idiosyncrasy, attribute specificness etc. *adj.;* singularity etc. (*unconformity*) 83; reading, version, lection; state; *trait;* distinctive feature; technicality; *differentia.*

particulars, details, minutiae, items, counts.

I, self, I myself, *ego*; my-, him-, her-, it-self.

V. specify, particularize, individualize, realize, specialize, designate, differentiate, determine, define, denote, indicate, itemize, detail.

descend to particulars, enter into detail, come to the point.

Adj. special; particular, individual, specific, proper, personal, intimate, original, private, respective, definite, concrete, determinate, especial, certain, esoteric, endemic, partial, party, peculiar, marked, appropriate, several, characteristic, diagnostic, exact, exclusive; singular etc. (*exceptional*) 83; idiomatic; typical, representative, distinctive.

this, that; yon, -der.

Adv. specially etc. *adj.;* in particular, *in propriâ personâ; ad hominem*; for my part.

each, apiece, one by one; severally, respectively, each to each; *seriatim*, in detail, bit by bit; *pro hac vice, − re natâ.*

namely, that is to say, *videlicet*, viz.; to wit.

80. Rule.—N. regularity, uniformity etc. 16; clock-work precision; punctuality etc. (*exactness*) 494; routine etc. (*custom*) 613; formula; system; rut; canon, convention, maxim; rule etc. (*form, regulation*) 697; key-note, standard, model; precedent etc. (*prototype*) 22; conformity etc. 82.

nature, principle; law; order of things; normal −, natural −, ordinary −, model- -state, − condition; standing -dish, − order; normality; Procrustean law; law of the Medes and Persians; hard and fast rule.

Adj. regular, uniform, symmetrical, constant, steady; according to rule etc. (*conformable*) 82; customary etc. 613; orderly etc. 58.

81. Multiformity.—N. multi-, omniformity; variety, diversity; multifariousness etc. *adj.*

Adj. multi-form, -fold, -farious, -generous; multiplex, variform, manifold, many-sided; multiplicate; omni-form, -genous, -farious; polymorphic; protean; heterogeneous, motley, mosaic; epicene, indiscriminate, desultory, irregular, diversified, different, divers; all manner of; of -every description, − all sorts and kinds; *et hoc genus omne;* and what not? *de omnibus rebus et quibusdam aliis.*

82. Conformity.—N. conform-ity, -ance; observance.

naturalization; conventionality etc. (*custom*) 613; agreement etc. 23.

example, instance, specimen, sample, quotation; exemplification, illustration, case in point; object lesson.

conventionalist, formalist, Philistine.

pattern etc. (*prototype*) 22.

V. conform to, − rule; accommodate − adapt- oneself to; rub off corners.

be -regular etc. *adj.;* move in a groove; follow
—, observe —, go by —, bend to —, obey- -rules,
— precedents; comply —, tally —, chime in —,
fall in-with; be -guided, — regulated- by; fall into
a -custom, — usage; follow the -fashion, — multitude; pass muster, do as others do, *hurler aves les
loups;* do at Rome as the Romans do; go —,
swim- with the -stream, — current, — tide; tread
the beaten track etc. (*habit*) 613; rubber-stamp;
keep one in countenance.

exemplify, illustrate, cite, quote, put a case;
produce an- instance etc. *n.*

Adj. conformable to rule, adaptable, compliant, consistent, agreeable; regular etc. 80;
according to -regulation, — rule, — Cocker; *en
règle, selon les règles,* well regulated, orderly;
symmetric etc. 242.

conventional commonplace etc. (*customary*)
613; of -daily, — every day- occurrence; in the
natural order of things; ordinary, common, — or
garden, prosaic, habitual, usual.

in the order of the day; naturalized.

typical, normal, formal; canonical, orthodox,
sound, strict, rigid, positive, uncompromising,
Procrustean; point device.

secundum artem, ship-shape, technical.

exemplary, illustrative, in point.

Adv. conformably etc. *adj.;* by rule; agreeably
to; in -conformity, — accordance, — keeping-
with; according to; consistently with; as usual, *ad
instar, instar omnium; more -solito, — major-
um.*

for the sake of conformity; of —, as a matter
of- course; *pro formâ,* for form's sake, by the
card; according to plan.

invariably etc. (*uniformly*) 16.

for -example, — instance; *exempli gratiâ; e.g.,
inter alia.*

Phr. *cela va sans dire, ex pede Herculem,
noscitur a sociis.*

83. Unconformity.—N. non-conformity etc.
82; un-, dis-conformity; unconventionality, informality, abnormity, anomaly; anomalousness
etc. *adj.;* exception, peculiarity, etc. 79; infraction —, breach —, violation —, infringe-
ment- of -law, — custom, — usage; eccentricity,
bizarrerie, oddity, *je ne sais quoi,* monstrosity,
rarity; freak of Nature.

individuality, idiosyncrasy, singularity,
oritinality, mannerism.

aberration; irregularity; variety; singularity;
exemption; salvo etc. (*qualification*) 469.

nonconformist; nondescript, character,
original, nonsuch, monster, prodigy, wonder,
miracle, curiosity, missing link, flying fish, black
swan, *lusus naturae, rara avis,* queer fish,
mongrel; half-caste, -blood, -breed; *métis,* cross
breed, hybrid, mule, mulatto, sacatra, marabou;
tertium quid, hermaphrodite, gynander, an-
drogyn.

phoenix, chimera, hydra, sphinx, minotaur;
griff-in, -on; centaur; hippogriff, -centaur; sagit-
tary; kraken, cockatrice, wyvern, roc, liver,
dragon, sea-serpent; mermaid; unicorn; Cyclops,
'men whose heads do grown beneath their
shoulders;. Teratolgy.

fish out of water; neither -one thing nor
another, — fish flesh nor fowl nor good red her-

ring; one in a -way, — thousand; out-cast, -law;
Ishmael, pariah; oasis.

V. be -unconformable etc. *adj.;* leave the
beaten -track, — path; infringe —, break —,
violate- a -law, — habit, — usage, — custom;
drive a coach and six through; stretch a point;
have no business there; baffle —, beggar- all description.

Adj. unconformable, exceptional; abnorm-al,
-ous; anomal-ous, -istic; out of -order, — place,
— keeping, — tune, — one's element; irregular,
arbitrary; lawless, informal, aberrant, stray,
wandering, wanton; peculiar, exclusive, unnatural, eccentric, crotchety, egregious; out of
the -beaten track, — common, — common run,
— pale of; misplaced; funny.

un-usual, -accustomed, -customary, -wonted, -
common; rare, singular, *unique,* curious, odd,
extraordinary, strange, monstrous; wonderful
etc. 870; unexpected, unaccountable; *outré,* out
of the way, remarkable, noteworthy; queer,
quaint, nondescript, none such, *sui generis;*
original, unconventional, Bohemian, unfashionable; un-described, -precedented, -paralleled, -
exampled, -heard of, -familiar; fantastic, new-
fangled, grotesque, *bizarre;* outlandish, exotic,
tombé de nues, preternatural; denaturalized.

heterogeneious, heteroclite, amorphous,
mongrel, amphibious, epicene, half-blood,
hybrid; androgyn-ous, -al; unsymmetric etc. 243.

qualified etc. 469.

Adv. unconformably etc. *adj.;* except, unless,
save, barring, beside, without, save and except,
let alone.

however, yet, but.

Int. what -on earth! — in the world!

Phr. never was -seen, — heard, — known- the
like.

84. Number.—N. number, symbol, numeral,
figure, cipher, digit, integer; counter; round
number; formula; function; series.

sum, total, aggregate, difference, complement, subtrahend; product; multipli-cand, -er, -
cator; coefficient, multiple; dividend, divisor,
factor, quotient, sub-multiple, fraction; mixed
number; numerator, denominator; decimal,
circulating decimal, repetend; common measure,
aliquot part; reciprocal; prime number; totitive,
totient.

permutation, combination, variation; election.

ratio, proportion; progression; arithmetical —,
geometrical —, harmonical- progression; percentage.

figurate —, pyramidal —, polygonal- numbers.

power, root, exponent, index, logarithm, antilogarithm; modulus.

differential, integral, fluxion, fluent.

Adj. numeral, complementary, divisible, aliquot, reciprocal, prime, fractional, decimal,
figurate, incommensurable.

proportional, exponential, logarithmic, logo-
metric, differential, fluxional, integral.

positive, negative; rational, irrational; surd,
radical, real, imaginary, impossible.

85. Numeration.—N. numeration, numbering
etc. *v.;* pagination; tale, tally, recension, enumer-

ation, summation, reckoning, computation, supputation; calcu-lation, -lus; algorithm, rhabdology, dactylonomy; measurement etc. 466; statistics.

arithmetic, analysis, algebra, fluxions; differential −, integral −, infinitesimal-calculus; calculus of differences.

[Statistics] dead reckoning, muster, poll, census, capitation, roll-call, recapitulation; account etc. (*list*) 86.

[Operations] notation, addition, subtraction, multiplication, division, proportion, rule of three, practice, equations, extraction of roots, reduction, involution, evolution, approximation, interpolation, differentiation, integration.

[Instruments] abacus, swan-pan, logometer, sliding −, slide- rule, tallies, Napier's bones, calculating −, adding- machine, difference engine; cash register.

arithmetician, calculator, abacist; mathematician, actuary, statistician, surveyor, geodesist.

V. number, count, tell; call −, run- over, take an account of, enumerate, call the roll, muster, poll, recite, recapitulate; sum; sum −, cast- up; tell off, score, cipher, compute, calculate, set a price, reckon, − up, estimate; suppute, add, subtract, multiply, divide, extract roots.

check, prove, demonstrate, balance, audit, overhaul, take stock; affix numbers to, page, foliate, paginate.

amount −, come- to.

Adj. numer-al, -ical; arithmetical, analytic, algebraic, statistical, numerable, computable, calculable; commensur-able, -ate; incommensur-able, -ate.

86. List.—N. list, catalogue, enumeration, inventory, schedule; register etc. (*record*) 551; account; bill, − of costs, syllabus; terrier, tally, file; almanac, calendar, index, table, atlas, contents, card index; rota, ticket; book, ledger; synopsis, *catalogue raisonné; tableau,* scroll, manifest, invoice, bill of lading; prospectus, *programme;* bill of fare, *menu, carte;* score, census, statistics, returns; Red −, Blue −, Domesday- book; *cadaster;* directory, gazetteer, dictionary, glossary, lexicon, thesaurus, gradus.

roll; check −, chequer −, bead- roll, − of honor; muster -roll, − book; roster, panel; cartulary, diptych.

V. list, enrol, schedule, register etc. *n.;* indent, post, docket; matriculate.

Adj. cadastral, listed etc. *v.*

87. Unity.—N. unity; oneness etc. *adj.;* individuality; solitude etc. (*seclusion*) 893; isolation etc. (*disjunction*) 44; unification etc. 48.

one, unit, ace; item; individual; solo, none else, no other, naught beside.

V. be -one, − alone etc. *adj.;* dine with Duke Humphrey.

isolate etc. (*disjoin*) 44.

render one; unite etc. (*join*) 43, (*combine*) 48.

Adj. one, sole, single, solitary, only- begotten; individual, apart, alone; kithless.

un-accompanied, -attended; *solus,* single-handed; singular, odd, unique, unrepeated, azygous, first and last; isolated etc. (*disjoined*) 44; insular; unitary.

lone; lone-ly, -some; desolate, dreary.

in-secable, -severable, -discerptible; compact, irresolvable.

Adv. singly etc. *adj.;* alone, by itself, *per se,* only, apart, in the singular number, in the abstract; one -by one, − at a time; simply; one and a half, *sesqui-.*

Phr. *natura il fece, e poi roppe la stampa.*

88. Accompaniment.—N. accompaniment; appurtenance, adjunct etc. 39; context.

coexistence, concomitance, company, association, companionship; part-, copart-nership; coefficiency.

concomitant, accessory, coefficient; companion, attendant, fellow, associate, consort, spouse, colleague, *fidus Achates;* part-, co-partner; satellite, hanger on, shadow; excort, *entourage,* suite, *cortège;* convoy, follower etc. 65; attribute.

V. accompany, coexist, attend, convoy, chaperon; hang −, wait- on; go hand in hand with; synchronize etc. 120; bear −, keep- company; row in the same boat; bring in its train, associate −, couple- with.

Adj. accompanying etc. *v.;* concomitant, fellow, twin, joint; associated −, coupled- with; accessory, attendant, *obbligato.*

Adv. with, withal; together −, along −, in company- with; hand in hand, side by side; cheek by -jowl, − jole; arm in arm; there-, here-with; and etc. (*addition*) 37.

together, in a body, collectively.

89. Duality.—N. dual-ity, -ism; duplicity; bi-plicity, -formity; span, polarity.

two, deuce, couple, couplet, doublet, brace, pair, cheeks, twins, Castor and Pollux, *gemini,* Siamese twins; fellows; yoke, conjugation, dyad, distich.

V. [unite in pairs] pair, couple, bracket, yoke; conduplicate, mate.

Adj. two, twain; dual, -istic; binary, binomial; twin, biparous; dyadic; conduplicate; duplex etc. 90; *tête-à-tête;* paired; dihedral.

coupled etc. *v.;* conjugate.

both, − the one and the other.

90. Duplication.—N. duplication, doubling etc. *v.;* gemi-, ingemi-nation; reduplication; iteration etc. (*repetition*) 104; renewal.

V. double; re-double, -duplicate; geminate; repeat etc. 104; renew etc. 660; duplicate, copy etc. 21.

Adj. double; doubled etc. *v.;* bicameral, bicapital, bi-fold, -form, -lateral, -farious, - facial; two-fold, -sided, -headed, -edged etc.; duplex; double-faced; twin, duplicate, ingeminate; second; dual etc. 29.

Adv. twice, once more; over again etc. (*repeatedly*) 104; as much again; twofold.

secondly, in the second place, again.

91. Bisection. [Division into two parts.]—N. bi-section, -partition; di-, subdi-chotomy; halving etc. *v.;* dimidiation; *hendiadis.*

bifurcation, forking, branching, furcation, ramification, divarication; fork, prong; fold.

half, moiety.

V. bisect, halve, divide, split, cut in two, cleave, dimidiate, dichotomize, divaricate.

go halves, divide with.

separate, fork, bifurcate; branch -off, — out; ramify.

Adj. bisected etc. v.; cloven, cleft; bipartite, biconjugate, bicuspid, bifid; bifur-cous, -cate, -cated; semi-, demi- hemi-

92. Triality.—N. triality, trinity,* triplicity.

three, triad, triplet, trey, trio, ternion, tri-nomial, leash; tierce; triennium; trefoil, triangle, trident, tripod, triumvirate, troika.

third power, cube.

Adj. three; tri-form, -nal, -nomial; tertiary; triune.

*Trinity is hardly ever used except in a theological sense; see Deity 976.

93. Triplication.—N. tripli-cation, -city; trebleness, trine, trilogy.

V. treble, triple, triplicate, cube.

Adj. treble, triple; tern, -ary; triplex, triplicate, threefold, trilogistic; third; trinal; trihedral.

Adv. three -times, — fold; thrice, in the third place, thirdly; trebly etc. adj.

94. Trisection. [Division into three parts.]—N. tri-section, -partition, -chotomy; third, — part.

V. trisect, divide into three parts, trifurcate.

Adj. trifid; trisected etc. v.; tripartite, -chotomous, -sulcate.

95. Quaternity.—N. quaternity, four, tetrad, quartet, quaternion, square, quadrature, quarter, quadruplet; quadrilateral, quadrangle, quatre-foil; quadriga.

V. reduce to a square, square.

Adj. four; quat-ernary, -ernal; quadratic; quar-tile, quartic, tetractic, tetrad, tetrahedral; quadrennial; quadrivalent.

96. Quadruplication.—N. quadruplication.

V. multiply by four, quadruplicate, bi-quadrate.

Adj. fourfold; quad-ruple, -ruplicate, -rible; quadruplex; fourth.

Adv. four times; in the fourth place, fourthly.

97. Quadrisection. [Division into four parts.]—N. quadri-section, -partition; quarter-ing etc. v.; fourth; quart, -er, -ern; farthing (i.e. fourthing); quarto.

V. quarter, divide into four parts, quadrisect.

Adj. quartered etc. v.; quadri-fid, -partite.

98. Five, etc.—N. five, cinque, quint, quin-cunx, quintuplet, quintet, pentagon, pentameter, Pentateuch; six, half-a-dozen; sextet, hexagon, hexameter, Heptarchy; eight, octet, octa-gon, octave; nine, three times three; ten, decade; eleven; twelve, dozen; thirteen; long —, baker's-dozen.

twenty, score; twenty-four, four and twenty, two dozen; twenty-five, five and twenty, quarter of a hundred; forty, two score; fifty, half a hundred; sixty, three score, sexagenarian; seven-ty, three score and ten, septuagenarian; eighty, four score, octogenarian; ninety, four score and ten, nonagenarian.

hundred, centenary, hecatomb, century; hundredweight, cwt.; one hundred and forty-four, gross; bicentenary, tercentenary etc.

thousand, chiliad; myriad, millennium, ten thousand; lac, lakh, one hundred thousand, plum; million; thousand million, milliard.

billion, trillion etc.

V. centuriate.

Adj. five, quinary, quintuple; fifth; senary, sextuple; sixth; seventh; octuple; eighth; nine-fold, ninth; tenfold, decimal, denary, decuple; tenth; eleventh; duo-denary, -denal; twelfth; in one's 'teens, thirteenth.

vices-, viges-imal; twentieth; twenty-fourth etc. n.

cent-uple, -uplicate, -ennial, -enary, -urial; secular, hundredth; thousandth; millenary etc.

99. Quinquesection, etc.—N. division by -five etc. 98; quinquesection etc.; fifth etc.; decima-tion.

V. decimate, quinquesect.

Adj. quinque-fid, -partite; quinquarticular; octifid; decimal, tenth, tithe, teind; duodecimal, twelfth; sexagesimal, -genary; hundredth, centesimal; millesimal etc.

100. Plurality. [More than one.]—N. plurality; a -number, — certain number; one or two, two or three etc.; a few, several; multitude etc. 102.

Adj. plural, more than one, upwards of, some, certain; not -alone etc. 87.

Adv. et cetera, &c., etc.

Phr. non deficit alter.

100a. Fraction [Less than one.]—N. fraction, fractional part, fragment; part etc. 51.

Adj. fractional, fragmentary, partial.

101. Zero.—N. zero, nothing, naught, nought, duck's egg, goose egg; cipher, none, nobody; not a soul; âme qui vive; absence etc. 187; unsubstantiality etc. 4.

Adj. not -one, — any.

102. Multitude.—N. multitude; numerousness etc. adj.; numer-osity, -ality; multiplicity; profu-sion etc. (plenty) 639; legion, host; great —, large —, round —, enormous- number; a quantity, numbers, array, sight, army, sea, galaxy; scores, peck, bushel, school, shoal, swarm, draft, bevy, cloud, flock, herd, drove, flight, covey, hive, brood, litter, farrow, fry, nest; mob, crowd etc. (assemblage) 72; lots, loads, heaps; all the world and his wife.

[Increase of number] greater number, ma-jority; multiplication, multiple.

V. be -numerous etc. adj.; swarm —, teem —, crawl —, creep -with; crowd, swarm, come thick upon; outnumber, multiply; people; swarm like locusts, — bees.

Adj. many, several, sundry, divers, various,

not a few; a -hundred, — thousand, — myriad, — million, — thousand and one; some -ten or a dozen, — forty or fifty etc.; half a -dozen, — hundred etc.; very —, full —, ever so- many; numer-ous, -ose; profuse, in profusion; manifold, multiplied, multitudinous, multiferous, multiple, multinomial, teeming, crawling, populous, peopled, crowded, thick, studded; galore.

thick coming, many more, more than one can tell, a world of; no end -of, — to; *cum multis aliis*; thick as -hops, — hail; plenty as blackberries; numerous as the -stars in the firmament, — sands on the sea-shore, — hairs on the head; and -what not, — heaven knows what; endless etc. (*infinite*) 105.

Phr. their name is 'Legion.'

103. Fewness.—N. fewness etc. *adj.*; paucity, small number; small quantity etc. 32; scarcity, sparsity; rarity; infrequency etc. 137; handfull; maniple; minority; exiguity.

[Diminution of number] reduction; weeding etc. *v.*; elimination, sarculation, decimation.

V. be -few etc. *adj.*

render -few etc. *adj.*; reduce, diminish the number, weed; eliminate, thin, decimate.

Adj. few; scarce; scant, -y; thin, rare, thinly scattered, few and far between; exiguous; infrequent etc. 137; *rari nantes*; hardly —, scarcely-any; to be counted on one's fingers; reduced etc. *v.*; unrepeated.

Adv. here and there.

104. Repetition.—N. repetition, iteration, reiteration, duplication, ding-dong, alliteration; *epistrophe*; harping, recurrence, succession, run; batto-, tauto-logy; monotony, tautophony; rhythm etc. 138; pleonasm, redundancy, diffuseness.

chimes, repetend, echo, *ritornello*, burden of a song, *refrain*; rehearsal; encore; *réchauffé, rifacimento*, recapitulation.

cuckoo etc. (*imitation*) 19; reverberation etc. 408; drumming etc. (*roll*) 407; renewal etc. (*restoration*) 660.

twice-told tale; old -story, — song, chestnut; second —, new- edition; reprint, new impression; return game, return match, reappearance, reproduction; periodicity etc. 138.

V. repeat, iterate, reiterate, reproduce, parrot, echo, re-echo, drum, harp upon, battologize, hammer, redouble.

recur, revert, return, reappear; renew etc. (*restore*) 660.

rehearse; do —, say- over again; ring the changes on; harp on the same string; din —, drum- in the ear; conjugate in all its moods, tenses and inflexions, begin again, go over the same ground, go the same round, never hear the last of; resume, return to, recapitulate, reword.

Adj. repeated etc. *v.*; repetition-al, -ary; recurrent, -ring; ever recurring, thick coming, frequent, incessant, redundant, pleonastic, tautological.

monotonous, harping, iterative; mocking, chiming; retold; aforesaid, -named; abovementioned, said; habitual etc. 613; another.

Adv. repeatedly, often, again, afresh, anew,

over again, once more; ditto, *encore, de novo, bis, da capo*.

again and again; over and over, — again; many times over; time- and again, — after time; year after year; day by day etc.; many —, several —, a number of- times; many —, full many- a time; times out of number, year in and year out, morning, noon and night; frequently etc. 136.

Phr. *ecce iterum Crispinus, toujours perdrix*, cut and come again; 'tomorrow and tomorrow.'

105. Infinity.—N. infini-ty, -tude, -teness etc. *adj.*; perpetuity etc. 112.

V. be -infinite etc. *adj.*; know —, have- no -limits, — bounds; go on for ever.

Adj. infinite, immense; number-, count-, sum-, measure-less; innumer-, immeasur-, incalcul-, illimit-, intermin-, unfathom-, unapproach-able; exhaustless, inexhaustible, indefinite; without -number, — measure, — limit, — end; incomprehensible; limit-, end-, bound-, termless; un-told, -numbered, -measured, -bounded, -limited; il-limited; perpetual etc. 112.

Adv. infinitely etc. *adj.*; *ad infinitum*.

106. Time.—N. time, duration; period, term, stage, space, span, spell, season; the whole -time, — period; course etc. 109.

intermediate, time, while, *interim*, interval, bit, pendency; inter-vention, -mission, -mittence, -regnum, -lude; respite.

era, epoch, eon, cycle; time of life, age, year, date; decade etc. (*period*) 108; moment, etc. (*instant*) 113; reign etc. 737.

glass —, ravages —, whirligig —, noiseless foot- of time; scythe.

V. continue, last, endure, go on, hold out, remain, stay, persist, abide, run; intervene; elapse etc. 109.

take —, take up —, fill —, occupy- time.

pass —, pass away —, spend —, while away —, consume —, talk against —, kill- time; tide over; use —, employ- time; tarry etc. 110; seize an opportunity etc. 134; waste time etc. (*be inactive*) 683.

Adj. continuing etc. *v.*; on foot; permanent etc. (*durable*) 110.

Adv. while, whilst, during, pending; during the -time, — interval; in the course of; for the time being, day by day; in the time of, when; meantime, -while; in the -meantime, — *interim; ad interim, pendente lite; de die in diem*; from -day to day, — hour to hour etc.; hourly, always; for a -time, — season; till, until, up to, yet; the whole —, all the- time; all along; throughout etc. (*completely*) 52; for good etc. (*diuturnity*) 110.

here-, there-, where-upon; then; *anno, — Domini;* A.D.; *ante Christum;* A.C.; before Christ; B.C.; *anno urbis conditae;* A.U.C.; *anno regni,* A.R.; once upon a time, one fine morning.

Phr. time -runs, — runs against; *tempus fugit.*

107. Neverness.—N. 'neverness;' absence of time, no time; *dies non;* Tib's eve; Greek Kalends.

Adv. never; at no -time, — period; on no occasion, never in all one's born days, nevermore, *sine die.*

108. Period. [Definite duration, or portion of time.]—N. period; second, minute, hour, day, week, sennight, octave, month, moon, quarter, semester, year, *lustrum, quinquennium,* decade, *decennium,* indiction, lifetime, generation, epoch, era, cycle.

century, age, *millennium; annus magnus.*

Adj. horary; hourly, annual etc. (*periodical*) 138.

108a. Contingent Duration.—**Adv.** during - pleasure, — good behavior; *quamdiu se bene gesserit.*

109. Course. [Indefinite duration.]—N. course —, progress —, process —, succession —, lapse —, flow —, flux —, effluxion, stream —, tract —, current —, sweep —, tide —, march —, step —, flight- of time; duration etc. 106.

[Indefinite time] aorist.

V. elapse, lapse, flow, run, proceed, advance, pass; roll —, wear —, press —, drag- on; flit, fly, slip, slide, glide, crawl; run -its course.

out; expire; go —, pass- by; be -past etc. 122.

Adj. elapsing etc. *v.;* aoristic; progressive, transient etc. 111.

Adv. in due -time, — season; in -course, — process, — the fulness- of time; in time.

Phr. *labitur et labetur; truditur dies die; fugaces labuntur anni;* 'tomorrow and tomorrow and tomorrow creeps in this petty pace from day to day.'

110. Diuturnity. [Long duration.]—N. diuturnity; a -long —, length of -time; an age, a century, an eternity, aeons; slowness etc. 275; perpetuity etc. 112; blue moon.

dura-bleness, -bility; persistence, lastingness etc. *adj.;* continuance, assiduity, endurance, standing; permanence etc. (*stability*) 150; survival, -vance; longevity etc. (*age*) 128; distance of time.

protraction —, prolongation —, extension- of time; delay etc. (*lateness*) 133.

V. last, endure, stand, remain, abide, continue, brave a thousand years.

tarry etc. (*be late*) 133; drag -on, — its slow length along, — a lengthening chain; protract, prolong; spin —, eke —, draw —, lengthen- out; temporize; gain —, make —, talk against- time.

out-last, -live; survive; live to fight again.

Adj. durable; perdurable; lasting etc. *v.;* of long -duration, — standing; permanent, chronic, long-standing; intransi-ent, -tive; intransmutable, persistent; life-, live-long; longeval, long-lived, macrobiotic, diuturnal, sempervirent, evergreen, perennial; unin-, ter-, unremitting; perpetual etc. 112.

lingering, protracted, prolonged, spun out etc. *v.;* long-pending, -winded; slow etc. 275.

Adv. long; for -a long time, — an age, — ages, — ever so long, — many a long day; long ago etc. (*in a past time*) 122; *longo intervallo.*

all the -day long, — year round; the livelong day, as the day is long, morning, noon and night; hour after hour, day after day, etc.; for good; permanently etc. *adj.*

111. Transientness. [Short duration.]—N. transientness etc. *adj.;* evanescence, impermanence, fugacity, transitoriness, volatility, caducity, mortality, span; flash in the pan, nine days' wonder, bubble, May-fly; spurt; temporary arrangement, interregnum.

velocity etc. 274; suddenness etc. 113; changeableness etc. 149.

V. be -transient etc. *adj.;* flit, pass away, fly, gallop, vanish, fade, fleet, melt away, evaporate; pass away like a -cloud, — summer cloud, — shadow, — dream.

Adj. transi-ent, -tory, -tive; passing, evanescent, fleeting; flying etc. *v.;* fug-acious, -itive; shifting, slippery; spasmodic.

tempor-al, -ary; provis-ional, -ory; cursory, short-lived, ephemeral, deciduous; perishable, mortal, precarious; impermanent.

brief, quick, brisk; cometary, meteoric, extemporaneous, summary; pressed for time etc. (*haste*) 684; sudden, momentary etc. (*instantaneous*) 113.

Adv. temporarily etc. *adj.; pro tempore;* for - the moment, — a time; awhile, *en passant, in transitu;* in a short time; soon etc. (*early*) 132; briefly etc. *adj.;* at short notice; on the -point, — eve -of; *in articulo;* between cup and lip.

Phr. one's days are numbered; the time is up; her to-day and gone tomorrow; *non semper erit aestas; eheu! fugaces labuntur anni; sic transit gloria mundi.*

112. Perpetuity. [Endless duration.]—N. perpetuity, eternity, timelessness; everness, aye, sempiternity, immortality, athanasia; everlastingness etc. *adj.;* perpetuation; infinite duration.

V. last —, endure —, go on- for ever; have no end.

eternize, eternify, perpetuate, immortalize.

Adj. perpetual, eternal, eterne; everlasting, -living, -flowing; continual, constant, sempiternal; co-eternal; endless, unending; ceaseless, incessant, uninterrupted, indesinent, unceasing; interminable, having no end; unfading, evergreen, amaranthine; neverending, -dying, -fading; deathless, immortal, undying, imperishable.

Adv. perpetually etc. *adj.;* always, ever, evermore, aye; for -ever, — aye, — evermore, — ever and a day, —, ever and ever; in all ages, from age to age; without end; world —, time- without end; *in saecula saeculorum;* to the -end of time, — crack of doom, — 'last syllable of recorded time;' till doomsday; constantly etc. (*very frequently*) 136.

Phr. *esto perpetuum; labitur et labetur in omne volubilis aevum.*

113. Instantaneity. [Point of time.]—N. instantane-ity, -ousness; sudden-, abrupt-ness.

moment, instant, second, minute, twinkling, trice, flash, breath, crack, jiffy, *coup,* burst, flash of lightning, stroke of time.

epoch, time; time of -day, — night; hour, minute; very -minute etc., — time, — hours; present —, right —, true —, exact —, correct-time.

V. be -instantaneous etc. *adj.,* twinkle, flash.

Adj. instantaneous, momentary, extempore, sudden, instant, abrupt; subitaneous, hasty, quick as- thought,* — lightning, — a flash; rapid as electricity.

Adv. instantaneously etc. *adj.*; in — in less than no time; *presto, subito, instanter,* suddenly, at a stroke, like- a shot, — greased lightning; in a trice, in a moment etc. *n.*; eftsoons, in the twinkling of - ar eye, — a bed post; at one jump, in the same breath, *per saltum, uno saltu;* at — , all at- once; in one's tracks; plump, slap; 'at one fell swoop;' at the same -instant etc. *n.*; immediately etc. (*early*) 132; *ex tempore,* on the -spot, — spur of the moment, — dot; just then, slap- dash etc. (*haste*) 684; before you could -turn round, — say -knife, — Jack Robinson.

Phr. touch and go; no sooner said than done.
*See note on 264.

114. Chronometry. [Estimation, measurement, and record of time.]—N. chrono-, horo-metry, -logy; date, epoch; style, era.

almanac, calendar, ephemeris; register, -try; chronicle, annals, journal, diary, chronogram.

[Instruments for the measurement of time] clock, watch; chrono-meter, -scope, -graph; repeater, alarum; time-keeper, -piece; dial, sun-dial, *gnomon, pendule,* horologe, pendulum, hourglass, water clock, clepsydra.

mean — , Greenwich — , solar — , sidereal — , local — , summer- time; daylight saving.

chrono-grapher, -loger, -logist; annalist.

V. fix — , mark- the time; date, register, chronicle; measure — , beat — , mark- time; bear date.

Adj. chrono-logical, -metrical, -grammatical; isochronal.

Adv. o'clock; *a.m., p.m.*

115. Anachronism. [False estimate of time.]—N. ana-, meta-, para-, prochronism; *prolepsis,* misdate; anticipation, antichronism.

disregard — , neglect — , oblivion- of time.

intempestivity etc. 135.

V. mis-, ante-, post-, over-date; anticipate; take no note of time.

Adj. misdated etc. *v.;* undated; overdue; out of date; anachronous etc. *n.*

116. Priority.—N. priority, antecedence, anteriority, pre-existence, - precedence etc. 62; precession etc. 280; precursor etc. 64; the past etc. 122; premises.

V. precede, come before; forerun; antecede, go before etc. (*lead*) 280; pre-exist; dawn; premise, presage etc. 511.

be -beforehand etc. (*be early*) 132; steal a march upon, anticipate, forestall; have — , gain- the start.

Adj. prior, previous; preced-ing, -ent; anterior, antecedent; pre-existing, -existent; foresighted; former, foregoing; afore — , before-, above-mentioned; aforesaid, said; introductory etc. (*precursory*) 64; pre-war.

Adv. before, prior to; earlier; previously etc. *adj.;* afore, ere, theretofore, erewhile, ere — , before- -then, — now; erewhile, already, yet, beforehand; aforetime; on the eve of, in anticipation.

117. Posteriority.—N. posteriority; succession, sequence; following etc. 281; subsequence,

supervention; futurity etc. 121; successor; sequel etc. 65; remainder, reversion.

V. follow etc. 281 —, come — , go- after; ensue, result; succeed, supervene; step into the shoes of.

Adj. subsequent, posterior, following, after, later, succeeding, postliminious, postnate; successive etc. 63; postdiluvial, -an; *puisné;* posthumous; post-war, future etc. 121.

Adv. subsequently, after, afterwards, since, later; at a -subsequent, — later- period; next, in the sequel, close upon, thereafter, thereupon, upon which, eftsoons; from that -time, — moment; after a -while, — time; in process of time.

postcenal, postcibal, postprandial, after-dinner.

118. The Present Time.—N. the present -time, — day, — moment, — juncture, — occasion; the times, existing time, time being; twentieth century; nonce, crisis, epoch, day, hour.

age, time of life.

Adj. present, actual, instant, current, latest, existing, that is.

Adv. at this -time, — moment etc. 113; at the - present time etc. *n.;* now, at present.

at this time of day, to-day, now-adays; already; even — , but — , just-now; on the present occasion; for the -time being, — nonce; *pro hâc vice;* on the -nail, — spot; on the spur of the -moment, — occasion.

until now; to -this, — the present day.

119. Different Time. [Time different from the present.]—N. different — , other- time.

[Indefinite time] aorist.

Adj. aoristic.

Adv. at that — , at which- -time, — moment, — instant; then, on that occasion, upon.

when; when-ever, -soever; upon which, on which occasion; at -another, — a different, — some other, — any - time; at various times; some — , one- -of these days, — fine morning, — day; sooner or later; some time or other; once upon a time, once.

120. Synchronism.—N. synchronism; coexistence, coincidence; simultaneousness etc. *adj.;* concurrence, concomitance, unity of time, interim.

[Having equal times] isochronism, syntony.

contemporary, coetanian.

V. coexist, concur, accompany, go hand in hand, keep pace with; synchronize, isochronize.

Adj. synchron-ous, -al, -ical, -istical; simultaneous, coexisting, coincident, concomitant, concurrent; coev-al, -ous; contempora-ry, - neous; coetaneous; coterminous, coeternal; isochronous.

Adv. at the same time; simultaneously etc. *adj.;* together, in concert, during the same time; in the same breath; *pari passu;* in the interim.

at the -very moment etc. 113; just as, as soon as; meanwhile etc. (*while*) 106.

121. Futurity. [Prospective time.]—N. futurity, -ition; future, hereafter, time to come; approaching — , coming — , after- -time, — age, — days, — hours, — years, — ages, — life;

morrow, to-morrow, bv and bv; millennium, doomsday, day of judgment, crack of doom, remote future.

approach of time, advent, time drawing on, womb of time; destiny etc. 152; eventuality.

heritage, heirs, posterity, descendants.

prospect etc. (*expectation*) 507; foresight etc. 510.

V. look forwards; anticipate etc. (*expect*) 507, (*foresee*) 510; forestall etc. (*be early*) 132.

come –, draw- on; draw near; approach, await, threaten; impend etc. (*be destined*) 152.

Adj. future, to come; coming etc. (*impending*) 152; next, near; near –, close- at hand; eventual, ulterior; expectant, prospective, in prospect etc. (*expectation*) 507.

Adv. prospectively, hereafter, on the knees of the gods, in future; to-morrow, the day after to-morrow; in -course, – process, – the fulness- of time; eventually, ultimately, sooner or later; *proximo; paulo post futurum;* in after time; one of these days; after a -time, – while.

from this time; hence-forth, -forwards; thence; thence-forth, -forward; whereupon, upon which.

soon etc. (*early*) 132; on the -eve, – point, – brink- of; about to; close upon.

122. Preterition. [Retrospective time.]—N. preterition, priority etc. 116; the past, past time; days –, times- -of yore, – of old, – past, – gone by; bygone days, good old days; old –, ancient –, former -times; fore time; yesterdays; the olden –, good old- time; auld lang syne; eld.

antiquity, antiqueness, *status quo;* time immemorial; distance of time; remote -age, – time; ancient history; remote past; rust of antiquity; ancientness.

pale-ontology, -ography, -ology; palaetiology,* archaeology; archaism, antiquarianism, mediaevalism, pre- Raphaelitism; retrospection, looking back, memory etc. 505.

laudator temporis acti; mediaevalist, pre-Raphaelite; antiqu-ary, -arian; archaeologist etc.; Oldbuck, Dryasdust.

ancestry etc. (*paternity*) 166.

V. be -past etc. *adj.;* have -expired etc. *adj.;* – run its course, – had its day; pass; pass –, go- -by, – away, – off; lapse, blow over.

look –, trace –, cast the eyes- back; exhume.

Adj. past, gone, gone by, over, passed away, bygone, foregone; elapsed, lapsed, preterlapsed, expired, no more, run out, blown over, that has been, whilom, extinct, never to return, exploded, forgotten, irrecoverable; obsolete etc. (*old*) 124; extinct as the dodo.

former, pristine, *quondam, ci-devant,* late; ancestral.

foregoing; last, latter; recent, overnight; past, preterite, preter-perfect, -pluperfect, past perfect.

looking back etc. *v.;* retro-spective, -active; archaelogical etc. *n.*

Adv. formerly; of -old, –yore; erst, whilom, erewhile; time was, ago, over; in -the olden time etc. *n.;* anciently, long -ago, – since; a long -while, – time- ago; years –, ages-ago; some time -ago, – since, – back.

yesterday, the day before yesterday; last -year, – season, – month etc.; *ultimo,* lately etc. (*newly*) 123.

retrospectively; ere –, before –, till- now; hitherto, heretofore; no longer; once, – upon a time; from time immemorial; in the memory of man; time out of mind; already, yet, up to this time; *ex post facto.*

Phr. time was; the time -has, – hath- been.

Whewell.

123. Newness.—N. newness etc. *adj.;* neologism, neoterism; novelty, recency; immaturity; youth etc. 127; gloss of novelty.

innovation; renovation etc. (*restoration*) 660.

modernist, neologist, neoteric.

modernism, modernity; mushroom; latest fashion, *dernier cri.*

upstart, *parvenu, nouveau riche.*

V. renew etc. (*restore*) 660; modernize.

Adj. new, novel, recent, fresh, green; young etc. 127; evergreen; raw, immature; virgin; untried, -handseled, -used, -trodden, -beaten; fledgling.

late, modern, neoteric; new-born, -fashioned, -fangled, -fledged; of yesterday; just out, brand –; span-new, up to date, topical; vernal, renovated; innovatory.

fresh as -a rose, – a daisy, – paint; spick and span.

Adv. newly etc. *adj.;* afresh, anew, lately, just now, only yesterday, the other day; latterly, of late.

not long –, a short time- ago.

124. Oldness.—N. oldness etc. *adj.;* age, antiquity; cobwebs of antiquity.

maturity, ripeness; decline, decay; senility etc. 128.

seniority, eldership, primogeniture.

archaism etc. (*the past*) 122; thing –, relic- of the past; megatherium.

tradition, prescription, custom, folklore, immemorial usage, common law.

V. be -old etc. *adj.;* have -had, – seen- its day; become -old etc. *adj.;* age, fade.

Adj. old, olden, ancient, antique; of long standing, time-honored, venerable; eld-er, -est; first-born.

prime; prim-itive, -eval, -igenous; primordi-al, -nate; aboriginal etc. (*beginning*) 66; diluvian, antediluvian; pre-historic; patriarchal, preadamite; paleocrystic; fossil, paleozoic, preglacial, ante-mundane; archaic, classic, mediaeval, pre-Raphaelite, ancestral, black-letter.

immemorial, traditional, prescriptive, customary, whereof the memory of man runneth not to the contrary; inveterate, rooted.

antiquated, of other times, rococo, of the old school, after-age, obsolete, fusty, moth-eaten; out of -date, – fashion; stale, old-fashioned, behind the -age, – times; exploded; gone out, – by; *passé,* outworn, run out; disused; senile etc. 128; time-worn; crumbling etc. (*deteriorated*) 659; second-hand.

old as -the hills, – Methuselah, – Adam, – history.

Adv. since the -world was made, – year one, – days of Methuselah.

125. Morning. [Noon.]—N. morning, morn, matins, forenoon, *a.m.,* prime, dawn, daybreak, daylight, sun-up, peep –, break- of day; aurora,

Eos; first blush —, prime- of the morning; twilight, crepuscule, sunrise, cockcrow.

spring; vernal equinox.

noon; mid-, noon-day; noontide, meridian, prime.

summer, midsummer; summer solstice.

Adj. matin, matutinal; vernal, aestival.

Adv. at -sunrise etc. *n.*; with the lark, when the morning dawns.

126. Evening. [Midnight.]—**N.** evening, eve; decline —, fall —, close- of day; eventide, evensong, vespers; candlelight; nightfall, curfew, dusk, twilight, blind man's holiday; eleventh hour; sun-set, -down; going down of the sun, cock-shut, dewy eve, gloaming, bed-time.

afternoon, *post meridiem, p.m.*

autumn; fall, — of the leaf; autumnal equinox, Indian summer, harvest-time.

midnight; dead —, witching time- of night; winter, — solstice.

Adj. vespertine, autumnal, nocturnal, wintry, brumal, hiemal.

127. Youth.—**N.** youth; juven- -ility, -escence; juniority; infancy; baby-, child-, boy-, girl-, youth-hood; *incunabula;* minority, immaturity, nonage, teens, tender age, bloom.

cradle, nursery, leading-strings, pupilage, puberty, *pucelage.*

prime —, flower —, spring-tide —, seedtime —, golden season - of life; heyday of youth, school days; rising generation, younger generation.

Adj. young, youthful, juvenile, green, callow, budding, sappy, *puisné,* beardless, unfledged, unripe, under age, in one's teens; *in statu pupillari;* younger, junior.

128. Age.—**N.** age; oldness etc. *adj.;* old —, advanced- age; sen-ility, -escence; years, anility, grey hairs, climacteric, grand climacteric, declining years, decrepitude, hoary age, caducity; superannuation; second childhood, -ishness; dotage; vale of years, decline of life, 'sear and yellow leaf;' three-score years and ten; green old age, ripe old age; longevity; time of life.

seniority, eldership; elders etc. (*veteran*) 130; firstling; *doyen,* dean, father; primogeniture; nostology.

V. be -aged etc. *adj.;* grow —, get- old etc. *adj.;* age; decline, wane.

Adj. aged; old etc. 124; elderly, senile; matronly, anile; in years; ripe, mellow, run to seed, declining, waning, past one's prime; grey, -headed; hoar, -y; venerable, time-worn, antiquated, *passé,* effete, doddering, decrepit, superannuated; advanced in -life, — years; stricken in years; wrinkled, marked with the crow's foot; having one foot in the grave; doting etc. (*imbecile*) 499.

old-, eld-er, -est; senior; first-born.

turned of, years old; of a certain age, no chicken, old as Methuselah; gerontic; ancestral; patriarchal etc. (*ancient*) 124.

129. Infant.—**N.** infant, babe, baby; nurse-, suck-, year-, wean-ling; *papoose, bambino.*

child, bairn, little- one, — tot, — mite, chick, brat, chit, pickaninny, kid, urchin; bant-, bratling; elf.

youth, boy, lad, slip, sprig, stripling, youngster, cub, unlicked cub, younker, callant, whipster, whipper-snapper, schoolboy, hobbledehoy, hopeful, cadet, minor, master.

scion; sap-, seed-ling; tendril, olive branch, nestling, chicken, duckling; larva, caterpillar, chrysalis, cocoon; tadpole, whelp, cub, pullet, fry, callow; codlin, -g; *foetus,* calf, colt, pup, foal, kitten; lamb, -kin.

girl; lass, -ie; wench, miss, damsel, *demoiselle,* damozel; maid, -en; virgin; nymph; colleen; minx, baggage, -school-girl; tomboy, flapper, hoyden.

Adj. infant-ine, -ile; puerile; boy-, girl-, child-, baby-, kitten-ish; baby; new-born, unfledged, new-fledged, callow.

in -the cradle, — swaddling clothes, — long clothes, — arms, — leading strings; at the breast; in one's teens; young etc. 127.

130. Veteran.—**N.** veteran, old man, seer, patriarch, greybeard, dugout, grand-father, -sire; grandam, beldam; gaffer, gammer; hag, crone; pantaloon; sexage-, octoge-, nonage-, cente-narian; old stager; dotard etc. 501.

preadamite, Methuselah, Nestor, Rip van Winkle, old Parr; elders; forefathers etc. (*paternity*) 166.

131. Adolescence.—**N.** adolescence, pubescence, majority; adultness etc. *adj.;* manhood, virility, maturity; flower of age; prime —, meridian- of life.

man etc. 373; woman etc. 374; adult, no chicken.

V. come -of age, — to man's estate, — to years of discretion; attain majority; assume the *toga virilis;* have -cut one's eye-teeth, — sown one's wild oats, settle down.

Adj. adolescent, pubescent, of age; of -full, — ripe- age; out of one's teens, grown up, mature, full- blown, — grown, in one's prime, in full bloom, manly, virile, adult; womanly, matronly; marriageable, nubile.

132. Earliness.—**N.** earliness etc. *adj.;* morning etc. 125.

punctuality; promptitude etc. (*activity*) 682; haste etc. (*velocity*) 274; suddenness etc. (*instantaneity*) 113.

prematurity, precocity, precipitation, anticipation; prevenience, a stitch in time.

V. be -early etc. *adj.;* — beforehand etc. *adv.;* keep time, take time by the forelock, anticipate, forestall; have —, gain- the start; steal a march upon; gain time, draw on futurity; bespeak, secure, engage, pre-engage.

accelerate; expedite etc. (*quicken*) 274; make haste etc. (*hurry*) 684.

Adj. early, prime, timely, in time, punctual, forward; prompt etc. (*active*) 682; summary.

premature, precipitate, precocious; prevenient, anticipatory; rathe.

sudden etc. (*instantaneous*) 113; unexpected etc. 508; impending, imminent; near, — at hand; immediate.

Adv. early, soon, anon, betimes, rathe; eft, -soons; ere —, before- long; punctually etc. *adj.;* to the minute; in time; in -good, — military, — pudding, — due- time; time enough.

beforehand; prematurely etc. *adj.;* precipitately etc. (*hastily*) 684; too soon; before -its, — one's- time; in anticipation; unexpectedly etc. 508.

suddenly etc. (*instantaneously*) 113; before one can say 'Jack Robinson,' at short notice, extempore; on the spur of the -moment, — occasion; at once; on the -spot, — instant; at sight; off —, out of- hand; *à vue d'oeil;* straight, -way, -forth; forthwith, incontinently, summarily, instanter, immediately, briefly, shortly, quickly, speedily, apace, before the ink is dry, almost immediately, presently, at the first opportunity, in no long time, by and by, in a while, directly.

Phr. touch and go, no sooner said than done.

133. Lateness.—N. lateness etc. *adj.;* tardiness etc. (*slowness*) 275.

de-lay, -lation; cunctation, procrastination; detention; deferring etc. *v.;* filibuster, postponement, adjournment, prorogation, retardation, respite, reprieve, stay; protraction, prolongation, moratorium; contango; demurrage; remand; Fabian policy, *médecine expectante,* chancery suit; leeway; high time.

V. be -late etc. *adj.;* tarry, wait, stay, bide, take time; dawdle etc. (*be inactive*) 683; linger, loiter, saunter, lag behind; bide —, take- one's time; hang -about, — around, — back, — in the balance; gain time; hang fire; stand —, lie-over.

put off, defer, delay, lay over, suspend; shift —, stave- off; waive, retard, remand, postpone, adjourn; procrastinate; dally; prolong, protract; spin —, draw —, lengthen- out; prorogue; keep back; tide over; push —, drive- to the last; let the matter stand over; reserve etc. (*store*) 636; temporize; consult one's pillow, sleep upon it.

shelve, table, lay on the table.

lose an opportunity etc. 135; be kept waiting, dance attendance; kick —, cool- one's heels; *faire antichambre;* wait impatiently; await etc. (*expect*) 507; sit up, — at night.

Adj. late, tardy, slow, behindhand, belated, postliminious, posthumous, backward, unpunctual; dilatory etc. (*slow*), overdue 275; delayed etc. *v.;* in abeyance.

Adv. late; late-, back-ward; late in the day; at -sunset, — the eleventh hour, — length, — last, — long; ultimately; after —, behind- time; too late; too late for etc. 135.

slowly, leisurely, deliberately, at one's leisure; *ex post facto; sine die.*

Phr. *nonum prematur in annum.*

134. Occasion.—N. occasion, opportunity, opening, room, scope, field; suitable —, proper- -time, — season; high time; opportuneness etc. *adj.;* tempestivity.

crisis, turn, juncture, emergency, conjuncture; turning point; given time.

nick of time; golden —, well-timed —, fine —, favorable- opportunity; clear stage, fair field; *mollia tempora; fata Morgana;* spare time etc. (*leisure*) 685.

V. seize etc. (*take*) 789 —, use etc. 677 —, give etc. 784- an -opportunity, — occasion; improve the occasion.

suit the occasion etc. (*be expedient*) 646.

strike the iron while it is hot, *battre le fer sur l'enclume,* make hay while the sun shines, take time by the forelock, *prendre la balle au bond.*

Adj. opportune, timely, well-timed, timeous, timeful, seasonable.

providential, lucky, fortunate, happy, favorable, propitious, auspicious, critical; suitable etc. 23; *obiter dicta.*

Adv. opportunely etc. *adj. ;* in -proper, — due- -time, — course, — season; for the nonce; in the -nick, — fulness- of time; all in good time; just in time, at the eleventh hour, now or never.

by the -way, — by; *en passant, à propos; pro re natâ,* — *hac vice; par parenthèse,* parenthetically, by way of parenthesis; while -speaking of, — on this subject; *ex tempore;* on the spur of the -moment, — occasion; on the spot etc. (*early*) 132.

Phr. *carpe diem; occasionem cognosce;* one's hour is come, the time is up; that reminds me.

135. Intempestivity.—N. intempestivity; unseasonableness; unsuitable —, improper-time; unreasonableness etc. *adj.;* evil hour; *contretemps;* intrusion; anachronism etc. 115.

V. be -ill timed etc. *adj.;* mistime, intrude, come amiss, break in upon; have other fish to fry; be -busy, — engaged, — tied up, — occupied.

lose —, throw away —, waste —, neglect etc. 460- an opportunity; allow —, suffer- the -opportunity, — occasion- to -pass, — slip, — go by, — escape, — lapse; waste time etc. (*be inactive*) 683; let slip through the fingers, lock the stable door when the steed is stolen.

Adj. ill-, mis-timed; untimely, intrusive, unseasonable; out of -date, — season; inopportune, timeless, untoward, *mal à propos,* unlucky, inauspicious, unpropitious, unfortunate, unfavorable; unsuited etc. 24; inexpedient etc. 647.

unpunctual etc. (*late*) 133; too late for; premature etc. (*early*) 132; too soon for; wise after the event.

Adv. inopportunely etc. *adj.;* as ill luck would have it, in an evil hour, the time having gone by, a day after the fair.

Phr. after meat mustard, after death the doctor.

136. Frequency.—N. frequency, oftness; repetition, etc. 104.

V. recur etc. 104; do nothing but; keep, — on.

Adj. frequent, many times, not rare, thickcoming, incessant, perpetual, continual, constant, recurrent, repeated etc. 104; habitual etc. 613; hourly, etc. 138.

Adv. often, often to be met with, oft; oft-, often-times; frequently; repeatedly etc. 104; unseldom, not unfrequently; in -quick, — rapid- succession; many a time and oft; daily, hourly etc.; every -day, — hour, — moment etc.

perpetually, continually, constantly, incessantly, without ceasing, at all times, daily and hourly, night and day, day and night, day after day, morning, noon and night, ever and anon.

most often; commonly etc. (*habitually*) 613.

sometimes, occasionally, at times, now and then, from time to time, there being times when, *toties quoties*, often enough, again and again etc. 104.

137. Infrequency. —N. infrequency, infrequence, rareness, rarity; fewness etc. 103; seldomness, uncommonness.

V. be -rare etc. *adj.*

Adj. un-, in-frequent; uncommon, sporadic, rare, — as a blue diamond; few etc. 103; scarce; almost unheard of, unprecedented, which has not occurred within the memory of the oldest inhabitant, not within one's previous experience.

Adv. seldom, rarely, scarcely, hardly; not often, unfrequently, infrequently, unoften; scarcely —, hardly- ever; once in a blue moon.

once; once -for all, — in a way; *pro hac vice;* like angels' visits, few and far between.

138. Regularity of recurrence. **Periodicity.**—N. periodicity, intermittence; beat; oscillation etc. 314; pulse, pulsation; rhythm; alternation, -nateness, -nativeness, -nity.

bout, round, revolution, rotation, turn.

anniversary, birthday, jubilee, centenary, bi-, ter-centenary.

[Regularity of return] rota, cycle, period, stated time, routine; days of the week; Sunday, Monday etc.; months of the year; January etc.; feast, fast, saint's day etc.; Christmas, Easter, New Year's Day etc. 998; quarter-, Lady-, Midsummer-, Michaelmas-day; May Day, the King's Birthday; leap year, seasons.

punctuality, regularity, steadiness.

V. recur in regular -order, — succession; return, revolve, rotate; come -again, — in its turn; come round, — again; beat, pulsate; alternate; intermit.

Adj. periodic, -al; serial, recurrent, cyclic-, -al, rhythmic-, -al, even; recurring etc. *V.;* inter-, remittent; alternate, every other.

hourly; diurnal, daily; quotidian, tertian, weekly; hebdomad-al, -ary; bi-weekly, fortnightly; monthly, menstrual, catamenial; yearly, annual; biennial, triennial, etc.; bissextile; centennial, secular; paschal, lenten, etc.

regular, steady, punctual, constant, methodical, regular as clockwork.

Adv. periodically etc. *adj.;* at -regular intervals, — stated times; at -fixed, — established-periods; punctually etc. *adj.; de die in diem;* from day to day, day by day.

by turns, in -turn, — rotation; alternately, every other day, off and on, ride and tie, round and round.

139. Irregularity of recurrence.—N. irregularity, uncertainty, unpunctuality; fitfulness etc. *adj.*

Adj. irregular, uneven, uncertain, unpunctual, capricious, erratic, desultory, fitful, flickering; rambling, rhapsodical; spasmodic, unsystematic, unequal, variable, halting.

Adv. irregularly etc. *adj.;* by fits and starts etc. (*discontinuously*) 70.

140. Change. [Difference at different times.]—N. change, alteration, mutation, permutation, variation, modification, modulation, inflexion, mood, qualification, innovation, *metastasis*, deviation, shift, turn; diversion; break.

transformation, transfiguration; metamorphosis; metabolism; transmutation; transsubstantiation; metagenesis, transanimation, transmigration, metempsychosis; version, metathesis, transmogrification; catalysis; *avatar*; alterative.

conversion etc. (*gradual change*) 144; revolution etc. (*sudden or radical change*) 146; inversion etc. (*reversal*) 218; displacement etc. 185; transference etc. 270.

changeableness etc. 149; tergiversation etc. (*change of mind*) 607.

V. change, alter, vary, wax and wane; modulate, diversify, qualify, tamper with; turn, shift, veer, jibe, tack, chop, shuffle, swerve, dodge, warp, deviate, turn aside, evert, intervert; pass to, take a turn, turn the corner, resume.

work a change, modify, vamp, revamp, superinduce; trans-form, —mute, -ume, -figure etc. *n.;* metamorphose, ring the changes; convert, resolve; revolutionize; chop and change; patch, re-shape.

innovate, introduce new blood, shuffle the cards, spin the wheel; give a -turn, — color- to; influence, turn the scale; shift the scene, turn over a new leaf.

recast etc. 146; reverse etc. 218; disturb etc. 61; convert into etc. 144.

Adj. changed etc. *v.;* new-fangled; changeable etc. 149; transitional; modifiable; alterative.

Adv. *mutatis mutandis.*

Int. *quantum mutatus!*

Phr. 'a change came o'er the spirit of my dream;' *nous avons changé tout cela; tempora mutantur et nos mutamur in illis; non sum qualis eram.*

141. Permanence. [Absence of change.]—N. stability etc. 150; quiescence etc. 265; obstinacy etc. 606.

permanence, -cy, persistence, fixity, fixity of purpose, endurance, durability; standing, *status quo;* maintenance, preservation, conservation; conservatism; *laissez-faire;* law of the Medes and Persians; standing dish.

V. let -alone, — be; persist, remain, stay, tarry, rest; hold, — on; last, endure, bide, abide, aby, dwell, maintain, keep; stand, — still, — fast; subsist, live, outlive, survive; hold —, keep- one's ground, — footing; hold good.

Adj. stable etc. 150; persisting etc. *v.;* permanent; established, fixed; durable; unchanged etc. (change etc. 140); unrenewed; intact, inviolate; persistent; monotonous, uncheckered; unfailing.

un-destroyed, -repealed, -suppressed; conservative, *qualis ab incepto;* prescriptive etc. (*old*) 124; stationary etc. 265.

Adv. *in statu quo;* for good, finally; at a stand, -still; *uti possidetis;* without a shadow of turning.

Phr. as you were!; *j'y suis j'y reste; esto perpetua; nolumus leges Angliae mutari;* let sleeping dogs lie.

142. Cessation. [Change from action to

rest.]—N. cessation, discontinuance, desistance, desinence.

inter-, re-mission; sus-pense, -pension, interruption, hitch; hartal; stop; stopping etc. *v.*; closure, stoppage, halt; arrival etc. 292.

pause, rest, lull, respite, truce, armistice, drop; interregnum, abeyance.

closure etc. 261.

dead -stop, — stand, — lock; checkmate; comma, colon, semicolon, period, full stop; end etc. 67; death etc. 360; *caesura*.

V. cease, discontinue, desist, stay; break —, leave- off; hold, stop, pull up, stall, stop short, check; stick, deadlock, hand fire; halt; pause, rest

have done with, give over, surcease, shut up shop; give up etc. (*relinquish*) 624.

hold —, stay- one's hand; rest on one's oars, repose on one's laurels.

come to a -stand, — standstill, — dead lock, — full stop; arrive etc. 292; go out, die away, peter out; wear -away, — off; pass away etc. (*be past*) 122; be at an end.

intromit, interrupt, suspend, interpel; inter-, re-mit; put -an end, — a stop, — a period- to; bring to a stand, -still; stop, cut out, cut short, arrest, avast; stem the -tide, — torrent; pull the check string; switch off.

Int. halt! hold! stop! enough! avast! have done! a truce to! soft! leave off! shut up! give over! chuck it!

143. Continuance in action.—N. continu-ance, -ation; run; extension, prolongation; maintenance, perpetuation; persistence etc. (*perseverance*) 604a; repetition etc. 104.

V. continue, persist; go —, jog —, keep —, carry —, run — hold- on; abide, keep, pursue, stick to; endure; take —, maintain- its course; keep up.

sustain, uphold, hold up, keep on foot; follow up, perpetuate, prolong; maintain; preserve etc. 604a; harp upon etc. (*repeat*)104.

keep -going, — alive, — at it, — the pot boiling, — the ball rolling, — up the ball; plod-, plug-along; slog on; die in harness; hold on —, pursue the even tenor of one's way.

let be; *stare super antiquas vias; quieta non movere;* let things take their course.

Adj. continuing etc. *v.*; uninterrupted, unintermitting, unremitting, unvarying, unshifting; unreversed, unstopped, unrevoked, unvaried; sustained; undying etc. (*perpetual*) 112; inconvertible.

follow-up.

Int. carry on! right away!

Phr. *vestigia nulla retrorsum; labitur et labetur.*

144. Conversion. [Gradual change to something different.]—N. conversion, reduction, transmutation, transformation, development, resolution, assimilation; assumption; naturalization.

chemistry, alchemy; progress, growth, lapse, flux.

passage; transit, -ion; transmigration, shifting etc. *v.*; conjugation; convertibility.

crucible, alembic, caldron, retort, test tube etc.

convert, neophyte, proselyte, pervert, renegade, deserter, apostate, turncoat.

V. be converted into; become, get, wax; come —, turn- -to, — into; turn out, lapse, shift; run —, fall —, pass —, slide —, glide —, grow —, ripen —, open —, resolve itself —, settle —, merge- into; melt, grow, come round to, mature, mellow; assume the -form, — shape, — state. — nature, — character- of; illapse; assume a new phase, undergo a change.

convert —, resolve- into; make, render; mold, form etc. 240; remodel, new model, refound, reform, reorganize; assimilate —, bring — reduce- to; transform.

Adj. converted into etc. *v.*; convertible, resolvable into; transitional; naturalized.

Adv. gradually etc. (*slowly*) 275; *in transitu* etc. (*transference*) 270.

145. Reversion.—N. reversion, return; revulsion, reaction.

turning point, turn of the tide; *status quo ante bellum;* calm before a storm

alternation etc. (*periodicity*) 138; inversion etc. 219; recoil etc. 277; regression etc. 283; restoration etc. 660; relapse etc. 661; vicinism, atavism, throwback.

V. revert, turn back, return; relapse etc. 661; recoil etc. 277; retreat etc. 283; restore etc. 660; undo, unmake; turn the -tide, — scale; escheat.

Adj. reverting etc. *v.*; revulsive, reactionary.

Adv. *à rebours,* wrong side out.

146. Revolution. [Sudden or violent change.]—N. revolution, *bouleversement,* subversion, break up; destruction etc. 162; sudden —, radical —, sweeping —, organic- change; clean sweep, *coup d'état,* overthrow, *débâcle;* counter-revolution, rebellion etc. 742.

transilience, jump, leap, plunge, jerk, start; explosion; spasm, convulsion, throe, revulsion; storm, earthquake, eruption, upheaval, cataclysm.

legerdemain etc. (*trick*) 545.

V. revolutionize; new model, remodel, recast; strike out something new, break with the past; change the face of, unsex; revert etc. 742.

Adj. unrecognizable.

Revolutionary, Bolshevik etc. 742.

147. Substitution. [Change of one thing for another.]—N. substitution, subrogation, commutation; supplanting etc. *v.*; supersession, metonymy etc. (*figure of speech*) 521.

[Thing substituted.] substitute, *succedaneum,* make-shift, temporary expedient, shift, *pis aller,* stop-gap, jury-mast, *locum tenens,* warming-pan, dummy, goat, scape-goat; double; change-ling; *quid pro quo,* alternative; remount; representative etc. (*deputy*) 759; palimpsest.

price, purchase-money, consideration, equivalent.

V. substitute, put in the place of, change for; make way for, give place to; supply —, take- the place of; supplant, supersede, replace, cut out, serve as a substitute; step into —, stand in- the shoes of; make a shift —, put up- with; borrow of Peter to pay Paul; commute, redeem, compound for.

Adj. substituted etc.. v.; vicarious, subdititious; substitutional.

Adv. instead; in -place, − lieu, − the stead, − the room- of; faute de mieux.

148. Interchange. [Double or mutual change.]—N. inter-, ex-change; com-, per-, intermutation; reciprocation, transposal, transposition, shuffling; reciprocity, castling [at chess]; hocus-pocus.

interchange-ableness, -ability.

barter etc. 794; tit for tat etc. (retaliation) 718; cross fire, battledore and shuttlecock; quid pro quo.

V. inter-, ex-, counter-change; bandy, transpose, shuffle, change hands, swap, trade, permute, reciprocate, commute; give and take, return the compliment; play at -puss in the corner, − battledore and shuttlecock; retaliate etc. 718; barter etc. 794.

Adj. interchanged etc. v.; reciprocal, mutual, commutative, interchanged etc. v.; interchangeable, intercurrent.

Adv. in exchange, vice versâ, mutatis mutandis, backwards and forwards, by turns, turn and turn about, turn about; each −, every one- in his turn.

149. Changeableness.—N. changeableness etc. adj.; mutability, inconstancy; versatility, mobility; instability, unstable equilibrium; vacillation etc. (irresolution) 605; fluctuation, vicissitude; alternation etc. (oscillation) 314.

restlessness etc. adj.; fidgets, disquiet; dis-, inquietude; unrest; agitation etc. 315.

moon, Proteus, chameleon, kaleidoscope, quicksilver, shifting sands, weathercock, harlequin, Cynthia of the minute, April showers; wheel of Fortune; transientness etc. 111.

V. fluctuate, vary, waver, flounder, flicker, flitter, flit, flutter, shift, shuffle, shake, totter, tremble, vacillate, wamble, turn and turn about, ring .the changes; sway −, shift- to and fro; change and change about; oscillate etc. 314; vibrate −, oscillate- between two extremes; alternate; have as many phases as the moon.

Adj. change-able, -ful; changing etc. 140; mutable, variable, checkered, ever changing, kaleidoscopic, prote-an, -iform; versatile.

unstaid, inconstant; un-steady, -stable, -fixed, -settled; fluctuating etc. v.; restless; mercurial; agitated etc. 315; erratic, fickle; irresolute etc. 605; capricious etc. 608; touch-and-go; inconsonant, fitful, spasmodic; vibratory; afloat; alternating; alterable, plastic, mobile; fleeting, transient etc. 111.

Adv. see-saw etc. (oscillation) 314; off and on.

150. Stability.—N. stability; immutability etc. adj.; unchangeableness etc. adj.; constancy; stable equilibrium, immobility, soundness, vitality, stabiliment, stabilization, stiffness, ankylosis, solidity, aplomb.

establishment, fixture; rock, pillar, tower, foundation, leopard's spots, Ethiopian's skin, law of the Medes and Persians.

stabilimeter, stabilizator.

permanence etc. 141; obstinacy etc. 606.

V. be -firm etc. adj.; stick fast; stand −, keep −, remain- firm; weather the storm.

settle, establish, stablish, ascertain, fix, set, stabilitate, stabilize; retain, stet, keep hold; make -good, − sure; fasten etc. (join) 43; set on its legs, float; perpetuate.

settle down; strike −, take- root; take up one's abode etc. 184; build one's house on a rock.

Adj. unchangeable, immutable; unalter-ed, -able; not to be changed, constant; permanent etc. 141; invariable, undeviating; stable, durable; perennial etc. (diuturnal) 110.

fixed, steadfast, firm, fast, steady, balanced; confirmed, valid, fiducial, immovable, irremovable, riveted, rooted; settled, established etc. v.; vested; incontrovertible, stereotyped, indeclinable.

tethered, anchored, moored, at anchor, on a rock, firm as a rock; firmly -seated, − established etc. v.; deep-rooted, ineradicable; inveterate; obstinate etc. 606.

transfixed, stuck fast, aground, high and dry, stranded.

indefeasible, irretrievable, intransmutable, incommutable, irresoluble, irrevocable, irreversible, reverseless, inextinguishable, irreducible; indissol-uble, -vable; indestructible, undying, imperishable, indelible, indeciduous; insusceptible, − of change.

Int. stet.

151. Eventuality.—N. eventuality, event, occurrence, incident, affair, transaction, proceeding, fact; matter of −, naked- fact; phenomenon; advent.

business, concern; circumstance, particular, casualty, happening, accident, adventure, passage, crisis, pass, emergency, contingency, consequence etc. 154.

the world, life,. things, doings, affairs, matters; things −, affairs- in general; the times, state of affairs, order of the day; course −, tide −, .stream −, current −, run −, march- of -things, − events; ups and downs of life; chapter of accidents etc. (chance) 156; situation etc. (circumstances) 8.

V. happen, occur; take -place, − effect; come, become of; come -off, − about, − round, − into existence, − forth, − to pass, − on; pass, present itself; fall; fall −, turn- out; run, be on foot, fall in; be-fall, -tide, -chance; prove, eventuate, draw on; turn −, crop −, spring −, cast- up; super-, sur-vene; issue, emanate, arrive, ensue, arise, start, hold, take its course; pass off etc. (be past) 122.

meet with; experience; fall to the lot of; be one's -chance, − fortune, − lot; find; encounter, undergo; pass −, go- through; endure etc. (feel) 821.

Adj. happening etc. v.; going on, doing, current; in the wind, afloat; on -foot, − the tapis; at issue, in question; incidental.

eventful, momentous, signal; stirring, bustling, full of incident.

Adv. eventually, ultimately, in -the event of, − case; in the course of things; in the -natural, − ordinary- course of things; as -things, − timesgo; as the world -goes, − wags; as the -tree falls, − cat jumps; as it may -turn out, − happen.

Phr. the plot thickens.

152. Destiny.—N. destiny etc. (*necessity*) 601; hereafter, future −, post- existence; future state, next world, world to come, after life; futurity etc. 121; everlasting -life, − death; prospect etc. (*expectation*) 507.

V. impend; hang −, lie −, hover-·over; threaten, loom, await, come on, approach, stare one in the face; fore-, pre-ordain; predestine, doom, foredoom, foreshadow, have in store for.

Adj. impending etc. *v.;* destined; about to -be, − happen; coming, in store, to come, going to happen, instant, at hand, near; near −, close- at hand; overhanging, hanging over one's head, imminent; brewing, preparing, forthcoming; in the wind, on the cards, in reserve; that -will, − is to- be; in prospect etc. (*expected*) 507; looming in the -distance, − horizon, − future; unborn, in embryo; in the womb of -time; − futurity; on the knees of the gods; pregnant etc. (*producing*) 161.

Adv. in -time, − the long run; all in good time; eventually etc. 151; whatever may happen etc. (*certainly*) 474; as -chance etc. 156- would have it.

153. Cause. [Constant antecedent.]—N. cause, origin, source, principle, element; occasioner, prime mover, engine, turbine, motor, *primum mobile; vera causa*; author etc. (*producer*) 164; main-spring, agent; dynamo, generator, battery (electric); leaven; groundwork, foundation etc. (*support*) 215.

spring, fountain, well, font; fountain −, spring- head; *fons et origo*, genesis; descent etc. (*paternity*) 166; remote cause; influence.

pivot, hinge, turning-point, lever; key; kernel, core; proximate cause, *causa causans;* last straw that breaks the camel's back.

ground; reason, − why; why and wherefore, rationale, occasion, derivation; final cause etc. (*intention*) 620; *le dessous des cartes;* undercurrents.

rudiment, egg, germ, embryo, fetus, bud, root, *radix*, radical, etymon, nucleus, seed, stem, stalk, stock, *stirps*, trunk, tap-root; latent organism.

nest, cradle, nursery, womb, *nidus*, birth-, breeding-place, hot-bed.

caus-ality, -ation; origination; production etc. 161.

V. be the -cause etc. *n.-* of; originate; give -origin, − rise, − occasion- to; cause, occasion, sow the seeds of, kindle, suscitate; bring -on, − to pass, − about; produce; create etc. 161; set -up, − afloat, − on foot; found, broach, institute, lay the foundation of, inaugurate; lie at the root of.

procure, induce, draw down, open the door to, superinduce, evoke, entail, operate; elicit, provoke.

conduce to etc. (*tend to*) 176; contribute; promote; have a -hand in, − finger in- the pie; determine, decide, turn the scale, give the casting vote; have a common origin; derive its origin etc. (*effect*) 154.

Adj. caused etc. *v.;* causal, original; prim-ary, -itive, -ordial; aboriginal; radical; inceptive, embry-onic, -otic; *in -embryo*, − *ovo;* seminal, germinal; formative, productive etc. 168; at the bottom of; connate, having a common origin.

Adv. because etc. 155; behind the scenes.

154. Effect. [Constant sequent.]—N. effect,

consequence, sequela; derivative, -tion; result; result-ant, -ance; upshot, issue, *dénouement;* outcome; termination, end etc. 67; development, outgrowth, fruit, crop, harvest, product, bud, blossom, florescence, ear.

production, produce, product, finished product, work, handiwork, fabric, performance; creature, creation; offspring, -shoot; first-fruits, -lings; *prémices*.

V. be the -effect etc. *n.-* of; be -due, − owing-to; originate -in, − from; rise −, arise −, take its rise −, spring −, proceed −, emanate −, come −, grow −, bud −, sprout −, germinate −, issue −, flow −, result −, follow −, derive its origin −, accrue- from; come -:to, − of, − out of; depend −, hand −, hinge −, turn- upon.

take the consequences, sow the wind and reap the whirlwind.

Adj. owing to; resulting from etc. *v.;* resultant; derivable from; due to; caused etc. by, 153; dependent upon; derived −, evolved- from; derivative; hereditary.

Adv. of course, it follows that, naturally, consequently; as a −, in- consequence; through all, all along of, necessarily, eventually.

Phr. *cela va sans dire,* thereby hangs a tale.

155. Attribution. [Assignment of cause.]—N. attribution, theory, etiology, ascription, reference to, rationale;·accounting for etc. *v.;* imputation, derivation from.

fil-, affil-iation; pedigree etc. (*paternity*) 166. explanation etc. (*interpretation*) 522; reason why etc. (*cause*) 153.

V. attribute −, ascribe −, impute −, refer −, lay −, point −, trace −, bring home- to; put −, set- down- to; charge −, ground- on; invest with, assign as cause, charge with, blame, lay at the door of, father upon; saddle with; affiliate; account-for, derive from, point out the -reason etc. 153; theorize; tell how it comes; put the saddle on the right horse.

Adj. attributed etc. *v.;* attributable etc. *v.;* refer-able, -rible; due to, derivable from; owing to etc. (*effect*) 154; putative.

Adv. hence, thence, therefore, for, since, on account of, because, owing to; on that account; from -this, − that- cause; thanks to, forasmuch as; whence; *propter hoc.*

why? wherefore? whence? how -comes, − is, − happens- it? how does it happen?

in -some, − some such- way; somehow, − or other.

Phr. that is why; *hinc illae lachrymae; cherchez la femme.*

156. Chance.† [Absence of assignable cause.]—N. chance, indetermination, accident, fortune, hazard, hap, haphazard, chance-medley, random, luck, *raccroc*, casualty, fortuity, contingence, coincidence, adventure, hit; fate etc. (*necessity*) 601; equal chance; lottery, raffle, tombola, sweepstake; toss up etc. 621; turn of the -table, − cards; hazard of the die, chapter of accidents; cast −, throw- of the dice; heads or tails, wheel of Fortune, whirligig of chance; *sortes; − Virgilianae.*

probability, possibility, contingency, odds, long odds, run of luck; main- chance.

theory of -probabilities, — chances; book-making; assurance; speculation, gamble, gaming etc. 621.

V. chance, hap, turn up; fall to one's lot; be one's -fate etc. 601; stumble on, light —, blunder —, hit- upon; take one's chance etc. 621.

Adj. casual, fortuitous, accidental, haphazard, random, stray, adventitious, adventive, causeless, incidental. contingent, uncaused, undetermined, indeterminate; possible etc. 470; unintentional etc. 621.

Adv. by -chance, — accident; casually; perchance etc. (*possibly*) 470; for aught one knows; as -good, — bad, — ill-luck etc. *n*.- would have it; as it may -be, — chance, — turn up, — happen; as the case may be.

†The word *Chance* has two distinct meanings: the first, the absence of assignable *cause*, as above; and the second, the absence of *design*—for the latter see 621.

157. Power.—N. power; poten-cy, -tiality; puissance, might, force; energy etc. 171; dint; right -hand, — arm; ascendency, sway, control; pre-potency, -pollence; almightiness, omnipotence; authority etc. 737; strength etc. 159.

ability; ableness etc. *adj*.; competency; efficiency, -cacy; validity, cogency; enablement; vantage ground; influence etc. 175; horse power; dynamometer.

pressure; elasticity; gravity; attraction, repulsion; *vis -inertiae, — mortua, — viva;* friction, suction.

electricity, magnetism, galvanism, voltaic electricity, voltaism, electro-magnetism, electrostatics, electrification; electric — current, — power; potential —, dynamic —, kinetic —, electrical —, chemical —, atomic- energe; electric field, circuit, charge, discharge, shock, polarity, pole; amperage, voltage, wattage, resistance, conduction, induction, electrification, electrolysis.

electronics, radionics, electron physics, electrophysics, avionics, radiometry, photoelectronics; electron, negatron, positron, photoelectron, thermion, barytron; electronic effect; electron emission; electron —, cathode —, anode —, positive — ray; electron — current, — flow — stream, — beam, — volt; electronic circuit; conductance; electron tube, tube, vacuum tube, photoelectric tube, call; transistor.

capability, capacity; *quid valeant humeri quid ferre recusent;* faculty, quality, attribute, endowment, virtue, gift, property, qualification, susceptibility.

V. be -powerful etc. *adj*.; gain -power etc. *n*. belong —, pertain- to; lie —, be- in one's power; can.

electrify, generate, magnetize.

give —, confer —, exercise- power etc. *n*.; empower, enable, invest; in-, en-due; endow, arm; strengthen etc. 159; compel etc. 744.

Adj. powerful, puissant; potent, -ial; capable, able; equal —, up- to; cogent, valid; effect-ive, -ual; efficient, efficacious, adequate, competent; multi-, pleni-, omni-, armi- potent; mighty, ascendent; almighty.

electric, electrical, electronic etc.

forcible etc. *adj*. (*energetic*) 171; influential etc. 175; productive etc. 168.

Adv. powerfully etc. *adj*.; by -virtue, — dint-of.

158. Impotence.—N. impotence; in-, dis-ability; disablement, impuissance, imbecility, caducity; incapa-city, -bility; inapt-, inept-itude; indocility; invalidity, inefficiency, incompetence, disqualification.

telum imbelle, brutum fulmen, blank cartridge, flash in the pan, *vox et praeterea nihil,* dead letter, bit of waste paper, dummy; scrap of paper.

inefficacy etc. (*inutility*) 645; failure etc. 732.

helplessness etc. *adj*.; prostration, paralysis, palsy, ataxia, apoplexy, syncope, sideration, *deliquium,* collapse, exhaustion, softening of the brain, emasculation, inanition, senility etc. 128; castrato, eunuch.

cripple, old woman, muff, molly-coddle, milk-sop.

V. be -impotent etc. *adj*.; not have a leg to stand on.

vouloir -rompre l'anguille au genou, — prendre la lune avec les dents.

collapse, faint, swoon, fall into a swoon, drop; go by the board; end in smoke etc. (*fail*) 732.

render -powerless etc. *adj*.; deprive of power; decontrol; dis-able, -enable; disarm, incapacitate, disqualify, unfit, invalidate, undermine, deaden, cramp, tie the hands; double up, prostrate, paralyze, muzzle, cripple, becripple, maim, lame, hamstring, draw the teeth of; throttle, strangle, *garrotte;* ratten, silence, sprain, clip the wings of, render *hors de combat,* spike the guns; take the wind out of one's sails, scotch the snake, put a spoke in one's wheel; break the -neck, — back; un-hinge, -fit; put out of gear.

unman, unnerve, devitalize, attenuate, enervate; emasculate, spay, caponize, castrate, geld; effeminize.

shatter, exhaust; weaken etc. 160.

Adj. powerless, impotent, unable, incapable, incompetent; ineff-icient, -ective; inept; un-fit, -fitted; un-, dis-qualified; unendowed; in-, un-apt; crippled, decrepit; disabled etc. *v*.; armless.

harmless, unarmed, weaponless, defenceless, *sine ictu,* unfortified, indefensible, vincible, pregnable, untenable.

para-lytic, -lyzed; palsied, imbecile; nerve-, sinew-, marrow-, pith-, lust-less; emasculate, disjointed, out of -joint, — gear; un-nerved, -hinged; water-logged, on one's beam ends, rudderless; laid on one's back; done up, dead beat, exhausted, shattered, demoralized; gravelled etc. (*in difficulty*) 704; helpless, unfriended, fatherless; without a leg to stand on, *hors de combat,* laid on the shelf.

null and void, nugatory, imoperative, good for nothing; dud; invertebrate; ineffectual etc. (*failing*) 732; inadequate etc. 640; inefficacious etc. (*useless*) 645.

159. Strength. (Degree of power.)—N. strength; power etc. 157; energy etc. 171; vigor, force; main —, physical —, brute- force; spring, elasticity, tone, tension, tonicity.

stoutness etc. *adj*.; lustihood, stamina, nerve,

muscle, sinew, thews and sinews, *physique;* pith, - iness; virility, vitality.

athlet-ics, -icism; gymnastics, feats of strength.

adamant, steel, iron, oak, heart of oak; iron grip; grit, bone.

athlete, gymnast, tumbler, acrobat; Atlas, Hercules, Antaeus, Samson, Cyclops, Goliath, Titan; tower of strength; giant refreshed.

strengthening etc. *v.;* invigoration, refreshment, refocillation.

[Science of forces] dynamics, statics.

V. be -strong etc. *adj.,* − stronger; overmatch.

render -strong etc. *adj.;* give -strength etc. *n.;* strengthen, invigorate, brace, nerve, fortify, buttress, sustain, harden, case-harden, steel; gird; screw −, wind −, set- up; gird −, brace- up one's loins; recruit, set on one's legs; vivify; refresh etc. 689; refect; reinforce etc. (*restore*) 660.

Adj. strong, mighty, vigorous, forcible, hard, adamantine, stout, robust, sturdy, hardy, powerful, potent, puissant, valid.

resistless, irresistible, invincible, proof a-gainst, impregnable, unconquerable, indomitable, inextinguishable, unquenchable; incontestable; more than a match for; over-powering, - whelming; all-powerful; sovereign.

able-bodied; athletic, gymnastic; Herculean, Cyclopean, Atlantean; muscular, husky, brawny, wiry, well-knit, broad-shouldered, sinewy, strapping, stalwart, gigantic.

man-ly, -like, -ful; masculine, male, virile, in the prime of manhood.

un-weakened, -allayed, -withered, -shaken, - worn, -exhausted; in full -force, − swing; in the plenitude of power.

stubborn, thick-ribbed, made of iron, deep-rooted; strong as -a lion, − a horse, − brandy; sound as a roach; in -fine, − high- feather; in fine fettle; like a giant refreshed.

Adv. strongly etc. *adj.;* by -force etc. *n.;* by main force etc. (*by compulsion*) 744.

Phr. 'our withers are unwrung.'

160. Weakness.—N. weakness etc. *adj.;* debility, atony, relaxation, languor, enervation; impotence etc. 158; infirmity; effeminacy, feminality; fragility, flaccidity; inactivity etc. 683.

declension −, loss −, failure- of strength; delicacy, invalidation, decrepitude, asthenia, adynamy, cachexy, *cachexia,* anemia, bloodlessness, sprain, strain.

reed, thread, rope of sand, broken reed, house -of cards, − built on sand.

soft-, weak-ling; infant etc. 129; youth etc. 127.

V. be -weak etc. *adj.;* drop, crumble, give way, totter, tremble, shake, halt, limp, fade, languish, decline, flag, fail, have one foot in the grave.

render -weak etc. *adj.;* weaken, enfeeble, debilitate, shake, deprive of strength, relax, enervate; un-brace, -nerve; cripple, unman, etc. (*render powerless*) 158; cramp, reduce, sprain, strain, blunt the edge of; dilute, impoverish; deci-mate; extenuate; reduce -in strength, − the strength of; invalidate; *mettre de l'eau dans son vin.*

Adj. weak, feeble, debile; impotent etc. 158; relaxed, unnerved etc. *v.;* sap-, strength-, power-less; weakly, unstrung, flaccid, adynamic, asthenic; nervous.

soft, effeminate, feminate, womanish.

frail, fragile, shattery, frangible, brittle etc. 328; flimsy, unsubstantial, gimcrack, ginger-bread; rickety, cranky; creachy; drooping, tottering etc. *v.;* broken, lame, halt, game, withered, shattered, shaken, crazy, shaky, tumble-down; palsied etc. 158; decrepit; C3.

languid, poor, poorly, infirm; faint, -ish; sickly etc. (*disease*) 655; dull, slack, evanid, spent, short-winded, effete; weatherbeaten; decayed, rotten, worn, seedy, languishing, wasted, washy, wishy-washy, laid low, pulled down, the worse for wear.

un-strengthened etc. 159, -supported, -aided, - assisted; aidless, defenceless etc. 158.

on its last legs; weak as a -child, − baby, − chicken, − cat, − rat; weak as -water, − water gruel, − gingerbread, − milk and water; color-less etc. 429.

Phr. *non sum qualis eram.*

161. Production.—N. production, creation, construction, formation, fabrication, manufacture; building, architecture, erection, edification; coinage; organization; *nisus formativus;* putting together etc. *v.;* establishment; workmanship, performance; achievement etc. (*completion*) 729; effect etc. 154.

flowering, fructification fruition.

bringing forth etc. *v.;* parturition, birth, birth-throe, child-birth, delivery, confinement, *accouchement,* travail, labour, midwifery, obstetrics; geniture; gestation etc. (*maturation*) 673; evolution, development, growth; genesis, fertilization, breeding, conception, germination, generation, *epigenesis,* pro-creation, -genera-tion, -pagation; fecundation, impregnation; spontaneous generation; arche-genesis, -biosis; bio-, abio-, homo-, xeno-genesis.

authorship, publication; works, *oeuvre, opus.*

edifice, building, structure, fabric, erection, pile, tower, flower, fruit.

V. produce, perform, operate, do, make, gar, form, construct, fabricate, frame, contrive, manufacture; weave, forge, coin, carve, chisel; build, raise, edify, rear, erect, put together; set −, run- up; establish, constitute, compose, organize, institute, get up; achieve, accomplish etc. (*complete*) 729.

flower, sprout, blossom, burgeon, bear fruit, fructify, spawn, teem, ean, yean, farrow, drop, calf, pup, whelp, kitten, kindle; bear, lay, bring forth, give birth to, lie in, be brought to bed of, evolve, pullulate, usher into the world.

make productive etc. 168; create; beget, conceive, get, generate, fecundate, impregnate; pro-create, -generate, -pagate; engender; bring −, call- into -being, − existence; breed, hatch, develop, bring up.

induce, superinduce; suscitate; cause etc. 153; acquire etc. 775.

Adj. produc-ed, -ing etc. *v.;* productive of; prolific etc. 168; creative; formative; gen-etic, -ial, -ital; fertile, pregnant; *enceinte,* big −, fraught-with; with child, in the family way, teeming, parturient, in the straw, brought to bed of; puerper-al, -ous.

architectonic; constructive.

162. Destruction. [Non-production.]—N. destruction; waste, dissolution, breaking up; di-, dis-ruption; consumption; disorganization.

fall, downfall, ruin, perdition, crash, smash, havoc, *délabrement, débâcle;* break -down, — up; prostration; desolation, *bouleversement*, wreck, crack-up, crash, wrack, shipwreck, cataclysm; Caudine Forks, Sedan.

extinction, annihilation; destruction of life etc. 361; knock-out, knock-down blow; doom, crack of doom.

destroying etc. *v.;* demo-lition, -lishment; biblioclasm; overthrow, subversion, suppression; abolition etc. (*abrogation*) 756; sacrifice; ravage, devastation, *sabotage, razzia;* incendiarism; revolution etc. 146; extirpation etc. (*extraction*) 301; *commencement de la fin*, road to ruin; dilapidation etc. (*deterioration*) 659.

V. be -destroyed etc.; perish; fall, — to the ground; tumble, topple; go —, fall- to pieces; break up; crumble, — to dust; go to -the dogs, — the wall, — smash, — shivers, — wreck, — pot, — wrack and ruin; go -by the board, — all to smash, — to pieces, — under; be all -over, — up- with; totter to its fall.

destroy; do —, make- away with; nullify; annul etc. 756; sacrifice, demolish; tear up; over-turn, -throw, -whelm; upset, subvert, put an end to; seal the doom of, do for, dish, undo; break -, cut- up; break —, cut —, pull —, mow —, blow —, beat-down; suppress, quash, put down; cut short, take off, blot out; dispel, dissipate, dissolve; consume.

smash, — to smithereens, quell, squash, squelch, crumple up, shatter, shiver; batter; tear —, crush —, cut —, shake —, pull —, pick- to pieces; nip; tear to -rags, — tatters; crush —, knock- to atoms; pulverize; ruin; strike out; throw —, knock- -down, — over; lay by the heels; fell, sink, swamp, scuttle, wreck, crash, shipwreck, engulf, submerge; lay in -ashes, — ruins; sweep away, erase, expunge, strike out, delete, efface, raze; level, — with the -ground, — dust.

deal destruction, lay waste, ravage, gut; disorganize; dismantle etc. (*render useless*) 645; devour, swallow up, desolate, devastate, sap, mine, blast, confound; exterminate, extinguish, quench, annihilate; snuff —, put —, stamp —, trample- out; lay —, trample- in the dust; prostrate; tread —, crush —, trample- under foot; lay the axe to the root of; make -short work, — a clean sweep, — mincemeat- of; cut up root and branch; fling —, scatter- to the winds; throw overboard; strike at the root of, sap the foundations of, spring a mine, blow up; ravage with fire and sword; cast to the dogs; eradicate etc. 301.

Adj. destroyed etc. *v.;* perishing etc. *v.;* trembling —, nodding —, tottering- to its fall; in course of destruction etc. *n.;* extinct.

destructive, subversive, ruinous, incendiary, deletory; destroying etc. *v.;* suicidal; deadly etc. (*killing*) 361.

Adv. with -crushing effect, — a sledge-hammer.

Phr. *delenda est Carthago.*

163. Reproduction.—N. reproduction, renovation; restoration etc. 660; renewal; new edition, reprint etc. 21; revival, regeneration, palingenesia, revivification; apotheosis; resuscitation, reanimation, resurrection, resurgence, reappearance, atavism; Phoenix; reincarnation.

generation etc. (*production*) 161; multiplication.

V. reproduce; restore etc. 660; revive, renovate, renew, regenerate, revivify, resuscitate, reanimate, refashion, stir the embers, put into the crucible; multiply, repeat, resurge.

crop up, spring up like mushrooms.

Adj. reproduced etc. *v.;* renascent, reappearing; reproductive; resurgent; progenitive; Hydra-headed.

164. Producer.—N. producer, creator, deviser, designer, originator, inventor, author, founder, generator, mover, architect; grower, constructor, maker etc. (*agent*) 690.

165. Destroyer.—N. destroyer etc. (destroy etc. 162); cankerworm etc. (*bane*) 663; iconoclast; assassin etc. (*killer*) 361; executioner etc. (*punish*) 975; Hun, Vandal, nihilist, anarchist.

166. Paternity.—N. paternity; parentage; fatherhood; consanguinity etc. 11.

parent, father, sire, dad, daddy, papa, governor, *pater, paterfamilias, abba;* genitor, progenitor, procreator, begetter; ancestor; grandsire, -father; great-grandfather.

house, stem, truck, tree, stock, *stirps,* pedigree, lineage, line, family, tribe, sept, race, clan; genealogy, descent, extraction, birth, ancestry; forefathers, forbears, patriarchs.

motherhood, maternity; mother, dam, mamma, *materfamilias;* grand-mother; matriarch.

Adj. paternal, parental; maternal; family, ancestral, linear, matrilinear, patrilineal, patriarchal.

167. Posterity.—N. posterity, progeny, breed, issue, offspring, brood, litter, seed, farrow, spawn, spat; family, children, grandchildren, heirs; great-grandchild.

child, son, daughter; kid; infant etc. 129; bantling, scion; shoot, sprout, olive branch, sprit, branch; off-shoot, -set; ramification; descendant; heir, -ess; heir -apparent, — presumptive; chip of the old block; heredity; rising generation.

straight descent, sonship, line, lineage, filiation, promogeniture

Adj. filial.

168. Productiveness.—N. productiveness etc. *adj.;* fecundity, fertility, luxuriance, uberty.

pregnancy, pullulation, fructification, multiplication, propagation, procreation; superfetation.

milch cow, rabbit, hydra, warren, seed-plot, land flowing with milk and honey; second crop, after-crop, -growth, -math; fertilization.

V. make -productive etc. *adj.;* fructify; pro-create, generate, fertilize, spermatize, impregnate; fecund-ate, -ify; teem, ,pullulate, multiply; produce etc. 161; conceive.

Adj. productive, prolific; teem-ing, -ful; fertile, fruitful, frugiferous, fruit-bearing; fructiferous; fecund, luxuriant; pregnant, uberous.

procre-ant, -ative; generative, life-giving, spermatic; originative; multiparous; omnific; propagable.

parturient etc. (*producing*) 161; profitable etc. (*useful*) 644.

169. Unproductiveness.—N. unproductiveness etc. *adj.;* infertility, steril; ity, infecundity; impotence etc. 158- unprofitableness etc. (*inutility*) 645.

waste, desert, Sahara, wild, wilderness, howling wilderness.

V. be -unproductive etc. *adj.;* hang fire, flash in the pan, come to nothing.

Adj. unproductive, inoperative, barren, addle, unfertile, unprolific, arid, sterile, unfruitful, acarpous, infecund; *sine prole;* fallow; teem-, issue-, fruitless; unprofitable etc. (*useless*) 645; null and void, of no effect.

170. Agency.—N. agency, operation, force, working, strain, function, office, maintenance, exercise, work, swing, play; inter-working, -action, procuration, procurement.

causation etc. 153; instrumentality etc. 631; influence etc. 175; action etc. (*voluntary*) 680; *modus operandi* etc. 627.

quickening —, maintaining- power; home stroke.

V. be -in action etc. *adj.;* operate, work; act, — upon; perform, play, support, sustain, strain, maintain, take effect, quicken, strike.

come —, bring- into -operation, — play; have -play, — free play; bring to bear upon.

Adj. operative, efficient, efficacious, practical, effectual.

at work, on foot; acting etc. (*doing*) 680; in -operation, — force, — action,— play, — exercise; acted —, wrought- upon.

Adv. by the -agency etc. *n.*- of; through etc. (*instrumentality*) 631; by means of etc. 632.

171. Physical Energy.—N. energy, physical energy, force; keenness etc. *adj.;* intensity, vigor, strength, elasticity; go; pep, live wire, high pressure; backbone, mettle, fire, vim.

acri-mony, -tude, -dity; causticity, virulence, poignancy; harshness etc. *adj.;* severity, edge, point; pungency etc. 392.

cantharides; Spanish fly; seasoning etc. (*condiment*) 393, stimulant, excitant.

activity, agitation, effervescence; ferment, -ation; ebullition, splutter, perturbation, stir, bustle; voluntary energy etc. 682; quicksilver.

resolution etc. (*mental energy*) 604; exertion etc. (*effort*) 686; excitation etc. (*mental*) 824.

V. give -energy etc. *n.;* energize, stimulate, kindle, excite, activate, exert; sharpen, pep up, intensify; inflame etc. (*render violent*) 173; wind up etc. (*strengthen*) 159.

strike, — into, — hard, — home; make an impression.

Adj. strong, energetic, forcible, active; strenuous, forceful, mettlesome, enterprising, go ahead; intense, deep-dyed, severe, keen, vivid, sharp, acute, incisive, trenchant, brisk, vigorous, live.

rousing, irritating; poignant; virulent, caustic, corrosive, mordant, harsh, stringent; double-edged, — shotted, — distilled; drastic, escharotic; racy etc. (*pungent*) 392; sarcastic etc. 932.

potent etc. (*powerful*) 157; radio-active.

Adv. strongly etc. *adj.; fortiter in re;* with telling effect.

Phr. the steam is up; *vires acquirit eundo.*

172. Physical Inertness.—N. inertness, dulness etc. *adj.;* inertia, *vis inertiae,* inertion, inactivity, torpor, languor; dormancy, quiescence etc. 265; latency, inaction, passivity.

mental inertness; sloth etc. (*inactivity*) 683; inexcitability etc. 826; irresolution etc. 605; obstinacy etc. 606; permanence etc. 141.

V. be -inert etc. *adj.;* hang fire, smoulder.

Adj. inert, inactive, passive, pacific; torpid etc. 683; sluggish, stagnant, dull, heavy, flat, slack, tame, slow, blunt; lifeless, dead, uninfluential.

latent, dormant, smouldering, unexerted.

Adv. inactively etc. *adj.;* in -suspense, -abeyance.

173. Violence.—N. violence, inclemency, vehemence, might, impetuosity; boisterousness etc.; *adj.;* effervescence, ebullition; turbulence, bluster; uproar, riot, row, rumpus, *le diable à quatre,* devil to pay, all the fat in the fire.

severity etc. 739; ferocity, rage, berserk, fury; exacerbation, exasperation, malignity; fit, paroxysm, orgasm; force, brute force; outrage; *coup de main;* strain, shock, shog; spasm, convulsion, 'throe; hysterics, passion etc. (*state of excitability*) 825.

out-break, -burst; burst, bounce, dissilience, discharge, volley, explosion, blow up, blast, detonation, rush, eruption, displosion, torrent.

turmoil etc. (*disorder*) 59; ferment etc. (*agitation*) 315; storm, tempest, rough weather; squall etc. (*wind*) 349; earthquake, volcano, thunderstorm.

fury, dragon, demon, tiger, beldame, Tisiphone, Megaera, Alecto, madcap, wild beast; fire-eater etc. (*blusterer*) 887.

V. be -violent etc. *adj.;* run high; ferment, effervesce; romp, rampage; run -wild, — riot; break the peace; rush, tear; rush head-long, -foremost; run amuck, raise a storm, make a riot; make —, kick up- a row, — a fuss; bluster, rage, roar, riot, storm; boil, — over; fume, foam, come in like a lion, wreak, bear down, ride roughshod, out-Herod Herod; spread like wildfire.

break —, fly —, burst- out; bounce, shock, strain; break-, pry-, force-, prize- open.

render -violent etc. *adj.;* sharpen, stir up, quicken, excite, incite, urge, lash, stimulate; irritate, inflame, exacerbate, kindle, suscitate; foment; accelerate, aggravate, exasperate, convulse, infuriate, madden, lash into fury; fan —, add fuel to- the flame; *oleum addere camino.*

explode, go off, displode, fly, detonate, thunder, blow up, flash, flare, erupt, burst; let - off, − fly; discharge, detonize, fulminate.

Adj. violent, vehement, forcible; warm; acute, sharp; rough, rude, ungentle, bluff, boisterous, wild, vicious; brusque, abrupt, waspish; impetuous; rampant.

turbulent; disorderly; blustering, raging etc. *v.;* troublous, riotous; tumultu-ary, -ous; obstreperous, uproarious; extravagant; unmitigated; ravening, tameless; frenzied etc. (*insane*) 503; desperate etc. (*rash*) 863; infuriate, towering, furious, outrageous, frantic, hysteric, in hysterics.

fiery, flaming, scorching, hot, red-hot, ebullient.

savage, fierce, ferocious, fierce as a tiger.

excited etc. *v.;* un-quelled, -quenched, -extinguished, -repressed, -bridled, -ruly; headstrong; un-governable, -appeasable, -mitigable; un-, in-controllable; insup-, irre-pressible.

spasmodic, convulsive, explosive; detonating etc. *v.;* volcanic, meteoric; stormy etc. (*wind*) 349.

Adv. violently etc. *adj.;* amain; by -storm, − force, − main force; with might and main; tooth and nail, *vi et armis*, at the point of the -sword, − bayonet; at one fell swoop; with a high hand, through thick and thin; in desperation, with a vengeance; à −. à *touteoutrance;* head-long, - foremost, -first; like a bull at a gate.

174. Moderation.—N. moderation; lenity etc. 740; temperance, temperateness, gentleness etc. *adj.;* sobriety; quiet; · mental calmness etc. (*inexcitability*) 826.

moderating etc. *v.;* relaxation, remission, mitigation etc. 834; tranquilization, alleviation, assuagement, appeasement, contemporation, pacification.

measure, *juste milieu*, golden mean etc. 29.

moderator; lullaby, sedative, lenitive, demulcent, rose-water, balm, soothing syrup, poppy, opiate, anodyne, milk, opium, laudanum, 'poppy or mandragora;' wet blanket; palliative, calmative.

V. be -moderate etc. *adj.;* keep within -bounds, − compass; sober −, settle- down; keep· the pease, remit, relent; take in sail.

moderate, soften, mitigate, temper, accoy; at-, con-temper; mollify, lenify, dull, take off the edge, blunt, obtund, sheathe, subdue, chasten; sober −, tone −, smooth- down; censor, blue-pencil, weaken etc. 160; lessen etc. (*decrease*) 36; check; palliate.

tranquilize, assuage, appease, dulcify, swage, lull, soothe, compose, still, calm, cool, quiet, hush, quell, sober, pacify, tame, damp, lay, allay, rebate, slacken, smooth, alleviate, rock to sleep, deaden, smother; throw -cold water on, − a wet blanket over; slake; curb etc. (*restrain*) 751; tame etc. (*subjugate*) 749; smooth over; pour oil on the -waves, − troubled waters; pour balm into, *mettre de l'eau dans son vin*.

go out like a lamb, 'roar you as gently· as any sucking dove.'

Adj. moderate; lenient etc. 740; gentle, mild; cool, sober, temperate, reasonable, measured; tempered etc. *v.;* calm, unruffled, quiet, tranquil,

still; slow, smooth, untroubled; tame; peaceful, - able; pacific, halcyon.

un-exciting, -irritating; soft, bland, oily, demulcent, lenitive, anodyne; hypnotic etc. 683; sedative; assuaging.

mild as mother's milk; milk and water; gentle as a lamb.

Adv. moderately etc. *adj.;* gingerly; *piano;* under easy sail, at half speed; within -bounds, − compass; in reason.

Phr. *est modus in rebus*.

175. Influence.—N. influence; importance etc. 642; weight, pressure, preponderance, prevalence, sway, pull; predomi-nance, -nancy; ascendency; control, dominance, reign; authority etc. 737; capability etc. (*power*) 157; interest; spell, magic, magnetism.

footing; purchase etc. (*support*) 215; play, leverage, vantage ground.

tower of strength, host in himself; protection, patronage, auspices.

V. have -influence etc. *n.;* be -influential etc. *adj.;* carry weight, actuate, sway, bias, weigh, tell; have a hold upon, magnetize, bear upon, gain a footing, work upon; take -root, − hold; strike root in.

run through, pervade, prevail, dominate, predominate, subject; out-, over-weigh; over-ride, - bear, − come; gain head; rage; be -rife etc. *adj.;* spread like wildfire; have −, get −, gain- -the upper hand, − full play.

be -recognized, − listened to; make one's voice heard, gain a hearing; play a -part, − leading part- in; lead, control, rule, master; get the mastery over; make one's influence felt, cut ice with; take the lead, pull the strings; turn −, throw one's weight into- the scale; set the fashion, lead the dance.

Adj. influential; important etc. 642; weighty; prevailing etc. *v.;* prevalent, rife, rampant; dominant, regnant, predominant, in the ascendant, hegemonical; authoritative, recognized, telling, with authority.

Adv. with telling effect.

175a. Absence of Influence.—N. impotence etc. 158; inertness etc. 172; irrelevancy etc. 10.

V. have no -influence etc. 175.

Adj. uninfluential; unconduc-ing, -ive, -ting to; powerless etc. 158; irrelevant etc. 10.

176. Tendency.—N. tendency; apt-ness, -itude; proneness, proclivity, bent, turn, tone, bias, set, warp, leaning to, predisposition, inclination, conatus, propensity, susceptibility; liability etc. 177; quality, nature, temperament; characteristic, idio-crasy, -syncrasy; cast, vein, grain; humor, mood; drift etc. (*direction*) 278; conduciveness, -ducement; applicability etc. (*utility*) 644; subservience etc. (*instrumentality*) 631.

V. tend, contribute, conduce, lead, dispose, incline, verge, bend to, warp, turn, trend, affect, carry, redound to, bid fair to, gravitate towards; promote etc. (*aid*) 707.

Adj. tending etc. *v.;* conducive, working to-

wards, in a fair way to, calculated to; liable etc.
177; subservient etc. (*instrumental*) 631; useful
etc. 644; subsidiary etc. (*helping*) 707.

Adv. for, whither.

177. Liability.—N. lia-bility, -bleness; possibility, contingency; suscepti-vity, -bility.

V. be -liable etc. *adj.*; incur, lay oneself open
to; run the —, stand a- chance; lie under, expose
oneself to, open a door to.

Adj. liable, subject; in danger etc. 665; open —,
exposed —, obnoxious- to; answerable, responsible, accountable, amenable; unexempt from; apt
to; dependent on; incident to.

contingent, incidental, possible, on the cards,
within range of, at the mercy of.

178. Concurrence.—N. concurrence, co-
operation, coagency; coincidence, consilience;
union; agreement etc. 23; consent etc. (*assent*)
488; alliance; concert etc. 709; partnership etc.
712; collaboration, conformity.

V. con-cur, -duce, -spire, -tribute; agree, unite,
harmonize; hang —, pull- together etc. (*co-
operate*) 709; help to etc. (*aid*) 707.

keep pace with, run parallel to; go —, go along
—, go hand in hand- with.

Adj. concurring etc. *v.*; concurrent, conformable, joint, co-operative, concordant, coincident, concomitant, harmonious; in alliance with,
banded together, of one mind, at one with;
parallel.

Adv. with one consent.

179. Counteraction.—N. counteraction, opposition; contrariety etc. 14; antagonism, polarity; clashing etc. *v.*; collision, interference,
resistance, renitency, friction; reaction; retro-
action; repercussion etc. (*recoil*) 277; counterblast; neutralization etc. (*compensation*) 30; *vis
inertiae*; check etc. (*hindrance*) 706.

voluntary -opposition etc. 708. — resistance
etc. 719; repression etc. (*restraint*) 751.

V. counteract; run counter, clash, cross; interfere —, conflict- with; jostle; go —, run —, beat
—, militate- against; stultify; antagonize, frustrate, oppose etc. 708; withstand etc. (*resist*) 719;
hinder etc. 706; repress etc. (*restrain*) 751; react
etc. (*recoil*) 277.

undo, neutralize, cancel; counterpoise etc.
(*compensate*) 30; overpoise.

Adj. counteracting etc. *v.*; antagonistic, conflicting, retroactive, renitent, reactionary; contrary etc. 14.

Adv. although etc. 30; in spite of etc. 708;
malgré; against.

180. Space. [Indefinite space.]—N. space,
extension, extent, superficial extent, expanse,
stretch; capacity, volume, room, accommodation,
scope, range, latitude, field, way, expansion, compass, sweep, play, swing, spread.

dimension, fourth dimension; relativity, geo-
metry.

spare —, elbow —, house- room; stowage,
roomage, margin; opening, sphere, arena; lee-,
sea-, head-way.

open —, free- space; wide open spaces, void etc.
(*absence*) 187; waste; wild-, wilder-ness; up-, bot-
tom-, moor -land; *campagna, veldt,* prairie,
steppe.

abyss etc. (*interval*) 198; unlimited space;
infinity etc. 105; world, wide world; ubiquity etc.
(*presence*) 186; length and breadth of the land.

proportions, acreage; acres, — roods and
perches; square -inches, — yards etc.

V. reach, extend, stretch, sweep, spread,
range, cover, thrust out, reach forth.

Adj. spacious, roomy, extensive, expansive,
capacious, ample; wide-spread, vast, world-wide,
uncircumscribed; boundless etc. (*infinite*) 105;
shore-, track-, path-less; large etc. 192.

spatial, dimensional, proportional; two-,
three-, four-dimensional; stereoscopic.

Adv. extensively etc. *adj.*; wherever; everywhere; far and -near, — wide; right and left, all
over, all the world over; throughout the -world,
— length and breadth of the land; under the sun,
in every quarter; in all -quarters, — lands; here,
there and everywhere; from -pole to pole, —
China to Peru, — Indus to the pole, — Dan to
Beersheba, — end to end; on the face of the earth,
in the wide world, from all points of the compass; to the -four winds, — uttermost parts of the
earth.

180a. Inextension.—N. in-, non-extension;
point; atom etc. (*smallness*) 32; pinprick; limitation etc. 229.

181. Region. [Definite space.]—N. region,
sphere, sphere of influence, corridor, ground,
soil, area, realm, hemisphere, quarter district,
beat, orb, orbit, zone, belt, circuit, circle; pale etc.
(*limit*) 233; com-, department; domain, tract,
territory, terrain, country, canton, county, shire,
province, *arrondissement,* diocese, parish, township, borough, constituency, *commune,* ward,
wapentake, hundred, riding, lathe, garth, soke,
tithing, bailiwick; empire, kingdom, principality,
duchy, grand —, arch- duchy, palatinate, republic,
commonwealth, dominion, colony, state, island.

arena, precincts, *enceinte,* walk, march; patch,
plot, enclosure, etc. 232; close, *enclave,* field,
court; street etc. (*abode*) 189.

clime, climate, zone, meridian, latitude.

Adj. territorial, local, parochial, provincial,
insular.

182. Place. [Limited space.]—N. place, lieu,
spot, point, dot; niche, nook, etc. (*corner*) 244;
hole; pigeonhole etc. (*receptacle*) 191; compartment; premises, precinct, station, confine; area,
court, yard, quadrangle, square, compound;
abode etc. 189; locality etc. (*situation*) 183.

ins and outs; every hole and corner.

Adv. somewhere, in some place, wherever it
may be, here and there, in various places,
passim.

183. Situation.—N. situation, position, locality, *locale*, *status*, latitude and longitude; footing, standing, standpoint, post; stage, aspect, attitude, posture, *pose*.

place, site, base, station, seat, *venue*, whereabouts, environment, neighborhood; bearings etc. (*direction*) 278; spot etc. (*limited space*) 182.

top-, ge-, chor-ography; map etc. 554.

V. be -situated, – situate; lie; have its seat in.

Adj. situ-ate, -ated; local, topical, topographical etc. *n*.

Adv. *in -situ*, – *loco;* here and there, *passim;* here-, there-, whereabouts; in place, here, there. in – , amidst- such and such- -surroundings, – *environs*, – *entourage*.

184. Location.—N. loca-tion, -lization; lodgement; de-, re-position; stow-, pack-age; collocation; packing, lading; establishment, settlement, installation; fixation; insertion etc. 300.

anchorage, roadstead, mooring, mooring mast, encampment, camp, bivouac.

plantation, colony, settlement, cantonment, encampment, reservation; colonization, domestication, situation; habitation etc. (*abode*) 189; cohabitation; 'a local habitation and a name;' indenization, naturalization.

. V. place, situate, locate, localize, make a place for, put, lay, set, seat, station, lodge, quarter, post, install; storehouse, stow; extablish, fix, pin, root; graft; plant etc. (*insert*) 300; shelve, pitch, camp, lay down, deposit, reposit; cradle; moor, tether, picket; pack, tuck in; embed; vest, invest in.

billet on, quarter upon, saddle with; load, lade, freight; pocket, put up, bag.

inhabit etc. (*be present*) 186; domesticate, colonize, populate people; take – , strike-root; anchor; cast –, come to an- anchor; sit –, settle-down; settle; take up one's -abode, – quarters; plant –, establish –, locate- oneself; squat, perch, hive, *se nicher*, bivouac, burrow, get a footing; encamp, pitch one's tent; put up -at, – one's horses at; keep house.

indenizen, naturalize, adopt.

put back, replace etc. (*restore*) 660.

Adj. placed etc. *v.;* situate, posited, ensconced, embedded, embosomed, rooted; . domesticated; vested in unremoved; settled, stationed, established.

moored etc. *v.;* at anchor.

185. Displacement.—N. displacement, elocation, transposition.

ejectment etc. 297; exile etc. (*banishment*) 893; removal etc. (*transference*) 270; unshipment.

misplacement, dislocation etc. 61; fish out of water.

V. dis-place, -plant, -lodge, -nest, -establish; misplace, unseat, disturb; exile etc. (*seclude*) 893; ablegate, set aside, remove; take –, cart- away; take – , draft- off; lade etc. 184, unship.

unload, empty etc. (*eject*) 297; transfer etc. 270; dispel.

vacate; depart etc. 293.

Adj. displaced etc. *v.;* un-placed, -housed, -harbored, -established, -settled; house-, home-less; out of -place, – a situation.

misplaced, out of its element.

186. Presence.—N. presence; occupancy, ation; attendance; whereness.

permeation, pervasion; diffusion etc. (*dispersion*) 73.

ubi-ety, -quity, -quitariness; omnipresence.

bystander etc. (*spectator*) 444.

V. exist in space, be -present etc. *adj.;* assist at; make one -of, – at; look on, attend, remain; find –, present- oneself; show one's face; fall in the way of, occur in a place; lie, stand; occupy.

people; inhabit, dwell, reside, stay, sojourn, live, room, abide, bunk, lodge, nestle, roost, perch; take up one's abode etc. (*be located*) 184; tenant, occupy.

resort to, frequent, haunt; revisit.

fill, pervade, permeate; be -diffused, – disseminated- through; over-spread, -run; run through; meet one at every turn.

Adj. present; occupying, inhabiting etc. *v.;* moored etc. 184; residential, resi-ant, -dent, -dentiary; domiciled.

ubiquit-ous, -ary; omnipresent.

peopled, populous, full of people, inhabited.

Adv. here; there, where, everywhere, aboard, on board, at home, afield; on the spot; here, there and everywhere etc. (*space*) 180; in presence of, before; under the -eyes, –nose- of; in the face of; *in propriâ personâ*.

187. Absence. [Nullibiety.]—N. absence; inexistence etc. 2; non-residence, absenteeism; non-attendance, *alibi*.

emptiness etc. *adj.;* void, *vacuum;* vac-uity, -ancy; *tabula rasa;* exemption; *hiatus* etc. (*interval*) 198; no man's land.

truant, absentee.

nobody; nobody -present, – on earth; no one; not a soul; *âme qui vive*.

V. be -absent etc. *adj.;* keep -away, – out of the way; play truant, absent oneself, stay away.

withdraw, make oneself scarce, vacate; go away, slip out, slip away, retreat etc. 293.

Adj. absent, not present, away, nonresident, gone, from home; missing; lost; wanted, wanting; omitted; nowhere to be found; inexistent etc. 2.

empty, void; blank, vac-ant, -uous; untenanted, -occupied, -inhabited; tenantless; desert, -ed; devoid; un-, uninhabitable.

exempt from, not having.

Adv. without, *minus*, nowhere; elsewhere; neither here nor there; in default of; *sans;* behind one's back.

Phr. the bird has flown, *non est inventus*.

188. Inhabitant.—N. inhabitant; habitant, resident, -iary; dweller, in-dweller; occup-ier, ant, farmer, planter; householder, lodger, boarder, paying guest; inmate, tenant, renter, incumbent, sojourner, *locum tenens*, commorant; settler, squatter, backwoodsman, colonist; islander; denizen, citizen; burgher, oppidan, cockney, cit, townsman, burgess; villager; cottager, -tier, -ter; compatriot.

native, indigene, aboriginal, aborigines, auto-chthones; Briton, Englishman, John Bull; new comer etc. (*stranger*) 57.

garrison, crew; population; people etc. (*mankind*) 372; colony, settlement; household.

V. inhabit etc. (*be present*) 186; indenizen etc. (*locate oneself*) 184.

Adj. indigenous; enchorial; national, nat-ive, -al; autochthonous; British, English; colonial; domestic, domiciliated, -ed; naturalized, vernacular, domesticated; domiciliary.

. in the occupation of; garrisoned —, occupied-by.

189. Abode. [Place of habitation, or resort.]—N. abode, dwelling, lodging, -s; diggings, domicile, residence, address, habitation, where one's lot is cast, local habitation, berth, seat, lap, sojourn, housing, quarters, headquarters, resiance, tabernacle, throne, ark.

home, fatherland, mother country, country etc. 181; home-stead, -stall; fireside, chimney corner; hearth, — stone; household gods, *lares et penates*, roof, household, housing, *dulce domum*, paternal domicile; native -soil, — land, blighty.

nest, *nidus*, snuggery; arbor, bower etc. 191; lair, den, cave, hole, hidingplace, cell, *sanctum sanctorum*, aerie, eyry, rookery, hive; *habitat*, haunt, covert, resort, retreat, perch, roost; nidification.

bivouac, camp, encampment, cantonment, castrametation; barrack, casemate, casern.

tent etc. (*covering*) 223; building etc. (*construction*) 161; chamber etc. (*receptacle*) 191.

tenement, messuage, farm, farmhouse, grange, *hacienda*.

cot, cabin, log cabin, shack, hut, *châlet*, croft, shed, booth, stall, hovel, bothy, shanty, igloo, tepee, wigwam; pen etc. (*inclosure*) 232; barn, bawn; kennel, sty, dog-hole, cote, coop, hutch, byre; cowhouse, -shed; stable, dove-cote, shippen.

house, mansion, place, villa, cottage, box, lodge, hermitage, *rus in urbe*, folly, rotunda, tower, *château*, castle, pavilion, hotel, court, manor-house, capital messuage, hall, palace, alcazar; country seat; kiosk, bungalow; temple etc. 1000; home of rest, alms-, poor-, work-house, asylum; boarding-, lodging-house; flat, maisonette, duplex, penthouse, suite of rooms, apartments, rooms, room building etc. 161; Mansion House, town hall, Capitol.

assembly-room, auditorium, coliseum, meeting-house, pump-room, spa, health resort, watering-place; club; theatre etc. 840; drill hall, gymnasium, church etc. 1000; Houses of Parliament etc. 696; school etc. 542; inn; hostel, -ry; hotel, tavern, caravansary, khan, hospice; public-, ale-, pot-, mug-house; gin-palace, gin mill; coffee-, eating-house; canteen, *restaurant*, *rotisserie*, cafeteria, grill-room, *buffet*, *cafe*, *estaminet*, *posada*, *bodega*; bar; saloon, speakeasy, shebeen.

hamlet, village, thorp, dorp, ham, kraal; borough, burgh, town, county-seat, — town, city, capital, metropolis; suburb, quarter, parish etc. 181; ghetto; province, country.

street, place, terrace, parade, esplanade, promenade, pier, embankment, road, villas, row, walk, lane, alley, court, quadrangle, quad, wynd, close, yard, passage, rents, mansions, buildings, mews.

square, polygon, circus, crescent, mall, *piazza*, arcade, colonnade, peristyle, cloister; gardens, grove, residences; block of buildings, market-place, *place*.

anchorage, roadstead, roads; dock, basin, wharf, quay, port, harbor; dry-, graving-, floating-dock.

garden, park, pleasure-ground, pleasance, demesne.

V. take up one's abode etc. (*locate oneself*) 184; inhabit etc. (*be present*) 186.

Adj. urban, oppidan, metropolitan; suburban; provincial, rural, rustic; countrified; regional, parochial, domestic; cosmopolitan; palatial.

190. Contents. [Things contained.]—N. contents; cargo, lading, freight, shipment, load, bale, burden; cart-, ship-load; cup —, basket —, etc. (*receptacle*) 191 - of; inside etc. 221; stuffing, ullage.

V. load, lade, ship, charge, fill, stuff.

191. Receptacle.—N. receptacle, container; inclosure etc. 232; recipient, receiver, reservatory.

compartment; cell, -ule; follicle; hole, corner, niche, recess, nook; crypt, stall, pigeon-hole, cove, oriel; cave etc. (*concavity*) 252.

capsule, vesicle, cyst, pod, calyx, *cancelli*, utricle, bladder, udder.

stomach, paunch, *venter*, abdomen, ventricle, crop, craw, ingluvies, maw, gizzard, bread-basket, belly, little Mary; mouth.

pocket, pouch, fob, sheath, scabbard, socket, bag, vanity bag, compact, sac, sack, saccule, despatch —, attaché-, tachy- case, wallet, scrip, card-, note-, case, billfold, poke, knit, knap-, haver-, ruck-sack, sachel, satchel, reticule, budget, net; ditty-, -box, -bag, kitbag, portfolio; saddlebags, holster; quiver etc. (*magazine*) 636.

chest, box, coffer, caddy, case, casket, pyx, pix, *caisson*, desk, *bureau*, reliquary, shrine; trunk, portmanteau, band-box, *valise*, suitcase, hand-traveling-, overnight-, Gladstone-, carpet-bag, brief case; boot, imperial; *vache*; cage, manger, rack.

vessel, vase, bushel, barrel; canister, jar; pottle, basket, punnet, pannier, buck-basket, hopper, maund, creel, cran, crate, cradle, bassinet, wisket, whisket, *jardinière*, *corbeille*, hamper, wastepaper basket, dosser, dorser, tray, hod, scuttle, utensil, spittoon, cuspidor.

[For liquids] cistern etc. (*store*) 636; vat, caldron, barrel, cask, puncheon, keg, rundlet, tun, butt, firkin, hogshead, kilderkin, carboy, amphora, ampulla, bottle, jar, leather bottle, decanter, ewer, cruse, carafe, crock, kit, canteen, flagon; demijohn; flask, -et; stoup, noggin, vial, phial, ampoulé, cruet, caster; gourd; urn, *épergne*, salver, *patella, tazza, patera*; pig-, big-gin; tea-, coffee-pot, percolator, *samovar*, tyg, nipperkin, pocket-pistol; tub, bucket, pail, skeel, pot, tankard, jug, pitcher, toby, mug, pipkin; gal-, gall-ipot, pannikin; matrass, receiver, retort, alembic, bolthead, can, kettle; bowl, basin, jorum, punch-bowl, cup, goblet, chalice, tumbler, glass, wineglass, rummer, beaker, tass, horn, saucepan, skillet, posnet, tureen, terrine, *casserole*, sauce-, gravy-boat.

plate, platter, paten, dish, vegetable —, *entrée*-dish, trencher, calabash, porringer, potager, saucer, pan, crucible.

shovel, trowel, spoon; table-, dessert-, tea-, egg-salt-spoon, spatula, ladle; dipper; baler; watch-glass, thimble.

closet, commode, cupboard, cellaret, *chiffonniere*, locker, bin, bunker, *buffet*, press, safe, sideboard, drawer, chest of drawers, till, *scrutoire*, *secretaire*, *escritoire*, davenport, book-case, cabinet, canterbury, corner cupboard, wardrobe.

chamber, apartment, room, cabin; office, court, hall, atrium; suite of rooms, flat, story, saloon, *salon*, parlor; presence-chamber; sitting-, drawing-reception-, state-; living-, work-room; gallery, cabinet, closet, cubicle; pew, box; *boudoir*; *adytum*, *sanctum*, bed-room, dormitory, dressing-room, refectory, dining-room, *salle-à-manger*; nursery, schoolroom; library, study; *studio*; billiard-, bath-, smoking-room; den, canteen, mess, officers' mess; gun-, ward-, mess-room.

attic, loft, garret, cockloft, clerestory; cellar, vault, hold, cockpit; *entre-sol*; mezzanine floor; ground-floor, *rez-de-chaussée*; basement, kitchen, cook-house, galley, pantry, scullery, offices; store-room etc. (*depository*) 636; lumber-room; dust-hole, -bin; dairy, laundry, coachhouse; *garage*; *hangar*; out-, pent-house, lean-to.

portico, porch, piazza, verandah, lobby, court, hall, vestibule, corridor, passage; ante-room, chamber; lounge; *foyer*, *loggia*.

conservatory, green-house, glass-house, vinery, bower, arbor, summer-house, alcove, grotto, hermitage, pergola.

lodging etc. (*abode*) 189; bed etc. (*support*) 215; carriage etc. (*vehicle*) 272.

Adj. capsular; saccu-lar, -lated; recipient; ventricular, cystic, vascular, vesicular, cellular, camerated, locular, multilocular, poly-gastric; marsupial, siliqu-ose, -ous.

192. Size.—N. size, magnitude, dimension, bulk, volume; largeness etc. *adj.*; greatness etc. (*of quantity*) 31, expanse etc. (*space*) 180; amplitude, mass; proportions.

capacity; ton-, tun-nage; caliber, scantling.

turgidity etc. (*expansion*) 194; corpulence, obesity; plumpness, etc. *adj.*, *embonpoint*, corporation, flesh and blood, lustihood.

hugeness, etc. *adj.*; enormity, immensity, monstrosity.

giant, Brobdingnagian, Antaeus, Goliath, Gog and Magog, Gargantua, monster, mammoth, Cyclops; whale, porpoise, behemoth, leviathan, elephant, hippopotamus; colossus; tun, Jump, bulk, block, loaf, mass, clod, nugget, bushel, thumper, whopper, spanker, strapper; Triton among the minnows.

mountain, mound; heap etc. (*assemblage*) 72.
largest portion etc. 50; full-, life-size.

V. ve- large etc. *adj.*; become -large etc. (*expand*) 194.

Adj. large, big; great etc. (*in quantity*) 31; considerable, bulky, voluminous, ample, massive, massy; capacious, comprehensive; spacious etc. 180; mighty, towering, fine, magnificent.

corpulent, stout, fat, plump, squab, full, lusty, strapping, bouncing; portly, burly, well-fed, full-grown; stalwart, brawny, fleshy; goodly; in good -case, — condition; in condition; chopping, jolly; chub-, chubby-faced.

lubberly, hulky, unwieldy, lumpish, gaunt, spanking, whacking, whopping, thumping, thundering, hulking; overgrown; puffy etc. (*swollen*) 194.

huge, immense, enormous, mighty; vast, -y; amplitudinous, stupendous; monst-er, -rous; gigantic, elephantine; 'giant, -like; colossal, Cyclopean, Brobdingnagian, Garguantuan, Titanic; infinite etc. 105.

large as life; plump as a dumpling, — partridge; fat as -a pig, — a quail, — butter, — brawn, — bacon.

193. Littleness.—N. littleness etc. *adj.*; smallness etc. (*of quantity*) 32; exiguity, inextension; parvi-tude, -ty; duodecimo; Elzevir edition, epitome, microcosm; rudiment; vanishing point; thinness etc. 203.

dwarf, pigmy, atomy, Liliputian, midget, chit, pigwidgeon, urchin, elf; doll, puppet; Tom Thumb, Hop-o'-my thumb, Humpty-dumpty; man-, mannikin; *homunculus*, dapperling, fingerling, dandiprat, cock-sparrow, scalawag.

animalcule, monad, mite, insect, emmet, fly, midge, gnat, shrimp, minnow, worm, maggot, entozoon; *bacillus*, microbe, micro-organism, *bacteria*; *infusoria*; microbe; grub; tit, tomtit, runt, mouse, small fry; millet-, mustard-seed; barleycorn; pebble, grain of sand; mole-hill, button, bubble.

point; atom etc. (*small quantity*) 32; fragment etc. (*small part*) 51; powder etc. 330; point of a pin, mathematical point; *minutiae* etc. (*unimportance*) 643.

micro-graphy, -meter, -scope; vernier; scale.

V. be -little etc. *adj.*; lie in a nutshell; become small etc. (*decrease*) 36, (*contract*) 195.

Adj. little; small etc. (*in quantity*) 32; minute, diminutive, microscopic; inconsiderable etc. (*unimportant*) 643; exiguous, puny, tiny, wee, petty, minikin, miniature, pigmy, elfin; under sized; dwarf, -ed, -ish; spare, stunted, limited; cramp, -ed; pollard, Liliputian, dapper, pocket; port-ative, -able; duodecimo; dumpy, squat; compact, handy; short etc. 201.

impalpable, intangible, evanescent, imperceptible, invisible, inappreciable, infinitesimal, homeopathic; atomic, corpuscular, molecular; rudiment-ary, -al; embryonic.

weazen, scant, scraggy, scrubby; thin etc. (*narrow*) 203; granular etc. (*powdery*) 330; shrunk etc. 195.

Adv. in a -small compass, — nutshell; on a small scale.

194. Expansion.—N. expansion; increase etc. 35 -of size; enlargement, extension, augmentation; ampli-fication, -ation; aggrandizement, spread, increment, growth, development, pullulation, swell, dilation, dilatation, rarefaction; turg-escence, -idness, -idity; obesity etc. (*size*) 192; dropsy, tumefaction, intumescence, swelling, tumor, *diastole*, distension; puff-ing, -iness; inflation; pandiculation.

dilatability, expansibility.

germination, growth, upgrowth; accretion etc. 35.

over-growth, -distension; hypertrophy, tympany.

bulb etc. (*convexity*) 250; plumper; superiority of size.

V. become -larger etc. (large etc. 192); expand, widen, enlarge, extend, grow, increase, incrassate, swell, gather; fill out; deploy, take open order, dilate, stretch, spread; mantle, wax; grow −, spring- up; bud, bourgeon, shoot, sprout, germinate, put forth, vegetate, pullulate, open, burst forth, flower, blow etc. 734; gain −, gather- flesh; outgrow; spread like wildfire, overrun.

be larger than; surpass etc. (*be superior*) 33.

render -larger etc. (large etc. 192); expand, spread, extend, aggrandize, distend, develop, amplify, spread out, widen, magnify, rarefy, inflate, puff, puff out, blow up, stuff, pad, cram; exaggerate; fatten.

Adj. expanded etc. *v.*; larger etc. (large etc. 192); swollen; expansive; wide-open, -spread; fan-shaped; flabelliform; overgrown exaggerated, bloated, fat, turgid, tumid, hypertrophied, dropsical; pot-, swag-bellied; edematous, obese, puffy, pursy, blowzy, distended; patulous; bulbous etc. (*convex*) 250; full-blown, -grown, -formed; big etc. 192.

195. Contraction.—N. contraction, reduction, diminution; decrease etc. 36- of size; defalcation, decrement; lessening, shrinkage; collapse; emaciation, attenuation, tabefaction, comsumption, marasmus, atrophy; systole, neck, hourglass.

condensation, compression, constraint, compactness; compendium etc. 596; squeezing etc. *v.*; strangulation; corrugation; astringency, constringency; astringents, sclerotics; contractility, compressibility; coarctation.

inferiority in size.

V. become -small, − smaller; lessen, decrease etc. 36; grow less, dwindle, shrink, contract, narrow, shrivel, collapse, wither, lose flesh, wizen, fall away, waste, wane, ebb; decal etc. (*deteriorate*) 659.

be smaller than, fall short of; not come up to etc. (*be inferior*) 34.

render smaller, lessen, diminish, contract, draw in, shrink, shrivel, narrow, coarctate; constrict, constringe; condense, compress, boil down, deflate, exhaust, empty; squeeze, corrugate, crush, crumple up, warp, purse up, pack, stow; pinch, tighten, strangle; cramp; dwarf, bedwarf; shorten etc. 201; circumscribe etc. 229; restrain etc. 751; fold etc. 258.

pare, reduce, attenuate, rub down, scrape, file, grind, chip, shave, shear.

Adj. contracting etc. *v.*; astringent; shrunk, contracted etc. *v.*; strangulated, tabid, wizened, stunted, tabescent; marasmic; waning etc. *v.*; neap; compact; shriveled, preshrunk.

unexpanded etc. (expand etc. 194); inswept; contractile; compressible; smaller etc. small etc. 193).

196. Distance.—N. distance; space etc. 180; remoteness, farness; far- cry to; longinquity, elongation; offing, background; removedness; parallax; reach, span, stride; drift.

out-post, -skirt; horizon, sky-line; aphelion; foreign parts, *ultima Thule*, *ne plus ultra*, antipodes; long range, giant's stride.

dispersion etc. 73.

V. be -distant etc. *adj.*; extend −, stretch −, reach −, spread −, go −, get −, stretch away- to; range, outrange, outreach.

remain at a distance; keep −, stand- -away, - off, − aloof, − clear of.

Adj. distant; far -off, away; remote, telescopic, distal, wide of; stretching to etc. *v.*; yon, -der; ulterior; trans-marine, -pontine, -atlantic, -pacific, -continental, -polar, -equatorial, -alpine; tramontane; ultra-montane, -mundane; hyperborean, antihodean; inaccessible, out of the way; unapproached, -able; incontiguous.

Adv. far -off, − away; afar, -off; off; away; a-long, − great, − good- way off; wide away, aloof; wide −, clear- of; out of -the way. − reach; abroad, yonder, farther, further, beyond; *outre mer*, over the border, far and wide, over the hills and far away; from pole to pole etc. (*over great space*) 180; to the -uttermost parts. − ends- of the earth; out of -hearing, − range, nobody knows where, *à perte de vue*, out of the sphere of, wide of the mark; a far cry to.

apart, asunder; wide -apart, − asunder; *longo intervallo*; at arm's length.

197. Nearness.—N. nearness etc. *adj.*; proximity, propinquity; vicinity, -age; neighborhood, adjacency; contiguity etc. 199.

short -distance, − step, − cut; earshot, close quarters, brief span; stone's throw; bow −, gun −, pistol- shot; hair's breadth, span; close-up.

purlieus, neighborhood, vicinage, *environs*, *alentours*; suburbs, confines, *banlieue*, borderland; whereabouts.

bystander; neighbor, borderer.

approach etc. 286; convergence etc. 290; perihelion.

V. be -near etc. *adj.*; adjoin, hang about, trench on; border-, verge upon; stand by, approximate, tread on the heels of, cling to, clasp, hug; cuddle, huddle; hang about the skirts of, hover over; burn; abut.

bring −, draw- -near etc. 286; converge etc. 290; crowd etc. 72; place -side by side etc. *adv.*

Adj. near, nigh; close-, near- at hand; close, neighboring, propinquent, bordering upon; adjacent, adjoining, limitrophe; proxim-ate, -al; at hand, handy; near the mark, near run; home, intimate.

Adv. near, nigh; hard −, fast- by; close -to, upon, − up; at the point of; next door to; within -reach, − call, − hearing, − earshot, − range within an ace of; but a step, not far from, at no great distance; on the -verge, − brink, − skirts- of; in the -environs etc. *n.*; at one's -door, − feet, − elbow, − finger's end, − side; on the tip of one's tongue; under one's nose; within a -stone's throw etc. *n.*; in -sight, − presence- of; at close quarters; cheek by -jole, − jowl; beside, alongside, side by side, *tête-à-tête*; in juxtaposition etc. (*touching*) 199; yard-arm to yard-arm; at the heels of; on the confines of, at the threshold, bordering upon, verging to; in the way.

about; here- there-abouts; roughly, in round

numbers; approxim- -ately, – atively; as good as, well nigh.

198. Interval.—N. interval, interspace; separation etc. 44; break gap, opening; hole etc. 260; chasm, *hiatus,* caesura; inter-ruption,- regnum; interstice, *lacuna,* cleft, mesh, crevice, chink, rime, creek, cranny, crack, chap, slit, slot, fissure, scissure, rift, flaw, breach, fracture, rent, gash, cut, leak, dike, ha-ha.

gorge, defile, ravine, canon, *crevasse,* abyss, abysm; gulf; inlet, frith, strait, gully, gulch, nullah; pass; notch; furrow etc. 259; yawning gulf; *hiatus - maxime, – valde- deflendus;* parenthesis etc. (*interjacence)* 228; void etc. (*absence)* 187; incompleteness etc. 530.

V. gape etc. (*open)* 260; part, remove.

Adj. with an interval, far between; separated, spaced, split.

Adv. at intervals etc. (*discontinuously)* 70; *longo intervallo.*

199. Contiguity.—N. contiguity, contact, proximity, apposition, juxtaposition, touching etc. *v.;* abutment, osculation; meeting, appulse, appulsion, *rencontre,* rencounter, syzygy, coincidence, conjunction, coexistence; adhesion etc. 46.

border-land; frontier etc. (*limit)* 233; tangent.

V. be -contiguous etc. *adj.;* join, adjoin, abut on, march with, border; tick, graze, touch, meet, osculate, kiss, come in contact; coincide; coexist; adhere etc. 46.

Adj. contiguous; touching etc. *v.;* in -contact etc. *n.,* conterminous, end to end, osculatory; pertingent; tangential.

hand to hand; close to etc. (*near)* 197; with no - interval etc. 198.

200. Length.—N. length, longitude, span, extent, mileage.

line, bar, rule, stripe, streak, spoke, radius.

lengthening etc. *v.;* pro-longation, -duction, - traction; ten-sion, -sure; extension.

[Measures of length] line, nail, inch, hand, palm, foot, cubit, yard, ell, fathom, rod, pole, perch, furlong, mile, league; chain, meter, kilo-, centi-, milli- etc meter.

pedometer, perambulator, odometer, odograph, speedometer, cyclometer, log, telemeter, range finder; scale etc. (*measurement)* 466.

V. be -long etc. *adj.;* stretch out, sprawl; extend –, reach –, stretch -to; make a long arm, 'drag its slow length along.'

render -long etc. *adj.;* lengthen, extend, elongate; stretch; pro-long, -duce, -tract; let –, pay –, draw –, spin- out; drawl.

enfilade, look along, view in perspective.

Adj. long, -some; lengthy, lank, wiredrawn, outstretched; stretched, drawn out, lengthened etc. *v.,* sesquipedalian etc. (*words)* 577; interminable, no end of.

line-ar, -al; longitudinal, oblong.

as long as -my arm, –to-day and to-morrow; unshortened etc. (*shorten* etc. 201).

Adv. lengthwise, at length, longitudinally, endlong, along; *tandem;* in a line etc. (*continuously)* 69; in perspective.

from -end to end; –stem to stern, –head to foot, –the crown of the head to the sole of the foot, – top to toe, –head to heels; fore and aft.

201. Shortness.—N. shortness etc. *adj.;* brevity; littleness etc. 193; a span.

shortening etc. *v.;* abbrevia-tion, -ture; abridgment, concision, retrenchment, curtailment, decurtation; reduction etc. (*contraction)* 195; epitome etc. (*compendium)* 596.

abridger, abstractor, epitomiser.

elision, ellipsis; conciseness etc. (*in style)* 572.

V. be -short etc. *adj.;* render -short etc. *adj.;* shorten, curtail, abridge, abbreviate, take in, reduce; compress etc. (*contract)* 195; epitomize etc. 596.

retrench, cut short, obtruncate; scrimp, cut, chop up, hack, hew; cut –, pare- down; clip, snip, dock, lop, prune; shear, shave, mow, reap, crop; snub; truncate, pollard, stunt, nip, nip in the bud, check the growth of; [in drawing] foreshorten.

Adj. short, brief, curt; compendious, compact; stubby, scrimp; shorn, stubbed; stumpy, thickset, podgy, stocky, pug; squab, -by; squat, dumpy; little etc. 193; curtailed of its fair proportions; short by; oblate; concise etc. 572; summary.

Adv. shortly etc. *adj.;* in short etc. (*concisely)* 572.

202. Breadth. Thickness.—N. breadth, width, latitude, amplitude; diameter, bore, calibre, radius; superficial extent etc. (*space)* 180.

thickness, crassitude, corpulence etc. (*size)* 192; dilatation etc. (*expansion)* 194.

V. be -broad etc. *adj.;* become –, render- - broad etc. *adj.;* expand etc. 194; thicken, widen.

Adj. broad, wide, ample, extended; discous; fanlike; out-spread, -stretched; wide as a church-door.

thick, dumpy, squab, squat, thickset, tubby; thick as a rope, stubby etc. 201.

203. Narrowness. Thinness.—N. narrowness etc. *adj.,* closeness, exility; exiguity etc. (*little)* 193.

line; hair's –, finger's -breadth; strip, streak, vein.

thinness etc. *adj.;* tenuity; emaciation, slenderness, macilency, *marcor.*

shaving, slip etc. (*filament)* 205; threadpaper; skeleton, shadow, scrag, anatomy, spindle-shanks, barebones, lantern jaws, mere skin and bone.

middle construction, stricture, neck, waist, isthmus, wasp, hour-glass; ridge, *ghaut,* pass; ravine etc. 198.

narrowing, coarctation, angustation, tapering, contraction etc. 195.

V. be-narrow etc. *adj.;* narrow, taper, diminish, contract etc 195; render -narrow etc. *adj.*

Adj. narrow, close; slender, thin, fine; *svelte;* thread-like etc. (*filament)* 205; finespun, taper, slim, gracile, slight, slight-made; scant, -y; spare, delicate, incapacious; contracted etc. 195; unexpanded etc. (expand etc. 194); slender as a thread, capillary.

emaciated, lean, meager, gaunt, macilent; lank, -y; weedy, skinny, scrawny, scraggy; starv-ed, -cling; attenuated, shrivelled; wizened, pinched, peaky; skeletal, spindling, spindle- -legged, -shanked; extenuated, tabid, marcid, bare-bone, raw-boned; herring-gutted; worn to a shadow, lean as a rake; thin as a -lath,—whipping post.—wafer; hatchet-faced; lantern-jawed.

204. Layer.—N. layer, stratum, course, bed, zone, *substratum,*floor, flag, stage, story, tier, slab, escarpment, table, tablet, panel, plaque; board, plank; trencher, platter.

plate; lam-ina, -ella; sheet, flake, foil, wafer, scale, coat, peel, pellicle, ply, thickness, membrane, film, leaf, slice, shive, cut, rasher, shaving, integument etc. (*covering*) 223.

V. slice, shave, pare, peel; plate, coat, veneer; cover etc. 223.

Adj. lamell-ar, -ated, -iform; laminated, -iferous; micaceous; schist-ose, -ous; scaly; filmy, membranous, flaky, squamous; folia-ted, -ceous; stratified, -form; tabular, discoid, spathic.

205. Filament.—N. filament, line; fiber, fibril, funicle, vein, hair, capillament, *cilium*, tendril, gossamer; hair-stroke; harl.

wire, string, thread, packthread, cotton, sewing-silk, twine, twist, whip-cord, cord, rope, cable, yarn, hemp, oakum, jute, wool, worsted.

strip, shred, slip, spill, list, band, fillet, *fascia*, ribbon, riband, tape, roll, lath, slat, strake, splinter, shiver, shaving.

beard etc. (*roughness*) 256; ramification; strand.

Adj. fil-amentous, -aceous, -iform; fibr-ous, -illous; thread-like, wiry, stringy, ropy; capill-ary, -iform; funicular, wire-drawn; anguilliform; flagelliform; hairy etc. (*rough*) 256; ligulate.

206. Height.—N. height, altitude, elevation, ceiling; eminence, pitch; loftiness etc. *adj.*; sublimity.

tallness etc. *adj.*; stature, procerity; prominence etc. 250.

colossus etc. (*size*) 192; giant, grenadier, giraffe.

mount, -ain; hill, butte, monticle, fell, knap; -cape; head-, fore-land; promontory; ridge, hog's back, dune; rising - - vantage- ground; down; moor, -land; Alp, up-, table-, high-lands; heights etc. (*summit*) 210; knoll, hummock, hillock, barrow, mound, mole, *kopje*; steeps, bluff, cliff, craig, tor, peak, pike, clough; escarpment, edge, ledge, brae; dizzy height.

tower, pillar, column, pylon, obelisk, monument, steeple, spire, minaret, *campanile*, belfry, turret, roof, dome, cupola, pagoda, pyramid; sky scraper; Eiffel tower.

pole, pikestaff, maypole, flagstaff; mast, top—, topgallant- mast.

ceiling etc (*covering*) 223.

high water, high—, flood—, spring-tide.

altimetry etc (*angle*) 244; altimeter, height-finder, hypsometer, barograph.

V. be -high etc *adj*.; tower, soar, command; hover; cap, culminate; overhang, hang over, impend, beetle; bestride, ride, mount; perch, surmount; cover etc. 233; overtop etc. (*be superior*) 33; stand on tiptoe.

become -high etc. *adj.*; grow, - higher, - taller; upgrow; rise etc. (*ascend*) 305.

render -high etc. *adj.*; heighten etc. (*elevate*) 307.

Adj. high, elevated, eminent, exalted, lofty, supernal; tall; gigantic etc. (*big*) 192; Patagonian; towering, beetling, soaring, hanging [gardens]; elevated etc. 307; upper; highest etc. (*topmost*) 210; monticulous, perching, hill-dwelling.

up-, moor-land; hilly, mountainous, alpine, subalpine, heaven-kissing; cloud-topt, -capt, -touching; aerial.

overhanging etc. *v.*; incumbent, overlying; super-incumbent, -natant, -imposed; prominent etc. 250.

tall as a -maypole, —poplar,—steeple; lanky etc. (*thin*) 203.

Adv. on high, high up, aloft, up, above, aloof, overhead; up—, above- stairs; in the clouds; on -tiptoe, —stilts,—the shoulders of; over head and ears; breast high.

over, upwards; from top to bottom etc. (*completely*) 52.

207. Lowness.—N. lowness etc. *adj.*; debasement, depression; prostration etc. (*horizontal*) 213; depression etc. (*concave*) 252.

molehill; lowlands; bottomlands; basement-ground-floor; *rez de chaussée* etc. 211; hold; feet, heels.

low water; low—, ebb—, neap—, spring- tide.

V. be -low etc. *adj.*; lie -low, —flat; underlie; crouch, slouch, wallow, grovel; lower etc. (*depress*) 308.

Adj. low, neap, debased; nether, -most; flat, level with the ground; lying low etc. *v.*; crouched, subjacent, squat, prostrate etc. (*horizontal*) 213.

Adv. under; be-, under-neath; below; down, -wards; adown, at the foot of; under-foot, -ground; down—, below-stairs; at a low ebb; below par.

208. Depth.—N. depth; deepness etc. *adj.*; profundity, depression etc. (*concavity*) 252.

hollow, pit, shaft, well, crater, abyss; gulf etc. 198; bowels of the earth, bottomless pit, hell.

soundings, sonar, depth of water, water, draught; submersion; plummet, sound, probe; sounding -rod, - line, - machine; lead; submarine, diving bell, bathysphere; diver.

V. be -deep etc. *adj.*; render -deep etc. *adj.*; deepen.

plunge etc. 310; sound, heave the lead, take soundings; dig etc. (*excavate*) 252.

Adj. deep, -seated; profound, sunk, buried; submerged etc. 310; sub-aqueous, -marine, -terranean, -terrene; underground.

bottom-, sound-, fathom-less; unfathom-ed, -able; abysmal; deep as a well, deep-sea.

knee-, ankle-deep.

Adv. beyond—, out of- one's depth; over head and ears, over one's head.

209. Shallowness.—N. shallowness etc. *adj.*; shoals; mere scratch; veneer, gloss, pinprick.

Adj. shallow, superficial; skin-, ankle-, knee-deep; just enough to wet one's feet; shoal, -y.

V. shallow, shoal, skim— over, —the surface, touch on.

210. Summit.—N. summit, -y; top, vertex, apex, zenith, pinnacle, acme, acropolis, culmination, meridian, utmost height, *ne plus ultra*, height, pitch, maximum, climax, apogee; culminating —, crowning —, turning- point; turn of the tide, fountain head; water-shed, -parting; sky, pole.

tip, -top; crest, crow's nest, cap, truck, peak, nib; end etc. 67; crown, brow; head, nob, noddle, pate, skull, cranium.

high places, heights.

top-, top-gallant mast, sky scraper; quarter — hurricane- deck.

architrave, frieze, cornice, coping, coping-stone, zoophorus, capital, headpiece, capstone, epistyle, sconce, pediment, entablature; tympanum; ceiling etc. (*covering*) 223.

attic, loft, garret, house-top, upper story, roof, topping, icing, frosting.

V. culminate, cap, crown, top; overtop etc. (*be superior to*) 33.

Adj. highest etc. (high etc. 206); top; top-, upper-most; tip-top; culminating etc. *v.*; meridi-an, -onal; capital, head, polar, supreme, supernal, top-gallant.

Adv. a-top, at the top of — the tree, — the heap.

211. Base.—N. base, -ment; plinth, dado, wainscot, baseboard; foundation etc. (*support*) 215; substructure, *sub stratum*, sump, ground, earth, pavement, floor, paving, flag, carpet, ground-floor, deck; footing, groundwork, basis; hold, bilge, orlop deck.

bottom, nadir, foot, sole, toe, hoof, keel, kelson, root.

Adj. bottom; under-, nether-most; fundamental; founded —, based —, grounded —, built- on.

212. Verticality.—N. verticality; erectness etc. *adj.*; perpendicularity; right angle, normal; azimuth circle.

wall, palisade, precipice, cliff, steep, bluff.

elevation, erection; square, plumb-line, plummet.

V. be -vertical etc. *adj.*; stand -up, — on end, — erect, — upright; stick —, cock-up.

render -vertical etc. *adj.*; set —, stick —, raise —, cock- up; erect, rear, raise, pitch, raise on its legs.

Adj. vertical, upright, erect, perpendicular, normal, plumb, straight, bolt upright; rampant; straight —, standing- up etc. *v.*; rectangular, orthogonal.

Adv. vertically etc. *adj.*; up, on end; up —, right- on end; *à plomb*, endwise; on one's legs; at right angles.

213. Horizontality.—N. horizontality; flatness; level, plane; stratum etc. 204; dead -level, — flat; level plane.

recumbency; lying down etc. *v.*; reclination, decumbence; de-, discumbency; proneness etc. *adj.*; accubation, supination, resupination, prostration; azimuth.

plain, floor, platform, bowling-green; cricket--ground; court; gridiron; base-ball diamond; hockey rink; tennis-, croquet-ground, — lawn; billiard table; terrace, estrade, esplanade, *parterre*, table-land, *plateau*, ledge.

spirit-, level; T-square.

V. be -horizontal etc. *adj.*; lie, recline, couch; lie -down, — flat, — prostrate; sprawl, loll; sit down.

render -horizontal etc. *adj.*; lay, — down, — out; level, flatten, even, raze, equalize, smooth, align; prostrate, knock down, floor, fell, ground.

Adj. horizontal, level, even, plane; flat etc. 251; flat as a -billiard table, — bowling green; alluvial; calm, — as a mill-pond; smooth, —as glass.

re-, de-, pro-, ac-cumbent; lying etc. *v.*; prone, supine, couchant, jacent, prostrate.

Adv. horizontally etc. *adj.*; on -one's back. —all fours, — its beam ends.

214. Pendency.—N. pend-, dependency; suspension, hanging etc. *v.*

pendant, drop, tippet, tassel, lobe, tail, train, flap, lappet, skirt, pig-tail, queue, pendulum, hanger, suspender, supporter.

peg, knob, button, hook, nail, stud, ring, staple, tenterhook; davit; fastening etc. 45; spar, horse, chande-, gase-, electro-lier.

V. be -pendent etc. *adj.*; hang, depend, swing, dangle, droop; sag; swag; daggle, flap, trail, flow, suspend, hang, sling, hook up, hitch, fasten to, append.

Adj. pend-ent, -ulous; pensile; hanging etc. *v.*; dependent; suspended etc. *v.*; lowering, overhanging, beetling, decumbent; loose, flowing, having a -peduncle etc. *n.*; pedunculate, tailed, caudate.

215. Support.—N. support, backing, ground, foundation, base, basis; *terra firma*; bearing, fulcrum, *point d'appui*, caudex, purchase, footing, hold, -*locus standi*; landing, — stage, — place; stage, platform; block; rest, resting-place; ground--work, *substratum*, sustentation, subvention; floor etc. (*basement*) 211.

supporter; aid etc. 707; prop, stand, anvil, fulciment; hod, stay, shore, skid, rib, sprag, truss, bandage; sleeper; stirrup, stilts, shoe, sole, heel, splint, lap; bar, rod, boom; sprit, outrigger.

staff, stick, crutch, alpenstock, bourdon; *bâton*, maulstick, colstaff, cowlstaff, staddle; stalk, ped-icel, -icle, — uncle.

post; pillar, shaft, column, pilaster; pediment, pedestal; plinth, shank, leg, socle, zocle; buttress, jamb, mullion, abutment; pile, baluster, banister, stanchion, king post; balustrade.

frame, -work, body, *chassis, fuselage*; scaffold, skeleton, beam, rafter, girder, lintel, joist, cantilever, travis, trave, corner-stone, summer, transom; rung, round, step, sill.

columella, back-bone; key-stone; axle, -tree; axis; arch, ogive, mainstay.

trunnion, pivot, rowlock; peg etc. (*pendency*)

214; tie-beam etc. (*fastening*) 45; thole pin.

board, ledge, shelf, hob, bracket, trevet, trivet, arbor, rack, hatrack; mantel, -piece, -shelf; slab, console; counter, dresser, flange, corbel; table, trestle, teapoy; shoulder; perch; horse; easel, desk; retable, predella.

seat, throne, dais; divan, musnud; chair, bench, form, stool, camp-stool, sofa, settee, davenport, stall, miserere, arm –, easy –, elbow –, rocking-chair; couch, day bed, *fauteuil*, woolsack, ottoman, settle, squab, bench, box, dicky;- saddle, pannel, pillion; side –, pack- saddle; pommel.

bed, berth, pallet, tester, crib, cot, bassinet, hammock, shakedown, camp bed, bunk, truckle-bed, cradle, litter, stretcher, bedstead; four-poster, French bed; bedding, mattress, *paillasse;* pillow, bolster; mat, rug, cushion.

stool, footstool, hassock, faldstool, *prie-dieu;* tabouret; tripod.

Atlas, Persides, Atlantes, Caryatides, Hercules.
V. be -supported etc.; lie –, sit –, recline –, lean –, loll –, rest –, stand –, step –, repose – , abut –, beat –, be based etc.- on; have at one's back; be-stride, -straddle.

support, bear, carry, hold, sustain, shoulder; hold –, back –, bolster –, shore- up; up-hold, -bear; prop; under-prop,-pin, -set; bandage, etc. 43; brace, truss; cradle, pillow.

give –, furnish –, afford –, supply –, lend- -support, – foundations; bottom, found, base, ground, embed.

maintain, keep on foot; aid etc. 707.
Adj. support-ing, -ed, etc.*v.*; atlantean, columellar; sustentative, fundamental, basal.
Adv. astride on, astraddle; pick-a-back.

216. Parallelism.—**N.** parallelism; coextension, concentricity, collimation.
V. be –, lie- parallel to; collimate; equate, match.
Adj. parallel; coextensive, collateral, concentric, concurrent, abreast, aligned.
Adv. alongside, abreast etc. (*laterally*) 236.

217. Obliquity.—**N.** obliquity, inclination, skew, slope, slant; crookedness etc. *adj.*; slopeness; leaning etc. *v.*; bevel, bezel, ramp, tilt; bias, list, twist, warp, swag, cant, lurch; distortion etc. 243; bend etc. (*curve*) 245; tower of Pisa.

acclivity, rise, ascent, grade, gradient, *glacis*, rising ground, hill, bank, declivity, downhill, dip, fall, devexity; gentle –, rapid- slope; easy -ascent, – descent; shelving beach; *talus; montagne Russe; facilis descensus Averni.*

steepness etc. *adj.*; cliff, precipice etc. (*vertical*) 212; escarpment, scarp.

[Measure of inclination]clinometer, theodolite, level, sextant, quadrant, protractor; angle, sine, cosine, tangent etc. hypothenuse.

diagonal; zigzag, chevron.
V. be -oblique etc. *adj.*; slope, slant, lean, incline, shelve, stoop, decline, descent, bend, heel, careen, sag, swag, seel, slouch, cant, sidle.

render -oblique etc. *adj.*; sway, bias; slope, slant; incline, bend, crook; cant, tilt; distort etc. 243.
Adj. oblique, inclined; sloping etc. *v.*; tilted etc.

v.; recumbent, clinal, skew, askew, slant, aslant, bias, plagiedral, indirect, wry, awry, ajee, crooked; knock-kneed etc. (*distorted*) 243; bevel, out of the perpendicular.

uphill, rising, ascending, acclivous; downhill, falling, descending; declining, declivous, devex, anticlinal; steep, abrupt, precipitous, breakneck.

diagonal; trans-verse, -versal; athwart, antiparallel; curved etc. 245.
Adv. obliquely etc. *adj.*; on –, all on- one side; askew, askant, askance, aslope, asquint, edgewise, at an angle; side-long, -ways; slope-, slant-wise; by a side wind.

218. Inversion.—**N.** in-, e-, sub-, re-, retro-, intro-version; contraposition etc. 237; contrariety etc. 14; reversal; turn of the tide.

overturn, upset, capsize; somer-sault, -set; summerset; *culbute;* revulsion; *pirouette.*

transposition, transposal, anastrophy, *metastasis, hyperbaton, anastrophe, hysteron--proteron,* hypallage, *synchysis, tmesis,* parenthesis; *metathesis;* palindrome; Spoonerism.

pronation and supination.
V. be -inverted etc.; turn –, go –, wheel- -round, – about, – to the right about; turn –, go –, tilt –, topple-over; capsize, turn turtle.

in-, sub-, retro-, intro-vert; reverse; up-, over-turn, -set; turn -topsy turvy etc. *adj.; culbuter;* transpose, put the cart before the horse, turn the tables.
Adj. inverted etc. *v.*; wrong side -out, – up; inside out, upside down; bottom –, keel- upwards, supine, on one's head, topsy turvy, *sens dessus sens dessous.*

inverse; reverse etc. (*contrary*) 14; opposite etc. 237.

topheavy, unstable.
Adv. inversely etc.*adj.*; hirdie-girdie; heels over head, head over heels.

219. Crossing.—**N.** crossing etc. *v.*; intersection, – lacement, – twinement, -digitation; decussation, transversion; convolution etc. 248.

reticulation, meshwork, network; inosculation, anastomosis, inter-texture, mortise.

net, *plexus,* web, mesh, twill, skein, sleeve, felt, lace; wicker; mat, ting; plait, trellis, wattle, lattice, grating, *grille,* gridiron, tracery, fretwork, filigree, reticle; tissue, netting, mokes.

cross, crucifix, rood, crisscross, crux; chain, wreath, braid, cat's cradle,knot; entanglement etc. (*disorder*) 59.

[woven fabrics] cloth, linen, muslin, cambric, drill, homespun, tweed, broadcloth etc.
V. cross, decussate; inter-sect, -lace, -twine, twist, -weave, -digitate, -link.

twine, entwine, weave, inweave, twist, wreathe; anastomose, inosculate, dovetail, splice, link.

mat, plait, plat, braid, felt, twill; tangle, entangle, ravel, net, knot; dishevel, raddle.
Adj. crossing etc.*v.*; crossed, matted etc. *v.*, transverse.

cross, cruciform, crucial, reti-form, -cular, culated; areolar, cancellated, mullioned, latticed, grated, barred, streaked; textile, secant, plexal, interfretted.
Adv. across, thwart, athwart, transversely, crosswise.

220. Exteriority.—N. exteriority; outside, exterior; surface, superficies; skin etc. (*covering*) 223; *superstratum*; disk, disc; face, facet, external, the open.

excentricity; circumjacence etc. 227.

V. be -exterior etc. *adj.*; lie around etc. 227.

place -exteriorly, — outwardly, — outside; put —, turn- out.

Adj. exter-ior, -nal; extraneous, outer, -most; out-ward, -lying, -side, -door; round about etc. 227; extramural.

superficial, skin-deep; frontal, discoid.

extraregarding; eccentric; outstanding; extrinsic etc. 6.

Adv. externally etc. *adj.*; out, without, over, outwards, *ab extra*, out of doors; *extra muros*.

in the open air; *sub -Jovè*, — *dio; à la belle étoile, al fresco.*

221. Interiority.—N. interiority; inside, -land, interior, endocrine; interspace, subsoil, *sub-stratum*.

contents etc. 190; substance, pith, marrow; backbone etc. (*center*) 222; heart, bosom, breast, abdomen; vitals, viscera, entrails, bowels, belly, intestines, guts, chitterlings, womb, lap; gland, cell; internal organs, *penetralia*, recesses, innermost recesses; cave etc. (*concavity*) 252.

inhabitant etc. 188.

V. be -inside etc. *adj.*, — within etc. *adv.*

place —, keep- within; enclose etc. (*circumscribe*) 229; intern; embed etc. (*insert*) 300.

Adj. inter-ior, -nal; inner, inside, intimate, inward, intraregarding; in-, inner-most; deep-seated; visceral, intestine, -tinal; inland; subcutaneous; interstitial etc. (*interjacent*) 228; inwrought etc. (*intrinsic*) 5; enclosed etc. *v.*

home, domestic, indoor, intramural, vernacular; endemic.

Adv. internally etc. *adj.*; inwards, within, in, inly; here-, there-, where-in; *ab intra*, withinside; in —, within- doors; at home, in the bosom of one's family.

222. Centrality.—N. centrality, centricalness, center; middle etc. 68; focus etc. 74.

core, kernel; nucleus, nucleolus; heart, pole, axis, pivot, fulcrum, bull's eye; hub, nave, navel; *umbilicus*, spine, backbone, marrow, pith; hot-bed; concentration etc. (*convergence*) 290; centralization; symmetry.

center of -gravity, — pressure, — percussion, — oscillation, — buoyancy etc. metacenter.

V. be -central etc. *adj.*; converge etc. 290.

render central, centralize, concentrate; bring to a focus.

Adj. centr-al, -ical; middle etc. 68; axial, pivotal, focal, umbilical, concentric; middlemost; nuclear, centric, centraidal; spinal, vertebral.

Adv. middle; midst; centrally etc. *adj.*

223. Covering.—N. covering, cover; canopy, tilt, awning, baldachin, tent, marquee, *tente d'abri*, umbrella, parasol, sunshade; veil (*shade*) 424; shield etc. (*defense*) 717; hall.

roof, dome, cupola, mansard roof; ceiling; thatch, tile; pan-, pen-tile; tiling, shingles, slates, slating, leads; shed etc. (*abode*) 189.

top, lid, covercle, door, *operculum*, eyelid, blind, curtain.

bandage, plaster, lint, wrapping, dossil, finger stall.

coverlet, counterpane, sheet, quilt, comforter, eiderdown; tarpaulin, blanket, rug, drugget, linoleum, oilcloth; housing.

in-, tegument; skin, pellicle, fleece, fell, fur, ermine, miniver, sable, sealskin etc.; fabrikoid; leather, morocco, calf, pigskin, elk, kid, cowhide etc.; shagreen, hide; pelt, -ry; cuticle, *dermis*, scarf-skin, *epidermis*.

clothing etc. 225; mask etc. (*concealment*) 530.

peel, crust, bark, rind, *cortex*, husk, shell, coat.

capsule; ferrule; sheath, -ing; pod, cod; casing, case, theca; *elytrqn; involucrum;* wrapp-ing, -er, cellophane; envelope, vesicle; dermatology, conchology.

armor, -plate, armoring; veneer, facing; pavement; scale etc. (*layer*) 204; coating, paint, stain; varnish etc. (*resin*) 356a; anointing etc. *v.*; inunction; incrustation, superposition, obduction, ground, enamel, whitewash, plaster, stucco, rough cast, pebble dash, compo; rendering; cerement; ointment etc. (*grease*) 356.

V. cover; super-pose, -impose; over-lay, -spread; wrap etc. 225; incase; face, case, veneer, pave, paper; tip, cap, bind, revet.

coat, paint, varnish, pay, incrust, stucco, cement, dab, plaster, tar; wash; be-, smear; be-, daub; anoint, do over; gild, plate, electroplate, japan, laquer, lacker, enamel, whitewash; lay it on thick.

over-lie, -arch; conceal etc. 528.

Adj. covering etc. *v.*; cutaneous, dermal, cortical, cuticular, tegumentary, skinny, scaly, squamous; covered etc. *v.*; imbricated, loricated, armor-plated, iron-clad; under cover, hooded, cloaked, cowled.

224. Lining.—N. lining, inner coating; coating etc. (*covering*) 223; stalactite, -agmite.

filling, stuffing, wadding, padding, bushing, wainscot, *parietes*, wall brattice.

V. line, stuff, incrust, wad, pad, fill.

Adj. lined etc. *v.*

225. Investment.—N. investment; covering etc. 223; dress, clothing, raiment, drapery, costume, attire, guise, toilet, *toilette*, trim; habiliment; vesture, -ment; garment, garb, palliament, apparel, wardrobe, wearing apparel, clothes, things.

array; tailoring, millinery; best bib and tucker; finery etc. (*ornament*) 847; full dress etc. (*show*) 882; garniture; theatrical properties.

outfit, equipment, *trousseau*; uniform, khaki, regimentals; academicals, canonicals etc. 999; livery, gear, harness, turn out, accoutrement, caparison, suit, rigging, trappings, traps, slops, togs, toggery; masquerade.

dishabille, morning dress, lounge suit, tea-gown, *kimono, négligé*, dressing-gown, *peignoir*, wrapper, undress; shooting-coat; smoking jacket, mufti; rags, tatters, old clothes; mourning, weeds; duds; slippers.

robe, tunic, dolman, *paletot*, habit, gown, coat, coatee, frock, blouse, *pelisse*, middy, sagum, *toga*, smock-frock; frock-, dress-, morning-, tail- coat; dress-suit, – clothes, swallow-tail coat, dinner-, Eton-jacket.

cloak, pall; mantle, mantlet, mantua, shawl, *pelisse*, veil, yashmak; cape, tippet, kirtle, plaid, muffler, comforter, Balaclava helmet, haik, huke, chlamys, mantilla, tabard, housing, horse-cloth, burnous, *roquelaure*, *houppelande*; sur-, top-, over-, great-coat; *surtout*, spencer, cardigan, sweater, blazer; mackintosh, waterproof, slicker, raincoat, oilskin, trench coat, ulster, monkey-, pea-pilot-jacket, redingote; wraprascal, poncho, cardinal, pelerine, talma.

jacket, jumper, vest, jerkin, waistcoat, doublet, *camisole*, gabardine; stays, *corsage*, corset, corselet, bodice; stomacher, skirt, petticoat, slip, farthingale, kilt, jupe, crinoline, bustle, hobble skirt, *panier*, apron, pinafore; loin cloth.

trousers; breeches, trews, pantaloons, unmentionables, inexpressibles, overalls, pajamas, smalls, small-clothes; tights, pants, shorts, drawers; knickerbockers, knickers, plus fours, bloomers, divided skirt; phil-, fill-ibeg.

head-dress, -gear; cap, *béret*, tam o' shanter, glengarry, topee-sombrero, hat; cocked –, high –, tall –, top –, silk –, opera –, crush - hat, *gibus*, beaver, castor, bonnet, tile, wideawake, billy-cock; bowler; soft felt –, straw –, leghorn- hat, panama; toque, wimple; night-, mob-, skull-cap, biretta; hood, cowl, coif; capote, calash; scull-cap; kerchief, snood; head, *coiffure*; crown etc. (*circle*) 247; *chignon*, pelt, wig, front, peruke, periwig; caftan, turban, fez, *tarboosh*, taj, shako, csako, busby, *képi*, forage cap, bearskin; helmet etc. 717; mask, domino.

body clothes; linen; shirt, sark, smock, shift, *chemise*, *lingerie*; night-gown, -shirt; bed-gown, *sac de nuit*; jersey, guernsey; underclothing, - waistcoat.

neck-erchief, -cloth, tie, ruff, collar, cravat, stock, handkerchief, bandana, scarf, bib, tucker; dicky, boa; girdle etc. (*circle*) 247; cummerbund.

shoe, pump, brogue, boot, slipper, sandal, galoche, galoshes, arctics, rubber boots, overshoes, patten, clog, sabot, high-low; Blucher –, Wellington –, Hessian –, jack –, top- boot; Balmoral; legging, puttee, buskin, greave, galligaskin, moccasin, *gamache*, gambado, gaiter, spatter-dash, spat, antigropeles; stocking, hose, gaskins, trunk-hose, sock, hosiery.

glove, gauntlet, mitten, cuff, muffettee, wristband, sleeve.

swaddling cloth, baby-linen, *layette*; pocket-handkerchief.

shroud, etc. 363.

clothier, tailor, milliner, *costumier*, sempstress, seamstress, snip; dress-, habit-, breeches-, shoe-maker; cordwainer, cobbler, Crispin, hosier, hatter; draper, linendraper, haberdasher, mercer.

V.invest, cover etc. 223; envelop, lap, involve; in-, en-wrap, wrap, fold –, wrap –, lap –, muffle-up, overlap, sheathe, swathe, swaddle, roll up in, shroud, circumvest.

vest, clothe, array, dress, dight, drape, robe, enrobe, attire, tire, garb, habilitate, apparel, accouter, rig, fit out; bedizen, deck etc. (*ornament*) 847, perk, equip, harness, caparison; dress up.

wear; don; put –, huddle –, slip- on; mantle.

Adj. invested etc. v.; habited; dight, -ed; clad, *costumé*, shod, *chaussé*; *en grande tenue* etc. (*show*) 882.

sartorial.

226. Divestment.—N. divestment; taking off, stripping, removal etc. *v.*

nudity; bareness etc. *adj.*; undress; dishabille etc. 225, altogether; nu-, denu-dation; decortication, depilation, excoriation, desquamation; molting; exfoliation.

baldness, alopecia, acomia.

V. divest; uncover etc. (*cover* etc. 223); denude, bare, strip; undress, unclothe, disrobe etc. (dress, enrobe, etc. 225); uncoif; dismantle; uncase; put –, take –, cast- off; shed, doff; husk, peel, pare, decorticate, desquamate; excoriate, skin, scalp, flay, bark, expose, lay open; exfoliate, molt, mew; cast the skin.

Adj. divested etc. *v.*; bare, naked, nude; undressed, -draped, -clad, -clothed, -appareled; exposed; in dishabille; *décolleté*; bald, threadbare, ragged, callow, roofless.

in -a state of nature, – nature's garb, – buff, – native buff, – birthday suit; *in puris naturalibus*; with nothing on, stark naked; bald as a coot, bare as the back of one's hand; out at elbows; barefoot; bareback; leaf-, nap-, hairless, shaved, clean shaven, tonsured, beardless, bald-headed, acomous.

227. Circumjacence.—N. circumjacence, ambience; environment, encompassment; atmosphere, medium; surroundings, *entourage*.

outpost, border etc. (*edge*) 231; girdle etc. (*circumference*) 230; outskirts, *boulevards*, suburbs, purlieus, precincts, *faubourgs*, *environs*, *banlieue*, neighborhood, vicinity.

V.lie -around etc. *adv.*; surround, beset, compass, encompass, environ, inclose, enclose, encircle, circle, embrace, circumvent, lap, gird; begird, girdle, engird; skirt, twine round; hem in etc. (*circumscribe*) 229; besiege, invest, blockade.

Adj. circum-jacent, -ambient, -fluent; ambient; surrounding etc. *v.*, circumferential, suburban.

Adv. around, about; without; on -every side, – all sides, right and left, all round, round about; in the neighborhood.

228. Interjacence.—N. inter-jacence, -currence, -venience, -location, -digitation, - penetration, permeation.

inter-jection, -polation, -lineation, -spersion, - calation; embolism.

inter-vention, -ference, -position, in-, ob-trusion; insinuation, insertion etc. 300; dovetailing; infiltration; intromission.

intermedi-um, -ary, go-between, agent, middleman, medium, bodkin, intruder, interloper; parenthesis, episode, fly-leaf.

partition, *septum*, diaphragm, mid-riff; party wall, panel, vail, bulkhead, brattice, *cloison*; half way house.

V.lie –, come –, get- between; intervene, slide in, interpenetrate, permeate.

put between, introduce, intromit, import; throw –, wedge –, edge –, jam –, worm –, foist –, run –, plough –, work- in; interpose, -ject, -calate. -polate, -line, -leave, -sperse, -weave, -lard, -digitate; let in, dovetail, splice, mortise; insinuate, smuggle; infiltrate, ingrain.

interfere, put in an oar, thrust one's nose in; intrude, obtrude; have a finger in the pie; introduce the thin end of the wedge; thrust in etc. (*insert*) 300.

Adj. inter-jacent, -current, -venient, -vening etc. *v.*, -mediate, -mediary, -calary, -stitial, -costal, -mural, -planetary, -stellar; embolismal.

parenthetical, episodic: mediterranean; intrusive; embosomed; merged, mean, middle, medium, median.

Adv. between, betwixt; 'twixt; among, -st; amid, st; 'mid, -st; in the thick of; betwixt and between; sandwich-wise; parenthetically, *obiter dictum*.

---

229. Circumscription.—N. circumscription, limitation, inclosure; confinement etc. (*restraint*) 751; circumvallation, encincture; envelope etc. 232.

V. circumscribe, limit, bound, confine, restrict, enclose; surround etc. 227; compass about; imprision etc. (*restrain*) 751; hedge –, wall –, rail-in; fence –, hedge- round; embar; picket, corral.

enfold, bury, incase, pack up, enshrine, inclasp; wrap up etc. (*invest*) 225; embosom.

Adj. circumscribed etc. *v.*; begirt, lapt; circumambient; buried –, immersed- in; embosomed, in the bosom of, imbedded, encysted, mewed up; imprisoned etc. 751; land-locked, in a ring fence

---

230. Outline.—N. outline, circumference; perimeter, -phery; ambit, circuit, lines, *tournure, contour,* profile, *silhouette,* lineaments; bounds, coastline.

zone, belt, girth, band, baldric, zodiac, girdle, tire, cingle, clasp, girt; *cordon* etc. (*inclosure*) 232; circlet etc. 247.

V. outline, delineate, *silhouette,* circumscribe etc. 229; profile, block out.

Adj. outlined etc. *v.*; circumferential, perimetric, peripheral.

---

231. Edge.—N. edge, verge, brink, brow, brim, margin, border, confines, skirt, rim, felloe, felly, flange, side, mouth; jaws, chops, chaps, *fauces*; lip, muzzle.

threshold, door, porch; portal etc. (*opening*) 260; coast, shore, strand, beach, bank, wharf, quay, dock.

frame, fringe, flounce, frill, list, trimming, edging, skirting, hem, selvedge, welt; furbelow, valance, exergue.

Adj. border, marginal, skirting; labial; labiated, marginated.

---

232. Inclosure.—N. inclosure, enclosure, envelope; package, box, crate, case etc. (*receptacle*) 191; wrapper; girdle etc. 230.

pen, fold, croft, sty; pen-, in-, sheep-fold; paddock, pound, corral, kraal; yard, compound; net, seine net.

wall; hedge, -row; *espalier;* fence etc. (*defence*) 717; pale, paling, balustrade, rail, railing, gunwale; quickset hedge, park paling, circumvallation, *enciente*, ring fence.

barrier, barricade; gate; -way; door, hatch, *cordon;* prison etc. 752.

dike, dyke, ditch, fosse, moat, trench.

V. inclose; circumscribe etc. 229.

---

233. Limit.—N. limit, boundary, bounds, confine, *enclave*, term, bourn, verge, kerb-stone, curbstone, but, pale; termin-ation, -us; stint, frontier, precinct, marches.

boundary line, landmark; line of -demarcation, – circumvallation; pillars of Hercules; Rubicon, turning-point; *ne plus ultra;* sluice, flood-gate.

V. limit, bound, confine, define, circumscribe, demarcate, delimit, encompass.

Adj. definite; contermin-ate, -able, terminable, limitable; terminal, frontier, border, bordering, boundary.

Adv. thus far, – and no further.

---

234. Front.—N. front; fore, – part; foreground; forefront, face, disk, disc, frontage, *façade, proscenium,* facia, frontispiece; priority, anteriority; obverse [of a medal].

fore –, front- rank, first line; van, -guard; advanced guard; outpost, scout.

brow, forehead, visage, physiognomy, phiz, features, countenance, map, mug; rostrum, beak, bow, stem, prow, prore, jib, bowsprit; forecastle.

pioneer etc. (*precursor*) 64; metoposcopy.

V. be –, stand- in front etc. *adj.*; front, face, confront, breast, brave; bend forwards; come to the -front, – fore.

Adj. fore, forward, anterior, front, frontal, head-on, leading, first, primary.

Adv. before; in -front, – the van, – advance; ahead, right ahead; fore-, head-most; in the foreground; before one's -face, – eyes; face to face, *vis-à-vis*.

---

235. Rear.—N. rear, back, posterior-ity; rear -rank, – guard; background, *hinterland*.

occiput, nape, scruff, chine; heels; tail, rump, croup, buttock, posteriors, bottom, seat, backside, scut, breech, *dorsum*, loin; dorsal –, lumbar-region; hind quarters.

stern poop, after-part, counter; postern, heel-, tail-piece, crupper.

wake; train etc. (*sequence*) 281.

reverse; other side of the shield.

V. be -behind etc. *adv.*; fall astern; bend backwards; bring up the rear; follow etc. 622; tail, shadow.

Adj. back, rear; hind, -er, -most, -ermost; postern, -erior; dorsal, after; caudal, lumbar; mizzen.

Adv. behind; in the -rear, – ruck, – back-

ground; behind one's back; at the -heels. – tail. –
back- of; back to back.

after, -most, aft, abaft, astern, stern- most,
aback, rear-, hind-, back-ward.

236. Laterality.—N. laterality; side, flank,
beam, quarter, lee; hand; cheek, jowl, jole, wing;
profile; temple, *parietes*, loin, haunch, hip.

gable, -end; broadside; lee side.

points of the compass; East, Orient, Levant;
West, occident; orientation.

V. be -on one side etc. *adv.*; flank, outflank;
sidle; skirt, border.

Adj. lateral, sidelong; collateral; parietal,
flanking, skirting, flanked; sideling.

many-sided; multi-, bi-, tri-, quadri- lateral.

East-ern, -ward, -erly; orient, -al, auroral,
Levantine; West-ern, -ward, -erly; occidental,
Hesperian; equatorial.

Adv. side-ways, -long; broadside on; on one
side, abreast, abeam, alongside, beside, aside;
by, – the side of; side by side; cheek by jowl
etc. (*near*) 197; to -windward, – leeward;
laterally etc. *adj.*; right and left; on her beam
ends.

237. Contraposition.—N. contraposition, opposition; polarity; inversion etc. 218; opposite side,
antithesis; reverse, inverse; counterpart; antipodes;
opposite poles, North and South.

V. be -opposite etc. *adj.*; subtend.

Adj. opposite, reverse, inverse; antipodal, subcontrary, fronting, facing, diametrically opposite.

Northern, Septentrional, Boreal, arctic;
Southern, Austral, antarctic, polar.

Adv. over, – the way, – against; against; face to
face, vis-à-vis; as poles asunder.

238. Dextrality.—N. dextrality; right, – hand;
dexter, offside, starboard.

Adj. dextral, right-handed; ambidextral; dexterous, dextrorsal etc.

239. Sinistrality.—N. sinistrality; left, – hand;
sinister, nearside, larboard, port.

Adj. sinistral, sinister, sinistrorsal etc., left-
handed, sinistromanual, sinistrous.

240. Form.—N. form, figure, shape, physique;
con-formation, -figuration; make, formation,
frame, construction, design, cut, set, build, trim,
cut of one's jib; stamp, type, cast, mold; fashion;
contour etc. (*outline*) 230, structure etc. 329.

feature, lineament, outline, turn; phase etc.
(*aspect*) 448; posture, attitude, *pose*.

[Science of form] morphology.

[Similarity of form] isomorphism.

forming etc. *v.*; form-, figur-, efform- ation;
sculpture.

V. form, shape, figure, fashion, efform, carve,
cut, chisel, hew, cast; rough-hew, -cast; sketch;
block –, hammer- out; trim; lick –, put- into

shape; model, knead, work up into, set, mold,
sculpture; cast, stamp; built etc. (*construct*) 161.

Adj. formed etc. *v.*

[Receiving form] plastic, fictile, full- fashioned
etc.

[Giving form] plasmic, etc.

[Similar in form] isomorphous etc.

241. Amorphism. [Absence of form.]—**N.**
amorphism, informity, uncouthness; unlicked cub,
rough diamond; *rudis indigestaque moles*; disorder etc. 59; deformity etc. 243.

disfigure-, deface-ment, deformation; mutilation.

V. [Destroy form] deface, disfigure, deform,
mutilate, truncate; derange etc. 61.

Adj. shapeless, amorphous, malformed, formless; un-formed, -hewn, -fashioned, -shapen;
rough, rude, Gothic, barbarous, rugged, in the
rough; misshapen etc. 243.

242. Symmetry. [Regularity of form.]—**N.**
symmetry, shapeliness, finish; beauty etc. 845;
proportion, eurythmy, eurythmic, uniformity,
parallelism; bi-, tri-, multi-lateral symmetry;
centrality etc. 222.

arborescence, branching, ramification.

Adj. symmetrical, shapely, well set, finished;
beautiful etc. 845; classic, chaste, severe.

regular, uniform, balanced; equal etc. 27;
parallel, coextensive.

arbor-escent, -iform; dendr-iform, -oid; branching; ramous, ramose.

243. Distortion. [Irregularity of form.]—**N.**
dis-, de-, con-tortion; knot, mop, warp, buckle,
screw, twist; crookedness etc. (*obliquity*) 217;
grimmace; deformity; mal-, malcon-formation;
monstrosity, misproportion, want of symmetry,
anamorphosis; ugliness etc. 846; teratology.

V. distort, contort, twist, warp etc. *n.*; wrest,
writhe, make faces, deform, misshape.

Adj. distorted etc. *v.*; out of shape, irregular, unsymmetric, awry, wry, askew, crooked, sinuous;
anamorphous; not -true, – straight; on one side,
crump, deformed; mis-shapen, -begotten; mis-, ill-
proportioned; ill-made; grotesque, crooked as a
ram's horn; hump-, hunch-, bunch-, crook-backed;
bandy; bandy-, bow-legged; bow-, knock-kneed;
splay-, club-footed; taliped; round-shouldered;
snub-nosed; curtailed of one's fair proportions;
scalene, stumpy etc. (*short*) 201; gaunt etc. (*thin*)
203; bloated etc. 194.

Adv. all manner of ways.

244. Angularity.—N. angular-ity, -ness; aduncity; angle, cusp, bend; fold etc. 258; notch etc.
257; fork, bifurcation.

elbow, knee, knuckle, ankle, groin, crotch,
crane, fluke, scythe, sickle, zigzag, kimbo.

corner, nook, recess, niche, oriel.

right angle etc. (*perpendicular*) 212; obliquity
etc. 217; angle of 45 degrees, miter; acute –, obtuse –, salient –, re-entrant –, spherical –,
solid –, dihedral- angle.

angular -measurement, − elevation, − distance, − velocity; trigon-, goni-ometry; altimetry; clin-, graph-, goni-ometer; theodolite; transit circle; sextant, quadrant; dichotomy.

triangle, trigon, wedge; rectangle, square, lozenge, diamond; rhomb, -us; quadr-angle, - ilateral; parallelogram; quadrature; poly-, penta-, hexa-, hepta-, octa-, deca-gon.

Platonic bodies; cube, rhomboid; tetra-, penta-, hexa-, octa-, dodeca-, icosa-hedron; prism, pyramid; parallelopiped.

V. bend, fork, bifurcate, crinkle, divaricate, branch, ramify.

Adj. angular, bent, crooked, aduncous, un-cinated, aquiline, jagged, serrated; falc-iform, - ated; furcular, furcated, forked, bifurcate, crotched; zigzag; dovetailed; knock-kneed, crinkled, akimbo, kimbo, geniculated; oblique etc. 217.

fusiform, wedge-shaped, cuneiform; tri-angular, -gonal, -lateral; quadr-angular, -ilateral; rectangular, square, foursquare, multilateral; polygonal etc. n.; cubical, rhomboidal, pyramidal.

245. Curvature.—N. curv-ature, -ity, -ation; incurv-ity, -ation; bend; flex- ure, -ion; conflexure; crook, hook, bought, bending; de-, inflexion; arcuation, devexity, turn; deviation, *détour*, sweep; curl, -ing; bough; recurv-ity, -ation; sinuosity etc. 248; aduncity.

curve, arc, arch, arcade, vault, dome, bow, crescent, *meniscus*, half-moon, lunule, horse-shoe, loop, crane-neck; para-, hyper-bola; catenary, festoon; conch-, cardi-oid; caustic, instep; tracery.

V. be -curved etc. *adj.*; sweep, swag, sag; deviate etc. 279; turn; re-enter.

render -curved etc. *adj.*; bend, curve, incurvate; de-, in-flect; crook; turn, round, arch, arcuate, arch over, loop the loop, concamerate; bow, coil, curl, recurve, frizzle.

Adj. curved etc. *v.*; curvi-form, -lineal, -linear, devex, devious; recurv-ed, -ous; *retroussé*; crump; bowed etc. *v.*; vaulted; hooked; falc-iform, -ated; semicircular, crescentic; lun-iform, -ular; semi-lunar, meniscal; conchoidal; cord-iform, -ated; cardioid; heart-, bell-, pear-, fig-shaped; reniform; lenti-form, -cular; bow-legged etc. (*distorted*) 243; oblique etc. 217; circular etc. 247.

246. Straightness.—N. straightness, rectilinearity, directness; inflexibility etc. (*stiffness*) 323; straight −, right −, direct-, bee- line; short cut.

V. be -straight etc. *adj*; have no turning; not - incline, − bend, − turn, − deviate- to either side; go straight; steer for etc. (*direction*) 278

render straight, straighten, rectify; set −, put-straight; un-bend, -fold, -curl etc. 248, -ravel etc. 219, -wrap.

Adj. straight; rectiline-ar, -al; direct, even, right, true, in a line; unbent etc. *v.*; un-deviating, -turned, -distorted, -swerving; straight as an arrow etc. (*direct*) 278; inflexible etc. 323.

247. Circularity. [Simple circularity.]—N. circularity, roundness; rotundity etc. 249.

circle, circlet, ring, washer, areola, hoop, round-let, *annulus*, annulet, bracelet, armlet, armilla; ringlet; eye, loop, wheel; cycle, orb, orbit, rundle, zone, belt, *cordon*, band; sash, girdle, cestus, cincture, baldric, fillet, *fascia*, wreath, garland; crown, corona, coronet, chaplet, snood, necklace, collar; noose, lasso, lariat.

ellipse, oval, ovule; ellipsoid, cycloid; epicycloid, -cycle; semi-circle; quadrant, sextant, sector.

V. make -round etc. *adj.*; round.

go round; encircle etc. 227; describe -a circle etc. 311.

Adj. round, rounded, circular, annular, orbicular; oval, ovate; elliptic, -al; ovoid, egg-shaped; pear-shaped etc. 245; cycloidal etc. *n.*; spherical etc. 249.

248. Convolution. [Complex circularity.]—N. winding etc. *v.*; con-, in-, circum-volution; wave, undulation, tortuosity, anfractuosity; sinu-osity, - ation, sinuousness; meandering, circuit, circumbendibus, twist, twirl, windings and turnings, *ambages*; torsion; inosculation; reticulation etc. (*crossing*) 219.

coil, roll, curl, buckle, spire, spiral, helix, corkscrew, worm, volute, whorl, rundle; tendril; scollop, scallop, escalop; kink.

serpent, snake, eel, maze, labyrinth.

V. be -convoluted etc. *adj.*; wind, twine, turn and twist, twirl; wave, undulate, meander; inosculate; entwine, intwine; twist, coil, roll; wrinkle, curl, crisp, twill; frizz, -le; crimp, crape, indent, scollop, scallop; wring, intort; contort; wreathe etc. (*cross*) 219.

Adj. convoluted; winding, twisted etc. *v.*; tortile, tortive; wavy; und-ated, -ulatory; circling, snaky, snake-like, serpentine; serpent-, anguill-, vermiform; vermicular; mazy, tortuous, anfractuous, sinuous, flexuous, wavy, sigmoidal.

involved, intricate, complicated, perplexed; labyrinth-ic, -ian, -ine; circuitous; peristaltic; daedalian, curly.

wreathy, frizzly, *crêpé*, buckled; ravelled etc. (*in disorder*) 59.

spiral, coiled, helical, turbinated.

Adv. in and out, round and round.

249. Rotundity.—N. rotundity; roundness etc. adj.; cyclindricity; spher-icity, -oidity; globosity.

cylin-der, -droid, barrel, drum; roll, -er; *rouleau*, column, rolling-pin, rundle; chimney-pot, drain-pipe.

cone, conoid; pear-, egg-, bell-shape.

sphere, globe, orb, orbit, ball, boulder, bowlder; spher-, ellips-, ge-, glob-oid, oblong −, oblate-spheroid; drop, spherule, globule, vesicle, bulb, bullet, pellet, *pelote*, clew, pill, marble, pea, knob, pommel, knot.

V. render -spherical etc. *adj.*, form into a sphere, sphere, roll into a ball; give -rotundity etc. *n.*, round.

Adj.rotund; round etc. (*circular*) 247; cylindric, -ical, -oid; columnar, lumbriciform; conic, -al; spher-ical, -oidal; glob-ular, -ated, -ous, -ose; egg-, bell-, pear-shaped; ov-oid, -iform; gibbous; campaniform, -ulate, -iliform; fungiform, bead-like, moniliform, pyriform, bulbous; *teres atque rotundus*; round as -an orange, — an apple, — a ball, — a billiard ball, — a cannon ball.

250. Convexity.—N. convexity, prominence, projection, swelling, gibbosity, bilge, bulge, protuberance, protrusion; excrescency, camber.

intumescence; tumor; tubercle, -osity; excrescence; hump, hunch, bunch, gnarl.

tooth, knob, elbow, process, *apophysis*, condyle, bulb, node, nodule, nodosity, tongue, *dorsum*, boss, embossment, bump, clump; sugar-loaf etc. (*sharpness*) 253; bow; mamelon.

pimple, wen, wheal, *papula*, postule, pock, proud flesh, growth, goiter, *sarcoma*, caruncle, corn, bunion, wart, furnuncle, polypus, adenoid, fungus, fungosity, *exostosis*, bleb, blister, blain; boil etc. (*disease*) 655; bubble, blob.

papilla, nipple, teat, pap, breast, dug, mammilla; proboscis, nose, neb, beak, snout, nozzle, snozzle; Adam's apple; belly, paunch, corporation; withers, back, shoulder, lip, flange.

peg, button, stud, ridge, rib, jutty, trunnion, snag.

cupola, dome, bee-hive; arch, balcony, eaves; pilaster.

relief, relievo, *cameo; basso-, mezzo-, alto-rilievo*; low-, bas-, high-relief.

hill etc. (*height*) 206; cape, promontory, mull; fore-, head-land; point of land, naze, ness, mole, jetty, hummock, ledge, spur.

V. be -prominent etc. *adj.*; project, bulge, protrude, bag, belly, pout, bouge, bunch; jut —, stand —, stick —, poke- out; stick —, bristle —, start —, cock —, shoot- up; swell —, hang —, bend-over; beetle.

render -prominent etc. *adj.*; raise 307; emboss, chase.

Adj. convex, prominent, protuberant, underhung, undershot; projecting etc. *v.*; bossed, bossy, nodular, bunchy; clav-ate, -ated; hummocky, *moutonné*, mammiform; papul-ous, -ose; hemispheric, bulbous; bowed, arched; bold; bellied; tuber-ous, -culous; tumorous; cornute, knobby, odontoid; lenti-form, -cular; gibbous.

salient, in relief, raised, *repoussé*; bloated etc. (*expanded*) 194.

251. Flatness.—N. flatness etc *adj.*; smoothness etc. 255.

plane; level etc. 213; plate, platter, table, tablet, slab.

V. render flat, flatten, squash; level etc. 213.

Adj. flat, plane, even, flush, scutiform, discoid; level etc. (*horizontal*) 213; smooth; flat as -a pancake, — a fluke, — a flounder, — a board, — my hand.

252. Concavity.—N. concavity, depression, dip; hollow, -ness; indentation, *intaglio*, cavity, antrum, dent, dint, dimple, follicle, pit, *sinus, alveolus, lacuna*; excavation, trench, shaft, sap, mine, tunnel, burrow; trough etc. (*furrow*) 259; honeycomb.

cup, basin, crater, punch-bowl; cell etc. (*receptacle*) 191; socket, faucet.

valley, vale, dale, dell, gap, dingle, combe, bottom, slade, strath, glade, grove, glen, cave, cavern, cove; grot, -to; alcove, *cul-de-sac*, blind alley; gully etc. 198; arch etc. (*curve*) 245; bay etc. (*of the sea*) 343.

excavator, sapper, miner.

V. be -concave etc. *adj.*; retire, cave in.

render -concave etc. *adj.*; depress, hollow; scoop, — out; gouge, dig, delve, excavate, dent, dint, mine, sap, undermine, burrow, tunnel, stave in.

Adj. depressed etc. *v.*; concave, hollow, stove in; dished; spoon-like; retiring; retreating; cavernous; porous etc. (*with holes*) 260; cellular, spongy, spongious; honeycombed, alveolar; infundibul-ar, -iform; funnel-, bell-shaped; campaniform, capsular; vaulted, arched.

253. Sharpness.—N. sharpness etc. *adj.*; acuity, acumination; spinosity.

point, spike, spine, *spiculum*, tine; needle, pin; tack, nail; prick, -le; spur, rowel, barb; spit, cusp; horn, antler; snag; tag; thorn, bristle.

nib, tooth, incisor, tusk; spoke, cog, ratchet.

crag, crest *arête*, cone, peak, sugar-loaf, pike, *aiguille*; spire, pyramid, steeple.

beard, *chevaux de frise*, porcupine, hedgehog, brier, bramble, thistle; comb, awn, bur.

wedge; knife-, cutting- edge; blade, edge-tool, cutlery, knife, penknife, whittle, razor; scalpel, bistoury, lancet; chisel; ploughshare, coulter; hatchet, axe, pick-axe, mattock, pick, adze, bill; bill-hook, cleaver, cutter; skiver; scythe, sickle, scissors, shears; sword etc. (*arms*) 727; bodkin etc. (*perforator*) 262.

sharpener, hone, strop; grind-, whet-stone; steel, emery.

V. be -sharp etc. *adj.*; taper to a point; bristle with.

render -sharp etc. *adj.*; sharpen, point, aculeate, acuminate, whet, barb, spiculate, set, strop, grind.

cut etc. (*sunder*) 44.

Adj. sharp, keen; acute; aci-cular, -form; aculeated, -minated; pointed; tapering; conical, pyramidal, mucron-ate, -ated; spindle-, needle-shaped; spiked, spiky, ensiform, peaked, salient, cusp-ed; -idate, -idated; corn-ute, -uted, -iculate; prickly; spiny, spinous; thorny, bristling, muricated, pectinated, studded, thistly, briery; craggy etc. (*rough*) 256; snaggy; digitated, two-edged, fusiform; denti-form, -culated; toothed; odontoid; star-like; stell-ated, -iform; arrow-headed; arrowy, barbed, spurred, sagittal; spear-shaped, hastate; horned; conical.

cutting; sharp-, knife-edged; sharp —, keen-as a razor; sharp as a needle; sharpened etc. *v.*; set.

254. Bluntness.—N. bluntness etc. *adj.*; abruptness, dullness.

V. be —, render- blunt etc. *adj.*; obtund, dull; take off the -point, — edge; turn.

Adj. blunt, obtuse, dull, bluff.

255. Smoothness.—N. smoothness etc. *adj.*; polish, gloss; lubric-ity, -ation.

down, velvet, silk, satin; slide; bowling green etc. (*level*) 213; glass, ice; asphalt, pavement, flags.

roller, steam-roller; iron, flat-iron, tailor's goose; sand-, emery-paper; burnisher, turpentine and bees-wax.

V. smooth, -en; plane; file; mow, shave; level, roll; macadamize; polish, burnish, planish, levigate, calender, glaze; iron, hot-press, mangle; lubricate etc. (*oil*) 332.

Adj. smooth; polished etc. *v.*; even; level etc. 213; plane etc. (*flat*) 251; sleek, glossy, silken, silky; lanate, downy, velvety; glabrous, slippery, glassy, lubricous, oily, soft; unwrinkled; smooth as -glass, — ice, — velvet, — oil; slippery as an eel; wooly etc. (*feathery*) 256.

256. Roughness.—N. roughness etc. *adj.*; tooth, grain, texture, ripple; asperity, rugosity, salebrosity, corrugation, nodosity; arborescence etc. 242.

brush, hair, beard, shag, mane, whisker, mutton-chops, *moustache, mustachio*, imperial, Van Dyke, tress, lock, curl, ringlet, *fimbriae, cilia, villi*; eye-lashes, eye-brows, love-lock.

plum-age, -osity; plume, *panache*, crest; feather, tuft, tussock, fringe, toupee.

wool, velvet, plush, nap, pile, floss, fluff, fur, down; byssus, moss, bur.

V. be -rough etc. *adj.*; go against the grain.

render -rough etc. *adj.*; roughen, rough cast, knurl; ruffle, crisp, crumple, crinkle, corrugate, engrail; set on edge, stroke — , rub- the wrong way, rumple.

Adj. rough, uneven; scabrous, knotted; nodular; rug-ged, -ose, -ous; asperous, crisp, salebrous, gnarled, unpolished, unsmooth, rough-hewn; knurled, cross-grained, crag-gy, -ged; crankling, scraggy, jagged, unkempt, prickly etc. (*sharp*) 253; arborescent etc. 242; leafy, well-wooded; feathery; plum-ose, -igerous; tufted, fimbriated, hairy, bristly, ciliated, filamentous, hirsute; crin-ose, -ite; bushy, hispid, villous, pappous, bearded, pilous, shaggy, shagged; fringed, befringed; set-ous, -ose, -aceous; 'like quills upon the fretful porcupine;' rough as a -nutmeg grater, — bear.

downy, velvety, flocculent, wolly; lan-ate, -ated; lanugin-ous, -ose; tomentous.

Adv. against the grain, in the rough, on edge.

257. Notch.—N. notch, dent, nick, cut; indent, -ation; serration; dimple.

embrasure, battlement, machicolation; saw, tooth, crenelle, scallop, scollop, vandyke.

V. notch, nick, cut, pink, mill, score, dent, indent, jag, scarify, scotch, crimp, scollop, crenulate, vandyke.

Adj. notched etc. *v.*; crenate, -d; dentate, -d; denticulate, -d; toothed, palmated, serrated.

258. Fold.—N. fold, plicature, pleat, plait, ply, crease; tuck, gather; flexion, flexure, joint, elbow, doubling, duplicature, wrinkle, rimple, crinkle, crankle, crumple, rumple, rivel, ruck, ruffle, dog's ear, corrugation, frounce, flounce, lapel; pucker, crow's feet.

V. fold, double, plicate, pleat, plait, crease, wrinkle, crinkle, crankle, curl, smock, cockle up, crocker, rimple, rumple, frizzle, frounce, rivel, twill, corrugate, ruffle, crimple, crumple, pucker; turn —, double- -down, — under; tuck, ruck, hem, gather.

Adj. folded etc. *v.*

259. Furrow.—N. furrow, groove, rut, *sulcus*, scratch, streak, *striae*, crack, score, incision, slit; chamfer, fluting.

channel, gutter, trench, ditch, dike, dyke, moat, fosse, trough, kennel; ravine etc. (*interval*) 198.

V. furrow etc. *n.*; flute, groove, carve, corrugate, plough; incise, chase, enchase, grave, engrave, etch, bite in, cross-hatch.

Adj. furrowed etc. *v.*; ribbed, straited, sulcated, fluted, canaliculated; biscule-ous, -ate; trisulcate; corduroy

260. Opening.—N. hole, foramen; puncture, blow-out, perforation; pin-, key-, loop-, port-, peep-, mouse-, pigeon-hole; eye, — of a needle; eyelet; slot.

opening; apert-ure, -ness; hiation, yawning, oscitancy, dehiscence, patefaction, pandiculation; gap, chasm etc. (*interval*) 198.

embrasure, window, casement, light; sky-, fan-light; lattice; bay-, bow-window; oriel; dormer, lantern.

out-, in-let; vent, vomitory; *embouchure*; orifice, mouth, sucker, muzzle, throat, gullet, placket, weasand, wizen, nozzle, *esophagus*.

portal, porch, gate, ostiary, postern, wicket, trap-door, hatch, door; arcade; gate-, door-, hatch-, gang-way; lych-gate.

way, path etc. 627; thoroughfare; channel, passage, tube, pipe; waterpipe etc. 350; air-pipe etc. 351; vessel, tubule, canal, gut, fistula; adjutage, ajutage; chimney, smoke stack, flue, tap, funnel, gully, tunnel, main; mine, pit, adit, shaft; gallery, alley, aisle, glade, lane, vista.

bore, caliber; pore; blind orifice.

por-ousness, -osity; sieve, cullender, colander; grater, shredder; cribble, riddle, screen; honeycomb.

aperture, perforation; piercing etc. *v.*; terebration, empalement, pertusion, puncture, acupuncture, penetration.

opener, corkscrew, can opener, key, master-key, *passe-partout*.

V. open, ope, gape, dehisce, yawn, bilge; fly open.

perforate, pierce, empierce, tap, bore, drill; mine etc. (*scoop out*) 252; tunnel; trans-pierce, -fix; en-filade, impale, spike, spear, gore, spit, stab, pink, puncture, lance, trepan, trephine, stick, prick, rid-dle, punch; stave in.

cut a passage through; make -way, — room- for. un-cover, -close, -rip; lay —, cut —, rip —, throw- open.

Adj. open; perforated etc. *v.*; perforate; wide open, agape, ajar; un-closed, -stopped; oscitant, gaping, yawning; patent.

tubular, cannular, fistulous; per-vious, -meable; foraminous; vesi-, vas-cular; porous, follicular.

cribriform, honeycombed, infundibular, riddled; tubul-ous, -ated, piped.

opening etc. *v.*; aperient.

Int. *open sesame!*

261. Closure.—N. closure, occlusion, blockade; shutting up etc. *v.*; obstruction etc. (*hindrance*) 706; gag; embolism; contraction etc. 195; infarction; con-, ob-stipation; blind -alley, – corner; *cul-de-sac*, *caecum*; imperforation, -viousness etc. *adj.*; -meability; stopper etc. 263; *operculum*.

V. close, occlude, plug; block –, stop –, fill –, bung –, cork –, button –, stuff –, shut –, damup, obturate; blockade; obstruct etc. (*hinder*) 706; bar, bolt, stop, seal, plumb; choke, throttle; ram down, tamp, dam, cram; trap, clinch; put to –, shut- the door; batten down the hatches.

Adj. closed etc. *v.*; shut, operculated; unopened.

unpierced, imporous, caecal; imperforate, -vious, -meable; impenetrable; un-, im-passable; invious; path-, way-less; untrodden.

unventilated; air-, water-tight; hermetically sealed; tight, snug.

262. Perforator.—N. perforator, piercer, borer, auger, gimlet, stylet, drill, wimble, awl, bradawl, scoop, terrier, corkscrew, dibble, trocar, trepan, trephine, probe, bodkin, needle, stiletto, broach, reamer, rimer, warder, lancet; punch, -eon; spikebit, gouge; spear etc. (*weapon*) 727.

263. Stopper.—N. stopper, stopple; plug, cork, bung, spike, spill, stop-cock, tap; rammer; ram, -rod; piston; stopgap; wadding, stuffing, padding, stopping, dossil, pledget, tompion, tourniquet, obturator; wad.

cover etc. 223; valve, slide valve; vent-peg, spigot.

janitor, door –, gate- keeper, porter, commissionaire, *concierge*, warder, beadle, Cerberus, usher, guard, sentry, sentinel; ostiary.

264. Motion. [Successive change of place. *]—N.** motion, movement, move; motivity, motility, going etc. *v.*; unrest.

stream, current, flow, flux, run, course, stir; conduction, evolution; kinematics.

step, rate, pace, tread, stride, gait, clip, port, footfall, cadence,. carriage, velocity, angular velocity; progress, locomotion; journey etc. 266; voyage etc. 267; transit etc. 270.

restlessness etc. (*changeableness*) 149; mobility; movableness, motive power; laws of motion; mobilization.

V. be -in motion etc. *adj.*; move, go, hie, gang, budge, stir, pass, flit; hover -round, – about; shift, slide, slither, glide; roll, – on; flow, stream, run, drift, sweep along; wander etc. (*deviate*) 279; walk etc. 266; change –, shift- one's -place, – quarters; dodge; keep -going, – moving.

put – , set- in motion; move; impel etc. 276; propel etc. 284; render movable, mobilize.

Adj. moving etc. *v.*; in motion; motile, transitional; motory, motive; shifting, movable, mobile, mercurial, unquiet; restless etc. (*changeable*) 149; nomadic etc. 266; erratic etc. 279.

Adv. under way; on the -move, – wing, – tramp, – march.

'A thing cannot be said to *move* from one place to another, unless it passes in succession through every intermediate place; hence motion is only such a change of place as is *successive.* 'Rapid, swift, etc., as thought' are therefore incorrect expressions.

265. Quiescence.—N. rest; stillness etc. *adj.*; quiescence; stag-nation, -nancy; fixity, immobility, catalepsy; indisturbance; quietism.

quiet, tranquillity, calm; repose etc. 687; peace; dead calm, anticyclone; statue-like repose; silence etc. 403; not a -breath of air, – mouse stirring; sleep etc. (*inactivity*) 683.

pause, lull etc. (*cessation*) 142; stand, – still; standing still etc. *v.*; lock; dead -lock, – stop, – stand; full stop; fix; embargo.

resting-place; bivouac; home etc. (*abode*) 189; pillow etc. (*support*) 215; haven etc. (*refuge*) 666; goal etc. (*arrival*) 292.

V. be -quiescent etc. *adj.*; stand –, lie- still; keep quiet, repose, hold the breath.

remain, stay; stand, lie to, ride at anchor, remain *in situ.* mark time, tarry; bring –, heave –, lay- to; pull –, draw- up; hold, halt; stop, – short; rest, pause, anchor; cast –, come to an- anchor; rest on one's oars; repose on one's laurels, take breath; stop etc. (*discontinue*) 142.

stagnate, vegetate; *quieta non movere*; let - alone, – well alone; abide, rest and be thankful; keep within doors, stay at home, go to bed.

dwell etc. (*be present*) 186, settle etc. (*be located*) 184; alight etc. (*arrive*) 292.

stick, – fast; stand, – like a post; not stir a -peg, – step; be at a -stand etc. *n.*

quell, becalm, hush, stay, lull to sleep, lay an embargo on; put the brake on.

Adj. quiescent, still; motion-, move-less; fixed; stationary; at -rest, – a stand, – a stand-still, – anchor; stock-still; immotile; standing still etc. *v.*; sedentary, untravelled, stay-at-home; becalmed, stagnant, quiet; un-moved, -disturbed, -ruffled; calm, restful; cataleptic; immovable etc. (*stable*) 150; sleeping etc. (*inactive*) 683; silent etc. 403; still as -a statue; – a post, – a mouse, – death.

Adv. at a stand etc. *adj.*; *tout court*; at the halt.

Int. stop! stay! avast! halt! hold, – hard! whoa!

Phr. *requiescat in pace.*

266. Journey. [Locomotion by land.]—**N.** travel; traveling etc. *v.*; wayfaring, campaigning.

journey, excursion, expedition, tour, trip, grand tour, circuit, peregrination, discursion, ramble, pilgrimage, *trek*, course, ambulation, march, walk, hike, promenade, constitutional, stroll, saunter, tramp, jog-trot, turn, stalk, perambulation; noctambulation; somnambulism, sleep walking; outing, ride, drive, airing, jaunt.

equitation, horsemanship, riding, *manège*, ride and tie.

roving, vagrancy, pererration; marching and countermarching; nomadism; vagabond-ism, -age; gadding; flit, -ting; migration; e-, im-, de-, intermigration.

plan, itinerary, guide; hand-, road- book; Baedeker, Murray, Bradshaw, time table.

procession, parade, cavalcade, caravan, file, *cortège*, column.

[Organs and instruments of locomotion] vehicle etc. 272; locomotive etc. 271; legs, feet, pegs, pins, trotters.

traveler etc. 268.

V. travel, journey, course; tour; take —, go- a journey, take —, go out for- -a walk etc. *n.*; have a run; take the air.

flit, take wing; migrate, emigrate, *trek*; rove, prowl, roam, range, patrol, pace up and down, traverse; scour —, traverse- the country; peragrate; per-, circum-ambulate; nomadize, wander, ramble, stroll, saunter, hover, go one's rounds, straggle; gad; — about; expatiate.

walk, march, step, tread, pace, plod, wend; promenade; trudge, tramp; stalk, stride, straddle, strut, foot it, stump, bundle, bowl along, toddle; paddle; tread —, follow —, pursue- a path.

take horse, ride, drive, trot, amble, canter, prance, fisk, frisk, *caracoler*; gallop etc. (*move quickly*) 274; motor, cycle, taxi; go by -car, — train, — tram, — bus, — plane.

peg —, jog —, wag —, shuffle- on; stir one's stumps; bend one's -steps, — course; make —, find —, wend —, pick —, thread —, plough- one's way; coast, slide, glide, skim, skate, ski; march in procession, file off, defile.

go —, repair —, resort —, hie —, betake oneself- to.

Adj. traveling etc. *v.*; ambulatory, itinerant, peripatetic, perambulatory, roving, rambling, gadding, discursive, vagrant, migratory, nomadic; circumforane-an, -ous; somnambular, nocti-, mundivagant; locomotive, automotive, self-moving.

way-faring, -worn; travel-stained.

Adv. on -foot, — horseback, — Shanks's mare; by the Marrowbone-stage; *in transitu* etc. 270; *en route* etc. 282.

Int. come along!

267. Navigation. [Locomotion by water, or air.]—N. navigation; aquatics; boating, cruising, yachting; ship etc. 273; oar, scull, sweep, punt pole, paddle, — wheel, screw, propeller, stern wheel, sail, canvas.

natation, swimming; fin, flipper, fish's tail.

aeronautics, aviation, flying, winging, cruising, gliding, ballooning; blind —, instrument — flying; avigation, take-off.

flight, trip, run; solo —, nolo (pilotless) —, supersonic —, test — flight; air -lift, -drop; shuttle, reconnaisence, mission, dry run (coll.), search mission, combat flight, sortie, air raid, bombing mission; air — support, — cover, — umbrella; formation flying, maneuvers, aerobatics, stunt flying (coll.), diving, rolling, barrel roll, spin, tail spin, loop, buzzing.

landing, instrument —, crash — landing.

angle, center, axis, stability, load, pressure, torsion, torque, thrust, propulsion, jet propulsion, pitch, lift, dray, yaw, resistance, drift, flow, wash.

course, heading, altitude; air -route, -lane.

voyage, sail, cruise, passage, circumnavigation, *periplus*; head-, stern-, lee-way.

astro-, cosmo- nautics; space —, interplanetary — travel; space — exploration, — flight.

mariner, aeronaut etc. 269.

V. sail; put to sea etc. (*depart*) 293; take ship, get under way; spread -sail, — canvas; gather way, have way on; make —, carry- sail; plough the waves, — deep, — main, — ocean; walk the waters.

navigate, warp, luff, scud, boom, kedge; drift, course, cruise, coast; hug the -shore, — land; circumnavigate.

ply the oar, row, paddle, pull, scull, punt, steam.

swim, float; buffet the waves, ride the storm, skim, *effleurer*, dive, wade.

fly, pilot, copilot, astronavigate, solo, take off, taxi, ascend, climb, stunt, spin, loop, roll, dive, buzz, land, descend, level off, bail out, parachute.

Adj. sailing etc. *v.*; seafaring, nautical, maritime, naval; sea-going, coasting; afloat; navigable, aquatic, natatory.

volitant, volant, aerostatic, aerial, aeronautic; alar, alate, pennate.

Adv. under -way, — sail, — canvas, — steam; on the wing.

268. Traveler.—N. traveler, wayfarer, voyager, itinerant, passenger.

tourist, excursionist, globe-trotter; explorer, adventurer, mountaineer, Alpine Club; peregrinator, wanderer, rover, straggler, rambler; bird of passage; gad-about, -ling; vagrant, scattering, landloper, waifs and estrays, wastrel, stray; loafer; tramp, -er, hobo, beachcomber, vagabond, nomad, Bohemian, gipsy, Arab, Wandering Jew, Hadji, pilgrim, palmer; peripatetic; somnambulist; sleep walker, noctambulist; emigrant, fugitive, refugee, *émigré*.

runner, courier, King's messenger; Mercury, Iris, Ariel, comet.

pedestrian, walker, foot-passenger; cyclist; wheelman.

rider, horseman, equestrian, cavalier, jockey, rough rider, trainer, breaker, huntsman.

driver, coachman, whip, Jehu, charioteer, postilion, post-boy, carter, wagoner, drayman, truckman; cab-man, -driver; *voiturier, vetturino, condottiere*; engine-driver; stoker, fireman, guard, brakeman, conductor; chauffeur, automobilist, motorist, motor —, truck —, taxi- driver.

269. Mariner.—N. sailor, mariner, navigator, argonaut; sea-man, -farer, -faring man; yachtsman; tar, jack tar, salt, gob, sea-dog, shellback, able seaman, A.B.; man-of-war's man, bluejacket, marine, jolly; midshipman, middy, reefer; captain, commander, master mariner, skipper, mate; ship-, boat-, ferry-, water-, lighter-, barge- longshoreman, hoveller; bargee, gondolier; oar-, -sman; rower; boat-, cock-swain; coxswain; steersman, helmsman, pilot; crew; lascar.

aerial navigator; aero-, astro-, cosmonaut; balloonist, Icarus, aviator, pilot, flyer, copilot, spaceman; fighter —, bomber — pilot; bombardier, gunner; meteorologist; stewardess, aviatrix, aviatress; ground crew, aeromechanic, aeronautical engineer; parachutist, paratrooper.

270. Transference.—N. transfer; -ence; trans-, e-location; displacement; *meta-stasis, -thesis*; removal; re-, a-motion; relegation; de-, asportation; extradition, conveyance, draft; carrying, carriage; convection, -duction, -tagion, infection; transfusion; transfer etc. (*of property*) 783.

transit, transition; passage, ferry, gestation; portage, porterage, carting, cartage; shoveling etc. *v.*; vect-ion, -ure, -itation; shipment, freight, wafture; trans-mission, -port, -portation, -umption, -plantation, -lation; shift-, dodg-ing; dispersion etc. 73; transposition etc. (*interchange*) 148; traction etc. 285.

[Thing transferred] drift, alluvium, detritus, *moraine*; gift, legacy, bequest, lease; freight, mails, cargo, luggage, baggage, goods.

V. trans-fer, -mit, -port, -place, -plant; convey, assign, carry, bear, fetch and carry; carry —, ferry-over; hand, pass, forward; shift; conduct, convoy, bring, fetch, reach.

send, delegate, consign, mail post, relegate, turn over to, pass the buck, deliver; ship, embark; waft; switch, shunt; transpose etc. (*interchange*) 148; displace etc. 185; throw etc. 284; drag etc. 285.

shovel, lade, dip, ladle, bale, decant, draft off, transfuse.

Adj. transferred etc. *v.*; drifted; movable, portable, -ative; conductive; contagious, infectious.

transferable, assignable, conveyable, devisable, negotiable, transmissible.

Adv. from -hand to hand, — pillar to post. on —, by- the way; on the -road, — wing; as one goes; *in transitu, en route, chemin faisant, en passant*, in mid-progress.

271. Carrier.—N. carrier, porter, red cap, bearer, messenger, postman, tranter, conveyer; stevedore; coolie; conductor, locomotive, tractor, caterpillar tractor, motor.

beast of burden, cattle, horse steed, nag, palfrey, Arab, blood horse, thorough-bred, galloway, charger, courser, racer, hunter, jument, pony, filly, colt, foal, barb, roan, jade, hack, *bidet*, pad, cob, tit, punch, roadster, goer; race-, pack-, draft-, cart-, dray-, post-horse, mount; Shetland pony, sheltie; garran; jennet, genet, bayard, mare, stallion, gelding; stud.

Pegasus, Bucephalus, Rozinante.

ass, donkey, jackass, mule, hinny; sumpter- horse, — mule; reindeer; camel, dromedary, mehari, llama, elephant; carrier pigeon.

carriage etc. (*vehicle*) 272; ship etc. 273.

Adj. equine, asinine.

272. Vehicle.—N. vehicle, conveyance, carriage, car, caravan, van, furniture van, pantechnicon; wagon, wain, dray, cart, lorry.

carriole, sledge, sled, sleigh, bob-sleigh, toboggan, *luge*, truck, tram; limber, tumbrel, pontoon, barrow; wheel-, hand- -barrow, — cart, trolley, perambulator; Bath —, wheel —, sedan-chair, jinriksha, rickshaw, ekka; chaise; palankeen, -quin; litter, horse-litter, brancard, crate, hurdle, stretcher, ambulance; velocipede, hobbyhorse, coaster, scooter, go-cart; cycle; bi-, tri-, quadri-cycle; tandem, safety; skate, roller —, ice —skate; sled, sleigh, ski, snow-shoe.

equipage, turn-out; coach, chariot; *quadriga*, chaise, phaëton, break, brake, mail-phaëton, wagonette, drag, curricle, tilbury, whisky, landau, *barouche*, victoria, brougham, clarence, calash, *calèche*, britzska, *araba*, kibitka; berlin; sulky, *désobligeant*, sociable, *vis-à-vis, dormeuse*; jaunting —, outside- car; *tarantass*; runabout; shay.

post-chaise; diligence, stage; stage —, mail —, hackney —, glass- coach; stage-wagon; car, omnibus, bus, fly, *cabriolet*, cab, hansom, shofle, fourwheeler, growler, *droshki*, drosky.

dog-cart, trap, gig, whitechapel, buggy, four-in-hand, unicorn, random, tandem; shandredhan, *char-à-banc*.

automobile, motor-, auto-, touring-, racing-, cycle-, side-, steam-, electric- car; motor —cycle, — bike; motorized vehicle; bus, minibus; buggy, crate, tub, flivver, jalopy, wreck, clunker, dog, heap (all. slang); coupe, coup, sedan, convertible, hard-top; camper, trailer, **mobile home**; limosine, **landaulette**, cabriolet, *coupé, voiturette*, runabout, electromobile, taxi, -cab.

train; passenger —, express —, freight —, subway —, special —, corridor —, parliamentary —, luggage —, goods- train, *train de luxe*; 1st-, 2nd-, 3rd- class- -train, — carriage, — compartment; Pullman —, sleeping-, club-, observation-, dining-, restaurant-car; mail-, luggage-, brake-van, coach, car, carriage; rolling stock; horse-box, cattle- truck.

273. Ship.—N. ship, vessel, sail; craft, bottom, navy, marine, fleet, flotilla, squadron; shipping, man of war etc. (*combatant*) 726; transport, tender, store-ship; merchant ship, merchantman; packet, liner; whaler, slaver, collier, coaster, tanker, freighter, freight steamer, cargo boat, lighter; fishing-, pilot- boat; trawler, drifter; cable ship; hulk; yacht; floating palace, ocean greyhound.

ship, bark, barque, brig, snow, hermaphrodite brig; brigantine, barquentine; schooner; topsail —, fore and aft —, three masted- schooner; *chasse-marée*; sloop, cutter, corvette, clipper, foist, yawl, dandy, ketch, smack, lugger, barge, hoy, cat-, -boat, buss; sail-er, -ing vessel, wind jammer; steamer, -boat, -ship; mail—, paddle —, screw —, stern-wheel- steamer; tug; train-ferry; line of steamers etc.

boat, pinnace, launch, motor-boat, picket-boat; hydroplane; life-, long-, jolly-, bum-, fly-, cock-ferry-, canal- boat, dory, dugout, galliot; shallop, gig, funny, skiff, dingy, scow, cockleshell, wherry, coble, punt, cog, lerret; eight-, four-, pair- oar; randan; out- rigger; float, raft, pontoon; prame, ice-yacht.

state barge, bucentaur.

catamaran, coracle, gondola, carvel, caravel; felucca, caique, canoe; trireme; galley, — foist; bilander, dogger, hooker, howker; argosy, carack; galliass, galleon; galliot, polacca, polacre, corsair, tartane, junk, lorcha, praam, proa, prahu, saïck, sampan, xebec, dhow; dahabeah; nuggar, cayak, piroque; trireme.

submarine, submersible.

aircraft (*combatant*) etc. 726; flying machine, air mail, aero-, air-, mono-, bi-, tri-, hydro aeroplane, plane, cabin —, transport —, propeller — plane; *avion*, flying boat, glider: helicopter, rotor —, gyro-plane, whirlybird, autogyro, gyrodine; sea-, hydro-plane; amphibian; jet. — plane; turbo-, ram-, pulse-, subsonic —, supersonic —, strato- jet; rocket — plane, — ship.; space ship; war-, combat — plane; kamikaze, fleet, armada; trainer, fliight simulator; aerostat, dirigible, blimp (coll.), zeppelin; parachute, chute (coll.); kite.

rocket, flying —, ballistic —, guided — missile, projectile; rocket —, robot —, buzz-bomb; multistage —, step —, test — rocket; booster; satellite; flying saucer, unidentified flying object. (UFO).

nacelle, car, gondola, aileron; hangar, airport, landing field, airdrome; catwalk, controls, rudder, tail.

Adj. marine, maritime, naval, nautical, seafaring, sea-, ocean-going, sea-worthy.

aerial, aeronautical, air-worthy, flying etc. *n*.

Adv. afloat, aboard; on -board, — ship board, — board ship.

274. Velocity.—N. velocity, speed, celerity; swiftness etc. *adj*.; rapidity, eagle speed; expedition etc. (*activity*) 682; pernicity; acceleration; haste etc. 684.

spurt, rush, dash, race, steeplechase; smart —, lively —, swift etc. *adj*. —, rattling —, spanking —, strapping- -rate, — pace: round pace; flying, flight.

gallop, canter, trot, round trot, run, scamper; hand —, full- gallop; swoop.

lightning, light, electricity, wind; cannon-ball, rocket, arrow, dart, quicksilver; telegraph, express train; torrent; swallow flight.

eagle, antelope, courser, race-horse, gazelle; greyhound, hare, doe, squirrel.

Mercury, Ariel, Camilla, Harlequin.

[Measurement of velocity.] speedometer, log, -line, tachometer.

air speed, speed of sound, sonic —, subsonic —, supersonic —, ultrasonic —, hypersonic —, transonic — speed.

V. move quickly, trip, fisk; speed, hie, hasten, sprint, spurt, post, spank, scuttle; scud, -dle, scurry; scour, — the plain; scamper, sprint, dash, run, — like mad; fly, race, run a race, cut away, cut and run, shoot, tear, whisk, whiz, sweep, skim, brush; cut —, bowl- along; rush etc. (*be violent*) 173; dash -on, — off, — forward; bolt; trot, gallop, bound, flit, spring, dart, boom; march in -quick, — double-time; ride hard; et over the ground, scorch.

hurry etc. (*hasten*) 684; accelerate, put on; quicken; quicken —, mend- one's pace; clap spurs to one's horse; make-haste, — rapid strides, — forced marches, — the best of one's way; put one's best leg foremost, stir one's stumps, wing one's way, set off at a score; carry —, crowd- sail; go off like a shot, go ahead, gain ground; outstrip the wind, fly on the wings of the wind.

keep -up, — pace- with; outstrip etc. 303.

Adj. fast, speedy, swift, rapid, quick, fleet; nimble, agile, expeditious; express; active etc. 682; flying, galloping etc. *v*.; light- nimble-footed; winged; eagle-winged, mercurial, electric telegraphic; light-legged; light of heel; swift as -an arrow etc. *n*.; quick as -lightning etc. *n*., — thought.*

Adv. swiftly etc. *adj*.; with -speed etc. *n*.; apace; at -a great rate, — full speed, — railway speed; full -drive, — gallop; post-haste, in full sail, tantivy; trippingly; instantaneously etc. 113; like a shot.

under press of -sale, — canvas, — sail and steam; *velis et remis*, on eagle's wing, in double quick time; with -rapid, — giant- strides; *à pas de géant*; in seven league boots; whip and spur; *ventre à terre*; as fast as one's -legs, — heels- will carry one; as fast on one can lay feet to the ground, at the top of one's speed; by leaps and bounds; with haste etc. 684; in- high — gear, — speed.

Phr. *vires acquirit eundo.*

*See note on 274.

275. Slowness.—N. slowness etc. *adj*.; languor etc. (*inactivity*) 683; drawl; creeping etc. *v*., lentor.

retardation; slackening etc. *v*.; delay etc. (*lateness*) 133; claudication.

jog-, dog-trot, walk; mincing steps; slow -march, — time.

slow -goer, — coach, — back; lingerer, loiterer, sluggard, tortoise, snail; dawdle etc. (*inactive*) 683.

V. move -slowly, etc. *adv*.; creep, crawl, lag, slug, walk, drawl, linger, loiter, saunter; plod, trudge, stump along, lumber; trail; drag; dawdle etc. (*be inactive*) 683; grovel, worm one's way, steal along; jog -, rub -, bundle- on; toddle, waddle, wabble, slug; traipse, slouch, shuffle, halt, hobble, limp, claudicate, shamble; flag, falter, totter, stagger; mince, step short; march in -slow time, — funeral procession; take one's time; hang fire etc. (*be late*) 133.

retard, relax; slacken, check, moderate, rein in, curb; reef; strike -, shorten -, take in- sail; put on the drag, apply the brake; clip the wings; reduce the speed, decelerate; slacken -speed, — one's pace, lose ground; back -water, — pedal, put the engines astern, throttle down.

Adj. slow, slack; tardy; dilatory etc. (*inactive*) 683; gentle, easy; leisurely; deliberate, gradual; insensible, imperceptible; languid, sluggish, apathetic, phlegmatic, slow-paced, tardigrade, snail-like; creeping etc. *v*.

Adv. slowly etc. *adj*.; leisurely; *piano, adagio; largo, larghetto*; at half speed, under easy sail; at a -foot's, — snail's- pace; — funeral- pace; slower than molasses in January; in slow time; with -mincing steps, — clipped wings; *haud passibus aequis*; in low —, gear, — speed.

gradually etc. *adj*.; *gradatim*; by -degrees, — slow degrees, — inches, — little and little; step by step; inch by inch, bit by bit, little by little, *seriatim*; consecutively.

276. Impulse.—N. impulse, impulsion, impetus; momentum; push, pulsion, thrust, shove, jog, jolt, brunt, booming, boost, throw; explosion etc. (*violence*) 173; propulsion etc. 284, jet propulsion; firing, launching, projection, trajection.

percussion, concussion, collision, occursion, clash, encounter, cannon, *carambole*, appulse, shock, crash, bump; impact; *élan*; charge etc. (*attack*) 716; beating etc. (*punishment*) 972.

blow, dint, stroke, knock, tap, rap, slap, smack, pat, dab; fillip; slam, bang; hit, whack, thwack, clout; cuff etc. 972; squash, dowse, whap, swap, punch, thump, swipe, jab, pelt, kick, punce, calcitration; *ruade*; arietation; cut, thrust, lunge, yerk.

hammer, sledge-hammer, mall, maul, mallet, flail; ram, -mer; battering-ram, monkey, pile-driver, punch, bat, tamper, tamping iron; cudgel etc. (*weapon*) 727; axe etc. (*sharp*) 253.

[Science of mechanical forces] mechanics, dynamics etc.

V. give an -impetus etc. *n.*; impel, push; start, give a start to, set going; drive, urge, boom; thrust, prod, foin; cant; elbow, shoulder, jostle, justle, hustle, hurtle, shove, jog, jolt, bean, encounter; run –, bump –, butt- against; knock –, run- one's head against; impinge.

fire, launch, project, traject, propel, 284.

strike, knock, hit, hash, tap, rap, bat, slap, flap, dab, pat, thump, beat, bang, slam, dash; punch, thwack, whack; hit –, strike- hard; swap, batter, dowse, baste; pelt, patter, skelter, buffet, belabor, tamp; fetch one a blow, swat; poke at, pink, lunge, yerk; kick, calcitrate; butt; strike at etc. (*attack*) 716; whip etc. (*punish*) 972; propel etc. 284.

come –, enter- into collision; collide; foul; fall –, run- foul of.

throw etc.

Adj. impelling etc. *v.*; im-pulsive, -pellent; booming; dynamic, -al; impelled etc. *v.*

277. Recoil.—**N.** recoil; re-, retro-action; revulsion; rebound, *ricochet*; re-percussion, - calcitration; kick, *contre-coup*; springing back etc. *v.*; elasticity etc. 325; reflexion, reflex, reflux; reverberation etc. (*resonance*) 408; rebuff, repulse; return.

ducks and drakes; boomerang; spring; reactionist, reactionary.

V. recoil, resile, react; spring –, fly –, bound-back; rebound, reverberate, repercuss, recalcitrate, echo, *ricochet*.

Adj. recoiling etc. *v.*; re-fluent, -percussive, - calcitrant, -actionary; retroactive.

Adv. on the -recoil etc. *n.*

278. Direction.—**N.** direction, bearing, course, set, drift, tenor; tendency etc.176; incidence; bending, trending etc *v.*; dip, tack, aim, collimation; steer-ing, -age.

point of the compass, cardinal –, half –, quarter- points; North, East, South, West; N by E, ENE, NE by N, NE etc; rhumb, azimuth, line of collimation.

line, path, road, range, quarter, line of march; alignment; straight shot, bee-line.

course, bearing, heading, altitude, air -route, - lane, angle, center, axis, torsion, torque, pitch, lift, drift, flow, wash.

V. tend –, bend –, point- towards; conduct –, go- to; point -to, – at; bend, trend, verge, incline, dip, determine.

steer –, make- -for, – towards; aim –, level- at; take aim; keep –, hold- a course; be bound for; bend one's steps towards; direct –, steer –, bend –, shape- one's course; align –, align- one's march; go straight, – to the point; march -on, – on a point.

ascertain one's -direction etc. *n.*; *s'orienter*, see which way the wind blows; box the compass.

Adj. directed etc. *v.*, – towards; pointing towards etc. *v.*; bound for; aligned –, with; direct, straight; un-deviating, -swerving; straightforward; North, -ern, -erly, etc. *n.* -

directable etc. *v.*

Adv. towards; on the -road, – high road- to; versus, to; hither, thither, whither; directly; straight, – forwards; – as an arrow; point blank; in a direct, – straight- line -to, – for, – with; in a line with; full tilt at, as the crow flies.

before –, near –, close to –, against- the wind; windwards, in the wind's eye.

through, *via*, by way of; in all -directions, – manner of ways; *quaqua-versum*, from the four winds.

279. Deviation.—**N.** deviation; swerving etc. *v.*; obliquation, warp, refraction; flection, flexion; sweep; de-flection, -flexure; declination.

diversion, digression, departure from, aberration, drift, sheer; divergence etc. 291; zigzag, *détour* etc. (*circuit*) 629.

[Desultory motion] wandering etc. *v.*; vagrancy, evagation; by-paths and crooked ways.

[Motion sideways, oblique motion] sidling etc. *v.*; *échelon*, leeway; knight's move (at chess).

V. alter one's course, deviate, depart from, turn, trend; bend, curve, etc. 245; swerve, heel, bear off.

intervert; deflect; divert, – from its course; put on a new scent, shift, shunt, switch, wear, draw aside, crook, warp, short circuit.

stray, straggle; sidle, edge; diverge etc. 291; tralineate, digress, divagate; wander; wind, twist, meander, meander around Robin Hood's barn; veer, tack, sheer; turn -aside, – a corner, – away from; wheel, steer clear of; ramble, rove, drift; go -astray, – adrift; yaw, dodge; step aside, case off, make way for, shy.

fly off at a tangent; glance off; turn, wheel –, face- about; turn –, face- to the right about; wabble etc. (*oscillate*) 314; go out of one's way etc. (*perform a circuit*) 629; lose one's way.

Adj. deviating etc. *v.*; aberrant, errant; ex-, dis-cursive; devious, desultory, loose; rambling; stray, erratic, vagrant, undirected; circuitous, in-direct, zigzag; crab-like.

Adv. astray from, round about, wide of the mark; to the right about; all manner of ways, circuitously etc. 629.

obliquely, sideling, like the move of the knight on a chessboard.

280. Precession. [Going before.]—**N.** precession, leading, heading, precedence etc. 62; priority etc. 116; the lead, *le pas*; van etc. (*front*) 234; precursor etc. 64.

V. go -before, – ahead, – in the van, – in advance; precede, forerun; usher in, introduce, herald, head, take the lead; lead, – the way, – the dance; get –, have- the start, steal a march; get -before, – ahead, – in front of, outstrip etc. 303; take precedence etc. (*first in order*) 62.

Adj. foremost, first, leading etc. *v.*

Adv. in advance, before, ahead, in the van; fore-head-most, in front.

Phr. *seniores priores.*

281. Sequence. [Going after.]—N. sequence, run; coming after etc. (*order*) 63; (*time*) 117; following; pursuit etc. 622.

follower, attendant, satellite, shadow, dangler, train.

V. follow; pursue etc. 622; go –, fly- after, attend, beset, dance attendance on, dog, be-dog; tread -in the steps of, – close upon; be –, go –, follow- in the -wake, – trail, – rear- of; trail, follow as a shadow, hang on the skirts of; tread –, follow- on the heels of, tag- after.

lag, get behind.

Adj. following etc. *v.*

Adv. behind; in the -rear etc. 235, – train of, wake of; after etc. (*order*) 63, (*time*) 117.

282. Progression. [Motion forwards; progressive motion.]—N. progress, -ion, -iveness; advancing etc. *v.*; advance, -ment; ongoing; flood-tide, headway; march etc. 266; rise; improvement etc. 658.

V. advance; proceed, progress; get -on, – along, – over the ground; gain ground; jog –, rub –, wag- on; go with the stream; keep –, hold on-one's course; go –, move –, come –, get –, pass –, push –, press--on, – forward, – forwards, – ahead; press onwards, step forward; make –, work –, carve –, push –, force –, edge –, elbow-one's way; make -progress, – head, – way, – headway, – advances, – strides, – rapid strides etc. (*velocity*) 274; go –, shoot- ahead; distance; make up leeway.

Adj. advancing etc. *v.*; pro-gressive, -fluent; advanced.

Adv. forward, onward; forth, on ahead, under way, *en route* for, on -one's way, – the way, – the road, – the high road- to; in -progress, – mid progress; *in transitu* etc. 270.

Phr. *vestigia nulla retrorsum*.

283. Regression. [Motion backwards.]—N. regress, -ion; retro-cession, -gression, -gradation, -action; *reculade*; retreat, withdrawal, retirement, remigration; recession etc. (*motion from*) 287; recess; crab-like motion.

re-fluence, -flux; backwater, regurgitation, ebb, return; resilience; reflexion (*recoil*) 277; *volte-face*.

counter -motion, – movement, – march; veering, tergiversation, recidivation, backsliding, fall, relapse; deterioration etc. 659.

turning point etc. (*reversion*) 145.

V. re-cede, -grade, -turn, -vert, -treat, -tire; retro-grade, -cede; back, – down, – out, crawl; withdraw; rebound etc. 277; go –, come –, turn –, hark –, draw –, fall –, get –, put –, run-back; lose ground; fall –, drop- astern; back water, put about; veer, – round; double, wheel, counter-march; ebb, regurgitate; *jib*, shrink, shy, turn -tail, – round, – upon one's heel, – one's back upon; retrace one's steps, dance the back step; sound –, beat- a retreat; go home.

Adj. receding etc. *v.*; retro-grade, -gressive; re-gressive, -fluent, -flex, -cidivous, -silient; crab-like; reactionary etc. 277; counter-clockwise.

Adv. back, -wards; reflexively, to the right about, *à reculons*, *à rebours*.

Phr. *revenons à nos moutons*, as you were.

284. Propulsion. [Motion given to an object situated in front.]—N. pro-pulsion, -jection; *vis a tergo*; push etc. (*impulse*) 276; e-, jaculation; ejection etc. 297; throw, fling, toss, shot, discharge, shy.

[Science of propulsion] steam –, gas –, diesel –, jet –, rocket – propulsion, gunnery, ballistics, archery.

missile, projectile, ball, *discus*, javelin, hammer, quoit, brickbat, shot, bullet; arrow, shaft, gun etc. (*arms*) 727.

shooter, shot; gunner, gun-layer; archer, toxophilite; bow-, rifle-, marks- man; good –, crack- shot; sharpshooter etc. (*combatant*) 726

V. propel, project, throw, fling, cast, pitch, chuck, toss, jerk, heave, shy, hurl; flirt, fillip, dart, lance, tilt; e-, jaculate; fulminate, bolt, drive, sling, pitchfork.

send; send –, let –, fire- off; discharge, shoot; launch, send forth, let fly; dash.

put –, set- in motion; set agoing, start; give -a start, – an impulse- to; push, impel etc. 276; trundle etc. (*set in rotation*) 312; expel etc. 297.

carry one off one's legs; put to flight.

Adj. propelled etc. *v.*; propelling etc. *v.*; propulsive, -jectile.

285. Traction. [Motion given to an object situated behind.]—N. traction; drawing etc. *v.*; draft, pull, tug, haul; rake; 'a long pull, a strong pull and a pull all together;' towage, haulage.

V. draw, pull, haul, lug, rake, drag, draggle, tug, tow, trail, trawl, train; take in tow.

wrench, jerk, twitch.

Adj. drawing etc. *v.*; tractive, tractile; ductile; pulling, hauling, tugging, towing.

286. Approach. Motion towards.]—N. approach, approximation, appropinquation; access; appulse; afflux, -ion; advent etc. (*approach of time*) 121; pursuit etc. 622; convergence etc. 290.

V. approach, approximate; near; get –, go –, draw- near; come, – near, – to close quarters; move –, set in- towards; draw; make up to; gain upon; pursue etc. 622, tread on the heels of; bear up; make the land; hug the -shore, – land.

Adj. approaching etc. *v.*; approximative; convergent; affluent; impending, imminent etc. (*destined*) 152.

Adv. on the road.

Int. come hither! approach! here! come! come near!

287. Recession. [Motion from.]—N. recession, retirement, withdrawal; retreat; retrocession etc. 283; departure etc. 293; recoil etc. 277; flight etc. (*avoidance*) 623.

V. recede, go, move from, retire, ebb, withdraw, shrink; come –, move –, go –, get –, drift-away; depart etc. 293; retreat etc. 283; move –, stand –, sheer- off; swerve from; fall back, stand aside; run away etc. (*avoid*) 623.

remove, shunt, side track, switch off.

Adj. receding etc. *v.*

288. Attraction. [Motion towards, actively.]—N. attract-ion, -iveness; pull; drawing to, pulling towards, adduction, magnetism, gravity, attraction of gravitation; lure, bait, decoy.

lode-stone, -star; magnet, siderite, magnetite.

V. attract; draw –, pull –, drag- towards; adduce.

lure, bait, decoy.

Adj. attracting etc. *v.*; attrahent, attractive, adducent, adductive, alluring.

289. Repulsion. [Motion from, actively.]—**N.** repulsion; driving from etc. *v.*; repulse; abduction.

V. repel; push –, drive – etc. 276; from; chase, dispel; retrude; abduce, abduct, send away, repulse, dismiss.

keep at arm's length, turn one's back upon, give the cold shoulder; send packing; send -off, – away- with a flea in one's ear. – about one's business.

Adj. repelling etc. *v.*; repellant, repulsive; abducent, abductive.

290. Convergence. [Motion nearer to.]—**N.** con-vergence, -fluence, -course, -flux, -gress, - currence, -centration; appulse, meeting; corradiation.

assemblage etc. 72; resort etc. (*focus*) 74; asymptote.

V. converge, concur; come together, unite, meet, fall in with; close -with, – in upon; center - round, – in; enter in; pour in.

gather together, unite, concentrate, bring into a focus.

Adj. converging etc. *v.*, con-vergent, -fluent, - current; centripetal; asymptotical.

291. Divergence. [Motion further off.]—**N.** diverg-ence, -ency; divarication, ramification, radiation; separation etc. (*disjunction*) 44; dispersion etc. 73; deviation etc. 279; aberration, declination.

V. diverge, divaricate, radiate; ramify; branch –, glance –, file- off, fly off, – at a tangent; spread, scatter, disperse etc. 73; deviate etc. 279; part etc. (*separate*) 44; splay apart.

Adj. diverging etc. *v.*; divergent, radiant, centrifugal; aberrant.

292. Arrival. [Terminal motion at.]—**N.** arrival, advent, landing, de-, disem-barkation; reception, welcome, *vin d'honneur.*

home, goal, bourn, landing-place, -stage; resting –, stopping -place; destination, harbor, haven, port, terminal, terminus, railway station, depot, airport, halt, halting -place, – ground, anchorage etc. (*refuge*) 666.

return, recursion, remigration; meeting, ren-, encounter.

completion etc. 729.

V. arrive; get to, come to; come; reach, attain; come up, – with, – to; overtake, make, fetch, complete etc. 729, join, rejoin.

light, alight, dismount, land, go ashore, debark, disembark, put -in, – into, visit, cast anchor, pitch one's tent; sit down etc. (*be located*) 184; get to one's journey's end; make the land; be in at the death; come –, get- -back, – home; return; come in etc. (*ingress*) 294; make one's appearance etc. (*appear*) 446; drop in; detrain; outspan.

come to hand; come -at, – across; hit; come –, light –; pop –, bounce –, plump –, burst –, pitch- upon; meet; en- ren-counter; come in contact.

Adj. arriving etc. *v.*; homewardbound; terminal.

Adv. here, hither.

Int. welcome! hail! all hail! good- day, – morrow; greetings! hullo! well!

293. Departure. [Initial motion from.]—**N.** departure, decession, decampment; embarkation; take-off; outset, start; removal; exit etc. (*egress*) 295; exodus, Hejira, flight.

leave-taking, *congé,* valediction, valedictory, adieu, farewell, good-bye, stirrup-cup.

starting -point, – post; point –, place- of - departure, – embarkation; port of embarkation.

V. depart; go, – away; take one's departure, set out; set –, march –, put –, start –, be –, move –, get –, whip –, pack –, go –, take oneself-off; start, issue, march out, debouch; go –, sallyforth; sally, set forward; be gone.

leave a place, quit, vacate, evacuate, abandon; go off the stage, make ones' exit; retire, withdraw, remove; go -one's way, – along, – from home; take -flight, – wing; spring, fly, flit, wing one's flight; fly –, whip- away; take off, hop off; embark; go -on board, – aboard; set sail; put –, go- to sea; sail, take ship; hoist blue Peter; get under way, weigh anchor; strike tents, break camp, decamp; walk one's chalks, make tracks, cut one's stick; cut and run; take leave; say –, bid- -goodbye etc. *n.*; disappear etc. 449; abscond etc. (*avoid*) 623; entrain, embus, emplane; saddle –, harness –, hitch- up; inspan.

Adj. departing etc. *v.*; valedictory; outward bound.

Adv. whence, hence, thence; with a foot in the stirrup; on the -wing, – move.

Int. begone! etc. (*ejection*) 297; to horse! all aboard! farewell! adieu! good-bye, – day! *au revoir! auf wiedersehen!* fare you well! so long! God -bless you, – speed! *bon voyage!*

294. Ingress. [Motion into.]—**N.** ingress; entrance, entry; introgression; influx, intrusion, inroad, incursion, invasion, irruption; pene-, interpene- tration, illapse, import, importation, infiltration; immigration, admission etc. (*reception*) 296, insinuation etc. (*interjacence*) 228; insertion etc. 300.

inlet; way in; mouth, door etc. (*opening*) 260; path etc. (*way*) 627, conduit etc. 350; immigrant, visitor, incomer, newcomer, colonist.

V. have the *entrée*; enter; go –, come –, pour –, flow –, creep –, slip –, pop –, break –, burst- -into, – in; set foot on; burst in, break-in upon, invade, intrude, butt in, horn in, crash, insinuate itself; inter-, penetrate, infiltrate; find one's way –, wriggle –, worm oneself- into.

give entrance to etc. (*receive*) 296; insert etc. 300.

Adj. incoming, ingressive etc. *n.*; inward bound.

Adv. inward.

295. Egress. [Motion out of.]—**N.** egress, exit, issue; emer-sion, -gence; disemboguement; out-break, -burst; e-, pro-ruption; emanation; evacuation; ex, trans-udation; extravasation, per-spiration, sweating, leakage, percolation, distillation, oozing; gush etc. (*water in motion*) 348; outpour, -ing; effluence, effusion; efflux, -ion; drain; dribbling etc. *v.*; defluxion; drainage; out-come, -put; discharge etc. (*excretion*) 299.

export; expatriation; e-, re-migration; *débouche*; exodus etc. (*departure*) 293; emigrant, migrant, *émigré*, colonist.

outlet, vent, spout, tap, sluice, floodgate; pore; vomitory, out-gate, sally-port; way out; mouth, door etc. (*opening*) 260; path etc. (*way*) 627; con-duit etc. 350; air-pipe etc. 351.

V. emerge, emanate, issue; go –, come –, move –, pass –, pour –, flow- out of; pass off, evacuate; migrate.

ex-, trans-ude; leak; run, – out, – through; per-, trans-colate; seep; strain, distil; perspire, sweat, drain, ooze; filter, filtrate; dribble, gush, spout, flow out; well, – out; pour, trickle etc. (*water in motion*) 348; effuse, extravasate, disem-bogue, discharge itself, debouch; come –, break-forth; burst- out, – through; find vent, escape etc. 671.

Adj. effused etc. *v.*; outgoing, outward bound.

Adv. outward.

296. Reception. [Motion into, actively.]—**N.** reception; admission, admittance, *entrée*, im-portation; initiation; intro-duction, -mission, -ception; immission, ingestion, imbibition, ab-sorption, ingurgitation, inhalation; suction, sucking; eating, drinking etc. (*food*) 298; insertion etc. 300; interjection etc. 228.

V. give -entrance to, – admittance to, – the *entrée*; intro-duce, -mit; usher, admit, receive, im-port, initiate, bring in, open the door to, throw open, ingest, absorb, imbibe, inhale, infiltrate; let –, take –, suck- in; re-admit, -sorb, -absorb; snuff up; swallow, ingurgitate; engulf, engorge; gulp; eat, drink etc. (*food*) 298.

Adj. admit-ting etc. *v.*, -ted etc. *v.*; admissible; absorbent; introductory, introceptive, intromittent, initiatory.

297. Ejection. [Motion out of, actively.]—**N.** ejection, emission, effusion, rejection, expulsion, eviction, extrusion, trajection; discharge.

egestion, evacuation, vomition, disgorgement, voidance, eruption, eruptiveness; ruc-, cruc-tation, blood-letting, venesection, phlebotomy, paracen-tesis; tapping, drainage; clear-ance, -age, voidance; vomiting, excretion etc. 299.

deportation; banishment etc. (*punishment*) 972; rogue's march; relegation, extradition; dislodgment.

V. give -exit, – vent- to; let –, give –, pour –, send- out; des-, dis-patch; exhale, excern, ex-crete, disembogue, secrete, secern; extravasate,

shed, void, evacuate, egest, emit; open the -sluices, – floodgates; turn on the tap; extrude, detrude; ef-fuse, spend, expend; pour forth; squirt, spirt, spill, slop; perspire etc. (*exude*) 295; breathe, blow etc. (*wind*) 349.

tap, draw off; bale –, lade- out; let blood, broach.

eject, reject; expel, discard; cut, send to Coven-try, boycott, ostracize; *chasser*; banish etc. (*punish*) 972; throw etc. 284 -out, – up, – off, – away, – aside; push etc. 276 -out, – off, – away, – aside; shovel –, sweep- -out, – away; brush –, whisk –, turn –, send- -off, – away; discharge; send –, turn –, cast- adrift; turn –, bundle- out; throw overboard; give the sack to; send -packing, – about one's business, – to the right about; strike off the roll etc. (*abrogate*) 756; turn out-neck and heels, – head and shoulders, – neck and crop; pack off; send away with a flea in the ear; send to Jericho; bow out, show the door to, dismiss, fire, sack.

turn out of -doors, – house and home; evict, oust; exorcise, un-house, -kennel; dislodge; un-, dis-people; depopulate; relegate, deport.

empty; drain, – to the dregs; sweep off; clear, – off, – out, – away; such, draw off, extract; clean out, make a clean sweep of, clear decks, purge.

em-, dis-, disem-bowel; eviscerate, gut; unearth, root -out, – up; averruncate; weed –, get out; eliminate, get rid of, do away with, shake off; exen-terate.

vomit, spew, puke, keck, retch; belch, – out, eruct, eructate; cast –, bring- up; disgorge; ex-pectorate, salivate, clear the throat, hawk, spit, sputter, splutter, slobber, drool, drivel, slaver, slab-ber.

unpack, unlade, unload, unship; break bulk.

be let out; ooze etc. (*emerge*) 295.

Adj. emitt-ing, -ed etc. *v.*

begone! get you gone! get –, go- away, – along, – along with you! go your way! away, – with! off with you! go, – about your business! be off! avaunt! aroynt! get out!

298. Food. [Eating.]—**N.** eating etc. *v.*; deglutition, gulp, epulation, mastication, man-ducation, rumination, gastronomy, gastrology; panto-, hippo-, ichthyo-phagy etc.; gluttony etc. 957; carnivorousness, vegetarianism.

mouth, jaws, mandible, mazard, chops.

drinking etc. *v.*; potation, draught, libation; carousal etc. (*amusement*) 840; drunkenness etc. 959.

food, *pabulum*; aliment, nourishment, nutriment; susten-ance, -tation; nurture, sub-sistence, provender, feed, fodder, provision, ration, keep, commons, board; commissariat etc. (*provision*) 637; prey, forage, pasture, pasturage; fare, cheer; diet, -ary; regimen; belly timber, staff of life; bread, and cheese; proteins, carbohydrates, vitamines.

comestibles, eatables, victuals, edibles, *ingesta*; grub, prog, tack, hard tack, meat; bread, -stuffs; cereals; viands, cates, delicacy, dainty, creature comforts, contents of the larder, flesh-pots; festal board; ambrosia; good -cheer, – living.

hors-d'oeuvre; soup, pottage, *potage*, broth,

bouillon, consommé, purée, borsch, stock, skilly, gumbo; fish, – cakes, – pie; joint, *rôti, pièce de résistance, relevé,* hash, *réchauffé,* stew, *ragoût,* fricassee, mince, *salim, goulash, bouillabaisse, remove, entrée, croquette, rissole,* sausage, curry, bubble and squeak; haggis, collops, giblets; poultry, game etc.; biscuit, bun, scone, rusk, pancake, pie, pastry, pasty, patty, *patisseria,* tart, turnover, *vol-au-vent, soufflé,* dumpling, pudding, duff, *compote,* fritters, cake, napoleon, *blancmange,* custard, jelly, jam, sweets etc. 396; *entremet;* oatmeal, porridge, hasty pudding, gruel; eggs, omelet, cheese, matzoon, savory, vegetable, salad, *mayonnaise,* fruit; sauce, condiment etc. 393; kickshaws.

    table, *cuisine,* bill of fare, *menu, table d'hôte,* ordinary, *à la carte;* cover.

    meal, repast, feed, spread; mess; dish, plate, course, side dish; regale, regale-, refresh-, entertain-ment; refection, collation, picnic, feast, banquet, junket; breakfast; lunch, -eon, *déjeuner,* bever, tiffin, tea, dinner, supper, snack, whet, bait, dessert; pot-luck, *table d'hôte, déjeuner à la fourchette;* hearty –, square –, substantial –, fullmeal; blow out; light refreshment; pemmican.

    mouthful, bolus, gobbet, tit-bit, morsel, sop, sippet.

    drink, beverage, liquor, broth, soup; potion, dram, draft, drench, swill; nip, peg, sip, sup, gulp.

    wine, champagne, spirits, *liqueur* beer, porter, stout, ale, malt liquor, julep, Sir John Barleycorn, stingo, heavy wet, bitter, lager- beer, cider; grog, toddy, flip, purl, punch, negus, cup, bishop, posset, wassail; bitters, *apéritif,* high-ball, cocktail; whisky, rum, absinthe; gin etc. *(intoxicating liquor)* 959; coffee, chocolate, cocoa, tea, *maté,* the cup that cheers but not inebriates.

    eating-house etc. 189.

    V. eat, feed, fare, devour, swallow, take; gulp, bolt, snap; fall to; despatch, dispatch; discuss; take –, get –, gulp-down; lay –, tuck- in; lick, pick, peck; gormandize etc. 957; bite, champ, munch, cranch, craunch, crunch, chew, masticate, nibble, gnaw, mumble.

    live on; feed –, batten –, fatten –, feast- upon; browse, graze, crop, regale; carouse etc. *(make merry)* 840; eat heartily, do justice to, play a good knife and fork, banquet.

    break -bread, – one's fast; breakfast; lunch, dine, take tea, sup.

    drink, – in, – up, – one's fill; quaff, sip, sup; suck, – up; lap; swig; swill; tipple etc. *(be drunken)* 959; empty one's glass, drain the cup; toss -off, – one's glass; wash down, crack a bottle, wet one's whistle.

    cater, purvey etc. 637.

    Adj. eatable, edible, esculent, comestible, alimentary; cereal, cibarious; dietetic; culinary; nutri-tive, -tious; succulent; drinkable, pot-able, -ulent; bibulous.

    omn-, carn-, herb-, frug-, gran-, gramin-, phytivorous; ichthyophagous.

    prandial.

299. Excretion.—**N.** excretion, discharge, emanation; ejection etc. 297; exhalation, exudation, extrusion, secretion, effusion, extravasation, *ecchymosis,* evacuation, cacation, defecation, dysentery, dejection, *feces,* excrement;

perspiration, sweat; sub-, exud-ation; *diaphoresis;* sewage.

    saliva, spittle, rheum; ptyalism, salivation, catarrh, distemper; diarrhea; *ejecta, egesta, sputum, sputa; excreta;* lava; *exuviae* etc. *(uncleanness)* 653.

    hemorrhage, bleeding; catamenia, menses; outpouring etc. *(egress)* 295; leucorrhea.

    V. excrete etc. *(eject)* 297; emanate etc. *(come out)* 295.

    Adj. excretory, fecal, secretory; ejective, eliminant.

300. Insertion. [Forcible ingress.]—**N.** insertion, implantation, intercalation, embolism, introduction; interpolation, insinuation etc. *(intervention)* 228; planting etc. *v.;* injection, inoculation, importation, infusion; forcible -ingress etc. 294; immersion; submersion, -gence; dip, plunge; bath etc. *(water)* 337; interment etc. 363.

    V. insert; intro-duce, -mit; put –, run- into; import; inject; interject etc. 228; infuse, instil, inoculate, impregnate, imbue, imbrue.

    graft, ingraft, bud, plant, implant; dovetail obtrude; thrust –, stick –, ram –, stuff –, tuck –, press –, drive –, pop –, whip –, drop –, put- in; impact; empierce etc. *(make a hole)* 260.

    embed; immerse, immerge, merge; bathe, soak etc. *(water)* 337; dip, plunge etc. 310.

    bury etc. *(inter)* 363.

    insert etc. -itself; plunge *in medias res.*

    Adj. inserted etc. *v.*

301. Extraction. [Forcible egress.]—**N.** extraction; extracting etc. *v.;* removal, elimination, extrication, eradication, evolution.

    evulsion, avulsion; wrench; expression, squeezing; extirpation, extermination; ejection etc. 297; export etc. *(egress)* 295; distillation.

    extractor, corkscrew, forceps, pliers.

    V. extract, draw, pit; take –, draw –, pull –, tear –, pluck –, pick –, get- out; wring from, wrench; extort; root –, weed –, grub –, rakeup, – out; eradicate; pull –, pluck- up by the roots; averruncate; unroot; uproot, pull up, extirpate, dredge.

    remove; educe, elicit; evolve, extricate; eliminate etc. *(eject)* 297; eviscerate etc. 297.

    express, squeeze –, press- out; distil.

    Adj. extracted etc. *v.*

302. Passage. [Motion through.]—**N.** passage, transmission; permeation; pene-, interpene-tration; transudation, infiltration; *osmosis,* osmose, endos-, exos-mose; intercurrence; ingress etc. 294; egress etc. 295; path etc. 627; conduit etc. 350; opening etc. 260; journey etc. 266; voyage etc. 267.

    V. pass, – through; perforate etc. *(hole)* 260; penetrate, permeate, thread, thrid, enfilade; go through, – across; go –, pass- over; cut across; ford, cross; pass and repass, work; make –, thread –, worm –, force- one's way; make –, force- a passage; cut one's way through; find its -way, –

vent; transmit, make way, clear the course; traverse, go over the ground.

Adj. passing etc. *v.*; intercurrent; osmotic etc. *n.*

Adv. *en passant* etc. (*transit*) 270.

303. Overstep. [Motion beyond.]—**N.** transcursion, -ilience, -gression; infraction, intrusion; trespass; encroach-, infringe-ment; extravagation, transcendence; redundance etc. 641; ingress etc. 294.

V. transgress, surpass, pass; go- beyond, – by; show in –, come to the- front; shoot ahead of; steal a march –, gain- upon.

over-step, -pass, -reach, -go, -ride- -leap, -jump, -skip, -lap, -shoot the mark; out-strip, -leap, -jump, -go, -step, -run, -ride, -do; beat, – hollow; distance; leave in the -lurch, – rear; go one better, throw into the shade; exceed, transcend, surmount; soar etc. (*rise*) 305.

encroach, intrude, trespass, infringe, invade, trench upon, intrench on; strain; stretch –, strain- a point; pass the Rubicon.

Adj. surpassing etc. *v.*

Adv. beyond the mark, ahead.

304. Shortcoming. [Motion short of.]—**N.** shortcoming, failure; delinquency; falling short etc. *v.*; de-fault, -falcation; leeway; labor in vain, no go.

incompleteness etc. 53; imperfection etc. 651; insufficiency etc. 640; noncompletion etc. 730; failure etc. 732.

V. come –, fall –, stop- -short, – short of; not reach; want; keep within -bounds, – the mark, – compass.

break down, stick in the mud, collapse, come to nothing; fall -through, – to the ground, – down; cave in, end in smoke, fizzle out, miss the mark, fail; lose ground; miss stays, slump.

Adj. unreached; deficient; short, – of; *minus*; out of depth; perfunctory etc. (*neglect*) 460.

Adv. within -the mark, – compass, – bounds; behindhand; *re infectâ*; to no purpose; far from it.

Phr. the bubble burst.

305. Ascent. [Motion upwards.]—**N.** ascent, ascension; rising etc. *v.*; rise, upgrowth; leap etc. 309; acclivity, hill etc. 217; stair, stairs, stair-case, - way, flight of -steps, – stairs; ladder, companion, – way; lift, elevator etc. 307.

rocket, lark; sky-rocket, -lark; Alpine Club.

V. ascend, rise, mount, arise, uprise; go- –, get –, work one's way –, start –, spring –, shoot- up; zoom; aspire.

climb, clamber, ramp, scramble, swarm, *escalade*, surmount; scale, – the heights.

tower, soar, hover, spire, plane, swim, float, surge; leap etc. 309.

Adj. rising etc. *v.*; scandent, buoyant; supernatant, -fluitant; excelsior.

Adv. uphill.

306. Descent. [Motion downwards.]—**N.** descent, descension, declension, declination; fall;

falling etc. *v.*; drop, cadence; subsidence, lapse; come-down, downfall, tumble, slip, tilt, trip, lurch; cropper, *culbute*; titubation, stumble; fate of Icarus; dive, nose-dive, *volpané*.

avalanche, *débâcle*, landslip, slide.

V. descend; go –, drop –, come-down; fall, gravitate, drop, slip, slide, glissade, dive, plunge, settle; decline, slump, set, sink, droop, come down a peg.

dismount, alight, light, get down; swoop; stoop etc. 308; fall prostrate, precipitate oneself; let fall etc. 308.

tumble, trip, stumble, titubate, lurch, pitch, swag, topple; topple –, tumble- -down, – over; tilt, sprawl, plump down, come a cropper.

Adj. descending etc. *v.*; descendent, declivitous; downcast; decur-rent, sive; labent, deciduous; nodding to its fall.

Adv. down, -hill, -wards.

307. Elevation.—**N.** elevation; raising etc. *v.*; erection, lift; sublevation, upheaval; sublimation, exaltation; prominence etc. (*convexity*) 250.

lever etc. 633; crane, derrick, windlass, capstan, winch, dredger, lift, elevator, escalator, dumb waiter.

V. heighten, elevate, raise, lift, erect; set –, stick –, perch –, perk –, tilt- up; rear, hoist, heave; up-lift, -raise, -rear, -bear, -cast, -hoist, - heave; buoy, weigh, mount, give a lift; exalt, sublimate; place –, set- on a pedestal.

take –, drag –, fish- up; dredge.

stand –, rise –, get –, jump- up; spring to one's feet; hold -oneself, – one's head- up; draw oneself up to his full height.

Adj. elevated etc. *v.*; standing up; stilted, attollent, rampant.

Adv. on -stilts, – the shoulders of, – one's legs, – one's hind legs.

308. Depression.—**N.** lowering etc. *v.*; depression; dip etc. (*concavity*) 252; abasement; detrusion; reduction.

over-throw, -set, -turn; upset; prostration, subversion, precipitation.

bow; courtesy, curtsy; genuflexion, *kowtow*; obeisance, *salaam*.

V. depress, lower; let –, take- -down, – down a peg; cast; let -drop, – fall; -sink, debase, bring low, abase, slash, reduce, detrude, pitch, precipitate.

over-throw, -turn, -set; upset, subvert, prostrate, level, fell; cast –, take –, throw –, fling –, dash –, pull –, cut –, knock –, hew- down; raze, – to the ground; humiliate, trample in the dust, pull about one's ears.

sit, – down; couch, squat, crouch, stoop, bend, bow, courtesy, curtsy; bob; duck, dip, genuflect, kneel; *kowtow*, *salaam*, make obeisance, prostrate oneself; bend, bow- the -head, – knee; incline the head; bow down; cower; recline etc. (*be horizontal*) 213.

Adj. depressed etc. *v.*; at a low ebb; prostrate etc. (*horizontal*) 213; detrusive.

309. Leap.—**N.** leap, jump, hop, spring, bound, vault, saltation.

dance, caper, gambol; curvet, caracole; *gambade*, *-bado*; capriole, demivolt; buck, – jump; hop, skip and jump.

kangaroo, jerboa, chamois, goat, frog, grasshopper, flea.

V. leap; jump -up, – over the moon; hop, spring, bound, vault, ramp, cut capers, gambol, trip, skip, dance, caper, curvet, *caracole*; foot it, bob, bounce, flounce, start, frisk etc. (*amusement*) 840; jump about etc. (*agitation*) 315; trip it on the light fantastic toe, dance oneself off one's legs.

Adj. leaping etc. *v.*; saltatory, frisky.

Adv. on the light fantastic toe.

310. Plunge.—**N.** plunge, dip, dive, header; ducking etc. *v.*; submergence, immersion, diver.

V. plunge, dip, souse, duck; dive, plump; take a -plunge, – header, make a plunge; bathe etc. (*water*) 337

sub-marge, -merse; immerse, douse, sink, engulf, send to -the bottom, – Davy Jones' locker.

get out of one's depth; go -to the bottom, – down like a stone; founder, welter, wallow.

311. Circuition. [Curvilinear motion.]—**N.** circuition, circulation; turn, curvet; excursion; circum-vention, -navigation, -ambulation; north-west passage; ambit, gyre, lap, circuit etc. 629.

turning etc. *v.*; wrench; evolution; coil, helix, spiral; corkscrew.

V. turn, bend, wheel; go –, put- about; heel; go –, turn -round, – to the right about; turn on one's heel; make –, describe- a -circle, – complete circle; encircle; go –, pass- through -180°, – 360°

circum-navigate, -aviate, -ambulate, -vent; put a girdle round the earth, go the round, make the round of.

turn –, round- a corner; double a point.

wind, circulate, meander; whisk, twirl; twist etc. (*convolution*) 248; make a *détour* etc. (*circuit*) 629.

Adj. turning etc. *v.*; circuitous; circum-foraneous, -fluent; devious, roundabout, circum-ambient, -flex. -navigable.

Adv. round about.

312. Rotation. [Motion in a continued circle.]—**N.** rotation, revolution, gyration, circulation, roll, circum-rotation, -volution, -gyration; volutation, circination, turbination, *pirouette*, convolution.

verticity; whir, whirl, swirl, eddy, vortex, whirlpool, gurge; cyclone, tornado; surge; *vertigo*, dizzy round; Maelstrom, Charybdis; Ixion; wheel of Fortune.

wheel, screw, propeller, whirligig, rolling stone, windmill; top, teetotum, merry-go-round; roller; cog-, fly-wheel, spit; jack; caster.

axis, axle, spindle, spool, pivot, pin, hinge, pole, swivel, gimbals, arbor, bobbin, mandrel, shaft.

[Science of rotatory motion] trochilics, gyrostatics.

V. rotate; roll, – along; revolve, spin; turn, – round; circumvolve; circulate; gyre, gyrate, wheel,

whirl, swirl, twirl, trundle, troll, bowl; slew round.

roll up, furl; wallow, welter; box the compass; spin like a -top, – teetotum.

Adj. rotating etc. *v.*; rota-tory, -ry; circumrotatory, trochilic, vertiginous, gyratory; vortic-al, -ose.

Adv. head over heels, round and round, like a horse in a mill.

313. Evolution. [Motion in a reverse circle.]—**N.** evolution, unfolding, development; eversion etc. (*inversion*) 218.

V. evolve; un-fold, -roll, -wind, -coil, -twist, - furl, -twine, -ravel; disentangle; develop.

Adj. evolving etc. *v.*; evolved etc. *v.*

314. Oscillation. [Reciprocating motion, motion to and fro.]—**N.** oscillation; vibration, libration; motion of a pendulum; nutation; undulation; pulsation; pulse; throb; seismic disturbance.

alternation; coming and going etc. *v.*; ebb and flow, flux and reflux, ups and downs; wave, vibratiuncle, swing, beat, shake, wag, see-saw, dance, lurch, dodge; fluctuation; vacillation etc. (*irresolution*) 605.

seismometer, vibroscope, seismograph.

V. oscillate; vi-, li-brate; alternate, undulate, wave; sway, rock, swing; pulsate, beat; wag, -gle; nod, bob, courtesy, curtsy; tick; play; chatter, wamble, wabble; teeter, dangle, swag.

fluctuate, dance, curvet, reel, quake; quiver, quaver, shake, flicker; wriggle; roll, toss, pitch; flounder, stagger, totter, waddle; move –, bob- up and down etc. *adv.*; pass and repass, ebb and flow, come and go, shuttle; vacillate etc. 605.

brandish, shake, flourish.

Adj. oscillating etc. *v.*; oscill-, undul-, puls-, libr-atory; vibrat-ory, -ile; pendulous, shutterwise, seismic.

Adv. to and fro, up and down, backwards and forwards, see-saw, zigzag, wibble-wabble, in and out, from side to side, like buckets in a well.

315. Agitation. [Irregular motion.]—**N.** agitation, stir, tremor, shake, ripple, jog, jolt, jerk, shock, succussion, trepidation, . quiver, quaver, dance; jactit-ation, -ance; shuffling etc. *v.*; twitter, flicker, flutter.

disquiet, perturbation, commotion, turmoil, turbulence; tumult, -uation; hubbub, rout, bustle, fuss, racket, *subsultus*, staggers, megrims, epilepsy, fits, twitching, vellication, St. Vitus' dance.

spasm, throe, throb, palpitation, convulsion, paroxysm; tetanus.

disturbance etc. (*disorder*) 59; restlessness etc. (*changeableness*) 149.

ferment, -ation; ebullition, effervescence, hurly burly, *cahotage*; tempest, storm, ground swell, heavy sea, whirlpool, vortex etc. 312; whirlwind etc. (*wind*) 349.

V. be -agitated etc.; shake; tremble, – like an aspen leaf; quiver, quaver, quake, shiver, twitter, twire, dither, dodder; twitch, writhe, toss, shuffle, tumble, stagger, bob, reel, sway; wag, -gle, wiggle; wriggle, – like an eel; squirm; dance, stumble, shamble, flounder, totter, flounce, flop, curvet, prance.

throb, pulsate, beat, palpitate, go pit-a-pat; flutter, flitter, flicker, bicker; bustle.

ferment, effervesce, foam; boil, – over; bubble, – up; simmer.

toss –, jump- about; jump like a parched pea; shake like an aspen leaf; shake to its -center, – foundations; be the sport of the winds and waves; reel to and fro like a drunken man; move –, drive- from post to pillar and from pillar to post; keep between hawk and buzzard.

agitate, shake, convulse, toss, tumble, bandy, wield, brandish, flap, flourish, whisk, jerk, hitch, jolt; jog, -gle; hostle, buffet, hustle, disturb, stir, shake up, churn, jounce, wallop, whip, vellicate.

Adj. shaking etc. v.; agitated, tremulous; de-, sub-sultory; shambling; giddy-paced, saltatory, convulsive, jerky, unquiet, restless, all of a twitter.

Adv. by fits and starts; subsultorily etc. adj.; per saltum; hop, skip and jump; in -convulsions, – fits, pit-a-pat.

316. Materiality.—N. material-ity, -ness; materialization; corpor-eity, -ality; substantiality, material existence, incarnation, flesh and blood, plenum; physical condition.

matter, body, substance, brute matter, stuff, element, principle, protoplasm, plasma, parenchyma, material, substratum, hyle, corpus, pabulum; frame.

object, article, thing, something; still life; stocks and stones; materials etc. 635.

[Science of matter] physics; somatology, -ics; natural –, experimental- philosophy; physical science, philosophie positive, materialism, hylism; applied –, micro-, molecular –, nuclear – physics.

atomics, atomic science, nucleonics, quantum mechanics, radiology.

atom, radical, tracer, isotope, pleiad; atomic – nucleus, – cluster; nuclear particle, neutron, protron, shell, valence electron.

materialist, physicist, atomic scientist, radiologist.

V. materialize, incorporate, incarnate, substantiate, embody.

atomize, split –, smash – the atom; radio-activate.

Adj. material, bodily; corpor-eal, -al; physical; somat-ic, -oscopic; sensible, tangible, ponderable, palpable, substantial; fleshly, incarnate.

physical, bio-, electro-, geo-physical; atomic, nuclear, thermonuclear, radio-active.

objective, impersonal, neuter, unspiritual, materialistic.

317. Immateriality.—N. immaterial-ity, -ness; incorporeity, dematerialization, unsubstantiality, spirituality; inextension; astral plane.

personality; I, myself, me; ego, spirit etc. (soul) 450; astral body; immaterialism; spiritual-ism, -ist; subliminal –, subconscious- self.

V. disembody, spiritualize, dematerialize.

Adj. immateri-al, -ate; incorpor-eal, -al; asomatous, unextended; un-, dis-embodied; extramundane, supersensible, unearthly;

pneumatoscopic; spiritual etc. (psychieal) 450; aery.

personal, subjective.

318. World.—N. world, creation, nature, universe; earth, globe, wide world; cosmos; terraqueous globe, sphere; macro-, mega-cosm; music of the spheres; strato-, tropo-sphere.

heavens, sky, welkin, empyrean; starry -heaven, – host; firmament; vault –, canopy- of heaven; celestial spaces.

heavenly bodies, stars, luminaries, nebulae; galaxy, milky way, galactic circle, via lactea.

sun, orb of day, Apollo, Phoebus; photo-, chromo-sphere; solar system; planet, -oid, asteroid; comet; satellite; moon, orb of night, Diana, Luna; aerolite, meteor; falling –, shooting-star; meteorite.

constellation, zodiac, signs of the zodiac, Charles's wain, Great Bear, Southern Cross, Orion's belt, Cassiopeia's chair, Pleiades etc.

colures, equator, ecliptic, orbit.

[Science of heavenly bodies] astronomy; uranography, -logy; cosmo-logy, -graphy, -gony; eidouranion, orrery; geography; geodesy etc. (measurement) 466; star-gazing, -gazer; astronomer; cosmogonist, geodesist, geographer; observatory.

Adj. cosmic, cosmical, mundane; terr-estrial, -estrious, -aqueous, -ene, -eous; telluric, earthly, geotic, geodetic, cosmogonal, under the sun; sublunary, -astral.

solar, heliacal; lunar; celestial, heavenly, empyreal, sphery; starry, stellar; sider-eal, -al; astral; nebular.

Adv. in all creation, on the face of the globe, here below, under the sun.

319. Gravity.—N. gravi-ty, -tation; weight; heaviness etc. adj.; specific gravity; ponderosity, pressure, load; bur-den, -then; ballast, counterpoise; lump –, mass –, weight- of.

lead, millstone, mountain, Ossa on Pelion.

weighing, ponderation, trutination; weights; avoirdupois –, troy –, apothecaries'- weight; grain, scruple, drachm, ounce, pound, lb., load, stone, hundredweight, cwt., ton, quintal, carat, penny weight, tod, gram, kilogram etc.

[Weighing instrument] balance, scales, steelyard, beam, weighbridge, spring balance, weighing machine.

[Science of gravity] statics.

V. be -heavy etc. adj.; gravitate, weigh, press, cumber, load.

[Measure the weight of] weigh, poise.

Adj. weighty; weighing etc. v.; heavy, – as lead; ponder-ous, -able; lump-ish, -y; cumber-, burden-some; cumbrous, unwieldy, massive.

in-, superin-cumbent.

320. Levity.—N. levity; lightness etc. adj.; imponderability, imponderables, buoyancy, volatility.

feather, dust, mote, down, thistledown, flue, cobweb, gossamer, straw, cork, bubble; float, bouy; ether, air.

leaven, ferment, barm, yeast, enzyme.

V. be -light etc. *adj.*; float, swim, be buoyed up. render -light etc. *adj.*; lighten, levitate; leaven.

Adj. light, subtile, subtle, airy; imponder-ous, - able; astatic, weightless, ethereal, sublimated; uncompressed, volatile; buoyant, floating etc. *v.*; barmy, frothy; portable.

light as -a feather, – thistle down, – air. fermenting etc. *n.*

321. Density.—N. density, solidity; solidness etc. *adj.*; impenetra-, impermea-bility; incompressibility; imporosity; cohesion etc. 46, constipation, consistence, spissitude.

specific gravity; hydro-, areo-meter.

condensation; solid-ation, -ification; consolidation; concretion, caseation, coagulation; petrifaction etc. (*hardening*) 323; crystallization, precipitation; deposit, precipitate, silt; inspissation; thickening etc. *v.*

indivisibility, indiscerptibility, indissolvableness. solid body, mass, block, knot, lump; con-cretion, -crete, -glomerate; cake, clot, stone, curd, coagulum, grume; bone, gristle, cartilage.

V. be -dense etc. *adj.*; become – , render- solid etc. *adj.*; solid-ify, -ate; concrete, set, take a set, consolidate, congeal, coagulate; curd, -le; fix, clot, cake, candy, precipitate, deposit, cohere, crystallize; petrify etc. (*harden*) 323.

condense, thicken, inspissate, incrassate; compress, squeeze, ram down, constipate.

Adj. dense, solid, solidified etc. *v.*; cohe-rent, - sive etc. 46; compact, close, serried, thickset; substantial, massive, lumpish; impenetrable, impermeable, imporous; incompressible; constipated; concrete etc. (*hard*) 323; knot-ted, -ty; gnarled; crystal-line, -lizable; thick, grumous, stuffy.

un-dissolved, -melted, -liquified, -thawed. in-divisible, -discerptible, -frangible, dissolvable, -dissoluble, -soluble, -fusible.

322. Rarity.—N. rarity; tenuity; absence of - solidity etc. 321; subtility; sponginess, compressibility.

rarefaction, expansion, dilatation, inflation, subtilization.

ether etc. (*gas*) 334.

V. rarefy, expand, dilate, subtilize, attenuate, thin.

Adj. rare, subtile, thin, fine, tenuous, compressible, flimsy, slight; light etc. 320; cavernous, spongy etc. (*hollow*) 252.

rarefied etc. *v.*; unsubstantial; uncom-pact, - pressed.

323. Hardness.—N. hardness etc. *adj.*; rigidity, renitence, inflexibility, temper, callosity, durity.

induration, petrifaction; lapid-ification, -escence; vitri-, ossi-, corni-fication; crystallization.

stone, pebble, flint, marble, rock, fossil, crag, crystal, quartz, granite, adamant; bone, cartilage; heart of oak, block, board, deal board; iron, steel; cast –, wrought- iron; nail; brick, concrete; cement.

V. render -hard etc. *adj.*; harden, stiffen, indurate, petrify, temper, ossify, vitrify.

Adj. hard, rigid, stubborn, stiff, firm; starch, - ed; stark, unbending, unlimber, unyielding; inflexible, tense; indurate, -d; gritty, proof.

adamant-ine, -ean; concrete, stony, rocky, lithic, granitic, vitreous; crystalline; horny, corneous; bony; oss-eous, -ific; cartilaginous, hard as a -stone etc. *n.*; stiff as -buckram, – a poker.

324. Softness.—N. softness, pliableness etc. *adj.*; flexibility; pli-ancy, -ability; sequacity, malleability; flabbiness; duct-, tract-ility; extend-, extensibility; plasticity; inelasticity; flaccidity, laxity.

clay, wax, butter, dough, pudding; cushion, pillow, feather-bed, pad, down, padding, wadding. mollification; softening etc. *v.*

V. render -soft etc. *adj.*; soften, mollify, mellow, relax, temper; mash, knead, squash, *massage*.

bend, yield, relent, relax, give.

Adj. soft, tender, supple; pli-ant, -able; flexible, -ile; lithe, -some; lissom, limber, plastic; ductile; tract-ile, -able; malleable, extensile, sequacious, inelastic, mollient.

yielding etc. *v.*; flabby, limp, flimsy.

flaccid, flocculent, downy; spongy, edematous, medullary, doughy, argillaceous, mellow.

soft as -butter, – down, – silk; yielding as wax; tender as a chicken.

325. Elasticity.—N. elasticity, springiness, spring, resilience, renitency, buoyancy.

india-rubber, caoutchouc, gutta-percha, whalebone, gum elastic.

V. be -elastic etc. *adj.*; spring back etc. (*recoil*) 227.

Adj. elastic, tensile, springy, ductile, resilient, renitent, buoyant.

326. Inelasticity.—N. want of – , absence of-elasticity etc. 325; inelasticity etc. (*softness*) 324.

Adj. inelastic etc. (*soft*) 324.

327. Tenacity.—N. tenacity, toughness, strength; cohesion etc. 46; sequacity; stubbornness etc. (*obstinacy*) 606; viscidity etc. 352.

leather; gristle, cartilage.

V. be -tenacious etc. *adj.*; resist fracture.

Adj. tenacious, tough, cohesive, adhesive, strong, resisting, sequacious, stringy, gristly, cartilaginous, leathery, coriaceous, tough as whit-leather; stubborn etc. (*obstinate*) 606.

328. Brittleness.—N. brittleness etc. *adj.*; frag-, friab-, frangib-, fiss-ility; frailty; house of -cards, – glass.

V. be -brittle etc. *adj.*; live in a glass house. break, crack, snap, split, shiver, splinter, crumble, break short, burst, fly, give way; fall to pieces; crumble -to, – into- dust.

Adj. breakable, brittle, frangible, fragile, frail, friable, delicate, gimcrack, shivery, fissile; splitting etc. *v.*; lacerable, splintery, crisp, crimp, short, brittle as glass.

329. Texture. [Structure.]—**N.** structure, organization, anatomy, frame, mold, fabric, construction; frame-work, carcass, architecture; stratification, cleavage.

substance, stuff, *compages, parenchyma*; constitution, staple, organism.

[Science of structures]organ-, oste-, my- splanchn-, neur-, angi-, aden-ology; angi-, aden-ography.

texture; inter-, con-texture; tissue, grain, web, surface; warp and -woof, − weft; tooth, nap etc. (*roughness*) 256; fineness −, coarseness- of grain.

[Science of textures] histology.

Adj. structural, organic; anatomic, -al.

text-ural, -ile; fine-, coarse-grained; fine, delicate, subtile, gossamery, filmy; coarse; homespun; linsey-woolsey.

330. Pulverulence. [State of powder.]—**N.** pulverulence; sandiness etc. *adj.*; efflorescence; friability.

powder, dust, sand, shingle; sawdust; grit; attrition; meal, bran, flour, *farina*, spore, sporule; crumb, seed, grain; particle etc. (*smallness*) 32; thermion; limature, filings, *débris, detritus*, scobs, magistery, fine powder; *flocculi*.

smoke; cloud of -dust, − sand, − smoke; puff −, volume -of smoke; sand −, dust- storm.

[Reduction to powder] pulverization, comminution, attenuation, granulation, disintegration, subaction, contusion, trituration, levigation, abrasion, detrition, multure; limâtion; filing etc. *v.*

[Instruments for pulverization] mill, millstone, grater, rasp, file, pestle and mortar, nutmeg grater, teeth, molar, grinder, chopper, grindstone, kern, quern, muller.

V. come to dust; be -disintegrated, − reduced to powder etc.

reduce −, grind- to powder; pulverize, comminute, granulate, triturate, levigate; scrape, file, abrade, rub down, grind, grate, rasp, pound, bray, bruise; con-tuse, -tund; beat, crush, cranch, craunch, crunch, muller, scranch, crumble, disintegrate; attenuate etc. 195.

Adj. powdery, pulverulent, granular, mealy, floury, farinaceous, branny, furfuraceous, flocculent, dusty, sandy, sabulous; aren-ose, -arious, -aceous; gritty; efflorescent, impalpable.

pulverizable; friable, crumbly, shivery; pulverized etc. *v.*; attrite; in pieces.

331. Friction.—**N.** friction, attrition; rubbing etc. *v.*; erasure; con-frication, -trition; affriction, abrasion, arrosion, limature, frication, rub; elbowgrease; rosin; *massage*.

V. rub, scratch, abrade, scrape, scrub fray, rasp, graze, curry, scour, polish, rub out, erase, gnaw; file, grind etc. (*reduce to powder*) 330; *massage*. set one's teeth on edge; rosin.

Adj. anâtriptic, abrasive.

332. Lubrication. [Absence of friction. Prevention of friction.]—**N.** smoothness etc. 255; unctuousness etc. 355.

lubri-cation, -fication; anointment; oiling etc. *v.* synovia; lubricant, graphite, glycerine, oil etc. 356; saliva; lather.

V. lubri-cate, -citate; oil, grease, lather, soap; wax.

Adj. lubricated etc. *v.*

333. Fluidity.—**N.** fluidity, liquidity; liquidness etc. *adj.*; gaseity etc. 334; liquefaction etc. 334.

fluid, inelastic fluid; liquid, liquor; lymph, humor, juice, sap, serum, blood, serosity, gravy, rheum, ichor, sanies.

solu-bility, -bleness.

[Science of liquids] hydro-logy, -statics, dynamics, hydraulics. etc.

V. be -fluid etc. *adj.*; flow etc. (*water in motion*) 348; liquefy etc. 335.

Adj. liquid, fluid, serous, juicy, succulent, sappy; fluent etc. (*flowing*) 348.

liquefied etc. 335; uncongealed; soluble, hydrostatic etc. *n.*

334. Gaseity.—**N.** gaseity, gaseousness, vapourousness etc. *adj.*; flatulence, -lency; volatility, aeration, gasification.

elastic fluid, gas, air, vapor, ether, steam, fume, reek, *effluvium, flatus*; cloud etc. 353.

[Science of elastic fluids] pneumat-ics, -ostatics; aero-statics, -dynamics etc.

gas-, gaso-meter.

V. gassify, aerate, aerify; emit vapor etc. 336.

Adj. gaseous, aeriform, ethereal, aerial, airy, vaporous, volatile, evaporable; flatulent; aerostatic etc. *n.*

335. Liquefaction.—**N.** liquefaction; liquescen-ce, -cy, deliquescence; melting etc. (*heat*) 384; colliqu-ation, -efaction; thaw; de-, liquation; lixiviation, dissolution.

solution, apozem, lixivium, infusion, decoction, flux.

solvent, diluent, menstruum, alkahest, *aqua fortis*.

V. render -liquid etc 333; liquefy, run, deliquesce; melt etc. (*heat*) 384; solve; dissolve, resolve; liquate; hold in solution; leach, lixiviate.

Adj. lique-fied etc. *v.*, -scent, -fiable; deliquescent, soluble, colliquative; solvent.

336. Vaporization.—**N.** vapor-, volatilization; gasification; e-, vaporation; distillation, cohobation, sublimation, exhalation, volatility.

vaporizer, still, retort, spray, atomizer; fumigation, steaming.

V. render -gaseous etc. 334; vaporize, volatilize; distil, sublime, evaporate, exhale, smoke, transpire, emit vapor, fume, reek, steam, fumigate.

Adj. volatilized etc *v.*, reeking etc *v.*; volatile; evaporable, vaporizable.

337. Water.—**N.** water; serum, serosity; lymph; rheum; diluent.

dilution, maceration, lotion; washing etc. *v.*; im-, mersion; humectation, infiltration, spargefaction, affusion, irrigation, *douche*, balneation, bath.

deluge etc. (*water in motion*) 348; high water, flood-, spring-tide.

V. be -watering etc. *adj.*; reek.

add water, water, wet; moisten etc. 339; dilute, dip, immerse; merge; im-, sub-merge; plunge, souse, duck, drown; soak, steep, macerate, pickle, wash, sprinkle, sparge, lave, bathe, affuse, splash, swash, douse, slosh, drench; dabble, slop, slobber, irrigate, inundate, deluge; syringe, inject, gargle; infiltrate, percolate.

Adj. watery, aqueous, aquatic, lymphatic; balneal, diluent; drenching etc. *v.*; diluted etc. *v.*; weak; wet etc. (*moist*) 339.

Phr. the waters are out.

338. Air.—**N.** air etc. (*gas*) 334; common —, atmospheric- air; atmosphere, stratosphere, isothermal layer, troposphere, Heaviside layer.

open; – air; sky, welkin; blue, – sky; cloud etc. 353.

weather, climate, rise and fall of the barometer, isobar.

[Science of air] pneumatics, aero-logy, -scopy, -graphy; meteorology, climatology; eudio-, baro-, aero-meter; aneroid, baro-graph, -scope; weather-gauge, -glass, -cock.

exposure to the -air, — weather; ventilation; aero-station; -nautics; -naut etc. 265 and 269.

V. air, ventilate; fan etc. (*wind*) 349.

Adj. containing air, flatulent, effervescent; windy etc. 349.

atmospheric, airy; aeri-al, -form; pneumatic; meteorological; weather-wise.

Adv. in the open air, out of doors, *à la belle étoile, al fresco; sub -Jove, – dio.*

339. Moisture.—**N.** moisture; moistness etc. *adj.*; hum-idity, -ectation; madefaction, dew; *serein*; marsh etc. 345; Hygrometr-ry, -er.

V. moisten, wet; humect, -ate; sponge, damp, dampen, bedew; imbue, imbrue, infiltrate, saturate; seethe, sop; soak, drench etc. (*water*) 337.

be -moist etc. *adj.*; not have a dry thread; perspire etc. (*exude*) 295.

Adj. moist, damp; watery etc. 337; undried, humid, wet, dank, muggy, dewy; roric; roscid; juicy.

wringing wet; wet -through, — to the skin; saturated etc. *v.*

swashy, soggy, dabbled; reeking, seething, dripping, soaking, soft, sodden, sloppy, muddy; swampy etc. (*marshy*) 345; irriguous.

340. Dryness.—**N.** dryness etc. *adj.*; siccity, aridity, drought, ebb-, neap-tide, low water.

drying, ex-, de-siccation; evaporation; dehydration; arefaction, dephlegmation, drainage.

drier, desiccator.

V. be -dry etc. *adj.*; render -dry etc. *adj.*; dry;

dry –, soak- up; sponge, swab, wipe; ex-, desiccate, dehydrate, anhydrate; drain, parch.

be fine, hold up.

Adj. dry, anhydrous, arid, waterless; dried etc. *v.*; undamped; juice-, sap- less; sear; husky; rainless, without rain, fine; dry as -a bone, – dust, – a stick, – a mummy, – a biscuit; disiccated; dehydrated; water-proof, -tight.

341. Ocean.—**N.** sea, ocean, main, deep, brine, salt water, waters, waves, billows, high seas, offing, great waters, watery waste, 'vasty deep,' briny ocean, herring pond, steamer track, the seven seas; wave, tide etc. (*water in motion*) 348.

hydrograph-y, -er, oceanography; Neptune, Thetis, Triton, Naiad, Nereid; sea-nymph, Siren, mer-maid, -man; trident, dolphin.

Adj. oceanic; mar-ine, -itime; pleagic, -ian; sea-going, -worthy; hydrographic.

Adv. at –, on- sea; afloat, on the high seas.

342. Land.—**N.** land, earth, ground, dry land, *terra firma.*

continent, mainland, peninsula, delta; tongue –, neck- of land; isthmus; oasis; promontory etc. (*projection*) 250; highland etc. (*height*) 206.

coast, shore, scar, strand, beach; bank, lea; sea-board, -side, -shore, -bank, -coast, -beach; rock-, iron- bound coast; loom of the land; derelict; innings; *alluvium*, alluvion.

soil, glebe, clay, loam, marl, clodge, chalk, gravel, mold, subsoil, clod, clot; rock, crag, cliff.

acres; real estate etc. (*property*) 780; landsman, land-lubber, farmer.

geography etc. 318; agriculture etc. 371.

V. land, come to land; set foot on -the soil, – dry land; come –, go- ashore.

Adj. earthy; continental, midland; littoral, riparian, ripuarian; alluvial; terrene etc. (*world*) 318; landed, predial, territorial.

Adv. ashore; on -shore, – land.

343. Gulf. Lake.—**N.** land covered with water, gulf, gulph, bay, inlet, bight, estuary, arm of the sea, fiord, armlet; frith, firth, ostiary, mouth; lagune, lagoon; indraught; cove, creek; natural harbor; roads; strait, narrows; Euripus; sound, belt, gut, kyles.

lake, loch, lough, mere, tarn, plash, broad, pond, pool, lin, puddle, well, artesian well, tank, sump; standing -, dead –, sheet of- water; fish – mill-pond; race; ditch, dike, dyke, dam; reservoir etc. (*store*) 636.

Adj. lacustrine; land locked.

344. Plain.—**N.** plain, table land, mesa, face of the country; open -, champaign-country; basin, downs, waste, weary waste, desert, tundra, wild, steppe, pampas, savanna, prairie, champaign, heath, common, wold, veld; moor, -land, uplands, fell; bush; *plateau* etc. (*level*) 213; *campagna.*

meadow, mead, haugh, pasturage, park, field,

lawn, green, plat, plot, grass-plat, greensward, sward, grass, turf, sod, heather; lea, ley, lay; grounds.

Adj. campestrian, champaign, alluvial.

345. Marsh.—**N.** marsh, swamp, morass, marish, moss, fen, bog, quagmire, slough, sump, wash; mud, squash, slush.

Adj. marsh, -y; swampy, boggy, plashy, poachy, quaggy, soft; muddy, sloppy, squashy, spongy; paludal; moor-ish, -y; fenny.

346. Island.—**N.** island, isle, islet, eyot, ait, holm, reef, atoll, breaker; archipelago; islander.

Adj. insular, sea-girt.

347. Stream. [Fluid in motion.]—**N.** stream etc. (of water) 348, (of air) 349.

V. flow etc. 348; blow etc. 349.

348. River. [Water in motion.]—**N.** running water.

jet, spirt, squirt, spout, splash, swash, rush, gush, jet d'eau; sluice, chute.

water-spout, -fall; fall, cascade, force, foss; lin, -n, ghyll, Niagara; cata-ract, -dupe, -clysm; débâcle, inundation, deluge.

rain, -fall; serein; shower, scud; downpour, cloud burst; driving -, pouring -, drenching-rain; hyeto-logy, -graphy; rainy season, monsoon; predominance of Aquarius, reigh of St. Swithin; mizzle, drizzle, stilliciduum, plash; dropping etc. v.

stream, course, flux, flow, profluence; effluence etc. (egress) 295; defluxion; flowing etc. v.; current, tide, race.

spring; fount, -ain; rill, rivulet, gill, gullet, rillet; stream-, brook-let; runnel, sike, burn, beck, brook, stream, river; reach; tributary.

body of water, torrent, rapids, flush, flood, swash, spate; spring -, high -, full-tide; bore; eagre, hugre; fresh, -et; undertow, indraught, reflux, undercurrent, eddy, vortex, gurge, whirlpool, Maelstrom, regurgitation, overflow; confluence, corrivation.

wave, billow, surge, swell, ripple; roller, ground swell, surf, breaker, white horses; comber, beach-comber; rough -, heavy -, cross -, long -, short -, chopping -, choppy- sea, choppiness; tidal wave.

[Science of fluids in motion] Hydrodynamics; Hydraul-ics etc.; raingauge etc.

water-bearer, - carrier, Aquarius.

irrigation etc. (water) 337; pump; watering-pot, - cart; hydrant, standpipe, hose, sprinkler, drencher; fire engine, squirt, syringe.

V. flow, run; meander; gush, pour, spout, roll, jet, well, issue; drop, drip, dribble, plash, squirt, spurt, spirtle, trill, trickle, distil, percolate; stream, overflow, inundate, deluge, flow over, splash, swash, guggle, murmur, babble, bubble, purl, gurgle, sputter, regurgitate; ooze, flow out etc. (egress) 295.

rain, - hard, - in torrents, - cats and dogs, - pitchforks; come down in sheets; pour with rain, drizzle, mizzle, spit, sprinkle, set in.

flow -, fall -, open -, drain- into; discharge itself, desembogue.

[Cause a flow] pour; pour out etc. (discharge) 297; shower down; irrigate, drench etc. (wet) 337; spill, splash.

[Stop a flow] stanch; dam, -up etc. (close) 261; obstruct etc. 706.

Adj. fluent; dif-, pro-, af-fluent; tidal; flowing etc. v.; meand-ering, -ry, -rous; fluvi-al, -atile; streamy, showery, rainy, drizzly, drizzling, pluvial, pluviose, stillicidous.

349. Wind. [Air in motion.]—**N.** wind, draught, flatus, afflatus, air; breath, - of air; puff, whiff, zephyr; blow, drift; aura; stream, current; under-current.

gust, blast, breeze, squall, gale, half a gale, storm, tempest, hurricane, whirlwind, tornado, samiel, cyclone, typhoon; simoon; harmattan, monsoon, trade wind, sirocco, mistral, bise, föhn, tramontane, levanter; capful of wind; fresh -, stiff- breeze; keen blast; blizzard.

windiness etc. adj.; ventosity; rough -, dirty -, ugly -, stress of- weather; dirty-, windy-, mackerel- sky; mare's tail; thick -, black -, white- squall.

anemography, aerodynamics; windgauge, anemometer, weather-cock, vane.

suf-, insuf-, per-, in-, af-flation; blowing, fanning etc. v.; ventilation.

sneezing etc. v.; sternutation; hic-cup, -cough; catching of the breath; breathing etc.

Eolus, Eurus, Boreas, Zephyr, cave of Eolus.

air-pump, lungs, bellows, blow-pipe, fan, blower; pulmotor, ventilator, punkah, aspirator, exhauster, ejector.

V. blow, waft; blow -hard, - great guns, - a hurricane etc. n.; whistle, roar, howl, ring in the shrouds; stream, issue.

respire, breathe, in-, ex-hale, puff; whif, -fle; gasp, wheeze; snuff, -le; sniff, -le; sneeze, cough, belch.

fan, ventilate; in-, per-flate; blow -, pump- up.

Adj. blowing etc. v.; windy, airy, aeolian, flatulent; breezy, gusty, squally; stormy, tempestuous, blustering; boisterous etc. (violent) 173.

pulmon-ic, -ary.

350. Conduit. [Channel for the passage of water.]—**N.** conduit, channel, duct, watercourse, race; head -, tail- race; adit, aqueduct, canal, trough, flume, gutter, pantile; dike, canyon, ravine, gorge, hollow, main, gully, moat, ditch, drain, sewer, culvert, cloaca, sough, kennel, siphon, piscina; pipe etc. (tube) 260; funnel; tunnel etc. (passage) 627; water -, waste- pipe; emunctory, gully-hole, artery, aorta, vein, blood vessel; lymphatic; throat, alimentary canal, intestine; pore, spout, scupper; ad-, a-jutage; hose; gar-, gur-goyle; penstock, weir; flood-, water-gate; sluice, lock, valve; rose; waterworks.

Adj. vascular etc. (with holes) 260.

351. Air-pipe. [Channel for the passage of air.]—**N.** air-pipe, - shaft, - way, - passage, -

tube; shaft, flue, chimney, funnel, vent, blow-hole, nostril, nozzle, throat, weasand, *trachea*; *bronchus*, *-ia*; larynx, tonsils, wind-pipe, spiracle; venti-duct, -lator; louvre, Venetian blinds; blow-pipe etc. (*wind*) 349; pipe etc. (*tube*) 260.

352. Semiliquidity.—N. semiliquidity; stickiness etc. *adj.*; visc-idity, -osity; gumm-, glutin-, muc-osity; spiss-, crass-itude; lentor; adhesiveness etc. (*cohesion*) 46.

inspiss-, incrass-ation; thickening, coagulation.

jelly, aspic, mucilage, gelatin, isinglass; colloid, mucus, phlegm; pituite, lava; glair, starch, gluten, albumen, milk, cream, protein; syrup, treacle; gum, size, glue, paste; wax, bee's-wax; emulsoid, emulsion, soup; squash, mud, slush, slime, ooze; moisture etc. 339; marsh etc. 345.

V. inspiss-, incrass-ate; coagulate, gelatinize, gelatinify, gel, jell, emulsify, thicken; mash, squash, churn, beat up.

Adj. semi-fluid, -liquid; half-melted, -frozen; milky, muddy etc. *n.*; lact-eal, -ean, -eous, -escent, -iferous; emulsive, curdled, thick, succulent, uliginous.

gelat-, album-, mucilag-, glut-inous; gelatine, mastic, amylaceous, ropy, clammy, clotted; vis-cid, -cous; sticky, tacky; slab, -by; lentous, pituitous; mu-cid, -culent, -cous.

353. Bubble. [Mixture of air and water.] [Cloud.]—N. bubble; foam, froth, head, fume, spume, lather, suds, spray, surf, yeast, barm, spin-drift.

cloud, vapor, fog, mist, haze, steam; scud, rack, *nimbus*; *cumulus*, woolpack, *cirrus*, *stratus*; cirro-, *cumulo-stratus*; *cirro-cumulus*; mackerel sky, mare's tail, dirty sky.

[Science of clouds] nephelognosy, nephology.

effervescence, fermentation; bubbling etc. v.

nebula; cloudiness etc. (*opacity*) 426; nebulosity etc. (*dimness*) 422.

V. bubble, boil, foam, froth, spume, mantle, sparkle, guggle, gurgle; effervesce, ferment, fizzle; aerate; cloud, overcast, befog.

Adj. bubbling etc. v.; frothy, nappy, ef-fervescent, sparkling, *mousseux*, up, fizzy, with a head on.

cloudy etc. *n.*; vaporous, nebulous, overcast; nubiferous, nephological; foggy, brumous.

354. Pulpiness.—N. pulpiness etc. *adj.*; pulp, paste, dough, sponge, curd, pap, rob, jam, pudding, mush, fool, poultice, grume.

Adj. pulpy etc. *n.*; pultaceous, grumous.

V. pulp, pulpify, mash.

355. Unctuousness.—N. unctuousness etc. *adj.*; unctuosity, lubricity; ointment etc. (*oil*) 356; anointment; lubrication etc. 332.

V. oil etc. (*lubricate*) 332.

Adj. unctuous, oily, oleaginous, adipose, sebaceous; fat, -ty; greasy, waxy, butyraceous, soapy, saponaceous, pinguid, lardaceous; slippery.

356. Oil.—N. oil, fat, butter, cream, grease, tallow, suet, lard, dripping, margarine, oleomargarine, exunge, blubber; glycerine, stearine, elaine, oleagine; soap; soft soap, wax, cerement; paraffin, spermaceti, adipocere; petroleum, mineral —, rock —, crystal- oil, kerosene, vegetable —, colza —, olive —, linseed —, cotton seed —, rape —, nut —, fusel- oil; animal —, neat's foot —, signal —, train- oil; ointment, unguent, liniment, salve, pomade, pomatum, brilliantine, spike —, nard.

356a. Resin.—N. resin, rosin, colophony; gum; lac, shellac, sealing-wax; amber, -gris; bitumen, pitch, tar, asphalt, -e, -um; varnish, copal, mastic, magilp, lacquer, japan.

V. varnish etc. (*overlay*) 223.

Adj. resinous, bituminous, pitchy, tarry.

357. Organization.—N. organized -world, — nature; living —, animated- nature; living beings; organic remains, organism; fossils; animal and vegetable kingdom, *fauna* and *flora*, biota.

prot-oplasm, -ein; albumen; structure etc. 329; organ-ization, -ism.

[Science of living beings] biology; natural history,* organic —, bio-chemistry, anatomy, physiology, embryology, morphology, evolution, Darwinism, Lamarkism, zoology etc. 368; botany etc. 369; naturalist, biologist etc.

Adj. organ-ic, -ized.

*The term *Natural History* is also used as relating to all the objects in Nature whether organic or inorganic, and in-cluding therefore *Mineralogy, Geology, Meteorology*, etc.

358. Inorganization.—N. mineral -world, — kingdom; unorganized —, inorganic —, brute —, inanimate- matter.

[Science of the mineral kingdom] mineralogy; geo-logy, -gnosy, -scopy; metall-urgy, -ography; lithology; orycto-logy, -graphy.

V. turn to dust, pulverize.

Adj. in-organic, -animate; unorganized; azoic; mineral.

359. Life.—N. life; vi-tality, -ability; animation; vital -spark, — flame, — force.

respiration, wind; breath -of life, — of one's nostrils; life-blood; Archeus; existence etc. 1.

vivification, vitalization; revivification etc. 163; Prometheus; life to come etc. (*destiny*) 152.

[Science of life] physiology, etiology, em-bryology, biology; animal economy.

nourishment, staff of life etc. (*food*) 298.

V. be -alive etc. *adj.*; live, breathe, respire; sub-sist etc. (*exist*) 1; walk the earth; strut and fret one's hour upon a stage; be spared.

see the light, be born, come into the world; fetch —, draw- -breath, — the breath of life; quicken; revive; come to, — life.

give birth to etc. (*produce*) 161; bring to life, put into life, vitalize; vivi-fy, -ficate; reanimate etc. (*restore*) 660; keep -alive, — body and soul together, — the wolf from the door; support life.

have nine lives like a cat.

Adj. living, alive; in -life, – the flesh, – the land of the living; on this side of the grave, above ground, breathing, quick, animated, viable; lively etc. (*active*) 682; alive and kicking; tenacious of life.

vital; vivi-fying; -fied etc. *v.*; Promethean.

Adv. *vivendi causâ.*

---

360. Death.—N. death, dying etc. *v.*; de-cease, -mise; dissolution, departure, *obit*, release, rest, *quietus*, fall; loss, bereavement.

end etc. 67 –, cessation etc. 142 –, loss –, ex-tinction –, ebb- of -life etc. 359.

death-warrant, -watch, -rattle, -bed; stroke –, agonies –, shades –, valley of the shadow –, jaws –, hand- of death; last -breath, – gasp, – agonies; dying -day, – breath, – agonies; swan song, *chant du cygne*; *rigor mortis*; Stygian shore; crossing the bar, the great adventure.

King -of terrors, – Death; Death, Angel of Death; mortality; doom etc. (*necessity*) 601.

euthanasia; happy release; break up of the system; natural -death, – decay; sudden –, violent- death; untimely end, watery grave; suf-focation, *asphyxia*; heart failure; fatal disease etc. (*disease*) 655; death-blow etc. (*killing*) 361.

necrology, bills of mortality, obituary; death-song etc. (*lamentation*) 839.

V. die, expire, perish; meet one's -death, – end; pass away, be taken; yield –, resign- one's breath; resign one's -being, – life; end one's -days, – life, – earthly career; breathe one's last; cease to -live, – breathe; depart this life; be -no more etc. *adj.*; go –, drop –, pop -off; lose –, lay down –, relinquish –, surrender- one's life; drop –, sink- into the grave; close one's eyes; fall –, drop- dead, – down dead; break one's neck; give –, yield- up the ghost; be all over with one.

pay the debt to nature, shuffle off this mortal coil, take one's last sleep; go the way of all flesh; join the -greater number, – majority, – choir in-visible, to life immortal awake; come –, turn- to dust; cross the Stygian ferry; go to -one's long ac-count, – one's last home, – Davy Jones's locker, – the wall; receive one's death warrant, make one's will, die a natural death, go out like the snuff of a candle; come to an untimely end; catch one's death; go off the hooks, kick the bucket, pet out; go West; hop the twig, turn up one's toes; die a violent death etc. (*be killed*) 361; make the supreme sacrifice.

Adj. dead, lifeless; deceased, demised, departed, defunct; late, gone, no more; ex-, in-animate; out of the world, taken off, released; departed this life etc. *v.*; dead and gone; bereft of life, stone dead, dead as -a door nail, – a door post, – mutton, – a herring, – nits; launched into eternity, gathered to one's fathers, numbered with the dead, gone to a better land, behind the veil, beyond the grave, – mortal ken.

dying etc. *v.*; mori-bund, -ent, Acherontic; hip-pocratic; *in -articulo*, – *extremis*; in the -jaws, – agony- of death; going, – off; *aux abois*; on one's -last legs, – death bed; at -the point of death, – death's door, – the last gasp; near one's end, given over, booked, fey; with one foot in –, tottering on the brink of- the grave.

still-born; mortuary; deadly etc. (*killing*) 361.

Adv. *post -obit*, – *mortem*.

Phr. life -ebbs, – fails, – hangs by a thread; one's -days are numbered, – hour is come, – race is run, – doom is sealed; Death -knocks at the door, – stares one in the face; the breath is out of the body; the grave closes over one; *sic itur ad astra.*

---

361. Killing. [Destruction of life; violent death.]—N. killing etc. *v.*; homicide, man-slaughter, murder, assassination, trucidation, oc-cision; lynching, effusion of blood; blood, -shed; gore, slaughter, carnage, butchery; *battue*, gladiatorial combat.

massacre; *fusillade, noyade, pogrom*; thuggism; racketeering.

death blow, finishing stroke, *coup de grâce*, *quietus*; execution etc. (*capital punishment*) 972; judicial murder; martyrdom.

butcher, slayer, murderer, Cain, assassin, cut-throat, garrotter, *bravo*, thug, racketeer, gunman, mobster, gangster, Moloch, *matador, sabreur, guet-à-pens*; gallows, executioner etc. (*punishment*) 975; man-eater.

regicide, parricide, fratricide, infanticide, abor-ticide etc.

suicide, *felo de se, suttee, hara kiri*, Juggernaut; immolation, holocaust.

suffocation, strangulation, *garrotte*; hanging etc. *v.*

deadly weapon etc. (*arms*) 727; Aceldama; the potter's field, the field of blood.

fatal accident, violent death, casualty.

[Destruction of animals] slaughtering; phthiozoics;* sport, -ing; the chase, venery; hunt-ing, coursing, shooting, fishing; pig-sticking; sports-, hunts-, fisher-man; hunter, Nimrod; slaughterer, knacker, slaughter-house, shambles, *abattoir.*

V. kill, put to death, slay, shed blood; murder, assassinate, butcher, slaughter; victimize, im-molate; massacre; take away –, deprive of- life; make away with, put an end to; despatch, dispatch; burke settle, do, – to death, – for.

strangle, garrotte, hang, lynch, throttle, choke, stifle, suffocate, stop the breath, smother, asphyxiate, drown.

saber; cut -down, – to pieces, – the throat; jugulate; stab, run through the body, bayonet; put to the -sword, – edge of the sword.

shoot, – dead; blow one's brains out; brain, knock on the head; stone, lapidate; give –, deal- a death blow; give a -quietus, – coup de grâce.

behead, bowstring etc. (*execute*) 972.

hunt, shoot etc. *n.*

cut off, nip in the bud, launch into eternity, send to one's last account, bump off, rub out, sign one's death warrant, strike the death knell of.

give no quarter, pour out blood like water; decimate; run amuck, wade knee-deep –, imbrue one's hands- in blood.

die a violent death, welter in one's blood; dash –, blow- out one's brains; commit suicide; kill -–make away with –, put an end to- oneself.

Adj. killing etc. *v.*; murd-, slaught-erous; sanguin-ary, -olent; blood-stained, -thirsty;

homicidal, red-handed; bloody, -minded; ensanguined, gory, sanguineous.

mortal fatal, lethal; dead-, death-ly; mort-, lethiferous; unhealthy etc. 657; internecine; suicidal.

sporting; piscator-ial, -y.

Adv. in at the death.

*Bentham, 'Chrestomathia.'

362. Corpse.—N. corpse, corse, carcass, bones, skeleton, dry-bones; defunct, relics, *relinquiae*, remains, mortal remains, dust, ashes, earth, clay; mummy; carrion; food for- worms, — fishes; tenement of clay, this mortal coil.

shade, ghost, *manes*, apparition etc. 980.

organic remains, fossils.

Adj. cadaverous, corpse-like; unburied etc. 363.

363. Interment.—N. interment, burial, inhumation, sepulture, entombment; in-, humation; obs-, ex-equies; funeral, wake, pyre, funeral pile; cremation.

funeral -rite, — solemnity; knell, passing bell, tolling; dirge etc. (*lamentation*) 839; cypress; *obit*, dead march, muffled drum; coroner, mortician, undertaker, mute, mourner, professional mourner, pallbearer; elegy; funeral -oration, — sermon; epitaph.

grave clothes, shroud; winding-sheet, cere-cloth; cerement.

coffin, shell, sarcophagus, urn, pall, bier, hearse, catafalque, cinerary urn.

grave, pit, sepulcher, tomb, vault, crypt, catacomb, mausoleum, *Golgotha*, house of death, narrow house, long home; cemetery, necropolis, boneyard; burial-place, -ground; grave-, churchyard; God's acre; mortuary, tope, cromlech, dolmen, menhir, barrow, tumulus, cairn; ossuary; bone-, charnel-, dead-house; *Morgue*; lich-gate; crematorium.

sexton, grave-digger.

monument, memorial, cenotaph, shrine; grave-, head-, tomb-stone; *memento mori*; hatchment, stone, cross.

exhumation, disinterment; necropsy, autopsy, *post mortem* examination.

V. inter, bury, lay in —, consign to- the -grave, — tomb; en-, in-tomb; inhume; lay out, prepare for burial, embalm, mummify; conduct a funeral, hold services; toll the knell; put to bed with a shovel.

exhume, disinter, unearth.

Adj. buried etc. v.; burial; fune-real, -brial; mortuary, sepulchral, cinerary; elegiac; necroscopic.

Adv. in memoriam; post-obit, -mortem; beneath —, under- the sod.

Phr. hic jacet, ci-git, requiescat in pace.

364. Animality.—N. animal life; anima-tion, -lity, -lization; breath.

flesh, — and blood; corporeal nature; *physique*, strength etc. 159.

V. animalize, incorporate.

Adj. fleshly, incarnate, carnal, corporeal, human.

365. Vegetability.—N. vegetable life, vegetation, -bility; herbage.

V. vegetate, germinate, sprout, shoot; cultivate.

Adj. vegetable etc. 367; rank, lush.

366. Animal.*—N. animal, — kingdom; *fauna*; brute creation.

beast, brute, creature, created being; creeping —, living- thing; dumb -animal, — creature.

flocks and herds, live stock; domestic —, wild-animals; game, *ferae naturae*; beasts of the fields, fowls of the air, denizens of the day.

vertebrate, bi-, quadru-ped, mammal, marsupial, bird, reptile, batrachian, amphibian, fish, crustacean, shell fish, articulate, mollusc, worm, insect, zoophyte; protozoon, animalcule etc. 193.

horse etc. (*beast of burden*) 271; cattle, kine, ox; bull, -ock; steer, stot; cow, milch-cow, calf, heifer, shorthorn; sheep; lamb, -kin; ewe —, pet-lamb; ewe, ram, tup; pig, swine, boar, hog, shoat, sow; tag, teg, wether.

dog, bitch, hound; pup, -py; whelp, cur, mutt, mongrel; house-, watch-, sheep-, shepherd's, sporting-, fancy-, lap-, toy-, bull-, badger-dog; mastiff; blood-, grey-, stag-, deer-, fox-, otter-, hound; harrier, beagle, spaniel, pointer, setter, retriever; Newfoundland; water -dog, — spaniel; pug, poodle; dachshund; Pinscher; turnspit; terrier; fox —, Skye- terrier; Dandie Dinmont; colley.

cat; puss,-y; kitten; grimalkin; gib-, tom-cat; mouser; fox, Reynard, vixen, stag, deer, hart, buck, doe, roe, antelope.

bird; poultry, fowl, cock, hen, chicken, chanticleer, partlet, rooster, dunghill cock, barn-door fowl; feathered -tribes, — songster; singing —, dicky- bird; canary, finch, auk, dodo, moa, roc, phoenix.

snake, serpent, viper, adder; newt, eft; asp, vermin.

Adj. animal, zoological.

equine, bovine, vaccine, canine, feline; fishy; piscator-y, -ial; molluscous, vermicular.

* *Extended lists of names of specific varieties of animals, vegetables, etc., are beyond the scope of this work.*

367. Vegetable.*—N. vegetable, — kingdom; *flora*, verdure.

plant; tree, shrub, bush; creeper; vine; herb, -age; grass.

annual; per-, bi-, tri-ennial; exotic.

timber; primeval —, virgin- forest, wood, -lands; hurst; frith, holt, weald, park; chase, greenwood, brake, grove, copse, coppice, *bocage*, *tope*, clump of trees, thicket, spinet, spinney; under-, brush-wood, boscage, scrub; the oak and the ash and the bonny ivy tree.

bush, jungle, prairie; heath, -er; fern, bracken, furze, gorse, whin, broom; grass, turf, grassland, greensward, green, lawn, meadow; pas-ture, -turage; turbary; sedge, rush, weed; fungus, mushroom, toadstool, lichen, moss, conferva, mold; seaweed etc., growth, crop.

foliage, leafage, branch, bough, ramage; spray etc. 51; leaf, frond, flag, petal, shoot, tendril.

flower, blossom, bud, bloom, bine; flowering plant; tree, sapling, pollard, timber-, fruit-tree; palm-, gum-tree, pulse, legume.

Adj. veget-able, -ous; herb-aceous, -al; botanic; sylvan, silvan, arbor- ary, -eous, -escent, -ical; dendritic, dendriform; woooy, grassy; ver-dant, - durous; floral, mossy; lign-ous, -eous; wooden, leguminous; end-, ex-ogenous.

*Extended lists of names of specific varieties of animals, vegetables, etc., are beyond the scope of this work.

368. Zoology. [The science of animals.]—N. zoo-logy, -nomy. -graphy, -tomy; anatomy; comparative anatomy; animal –, comparative-physiology; morphology.

anthrop-, ornith-, ichthy-, herpet-, ophi-, malac-, helminth-, entom-, oryct-, paleont-ology; ichthy- etc. -otomy; taxidermy.

zo- etc. -ologist.

Adj. zoological etc. n.

369. Botany. [The science of plants.]—N. botany; phyto-graphy, -logy, -tomy; vegetable physiology, herborization, dendr-, myc-, fung-, alg-ology; flora, pomona; botanist etc.; botanic garden etc. (*garden*) 371; *hortus siccus, herbarium*, herbal.

herb-ist, -arist, -alist, -orist, -arian etc.

V. botanize, herborize.

Adj. botanical etc. n.

370. Cicuration. [The economy or management of animals.]—N. taming etc. v.; cicuration, zoohygiantics; domestication, -ity; *manège*; veterinary art; breeding, pisciculture, apiculture etc.

menagery, vivarium, zoological garden, zoo; bear-pit; aviary, apiary, hive; aquarium, fishery, fish hatchery; duck-, fish-pond; stud-farm; stock farm, dairy.

[Destruction of animals] phthisozoics etc. (*killing*) 361.

neat-, cow-, shep-herd, shepherdess; grazier; drover, cowboy, cowkeeper; trainer, breeder, groom, ostler etc. 746; veterinary surgeon, vet, horse doctor; farrier; keeper; game keeper.

cage etc. (*prison*) 752; hen-coop, bird-cage, cauf; sheep-fold etc. (*inclosure*) 232.

V. tame, domesticate, acclimatize, breed, tend, break in, train, corral, round up; cage, bridle etc. (*restrain*) 751; ride etc. 266.

drive, yoke, harness, hitch; groom, eurry-comb; milk; shear; hatch; incubate.

Adj. pastoral, bucolic; tame, domestic, domesticated, broken in, gentle, docile.

371. Agriculture. [The economy or management of plants.]—N. agriculture, cultivation, husbandry, farming; georgics, geoponics; tillage, tilth, agronomy, gardening, spade husbandry. vintage; hort-, arbor-, silv-, citr-, vit-, flor-iculture; intensive culture; landscape gardening; forestry, afforestation.

husbandman, horticulturist, citriculturist, gardener, florist, agricult-or, -urist; yeoman, farmer, cultivator, tiller of the soil, ploughman, sower, reaper; woodcutter, backwoodsman, forester; vine grower, vintager; Boer; Triptolemus.

field, meadow, garden; botanic –, winter –, or-namental –, flower –, kitchen –, truck –, market –, hop- garden; nursery; green-, hot-, glass-house; conservatory, cucumber frame, *cloche*, bed, border, seed-plot; grass-plat, lawn; park etc. (*pleasure ground*) 840; *partere*, shrubbery, plantation, avenue, *arboretum*, pinery, *pinetum*, orchard, vineyard, vinery; orangery; farm etc. (*abode*) 189.

V. cultivate; till, – the soil; farm, garden; sow, plant; reap, mow, cut; manure, dress the ground, dig, delve, dibble, hoe, plough, plow, harrow, rake, weed, lop and top, force, transplant, thin out, bed out, prune, graft.

Adj. agr-icultural, -airan. -estic.

arable; predial, rural, rustic, country, bucolic, Boeotian; horticultural.

372. Mankind.—N. man, -kind; human -race, – species, – nature; humanity, mortality, flesh, generation.

[Science of man] anthropo-logy, -graphy, sophy; ethno-logy, -graphy; humanitarianism.

human being, person, -age; individual, creature, fellow creature, mortal, body, somebody, one; such a –, someone; soul, living soul; earthling; party, head, hand; *dramatis personae*.

people, persons, folk, public, society, world; community, – at large; general public; nation, - ality; state, realm; common-weal, -wealth; republic, body politic; million etc. (*commonalty*) 876; population etc. (*inhabitant*) 188.

cosmopolite; lords of the creation; ourselves.

Adj. human, mortal, personal, individual, national, civic, public, cosmopolitan; anthropoid.

373. Man.—N. man, male, he; manhood etc. (*adolescence*) 131; , gentleman, sir, master; yeoman, wight, swain, fellow, guy, blade, *beau*, chap, gaffer, good man; husband etc. (*married man*) 903; Mr., mister, *monsieur, sahib, Herr, señor, signor*; boy etc. (*youth*) 129; Adonis.

[Male animal] cock, drake, gander, dog, boar, stag, hart, buck, horse, entire horse, stallion; gib-, tom-cat; he-, Billy-goat; ram, tup; bull, -ock; capon, ox, gelding; steer, stot.

Adj. male, he, masculine; manly, virile; un-womanly, -feminine.

374. Woman.—N. woman, she, female, petticoat, skirt, moll, broad.

feminality, feminity, muliebrity; womanhood etc. (*adolescence*) 131; feminism; gynecology, gyniatrics, gynics.

womankind; the -sex, – fair; fair –, softer- sex; weaker vessel; the distaff side.

dame, madam, *madame*, mistress, Mrs., lady, *mem-sahib, Frau, señora, signora, donna, belle*, matron, dowager, goody, gammer; good -woman, – wife; squaw; wife etc. (*marriage*) 903; matronage, -hood.

Venus, nymph, wench, *grisette*; little bit of fluff; girl etc. (*youth*) 129.

inamorata (love) etc. 897; courtesan etc. 962. spinster, old maid, virgin, bachelor girl, new woman, amazon.

[Female animal] hen, slut, bitch, sow, doe, roe, mare; she-, Nanny-goat; ewe, cow; lioness, tigress; vixen.

gynecaeum, harem, seraglio, zenana, purdah.

Adj. female, she; feminine, womanly, ladylike, matronly, maidenly; womanish, effeminate, unmanly, gynecic.

375. Physical Sensibility.—N. sensibility; sensitiveness etc. adj.; physical sensibility, feeling, perceptivity, anaphylaxis, susceptibility, esthetics; moral sensibility etc. 882.

sensation, impression, effect; consciousness etc. (knowledge) 490.

external senses.

V. be -sensible etc. adj. -of; feel, perceive.

render, -sensible etc. adj.; excite, stir, sharpen, cultivate, tutor.

cause sensation, impress; excite -, produce- an impression.

Adj. sens-ible, -itive, -uous; esthetic, perceptive, sentient; conscious etc. (aware) 490; impressionable, responsive, alive to.

acute, sharp, keen, vivid, lively, impressive, thinskinned.

Adv. to the quick.

376. Physical Insensibility.—N. insensibility, physical insensibility; obtuseness etc. adj.; palsy, paralysis, anesthesia, analgesia, narcosis, hypnosis, twilight sleep, stupor, coma, trance, catalepsy; sleep etc. (inactivity) 683; moral insensibility etc. 823; numbness etc. 381.

anesthetic agent, general -, local- anesthetic, opium, ether, chloroform, cocaine, novocaine, chloral; nitrous oxide, laughing gas; refrigeration.

V. be -insensible etc. adj.; have a -thick skin, - rhinoceros hide.

render -insensible etc. adj.; blunt, pall, obtund, benumb, deaden, paralyze; anesthetize, drug, dope; put under the influence of -chloroform etc. n.; hypnotize; stupefy, stun, narcotize.

Adj. insensible, unfeeling, senseless, comatose, dazed, impercipient, callous, thick-skinned, pachydermatous; hard, -ened; case-hardened; proof; obtuse, dull; anesthetic; paralytic, palsied, numb, dead.

377. Physical Pleasure.—N. pleasure; physical -, sensual -, sensuous- pleasure; bodily enjoyment, animal gratification, sensuality; hedonism, luxuriousness etc. adj.; dissipation, round of pleasure; titillation, gusto, creature comforts, comfort, ease; pillow etc. (support) 215; luxury, lap of luxury; purple and fine linen; bed of -down, - roses; velvet, clover; cup of Circe etc. (intemperance) 954.

treat; diversion, divertisement, entertainment; refreshment, regale; feast; délice; dainty etc. 394; bonne bouche.

source of pleasure etc. 829; happiness etc. (mental enjoyment) 827.

V. feel -, experience -, receive- pleasure; enjoy, relish; luxuriate -, revel -, riot -, bask -,

swim -, wallow- in; feast on; gloat -over, - on; smack the lips.

live -on the fat of the land, - in comfort etc. adv., bask in the sunshine, faire ses choux gras.

give pleasure etc. 829.

Adj. enjoying etc. v.; luxurious, voluptuous, sensual, hedonistic, comfortable, cosy, snug, in comfort, at ease.

agreeable etc. 829; grateful, refreshing, comforting, cordial, genial; sensuous; palatable etc. 394; sweet etc. (sugar) 396; fragrant etc. 400; melodious etc. 413; lovely etc. (beautiful) 845.

Adv. in -comfort etc. n.; on -a bed of roses etc. n.; at one's ease.

378. Physical Pain.—N. pain; suffering, -ance; bodily - physical -pain, - suffering; mental suffering etc. 828; dolor, ache, aching etc. v.; smart, shoot, -ing; twinge, twitch, gripe, head-, ear-, toothache; migraine, neuralgia, neuritis, lumbago, gout, sciatica; hurt, cut; sore, -ness; discomfort, malaise; tic douloureux.

spasm, cramp; nightmare, ephialtes; crick, stitch, kink; thrill, convulsion, throe; throb etc. (agitation) 315; pang.

sharp -, piercing -, throbbing -, shooting - gnawing -, burning- pain; anguish, agony.

torment, torture; rack; cruci-ation, -fixion; martyrdom; martyr, toad under a harrow, vivisection.

V. feel -, experience -, suffer -, undergo- pain etc. n.; suffer, ache, smart, bleed; tingle, shoot; twinge, twitch, lancinate; writhe, wince, make a wry face; sit on -thorns, - pins and needles.

give -, inflict- pain; pain, hurt, chafe, sting, bite, gnaw, gripe, stab, grind; pinch, tweak; grate, gall, fret, prick, pierce, wring, convulse; torment, torture; rack, agonize; crucify; excruciate; break on the wheel, put to the rack; flag etc. (punish) 972; grate on the ear etc. (harsh sound) 410.

Adj. in -pain etc. n.; - a state of pain; pained etc. v.

painful; aching etc. v.; biting, poignant; sore, raw, tender, with exposed nerve.

379. Touch. [Sensation of pressure.] —N. touch; tact, -ion, -ility; feeling; palp-ation, -ability; manipulation; brush, tick, graze, contact etc. 199.

[Organ of touch] hand, finger, fore-finger, thumb, paw, teeler, antenna.

V. touch, teel, handle, finger, thumb, paw, fumble, grope, grabble; twiddle, tweedle; pass -, run- the fingers over, massage, rub, knead; palpate, stroke, manipulate, wield; throw out a feeler.

Adj. tact-ual, -ile; tangible, palpable; lambent.

380. Sensations of Touch.—N. itching etc. v.; titillation, formication, aura.

V. itch, tingle, creep, thrill, sting; prick, -le; tickle, titillate.

Adj. itching etc. v.

381. Numbness. [Insensibility to touch.] —N.

numbness etc. (*physical insensibility*) 376; pins and needles.

local anesthetic,cocaine novocaine etc.; morphia.

V. benumb etc. 376; freeze, dull, deaden.

Adj. numb; benumbed etc. *v.*; intangible, impalpable.

382. Heat.—**N.** heat, caloric; temperature, warmth, fervor, calidity; incal-, incand-, recal-, decal-escence; glow, flush, blush; fever, hectic.

phlogiston; fire, spark, scintillation, flash, flame, blaze; arc; bonfire; firework, pyrotechny; wild-fire; sheet of fire, lambent flame; devouring element; conflagration.

summer, dog-days, canicule; baking etc. 384 –, white –, tropical –, Afric –, Bengal –, summer –, blood- heat; heat wave, sirocco, simoon; broiling sun; isolation, warming etc. 384.

sun etc. (*luminary*) 423; fire worshipper etc. 991; furnace etc. 386.

geyser, hot spring, volcano.

: Science of heat. pyrology; thermology, -otics; thermometer etc. 389.

V. be -hot etc. *adj.*; glow, incandesce, flush, sweat, swelter, bask, smoke, reek, stew, simmer, seethe, boil, burn, singe, scorch, scald, grill, broil, blaze, flame; smoulder; parch, fume, pant.

heat etc. (*make hot*) 384; thaw, fuse, melt, give.

Adj. hot, heated, warm, mild, genial, tepid, lukewarm, unfrozen; therm-al, -ic; calorific; fervent, -id; ardent; aglow.

sunny, torrid, tropical, estival, canicular; close, sultry, stifling, stuffy, suffocating, oppressive; reeking etc. *v.*; baking etc. 384.

red –, white –, smoking –, bruning etc. *v.* –, piping- hot; like -a furnace, – an oven; hot as -fire, – pepper; hot enough to roast an ox.

fiery; incand-, incal-escent; candent, ebullient, glowing, smoking; on fire; blazing etc. *v.*; in -flames, – a blaze; alight, afire, ablaze; unquenched, -extinguished; smouldering; in a -heat, – glow, – fever, – perspiration, – sweat; sudorific; swelter-ing, -ed; blood-hot, -warm; warm as -a toast, – wool recalescent, thermogenic, pyrotechnic, feverish, febrile, inflamed.

volcanic, plutonic, igneous; isother-mal, -mic, -al.

Phr. Not a breath of air.

383. Cold.—**N.** cold, -ness etc. *adj.*; frigidity, gelidity, algidity, inclemency, *fresco*..

winter; depth of –, hard- winter, Siberia, Nova Zembla; Ant-, arctic, North –, South- Pole.

ice; snow, – flake, – crystal – drift; sleet; hail, -stone; rime, frost, hoar –, white –, hard –, sharp- frost; icicle, thick-ribbed ice; fall of snow, snow storm, heavy fall, *avalanche*; ice-berg, -floe; floe, berg; *glacier*; *nevée*, serac

[Sensation of cold] chilliness etc. *adj.*; chill shivering etc. *v.*, goose- skin, -flesh; *rigor*, horripilation, chattering of teeth, frostbite, chilblain.

V. be -cold etc. *adj.*; shiver, starve, quake, shake, tremble, shudder, didder, quiver; perish with cold; chill etc. (*render cold*) 385.

Adj. cold, cool, chill, -y, gelid, frigid, algid; fresh, keen, bleak, raw, inclement, bitter, biting,

niveous, cutting, nipping, piercing, pinching; clay-cold; starved etc. (*made cold*) 385; shivering etc. *v.*; aguish, *transi de froid*; frost- bitten, -bound, -nipped.

cold as -a stone, – marble, – lead, – iron, – a frog, – charity, – Christmas; cool as -a cucumber, – custard.

icy, glacial, frosty, freezing, wintry, brumal, hibernal, boreal, arctic, antarctic, polar, Siberian, hyemal; hyperbore-an, -al; ice-bound; frozen out.

un-warmed, -thawed, -heated; isocheimal, chimenal.

Adv. coldly, bitterly etc. *adj.*; *à pierre fendre*.

384. Calefaction.—**N.** increase of temperature; heating etc. *v.*; cale-, tepe-, torre-faction; melting, fusion; liquefaction etc. 335; burning etc. *v.*; kindling, combustion; in-, ac-cension; con-, cremation; scorification; cauter-y, -ization; ustulation, calcination; in-, cineration; cupellation; carbonization.

ignition, inflammation, adustion, flagration; de-, con-flagration; empyrosis, incendiarism; arson; *auto da fé*; suttee.

boiling etc. *v.*; coction, ebullition, estuation, elixation, decoction.

furnace etc. 386; blanket, flannel, fur, muffler, wrap; wadding etc. (*lining*) 224; clothing etc. 225.

match etc. (*fuel*) 388; incendiary, pryomaniac; *pétroleur, pétroleuse*; cauterant, caustic, lunar caustic, apozem, moxa.

sunstroke, *coup de soleil*; insolation, sunburn.

pottery, ceramics, crockery, porcelain, china; earthen-, stone-ware; pot, mug, *terra-cotta*, brick, clinker; cinder, ash, *scoriae*; embers, dress, slag, products of combustion, coke, carbon, charcoal.

inflamma-, combusti-bility.

[Transmission of heat] diathermancy, trans-calency, diathermy.

V. heat, warm, chafe, stive, foment; make -hot etc. 382; sun oneself, bask in the sun.

fire; set -fire to, – on fire; kindle, enkindle, light, ignite, strike a light; apply the -match, – torch- to; re-kindle, -lume; fan –, add fuel to- the flame; poke –, stir –, blow- the fire; make a bonfire of; burn at the stake.

melt, thaw, fuse; liquefy etc. 335.

burn, inflame, roast, toast, fry, grill, singe, parch, bake, torrefy, scorch; brand, cauterize, sear, burn in, corrode, char, carbonize, calcine, incinerate; smelt, cupel, scorify; reduce to ashes; burn to a cinder; commit –, consign- to the flames.

boil, digest, stew, cook, seethe, scald, parboil, simmer; do to rags.

take –, catch- fire; blaze etc. (*flame*) 382

Adj. heated etc. *v.*, molten, sodden; réchauffe; heating etc. *v.*

inflammable, burnable, inflammatory, combustible, diatherm-al, -anous, burnt etc. *v.*, volcanic

386. Refrigeration.—**N.** refrigeration, in-frigidation, reduction of temperature, cooling etc. *v.*; con-gelation, -glaciation; ice etc. 383, solidification etc. (*density*) 321; refrigerator etc. 387.

extincteur; fire, – engine, – extinguisher, – annihilator, – brigade, – man; sprinkler, hose, hydrant, standpipe.

incombusti-bility, -bleness etc. *adj.*

V. cool, fan, refrigerate, refresh, ice; congeal, freeze, glaciate; benumb, starve, pinch, chill, petrify, chill to the marrow, nip, cut, pierce, bite, make one's teeth chatter; damp, slack; quench; put –, stamp- out; extinguish.

go –, burn- out.

Adj. cooled etc. *v.*; frozen out; cooling etc. *v.*; frigorific.

incombustible; un-, unin-flammable; fire-proof.

386. Furnace.—N. furnace, blast furnace, fire-box, stove, incinerator, destructor, crematorium, crematory, kiln, oven, oast-house; hot-, bake-, wash-house; laundry; conservatory; hearth, focus; athanor, hypocaust, reverberatory; volcano; forge, fiery furnace; *tuyère*, brasier, salamander, heater, warming-pan, foot-warmer, hot-water bottle; radiator; boiler, geyser, caldron, seething caldron, pot; urn, kettle; chafing-dish; retort, crucible, alembic, still; saggar.

fire-place, -dog, -irons; hearth, ingle, grate, range, kitchener; kitchen range; oil-, gas-, electric, -cooker, -stove; fireless cooker; fire; galley; ca-, cam-boose; poker, tongs, shovel, hob, trivet; and-, grid-iron; frying-, stew-pan etc.

hot –, Turkish –, Russian –, vapor –, shower –, warm- bath; *calidarium*, *tepidarium*, *sudatorium*, sudatory; *hammam*.

387. Refrigerator.—N. refrigerator, -y; *frigidarium*; cold storage; refrigerating-plant, – machine; ice-house, -pail, -bag, -chest, -pack; cooler, damper; wine-cooler, freezing mixture.

388. Fuel.—N. fuel, firing, combustible, coal, wallsend, anthracite, bituminous coal, slack, culm, cannel coal, lignite, briquette, coke, carbon, char-coal; turf, peat, fire-wood, bobbing, faggot, log, yule log, ember, cinder etc. (*products of combustion*) 384; kindling wood, tinder, touch-wood; fumigator, sulphur, brimstone; incense; port-fire; fire-barrel, -ball, -brand.

fuel oil, gas, gasoline, electricity.

brand, torch, fuse; wick; spill, match, safety match, light, lucifer, congreve, vesuvian, vesta, fusee, locofoco; linstock; illuminant.

candle etc. (*luminary*) 423; oil etc. (*grease*) 356; petrol, gasoline, methylated –, spirit; gas, acetylene.

Adj. carbonaceous; combustible, inflammable.

V. stoke, fire, feed, add fuel to the flames.

389. Thermometer.—N. thermo-meter, -scope, -stat, -pile, differential thermometer; pyro-, calori-meter; radio micrometer etc.

390. Taste.—N. taste, flavor, gust, *gusto*, relish, savor; sapor, sapidity; twang, smack, smatch; after-taste, tang.

tasting; de-, gustation.

palate, tongue, tooth, stomach.

V. taste, savor, smatch, smack, flavor, twang; tickle the palate etc. (*savory*) 394; smack the lips.

Adj. sapid, saporific; gusta-ble, -tory; strong; flavored, spiced, savory; palatable etc. 394

391. Insipidity.—N. insipidity; tastlessness etc. *adj.*

V. be -tasteless etc. *adj.*

Adj. void of -taste etc. 390; insipid; jejune; taste-, gust-, savor-less; ingustible, mawkish, milk -and water, weak, stale, flat, vapid, *fade*, wishy-washy, mild; untasted.

392. Pungency.—N. pungency, piquancy, poignancy, *haut-goût*, strong taste, twang, race, tang.

sharpness etc. *adj.*; acrimony, acridity; roughness etc. (*sour*) 397; unsavoriness etc. 395.

niter, saltpeter; mustard, cayenne, caviar; seasoning etc. (*condiment*) 393; brine.

dram; cordial, nip, pick-me-up, bracer, potion.

nicotine, tobacco, snuff, quid; segar; cigar, -ette, gasper, fag; cheroot; weed; fragrant –, Indian-weed; pipe, clay pipe, churchwarden, brier, meer-schaum, hookah, hubble-bubble.

V. be -pungent etc. *adj.*; bite the tongue.

render -pungent etc. *adj.*; season, spice, salt, pepper, pickle, brine, devil, curry.

smoke, chew, take snuff.

Adj. pungent, strong; high-, full-flavored; high-tasted, -seasoned; gamy; sharp, stinging, rough, *piquant*, racy; biting, mordant; spicy; seasoned etc. *v.*; hot, – as pepper; peppery, vellicating, escharotic, meracious; acrid, acrimonious, bitter; rough etc. (*sour*) 397; unsavory etc. 395.

salt, saline, brackish, briny; salt as -brine, – a herring, – Lot's wife.

393. Condiment.—N. condiment, flavoring, salt, mustard, pepper, cayenne, curry, seasoning, sauce, spice, cinnamon, chillies, relish, *sauce piquante*, caviare, pot-herbs, onion, garlic, pickle, chutney, nutmeg etc.

V. season etc. (*render pungent*) 392.

394. Savoriness.—N. savoriness etc. *adj.*; relish, zest.

tit-bit, dainty, delicacy, ambrosia, nectar, *bonne bouche*; game, turtle, venison.

V. taste good, be -savory etc. *adj.*; tickle the -palate, – appetite; flatter the palate.

render -palatable etc. *adj.*

relish, like, smack the lips.

Adj. savory, well-tasted, to one's taste, tasty, good, palatable, nice, dainty, delectable; tooth-ful, -some; gustful, appetizing, lickerish, delicate, delicious, exquisite, rich, luscious, ambrosial.

Adv. *per amusare la bocca*.

Phr. *cela se laisse manger.*

395. Unsavoriness.—N.unsavoriness etc. *adj.*; amaritude; acri-mony. -tude; roughness etc. (*sour*) 397; acerbity, austerity; gall and worm-wood, rue, quassia, aloes; sickener.

V. be -unpalatable etc. *adj.*; sicken, disgust, nauseate, pall, turn the stomach.

Adj. un-savory. -palatable, -sweet; ill-flavored, un-appetizing, -eatable, inedible; bitter, — as gall; acrid, acrimonious; rough.

offensive, repulsive, nasty; sickening etc. *v.*; nauseous; loath-, ful-some; unpleasant etc. 830.

396. Sweetness.—N. sweetness, dulcitude, saccharinity.

sugar, cane-, beet-sugar; saccharine, glucose, syrup, treacle, molasses, honey, manna; confection, -ary; sweets, grocery, conserve, preserve, *confiture*, jam, marmalade, julep; sugar-candy, -plum; licorice, liquorice, plum, lollipop, *bon bon, jujube,* comfit, sweetmeat, caramel, toffee, butterscotch.

nectar; hydromel, mead, metheglin, honeysuckle, *liqueur*, sweet wine.

pastry, pie, tart, puff, pudding, cake.

dulc-ification, -oration.

V. be sweet etc. *adj.*

render -sweet etc. *adj.*; sugar, saccharize, sweeten; edulcorate; dulc-orate, -ify; candy; mull.

Adj. sweet, sugary; sacchar-ine, -iferous; dulcet, honied, candied, luscious, nectarious, melliferous; sweetened etc. *v.*

sweet as -a nut, — sugar, — honey.

397. Sourness.—N. sourness etc. *adj.*; acid, -ity; acetous fermentation; acerbity.

vinegar, verjuice, crab, alum.

V. be —, turn- -sour etc. *adj.*; set the teeth on edge.

render -sour etc. *adj.*; acid-ify, -ulate.

Adj. sour; acid, -ulous, -ulated; acerb; tart, crab-bed; acet-ous, -ose; sour as vinegar, sourish, acescent, sub-acid; styptic, hard, rough; unripe, green.

398. Odor.—N. odor, smell, odorament, scent, effluvium; eman-, exhal-ation; fume, essence, trail, nidor, redolence.

sense of smell; scent; act of -smelling etc. *v.*

V. have an -odor etc. *n.*; smell, — of, — strong of; exhale; give out a -smell etc. *n.*; scent.

smell, scent; snuff, — up; sniff, nose, inhale.

Adj. odor-ous, -iferous; smelling, strong-scented; redolent, graveolent, nidorous, pungent.

[Relating to the sense of smell] olfactory, quick-scented..

399. Inodorousness.—N. inodorousness; absence —, want- of smell.

V. be -inodorous etc. *adj.*; not smell.

deodorize.

Adj. inodor-ous, -ate; scentless; without — , wanting- smell etc. 398.

deodoriz-ed, -ing.

400. Fragrance.—N. fragrance, aroma, redolence, perfume, *bouquet*; sweet smell, aromatic perfume.

perfumery; incense; musk, frankincense; pastil, -le; myrrh, perfumes of Arabia, chypre; otto, ottar, attar; bergamot, balm, civet, *pot-pourri*, pulvil; nosegay, *boutonnière*; scent, -bag; *sachet*, scent-bottle, smelling bottle, *vinaigrette*; toilet water, *eau de Cologne*; thurible, censer, thurification.

perfumer; incense bearer.

V. be -fragrant etc. *adj.*; have a -perfume etc. *n.*; smell sweet, scent, perfume, thurify, embalm.

Adj. fragrant, aromatic, redolent, spicy, balmy, scented; sweet-smelling, -scented; perfum-ed, -atory; thuriferous; fragrant as a rose, muscadine, ambrosial.

401. Fetor.—N. fetor, fetidness; bad etc. *adj.*; -smell, — odor; stench, stink; mephitis, foul —, mal- odor; *empyreuma*; mustiness etc. *adj.*; rancidity; foulness etc. (*uncleanness*) 653.

stoat, polecat, skunk; asafetida; fungus, garlic; stink-pot, -bomb.

V. have a -bad smell etc. *n.*; smell; stink, — in the nostrils, — like a polecat; smell -strong etc. *adj.*; — offensively.

Adj. fetid; strong-smelling; high, bad, strong, fulsome, offensive, noisome, rank, rancid, reasty, tainted, musty, fusty, frouzy; olid, -ous; nidorous; smelling, stinking; putrid etc. 653; suffocating, mephitic; empyreumatic.

402. Sound.—N. sound, noise, strain; accent, twang, intonation, tone, tune; cadence; sonority, sonorousness etc. *adj.*; audibility; resonance etc. 408; voice etc. 580.

[Science of sound] acou-, acu-stics; catacoustics; cataphonics; phon-ics, -etics, -ology, -ography; diacoustics, -phonics.

telephone, phonograph etc. 418.

V. produce sound; sound, make a noise; give out —, emit- sound; phonetize, phonate; resound etc. 408.

Adj. sounding; soniferous; sonorific; resonant, audible, acoustic, auditory, distinct; stertorous; phonic, sonant; phonetic.

403. Silence.—N. silence; stillness etc. (*quiet*) 265; peace, hush, lull, rest; muteness etc. 581; solemn -, awful -, dead -, deathlike-silence.

V. be -silent etc. *adj.*; hold one's tongue etc. (*not speak*) 585.

render -silent etc. *adj.*; silence, still, hush; stifle, muffle, gag, stop; muzzle, put to silence etc. (*render mute*) 581.

Adj. silent; still, -y; calm, quiet; noise-, sound-, speech-less; hushed etc. *v.*; mute etc. 581; aphonic.

soft, solemn, awful, deathlike, silent as the grave; inaudible etc. (*faint*) 405.

Adv. silently etc. *adj.*; *sub silentio*; in perfect silence.

Int. hush! `sh! silence! soft! whist! tush! chut! tut! *pax!* mum's the word! hold your tongue! shut up! be silent! be quiet! stop that noise! hold your row! dry up! peace, be still!

Phr. one might hear a -feather, – pin- drop.

404. Loudness.—N. loudness, power; loud noise, din; clang, -or; clatter, noise, bombilation, roar, uproar, racket, static, grinders, hubbub, *fracas*, *charivari*, trumpet blast, blare, flourish of trumpets, fanfare, *tintamarre*, peal, swell, blast, alarum, boom; resonance etc. 408.

vociferation; pandemonium, hullaballoo etc. 411; lungs; Stentor; megaphone; siren.

artillery, cannon, gunfire, shellburst, bomb; thunder.

V. be -loud etc. *adj.*; peal, swell, clang, boom, thunder, fulminate, roar; resound etc. 408; speak up, shout etc. (*vociferate*) 411; bellow etc. (*cry as an animal*) 412; give tongue.

rend the -air, – skies; fill the air; din –, ring –, thunder- in the ear; pierce –, split –, rend-the-ears. – head; deafen, stun; *faire le diable a quatre*; make one's windows shake; awaken – startle- the echoes; make the welkin ring.

Adj. loud, sonorous, high-, big- sounding; blatant; deep, full, powerful, noisy, clangorous, multisonous, *fortisimo*; thundering, deafening etc. *v.*; trumpet-tongued; ear-splitting, -rending, - deafening; piercing; obstreperous, rackety, uproarious; enough to wake the -dead, – seven sleepers.

shrill etc. 410; clamorous etc. (*vociferous*) 411; stentor-ian, -ophonic.

Adv. loudly etc. *adj.*; aloud; at the top of one's voice, lustily, in full cry.

Phr. the air rings with.

405. Faintness.—N. faintness etc. *adj.*; faint sound, whisper, breath; under-tone, -breath; murmur, hum, rustle, buzz, purr; plash; sough, moan, sigh, susurration; tinkle; 'still small voice.'

hoarseness etc. *adj.*; raucity.

silencer, soft pedal, damper, mute, *sourdine*.

V. whisper, breathe, murmur, purl, hum, gurgle, ripple, babble, flow; tinkle; mutter etc. (*speak imperfectly*) 583.

steal on the ear; melt in –, float on- the air. muffle, mute, deaden, damp, stifle.

Adj. inaudible; scarcely –, just- audible; low, dull; stifled, muffled; hoarse, husky; gentle, soft, faint; floating; purling, flowing etc. *v.*; whispered etc. *v.*; liquid; soothing; dulcet etc. (*melodious*) 413.

Adv. in a whisper, with bated breath, *sotto voce*, between the teeth, aside; *pian-o, -issimo*; *à la sourdine*; *con sourdine*; out of earshot, inaudibly etc. *adj.*

406. Snap. [Sudden and violent sounds.]**—N.** snap etc. *v.*; rapping etc. *v.*; de-, crepitation; smack, clap, report; thud; burst, explosion, discharge, detonation, blow-out, back-fire, firing, salvo, volley, pistol-shot.

squib, cracker, gun, rifle, pop-gun.

V. rap, snap, tap, knock; click; clash; crack, -

le; crash; pop; slam, bang, clap, thump, plump; toot; back-fire, explode, burst on the ear.

Adj. rapping etc. *v.*

Int. crash! bang!

407. Roll. [Repeated and protracted sounds.]**—N.** roll etc. *v.*; drumming etc. *v.*; tattoo; ding-dong; tantara; rataplan; whirr; rat-a-tat; rub-a-dub; pit-a-pat, quaver, clutter, *charivari*, racket; cuckoo; repetition etc. 104; peal of bells, devil's tattoo; reverberation etc. 408.

drumfire, barrage.

machine gun.

V. roll, drum, rumble, rattle, clatter, rustle, roar, drone, patter, clack.

hum, trill, shake; chime, peal, toll; tick, beat. drum –, din- in the ear.

Adj. rolling etc. *v.*; monotonous etc. (*repeated*), 104; like a bee in a bottle.

408. Resonance.—N. resonance; ring etc. *v.*; ringing etc. *v.*; tintinnabulation; reflection, reverberation, clangor.

low –, base –, bass –, flat –, grave –, deep –, pedal- note; bass; *basso*, – *profondo*; bari-, bary-tone; *contralto*.

V. re-sound. -verberate, -echo; ring, ding, sing, jingle, gingle, chink, clink; tink, -le; chime; gurgle etc. 405; plash, guggle, echo, ring in the ear.

Adj. resounding etc. *v.*; resonant, tinnient; tintinnabulary; deep-toned, -sounding, -mouthed; hollow, sepulchral; gruff etc. (*harsh*) 410.

408a. Non-resonance.—N. thud, thump, dead sound; non-resonance; muffled drums, cracked bell; silencer, damper; mute, *sourdine*.

V. sound dead; stop –, damp- the -sound, – reverberations; deaden, muffle.

Adj. non-resonant, dead, muted, muffled.

409. Sibilation. [Hissing sounds.]**—N.** sibilation; hiss etc. *v.*; sternutation; high note etc. 410.

goose, serpent, snake.

V. hiss, buzz, whiz, rustle; fizz, -le, sizzle, swish; wheeze, whistle, snuffle; squash; sneeze.

Adj. sibilant; hissing etc. *v.*; wheezy.

410. Stridor. [Harsh sounds.]**—N.** creak etc. *v.*; creaking etc. *v.*; discord etc. 414; stridor; harshness, roughness, sharpness etc. *adj.*; cacophony.

acute –, high- note; *soprano*, treble, tenor, *alto*, falsetto, *voce di testa*; shriek, cry etc. 411.

piccolo, fife, penny -whistle, – trumpet.

V. creak, grate, jar, burr, pipe, twang, jangle, clank, clink; scream etc. (*cry*) 411; yelp etc. (*animal sound*) 412; buzz etc. (*hiss*) 409.

set the teeth on edge, écorcher les orielles; pierce –, split- the -ears, – head; offend –, grate upon –, jar upon- the ear.

Adj. creaking etc. *v.*; strident, stridulous, harsh,

coarse, hoarse, horrisonous, raucous, metallic, rough. gruff, grum, sepulchral.

sharp, high, acute, shrill, high-pitched; trumpet-toned; piercing, ear-piercing; cracked; discordant etc. 414; cacophonous.

411. Cry.—N. cry etc. v.; voice etc. (*human*) 580; bark etc. (*animal*) 412.

vociferation, outcry, hullaballoo, chorus, clamor, hue and cry, plaint; lungs; stentor.

V. cry, roar, shout, bawl, brawl, halloo, halloa, hail, hoop, whoop, yell, bellow, howl, scream, screech, screak, shriek, shrill, squeak, squeal, squall, whine, whinny, pule, pipe, yaup.

cheer, hurrah; hoot; grumble, maon, groan.

snore, snort; grunt etc. (*animal sounds*) 412.

vociferate; raise −, lift up- the voice; call −, sing −, cry- out; exclaim; rend the air; thunder −, shout- at the -top of one's voice, − pitch of one's breath; s'égosiller; strain the -throat, − voice, − lungs; give a -cry etc.

Adj. crying etc. v.; clam-ant, -orous; vociferous; stentorian etc. (*loud*) 404; open-mouthed.

412. Ululation. [Animal sounds.]—**N.** cry etc. v.; crying etc. v.; ululation, latration, belling; reboation; call, note; bark, howl, yelp; twittering, woodnote; insect cry, fritinancy, drone; screech; cuckoo.

V. cry, ululate, howl, roar, bellow, blare, rebellow, bark, yelp; bay, − the moon; yap, growl, yarr, yawl, snarl, howl; grunt, -le; snort, squeak; neigh, bray; mew, mewl; purr, caterwaul, pule; bleat, low, moo; troat, croak, crow, screech, caw, coo, gobble, quack, cackle, gaggle, guggle; chuck, -le; cluck; clack; cheep, chirp, chirrup, twitter, sing, cuckoo; pout, wail, hum, buzz; hiss, blatter; hoot.

Adj. crying etc. v.; blatant, latrant; re-, mugient; deep-, full-mouthed.

Adv. in full cry.

413. Melody. Concord.—N. melody, rhythym, measure; rhyme etc. (*poetry*) 597.

pitch, *timbre*, intonation, tone, overtone.

scale, gamut; diapason; diatonic −, chromatic −, enharmonic- scale; key, clef, chords.

modulation, temperament, syncope, syncopation, preparation, suspension, resolution.

staff, stave, line, space, brace; bar, rest; *appogiato, -tura; acciaccatura*, shake, *arpeggio*.

note. musical note, notes of a sclae; sharp, flat, natural; high note etc. (*shrillness*) 410; low note etc. 408; interval; semitone; second, third, fourth etc.; diatessaron.

breve, semibreve, minim, crotchet, quaver; semi-demisemi- quaver; sustained note, drone, burden.

tonic; key-, leading-, fundamental-, note; super-tonic, mediant, dominant; sub-mediant, -dominant, organ-, pedal-point; octave, tetrachord; major −, minor- -mode, − scale, − key; Doric mode, passage, phrase.

concord, harmony; unison, -ance; chime, homophony, euphon-y, -ism; tonality; consonance; concent; part.

orchestration; harmonization, − phrasing.

[Science of harmony] harmon-y, -ics; thorough-fundamental- bass; counterpoint; faburden.

piece of music etc. 415; composer, harmonist, contrapuntist.

V. be -harmonious etc. *adj.*; harmonize, chime, symphonize, transpose; put in tune, tune, accord, string; score, arrange, orchestrate.

Adj. harmoni-ous, -cal; in -concord etc. *n.*, − tune, − concert; unisonant, concentual, symphonizing, isotonic, homophonous, assonant, consonant.

measured, rhythmical, diatonic, chromatic, enharmonic.

melodious, musical; tuneful, tunable; sweet, dulcet, canorous; mell-ow, -ifluous; soft; clear, − as a bell; silvery; euphon-ious, -ic, -ical; symphonious; enchanting etc. (*pleasure-giving*) 829; fine-, full-, silver-toned.

Adv. harmoniously etc. *adj.*

414. Discord.—N. discord, -ance; dissonance, cacaphony, caterwauling; harshness etc. 410; consecutive fifths.

[Confused sounds] Babel, pandemonium; Dutch −, cat's- concert; marrow-bones and cleavers.

V. be -discordant etc. *adj.* : jar etc. (*sound harshly*) 410.

Adj. discordant; dis-, ab-sonant; out of tune, tuneless; un-musical, -tunable; un-, im-melodious; un-, in-harmonious; sing-song; cacophonous; jarring, harsh etc. 410.

415. Music.—N. music, classical −, modern −, descriptive- music; concert, recital; strain, tune, air, *motif*; melody etc. 413; *aria, arietta*; piece of music, *sonata; rond-o, -eau; pastorale, cavatina, roulade, fantasia, toccata, concerto*, overture, symphony, symphonic poem, tone poem, prelude, voluntary, *intermezzo*, variations, *cadenza*; cadence; fugue, canon, serenade, *nocturne, notturno*, rhapsody, romance, *aubade*, dithyramb; opera, operetta; oratorio; composition, movement, stave.

instrumental music; full-, orchestral- score; minstrelsy, tweedledum and tweedledee, band, orchestra etc. 416; concerted piece, *potpourri, medley, capriccio*, incidental music; improvisation; peal.

vocal music, vocalism; chaunt, chant; psalm, -ody; hymn; song etc. (*poem*) 597; canticle, canzonet, *cantata, bravura, coloratura*; lay, ballad, ditty, carol, barcarolle, pastoral, recitative, *recitativo, solfeggio*, tonic sol-fa.

Lydian measures; slow -music. − movement; *adagio* etc. *adv.*; minuet; siren strains, soft music, lullaby; *berceuse*, cradle song, dump; dirge etc. (*lament*) 839; pibroch; martial music, march, funeral-, dead- march; dance 'music; waltz etc. (*dance*) 840; rag-time, syncopation, jazz.

solo, duet, *duo, trio*; quartet; quintet, sextet, septet; part song, descant, glee, madrigal, catch, round, chorus, *chorale*; antiphon, -y; accompaniment, second −, alto −, tenor −, bass-part; score, thorough bass; counterpoint.

composer etc. 413; musician etc. 416.

V. compose, perform etc. 416; attune.

Adj. musical; instrumental, orchestral, vocal, choral, lyric, operatic; harmonious etc. 413.

Adv. *adagio; largo, larghetto, andan-te, -tino; alla capella; maestoso, moderato; allegr-o, -etto; spiritoso, vivace, veloce; prest-o, -issimo; pian-o, -issimo, fort-e, -issimo, sforzando; con brio; capriccioso; scherz-o, -ando; legato, sostenuto, staccato, crescendo, diminuendo, rallentando, affettuoso, arioso; parlante, cantabile; obbligato; pizzicato, tremolo, vibrato.*

416. Musician. [Performance of Music.]—**N.** musician, *artiste, virtuoso*, performer, player, minstrel; bard etc. (*poet*) 597; instrumental-, organ-, accompan-, pian-, violin-, flaut-, harp-ist; harper, fiddler, fifer, trumpeter, piper, drummer; catgut scraper.

band, orchestra, waits.

vocal-, melod-ist; singer, warbler; songst-, chaunt-er, -ress; *diva, cantatrice*, coloratura, soprano, mezzo-soprano, alto, contralto, tenor, baritone, bass, *basso, -profundo.*

choir, quire, chorister; chorus, — singer; choral society, festival, *eisteddfod.*

nightingale, philomel, thrush; siren; Orpheus, Apollo, the Muses, Erato, Euterpe, Terpsichore; tuneful -nine, — quire.

composer etc. 413.

performance, virtuosity, execution, touch, expression, solmization.

V. play, pipe, strike — , tune-up, sweep the chords, tickle — , paw- the ivories, vamp, tweedle, fiddle; strike the lyre, beat the drum; blow — , sound — , wind- the horn; grind the organ; touch the -guitar etc. (*instruments*) 417; thrum, strum, twang, drum, beat — , keep- time, conduct.

execute, perform; accompany; sing — , play- a second; compose, write music, set to music, arrange, harmonize, orchestrate.

sing, chaunt, chant, hum, warble, carol, chirp, chirrup, lilt, purl, quaver, trill, shake, twitter, whistle; sol-fa; intone.

have -an ear for music, — a musical ear, — a correct ear, — absolute pitch.

Adj. playing etc. *v.*; musical, lyric.

Adv. *adagio, andante* etc. (*music*) 415.

417. Musical Instruments.—**N.** musical instruments; band; string-, brass-, drum and fife-, military-, bugle-, German-, dance-, jazz-band; orchestra, string quartet; orchestration, orchestrelle.

[Stringed instruments] mono-, poly-chord; harp, lyre, lute, archlute, thearbo; mandol-a, -in, -ine; guitar; *ukulele*; psaltery, zither; bandore, cither, -n; gittern, rebeck, *bandurria*, banjo, zither banjo, *balalaika, samisen*; plectrum.

viol, -in, Cremona, Stradivarius; fiddle; kit; *vielle, viola, — d'amore, — di gamba*; tenor, *violoncello*, cello; bass, bass-, bass-viol; double-bass, *contrabasso, violone*, hurdy-gurdy; strings, catgut; bow, fiddlestick.

piano, -forte; grand — , concert grand — , baby — , upright — , cottage- piano; pianino, pianette; harpsi-, clavi-, clari-, mani-chord; *clavier*, spinet, virginals; dulcimer, *cymbalo*; Eolian harp; piano-

organ, -player, electric piano, player-piano, pianola.

[Wind instruments] organ, church — , pipe — , American- organ; harmoni-um, -phon; accordion, seraphina, concertina; melodeon; barrel- organ; humming top.

flute, fife, piccolo, flageolet, penny-whistle, reed instrument; clari-net, -onet; bass clarionet; saxophone; basset horn, *corno di bassetto*; musette, shawm, oboe, hautboy, *cor Anglais, corno Inglese*, bassoon, double bassoon, *contrafagotto*; bag-, union-pipes; ocarina, Pandean pipes; calliope; sirene, pipe, pitch-pipe; sourdet; whistle, catcall.

horn, bugle, key bugle, cornet, *cornet-à-pistons*, cornopean, clarion, trumpet, trombone, ophicleide, serpent; English-, French-, bugle-, sax-, flugel-, alt-, helicon-, post-horn; sackbut, euphonium, bombardon, tuba, bass tuba.

[Vibrating surfaces] cymbal, bell, gong, peal of bells, *carillon*; tambour, -ine; drum, tom-tom, tabor, -ret, -ourine, -orin; *sistrum, grand caisse*, bass-, big-, side-, kettle-drum; *tympani*; war drums; tymbal, timbrel, castanet, bones; musical-glasses, -stones; harmonica, sounding— board, rattle; gramophone, phonograph.

[Vibrating bars] reed, tuning-fork, triangle, Jew's harp, musical box, harmonicon, xylophone, marimba, *celeste.*

sord-ine, -et; *sourd-ine, -et*; mute.

418. Hearing. [Sense of sound.]—**N.** hearing etc. *v.*; audition, auscultation; eavesdropping; audibility; acoustics etc. 402.

acute — , nice — , delicate — , quick — , sharp — , correct — , musical -ear; ear for music.

ear, auricle, lug, acoustic organs, auditory apparatus, ear-drum, tympanum; ear-, speaking-trumpet, megaphone; telephone, radiophone, stethoscope, phonograph, gramophone, microphone.

hearer, auditor, listener, eavesdropper; audi-tory, -ence.

V. hear, overhear; hark, -en; list, -en; give — , lend — , bend- an ear; give attention; catch a sound, prick up one's ears; give -a hearing, — audience -to.

hang upon the lips of, be all ear, listen with both ears, monitor.

become audible; meet — , fall upon — , catch — , reach- the ear; be heard; ring in the ear etc. (*resound*) 408.

Adj. hearing etc. *v.*; auditory, auricular, aural, auditive, acoustic.

Adv. *arrectis auribis.*

Int. hark, — ye!-hear! list, -en! *Oyez!* attention! lend me your ears!

419. Deafness.—**N.** deafness, hardness of hearing, surdity; inaudibility.

V. be -deaf etc. *adj.*; have no ear; shut — , stop — , close- one's ears; turn a deaf ear to.

render deaf, stun, deafen.

Adj. deaf, earless, surd; hard — , dull- of hearing; deaf-mute, stunned, deafened; stone deaf; deaf as -a post, — an adder, — a beetle, — a trunk-maker.

inaudible etc. 405; out of hearing.

420. Light.—N. light, ray, beam, stream, gleam, streak, pencil; sun-, moon-beam; dawn, aurora.

day; sunshine; light of -day, – heaven; sun etc. (*luminary*) 432, day-, broad day-, noontide- light; noon-tide, -day; glare.

glow etc. *v.*; afterglow, sunset; glimmering etc. *v.*; glint; play –, flood- of light; phosphorescence, flush, halo, glory, nimbus, aureole, *aureola*.

spark, *scintilla*; *facula*; sparkling etc. *v.*; emication, scintillation, flash, blaze, coruscation, fulguration; flame etc. (*fire*) 382; lightning, *ignis fatuus*, etc. (*luminary*) 423, radio-activity.

luster, sheen, shimmer, reflection; gloss, tinsel, spangle, brightness, brilliancy, splendor; ef-, refulgence; ful-gor, -gidity; dazzlement, resplendence, transplendency; luminousness etc. *adj.*; luminosity; lucidity; renitency; radi-ance, -ation; irradiation, illumination, phosphorescence, luminescence.

radiation, radiant heat, infra-red rays, visible radiation, ultra-violet –, actinic- rays, actinism; X –, Roentgen- rays; phot-, heli-ography; optical instruments etc. 445.

[Science of light] optics; photo-logy, -metry; di-, cat-optrics.

[Distribution of light] *chiaroscuro*, *clair-obscur*, clear obscure, breadth, light and shade, black and white, tonality, half-tone, mezzotint.

reflection, refraction, dispersion, double refraction, polarization, diffraction, interference.

illuminant etc. 423.

V. shine, glow, glitter, phosphoresce; glis-ter, – ten; twinkle, gleam, flare, – up; glare, beam, shimmer, glimmer, flicker, sparkle, scintillate, coruscate, flash, fulgurate, blaze; be -bright etc. *adj.*; reflect light, daze, dazzle, bedazzle, raidate, shoot out beams.

clear up, brighten.

lighten, enlighten; light, – up; irradiate, shine upon; give –, hang out- a light; cast –, throw –, shed- -luster, – light- upon; illum-e, -ine, -inate; relume, strike a light; kindle etc. (*set fire to*) 384.

Adj. shining etc. *v.*; lumin-ous, -iferous; luc-id, -ent, -ulent, -ific, -iferous; illuminating, light, -some; bright, vivid, splendent, nitid, lustrous, shiny, brilliant, beamy, scintillant, radiant, lambent; sheen, -y; glossy, burnished, glassy, sunny, orient, meridian; noon-day, -tide; cloudless, clear; unclouded, -obscured.

garish; re-, tran-splendent; re-, effulgent; ful-gid, -gent; relucent, splendid, blazing, in a blaze, ablaze, rutilant, meteoric, phosphorescent; aglow.

bright as silver; light –, bright- as -day, – noonday, – the sun at noonday.

optical, actinic; photo-genic, -graphic; heliographic, radioactive.

421. Darkness.—N. darkness etc. *adj.*; olackness etc. (*dark color*) 431; obscurity, gloom, murk; dusk etc. (*dimness*) 422; tenebrosity, umbrageousness.

Cimmerian –, Stygian –, Egyptian- darkness; night; midnight; dead of –, witching time of-night; blind man's holiday; darkness -visible; – that can be felt; palpable, obscure; Erebus.

shade, shadow, umbra, penumbra; sciagraphy; *silhouette*; radiograph, skiagraph.

obscuration; ad-, ob-umbration; obtenebration, offuscation, caligation; extinction; eclipse, total eclipse; gathering of the clouds.

shading; distribution of shade; *chiaroscuro* etc. (*light*) 420.

noctivagation, noctograph, noctuary.

obscurantist.

V. be -dark etc. *adj.*

darken, obscure, shade; dim; tone down, lower; over-cast, -shadow; cloud, eclipse; ob-, of-fuscate; ob-, ad-umbrate, cast into the shade; be-cloud, -dim, -darken; cast –, throw –, spread- a -shade, – shadow, – gloom.

extinguish; put –, blow –, snuff- out; doubt.

Adj. dark, -some, -ling; obscure, tenebrous, tenebrious, sombrous, pitch dark, pitchy, caliginous; black etc. (*in color*) 431.

sunless, lightless etc. (*see* sun, light etc. 423); somber, dusky; unilluminated etc. (*see* illuminate etc. 420); nocturnal; dingy, lurid, gloomy; murk-y, -some; shady, umbrageous; overcast etc. (*dim*) 422; cloudy etc. (*opaque*) 426; darkened etc. *v.*

dark as -pitch, – a pit, – Erebus.

benighted; noctivag-ant, -ous.

Adv. in the -dark, – shade; at night.

422. Dimness.—N. dimness etc. *adj.*; darkness etc. 421; paleness etc. (*light color*) 429.

half-light, *demi-jour*; partial -shadow, – eclipse; shadow of a shade; glimmer, -ing; nebulosity; cloud etc. 353; eclipse.

aurora, dusk, twilight, gloaming, blind man's holiday, shades of evening, crepuscule, cockshut time; break of day, daybreak, dawn.

moon-light, -beam, -shine; star- owl's-, candle-, rush-, fire-light; farthing candle.

V. be – ,grow- -dim etc. *adj.*; flicker, twinkle, glimmer; loom, lower; fade; darken; pale, – its ineffectual fire.

render -dim etc. *adj.*; dim, bedim, obscure.

Adj. dim, dull, lack-luster, dingy, darkish, shorn of its beams; dark 421.

faint, shadowed forth; glassy; bleary; cloudy; misty etc. (*opaque*) 426; muggy, fuliginous; nebulous, -ar; obnubilated, overcast, crepuscular, twilight, muddy, lurid, leaden, dun, dirty; looming etc. *v.*

pale etc. (*colorless*) 429; confused etc. (*invisible*) 447.

423. Luminary. [Source of light.]—**N.** luminary; light etc. 420; flame etc. (*fire*) 382.

spark, *scintilla*; phosphorescence.

sun, orb of day, day star, Phoebus, Apollo, Helios, Phaethon, Hyperion, Ra, Aurora; star, orb, meteor; falling –, shooting- star; blazing –, dog-star; Sirius, canicula, Aldebaran; morning star, Lucifer, Phosphor, evening star; Hesperus, Venus, planet, moon etc. 318; constellation, galaxy; northern light, *aurora -borealis*, – *australis*, zodiacal light; mock sun, parhelion.

lightning; fork –, sheet –, summer- lightning, St. Elmo's fire; phosphorus; *ignis fatuus*; Jack o' – Friar's- lantern; Will o' the wisp, fire-drake, *Fata Morgana*.

glow-worm, fire-fly.

radium, luminous paint.

[Artificial light] gas; gas –, lime –, electric –, head –, search –, spot –, flash –, flood –, footlight; lamp, oil –, gas –, arc –, incandescent-lamp; flare; lant-ern, -horn; dark lantern, bull's eye, projector; candle, *bougie*, tallow –, wax- candle; dip, farthing dip; taper, rush-light; oil etc. (*grease*) 356; wick, burner; Argand, moderator, duplex; torch, *flambeau*, link, brand; cresset; gase-, chande-, electro-lier; candelabrum, *girandole*, sconce, luster, candle-stick.

firework, fizgig; pyrotechnics; Roman candle, Very light, star shell, parachute light; rocket, lighthouse etc. (*signal*) 550.

V. illuminate etc. (*light*) 420.

Adj. self-luminous, incandescent; phosphor-ic, -escent; luminescent, fluorescent, radiant etc. (*light*) 420.

424. Shade.—N. shade; awning etc. (*cover*) 223; parasol, sunshade, umbrella; screen, curtain, shutter, blind, gauze, veil, mantle, mask; cloud, mist, gathering of clouds; smoke screen; smoked glasses, colored spectacles; blinkers, blinders.

umbrage, glade; shadow etc. 421.

V. draw a curtain; put up –, close- a shutter; veil etc. *v.*; cast a shadow etc. (*darken*) 421; screen, obstruct the view.

Adj. shady, umbrageous, bowery.

425. Transparency.—N. transparen-ce, -cy; translucen-ce, -cy; diaphaneity; luc-, pelluc-, limpidity.

transparent medium, glass, crystal, mica; lymph, water.

v. be -transparent etc. *adj.*; transmit light.

Adj. transparent, pellucid, lucid, diaphanous; trans-, tra-lucent; limpid, clear, serene, crystalline, clear as crystal, vitreous, transpicuous, glassy, hyaline.

426. Opacity.—N. opacity; opaqueness etc. *adj*

film; cloud etc. 353.

V. be -opaque etc. *adj.*; obstruct the passage of light; ob-, of-fuscate.

Adj. opaque, impervious to light.

dim etc. 422; turbid, thick, muddy, opacous, obfuscated, fuliginous, cloudy, hazy, foggy, vaporous, nubiferous, muggy.

smoky, fumid, murky, dirty.

427. Semitransparency.—N. semitransparency, opalescence, milkiness, pearliness; gauze, muslin; film; mist etc. (*cloud*) 353; frosted glass.

Adj. semi-transparent, -pellucid, -diaphanous, -opacous, -opaque; opal-escent, -ine; pearly, milky, frosted, mat; misty.

428. Color.—N. color, hue, tint, tinge, dye, complexion, shade, tincture, cast, livery, coloration, chromatism, glow, flush; tone, key.

pure –, positive –, primary –, primitive –, complementary- color; three primaries; spectrum, chromatic dispersion; broken –, secondary –, tertiary- color.

local color, coloring, keeping, tone, value, aerial perspective.

[Science of color] chromatics, spectrum analysis; prism, spectroscope.

pigment, coloring matter, paint, dye, wash, distemper, stain; medium; mordant; oil-paint etc. (*painting*) 556.

V. color, dye, tinge, stain, tint, tinct, tone, paint, wash, ingrain, grain, illuminate, emblazon, imbue; paint etc. (*fine art*) 556; daub.

Adj. colored etc. *v.*; colorific, tingent, tinctorial; chormatic, prismatic; full-, high-, deep-colored; doubly-dyed; polychromatic.

bright, vivid, intense, deep; fresh, unfaded; rich, gorgeous; highly colored; gay; variegated etc. 440.

gaudy, florid; garish, showy, flaunting, flashy; raw, crude; glaring, flaring; discordant, inharmonious.

mellow, harmonious, pearly, sweet, delicate, tender, refined.

429. Achromatism. [Absence of color.]—N. achromatism; de-, dis-coloration; pall-or, -idity; paleness etc. *adj.*; etiolation; neutral tint, monochrome, black-and-white.

V. lose -color etc. 428; fade, fly, go; become -colorless etc. *adj.*; turn pale, pale, whiten.

deprive of color, decolorize, bleach, tarnish, achromatize, blanch, etiolate, wash out, tone down.

Adj. uncolored etc. (*see* color etc. 428); colorless, achromatic, hueless, pale, pallid; pale-, tallow-faced; faint, dull, cold, muddy, leaden, dun, wan, sallow, dead, dingy, ashy, ashen, ghastly, cadaverous, glassy, lack-luster; discolored etc. *v.* light-colored, fair, *blond*; white etc. 430.

pale as -death, – ashes, – a witch, – a ghost, – a corpse.

430. Whiteness.—N. whiteness etc. *adj.*; argent.

albification, albescence, albinism, etiolation.

snow, paper, chalk, milk, lily, ivory, silver, alabaster; white lead, chinese –, flake –, ivory –, zinc- white, white-wash, -ning, whiting.

V. be -white etc. *adj.*

render -white etc. *adj.*; whiten- bleach, blanch, etiolate, whitewash, silver, frost.

Adj. white; milky, milk-, snow-white; snowy, niveous, candid, chalky; hoar, -y; frosted, silvery; argent, -ine; canescent.

– whitish, creamy, pearly, ivory, fair, *blond*, ash-blond, platinum blond; blanched etc. *v.*; high in tone, light.

white as -a sheet, – driven snow, – a lily, – silver; like -ivory etc. *n.*

431. Blackness.—N. blackness etc. *adj.*; darkness etc. (*want of light*) 421; swarthness, lividity, dark color, tone, color; *chiaroscuro* etc. 420.

nigrification, infuscation, denigration.

jet, ink, ebony, coal, pitch, soot, smudge, charcoal, sloe, raven, crow; black.

[Pigments] lamp –, ivory –, blue-black; writing –, printing –, printer's –, Indian- ink.

V. be -black etc. *adj.*

render -black etc. *adj.*; blacken, infuscate, denigrate; blot, -ch; smutch; smirch; darken etc. 421.

Adj. black, sable, swarthy, somber, dark, inky, ebon, atramentous, jetty; coal-, jet-black; fuliginous, pitchy, sooty, swart, dusky, dingy, murky, low-toned, low in tone; of the deepest dye.

black as -jet etc. *n.*, – my hat, – a shoe, – a tinker's pot, – November, – thunder, – midnight; nocturnal etc. (*dark*) 421; nigrescent; gray etc. 432; obscure etc. 421.

Adv. in mourning.

432. Gray.—N. gray etc. *adj.*; neutral tint, silver, pepper and salt, *chiaroscuro*, *grisaille*, grayness.

[Pigments] Payne's gray; black etc. 431.

Adj. gray, grey; steel –, iron- gray, dun, drab, dingy, leaden, livid, somber, sad, pearly; silver, -y, -ed; ash-en, -y; ciner-eous, -itious; grizzl-y, -ed; dove-, slate-, stone-, mouse-, ash-colored; mole; cool.

433. Brown.—N. brown etc. *adj.*

[Pigments] bister, ocher, sepia, Vandyke brown.

Adj. brown, adust, bay, dapple, auburn, chestnut, nutbrown, cinnamon, hazel, fawn, puce, *écru*, russet, tawny, fuscous, chocolate, maroon, foxy, tan, brunette, whitey-brown; snuff-, liver-colored; brown as -a berry, – mahogany; reddish brown; copper-, rust- colored; henna, bronze, khaki; russet, roan, sorrel.

sub-burnt; tanned etc. *v.*

V. render -brown etc. *adj.*; tan, embrown, bronze.

434. Redness.—N. red, scarlet, vermilion, cardinal, Post Office, red, carmine, crimson, pink, lake, *cerise*, cherry red, maroon, carnation, *couleur de rose, rose du Barry*; magenta, damask; flesh -color, – tint; color; fresh –, high- color; warmth; gules.

ruby, garnet, carbuncle; rose; rust, iron-mold.

[Dyes and pigments] cinnabar, cochineal; fuchsine; ruddle, madder, redlead; light –, Venetian- red; red ink, annotto.

redness etc. *adj.*; rub-escence, -icundity, -.ication; erubescence, blush.

V. be –, become- -red etc. *adj.*; blush, flush, color up, mantle, redden.

render- red etc. *adj.*; redden, rouge; rub-ify, -ricate; incarnadine; ruddle.

Adj. red etc. *n.*; -dish; rufous, ruddy, florid, incarnadine, sanguine, bloody, gory; ros-y, -eate; blowz-y, -ed; brunt; rubi-cund, -form; lurid, stammel, blood-red; russet, murrey, carroty, sorrel, lateritious.

rose-, ruby-, cherry-, claret-, wine-, plum-,

flame-, flesh-, peach-, salmon-, brick-, brickdust-colored, reddish brown etc. 433.

red as -fire, – blood, – scarlet, – a turkeycock, – a lobster; warm, hot; foxy.

435. Greenness.—N. green etc. *adj.*; blue and yellow; vert.

emerald, verd antique, verdigris, malachite, beryl, aquamarine, reseda.

[Pigments] *terre verte*, verditer, bice, chlorophyl.

greenness, verdure, verdancy; viridity, -escence.

Adj. green, verdant; glaucous, olive; porraceous; green as grass.

emerald –, pea –, grass –, apple –, sea –, olive –, bottle –, leaf- green.

greenish; vir-ent, -escent.

436. Yellowness.—N. yellow etc. *adj.*; or.

[Pigments] gamboge; cadmium –, chrome –, Indian –, lemon- yellow; orpiment, yellow ocher, Claude tint, aureolin.

crocus, saffron, topaz, gold.

jaundice; London fog; yellowness etc. *adj.*

Adj. yellow, aureate, gold, golden, gilt, gilded, flavous, citrine, fallow; fulv-ous, -id; sallow, luteous, fawny, creamy, sandy; xanth-ic, -ous; jaundiced.

gold-, citron-, saffron-, lemon-, sulphur-, amber-, straw-, primrose-, cream-colored; flazen, yellowish, buff.

yellow as a -quince, – guinea, – crow's foot.

437. Purple.—N. purple etc. *adj.*; blue and red, bishop's purple; aniline dyes, gridelin, amethyst; purpure.

livid-ness, -ity.

V. empurple.

Adj. purple, violet, plum-colored, lavender, lilac, puce, *mauve*; livid.

438. Blueness.—N. blue etc. *adj.*; garter-blue; watchet.

[Pigments] ultramarine, smalt, cobalt, cyanogen; Prussian –, syenite- blue; bice, indigo, woad.

lapis lazuli, sapphire, turquoise.

blue-, bluish-ness; bloom.

Adj. blue, azure, cerulean; sky-blue, -colored, -dyed; navy-blue, aquamarine, electric blue, royal blue, cyanic; bluish; atmospheric, retiring; cold.

439. Orange.—N. orange, red and yellow; gold; or; flame etc. color, *adj.*

[Pigments] ochre, Mars orange, cadmium.

V. gild, warm.

Adj. orange; ocherous; orange-, gold-, flame-, copper-, brass-, apricot-colored; warm, hot, glowing.

440. Variegation.—N. variegation; di-, tri-chromism; iridescence, irisation, play of colors, polychrome, maculation, spottiness, striae.

spectrum, rainbow, iris, tulip, peacock, chameleon, butterfly, tortoiseshell; mackerel, − sky; zebra, leopard, mother-of-pearl, nacre, opal, marble, batik.

check, plaid, tartan, patchwork; mar-, par-quetry; mosaic, *tesserae*, tesselation, chess-board, checkers, chequers; harlequin; Joseph's coat; tricolor; patchès, bands, stripes, spots etc of color.

V. be -variegated etc. *adj.*; variegate, stripe, streak, checker, chequer; be-, speckle, fleck; be-, sprinkle; stipple, maculate, dot, bespot; tattoo, inlay, tesselate, damascene; embroider, braid, quilt.

Adj. variegated etc. *v.*; many-colored, -hued; divers-, parti-colored; di-, poly-chromatic; bi-, tri-, versi-color; of all -the colors of the rainbow, − manner of colors; kaleidoscopic.

iridescent; opal-ine, -escent; prismatic, nacreous, pearly, shot, *gorge de pigeon*, *chatoyant*, irisated.

pied, piebald, skewbald; motley; mottled, mar-bled; pepper and salt, paned, dappled, clouded, cymophanous.

mosiac, tesselated, chequered, plaid; tortoiseshell etc. *n.*

spott-ed, -y; punctuated, powdered; speckled etc. *v.*; freckled, fleabitten, studded; fleck-ed, -ered; striated, barred, veined; brind-ed, -led; tabby; watered; grizzled; listed; embroidered etc. *v.*; daedal.

441. Vision.—N. vision, sight, optics, eye-sight.

view, look, espial, glance, ken, *coup d'oeil*; glimpse, peep, glint; gaze, stare, leer; perlustration, contemplation; conspect-ion, -uity; regard, survey; in-, intro-spection; *reconnaissance*, speculation, watch, espionage, *espionnage*, autopsy; ocular -inspection, − demonstration; sight-seeing.

macrography, micrography.

point of view; view-, stand- point; gazebo, loop-hole, *belvedere*, watchtower.

field of view; theater, amphitheater, arena, vista, horizon; commanding −, bird's eye −, panoramic- view; periscope.

visual organ, organ of vision; eye; naked −, unassisted- eye; eye-ball, retina, pupil, iris, cornea, white; optics, orbs; saucer −, goggle −, gooseberry-eyes.

short sight etc. 443; clear −, sharp −, quick −, eagle −, piercing-, −, penetrating- -sight, − glance, − eye; perspicacity, discernment; catopsis.

eagle, hawk; cat, lynx; Argus.

evil eye; basilisk, cockatrice.

spectacles, telescope etc. 445.

V. see, behold, discern, perceive, have in sight, descry, sight, make out, discover, distinguish, recognize, spy, espy, ken; get −, have −, catch- a -sight, − glimpse- of; command of view of; witness, contemplate, speculate; cast −, set- the eyes on; be a -spectator etc. 444- of; look on etc. (*be present*) 186; see sights etc. (*curiosity*) 445; see at a glance etc. (*intelligence*) 498.

look, view, eye; lift up the eyes, open one's eye; look -at, − on, − upon, − over, − about one, − round; survey, scan, inspect; run the eye -over, − through; reconnoiter, glance -round, − on, − over; turn −, bend- one's looks upon; direct the eyes to, turn the eyes on, cast a glance, make eyes at.

observe etc. (*attend to*) 457; watch etc. (*care*) 459; see with one's own eyes; watch for etc. (*expect*) 507; peek, peep, peer, pry, take a peep; play at bo-peep.

look -full in the face, − hard at, − intently; strain one's eyes; fix −, rivet- the eyes upon; stare, gaze; pore over, gloat -over, − on; leer, ogle, glare; goggle; cock the eye, squint, gloat, look askance; give the glad eye.

Adj. seeing etc. *v.*; visual, ocular, -al; ophthalmic.

far-, clear-sighted etc. *n.*; eagle-, hawk-, lynx-, keen-, Argus-eyed.

visible etc. 446.

Adv. visibly etc. 446; in sight of, with one's eyes open.

at -sight, − first sight, − a glance, − the first blush; *primâ facie*.

Int. look! etc. (*attention*) 457.

Phr. the scales falling from one's eyes.

442. Blindness.—N. blindness, anopsia, cecity, excecation, *amaurosis*, cataract, ablepsy, prestriction; dim-sightedness etc. 443.

V. be -blind etc. *adj.*; not see; lose sight of; have the eyes bandaged; grope in the dark.

not look; close −, shut −, turn away −, avert-the eyes; look another way; wink etc. (*limited vision*) 443; shut the eyes −, be blind- to; wink −, blink- at.

render -blind etc. *adj.*; blind, -fold; hoodwink, dazzle; put one's eyes out; throw dust into one's eyes; *jeter de la poudre aux yeux*; screen from sight etc. (*hide*) 528.

Adj. blind; eye-, sight-, vision-less; dark; stone-, sand-, stark-blind; undiscerning; dim-sighted etc. 443.

blind as -a bat, − a buzzard, − a beetle, − a mole, − an owl; wall-eyed.

blinded etc. *v.*

Adv. blind-ly, -fold; darkly.

443. Dim-sightedness. [Imperfect vision.] [Fallacies of vision.]**—N.** dim −, dull −, half −, short −, near −, long −, double −, astigmatic−, failing- sight; dim etc -sightedness; snow blindness; purblindness, lippitude; my-, presby-opia; confusion of vision; astigmatism; nystagmus; color-blindness, dichromism, chromato-pseudo-blepsis, Daltonism; nyctalopy; *strabismus*, strabism, squint, cast in the eye, swivel eye, goggle eyes; obliquity of vision.

winking etc. *v.*; nictitation; blinkard, albino.

dizziness, swimming, scotomy; cataract; ophthalmia.

[Limitation of vision] eye shade, blinker, blinder; screen etc. (*hider*) 530.

[Fallacies of vision] *deceptio visûs*; refraction, distortion, illustion, false light, *anamorphosis*, virtual image, *spectrum*, *mirage*, looming, phasma; phant-asm, -asma, -om; vision; specter, apparition, ghost; *ignis fatuus* etc. (*luminary*) 423; specter of the Brocken; magic mirror; magic lantern etc. (*show*) 448; mirror, lens etc. (*instrument*) 445.

V. be -dim-sighted etc. **e.**; see double; have a - mote in the eye, − mist before the eyes, − film over the eyes; see through a -prism, − glass darkly; wink, blink, nictitate; squint; look ask-ant, -ance; screw up the eyes, glare, glower.

dazzle, glare, blur, swim, loom.

Adj. dim-sighted etc. *n.*; my-, presby-opic; astigmatic; moon-, mope-, blear-, goggle-, gooseberry-, one-eyed; blind of one eye, monoculous; half-, pur-, color-blind; dichromatic.

blind as a bat etc. (*blind*) 442; winking etc. *v.*

444. Spectator.—N. spectator, beholder, observer, inspector, viewer, looker-on, onlooker, witness, eye-witness, bystander, passer by; sight-seer.

spy, scout; sentinel etc. (*warning*) 668.

v. witness, behold etc. (*see*) 441; look on etc. (*be present*) 186.

445. Optical Instruments.—N. optical instruments; lens, meniscus, magnifier, reading −, burning- glass; micro-, mega-, teino-scope; spectacles, glasses, barnacles, goggles, giglamps, eyeglass, *pince-nez*, monocle; periscopic lens; telescope, glass, lorgnette, binocular; spy-, opera-, field-glass, periscope, range finder.

mirror, reflector, speculum; looking-, pier-, cheval-, hand-glass.

prism; camera, *camera-lucida*, *-obscura*; projector, stereopticon, magic lantern etc. (*show*) 448; chro-, thau-matrope; stereo-, pseudo-, poly-, kaleido-scope.

photo-, opto-, erio-, actino-, luci-, radio-, spectro-meter; polari-, polemo-, spectro-scope, diffraction grating.

optics, optician, optometry, optometrist; microscop-y, -ist; photometry, photography; photographer.

446. Visibility.—N. visibility, perceptibility; conspicuousness, distinctness etc. *adj.*; conspicuity; appearance etc. 448; exposure; manifestation etc. 525; ocular -proof, − evidence, − demonstration; field of view etc. (*vision*) 441.

V. be −, become- -visible etc. *adj.*; appear, emerge, open to the view; meet −, catch- the eye; present −, show −, manifest −, produce −, discover −, reveal −, expose −, betray- itself; stand -forth, − out; show; arise; peep −, peer −, crop- out; start −, spring −, show −, turn −, crop- up; glimmer, glitter, glow, loom; glare; burst forth, scintillate; burst upon the -view, − sight; heave in sight; come -in sight, − into view, − out, − forth, − forward, see the light of day; break through the clouds; make its appearance, show its face, materialize, appear to one's eyes, come upon the stage, enter; float before the eyes, speak for itself. etc. (*manifest*) 525; attract the attention etc. 457; reappear; live in a glass house.

expose to view etc. 525.

Adj. visible, perceptible, perceivable, discernible, apparent; in -view, − full view, − sight; exposed to view, *en evidence*; unclouded.

obvious etc. (*manifest*) 525; plain, clear,

distinct, definite; well-defined, -marked; in focus; recognizable, palpable, autoptical; glaring, staring, conspicuous; stereoscopic; in -bold, − strong, − high- relief.

periscopic, panoramic.

before −, under- one's eyes; before one, *à vue d'oeil*, in one's eye, *oculis subjecta fidelibus*.

Adv. visibly etc. *adj.*; in sight of; before one's eyes etc. *adj.*; *veluti in speculum*.

447. Invisibility.—N. invisibility, nonappearance, imperceptibility; indistinctness etc. *adj.*; mystery, delitescence.

concealment etc. 528; latency etc. 526.

V. be -invisible etc. *adj.*; be hidden etc. (*hide*) 528; lurk etc. (*lie hidden*) 526; escape notice.

render -invisible etc. *adj.*; conceal etc. 528; put out of sight.

not see etc. (*be blind*) 442; lose sight of.

Adj. invisible, imperceptible; un-, in-discernible; un-, non-apparent; out of −, not in- sight; *à perte de vue*; behind the -scenes, − curtain; view-, sightless; in-, un-conspicuous; unseen etc. (*see see* etc. 441); covert etc. (*latent*) 526; eclipsed, under an eclipse.

dim etc. (*faint*) 422; mysterious, dark, obscure, confused; indistin-ct, -guishable; shadowy, indefinite, undefined; ill-defined, -marked; blurred, fuzzy, out of focus; misty etc. (*opaque*) 426; veiled etc. (*concealed*) 528; delitescent.

448. Appearance.—N. appearance, phenomenon, sight, spectacle, show, premonstration, scene, species, view, *coup d'oeil*; look-out, out-look, prospect, vista, perspective, bird's-eye view, scenery, landscape, picture, *tableau*; display, exposure, *mise en scène*; scenery, *décor*; rising of the curtain.

phant-asm, -om etc. (*fallacy of vision*) 443.

pageant, *spectacle*; peep-, raree-, gallanty-show; *ombres chinoises*; projector, optical −, magic-lantern, phantasmagoria, dissolving views; cinema, -tograph; bio-scope, -graph; moving pictures, movies, film, screen etc.; pan-, di-, cosm-, georama; *coup* −, *jeu- de théâtre*; pageantry etc. (*ostentation*) 882; insignia etc. (*indication*) 550.

aspect, phase, *phasis*, seeming, shape etc. (*form*) 240; guise, look, complexion, color, image, mien, air, cast, carriage, port, demeanor; presence, expression, first blush, face of the thing; point of view, light.

lineament, feature, trait, lines; out-line, -side; contour, *silhouette*, face, countenance, physiognomy, visage, phiz, mug, cast of countenance, profile, *tournure*, cut of one's jib, metoposcopy; outside etc. 220.

V. appear; be −, become- visible· etc. 446; seem, look, show; present −, wear −, carry −, have −, bear −, exhibit −, take −, take on −, assume- the -appearance, − semblance- of; look like; cut a figure, figure; present to the view; show etc. (*make manifest*) 525.

Adj. apparent, seeming, ostensible; on view.

Adv. apparently; to all -seeming, − appearance; ostensibly, seemingly, as it seems, on the face of it, *primâ facie*; at the first blush, at first sight; in the eyes of; to the eye.

449. Disappearance.—N. disappearance, evanescence, eclipse, occultation.

departure etc. 293; exit, vanishing point; dissolving views.

V. disappear, vanish, dissolve, fade, melt away, pass, go, avaunt; be -gone etc. *adj.*; leave -no trace, — 'not a rack behind;' go off the stage etc. (*depart*) 293; suffer —, undergo- an eclipse; be lost to — retire from- -sight, — view.

lose sight of.

efface etc. 552.

Adj. disappearing etc. *v.*; evanescent; missing, lost; lost to -sight, — view; gone; *spurlos versenki.*

Int. vanish! disappear! avaunt! etc. (*ejection*) 297.

450. Intellect.—N. intellect, mind, understanding, reason, thinking principle; rationality; cogitative —, cognitive —, intellectual- faculties; faculties, senses, consciousness, observation, percipience, apperception, mentality, intelligence, intellection, intuition, association of ideas, instinct, flair, conception, judgment, wits, parts, capacity, intellectuality, reasoning power, brains, genius; wit etc. 498; ability etc. (*skill*) 698; wisdom etc. 498.

soul, spirit, ghost, inner man, heart, breast, bosom, *penetralia mentis, divina particula aurae,* heart's core; ego, psyche, pneuma, subconsciousness, subconscious, subliminal self; dual personality.

organ —, seat- of thought; *sensorium,* sensory, brain, gray matter; head, -piece; pate, noddle, skull, scull, *pericranium, cerebrum, cranium,* brain-pan, -box; sconce, upper story.

[Science of mind] metaphysics; psychics, psycho-logy, -metry, -genesis, -analysis, -physics, psychi-atry, -cal research, thought reading etc. 992; ideology; mental —, moral- philosophy; philosophy of the mind; pneumat-, phren-ology; no —, cranio-logy, -scopy.

ideal-ity, -ism; transcendental-, spiritual-ism; immateriality etc. 317.

metaphysician, psychologist etc.

V. note, notice, mark; take -notice, — cognizance- of; be -aware, — conscious- of; realize; appreciate; ruminate etc. (*think*) 451; fancy etc. (*imagine*) 515; conceive, reason, understand.

Adj. [Relating to intellect] intellectual, mental, rational, subjective, metaphysical, nooscopic, spiritual; ghostly; psych-ical, -ological; cerebral.

immaterial etc. 317; endowed with reason.

Adv. *in petto.*

450a. Absence or want of Intellect.—N. absence —, want- of -intellect etc. 450; imbecility etc. 499; brutality; brute -instinct, — force.

Adj. unendowed with reason.

451. Thought.—N. thought; exercitation —, exercise- of the intellect; reflection, cogitation, consideration, meditation, study, lucubration, speculation, deliberation, pondering; head-, brain-work; cerebration; mentation, deep reflection; close study, application etc. (*attention*) 457.

abstract thought, abstraction, contemplation, musing; brown study etc. (*inattention*) 458; reverie, Platonism; depth of thought, workings of the mind, thoughts, inmost thoughts; self-counsel, communing, -consultation.

association —, succession —, flow —, train —, current- of -thought, — ideas.

after —, mature- thought; reconsideration, second thoughts; retrospection etc. (*memory*) 505; excogitation; examination etc. (*inquiry*) 461; invention etc. (*imagination*) 515.

thoughtfulness etc. *adj.*

V. think, reflect, reason, cogitate, excogitate, consider, deliberate; bestow -thought, — consideration- upon; speculate, contemplate, meditate, ponder, muse, dream, ruminate; brood —, con-over; animadvert, study; bend—, apply- the mind etc. (*attend*) 457; digest, discuss, hammer at, weigh, perpend; realize, appreciate; fancy etc. (*imagine*) 515; trow.

take into consideration; take counsel etc. (*be advised*) 695; commune with —, bethink- oneself; collect one's thoughts; revolve —, turn over —, run over- in the mind; chew the cud —, sleep- upon; take counsel of —, advise with- one's pillow.

rack —, ransack —, crack —, beat —, cudgel-one's brains; set one's -brain, — wits- to work.

harbor —, entertain —, cherish —, nurture- an idea etc. 453; take into one's head; bear in mind; reconsider.

occur; present —, suggest- itself; come —, get-into one's head; strike one, flit across the view, come uppermost, run in one's head; enter —, pass in —, cross —, flash on —, flash across —, float in —, fasten itself on —, be uppermost in —, occupy- the mind; have in one's mind.

make an impression; sink —, penetrate- into the mind; engross the thoughts.

Adj. thinking etc. *v.*; thoughtful, pensive, meditative, reflective, cogitative, museful, wistful, contemplative, speculative, deliberative, studious, sedate, introspective, Platonic, philosophical.

lost —, engrossed —, rapt —, absorbed- in thought etc. (*inattentive*) 458; deep musing etc. (*intent*) 457.

in the mind, under consideration, in contemplation.

Adv. all things considered; taking everything into account.

Phr. the mind being on the stretch; the -mind, — head- -turning, — running- upon.

452. Incogitancy. [Absence or want of thought.]—N. incogitancy, vacancy, inunderstanding; inanity, fatuity etc. 499; thoughtlessness etc. (*inattention*) 458.

V. not -think etc. 451; not think of; dismiss from the -mind, — thoughts etc. 451.

indulge in reverie etc. (*be inattentive*) 458.

put away thought; unbend —, relax —, divert- the mind.

Adj. vacant, unintellectual, unideal, unoccupied, unthinking, inconsiderate, thoughtless; absent etc. (*inattentive*) 458; diverted; irrational etc. 499; narrow-minded etc. 481.

un-thought of, -dreamt of, -considered; off one's mind; incogitable, not to be thought of, inconceivable.

453. Idea. [Object of thought.]—**N.** idea, notion, conception, thought, apprehension, impression, perception, image, sentiment, reflection, observation, consideration; abstract idea, principle; archetype.

view etc. (*opinion*) 484; theory etc. 514; conceit, fancy; phantasy etc. (*imagination*) 515.

point of view etc. (*aspect*) 448; field of view.

454. Topic. [Subject of thought.]—**N.** subject of –, material for- thought; food for the mind, mental *pabulum.*

subject, -matter; matter, theme, topic, what it is about, *thesis,* text, business, affair, matter in hand, argument; motion, resolution; head, chapter; case, point; proposition, theorem; field of inquiry; moot point, problem, etc. (*question*) 461.

V. float –, pass- in the mind etc. 451.

Adj. thought of; uppermost in the mind; *in petto.*

Adv. under -discussion, – consideration, – advisement; in -question, – the mind; on -foot, – the carpet, – the *tapis*; before the house, relative to etc. 9.

455. Curiosity. [The desire of knowledge.]—**N.** interest, thirst for knowledge; curi-osity, -ousness; inquiring mind; inquisitiveness.

sight-seer, quidnunc, newsmonger, Paul Pry, peeping Tom, eavesdropper; gossip etc. (*news*) 532; questioner, *enfant terrible.*

V. be -curious etc. *adj.*; take an interest in, stare, gape; prick up the ears, see sights, lionize; pry, speer; dig up.

Adj. curious, inquisitive, burning with curiosity, overcurious, nosey; inquiring etc. 461; prying; inquisitorial; agape etc. (*expectant*) 507; attentive etc. 457.

Phr. what's the matter? what next?

456. Incuriosity. [Absence of curiosity.]—**N.** incuriosity; incuriousness etc. *adj.*; *insouciance* etc. 866; indifference, apathy.

V. be -incurious etc. *adj.*; have no -curiosity etc. 455; take no interest in etc. 823; mind one's own business.

Adj. incurious, uninquisitive, uninterested, indifferent, bored; impassive etc. 823.

457. Attention.—N. attention; mindfulness etc. *adj.*; intent-ness, -iveness; thought etc. 451; adverten-ce, -cy, observ-ance, -ation; consideration, reflection, perpension; heed; particularity; notice, regard etc. *v.*; circumspection etc. (*care*) 459; study, scrutiny, once-over; in-, intro-spection; revision, -al.

active –, diligent –, exclusive –, minute –, close –, intense –, deep –, profound –, abstract –, labored –, deliberate- -thought, – attention, – application, – study.

minuteness, attention to detail etc. 459. absorption of mind etc. (*abstraction*) 458. indication, calling attention to etc. *v.*

V. be -attentive etc. *adj.*; attend, advert to, observe, look, see, view, remark, notice, regard, take notice, mark; give –, pay- -attention, – heed to; listen in, incline –, lend- an ear to; trouble one's head about; give a thought –, animadvert- to; occupy oneself with; contemplate etc. (*think of*) 451; look -at, – to, – after, – into, – over; see to; turn –, bend –, apply –, direct –, give- the -mind, – eye, – attention- to; have -an eye to, – in one's eye; bear in mind; take into -account, – consideration; keep in -sight, – view; have regard to, heed, mind, take cognizance of, be engaged in, entertain, recognize; make –, take- note of; note.

examine cursorily; glance -at, – upon, – over; cast –, pass- the eyes over; run over, turn over the leaves, dip into, perstringe; skim etc. (*neglect*) 460; take a cursory view of.

examine –, closely, – intently; scan, scrutinize, consider; give –, bend- one's mind to; overhaul, revise, pore over; inspect, review, pass under review; take stock of; fix –, rivet –, focus –, devote- the -eye, – mind, – thoughts, – attention- on *or* to; hear –, think- out; mind one's business.

revert –, hark back- to; watch etc. (*expect*) 507, (*take care of*) 459; hearken –, listen- to; prick up the ears; have –, keep- the eyes open; come to the point.

meet with attention; fall under one's -notice, – observation; be -under consideration etc. (*topic*) 454.

catch –, strike- the eye; attract notice; catch –, awaken –, wake –, invite –, solicit –, attract –, claim –, excite –, engage –, occupy –, strike –, arrest –, fix –, engross –, absorb –, rivet-the- attention, – mind, – thoughts; be -present to, – uppermost in- the mind.

bring under one's notice; point -out, – to, – at, – the finger at; lay the finger on, indigitate, indicate; direct –, call- attention to; show; put a mark etc. (*sign*) 550- upon; call soldiers to 'attention;' bring forward etc. (*make manifest*) 525.

Adj. attentive, mindful, heedful, observant, regardful; alive –, awake- to, alert; observing etc. *v.*; taken up –, occupied- with; engaged –, engrossed –, interested –, wrapped- in; absorbed, rapt; breathless; pre-occupied etc. (*inattentive*) 458; watchful etc. (*careful*) 459; intent on, open-eyed, breathless, undistracted, upon the stretch; on the watch etc. (*expectant*) 507.

steadfast.

Int. see! look, – here, – out, – alive, – you, – to it! mark! lo! behold! soho! hark, – ye! mind! halloo! observe! lo and behold! attention! *nota bene*;N.B.; °,†; I'd have you to know; notice! take notice! O yes! *Oyez!*

Phr. this is –, these are- to give notice.

458. Inattention.—N. in-attention, – consideration; inconsiderateness etc. *adj.*; oversight; inadverten-ce, -cy; non-observance, disregard.

supineness etc. (*inactivity*) 683; *étourderie*; want of thought; heedlessness etc. (*neglect*) 460; *insouciance* etc. (*indifference*) 866.

abstraction; absence —, absorption- of mind; preoccupation, distraction, reverie, brown study, deep musing, fit of abstraction, woolgathering.

V. be -inattentive etc. *adj.*; overlook, disregard; pass by etc. (*neglect*) 460; not -observe etc. 457; think little of.

close —, shut- one's eyes to; wink at; pay no attention to; dismiss —, discard —, discharge- from one's -thoughts, — mind; drop the subject, think no more of; set —, turn —, put- aside; turn -away from, — one's attention from, — a deaf ear to, — one's back upon.

abstract oneself, dream, indulge in reverie.

escape -notice, — attention; come in at one ear and go out at the other; forget etc. (*have no remembrance*) 506.

call off —, draw off —, call away —, divert —, distract- the -attention, — thoughts, — mind; put out of one's head; dis-concert, -compose; put out, confuse, perplex, bewilder, fluster, muddle, dazzle; throw a sop to Cerberus.

Adj. inattentive; un-observant, -mindful, heeding, -discerning; inadvertent; mind-, regard-, respect-less; listless etc. (*indifferent*) 866; blind, deaf; flighty, hand over head; cur-, percur-sory; giddy-, scatter-, hare-brained; unreflecting, *écervelé*, inconsiderate, off-hand, thoughtless, dizzy, muzzy, brainsick; giddy, — as a goose; wild, harum-scarum, ranipole, high-flying; heed-, careless etc. (*neglectful*) 460.

absent, absent-minded, abstracted, *distrait*; lost; lost —, wrapped- in thought, woolgathering; rapt, in the clouds, bemused; dreaming —, musing- on other things; pre-occupied; engrossed etc. (*attentive*) 457; in a -reverie etc. *n.*; off one's guard etc. (*inexpectant*) 508; napping; dreamy.

disconcerted, put out etc. *v.*; rattled.

Adv. inattentively, inadvertently etc. *adj.*; *per incuriam, sub silentio.*

Int. stand -at ease, — easy!

Phr. the attention wanders; one's wits gone a -woolgathering; — bird's nesting; it never entered into one's head; the mind running on other things; one's thoughts being elsewhere; had it been a bear it would have bitten you.

459. Care. [Vigilance.]—**N.** care, solicitude, heed; heedfulness etc. *adj.*; scruple etc. (*conscientiousness*) 939.

watchfulness etc. *adj.*; vigilance, *surveillance*, eyes of Argus, watch, vigil, look out, watch and ward, *l'oeil du maître*.

alertness etc. (*activity*) 682; attention etc. 457; prudence etc., circumspection etc. (*caution*) 864; forethought etc. 510; precaution etc. (*preparation*) 673; tidiness etc. (*order*) 58, (*cleanliness*) 652; accuracy etc. (*exactness*) 494; minuteness, attention to detail; meticulousness, nicety, circumstantiality.

V. be -careful etc. *adj.*; reck; take care etc. (*be cautious*) 864; pay attention to etc. 457; take care of; look —, see- -to, — after; keep -an eye, — a sharp eye- upon; keep -watch, — watch and ward; mount guard, set watch, watch; keep in -sight, — view; chaperon, play gooseberry; mind, — one's business.

look -sharp, — about one; look with one's own eyes; keep a -good, — sharp- look-out; have all one's -wits, — eyes- about one; watch for etc. (*expect*) 507; stand to; keep one's eyes —, have the eyes —, sleep with one eye- open.

take precautions etc. 673; protect etc. (*render safe*) 664.

do one's best etc. 682; mind one's Ps and Qs, speak by the card, pick one's steps.

Adj. care-, regard-, heed-ful; taking care etc. *v.*; particular; prudent etc. (*cautious*) 864; considerate; thoughtful etc. (*deliberative*) 451; provident etc. (*prepared*) 673; alert etc. (*active*) 682; sure-footed.

guarded, on one's guard; on the *-qui vive, -* alert, — watch, — look-out; awake, broad awake, vigilant; watch-, wake-, wist-ful; Argus-, lynx-eyed; wide awake etc. (*intelligent*) 498; on the watch for etc. (*expectant*) 507.

tidy etc. (*orderly*) 58, (*clean*) 652; accurate etc. (*exact*) 494; scrupulous etc. (*conscientious*) 939; *cavendo tutus* etc. (*safe*) 664.

Adv. carefully etc. *adj.*; with care, gingerly.

Phr. *quis custodiet ipsos custodes?*

460. Neglect.—**N.** neglect; carelessness etc. *adj.*; trifling etc. *v.*; negligence; omission, laches, default; remissness, slackness, procrastination; supineness etc. (*inactivity*) 683; inattention etc. 458; *nonchalance* etc. (*insensibility*) 823; imprudence, recklessness etc. 863; slovenliness etc. (*disorder*) 59; (*dirt*) 653; improvidence etc. 674; non-completion etc. 730; inexactness etc. (*error*) 495.

paraleipsis [in rhetoric].

trifler, slacker, waster, waiter on Providence; Micawber.

V. be -negligent etc. *adj.*; take no care of etc. (take care of etc. 459); neglect; let -slip, — go; lay —, set —, cast —, put- aside; keep —, leave- out of sight; lose sight of.

overlook, disregard; pass -over, — by; let pass; blink; wink —, connive- at; gloss over; take no -note, — notice, — thought, — account- of; pay no regard to; *laisser aller*; allow to lie on the table.

scamp; trifle, fribble; do by halves; skimp; cut; slight etc. (*despise*) 930; play — trifle- with; slur; skim, — the surface; *effleurer*; take a cursory view of etc. 457.

slur —, slip —, skip —, jump- over; pertermit, miss, skip, jump, omit, give the go-by to, push aside, throw into the background, shelve, sink; ignore, shut one's eyes to, refuse to hear, turn a deaf ear to; leave out of one's calculation; not -attend to etc. 457, — mind; not trouble -oneself, — one's head- -with, — about; forget etc. 506; be caught napping etc. (*not expect*) 508; leave a loose thread; let the grass grow under one's feet.

render -neglectful etc. *adj.*; put —, throw- off one's guard.

Adj. neglecting etc. *v.*; unmindful, negligent, neglectful; heedless, careless, thoughtless; perfunctory, remiss, slack.

inconsiderate; un-, in-circumspect; off one's guard; un-wary, -watchful, -guarded; offhand.

supine etc. (*inactive*) 683; inattentive etc. 458; *insouciant* etc. (*indifferent*) 823; imprudent, reckless etc. 863; slovenly etc. (*disorderly*) 59, (*dirty*) 653; inexact etc. (*erroneous*) 495; improvident etc. 674.

neglected etc. *v.*; un-heeded, -cared for, -

perceived, -seen, -observed, -noticed, -noted, - marked, -attended to, -thought of, -regarded, - remarked, -missed; shunted, shelved.

un-examined, -studied, -searched, -scanned, - weighed, -sifted, -explored.

Adv. negligently etc. *adj.*; hand over head, anyhow; in an unguarded moment etc. (*unexpectedly*) 508; *per incuriam.*

Int. never mind, no matter, let it pass; it will be all the same a hundred years hence.

461. Inquiry. [Subject of Inquiry. Question.]—**N.** inquiry; request etc. 765; search, research, quest; pursuit etc. 622.

examination, review, scrutiny, investigation, indagation; per-quisition, -scrutation, -vestigation; inqu-est, -isition; exploration; *exploitation*, ventilation.

sifting; calculation, analysis, dissection, resolution, induction; Baconian method.

strict -, close -, searching -, exhaustive- inquiry; narrow -, strict- search; study etc. (*consideration*) 451.

scire facias, ad referendum; trial.

questioning etc. *v.*; interroga-tion, -tory; third degree; interpellation; challenge, examination, cross-examination, catechism; feeler, Socratic method, zetetic philosophy; leading question; discussion etc. (*reasoning*) 476; questionnaire, questionary.

reconnoitering, *reconnaissance*; prying etc. *v.*; espionage, *espionnage*; domiciliary visit, peep behind the curtain; lantern of Diogenes.

question, query, problem, *desideratum*, point to be solved, porism; subject -, field- of -inquiry, - controversy; point -, matter- in dispute; moot-point; issue, question at issue; bone of contention etc. (*discord*) 713; plain -, fair -, open- question; enigma etc. (*secret*) 533; knotty point etc. (*difficulty*) 704; *quod-libet*; threshold of an inquiry.

inquirer, investigator, experimenter, inquisitor, inspector, querist, examiner, catechist; scrut-ator, - ineer; analyst; quidnunc etc. (*curiosity*) 455.

V. make -inquiry etc. *n.*; inquire, seek, search, frisk, speer, look -for, — about for, — out for; scan, reconnoiter, explore, sound, rummage, ransack, pry, peer, look round; look -, go- -over, — through; spy, over-haul.

scratch the head, slap the forehead.

look -, peer -, pry- into every hole and corner; look behind the scenes; trace up; hunt -, fish -, dig -, ferret- out; unearth; leave no stone unturned.

seek a -clue, — clew; hunt, track, trail, shadow, mouse, dodge, trace; follow the -trail, — scent; pursue etc. 622; beat up one's quarters; fish for; feel for etc. (*experiment*) 463.

investigate; take up -, institute -, pursue -, follow up -, conduct -, carry on -, prosecute- -an inquiry etc. *n.*; look -at, — into; pre-examine; discuss, canvass, agitate.

examine, study, consider, calculate; dip -, dive -, delve -, go deep- into; make sure of, probe, sound, fathom; probe to the -bottom, — quick; scrutinize, analyze, anatomize, dissect, parse, resolve, sift, winnow; view -, try- in all its phases; thresh out.

bring in question, subject to examination; put to

the proof etc. (*experiment*) 463; audit, tax, pass in review; take into consideration etc. (*think over*) 451; take counsel etc. 695.

ask, question, demand; put -, pop -, propose -, propound -, moot -, start -, raise -, stir -, suggsst -, put forth -, ventilate -, grapple with -, go into- a question.

put to the question, interrogate, catechize, pump, grill; cross-question, -examine; dodge; require an answer; pick -, suck- the brains of; feel the pulse. be -in question etc. *adj.*, undergo examination.

Adj. inquiry etc. *v.*; inquisitive etc. (*curious*) 455; requisit-ive, -ory; catechetical, inquisitorial, analytic; in -search, — quest- of; on the look-out for, interrogative, zetetic; all-searching.

un-determined, -tried, -decided; in -question, - dispute, — issue, — course of inquiry; under - discussion, — consideration, — investigation etc. *n.*, *sub judice*, moot, proposed; doubtful etc. (*uncertain*) 475.

Adv. what? why? wherefore? whence? whither? where? *quaere?* how -comes, — happens, — is- it? what is the reason? what's -the matter, — up, in the wind? what on earth? when? who?

462. Answer.—**N.** answer, response, reply, replication, *riposte*, rejoinder, surrejoinder, rebutter, surrebutter, counter-evidence etc. 468, counter-charge, defence, plea; retort, repartee; contradiction etc. 536; rescript, -ion; antiphon, -y; acknowledgment; password; echo.

discovery etc. 480a; solution etc. (*explanation*) 522; rationale etc. (*cause*) 153; clue etc. (*indication*) 550.

Oedipus; oracle, etc. 513; return etc. (*record*) 551.

V. answer, respond, reply, rebut, retort, rejoin; give -, return for- answer; acknowledge, echo.

explain etc. (*interpret*) 522; solve etc. (*unriddle*) 522; discover etc. 480a; fathom, hunt out etc. (*inquire*) 461; satisfy, set at rest, determine.

Adj. answering etc. *v.*; respon-sive, -dent; oracular; antiphonal; conclusive.

Adv. because etc. (*cause*) 153; on the -scent, - right scent.

Int. *eureka!*

463. Experiment.—**N.** experiment; essay etc. (*attempt*) 675; research etc. (*investigation*) 461; trial, tentative method, *tâtonnement*.

verification, probation, *experimentum crucis*, proof, criterion, diagnostic test, tryout, crucial test, acid test.

crucible, reagent, check, touchstone, pix; assay; ordeal; ring.

empiricism, rule of thumb.

feeler; pilot -, messenger- balloon, *ballon d'essai*; pilot engine; scout; straw to show the wind. speculation, random shot, leap in the dark.

analy-zer, -st; adventurer, explorer, sourdough, prospector; experiment-er, -ist, -alist; assayer.

V. experiment; essay etc. (*endeavor*) 675; try, assay, sample; make -an experiment, — trial of; give a trial to; put upon -, subject to- trial; experiment upon; rehearse; put -, bring -, submit-to the -test, — proof; prove, verify, test, touch, practise upon, try one's strength.

grope; feel —, grope- -for, — one's way; fumble; *tâttonner, aller à tâtons*; put —, throw- out a feeler; send up a pilot balloon; see how the -land lies, — wind blows; consult the barometer; feel the pulse; fish —, bob- for; cast —, beat- about for; angle, trawl, cast one's net, beat the bushes.

venture, try one's fortune etc. (*adventure*) 675; explore etc. (*inquire*) 461.

Adj. experimental; probat-ive, ory, -ionary; analytic, docimastic; tentative; empirical; speculative, tentive.

under probation, on one's trial, on trial, on approval.

464. Comparison.—N. comparison, collation, contrast; identification.

sim-ile, -ilitude; allegory etc. (*metaphor*) 521.

V. compare -to, — with; collate, confront; place side by side etc. (*near*) 197; set —, pit- against one another; contrast balance.

identify, draw a parallel, parallel.

compare notes; institute a comparison; *parva componere magnis*.

Adj. comparative, relative; metaphorical etc. 521.

compared with etc. *v.*; comparable.

Adv. relatively etc. (*relation*) 9; as compared with etc. *v.*

465. Discrimination.—N. discrimination, distinction, differentiation, diagnosis, diorism; nice perception; perception —, appreciation- of difference; acuteness; estimation etc. 466; nicety, refinement; taste etc. 850; *critique*, judgement, tact; insight, discernment etc. (*intelligence*) 498; *nuances*.

V. discriminate, distinguish, differentiate, severalize; separate; draw the line, sift; separate —, winnow- the chaff from the wheat; split hairs.

estimate etc. (*measure*) 466; know -which is which, — one's stuff, — one's way about, — what is what, — 'a hawk from a handsaw.'

take into -account, — consideration; give — allow- due weight to; weigh carefully.

Adj. discriminating etc. *v.*; dioristic, discriminative, critical, distinctive; nice.

Phr. *il y a fagots et fagots*; *rem acu tetigisti*.

465a. Indiscrimination.—N. indiscrimination; promiscuity; indistinctness, -ion; uncertainty etc. (*doubt*) 475; obtuseness.

V. not -indiscriminate etc. 465; overlook etc. (*neglect*) 460- a distinction; con-found, -fuse, jumble; swallow whole.

Adj. indiscriminate, undiscriminating, promiscuous; undistinguish-ed, -able, -ing; unmeasured.

466. Measurement.—N. measurement, admeasurement, mensuration, survey, valuation, appraisment, assessment, assize; estim-ate, -ation; dead reckoning; reckoning etc. (*numeration*) 85; gauging etc. *v.*

metrology, weights and measures, compound arithmetic.

measure, yard measure, standard, rule, foot-rule, chain, tape, staff, compass, callipers; dividers; gage, gauge, planimeter; meter, line, rod, check.

volt, kilowatt, ampere, candle power; horse power; axle load; foot pound.

flood —, high water- mark; Plimsoll mark; index etc. 550.

scale; gradu-ation, -ated scale; nonius; vernier etc. (*minuteness*) 193; pedo (*length*)- 200, sounding line etc. (*depth*) 208, thermo (*heat* etc. 398)-, baro (*air* etc. 338)-, dynamo (*power*)- 276, anemo (*wind* 349)-, gonio (*angle* 244)- meter; landmark etc. (*limit*) 233; balance etc. (*weight*) 310; optical instruments etc. 445.

co-ordinates, ordinate and abscissa, polar co-ordinates, latitude and longitude, declination and right ascension, altitude and azimuth.

geo-, stereo-, hypso-metry; metage; surveying, land surveying; geo-desy, -detics, -desia; ortho-, alti-metry; *cadastre*.

astrolabe, armillary sphere.

land, -surveyor; geometer, topographer, cartographer, hydrographer.

V. measure, meter, mete; value, assess, rate, appraise, estimate, form as estimate, set a value on; appreciate; standardize.

span, pace, step; apply the -compass etc. *n.*; gauge, plumb, probe, calliper, sound, fathom etc. 208; heave the -log, — lead; weigh etc. 319; survey.

take an average etc. 29; graduate.

Adj. measuring etc. *v.*; metric, -al; measurable; geodetical, cadastral, topographical.

467. Evidence. [on one side]—N. evidence; facts, premises, *data, praecognita,* grounds.

indication etc. 550; criterion etc. (*test*) 463.

testi-mony, -fication; attestation; deposition etc. (*affirmation*) 535; examination.

admission etc. (*assent*) 488; authority, warrant, credential, diploma, voucher, certificate, docket; record etc. 551; document, muniments; *pièce justificative*; deed, warranty etc. (*security*) 771; signature, seal etc. (*identification*) 550; exhibit, citation, reference.

witness, indicator; eye-, ear-witness; deponent; sponsor.

oral —, documentary —, hearsay —, external —, extrinsic —, internal —, intrinsic —, circumstantial —, cumulative —, *ex parte* —, presumptive —, collateral —, constructive- evidence; proof etc. (*demonstration*) 478; evidence in chief; finger prints, dactylogram.

secondary evidence; confirmation, corroboration, adminicle, support; ratification etc. (*assent*) 488; authentication, verification; compurgation, wager of law, comprobation.

citation, reference.

V. be -evidence etc. *n.*; evince, show, betoken, tell of; indicate etc. (*denote*) 550; imply, involve, argue, bespeak, breathe.

have —, carry- weight; tell, speak volumes; speak for itself etc. (*manifest*) 525.

rest −, depend- upon; repose on.

bear -witness etc. *n.*; give -evidence etc. *n.*; testify, depose, witness, vouch for; sign, seal, undersign, set one's hand and seal, sign and seal, deliver as one's act and deed, certify, attest; acknowledge etc. (*assent*) 488.

make absolute, confirm, ratify, corroborate, endorse, countersign, support, bear out, vindicate, uphold, warrant.

adduce, attest, cite, quote; refer −, appeal- to; call, − to witness; bring -forward, − into court; allege, plead; produce −, confront- witnesses; collect −, bring together −, rake up- evidence.

have −, make out- a case; establish, circumstantiate, authenticate, substantiate, verify, make good, quote chapter and verse; bring -home to, − to book.

Adj. showing etc. *v.*; evidential, indica-tive, -tory; deducible etc. 478; grounded −, founded −, based- on; first hand, authentic, verifiable; corroborative, confirmatory; significant, conclusive.

Adv. by inference; according to, witness, *a fortiori*; still -more, − less; *raison de plus*; in corroboration etc. *n.* of; *valeat quantum*; under - seal, − one's hand and seal.

468. Counter-evidence. [Evidence on the other side, on the other hand.]—**N.** counter-evidence, evidence on the other -side, − hand; disproof; refutation etc. 479; negation etc. 536; conflicting evidence.

plea etc. 617; vindication etc. 937; counter-protest; *tu quoque* argument; other side −, reverse- of the shield.

V. countervail, oppose; run counter; rebut etc. (*refute*) 479; subvert etc. (*destroy*) 162; check, weaken; contravene; contradict etc. (*deny*) 536; tell another story, turn the -tables, − scale; alter the case; cut both ways; prove a negative.

audire alteram partem.

Adj. countervailing etc. *v.*; contradictory, in rebuttal.

un-attested, -authenticated, -supported by evidence; supposititious, trumped up.

Adv. *per contra*, conversely, on the other hand.

469. Qualification.—**N.** qualification, limitation, modification, coloring.

allowance, grains of allowance, consideration, extenuating circumstances.

condition, proviso, exception; exemption; salvo, saving clause; discount etc. 813.

V. qualify, limit, modify, affect, temper, leaven, give a color to, introduce new conditions.

allow −, make allowance- for; admit exceptions, take into account.

take exception, object.

Adj. qualifying etc. *v.*; conditional; extenuatory; exceptional etc. (*unconformable*) 83.

hypothetical etc. (*supposed*) 514; contingent etc. (*uncertain*) 475.

Adv. provided, − always; if, unless, but, yet; according as; conditionally, admitting, supposing; on the supposition of etc. (*theoretically*) 514; with the understanding, even, although, though, for all that, after all, at all events.

with grains of allowance, *cum grano salis*; *exceptis excipiendis*; wind and weather permitting; if possible etc. 470.

subject to; with this -proviso etc. *n.*

470. Possibility.—**N.** possibility, potentiality; what -may be, − is possible etc. *adj.*; compatibility etc. (*agreement*) 23.

practicability, feasibility; practicableness etc. *adj.*

contingency, chance etc. 156.

V. be -possible etc. *adj.*; stand a chance, have a leg to stand on; admit of, bear.

render -possible etc. *adj.*; put in the way of.

Adj. possible; on the -cards, − dice; *in posse*, within the bounds of possibility, conceivable, credible, imaginable; compatible etc. 23.

practicable, feasible, workable, performable, achievable; within -reach, − measurable distance; accessible, superable, surmountable; at-, obtainable; contingent etc. (*doubtful*) 475.

Adv. possibly, by possibility; perhaps, -chance, -adventure; may be, haply, mayhap.

if possible, wind and weather permitting, God willing, *Deo volente*, D.V.

471. Impossibility.—**N.** impossibility etc. *adj.*; what -cannot, − can never- be; sour grapes; infeasibility, impracticability; hopelessness etc. 859.

V. be -impossible etc. *adj.*; have no chance whatever.

attempt impossibilities; square the circle; discover the -philosopher's stone − elixir of life, − secret of perpetual motion; wash a blackamoor white; skin a flint; make -a silk purse out of a sow's ear, − bricks without straw; have nothing to go upon; weave a rope of sand, build castles in the air, *prendre la lune avec les dents*, extract sunbeams from cucumbers, set the Thames on fire, milk a he-goat into a sieve, catch a weasel asleep, *rompre l'anguille au genou*, be in two places at once.

Adj. impossible; not -possible etc. 470; absurd, contrary to reason; unlikely, at variance with facts; unreasonable etc. 477; incredible etc. 485; beyond the bounds of -reason, − possibility; from which reason recoils; visionary; inconceivable etc. (*improbable*) 473; prodigious etc. (*wonderful*) 870; un-, in-imaginable, unthinkable, not a Chinaman's chance.

impracticable, unachievable; un-, in-feasible; insuperable; un-, in-surmountable; unat-, unobtainable; out of -reach, − the question; not to be -had, − thought of; beyond control; desperate etc. (*hopeless*) 859; incompatible etc. 24; inaccessible, uncomeatable, impassable, impervious, in-navigable, inextricable.

out of −, beyond- one's -power, − depth, − reach, − grasp; too much for; *ultra crepidam*.

Phr. the grapes are sour; *non possumus*; *non nostrum tantas componere lites.*

472. Probability.—**N.** probability, likelihood; likeliness etc. *adj.*

vraisemblance, verisimilitude, plausibility;

color, semblance, show of; presumption; presumptive –, circumstantial- evidence; credibility.

reasonable –; fair –, good –, favorable- -chance, – prospect; prospect, well-grounded hope; chance etc. 156.

V. be -probable etc. *adj.*; give –, lend- color to; point to; imply etc. (*evidence*) 467; bid fair etc. (*promise*) 511; stand fair for; stand –, run- a good chance.

presume, infer, suppose, take for granted.

think likely, dare say, flatter oneself; expect etc. 507; count upon etc. (*believe*) 484.

Adj. probable, likely, hopeful, to be expected, in a fair way.

plausible, specious, ostensible, colorable, *ben trovato*, well-founded, reasonable, credible, easy of belief, presumable, presumptive, apparent.

Adv. probably etc. *adj.*; belike; in all -probability, – likelihood; very –, most- likely; as likely as not; like enough; ten etc. to one; apparently, seemingly, according to every reasonable expectation; *primâ facie*; to all appearance etc. (*to the eye*) 448.

Phr. the -chances, – odds- are; appearances –chances- are in favor of; there is reason to -believe, – think, – expect; I dare say; all Lombard Street to a China orange.

473. Improbability.—N. improbability, unlikelihood; unfavorable –, bad –, little –, small –, poor –, scarcely any –, no –, not a ghost of a- chance; bare possibility; long odds; incredibility etc. 485.

V. be -improbable etc. *adj.*; have a -small chance etc. *n.*

Adj. improbable, unlikely, contrary to all reasonable expectation, implausible.

rare etc. (*infrequent*) 137; unheard of, inconceivable; un-, in-imaginable; incredible etc. 485; more than doubtful.

Int. not likely! no fear!

Phr. the chances are against.

474. Certainty.—N. certainty; necessity etc. 601; certitude, certainness, surety, assurance, sureness; dead –, moral- certainty; infallibleness etc. *adj.*; infallibility, reliability.

gospel, scripture, church, pope, court of final appeal; *res judicata, ultimatum*.

positiveness; dogmat-ism, -ist, -izer; *doctrinaire*, know-all, bigot, -ry; opinionist, Sir Oracle; *ipse dixit*; zealot.

fact; positive –, matter of- fact; *fait accompli*.

V. be -certain etc. *adj.*, stand to reason.

render -certain etc. *adj.*; in-, en-, as-sure; clinch, make sure; determine, decide, set at rest, 'make assurance double sure;' know etc. (*believe*) 484; dismiss all doubt.

dogmatize, lay down the law.

Adj. certain, sure; assured etc. *v.*; solid, well-founded.

unqualified, absolute, positive, determinate, definite, clear, unequivocal, categorical, unmistakable, decisive, decided, ascertained.

inevitable, unavoidable, ineluctable, avoidless.

unerring, infallible; unchangeable etc. 150; to be depended on, trustworthy, reliable, bound.

un-impeachable, -deniable, -questionable; indisputable, -contestable, -controvertible, - defeasible, -dubitable; irrefutable etc. (*proven*) 478; conclusive, without power of appeal, final.

indubious; without –, beyond a –, without a shade or shadow or- -doubt – question; past dispute; beyond all -question, – dispute; undoubted, -contested, -questioned, -disputed; question-, doubt-less.

bigoted, fanatical, dogmatic, opinionat-ed, -ive, *doctrinaire*.

authoritative, authentic; official

sure as -fate, – death and taxes, – a gun.

evident, self-evident, axiomatic; clear, – as day, – as the sun at noonday; obvious.

Adv. certainly etc. *adj.*; for certain, certes, sure, no doubt, doubtless, and no mistake, *flagrante delicto*, sure enough, to be sure, of course, as a matter of course, *à coup sur*, to a certainty, undoubtedly; in truth etc. (*truly*) 494; at -any rate, – all events; without fail; *coûte que coûte*; whatever may happen, if the worst come to the worst; come –, happen- what -may, – will; sink or swim; rain or shine.

Phr. *cela va sans dire*; there is -no question, – not a shadow of doubt; the die is cast etc (*necessity*) 601.

475. Uncertainty.—N. uncertainty, incertitude, doubt; doubtfulness etc *adj*; dubi-ety, tation, -tancy, -ousness.

hesitation, suspense; perplexity, embarrassment, dilemma, quandary, Morton's fork, bewilderment; timidity etc. (*fear*) 860; indecision, vacillation etc 605; *diaporesis*, indetermination.

vagueness etc. *adj.*; haze, fog; obscurity etc. (*darkness*) 421; ambiguity etc. (*double meaning*) 520; contingency, double contingency, possibility upon a possibility; conjecture; open question etc. (*question*) 461; *onus probandi*, blind bargain, pig in a poke, leap in the dark, something or other- needle in a bottle of hay; roving commission.

fallibility, unreliability untrustworthiness, precariousness.

V. be -uncertain etc. *adj*, wonder whether.

lose the -clue, – clew, – scent; miss one's way.

not know -what to make of etc. (*unintelligibility*) 519, – which way to turn, – whether one stands on one's head or one's heels; float in a sea of doubt, hesitate, flounder; lose -oneself, – one's head, – one's way, wander aimlessly; muddle one's brains.

render -uncertain etc. *adj.*; put out, pose, puzzle, perplex, embarrass; confuse, -found; bewilder, mystify, bother, nonplus, addle the wits, throw off the scent; *ambiguas in vulgus spargere voces*; keep in suspense.

doubt etc. (*disbelieve*) 485; hang –, tremble- in the balance; depend.

Adj. uncertain; casual; random etc. (*aimless*) 621; changeable etc. 149.

doubtful, dubious; indecisive; unsettled, -decided, -determined; in suspense, open to discussion; controvertible; in question etc. (*inquiry*) 461; insecure, unstable.

vague; in-determinate, -definite; ambiguous, equivocal; undefin-ed, -able; confused etc. (*indistinct*) 447; mystic, mysterious, veiled, obscure, cryptic, oracular.

perplexing etc. *v.*; enigmatic, paradoxical; apocryphal, problematical, hypothetical; experimental etc. 463.

fallible, questionable, precarious, slippery, ticklish, debatable, disputable; un-reliable, -trustworthy.

contingent, — on, dependent on; subject to; dependent on circumstances; occasional; provisional.

unauth-entic, -enticated, -oritative; un-ascertained, confirmed; undemonstrated; un-told, -counted.

in a -state of uncertainty, — cloud, — maze; ignorant etc. 491; on the horns of a dilemma; afraid to say; out of one's reckoning, astray, adrift; as -sea, — fault, — a loss, — one's wit's end, — a *nonplus*; puzzled etc. *v.*; lost abroad, *désorienté*; dis-tracted, -traught.

Adv. *pendente lite; sub spe rati.*

Phr. Heaven knows; who can tell? who shall decide when doctors disagree?

476. Reasoning.—N. reasoning; ratio-cination, -nalism; dialectics, induction, generalization.

discussion, comment, ventilation; inquiry etc. 461.

argumentation, controversy, debate; polemics, wrangling; contention etc. 720; logomachy; disputation, -ceptation; paper war.

art of reasoning, logic.

process —, train —, chain- of reasoning; de-, induction; systhesis, analysis.

argument; case, plea, *plaidoyer*, opening; *lemma*, proposition, terms, premises, postulate, *data*, starting point, principle; inference etc. (*judgment*) 480.

pro-, syllogism; enthymeme, sorites, dilemma, *perilepsis, a priori* reasoning, *reductio ad absurdum*, horns of a dilemma, *argumentum ad hominem*, comprehensive argument.

reasoner, logician, dialectician; disputant; controver-sialist, -tist; wrangler, arguer, debater, polemic, casuist, rationalist; scientist.

logical sequence; good case; correct —, just —, sound —, valid —, cogent —, logical —, forcible —, persuasive —, persuasory —, consectary —, conclusive etc. 478 —, subtle- reasoning; force of argument; strong -point, — argument.

arguments, reasons, pros and cons.

V. reason, argue, discuss, debate, dispute, wrangle; bandy -words, — arguments; chop logic; hold —, carry on- an argument; controvert etc. (*deny*) 536; canvass; comment —, moralize-upon; consider etc. (*examine*) 461.

open a -discussion, — case: join —, be at- issue; moot; come to the point; stir —, agitate —, ventilate —, torture- a question; try conclusions; take up a -side, — case.

contend, take one's stand upon, insist, lay stress on; infer etc. 480.

follow from etc. (*demonstration*) 478.

Adj. rational; reasoning etc. *v.*; rationalistic; argumentative, controversial, dialectic, polemical; discurs-ory, -ive; disputations.

debatable, controvertible.

logical; in-, de-ductive; synthetic, analytic; relevant etc. 23.

Adv. for, because, hence, whence, seeing that, since, sith, then, thence, so; for -that, — this, — which- reason; for-, inasmuch as; whereas, *ex concesso*, considering, in consideration of; there-, where-fore; consequently, *ergo*, thus, accordingly; *a fortiori*.

in -conclusion, — fine; finally, after all, *au bout du compte*, on the whole, taking one thing with another.

rationally etc. *adj.*

477. Sophistry. [The absence of reasoning.] **Intuition.** [False or vicious reasoning; show of reason.]—N. intuition, instinct, association; presentiment; rule of thumb.

sophistry, paralogy, perversion, casuistry, jesuitry, equivocation, evasion, mental reservation; chicane, -ry; quiddit, quiddity; mystification; special pleading; speciousness etc. *adj.*; nonsense etc. 497; word-, tongue-fence.

false —, vicious- reasoning; *petitio principii, ignoratio elenchi; post hoc ergo propter hoc; non sequitur, ignotum per ignotius.*

misjudgment etc. 481; false teaching etc. 538.

sophism, solecism, paralogism; quibble, quirk, *elenchus*, elench, fallacy, *quodlibet*, subterfuge, subtlety, quillet; inconsistency, antilogy; 'a mockery, a delusion and a snare;' claptrap, mere words; 'lame and impotent conclusion.'

meshes —, cobwebs- of sophistry; flaw in an argument; weak point, bad case.

over-refinement; hair-splitting etc. *v.*

sophist, casuist, paralogist.

V. judge -intuitively. — by intuition; hazard a proposition, talk at random.

reason -ill, — falsely etc. *adj.*; paralogize; misjudge etc. 481.

pervert, quibble; equivocate, mystify, evade, elude; gloss over, varnish; misteach etc. 538; mislead etc. (*error*) 495; cavil, refine, subtilize, split hairs; misrepresent etc. (*lie*) 544.

beg the question, reason in a circle, cut blocks with a razor, beat about the bush, play fast and loose, blow hot and cold, prove that black is white and white black, travel out of the record, *parler à tort et à travers*, put oneself out of court, not have a leg to stand on.

Adj. intuitive, instinctive, impulsive; independent of —, anterior to- reason; gratuitous; hazarded; unconnected.

unreasonable, illogical, false, unsound, invalid; unwarranted, not following; inconsequent, -ial; inconsistent, incongruous, abson-ous, -ant; unscientific; untenable, inconclusive, incorrect; fall-acious, -ible; groundless, unproved.

deceptive, sophistical, sophisticated, casuistical, jesuitical; illus-ive, -ory; specious, hollow, plausible, *ad captandum*, evasive; irrelevant etc. 10.

weak, feeble, poor, flimsy, loose, vague, irrational; nonsensical etc. (*absurd*) 497; foolish etc. (*imbecile*) 499; frivolous, pettifogging, quibbling; finespun, over-refined.

at the end of one's tether, *au bout de son latin.*

Adv. intuitively etc. *adj.*; by intuition; illogically etc. *adj.*

Phr. *non constat*; that goes for nothing.

478. Demonstration.—N. demonstration, proof; conclusiveness etc *adj.*; *apodixis*, probation, comprobation.

logic of facts etc. (*evidence*) 467; *experimentum curcis* etc. (*test*) 463; argument etc. 476; irrefragability.

V. demonstrate, prove, establish, make good; show; evince etc. (*be evidence of*) 467; verify etc. 467; settle the question, reduce to demonstration, set the question at rest.

make out, — a case; prove one's point, have the best of the argument; draw a conclusion etc. (*judge*) 480.

follow, — of course; stand to reason; hold -good, — water.

Adj. demonstra-ting etc. *v.*, -tive, -ble; probative, unanswerable, conclusive; apodictic, -al; irre-sistible, -futable, -fragable, undeniable.

categorical, decisive, crucial.

demonstrated etc. *v.*; proven; unconfuted, -answered, -refuted; evident etc. 474.

deducible, consequential, consectary, inferential, following.

Adv. of course, in consequence, consequently, as a matter of course.

Phr. *probatum est*; there is nothing more to be said, Q.E.D., it must follow.

479. Confutation.—N. con-, re-futation; answer, complete answer; disproof, conviction, redargution, invalidation; expos-ure, -ition; clincher; retort; *reductio ad absurdum*; knock down —, *tu quoque*- argument.

V. con-, re-fute; parry, negative, disprove, redargue, expose, show the fallacy of, rebut, defeat; demolish etc. (*destroy*) 162; over-throw, -turn; scatter to the winds, explode, invalidate; silence; put —, reduce- to silence; clinch -an argument, — a question; give one a set down, stop the mouth, shut up; have, — on the hip; get the better of; confound, convince.

not leave a leg to stand on, cut the ground from under one's feet.

be confuted etc.; fail; expose —, show- one's weak point.

Adj. confut-ing, -ed etc. *v.*; capable of refutation; re-, con-futable.

condemned -on one's own showing, — out of one's own mouth.

Phr.the argument falls to the ground, *cadit quaestio*, it does not hold water, '*suo sibi gladio hunc jugulo*.'

480. Judgment. [Conclusion.]—N. result, conclusion, upshot; deduction, inference, ergotism; illation; corollary, porism; moral.

estimation, valuation, appreciation, judication; di-, ad-judication; arbitr- ament, -ement, -ation; assessment, ponderation.

award, estimate; review, criticism, *critique*, notice, report.

decision, determination, judgment, finding, verdict, sentence, decree, — nisi, — absolute, — interlocutory; dictum; *res judicata*.

plébiscite, referendum, voice, casting vote; vote etc. (*choice*) 609; opinion etc. (*belief*) 484; good judgment etc. (*wisdom*) 498.

judge, jurist, umpire; arbi-ter, -trator; assessor, referee; censor, reviewer, critic; *connoisseur*; commentator etc. 524; inspector, inspecting officer.

V. judge, conclude; come to —, draw —, arrive at- a conclusion; ascertain, determine, make up one's mind.

deduce, derive, gather, collect, draw an inference, make a deduction, weet, ween.

form an estimate, estimate, size up, appreciate, value, count, assess, rate, rank, account; regard, consider, think of; look upon etc. (*believe*) 484.

settle; pass —, give- an opinion; decide, try, pronounce, rule; pass -judgment, — sentence; sentence, doom; find; give —, deliver- judgment; adjud-ge, -icate; arbitrate, award, report; bring in a verdict; make absolute, set a question ar rest; confirm etc. (*assent*) 488.

comment, criticize; review, pass under review etc (*examine*) 457; investigate etc. (*inquire*) 461.

hold the scales, sit in judgment; try —, hear- a cause.

Adj. judging etc. *v.*; judicious etc. (*wise*) 498; determinate, conclusive, censorious, critical etc. 932.

Adv. on the whole, all things considered.

480a. Discovery. [Result of search or inquiry.]—N. discovery, invention, detection, disenchantment, disclosure, find, ascertainment, revelation.

trover etc. 775.

V. discover, find, determine, evolve; fix upon; find —, trace —, make —, hunt —, fish —, worm —, ferret —, root-out; fathom; bring —, drawout; educe, elicit, bring to light, invent; dig —, grub —, fish- up; unearth, disinter.

solve, resolve; un-riddle, -ravel, -lock; pick —, open- the lock; find a -clue, — clew- to; interpret etc. 522; disclose etc. 529.

trace, get at; hit it, have it; lay one's -finger, — hands- upon; spot; get —, arrive- at the -turth etc. 494; put the saddle on the right horse, hit the right nail on the head.

be near the truth, burn; smoke, scent, sniff, smell a rat.

open the eyes to; see -through, — daylight, — in its true colors, — the cloven foot; detect; catch, — tripping.

pitch —, fall —, light —, hit —, stumble —, pop- upon; come across; meet —, fall in- with.

recognize, realize, verify, make certain of, identify.

Int. *eureka!*

481. Misjudgment.—N. misjudgment, obliquity of —, warped- judgment; mis-calculation, -computation, -conception etc. (*error*) 495; hasty conclusion.

prejud-gment, -ication, -ice; foregone conclusion; pre-notion, -vention, -conception, -
dilection, -possession, -apprehension, -sumption, -
sentiment; fixed –, preconceived- idea; *idée fixe*;
mentis gratissimus error; fool's paradise.

esprit de corps, party spirit, race –, class-
prejudice, partisanship, clannishness, *prestige*.

bias, warp, twist; hobby, fad, whim, craze, quirk,
crotchet, partiality, infatuation, blind side, mote in
the eye.

one-sided –, partial –, narrow –, confined –,
superficial- views, – ideas,– conceptions, –
notions; narrow mind; bigotry etc. (*obstinacy*)
606; *odium theologicum*; pedantry; hypercriticism.
doctrinaire etc. (*positive*) 474.

V. mis-judge, -estimate, -think, -conjecture, -
conceive etc. (*error*) 495; fly in the face of facts;
mis-calculate, -reckon, -compute.

overestimate etc. 482; underestimate etc. 483.

pre-, fore-judge; pre-suppose, -sume, -judicate;
dogmatize; have a -bias etc. *n.*; have only one idea;
jurare in verba magistri, run away with the notion;
jump –, rush- to a conclusion; look only at one
side of the shield; view -with jaundiced eye, –
through distorting spectacles; not see beyond one's
nose; *dare pondus fumo*; get the wrong sow by the
ear etc. (*blunder*) 699.

give a -bias, – twist; bias, warp, twist; prejudice, -possess.

Adj. misjudging etc. *v.*; ill-judging, wrong-
headed; prejudiced, prejudicial, etc. *v.*; jaundiced;
short-sighted, pur-blind; partial, one-sided, superficial.

narrow-minded; confined, insular, provincial,
parochial, illiberal, intolerant, narrow, besotted,
infatuated, fanatical, cracked, warped, *entêté*,
positive, dogmatic, dictatorial; conceited; opin-,
opini-ative; opinion-ed, -ate, -ative, -ated; self-
opinioned, wedded to an opinion, *opinâtre*;
bigoted, etc. (*obstinate*) 606; crotchety, fussy, impracticable; unreason-able, -ing; stupid etc. 499;
credulous etc. 486.

misjudged etc. *v.*

Adv. *ex parte*.

Phr. nothing like leather; the wish the father to
the thought.

482. Overestimation.—**N.** overestimation etc.
v.; exaggeration etc. 549; vanity etc. 880; optim-,
pessim-ism, -ist; megalomania.

much -cry and little wool, – ado about nothing;
storm in a teacup; fine talking, rodomontade, gush,
hot air, gas, bombast.

egotism etc. 880; boasting etc. 884.

V. over-estimate, -rate, -value, -prize, -weigh, -
reckon, -strain, -praise; estimate too highly, attach
too much importance to, make mountains of
molehills, catch at straws; strain, magnify;
exaggerate etc. 549; set too high a value upon;
think –, make- -much, – too much- of;
outreckon.

extol, – to the skies; make the -most, – best, –
worst- of, eulogize, panegyrize, gush, puff, boost;
make two bites of a cherry.

have too high an opinion of oneself etc. (*vanity*) -
880.

Adj. overestimated etc. *v.*; oversensitive etc.

(*sensibility*) 822; inflated, puffed up, exaggerated
etc. 549.

Phr. all his geese are swans; *parturiunt montes*.

483. Underestimation.—**N.** underestimation;
depreciation etc. (*detraction*) 934; pessim-ism, -ist;
undervaluing etc. *v.*; modesty etc. 881.

V. under-rate, -estimate, -value, -reckon;
depreciate; disparage etc. (*detract*) 934; not do
justice to; mis-, dis-prize; ridicule etc. 856; slight
etc. (*despise*) 930; neglect etc. 460; slur over, un-
der-state.

make -light, – little, – nothing, – no account-
of; minimize, belittle, run down, think nothing of;
set -no store by, – at naught; shake off as
dewdrops from the lion's mane.

Adj. depreciat-ing, -ed, -ive, -ory, etc. *v.*; un-
appreciated, -valued, -prized; pejorative.

484. Belief.—**N.** belief; credence; credit;
assurance; faith, trust, troth, confidence, presumption, sanguine expectation etc. (*hope*) 858; depen-
dence on, reliance on.

persuasion, conviction, convincement,
plerophory, self-conviction; certainty etc. 474;
opinion, mind, view; conception, thinking; impression etc. (*idea*) 453; surmise etc. 514; conclusion etc. (*judgment*) 480.

tenet, dogma, principle, way of thinking;
popular belief etc. (*assent*) 488.

firm –, implicit –, settled –, fixed –, rooted
–, deep-rooted –, staunch –, unshaken –,
steadfast –, inveterate –, calm –, sober –,
dispassionate –, impartial –, well-founded- -
belief, – opinion etc.; *uberrima fides*.

system of opinions, school, doctrine, articles,
canons; declaration –, profession- of faith; tenets,
credenda, creed; thirty-nine articles etc. (*orthodoxy*) 983a; catechism; assent etc. 488;
propaganda etc. (*teaching*) 537.

credibility etc. (*probability*) 472.

V. believe, credit; give -faith, – credit, –
credence- to; see, realize; assume, receive; set down
–, take- for; have –, take- it; consider, esteem,
presume.

count –, depend –, calculate –, pin one's faith
–, reckon –, lean –, build –, rely –, rest-
upon; lay one's account for; make sure of.

make oneself easy -about, – on that score; take
on -trust, – credit; take for -granted, –; gospel;
allow –, attach- some weight to.

know, – for certain; have –, make- no doubt;
doubt not; be – rest- -assured etc. *adj.*; persuade
–, assure –, satisfy- oneself; make up one's mind.

give one credit for; confide –, believe –, put
one's trust- in; place –, repose- implicit confidence
in; take -one's word for, – at one's word; place
reliance on, rely upon, swear by, regard to.

think, hold; take, – it; opine, be of -opinion,
conceive, trow, ween, fancy, apprehend; have –,
hold –, possess –, entertain –, adopt –, imbibe
–, embrace –, get hold of –, hazard –, foster
–, nurture –, cherish- -a belief, – an opinion etc.
n.

view –, consider –, take –, hold –, conceive
–, regard –, esteem –, deem –, look upon –,
account –, set down- as; surmise etc. 514.

get —, take- it into one's head; come round to an opinion; swallow etc. (*credulity*) 486.

cause to -be believed etc. *v.*; satisfy, persuade, have the ear of, gain the confidence of, assure; convince, -vict, -vert; put across, sell; wean, bring round; bring —, put —, win- over; indoctrinate etc. (*teach*) 537; cram down the throat; produce —, carry- conviction; bring —, drive- home to.

go down, find credence, pass current; be - received etc. *v.*, — current etc. *adj.*; possess —, take hold of —, take possession of- the mind.

Adj. believing etc. *v.*; certain, sure, assured, positive, cocksure, satisfied, confident, unhesitating, convinced, secure.

under the impression; impressed —, imbued —, penetrated- with.

confiding, trustful, suspectless; unsusp-ecting, - icious; void of suspicion; credulous etc. 486; wedded to.

believed etc. *v.*; accredited, putative, unsuspected.

worthy of —, deserving of —, commanding- - belief, — confidence; credible, reliable, trusted, trustworthy, to be depended on, undoubted; satisfactory; probable etc. 472; fiduci-al, -ary; persuasive, impressive.

relating to belief, doctrinal.

Adv. in the -opinion, — eyes- of; *me judice*; me-seems, -thinks; to the best of one's belief; I - dare say, — doubt not, — have no doubt, — am sure; in my opinion; sure enough etc. (*certainty*) 474; depend —, rely- upon it; be —, rest- assured; I'll warrant you etc. (*affirmation*) 535.

485. Unbelief. Doubt.—N. un-, dis-, misbelief; discredit, miscreance; infidelity etc. (*irreligion*) 989; dissent etc. 489; change of -opinion etc. 484; retraction etc.´ 607.

doubt etc. (*uncertainty*) 475; skepticism, mis̓giving, demur; dis-, mis-trust; misdoubt, suspicion, jealousy, scruple, qualm; *onus probandi*.

incredib-ility, -leness; incredulity; unbeliever etc. 487.

V. dis-believe, -credit; not -believe etc. 484; misbelieve; refuse to admit etc. (*dissent*) 489; refuse to believe etc. (*incredulity*) 487.

doubt; be -doubtful etc. (*uncertain*) 475; doubt the truth of; be -skeptical as to etc. *adj.*; diffide; dis-, mis-trust; suspect, smoke, scent, smell a rat; have —, harbor —, entertain- -doubts, — suspicions; have one's doubts.

demur, stick at, pause, hesitate, scruple, waver, stop and consider.

hang in -suspense, — doubt.

throw doubt upon, raise a question; bring —, call- in question; question, challenge, query; dispute; deny etc. 536; cavil; cause —, raise —, start —, suggest —, awake- a -doubt, — suspicion; ergotize.

startle, stagger; shake —, stagger- one's faith, — belief.

Adj. unbelieving; incredulous —, skeptical- as to; distrustful —, shy —, suspicious- of; doubting etc. *v.*

doubtful etc. (*uncertain*) 475; disputable; unworthy —, undeserving- of -belief etc. 484; questionable; sus-pect, -picious; open to -suspicion,

— doubt; staggering, hard to believe, incredible, not to be believed, inconceivable.

fallible etc. (*uncertain*) 475; undemonstrable; controvertible etc. (*untrue*) 495.

Adv. *cum grano salis.*

Phr. *fronti nulla fides; nimium ne crede colori;* *'timeo Danaos et dona ferentes;' credat Judaeus Apella*; let those believe who may.

486. Credulity.—N. credul-ity, -ousness etc. *adj.*; gull-, cull-ibility; gross credulity, infatuation; self-delusion, -deception; blind reasoning; superstition; one's blind side; bigotry etc. (*obstinacy*) 606; hyper-orthodoxy etc. 984; misjudgment etc. 481.

credulous person etc. (*dupe*) 547.

V. be -credulous etc. *adj.*; *jurare in verba magistri;* follow implicitly; swallow, — whole, gulp down; take on trust; take for -granted, — gospel; run away with -a notion, — an idea; jump —, rush- to a conclusion; think the moon is made of green cheese; take —, grasp- the shadow for the substance; catch at straws.

impose upon etc. (*deceive*) 545.

Adj. credulous, gullible; easily -deceived etc. 545; simple, green, soft, childish, silly, stupid; over-credulous, -confident; infatuated, superstitious; confiding etc. (*believing*) 484.

Phr. the wish the father to the thought; *credo quia impossibile.*

487. Incredulity.—N. incredul-ous-ness, -ity; skepticism, pyrrhonism; want of faith etc. (*irreligion*) 989.

suspiciousness etc. *adj.*; scrupulosity; suspicion etc. (*unbelief*) 485; dissent etc. 489.

unbeliever, skeptic, aporetic; atheist, agnostic, infidel, disbeliever, misbeliever, pyrrhonist etc. 989; heretic etc. (*heterodox*) 984.

v. be -incredulous etc. *adj.*; distrust etc. (*disbelieve*) 485; refuse to believe; shut one's -eyes, — ears- to; turn a deaf ear to; hold aloof; ignore; *nullis jurare in verba magistri.*

Adj. incredulous, skeptical, unbelieving, inconvincible; hard —, shy- of belief; suspicious, scrupulous, distrustful, heterodox etc. 984.

488. Assent.—N. assent, -ment; acquiescence, admission; nod; ac-, con-cord, -cordance; agreement etc. 23; affirm-ance, -ation; recognition, acknowledgment, avowal; confession, — of faith.

unanimity, common consent, *consensus*, acclamation, chorus, *vox populi*; popular —, current- -belief, — opinion; public opinion; concurrence etc. (*of causes*) 178; co-operation etc. (*voluntary*) 709.

ratification, confirmation, corroboration, approval, acceptance, *visa*; indorsement etc. (*record*) 551.

consent etc. (*compliance*) 762.

affirmant, consenter, covenantor, subscriber, endorser, upholder.

V. assent; give —, yield —, not- assent; acquiesce; agree etc. 23; receive, accept, accede, accord, concur, lend oneself to, consent, coincide, reciprocate, go with; be -at one with etc. *adj.*; go along −, chime in −, strike in −, close- with; echo, enter into one's views, agree in opinion; vote −, give one's voice- for; recognize; subscribe −, conform −, 'defer- to;' say -yes, − ditto, − amen; − aye- to.

acknowledge, own, admit, allow, avow, confess; concede etc. (*yield*) 762; come round to; abide by; permit etc. 760.

come to − , arrive at- -an understanding, − terms, − an agreement.

con−, af-firm; ratify, approve, endorse, countersign; visa; corroborate etc. 467.

go −, swim- with the stream, float with the current; be in the fashion, join in the chorus; be in every mouth.

Adj. assenting etc. *v.*; of one -accord, − mind; of the same mind, at one with, agreed, acquiescent, content; willing etc. 602.

un-contradicted, -challenged, -questioned, - controverted.

carried −, agreed- *-nem. con.* etc. *adv.*; unanimous; agreed on all hands, carried by acclamation.

affirmative etc. 535.

Adv. yes, yea, ay, aye, true; good; well; very - well, − true; well and good; granted; *placet*; even −, just- 'so; to be sure, surely, 'thou hast said;' truly, exactly, precisely, that's just it, indeed, certainly, certes, *ex concesso*; of course, unquestionably, assuredly, no doubt, doubtless, undoubtedly.

be it so; so -be it, − let it be, so mote it be; amen; with all my heart; willingly etc. 602.

with one -consent, − voice, − accord; unanimously, *una voce*, by common consent, in chorus, to a man, *nem. con.*; *nemine contradicente*, − *dissentiente*; without a dissentient voice; as one man, one and all, on all hands.

---

489. Dissent.—N. dissent; discordance etc. (*disagreement*) 24; difference −, diversity- of opinion.

non-conformity etc. (*heterodoxy*) 984; protestantism, recusancy, schism; disaffection; secession etc. 624; recantation etc. 607.

dissension etc. (*discord*) 713; discontent etc. 832; cavilling.

protest; contradiction etc. (*denial*) 536; noncompliance etc. (*rejection*) 764; disapprobation etc. 932; hartal.

dissent-ient, -er; non-juror, -content; recusant, sectary, schismatic, protestant, non-conformist, separatist, non-co-operator, conscientious objector, passive resister.

V. dissent, demur; call in question etc. (*doubt*) 485; differ in opinion, disagree; say -no etc. 536; refuse -assent, − to admit; cavil, protest, raise one's voice against, make bold to differ; repudiate; contradict etc. (*deny*) 536; agree to differ.

have no notion of, differ *toto caelo*; revolt -at, − from the idea.

shake the head, shrug the shoulders; look - askance, − askant.

secede; recant etc. 607.

Adj. dissenting etc. *v.*; negative etc. 536; dissident, -entient; unconsenting etc. (*refusing*) 764;

non-content, -juring; protestant, recusant; unconvinced, -verted.

unavowed, unacknowledged; out of the question.

discontented etc. 832; unwilling etc. 603; extorted.

sectarian, denominational, schismatic, heterodox, intolerant.

Adv. no etc. 536; at -variance, − issue- with; under protest; *non placet*.

Int. God forbid! not for the world; not on your life; I beg to differ; I'll be hanged if; never tell me; your humble servant, pardon me; tell that to the marines.

Phr. many men many minds; *quot homines tot sententiae; tant s'en faut; il s'en faut bien.*

---

490. Knowledge.—N. knowledge; cogn-izance, -ition, -oscence; acquaintance, experience, ken, privity, insight, familiarity; com−, ap-prehension; recognition; appreciation etc. (*judgment*) 480; intuition; consci-ence, -ousness; preception, precognition; acroamatics.

light, enlightenment; glimpse, inkling; side light; glimmer, -ing; dawn; scent, suspicion; impression etc. (*idea*) 453; discovery etc. 480a.

system −, body- of knowledge; science, philosophy, pansophy; theory, Etiology; circle of the sciences; pandect, doctrine, body of doctrine; cy-, ency-clopedia; school etc. (*system of opinions*) 484.

tree of knowledge; republic of letters etc. (*language*) 560.

erudition, learning, lore, scholarship, reading, letters; literature; booklearning, bookishness; biblio-mania, -latry; information, general information; store of -knowledge etc.; education etc. (*teaching*) 537; culture, attainments; acquirements, -sitions; accomplishments, proficiency; practical knowledge etc. (*skill*) 698; higher education, liberal education; dilettantism; rudiments etc. (*beginning*) 66.

deep −, profound −, solid −, accurate −, acroatic −, acroamatic −, vast −, extensive −, encyclopedical- -knowledge, − learning; omniscience, pantology.

march of intellect; progress −, advance- of - science, − learning; schoolmaster abroad.

V. know, ken, scan, wot; wot −, be aware etc. *adj.*- of; ween, weet, trow, have, possess.

conceive; ap-, com-prehend; take, realize, understand, appreciate; fathom, make out; recognize, discern, perceive, see, get a sight of, experience.

know full well; have −, possess- some knowledge of; be *-au courant* etc. *adj.*; have -in one's head, − at one's fingers' ends; know by -heart, − rote; be master of; *connaître le dessous des cartes*, know what's what etc. 698.

see one's way; learn, discover etc. 480a.

come to one's knowledge etc. (*information*) 527.

Adj. knowing etc. *v.*; cognitive; acroamatic.

aware −, cognizant −, conscious- of; acquainted −, made acquainted- with; privy −, no stranger- to; *au -fait*, − *courant*; in the secret; up −, alive- to; sensible of; behind the -scenes, − curtain; let into; apprized −, informed- of; undeceived.

proficient −, versed −, read −, forward −,

strong –, at home- in; conversant –, familiar-
with.

erudite, instructed, learned, lettered, educated;
high-brow; well-conned, -informed, -read, -
grounded, -educated; enlightened, shrewd, in-
sightful, *savant*, blue, bookish, scholastic, solid,
profound, deep-read, book-learned; accomplished
etc. (*skilful*) 698; omniscient; self-taught, -
educated. .

known etc. *v.*; ascertained, well-known,
recognized, received, notorious, noted; proverbial;
familiar, – as household words, to every
schoolboy; hackneyed, trite, commonplace.

knowable, cogn-oscible, -izable.

Adv. to –, to the best of- one's knowledge.

Phr. one's eyes being opened etc. (*disclosure*)
529.

491. Ignorance.—N. ignorance, nescience,
tabula rasa, crass ignorance, *ignorance crasse*;
unacquaintance; unconsciousness etc. *adj.*; dark-,
blind-ness; incomprehension, inexperience, simplicity.

unknown quantities, *x*, *y*, *z*.

sealed book, *terra incognita*, virgin soil, unexplored ground; dark ages.

[Imperfect knowledge] smattering, super-
ficiality, half-learning, sciolism, glimmering;
bewilderment etc. (*uncertainty*) 475; incapacity.

[Affectation of knowledge] pedantry; charlatan-
ry, -ism.

V. be -ignorant etc. *adj.*; not -know etc. 490;
know -not, – not what, – nothing of; have no -
idea, – notion, – conception; not have the
remotest idea; not know chalk from cheese.

ignore, be blind to; keep in ignorance etc. (*conceal*) 528.

see through a glass darkly; have a -film over the
eyes, – glimmering etc. *n.*; wonder whether; not
know what to make of etc. (*unintelligibility*) 519;
not pretend –, not take upon oneself- to say.

Adj. ignorant, nescient; un-knowing, -aware, -
acquainted, -apprized, -witting, -weeting, -
conscious; wit-, weet-less; a stranger to; unconversant.

un-informed, -cultivated, -versed, -instructed, -
taught, -initiated, -tutored, -schooled, -guided, -
enlightened; Philistine; behind the age.

shallow, superficial, green, rude, empty, half-
learned, illiterate; un-read, -informed, -educated, -
learned, -lettered, -bookish; empty-headed;
lowbrow; pedantic.

in the dark; be-nighted, -lated; blind-ed, -fold;
hoodwinked; misinformed; *au bout de son latin*, at
the end of his tether; at fault; at sea etc. (*uncertain*)
475; caught tripping.

un-known, -apprehended, -explained,
ascertained, -investigated, -explored, -heard of, -
perceived; concealed etc. 528; novel.

Adv. ignorantly etc. *adj.*; unawares; for -
anything, – aught- one knows; not that one knows.

Int. God –, Heaven –, the Lord –, nobody-
knows.

Phr. a little learning is a dangerous thing.

492. Scholar.—N. scholar, *connoisseur*,
savant, pundit, schoolman, professor, graduate,
wrangler, moonshee; academ-ician, -ist; fellow,
don, post graduate, advanced student; master –,
bachelor- of arts; doctor, licentiate, gownsman;
philo-sopher, -math; scientist, clerk; soph, -ist, -
ister; linguist, classicist; glosso-, etymo-, philologist;
philologer; lexico-, glosso-grapher; scholiast, commentator, annotator, grammarian; *littérateur*,
literati, *dilettanti*, *illuminati*; Mezzofanti, admirable Crichton, Maecenas.

book-worm, *helluo librorum*, biblio-phile, -
maniac; blue-stocking, *bas-bleu*; big-wig, learned
Theban.

learned –, literary- man; *homo multarum
literarum*; man of -learning, – letters, –
education; high-brow, intelligentsia.

antiquar-ian, -y; archeologist; sage etc. (*wise
man*) 500.

pendant, *doctrinaire*; pedagogue, Dr. Pangloss;
pantologist.

teacher etc. 540; schoolboy etc. (*learner*) 541.

Adj. learned etc. 490; brought up at the feet of
Gamaliel.

493. Ignoramus.—N. ignoramus, illiterate,
moron, dunce, numskull; wooden spoon; no -
scholar.

sciolist, smatterer, dabbler, half-scholar;
charlatan; wiseacre.

novice, griffin; greenhorn etc. (*dupe*) 547; tyro
etc. (*learner*) 541.

lubber etc. (*bungler*) 701; fool etc. 501; pedant
etc. 492.

Adj. bookless, shallow, simple, dense, dumb,
thick, dull, ignorant etc. 491.

494. Truth. [Object of knowledge.]—N. fact,
reality etc. (*existence*) 1; plain matter of fact;
nature etc. (*principle*) 5; truth, verity; gospel; orthodoxy etc. 983a; authenticity; veracity etc. 543.

accuracy, exactitude; exact-, precise-ness etc.
adj.; precision, delicacy; rigor, mathematical
precision, punctuality; clockwork precision etc.
(*regularity*) 80.

orthology; *ipsissima verba*; letter of the law,
realism.

plain –, honest –, sober –, naked –,
unalloyed –, unqualified –, stern –, exact –, in-
trinsic- truth; *nuda veritas*; the very thing; not an -
illusion etc. 495; real Simon Pure; unvarnished
tale; the truth, the whole truth and nothing but the
truth; just the thing.

V. be -true etc. *adj.*, – the case; stand the test;
have the true ring; hold -good, – true, – water;
conform to- rule.

render –, prove- -true etc. *adj.*; substantiate etc.
(*evidence*) 467.

get at the truth etc. (*discover*) 480a.

Adj. real, actual etc. (*existing*) 1; veritable, true;
certain etc. 474; substantially –, categorically-
true etc; true -to the letter; – to life, – to scale, –
the facts, – as gospel; unimpeachable; veracious
etc. 543; unre-, uncon-futed; un-ideal -imagined;
realistic.

exact, accurate, definite, precise, well defined,
just, right, correct, strict, severe; close etc. (*similar*)
17; literal; rigid, rigorous; scrupulous etc. (*con-

scientious) 939; religiously exact, punctual, mathematical, scientific; faithful, constant, unerring; curious, particular, punctilious, meticulous, nice, delicate, fine.

genuine, authentic, legitimate, pukka: orthodox etc. 983a; official, *ex officio*.

pure, natural, sound, sterling; un-sophisticated, -adulterated, -varnished, -colored; in its true colors.

well-grounded, -founded; solid, substantial, tangible, valid; undis-torted, -guised; un-affected, -exaggerated, -romantic, -flattering.

Adv. truly etc.*adj.*; verily, indeed, in reality; as a matter of fact; beyond -doubt, − question; with truth etc. (*veracity*) 543; certainly etc. (*certain*) 474; actually etc. (*existence*) 1; in effect etc. (*intrinsically*) 5.

exactly etc. *adj.* ; *ad amussim*; *verbatim*, − *et literatim*; word for word, literally, *literatim*, *totidem verbis*, *sic*, to the letter, chapter and verse, *ipsissimis verbis*; *ad unguem*; to an inch; to a -nicety, − hair, − tittle, − turn, − T; *au pied de la lettre*; neither more nor less; in -every respect, − all respects; *sous tous les rapports*; at -any rate, − all events; strictly speaking.

Phr. the -truth, − fact- is; *rem acu tetigisti*.

495. Error.—**N.** error, fallacy; misconception, -apprehension, -understanding; inexactness etc. *adj.*; laxity; misconstruction etc. (*misinterpretation*) 523; miscomputation etc. (*misjudgment*) 481; *non-sequitur* etc. 477; misstatement, -report; anachronism; malapropism.

mistake; miss, fault, blunder, boner, bloomer, howler, *quid pro quo*, cross purposes, oversight, misprint, *erratum*, *corrigendum*, slip, blot, flaw, loose thread; trip, stumble etc. (*failure*) 732; botchery etc. (*want of skill*) 699; slip of the -tongue, − pen; *lapsus -linguae*, − *calami*, clerical error; bull etc. (*absurdity*) 497.

il-, de-lusion; false -impression, − idea; bubble; self-deceit, -deception; warped notion; mists of error; superstition, exploded notion.

heresy etc. (*heterodoxy*) 984; hallucination etc. (*insanity*) 503; false light etc. (*fallacy of vision*) 443; dream etc. (*fancy*) 515; fable etc. (*untruth*) 546; bias etc. (*misjudgment*) 481; misleading etc. *v.*

V. be -erroneous etc. *adj.*

cause error; mis-lead, -guide; lead -astray, − into error; beguile, misinform etc. (*misteach*) 538; delude; give a false -impression, − idea; falsify, garble, misstate; deceive etc. 545; lie etc. 544.

err; be -in error etc. *adj.*; − mistaken etc. *v.*; be deceived etc. (*duped*) 547; mistake, receive a false impression, deceive oneself; fall into −, lie under −, labor under- -an error etc. *n.*; be in the wrong, blunder; mis-apprehend, -conceive, -understand, -reckon, -count, -calculate etc. (*misjudge*) 481.

play −, be- at cross purposes etc. (*misinterpret*) 523.

trip, stumble; lose oneself etc. (*uncertainty*) 475; go astray; fail etc. 732; take the wrong sow by the ear etc. (*mismanage*) 699; put the saddle on the wrong horse; reckon without one's host; take the shadow for the substance etc. (*credulity*) 486; dream etc. (*imagine*) 515.

Adj. erroneous, untrue, false, devoid of truth, fallacious, faulty, apocryphal, unreal, ungrounded,

groundless; unsubstantial etc. 4; heretical etc. (*heterodox*) 984; unsound; illogical etc. 477; wrong.

in-, un-exact; in-accurate, -correct; indefinite etc. (*uncertain*) 475.

illus-ive, -ory; delusive; mock; ideal etc. (*imaginary*) 515; spurious etc. 545; deceitful etc. 544; perverted.

controvertible, unsustain-able, -ed; unauthenticated, untrustworthy.

exploded, refuted, discarded.

in −, under an- error etc. *n.*; mistaken etc. *v.*; tripping etc. *v.*; out, − in one's reckoning; aberrant; beside −, wide of the- -mark, − truth; astray etc. (*at fault*) 475; on -a false, − the wrong- scent; in the wrong box; at cross purposes, all in the wrong, all abroad, at sea.

Adv. more or less.

496. Maxim.—**N.** maxim, aphorism; apo-, apoph-thegm; *dictum*, saying, gnome, adage, saw, proverb, epigram; sentence, *mot*, motto, word, by-word, precept, moral, phylactery, *protasis*, brocard.

axiom, postulate, theorem, *scholium*, truism.

reflection etc. (*idea*) 453; conclusion etc. (*judgment*) 480; golden rule etc. (*precept*) 697; principle, *principia*; profession of faith etc. (*belief*) 484; formula.

wise −, sage −, received −, admitted −, recognized- maxim etc.; true −, common −, hackneyed −, trite −, commonplace- saying etc.

Adj. aphoristic, proverbial, phylacteric; axiomatic, gnomic.

Adv. as -the saying is, − they say.

497. Absurdity.—**N.** absurd-ity, -ness etc. *adj.*; imbecility etc. 499; alogy, nonsense, paradox, inconsistency; stultiloqu-y, -ence, futility.

blunder, muddle, bull; Irish-, Hibernic-ism; slip-slop; anti climax; bathos; sophism etc. 477.

farce, burlesque, *galimatias*, *amphigouri*, rhapsody; farrago etc. (*disorder*) 59; extravagance, romance; sciomachy.

joke, catch, sell, pun, verbal quibble, macaronic; jargon, fustian, twaddle etc. (*no meaning*) 517; exaggeration etc. 549; moonshine, stuff; mare's nest.

vagary, tomfoolery, mummery, monkey trick, practical joke, *boutade*, *escapade*.

V. play the fool etc. 499; stultify, blunder, muddle; joke; talk nonsense, *parler à tort et à travers*; *battre la campagne*; be -absurd etc. *adj.*

Adj. absurd, nonsensical, preposterous, egregious, senseless, farcical, inconsistent, ridiculous, extravagant, quibbling, futile; macaronic, punning, paradoxical.

foolish etc. 499; sophistical etc. 477; unmeaning etc. 517; without rhyme or reason; fantastic.

Int. fiddle-de-dee! pish! pish and tush! pho! stuff and nonsense! rubbish! !rot! bosh! in the name of the Prophet—figs!

Phr. *credat Judaeus Apella*; tell it to the marines.

498. Intelligence. Wisdom.—**N.** intelligence, capacity, comprehension, understanding, intellect etc. 450; nous, parts, sagacity, mother wit, wit, *esprit*, gumption, quick parts, grasp of intellect; acuteness etc. *adj.*; acumen, subtlety, penetration; perspica-cy, -city; discernment; long-headedness, due sense of, good judgment; discrimination etc. 465; craftiness, cunning etc. 702; refinement etc. (*taste*) 850.

head, brains, gray matter, headpiece, upper story, long head; eagle -eye, — glance; eye of a -lynx, — hawk.

wisdom, sapience, sense; good —, common —, plain —, horse- sense; clear thinking; rationality, reason; reasonableness etc. *adj.*; judgment; solidity, depth, profundity, caliber; enlarged views; reach —, compass- of thought; enlargement of mind.

genius, inspiration, *geist*, fire of genius, heaven-born genius, soul; talent etc. (*aptitude*) 698.

[Wisdom in action] prudence etc. 864; vigilance etc. 459; tact etc. 698; foresight etc. 510; sobriety, self-possession, *aplomb*, ballast, mental -poise, — balance.

a bright thought, inspiration, brainwave, not a bad idea.

V. be -intelligent etc. *adj.*; have all one's wits about one; understand etc. (*intelligible*) 518; catch —, take in- an idea; take a -joke, — hint.

see -through, — at a glance, — with half an eye, — far into, — through a millstone; penetrate; discern etc. (*descry*) 441; foresee etc. 510.

discriminate etc. 465; know what's what etc. 698; listen to reason.

Adj. [Applied to persons] intelligent, quick of apprehension, keen, acute, alive, brainy, awake, bright, quick, sharp; quick-, keen-, clear-, sharp-eyed, -sighted, -witted; wide awake; canny, shrewd, astute; clear-headed; far-sighted etc. 510; discerning, perspicacious, penetrating, piercing; argute nimble-, needle-witted; sharp as a needle; alive to etc. (*cognizant*) 490; clever etc. (*apt*) 698; arch etc. (*cunning*) 702; *pas si bête*; acute etc. 682.

wise, sage, sapient, sagacious, reasonable, rational, sound, in one's right mind, sensible, *abnormis sapiens*, judicious, strong-minded.

un-prejudiced, -biassed, -bigoted, -prepossessed; un-dazzled, -perplexed; of unwarped judgment, impartial, equitable, fair, broad-minded.

cool; cool-, long-, hard-, strong-headed; long-sighted, calculating, thoughtful, reflecting; solid, deep, profound.

oracular; heaven-directed, -born.

prudent etc. (*cautious*) 864; sober, staid, solid; considerate, politic, wise in one's generation; watchful etc. 459; provident etc. (*prepared*) 673; in advance of one's age; wise as a serpent, — Solomon, — Solon.

[Applied to actions] wise, sensible, reasonable, judicious; well-judged, -advised; prudent, politic; expedient etc. 646.

499. Imbecility. Folly.—N. want of -intelligence etc. 498, — intellect etc. 450; shallow-, silli-, foolish-ness etc. *adj.*; imbecility, incapacity, vacancy of mind, poverty of intellect, clouded perception, poor head, apartments to let; stup-, stolidity; hebetude, dull understanding, meanest capacity; short-sightedness; incompetence etc. (*unskilfulness*) 699.

one's weak side; bias etc. 481; infatuation etc. (*insanity*) 503.

simplicity, puerility, babyhood; dotage, anility, second childishness, senile dementia, fatuity; idiocy, -tism; driveling.

folly, frivolity, desipience, irrationality, trifling, ineptitude, nugacity, inconsistency, lip-wisdom, conceit; sophistry etc. 477; giddiness etc. (*inattention*) 458; eccentricity etc. 503; extravagance etc. (*absurdity*) 497; rashness etc. 863.

act of folly etc. 699.

V. be -imbecile etc. *adj.*; have no -brains, — sense etc. 498.

trifle, drivel, *radoter*, dote; ramble etc. (*madness*) 503; play the -fool, — monkey, — goat, take leave of one's senses; not see an inch beyond one's nose; stultify oneself etc. 699; talk nonsense etc. 497.

Adj. [Applied to persons] un-intelligent, -intellectual, -reasoning; mind-, wit-, reason-, brain-less; having no -head etc. 498; not -bright etc. 498; inapprehensible.

weak-, addle-, puzzle-, blunder-, muddle-, muddy-, pig-, beetle-, maggotty-, gross-headed; beef-, fat- -witted, -headed.

weak, feeble-minded; dull-, shallow-, rattle-, lack-brained; half-, nit-, short-, dull-, blunt-witted; shallow-, clod-, addle-pated; dim-, short-sighted; thick-skulled; weak in the upper story.

shallow, *borné*, weak, wanting, soft, nutty, sappy, spoony; dull, — as a beetle; stupid, heavy, insulse, obtuse, blunt, stolid, doltish, asinine; inapt etc. 699; prosaic etc. 843.

child-ish, -like; infant-ine, -ile; baby-, bab-ish; puerile, anile; simple etc. (*credulous*) 486.

fatuous, idiotic, imbecile, moronic, driveling; blatant, babbling; vacant; sottish; bewildered etc. 475.

blockish, unteachable; Boeot-ian, -ic; bovine; un-gifted, -discerning, -enlightened, -wise, philosophical; apish.

foolish, silly, senseless, irrational, insensate, nonsensical, inept; maudlin.

narrow-minded etc. 481; bigoted etc. (*obstinate*) 606; giddy etc. (*thoughtless*) 458; rash etc. 863; eccentric etc. (*crazed*) 503.

[Applied to actions] foolish, unwise, indiscreet, injudicious, improper, unreasonable, without reason, ridiculous, silly, stupid, asinine; ill-imagined, -advised, -judged, -devised; inconsistent, irrational, unphilosophical; extravagant etc. (*nonsensical*) 497; sleeveless, idle, useless etc. 645; inexpedient etc. 647; frivolous etc. (*trivial*) 643; absurd etc. 497.

Phr. *Davis sum non Oedipus.*

500. Sage.—N. sage, wise man; pundit; master -mind, — spirit of the age; longhead, thinker, philosopher.

authority, oracle, mentor, luminary, shining light, *esprit fort*, *magnus Apollo*, Solon, Solomon, Nestor, Magi, 'second Daniel.'

man of learning etc. 492; expert etc. 700; wizard etc. 994.

[Ironically] wiseacre, bigwig.

Adj. wise, learned; authoritative, oracular; erudite etc. 490; venerable, reverenced, revered, *emeritus*.

501. Fool.—N. fool, idiot, tomfool, wiseacre, simpleton, Simple Simon, nit-wit, witling, dizzard, donkey, ass; ninny, -hammer; moron, dolt, booby, Tom Noddy, looby, hoddy-doddy, noddy, nonny, noodle, nizy, owl; goose, -cap; *imbécile*; gaby, *radoteur*, nincompoop, *badaud*, zany; trifler, -babbler; pretty fellow; natural, *niais*.

child, baby, infant, innocent, milksop, sop.

oaf, lout, loon, lown, dullard, doodle, calf, colt, buzzard, block, put, stick, stock, numps, tony.

bull-, dunder-, addle-, block-, dull-, logger-, jolt-, jolter-, beetle-, gross-, thick-, giddy-head; num-, thick- skull; lack-, shallow-brain; half-, lack-wit; dunder-pate; fat-head, poor stick.

sawney, gowk; clod, -hopper; clod-, clot-poll, -pate; bull-calf; men of Boeotia, wise men of Gotham.

un sot à triple étage, sot; jobbernowl, changeling, mooncalf, *gobemouche*.

dotard, driveller; old -fogey, – woman; crone, grandmother.

greenhorn etc. (*dupe*) 547; dunce etc. (*ignoramus*) 493; lubber etc. (*bungler*) 701; madman etc. 504.

one who -will not set the Thames on fire, – did not invent gunpowder; *qui n'a pas inventé la poudre*; no conjuror.

502. Sanity.—N. sanity; soundness etc. *adj.*; rationality, normality, sobriety, lucidity, lucid interval; senses, sober senses, sound mind, *mens sana*.

V. be -sane etc. *adj.*; retain one's senses, – reason.

become -sane etc. *adj.*; come to one's senses, sober down.

render -sane etc. *adj.*; bring to one's senses, sober.

Adj. sane, rational, reasonable, *compos mentis*, of sound mind; sound, -minded.

self-possessed; sober, -minded.

in one's -sober senses, – right mind; in possession of one's faculties.

Adv. sanely etc. *adj.*

503. Insanity.—N. disordered -reason, – intellect; diseased –, unsound –, abnormal- mind; derangement, unsoundness.

insanity, lunacy; madness etc. *adj.*; mania, *rabies*, *furor*, mental aliénation, paranoia, aberration; *amentia*, dementation, -tia, -cy; *dementia praecox*; *morosis*, idiocy, phrenitis, frenzy, raving, incoherence, wandering, delirium, calenture of the brain, delusion, hallucination; lycanthropy, brain storm, *delirium tremens*, D.T.'s.

vertigo, dizziness, swimming; sunstroke, *coup de soleil*, siriasis.

fanatisism, infatuation, craze; oddity, eccentricity, twist, monomania; klepto-, dipso-mania; hypochondriasis etc. (*low spirits*) 837; *melancholia*, hysteria.

screw –, tile –, slate- loose; bee in one's bonnet, rats in the upper story.

dotage etc. (*imbecility*) 499.

V. be –, become- -insane etc. *adj.*; lose one's senses, – reason, – faculties, – wits; go –, run-

mad, run amuck; rave, dote, ramble, wander; drivel etc. (*be imbecile*) 499; have a -screw loose etc. *n.*, – devil; *avoir le diable au corps*; lose one's head etc. (*be uncertain*) 475.

derange, render –, drive- -mad etc. *adj.*; madden, dementate, addle the wits, derange the head, infatuate, befool; turn -the brain, – one's head.

Adj. insane, mad, lunatic; crazy, crazed, *aliéné*, *non compos mentis*; not right, cracked, touched; bereft of reason; unhinged, deranged, unsettled in one's mind; insensate, reasonless, beside oneself, demented, daft; phren-, fren-zied. -etic; possessed, – with a devil; far gone, maddened, moonstruck; shatterpated; barmy; mad-, scatter-, shatter-, crackbrained, off one's head; bug-house, *loco*.

maniacal; manic, manic-depressive; delirious, light-headed, incoherent, rambling, doting, wandering; frantic, raving, stark staring mad, amok, amuck.

corybantic, dithyrambic; rabid, giddy, vertiginous, dizzy, wild, haggard, mazed; flighty; distracted, -aught; bewildered etc. (*uncertain*) 475.

mad as a -March hare, – hatter; of -unsound mind etc. *n.* touched –, wrong –, not right- in one's -head, – mind, – wits, – upper story; out of one's -mind, – senses, – wits; not in one's right mind.

fanatical, infatuated, odd, eccentric; hypp-ed, -ish.

imbecile, silly etc. 499.

Adv. like one possessed.

Phr. the mind having lost its balance; the reason under a cloud; *tête -exaltée, -montée*.

504. Madman—N. madman, lunatic, maniac, bedlamite, candidate for Bedlam, raver, madcap; energumen; paranoiac; auto-, mono-, pyro-, megalo-, dipso-, klepto-maniac; hypochondriac etc. (*low spirit*) 837.

dreamer etc. 515; rhapsodist, seer, high-flier, enthusiast, crank, eccentric, nut, fanatic, *fanatico*; *exalté*; knight errant, Don Quixote.

idiot etc. 501.

505. Memory.—N. memory, remembrance; reten-tion, -tiveness; tenacity; *veteris vestigia flammae*; tablets of the memory; readiness.

reminiscence, recognition, recurrence, recollection, rememoration; retrospect, -ion; after-thought.

suggestion etc. (*information*) 527; prompting etc. *v.*; hint, reminder; token of remembrance, *memento*, *souvenir*, keepsake, relic, *memorandum*; remembrancer, flapper; memorial etc. (*record*) 551; commemoration etc. (*celebration*) 883.

things to be remembered, *memorabilia*.

art of –, artificial- memory; *memoria technica*; mnemo-nics, -technics; phrenotypics; Mnemosyne; memorandum-, note-, engagement-, prompt-book.

retentive –, tenacious –, green –, trustworthy –, capacious –, faithful –, correct –, exact –, ready –, prompt- memory.

V. remember, mind; retain the -memory, – remembrance- of; keep in view.

have –, hold –, bear –, carry –, keep –, retain- in or in the -thoughts, – mind, – memory, – remembrance; be in –, live in –, remain in –, dwell in –, haunt –, impress- one's -memory, – thoughts, – mind.

sink in the mind; run in the head; not be able to get it out of one's head; be deeply impressed with; rankle etc. (*revenge*) 919.

recur to the mind; flash -on the mind, – across the memory.

recognize, recollect, bethink oneself, recall, call up, conjure up, retrace; look –, trace- -back, – backwards; think –, look back- upon; review; call –, recall –, bring- to mind; remembrance; carry one's thoughts back; rake up the past.

suggest etc.'(*inform*) 527; prompt; put –, keep- in mind; remind; fan the embers; call –, summon –, rip- up; renew; *infandum renovare dolorem*; task –, tax –, jog –, flap –, refresh –, rub up –, awaken- the memory; pull by the sleeve; bring back the memory, put in remembrance, memorialize.

get –, have –, learn –, know –, say –, repeat- by -heart, – rote; drive –, get- into -one's head; say one's lesson; repeat, – as a parrot; have at one's finger's ends.

commit to memory; memorize; con, – over; fix –, rivet –, imprint –, impress –, stamp –, grave –, engrave –, store –, treasure up –, bottle up –, embalm –, enshrine- in the memory; load –, store –, stuff –, burden- the memory with.

redeem from oblivion; keep the memory -alive, – green; *tangere ulcus*; keep up the memory of; commemorate etc. (*celebrate*) 883.

make a note of etc. (*record*) 551.

Adj. remember-ing, -ed etc. *v.*; mindful, reminiscential; retained in the memory etc. *v.*; pent up in one's memory; fresh; green, – in remembrance, still vivid; unforgotten, present to the mind; within one's -memory etc. *n.*; indelible; not to be forgotten, unforgettable, enduring; uppermost in one's thoughts; memorable etc. (*important*) 642.

Adv. by -heart, – rote; without book, *memoriter.*

in memory of; *in memoriam*; suggestive.

Phr. *manet altâ mente repostum*; *forsan et haec olim meminisse juvabit.*

506. Oblivion.—N. oblivion; forgetfulness etc. *adj.*; obliteration etc. 552, of –, insensibility etc. 823 to- the past.

short –, treacherous –, loose –, slippery –, failing- memory; decay –, failure –, lapse- of memory; memory like a sieve; waters of -Lethe, – oblivion, *amnesia.*

pardon, acquittal, amnesty, oblivion; absolution.

V. forget; be -forgetful etc. *adj.*; fall –, sink- into oblivion; have -a short memory etc. *n.* – no head.

forget one's own name, have on the tip of one's tongue, come in at one ear and go out at the other.

slip –, escape –, fade from –, die away from- the memory; lose, – sight of.

unlearn; efface etc. 552 –, discharge- from the memory; consign to -oblivion, – the tomb of the Capulets; think no more of etc. (*turn the attention from*) 458; cast behind one's back, wean one's thoughts from; let bygones be bygones etc. (*forgive*) 918.

Adj. forgotten etc. *v.*; unremembered, past recollection, bygone. out of mind; buried –, sunk-

in oblivion; clean forgotten; gone out of one's -head, – recollection.

forgetful, oblivious, mindless, heedless, Lethean; insensible etc. 823- to the past.

Phr. *non mi ricordo*; the memory -failing, – deserting one, – being at (*or* in) fault.

507. Expectation.—N. expect-ation, -ance, -ancy; anticipation, reckoning, calculation; contingency; foresight etc. 510.

contemplation, prospection, look out; prospect, perspective, horizon, vista; destiny etc. 152.

suspense, waiting, abeyance; curiosity etc. 455; anxious –, ardent –, eager –, breathless –, sanguine- expectation; torment of Tantalus.

presumption, hope etc. 858; trust etc. (*belief*) 484; prognostication, auspices etc. (*prediction*) 511.

V. expect; look -for, – out for, – forward to; hope for, anticipate; have in -prospect, – contemplation; keep in view; contemplate, promise oneself; not -wonder etc. 870 -at, – if.

wait –, tarry –, lie in wait –, watch –, bargain- for; keep a -good, – sharp- look-out for; await; stand at 'attention,' abide, bide one's –, mark- time, watch.

foresee etc. 510; prepare for etc. 673; forestall etc. (*be early*) 132; count upon etc. (*believe in*) 484; think likely etc. (*probability*) 472; make one's mouth water.

lead one to expect etc. (*predict*) 511; have in store for etc. (*destiny*) 152.

prick up one's ears, hold one's breath.

Adj. expectant; expecting etc. *v.*; in -expectation etc. *n.*; on the watch etc. (*vigilant*) 459; open -eyed, -mouthed; agape, gaping, all agog; on -tenterhooks, – tiptoe, – the tiptoe of expectation; *aux aguets*; ready; curious etc. 455; looking forward to; prepared for; on the rack.

expected etc. *v.*; long expected, foreseen; in prospect etc. *n.*; prospective; in -one's eye, – view, – the horizon; impending etc. (*destiny*) 152.

Adv. expectantly; in the event of; on the watch etc. *adj.*; with -breathless expectation etc. *n.*; – bated breath, – eyes, – ears strained; *arrectis auribus*; on edge.

Phr. we shall see; *nous verrons.*

508. Inexpectation.—N. in-, non-expectation; false expectation etc. (*disappointment*) 509; miscalculation etc. 481; unforeseen contingency, the unforeseen, the unexpected.

surprise, sudden burst, thunderclap, blow, shock; bolt out of the blue; eye-opener; wonder etc. 870.

V. not -expect etc. 507; be taken by surprise; start; miscalculate etc. 481; not bargain for; come –, fall- upon.

be -unexpected etc. *adj.*; come -unawares etc. *adv.*; turn up, pop, drop from the clouds; come –, burst –, flash –, bounce –, steal –, creep- upon one; come –, burst- like a thunder-clap; -bolt; take –, catch- -by surprise, – unawares, – napping. pounce –, spring a mine- upon.

surprise, startle, take aback, electrify, stun, stagger, take away one's breath, throw off one's guard; astonish etc. (*strike with wonder*) 870.

Adj. non-expectant; surprised etc. *v.*; un-warned, -aware; off one's guard; inattentive etc. 458.

un-expected, -anticipated, -prepared for, -looked for, -foreseen, -hoped for; dropped from the clouds; beyond –, contrary to –, against- expectation; out of one's reckoning; unheard of etc. (*exceptional*) 83; startling; sudden etc. (*instantaneous*) 113.

Adv. abruptly, unexpectedly, plump, pop, *à l'improviste*, unawares; without -notice, – warn-ing, – saying 'by your leave;' like a -thief in the night, – thunderbolt; in an unguarded moment; suddenly etc. (*instantaneously*) 113.

Int. heyday! etc. (*wonder*) 870.

Phr. little did one -think, – expect; nobody would ever -suppose, – think, – expect; who would have thought?'

509. Disappointment. [Failure of ex-pectation.]—**N.** disappointment, disillusionment; blighted hope, balk; blow; slip 'twixt cup and lip; non-fulfilment of one's hopes; sad –, bitter- disap-pointment; trick of fortune; afterclap; false –, vain- expectation; miscalculation etc. 481; fool's paradise; much cry and little wool.

V. be disappointed; look -blank, – blue; look –, stand- -aghast etc. (*wonder*) 870; find to one's cost; laugh on the wrong side of one's mouth; find one a false prophet.

disappoint; crush –, dash –, balk –, disap-point –, blight –, falsify –, defeat –, not realize- one's -hope, – expectation; balk, jilt, bilk; play one -false, – a trick; dash the cup from the lips; tantalize; dumb-found, -founder; disillusion, -ize; dissatisfy, disgruntle.

Adj. disappointed etc. *v.*; disconcerted, aghast; out of one's reckoning; disgruntled.

Phr. the mountain brought forth a mouse; *nascitur ridiculus mus; parturiunt montes; diis aliter visum,* the bubble burst; one's countenance falling.

510. Foresight.—**N.** foresight, prospicience, prevision, longsightedness; anticipation; providence etc. (*preparation*) 673.

fore-thought, -cast; pre-deliberation, -surmise; foregone conclusion etc. (*prejudgment*) 481; prudence etc. (*caution*) 864.

foreknowledge; *prognosis*; pre-cognition, -science, -notion, -sentiment; second sight; sagacity etc. (*intelligence*) 498.

prospect etc. (*expectation*) 507; foretaste; prospectus etc. (*plan*) 626.

V. foresee; look -forwards to, – ahead, – beyond; scent from afar; feel in one's bones; look –, pry –, peep into the future.

see one's way; see how the -land !ies, – wind blows, – cat jumps.

anticipate; expect etc. 507; be beforehand etc. (*early*) 132; predict etc. 511; fore-know, -judge, -cast; surmise; have an eye to the -future, – main chance; *respicere finem*; keep a sharp look-out etc. (*vigilance*) 459; forewarn etc. 668.

Adj. foreseeing etc. *v.*; prescient; anticipatory; far-seeing, -sighted; sagacious etc. (*intelligent*) 498; weather-wise; provident etc. (*prepared*) 673; prospective etc. 507.

Adv. against the time when.

511. Prediction.—**N.** prediction, an-nouncement; program, programme etc. (*plan*) 626; premonition etc. (*warning*) 668; *prognosis*, prophecy, vaticination, Mantology, prognostication, premonstration, augur-y, -ation; a-ha-riolation; fore-, a-boding; bode-, abode-ment; omin-ation, -ousness;· auspices, forecast; sign, presage, prognostic; omen etc. 512; horoscope, nativity; sooth, -saying; fortune-telling; divination; crystal gazing, necromancy etc. 992; prophet etc. 512.

[Divination by the stars] astrology, horoscopy, astramancy, judicial astrology.*

[Place of prediction] *adytum.*

prefigur-ation, -ement; prototype, type.

V. predict, prognosticate, prophesy, vaticinate, divine, foretell, soothsay, augurate, tell fortunes; cast a -horoscope, – nativity; advise; forewarn etc. 668.

presage, augur, bode; a-, fore-bode, -cast; fore-be-token; pre-figure, -show; portend; fore-show, -shadow, shadow forth, typify, ominate, signify, point to, precurse.

usher in, herald, premise, announce; lower.

hold out –, raise –, excite- -expectation, – hope; bid fair, promise, lead one to expect; be the -precursor etc. 64.

Adj. predicting etc. *v.*; predictive, prophetic, fatidical, vaticinal, oracular, Sibylline, haruspical, weatherwise.

ominous, presageful, portentous; augur-ous, -al, -ial;· auspici-al, -ous; prescious, monitory, ex-tispicious, premonitory, precusory, significant of, pregnant with, big with the fate of.

Phr. 'coming events cast their shadows before.'

*The following terms, expressive of different forms of divination, have been collected from various sources, and are here given as a curious illustration of bygone super-stitions:

Divination *by oracles,* Theomancy; *by the Bible,* Bibliomancy; *by ghosts,* Psychomancy; *by spirits seen in a magic lens,* Cristallomantia; *by shadows or manes,* Sciomancy; *by appearances in the air,* Aeromancy, Chaomancy, *by the stars at birth,* Genethliacs; *by meteors,* Meteoromancy; *by winds,* Austromancy; *by sacrificial ap-pearances,* Aruspicy (or Haruspicy), Hieromancy, Hieroscopy; *by the entrails of animals sacrificed,* Hieromancy; *by the entrails of a human sacrifice,* An-thropomancy; *by the entrails of fishes,* Ichthyomancy; *by sacrificial fire,* Pyromancy; *by red-hot iron,* Sideromancy; *by smoke from the alter,* Capnomancy; *by mice,* Myomancy; *by birds,* Orniscopy, Ornithomancy; *by a cock picking up grains,* Alectryomancy (or Alectoromancy); *by fishes,* Ophiomancy; *by herbs,* Botanomancy; *by water,* Hydromancy; *by fountains,* Pegomancy; *by a wand,* Rhab-domancy; *by dough of cakes,* Crithomancy; *by meal,* Aleuromancy, Alphitomancy; *by salt,* Halomancy; *by dice,* Cleromancy; *by arrows,* Belomancy; *by a balanced hatchet,* Axinomancy; *by a balanced sieve,* Coscinomancy; *by a suspended ring,* Dactyliomancy; *by dots made at random on paper,* Geomancy; *by precious stones,* Lithomancy; *by pebbles,* Pessomancy; *by pebbles drawn from a heap,* Psephomancy; *by mirrors,* Catoptromancy; *by writings in ashes,* Tephramancy; *by dreams,* Oneiromancy; *by the hand,* Palmistry, Chiromancy; *by nails reflecting the sun's rays,* Onychomancy; *by finger rings,* Dactylomancy; *by numbers,* Arithmancy; *by drawing lots,* Sortilege; *by passages in books,* Stichomancy; *by the letters forming the name of the person,* Onomancy, Nomancy; *by the*

features. Anthroposcopy; *by the mode of laughing.*
Geloscopy; *by ventriloquism.* Gastromancy; *by walking in
a circle.* Gyromancy; *by dropping melted wax into water.*
Ceromancy; *by currents.* Bletonism.

512. Omen.—N. omen, portent, presage,
prognostic, augury, auspice; sigh etc. (*indication*)
550; herald, forerunner, harbinger etc. (*precursor*)
64.

bird of ill omen, signs of the times; gathering
clouds; warning etc. 668.

prefigurement etc. 511.

513. Oracle.—N. oracle; prophet, -ess; seer,
soothsayer, augur, fortune-teller, palmist, medium,
clairvoyant, crystal gazer, witch, geomancer,
aruspex; a-, ha-ruspice; Sibyl; Python, -ess; Pythia;
Pythian –, Delphian- oracle; Monitor, Sphinx,
Tiresias, Cassandra, Sibylline leaves; Zadkiel, Old
Moore; sorcerer etc. 994; interpreter etc. 524.

514. Supposition.—N. supposition, assumption, postulation, condition, pre-supposition,
hypothesis, postulate, *postulatum*, theory, *data*;
pro-, position; *thesis*, theorem; proposal etc. (*plan*)
626.

bare –, vague –, loose- -supposition, –
suggestion; conceit; conjecture; guess, – work;
rough guess, shot; conjecturality; surmise,
suspicion, inkling, suggestion, suggestiveness,
association of ideas, hint; presumption etc. (*belief*)
484; divination, speculation.

theorist, speculator, doctrinarian, hypothesist.

V. suppose, conjecture, surmise, suspect, guess,
divine; theorize; pre-sume, -surmise, -suppose;
assume, fancy, wis, take it; give a guess, speculate,
believe, dare say, take it into one's head, take for
granted.

put forth; pro-pound, -pose; moot; hypothesize;
start, put a case, submit, move, make a motion;
hazard –, throw out –, put forward- a -
suggestion, – conjecture.

allude to, suggest, hint, put it into one's head.

suggest itself etc. (*thought*) 451; run in the head
etc. (*memory*) 505; marvel –, wonder- -if, –
whether.

Adj. supposing etc. *v.*; given, mooted,
postulatory; assumed etc. *v.*; supposit-ive, -itious;
gratuitous, speculative, conjectural, hypothetical,
suppositional, theoretical, academic, supposable,
presumptive, putative.

suggestive, allusive, stimulating.

Adv. if, – so be; an; on the -supposition etc. *n.*;
ex hypothesi; in -case, – the event of; *quasi*, as if,
provided; perhaps etc. (*by possibility*) 470; for
aught one knows.

515. Imagination.—N. imagination;
originality; invention; fancy; inspiration; *verve*;
empathy.

warm –, heated –, excited –, sanguine –, ardent –, fiery –, boiling –, wild –, bold –,

daring –, playful –, lively –, fertile- -
imagination, – fancy.

'mind's eye;' 'such stuff as dreams are made of.'

ideal-ity, -ism; romanticism, utopianism, castle-
building; dreaming; frenzy; ecs-, ex-tasy; calenture
etc. (*delirium*) 503; reverie, brown study, trance;
somnambulism.

conception, *vorstellung*, ercogitation, 'a fine
frenzy,' poetic frenzy, divine afflatus; cloud-,
dream-land; flight –, fumes- of fancy; 'thickcoming fancies;' creation –, coinage- of the brain;
imagery, word painting.

conceit, maggot, figment, myth, dream, vision,
shadow, chimera; phan-tasm, -tasy; fantasy, fancy;
whim, -sey; vagary; rhapsody, romance, *extravaganza*; air-drawn dagger, bugbear, nightmare;
flying Dutchman, great sea-serpent, man in the
moon, castle in the air, *château en Espagne*;
Utopia, Atlantis, happy valley, millennium, fairy
land; land of Prester John, kingdom of Micomicon;
work of fiction etc. (*novel*) 594; poetry etc. 597;
drama etc. 599; Arabian nights; *le pot au lait*;
dream of Alnaschar etc. (*hope*) 858; day –
golden- dream

illusion etc. (*error*) 495; phantom etc. (*fallacy
of vision*) 443; *Fata Morgana* etc. (*ignis fatuus*)
423; vapor etc. (*cloud*) 353; stretch of the
imagination etc. (*exaggeration*) 549.

idealist, romanticist, visionary; mopus; romancer, dreamer; somnambulist; rhapsodist etc.
(*fanatic*) 504.

V. imagine, fancy, conceive; ideal-, real-ize;
dream, – of; 'give to airy nothing a local
habitation and a name.'

create, originate, devise, invent, coin, fabricate;
improvise, strike out something new.

set one's wits to work; strain –, crack- one's invention; rack –, ransack –, cudgel- one's brains;
excogitate.

give -play, – the reins, – a loose- to the -
imagination, – fancy; empathize; indulge in
reverie.

conjure up a vision; fancy –, represent –, picture –, figure- to oneself; envisage.

float in the mind; suggest itself etc. (*thought*)
451.

Adj. imagined etc. *v.*; *ben trovato*; air-drawn, -
built.

imagin-ing etc. *v.*, -ative; original, inventive,
creative, fertile, productive; ingenious.

romantic, high-flown, flighty, extravagant,
fanatic, enthusiastic, Utopian, Quixotic;
preposterous, rhapsodical.

ideal, unreal; in the clouds, *in nubibus*; unsubstantial etc. 4; illusory etc. (*fallacious*) 495; fictitious, theoretical, hypothetical.

fabulous, legendary; myth-ic, -ological;
chimerical; imagin-, vision-ary; notional; fan-cy, -
ciful, -tastic, -tastical; whimsical; fairy, -like.

dreamy, entranced, vaporous.

516. Meaning. [Idea to be conveyed.] [Thing
signified.]—**N.** meaning; signific-ation, -ance;
sense, expression; im-, pur-port; drift, tenor, implication, connotation, essence, force, spirit
bearing, coloring; scope.

matter; subject, -matter; argument, text, sum and
substance; gist etc. 5.

general –, broad –, substantial – colloquial –, literal –, plain –, simple –, accepted –, natural –, unstrained –, true etc. (*exact*) 494 –, honest etc. 543 –, *primâ facie* etc. (*manifest*) 525- meaning.

literality; literal interpretation; after acceptation; allusion etc. (*latency*) 526; suggestion etc. (*information*) 527; synonym; figure of speech etc. 521; acceptation etc. (*interpretation*) 522.

V. mean, signify, express, connote, denote; im-, pur-port; convey, imply, breathe, indicate, bespeak, bear a sense; tell –, speak- of; touch on; point –, allude- to; drive at; involve etc. (*latency*) 526; delcare etc. (*affirm*) 535.

understand by etc. (*interpret*) 522.

Adj. meaning etc. *v.*; expressive, suggestive, meaningful, allusive; signific-ant, -ative, -atory; pithy; full of –, pregnant with- meaning.

declaratory etc. 535; intelligible etc. 518; literal, metaphrastic; synonymous; tantamount etc. (*equivalent*) 27; implied etc. (*latent*) 526; explicit etc. 525; literal etc. 562.

Adv. to that effect; that is to say etc. (*being interpreted*) 522.

literally; evidently, from the context.

517. Unmeaningness. [Absence of meaning.]—**N.** unmeaningness etc. *adj.*; scrabble, scribble, scrawl, daub, (*painting*), strumming (*music*).

empty sound, dead letter, *vox et praeterea nihil*; 'a tale told by an idiot, full of sound and fury, signifying nothing;' 'sounding brass and a tinkling cymbal.'

nonsense, jargon, gibberish, jabber, mere words, hocus-pocus, fustian, rant, bombast, balderdash, palaver, patter, flummery, *verbiage*, babble, *bavardage*, *baragouin*, platitude, *niaiserie*; inanity; rigmarole, rodomontade; truism; *nugae canorae*; twaddle, twattle, fudge, trash; stuff, – and non-sense; bosh, rubbish, rot, drivel, moonshine, wish-wash, fiddle-faddle, flapdoodle; absurdity etc. 497; vagueness etc. (*unintelligibility*) 519.

V. mean nothing; be -unmeaning etc. *adj.*; twaddle, quibble, rant, gabble, scrabble etc. *n.*

Adj. unmeaning; meaning-, sense-less; non-sensical; void of -sense etc. 516.

in-, un-expressive; vacant, fatuous; not significant; insignificant,.

trashy, washy, inane, vague, trumpery, trivial, fiddle-faddle, twaddling, quibbling.

unmeant, not expressed; tacit etc. (*latent*) 526.

inexpressible, undefinable, incommunicable.

Int. rubbish! etc. 497.

518. Intelligibility.—**N.** intelligibility, clear-ness, clarity, explicitness etc. *adj.*; lucidity, per-spicuity; legibility, plain speaking etc. (*manifestation*) 525; precision etc. 494; a word to the wise.

V. be -intelligible etc. *adj.*; speak -for itself, – volumes; tell its own tale, lie on the surface.

render -intelligible etc. *adj.*; popularize, sim-plify, clear up; elucidate etc. (*explain*) 522.

understand, comprehend; take, – in; catch, grasp, recognize, follow, collect, master, make out;

see -with half an eye, – daylight, – one's way; en-ter into the ideas of; come to an understanding.

Adj. intelligible; clear, – as -day, – crystal, – noonday; lucid; per-, tran-spicuous; luminous, transparent; comprehensible.

easily understood, easy to understand, for the million, intelligible to the meanest capacity, popularized.

plain, distinct, explicit, clear-cút; positive; definite etc. (*precise*) 494.

graphic, vivid, telling; expressive etc. (*meaning*) 516; illustrative etc. (*explanatory*) 522.

un-ambiguous, -equivocal, -mistakable etc. (*manifest*) 525, -confused; legible, recognizable; obvious etc. 525.

Adv. in plain -terms, – words, – English.

Phr. he that runs may read etc. (*manifest*) 525.

519. Unintelligibility.—**N.** unintelligibility, incomprehensibility, imperspicuity; in-conceivableness, vagueness etc. *adj.*; obscurity; am-biguity etc. 520; doubtful meaning; uncertainty etc. 475; perplexity etc. (*confusion*) 59; spinosity; *ob-scurum per obscurius*; mystification etc. (*con-cealment*) 528; latency etc. 526; tran-scendentalism.

paradox; enigma, riddle etc. (*secret*) 533; *dignus vindice nodus*; sealed book; steganography, freemasonry.

pons asinorum, asses' bridge; double –, high-Dutch, Greek, Hebrew; jargon etc. (*unmeaning*). 517.

obscurantist.

V. be -unintelligible etc. *adj.*; require - explanation etc. 522; have a doubtful meaning, pass comprehension.

render -unintelligible etc. *adj.*; conceal etc. 528; darken etc. 421; confuse etc. (*derange*) 61; perplex etc. (*bewilder*) 475.

not -understand etc. 518; lose, -- the clue; miss; not know what to make of, be able to make nothing of, give it up; not be able to -account for, – make either head or tail of; be at sea etc. (*un-certain*) 475; wonder etc. 870; see through a glass darkly etc. (*ignorance*) 491.

not understand one another; play at cross pur-poses etc. (*misinterpret*) 523.

Adj. un-intelligible, -accountable, -decipherable, -discoverable, -knowable, -fathomable; in-cognizable, -explicable, -scrutable; inap-, incom-prehensible; insol-vable, -uble; impenetrable.

illegible, indecipherable, as Greek to one, unexplained, paradoxical; enigmatic, -al; puzzling, baffling.

obscure, dark, muddy, clear as mud, seen through a mist, dim, nebulous, shrouded in mystery; undiscernible etc. (*invisible*) 447; misty etc. (*opaque*) 426; hidden etc. 528; latent etc. 526.

indefinite etc. (*indistinct*) 447; perplexed etc. (*confused*) 59; undetermined, vague, loose, am-biguous; mysterious, mystic, -al; transcendental; oc-cult, recondite, esoteric, abstruse, crabbed.

incon-ceivable, -ceptible; searchless; above –, beyond –, past- comprehension; beyond one's depth; unconceived.

inexpressible, undefinable, incommunicable, unutterable, ineffable, unpronounceable.

520. Equivocalness. [Having a double sense.]—**N.** equivocalness etc. *adj.*; double - meaning etc. 516; ambiguity, *double entendre*, pun, paragram, *calembour*, quibble, *équivoque*, anagram; conundrum etc. (*riddle*) 533; word-play etc. (*wit*) 842; homonym, -y; amphibo-ly, -logy; ambiloquy.

Sphinx, Delphic oracle.

equivocation etc. (*duplicity*) 544; white lie, mental reservation etc. (*concealment*) 528.

V. be -equivocal etc. *adj.*; have two -meanings etc. 516; equivocate etc. (*palter*) 544.

Adj. equivocal, ambiguous, amphibolous, homonymous; double-tongued etc. (*lying*) 544.

521. Metaphor.—**N.** figure of speech; *façon de parler*, way of speaking, colloquialism.

phrase etc. 566; figure, trope, metaphor, tralatition, metonymy, enallage, *catachresis*, *synecdoche*, *autonomasia*; irony, satire, figurativeness etc. *adj.*; image, -ry; *metalepsis*, type, anagoge, simile, personification, *prosopopaeia*, allegory, apologue, parable, fable; allusion, adumbration; application; euphemism; euphuism.

V. employ -metaphor etc. *n.*; personify, allegorize, adumbrate, shadow forth, apply, allude -, refer- to.

Adj. metaphorical etc. *n.*; figurative, catachrestical, typical, tralatitious, parabolic, allegorical, allusive, anagogical; ironical; colloquial.

Adv. so to -speak, - say, - express oneself; as it were.

Phr. *mutato nomine de te fabula nattatur.*

522. Interpretation.—**N.** interpretation, definition; explan-, explic-ation; solution, answer; rationale; plain -, simple -, strict- interpretation; meaning etc. 516.

translation, rend-ering, -ition; reddition; literal -, free- translation; key, crib; secret; clew etc. (*indication*) 550; Rosetta stone.

exegesis; ex-pounding, -position; Hermeneutics; comment, -ary; inference etc. (*deduction*) 480; illustration, exemplification; gloss, annotation, *scholium*, note; e-, di-lucidation, enucleation; *éclaircissement*, *mot de l'énigme*.

symptomat-, semei-ology; metoposcopy, physiognomy; diagnosis, prognosis; paleography etc. (*philology*) 560.

accept-ion, -ation, -ance; light, reading, lection, construction, version.

equivalent, - meaning etc. 516; synonym; para-, meta-phrase; convertible terms, apposition; dictionary etc. 562; polyglot.

V. interpret, explain, define, construe, translate, render; do -, turn- into; transfuse the sense of.

find out etc. 480*a*- -the meaning etc. 516- of; read; spell -, figure -, make- out; decipher, decode, unravel, disentangle, puzzle out; find the key of, enucleate, resolve, solve; read between the lines.

account for; find -, tell- the cause etc. 153- of; throw -, shed- light, - new light, - a fresh light- upon; clear up, elucidate.

illustrate, exemplify; unfold, expound, comment upon, annotate; popularize etc. (*render intelligible*) 518.

take -, understand -, receive -, accept- in a particular sense; understand by, put a construction on, be given to understand.

Adj. explanatory, expository; explica-tive, -tory; exegetical; hermeneutic, interpretive, illustrative, elucidative, annotative, scholiastic.

polyglot; literal; para-, meta-phrastic; cosignificative, synonymous; equivalent etc. 27.

Adv. in -explanation etc. *n.*; that is to say, *id est*, *videlicet*, to wit, namely, in other words.

literally, strictly speaking; in -plain, - plainer- terms, - words, - English; more simply.

523. Misinterpretation.—**N.** misinterpretation, -apprehension, -understanding, - acceptation, -construction, -application; *catachresis*; cross -reading, - purposes; mistake etc. 495.

misrepresentation, perversion, exaggeration etc. 549; false -coloring - construction; abuse of terms; parody, travesty; falsification etc. (*lying*) 544.

V. mis-interpret, -apprehend, -understand, - conceive, -judge, -doubt, -spell, -translate, - construe, -apply; mistake etc. 495.

misrepresent, pervert; garble etc. (*falsify*) 544; distort, detort; travesty, play upon words; stretch -, strain -, wrest- the -sense, - meaning; explain away; put a -bad, - false- construction on; give a false coloring, look through -rose colored -, - dark - spectacles.

be -, play- at cross purposes.

Adj. misinterpreted etc. *v.*; untranslat-ed, -able.

Adv. at cross purposes.

524. Interpreter.—**N.** interpreter, translator, ex-positor, -pounder, -ponent, -plainer; demonstrator.

scholiast, commentator, annotator; meta-, para-phrast.

spokesman, speaker, mouthpiece, prolocutor; diplomat etc. 758.

guide, courier, dragoman, *valet de place*, *cicerone*, showman; oneirocritic; Oedipus; oracle etc. 513.

525. Manifestation.—**N.** manifestation; unfolding; plainness etc. *adj.*; plain speaking; expression; showing etc. *v.*; exposition, demonstration, *séance*; exhibition, production; display, showing off etc. 882; premonstration. [Thing shown] exhibit, show.

indication etc. (*calling attention to*) 457; publicity etc. 531; disclosure etc. 529; openness etc. (*honesty*) 543, (*artlessness*) 703; *épachement*, prominence.

V. make -, render- -manifest etc. *adj.*; bring forth, - forward, - to the front, - into view; give notice, express; represent, set forth, exhibit; show,

– up; expose; produce; hold up –, expose- to view; set –, place –, lay- before -one, – one's eyes; tell to one's face; trot out, put through one's paces, unfold, show off, show forth, unveil, bring to light, display, demonstrate, unroll; lay open; draw –, bring- out; bring out in strong relief; call – , bring- into notice; hold up the mirror; wear one's heart upon his sleeve; show one's -face, – colors; manifest oneself; speak out; make no -mystery, – secret- of; unfurl the flag; proclaim etc. (*publish*) 531.

indicate etc. (*direct attention to*) 457; disclose etc. 529; elicit etc. 480*a*; interpret etc. 522.

be -manifest etc. *adj.*; appear etc. (*be visible*) 446; transpire etc. (*be disclosed*) 529; speak for itself, stand to reason; stare one in the face; loom large, appear on the horizon, rear its head; give - token, – sign, – indication of; tell its own tale etc. (*intelligible*) 518; go without saying.

Adj. manifest, apparent; salient, striking, demonstrative, prominent, in the foreground, notable, pronounced.

flagrant; notorious etc. (*public*) 531; arrant; stark staring, unshaded, glaring.

defin-ed, -ite; distinct, conspicuous etc. (*visible*) 446; obvious, evident, incontestable, unmistakable, not to be mistaken, plain, clear, palpable, self-evident, autoptical; intelligible etc. 518; clear as -day, – daylight, – noonday; plain as -a pikestaff, – the sun at noonday, – the nose on one's face, – the way to the parish church.

ostensible; open, – as day; overt, patent, express, explicit; naked, bare, literal, downright, undisguised, exoteric.

unreserved; frank, plain spoken etc. (*artless*) 703; barefaced, brazen, bold, shameless, daring, flaunting, loud.

manifested etc. *v.*; disclosed etc. 529; expressible, capable of being shown, producible; in-, un-concealable.

Adv. manifestly, openly etc. *adj.*; before one's eyes, under one's nose, to one's face, face to face, above board, *cartes sur table*, on the stage, in plain sight, in open court, in the open, – streets; at the cross roads; in market overt; in the face of -day, – heaven; in -broad –, open- daylight; without reserve; at first blush, *primâ facie*, on the face of; in set terms.

Phr. *cela saute aux yeux*; he that runs may read; you can see it with half an eye; it needs no ghost to tell us; the meaning lies on the surface; *cela va sans dire*; *res ipsa loquitur*.

526. Latency.—N. latency, inexpression; hidden –, occult- meaning; occultness, occultism, mysticism, mystery, cabala, symbolism, anagoge; silence etc. (*taciturnity*) 585; concealment etc. 528; more than meets the -eye, – ear; Delphic oracle; *les dessous des cartes*, undercurrent.

allusion, insinuation, implication; innuendo etc. 527; adumbration; 'something rotten in the state of Denmark.'

snake in the grass etc. (*pitfall*) 667; secret etc. 533.

darkness, invisibility, imperceptibility.

latent influence, power behind the throne; friend at court, wire puller.

V. be -latent etc. *adj.*; lurk, smoulder, underlie, make no sign; escape -observation, – detection, – recognition; lie hid etc. 528.

laugh in one's sleeve; keep back etc. (*conceal*) 528.

involve, imply, implicate, connote, import, understand, allude to, infer, leave an inference; symbolize; whisper etc. (*conceal*) 528.

Adj. latent; lurking etc. *v.*; secret etc. 528; occult, symbolic, mystic; implied etc. *v.*; dormant.

un-apparent, -known, -seen etc. 441; in the background; invisible etc. 447; indiscoverable, dark; impenetrable etc. (*unintelligible*) 519; un-spied, -suspected.

un-said, -written, -published, -breathed, -talked of, -told etc. 527, -sung, -exposed, -proclaimed, -disclosed etc. 529, -pronounced, -mentioned, -expressed; not expressed, tacit.

un-developed, -solved, -explained, -traced, -discovered etc. 480*a*, -tracked, -explored, -invented.

indirect, crooked, inferential; by -inference, – implication; implicit, constructive; allusive, covert, muffled, steganographic; under-stood, -hand, -ground; concealed etc. 528; delitescent.

Adv. by a side wind; *sub silentio*; in the background; behind the scenes, – one's back, – the veil; below the surface; on the tip of one's tongue; secretly etc. 528; between the lines; by a mutual understanding.

Phr. 'thereby hangs a tale.' 'that is another story.'

527. Information.—N. information, enlightenment, acquaintance, knowledge etc. 490; publicity etc. 531.

communication, intimation; not-ice, -ification; e-an-nunciation; announcement; representation, round robin, presentment.

case, estimate, specification, report, advice, monition; news etc. 532; return etc. (*record*) 551; account etc. (*description*) 594; statement etc. (*affirmation*) 535.

mention; acquainting etc. *v.*; instruction etc. (*teaching*) 537; outpouring; intercommunication, communicativeness.

informant, authority, teller, announcer, annunciator, harbinger, herald, intelligencer, commentator, columnist, reporter, exponent, mouthpiece; informer, keek, eavesdropper, delator, detective, sleuth; *mouchard*, spy, stool pigeon, newsmonger; messenger etc. 534; *amicus curiae*.

valet de place, *cicerone*, pilot, guide; guide-, hand-book; *vade mecum*; manual; map, plan, chart, gazetteer; itinerary etc. (*journey*) 266.

hint, suggestion, wrinkle, innuendo, inkling, whisper, passing word, word in the ear, subaudition, cue, by-play; gesture etc. (*indication*) 550; gentle – broad- hint; *verbum sapienti*; word to the wise; insinuation etc. (*latency*) 526.

V. tell; inform, – of; acquaint, – with; impart, – to; make acquainted with, bring to the ears of, apprise, advise, enlighten, awaken.

let fall, mention, express, intimate, represent, communicate, make known; publish etc 531; notify, signify, specify, convey the knowledge of.

let one –, have one to- know; serve notice, give one to understand; give notice; set –, lay –, put-before; point out, put into one's head; put one in possession of; instruct etc. (*teach*) 537; direct the attention to etc. 457.

an-nounce, -nunciate; report, – progress; bring –, send –, leave –, write- word; tele-graph, - phone; ring –, call- up; wire; retail, render an account; give an account etc. (*describe*) 594; state etc. (*affirm*) 535.

disclose etc. 529; show cause; explain etc. (*interpret*) 522.

hint; give an inkling of; give –, drop –, throw out- a hint; insinuate; allude –, make allusion- to; glance at; tip off, tip the wink etc. (*indicate*) 550; suggest, prompt, give the cue, breathe; whisper, – in the ear.

give a bit of one's mind; tell one plainly, – once for all; speak volumes.

un-deceive, -beguile; set right, correct, open the eyes of, disabuse.

be -informed of etc.; know etc. 490; learn etc. 539; get scent of, gather from; awaken –, open one's eyes- to; become -alive, – awake- to; keep posted; hear, overhear, understand.

come to one's -ears, – knowledge; reach one's ears.

Adj. informed etc. *v.*; *communiqué*; reported etc. *v.*; published etc. 531; advisory.

expressive etc. 516; explicit etc. (*open*) 525, (*clear*) 518; plain-spoken etc. (*artless*) 703.

declara-, nuncupa-, expository; declarative, enunciative, communicat-ive, -ory; oral.

Adv. from information received; according to - rumor, – report; in the air; from what one can gather.

Phr. a little bird told me.

528. Concealment.—**N.** concealment; hiding etc. *v.*; occultation, mystification.

seal of secrecy; screen etc. 530; disguise etc. 530; masquerade; masked battery; hiding place etc. 530; cipher, code, crypt-, stegan-ography; invisible –, sympathetic- ink; palimpsest; freemasonry.

stealth, -iness; obreption; slyness etc. (*cunning*) 702.

latit-ancy, -ation; seclusion etc. 893; privacy, secrecy, secretness; *incognita*.

reticence; reserve; mental –, reservation, aside; *arrière pensée*, suppression, evasion, white lie, misprision; silence etc. (*taciturnity*) 585; suppression of truth etc. 544; underhand dealing; close-, secretive-ness etc. *adj.*; mystery.

latency etc. 526; snake in the grass; secret etc. 533.

V. conceal, hide, secrete, stow away, put out of sight; lock –, seal –, bottle- up.

cover, screen, cloak, veil, shroud; screen from - sight, – observation; draw the veil; draw –, close- the curtain; curtain, shade, eclipse, throw a veil over; be-cloud, -fog, -mask; mask, disguise; ensconce, muffle, smother; whisper.

keep -from, – back, – to oneself; keep -snug, – close, – secret, – dark; bury; sink, suppress; keep -from, – out of- -view, – sight; keep in –, throw into- the -shade, – background; cover up one's tracks; stifle, hush up, withhold, reserve; fence with a question; ignore etc. 460.

code, codify, use a cipher.

keep -a secret, – one's own counsel; hold one's

tongue etc. (*silence*) 585; make no sign, not let it go further; not breathe a -word, – syllable- about; not let the right hand know what the left is doing; hide one's light under a bushel, bury one's talent in a napkin.

keep –, leave- in -the dark, – ignorance; blind, – the eyes; blindfold, hoodwink, mystify; puzzle etc. (*render uncertain*) 475; bamboozle etc. (*deceive*) 545.

be -concealed etc. *v.*; suffer an eclipse; retire from sight, couch; hide oneself; lie -hid, – in ambush, – low, – *perdu*, – snug, – close; seclude oneself etc. 893; lurk, sneak, skulk; slink, pussyfoot, prowl; steal -into, – out of, – by, – along; play at -bopeep, – hind and seek; hide in holes and corners.

Adj. concealed etc. *v.*; hidden; veiled, secret, recondite, mystic, cabalistic, occult, dark; cryptic, -al, private, privy, *in petto*, auricular, clandestine, close, inviolate.

behind a -screen etc. 530; under -cover, – an eclipse; in -ambush, – hiding, – disguise; in a - cloud, – fog, – mist, – haze, – dark corner; in the -shade, – dark; clouded, wrapt in clouds; invisible etc. 447; buried, underground, *perdu*; incommunicado; secluded etc. 893.

un-disclosed etc. 529; -told etc. 527; covert etc. (*latent*) 526; mysterious etc. (*unintelligible*) 519.

irrevealable, inviolable; confidential; esoteric; not to be spoken of.

obreptitious, furtive, stealthy, feline; skulking etc. *v.*; surreptitious, underhand, hole and corner; sly etc. (*cunning*) 702; secretive, evasive, noncommittal, reserved, reticent, uncommunicative, buttoned up; close, – as wax; taciturn etc. 585.

Adv. secretly etc. *adj.*; in -secret, – private, – one's sleeve, – holes and corners; in the dark etc. *adj.*

januis clausis, with closed doors, *a huis clos*; hugger-mugger, *à la dérobée*; under the -cloak of, – rose, – table; *sub rosâ, en tapinois*, in the background, aside, on the sly, with bated breath, *sotto voce*, in a whisper, without beat of drum, *à la sourdine*.

in –, strict- confidence; confidentially etc. *adj.*; between -ourselves, – you and me; *entre nous, inter nos*, under the seal of secrecy; in -code, – cipher.

underhand, by stealth, like a thief in the night; stealthily etc. *adj.*; behind -the scenes, – the curtain, – one's back, – a screen etc. 530; *incognito*; *in camerâ*.

Phr. it -must, – will- go no further; 'tell it not in Gath,' nobody the wiser.

529. Disclosure.—**N.** disclosure; retection; unveiling etc. *v.*; deterration, revealment, revelation; divulgence, expos-ition, -ure; *exposé*; whole truth; tell-tale etc. (*news*) 532.

acknowledgment, avowal; confession, -al; shrift. bursting of a bubble; *dénouement*.

V. dis-close, -cover, -mask; draw –, draw aside –, lift –, raise –, lift up –, remove –, tear- the -veil, – curtain; un-mask, -veil, -fold, -cover, -seal, -kennel; take off –, break- the seal; lay -open, – bare; expose; open, – up; bare, bring to light; evidence; make -clear, – evident, – manifest; evince.

divulge, reveal, break; let into the secret; reveal the secrets of the prison-house; tell etc. (*inform*) 527; breathe, utter, blab, peach; let -out, – fall, – drop, – the cat out of the bag; betray; tell tales, – out of school; come out with; give -vent, – utterance- to; open the lips, blurt out, vent, whisper about; speak out etc. (*make manifest*) 525; make public etc. 531; unriddle etc. (*find out*) 480a; split; blow the gaff; break the news.

acknowledge, allow, concede, grant, admit, own, confess, avow, throw off all disguise, turn inside out, make a clean breast; show one's -hand, – cards; unburden –, disburden- one's -mind, – conscience, – heart; open –, lay bare –, tell a piece of- one's mind; unbosom oneself, own to the soft impeachment; say –, speak- the truth; turn - King's, – Queen's, – States's- evidence.

raise –, drop –, lift –, remove –, throw off- the mask; expose; debunk; lay open; un-deceive, -beguile; disabuse, set right, correct, open the eyes of; *désillusionner*.

be -disclosed etc.; transpire, come to light; come in sight etc. (*be visible*) 446; become known, escape the lips; come –, ooze –, creep –, leak –, peep –, crop- out; show its -face, – colors; discover etc. itself; break through the clouds, flash on the mind.

Adj. disclosed etc. *v.*

Int. out with it!

Phr. the murder is out; a light breaks in upon one; the scales fall from one's eyes; the eyes are opened.

530. Ambush. [Means of concealment.]—**N.** hiding-place; secret -place, drawer; recess, hole, funk hole, holes and corners; closet, crypt, *adytum*, abditory, *oubliette*, safe, – deposit.

am-bush, -buscade; stalking horse; lurking-hole, -place; secret path, backstairs; retreat etc. (*refuge*) 666.

screen, cover, shade, blinder; veil, curtain, blind, *purdah*, cloak, cloud.

mask, vizor, visor, disguise, masquerade dress, domino; *camouflage*.

pitfall etc. (*source of danger*) 667; trap etc. (*snare*) 545.

v. ambush, ambuscade, lie in ambush etc. (*hide oneself*) 528; lie in wait for; set a trap for etc. (*deceive*) 545.

Adv. *aux aguets*.

531. Publication.—**N.** publication; public -announcement etc. 527; promulgation, propagation, proclamation, pronouncement, encylical, *pronunciamento*; circulation, indiction, edition, imprint, impression, printing; hue and cry.

publicity, notoriety, currency, flagrancy, cry, *bruit*; *vox populi*; report etc. (*news*) 532.

the Press, fourth estate, public press, newspaper, periodical, journal, gazette; house organ, trade publication, tabloid, daily, weekly, monthly, quarterly, annual, magazine, monograph, book; review; news sheet, special edition, supplement, feature, rotogravure, comic strips; leaflet, pamphlet; telegraphy; publisher etc. *v.*

circular, – letter; manifesto, advertisement,

puff, placard, bill, *affiche*, broadside, poster; notice etc. 527; program.

V. publish; make -public, – known etc. (*information*) 527; speak –, talk- of; broach; utter; put forward; circulate, propagate, promulgate; spread –, abroad; rumor, diffuse, disseminate, evulgate; put –, give –, send- forth; emit, edit, get out; issue; cover, report; bring –, lay –, drag- before the public; give -out, – to the world; put –, bandy –, hawk –, buzz –, whisper –, bruit –, blaze- about; drag into the -open day, – limelight; voice.

proclaim, herald, blazon; blaze –, noise- abroad; sound a trumpet; trumpet –, thunder- forth; give tongue; announce with -beat of drum, – flourish of trumpets; proclaim -from the housetops, – at Charing Cross, at the cross roads; declare, declaim.

advertise, placard; post, – up; *afficher*, publish in the Gazette, send round the crier.

raise a -cry, – hue and cry, – report; set news afloat.

telegraph, cable, wireless, broadcast.

be -published etc; be –, become- public etc. *adj.*; come out; go –, fly –, buzz –, blow- about; get -about, – abroad, – afloat, – wind; find vent; see the light; go forth, take air, acquire currency, pass current; go -the rounds, – the round of the newspapers, – through the length and breadth of the land; *virum volitare per ora*; pass from mouth to mouth; spread; run –, spread- like wildfire.

Adj. published etc. *v.*; current etc. (*news*) 532; in circulation, public; notorious; flagrant, arrant; open etc. 525; trumpet-tongued; encyclical, promulgatory; exoteric.

Adv. publicly etc. *adj.*; in open court, with open doors; in the limelight.

Int. *Oyez!* O yes! notice!

Phr. notice is hereby given; this is –, these are- to give notice.

532. News.—**N.** news; information etc. 527; piece –, budget- of -news, – information; report, story, yarn, copy, filler, intelligence, tidings; stop press news.

word, advice, *aviso*, message; dis-, des-patch; telegram, cable, wireless telegram, radio-gram, marconi-gram, communication, errand, embassy; *bulletin*.

microphone; public address system, P.A.; walkie talkie, radio -telephone, -phone.

radio, wireless (Eng.), high fidelity, hi fi, radio set, transistor, receiver; speaker, loudspeaker, amplifier, tweeter, woofer; transmitter, broadcaster; AM –, FM –, short wave – transmitter; radio station, studio, control room, network, hookup, circuit; frequency, kilocycles, megacycles; band, channel, modulation, amplification; broadcast, program, newscast, network show, commerical announcement, serial, sound effects; signature, station – identification, – break, radio listener, audiophile.

television, TV, video, color television; television –, live – broadcast, telecast, TV show; televising, telecasting, transmission, television channel, video, audio, beam, reception, image, test pattern; rain, snow, ghost; television –, TV – station, mobile unit, TVmobile, transmitter, televisor, boost, camera; set, monitor, tube, screen.

rumor, hearsay, *on dit*, flying rumor, news stirring, cry, buzz, *bruit*, fame; talk, *ouï-dire*, scandal, eavesdropping; town –, table- talk; tittletattle; *canard*, topic of the day, idea afloat.

fresh –, stirring –, old – stale- news; glad tidings; old –, stale- story.

narrator etc. (*describe*) 594; news-, scandalmonger; tale-bearer; tell-tale, gossip, tattler, busybody, chatterer; informer.

broad-, news-, sports-caster; commentator, announcer, master of ceremonies, M.C., programmer, sound man, radioman, ham, radioperator.

television technician, TV man, cameraman, soundman.

V. transpire etc. (*be disclosed*) 529; rumor etc. (*publish*) 531.

broadcast, radio, transmit, send, release, beam; sign – on, – off; go on –, go off – the air, monitor; listen –, tune – in.

tele-vise, -cast; color cast.

Adj. many-tongued; rumored; publicly –, currently- -rumored, – reported; rife, current, floating, afloat, going about, in circulation, in everyone's mouth, all over the town.

Adv. as the story -goes, – runs; as they say, it is said.

533. Secret.—**N.** secret; dead –, profoundsecret; *arcanum*, mystery; latency etc. 526; Asian mystery; sealed book, secrets of the prison-house; *le dessous des cartes*.

enigma, riddle, puzzle, nut to crack, conundrum, charade, rebus, logogriph; mono-, ana-gram; acrostic, cross-word puzzle; Sphinx; *crux criticorum*.

maze, labyrinth, Hyrcynian wood.

problem etc. (*question*) 461; paradox etc. (*difficulty*) 704; unintelligibility etc. 519; *terra incognita* etc. (*ignorance*) 491.

Adj. secret etc. (*concealed*) 528.

534. Messenger.—**N.** messenger, envoy, emissary, legate; nuncio, internuncio; intermediary; ambassador etc. (*diplomatist*) 758.

marshal, flag-bearer, herald, crier, trumpeter, bellman, pursuivant, *parlementaire*, *apparitor*.

courier, runner, dawk, *estafette*; Hermes, Mercury, Iris, Ariel.

postman, letter carrier, telegraph boy, messenger boy, district messenger; despatch rider, commissionaire, errand-boy.

mail; post, -office; letter-bag; mail -boat, - train, – coach, – van, aerial mail; tele-graph, - phone; cable, wire; carrier-pigeon; wireless telegraph, -phone; radiotele-graph, -phone.

journalist, newspaperman, reporter; gentleman –, representative- of the press; sob sister; penny-aliner; special –, war –, own- correspondent; spy, scout; informer etc. 527.

535. Affirmation.—**N.** affirm-ance, -ation; statement, allegation, assertion, predication, declaration, word, averment.

asseveration, adjuration, swearing, oath, affidavit; deposition etc. (*record*) 551; avouchment, assurance; protest, -ation; profession; acknowledgment etc. (*assent*) 488; pledge.

vote, voice, suffrage, ballot.

remark, observation; position etc. (*proposition*) 514; saying, *dictum*, sentence, *ipse dixit*.

emphasis, positiveness, peremptoriness; dogmatism etc. (*certainty*) 474; dogmatist etc. 887.

V. assert; make -an assertion etc. *n.*; have one's say; say, affirm, predicate, declare, state, represent; protest, profess.

put -forth, – forward; advance, allege, propose, propound, enunciate, enounce, broach, set forth, hold out, maintain, contend, pronounce, pretend.

depose, depone, aver, avow, avouch, asseverate, swear; make –, take one's- oath; make –, swear –, put in- an affidavit; take one's Bible oath, kiss the book, vow, *vitam impendere vero*; swear till - one is black in the face, – all's blue; be sworn, call Heaven to witness; vouch, warrant, certify, assure, swear by bell, book and candle.

swear by etc. (*believe*) 484; insist –, take one's stand- upon; emphasize, lay stress on; assert - roundly, – positively; lay down, – the law; raise one's voice, dogmatize, have the last word; rap out; repeat; re-assert, -affirm.

announce etc. (*information*) 527; acknowledge etc. (*assent*) 488; attest etc. (*evidence*) 467; adjure etc. (*put to one's oath*) 768.

Adj. asserting etc. *v.*; declaratory, predicatory, pronunciative, affirmative, *soi-disant*; positive; certain etc. 474; express, explicit etc. (*patent*) 525; absolute, emphatic, flat, broad, round, pointed, marked, distinct, decided, confident, assertive, insistent, trenchant, dogmatic, definitive, formal, solemn, categorical, peremptory; unretracted; predicable, affirmable.

Adv. affirmatively etc. *adj.*; in the affirmative. with emphasis, *ex cathedrâ*, without fear of contradiction.

I must say, indeed, i' faith, let me tell you, why, give me leave to say, marry, you may be sure, I'd have you to know; upon my -word, – honor; by my troth, egad, I assure you; by -jingo, – Jove, – George, – etc.; troth, seriously, sadly; in –, in sober- -sadness, – truth, – earnest; of a truth, truly, pardi, perdy; in all conscience, upon oath; be assured etc. (*belief*) 484; yes etc. (*assent*) 488; I'll -warrant, – warrant you, – engage, – answer for it, – be bound, – venture to say, – take my oath; in fact, as a matter of fact, forsooth, joking apart; so help me God; not to mince the matter.

Phr. quoth he; *dixi*.

536. Negation.—**N.** ne-, abne-gation; denial; dis-avowal, -claimer; abjuration; contra-diction, - vention; recusation, protest; rebuttal; recusancy etc. (*dissent*) 489; flat –, emphatic- -contradiction, – denial; *démenti*.

qualification etc. 469; repudiation etc. 610; retraction etc. 607; confutation etc. 479; refusal etc. 764; prohibition etc. 761.

V. deny; contra-dict, -vene; controvert, give denial to, gainsay, negative, shake the head.

dis-own, -affirm, -claim, -avow; recant etc. 607; revoke etc. (*abrogate*) 756.

dispute, impugn, traverse, rebut, join issue upon; bring –, call- in question etc. (*doubt*) 485.

deny -flatly, – peremptorily, – emphatically, – absolutely, – wholly, – entirely; give the lie to, belie.

repudiate etc. 610; set aside, ignore etc. 460; rebut etc. (*confute*) 479; qualify etc. 469; refuse etc. 764.

Adj. denying etc. *v.*; denied etc. *v.*; contradictory; negat-ive, -ory; revocatory; recusant etc. (*dissenting*) 489; at issue upon.

Adv. no, nay, not, nowise; not a -bit, – whit, – jot; not -at all, – in the least, – so; no such thing; nothing of the -kind, – sort; quite the contrary, *tout au contraire*, far from it; *tant s'en faut*; on no account, in no respect; by -no, – no manner of- means; negatively.

phr. there never was a greater mistake; I know better; *non haec in foedera*.

537. Teaching.—N. teaching etc. *v.*; instruction; edification; education; pedagogy; tuition; tutor-, tutel-age; direction, guidance.

qualification, preparation; train-, school-ing etc. *v.*; discipline; exer-cise, -citation; drill, practice.

persuasion, proselytism, propagandism, *propaganda*; in-doctrination, -culcation, oculation.

explanation etc. (*interpretation*) 522; lesson, lecture, sermon, homily; apologue, parable; discourse, prelection, preachment, disquisition.

exercise, task; *curriculum*; course, – of study; grammar, three R's, initiation, A.B.C. etc. (*beginning*) 66.

elementary –, primary –, secondary –, grammar school –, high school –, college –, university –, technical –, liberal –, classical –, religious –, denominational –, moral –, secular-education; technical –, vocational- training; university extension lectures; propaedeutics, moral tuition; evening classes, correspondence course.

physical education, gymnastics, calisthenics, eurythmics; *sloyd*.

V. teach, instruct, edify, school, tutor; cram, prime, coach; enlighten etc. (*inform*) 527.

in-culcate, -doctrinate, -oculate, -fuse, -stil, -fix, -graft, -filtrate; im-bue, -pregnate, -plant; graft, sow the seeds of, disseminate, propagandize.

give an idea of; put -up to, – in the way of; set right.

sharpen the wits, enlarge the mind; give new ideas, open the eyes, bring forward, 'teach the young idea how to shoot;' improve etc. 658.

expound etc. (*interpret*) 522; lecture; prelect; read –, give- a -lesson, – lecture – sermon, – discourse; hold forth, preach; sermon-, moral-ize; point a moral.

train, discipline; bring up, – to; educate, form, ground, prepare, qualify, drill, exercise, practice, habituate, familiarize with, nurture, dry-nurse, breed, rear, take in hand; break, – in; tame; pre-instruct; initiate; inure etc. (*habituate*) 613.

put to nurse, send to school.

direct, guide; direct attention to etc. (*attention*) 457; impress upon the -mind, – memory; beat into, – the head; convince etc. (*belief*) 484.

Adj. teaching etc. *v.*; taught etc. *v.*; educational;

scholastic, academic, doctrinal; disciplinal; instructive, didactic, hortative, pedagogic, tutorial.

Phr. the schoolmaster abroad.

538. Misteaching—N. mis-teaching, -information, -intelligence, -guidance, -direction, -persuasion, -instruction, -leading etc. *v.*; perversion, false teaching; sophistry etc. 477; college of Laputa; the blind leading the blind.

V. mis-inform, -teach, -direct, -guide, -instruct, -correct; pervert; put on a false –, throw off the-scent; deceive etc. 545; mislead etc. (*error*) 495; misrepresent; lie etc. 544; *ambiguas in vulgum spargere voces*, preach to the wise, teach one's grandmother to suck eggs.

render unintelligible etc. 519; bewilder etc. (*uncertainty*) 475; mystify etc. (*conceal*) 528; un-teach.

Adj. misteaching etc. *v.*; unedifying.

Phr. *piscem natare doces*.

539. Learning.—N. learning; acquisition of -knowledge etc. 490, – skill etc. 698; acquirement, attainment; edification, scholarship, erudition; lore; information; self-instruction; study, reading, perusal; inquiry etc. 461.

ap-, prenticeship; pupil-age, -arity; tutelage, novitiate, matriculation.

docility etc. (*willingness*) 602; aptitude etc. 698.

V. learn; acquire –, gain –, receive –, take in –, drink in –, imbibe –, pick up –, gather –, get –, obtain –, collect –, glean- -knowledge, – information, – learning.

acquaint oneself with, master; make oneself -master of, – acquainted with; grind, cram; get –, coach- up; learn by -heart, – rote.

read, spell, peruse; con –, pore – thumb- over; wade through; dip into; run the eye -over, – through; turn over the leaves.

study; be -studious etc. *adj.*; consume the midnight oil, mind one's book.

go to -school, – college, – the university; serve -an (*or* one's) apprenticeship, – one's time; learn one's trade; be -informed etc. 527; be -taught etc. 537.

Adj. studious; schol-astic, -arly; teachable; docile etc. (*willing*) 602; apt etc. 698; industrious etc. 682; learned erudite.

Adv. at one's books; *in statu pupillari* etc. (*learner*) 541.

540. Teacher.—N. teacher, trainer, instructor, institutor, master, tutor, don, director, Corypheus, dry nurse, coach, grinder, crammer; governor, bear-leader; governess, duenna; disciplinarian.

professor, lecturer, reader, prelector, prolocutor, preacher; Boanerges; pastor etc. (*clergy*) 996; schoolmaster, dominie, usher, pedagogue, abecedarian; schoolmistress, dame, monitor, proctor, pupil-teacher.

expositor etc. 524; preceptor, guide; mentor etc. (*adviser*) 695; pioneer, apostle, missionary, propagandist, moonshee; example etc. (*model for imitation*) 22.

professorship etc. (*school*) 542.

tutelage etc. (*teaching*) 537.

Adj. professorial, tutorial etc. 537.

541. Learner.—N. learner, scholar, student, *alumnus*, *élève*, pupil; ap-, prentice; articled clerk; school-boy, -girl, beginner, tyro, abecedarian, alphabetarian.

recruit, novice, neophyte, tenderfoot, inceptor, *débutant*, catechumen, probationer; undergraduate; freshman, frosh; sophomore, junior, senior; junior −, senior- soph; sophister, questionist, fellow-, commoner, pensioner, exhibitioner, sizar, scholar, fellow, advanced −, post graduate −, research- student.

class, form, grade, standard, remove; pupilage etc. (*learning*) 539.

disciple, follower, apostle, proselyte; fellow student, school-mate, -fellow, class mate, condisciple.

Adj. *in statu pupillari*, in leading strings, sophomoric.

542. School.—N. school, academy, university, *alma mater*, college, seminary, Lyceum; instit-ute, -ution, *conservatoire*; *palaestra*, *gymnasium*.

day −, boarding −, public −, preparatory −, elementary −, primary −, nursery −, dame's −, grammar −, Board −, County −, Council −, parochial −, denominational −, Sunday −, religious −, collegiate −, secondary −, continuation −, night −, correspondence −, secretarial −, military −, law −, medical −, business −, technical- school; technical −, training- college; Polytechnic; training ship; *Kindergarten*, nursery, *crèche*, reformatory.

pulpit, desk, reading desk, ambo, class-, lecture-room, theater, amphitheater, forum, stage, rostrum, platform, hustings, tribune.

school −, horn −, text-book; grammar, primer, abecedary, rudiments, manual, *vade mecum*, Lindley, Murray, Cocker.

professor-, lecture-, reader-ship; chair; schoolmaster etc. 540.

School Board, Council of Education; *propaganda*.

Adj. scholastic, academic, collegiate; educational.

Adv. *ex cathedrâ*.

543. Veracity.—N. veracity; truthfulness, frankness etc. *adj.*; truth, sooth, sincerity, candor, honesty, fidelity; plain dealing, *bona fides*; love of truth; probity etc. 939; ingenuousness etc. (*artlessness*) 703.

the truth the whole truth and nothing but the truth; honest −, sober- truth etc. (*fact*) 494; unvarnished tale; light of truth.

V. speak −, tell- the truth; speak by the card; paint in its −, show oneself in ones -true colors; make a clean breast etc. (*disclose*) 529; speak one's mind etc. (*be blunt*) 703; not -lie etc. 544, − deceive etc. 545.

Adj. truthful, true; ver-acious, -edical; scrupulous etc. (*honorable*) 939; sincere, candid, frank, open, straightforward, unreserved; open-, true-, simple- hearted; honest, trustworthy; undissembling etc. (dissemble etc. 544); guileless, pure; unperjured, ture blue, as good as one's word;

unaffected, unfeigned, *bonâ fide*; outspoken, ingenuous etc. (*artless*) 703; undisguised etc. (*real*) 494.

Adv. truly etc. (*really*) 494; on oath; in plain words etc. 703; in −, with −, of a −, in good −, very- truth; as the -dial to the sun, − needle to the pole; honor bright; troth; in good -sooth, − earnest; unfeignedly, with no nonsense, in sooth, sooth to say, *bonâ fide*, *in foro conscientiae*; without equivocation; *cartes sur table*, from the bottom of one's heart; by my troth etc. (*affirmation*) 535.

544. Falsehood.—N. false-hood, -ness; fals-ity, -ification; misrepresentation; deception etc. 545; untruth etc. 546; guile; bad faith; lying etc. *v.*; misrepresentation; mendacity, perjury, false swearing; forgery, invention, fabrication; subreption; covin.

perversion −, suppression- of truth; *suppressio veri*; perversion, distortion, false coloring; exaggeration etc. 549; prevarication, equivocation, shuffling, fencing, evasion, fraud; *suggestio falsi* etc. (*lie*) 546; mystification etc. (*concealment*) 528; simulation etc. (*imitation*) 19; dis-simulation, -sembling; deceit.

sham; pretence, pretending, malingering.

lip-homage, − service; mouth honor; hollowness; mere -show, − outside, eye-wash, window dressing; duplicity, double dealing, insincerity, hypocrisy, cant, humbug, casuistry; jesuit-ism, -ry; pharisaism; Machiavelism, 'organized hypocrisy;' crocodile tears, mealy-mouthedness, quackery; charlatan-ism, -ry; gammon; bun-kum, -come; flam, ban, flim-flam, cajolery, flattery; Judas kiss; perfidy etc. (*bad faith*) 940; *il volto sciolto i pensieri stretti*.

unfairness etc. (*dishonesty*) 940; artfulness etc. (*cunning*) 702; misstatement etc. (*error*) 495.

V. be -false etc. *adj.*, − a liar etc. 548; speak -falsely etc. *adv.*; tell a -lie etc. 546; lie, fib; lie like a trooper; swear falsely, forswear, perjure oneself, bear false witness.

mis-state, -quote, -cite, -report, -represent; belie, falsify, pervert, distort; put a false construction upon etc. (*misinterpret*) 523.

prevaricate, equivocate, quibble; palter, − to the understanding; *répondre en Normand*; trim, shuffle, fence, mince the truth, beat about the bush, blow hot and cold, play fast and loose.

garble, gloss over, disguise, give a color to; give −, put- a -gloss, − false coloring- upon; color, varnish, cook, dress up, embroider; varnish right and puzzle wrong, exaggerate etc. 549.

invent, fabricate; trump −, get- up; forge, hatch, concoct; romance etc. (*imagine*) 515; cry 'wolf!'

dis-semble, -simulate; feign, assume, put on, pretend, màke believe; play -false, − a double game; coquet; act −, play-, a part; affect etc. 855; simulate, pass off for; counterfeit, fake, sham, make a show of; malinger; swing the lead; say the grapes are sour.

cant, play the hypocrite, sham Abraham, *faire pattes de velours*, put on the mask, clean the outside of the platter, lie like a conjuror; hang out −, hold out −, sail under- false colors; 'commend the poisoned chalice to the lips;' *ambiguas in vulgus spargere voces*; deceive etc. 545.

Adj. false, deceitful, mendacious, unveracious,

fraudulent, untruthful, dishonest; faith-, truth-, troth-less; un-fair, -candid; evasive; un-, disingenuous; hollow, insincere, *Parthis mendacior*; forsworn.

canting; hypocrit-, jesuit-, pharisa-ical; tartuffish; Machiavelian; double-tongued, -faced, -handed, -minded, -hearted, -dealing; two-faced, bare-faced; Janus-faced; smooth-faced, -spoken, -tongued; plausible; mealy-mouthed; affected etc. 855.

collus-ive; -ory; artful etc. (*cunning*) 702; perfidious etc. 940, spurious etc. (*deceptive*) 545; untrue etc. 546; falsified etc. *v.*; covinous.

Adv. falsely etc. *adj.*; *à la Tartufe*, with a double tongue; out of whole cloth; slily etc. (*cunning*) 702.

545. Deception.—N. deception; falseness etc. 544; untruth etc. 546; impos-ition, -ture; fraud, deceit, guile; fraudulen-ce, -cy; covin; knavery etc. (*cunning*) 702; misrepresentation etc. (*falsehood*) 544.

delusion, gullery, bluff, spoof, *blague*; juggl-ing, -ery; sleight of hand, legerdemain; presti-giation, -digitation; magic etc. 992; conjur-ing, -ation; hocus pocus, jockeyship; trickery, coggery, hanky-panky, chicanery, pettifogging, sharp practice; *supercherie*, cozenage, circumvention, ingannation, collusion; treachery etc. 940; practical joke.

trick, cheat, wile, ruse, blind, feint, plant, bubble fetch, catch, chicane, juggle, reach, hocus, bite; thimble-rig, card-sharping, artful dodge, machination, swindle, hoax; tricks upon travellers; confidence trick; strategem etc. (*artifice*) 702; theft etc. 791.

snare, trap, pitfall, decoy, gin; sprin-ge, -gle; noose, hook; bait, decoy-duck, tub to the whale, baited trap, *guet-à-pens*; cobweb, net, meshes, toils, mouse-trap, bird-lime; ambush etc. 530; trap-door, sliding panel, false bottom; spring-net, -gun; mask, -ed battery; mine; booby trap.

Cornish hug; wolf in sheep's clothing etc. (*deceiver*) 548; disguise, -ment; false colors, masquerade, mummery, borrowed plumes; *pattes de velours*.

mockery etc. (*imitation*) 19; copy etc. 21; counterfeit, sham, brummagem, make-believe, forgery, fraud, fake; lie etc. 546; 'a mockery, a delusion, and a snare,' hollow mockery.

whited -, painted- sepulcher; tinsel, paste, false jewelry, scagliola, ormolu, German silver, Britannia metal, paint; jerry building; man of straw.

illusion etc. (*error*) 495; *ignis fatuus* etc. 423; *mirage* etc. 443.

V. deceive, take in; defraud, cheat, jockey, do, cozen, diddle, nab, gyp, chouse, double cross, play one false, bilk, cully, jilt, bite, pluck, swindle, victimize; abuse; mystify; blind one's eyes; blindfold, hoodwink, spoof, bluff; throw dust into the eyes, 'keep the word of promise to the ear and break it to the hope,' 'draw a herring across the trail.'

impose -, practice -, play -, put -, palm -, foist- upon; snatch a verdict.

circumvent, overreach; out-reach, -wit, maneuvre; steal a march upon, give the go-by to, leave in the lurch.

set -, lay- a -trap, - snare- for; bait the hook, forlay, spread the toils, lime; decoy, waylay, lure,

beguile, delude, inveigle; tra-, tre-pan; kidnap; let-, hook-in; trick; en-, in-trap, -snare, entoil, benet; nick, springe; catch, - in a trap; sniggle, entangle, illaqueate, hocus, practice on one's credulity, dupe, gull, hoax, fool, befool, bamboozle; hum, -bug; gammon, stuff up, dope, sell; play a -trick, - practical joke- upon one; balk, trip up, throw a tub to a whale; fool to the top of one's bent, send on -a wild goose chase, - a fool's errand; make -game, - a fool, - an April fool, - an ass- of; trifle with, cajole, flatter; come over etc. (*influence*) 615; gild the pill, make things pleasant, divert, put a good face upon; dissemble etc. 544.

cog, - the dice, play with marked cards; live by one's wits, play at hide and seek; obtain money under false pretences etc. (*steal*) 791; conjure, juggle, practice chicanery; gerrymander.

play -, palm -, foist -, fob- off.

lie etc. 544; misinform etc. 538; mislead etc. (*error*) 495; betray etc. 940; be -deceived etc. 547.

Adj. deceived etc. *v.*; deceiving etc. *v.*; cunning etc. 702; prestigi-ous, -atory; decept-ive, -ious; deceitful, covinous; delus-ive, -ory; illus-ive, -ory; elusive, insidious, *ad captandum vulgus*.

untrue etc. 546; mock, sham, make-believe, counterfeit, faked, pseudo, spurious, so-called, pretended, feigned, trumped up, bogus, scamped, fraudulent, tricky, factitious, artificial, bastard; surreptitious, illegitimate, contraband, adulterated, sophisticated; unsound, rotten at the core; colorable; disguised; meretricious; tinsel, pinchbeck, plated; catch-penny; Brummagem; simulated etc. 544.

Adv. under -false colors, -- the garb of, -- cover of; over the left.

Phr. *fronti nulla fides.*

546. Untruth.—N. untruth, falsehood, lie, story, thing that is not, fib, bounce, crammer, taradiddle, whopper.

forgery, fabrication, invention; mis-statement, -representation; perversion, falsification, gloss, *suggestio falsi*; exaggeration etc. 549.

fiction; fable, nursery tale; romance etc. (*imagination*) 515; untrue -, false -, trumped up- -story, - statement; thing devised by the enemy; *canard*; shave, sell, hum, yarn, traveler's tale, Canterbury tale, cock and bull story, fairy tale, clap-trap.

myth, moonshine, bosh, all my eye, -and Betty Martin, mare's nest, farce.

irony; half truth, white lie, pious fraud; mental reservation etc. (*concealment*) 528.

pretence, pretext; false -plea etc. 617; subterfuge, evasion, shift, shuffle, make-believe; sham etc. (*deception*) 545.

profession, empty words; Judas kiss etc. (*hypocrisy*) 544; disguise etc. (*mask*) 530.

V. have a false meaning; not ring true.

pretend, sham, feign, counterfeit, make believe.

Adj. untrue, false, trumped up; void of -, without- foundation; far from the truth, false as dicer's oaths; unfounded, *ben trovato*, invented, fabulous, fabricated, forged; fict-, fact-, supposit-, surrept-itious; e-, il-lusory; ironical; satirical; evasive; *soi-disant* etc. (*misnamed*) 565.

Phr. *se non e vero e ben trovato.*

547. Dupe.—N. dupe, gull, gudgeon, *gobemouche*, cull, cully, victim, sucker, pigeon, April fool; laughing stock etc. 857; Cyclops, simple Simon, flat, mug, greenhorn; fool etc. 501; puppet, cat's paw.

V. be -deceived etc. 545, − the dupe of; fall into a trap; swallow −, nibble at- the bait; bite; catch a Tartar.

Adj. credulous etc. 486; mistaken etc. (*error*) 495.

548. Deceiver.—N. deceiver etc. (deceive etc. 545); dissembler, hypocrite; sophist, Pharisee, Jesuit, Mawworm, Pecksniff, Joseph Surface, Tartufe, Janus; serpent, snake in the grass, cockatrice, Judas, wolf in sheep's clothing; Molly Maguire; jilt; shuffler.

liar etc. (lie etc. 544; story-teller, perjurer, false-witness, *mentuer à triple étage*, Scapin.

imposter, pretender, capper, decoy, fraud, *soi-disant*, humbug; adventurer; Cagliostro, Fernam Mendez Pinto; ass in lion's skin etc. (*bungler*) 701; actor etc. (*stage player*) 599.

quack, *charlatan*, mountebank, saltimbanco, *saltimbanque*, empiric, quacksalver, medicaster.

conjuror, juggler, magician, necromancer, trickster, prestidigitator, medium, jockey; crimp; decoy-duck, stool pigeon; rogue, knave, cheat; swindler etc. (*thief*) 792; jobber.

549. Exaggeration.—N. exaggeration; expansion etc. 194; hyperbole, stretch, strain, coloring; high coloring, caricature, *caricatura*; extravagance etc. (*nonsense*) 497; Baron Munchausen; men in buckram, yarn, fringe, embroidery, traveler's tale; Pelion upon Ossa.

storm in a teacup; much ado about nothing etc. (*over-estimation*) 482; puffery etc. (*boasting*) 884; rant etc. (*turgescence*) 577.

figure of speech, *façon de parler*; stretch of-fancy, − the imagination; flight of fancy etc. (*imagination*) 515.

false coloring etc. (*falsehood*) 544; aggravation etc. 835.

V. exaggerate, magnify, pile up, aggravate; amplify etc. (*expand*) 194; overestimate etc. 482; hyperbolize; over-charge, -state, -draw, -lay, -shoot the mark, -praise; make -much, − the most- of; strain, − a point; stretch, − a point; go great lengths; spin a long yarn; draw −, shoot with- a long-bow; deal in the marvelous.

out -Herod Herod, run riot, talk at random. heighten, overcolor; color -highly, − too highly; embroider, *broder*; flourish; color etc. (*misrepresent*) 544; puff etc. (*boast*) 884.

Adj. exaggerated etc. *v.*; overwrought; bombastic etc. (*magniloquent*) 577; hyperbolical, on stilts; fabulous, extravagant, preposterous, egregious, *outré*, high-flying.

Adv. hyperbolically etc. *adj*.

550. Indication.—N. indication; symbol-ism, -ization; semeio-logy, -tics; sign of the times.

lineament, feature, *trait*, characteristic, trick,

diagnostic; divining-rod; cloven hoof; footfall; means of recognition; earmark.

sign, symbol; ind-ex, -ice, -icator; point, -er; marker; exponent, note, token, symptom.

type, figure, emblem, cipher, device; representation etc. 554; epigraph, motto, posy.

gest-ure, -iculation; pantomime; wink, glance, leer; nod, shrug, beck; touch, nudge; grip; dactylology, -nomy; freemasonry, telegraphy, chirology, by-play, dumb-show; cue; hint etc. 527; clue, clew, key, scent, tract etc. 551.

signal, -post; rocket, blue light; watch-fire, -tower; telegraph, semaphore, flag-staff; cresset, fiery cross; calumet; heliograph, signal-, flash-lamp; radar, radar signal, pulse −, microwave −, radar; tracing, blips, pips.

mark, line, stroke, dash, score, stripe, streak, scratch, tick, dot, point, notch, nick, blaze; asterisk, red letter, Italics, heavy type, inverted commas, quotation marks, sublineation, underlining, jotting; print; impr-int, -ess, ession; note, annotation, mark of exclamation.

[For identification] badge, criterion; counter-check, -mark, -sign, -foil, duplicate, tally; label, tab, ticket, stub, billet, letter, counter, *tessera*, card, bill, check; witness, voucher; stamp; *cachet*; trade −, Hall- mark; broad arrow; signature; address − , visiting- card; *carte de visite*; credentials etc. (*evidence*) 467; passport, identity book; attestation; hand, − writing, sign-manual; cipher; monogram, − mark, seal, sigil, signet; autograph, -y, paraph, brand; superscription; in-, en-dorsement; title, heading, rubric, docket; *mot -de passe*, − *du guet*; *passe-parole*; shibboleth; watch-, catch-, pass-word; open *sesame*.

insignia, banner, -et, -ol; bandrol; flag, colors, streamer, standard, eagle, labarum, oriflamb, *oriflamme*; figure-head; ensign; pen-non, -nant, -dant; burgee, blue Peter, jack, ancient, gonfalon, union-jack; tricolor, stars and stripes; bunting.

hearldry, crest; coat of − , arms; armorial bearings, hatchment; e-, scutcheon; shield, supporters; livery, uniform; cockade, *epaulette*, brassard, chevron; garland, chaplet, love-knot, fillet, favor.

[Of locality] beacon, cairn, post, staff, flagstaff, hand, pointer, vane, cock, weathercock; guide-hand-, finger-, directing-, sign-post; pillars of Hercules, pharos, signal fire; land−, sea-mark; lighthouse, balize; pole-, load-, lode-star; cynosure, guide; address, direction, name; sign, -board.

[Of the future] warning etc. 668; omen etc. 512; prefigurement etc. 511. [Of the past] trace record etc. 551. [Of danger] warning etc. 668; alarm etc. 669. [Of authority] scepter etc. 747. [Of triumph] trophy etc. 733. [Of quantity] gauge etc. 466. [Of distance] mile-stone, -post. [Of disgrace] brand, fool's cap, stigma, mark of Cain. [For detection] check, tell-tale; test etc. (*experiment*) 463.

notification etc. (*information*) 527; advertisement etc. (*publication*) 531.

word of command, call; bugle-, trumpet-call; reveille, taps; bell, alarum, cry; battle − , rallying-cry.

church, bell, angelus, sacring bell; muezzin.

exposition etc. (*explanation*) -522; proof etc. (*evidence*) 463; pattern etc. (*prototype*) 22.

V. indicate; be the -sign etc. *n*.- of; denote,

betoken; argue, testify etc. (*evidence*) 467; bear the -impress etc. *n.*- of; con-note, -notate.

represent, stand for; typify etc. (*prefigure*) 511; symbolize.

put -an indication, - a mark, - etc. *n.*; note, mark, tick, blaze, stamp, earmark; set one's seal upon; label, ticket, docket; dot, spot, score, dash, trace, chalk; print; im-print, -press, surprint; engrave, stereotype, electrotype.

signal, transmit, send, radiate, beam, deflect, echo, bounce back, return.

make a -sign etc. *n.*; signalize; give -, hang out- a signal; beck, -on; gesture; not; wink, glance, leer, nudge, shrug, tip the wink; gesticulate; raise -, hold up- the-finger, - hand; saw the air, suit the action to the word.

wave -, unfurl -, hoist -, hang out- a banner etc. *n.*; wave -the hand, - a kerchief; give the cue etc. (*inform*) 527; show one's colors; give -, sound- an alarm; beat the drum, sound the trumpets, raise a cry.

sign, seal, attest etc. (*evidence*) 467; underline etc. (*give importance to*) 642; call attention to etc. (*attention*) 457; give notice etc. (*inform*) 527.

Adj. indicat-ing etc. *v.*; -ive, -ory; de-, connotative; diacritical, representative, typical, symbolic, pantomimic, pathognomonic, symptomatic, ominous, characteristic, demonstrative, diagnostic, exponential, emblematic, armorial; individual etc. (*special*) 79.

known -, recognizable- by; indicated etc. *v.*; pointed, marked.

[Capable of being denoted] denotable; indelible.

Adv. in token of; symbolically etc. *adj.*; in dumb show.

Phr. *ecce signum*; *ex ungue leonem, ex pede Herculem.*

551. Record.—N. trace, vestige, relic, remains; scar, *cicatrix*; foot-step, -mark, -print; track, mark, wake, trail, spoor, scent, *piste.*

monument, hatchment, escutcheon, slab, tablet, trophy, achievement; obelisk, pillar, column, monolith, cromlech, dolmen; memorial; *memento* etc. (*memory*) 505; testimonial, medal, ribbon, order; commemoration etc. (*celebration*) 883.

record, note, minute; *dossier*; register, -try; census, roll etc. (*list*) 86; cartulary, diptych, Domesday book; entry, memorandum, indorsement, inscription, copy, duplicate, docket; notch etc. (*mark*) 550; muniment, deed etc. (*security*) 771; document; deposition, *procès-verbal*; affidavit; certificate etc. (*evidence*) 467.

note-, memorandum-, pocket-, commonplace-book; portfolio; scoring-board, -sheet; bulletin board; card index, file; pigeon-holes, *excerpta, adversaria*, jottings, dottings.

gazette, -er; newspaper, magazine etc. 531; alman-ac, -ack; calendar, ephemeris, noctuary, diary, log, journal, account-, cash-, day-book, ledger.

archive, scroll, state-paper, Congressional Record, return, blue-book; statistics etc. 86; *compte rendu*; Acts -, Transactions -, Proceedings- of; Hansard's Debates; chronicle, annals; legend; history, biography etc. 594.

registration; en-, in-rolment; tabulation; entry,

booking; signature etc. (*identification*) 550; recorder etc. 553; journalism.

drawing, photograph etc. 554; phonograph -, gramophone- record; music roll.

V. record; put -, place- upon record; go on record; chronicle, calendar, hand down to posterity; keep up the memory of etc. (*remember*) 505; commemorate etc. (*celebrate*) 883; report etc. (*inform*) 527; commit to -, reduce to-writing; put -, set down- -in writing, - in black and white; put -, jot -, take -, write -, note -, set-down; note, minute, put on paper; take -, make- a -note, - minute, - memorandum; make a return.

mark etc. (*indicate*) 550; sign etc. (*attest*) 467.

enter, book; post, - up; insert, make an entry of; mark -, tick- off; register, list, docket, enroll, inscroll; file etc. (*store*) 636.

Adv. on record.

552. Obliteration. [Suppression of sign.]—N. obliteration; erasure, rasure; effacement; interference; cancel, -lation; cassation; circumduction; deletion, blot; *tabula rasa.*

V. efface, obliterate, erase, rase, expunge, cancel; blot -, take -, rub -, scratch -, strike -, wipe -, wash -, sponge- out; wipe -, rub- off; wipe away; deface, render illegible; draw the pen through, apply the sponge.

interfere, jam, black-, block-out; clutter, screen. be -effaced etc.; leave no -trace etc. 449; 'leave not a rack behind.'

Adj. obliterated etc. *v.*; out of print; printless; leaving no trace; intestate; un-recorded, -registered, -written.

Int. *dele*; out with it!

553. Recorder.—N. recorder, notary, clerk; regis-trar, -trary. -ter; prothonotary; amanuensis, secretary, scribe, stenographer, remembrancer, book-keeper, *custos rotulorum*, Master of the Rolls.

annalist; historian, -ographer; chronicler, journalist, reporter, columnist; biographer etc. (*narrator*) 594; antiquary etc. (*antiquity*) 122; memorialist.

draughtsman etc. 559; engraver 558; photographer, cinematographer, camera man.

Recording instrument, recorder, camera, phonograph, gramophone, dictaphone, telegraphone, telautograph, printing telegraph, tape recorder, ticker, time recorder, cash register, turnstile, speedometer, voting machine, seismograph, radar, oscilloscope, teletypewriter, pari-mutuel, photostat.

554. Representation.—N. represent-ation, -ment; imitation etc. 19; illustration, delineation, depictment, portrayal; imagery, portraiture, iconography; design, -ing; art, fine arts; painting etc. 556; sculpture etc. 557; engraving etc. 558; photography, radiography, skiagraphy.

person-ation, -ification; impersonation; drama etc. 599.

picture, drawing, sketch, draught, draft; tracing; copy etc. 21; photo-, helio-graph; daguerreo-, talbo-, calo-, helio-type; cabinet, *carte-de-visite*, snapshot; X-ray photograph; radio-gram, -graph, skia-graph, -gram.

image, likeness, icon, portrait; striking −, speaking- likeness; very image; effigy, fac-simile.

figure, − head; puppet, doll, *figurine*, aglet, manikin, lay-figure, model, *marionnette*, *fantoccini*, bust; waxwork, statue, -tte, automaton, Robot.

hieroglyphic, anaglyph; dia-, mono-gram, graph.

map, plan, chart; ground plan, projection, elevation; ichno-, carto-graphy; atlas; outline, scheme; view etc. (*painting*) 556.

artist, draughtsman etc. 559.

V. represent, delineate; depict, -ure; portray; picture; take −, catch- a likeness etc. *n.*; hit off, photograph, daguerreotype; figure; shadow -forth, − out; adumbrate; body forth; describe etc. 594; trace, copy; mold.

dress up; illustrate, symbolize.

paint etc. 556; carve etc. 557; engrave etc. 558.

person-ate, -ify; impersonate; assume a character; pose as; act; play etc. (*drama*) 599; mimic etc. (*imitate*) 19; hold the mirror up to nature.

Adj. represent-ing etc. *v.*, -ative; illustrative; represented etc. *v.*; imitative, figurative.

like etc. 17; graphic etc. (*descriptive*) 594.

555. Misrepresentation.—N. misrepresentation, distortion, exaggeration; daubing etc. *v.*; bad likeness, daub, sign-painting; scratch, caricature; *anamorphosis*.

V. misrepresent, distort, overdraw, travesty, parody, burlesque, exaggerate, caricature, daub.

Adj. misrepresented etc. *v.*

556. Painting.—N. painting; depicting; drawing etc. *v.*; design; perspective, skiagraphy; *chiaroscuro* etc. (*light*) 420; composition; treatment, values, atmosphere, tone, technique.

historical −, portrait −, miniature −, landscape −, marine −, flower −, scene- painting; scenography.

school, style; the grand style, high art, *genre*, portraiture; ornamental art etc. 847.

mono-, poly-chrome; *grisaille*.

pallet, palette; easel; brush, pencil, stump; blacklead, charcoal, crayons, chalk, pastel; paint etc. (*coloring matter*) 428; water-, body-, oil-color; oils, oil-paint; varnish etc. 356a; *gouache*, tempera, distemper, fresco, water-glass; enamel; encaustic painting; *graffito, gesso;* mosiac; tapestry.

picture, painting, piece, *tableau*, canvas; oil etc.- painting; fresco, cartoon; easel − cabinet- picture; drawing, draught, draft; pencil etc. −, watercolordrawing; sketch; outline; study.

portrait etc. (*representation*) 554; whole −, full −, half- length; kitcat; head; miniature, shade, *silhouette*; profile.

landscape, sea-piece, -scape; view, scene, prospect; interior; bird's- eye view; pan-, di-orama; still life.

picture −, art- gallery; *studio, atelier.*

V. paint, design, limn, draw, sketch, pencil, scratch, shade, stipple, hatch, dash off, chalk out, square up; color, dead-color, wash, varnish; draw in -pencil etc. *n.*; paint in -oils etc. *n.*; stencil; depict etc. (*represent*) 554.

Adj. painted etc. *v.*; pictorial, graphic, picturesque, decorative; classical, romantic, pre-Raphaelite, modern, cubist, futurist, vorticist.

pencil, oil etc. *n.*

Adv. in -pencil etc. *n.*

Phr. *fecit, delineavit.*

557. Sculpture.—N. sculpture, insculpture; carving etc. *v.*; statuary, ceramics, plastic arts.

high −, low −, bas- relief; relievo; *basso-, alto-, mezzo-relievo; intaglio*, anaglyph; medal, -lion; *cameo.*

marble, bronze, *terra cotta*; ceramic ware, pottery, porcelain, china, earthenware, faïence, enamel, *cloisonné.*

statue etc. (*image*) 554; cast etc. (*copy*) 21; glyptotheca.

V. sculpture, carve, cut, chisel, model, mold; cast.

Adj. sculptured etc. *v.*; in relief, anaglyptic, ceroplastic, ceramic; parian; marble etc. *n.*

558. Engraving.—N. engraving, chalcography; line −, mezzotint −, stipple −, chalk- engraving; dry-point, bur; etching, aquatinta; plate −, copper-plate −, steel −, wood-, process-, photoengraving; xylo-, ligno-, glypto-, cero-, litho-, chromolitho-, photolitho-, zinco-, glypho- -graphy, -graph.

impression, print, engraving, plate; steel-, copper-plate; etching; mezzo-, aqua-, litho-tint; cut, woodcut, block; stereo-, grapho-, auto-, helio-type; half-tone; *photogravure, rotogravure.*

graver, *burin*, etching-point, style; plate, stone, wood-block, negative; die, punch, stamp.

printing; plate −, copper-plate −, intaglio −, anastatic −, lithographic −, color −, three colorprinting; type-printing etc. 591.

illustr-, illumin-ation; *vignette*, initial letter, *cul de lampe*, tail-piece.

V. engrave, grave, stipple, scrape, etch; bite, − in; lithograph etc. *n.*; print.

Adj. insculptured; engraved etc. *v.*

Phr. *sculpsit, imprimit.*

559. Artist.—N. artist; painter, limner, drawer, sketcher, delineator; cartoon-, caricatur-ist, designer, engraver; draughtsman; copyist; enameller, -list.

historical −, landscape −, genre −, marine −, flower −, portrait −, miniature −, scene −, signpainter; engraver; Apelles; sculptor, carver, chaser, modeller, lapidary, *figuriste*, statuary; Phidias, Praxiteles; Royal Academician.

photographer, retoucher.

560. Language.—N. language; phraseology etc. 569; speech etc. 582; tongue, lingo, vernacular, slang; mother –, vulgar –, native- tongue; household words; King's or Queen's English; idiom; dialect etc. 563.

volapuk, esperanto, ido, occidental, Ro.

confusion of tongues, Babel, *pasigraphie*; pantomime etc. (*signs*) 550; *onomatopaeia*.

phil-, gloss-, glott-ology; linguistics, chrestomathy; paleo-logy; -graphy; comparative grammar.

literature, letters, polite literature, *belles lettres*, muses, humanities, *literae humaniores*, republic of letters, dead languages, classics; genius of a language; scholarship etc. (*knowledge*) 490.

linguist etc. (*scholar*) 492.

V. speak, say, express by words etc. 566.

Adj. lingu-al, -istic; dialectic; vernacular, current, colloquial, slangy; bilingual, polyglot; literary.

561. Letter.—N. letter; character; hieroglyphic etc. (*writing*) 590; type etc. (*printing*) 591; capitals; majus-, minus-cule; alphabet, ABC, abecedary, christcross row, chrisscross row.

consonant, vowel, diphthong; mute, surd; sonant, liquid, labial, dental, palatal, gutteral.

syllable; mono-, dis-, poly-syllable; affix, prefix, suffix.

spelling, orthography; phon-ography, -etic spelling; ana-, meta-grammatism.

cipher, monogram, anagram; double – acrostic.

V. spell.

Adj. literal; alphabetical, abecedarian; syllabic; uncial etc. (*writing*) 590; phonetic, voiced, mute etc. *n*.

562. Word.—N. word, term, vocable; name etc. 564; phrase etc. 566; root, etymon; derivative; part of speech etc. (*grammar*) 567.

dictionary, vocabulary, word book, lexicon, index, glossary, thesaurus, *gradus, delectus*, concordance.

etymology, lexicology, derivation; phonology, orthoepy; gloss-, termin-, orism-ology; paleology etc. (*philology*) 560; comparative philology.

lexicograph-er, -y; glossographer etc. (*scholar*) 492; etymologist; logolept.

verbosity, verbiage, loquacity etc. 584.

Adj. verbal, literal; titular, nominal. [Similarly derived] conjugate, paraonymous; derivative.

Adv. verbally etc. *adj.*; *verbatim* etc. (*exactly*) 494.

563. Neology.—N. neolo-gy; -gism; new-fangled expression; barbarism; caconym; archaism, black letter, monkish Latin; corruption; missaying, antiphrasis.

paronomasia, play upon words; wordplay etc. (*wit*) 842; *double-entente* etc. (*ambiguity*) 520; palindrome, paragram, clinch; abuse of -language, – terms.

dialect, brogue, *patois*, provincialism, broken English, *lingua franca*; Brit-, Gall-, Scott-, Hibernicism; American-ism; Gipsy lingo, Romany, pidgin English.

dog Latin, macaronics, gibberish, confusion of tongues, Babel; jargon.

colloquialism etc. (*figure of speech*) 521; by-word; technicality, lingo, slang, cant, *argot*, St. Giles's Greek, thieves' Latin, peddler's French, flash tongue, Billingsgate, Wall Street slang.

pseudonym etc. (*misnomer*) 565; Mr. So-and-so; what d'ye call 'em, what's his name; thingum-my, -bob; *je ne sais quoi.*

neologist, coiner of words.

V. coin words.

Adj. neologic, -al; rare; archaic; obsolete etc. (*old*) 124; colloquial, dialectic, slang, cant.

564. Nomenclature.—N. nomenclature; naming etc. *v.*; nuncupation, nomination, baptism; orismology; *onomatopaeia*; antonomasia.

name; appella-tion, -tive; designation; title; head, -ing, caption; denomination; by-name, epithet.

style, proper name; prae-, ag-, cog-nomen; patronymic, surname; cognomination; compellation, description; empty -title, – name; handle to one's name; namesake, eponym.

synonym, antonym.

term, expression, noun; by-word; convertible terms etc. 522; technical term; cant etc. 563.

V. name, call, term, denominate, designate, style, entitle, intitule, clepe, dub, christen, baptize, nickname, characterize, specify, define, distinguish by the name of; label etc. (*mark*) 550.

be -called etc. *v.*; take – , bear – , go (*or be known*) by – , go (*or pass*) under – , rejoice in- the name of.

Adj. named etc. *v.*; hight, yclept, known as; what one may -well, – fairly, – properly, – fitly-call.

nuncupa-tory, -tive; cognominal, titular, nominal; orismological.

565. Misnomer.—N. misnomer; *lucus a non lucendo*; Mrs. Malaprop; what d'ye call 'em etc. (*neologism*) 563.

nickname, *sobriquet*, by-name, handle, moniker; assumed -name, – title; *alias; nom de guerre*, – *plume*, – *theâtre*; pseudonym, pen name, stage name.

V. mis-name, -call, - term; nickname; assume -a name, – an alias.

Adj. misnamed etc. *v.*; pseudonymous; *soi-disant*; self-called, -styled, -christened; so-called.

nameless, anonymous; without a – , having no-name; innominate, unnamed.

Adv. in no sense.

566. Phrase.—N. phrase, expression, set phrase; sentence, paragraph; figure of speech etc. 521; idi-om, -otism; turn of expression.

paraphrase etc. (*synonym*) 522; periphrase etc. (*circumlocution*) 573; motto etc. (*proverb*) 496. phraseology etc. 569.

V. express, phrase; word, – it; give -words, – expression- to; voice; arrange in –, clothe in –, put into –, express by- words; couch in terms; find words to express; speak by the card.

Adj. expressed etc. *v.*; idiomatic.

Adv. in -round, – set, – good, set- terms; in set phrases.

567. Grammar.—**N.** grammar, accidence, syntax, *praxis*, analysis, paradigm, punctuation; parts of speech, inflexion, case, declension, conjugation; *jus et norma loquendi*; Lindley Murray etc. (*school-book*) 542; correct style; philology etc. (*language*) 560.

V. parse, analyze; decline, conjugate; punctuate.

Adj. grammatical; syntactic; inflexional.

568. Solecism.—**N.** solecism; bad –, false –, faulty- grammar; slip, error; slip of the -pen, – tongue; *lapsus calami*-, – *linguae*; *faux pas*; slipslop; bull.

V. use -bad, – faulty- grammar; solecize, commit a solecism; murder the -King's, – Queen's-English; break Priscian's head.

Adj. ungrammatical; in-correct, -accurate; faulty, improper, incongruous, abnormal.

569. Style.—**N.** style, diction, phraseology, wording; manner, strain; composition; mode of expression, choice of words, literary power, ready pen, pen of a ready writer; command of language etc. (*eloquence*) 582; authorship; *la morgue littéraire*.

V. express by words etc. 566; write.

570. Perspicuity.—**N.** perspicuity etc. (*intelligibility*) 518; plain speaking etc. (*manifestation*) 525; defin-iteness, -ition; exactness etc. 494; perspicuousness, logical acuteness.

Adj. lucid etc. (*intelligible*) 518; explicit etc. (*manifest*) 525; exact etc. 494.

571. Obscurity.—**N.** obscurity etc. (*unintelligibility*) 519; involution; hard words; ambiguity etc. 520; vagueness etc. 475; inexactness etc. 495; what d'ye call 'em etc. (*neologism*) 563; cloudiness, confusion.

Adj. obscure etc. *n.*; crabbed, involved, confused.

572. Conciseness.—**N.** conciseness etc. *adj.*; brevity, 'the soul of wit,' laconism; Tacitus; ellipsis; syncope; abridgment etc. (*shortening*) 201; compression etc. 195; epitome etc. 596; monostitch; portmanteau word, telescope word, protogram.

V. be -concise etc. *adj.*; condense etc. 195; abridge etc. 201; abstract etc. 596; come to the point.

Adj. concise, brief, short, terse, close; to the point, exact; neat, compact, condensed, pointed; laconic, curt, pithy, trenchant, summary; pregnant; compendious etc. (*compendium*) 596; succinct; elliptical, epigrammatic, crisp, sententious.

Adv. concisely etc. *adj.*; briefly, summarily; in brief, – short, – a word, – few words, – a nutshell; for shortness sake; to -come to the point, – make a long story short, – cut the matter short, – be brief; it comes to this, the long and short of it is.

573. Diffuseness.—**N.** diffuseness etc. *adj.*; amplification etc. *v.*; dilating etc. *v.*; verbosity, *verbiage*, wordiness, cloud of words, *copia verborum*; flow of words etc. (*loquacity*) 584.

poly-, tauto-, batto-, perisso-logy; pleonasm, exuberance, redundance; thrice-told tale; prolixity; circumlocution, *ambages*; periphra-se, -sis; roundabout phrases; episode; expletive; penny-a-lining; padding, drivel, twaddle, rigmarole; richness etc. 577.

V. be -diffuse etc. *adj.*; run out on, descant, expatiate, enlarge, dilate, amplify, expand, inflate, pad; launch –, branch- out; rant.

maunder, prose; harp upon etc. (*repeat*) 104; dwell on, insist upon.

digress, ramble, *battre la campagne*, beat about the bush, perorate, spin a long yarn, protract; spin –, swell –, draw- out, drivel.

Adj. dif-, pro-fuse; wordy, verbose, largiloquent, copious, exuberant, effusive, pleonastic, lengthy; long, -some, -winded, -spun, -drawn out; diffusive, spun out, protracted, prolix, prosing, maundering; circumlocutory, periphrastic, ambagious, roundabout; digressive; dis-, ex-cursive; rambling, episodic; flatulent, frothy.

Adv. diffusely etc. *adj.*; at large, *in extenso*; about it and about it.

574. Vigor.—**N.** vigor, power, force; boldness, raciness etc. *adj.*; spirit, point, antithesis, piquancy; *verve*, glow, fire, warmth, ardor, enthusiasm; 'thoughts that breathe and words that burn;' strong language; punch; gravity, sententiousness; elevation, loftiness, sublimity.

eloquence; command of -words, – language.

Adj. vigorous, nervous, powerful, forcible, trenchant, mordant, biting, incisive, impressive; sensational.

spirited, lively, glowing, sparkling, racy, bold, slashing; pungent, *piquant*, full of point, pointed, pithy, antithetical; sententious.

lofty, elevated, sublime, grand, weighty, ponderous; eloquent; vehement, petulant, impassioned; poetic.

Adv. in -glowing, – good set, – no measured-terms.

575. Feebleness.—**N.** feebleness etc. *adj.*;

Adj. feeble, bald, tame, meager, insipid, nerve-les, jejune, vapid, trashy, cold, frigid, poor, dull, dry, languid; pros-ing, -y, -aic; unvaried, monotonous, weak, frail, washy, wishy-washy, sloppy; sketchy, slight; careless, slovenly, loose, lax; slip-shod, -slop; inexact; dis-jointed, -connected; puerile, childish; flatulent; rambling etc. (*diffuse*) 573.

576. Plainness.—N. plainness etc. *adj.*; simplicity, severity; plain -terms, – English; Saxon English; household words.

V. speak plainly; call a spade 'a spade;' plunge *in medias res*; come to the point.

Adj. plain, simple; un-ornamented, -adorned, -varnished; home-ly, -spun; neat; severe, chaste, pure, Saxon; commonplace, matter of fact, natural, prosaic, sober, unimaginative.

dry, unvaried, monotonous etc. 575.

Adv. in plain -terms, – words, – English, – common parlance; point blank.

577. Ornament.—N. ornament; floridness etc. *adj.*; turg-idity, -escence; altiloquence etc. *adj.*; orotundity; declamation, teratology; well-rounded periods; elegance etc. 578.

inversion, antithesis, alliteration, *paronomasia*; figurativeness etc. (*metaphor*) 521.

flourish; flowers of -speech, – rhetoric; euphuism, -emism.

big-, high-sounding words; macrology, *sesquipedalia verba*, sesquipedalianism; Alexandrine; inflation, pretension; rant, bombast, fustian, bunkum, balderdash, prose run mad; fine writing; Minerva press.

phrasemonger; euph-uist, -emist.

V. ornament, overlay with ornament, overcharge; smell of the lamp.

Adj. ornamented etc. *v.*; beautified etc. 847; ornate, florid, rich, flowery; euph-uistic, -emistic; sonorous; high-, big-sounding; inflated, swelling, tumid; turg-id, -escent; pedantic, pompous, stilted; high-flown, -flowing; sententious, rhetorical, declamatory; grandiose; grand-, magn-, alt-iloquent; sesquipedal, -ian; Johnsonian, mouthy; bombastic; fustian; frothy, flashy, flaming, flamboyant.

antithetical, alliterative; figurative etc. 521; artificial etc. (*inelegant*) 579.

Adv. *ore rotundo*; with rounded phrase.

578. Elegance.—N. elegance, purity, grace, ease, felicity, distinction, gracefulness, refinement, readiness etc. *adj.*; concinnity, euphony, numerosity, balance, rythym, symmetry, proportion; restraint; good taste, propriety.

well rounded –, well turned –, flowing-periods; the right word in the right place; antithesis etc. 577.

purist, stylist.

V. point an antithesis, round a period.

Adj. elegant, polished, classical, Attic, correct, Ciceronian, artistic; chaste, pure, Saxon, academical.

graceful, easy, readable, fluent, flowing, tripping; unaffected, natural, unlabored; mellifluous; euph-onious, -emistic; rhythmical, balanced, symmetrical.

felicitous, happy, neat; well –, neatly- put, – expressed.

579. Inelegance.—N. inelegance; vulgarity, bad taste; stiffness etc. *adj.*; unlettered Muse; barbarism; slang etc. 563; solecism etc. 568; mannerism etc. (*affectation*) 855; euphuism; fustian etc. 577; cacophony; want of balance; words that - break the teeth, – dislocate the jaw.

V. be -inelegant etc. *adj.*

Adj. inelegant, graceless, ungraceful, unpolished; harsh, abrupt; dry, stiff, cramped, formal, *guindé*; forced, labored, awkward; artificial, mannered, ponderous; turgid etc. 577; affected, euphuistic; barbarous, uncouth, grotesque, rude, crude, halting; vulgar, offensive to ears polite.

580. Voice.—N. voice; vocality; organ, lungs, bellows; good –, fine –, powerful etc. (*loud*) 404 –, musical etc. 413- voice; intonation; tone etc. (*sound*) 402- of voice.

vocalization; cry etc. 411; strain, utterance, prolation; exclam-, ejacul-, vocifer-ation; enunci-, articul-ation; articulate sound; distinctness; clearness, – of articulation; stage whisper; delivery; attack.

accent, -uation; emphasis, stress; broad –, strong –, pure –, native –, foreign- accent; pronunciation.

[Word similarly pronounced] homonym.

orthoepy; euphony etc. (*melody*) 413.

gastri-, ventri-loquism; ventriloquist; polyphonism, -ist.

[Science of voice] phonology etc. (*sound*) 402.

V. sing, speak, utter, breathe, voice; give -utterance, – tongue; cry etc. (*shout*) 411; ejaculate, rap out; vocalize, prolate, articulate, enunciate, enounce, pronounce, accentuate, aspirate, deliver, mouth; emit, murmur, whisper, – in the ear, croon, yodel.

Adj. vocal, phonetic, oral; ejaculatory, articulate, distinct, stertorous; enunciative; accentuated, aspirated; euphonious etc. (*melodious*) 413.

581. Aphony—N. aphony, *aphonia*; dumbness etc. *adj.*; obmutescence; absence –, want- of voice; dysphony; silence etc. (*taciturnity*) 585; raucity; harsh etc. 410 –, unmusical etc. 414- voice; *falsetto*, 'childish treble;' mute, dummy, deaf mute.

V. keep silence etc. 585; speak -low, – softly; whisper etc. (*faintness*) 405.

silence; render -mute, – silent etc. 403; muzzle, muffle, suppress, smother, gag, strike dumb, dumbfound, -founder; drown the voice, put to silence, stop one's mouth, cut one short.

stick in the throat.

Adj. aphon-ous, -ic, dumb, mute; deaf-mute, –

and dumb; mum; tongue-tied; breath-, tongue-, voice-, speech-, word-less; mute as a ;fish, – stock-fish, – mackerel; silent etc. (*taciturn*) 585; muz-zled; in-articulate, -audible.

croaking, raucous, hoarse, husky, dry, hollow, sepulchral, hoarse as a raven.

Adv. with -bated breath, – the finger on the lips; *sotto voce*; in a -low tone, – cracked voice, – broken voice; in an aside.

Phr. *vox faucibus haesit.*

582. Speech.—N. speech, faculty of speech; locution, talk, parlance, verbal intercourse, prolation, oral communication, word of mouth, *parole*, palaver, prattle; effusion.

oration, recitation, delivery, say, address, speech, lecture, harangue, sermon, *tirade*, screed, formal speech, salutatory, peroration; prelection; speechifying; soliloquy etc. 589; allocution etc. 586; interlocution etc. 588.

oratory; elo-cution, -quence; rhetoric, declamation; grandi-, multi-loquence; burst of eloquence; facundity; talkativeness; flow –, com-mand- of -words, – language; *copia verborum*; power of speech, gift of the gab; *usus loquendi*.

speaker etc. *v.*; spokesman, pro-, inter-locutor; mouthpiece, Hermes; ora-tor, -trix, -tress; Demosthenes, Cicero; rhetorician; stump –, plat-form- orator, tub-thumper; elocutionist; speech-maker, patterer, *improvisatore*.

V. speak, – of; say, utter, pronounce, deliver, give utterance to; utter –, pour- forth; breathe, let fall, come out with; rap –, blurt- out; have on one's lips; have at the -end, – tip- of one's tongue.

break silence; open one's -lips, – mouth; lift –, raise- one's voice; give –, wag the- tongue; talk, outspeak; put in a word or two.

hold forth; make –, deliver- -a speech etc. *n.*; speechify, harangue, declaim, stump, flourish, spout, rant, recite, lecture, preach, sermonize, discourse, be on one's legs; have –, say- one's say; expatiate etc. (*speak at length*) 573; speak one's mind.

soliloquize etc. 589; tell etc. (*inform*) 527; speak to etc. 586; talk together etc. 588.

be -eloquent etc. *adj.*; have -a tongue in one's head, – the gift of the gab etc. *n.*

pass –, escape- one's lips; fall from the -lips, – mouth.

Adj. speaking etc., spoken etc. *v.*; oral, lingual, phonetic, not written, unwritten, outspoken; elo-quent, -cutionary; orat-, rhetorical; declamatory; grandiloquent etc. 577; talkative etc. 584.

Adv. orally etc. *adj.*; by word of mouth, *viva voce*, from the lips of.

Phr. quoth –, said- he etc.

583. Stammering. [Imperfect Speech.]—N. inarticulateness; stammering etc. *v.*; hesitation etc. *v.*; impediment in one's speech; aphasia, titubancy, traulism; whisper etc. (*faint sound*) 405; lisp, drawl, tardiloquence; nasal -tone, – accent; twang; *falsetto* etc. (*want of voice*) 581; broken -voice, – accents, – sentences.

brogue etc. 563; slip of the tongue, *lapsus linguae.*

V. stammer, stutter, hesitate, falter, hammer; balbu-tiate, -cinate; haw, hum and haw, be unable to put two words together.

mumble, mutter; maund, -er; whisper etc. 405; mince, lisp; jabber, gabble, gibber; sp-, spl-utter; muffle, mump; drawl, mouth; croak; speak -thick, – through the nose; snuffle, clip one's words; mur-der the -language, – King's (*or* Queen's) English; mis-pronounce, -say.

Adj. stammering etc. *v.*; inarticulate, guttural, nasal; tremulous.

Adv. *sotto voce* etc. (*faintly*) 405.

584. Loquacity.—N. loquac-ity, -iousness; talkativeness etc. *adj.*; garrulity; multiloquence, much speaking, effusion, wordiness.

jaw; gab, -ble; jabber, chatter; prate, prattle, cackle, clack; twaddle, trattle, rattle; *caquet, -terie*; blabber, *bavardage*, bibble-babble, gibble-gabble; small talk etc. (*converse*) 588.

fluency, flippancy, volubility, flowing tongue; flow, – of words; *flux de -bouche*, – *mots*, – *paroles*; *copia verborum, cacoëthes loquendi*; verbosity etc. (*diffuseness*) 573; gift of the gab etc. (*eloquence*) 582.

talker; chatter-er, -box; babbler etc. *v.*; rattle; ranter; sermonizer, proser, driveller; wind bag; gossip etc. (*converse*) 588; magpie, jay, parrot, poll, Babel; *moulin à paroles.*

V. be -loquacious etc. *adj.*; talk glibly, pour forth, patter; prate, palaver, prose, chatter, prattle, clack, jabber, jaw; rattle, – on; twaddle, twattle, babble, gabble; out-talk; talk oneself -out of breath, – hoarse; maunder, gush, blatter; talk a donkey's hind leg off; expatiate etc. (*speak at length*) 573; gossip etc. (*converse*) 588; din in the ears etc. (*repeat*) 104; talk -at random, – nonsense etc. 497; be hoarse with talking.

Adj. loquacious, talkative, conversational, garrulous, linguacious, multiloquous; chattering etc. *v.*; chatty etc. (*sociable*) 892; declamatory etc. 582; open-mouthed.

fluent, voluble, glib, flippant; long-tongued, -winded etc. (*diffuse*) 573.

Adv. trippingly on the tongue; glibly etc. *adj.*

Phr. the -tongue running -fast, – loose, – on wheels.

585. Taciturnity.—N. silence, muteness, ob-mutescence; taciturnity, pauciloquy, costiveness, curtness; reserve, reticence etc. (*concealment*) 528; *aposiopesis.*

man of few words.

V. be -silent etc. *adj.*; keep silence; hold one's -tongue, – peace, – jaw; not speak etc. 582; say nothing; seal –, close –, put a padlock on- the -lips, – mouth; put a bridle on one's tongue; keep one's tongue between one's teeth; make no sign, not let a word escape one; keep a secret etc. 528; not have a word to say; lay –, place- the finger on the lips; render mute etc. 581.

stick in one's throat.

Adj. silent, mute, mum; silent as -a post, – a stone, – the grave etc. (*still*) 403; dumb etc. 581.

taciturn, sparing of words; close, – mouthed –

tongued; laconic, costive, inconversable, curt; reserved; reticent etc. (*concealing*) 528.

Int. tush! silence! mum! hush! *chut!* hist! tut! etc. 403.

586. Allocution.—**N.** allocution, alloquy, address; speech etc. 582; apostrophe, interpellation, appeal, invocation, salutation; word in the ear. [Feigned dialogue] dialogism.

platform etc. 542; audience etc. (*interview*) 588.

V. speak to, address, accost, make up to, apostrophize, appeal to, invoke; hail, salute; call to, halloo.

take -aside, − by the button, button-hole; talk to in private.

lecture etc. (*make a speech*) 582.

Int. soho! halloo! hey! hist! hi!

587. Response etc.; *see* Answer 462

588. Interlocution.—**N.** interlocution; collocution, colloquy, converse, conversation, confabulation, talk, discourse, verbal intercourse; communion, oral communication, commerce; dia-, duo-, tria-logue.

causerie, chat, chit-chat; small −, table −, teatable −, town −, village −, idle- talk; tattle, gossip, tittle-tattle; babble, -ment; *tripotage*, cackle, prittle-prattle, *on dit*; talk of the -town, − village.

conference, parley, interview, audience, *pourparler*; *tête-à-tête*; reception, *conversazione*; congress etc. (*council*) 696; pow-wow.

hall of audience, *durbar*, coliseum, assembly hall, auditorium.

palaver, debate, logomachy, war of words, controversy.

talker, gossip, tattler; Paul Pry; tabby; chatterer etc. (*loquacity*) 584; interlocutor etc. (*spokesman*) 582; conversation-ist, -alist; dialogist.

'the feast of reason and the flow of soul;' *mollia tempora fandi*.

V. talk together, converse, confabulate; hold −, carry on −, join in −, engage in- a conversation; put in a word; shine in conversation; bandy words; parley; palaver; chat, gossip, tattle; prate etc. (*loquacity*) 584.

discourse −, confer −, commune −, commerce- with; hold -converse, − conference, − intercourse; talk it over; be closeted with; talk with one -in private, − *tête-à-tête*.

Adj. conversing etc. *v.*; interlocutory; conversational, -able; discursive, -coursive; chatty etc. (*sociable*) 892; colloquial, *tête-à-tête*, confabulatory.

589. Soliloquy.—**N.** soliloquy, monologue, apostrophe.

solilo-quist, -quizer, monologi 1.

V. soliloquize; say −, talk- to oneself; say aside, think aloud, apostrophize.

Adj. soliloquizing etc. *v.*

Adv. aside.

590. Writing.—**N.** writing etc. *v.*; chiro-, stelo-, cero-graphy, graphology; stylography; pen-craft, -script, -manship; quill-driving; typewriting.

writing, manuscript, MS., *literae scriptae*; these presents.

stroke −, dash- of the pen; *coup de plume*; line, pen and ink.

letter etc. 561; uncial writing, cuneiform character, arrow-head, Ogham, Runes, futhorc; hieroglyphic, hieratic, demotic; script; contraction.

short-hand; steno-, brachy-, tachy-graphy; secret writing, writing in cipher; crypt-, stegan-ography; phono-, pasi-, poly-, logo-graphy.

copy; tran-, re-script; draft, rough −, fair- copy; handwriting; signature, sign-manual; auto-, mono-, holo-graph; hand, fist; mark.

calligraphy; good −, running −, flowing −, cursive −, legible −, copperplate −, round −, bold-hand.

cacography, *griffonage*, *barbouillage*; bad −, cramped −, crabbed −, illegible- hand; scribble etc. *v.*; *pattes de mouche*; ill-formed letters; pot-hooks and hangers.

stationery; pen, quill, goose-quill, reed; stylographic-, fountain-pen; pencil, style, stylus; paper, foolscap, parchment, vellum, papyrus, pad, tablet, block, note book, slate, marble, pillar, table, black board.

ink-bottle, -pot, -stand, -well, -horn; typewriter.

transcription etc. (*copy*) 21; inscription etc. (*record*) 551; superscription etc. (*indication*) 550.

composition, authorship; *cacoethes scribendi*.

writer, scribe, amanuensis, scrivener, secretary, clerk, penman, copyist, transcriber, quill-driver; writer for the press etc. '(*author*) 593.

shorthand writer, stenographer; typewriter, typist.

V. write, pen; copy, engross; write out, − fair; transcribe; scribble, scrawl, scrabble, scratch; interline; stain paper; write down etc. (*record*) 551; sign etc. (*attest*) 467; take down, − in shorthand; typewrite, type.

compose, indite, draw up, redact, draft, formulate; dictate; inscribe, throw on paper, dash off; concoct.

take -up the pen, − pen in hand; shed −, spill −, dip one's pen in- ink.

Adj. writing etc. *v.*; written etc. *v.*; in -writing, − black and white; under one's hand.

uncial, Runic, cuneiform, hieroglyphical etc. *n.*

Adv. *currente calamo*; pen in hand.

591. Printing.—**N.** printing; block −, type-printing, lino-, mono-type; plate printing etc. (*engraving*) 558; the press etc. (*publication*) 531; composition.

print, letterpress, text, matter, standing type; context, note, page, column; over-running; head-, foot-line, title.

typography; stereo-, electro-, apro-type; type,

black letter, heavy type, font, fount; pi, pie; capitals etc. (*letters*) 561; diamond, pearl, nonpareil, minion, brevier, bourgeois, long primer, small pica, pica, english, great primer.

folio etc. (*book*) 593; copy, impression, pull, proof, galley –, author's –, page- proof, revise.

printer, compositor, reader; printer's devil.

V. print; compose; put –, go- to press; pass –, see- through the press; publish etc. 531; bring out; appear in –, rush into- print.

Adj. printed etc. *v.*; in type; typographical etc. *n.*

592. Correspondence.—**N.** correspondence, letter, epistle, note, *billet*, post-, letter-card, missive, circular, form letter; favor, *billet-doux*; des-, dis-patch; *bulletin*, communication etc. 532; these presents; rescript, -ion; post etc. (*messenger*) 534; letter writer, correspondent.

V. correspond, – with; write –, send a letter-to; keep up a correspondence; drop a line to; despatch; communicate with; circularize.

Adj. epistolary.

593. Book.—**N.** book, -let; writing, work, volume, tome, opuscule; tract, -ate; *livret*; *brochure, libretto*, handbook, treatise, text-book, codex, manual, pamphlet, monograph, enchiridion, circular, publication; book of poems; novel; chap-book.

part, issue, number, *livraison*; album, portfolio; periodical, serial, magazine, *ephemeris*, annual, journal.

paper, bill, sheet, broadsheet, screed; leaf, -let; fly-leaf, page; quire, ream.

chapter, section, head, article, paragraph, passage, clause, supplement, appendix; *feuilleton*.

folio, quarto, octavo; duo-, sexto-, octo-decimo.

en-, cyclopedia, dictionary, lexicon, thesaurus, concordance, anthology, bibliography; compilation, compendium, catalogue etc. 86; library, bibliotheca; the press etc. (*publication*) 531.

writer, author, *littérateur*, essayist, journalist, publicist; scribe, penman, war –, special –, correspondent; pen, scribbler, the scribbling race; ghost, hack, literary hack, Grub-street writer; writer for –, gentlemen of –, representative of-the press; reporter, penny-a-liner; editor, sub-editor; playwright etc. 599; poet etc. 597.

bookseller, publisher; biblio-pole, -polist, -grapher; librarian; book -collector, – worm.

book -shop, – club, circulating –, lending –, public- library; publishing house.

knowledge of books, bibliography; book-learning etc. (*knowledge*) 490.

594. Description.—**N.** description, account, statement, report; *exposé* etc. (*disclosure*) 529; specification, particulars, scenario, plot; state –, summary- of facts; brief etc. (*abstract*) 596; return etc. (*record*) 551; *catalogue raisonné* etc. (*list*) 86; guide-book etc. (*information*) 527.

delineation etc. (*representation*) 554; sketch, vignette; monograph; minute –, detailed –, particular –, circumstantial –, graphic- account; narration, recital, rehearsal, relation.

histori-, chron-ography; historic Muse, Clio; history; bi-, autobi-ography; necrology, obituary.

narrative, history; memoir, memorials; annals etc. (*chronicle*) 551; tradition, legend, saga, epic, epos, story, tale, historiette; personal narrative, journal, letters, life, adventures, fortunes, experiences, confessions; anecdote, ana, *trait*.

work of fiction, short story, novelette, novel, romance, penny dreadful, shilling, shocker, Minerva press; fairy –, nursery- tale; fable, allegory, parable, apologue.

relator etc. *v.*; *raconteur*; historian etc. (*recorder*) 553; biographer, fabulist, novelist, story teller, romancer, teller of tales, spinner of yarns, anecdotist.

V. describe; set forth etc. (*state*) 535; draw a picture, picture; portray etc. (*represent*) 554; characterize, particularize; narrate, relate, recite, recount, sum up, run over, recapitulate, rehearse, fight one's battles over again.

unfold etc. (*disclose*) 529- a tale; tell; give –, render- an account of; report, make a report, draw up a statement.

detail; enter into –, descend to- -particulars, – details.

Adj. descriptive, graphic, narrative, epic, suggestive, well-drawn; historic; auto-, biographical, realistic, expository, tradition-al, -ary; legendary; fabulous, mythical; anecdotic, storied; described etc. *v.*

595. Dissertation.—**N.** dissertation, treatise, essay; *thesis*, theme; tract, -ate, -ation, excursus; discourse, memoir, disquisition, lecture, sermon, homily, pandect.

commentary, review, *critique*, criticism, article; lead-er, -ing article, editorial; argument, running commentary.

investigation etc. (*inquiry*) 461; study etc. (*consideration*) 451; discussion etc. (*reasoning*) 476; exposition etc. (*explanation*) 522.

commentator, critic, essayist, pamphleteer; publicist, reviewer, leader writer, editor, annotator.

V. dissert –, descant –, write –, touch- upon a subject; dissertate; treat of –, take up –, ventilate –, discuss –, deal with –, go into –, canvass –, handle –, do justice to- a subject; comment, criticize, interpret-etc. 522.

Adj. dis-cursive, -coursive; disquisitional, disquisitionary; expository, critical.

596. Compendium.—**N.** compend, -ium; abstract, *précis*, epitome, *multum in parvo*, analysis, pandect, digest, sum and substance, brief, abridgment, summary, *aperçu*, draft, minute, note; synopsis, textbook, *conspectus*, outlines, syllabus, contents, heads, prospectus.

album; scrap –, note –, memorandum –, commonplace- book; extracts, *excerpta*, cuttings; fugitive -pieces, – writings; *spicilegium*, flowers, anthology, miscellany, *collectanea, analecta*; compilation.

recapitulation, *résumé*, review.

abbrevia-tion, -ture; contraction; shortening etc. 201; compression etc. 195.

V. abridge, abstract, epitomize, summarize; make –, prepare –, draw –, compile- an abstract etc. *n.*

recapitulate, review, skim, run over, sum up.

abbreviate etc. (*shorten*) 201; condense etc. (*compress*) 195; compile etc. (*collect*) 72; edit, blue pencil.

Adj. compendious, synoptic, analectic, analytical; abridged etc. *v.*

Adv. in -short, – epitome, – substance, – few words.

Phr. it lies in a nutshell.

597. Poetry.—**N.** poetry, poetics, poesy, Muse, Calliope, tuneful Nine, Parnassus, Helicon, Pierides, Pierian spring, afflatus, inspiration.

versification, rhyming, making verses; prosody, scansion, orthometry.

poem; epic, – poem; epopee, *epopaea*, ode, epode, idyl, lyric, eclogue, pastoral, bucolic, georgic, dithyramb, anacreontic, sonnet, roundelay, *rondel, rondoletto, rondeau, rondo,* triolet, madrigal, canzonet, *cento,* monody, elegy, palinode; rhapsody.

dramatic –, lyric- poetry; opera; posy, anthology.

song, ballad, lay; love –, drinking –, war –, folk –, sea- song; lullaby; music etc. 415; nursery rhymes.

[Bad poetry] doggerel, Hudibrastic verse, prose run mad; macaronics; macaronic –, leonine- verse; runes.

canto, stanza, distich, verse, line, couplet, triplet, quatrain, sestet; *strophe, antistrophe,* refrain, chorus, burden.

verse, rhyme, assonance, crambo, meter, measure, foot, numbers, strain, rhythm; accentuation etc. (*voice*) 580; iambus, dactyl, spondee, trochee, anapest etc.; hex-, pent-ameter; Alexandrine; blank verse, alliteration.

elegiacs etc. *adj.*; elegiac etc. *adj.* -verse, – meter, – poetry.

poet, – laureate; laureate; minor poet, bard, lyrist, scald, troubadour, *trouvère*; mistrel; minne-, meister-singer; *improvisatore*; versifier, sonneteer; ballad monger; rhym-er, -ist, -ester; poetaster.

V. poetize, sing, versify, make verses, rhyme, scan.

Adj. poetic, -al; lyric, -al; tuneful; epic; dithyrambic etc. *n.*; metrical; a-, catalectic; elegiac, iambic, trochaic, spondaic, anapest; Ionic, Sapphic, Alcaic, Pindaric.

598. Prose.—**N.** prose, – writer, pros-aism, -aist, -er.

V. prose, write prose.

write -prose, – in prose.

Adj. pros-y, -aic; unpoetical.

rhymeless, unrhymed, in prose, not in verse.

599. Drama.—**N.** drama, the -drama, – stage,

– theater, – play; theatricals, dramaturgy, histrionic art, buskin, sock, *cothurnus,* Melpomene and Thalia, Thespis.

play, stage-play, piece, five-act play, tragedy, comedy, opera, comic opera, *vaudeville, comedietta, lever de rideau,* curtain raiser, interlude, afterpiece, exode, farce, *divertissement, extravaganza,* burletta, harlequinade, pantomime, mimodrama, burlesque, *opéra bouffe,* musical comedy, review, revue, intimate revue, variety, cabaret entertainment, *ballet, spectacle,* masque, *drame, comédie drame;* melo-drama, -drame; *comédie larmoyante,* emotional drama, sensation drama, tragi-, farcical-comedy; mono-drame, -logue; duologue; trilogy; charade, *proverbe*; mystery, miracle –, morality-, play.

act, scene, *tableau*; in-, intro-duction; pro-, evilogue, curtain; *libretto,* book, script.

performance, representation, show, *mise en scène,* stagery, *jeu de théâtre,* stage-craft; acting; gesture etc. 550; impersonation etc. 554; stage business, gag, patter, buffoonery.

theater; play-, opera-house; house; music hall; *cabaret*; amphitheater, circus, hippodrome; puppet-show, *fantoccini; marionnettes,* Punch and Judy.

cinéma, -tograph-, picture –, theater, the pictures, the movies, the talkies.

auditory, *auditorium,* front of the house, stalls, boxes, balcony, dress –, upper- -circle, – boxes, amphitheater, pit, gallery; *foyer;* greenroom; dressing rooms, *coulisses.*

flat; drop, – scene; wing, screen, side-scene; transformation scene, curtain, act-drop, safety –, fire- curtain; *proscenium,* forestage.

stage, revolving stage, scene, the boards; star –, grave –, trap, mezzanine floor; flies; gridiron, floats, battens, footlights; lime –, spot –, flood –, bunch-lights; scenery, set, *décor;* orchestra.

theatrical -costume, – properties, props.

part, *rôle,* character, cast, *dramatis personae; répertoire.*

actor, player; stage –, strolling- player; old –, stager, performer; mime, -r; *artiste;* com-, tragedian, straight man; *tragédienne,* Thespian, Roscius, star.

pantomimist, clown, harlequin, *buffo,* buffoon, *farceur, grimacier,* pantaloon, columbine; *Pierrot, Pierrette*; punch, -inello; *pulcinell-o, -a*; mute, *figurante,* general utility; super, -numerary, extra.

mummer, guiser, guisard, gysart, masque.

mountebank, Jack Pudding; tumbler, posturemaster, acrobat, equilibrist, juggler, contortionist; *danseuse, ballerina,* ballet -dancer, – girl, *coryphée; bayadère, geisha*; chorus -singer, – girl.

company; first tragedian, *prima donna,* lead, leading lady, protagonist; *jeune premier*; juvenile lead, *débutant, -e*; light –, genteel –, low- -comedy, – comedian; *soubrette,* walking gentleman, *amoroso,* heavy, heavy father, *ingénue, jeune veuve, commère, compère.*

property man, *costumier,* machinist, stage hand, electrician, prompter, call-boy; director, manager; stage –, acting –, business- manager; *entrepreneur, impresario,* producer, press agent

dramatic -author, – writer; play-writer, -wright; dramatist, mimographer; dramatic critic.

V. act, play, perform; stage, produce, put on the stage; personate etc. 554; mimic etc. (*imitate*) 19; enact; play –, act –, go through –, perform- a part; rehearse, spout, gag, rant; 'strut and fret one's hour upon a stage;' tread the -stage, – boards; come out; star.

Adj. dramatic; theatric, -al; scenic, histrionic, anctorial, comic, tragic, buskined, farcical, tragi-comic, melodramatic, operatic; stagey spectacular; stagestruck.

Adv. on the -stage, – boards; before -the floats, – an audience; in the limelight, behind the footlights; behind the scenes.

600. Will.—N. will, volition, conation, velleity; will and pleasure, free-will; freedom etc. 748; discretion; choice, inclination, intent, purpose, option etc. (*choice*) 609; voluntariness; spontane-ity, -ousness; originality.

pleasure, wish, desire, mind; frame of mind etc. (*inclination*) 602; intention etc. 620; predeter-mination etc. 611; self-control etc. determination etc. (*resolution*) 604; will-power.

V. will, list; see –, think- fit; determine etc. (*resolve*) 604; settle etc. (*choose*) 609; volunteer.

have a will of one's own; do what one chooses etc. (*freedom*) 748; have it all one's own way; have one's -will, – own way.

use –, exercise- one's discretion; take -upon oneself, – one's own course, – the law into one's own hands; do -of one's own accord, – upon one's own -responsibility, – authority; take the bit between one's teeth; take responsibility; originate etc. (*cause*) 153.

Adj. voluntary, volitive, volitional, wilful; free etc. 748; optional; discretion-al, -ary; volitient; dic-tatorial.

minded etc. (*willing*) 602; prepense etc. (*predetermined*) 611; intended etc. 620; autocratic; unbidden etc. (bid etc. 741); spon-taneous; original etc. (*causal*) 153.

Adv. voluntarily etc. *adj.*; at -will, – pleasure; *à -volonté, – discrétion; al piacere; ad -libitum, – arbitrium;* as -one thinks proper, – it seems good to.

of one's own -accord, – free will; *proprio –, suo –, ex mero- motu;* out of one's own head; by choice etc. 609; purposely etc. (*intentionally*) 620; deliberately etc. 611.

Phr. *stet pro ratione voluntas; sic volo sic jubeo.*

601. Necessity.—N. involuntariness; instinct, blind –, natural- impulse; inborn –, innate-proclivity; the force of circumstances.

necessi-ty, -tation, necessarianism; obligation; compulsion etc. 744; subjection etc. 749; stern –, hard –, dire –, imperious –, inexorable –, iron –, adverse- -necessity, – fate; what must be.

desti-ny, -nation; fatality, fate, *kismet,* doom, foredoom, election, predestination; pre-, fore-ordination; lot, fortune; fatalism, determinism; inevitableness etc. *adj.*; spell etc. 993.

star, -s; planet, -s; astral influence; sky, Fates, Norns, *Parcae,* Sisters three, Clotho, Lachesis, Atropos; book of fate; God's will, will of Heaven; wheel of Fortune, Ides of March, Hobson's choice.

last -shift, – resort; *dernier ressort; pis aller*

etc. (*substitute*).147; necessaries etc. (*requirement*) 630.

necess-arian, -itarian; fatalist, determinist; automaton.

V. lie under a necessity; be -fated, – doomed – destined etc., – in for, – under the necessity of; have no -choice, – alternative; be- obliged –, forced –, driven –, one's -fate etc. *n.*- to; be -pushed to the wall, – driven into a corner, – unable to help, – drawn irresistibly.

destine, doom, foredoom, devote; pre-destine, -ordain; cast a spell etc. 992; necessitate; compel etc. 744.

Adj. necessary; needful etc. (*requisite*) 630.

fated; destined etc. *v.*; fateful; elect; spell-bound.

compulsory etc. (*compel*) 744; uncontrollable, inevitable, unavoidable, irrestible, irrevocable, inexorable, binding; avoid-, resist-less; written in the book of fate.

involuntary, instinctive, automatic, blind, mechanical; un-conscious, -witting, -thinking; unin-tentional etc. (*undesigned*) 621; impulsive etc. 612.

Adv. necessarily etc. *adv.*; of -necessity, – course; *ex necessitate rei;* needs must; perforce etc. 744; *nolens volens;* will he nil he, willy nilly, *bon gré mal gré,* willing or unwilling, *coûte que coûte,* forcefully.

faute de mieux; by stress of; if need be.

Phr. it cannot be helped; there is no- help for, – helping- it; it -will, – must, – must needs- be, – be so, – have its way; the die is cast; *jacta est alea; che sarà sarà;* 'it is written;' one's- days are numbered, – fate is sealed; *Fata obstant; diis aliter visum.*

602. Willingness.—N. willingness, volun-tariness etc. *adj.*; willing mind, heart.

disposition, inclination, leaning, *animus;* frame of mind, humor, mood, vein; bent etc. (*turn of mind*) 820; *penchant* etc. (*desire*) 865; aptitude etc. 698.

doc-ility, -ibleness, tractability; persuasi-bleness, -bility; pliability etc. (*softness*) 324.

geniality, cordiality; goodwill; alacrity, readiness, earnestness, forwardness, enthusiasm; zeal, eagerness etc. (*desire*) 865.

assent etc. 488; compliance etc. 762; pleasure etc. (*will*) 600.

labor of love, self-appointed task; volunteer, -ing, gratuitous service; unpaid worker, amateur.

V. be -willing etc. *adj.*; incline, lean to, mind, propend; had as lief; lend –, give –, turn- a willing ear; have -a, – half a, – a great- mind to; hold –, cling- to; desire etc. 865.

see –, think- -good, – fit, – proper; acquiescence etc. (*assent*) 488; comply with etc. 762.

swallow –, nibble at- the bait; gorge the hook; swallow hook, line and sinker; have –, make- no scruple of; make no bones of; jump –, catch- at; meet half way; volunteer, offer oneself etc. 763.

Adj. willing, minded, fain, disposed, inclined, favorable, favorably- minded, -inclined, -disposed; nothing loth; in the -vein, – mood, – humor, – mind.

ready, forward, enthusiastic, earnest, eager; bent upon etc. (*desirous*) 865; predisposed, propense.

docile; persua-dable, -sible; suasible, easily persuaded, facile, easy-going; amenable; tractable etc.
(*pliant*) 324; genial, gracious, cordial, hearty; content etc. (*assenting*) 488.

voluntary, gratuitous, spontaneous; unasked etc.
(ask etc. 765); unforced etc. (*free*) 748.

Adv. willing etc. *adj.*; fain, freely, as lief, heart
and soul; with -pleasure, – all one's heart, – open
arms; with -good, – right good- will; *de bonne
volonté*, *ex animo*; *con amore*, heart in hand,
nothing lofh, without reluctance, of one's own accord, graciously, with a good grace, without demur.

à la bonne heure; by all -means, – manner of
means; to one's heart's content; yes etc. (*assent*)
488.

Int. sure, -ly! of course!

603. Unwillingness.—N. unwillingness etc.
adj.; indispos-ition, -edness; disinclination, aver-
sation, aversion; nolleity, nolition; renitence; reluctance; indifference etc. 866; backwardness etc.
adj.; slowness etc. 275; want of -alacrity, –
readiness; indocility etc. (*obstinacy*) 606.

scrupul-ousness, -osity; qualms of conscience,
delicacy, demur, scruple, qualm, shrinking, recoil;
hesitation etc. (*irresolution*) 605; fastidiousness
etc. 868.

averseness etc. (*dislike*) 867; dissent etc. 489;
refusal etc. 764.

slacker, scrimshanker, *embusqué*, unwilling
worker, forced labor.

V. be -unwilling etc. *adj.*; nill; dislike etc. 867;
grudge, begrudge; not be able to find it in one's
heart to, not have the stomach to.

demur, stick at, scruple, stickle; hang fire, run
rusty, slack, shirk, scamp, give up, fight shy of, not
pull fair; recoil, shrink, swerve; hesitate etc. 605;
avoid etc. 623.

oppose etc. 708; dissent etc. 489; refuse etc.
764.

Adj. unwilling; not in the vein, loth, shy of,
disinclined, indisposed, averse, reluctant, not content; adverse etc. (*opposed*) 708; laggard, back-
ward, remiss, slack, slow to; renitent; indifferent
etc. 866; scrupulous; squeamish etc. (*fastidious*)
868; repugnant etc. (*dislike*) 867; rest-iff, -ive;
demurring etc. *v.*; unconsenting etc. (*refusing*)
764; involuntary etc. 601; grudging, irreconcilable.

Adv. unwilling etc. *adj.*; grudgingly, with a
heavy heart; with -á bad, – an ill- grace; against
–, sore against- -one's wishes, – one's will, – the
grain; *invitâ Minervâ*; *à contre coeur*; *malgré* soi;
in spite of -one's teeth, – oneself; *nolens volens*
etc. (*necessity*) 601; perforce etc. 744; under
protest; no etc. 536; not for the world, far be it
from me; not if I can help it; if I must I must.

604. Resolution.—N. determination, will; iron
–, unconquerable- will; will of one's own,
decision, resolution, backbone, grit; strength of -
mind, – will; resolve etc. (*intent*) 620; *in-
transigence*; firmness etc. (*stability*) 150; energy,
manliness, vigor; game, pluck; resoluteness etc.
(*courage*) 861; zeal etc. 682; *aplomb*; desperation;
devot-ion, -edness.

mastery over self; self-control, -command, -

mastery, -possession, -reliance, -government, -
restraint, -conquest, -denial; moral -courage, –
strength, – fiber; perseverance etc. 604*a*; tenacity;
obstinacy etc. 606; bull-dog; British lion.

V. have -determination etc. *n.*; know one's own
mind; be -resolved etc. *adj.*; make up one's mind,
will resolve, determine; decide etc. (*judgment*)
480; form –, come to- a -determination, –
resolution, – resolve; conclude, fix, seal, determine once for all, bring to a crisis, drive matters to
an extremity; take a decisive step etc. (*choice*) 609;
take upon oneself etc. (*undertake*) 676.

devote oneself –, give oneself up- to; throw
away the scabbard, kick down the ladder, nail
one's colors to the mast, set one's back against the
wall, set one's teeth, put one's foot down, burn
one's bridges, take one's stand; stand firm etc.
(*stability*) 150; steel oneself; stand no nonsense,
not listen to the voice of the charmer.

buckle to; put –, lay –, set- one's shoulder to
the wheel; put one's heart into; run the gantlet,
make a dash at, take the bull by the horns; beard
the lion in his den; rush –, plunge- *in medias res*;
go in for; insist upon, make a point of; set one's
heart, – mind- upon.

stick at nothing; make short work of etc. (*activity*) 682; not stick at trifles; go -all lengths, –
the whole hog; persist etc. (*persevere*) 604*a*; go
down with colors flying, die game; go through fire
and water, ride in the whirlwind and direct the
storm.

Adj. resolved etc. *v.*determined; strong-willed, -
minded; resolute etc. (*brave*) 861; self-possessed,
plucky, tenacious; decided, definitive, peremptory;
un-hesitating, -flinching, -shrinking; firm, cast iron,
indomitable, game to the backbone; inexorable,
relentless, not to be -shaken, – put down; *tenax
propositi*; inflexible etc. (*hard*) 323; obstinate etc.
606; steady etc. (*persevering*) 604*a*; unbending,
unyielding, irrevocable; firm as a rock; grim.

earnest, serious; set –, bent –, intent- upon.

steeled –, proof- against; *in utrumque paratus*.

Adv. resolutely etc. *adj.*; in –, in good- earnest;
seriously, joking apart, earnestly, heart and soul; on
one's metal; manfully, like a man, with a high
hand; with a strong hand etc. (*exertion*) 686.

at any -rate, – risk, – hazard, – price, –
cost, – sacrifice; at all -hazards, – risks, –
events; cost what it may; *coûte que coûte*; *à tort et
à travers*; once for all; neck or nothing; rain or
shine; with colors nailed to the mast.

Phr. *spes sibi quisque*.

604a. Perseverance. —N. perseverance; continuance etc. (*inaction*) 143; permanence etc. (*absence of change*) 141; firmness etc. (*stability*) 150.

constancy, steadiness, singleness –, tenacity- of
purpose; persistence, plodding, patience; sedulity
etc. (*industry*) 682; pertina-cy, -city, -ciousness;
iteration etc. 104.

bottom, game, pluck, stamina, backbone, grit;
indefatiga-bility, -bleness; bulldog courage.

V. persevere, persist; hold -on, – out; die in the
last ditch, be in at the death; stick –, cling –,
adhere- to ; stick to one's text, keep on; keep to –,
maintain- one's -course, – ground; bear –, keep
–, hold-up; plod; stick to work etc. (*work*) 686;

continue etc. 143; follow up; die -in harness, − at one's post.

Adj. persevering, constant; stead-y, -fast; un-deviating, -wavering, -faltering, -swerving, - flinching, -sleeping, -flagging, -drooping; steady as time; uninter-, un-remitting; plodding; industrious etc. 682; strenuous etc. 686; pertinacious; persist-ing, -ent.

solid, sturdy, staunch, stanch, ture to oneself; un-changeable etc. 150; unconquerable etc. (*strong*) 159; indomitable, game to the last, indefatigable, untiring, unwearied, never tiring.

Adv. through -evil report and good report, − thick and thin, − fire and water; *per fas et nefas*; without fail, sink or swim, at any price, *vogue la galère*; in sickness and in health.

Phr. never say die; *vestigia nulla retrorsum.*

605. Irresolution.—N. irresolution, infirmity of purpose, indecision; in-, un-determination, loss of will power; unsettlement; uncertainty etc. 475; demur, suspense; hesi-tating etc. v., -tation, -tancy; vacillation; ambivalence; changeableness etc. 149; fluctuation; alternation etc. (*oscillation*) 314; caprice etc. 608; lukewarmness.

fickleness, levity, *légèreté*; pliancy etc. (*softness*) 324; weakness; timidity etc. 860; cowardice etc. 862; half measures.

waverer, ass between two bundles of hay; shut-tlecock, butterfly; timeserver, opportunist, turn coat.

V. be -irresolute etc. *adj.*; hang −, keep- in suspense; heave 'ad referendum;' think twice about, pause; dawdle etc. (*inactivity*) 683; remain neuter; dilly dally, hesitate, boggle, hover, wobble, shilly-shally, hum and haw, demur, not know one's own mind; debate, balance; dally −, coquet- with; will and will not, *chasser-balancer;* go half-way, compromise, make a compromise; be thrown off one's balance, stagger like a drunken man; be afraid etc. 860; let 'I dare not' wait upon 'I would;' falter, waver.

vacillate etc. 149; change etc. 140; retract etc. 607; fluctuate; alternate etc. (*oscillate*) 314; keep off and on, play fast and loose; blow hot and cold etc. (*caprice*) 608.

shuffle, palter, blink; trim.

Adj. irresolute, infirm of purpose, double-minded, half-hearted; un-decided, -resolved, - determined; drifting; shilly-shally; fidgety, tremulous; wobbly; hesitating etc. v.; off one's balance; at a loss etc. (*uncertain*) 475.

vacillating etc. v.; unsteady etc. (*changeable*) 149; unsteadfast, fickle, unreliable, irresponsible, unstable, without ballast; capricious etc. 608; volatile, frothy; light, -some, -minded; giddy; fast and loose.

weak, feeble-minded, frail; timid etc. 860; cowardly etc. 862; facile; pliant etc. (*soft*) 324; unable to say 'no,' easy-going.

revocable, reversible.

Adv. irresolutely etc. *adj.*; irresolvedly; in faltering accents; off and on; from pillar to post; see-saw etc. 314.

Int. 'how happy could I be with either!'

606. Obstinacy.—N. obstinateness etc. *adj.*; obstinacy, tenacity; perseverance etc. 604a; im-movability; old school; inflexibility etc. (*hardness*) 323; obdur-acy, -ation; dogged resolution; resolution etc. 604; ruling passion; blind side.

self-will, contumacy, perversity; pervica-cy, -city; indocility.

bigotry, intolerance, dogmatism; opinia-try, - tiveness; fixed idea etc.; intractibility, in-corrigibility; (*prejudgment*) 481; fanaticism, zealotry, infatuation, monomania, opinionativeness.

mule; opin-ionist, -ionatist, -iator, -ator; stickler, dogmatist, die-hard, bitter-ender; bigot; zealot, en-thusiast, fanatic.

V. be -obstinate etc. *adj.*; stickle, take no denial, fly in the face of facts; opinionate, be wedded to an opinion, hug a belief; have one's own way etc. (*will*) 600; persist etc. (*persevere*) 604a; have −, insist on having- the last word.

die -hard, − fighting, fight -against destiny, − to the last ditch; not yield an inch, stand out.

Adj. obstinate, tenacious, stubborn, obdurate, case-hardened; inflexible etc. (*hard*) 323; im-movable, not to be moved; inert etc. 172; un-changeable etc. 150; inexorable etc. (*determined*) 604; mulish, obstinate as a mule, pig-headed.

dogged; sullen, sulky; un-moved, -influenced, - affected.

wilful, self-willed, perverse; res-ty, -tive, -tiff; pervicacious, wayward, refractory, unruly; head-y, -strong; *entêté*; contumacious; cross-grained.

arbitrary, dogmatic, opinionated, positive, bigoted; prejudiced etc. 481; prepossessed, in-fatuated; stiff-backed, -necked, -hearted; hard-mouthed, hidebound; unyielding; im-pervious, - practicable, -persuasible; unpersuadable; in-, un-tractable; incorrigible, deaf to advice, impervious to reason; crotchety etc. 608.

Adv. obstinately etc. *adj.*

Phr. *non possumus*; no surrender.

607. Tergiversation.—N. change of -mind, − intention, − purpose; afterthought.

tergiversation, recantation; palinode, -ody; renunciation; abjur-ation, -ement; defection etc. (*relinquishment*) 624; going over etc. v.; apostasy; retract-ion, -ation; withdrawal, disavowal etc. (*negation*) 536; revo-cation, -kement; reversal; repentance etc. 950; *redintegratio amoris.*

coquetry, flirtation; vacillation etc. 605; back-sliding, recidivation.

turn-coat, -tippet; rat, apostate, renegade, mugwump; con-, per-vert; proselyte, deserter; backslider, recidivist; black leg.

time-server, -pleaser; timist, Vicar of Bray, trim-mer, ambidexter; weathercock etc. (*changeable*) 149; Janus.

V. change one's -mind, − intention, − purpose, − note; abjure, renounce; withdraw from etc. (*relinquish*) 624; wheel −, turn −, veer- round; turn a *pirouette*; go over −, pass −, change −, skip- from one side to another; go to the right about; box the compass, shift one's ground, go upon another tack; back down, crawl, crawfish.

apostatize, change sides, go over, rat; recant, retract; revoke; rescind etc. (*abrogate*) 756; recall, forswear, abjure, unsay; come -over, − round- to an opinion.

draw in one's horns, eat one's words; eat −

swallow- the leek; swerve, flinch, back out of, retrace one's steps, think better of it; come back —, return- to one's first love; turn over a new leaf etc. (*repent*) 950.

trim, shuffle, play fast and loose, blow hot and cold, coquet, flirt, hold with the hare but run with the hounds; straddle; *nager entre deux eaux*; wait to see how the -cat jumps, — wind blows.

Adj. changeful etc. 149; irresolute etc. 605; ductile, slippery as an eel, trimming, ambidextrous, timeserving; coquetting etc. *v.*

revocatory, reactionary.

Phr. 'a change came o'er the spirit of my dream.'

608. Caprice.—N. caprice, fancy, humor; whim, -sey, -wham; crotchet, *capriccio*, quirk, freak, maggot, fad, vagary, prank, fit, flim-flam, *escapade*, *boutade*, wild-goose chase; capriciousness etc. *adj.*; kink.

V. be -capricious etc. *adj.*; have a maggot in the brain; take it into one's head, strain at a gnat and swallow a camel; blow hot and cold; play -fast and loose, — fantastic tricks.

Adj. capricious; erratic, eccentric, fitful, hysterical; full of -whims etc. *n.*; maggoty; inconsistent, fanciful, fantastic, whimsical, crotchety, particular, humorsome, freakish, skittish, wanton, wayward; contrary; captious; arbitrary; unrestrained, undisciplined; not amenable to reason; uncomfortable etc. 83; penny wise and pound foolish; fickle etc. (*irresolute*) 605; frivolous, sleeveless, giddy, volatile.

Adv. by fits and starts, without rhyme or reason, at one's own sweet will.

Phr. *nil fuit unquam sic impar sibi*; the deuce is in him.

609. Choice.—N. choice, option; discretion etc. (*volition*) 600; preoption; alternative; dilemma; *ambarras de choix*; adoption, co-optation; novation; decision etc. (*judgment*) 480.

election, poll, ballot, vote, voice, suffrage, plumper, cumulative vote; *plebiscitum, plébiscite, vox populi; referendum,* electioneering; voting etc. *v.*; franchise; ballot box; slate; ticket.

selection, excerption, gleaning, eclecticism; *excerpta,* gleanings, cuttings, scissors and paste; pick etc. (*best*) 650.

preference, prelation; predilection etc. (*desire*) 865.

V. offer for one's choice, set before; hold out —, present —, offer- the alternative; put to the vote. use —, exercise —, one's- -discretion, — option; adopt, take up, embrace, espouse; choose, elect, co-opt; take —, make- one's choice; make choice of, fix upon.

vote, poll, hold up one's hand; divide.

settle; decide etc. (*adjudge*) 480; list etc. (*will*) 600; make up one's mind etc. (*resolve*) 604.

select; pick, — and choose; pick —, single- out, excerpt; cull, glean, winnow; sift —, separate —, winnow- the chaff from the wheat; pick up, pitch upon; pick one's way; indulge one's fancy.

set apart, reserve, mark out for; mark etc. 550.

prefer; have -rather, — as lief; fancy etc. (*desire*) 865; be persuaded etc. 615.

take a -decided, — decisive- step; commit oneself to a course; pass —, cross- the Rubicon; cast in one's lot with; take for better or for worse.

Adj. optional; co-optative; discretional etc. (*voluntary*) 600; on approval.

ecletic; choosing etc. *v.*; preferential; chosen etc. *v.*; choice etc. (*good*) 648.

Adv. optionally etc. *adj.*; at pleasure etc. (*will*) 600; either, — the one or the other; or; at the option of; whether or not; once for all; for one's money.

by -choice, — preference; in preference; rather, before.

609a. Absence of Choice.—N. no —, Hobson's- choice; first come, first served; necessity etc. 601; not a pin to choose etc. (*equality*) 27; any, the first that comes.

neutrality, indifference; indecision etc. (*irresolution*) 605.

V. be -neutral etc. *adj.*; have no choice; waive, not vote; abstain —, refrain- from voting; leave undecided; make a virtue of necessity.

Adj. neu-tral, -ter; indifferent; undecided etc. (*irresolute*) 605.

Adv. either etc. (*choice*) 609.

610. Rejection.—N. rejection, repudiation, exclusion; declination; refusal etc. 764.

V. reject; set —, lay- aside; give up; decline etc. (*refuse*) 764; exclude, except, eliminate; pluck, spin; cast.

repudiate, scout, set at naught; fling —, cast —, thrown —, toss- -to the winds, — to the dogs, — overboard, — away; send to the right about; disclaim etc. (*deny*) 536; discard etc. (*eject*) 297, (*have done with*) 678.

Adj. rejected etc. *v.*; reject-aneous, -itious; not -chosen etc. 609, — to be thought of; out of the question.

Adv. neither, — the one nor the other; no etc. 536.

Phr. *non haec in foedera.*

611. Predetermination.—N. premeditation, -deliberation, -determination, -destination; foreordination; foregone conclusion; *parti pris;* resolve, propendency; intention etc. 620; project etc. 626.

V. pre-determine, -destine, -meditate, -resolve, -concert; foreordain; resolve beforehand.

Adj. pre-pense, -meditated etc. *v.*, -designed; advised, studied, designed, calculated; aforethought; intended etc. 620; foregone.

well-laid, -devised, -weighed; maturely considered; cut and dried; cunning.

Adv. advisedly etc. *adj.*; with premeditation, deliberately, all things considered, with eyes open, in cold blood; intentionally etc. 620.

612. Impulse.—N. impulse, sudden thought; *impromptu,* improvisation; inspiration, hunch, flash, spurt.

improvisatore, *improvisatrice*, improviser, extemporizer; creature of impulse.

V. flash on the mind.

say what comes uppermost; improvise, extemporize; rise to the occasion; spurt.

Adj. extemporaneous, impulsive, indeliberate; improvis-ed, -ate, -atory; un-, unpre-meditated; *improvisé*; unprompted, -guided; natural, unguarded; spontaneous etc. (*voluntary*) 600; instinctive etc. 601.

Adv. extem-pore, -poraneously; offhand, *impromptu*, *à l'improviste*; improviso; on the spur of the -moment, – occasion.

613. Habit.—N. habit, -ude; assuetude, -faction; wont; run, way.

common –, general –, natural –, ordinary –, habitual- -course, – run, – state- of things; matter of course; beaten -path, – track, – ground.

prescription, custom, use, usage, immemorial usage, practice; tradition; prevalence, observance; conventionalism, -ity; mode, fashion, vogue; *etiquette* etc. (*gentility*) 852; order of the day, cry; conformity etc. 82.

habitué, addict.

one's old way, old school, consuetude, *veteris vestigia flammae*; *laudator temporis acti.*

rule, standing order, precedent, routine; red-tape, -tapism; pipe-clay; rut, groove.

cacoëthes; bad –, confirmed –, inveterate –, intrinsic etc. 5- habit; addiction, trick.

training etc. (*education*) 537; seasoning, hardening, inurement; radication; second nature, acclimatization; knack etc. (*skill*) 698.

V. be -wont etc. *adj.*

fall into a custom etc. (*conform to*) 82; tread –, follow- the beaten -track, – path; *stare super antiquas vias*; move in a rut, run on in a groove, go round like a horse in a mill, go on in the old job-trot way.

habituate, inure, harden, season, caseharden; accustom, familiarize; naturalize, acclimatize; keep one's hand in; train etc. (*educate*) 537.

get into the -way, – knack- of; learn etc. 539; cling –, adhere- to; repeat etc. 104; acquire –, contract –, fall into- a -habit, – trick; addict oneself –, take- to; accustom oneself to.

be -habitual etc. *adj.*; prevail; come into use, become a habit, take root; gain –, grow- upon one.

Adj. habitual, ac-, customary; prescriptive; accustomed etc. *v.*; traditional; of -daily, – every-day- occurrence; wonted, usual, general, ordinary, common, frequent, every-day, household, jog-trot; well-trodden, -known; familiar, vernacular, trite, commonplace, banal, bromidic, conventional, regular, set, stock, officinal, established, stereotyped; pre-vailing, -valent; current, received, acknowledged, recognized, accredited; of course, admitted, understood.

conformable etc. 82; according to -use, – custom, – routine; in -vogue, – fashion; fashionable etc. (*genteel*) 852.

wont; used – given – addicted –, attuned –, habituated etc. *v.*- to; in the habit of; *habitué*; at home in etc. (*skilful*) 698; seasoned; permeated –, imbued- with; devoted –, wedded- to; never free from.

hackneyed, fixed, rooted, deep-rooted, ingrafted, permanent, inveterate, besetting; naturalized; ingrained etc. (*intrinsic*) 5.

Adv. habitually etc. *adj.*; always etc. (*uniformly*) 16.

as -usual, – is one's wont, – things go, – the world goes, – the sparks fly upwards; *more -suo*, – *solito*.

as a rule, for the most part; generally etc. *adj.*; most often, – frequently.

Phr. *cela s'entend.*

614. Desuetude.—N. desuetude, disusage; disuse etc. 678; want of -habit, – practice; inusitation; newness to; new brooms.

infraction of usage etc. (*unconformity*) 83; non-prevalence; 'a custom more honored in the breach than the observance.'

V. be -unaccustomed etc. *adj.*; leave off –, cast off –, break off –, wean oneself of –, violate –, break through –, infringe- -a habit, – a custom, – a usage; break one's fetters; disuse etc. 678; wear off.

Adj. un-accustomed, -used, -wonted, -seasoned, -inured, -habituated, -trained; new; green etc. (*unskilled*) 699; fresh, original, unhackneyed.

unusual etc. (*unconformable*) 83; un-conventional,- non-observant; disused etc. 678.

Adv. just for once.

615. Motive.—N. motive, springs of action.

reason, ground, call, principle; mainspring, *primum mobile*, key-stone; the why and the wherefore; *pro* and *con*, reason why; secret –, ulterior- motive, *arrière-pensée*; intention etc. 620.

inducement, consideration; attraction etc. 288; loadstone; magnet, -ism, -ic force; allect-ation, -ive; temptation, enticement, *agacerie*, allurement; witchery; bewitch-ment, -ery; charm; spell etc. 993; fascination, blandishment, cajolery; seduc-tion, -ement; honeyed words, voice of the tempter, son of the Sirens; forbidden fruit, golden apple.

persuasi-bility, -bleness; attractability; impress-, suscept-ibility; softness; persuas-, attract-iveness; tantalization.

influence, prompting, dictate, instance; impuls-e, -ion; incit-ement, -ation; press, instigation; provocation etc. (*excitation of feeling*) 824; in-spiration; per-, suasion; encouragement, advocacy; exhortation, advice etc. 695; solicitation etc. (*request*) 765; lobbying.

incentive, stimulus, spur, fillip, whip, goad, rowel, provocative, whet, dram.

bribe, lure; decoy, – duck; bait, trail of a red herring; bribery and corruption; sop, – for Cerberus.

prompter, tempter; seduc-er, -tor; suggester; coaxer, wheedler; instigator, firebrand, incendiary; Siren, Circe; *agent provocateur*; lobbyist.

V. induce, move; draw, – on; bring in its train, give an -impulse etc. *n.*- to; inspire; put up to, prompt, call up; attract, beckon.

stimulate etc. (*excite*) 824; spirit up, inspirit; a-, rouse; ecphorize; animate, incite, provoke, in-stigate, set on, actuate; act –, work –, operate-upon; encourage; pat −, clap- on the -back, − shoulder.

influence, weigh with, bias, sway, incline, dispose, predispose,- turn the scale, inoculate; lead, − by the nose; have −, exercise- influence- -with, − over, − upon; go −, come- round one; turn the head, magnetize.

persuade; prevail -with, − upon; overcome, carry; bring -round, − to one's senses; draw −, win −, gain −, come −, talk- over; procure, enlist, engage; invite, court.

tempt, seduce, overpersuade, entice, allure, captivate, fascinate, intrigue, bewitch, carry away, charm, conciliate, wheedle, coax, lure, suggest; inveigle; tantalize; cajole etc. (*deceive*) 545.

tamper with, bribe, suborn, grease the palm, bait with a silver hook, gild the pill, make things pleasant, put a sop into the pan, throw a sop to, bait the hook.

enforce, force; impel etc. (*push*) 276; propel etc. 284; whip, lash, goad, spur, prick, urge; egg −, hound −, hurry- on; drag etc. 285; exhort; advise etc. 695; call upon etc.; press etc. (*request*) 765; advocate.

set -an example, − the fashion; keep in countenance; back up.

be -persuaded etc.; yield to temptation, come round; concede etc. (*consent*) 762; obey a call; follow -advice, − the bent, − the dictates of; act · on principle.

Adj. impulsive, motive; suas-,. persuas-, hortative, -ory; protreptical; inviting, tempting etc. *v.*; seductive, attractive, irresistible; fascinating etc. (*pleasing*) 829; provocative etc. (*exciting*) 824.

induced etc. *v.*; disposed; persuadable etc. (*docile*) 602; spellbound; instinct −, smitten- with; inspired etc. *v.*- by.

Adv. because, therefore etc. (*cause*) 155; from - this, − that- motive; for -this, − that- reason; for; by reason −, for the sake −, on the score −, on account- of; out of, from, as, forasmuch as.

for all the world; on principle.

615a. Absence of Motive.—N. absence of motive; caprice etc. 608; chance etc. (*absence of design*) 621.

V. have no motive; scruple etc. (*be unwilling*) 603.

Adj. without rhyme or reason; aimless etc. (*chance*) 621.

Adv. capriciously; out of mere caprice.

616. Dissuasion.—N. dissuasion, dehortation, expostulation, remonstrance; deprecation etc. 766.

discouragement, damper, wet blanket; warning.

cohibition etc. (*restraint*) 751; curb etc. (*means of restraint*) 752; check etc. (*hindrance*) 706.

reluctance etc. (*unwillingness*) 603; contraindication.

V. dissuade, dehort, cry out against, remonstrate, expostulate, warn, contraindicate.

disincline, indispose, shake, stagger; dispirit; discourage, -hearten, -enchant; deter; hold −, keepback etc. (*restraint*) 751; render -averse etc. 603;

repel; turn aside etc. (*deviation*) 279; wean from; act as a drag etc. (*hinder*) 706; throw cold water on, damp, cool, chill, blunt, calm, quiet, quench; deprecate etc. 766.

Adj. dissuading etc. *v.*; dissuasive; dehortatory, expostulatory; monit-ive, -ory.

dissuaded etc. *v.*; uninduced etc. (*induce* etc. 615); unpersuadable etc. (*obstinate*) 606; averse etc. (*unwilling*) 603; repugnant etc. (*dislike*) 867.

617. Plea. [Ostensible motive, ground, or reason assigned.]—N. plea, pretext; allegation, advocation; ostensible -motive, − ground, − reason; excuse etc. (*vindication*) 937; color; gloss, guise.

loop-, starting-hole; how to creep out of, salvo, come off.

handle, peg to hang on room, *locus standi*; stalking horse, *cheval de bataille*, cue.

pretence etc. (*untruth*) 546; put off, subterfuge, dust thrown in the eyes; blind; moonshine; mere −, shallow- pretext; lame -excuse, − apology, tub to a whale; flase plea, sour grapes; makeshift, shift, white lie; special pleading etc. (*sophistry*) 477; soft sawder etc. (*flattery*) 933.

V. plead, allege; shelter oneself under the plea of; excuse etc. (*vindicate*) 937; gloss over; lend a color to; furnish a -handle etc. *n.*; make a -pretext, − handle- of; use as a plea etc. *n.*; take one's stand upon, make capital out of; pretend etc. (*lie*) 544.

Adj. ostensible etc. (*manifest*) 525; excusing; alleged, apologetic; pretended etc. 545.

Adv. ostensibly; under -color, − the plea, − the pretence- of.

618. Good.—N. good, benefit, advantage; improvement etc. ⫲ 658; interest, service, behoof, behalf; weal; main chance, *summum bonum*, common weal; 'consummation devoutly to be wished;' gain, boot; profit, harvest.

boon etc. (*gift*) 784; good turn; blessing, benison; world of good; piece of good -luck, − fortune; nuts, prize, windfall, godsend, waif, treasure trove.

good fortune etc. (*prosperity*) 734; happiness etc. 827.

[Source of good] goodness etc. 648; utility etc. 644; remedy etc. 662; pleasure-giving etc. 829.

Adj. commendable etc. 931; useful etc. 644; good etc., beneficial etc. 648.

V. benefit, profit, advantage, serve, help, avail; do good to, gain, prosper, flourish.

Adv. well, aright, satisfactorily, favorably, not amiss; all for the best; to one's -advantage etc. *n.*; in one's -favor, − interest etc. *n.*

Phr. so far so good.

619. Evil.—N. evil, ill, harm, hurt, mischief, nuisance; machinations of the devil, Pandora's box, ills that flesh is heir to.

blow, buffet, stroke, scratch, bruise, wound, gash, mutilation; mortal -blow,. − wound; *im-*

medicabile vulnus; damage, loss etc. (*deterioration*) 659.

disadvantage, prejudice, drawback.

disaster, accident, casualty; mishap etc. (*misfortune*) 735; bad job, devil to pay; calamity, bale, woe, catastrophe, tragedy; ruin etc. (*destruction*) 162; adversity etc. 735.

mental suffering etc. 828. [Evil spirit] demon etc. 980. [Cause of evil] bane etc. 663. [Production of evil] badness etc. 649; painfulness etc. 830; evil doer etc. 913.

outrage, wrong, injury, foul play; bad –, ill-turn; disservice; spoliation etc. 791; grievance, crying evil.

V. be in trouble etc. (*adversity*) 735; harm, injure, hurt, do disservice to.

Adj. disastrous, bad etc. 649; awry, out of joint; disadvantageous, injurious, harmful.

Adv. amiss, wrong, ill, to one's cost.

620. Intention.—**N.** intent, -ion, -ionality; purpose; *quo animo*; project etc. 626; undertaking etc. 676; predetermination etc. 611; design, ambition.

contemplation, mind, *animus*, view, purview, proposal; study; look out.

final cause; *raison d'être*; *cui bono*; object, aim, end; 'the be all and the end all;' drift etc. (*meaning*) 516; tendency etc. 176; destination, mark, point, butt, goal, target, bull's-eye, quintain; prey, quarry, game.

decision, determination, resolve; set –, settled-purpose; *ultimatum*; resolution etc. 604; wish etc. 865; *arrière-pensée*; motive etc. 615.

[Study of final causes] teleology.

V. intend, purpose, design, mean; have to; propose to oneself; harbor a design; have in -view, – contemplation, – one's eye, – *petto*; have an eye to.

bid –, labor- for; be –, aspire –, endeavour-after; be –, aim –, drive –, point –, level- at; take aim; set before oneself; study to.

take upon oneself etc. (*undertake*) 676; take into one's head; meditate, contemplate; think –, dream –, talk- of; premeditate etc. 611; compass, calculate; dest-ine, -inate, propose.

project etc. (*plan*) 626; have a mind to etc. (*be willing*) 602; desire etc. 865; pursue etc. 622.

Adj. intended etc. *v.*; intentional, advised, express, determinate; prepense etc. 611; bound for; intending etc. *v.*; minded, disposed, inclined; bent upon etc. (*earnest*) 604; at stake, on the -anvil, – tapis; in -view; – prospect, – the breast of; *in petto*; teleological.

Adv. intentionally etc. *adj.*; advisedly, wittingly, knowingly, designedly, purposely, on purpose, by design, studiously, pointedly; with -intent etc. *n.*; deliberately etc. (*with premeditation*) 611; with one's eyes open, in cold blood.

for; with -a view, – an eye- to; in order -to, – that; to the end –, with the intent- that; for the purpose –, with the view –, in contemplation –, on account- of.

in pursuance of, pursuant to; *quo animo*; to all intents and purposes.

621. Chance.†[Absence of purpose in the succession of events.]—**N.** chance etc. 156; lot, fate etc. (*necessity*) 601; luck; good luck etc. (*good*) 618; bad luck etc. 735; wheel of fortune; mascot; swastika.

speculation, venture, stake, flutter, flier, gamble, game of chance; mere –, random- shot; blind bargain, leap in the dark; pig in a poke etc. (*uncertainty*) 475; fluke, pot-luck.

drawing lots; sorti-legy, -tion; . *sortes*, – *Virgilianae*; *rouge et noir*, hazard, *roulette*, pitch and toss, chuck-farthing, cup-tossing, heads or tails, cross and pile, wager; bet, -ting; risk, stake, plunge; gambling; the turf.

stock exchange, bourse, board of trade, curb exchange.

gaming-, gambling-, betting-house; hell; betting ring, totalizator; dice, – box; dicer; gam-bler, -ester, plunger, stock operator, manipulator, punter; man of the turf; adventurer, speculator; book-maker, layer, backer.

V. chance etc. (*hap*) 156; stand a chance etc. (*be possible*) 470.

toss up; cast –, draw- lots; leave –, trust- -to chance, – to the chapter of accidents; tempt fortune; chance it, take one's chance; run –, incur –, encounter- the -risk, – chance; stand the hazard of the die.

speculate, try one's luck, set on a cast, raffle, put into a lottery, buy a pig in a poke, shuffle the cards.

risk, venture, hazard, stake; lay, – a wager; make a bet, wager, bet, gamble; game, play for; play at chuck-farthing.

Adj. fortuitous etc. 156; unintentional, -ded; accidental; not meant; un-designed, -purposed; unpremeditated etc. 612; never thought of.

indiscrim.nate, promiscuous; undirected, random; aim-, drift-, design-, purpose-, cause-less; without purpose.

possible etc. 470.

Adv. casually etc. 156; unintentionally etc. *adj.*; unwittingly.

en passant, by the way, incidentally; as it may happen; at -random, – a venture, – haphazard; as luck would have it, by -chance, – good fortune; un-, -luckily.

† See note on 156.

622. Pursuit. [Purpose in action.]—**N.** pursuit; pursuing etc. *v.*; prosecution; pursuance; enterprise etc. (*undertaking*) 676; business etc. 625; adventure etc. (*essay*) 675; quest etc. (*search*) 461; scramble, hue and cry, game; hobby.

chase, hunt, *battue*, race, steeplechase, hunting, coursing; ven-ation, -ery; fox-chase; sport, -ing; shooting, angling, fishing, hawking.

pursuer; hunt-er, -sman; sportsman, Nimrod, the field; hound etc. 366.

V. pursue, prosecute, follow; run –, make –, be –, hunt – prowl- after; shadow; carry on etc. (*do*) 680; engage in etc. (*undertake*) 676; set about etc. (*begin*) 66; endeavor etc. 675; court etc: (*request*) 765; seek etc. (*search*) 461; aim at etc. (*intention*) 620; follow the trail etc. (*trace*) 461; fish for etc. (*experiment*) 463; press on etc. (*haste*) 684; run a race etc. (*velocity*) 274.

chase, give chase, course, dog, hunt, hound, stalk; tread –, follow- on the heels of etc. (*sequence*) 281.

rush upon; rush headlong etc. (*violence*) 173;

ride –, run- full tilt at; make a leap –, jump –, snatch- at; run down; start game.

tread a path; take –, hold- a course; shape –, direct –, bend- one's -steps, – course; play a game; fight –, elbow- one's way; follow up; take -to, – up; go in for; ride one's hobby.

Adj. pursuing etc. *v.*; in quest of etc. (*inquiry*) 461; in -pursuit, – full cry, – hot pursuit; on the scent.

Adv. in pursuance of etc. (*intention*) 620; after.

Int. tally-ho! yoicks! so-ho!

623. Avoidance. [Absence of pursuit.]—**N.** abst-ention, -inence; forbearance; refraining etc. *v.*; inaction 681; neutrality.

avoidance, evasion, elusion; seclusion etc. 893.

avolation, flight; escape etc. 671; retreat etc. 287; recoil etc. 277; departure etc. 293; rejection etc. 610.

shirker etc. *v.*; slacker; truant; fugitive, refugee; runa-way, -gate; renegade; deserter.

V. abstain, refrain, spare, not attempt; not do etc. 681; maintain the even tenor of one's way.

eschew, keep from, let alone, have nothing to do with; keep –, stand –, hold- -aloof, – off; take no part in, have no hand in.

avoid, shun, steer –, keep- clear of; fight shy of; keep -one's, – at a respectful- distance; keep –, get- out of the way; evade, elude, turn away from; set one's face against etc. (*oppose*) 708; deny oneself.

shrink; hang –, hold –, draw- back; recoil etc. 277; retire etc. (*recede*) 287; flinch, blink, blench, shy, shirk, dodge, parry, make way for, give place to.

beat a retreat; turn -tail, – one's back; take to one's heels; run, -away, – for one's life; cut and run; be off, – like a shot; fly, flee; fly –, flee –, run away- from; take –, take to- flight; desert, elope; make –, scamper –, sneak –, shuffle –, sheer- off; break –, burst –, tear oneself –, slip –, slink –, steal- -away, – away from; slip cable, part company, turn on one's heel; sneak out of, play truant, give one the go by, give leg bail, take French leave, slope, decamp, flit, bolt, abscond, levant, skedaddle, absquatulate, cut one's stick, walk one's chalks, show a light pair of heels, make oneself scarce; escape etc. 671; go away etc. (*depart*) 293; abandon etc. 624; reject etc. 610.

lead one a -dance, – a merry chase, – pretty dance; throw off the scent, play at hide and seek.

Adj. unsought, unattempted; avoiding etc. *v.*; neutral; shy of etc. (*unwilling*) 603; elusive, evasive, distant; fugitive, runaway; shy, wild.

Adj. lest, in order to avoid.

Int. forebear! keep –, hands- off! *sauve qui peut!* devil take the hindmost.

624. Relinquishment.—**N.** relinquish-, aban-don-ment; desertion, defection, secession, with-drawal; cave of Adullam; *nolle prosequi.*

discontinuance etc. (*cessation*) 142; renun-ciation etc. (*recantation*) 607; abrogation etc. 756; resignation etc. (*retirement*) 757; desuetude etc. 614; cession etc. (*of property*) 782.

V. relinquish, give up, abandon, desert, forsake, leave in the lurch; depart –, secede –, withdraw-from; back – out of, – down from, leave, go back on one's word, quit, take leave of, bid a long farewell; vacate etc. (*resign*) 757.

renounce etc. (*abjure*) 607; forego, have done with, drop; write off; disuse etc. 678; discard etc. 782; wash one's hands of; drop all idea of; *nolle-pros.*; lose interest in.

break –, leave- off; desist; stop etc. (*cease*) 142; hold –, stay- one's hand; quit one's hold; give over, shut up shop.

throw up the -game, – cards; give up the -point, – argument; pass to the order of the day, move the previous question, table the motion.

Adj. unpursued; relinquished etc. *v.*; relinquishing etc. *v.*

Int. avast etc.! (*stop*) 142.

625. Business.—**N.** business, occupation, em-ployment; pursuit etc. 622; what one is doing-, – about; affair, concern, matter, case, undertaking.

matter in hand, irons in the fire; thing to do, *agendum*, task, work, job, chore, errand, trans-action, commission, mission, charge, care; duty etc. 926.

part, *rôle*, cue; province, function, look-out, department, capacity, sphere, orb, field, line; walk, – of life; beat, round, routine; race, career.

office, place, post, incumbency, living situation, appointment, billet, berth, employ; service etc. (*servitude*) 749; engagement; undertaking etc. 676.

vocation, calling, profession, *métier*, cloth, faculty; industry, art; industrial arts; craft, mystery, handicraft; trade etc. (*commerce*) 794.

exercise; work etc. (*action*) 680; avocation; press of business etc. (*activity*) 682.

V. pass –, employ –, spend- one's time in; em-ploy oneself -in, – upon; occupy –, concern-oneself with; make it one's -business etc. *n.*; un-dertake etc. 676; enter a profession; betake oneself to, turn one's hand to; have to do with etc. (*do*) 680.

drive a trade; carry on –, do –, transact- -business, – a trade etc. *n.*; keep a shop; ply one's task, – trade; labor in one's vocation; pursue the even tenor of one's way; attend to -business, – one's work.

officiate, serve, act; act –, play- one's part; do duty; serve –, discharge –, perform- the -office, – duties, – functions- of; hold –, fill- -an office, – a place, – a situation; hold a portfolio.

be -about, – doing, – engaged in, – employed in, – occupied with, – at work on; have one's hands in, have in hand; have on one's -hands, – shoulders; bear the burden; have one's hands full etc. (*activity*) 682.

be -in the hands of, – on the stocks, – on the anvil; pass through one's hands.

Adj. business-like; work-a-day; professional; of-ficial, functional; busy etc. (*actively employed*) 682; on –, in- -hand, – one's hands; afoot; on -foot, – the anvil; going on; acting.

Adv. in the course of business, all in a day's work; professionally etc. *adj.*

626. Plan.—**N.** plan, scheme, design, project; propos-al, -ition; suggestion; resolution, motion;

precaution etc. (*provision*) 673; deep-laid etc. (*premeditated*) 611- plan etc.; racket.

system etc. (*order*) 58; organization etc. (*arrangement*) 60; germ etc. (*cause*) 153; Five Year Plan.

sketch, skeleton, outline, draught, draft, *ébauche, brouillon*; rough-cast, — draft, — draught, — copy; proof, revise.

forecast, *programme*, prospectus, scenario; *carte du pays*; card; bill, protocol; order of the day, list of agenda, *memorandum*; bill of fare etc. (*food*) 298; base of operations; platform, plank.

rôle; policy etc. (*line of conduct*) 692.

contrivance, invention, expedient, receipt, nostrum, artifice, device, gadget; stratagem etc. (*cunning*) 702; trick etc. (*deception*) 545; alternative, loophole, shift etc. (*substitute*) 147; last shift etc. (*necessity*) 601.

measure, step; stroke, — of policy; master stroke; trump-, court-card; *chaval de bataille*, great gun; *coup*, — d'*état*; clever —, bold —, good- -move, — hit, — stroke; bright -thought, — idea, great idea.

intrigue, cabal, plot, frame-up, conspiracy, complot, machination; under-, counter-plot.

schem-ist, -atist; stragetist, machinator, schemer; projector, author, builder, artist, promoter, designer etc. *v.*; conspirator; *intrigant* etc. (*cunning*) 702.

V. plan, scheme, design, frame, contrive, project, forecast, sketch; conceive, devise, invent etc. (*imagine*) 515; set one's wits to work etc. 515; spring a project; fall —, hit- upon; strike —, chalk —, cut —, lay —, map-out; lay down a plan; shape —, mark- out a course; predetermine etc. 611; concert, preconcert, preestablish; prepare etc. 673; hatch — a plot; concoct; take -steps, — measures.

cast, recast, systematize, organize; arrange etc. 60; digest, mature.

plot; counter-plot, -mine; dig a mine; lay a train; intrigue etc. (*cunning*) 702.

Adj. planned etc. *v.*; strategic, -al; planning etc. *v.*; in course of preparation etc. 673; under consideration; on the -*tapis*, — carpet, — table.

627. Method. [Path.]—N. method, way, manner, wise, gait, form, mole, fashion, tone, guise; *modus operandi*; procedure etc. (*line of conduct*) 692.

path, road, route, course; line of -way, — road; trajectory, orbit, track, beat, tack.

steps; stair, -case; flight of stairs, ladder, stile.

bridge, viaduct, gauntry, pontoon, stepping stone, plank, gangway, catwalk, drawbridge; pass, ford, ferry, tunnel, subway, elevated; pipe etc. 260.

door; gateway etc. (*opening*) 260; channel, passage, avenue, means of access, approach, perron, adit, entrance; artery, lane, alley, aisle, lobby, corridor, cloister; back- door, -stairs; secret passage; covert-way.

road-, path-, stair-way; thoroughfare; highway, pike, turnpike, trail, parkway, *boulevard*; turnpike —, royal —, coach- road; broad —, King's —, Queen's- highway; beaten -track, — path; horse —, bridle- road, — track, — path; pathway; walk, *trottoir*, foot-path, pavement, flags, side-walk; by —, cross- -road, — path, — way; cut; short -cut

etc. (*mid-course*) 628; carrefour; private —, occupation- road; highways and byways; rail-, tramroad, -way; funicular, ropeway, causeway; defile, cutting; canal etc. (*conduit*) 350; street etc. (*abode*) 189.

Adv. how; in what -way, — manner; by what mode; so, in this way, after this fashion, on these lines.

one way or another, anyhow; somehow or other etc. (*instrumentality*) 631; by way of; *viâ*; *in transitu* etc. 270; on the high road to.

Phr. *hae tibi erunt artes.*

628. Mid-course.—N. middle-, mid-course; moderation, mean etc. 29; middle etc. 68; *juste milieu, mezzo termine*, golden mean, *aurea mediocritas*.

straight etc. (*direct*) 278 -course, — path; short —, cross- cut; short- circuit; great circle sailing.

neutrality; half —, half and half- measures; compromise.

V. keep in —, steer —, preserve- -a middle, — an even- course; go straight etc. (*direct*) 278.

go half way, compromise, make a compromise.

Adj. neutral, average, even, impartial, moderate, straight etc. (*direct*) 278.

629. Circuit.—N. circuit, round-about way, digression, divagation, *détour*, circum-ambience, -ambulation, bendibus, *ambages*, loop; winding etc. (*circuition*) 311; zigzag etc. (*deviation*) 279.

V. perform —, make- a circuit; go -round about, — out of one's way; make a *détour*; meander etc. (*deviate*) 27; circumambulate.

lead a pretty dance; beat about, — the bush; make two bites of a cherry.

adj. circuitous, indirect, round-about; zig-zag etc. (*deviating*) 279; circum-ambient, -ambulatory.

Adv. by -a side wind, — an indirect course; in a roundabout way; from pillar to post.

630. Requirement.—N. requirement, need, wants, necessities; necessaries, — of life; stress, exigency, pinch, *sine quâ non*, matter of necessity; case of -need, — life or death.

needfulness, essentiality, necessity, indispensability, urgency, prerequisite.

requisition etc. (*request*) 765, (*exaction*) 741; run upon; demand —, call- for.

desideratum etc. (*desire*) 865; want etc. (*deficiency*) 640.

charge, claim, command, injunction, requisition, mandate, order, *ultimatum*.

V. require, need, want, have occasion for, entail; not be able to -do without, — dispense with; prerequire.

render necessary, necessitate, create a necessity for, call for, put in requisition; make a requisition etc. (*ask for*) 765, (*demand*) 741.

stand in need of; lack etc. 640; desiderate; desire etc. 865; be -necessary etc. *adj.*

Adj. required etc. *v.*; requisite, needful,

necessary, imperative, essential, indispensable, prerequisite; called for; in -demand, - request.

urgent, exigent, pressing, instant, crying, absorbing.

in want of; destitute of etc. 640.

Adv. *ex necessitate rei* etc. (*necessarily*) 601; of -, out of stern- necessity; at a pinch.

Phr. there is no time to lose; it cannot be -pared, - dispensed with.

631. Instrumentality.—N. instrumentality; aid tc. 707; subservien-ce, -cy; mediation, interention, -mediacy, medium, inter-medium, mediary, vehicle, hand; agency etc. 170.

minister, handmaid, servant, slave, maid, valet; midwife, *accoucheur*, obstetrician; go-between; at's paw; stepping-stone.

key; master -, pass -, latch- key; 'open eseme;' passport, *passe partout*, safe-conduct; influence.

instrument etc. 633; expedient etc. (*plan*) 626; means etc. 632.

V. subserve, minister, tend, mediate, intervene; ome -, go- between, interpose; pull the strings; be instrumental etc. *adj.*; pander to.

Adj. instrumental; useful etc. 644; ministerial; subservient, mediatorial; inter-mediate, -vening; conducive.

Adv. through, by, *per*; where-, there-, here-by; by the -agency etc. 170- of; by dint of; by -, in-irtue of; through the -medium etc. *n.*- of; along with; on the shoulders of; by means of etc. 632; by -, with- -the aid etc. (*assistance*) 707- of.

per fas et nefas, by fair means or foul; somehow, - or other; by hook or by crook.

632. Means.—N. means, resources, revenue, wherewithal, ways and means, income; capital etc. *money*) 800; stock in trade etc. 636; provision etc. 37; a shot in the locker; appliances etc. *machinery*) 633; means and appliances; coneniences; cards to play; expedients etc. *measures*) 626; two strings to one's bow; sheet anhor etc. (*safety*) 666; aid etc. 707; medium etc. 31.

V. find -, have -, possess- means etc. *n.*; provide the wherewithal.

Adj. instrumental etc. 631; mechanical etc. 633.

Adv. by means of, with; by -what, - all, - any, - some- means; where-, here-, there-with; wherewithal.

how etc. (*in what manner*) 627; through etc. (*by he instrumentality of*) 631; with -, by- the aid tc. (*assistance*) 707- of; by the -agency etc. 170-f.

633. Instrument.—N. machinery, mechanism, engineering.

instrument, organ, tool, implement, utensil, conrivance, machine, motor, engine, lathe, gin, mill, ump.

gear; tack-le, -ling, trice, rigging, gear, apaatus, appliances; plant, *matériel*; harness, trap-

pings, fittings, accouterments; equip-ment, -age; appointments, furniture, upholstery; chattels; paraphernalia etc. (*belongings*) 780; *impedimenta.*

mechanical -powers; lever, -age; mechanical advantage; crow, -bar; handspike, gavelock, jemmy, arm, limb, wing; oar, paddle; pulley, sheave; parbuckle; wheel and axle; wheel-, clock-work; wheels within wheels; pinion, gear wheel, spur -, bevel-gearing, chains, belting, crank, winch, capstan, windlass, crane, derrick, hoist, lift etc. 307; cam; pedal; wheel etc. (*rotation*) 312; inclined plane; wedge; screw; jack; spring, mainspring.

handle, hilt, haft, shaft, heft, shank, blade, trigger, tiller, helm, treadle, key; turnscrew, screwdriver, spanner, wrench.

hammer etc. (*impulse*) 276; edge tool etc. (*cut*) 253; borer etc. 262; vice, teeth etc. (*hold*) 781; nail, rope etc. (*join*) 45; peg etc. (*hang*) 214; support etc. 215; spoon etc. (*vehicle*) 272; arms etc. 727; oar etc. (*navigation*) 267.

Adj. instrumental etc. 631; mechanical, machinal, automatic, self-acting; brachial.

634. Substitute.—N. substitute etc. 147; deputy etc. 759; proxy, alternative, understudy.

635. Materials.—N. material, raw material, stuff, stock, staple; building materials, bricks and mortar; metal; stone; clay, brick; crockery etc. 384; compo-, -sition; reinforced -, ferro-, concrete; cement; wood, ore, timber; gravel, cobbles, macadam, asphalt, tarmac.

materials; supplies, munition, fuel, grist, household stuff; *pabulum* etc. (*food*) 298; ammunition etc. (*arms*) 727; contingents; relay, reinforcement; baggage etc. (*personal property*) 780; means etc. 632.

Adj. raw etc. (*unprepared*) 674; wooden etc. *n.*

636. Store.—N. stock, fund, mine, vein, lode, quarry; spring; fount, -ain; well, -spring; milch-cow.

stock in trade, supply; heap etc. (*collection*) 72; treasure; reserve, *corps de réserve*, reserve fund, nest-egg, savings, *bonne bouche.*

crop, harvest, mow, vintage; yield, product, gleanings.

store, accumulation, hoard, rick, stack; lumber; relay etc. (*provision*) 637.

store-house, -room, -closet; depository, *dépôt*, *cache*, safe deposit, vault, pantechnicon, repository, -servatory, -pertory; *repertorium*; promptuary, warehouse, *entrepôt*, magazine, dump, buttery, larder, pantry, panary, lanary, still-room, spence; crib, garner, granary, silo, barn; bunker; thesaurus; bank etc. (*treasury*) 802; armoury; arsenal; dock; gallery, museum, library, conservatory, hot-house; manag-ery, -erie, aquarium, zoological gardens.

reservoir, cistern, tank, sump, pond, mill-pond; gasometer.

budget, quiver, bandolier, portfolio; coffer etc. (*receptacle*) 191.

conservation; storing etc. *v.*; storage.

dictionary etc. 562; list etc. 86.

V. store; put –, lay –, set- by; stow away; set –, lay- apart; store –, hoard –, treasure –, lay –, heap –, put –, garner –, save- up; *cache*; accumulate, amass, hoard, fund, garner, save, bank.

conserve, reserve; keep –, hold- back; husband, – one's resources.

deposit; stow, stack, load, dump; harvest; heap, collect etc. 72; lay -in, – down, – by, store etc. *adj.*; keep, file [papers] lay in etc. (*provide*) 637; preserve etc. 670; put by for a rainy day.

Adj. stored etc. *v.*; in -store, – reserve, – ordinary; spare, supernumerary.

637. Provision.—N. provision, supply; grist, – to the mill; subvention etc. (*aid*) 707; resources etc. (*means*) 632.

provising etc. *v.*; purveyance; reinforcement; commissary, commissariat.

rations; iron –, emergency- rations; provender etc. (*food*) 298; *viaticum*; ensilage.

caterer, purveyor, commissary, quartermaster, steward, housekeeper, manciple, feeder, batman, victualler, storekeeper, grocer, provision merchant, green-, grocer, *comprador*, *restaurateur*; sutler etc. (*merchant*) 797; innkeeper, publican, confectioner, baker, butcher, wine merchant, vintner.

V. provide; make -provision, – due provision for; lay in, – a stock, – a store.

sup-ply, -peditate; furnish; find, – one in; arm.

cater, victual, provision, purvey, forage; beat up for; stock, – with; make good, replenish; fill, – up; recruit, feed, ration.

have in -store, – reserve; keep, – by one, – on foot; have to fall back upon; store etc. 636; provide against a rainy day etc. (*economy*) 817.

638. Waste.—N. consumption, expenditure, exhaustion; dispersion etc. 73; ebb; leakage etc. (*exudation*) 295; loss etc. 776; wear and tear; waste; prodigality etc. 818; misuse etc. 679; wasting etc. *v.*; rubbish etc. (*useless*) 645.

mountain in labor.

v. spend, expend, use, consume, swallow up, exhaust, deplete; impoverish; spill, drain, empty; disperse etc. 73.

cast –, throw –, fling –, fritter- away; burn the candle at both ends; waste; squander etc. 818.

'waste its sweetness on the desert air;' cast -one's bread upon the waters, – pearls before swine; employ a steam engine to crack a nut, waste powder and shot, break a butterfly on a wheel; labor in vain etc. (*useless*) 645; cut a whetstone with a razor, pour water into a sieve; tilt at windmills.

leak etc. (*run out*) 295; run to waste; ebb; melt away, run dry, dry up.

Adj. wasted etc. *v.*; at a low ebb.

wasteful etc. (*prodigal*) 818; penny wise and pound foolish.

Phr. *magno conatu magnas nugas; le jeu n'en vaut pas la chandelle.*

639. Sufficiency.—N. sufficiency, adequacy, enough, withal, *quantum sufficit*, satisfaction, competence; no less.

mediocrity etc. (*average*) 29.

fill; fullness etc (*completeness*) 52; plen-itude, -ty; abundance; copiousness etc. *adj.*; amplitude, galore, lots, profusion; full measure; 'good measure pressed down, shaken together and running over.'

luxuriance etc. (*fertility*) 168; affluence etc. (*wealth*) 803; fat of the land; 'a land flowing with milk and honey;' cornucopia; horn of -plenty, – Amalthaea; mine etc. (*stock*) 636.

outpouring; flood etc. (*great quantity*) 31; tide etc. (*river*) 348; repletion etc. (*redundance*) 641; satiety etc. 869; rich man etc. 803.

V. be -sufficient etc. *adj.*; suffice, do, just do, satisfy, pass muster; have -enough etc *n.*; eat –, drink –, have- one's fill; roll –, swim- in; wallow in etc. (*superabundance*) 641.

abound, exuberate, teem, flow, stream, rain, shower down; pour, – in; swarm; bristle with.

render -sufficient etc. *adj.*; replenish etc. (*fill*) 52.

Adj. sufficient, enough, adequate, up to the mark, commensurate, competent, satisfactory, valid, tangible.

measured; moderate etc. (*temperate*) 953.

full etc. (*complete*) 52; ample, plen-ty, -tiful, - teous; plenty as blackberries; copious, abundant; abounding etc. *v.*; replete, enough and to spare, flush; choke-full; well-stocked, -provided; liberal; unstint-ed, -ing; stintless; without stint; un-sparing, -measured; lavish etc. 641; wholesale.

rich, luxuriant etc. (*fertile*) 168; affluent etc. (*wealthy*) 803; wantless; big with etc. (*pregnant*) 161.

un-exhausted, -wasted; exhaustless, inexhaustible.

Adv. sufficiently, amply etc. *adj.*; full; in abundance etc. *n.*; with no sparing hand; to one's heart's content, *ad libitum*, without stint.

Phr. cut and come again.

640. Insufficiency.—N. insufficiency; inadequa-cy, -teness; incompetence etc. (*impotence*) 158; deficiency etc. (*incompleteness*) 53; imperfection etc. 651; shortcoming etc. 304; paucity; stint; scantiness etc. (*smallness*) 32; none to spare; bare subsistence.

scarcity, dearth; want, need, lack, poverty, exigency; inanition, starvation, famine, drought.

dole, pittance, mite; short -allowance, – commons; half-rations; banyan –, fast- day, Lent.

emptiness, poorness etc. *adj.*; depletion, vacancy, flaccidity; ebb-tide; low water; 'a beggarly account of empty boxes;' indigence etc. (*poverty*) 804; insolvency etc. (*non-payment*) 808; poor man etc. 804; bankrupt etc. 808.

V. be -insufficient etc. *adj.*; not -suffice etc. 639; come short of etc. 304; run dry.

want, lack, need, require; *caret*; be in want etc. (*poor*) 804; live from hand to mouth.

render- insufficient etc. *adj.*; drain of resources; impoverish etc. (*waste*) 638; stint etc. (*begrudge*) 819; put on short -commons, – allowance.

do -insufficiently etc. *adv.*; scotch the snake.

Adj. insufficient, inadequate; too -little etc 32; not -enough etc. 639; unequal to; incompetent etc. (*impotent*) 158; 'weighed in the balance and found wanting;' perfunctory etc. (*neglect*) 460; deficient etc. (*incomplete*) 53; wanting etc. *v.*; imperfect etc. 651; ill-furnished, -provided, -stored, -off.

slack, at a low ebb; empty, vacant, bare; short –, out –, destitute –, devoid –, bereft etc. 789 –, denuded- of; dry, drained.

un -provided, -supplied, -furnished; un-replenished, -fed; un-stored, -treasured; empty-handed.

meager, poor, thin, scrimp, sparing, spare, stint-ed, stunted; skimpy; starv-ed, -eling; half-starved, emaciated, famine-stricken, famished, underfed, undernourished; jejune.

scant etc. (*small*) 32; scarce; not to be had, – for love or money, – at any price; scurvy; stingy etc. 819; at the end of one's tether; without - resources etc. 632; in want etc. (*poor*) 804; in debt etc. 806.

Adv. insufficiently etc. *adj.*; in default –, for want- of; failing.

641. Redundance.—N. redundance; too - much, – many; superabundance, -fluity, -fluence, -saturation; nimiety, transcendency, exuberance, profuseness; profusion etc. (*plenty*) 639; repletion, enough in all conscience, *satis superque*, lion's share; more than -enough etc. 639; plethora, engorgement, congestion, load, surfeit, sickener; turgescence etc. (*expansion*) 194; over-dose, - measure, -supply, -flow; inundation etc. (*water*) 348; avalanche.

accumulation etc. (*store*) 636; heap etc. 72; drug, – in the market; glut; crowd; burden.

excess; sur-, over-plus, epact; margin; remainder etc. 40; duplicate; surplusage; expletive; work of –, supererogation; *bonus, bonanza.*

luxury; intemperance etc. 954; extravagance etc. (*prodigality*) 818; exorbitance, lavishness.

pleonasm etc. (*diffuseness*) 573; too many irons in the fire; embarrassment of riches; money to burn.

V. super-, over-abound; know no bounds, swarm; meet one at every turn; creep –, bristle-with; overflow; run –, flow –, well –, brim-over; run riot; over-run, -stock, -lay, -charge, -dose, - feed, -burden, -load, -do, -whelm, -shoot the mark etc. (*go beyond*) 303; surcharge, supersaturate, gorge, glut, load, drench, whelm, inundate, deluge, flood; drug, – the market.

choke, cloy, accloy, suffocate; pile up, lay it on, – with a trowel, lay on thick; impregnate with; lavish etc. (*squander*) 818.

send –, carry- coals to Newcastle, – owls to Athens; teach one's grandmother to suck eggs; *pisces natare docere*; kill the slain, 'gild refined gold,' 'paint the lily;' butter one's bread on both sides, put butter upon bacon; employ a steam-engine to crack a nut etc. (*waste*) 638.

exaggerate etc. 549; wallow in; roll in etc. (*plenty*) 639; remain on one's hands, hang heavy on hand, go a begging.

Adj. redundant; too -much, – many; exuberant, inordinate, superabundant, excessive, overmuch, replete, profuse, lavish; prodigal etc. 818; exor-bitant; overweening; extravagant, overcharged etc. *v.*; supersaturated, drenched, overflowing; running -over, – to waste, – down.

crammed –, filled- to overflowing; gorged, stuff-ed, ready to burst; dropsical, turgid, plethoric, full-blooded; obese etc. 194; voluminous.

superfluous, unnecessary, needless, super-vacaneous, uncalled for, to spare, in excess; over and above etc. (*remainder*) 40; *de trop*; adscititious etc. (*additional*) 37; supernumerary etc. (*reserve*) 636; on one's hands, spare, duplicate, supererogatory, expletive; *un peu fort.*

Adj. over, too, over and above; over – , too-much; too far; without – , beyond – out of-measure; with ... to spare; over head and ears; up to one's eyes, – ears; *extra*; beyond the mark etc. (*transcursion*) 303; over one's head.

Phr. It never rains but it pours.

642. Importance.—N. importance, consequence, moment, prominence, consideration, mark, materialness.

import, significance, concern; emphasis, interest.

greatness etc. 31; superiority etc. 33; notability etc. (*repute*) 873; weight etc. (*influence*) 175; value etc. (*goodness*) 648; usefulness etc. 644.

gravity, seriousness, solemnity; no -joke, – laughing matter; pressure, urgency, stress; matter of life and death.

memorabilia, notabilia, great doings; red-letter day.

great -thing, – point; main chance, 'the be all and end all,' cardinal point, outstanding feature; substance, gist etc. (*essence*) 5; sum and substance, *gravamen,* head and front; important –, principal –, prominent –, essential- part; half the battle; *sine quâ non*; breath of one's nostrils etc. (*life*) 359; cream, salt, core, kernel, heart, nucleus; key, - note, -stone; corner stone; trumpcard etc. (*device*) 626; salient points.

top-sawyer, first fiddle, *prima donna,* chief, big-wig; triton among the minnows.

V. be -important etc. *adj.*, – somebody, – something; import, signify, matter, be an object; carry weight etc. (*influence*) 175; make a figure etc. (*repute*) 873; be in the ascendant, come to the front, lead the way, take the lead, play first fiddle, throw all else into the shade; lie at the root of; deserve –, merit –, be worthy- -of notice, – regard, – consideration.

attach –, ascribe –, give- importance etc. *n.*-to; value, care for; set store -upon, – by; mark etc. 550; mark with a white stone, underline; write –, put –, print- in -italics, – capitals, – large letters, – large type, – letters of gold; accentuate, em-phasize, lay stress on.

make -a fuss, – a stir, – a piece of work, – much ado- about; make -of, – much of.

Adj. important; of -importance etc. *n.*; momen-tous, material; to the point; not to be -overlooked, – despised, – sneezed at; egregious; weighty etc. (*influential*) 175; of note etc. (*repute*) 873; notable, prominent, salient, signal; memorable, remarkable; worthy of -remark, – notice; never to be forgotten; stirring, eventful.

grave, serious, earnest, noble, grand, solemn, im-pressive, commanding, imposing.

urgent, pressing, critical, instant.

paramount, essential, vital, all-absorbing, radical, cardinal, chief, main, prime, primary, prin-cipal, leading, capital, foremost, overruling; of vital etc. importance.

in the front rank, first-rate, A1; superior etc. 33; considerable etc. (*great*) 31; marked etc. *v.*; rare etc. 137.

significant, telling, trenchant, emphatic, pregnant; *tanti*.

Adv. materially etc. *adj.*; in the main; above all, *par excellence*, to crown all.

643. Unimportance.—N. unimportance, insignificance, nothingness, immateriality.

triviality, trivia, fribble, levity, frivolity; paltriness etc. *adj.*; poverty; smallness etc. 32; vanity etc. (*uselessness*) 645; matter of indifference etc. 866; no object; side issue.

nothing, − to signify, − worth speaking of, − particular, − to boast of, − to speak of; small −, no great −, trifling etc. *adj.*-matter; mere -joke, − nothing; hardly −, scarcely- anything; nonentity, cipher, figurehead; no great shakes, *peu de chose*; child's play; small beer.

toy, plaything, popgun, paper pellet, gimcrack, geegaw, bauble, trinket, *bagatelle*, kickshaw, knicknack, whim-wham, trifle, 'trifles light as air.'

trumpery, trash, rubbish, stuff, *fatras*, frippery; 'leather or prunello;' chaff, drug, froth, bubble, smoke, cobweb; weed; refuse etc. (*inutility*) 645; scum etc. (*dirt*) 653.

joke, jest, snap of the fingers; fudge etc. (*unmeaning*) 517; fiddlestick, − end; pack of nonsense, mere farce.

straw, pin, fig, continental, button, rush; bulrush, feather, halfpenny, farthing, brass farthing, doit, peppercorn, jot, rap, pinch of snuff, old song.

minutiae, details, minor details, small fry; dust in the balance, feather in the scale, drop in the ocean, flea-bite, molehill; fingle-fangle.

nine days' wonder, *ridiculus mus*; flash in the pan etc. (*impotence*) 158; much ado about nothing etc. (*overestimation*) 482; storm in a teacup.

V. be -unimportant etc. *adj.*; not -matter etc. 642; go for −, matter −, signify- -little, − nothing; − little or nothing; not matter a -straw etc. *n.*

make light of etc. (*underestimate*) 483; catch at straws etc. (*overestimate*) 482.

Adj. unimportant; of -little, − small, − no- - account, − importance etc. 642; immaterial; un-, non-essential; not vital; irrelevant, incidental, indifferent.

subordinate etc. (*inferior*) 34; *médiocre* etc. (*average*) 29; passable, fair, respectable, tolerable, commonplace; uneventful, mere, common; ordinary etc. (*habitual*) 613; inconsiderable, so-so, insignificant, inappreciable, nugatory.

trifling, trivial; slight, slender, light, flimsy, frothy, idle; puerile etc. (*foolish*) 499; airy, shallow; weak etc. 160; powerless etc. 158; frivolous, petty, niggling; pid-, ped-dling; fribble, inane, ridiculous, farcical; fini-cal, -kin; fiddle-faddle, namby-pamby, wishy-washy, milk and water.

poor, paltry, pitiful; contemptible etc. (*contempt*) 930; sorry, mean, meager, shabby, miserable, wretched, vile, scrubby, scrannel, weedy, niggardly, scurvy, putid, beggarly, worthless, twopenny-half penny, cheap, trashy, catchpenny, gimcrack, trumpery, one-horse; toy.

not worth -the pains, − while, − mentioning, − speaking of, − a thought, − a curse, − a straw, − rap etc. *n.*; beneath −, unworthy of- -notice, −

regard, − consideration, − contempt; *de lanâ caprinâ*; vain etc. (*useless*) 645.

Adv. slightly etc. *adj.*; rather, somewhat, pretty well, fairly well, tolerably.

for aught one cares.

Int. no matter! pish! tush! tut! pshaw! pugh! pooh, -pooh! fudge! bosh! humbug! fiddle-stick, − end! fiddlededee! never mind! *n'importe!* what - signifies, − matter, − boots it, − of that, −'s the odds! a fig for! stuff ! nonsense! stuff and nonsense!

Phr. *magno conatu magnas nugas*; *le jeu n'en vaut pas la chandelle*; it -matters not, − does not signify; it is of no -consequence, − importance.

644. Utility.—N. utility; usefulness etc. *adj.*; efficacy, efficiency, adequacy; service, use, stead, avail; help etc. (*aid*) 707; applicability etc. *adj.*; subservience etc. (*instrumentality*) 631; function etc. (*business*) 625; value; worth etc. (*goodness*) 648; money's worth; productiveness etc. 168; *cui bono* etc. (*intention*) 620; utilization etc. (*use*) 677; step in the right direction.

common weal, public good; utilitarianism etc. (*philanthropy*) 910.

V. be -useful etc. *adj.*; avail, serve; subserve etc. (*be instrumental to*) 631; conduce etc. (*tend*) 176; answer −, serve- -one's turn, − a purpose.

act a part etc. (*action*) 680; perform −, discharge- -a function etc. 625; do −, render- a service, − good service, − yeoman's service; bestead, stand one in good stead; be the making of; help etc. 707.

bear fruit etc. (*produce*) 161; bring grist to the mill; profit, remunerate; benefit etc. (*do good*) 648.

find one's -account, − advantage- in; reap the benefit of etc. (*be better for*) 658.

render useful etc. (*use*) 677.

Adj. useful; of -use etc. *n.*; serviceable, usable, proficuous, good for; subservient etc. (*instrumental*) 631; conducive etc. (*tending*) 176; subsidiary etc. (*helping*) 707.

advantageous etc. (*beneficial*) 648; profitable, gainful, remunerative, worth one's salt; in-, valuable; prolific etc. (*productive*) 168.

adequate, ef-ficient, -ficacious; effect-ive, -ual; practicable, expedient etc. 646.

applicable, available, ready, handy, at hand, tangible; commodious, adaptable; of all work.

Adv. usefully etc. *adj.*; *pro bono publico*.

645. Inutility.—N. inutility; uselessness etc. *adj.*; inefficacy, futility; inep-, inap-titude; unsubservience; inadequacy etc. (*insufficiency*) 640; inefficiency etc. (*incompetence*) 158; unskilfulness etc. 699; disservice; unfruitfulness etc. (*unproductiveness*) 169; labor -in vain, − lost, − of Sisyphus; lost -trouble, − labor; work of Penelope; sleeveless errand, wild goose chase, mere farce.

tautology etc. (*repetition*) 104; supererogation etc. (*redundance*) 641.

vanitas vanitatum, vanity, inanity, worthlessness, nugacity; triviality etc. (*unimportance*) 643.

caput mortuum, waste paper, dead letter; blunt tool.

litter, rubbish, lumber, odds and ends, cast-off clothes; button-top; shoddy; rags, orts, trash, refuse, sweepings, scourings, off-scourings, dross, slag, waste, rubble, dottle, drast, *débris*; stubble, leavings; broken meat; dregs etc. (*dirt*) 653; weeds, tares; rubbish heap, dust hole; *rudera*, deads.

fruges consumere natus etc. (*drone*) 683.

V. be -useless etc. *adj.*; go a begging etc. (*redundant*) 641; fail etc. 732.

seek -, strive- after impossibilities; use vain efforts, labor in vain, roll the stone of Sisyphus, beat the air, lash the waves, *battre l'eau avec un bâton, donner un coup d'épée dans l'eau*, fish in the air, milk the ram, drop a bucket into an empty well, sow the sand; bay the moon; preach -, speak- to the winds; whistle jigs to a milestone; kick against the pricks, *se battre contre des moulins*; lock the stable door when the steed is stolen etc. (*too late*) 135; hold a farthing candle to the sun; cast pearls before swine etc. (*waste*) 638; carry coals to Newcastle etc. (*redundance*) 641; wash a blackamoor white etc. (*impossible*) 471.

render -useless etc. *adj.*; dis-mantle, -mast, -mount, -qualify, -able; unrig; cripple, lame etc. (*injure*) 659; spike guns, clip the wings; put out of gear.

Adj. useless, inutile, inefficacious, futile, unavailing, bootless; inoperative etc. 158; inadequate etc. (*insufficient*) 640; in-, un- subservient: inept, inefficient etc. (*impotent*) 158; of no -avail etc. (*use*) 644; ineffectual etc. (*failure*) 732; incompetent etc. (*unskilful*) 699; 'stale, flat and unprofitable;' superfluous etc. (*redundant*) 641; dispensable; thrown away etc. (*wasted*) 638; abortive etc. (*immature*) 674.

worth-, value-less; unsaleable; not worth a straw etc. (*trifling*) 643; dear at any price.

vain, empty, inane; gain-, profit-, fruit-less; unserviceable, -profitable; ill-spent; unproductive etc. 169; *hors de combat*; barren, sterile, impotent, unproductive; effete, past work etc. (*impaired*) 659; obsolete etc. (*old*) 124; fit for the -dust-hole, - wastepaper basket; good for nothing; of no earthly use; not worth -having, - powder and shot; leading to no end, uncalled for: un-necessary, - needed, superfluous.

Adv. uselessly etc. *adj.*; to -little, - no, - little or no- purpose.

Int. *cui bono?* what's the good!

646. Expedience. [Specific subservience.]—**N.** expedien-ce, -cy; desirableness, -bility etc. *adj.*; fitness etc. (*agreement*) 23; utility etc. 644; propriety; advantage; opportunism, pragmatism.

high time etc. (*occasion*) 134.

V. be -expedient etc. *adj.*; suit etc. (*agree*) 23; befit; suit -, befit- the -time, - season, - occasion.

conform etc. 82.

Adj. expedient; desir-, advis-, accept-able; convenient; worth while, meet; fit, -ting; due, proper, eligible, seemly, becoming; befitting etc. *v.*; opportune etc. (*in season*) 134; *in loco*; suitable etc. (*accordant*) 23; applicable etc. (*useful*) 644; practical, effective, pragmatical; suitable, handy.

Adv. in the right place; conveniently etc. *adj.*; in the nick of time.

Phr. *operae pretium est.*

647. Inexpedience.—**N.** enexpedien-ce, -cy; undesira-bleness, -bility etc. *adj.*; discommodity, impropriety; unfitness etc. (*disagreement*) 24; inutility etc. 645; inconvenience, inadvisability; disadvantage.

V. be -inexpedient etc. *adj.*; come amiss etc. (*disagree*) 24; embarrass etc. (*hinder*) 706; put to inconvenience; pay too dear for one's whistle.

Adj. inexpedient, undesirable; un-, in-advisable; objectionable; troublesome, in-apt, -eligible, -admissable, -convenient; in-, dis-commodious; disadvantageous; inappropriate, unsuitable, unfit etc. (*inconsonant*) 24.

ill-contrived, -advised; unsatsifactory; unprofitable etc., unsubservient etc. (*useless*) 645; inopportune etc. (*unseasonable*) 135; out of -, in the wrong- place; improper, unseemly.

clumsy, awkward; cum-brous, -bersome; lumbering, unwieldy, hulky; unmanageable etc. (*impracticable*) 704; impedient (*in the way*) 706.

unnecessary etc. (*redundant*) 641.

Phr. it will never do.

648. Goodness. [Capability of producing good. Good qualities.]—**N.** goodness etc. *adj.*; excellence, merit; virtue etc. 944; value, worth, price.

super-excellence, -eminence; superiority etc. 33; perfection etc. 650; *coup de maître*; master-piece, *chef d'oeuvre*, prime, flower, cream, *élite*, pick, A1, none such, *nonpareil, crême de la crême*, flower of the flock, cock of the roost, salt of the earth; champion.

tid-bit; gem, - of the first water; *bijou*, precious stone, jewel, pearl, diamond, ruby, brilliant, treasure; good thing; *rara avis*, one in a thousand.

beneficence etc. 906; good man etc. 948.

V. be -beneficial etc. *adj.*; produce -, do- good etc. 618; profit etc. (*be of use*) 644; benefit; confer a -benefit etc. 618.

be the making of, do a world of good, make a man of.

produce a good effect; do a good turn, confer an obligation; improve etc. 658.

do no harm, break no bones.

be -good etc. *adj.*; excel, transcend etc. (*be superior*) 33; bear away the bell.

stand the -proof, - test; pass -muster, - an examination.

challenge comparison, vie, emulate, rival.

Adj. harm-, hurt-less; unobnoxious; in-nocuous, -nocent, -offensive.

beneficial, valuable, of value; serviceable etc. (*useful*) 644; advantageous, profitable, edifying; salutzry etc. (*healthful*) 656.

favorable; propitious etc. (*hopegiving*) 858; fair, good, - as gold; excellent: better; superior etc. 33; above par; nice, fine; genuine etc. (*true*) 494.

best, choice, select, picked, elect, eximious, *recherché*, rare, priceless; unpara-goned, -lleled etc. (*supreme*) 33; superlatively etc. 33- good; super-fine, -excellent; bonzer; of the first water; first-rate, -class; high-wrought; exquisite, very best, crack, prime, tip-top, gilt-edged, capital, cardinal; standard etc. (*perfect*) 650; inimitable.

admirable, estimable; praiseworthy etc. (*approve*) 931; pleasing etc. 829; *couleur de rose*, precious, of great price; costly etc. (*dear*) 814; worth -its weight in gold, - a Jew's eye, - a king's ransom; matchless, peerless, invaluable, inestimable, precious as the apple of the eye.

tolerable etc. (not very good) 651; up to the mark, un-exceptionable, -objectionable; satisfactory, tidy.

in -good, - fair- condition; fresh; unspoiled; sound etc. (perfect) 650.

Adv. beneficially etc. adj.; well etc. 618.

649. Badness. [Capability of producing evil. Bad qualities.]—N. hurtfulness etc. adj.; virulence.

evil doer etc. 913; bane etc. 663; plague-spot etc. (insalubrity) 657; evil star, ill wind; snake in the grass, skeleton in the closet; amari aliquid, thorn in the side; Jonah, jinx, hoodoo.

malignity; malevolence etc. 907; tender mercies [ironically].

ill-treatment, annoyance, molestation, abuse, oppression, persecution, outrage; misusage etc. 679; injury etc. (damage) 659.

badness etc. adj.; peccancy, abomination; painfulness etc. 830; pestilence etc. (disease) 655; guilt etc. 947; depravity etc. 945.

V. be -hurtful etc. adj.; cause -, produce -, inflict -, work -, do- evil etc. 619; damnify, endamage, hurt, harm, scathe; injure etc. (damage) 659; pain etc. 830.

wrong, aggrieve, oppress, persecute; trample -, tread -, bear hard -, put-upon; overburden; weigh -down, - heavy on; victimize; run down; molest etc. 830.

maltreat, abuse; ill-use, -treat; thwart, buffet, bruise, scratch, maul; smite etc. (scourge) 972; do -violence, - harm, - a mischief; stab, pierce, outrage.

do -, make- mischief; bring -, get- into trouble.

destroy etc. 162.

Adj. hurt-, harm-, scath-, bane-, bale-ful; injurious, deleterious, detrimental, noxious, pernicious, mischievous, full of mischief, mischief-making, malefic, malignant, nocuous, noisome; prejudicial; dis-serviceable, advantageous; wide-wasting.

unlucky, sinister; obnoxious, untoward, disastrous.

oppressive, burdensome, onerous; malign etc. (malevolent) 907.

corrupting etc. (corrupt etc. 659) virulent, venomous, envenomed, corrosive; poisonous etc. (morbific) 657; deadly etc. (killing) 361; destructive etc. (destroying) 162; inauspicious etc. 859.

bad, ill, arrant, as bad bad can be, dreadful; horrid, -rible; dire; rank, peccant, foul, fulsome; rotten, - at the core.

vile, base, villainous; mean etc. (paltry) 643; injured etc., deteriorated etc. 659; unsatisfactory, exception, -able, indifferent; below par etc. (imperfect) 651; ill-contrived, -conditioned; wretched, sad, grievous, deplorable, lamentable; piti-ful, -able, woeful etc. (painful) 830.

evil, wrong; depraved etc. 945; shocking; reprehensible etc. (disapprove) 932.

hateful, - as a toad; abominable, detestable, execrable, cursed, accursed, confounded; damn-ed, -able; infernal; diabolic etc. (malevolent) 907.

inadvisable etc. (inexpedient) 647; unprofitable etc. (useless) 645; incompetent etc. (unskilful) 699; irremediable etc. (hopeless) 859.

Adv. badly etc. adj.; wrong, ill; to one's cost; where the shoe pinches.

Phr. bad is the best; the worst come to the worst.

650. Perfection.—N. perfection; perfectness etc. adj.; indefectibility; inpecc-ancy, -ability.

pink, beau idéal, phoenix, paragon; pink -, acme- of perfection; ne plus ultra; summit etc. 210.

cygne noir; philosopher's stone; chrysolite, Koh-i-noor, black tulip.

model, standard, pattern, mirror, admirable Chrichton; trump; very prince of.

master-piece, -stroke, super-excellence etc. (goodness) 648; transcendence etc. (superiority) 33.

V. be -perfect etc. adj.; transcend etc. (be supreme) 33.

bring to perfection, perfect, ripen, mature; consummate, complete etc. 729; put in trim etc. (prepare) 673; put the finishing touch to.

Adj. perfect, faultless, ideal; indefective, -ficient, -fectible; immaculate, spotless, impeccable; free from -imperfection etc. 651; un-blemished, -injured etc. 659; sound, - as a roach; in perfect condition; scathless, intact, harmless; seaworthy etc. (safe) 644; right as a trivet; in seipso totus teres atque rotundus; consummate etc. (complete) 52; finished etc. 729; complete in itself.

best etc. (good) 648; model, standard; inimitable, unparagoned, unparalleled etc. (supreme) 33; superhuman, divine; beyond all praise etc. (approbation) 931; sans peur et sans reproche.

Adj. to perfection, to the limit; perfectly etc. adj.; ad unguem; clean, - as a whistle.

651. Imperfection.—N. imperfection; imperfectness etc. adj.; deficiency; inadequacy etc. (insufficiency) 640; peccancy etc. (badness) 649; immaturity etc. 674.

fault, defect, weak point; screw loose; rift within the lute; fly in the ointment; flaw etc. (break) 70; gap etc. 198; twist etc. 243; taint, attainder; bar sinister, hole in one's coat; blemish etc. 848; weakness etc. 160; half-blood, touch of the tar brush; shortcoming etc. 304; drawback; seamy side.

mediocrity; no great -shakes, - catch; not much to boast of.

V. be -imperfect etc. adj.; have a -defect etc. n.; lie under a disadvantage; spring a leak.

not -, barely- pass muster; fall short etc. 304.

Adj. imperfect; not -perfect etc. 650; de-ficient, -fective; faulty, unsound, mutilated, tainted; out of -order, - tune; cracked, leaky; sprung; warped etc. (distort) 243; lame; injured etc. (deteriorated) 659; peccant etc. (bad) 649; frail etc. (weak) 160; inadequate etc. (insufficient) 640; crude etc. (unprepared) 674; incomplete etc. 53; found wanting; below par; shorthanded; below -, under- its full -strength, - complement.

indifferent, middling, ordinary, mediocre; average etc. 29; so-so; *cosi-cosi*, milk and water; tolerable, fair, passable; pretty -well, – good; rather –, moderately- good; good –, well-enough; decent; not -bad, – amiss; inobjectionable, admissable, bearable, only better than nothing.

secondary, inferior; second-rate, -best, one-horse.

Adv. almost etc.; to a limited extent, rather etc. 32; pretty, moderately; only; considering, all things considered, enough.

Phr. *surgit amari aliquid.*

652. Cleanness.—N. cleanness etc. *adj.*; purity; cleaning etc. *v.*; purification, defecation etc. *v.*; purgation, lustration; de-, abs-tersion; epuration, mundation, ablution, lavation, colature; disinfection etc. *v.*; drain-, sewerage.

lavatory, bath, -room; swimming pool, natatorium; public baths; hot –, cold –, Turkish –, Swedish –, Russian – vapor- bath; *hammam*, laundry, washhouse; washerwoman, laundress, laundryman; scavenger, cleaner, sweeper, goodie; crossing sweeper, white wings, dustman, sweep.

brush; broom, besom, carpet-sweeper, vacuum-cleaner, mop, squilgee, rake, shovel, sieve, riddle, screen, filter; scraper, strigil.

napkin, *serviette*, cloth, table-, carving-cloth, table-linen, napery, maukin, handkerchief, towel, sudary; doyley, doily, duster, sponge, mop, swab.

cover, drugget, mat, doormat.

soap, wash, lotion, detergent, cathartic, purgative; purifier etc. *v.*; dentifrice, tooth-powder, -paste; mouth wash; disinfectant.

V. be –, render- clean etc. *adj.*

clean, -se; mundify, rinse, wring, flush, full, wipe, mop, sponge, scour, swab, scrub, holystone, brush up.

'wash, shampoo, lave, launder, buck; abs-, de-terge; clear, purify; de-purate, -spumate, -fecate; purge, expurgate; Bowdlerize; elutriate, lixiviate, edulcorate, clarify, refine, rack; fil-ter, -trate; drain, strain.

disinfect, sterilize, pasteurize, fumigate, ventilate, deodorize; whitewash.

sift, winnow, screen, riddle, pick, weed, comb, rake, brush, sweep

rout –, clear –, sweep etc.- out; make a clean sweep of.

Adj. clean, -ly; pure; immaculate; spot-, stain-taint-less; without a stain, un-stained, -spotted, -soiled, -sullied, -tainted, -infected, -adulterated; aseptic; sweet, – as a nut.

neat, spruce, tidy, trim, gimp, clean as a new penny, like a cat in pattens; cleaned etc. *v.*; kempt.

Adv. neatly etc. *adj.*; clean as a whistle.

653. Uncleanness.—N. uncleanness etc. *adj.*; impurity; immundi-ty, -city; impurity etc. [of mind] 961.

defilement, contamination etc. *v.*; defedation; soil-ure, -iness; abomination; leaven; taint, -ure; fetor etc. 401.

decay; putre-scence, -faction; corruption; mold, must, mildew, dry-rot, *mucor*, rubigo, caries.

slovenry; slovenliness etc. *adj.*; squalor.

dowdy, drab, slut, malkin, slattern, sloven, slam-merkin, scrub, draggletail, mudlark, dustman, sweep; beast.

dirt, filth, soil, slop; dust, cobweb, flue; smoke, soot, smudge, smut, grime, raff.

sordes, dregs, grounds, lees; sedi-, settle-ment; heel-tap; dross, -iness; mother, precipitate, *scoria*, ashes, cinders, recrement, slag; scum, froth.

hog-wash, swill, ditch-, dish-, bilge-water; rins-ings, cheese-parings; sweepings etc. (*useless refuse*) 645; off-, out-scourings; off-scum; *caput mortuum*, *residuum*, sprue, feculence, clinker, draff; scurf, -iness; *exuviae*, morphew; fur, -fur; dandruff; tartar.

riffraff; vermin, louse, cootie, flea, bug.

mud, mire, quagmire, *alluvium*, silt, sludge, slime, slush, slosh.

spawn, offal, garbage, carrion; *excreta* etc. 299; slough, peccant humor, pus, matter, suppuration, *lienteria*; *feces*, excrement, ordure, dung; sew-sewer-age; muck, coprolite; guano, manure, com-post.

dunghill, *coluvies*, mixen, midden, bog, laystall, sink, w.c., water-, earth-closet, latrine, privy, jakes, John's, cess, -pool; sump, sough, *cloaca*, drain, sewer, common sewer; Cloacina; dust-hole.

sty, pig-sty, lair, den, Augean stable, sink of corruption; slum, rookery.

V. be –, become- unclean etc. *adj.*; rot, putrefy, fester, rankle, reek; stink etc. 401; mold, -er; go - bad etc. *adj.*

render -unclean etc. *adj.*; dirt, -y; soil, smoke, tarnish, slaver, spot, smear, daub, blot, blur, smudge, smutch, smirch; d-, dr-abble, -aggle; spat-ter, slubber; be-smear etc.; -mire, -slime, -grime, - foul; splash, stain, distain, maculate, sully, pollute, defile, debase, contaminate, taint, leaven; corrupt etc. (*injure*) 659; cover with -dust etc. *n.*; drabble in the mud.

wallow in the mire; slob-, slab-ber.

Adj. unclean, dirty, filthy, grimy, soiled etc. *v.*; not to be handled with kid gloves; dusty, snuffy, smutty, sooty, smoky; thick, turbid, dreggy; slimy.

uncleanly, slovenly, untidy, sluttish, dowdy, slat-ternly, draggletailed; un-combed, -kempt, -scoured, -swept, -wiped, -washed, -strained, -purified; squalid.

nasty, coarse, foul, impure, offensive, abominable, beastly, reeky, reechy; fetid etc. 401.

moldy, lentiginous, musty, mildewed, rusty, moth-eaten, mucid, rancid, bad, gone bad, touched, fusty, reasty, rotten, corrupt, tainted, high, fly-blown, maggoty; putr-id, -escent, -efied; purulent, carious, peccant, fec-al, -ulent; ster-coraceous, excrementitious; scurfy, impetiginous; gory, bloody; rotting etc. *v.*; rotten as -a pear, – cheese.

crapulous etc. (*intemperate*) 954; gross etc. (*impure in mind*) 961.

654. Health.—N. health, sanity; soundness etc. *adj.*; vigor; good –, perfect –, excellent –, rude –, robust- health; bloom, *mens sana in corpore sanò*; Hygeia; incorrupti-on, -bility; good state –, clean bill- of health; eupepsia

V. be in health etc. *adj.*; bloom, flourish.

keep -body and soul together, – on one's legs; enjoy -good, – a good state of - health; have a clean bill of health.

return to health; recover etc. 660; get better etc. (*improve*) 658; take a -new, – fresh- lease of life; convalesce, be convalescent, recruit; restore to health; cure etc. (*restore*) 660.

Adj. health-y, -ful; in -health etc. *n.*; well, sound, strong, fit, hearty, hale, fresh, blooming, green, whole; florid, flush, hardy, stanch, staunch, brave, robust, vigorous, weather-proof; convalescent.

un-scathed, -injured, -maimed, -marred, -tainted; sound of wind and limb, safe and sound; without a scratch.

on one's legs; sound as a -roach, – bell; fresh as -a daisy, – a rose, – April; picture of health; bursting with health; fit as a fiddle; hearty as a buck; in -fine, – high- feather; in -good case, – full bloom; in fine fettle; pretty bobbish, tolerably well, as well as can be expected.

sanitary etc. (*health-giving*) 656; sanatory etc. (*remedial*) 662.

655. Disease.°—N. disease, illness, sickness etc. *adj.*; ailing etc. *v.*; 'the ills that flesh is heir to;' morb-idity, -osity; infirmity, ailment, indisposition; complaint, disorder, malady; distemper, -ature.

visitation, attack, seizure, stroke, fit, epilepsy, apoplexy, shock, shell-shock.

delicacy, loss of health, valetudinarianism, invalidism, cachexy; *cachexia*, atrophy, *marasmus*; indigestion, *dyspepsia*; decay etc. (*deterioration*) 659; malnutrition, decline, consumption, palsy, paralysis, prostration; occupational diseases.

taint, pollution, infection, contagion, septicity, septicaemia, blood poisoning, pyaemia, epi-, endemic; murrain, plague, pestilence, virus, pox.

sore, ulcer, abscess, fester, boil; pimple etc. (*swelling*) 250; carbuncle, gathering, whitlow, imposthume, peccant humor, issue; rot, canker, cancer, *carcinoma*, *caries*, mortification, corruption, gangrene, *sphacelus*, leprosy, eruption, rash, breaking out, venereal disease.

fever, calenture; inflammation.

fatal etc. (*hopeless*) 859- -disease etc.; dangerous illness, galloping consumption, churchyard cough; general breaking up, break up of the system.

[Disease of the mind] neurasthenia; idiocy etc. 499; insanity etc. 503.

martyr to disease; cripple; 'the halt, the lame and the blind;' valetudinar-y, -ian; invalid, patient, case; sick-room, -chamber, hospital etc. 662.

[Science of disease] path-, eti-, nos-ology; therapeutics, diagnosis, prognosis.

V. be -ill etc. *adj.*; ail, suffer, labor under, be affected with, complain of; droop, flag, languish, halt; sicken, peak, pine, waste away, fail, lose strength; gasp.

keep one's bed; feign sickness etc. (*falsehood*) 544; malinger.

lay -by, – up; take –, catch- -a disease etc. *n.*, – an infection; be stricken by; break out.

Adj. diseased; ailing etc. *v.*; ill, – of; taken ill, seized with; indisposed, unwell, sick, squeamish, poorly, seedy; affected –, afflicted- with illness; laid up, confined, bed-ridden, invalided, in hospital, on the sick list; out of -health, – sorts; valetudinary.

un-sound, -healthy; sickly, morbose, healthless,

infirm, chlorotic, unbraced, drooping, flagging, lame, halt, crippled, halting.

morbid, tainted, vitiated, peccant, contaminated, poisoned, septic, tabid, mangy, leprous, cankered; rotten, – to, – at- the core; withered, palsied, paralytic, tuberculous; dyspeptic.

touched in the wind, broken-winded, spavined, gasping; *hors de combat* etc. (*useless*) 645.

weak-ly, -ened etc. (*weak*) 160; decrepit; decayed etc. (*deteriorated*) 659; incurable etc. (*hopeless*) 859; in declining health; cranky; in a bad way, in danger, prostrate; moribund etc. (*death*) 360.

morbific, epidemic etc. 657.

*Extended lists of different diseases are beyond the scope of this work.

656. Salubrity.—N. salubrity, salubriousness; healthiness etc. *adj.*

fine -air, – climate; eudiometer.

[Preservation of health] *hygiène*; valetudinarian, -ism, preventorium, sanitarian; *sanitarium, sanitorium,* immunity.

V. be -salubrious etc. *adj.*; agree with, be good for; assimilate etc. 23.

Adj. salu-brious, -tary, -tiferous, wholesome; health-y, -ful; sanitary, prophylactic, benign, bracing, tonic, invigorating, good for, nutritious, hyg-eian, -ienic.

in-noxious, -nocuous, -nocent; harmless, uninjurious, uninfectious; immune.

sanative etc. (*remedial*) 662; restorative etc. (*reinstate*) 660; useful etc. 644.

657. Insalubrity.—N. insalubrity, unhealthiness etc. *adj.*; non-naturals; plague spot; malaria etc. (*poison*) 663; death in the pot, contagion.

Adj. insalubrious; un-healthy, -wholesome; noxious, noisome, foul; morbi-fic, -ferous; mephitic, septic, azotic, deleterious, pesti-lent, -ferous, -lential; virulent, venomous, envenomed, poisonous, toxic, narcotic.

contagious, infectious, catching, taking, communicable, epidemic, zymotic, sporadic, endemic, pandemic, epizoötic.

innutritious, indigestible, ungenial; uncongenial etc. (*disagreeing*) 24.

deadly etc. (*killing*) 361.

658. Improvement.—N. improvement; a-, melioration; betterment; mend, amendment, emendation; mending etc. *v.*; advancement; advance etc. (*progress*) 282; ascent etc. 305; promotion, preferment; elevation etc. 307; increase etc. 35.

cultiv-, civiliz-ation; menticulture, culture, march of intellect; eugenics, euthenics, meliorism, telesis.

reform, -ation; revision, radical reform; second thoughts, correction, *limae labor*, refinement, elaboration; purification etc. 652; repair etc (*restoration*) 660; recovery etc. 660.

revise; revised –, new- edition.

reformer, radical, progressive.

V. improve; be —, become —, get- better; mend, amend.

advance etc. (*progress*) 282; ascend etc. 305; increase etc. 35; fructify, ripen, mature; pick up, come about, rally, take a favorable turn; turn -over a new leaf, — the corner; raise one's head, sow one's wild oats; recover etc. 660.

be -better etc. *adj.*, — improved by; turn to - right, — good, — best- account; profit by, reap the benefit of; make good use of, — capital out of; place to good account; take advantage of.

render better, improve, emend, make over, better; a-, meliorate; correct.

improve —, refine- upon; rectify; enrich, mellow, elaborate, fatten.

promote, cultivate, advance, forward, enhance; bring -forward, — on; foster etc. 707; invigorate etc. (*strengthen*) 159.

touch —, rub —, brush —, furbish —, bolster —, vamp —, brighten —, warm- up; polish, cook, make the most of, set off to advantage; prune; repair etc. (*restore*) 660; put in order etc. (*arrange*) 60.

review, revise, edit, redact; make -corrections, - improvements etc. *n.*; doctor etc. (*remedy*) 662; purify etc. 652.

relieve, refresh, revive, infuse new blood into, recruit, re-invigorate, renew, revivify, freshen; build -afresh, — anew; uplift, inspire.

re-form, -model, -organize; new model, civilize.

view in a new light, think better of, appeal from Philip drunk to Philip sober.

palliate, mitigate; lessen etc. 36- an evil.

Adj. improving etc. *v.*; progressive, improved etc. *v.*; better, — off, — for; all the better for; better advised.

reform-, emend-atory; reparatory etc. (*restorative*) 660; remedial etc. 662.

corrigible, improvable, curable, accultural.

Adv. on -consideration, — reconsideration, — second thoughts, — better advice; *ad melius inquirendum*; on the -mend, — up grade.

---

659. Deterioration.—N. deterioration, debasement; want, ebb; recession etc. 287; retrogradation etc. 283; decrease etc. 36.

degenera-cy, -tion, -teness; degradation; depravation, -ement; depravity etc. 945; demoralization, retrogression.

impairment, inquination, injury, damage, loss, detriment, delaceration, outrage, havoc, inroad, ravage, scath; perversion, prostitution, vitiation, discoloration, oxidation, pollution, defedation, poisoning, venenation, leaven, contamination, canker, corruption, adulteration, alloy.

decl-ine, -ension, -ination; decadence, -cy; falling off etc. *v.*; caducity, decrepitude, senility.

decay, dilapidation, ravages of time, wear and tear; cor-, e-rosion; mouldi-, rotten-ness; moth and rust, dry-rot, blight, marasmus, atrophy, collapse; disorganization; *délabrement* etc. (*destruction*) 162.

wreck, mere wreck, honeycomb, *magni nominis umbra*.

V. be —, become- -worse, — deteriorated etc. *adj.*; have seen better days, deteriorate, degenerate,

---

fall off; wane etc. (*decrease*) 36; ebb; retrograde etc. 283; decline, droop; go down etc. (*sink*) 306; go -downhill, — on from bad to worse, — farther and fare worse; jump out of the frying pan into the fire.

run to -seed, — waste; swale, sweal; lapse, be the worse for; break, — down; spring a leak, crack, start; shrivel etc. (*contract*) 195; fade, go off, wither, molder, rot, rankle, decay, go bad; go to — fall into- decay; 'fall into the sear and yellow leaf,' rust, crumble, shake; totter, — to its fall; perish etc. 162; die etc. 360.

[Render less good] deteriorate; weaken etc. 160; put back; taint, infect, contaminate, poison, empoison, envenom, canker; corrupt, exulcerate, pollute, vitiate, inquinate; de-, em-base; denaturalize, leaven; de-flower, -bauch, -file, - prave, -grade; stain etc. (*dirt*) 653; discolor; alloy, adulterate, sophisticate, tamper with, prejudice.

pervert, prostitute, demoralize, brutalize; render vicious etc. 945; compromise.

embitter, ex-, acerbate, aggravate.

injure, impair, labefy, damage, harm, hurt, shend, scathe; spoil, mar, despoil, dilapidate, waste; overrun; ravage; pillage etc. 791.

wound, stab, pierce, maim, lame, surbate, cripple, hough, hamstring, hit between the wind and water, scotch, mangle, mutilate, disfigure, blemish, deface, warp.

blight, rot; cor-, e-rode, eat away; wear -away, — out; gnaw, — at the root of; sap, mine, undermine, shake, sap the foundations of, break up; dis-organize, -mantle, -mast; destroy etc. 162.

damnify etc. (*aggrieve*) 649; do one's worst; knock down; deal a blow to; play -havoc, — sad havoc, — the mischief, — the deuce, — the very devil- -with, — among; decimate.

Adj. unimproved etc. (improve etc. 658); deteriorated etc. *v.*; altered, — for the worse; injured etc. *v.*; sprung; withering, spoiling, etc. *v.*; on the -wane, — decline; tabid; degenerate; worse; the —, all the- worse for; out of -repair, — tune; imperfect etc. 651; the worse for wear; battered; weather-ed, -beaten; stale, *passé*, shaken, dilapidated, frayed, faded, wilted, shabby, second-hand, second-rate, threadbare; worn, — to- -a thread, — a shadow, — the stump; rags; reduced, — to a skeleton, skeletonized; far gone.

decayed etc. *v.*; moth-, worn-eaten; mildewed, rusty, moldy, spotted, seedy, time-worn, moss-grown; discolored; effete, wasted, crumbling, moldering, rotten, cankered, blighted, tainted; depraved etc. (*vicious*) 945; decrep-id, -it; broken down; done, — for, — up; worn out, used up; fit for the -dust-hole, — wastepaper basket; past work etc. (*useless*) 645.

at a low ebb, in a bad way, on one's last legs, washed -up; — out; undermined, deciduous; nodding to its fall etc. (*destruction*) 162; tottering etc. (*dangerous*) 665; past cure etc. (*hopeless*) 859; fatigued etc. 688; backward, retrograde etc. (*retrogressive*) 283; deleterious etc. 649; behind the times.

Adv. on the down grade; beyond hope.

Phr. out of the frying pan into the fire; *aegrescit medendo*.

---

660. Restoration.—N. restor-ation, -al; re-instatement, -placement, -habilitation,

establishment, -construction; reporduction etc.
163; re-novation, -newal; reviv-al, -escence;
refreshment etc. 689; re-suscitation, -animation, -
vivification, -viction; Phoenix; reorganization.

renaissance, renascence, rebirth, second youth,
rejuvenation, rejuvenescence, new birth; regeneration, -cy, -teness; palingenesis, reconversion,
resurgence, resurrection.

redress, retrieval, reclamation, recovery; convalescence; resumption, *résumption*.

recurrence etc. (*repetition*) 104; *réchauffé,
rifacimento*.

cure, recure, sanation; healing etc. *v.*; redin-
tegration; rectification, instauration.

repair, reparation, mending; recruiting etc. *v.*;
cicatrization; disinfection; tinkering.

reaction; redemption etc. (*deliverance*) 672;
restitution etc. 790; relief etc. 834.

mender, repairer, renewer; tinker, cobbler; doctor etc. 662; *vis medicatrix* etc. (*remedy*) 662.
curableness.

V. return to the original state; recover, rally,
revive; come -to, – round, – to oneself; pull
through, weather the storm, be oneself again; get –
well, – round, – the better of, – over, – about;
rise from – one's ashes, – the grave; resurge,
resurrect; survive etc. (*outlive*) 110; resume, reappear; come to, – life again; live –, rise- again;
relive.

heal, skin over, cicatrize; right itself.

restore, put back, place *in statu quo*; re-instate, -
place, -seat, -habilitate, -establish, -estate, -install.

re-construct, -build, -organize, -constitute;
reconvert; re-new, -novate; recondition; regenerate;
rejuvenate.

re-deem, -claim, -cover, -trieve; rescue etc.
(*deliver*) 672.

redress, recure; cure, heal, remedy, doctor,
physic, medicate; break of; bring round, set on
one's legs.

re-suscitate, -vive, -animate, -vivify, -call to life;
reproduce etc. 163; warm up; reinvigorate, refresh
etc. 689.

redintegrate, make whole; recoup etc. 790; make
-good, – all square; rectify; put –, set- -right, –
to rights, – straight; set up, correct; put in order
etc. (*arrange*) 60; refit, recruit; fill up, – the ranks;
reinforce.

repair, mend; put in -repair, – thorough repair,
– complete repair; retouch, botch, vamp, tinker,
doctor, cobble; do –, patch –, plaster –, vamp-
up; darn, fine-draw, heel-piece; stop a gap, stanch,
staunch, caulk, calk, careen, splice, bind up
wounds.

Adj. restored etc. *v.*; *redivivus*, convalescent; in
a fair way; none the worse; rejuvenated, renascent.

restoring etc. *v.*; restorative, recuperative; sana-,
repara-tive, -tory; curative, remedial.

restor-, recover-, san-, remedi-, retriev-, cur-able.

Adv. *in statu qho*; as you were.

Phr. *revenons à nos moutons*.

661. Relapse.—**N.** relapse, lapse; falling back
etc. *v.*; retrogradation etc. (*retrogression*) 283;
deterioration etc. 659.

[Return to, or recurrence of a bad state]
backsliding, recidivation, recrudescence.

V. relapse, lapse; fall –, slide –, sink- back;

have a relapse; return; retrograde etc. 283;
recidivate; fall off etc. 659- again.

662. Remedy.—**N.** remedy, help, redress; antidote, anti-toxin, -biotic; anti-, counter-poison,
prophylactic, antiseptic, germicide, bactericide,
corrective, restorative, stimulant, pick-me-up,
tonic; sedative etc. 174; palliative; febrifuge; alter-
ant, -ative; specific; emetic, carminative; narcotic
etc. *adj.*; Nepenthe, Mithridate.

cure; radical –, perfect –, certain- cure;
sovereign remedy.

physic, medicine, patent medicine, Galenicals,
simples, drug, wonder –, miracle – drugs; potion,
draught, dose, pill, bolus, lozenge, tablet, tabloid,
capsule; electuary; linct-us, -ure; medicament.

nostrum, receipt, recipe, prescription;
catholicon, panacea, elixir, *elixir vitae*,
philosopher's stone; balm, balsam, cordial, theriac,
ptisan.

salve, ointment, cerate, oil, lenitive, lotion,
cosmetic; plaster; epithem, embrocation, liniment,
cataplasm, sinapism, arquebusade, traumatic,
vulnerary, pepastic, poultice, collyrium, depilatory.

compress, pledget; bandage etc. (*support*) 215.

treatment, medical treatment, regimen; diet-ary,
-etics; *vis medicatrix*, – *naturae*; *médicine expectante*; seton, blood-letting, bleeding, venesection, phlebotomy, cupping, leeches; operation,
surgical operation; tonsillectomy, appendectomy;
injection, electrolysis, massage.

pharma-cy, -cology, -ceutics; acology; materia
medica, pharmacopoeia, therapeutics, therapy,
posology, pathology etc. 655; home-, hetero-, all-,
hydr-opathy; cold water –, open air- cure;
dietetics; sur-, chirur-gery, osteopathy; healing art,
leechcraft, practice of medicine; ortho-paedy, -
praxy; dentistry, midwifery, obstetrics, gynecology.

faith -cure, – healing, Christian science; psycho-
therapy, -analysis, psychiatry.

hospital, infirmary, clinic; pest-, lazar-house;
lazaretto, lazaret; lock hospital; *maison de santé;
ambulance*; dispensary; *sanatorium, sanitarium*,
spa, baths, pump-room, well; *hospice*; Red Cross;
nursing home; asylum.

doctor, physician, surgeon; medical –, general-
practitioner, consultant, specialist; medical attendant; medical student, medico; chemist,
apothecary, pharmacopolist, druggist; leech;
Aesculapius, Hippocrates, Galen; *accoucheur*,
gynecologist, midwife, oculist, aurist, dentist;
operator; osteopath, bonesetter; nurse, monthly
nurse, sister; dresser; *masseur, masseuse*.

V. apply a -remedy etc. *n.*; doctor, dose, physic,
nurse, minister to, attend, dress the wounds,
plaster, bandage, poultice; heal, cure, work a cure,
kill or cure, remedy, stay (disease), snatch from the
jaws of death; prevent etc. 706; relieve etc. 834;
palliate etc. 658; restore etc. 660; drench with
physic; consult, operate, extract, deliver; bleed,
cup, let blood, transfuse; electrolyse; psycho-
analyse.

Adj. remedial; restorative etc. 660; corrective,
palliative, healing; sana-tory, -tive; prophylactic;
salutiferous etc. (*salutary*) 656; medic-al, -inal;
therapeutic, surgical, chirurgical, orthopedic,
epulotic, paregoric, tonic, corroborant, analeptic,
balsamic, anodyne, hypnotic, neurotic, narcotic,

sedative, lenitive, demulcent, emollient; depuratory; deter-sive, -gent; abstersive, disinfectant, febrifugal, alternative; traumatic, vulnerary.

dietetic, alimentary; nutrit-ious, -ive; peptic; alexi-pharmic, -teric; remedi-, cur-able.

663. Bane. —N. bane, curse, thorn in the -side, -flesh, bugbear, *bête noire*; evil etc. 619; hurtfulness etc. (*badness*) 649; painfulness etc. (*cause of pain*) 830; scourge etc. (*punishment*) 975; *damnosa hereditas*; white elephant.

sting, fang, thorn, tang, bramble, briar, nettle.

poison, leaven, virus, venom; intoxicant; arsenic, Prussic acid, antimony, tartar emetic, strychnine, nicotine, cyanide of potassium, corrosive sublimate; curare; hyoscine etc.; poison-, mustard-, tear-gas; carbon di-, mon-oxide; ptomaine poisoning, botulism; miasm, mephitis, malaria, azote, sewer gas; pest, stench etc. 401.

rust, worm, moth, moth and rust, fungus, mildew; dry-rot; canker, -worm; cancer; torpedo; viper etc. (*evil-doer*) 913; demon etc. 980.

hemlock, hellebore, nightshade, *belladonna*, henbane, aconite; Upas tree.

drugs, dope, opium, morphia, morphine, cocaine, heroin, hashish, bhang.

[*Science of poisons*] Toxicology.

Adj. baneful etc. (*bad*) 649; poisonous etc. (*unwholesome*) 657.

664. Safety. —N. safety, security, impregnability; invulnera-bility, -bleness etc. *adj.*; danger -past, − over; storm blown over; coast clear; escape etc. 671; means of escape, safetyvalve; safeguard, palladium, sheet anchor, rock, tower of strength.

guardian-, ward-, warden-ship; tutelage, custody, safe keeping; preservation etc. 670; protection, auspices.

safe-conduct, escort, convoy; guard, sheild etc. (*defense*) 717; guardian angel, tutelary -god, − deity, − saint; *genius loci*.

protector, guardian; ward-en, -er; preserver, custodian, *duenna chaperon*, third person.

watch-, ban-dog; Cerberus; watch-, patrol-, police-man, constable, peeler, bobby, copper, cop, bull, flat-foot, detective, armed guard; sentinel, sentry, scout etc. (*warning*) 668; garrison; guardship.

[*Means of safety*] refuge etc., anchor etc. 666; precaution etc. (*preparation*) 673; quarantine, *cordon sanitaire*. [Sense of security] confidence etc. 858.

V. be -safe etc. *adj.*; keep one's head above water, tide over, save one's bacon; ride out −, weather- the storm; light upon one's feet; bear a charmed life; escape etc. 671; possess nine lives.

make −, render- -safe etc. *adj.*; protect, watch over; take care of etc. (*care*) 459; preserve etc. 670; cover, screen, shelter, shroud, flank, ward; guard etc. (*defend*) 717; secure etc. (*restrain*) 751; intrench, fence round etc. (*circumscribe*) 229; house, nestle, ensconce; take charge of.

escort, convoy; garrison; watch, mount guard, patrol, scout, spy.

make assurance double sure etc. (*caution*) 864; take up a loose thread; take precautions etc. (*prepare for*) 673; take in a reef; double reef topsails.

seek safety; take −, find- shelter etc. 666; run into port.

Adj. safe, secure, sure; in -safety, − security; have an anchor to windward; on the safe side; under the -shield of, − shade of, − wing of, − shadow of one's wing; under -cover, − lock and key; out of -danger, − the meshes, − harm's way; in -harbor, − port; on sure ground, at anchor, high and dry, above water, on *terra firma*; unthreatened, -molested; protected etc. *v.*; cavendo tutus; panoplied etc. (*defended*) 717.

snug, sea-, air-worthy; weather-, water-, fire-, bomb-proof.

defensible, tenable, proof against, invulnerable; un-assailable, -attackable; im-pregnable, -perdible; founded on a rock; inexpugnable.

safe and sound etc. (*preserved*) 670; harmless; scathless etc. (*perfect*) 650; unhazarded; not -dangerous etc. 665.

protecting etc. *v.*; guardian, tutelary; perservative etc. 670; trustworthy etc. 939.

Adv. *ex abundanti cautela*; with impunity.

Phr. all's well; all clear; *salva res est*; *suave mari magno*; safety first.

665. Danger. —N. danger, peril, insecurity, jeopardy, risk, hazard, venture, precariousness, slipperiness; instability etc. 149; defenselessness etc. *adj.*

exposure etc. (*liability*) 177; vulnerability; vulnerable point, heel of Achilles; forlorn hope etc. (*hopelessness*) 859.

[Dangerous course] leap in the dark etc. (*rashness*) 863; road to ruin, *facilis descensus Averni*, hair-breadth escape.

cause for alarm; source of danger etc. 667. [Approach of danger] rock −, breakers- ahead; storm brewing; clouds -in the horizon, − gathering; warning etc. 668; alarm etc. 669. [Sense of danger] apprehension etc. 860.

V. be -in danger etc. *adj.*; be exposed to −, run into −, incur −, encounter- -danger etc. *n.*; run a risk; lay oneself open to etc. (*liability*) 177; lean on −, trust to- a broken reed; feel the ground sliding from under one, have to run for it; have the -chances, − odds- against one.

hang by a thread, totter; tremble on the -verge, − brink; sleep − stand -on a volcano; sit on a barrel of gunpowder, live in a glass house.

bring −, place −, put- in -danger etc. *n.*; endanger, expose to danger, imperil; jeopard, -ize; compromise; sail too near the wind etc. (*rash*) 863; put one's head in the lion's mouth.

adventure, risk, hazard, venture, stake, set at hazard; run the gauntlet etc. (*dare*) 861; engage in a forlorn hope.

threaten etc. 909- danger; run one hard; lay a trap for etc. (*deceive*) 545.

Adj. in -danger etc. *n.*; endangered etc. *v.*; fraught with danger; danger-, hazard-, peril-, parl-, pericul-ous; unsafe, unprotected etc. (safe, protect etc. 664); insecure, untrustworthy, unreliable; built upon sand, on a sandy basis.

defence-, fence-, guard-, harbor-less; unshielded; vulnerable, expugnable, unsheltered, exposed; open to etc. (*liable*) 177.

aux abois, at bay; on -the wrong side of the wall, – a lee shore, – the rocks.

at stake, in question; precarious, aleatory, critical, ticklish; slip-pery, -py; hanging by a thread etc. *v*.; with a halter round one's neck; between - the hammer and the anvil, – Scylla and Charybdis, – two fires; on the -edge, – brink, – verge of a- -precipice, – volcano; in the lion's den, on slippery ground, under fire; not out of the wood.

un-warned, -admonished, -advised; unprepared etc. 674; off one's guard etc. (*inexpectant*) 508.

tottering; un-stable, -steady; shaky, top-heavy, tumble-down, ramshackle, crumbling, waterlogged; help-, guide-less; in a bad way; reduced to –, at- the last extremity; trembling in the balance; nodding to its fall etc. (*destruction*) 162.

threatening etc. 909; ominous, ill-omened; alarming etc. (*fear*) 860; explosive; poisonous etc. 657.

adventurous etc. (*rash*) 863, (*bold*) 861.

Int. stop! look out! beware! take care!

Phr. *incidit in Scyllam qui vult vitare Charybdim; nam tua res agitur paries dum proximus ardet.*

666. Refuge. [Means of safety.]—**N.** refuge, sanctuary, retreat, fastness; stronghold, keep, last resort; ward; prison etc. 752; asylum, ark, home, almshouse, refuge for the destitute; hiding-place etc. (*ambush*) 530; *sanctum sanctorum* etc. (*privacy*) 893.

roadstead, anchorage; breakwater, mole, port, haven; harbor, – of refuge; sea-port; pier, jetty, embankment, quay.

covert, shelter, abri, screen, lee-wall, wing, shield, umbrella; splash-, dash-board, mudguard.

wall etc. (*inclosure*) 232; fort etc. (*defence*) 717.

anchor, kedge; grap-nel, -pling iron; sheet-, mushroom-anchor, main-stay; support etc. 215; check etc. 706; ballast.

jury-mast; vent-peg; safety -valve, – lamp; lightning conductor.

means of escape etc. (*escape*) 671; life-boat, swimming belt, cork jacket; life preserver, breeches buoy; parachute, plank, stepping-stone.

safeguard etc. (*protection*) 664.

V. seek –, take –, find- refuge etc. *n*.; seek –, find- safety etc. 664; throw oneself into the arms of; claim sanctuary; take to the -hills, – woods; make port, reach shelter, bar –, bolt –, lock -the door, – gete; let the portcullis down; raise the drawbridge.

667. Pitfall. [Source of danger.]—**N.** rocks, reefs, coral reef, sunken rocks, snags; sands, quicksands, Goodwin sands, sandy foundation; slippery ground; breakers, shoals, shallows, bank, shelf, flat, lee shore, iron-bound coast; rock –, breakers- ahead; derelict.

precipice; abyss, chasm, pit, crevasse; maelstrom, whirlpool, eddy, vortex, rapids, current, bore, tidal wave, storm, squall, hurricane, whirlwind; volcano;

ambush etc. 530; pitfall, trap-door; trap etc. (*snare*) 545.

sword of Damocles; wolf at the door, snake in the grass, viper in one's bosom, death in the pot; latency etc. 526.

ugly customer, dangerous person, *le chat qui dort*; firebrand, hornet's nest.

Phr. *latet anguis in herbâ; proximus ardet Ucalegon.*

668. Warning.—**N.** warning, caution, *caveat*; notice etc. (*information*) 527; premoni-tion, -shment; prediction etc. 511; contraindication; symptom; lesson, dehortation; admonition, monition; alarm etc. 669.

handwriting on the wall, *tekel upharsin*, yellow flag; fog-signal, -horn; siren; monitor, warning voice, Cassandra, signs of the times, Mother Carey's chickens, stormy petrel, bird of ill omen, gathering clouds, clouds in the horizon, cloud no bigger than a man's hand, death-watch.

watch-tower, beacon, signal-post; light-house etc. (*indication of locality*) 550.

sent-inel, -ry; watch, -man; watch and ward; watch-, ban-, house-dog; patrol, vedette, picket, bivouac, scout, spy, spial; advanced –, rear-guard, lookout, flagman.

cautiousness etc. 864.

V. warn, caution; fore-, pre-warn; ad-, premonish; give -notice, – warning; menace etc. (*threaten*) 909; put on one's guard; sound the alarm etc. 669; croak.

beware, ware; take -warning, – heed at one's peril; watch out for; keep watch and ward etc. (*care*) 459.

Adj. warning etc. *v*.; premonitory, monitory, cautionary; admonitory, -tive; ominous, threatening, lowering, minatory, symptomatic.

warned etc. *v*.; on one's guard etc. (*careful*) 459; (*cautious*) 864.

Adv. *in terrorem* etc. (*threat*) 909.

Int. beware! ware! take care! mind –, take care-what you are about; mind! look out!

Phr. *ne reveillez pas le chat qui dort; foenum habet in cornu.*

669. Alarm. [Indication of danger.]—**N.** alarm; alarum, larum, alarm bell, tocsin, *alerte*; beat of drum, sound of trumpet, note of alarm, hue and cry, signal of distress, S.O.S.; blue-lights; warcry, -whoop; warning etc. 668; fog-signal, -horn; siren; yellow flag; danger signal; red -light, – flag; fire -bell, – alarm; burglar alarm, police whistle, watchman's rattle.

false alarm, cry of wolf; bug-bear, -aboo.

V. give –, raise –, sound –, beat- the *or* an -alarm etc. *n*.; alarm; warn etc. 668; ring the tocsin, *battre la générale*; cry wolf.

Adj. alarming etc. *v*.

Int. *sauve qui peut! qui vive?* who goes there?

670. Preservation.—**N.** preservation; safe keeping; conservation etc. (*storage*) 636; maintenance, upkeep, support, sustentation, conservatism; *vis conservatrix*; salvation etc. (*deliverance*) 672; drying etc. *v.*

[Means of preservation] prophylaxis; preserv-er, -ative; canned goods; cold pack; hygi-astics, -antics; cover, durgget; *cordon sanitaire.*

[Superstitious remedies] charm etc. 993.

V. preserve, maintain, keep, sustain, support; keep -up, − alive; not willingly let die; shore −, bank- up; nurse; save, rescue; be −, make- safe etc. 664; take care of etc. (*care*) 459; guard etc. (*defend*) 717.

stare super antiquas vias; hold one's own; hold −, stand- -one's ground etc. (*resist*) 719.

embalm, dry, cure, smoke, salt, pickle, season, kyanize, bottle, pot, tin, can; husband etc. (*store*) 636.

Adj. preserving etc. *v.*; conservative; prophylatic; preserva-tory, -tive; hygienic.

preserved etc. *v.*; un-impaired, -broken, -injured, -hurt, -singed, -marred; safe, − and sound; intact, with a whole skin; without a scratch.

Phr. *nolumus leges Angliae mutari.*

671. Escape.—**N.** escape; scape; avolation, elopment, flight, get-away; evasion etc. (*avoidance*) 623; retreat; narrow −, hairbreadth- escape; close −, near- shave; come off, impunity.

[Means of escape] loophole etc. (*opening*) 260; path etc. 627; secret -door, − passage; refuge etc. 666; vent, − peg; safety-valve; drawbridge, fire-escape.

reprieve etc. (*deliverance*) 672; liberation etc. 750.

refugee etc. (*fugitive*) 623.

V. escape, scape; make −, effect −, make good- one's escape, make a get-away; get -off, − clear off, − well out of; *échapper belle*, save one's bacon; weather the storm etc. (*safe*) 664; escape scot-free.

elude etc., make off etc. (*avoid*) 623; march off etc. (*go away*) 293; give one the slip; slip through the -hands, − fingers; slip the collar, wriggle out of; break -loose, − from prison; break −, slip −, get- away; find -vent, − a hole to creep out of.

Adj. escap-ing, -ed etc. *v.*; stolen away, fled.

Phr. the bird has flown.

672. Deliverance.—**N.** deliverance, ex-trication, rescue; repriev-e, -al; respite; ransom; liberation etc. 750; truce, armistice; redemption, salvation; riddance; gaol delivery; exemption, day of grace; redeemableness.

V. deliver, extricate, rescue, save, redeem, ran-som, free, -liberate, release, set free, redeem, eman-cipate; bring -off, − through; *tirer d'affaire*, get the wheel out of the rut; snatch from the jaws of death, come to the rescue; rid; retrieve etc. (*restore*) 660; be −, get- rid of.

Adj. saved etc. *v.*; extric-, redeem-, rescu-able.

Phr. to the rescue!

673. Preparation.—**N.** preparation; providing etc. *v.*; provi-sion, -dence; anticipation etc. (*foresight*) 510; precaution, -concertation,

disposition; forecast etc. (*plan*) 626; rehearsal, not of preparation.

[Putting in order] arrangement etc. 60; clearance; adjustment etc. 23; tuning; equipment, outfit, accoutrement, armament, array.

ripening etc. *v.*; maturation, evolution; elaboration, concoction, digestion; gestation, hatch-ing, incubation, sitting.

groundwork, datum, first stone, cradle, stepping-stone; foundation, scaffold etc. (*support*) 215; scaf-folding, *échafaudage.*

[Preparation -of men] training etc. (*education*) 537; inurement etc. (*habit*) 613; novitiate; [− of food] cook-ing, -ery; brewing, culinary art; [− of the soil] till-, plough-, sow-ing; semination, cultivation.

[State of being prepared] prepared-, readi-, ripe-, mellow-ness; maturity; *un impromptu fait à loisir.*

[Preparer] preparer, teacher, coach, trainer, pioneer; *avant-courrier, -coureur*; sappers and miners, paver, navvy; packer, stevedore; warm-ingpan; precursor etc. 64.

V. prepare; get −, make- ready; make preparations, settle preliminaries, get up, sound the note of preparation; address oneself to.

set −, put- in order etc. (*arrange*) 60; forecast etc. (*plan*) 626; prepare −, plough −, dress- the ground; till −, cultivate- the soil; predispose, sow the seed, lay a train, dig a mine; lay −, fix- the -foundations, − basis, -groundwork; dig the foun-dations, erect the scaffolding; lay the first stone etc. (*begin*) 66.

rough-hew; cut out work; block −, hammer-out; lick into shape etc. (*form*) 240.

elaborate, mature, ripen, mellow, season, bring to maturity; nurture etc.

(*aid*) 707; hatch, cook, brew; temper; anneal, smelt; dry, cure etc. 670.

equip, arm, man; fit-out, -up; furnish, rig, dress, garnish, betrim, accouter, array, fettle, fledge; dress −, furbish −, brush −, vamp- up; refurbish; sharp-en one's tools, trim one's foils, set, prime, attune; whet the -knife, − sword; wind −, screw- up; ad-just etc. (*fit*) 27; put in- trim, − train, − gear, − working order, − tune, − a groove for, − har-ness; pack, stow away, store.

train etc. (*teach*) 537; inure etc. (*habituate*) 613; breed; prepare etc.- for; rehearse; make provision for; take -steps, − measures, − precautions; provide, − against; beat up for recruits; open the door to etc. (*facilitate*) 705.

set one's house in order, make all snug; clear -decks, − for action; close one's ranks; shuffle the cards.

prepare oneself; serve an apprenticeship etc. (*learn*) 539; lay oneself out for, get into harness, gird up one's loins, buckle on one's armor, *reculer pour mieux sauter*, prime and load, shoulder arms, get the steam up, put the horses to.

guard −, make sure- against; forearm, make sure, prepare for the evil day, have a rod in pickle, provide against a rainy day, feather one's nest; lay in provisions etc. 637; make investments; keep on foot.

be -prepared, − ready etc. *adj.*; hold oneself in readiness, watch and pray, keep one's powder dry; lie in wait for etc. (*expect*) 507; anticipate etc. (*foresee*) 510; *principiis obstare*; *veniente oc-currere morbo.*

Adj. preparing etc. *v.*; in -preparation, − course

of preparation, – agitation, – embryo, – hand, – train; afoot, afloat; on -foot, – the stocks, – the anvil; under consideration etc. (*plan*) 626; brewing, hatching, forthcoming, brooding; in -store for, – reserve.

precautionary, provident; prepara-tive, -tory; provisional, inchoate, under revision; preliminary etc. (*precedent*) 62.

prepared etc. *v.*; in readiness; ready, – to one's hand, – made, cut and dried; ready for use, reach me down, made to one's hand, handy, on the table, made to order; in gear; in working -order, – gear; snug, in practice.

ripe, mature, mellow; practiced etc. (*skillet*) 698; labored, elaborate, highly-wrought, smelling of the lamp, worked up.

in -full feather, – best bib and tucker; in –, at-harness; in – the saddle, – arms, – battle array, – war paint; up in arms; armed -at all points, – to the teeth, – *cap-à-pie*; sword in hand; booted and spurred.

in utrumque –, *semper- paratus*; on the alert etc. (*vigilant*) 459; at one's post.

Adv. in -preparation, – anticipation of; afoot, astir, abroad; abroach.

674. Non-preparation.—**N.** non-, absence of – , want of- preparation; unpreparedness; in-culture, inconcoction, improvidence.

immaturity, crudity; rawness etc. *adj.*; abortion; disqualification.

[Absence of art] nature, state of nature; virgin soil, unweeded garden; rough diamond, neglect etc. 460.

rough copy etc. (*plan*) 626; germ etc. 153; raw material etc. 635.

improvisation etc. (*impulse*) 612.

V. be -unprepared etc. *adj.*; want – , lack-preparation; lie fallow; *s'embarquer sans biscuits*; live from hand to mouth.

[Render unprepared] dismantle etc. (*render useless*) 645; undress etc. 226.

extemporize, improvise.

surprise, pay a surprise visit, take by surprise, drop in upon, take unawares; take pot-luck.

Adv. un-prepared etc. prepare etc. 673] without -preparation etc. 673; incomplete etc. 53; rudimental, embryonic, abortive; immature, unripe, raw, green, crude; coarse; rough, -cast, -hewn; in the rough; un-hewn, -formed, -fashioned, -wrought, - labored, -blown, -cooked, -boiled, -concocted, -cut, -polished.

callow, un-hatched, -fledged, -nurtured, -licked, -taught, -educated, -cultivated, -trained, -tutored, -drilled, -exercised; precocious, premature; un-, in-digested; un-mellowed, -seasoned, -leavened.

fallow; un-sown, -tilled; natural, in a state of na-ture; undressed; in dishabille, *en déshabille, en négligé*.

un-, dis-qualified; unfitted; ill-digested; un-begun, -ready, -arranged, -organized, -furnished, - provided, -equipped, -trimmed; out of -gear, – or-der; dismantled etc. *v.*

shiftless, improvident, unthrifty, thoughtless, unguarded; happy-go-lucky; caught napping etc. (*inexpectant*) 508; unpremeditated etc. 612.

Adv. extempore etc. 612.

675. Essay.—**N.** essay, trial, endeavor, aim, at-tempt; venture, adventure, speculation, *coup d'essai, début*; probation etc. (*experiment*) 463.

V. try, essay; experiment etc. 463; endeavor, strive; tempt, tackle, take on, attempt, make an at-tempt; venture, adventure, speculate, take one's chance, tempt fortune; try one's -fortune, – luck, – hand; use one's endeavor; feel –, grope –, pick- one's way.

try hard, push, make a bold push, use one's best endeavor; do one's best etc. (*exertion*) 686.

Adj. essaying etc. *v.*; experimental etc. 463; tentative, empirical, probationary.

Adv. experimentally etc. *adj.*; on trial, at a ven-ture; by rule of thumb.

if one may be so bold.

676. Undertaking.—**N.** undertaking, compact etc. 769; engagement etc. (*promise*) 768; enter-, em-prise; venture etc. 675; pilgrimage; matter in hand etc. (*business*) 625; move; first move etc. (*beginning*) 66.

V. undertake; engage –, embark- in; launch –, plunge- into; volunteer; apprentice oneself to; engage etc. (*promise*) 768; contract etc. 769; take upon -oneself, – one's shoulders; devote oneself to etc. (*determination*) 604.

take -up, – in hand; tackle; set – , go- about; set – , fall- -to, – to work; launch forth; set up shop; put in -hand, – execution; set forward; break the neck of a business, be in for; put one's hand to; betake oneself to, turn one's hand to, go to do; begin etc. 66; broach, institute, etc. (*originate*) 153; put – , lay- one's -hand to the plough, – shoulder to the wheel.

have in hand etc. (*business*) 625; have many irons in the fire etc. (*activity*) 682.

Adj. undertaking etc. *v.*; on the anvil etc. 625; adventurous, venturesome.

Int. here goes!

677. Use.—**N.** use; employ, -ment; exer-cise, - citation; appli-cation, -ance; adhibition, disposal; consumption; agency etc. (*physical*) 170; usufruct; usefulness etc. 644; recourse, resort, avail, pragmatism.

[Conversion to use] utilization, service, wear. [Way of using] usage.

V. use, make use of, employ, put to use; apply, put in -action, – operation, – practice; set -in motion, – to work.

ply, work, wield, handle, manipulate; play, – off; exert, exercise, practice, avail oneself of, profit by; resort –, have recourse – , recur –, take –, betake oneself- to; take -up with, – advantage of; lay one's hands on, try.

render useful etc. 644; mold; turn to -account, – use; convert to use, utilize, administer; work up; call – , bring- into play; put into requisition; call – , draw- forth; press –, enlist- into the service; bring to bear upon, devote, dedicate, consecrate, apply, adhibit, dispose of; make a -handle, – cat's paw- of.

fall beak upon, make a shift with; make the -most, – best- of.

use – , swallow- up; consume, absorb, expend; tax, task, wear, put to task.

Adj. in use; used etc. *v.*; well-worn, -trodden. useful etc. 644; subservient etc. (*instrumental*) 631· utilitarian; pragmatical.

678. Disuse.—N. forbearance, abstinence; disuse; relinquishment etc. 782; desuetude etc. (*want of habit*) 614.

V. not use; do without, dispense with, let alone, not touch, forbear, abstain, spare, waive, neglect; keep back, reserve.

lay -up, – by, – on the shelf, – up in a napkin; shelve; set –, put –, lay- aside; disuse, leave off, have done with; supersede; discard etc. (*eject*) 297; dismiss, give warning.

throw aside etc. (*relinquish*) 782; make away with etc. (*destroy*) 162; cast –, heave –, throw-overboard; cast to the -dogs, – winds; dismantle etc. (*render useless*) 645.

lie –, remain- unemployed etc. *adj.*

Adj. not used etc. *v.*; un-employed, -applied, -disposed of, -spent, -exercised, -touched, -trodden, -essayed, -gathered, -culled; uncalled for, not required.

disused etc. *v.*; done with;· run down, used up, cast off.

679. Misuse.—N. mis-use, -usage, employment, -application, -appropriation.

abuse, profanation, prostitution, desecration; waste etc. 638.

V. mis-use, -employ, -apply, -appropriate. desecrate, abuse, profane, prostitute; waste etc. 638; over-task, -tax, -work; squander etc. 818.

cut a whetstone with a razor, employ a steam-engine to crack a nut; catch at a straw

Adj. misused etc. *v.*

680. Action.—N. action, performance; doing etc. *v.*; perpetration; exercise, -citation; movement, operation, evolution, work; labor etc. (*exertion*) 686; *praxis*, execution; procedure etc. (*conduct*) 692; handicraft; business etc. 625; agency etc. (*power at work*) 170.

deed, act, overt act, stitch, touch, gest; trans-action, job, doings, dealings, proceeding, measure, step, maneuver, bout, passage, move, stroke, blow; *coup*, – *de main*, – *d'état*; *tour de force* etc. (*display*) 882; feat, exploit, stunt; achievement etc. (*completion*) 729; handiwork, workmanship, crafts-manship; manufacture; stroke of policy etc. (*plan*) 626.

actor etc. (*doer*) 690.

. **V.** do, perform, execute; achieve etc. (*complete*) 729; transact, enact; commit, perpetrate, inflict; exercise, prosecute, carry on, work, practice, play.

employ oneself, ply one's task; officiate, have in hand etc. (*business*) 625; labor etc. 686; be at work; pursue a course; shape one's course etc. (*conduct*) 692.

act, operate; take -action, – steps; strike a blow, lift a finger, stretch forth one's hand; take in hand etc. (*undertake*) 676; put oneself in motion; put in practice; carry into execution etc. (*complete*) 729; act upon.

be -an actor etc. 690; take –, act –, play –, perform- a part in; participate in; have a -hand in, – finger in the pie; have to do with; be a -party to, – participator in; bear –, lend- a hand; pull an oar, run in a race; mix oneself up with etc. (*meddle*) 682.

be in action; come into operation etc. (*power at work*) 170.

Adj. doing etc. *v.*; acting; in action; in harness; on duty; at work; in operation etc. 170; up to one's ears in work, in the midst of things.

Adv. in the -act, – midst of, – thick of; red-handed, *in flagrante delicto*; while one's hand is in.

681. Inaction.—N. inaction, passiveness, ab-stinence from action; non-interference; Fabian –, conservative- policy; neglect etc. 460; stagnation, vegetation; loafing.

inactivity etc. 683; rest etc. (*repose*) 687; quiescence etc. 265; want of –, in- occupation; unemployment; idle hours, time hanging on one's hands, *dolce far niente*; sinecure.

V. not -do, – act, – attempt; be -inactive etc. 683; abstain from doing, do nothing, hold, spare; not -stir, – move, – lift- a -finger, – foot, – peg; fold one's -arms, –. hands; leave –, let- alone; let -be, – pass, – things take their course, – it have its way, – well alone; *quieta non movere*; *stare super antiquas vias*; rest and be thankful, live and let live; lie –, rest- upon one's oars; *laisser -aller*, – *faire*; stand aloof; refrain etc. (*avoid*) 623; keep oneself from doing; remit –, relax- one's efforts; desist etc. (*relinquish*) 624; stop etc. (*cease*) 142; pause etc. (*be quiet*) 265.

wait, lie in wait, bide one's time, take time, tide it over.

cool –, kick- one's heels; loaf, while away the -time, – tedious hours; pass –, fill –, beguile- the time; talk against time; waste time etc. (*inactive*) 683.

lie -by, – on the shelf, – in ordinary, – idle, – to, – fallow; keep quiet, slug; have nothing to do, whistle for want of thought; twiddle one's thumbs.

undo, do away with; take -down, – to pieces; destroy etc. 162.

Adj. not doing etc. *v.*; not done etc. *v.*; undone; passive; un-occupied, -employed; out of -employ, – work, – a job; fallow; *désoeuvré*.

Adv. *re infectâ*, at a stand, *les bras croisés*, with folded arms; with the hands -in the pockets, – behind one's back; *pour passer le temps*.

Int. so let it be! stop! etc. 142; hands off!

Phr. nothing doing; *cunctando restituit rem*.

682. Activity.—N. activity; briskness, liveliness etc. *adj.*; animation, life, vivacity, spirit, verve, dash, energy, go.

nimbleness, agility; smartness, quickness etc. *adj.*; velocity etc. 274; alacrity, promptitude; des-, dis-patch; expedition; haste etc. 684; punctuality etc. (*early*) 132.

eagerness, zeal, ardor, *perfervidum ingenium*, *empressement*, earnestness, intentness; *abandon*; vigor etc. (*physical energy*) 171; devotion etc. (*resolution*) 604; exertion etc. 686.

industry, assiduity; assiduousness etc. *adj.*; sedulity; laboriousness; drudgery etc. (*labor*) 686; painstaking, diligence; perseverance etc. 604a; indefatigation; habits of business.

vigilance etc. 459; wakefulness; sleep-, restlessness; *pervigilium, insomnia*; racketing.

movement, bustle, hustle, stir, fuss, ado, bother, pottering; fidget, -iness; flurry etc. (*haste*) 684.

officiousness; dabbling, meddling; inter-ference, -position, -meddling, butting in, intrusiveness; tampering with, intrigue.

press of business, no sinecure, plenty to do, many irons in the fire, great doings, busy hum of men, battle of life, thick of -things, – the action; the madding corwd.

housewife, busy bee; new brooms; sharp fellow, blade; hustler, devotee, enthusiast, fan, zealot, fanatic; meddler, intermeddler, intriguer, busybody, kibitzer, pickthank.

V. be -active etc. *adj.*; busy oneself in; stir, -about, – one's stumps; bestir –, rouse- oneself; speed, hasten, peg away, lay about one, bustle, fuss; raise –, kick up- a dust; push; make a -push, -fuss, – stir; go ahead, push forward; flight –, elbow- one's way; make progress etc. 282; toil etc. (*labor*) 686; drudge, plod, persist etc. (*persevere*) 604a; keep -up the ball, – the pot boiling.

look sharp; have all one's eyes about one etc. (*vigilance*) 459; rise, arouse oneself, get up early, hustle, push; be about, keep moving, steal a march, kill two birds with one stone; seize the opportunity etc. 134; lose no time, not lose a moment, make the most of one's time, not suffer the grass to grow under one's feet, improve the shining hour, make short work of; dash off; make haste etc. 684; do one's best, take pains etc. (*exert oneself*) 686; do –, work- wonders.

have -many irons in the fire, – one's hands full, – much on one's hands; have other -things to do, – fish to fry; be busy; not have a moment -to spare, – that one can call one's own.

have one's fling, run the round of; go all lengths, stick at nothing, run riot.

outdo; over-do, -act, -lay, -shoot the mark; make a toil of a pleasure.

have a hand in etc. (*act in*) 680; take an active part, put in one's oar, have a finger in the pie, mix oneself up with, trouble one's head about, intrigue; agitate.

tamper with, meddle, moil; inter-meddle, -fere, -pose; obtrude; poke –, thrust- one's nose in, butt in.

Adj. active; brisk, – as a lark, – as a bee; lively, animated, vivacious; alive, – and kicking; frisky, spirited, stirring.

nimble, – as a squirrel; agile; light-, nimble-footed; featly, tripping.

quick, prompt, yare, instant, ready, alert, spry, sharp, smart, slick, go-ahead; fast etc. (*swift*) 274; quick as a lamplighter, expeditious; awake, broad awake; wide awake etc. (*intelligent*) 498.

forward, eager, ardent, strenuous, zealous, enterprising, pushing, in earnest; resolute etc. 604.

industrious, assiduous, diligent, sedulous, notable, painstaking; intent etc. (*attention*) 457; indefatigable etc. (*persevering*) 604a; unwearied; unsleeping, sleepless, never tired; plodding, hard-working etc. 686; business-like, workaday.

bustling; restless, – as a hyena; fussy, fidgety, pottering; busy, – as a hen with one chicken.

working, laboring, at work, on duty, in harness; up in arms; on one's legs, at call; up and -doing, – stirring.

busy, occupied; hard at -work, – it; up to one's ears in, full of business, busy as a bee.

meddling etc. *v.*; meddlesome, pushing, officious, overofficious, *intrigant*.

astir, stirring; a-going, -foot; on foot; in full swing; eventful; on the alert etc. (*vigilant*) 459.

Adv. actively etc. *adj.*; with -life and spirit, – might and main etc. 686, ÷ haste etc. 684, – wings; full tilt, *in mediis rebus*.

Int. be –, look- -alive, – sharp! move –, push-on! keep moving! go ahead! stir your stumps! *age quod agis!*

Phr. *carpe diem* etc. (*opportunity*) 134; *nulla dies sine lineâ; nec mora nec requies*; no sooner said than done etc. (*early*) 132; catch a weasel asleep.

683. Inactivity.—N. inactivity; inaction etc. 681; inertness etc. 172; obstinacy etc. 606.

lull etc. (*cessation*) 142; quiescence etc. 265; rust, -iness.

idle-, remiss-ness etc. *adj.*; sloth, indolence, indiligence; otiosity, dawdling etc. *v.*

dullness etc. *adj.*; languor; segni-ty, -tude; lentor; sluggishness etc. (*slowness*) 275; procrastination etc. (*delay*) 133; torp-or, -idity, -escence; stupor etc. (*insensibility*) 823; somnolence; drowsiness etc. *adj.*; nodding etc. *v.*; oscitation, -ancy; pandiculation, hyprotism, lethargy; heaviness, heavy eye-lids, sand in the eyes.

sleep, slumber; sound –, heavy –, balmy-sleep; Morpheus, dreamland; coma, trance, catalepsy, hypnosis, *ecstasis*, dream, hibernation, nap, doze, snooze, *siesta*, wink of sleep, forty winks, snore; Hypnology.

dull work; pottering; relaxation etc. (*loosening*) 47; Castle of Indolence.

[Cause of inactivity] lullaby, *berceuse*; anesthetic, sedative etc. 174; torpedo.

idler, drone, droil, dawdle, mopus; do-little, *fainéant*, dummy, sleeping partner; afternoon farmer; truant etc. (*runaway*) 623; lounger, *lazzarone*, floater, loafer, tramp, beggar, cadger; lubber, -bard; slow-coach etc. (*slow*) 275; opium –, lotus- eater; slug; lag-, slug-gard, lie-abed; slumberer, dormouse, marmot; waiter on Providence, *fruges consumere natus*.

V. be -inactive etc. *adj.*; do nothing etc. 681; move slowly etc. 275; let the grass grow under one's feet; take one's time, dawdle, poke, drawl, droil, lag, hang back, slouch; loll, -op; lounge, loaf, loiter; go to sleep over; sleep at one's post; *ne battre que d'une aile*.

take -it easy, – things as they come; lead an easy life, vegetate, swim with the stream, eat the bread of idleness; loll in the lap of -luxury, – indolence; waste –, consume –, kill –, lose time; burn daylight, waste the precious hours.

idle –, trifle –, fritter –, fool- away time; spend –, take- time in; ped-, pid-dle; potter, putter, dabble, faddle, fribble, fiddle-faddle; dally, dilly-dally.

sleep, slumber, be asleep; hibernate; oversleep; sleep like a -top, – log, – dormouse; sleep -soundly, – heavily; doze, drowze, snooze, nap; take a -nap etc. *n.*; dream; snore; settle –, go –, go off- to sleep; drop off; fall –, drop- asleep; close –, seal up- -the -eyes, – eyelids; weigh down the eyelids; get sleepy, nod, yawn; go to bed, turn in.

languish, expend itself, flag, hang fire; relax.

render -idle etc. *adj.*; sluggardize; mitigate etc. 174.

Adj. inactive; motionless etc. 265; unoccupied etc. (*doing nothing*) 681.

indolent, lazy, slothful, idle, otiose, lusk, remiss, slack, inert, torpid, sluggish, languid, supine, heavy, dull, leaden, lumpish; exanimate, soulless; listless; dron-y, -ish; lazy as Ludlam's dog.

dilatory, laggard; lagging etc. *v.*; slow etc. 275; rusty, flagging; lackadaisical, maudlin, fiddle-faddle; pottering etc. *v.*; shilly-shally etc. (*irresolute*) 605.

sleeping etc. *v.*; alseep; fast –, dead –, sound-alseep; in a sound sleep; sound as a top, dormant, comatose; in the -arms, – lap- of Morpheus.

sleep-y, -ful; dozy, drowsy, somnolent, torpescent; lethargic, -al; heavy, – with sleep; napping; somni-fic, -ferous; sopor-ous, -ific, -iferous; hypnotic; balmy, dreamy; un-, una-wakened.

sedative etc. 174.

Adv. inactively etc. *adj.*; at leisure etc. 685.

Phr. the eyes begin to draw straws.

684. Haste.—N. haste, urgency; des-, dis-patch; acceleration, spurt, spirt, forced march, rush, dash; velocity etc. 274; precipit-ancy, -ation, -ousness etc. *adj.*; impetuosity; *brusquerie*; hurry, scurry, scuttle drive, scramble, push, hustle, bustle, fuss, fidget, flurry, flutter, splutter.

V. haste, hasten; make -haste, – a dash etc. *n.*; hurry –, dash –, whip –, push –, press- -on, – forward; hurry, skurry, scuttle along, bundle on, dart to and fro, bustle, flutter, scramble; plunge, – headlong; run, race, speed; dash off; rush etc. (*violence*) 173.

bestir oneself etc. (*be active*) 682; lose -no time, – not a moment, – not an instant; make short work of; make the best of one's -time, – way.

be -precipitate etc. *adj.*; jump at; be in -haste, – a hurry etc. *n.*; have -no time, – not a moment- -to lose, – to spare; work -under pressure, – against time.

quicken etc. 274; accelerate, expedite, put on, precipitate, urge, whip, spur, flog, goad.

Adj. hasty, hurried, *brusque*; scrambling, cursory, precipitate, headlong, furious, boisterous, impetuous, hot-headed; feverish, fussy, pushing.

in -haste, – a hurry etc. *n.*; in -hot, – all- haste; breathless, pressed for time, hard pressed, urgent.

Adv. with -haste, – all haste, – breathless speed; in haste etc. *adj.*; apace etc. (*swiftly*) 274; amain; all at once etc. (*instantaneously*) 113; at short notice etc., immediately etc. (*early*) 132; posthaste; by -express, – telegraph, – wire. – wireless, – air mail.

hastily, precipitately etc. *adj.*; helter-skelter, hurry-skurry, holusbolus; slap-dash, -bang; full-tilt, -drive; heels over head, head and shoulders, headlong, *à corps perdu*.

by -fits and starts, – spurts; hop, skip and jump.

Phr. *sauve qui peut*, devil take the hindmost, no time to be lost; no sooner said than done etc. (*early*) 132; a word and a blow.

Int. hurry up! look alive! get a move on! buck up! double march! rush! urgent!

685. Leisure.—N. leisure; spare -time, – hours, – moments; vacant hour; time, – to spare, – on one's hands; holiday etc. (*rest*) 687; *otium cum dignitate*, ease.

V. have -leisure etc. *n.*; take one's -time, – leisure, – ease; repose etc. 687; move slowly etc. 275; while away the time etc. (*inaction*) 681; be - master of one's time, – an idle man; *desipere in loco*.

Adj. leisurely; slow etc. 275; deliberate, quiet,. calm, undisturbed; at -leisure, – one's ease, – a loose end.

Phr. time hanging heavy on one's hands.

686. Exertion.—N. exertion, effort, strain, tug, pull, stress, force, pressure, throw, stretch, struggle, spell, spurt, spirt; stroke –, stitch- of work.

'a stong pull, a long pull and a pull all together;' dead lift; heft; gymnastics, sports; exer-cise, - citation; wear and tear; ado; toil and trouble; uphill –, hard –, warm- work; harvest time.

labor, work, toil, travail, manual labor, sweat of one's brow, swink, operoseness, drudgery, slavery, fagging, hammering; *limae labor*.

trouble, pains, duty; resolution etc. 604; energy etc. (*physical*) 171.

V. exert oneself; exert –, tax- one's energies; use exertion.

labor, work, toil, moil, sweat, fag, drudge, slave, drag a lengthened chain, wade through, strive, strain; make –, stretch- a long arm; pull, tug, ply, ply –, tug at- the oar; do the work; take the laboring oar.

bestir oneself (*be active*) 682; take trouble, trouble oneself.

work hard; rough it; put forth -one's strength, – a strong arm; fall to work, bend the bow; buckle to, set one's shoulder to the wheel etc. (*resolution*) 604; work like a -Briton, – horse, – carthorse, – galley-slave, – coalheaver; labor –, work-day and night; redouble one's efforts; do double duty; work double -hours, – tides; sit up, burn the -midnight oil, – candle at both ends; stick to etc. (*persevere*) 604*a*; work –, fight- one's way; lay about one, hammer at.

take pains; do one's -best, – level best, – utmost; do -the best one can, – all one can, – all in one's power, – as much as in one lies, – what lies in one's power; use one's -best, – utmost- endeavor; try one's -best, – utmost; play one's best card; put one's -best, – right- leg foremost; have one's whole soul in one's work, put all one's strength into, strain every nerve; spare no -efforts, – pains; go all lengths; go through fire and water etc. (*resolution*) 604; move heaven and earth, leave no stone unturned.

Adj. laboring etc. *v.*

laborious, operose, elaborate; strained; toil-, trouble-, burden-, weari-some; uphill; herculean; gymnastic, athletic, palestric.

hardworking, painstaking, strenuous, energetic. hard at work, on the stretch.

Adv. laboriously etc. *adj.*; lustily; with -might and main, – all one's might, – a strong hand, – sledge-hammer; – much ado; to the best of one's abilities, *totis viribus, vi et armis, manibus pedibusque*, tooth and nail, *unguibus et rostro*, hammer and tongs, heart and soul; through thick and thin etc. (*perseverance*) 604a.

by the sweat of one's brow, *suo Marte*.

687. Repose.—N. repose, rest, silken repose; sleep etc. 683.

relaxation, breathing time; halt, pause etc. (*cessation*) 142; respite.

day of rest, *dies non*, Sabbath, Lord's day, holiday, red-letter day, vacation, recess.

V. repose; rest, – and be thankful; take -rest, – one's ease.

relax, unbend, slacken; take breath etc. (*refresh*) 689; rest upon one's oars; pause etc. (*cease*) 142; stay one's hand.

lie down; recline, – on a bed of down, – on an easy chair; go to -rest, – bed, – sleep etc. 683.

take a holiday, shut up shop; lie fallow etc. (*inaction*) 681.

Adj. reposing etc. *v.*; unstrained.

Adv. at rest.

688. Fatigue.—N. fatigue; weariness etc. 841; yawning, drowsiness etc. 683; lassitude, tiredness, fatigation, exhaustion; sweat.

anhelation, shortness of breath, panting; faintness; collapse, prostration, swoon, fainting, *deliquium*, syncope, lipothymy.

V. be -fatigued etc. *adj.*; yawn etc. (*get sleepy*) 683; droop, sink, flag; lose -breath, – wind; gasp, pant, puff, blow, drop, swoon, faint, succumb.

fatigue, tire, weary, bore, irk, fag, jade, harass, exhaust, knock up, wear out, prostrate.

tax, task, strain; over-task, -work, -burden, -tax, -strain.

Adj. fatigued etc. *v.*; weary etc. 841; drowsy etc. 683; drooping etc. *v.*; haggard; toil-, way-worn; footsore, surbated, weatherbeaten; faint; done –, used –, knock- up; exhausted, prostrate, spent; over-tired, -spent, -fatigued; forspent; unre-freshed, -stored.

worn, – out; battered, shattered, pulled down, seedy, altered.

breath-, wind-less; short of –, out of -breath, – wind; blown, puffing and blowing; short-breathed; anhelous; broken-, short-winded.

ready to drop, more dead than alive, dog -tired, – weary, walked off one's legs, tired to death, on one's last legs, played out, *hors de combat*.

fatiguing etc. *v.*; tire-, irk-, weari-some; weary; trying.

689. Refreshment.—N. bracing etc. *v.*; recovery of -strength etc. 159; restoration, revival etc. 660; repair, refection, refocillation, refreshment, regalement, bait; relief etc. 834.

V. brace etc. (*strengthen*) 159; reinvigorate; air, freshen up, refresh, recruit; repair etc. (*restore*) 660; fan, revocillate.

breathe, respire; draw –, take –, gather –, take a long –, regain –, recover- breath; get better, raise one's head; recover –, regain –, renew one's strength etc. 159; perk up.

come to oneself etc. (*revive*) 660; feel like a giant refreshed.

Adj. refreshing etc. *v.*; recuperative etc. 660. refreshed etc. *v.*; un-tired, -wearied.

690. Agent.—N. doer, actor, agent, performer, perpetrator, operator; execu-tor, -trix; practitioner, worker, stager.

bee, ant, working bee, laboring oar, shaft horse, servant –, maid- of all work, general servant, factotum.

workman, artisan; crafts-, handicrafts-man; mechanic, operative; working –, laboring- man; hewers of wood and drawers of water, laborer, navvy; hand, man, day laborer, journeyman, hack; mere -tool etc. 633; porter, docker, stevedore, beast of burden, drudge, fag.

maker, artificer, artist, wright, manufacturer, architect, contractor, builder, mason, bricklayer, smith, forger, Vulcan; black-, tin-smith; carpenter; ganger, platelayer.

machinist, mechanician, engineer, electrician, plumber, gasfitter etc.

semp-, sem-, seam-stress; needle-, char-, workwoman; tailor, cordwainer.

minister etc. (*instrument*) 631; servant etc. 746; representative etc. (*commissioner*) 758; (*deputy*) 759.

co-worker, fellow-worker, party to, participator in, co-operator, colleague, associate, collaborator, *particeps criminis, dramatis personae; personnel*.

Phrs. '*quorum pars magna fui.*'

691. Workshop.—N. work-shop, -house; laboratory; manufactory, mill, factory, armory, arsenal, mint, forge, loom; cabinet, *studio, bureau, atelier* hive, – of industry; nursery; hot-house, -bed; kitchen, kitchenette; dock, -yard; slip, yard, wharf; found-ry, -ery; furnace; vineyard, orchard, farm, kitchen garden.

melting pot, crucible, alembic, caldron, mortar, *matrix*.

692. Conduct.—N. dealing, transaction etc. (*action*) 680; business etc. 625.

tactics, game, policy, polity; general-, statesman-seaman-ship; strate-gy, -gics; plan etc. 626.

husbandry; house-keeping, -wifery; stewardship; *ménage*; regimen, *régime*; econom-y, -ics; political economy; management; government etc. (*direction*) 693.

execution, manipulation, treatment, campaign, career, life, course, walk, race.

conduct; behavior; de-, com-portment; carriage, *maintien*, demeanor, guise, bearing, manner, mien, air, observance.

course –, line- of -conduct, – action, – proceeding; *rôle*; process, ways, practice, procedure, *modus operandi*; method etc., path etc. 627.

V. transact, execute; des-, dis-patch; proceed with, discharge; carry -on, – through, – out, – into effect; work out; go –, get- through; enact; put into practice; officiate etc. 625.

behave –, comport –, demean –, carry –,
bear –, conduct –, acquit- oneself.

run a race, lead a life, play a game; take –,
adopt- a course; steer –, shape- one's course; play
one's- part, – cards; shift for oneself; paddle one's
own canoe.

conduct; manage etc. (*direct*) 693.

deal –, have to do- with; treat, handle a case;
take -steps, – measures.

Adj. conducting etc. *v.*; strategical, business-
like, practical, economic, executive.

693. Direction.—N. direction; manage-ment, -
ry; government, gubernation, conduct, legislation,
regulation, guidance; steer-, pilot-age; reins, – of
government; helm, rudder, controls, joy stick,
needle, compass, binnacle; guiding –, load –,
lode –, pole- star; cynosure.

super-vision, -intendence; *surveillance*, oversight;
eye of the master; control, charge, auspices; board
of control etc. (*council*) 696; command etc.
(*authority*) 737.

premier-, senator-ship; director etc. 694; chair,
seat, portfolio.

statesmanship; state-, king-craft.

minis-try, -tration; administration; steward-,
proctor-ship; agency.

V. direct, manage, govern, conduct; order,
prescribe, cut out work for; head, lead; lead –,
show- the way; take the lead, lead on; regulate,
guide, steer, pilot; take –, be at- the helm; have
–, handle –, hold –, take- the reins, handle the
ribbons; drive, tool; tackle.

super-intend, -vise; overlook, control, keep in
order, look after, see to, oversee, legislate for; administer, ministrate; patronize; have the -care, –
charge- of; have –, take- the direction; pull the -
strings, – wires; rule etc. (*command*) 737; have
–, hold- -office, – the portfolio; preside, – at the
board; take –, occupy –, be in- the chair; pull the
stroke oar.

Adj. directing etc. *v.*; executive, supervisory,
hegemonic.

Adv. at the -helm, – head of, in charge of; under the auspices of.

694. Director.—N. director, manager, governor, rector, comptroller; super-intendent, -visor;
intendant; over-seer, -looker; foreman, boss, straw
boss; supercargo, husband, inspector, visitor,
ranger, surveyor, aedile, moderator, monitor, taskmaster; master etc. 745; leader, ringleader,
demagogue, corypheus, conductor, fugleman,
precentor, bellwether, agitator.

guiding star etc. (*guidance*) 693; adviser etc.
695; guide etc. (*information*) 527; pilot; helmsman; steers-man, -mate; man at the wheel; wire-
puller.

driver, whip, Jehu, charioteer; coach-, car-, cab-
man, jarvey; postilion, *vetturino*, muleteer, teamster; whipper in; engineer, engine driver, motor-
man, *chauffeur*.

head, – man; principal, president, speaker;
chair, -man; captain etc. (*master*) 745; superior;
dean; mayor etc. (*civil authority*) 745; vice-

president, prime minister, premier, vizier, grand
vizier; dictator.

officer, functionary, minister, official, red-tapist,
bureaucrat; man –, Jack- in office; office-bearer;
person in authority etc. 745.

statesman, strategist, legislator, lawgiver, politician, administrator, statist, statemonger; Minos,
Draco; arbiter etc. (*judge*) 967; king maker, power
behind the throne.

board etc. (*council*) 696.

secretary, – of state; Reis Effendi; vicar etc.
(*deputy*) 759; steward; factor; agent etc. 758;
bailiff, middleman; ganger, clerk of. works; land-
reeve; factotum, major-domo, seneschal, housekeeper, shepherd, *croupier*; proctor, procurator,
curator, librarian.

Adv. *ex officio.*

695. Advice.—N. advice, counsel, adhortation;
word to the- wise; suggestion, submonition, recom-
mendation, advocacy, consultation.

exhortation etc. (*persuasion*) 615; expostulation
etc. (*dissuasion*) 616; admonition etc. (*warning*)
668; guidance etc. (*direction*) 693.

instruction, charge, injunction.

adviser, prompter; counsel, -lor; monitor, mentor, Nestor, *magnus Apollo*, senator; teacher etc.
540.

guide, manual, chart etc. (*information*) 527.

physician, leech, archiater; arbiter etc. (*judge*)
967.

refer-ence, -ment; consultation, conference,
parley, *pourparler* etc. 696.

V. advise, counsel; give -advice, – counsel, – a
piece of advice; suggest, prompt, submonish,
recommend, prescribe, advocate; exhort etc. (*persuade*) 615.

enjoin, enforce, charge, instruct, call; call upon,
etc. (*request*) 765; dictate.

expostulate etc. (*dissuasion*) 616; admonish etc.
(*warn*) 668.

advise with; lay heads –, consult- together;
compare notes; hold a council, deliberate, be
closeted with.

confer, consult, refer to, call in; take –, follow-
advice; follow implicitly; be advised by, have at
one's elbow, take one's cue from.

Adj. recommendatory; hortative etc. (*persuasive*) 615; dehortatory etc. (*dissuasive*) 616; admonitory etc. (*warning*) 668; consultative.

Int. go to!

696. Council.—N. council, committee, subcommittee, *comitia*, court, chamber, cabinet,
board, bench, staff; consultation.

senate, *senatus*, parliament, house, – of lords,
– Peers, – Commons, legislature, legislative
assembly, federal council, chamber of deputies,
directory, *reichsrath*, *rigsdag*, *cortes*, storthing,
witenagemote, *junta*, divan, *musnud*, *sanhedrim*,
Amphictyonic council; *duma*, *zemstvo*, *soviet*,
cheka, *ogpu*; Dail Eireann; caput, consistory,
chapter, syndicate; court of appeal etc. (*tribunal*)
966; board of -control, – works; vestry; county –,
borough –, district –, parish –, town- council,
local board.

cabinet –, privy- council, royal commission; cockpit, convocation, synod, congress, congregation, convention, diet, states-general, aulic council.

League of Nations, assembly, *caucus*, conclave, *clique*, conventicle; meeting, sitting, *séance*, conference, session, hearing, palaver, *pourparler*, *durbar*, pow-wow, house; *quorum*.

senator; member, – of parliament; councilor, M.P., representative of the people.

Adj. senatorial, curule, parliamentary.

697. Precept.—N. precept, direction, instruction, charge; prescript, -ion; *recipe*, receipt; golden rule; maxim etc. 496.

commandment, rule, ruling, canon, law, code, *corpus juris*, *lex scripta*, common –, unwritten –, canon- law; the Ten Commandments; act, statute, convention, rubric, stage direction, regulation; form, -ula, -ulary; technicality; nice point.

order etc. (*command*) 741.

698. Skill.—N. skill, skilfulness, address; dexter-ity, -ousness; adroitness, expertness etc. *adj* ; proficiency, competence, craft, callidity, facility, knack, trick, sleight; master-y, -ship; excellence, panurgy; ambidext-erity, -rousness; sleight of hand etc. (*deception*) 545.

sea-, air-, marks-, horse-manship; tight-, ropedancing.

accomplish-, acquire-, attain-ment; art, science; techn-icality, -ology, -ique; practical –, technicalknowledge; technocracy; finish, technic.

knowledge of the world, world wisdom, *savoirfaire*; tact; mother wit etc. (*sagacity*) 498; discretion etc. (*caution*) 864; *finesse*; craftiness etc. (*cunning*) 702; management etc. (*conduct*) 692; *ars celare artem*; self-help.

cleverness, talent, ability, ingenuity, capacity, parts, talents, faculty, endowment, *forte*, turn, gift, genius, flair, feeling; intelligence etc. 498; sharpness, readiness etc. (*activity*) 682; invention etc. 515; apt-ness, -itude; turn –, capacity –, geniusfor; felicity, capability, *curiosa felicitas*, qualification, habilitation.

proficient etc. 700.

masterpiece, *coup de maître*, *chef- d'oeuvre*, *tour de force*; good stroke etc. (*plan*) 626.

V. be -skilful etc. *adj* ; excel in, be master of; have -a turn for etc. *n*.

know -what's what, – a hawk from a handsaw, – what one is about, – on which side one's bread is buttered, – what's o'clock, – a thing or two; have cut one's -eye, – wisdom- teeth.

see -one's way, – where the wind lies, – which way the wind blows; have -all one's wits about one, – one's hand in; *savoir vivre*; *scire quid valeant humeri quid ferre recusent*

look after the main chance; cut one's coat according to one's cloth; live by one's wits; exercise one's discretion, feather the oar, sail near the wind; stoop to conquer etc. (*cunning*) 702; play one's - cards well, – best card; hit the right nail on the head, put the saddle on the right horse.

take advantage of, make the most of; profit by etc. (*use*) 677; make a hit etc. (*succeed*) 731; make a virtue of necessity; make hay while the sun shines etc. (*occasion*) 134.

Adj. skilful, dexterous, adroit, expert, apt, slick, handy, quick, deft, ready, resourceful, gain; smart etc. (*active*) 682; proficient, good at, up to, at home in, master of, a good hand, at, *au fait*, thoroughbred, masterly, crack, accomplished; conversant etc. (*knowing*) 490.

experienced, practiced, skilled; up –, well up-in; in -practice, – proper cue; competent, efficient, qualified, capable, fitted, fit for, up to the mark, trained, initiated, prepared, primed; finished.

clever, able, ingenious, felicitous, gifted, talented, endowed, cute, inventive etc. 515; shrewd, sharp etc. (*intelligent*) 498; cunning etc. 702; alive to, up to snuff, not to be caught with chaff; discreet.

neat-handed, fine-fingered, ambidextrous, surefooted; cut out –, fitted- for.

technical, artistic, scientific, daedalian, shipshape; workman-, business-, statesman-like.

Adv. skilfully etc. *adj* ; well etc. 618; artistically; with -skill, – consummate skill; *secundum artem*, *suo Marte*; to the best of one's abilities etc. (*exertion*) 686; like a machine.

699. Unskillfulness.—N. unskillfulness etc. *adj* ; want of -skill etc. 698; incompeten-ce, -cy; inability, -felicity, -dexterity, -experience; clumsiness; disqualification, unproficiency; quackery.

folly, stupidity etc. 499; indiscretion etc. (*rashness*) 863; thoughtlessness etc. (*inattention*) 458; (*neglect*) 460.

mis-management, -conduct; impolicy; maladministration; mis-rule, -government, -application, -direction, -feasance.

absence of rule, rule of thumb; bungling etc. ᴠ; failure etc. 732; screw loose; too many cooks.

blunder etc. (*mistake*) 495; *étourderie*, *gaucherie*, act of folly, *balourdise*; botch, -ery; bad job, sad work.

sprat sent out to catch a whale, much ado about nothing, wildgoose chase.

bungler etc. 701; fool etc. 501.

layman, amateur.

V. be -unskillful etc. *adj*; not see an inch beyond one's nose; blunder, bungle, boggle, fumble, muff, botch, bitch, flounder, loppet, stumble, trip; hobble etc. 275; put one's foot in it; make a -mess, – hash, – sad work- of; overshoot the mark.

play -tricks with, – Puck; mismanage, -conduct, -direct, -apply, -send.

stultify –, make a fool of –, commit- oneself; act foolishly; play the fool; put oneself out of court; lose one's -head, – cunning.

begin at the wrong end; do things by halves etc. (*not complete*) 730, make two bites of a cherry; play at cross purposes; strain at a gnat and swallow a camel etc. (*caprice*) 608; put the cart before the horse; lock the stable door when the horse is stolen etc. (*too late*) 135.

not know -what one is about, – one's own interest, – on which side one's bread is buttered; stand in one's own light, quarrel with one's bread and butter, throw a stone in one's own garden, kill the goose which lays the golden eggs, pay dear for one's whistle, cut one's own throat, burn one's fingers; knock –, run- one's head against a stone wall; fall into a trap, catch a Tartar, bring the house about one's ears; have too many -eggs in one basket (*imprudent*) 863, – irons in the fire.

mistake etc. 495; take the shadow for the substance etc. (*credulity*) 486; be in the wrong box, aim at a pigeon and kill a crow; take –, get- the wrong sow by the ear, – the dirty end of the stick; put -the saddle on the wrong horse, – a square peg into a round hole, – new wine into old bottles.

cut a whetstone with a razor; hold a farthing candle to the sun etc. (*useless*) 645; fight with –, grasp at- a shadow; catch at straws, lean on a broken reed, reckon without one's host, pursue a wildgoose chase; go on a fool's –, sleeveless-errand; go further and fare worse; loose –, miss-one's way; fail etc. 732.

Adj. un-skillful etc. 698; unskilled, inexpert; bungling etc. ꝟ ; awkward, clumsy, unhandy, lubberly, *gauche*, *maladroit*; left-, heavy-handed; slovenly, slatternly; gawky.

adrift, at fault.

in-, un-apt; inhabile; un-tractable, -teachable; giddy etc. (*inattentive*) 458; inconsiderate etc. (*neglectful*) 460; stupid etc. 499; inactive etc. 683; incompetent; un-, dis-, ill-qualified; unfit; quackish; raw, green, inexperienced, rusty, out of practice.

un-accustomed, -used, -trained etc. 537; -initiated, -conversant etc. (*ignorant*) 491; shiftless; unbusinesslike, unpractical; unstatesmanlike.

un-, ill-, mis-advised; ill-devised, -imagined, -judged, -contrived, -conducted; un-, mis-guided; misconducted, foolish, wild; infelicitous; penny wise and pound foolish etc. (*inconsistent*) 608.

Phr. one's fingers being all thumbs; the right hand forgets its cunning.

il se noyerait dans une goutte d'eau.

incidit in Scyllam qui vult vitare Charybdim; *out of the frying pan into the fire*

700. Proficient.—N. proficient, expert, adept, dab; *connoisseur* etc. (*scholar*) 492; master, -hand; top-sawyer, *prima donna*, first fiddle, *chef de cuisine*; protagonist; past master; profess-or, -ional, specialist.

picked man; medalist, prizeman.

veteran; old -stager, – campaigner, – soldier, – file, – hand; man of -business, – the world.

nice –, good –, clean- hand; practised –, experienced- -eye, – hand; marksman; good –, dead –, crack- shot; rope-dancer, funambulist, acrobat, contortionist; cunning man; conjuror etc. (*deceiver*) 548; wizard etc. 994.

genius; master-mind, – head, – spirit.

cunning –, sharp -blade, – fellow; jobber; cracksman etc. (*thief*) 792; politician, tactician, diplomat, -ist, strategist.

pantologist, admirable Crichton, Jack of all trades; prodigy of learning; walking encyclopedia; mine of information.

701. Bungler.—N. bungler; blunderer, -head; marplot, fumbler, lubber, lout, oaf, duffer, stick, clown; bad –, poor- -hand, – shot; butter-fingers.

no conjuror, flat, muff, slow coach, looby, lub-ber, swab; clod, yokel, hick, awkward squad, novice, greenhorn, jaywalker, *blanc-bec*.

land lubber; fresh water –, fair weather- sailor; horse-marine; fish out of water, ass in lion's skin, jackdaw in peacock's feathers; quack etc. (*deceiver*) 548; Lord of Misrule.

sloven, slattern, trapes.

Phr. *il n'a pas inventé la poudre*; he will never set the Thames on fire.

702. Cunning.—N. cunning, craft; cunningness, craftiness etc. *adj.*; subtlety, artificiality; maneuvring etc. *v.*; temporization; circumvention.

chicane, -ry; sharp practice, knavery, jugglery; concealment etc. 528; nigger in the woodpile; guile, duplicity etc. (*falsehood*) 544; foul play.

diplomacy, politics; Machiavellism; jobbery, back-stairs influence, gerrymandering.

art, -ifice; device, machination; plot etc. (*plan*) 626; maneuver, stratagem, dodge, artful dodge, wile; trick, -ery etc. (*deception*) 545; *ruse*, – *de guerre*; *finesse*, side-blow, thin end of the wedge, shift, go by, subterfuge, evasion; white lie etc. (*untruth*) 546; juggle, *tour de force*; tricks -of the trade, – upon travelers; imposture, deception; *expie-glerie*, net, trap etc. 545.

Ulysses, Machiavel, sly boots, fox, reynard; Scotch-, Yorkshire-man; Jew, Yankee; intriguer, *intrigant*, schemer, trickster.

V. be -cunning etc. *adj.*; have cut one's eyeteeth; contrive etc. (*plan*) 626; live by one's wits; maneuver; intrigue, gerrymander, *finesse*, double, temporize, stoop to conquer, *reculer pour mieux sauter*, circumvent, steal a march upon; overreach etc. 545; throw off one's guard; surprise etc. 508; outdo, get the better of, snatch from under one's nose; snatch a verdict; waylay, undermine, introduce the thin end of the wedge; play -a deep game, – tricks with; have an axe to grind; *ambiguas in vulgum spargere voces*; flatter, make things pleasant.

Adj. cunning, crafty, artful; skilful etc. 698; subtle, feline, vulpine; cunning as a -fox, – serpent; deep, – laid; profound; designing, contriving; intriguing etc. *v.*; strategic, diplomatic, politic, Machiavellian, time-serving; artificial; trick-y, -sy; wily, sly, slim, insidious, stealthy, foxy; underhand etc. (*hidden*) 528; subdolous; deceitful etc. 545; double-tongued, -faced; shifty; crooked, arch, pawky, shrewd, acute; sharp, – as a needle; canny, astute, leery, knowing, up to snuff, too clever by half, not to be caught with chaff.

Adv. cunningly etc. *adj.*; slily, on the sly, by a side wind.

Phr. diamond cut diamond.

703. Artlessness.—N. artlessness etc. *adj.*; nature, simplicity; innocence etc. 946; *bonhomie*, *naiveté*, *abandon*, candor, sincerity; singleness of -purpose, – heart; honesty etc. 939; plain speaking; *épanchement*.

rough diamond, matter of fact man; *le palais de vérité*; *enfant terrible*.

V. be -artless etc. *adj.*; look one in the face; wear one's heart upon his sleeves for daws to peck at; think aloud; speak -out, – one's mind; be free with one, call a spade a spade.

Adj. artless, natural, pure, native, simple, plain, martificial, untutored, unsophisticated, *ingenu*, unaffected, *naive*; sincere, frank; open, – as day; candid, ingenuous, guileless, unsuspicious, childlike; honest etc. 939; innocent etc. 946; Arcadian; undesigning, straightforward; unreserved, unvarnished, above-board; simple-, single-minded; frank-, open-, single-, simple-hearted; open and above-board.

free-, plain-, out-spoken; blunt, downright, direct, matter of fact, unpoetical; unflattering.

Adv. in plain -words. – English; without mincing the matter; not to mince the matter etc. *(affirmation)* 535.

Phr. *Davus sum non Oedipus; liberavi animam meam.*

704. Difficulty.—N. difficulty; hardness etc. *adj.*; impracticability etc. *(impossibility)* 471; tough –, hard –, uphill- work; hard –, Herculean –, Augean- task; task of Sisyphus, Sisyphean labor, tough job, teaser, rasper, dead lift.

dilemma, embarrassment; perplexity etc. *(uncertainty)* 475; involvement; intricacy; entanglement etc. 59; cross fire; awkwardness, delicacy, ticklish card to play, deadlock, knot, Gordian knot, *dignus vindice nodus*, net, meshes, maze; coil etc. *(convolution)* 248; crooked path.

nice –, delicate –, subtle –, knotty-point; vexed question, *vexata quaestio*, poser; puzzle etc. *(riddle)* 533; paradox; hard –, nut to crack; bone to pick, *crux, pons asinorum*, where the shoe pinches.

nonplus, quandary, strait, pass, pinch, pretty pass, stress, brunt; critical situation, crisis; trial, rub, emergency, exigency, scramble.

scrape, hobble, slough, quagmire, hot water, hornet's nest; sea –, peck- of troubles; pretty kettle of fish; pickle, stew, *imbroglio*, mess, muddle, botch, fuss, bustle, ado; false position; set fast, stand; dead -lock, – set; fix, horns of a dilemma, *cul de sac*; hitch; stumbling block etc. *(hindrance)* 706.

V. be -difficult etc. *adj.*; run one hard, go against the grain, try one's patience, put one out; put to one's -shifts, – wit's end; go hard with –, try- one; pose, perplex etc. *(uncertain)* 475; bother, nonplus, gravel, bring to a dead lock; be -impossible etc. 471; be in the way of etc. *(hinder)* 706.

meet with –, labor under –, get into –, plunge into –, struggle with –, contend with –, grapple with- difficulties; labor under a disadvantage; be -in difficulty etc. *adj.*

fish in troubled waters, buffet the waves, swim against the stream, scud under bare poles.

have -much ado with, – a hard time of it; come to the -push, – pinch; bear the brunt.

grope in the dark, lose one's way, weave a tangled web, walk among eggs.

get into a -scrape etc. *n.*; bring a hornet's nest about one's ears; be put to one's shifts; flounder, boggle, struggle; not know which way to turn etc. *(uncertain)* 475; get -tangled up, – wound up; *perdre son latin*; stick - at, – in the mud, – fast; come to a -stand, – dead lock; hold the wolf by the ears.

render -difficult etc. *adj.*; encumber, embarrass, ravel, entangle; put a spoke in the wheel etc. *(hinder)* 706; lead a pretty dance.

Adj. difficult, not easy, hard, tough; trouble-, toil-, irk-some; operose, laborious, onerous, arduous, Herculean, formidable; sooner –, more easily- said than done; difficult –, hard- to deal with; ill-conditioned, crabbed; not -to be handled with kid gloves, – made with rosewater.

awkward, unwieldy, unmanageable; intractable, stubborn etc. *(obstinate)* 606; perverse, refractory, plaguy, trying, thorny, rugged; knot-ted, -ty; invious; path-, track-less; labyrinthine etc. *(convoluted)* 248; intricate, complicated etc. *(tangled)* 59; impracticable etc. *(impossible)* 471; not -feasible etc. 470; desperate etc. *(hopeless)* 859.

embarrassing, perplexing etc. *(uncertain)* 475; delicate, ticklish, critical; beset with –, full -of –, surrounded by –, entangled by –, encompassed with- difficulties.

under a difficulty; in -difficulty, – hot water, – the suds, – a cleft stick, – a fix, – the wrong box, – a scrape etc. *n.*; – deep water, – a fine pickle; *in extremis*; between -two stools, – Scylla and Charybdis; surrounded by -shoals, – breakers, – quicksands; at cross purposes; not out of the wood.

reduced to straits; hard –, sorely- pressed; run hard; pinched, put to it, straitened; hard -up, – put to it, – set; put to one's shifts; puzzled, at a loss etc. *(uncertain)* 475; at -the end of one's tether, – one's wit's end, – a nonplus, – a standstill; graveled, nonplussed, stranded, aground; stuck –, set- fast; up a tree, at bay, *aux abois*, driven -into a corner, – from post to pillar, – to extremity, – to one's wit's end, – to the wall; *au bout de son latin*; out of one's -depth, – reckoning; put –, thrown -out.

accomplished with difficulty; hard-fought, -earned.

Adv. with -difficulty, – much ado; hardly etc. *adj.*; uphill; against the -stream, – grain; *à rebours; invitâ Minervâ*; in the teeth of; at –, upon- a pinch; at long odds.

Phr. ay there's the rub; *hic labor hoc opus*; things are come to a pretty pass.

705. Facility.—N. facility, ease; easiness etc. *adj.*; capability; feasibility etc. *(practicability)* 470; flexibility, pliancy etc. 324; smoothness etc. 255; convenience.

plain –, smooth –, straight- sailing; mere child's play, holiday task.

smooth water, fair wind; smooth – royal- road; clear -coast, – stage; *tabula rasa; full play* etc. *(freedom)* 748.

disen-cumbrance, -tanglement; deoppilation; permission etc. 760.

V. be -easy etc. *adj.*; go on –, run- smoothly; have -full play etc. *n.*; go –, run- on all fours; obey the helm, work well.

flow –, swim –, drift –, go- with the- -stream, – tide; see one's way; have -it all one's own way, – the game in one's own hands; walk over the course, win -at a canter, – hands down; make -light of, – nothing of; be at home in etc. *(skilful)* 698.

render -easy etc. *adj.*; facilitate, smooth, ease; popularize; lighten, – the labor; free, clear; disencumber, -embarrass, -entangle, -engage; deobstruct, unclog, extricate, unravel; untie –, cut- the knot; disburden, unload, exonerate, emancipate, free from, deoppilate; humor etc. (*aid*) 707; lubricate etc. 332; relieve etc. 834.

leave -a hole to creep out of, – a loophole, – the matter open; give -the reins to, – full play, – full swing; make way for; open the -door to, – way; prepare –, smooth –, clear- the -ground, – way, – path, – road; pave the way, bridge over; permit etc. 760.

Adj. easy, facile; feasible etc. (*practicable*) 470; easily -managed, – accomplished; within reach, accessible, easy of access, for the million, open to.

manageable, wieldy; towardly, tractable; submissive; yielding, ductile; pliant etc. (*soft*) 324; glib, slippery; smooth etc. 255; on -friction wheels, – velvet; convenient.

un-, dis-burdened, -encumbered, -embarrassed; exonerated; un-loaded, -obstructed, -trammeled, -impeded, -restrained etc. (*free*) 748; at ease, light.

at –, quite at- home; in -one's element, – smooth water.

Adv. easily etc. *adj.*; readily, smoothly, swimmingly, *ad lib.*, on easy terms, single-handed.

Phr. touch and go.

Int. all clear!

706. Hindrance.—N. prevention, preclusion, obstruction, stoppage; prohibition; inter-ruption, -ception, -clusion; hindrance, impedition; retardment, -ation; constriction; embarrassment, oppilation; coarctation, stricture, restriction; anchor etc. 666; restraint etc. 751 & 752; inhibition etc. 761; blockade etc. (*closure*) 261; picketing.

inter-ference, -position; obtrusion; discouragement, -countenance, -approval, approbation; opposition etc. 708.

impediment·, let, obstacle, obstruction, knot, knag; check, hitch, *contretemps*, *impasse*, screw loose, grit in the oil.

bar, stile, barrier; turn-stile, -pike; gate, portcullis; bulwark, parapet, barricade etc. (*defence*) 717; wall, dead wall, breakwater, groyne; bulkhead, block, buffer; stopper etc. 263; boom, dam, weir, burrock.

drawback, objection; stumbling-block, -stone; lion in the path; snag; snags and sawyers.

en-, in-cumbrance; clog, skid, shoe, spoke; brake, drag, – chain, – weight; stay, stop; preventive, prophylactic; contraception; load, burden, fardel, *onus*, millstone round one's neck, *impedimenta*; dead weight; lumber, pack; nightmare, Ephialtes, incubus, old man of the sea; remora.

difficulty etc. 704; insuperable etc. 471- obstacle; estoppel; ill wind; head wind etc. (*opposition*) 708; trammel, tether etc. (*means of restraint*) 752; hold back, counterpoise; damper, wet blanket, hinderer, marplot, kill-joy, dog in the manger, interloper; trail of a red herring; opponent etc. 710.

V. hinder, impede, impedite, embarrass.

keep –, stave –, ward- off; picket; obviate; a-, ante-vert; turn aside, draw off, prevent, forefend; nip in the bud; retard, slacken, check, let; counteract, -check; preclude, debar, foreclose, estop;

inhibit etc. 761; shackle etc. (*restrain*) 751; restrict, restrain, cohibit.

obstruct, filibuster, stop, stay, bar, bolt, lock; block, – up; belay, barricade; block –, stop- the way; dam up etc (*close*) 261; put on the -brake etc. *n.*; scotch –, lock –, put a spoke in- the wheel; put a stop to etc. 142; traverse, contravene; inter-rupt, -cept; oppose etc. 708; hedge -in, – round; cut off; interclude.

inter-pose, -fere, -meddle etc. 682.

cramp, hamper, clog, – the wheels; cumber; en-, in-cumber; handicap; choke; saddle –, load-with; overload, lay; lumber, trammel, tie one's hands, put to inconvenience; in-, discommode; discompose; hustle, drive into a corner; choke off.

run –, fall- foul of; cross the path of, break in upon.

thwart, frustrate, disconcert, balk, foil, baffle, snub, override, circumvent; defeat etc. 731; spike guns etc. (*render useless*) 645; spoil, mar, clip the wings of; cripple etc. (*injure*) 659; put an extinguisher on; damp; dishearten etc. (*dissuade*) 616; discountenance, throw cold water on, spoil sport; lay –, throw- a wet blanket on; cut the ground from under one, take the wind out of one's sails, undermine; be –, stand- in the way of; act as a drag; hang like a millstone round one's neck.

Adj. hindering etc. *v.*; obstr-uctive, -uent; impedi-tive, -ent; intercipient; prophylactic etc. (*remedial*) 662.

in the way of, unfavorable; onerous, burdensome; cumb-rous, -ersome; obtrusive.

hindered etc. *v.*; wind-bound, water-logged, heavy laden; hard pressed.

unassisted etc. (*see* assist etc. 707); single-handed, alone; deserted etc. 624.

707. Aid.—N. aid, -ance; assistance, help, opitulation, succor; support, lift, advance, furtherance, promotion; coadjuvancy etc. (*co-operation*); 709.

patronage, championship, countenance, favor, interest, advocacy, auspices.

sustentation, subvention, subsidy, bounty, alimentation, nutrition, nourishment, maintenance; manna in the wilderness; food etc. 298; means etc. 632.

ministr-y, -ation; subministration; acconodation.

relief, rescue; help at a dead lift; supernatural aid; *deus ex machinâ*.

supplies, reinforcements, succors, contingents, recruits; support etc. (*physical*) 215; adjunct, ally etc. (*helper*) 711.

V. aid, assist, help, succor, lend one's aid; come to the aid etc. *n*- of; contribute, subscribe to; bring –, give –, furnish –, afford –, supply- -aid etc. *n.*; render assistance; give –, stretch –, lend –, bear –, hold out- a -hand, – helping hand; give one a -lift, – cast, – turn; take -by the hand, – in tow; help a lame dog over a stile, lend wings to.

relieve, rescue; set -up, – agoing, – on one's legs; bear –, pull- through; give new life to, be the making of; reinforce, recruit; set –, put –, push-forward; give -a lift, – a shove, – an impulse- to; promote, further, forward, advance; speed, expedite, quicken, hasten.

support, sustain, uphold, prop, hold up, bolster.

cradle, nourish; nurture, nurse, dry nurse, suckle, put out to nurse; manure, cultivate, force; foster; cherish, foment; feed —, fan- the flame.

serve; do service to, tender to, pander to; ad-, sub-, minister to; tend, attend, wait on; take care of etc. 459; entertain; smooth the bed of death.

oblige, accomodate, consult the wishes of; humor, cheer, encourage.

second, stand by; back, — up; pay the piper, abet; work —, make interest —, stick up —, take up the cudgels- for; take up —, espouse —, adopt the cause of; advocate, beat up for recruits, press into the service; squire, give moral support to, keep in countenance, countenance, patronize; lend — oneself, — one's countenance- to; smile —, shine-upon; favor, befriend, take up, take in hand, enlist under the banners of; side with etc. (*co-operate*) 709.

be of use to; subserve etc. (*instrument*) 631; benefit etc. 648; render a service etc. (*utility*) 644; conduce etc. (*tend*) 176.

Adj. aiding etc. *v*; auxiliary, adjuvant, helpful; coadjuvant etc. 709; subservient, ministrant, ancillary, accessory, subsidiary.

at one's beck; friendly, amicable, favorable, propitious, well-disposed; neighborly; obliging etc. (*benevolent*) 906.

Adv. with —, by- -the aid etc. *n*.- of; on —, in-behalf of; in -aid, — the service, — the name, — favor, — furtherance- of; on account of; for the sake of, on the part of; *non obstante*.

Int. help! save us! to the rescue! S.O.S.!

708. Opposition.—**N.** opposition, antagonism, oppug-nancy, -nation; impugnation; contravention; counteraction etc. 179; counterplot.

cross-fire, under-current, head-wind.

clashing, collision, conflict, lack of harmony, contest.

competition, two of a trade, rivalry, emulation, race; war to the knife.

absence of -aid etc. 707; resistance etc. 719; restraint etc. 751; hindrance etc. 706.

V. oppose, contract, run counter to; withstand etc. (*resist*) 719; control etc. (*restrain*) 751; hinder etc. 706; antagonize, oppugn, fly in the face of, go dead against, kick against, fall foul of; set — , pit-against; face, confront, cope with; make a -stand, — dead set- against; set -oneself, one's face-against; protest —, vote —, raise one's voice-against; disfavor, turn one's back upon; set at naught, slap in the face, slam the door in one's face.

be —, play- at cross purposes; counter-work, -mine; thwart, overthwart.

stem, breast, encounter; stem —, breast- the -tide, — current, — flood; buffet the waves; beat up —, make head- against; grapple with; kick against the pricks etc. (*resist*) 719; contend etc. 720 —, do battle etc. (*warfare*) 722- -with, — against.

contra-dict, -vene; belie; go —, run —, beat —, militate- against; come in conflict with.

emulate etc. (*compete*) 720; rival, spoil one's trade.

Adj. oppos-ing, -ed etc. *v*; adverse, antagonistic; ambivalent; contrary etc. 14; at variance etc. 24; at issue, at war with; in opposition; 'agin the Government.'

un-favorable, -friendly; hostile, inimical, cross, unpropitious.

in hostile array, front to front, with crossed bayonets, at daggers drawn; up in arms; resistant etc. 791.

competitive, emulous.

Adv. against, *versus*, counter to, in conflict with, at cross purposes.

against the -grain, — current, — stream, — wind, — tide; with a headwind; with the wind -ahead, — in one's teeth.

in spite, in despite, in defiance; in the -way, — teeth, — face- of; across; a-, over-thwart; where the shoe pinches.

though etc. 30; even; *quand même*; *per contra*.

Phr. *nitor in adversum*.

709. Co-operation.—**N.** co-operation; coadjuvancy, -tancy; coagency, coefficiency; concert, concurrence, complicity, participation; union etc. 43; amalgamation, combination etc. 48; collusion.

association, alliance, colleagueship, jointstock, copartnership, trust, cartel, pool, ring, combine, interlocking directorate; confederation etc. (*party*) 712; federation, coalition, fusion; a long pull, a strong pull and a pull all together; log-rolling, freemasonry.

unanimity etc. (*assent*) 488; *esprit de corps*, party spirit; clan-, partisan-ship; reciprocity, concord etc. 714.

V. co-operate, co-adjute, concur; conduce etc. 178; combine, cartelize, unite one's efforts; keep —, draw —, pull —, club —, hang —, hold —, league —, band —, be banded- together; stand —, put- shoulder to shoulder; act in concert, join forces, fraternize, cling to one another, conspire, concert, lay one's heads together; confederate, be in league with; collude, understand one another, play into the hands of, hunt in couples.

side —, take side —, go along —, go hand in hand —, join hands —, make common cause —, strike in —, unite —, join —, mix oneself up —, take part —, play along —, cast in one's lot- with; join —, enter into- partnership with; rally round, follow the lead of; come to, pass over to, come into the views of; be —, row —, sail- in the same boat; sail on the same tack.

be a party to, lend oneself to; participate; have a -hand in, — finger in the pie; take —, bear- part in; second etc. (*aid*) 707; take the part of, play the game of; espouse a -cause, — quarrel.

Adj. co-operating etc. *v*; in -co-operation etc. *n*.— league etc. (*party*) 712; coadju-vant, -tant; hand and glove with.

favorable etc. 707- to; un-opposed etc. 708.

Adj. as one man etc. (*unanimously*) 488; shoulder to shoulder; in co-operation with.

710. Opponent.—**N.** opponent, antagonist, adversary; adverse party, opposition; enemy etc. 891; assailant.

oppositionist, obstructive; obscurantist; brawler, wrangler, brangler, disputant, extremist, irreconcilable, diehard, bitter-ender.

malcontent; Jacobin, Fenian etc. 742;
demagogue, reactionist.

passive resister, conscientious objector.

rival, competitor, contestant.

711. Auxiliary.—N. auxiliary; recruit;
assistant; adju-vant, -tant; adjunct; help, er, -mate,
ing hand; midwife; colleague, partner, mate, confrère, co-operator; coadju-tor, -trix; collaborator.

ally; friend etc. 890; confidant, fidus Achates,
al, chum, buddy, alter ego.

confederate; ac-, complice; accessory, — after
he fact; particeps criminis.

aide-de-camp, secretary, clerk, associate, mar-
hal; right-hand; candle-, bottle-holder; hand-maid;
ervant etc. 746; puppet, cat's-paw; stooge, depend-
nt. creature, jackal; tool, âme damnée; satellite,
dherent, parasite.

votary, disciple; secta-rian, -ry; seconder, backer,
pholder, supporter, abettor, advocate, partisan,
hampion, patron, friend at court, mediator.

friend in need, Jack at a pinch, deus ex
machinâ, guardian angel, fairy godmother; special
providence, tutelary genius.

712. Party.—N. party, faction, side,
denomination, class, communion, set, crowd, crew,
and, horde, posse, phalanx; regiment etc. 726;
amily, clan etc. 166.

Tories, Conservatives, Unionists, Whigs,
Liberals, Radicals, Labour party, Socialists, Com-
munists etc.; Republicans, Democrats, Farmer-
Labor; Fascisti, Revolutionaries etc. 742.

community, body, fellowship, sodality,
olidarity; con-, fraternity; sorority; brother-, sister-
ood.

Freemasons, Knights Templars, Odd Fellows,
Ku Klux Klan etx.

knot, gang, clique, ring, circle; coterie, club,
casino.

corporation, corporate body, guild; establish-
ent, company, copartnership, firm, house, joint
oncern, joint-stock company, trust, investment
ust, combine etc. 709.

society, association; instit-ute, -ution; union;
rade-union; league, syndicate, alliance, Verein,
und, Zollverein, combination; league —,
lliance- offensive and defensive; coalition;
ederation; confedera -tion, -cy; junto, cabal,
amarilla, camorra, brigue; freemasonry; party
pirit etc. (co-operation) 709.

staff; cast, dramatis personae.

V. unite, join; club together etc. (co-operate)
09; cement —, form- a party etc. n.; associate etc.
ssemble) 72.

Adj. in -league. — partnership, — alliance etc.

bonded —, banded —, linked etc. (joined) 43-
gether; embattled; confederated, federative, joint,
orporate, leagued, fraternal, masonic, cliquish.

Adv. hand in hand, side by side, shoulder to
houlder, en masse, in the same boat.

713. Discord.—N. disagreement etc. 24; dis-
ord, -accord, -sidence, -sonance; jar, clash, shock;
arring, jostling etc. v ; screw loose.

variance, difference, dissension, misun-
derstanding, cross purposes, odds, brouillerie;
division, split, rupture, disruption, division in the
camp, house divided against itself, rift within the
lute; disunion, breach; schism etc. (dissent) 489;
feud, faction.

quarrel, dispute, rippet, spat, tiff, tracasserie,
squabble, altercation, words, high words; wrangling
etc. v ; jangle, brabble cross questions and crooked
answers, snip-snap; family jars.

polemics; litigation; strife etc. (contention) 720;
warfare etc. 722; outbreak, open rupture; breaking
off of negotiations, recall of ambassadors;
declaration of war.

broil, brawl, row, racket, hubbub, rixation; embroilment, embranglement, imbroglio, fracas,
breach of the peace, piece of work, scrimmage,
rumpus; breeze, squall; riot, disturbance etc.
(disorder) 59; commotion etc. (agitation) 315;
bear garden, Donnybrook Fair.

subject of dispute, ground of quarrel, battle
ground, disputed point; bone -of contention, — to
pick; apple of discord, casus belli; question at issue
etc. (subject of inquiry) 461; vexed question,
vexata quaestio, brand of discord.

troublous times; cat-and-dog life; contentiousness etc. adj ; enmity etc. 889; hate etc.
898; Kilkenny cats; disputant etc. 710; strange
bedfellows.

V. be -discordant etc. adj ; disagree, come amiss
etc. 24; clash, jar, jostle, pull different ways, conflict, have no measures with, misunderstand one
another; live like cat and dog; differ; dissent etc.
489; have a -bone to pick, — crow to pluck- with.

fall out, quarrel, dispute; litigate; controvert etc.
(deny) 536; squabble, wrangle, jangle, brangle,
bicker, nag; spar etc. (contend) 720; have -words
etc. n. with; fall foul of.

split; break —, break squares —, part company-
with; declare war, try conclusions; join —, put in-
issue; pick a quarrel, fasten a quarrel on; sow —,
stir up- -dissension etc. n.; embroil, estrange, entangle, disunite, widen the breach; set -at odds, —
together by the ears; set —, pit- against; rub up the
wrong way.

get into hot water, fish in troubled waters, brawl;
kick up a -row, — dust; turn the house out of window.

Adj. discordant; disagreeing etc. v ; out of tune,
dissonant, inharmonious, harsh, grating, jangling,
ajar, on bad terms; dissentient etc. 489; inconsistent, contradictory, incongruous, discrepant;
un- reconciled, -pacified.

quarrelsome, unpacific; gladiatorial, controversial, polemic, disputatious; factious; liti-gious,
-gant; pettifogging.

at odds, at loggerheads, at daggers drawn, at
variance, at issue, at cross purposes, at sixes and
sevens, at feud, at high words; up in arms, together
by the ears, in hot water, embroiled.

torn, disunited.

Phr. quot homines tot sententiae; no love lost
between them, non nostrum tantas componere
lites.

714. Concord.—N. concord, accord, harmony,
symphony, homology; agreement etc. 23; sympathy etc. (love) 897; response; union, unison,

unity; bonds of harmony; peace etc. 721; unanimity etc. (*assent*) 488; league etc. 712; happy family.

rapprochement; *réunion*; amity etc. (*friendship*) 888; reciprocity; alliance, *entente cordiale*, good understanding, conciliation, arbitration, peacemaker etc. 724.

V. agree etc. 23; accord, harmonize with; fraternize; be -concordant etc. *adj.*; go hand in hand; blend —, tone in- with; run parallel etc. (*concur*) 178; understand one another; pull together etc. (*co-operate*) 709; put up one's horses together, sing in chorus.

side —, sympathize —, go —, chime in —, fall in- with; come round; be pacified etc. 723; assent etc. 488; enter into the -ideas, — feelings- of; reciprocate.

hurler avec les loups; go —, swim- with the stream.

pour oil on troubled waters, keep in good humor, render accordant, put in tune; come to an understanding, meet half-way; keep the —, remain at- peace.

Adj. concordant, congenial; agreeing etc. *v.*; in-accord etc. *n.*; harmonious, united, cemented; banded together etc. 712; allied; friendly etc. 888; fraternal; conciliatory; at one with; of one mind etc. (*assent*) 488.

at peace, in still water; tranquil etc. (*pacific*) 721.

Adv. with one voice etc. (*assent*) 488; in concert with, hand in hand; on one's side, unanimously.

715. Defiance.—**N.** defiance; daring etc. *v.*; dare, challenge, *cartel*; threat etc. 909; war-cry, -whoop.

V. defy, dare, beard; brave etc. (*courage*) 861; bid defiance to; set at -defiance, — naught; hurl defiance at; dance the war dance; snap the fingers at, laugh to scorn; disobey etc. 742.

show -fight, — one's teeth, — a bold front; bluster, look big, stand akimbo; double —, shake-the fist; threaten etc 909.

challenge, call out; throw —, fling- down the -gauntlet, — gage, — glove.

Adj. defiant; defying etc. *v.*; with arms akimbo; rebellious, insolent; reckless, greatly daring.

Adv. in -defiance, — the teeth- of; under one's very nose.

Int. do your worst! come if you dare! come on! marry come up! hoity toity!

Phr. *noli me tangere*; *nemo me impune lacessit*.

716. Attack.—**N.** attack; assault, — and battery; onset, onslaught, charge.

aggression, drive, offence; incursion, inroad; invasion; irruption; outbreak; *estrapade*, *ruade*; *coup de main*, sally, *sortie*, *camisade*; raid, foray; run -at, — against; dead set at.

storm, -ing; boarding, *escalade*; siege, investment, obsession, bombardment, cannonade; air raid.

fire, volley; platoon —, file —, rapid-fire; *fusillade*; sharp-shooting, sniping; broadside; raking —, cross —, machine gun- fire; — volley of grapeshot, *feu d'enfer*; salvo.

cut, thrust, lunge, pass, *passado*, *carte* and

tierce, home thrust, *coup de pied*; kick, punch, etc. (*impulse*) 276.

battue, *razzia*, *Jacquerie*, *dragonnade*; devastation etc. 162.

assailant, aggressor, invader.

base of operations, point of attack.

V. attack, assault, assail; set —, fall- upon; charge, impugn, break a lance with, enter the lists.

assume —, take- the offensive; be —, become-the aggressor; strike the first blow, fire the first shot, throw the first stone at; lift a hand —, draw the sword- against; take up the cudgels; advance —, march- against; march upon, invade, harry; come on, show fight.

strike at, poke at, thrust at; aim —, deal- a blow at; give —, fetch- one a -blow, — kick; have a -cut, — shot, — fling, — shy- at: be down —, pounce-upon; fall foul of, pitch into, launch out against; bait, slap on the face; make a -thrust, — pass, — set, — dead set- at; dunt; bear down upon.

close with, come to close quarters, bring to bay.

ride full tilt against; let fly at, dash at, run a tilt at, rush at, tilt at, run at, fly at, hawk at, have at, let out at; make a -dash, — rush at; attack tooth and nail; strike home; drive —, press- one hard; be hard upon, run down, strike at the root of.

lay about one, run amuck.

fire -upon, — at, — a shot at; shoot at, pop at, level at, let off a gun at; open fire, pepper, bombard, shell, pour a broadside into; fire -a volley, — red-hot shot; spring a mine.

throw -a stone, — stones- at; stone, lapidate, pelt; hurl -at, — against, — at the head of.

beset, besiege, beleaguer; lay siege to, invest, open the trenches, plant a battery, sap, mine; storm, board, scale the walls.

cut and thrust, bayonet, butt; kick, strike etc. (*impulse*) 276; whip etc. (*punish*) 972.

Adj. attacking etc. *v.*; aggressive, offensive, obsidional.

up in arms; on the warpath; over the top.

Adv. on the offensive.

Int. 'up and at them!'

717. Defense.—**N.** defense, protection, guard, ward; shielding etc. *v.*; propugnation; preservation etc. 670; guardianship.

self-defense, -preservation; resistance etc. 719.

safeguard etc. (*safety*) 664; screen etc. (*shelter*) 666, (*concealment*) 530; barrage; fortification; muni-tion, -ment; bulwark, fosse, moat, ditch, intrenchment, trench, dugout, gas mask; dike, dyke; parapet, parados, sunk fence, embankment, mound, mole, bank; earth- field-work, gabions; fence, wall, dead wall, contravallation; paling etc. (*inclosure*) 232; palisade, haha, stockade, *stoc-cado*, *laager*, *sangar*; barri-er, -cade; boom; portcullis, *chevaux de frise*; aba-, abat-, abba-tis; *vallum*, circumvallation, battlement, rampart, scarp; e-, counter-scarp; glacis, casemate.

mine, countermine.

buttress, abutment; shore etc. (*support*) 215.

breastwork, *banquette*, curtain, mantlet, bastion, demilune, redan, ravelin; advanced —, horn —, out- work, lunette; barb-acan, -ican; redoubt; fort-elage, -alice; lines; coast defense.

loop-hole, machicolation; sally-port, postern gate.

hold, stronghold, fastness; asylum etc. (*refuge*) 666; keep, donjon, fortress, citadel; capitol, castle; tower, – of strength; fort, barracoon, pah, sconce, martello tower, peel-house, block-house, rath; wooden walls; turret, barbette.

buffer, corner-stone, fender, apron, mask, gauntlet, thimble, carapace, armor, shield, buckler; target, targe, aegis, breastplate, cuirass, plastron, habergeon, mail, coat of mail, brigandine, hauberk, lorication, helmet, helm, basinet, sallet, salade, heaume, morion, murrion, armet, cabaset, vizor, casquetel, siege-cap, head-piece, casque, steel helmet, tin hat; *pickelhaube*, csako; shako etc. (*dress*) 225; bearskin; panoply; truncheon etc. (*weapon*) 727.

garrison, picket, piquet; defender, protector; guardian etc. (*safety*) 664; trabant, body guard, champion; knight-errant, Paladin; propugner.

V. defend, forfend, fend; shield, screen, shroud; fence round etc. (*circumscribe*) 229; fence, intrench; guard etc. (*keep safe*) 664; guard against; take care of etc. (*vigilance*) 459; bear harmless; keep –, ward –, beat- off; hinder etc. 706.

parry, repel, propugn, put to flight; give a warm reception to [*ironical*]; hold –, keep- at -bay, – arm's length.

stand –, act- on the defensive; show fight; maintain –, stand- one's ground; stand by; hold one's own; bear –, stand- the brunt; fall back upon, hold, stand in the gap.

Adj. defending etc. *v.*; defensive; mural; armed, – at all points, – *cap-à-pie*, – to the teeth; panoplied; accoutred, harnessed; iron-plated, -clad; loop-holed, castellated, machicolated; casemated; defended etc. *v.*; proof against, bomb-, bullet-proof; protective.

Adv. defensively; on the -defense, – defensive; in defense; at bay, *pro aris et focis*.

Int. no surrender! *il ne passeront pas!*

Phr. defense not defiance.

718. Retaliation.—N. retaliation, reprisal, retort; counter-stroke, -blast, -plot, -project; retribution, *lex talionis*; reciprocation etc. (*reciprocity*) 12.

requital, desert, tit for tat, give and take, blow for blow, *quid pro quo*, a Roland for an Oliver, measure for measure, an eye for an eye, diamond cut diamond, the biter bit, a game at which two can play; boomerang.

recrimination etc. (*accusation*) 938; revenge etc. 919; compensation etc. 30; reaction etc. (*recoil*) 277.

V. retaliate, retort, turn upon; pay -off, – back; pay in -one's own, – the same- coin; cap; reciprocate etc. 148; turn the tables upon, return the compliment; give -a *quid pro quo* etc. n., – as much as one takes; give and take, exchange -blows, – fisticuffs; be -quits, – even- with; pay off old scores.

serve one right, be hoist on one's own petard, throw a stone in one's own garden, cathch a Tartar.

Adj. retaliating etc. *v.*; retalia-tory, -tive; retributive, recriminatory, reciprocal.

Adv.. in retaliation; *en revanche.*

Phr. *mutato nomine de te fabula narratur; par pari refero; tu quoque*; you're another; *suo sibi gladio hunc jugulo.*

719. Resistance.—N. resistance, stand, front, oppugnation; opposition etc. 708; renitence, reluctation, recalcitration, recalcitrance; repugnance; kicking etc. *v.*

repulse, rebuff.

insurrection etc. (*disobedience*) 742; strike; turn –, lock –, barring- out; *levée en masse, Jacquerie*; riot etc. (*disorder*) 59.

V. resist; not -submit etc. 725; repugn, reluctate, withstand; stand up –, strive –, bear up –, be proof –, make head- against; stand, – firm, – one's ground, – the brunt of, – out; hold -one's ground, – one's own, – out.

breast the -wave, – current; stem the -tide, – torrent; face, confront, grapple with; show a bold front etc. (*courage*) 861; present a front; make a –, take one's- stand.

kick, – against; recalcitrate, kick against the pricks; oppose etc. 708; fly in the face of; lift the hand against etc. (*attack*) 716; rise up in arms etc. (*war*) 722; strike, turn out; draw up a round robin etc. (*remonstrate*) 932; revolt etc. (*disobey*) 742; make a riot.

prendre le mors aux dents; take the bit between the teeth; sell one's life dearly, die hard, keep at bay; repel, repulse.

Adj. resisting etc. *v.*; resist-ive, -ant; refractory etc. (*disobedient*) 742; recalcitrant, re-nitent, -pulsive, -pellant; up in arms.

proof against; unconquerable etc. (*strong*) 159; stubborn, unconquered; indomitable etc. (*persevering*) 604a; unyielding etc. (*obstinate*) 606.

Int. hands off! keep off!

720. Contention.—N. contention, strife; contest, -ation; struggle; belligerency; opposition etc. 708.

controversy, polemics; debate etc. (*discussion*) 476; war of words, logomachy, litigation; paper war, ink slinging; high words etc. (*quarrel*) 713; sparring etc. *v.*

competition, rivalry; corrival-ry, -ship; agonism, *concours*, match, race, horse-racing, heat, steeple chase, point-to-point race, handicap; boat race, regatta; field-day; sham fight, Derby day; turf, sporting, bull-fight, tauromachy, *gymkhana*, rodeo, Olympiad.

wrestling, *ju-jitsu*, pugilism; boxing, fisticuffs, spar, mill, set-to, scrap, round, bout, event; prize-fighting; quarter-staff, single stick; gladiatorship, gymnastics; athletic-s, – sports; games of skill etc. 840.

shindy; *fracas* etc. (*discord*) 713; clash of arms; tussle, scuffle, broil, fray; affray, -ment; velitation; col-, luctation; brabble, *brique*, scramble, *mêlée*, scrimmage, stramash, bush-fighting.

free –, stand up –, hand to hand –, running-fight.

conflict, skirmish; ren-, en-counter; *rencontre*, collision, affair, brush, fight; battle, – royal; combat, action, engagement, joust, tournament; tilt, -ing; tourney, list; pitched battle, guerilla warfare.

death-struggle, struggle for life or death, Armageddon; hard knocks, sharp contest, tug of war.

naval -engagement, – battle; *naumachia*, sea-fight.

duel, -lo; single combat, monomachy, satisfaction, *passage d'armes*, passage of arms, affair of honor; triangular duel; hostile meeting, digladiation; appeal to arms etc. (*warfare*) 722.

deeds –, feats- of arms; pugnacity; combativeness etc. *adj.*; bone of contention etc. 713.

V. contend; contest, strive, struggle, scramble, wrestle; spar, square; exchange -blows, – fisticuffs; scrap, mix with, fib, justle, tussle, tilt, box, stave, fence; skirmish; fight etc. (*war*) 722; wrangle etc. (*quarrel*) 713.

contend etc. –, grapple –, engage –, close –, buckle –, bandy –, try conclusions –, have a brush etc. *n.* –, tilt- with; encounter, fall foul of, pitch into, clapperclaw, run a tilt at; oppose etc. 708; reluct.

join issue, come to blows, be at loggerheads, set-to, come to the scratch, exchange shots, measure swords, meet hand to hand; take up the -cudgels, – glove, – gauntlet; enter the lists; couch one's lance; give satisfaction; appeal to arms etc. (*warfare*) 722.

lay about one; break the peace.

compete –, cope –, vie –, race- with; outvie, emulate, rival; run a race; contend etc. –, stipulate –, stickle- for; insist upon, make a point of.

Adj. contending etc. *v.*; together by the ears, at loggerheads, at war, at issue.

competitive, rival; belligerent; contentious, combative, bellicose, unpeaceful; warlike etc. 722; quarrelsome etc. 901; pugnacious; pugilistic, gladiatorial; palestric, -al.

Phr. *a verbis ad verbera*; a word and a blow.

721. Peace.—N. peace; amity etc. (*friendship*) 888; harmony etc. (*concord*) 714; tranquility etc. (*quiescence*) 265; truce etc. (*pacification*) 723; pacificism; pipe –, calumet- of peace.

piping time of peace, quiet life; neutrality.

V. be at peace; keep the peace etc. (*concord*) 714; make peace etc. 723.

Adj. pacific; peace-able, -ful; calm, tranquil, untroubled, halcyon; bloodless; neutral.

Phr. the storm blown over; the lion lies down with the lamb.

722. Warfare.—N. warfare; fighting etc. *v.*; hostilities; war, arms, the sword; Mars, Bellona, grim visaged war, *horrida bella*, Armageddon.

appeal to -arms, – the sword; ordeal –, wager- of battle; *ultima ratio regum*, arbitrament of the sword.

battle array, campaign, crusade, expedition; mobilization; state of siege; battle-field etc. (*arena*) 728; warpath.

art of war, tactics, strategy, castrametation; general-, soldier-ship; aerial –, submarine –, naval –, chemical-, atomic-, guerilla- warfare; military evolutions, ballistics, gunnery; chivalry; poison gas; gun-powder, shot, – and shell.

battle, tug of war etc. (*contention*) 720; service, campaigning, active service, tented field; fiery cross, trumpet, clarion, bugle, pibroch, slogan; war-cry, -whoop; battle cry, beat of drum, rappel, tom-tom; word of command; pass-, watch-word.

war to the -death, – knife; *guerre à -mort*, – *outrance*; open –, internecine –, civil- war.

V. arm; raise –, mobilize- troops; raise up in arms; take up the cudgels etc. 720; take up –, fly to –, appeal to- -arms, – the sword; draw –, unsheathe- the sword; dig up the hatchet; go to –, declare –, wage –, let slip the dogs of- war; cry havoc; kindle –, light- the torch of war; raise one's banner, send round the fiery cross; hoist the black flag; throw –, fling- away the scabbard; enrol, enlist, join up; take the field; take the law into one's own hands; do –, give –, join –, engage in –, go to- battle; flesh one's sword; set to, fall to, engage, measure swords with, draw the trigger, cross swords; come to -blows, – close quarters; fight; combat; contend etc. 720; battle –, break a lance- with.

serve; see –, be on- -service, – active service; campaign; wield the sword, shoulder a musket, smell powder, be under the fire; spill –, imbrue the hands in- blood; be on the warpath.

carry on -war, – hostilities; keep the field; fight the good fight; go over the top; cut one's way through; fight -it out, – like devils, – one's way, – hand to hand; sell one's life dearly.

Adj. conten-ding, -tious etc. 720; armed, – to the teeth, – cap-à-pie; sword in hand; in –, under –, up in- arms; at war with; bristling with arms; in -battle array, – open arms, – the field; embattled.

unpacific, unpeaceful; belligerent, combative, armigerous, bellicose, martial, warlike; mili-tary, -tant; soldier-like, -ly; chivalrous; strategical, internecine.

Adv. *flagrante bello*, in the -thick of the fray, – cannon's mouth; at the -swords's point, – point of the bayonet.

Int. *vae victis!* to arms! to your tents O Israel!

Phr. the battle rages.

723. Pacification.—N. pacification, conciliation; reconcil-iation, -ement; shaking of hands, accomodation, arrangement, adjustment; terms, compromise; amnesty, deed of release.

peace-offering, olive-branch; overtures; pipe –, calumet –, preliminaries- of peace.

truce, armistice; suspension of -arms, – hostilities; breathing-time; convention; *modus vivendi*; flag of truce, white flag, *parlementaire*, *cartel*.

hollow truce, *pax in bello*; drawn battle.

V. pacify, tranquilize, compose; allay etc. (*moderate*) 174; reconcile, propitiate, placate, conciliate, meet half-way, hold out the olive-branch, heal the breach, make peace, restore harmony, bring to terms.

settle –, arrange –, accommodate- -matters, – differences; set straight; make up a quarrel, *tantas componere lites*; come to -an understanding, – terms; bridge over, hush up; make -it, – matters-up; shake hands.

raise a siege; put up –, sheathe- the sword; bury the hatchet, lay down one's arms, turn swords into ploughshares; smoke the calumet of peace, close the temple of Janus; keep the peace etc. (*concord*) 714; be -pacified etc.; come round.

Adj. conciliatory, pacificatory; composing etc *v.*; pacified etc. *v.*

Phr. *requiescat in pace*.

724. Mediation.—N. media-tion, -torship, -tization; inter-vention, -position, -ference, - meddling, -cession; parley, negotiation, arbitration; flag of truce etc. 723; good offices, peace -offering; diploma-tics, -cy; compromise etc. 774.

mediator, intercessor, peacemaker, make-peace, negotiator, go-between; diplomatist etc. (*consignee*) 758; moderator, propitiator, umpire, arbitrator.

V. media-te, -tize; inter-cede, -pose, -fere, -vene; step in, negotiate; meet half-way; arbitrate; *magnas componere lites.*

Adj. mediatory, propitiatory, diplomatic.

725. Submission.—N. submission, yielding, acquiescence, compliance; non-resistance; obedience etc. 743; submissiveness, deference.

surrender, cession, capitulation, resignation.

obeisance, homage, kneeling, genuflexion, courtesy, curtsy, *salaam*, *kowtow*, prostration.

V. succumb, submit, yield, bend, resign, defer to, accede.

lay down -, deliver up- one's arms; hand over one's sword; lower -, haul down -, strike- one's flag, - colors; deliver the keys of the city.

surrender, - at discretion; cede, capitulate, come to terms, retreat, beat a retreat; draw in one's horns etc. (*humility*) 879; give -way, - ground, - in, - up; cave in; suffer judgment by default; bend, - to one's yoke, - before the storm; reel back; bend -, knuckle- -down, - to, - under; knock under.

humble oneself; eat -dirt, - the leek, - humble pie; bite -, lick- the dust; be -, fall- at one's feet; craven; crouch before, throw oneself at the feet of; swallow the -leek, - pill; kiss the rod; turn the other cheek; *avaler des couleuvres*, gulp down.

obey etc. 743; kneel to, bow to, pay homage to, cringe to, truckle to; bend the -neck, - knee; kneel, fall on one's knees, bow submission, courtesy, curtsy, *kowtow*; make obeisance.

pocket the affront; make -the best of, - a virtue of necessity; grin and abide, shrug the shoulders, resign oneself; submit with a good grace etc. (*bear with*) 826.

Adj. surrendering etc. *v.*; submissive, resigned, crouching; down-trodden; down on one's marrow bones; on one's bended knee; weak-kneed, un-, non-resisting; pliant etc. (*soft*) 324; undefended.

untenable, indefensible; humble etc. 879.

Phr. have it your own way; it can't be helped; amen etc. (*assent*) 488.

726. Combatant.—N. combatant; disputant, controversialist, polemic, litigant, belligerent; competitor, rival, corrival; fighter, assailant, aggressor; champion, Paladin; moss-trooper; swashbuckler, fire-eater, duellist, bully, bludgeon-man, rough, fighter, fighting-man, prize-fighter, pugilist, pug, boxer, bruiser, the fancy, gladiator, athlete, wrestler; fighting-, game-cock; swordsman, *sabreur.*

warrior, soldier, Amazon, man-at-arms, armigerent; campaigner, veteran; red-coat, military man, *rajpoot*, brave.

armed force, troops, soldiery, military, forces, sabaoth, the army, standing army, regulars, the line, troops of the line, militia, territorials, yeomanry, volunteers, trainband, fencible; auxiliary -, reserve- forces; reserves, *posse comitatus*, national guard, *gendarme*, beefeater; guards, -man; yeoman of the guard, life guards, household troops.

janissary; myrmidon; Mama-, Mame-luke; spahee, *spahi*, Cossack, Croat, Pandour; irregular, free lance, *franc-tireur*, *bashi-bazouk*, guerilla, *condottiere*; mercenary.

levy, draught, commando; *Land-wehr*, *-sturm*; conscript, recruit, rookie, cadet, raw levies.

private, - soldier; Tommy Atkins, rank and file, peon, trooper, doughboy, sepoy, *askari*, *legionnaire*, legionary, food for powder, cannon fodder; officer etc. (*commander*) 745; subaltern, ensign, shave-tail, standard bearer, non-com; spear-

pike-man; halberdier, lancer; musketeer, carabineer, rifleman, sharpshooter, yager, skirmisher; grenadier, fusileer; archer, bowman.

horse and foot; horse -, foot- soldier; cavalry, horse, artillery, horse -, field -, heavy -, mountain- artillery, infantry, light horse, *voltigeur*, *Uhlan*, mounted rifles, dragoon, hussar, trooper; light -, heavy- dragoon; heavy; *cuirassier*; gunner, cannoneer, bombardier, artillery-man, matross; sapper, - and miner; engineer; light infantry, rifles, *chasseur*, *zouave*; military train, supply and transport, coolie.

army, - corps, *corps d'armée*, host, division, column, wing, detachment, *escadrille*, garrison, flying column, brigade, regiment, corps, battalion, squadron, company, platoon, battery, subdivision, section, squad; piquet, picket, guard, rank, file; legion, phalanx, cohort; cloud of skirmishers; impi.

war-horse, charger, *destrier.*

armored -train, - car; tank.

marine, man of war's man etc. (*sailor*) 269; navy, first line of defense, wooden walls; naval forces, fleet, flotilla, armada, squadron.

man-of-war, warship; H.M.S., U.S.S.; capital ship; line-of-battle ship, battle ship; super-, dreadnought, battle -, armored -, protected - light-cruiser; scout, flotilla leader; destroyer, torpedo boat; submarine, submersible, U-boat; submarine chaser, eagle boat, mystery ship, Q-boat; mine-layer, -sweeper; ship of the line, iron-clad, turret-ship, ram, Monitor, floating battery; first-rate, frigate, sloop of war, corvette, gunboat, bomb-vessel, fire-boat; flag ship, guard ship, cruiser; air-plane carrier; privateer; tender; depot -, parent-ship; store -, troop- ship; transport, catamaran.

aircraft etc. 273; air force, scout, fighter, bomber, troop carrier, aerial patrol, seaplane, flying boat, torpedo plane; airship, Zeppelin; rigid -, semi-rigid -, non-rigid- airship; dirigible -, free -, captive -, kite -, observation- balloon.

anti-aircraft guns, searchlights, sound locators; catapult.

727. Arms.—N. arm, -s; weapon, deadly weapon; arma-ment, -ture; panoply, stand of arms; armor etc. (*defense*) 717; armory etc. (*store*) 636.

ammunition; powder, - and shot; explosive; propellant; gun-powder, -cotton; dynam-, melin-, cord-, lydd-ite; trinitrotoluene, T.N.T.; ammonal; cartridge; ball cartridge, *cartouche*, fire-ball; dud, black Marie; 'villainous saltpeter;' poison –, mustard –, lachrymatory –, tear- gas.

sword, saber, broadsword, cutlass, falchion, scimitar, cimeter, brand, whinyard, bilbo, glaive, glave, rapier, skean, Toledo, Ferrara, tuck, claymore, creese, kris, *kukri*, dagger, dirk, hanger, poniard, stiletto, stylet, dudgeon, bayonet; sword- bayonet, -stick; side arms, foil, blade, steel; axe, bill; pole-, battle-axe; gisarm, halberd, partisan, tomahawk, bowie-knife; at-, att-, yat-aghan; yatachan; good –, trusty –, naked- sword; cold –, naked-steel.

club, mace, truncheon, staff, bludgeon, cudgel, life-preserver, shillelagh, sprig; hand-, quarter-staff; bat, cane, stick, knuckle-duster, sand bag.

gun, piece; fire-arms; artillery, ordnance; siege –, battering-train; park, battery; cannon, gun of position, heavy –, siege –, field –, mountain –, anti-aircraft –, breech loading –, quick firing- gun; field piece, mortar, trench mortar; mine –, flame- -thrower, napalm; howitzer, carronade, culverin, basilisk; falconet jingal, swivel, *pederero, bouche à feu*; smooth bore, rifled cannon; Arm- strong –, Lancaster –, Paixhan –, Whitworth –, Parrott –, Krupp -–, Gatling –, Maxim –, Vickers –, Hotchkiss –, Lewis –, machine- gun; tommy gun, Thompson's submachine gun; *mitrailleu-r, -se*; pompom; blow pipe.

small arms; musket, -ry, firelock, flintlock, fowling-piece, shot gun, rifle, *fusil*, caliver, carbine, blunderbuss, musketoon, Brown Bess, matchlock, harquebuss, *arquebuse*, haguebut; petronel; smallbore; breech-, muzzle-loader; Minié –, En- field –, Westly Richards –, Snider –, Springfield –, Martini-Henry –, Lee-Metford –, Lee- Enfield –, Mauser –, Mannlicher –, magazine –, repeating- rifle; needle-gun, *chassepot*; pis-tol, -et; revolver, automatic pistol, automatic; wind-, air-gun; flame –, gas- projector.

bow, cross-bow, arbalest, balister, catapult, sling; battering-ram etc. (*impulse*) 276; gunnery; ballistics etc. (*propulsion*) 284.

missile, bolt, projectile, shot, pellet, ball; grape; grape –, canister –, bar –, cannon –, langrel –, langrage –, round –, chain- shot; explosive; incendiary –, expanding –, soft-nosed –, dum- dum- bullet; slug, stone, brickbat; hand –, rifle- grenade; high explosive –, incendiary –, stink-, A-, H-, atomic –, hydrogen – bomb; petard, torpedo, carcass, rocket; congreve, – rocket; shrapnel, *mitraille*; thunderbolt; mine, land mine, infernal machine.

pike, lance, spear, spontoon, javelin, assagai, throwing stick, dart, djerrid, arrow, reed, shaft, bolt, boomerang, harpoon, gaff.

728. Arena.—**N.** arena, field, platform; scene of action, theater; walk, course; hustings; stage, boards etc. (*playhouse*) 599; amphitheater; Coli-, Colos-seum; Flavian amphitheater, hippodrome, circus, race-course, track, *stadium, corso*, turf, cockpit, bear-garden, play-ground, playing fields, *gymnasium, palaestra*, ring, lists; tilt-yard, -ing ground; *Campus Martius, Champ de Mars*; aerodrome, airport, air base, flying field.

theater –, seat- of war; battle-field, -ground; field of -battle, – slaughter; no man's land; Aceldama, camp; the enemy's camp; trysting- place etc. (*place of meeting*) 74.

729. Completion.—**N.** completion; ac- complish-, achieve-, fulfil-ment; performance, execution; des-, dis-patch; consummation, culmination, climax; finish, conclusion, ef- fectuation; close etc. (*end*) 67; terminus etc. (*arrival*) 292; winding up; *finale, dénouement*, catastrophe, issue, upshot, result; final –, last –, crowning –, finishing- -touch, – stroke; last finish, *coup de grâce*; crowning of the edifice; coping-, keystone; missing link etc. 53; super- structure, *ne plus ultra*, work done, *fait accompli*. elaboration; finality; completeness etc. 52.

V. effect, -uate; accomplish, achieve, compass, consummate, hammer out; bring to -maturity, – perfection; perfect, complete; elaborate.

do, execute, make; go –, get- through; work out, enact; bring -about, – to bear, – to pass, – through, – to a head.

des-, dis-patch; knock –, finish –, polish- off; make short work of; dispose of, set at rest; perform, discharge, fulfil, realize; put in -practice, – force; carry -out, – into effect, – into execution; make good; be as good as one's word.

do thoroughly, not do by halves, go the whole hog; drive home; be in at the death etc. (*persevere*) 604a; carry through, play out, exhaust, deliver the goods, fill the bill.

finish, bring to a close etc. (*end*) 67; wind up, stamp, clinch, seal, set the seal on, put the seal to; give the -final touch etc. *n*. to; put the -last, – finishing- hand to; crown, – all; cap.

ripen, culminate; come to a -head, – crisis; come to its end; die -a natural death, – of old age; run -its course, – one's race; touch –, reach –, attain- the goal; reach etc. (*arrive*) 292; get in the harvest.

Adj. completing, final; conclu-ding, -sive; crowning etc, *v.*; exhaustive, complete, mature, perfect, consummate.

done, completed etc. *v.*; done for, sped, wrought out; highly wrought etc. (*preparation*)' 673; thorough etc. 52; ripe etc. (*ready*) 673.

Adv. completely etc. (*thoroughly*) 52; to crown all, out of hand.

Phr. the race is run; *actum est; finis coronat opus; consummatum est; c'en est fait*; it is all over; the game is played out, the bubble has burst.

730. Non-Completion.—**N.** non-completion, - fulfilment; shortcoming etc. 304; incompleteness etc. 53; drawn -battle, – game; work of Penelope, task of Sisyphus.

non-performance, inexecution; neglect etc. 460.

V. not -complete etc. 729; leave -unfinished etc. *adj.*, – undone; neglect etc. 460; let -alone, – slip; lose sight of.

fall short of etc. 304; do things by halves; scotch the snake, not kill it; hang fire; be slow to; collapse etc. 304.

Adj. not completed etc. *v.*; incomplete etc. 53; uncompleted, unfinished; unaccomplished; un- performed, unexecuted; sketchy, addle.

in progress, in hand; going on, proceeding; on one's hands; on the fire; on the stocks; in preparation; lacking the finishing touch.

Adv. *re infectâ*.

731. Success.—**N.** success, -fulness; speed; advance etc. (*progress*) 282.

trump card; hit, stroke; lucky —, fortunate —, good- -hit, — stroke; bold —, master- stroke; *coup de maître*, checkmate; half the battle, prize; profit etc. (*acquisition*) 775; best seller.

continued success; good fortune etc. (*prosperity*) 734; time well spent.

advantage over; edge; upper-, whiphand; ascendancy, mastery; expugnation, conquest, victory, subdual; subjugation etc. (*subjection*) 749.

triumph etc. (*exultation*) 884; proficiency etc. (*skill*) 698; conqueror, victor, winner, champion; master of the -situation, — position.

V. succeed; be -successful etc. *adj.*; gain one's -end, — ends; crown with success.

gain —, attain —, carry —, secure —, win- -a point, — an object; put over; make a go of; manage to, contrive to; accomplish etc. (*effect, complete*) 729; do —, work- wonders.

come off -well, — successfully, — with flying colors; make short work of; take —, carry- by storm; bear away the bell; win -one's spurs, — the battle; win —, carry —, gain- the -day, — prize, — palm; climb on the bandwagon; have -the best of it, — it all one's own way, — the game in one's own hands, — the ball at one's feet, — one on the hip; walk over the course; carry all before one, remain in possession of the field; score a success, win hands down.

speed; make progress etc. (*advance*) 282; win —, make —, work —, find- one's way; strive to some purpose; prosper etc. 734; drive a roaring trade; make profit etc. (*acquire*) 775; reap —, gather- the -fruits, — benefit of, — harvest; make one's fortune, get in the harvest, turn to good account; turn to account etc. (*use*) 677.

triumph, be triumphant; gain —, obtain- -a victory, — an advantage; chain victory to one's car.

surmount —, overcome —, get over- -a difficulty, — an obstacle etc. 706; *se tirer d'affaire*; make head against; stem the -torrent, — tide, — current; weather -the storm, — a point; turn a corner, keep one's head above water, tide over; master; get —, have —, gain- the -better of, — best of, — upper hand, — ascendancy, — whip hand, — start of; distance; surpass etc. (*superiority*) 33.

defeat, conquer, vanquish, discomfit; over-come, throw, -power, -master, -match, -set, -ride, -reach; out-wit, -do, -flank, -maneuver, -general, -vote; take the wind out of one's adversary's sails; beat, — hollow; rout, lick, drub, floor, worst; put -down, — to flight, — to the rout, — *hors de combat*; — out of court.

silence, quell, nonsuit, checkmate, upset, confound, nonplus, trump; baffle etc. (*hinder*) 706; circumvent, elude; trip up — the heels of; drive -into a corner, — to the wall; run hard, put one's nose out of joint.°

settle, do for; break the -neck of, — back of; capsize, sink, shipwreck, drown, swamp; subdue; subjugate etc. (*subject*) 749; reduce; make the enemy bite the dust; victimize, roll in the dust, trample under foot, put an extinguisher upon.

answer, — the purpose; avail, prevail, take effect, do, turn out well, work well, take, tell, bear fruit; hit -it, — the mark, — the right nail on the head; nick it; turn up trumps, make a hit; find one's account in.

Adj. succeeding etc. *v.*; successful; prosperous

etc. 734; triumphant; flushed —, crowned- with success; victorious; set up; in the ascendant; unbeaten etc. (*see* beat etc. *v.*); well-spent; felicitous, effective, in full swing.

Adv. successfully etc. *adj.*; with flying colors, in triumph, swimmingly; *à merveille*, beyond all hope; to some —, good- purpose; to one's heart's content.

Phr. *veni vidi vici*, the day being one's own, one's star in the ascendant; *omne tulit punctum*.

732. Failure.—**N.** failure; non-success, -fulfilment; dead failure, successlessness; abortion, miscarriage; *brutum fulmen* etc. 158; labor in vain etc. (*inutility*) 645; no go; inefficacy; inefficaciousness etc. *adj.*; vain —, ineffectual —, abortive- -attempt, — efforts; flash in the pan, 'lame and impotent conclusion;' frustration; slip 'twixt cup and lip etc. (*disappointment*) 509.

blunder etc. (*mistake*) 495; fault, omission, miss, oversight, slip, trip, stumble, claudication, footfall; false —, wrong- step; *faux pas*, titubation, *bévue*, *faute*, lurch; botchery etc. (*want of skill*) 699; scrape, jam, mess, muddle, foozle, *fiasco*, breakdown.

mishap etc. (*misfortune*) 735; split, collapse, smash, blow, explosion.

repulse, rebuff, defeat, rout, overthrow, discomfiture; beating, drubbing; *quietus*, nonsuit, subjugation; check-, fool's-mate.

fall, downfall, ruin, perdition; wreck etc. (*destruction*) 162; death-blow; bankruptcy etc. (*non-payment*) 808.

losing game, *affaire flambée*.

victim, prey; bankrupt.

V. fail; be -unsuccessful etc. *adj.*; not -succeed etc. 731; make -vain efforts etc. *n.*; do —, labor —, toil- in vain; lose one's labor, take nothing by one's motion; bring to naught, make nothing of; wash a blackamoor white etc. (*impossible*) 471; roll the stone of Sisyphus etc. (*useless*) 645; do by halves etc. (*not complete*) 730; lose ground etc. (*recede*) 283; flunk; fall short of etc. 304.

miss, — one's aim, — the mark, — one's footing; — stays; slip, trip, stumble; make a -slip etc. *n.*, — blunder etc. 495, — mess of, — botch of; bitch it, miscarry, abort, go up like a rocket and come down like the stick, reckon without one's host; get the wrong sow by the ear etc. (*blunder, mismanage*) 699.

limp, halt, hobble, titubate; fall, tumble; lose one's balance; fall -to the ground, — between two stools; flounder, falter, stick in the mud, run aground, split upon a rock; run —, knock —, dash- one's head against a stone wall; break one's back; break down, sink, drown, founder, have the ground cut from under one; get into -trouble, — a mess, — a scrape; come to grief etc. (*adversity*) 735; go to -the wall, — the dogs, — pot; lick —, bite- the dust; be -defeated etc. 731; have the worst of it, lose the day, come off second best, lose; fall a prey to; succumb etc. (*submit*) 725; not have a leg to stand on.

come to nothing, end in smoke; fall -to the ground, — through, — dead, — still-born, — flat; slip through one's fingers; hang —, miss- fire; flash in the pan, collapse; topple down etc. (*descent*) 305; go to wrack and ruin etc. (*destruction*) 162.

go amiss, go wrong, go cross, go hard with, go on a wrong tack; go on —, come off —, turn out

–, work- ill; take -a wrong, – an ugly- turn; gang agley.

be all -over with, – up with; explode; dash one's hopes etc. (*disappoint*) 509; defeat the purpose; upset the apple cart; sow the wind and reap the whirlwind, jump out of the frying pan into the fire.

Adj. unsuccessful, successless; failing, tripping etc. *v*.; at fault; unfortunate etc. 735.

abortive, addle, still-born; fruitless, sterile, bootless; ineffect-ual, -ive; inefficient etc. (*impotent*) 158; inefficacious; lame, hobbling, *décousu*; insufficient etc. 640; unavailing etc. (*useless*) 645; of no effect.

aground, grounded, swamped, stranded, cast away, wrecked, foundered, capsized, shipwrecked, non-suited; foiled; defeated etc. 731; struck –, borne –. broken- down; down-trodden; overborne, -whelmed; all up with; beaten to a frazzle.

lost, undone, ruined, broken; bankrupt etc. (*not paying*) 808; played out; done -up, – for; dead beat, ruined root and branch, *flambé*, knocked on the head; destroyed. etc. 162.

frustrated, thwarted, crossed, unhinged, disconcerted, dashed; thrown -off one's balance, – on one's back, – on one's beam ends; unhorsed, in a sorry plight; hard hit.

stultified, befooled, dished, hoist on one's own petard, victimized, sacrificed.

wide of the mark etc. (*error*) 495; out of one's reckoning etc. (*inexpectation*) 508; left in the lurch; thrown away etc. (*wasted*) 638; unattained; uncompleted etc. 730.

Adv. unsuccessfully etc. *adj*.; to little or no purpose, in vain, *re infectâ*.

Phr. the bubble has burst, the game is up, all is lost; the devil to pay; *parturiunt montes* etc. (*disappointment*) 509.

733. Trophy.—**N.** trophy; medal, prize, palm; ribbon, blue ribbon, *cordon bleu*; citation; cup, laurel, -s; bays, crown, chaplet, wreath, civic crown; Victoria Cross, V.C., *Croix de Guerre*, Iron Cross; Distinguished Service Cross, Medal of Honor, Congressional Medal; insignia etc. 550; feather in one's cap etc. (*honor*) 873; decoration etc. 877; garland, triumphal arch.

triumph etc. (*celebration*) 883; flying colors etc. (*show*) 882.

monumentum aere perennius.

734. Prosperity.—**N.** prosperity, welfare, well-being; affluence etc. (*wealth*) 803; success etc. 731; thrift, roaring trade; chicken in every pot, the full dinner paid; good –, smiles of- fortune; blessings, godsend.

luck; good –, run of- luck; sunshine; fair -weather, – wind; palmy –, bright –, halcyondays; piping times, tide, flood, high tide.

Saturnia regna, Saturnian age; golden -time, – age; bed of roses; fat of the land, milk and honey, loaves and fishes, fleshpots of Egypt.

made man, lucky dog, *enfant fâté*, spoiled child of fortune.

upstart, *parvenu, nouveau riche*, profiteer, skipjack, mushroom.

V. prosper, thrive, flourish; be -prosperous etc. *adj*.; drive a roaring trade; go on -well, – smoothly, – swimmingly; sail before the wind, swim with the tide; run -smooth, – smoothly, – on all fours.

rise –, get on- in the world; work –, make-one's way; look up; lift –, raise- one's head, make one's -fortune, – pile, feather one's nest.

flower, blow, blossom, bloom, fructify, bear fruit, fatten, batten.

keep oneself afloat; keep –, hold- one's head above water; light –, fall- on one's -legs, – feet; drop into a good thing; bear a charmed life; bask in the sunshine; have a -good, – fine- time of it; have a run, – of luck; have the -good fortune etc. *n*. to; take a favorable turn; live -on the fat of the land, – in clover.

Adj. prosperous; thriving etc. *v*.; in a fair way, buoyant; well -off, – to do, – to do in the world; set up, at one's ease; rich etc. 803; in good case; in -full, – high- feather; fortunate, lucky, in luck; born -with a silver spoon in one's mouth, – under a lucky star; on the sunny side of the hedge.

auspicious, propitious, providential.

palmy, halcyon; agreeable etc. 829; *couleur de rose*.

Adv. prosperously etc. *adj*.; swimmingly; as good luck would have it; beyond all -expectation, – hope, – one's wildest dreams.

Phr. one's star in the ascendant, all for the best, one's course runs smooth.

735. Adversity.—**N.** adversity, evil etc. 619; failure etc. 732; bad –, ill –, evil –, adverse –, hard- -fortune, – hap, – luck, – lot; frowns of fortune; evil -dispensation, – star, – genius; ups and downs of life, broken fortunes; hard -case, – lines, – life; sea –, peck- of troubles; hell upon earth; slough of despond; jinx.

trouble, humiliation, hardship, curse, blight, blast, load, pressure.

pressure of the times, iron age, evil day, time out of joint; hard –, bad –, sad- times; rainy day, cloud, dark cloud, gathering clouds, ill wind; visitation, infliction; affliction etc. (*painfulness*) 830; bitter -pill, – cup; care, trial; the sport of fortune.

mis-hap, -chance, -adventure, -fortune; disaster, calamity, catastrophe; accident, casualty, cross, reverse, check, *contretemps*, rub, pinch, setback.

losing game; falling etc. *v*.; fall, down-fall, come-down; ruin-ation, -ousness; undoing; extremity; ruin etc. (*destruction*) 162.

V. be -ill off etc. *adj*.; go hard with; fall on evil, – days; go on ill; not -prosper etc. 734.

go -downhill, – to rack and ruin etc. (*destruction*) 162, – to the dogs; fall, – from one's high estate; decay, sink, decline, go down in the world; have seen better days; bring down one's grey hairs with sorrow to the grave; come to grief; be all -over, – up- with; bring a -wasp's, – hornet's- nest about one's ears.

Adj. unfortunate, unblest, unhappy, unlucky; im-, un-prosperous; luck-, hap-less; out of luck; in trouble, in a bad way, in an evil plight; under a cloud; clouded; ill –, badly- off; in adverse circumstances; poor etc. 804; behindhand, down in the world, decayed, undone; on the road to ruin, on its last legs, on the wane; in one's utmost need.

planet-struck, devoted; born -under an evil star, — with a wooden ladle in one's mouth; ill-fated, -starred, -omened; inconspicuous, ominous, doomed, unpropitious.

adverse, untoward; disastrous, calamitous, ruinous, dire, deplorable.

Adv. if the worst come to the worst, as ill luck would have it, from bad to worse, out of the frying pan into the fire.

Phr. one's star is on the wane; one's luck -turns, — fails; the game is up, one's doom is sealed, the ground crumbles under one's feet, *sic transit gloria mundi, tant va la cruche à l'eau qu'à la fin elle se casse.*

736. Mediocrity.—**N.** moderate —, average-circumstances; respectability; middle classes, *bourgeoisie;* mediocrity; golden mean etc. (*midcourse*) 628, (*moderation*) 174.

V. jog on; go —, get on- -fairly, — quietly, — peaceably, — tolerably, — respectably; steer a middle course etc. 628.

Adj. middling, so-so, fair, medium, moderate, mediocre, second-, third- etc. -rate.

737. Authority.—**N.** authority; influence, patronage, power, preponderance, credit, *prestige,* prerogative, jurisdiction; right etc. (*title*) 924.

divine right, dynastic rights, authoritativeness; absolut-eness, -ism; despotism, tyranny; *jus nocendi.*

command, empire, sway, rule; domin-ion, -ation; sovereignty, supremacy, suzerainty; lord-, head-ship; chiefdom; seignior-y, -ity, hegemony, patriarchate, patriarchy; master-y, -ship, -dom; government etc. (*direction*) 693; dictation, control.

hold, grasp; grip, -e; reach; iron sway etc. (*severity*) 739; fangs, clutches, talons; rod of empire etc. (*scepter*) 747.

reign, regnancy, *régime,* dynasty; director-, dictator-ship; protector-ate, -ship; caliphate, pashalic, electorate; presiden-cy, -tship; administration; pro-, consulship; prefecture; seneschalship; magistra-ture, -cy; raj.

empire; monarchy; king-hood, -ship; royalty, regality, autocracy, monocracy, arist-archy, -ocracy; oligarchy democracy, demogogy; republic, -anism, federalism, socialism, collectivism; communism, bolshevism, syndicalism; mob law, mobocracy, ochlocracy, ergatocracy; *vox populi, imperium in imperio;* bureaucracy; beadle-, bumble-dom; stratocracy; martial law, military -power, — government; feudality, feudal system, feudalism.

Thearchy, diarchy; du-, tri-, heter-archy; du-, tri-umvirate; auto-cracy, -nomy; limited monarchy; constitutional -government, — monarchy; home rule, autonomy; self-government, -determination; representative government; Soviet government.

gyn-archy, -ocracy, -aeocracy; petticoat government, matriarchate, matriarchy.

[*Vicarious authority*] commission etc. 755; deputy etc. 759; permission etc. 760.

country, state, realm, commonwealth, canton,

constituency, toparchy, municipality, polity, body politic, *posse comitatus.*

person in authority etc. (*master*) 745; judicature etc. 965; cabinet etc. (*council*) 696; usurper; seat of -government, — authority; head-quarters.

[*Acquisition of authority*] accession; installation etc. 755; usurpation.

V. authorize etc. (*permit*) 760; warrant etc. (*right*) 924; dictate etc. (*order*) 741; have —, hold —, possess —, exercise —, exert —, wield- -authority etc. *n.*

be -at the head of etc. *adj.*; hold —, be in —, fill an- office; hold —, occupy- a post; be -master etc. 745.

rule, sway, command, control, administer; govern etc. (*direct*) 693; lead, preside over, reign; possess —, be seated on —, occupy- the throne; sway —, wield- the scepter; wear the crown.

have —, get- the -upper, — whip- hand; gain a hold upon, preponderate, dominate, boss, rule the roost; over-ride, -rule, -awe; lord it over, hold in hand, keep under, make a puppet of, lead by the nose, hold in the hollow of one's hand, turn round one's little finger, bend to one's will, hold one's own, wear the breeches; have -the ball at one's feet, — it all one's own way, — the game in one's own hand, — on the hip, — under one's thumb; be master of the situation; take the lead, play first fiddle, set the fashion; give the law to; carry with a high hand; lay down the law; 'ride in the whirlwind and direct the storm;' rule with a rod of iron etc. (*severity*) 739.

ascend —, mount- the throne, take the reins, — into one's hand; assume -authority etc. *n.,* — the reins of government; take —, assume the- command.

be -governed by, — in the power of; be under -the rule of, — the domination of.

Adj. ruling etc. *v.*; regnant, at the head, dominant, paramount, supreme, predominant, preponderant, in the ascendant, influential; gubernatorial; imperious; authoritative, executive, administrative, clothed with authority, official, *ex officio,* ministerial, bureaucratic, departmental, imperative, peremptory, overruling, absolute; hegemonic, -al; arbitrary; compulsory etc. 744; stringent.

regal, sovereign; royal, -ist; monarchical, kingly; imperial, -istic; princely; feudal; aristo-, auto-cratic; oligarchic etc. *n.*; democratic, republican, dynastic.

at one's command; in one's -power, — grasp; under control; authorized etc. (*due*) 924.

Adv. in the name of, by the authority of, *de par le Roi,* in virtue of; under the auspices of, in the hands of.

at one's pleasure; by a -dash', — stroke- of the pen; *ex mero motu; ex cathedrâ.*

Phr. the grey mare the better horse; 'every inch a king.'

738. Laxity. [Absence of authority.]—**N.** laxity; lax-, loose-, slack-ness; toleration etc. (*lenity*) 740; freedom etc. 748.

anarchy, interregnum; relaxation; loosening etc. *v.*; remission; dead letter, *brutum fulmen,* misrule; license, licentiousness; insubordination etc. (*disobedience*) 742; lynch law etc. (*illegality*) 964; nihilism.

[Deprivation of power.] dethronement, deposition, usurpation, abdication.

V. be -lax etc. *adj* ; *laisser -faire*, – *aller*; hold a loose rein; give -the reins to, – rope enough, – a loose to; tolerate; relax; misrule.

go beyond the length of one's tether; have one's - swing, – fling; act without -instructions, – authority; act on one's own responsibility, usurp authority.

dethrone, depose; abdicate.

Adj. lax, loose; slack; remiss etc. (*careless*) 460; weak.

relaxed; licensed; reinless, unbridled; anarchical; unauthorized etc. (*unwarranted*) 925.

739. Severity.—N. severity; strictness, formalism, harshness etc. *adj.*; rigor, stringency, austerity; inclemency etc. (*pitilessness*) 914a; arrogance etc. 885.

arbitrary power; absolut-, despot-ism; dictatorship, autocracy, tyranny, domineering, oppression; assumption, usurpation; inquisition, reign of terror, martial law; iron -heel, – rule, – hand, – sway; tight grasp; brute -force, – strength; coercion etc. 744; strong –, tight- hand.

hard -lines, – measure; tender mercies [ironical.]; sharp practice; bureaucracy, red tape; pipe-clay, officialism.

tyrant, disciplinarian, martinet, stickler, formalist, bashaw, despot, hard master, Draco, oppressor, inquisitor, extortioner, harpy, vulture, bird of prey.

V. be -severe etc. *adj.*

assume, usurp, arrogate, take liberties; domineer, bully etc. 885; tyrannize, inflict, wreak, stretch a point, put on the screw; be hard upon; bear –, lay-a heavy hand on; be –, come- down upon; illtreat; deal-hardly with, – hard measure to; rule with a rod of iron, chastise with scorpions; dye with blood; oppress, override; trample –, tread- -down, – upon, – under foot; crush under an iron heel, ride roughshod over; rivet the yoke; hold –, keep-a tight hand; force down the throat; coerce etc. 744; give no quarter etc. (*pitiless*) 914a.

Adj. severe; strict, hard, harsh, dour, rigid, stiff, stern, rigorous, uncompromising, exacting, exigent, *exigeant*, inexorable, inflexible, obdurate, austere, relentless, Spartan, Draconian, stringent, strait-laced, puritanical, prudish, searching, unsparing, ironhanded, hard-headed, peremptory, absolute, positive, arbitrary, imperative; coercive etc. 744; tyrannical, despotic, masterful, extortionate, grinding, withering, oppressive, inquisitorial; inclement etc. (*ruthless*) 914a; cruel etc. (*malevolent*) 907; haughty, arrogant etc. 885.

Adv. severely etc. *adj.*; with a -high, – strong, – tight, – heavy-hand.

at the point of the -sword, – bayonet.

Phr. *Delirant reges plectuntur Achivi.*

740. Leniency.—N. leni-ency, -ence, -ty; moderation etc. 174; toler-ance, -ation; mildness, gentleness; favor; indulgen-ce, -cy; clemency, mercy, forbearance, quarter; compassion etc. 914.

V. be -lenient etc. *adj.*; tolerate, bear with; *parcere subjectis*, give quarter.

indulge, allow one to have his own way, spoil.

Adj. lenient; mild, – as milk; gentle, soft; tolerant, indulgent, easy-going; clement etc. (*compassionate*) 914; forbearing; complaisant, long-suffering.

741. Command.—N. command, order, ordinance, act, *fiat*, bidding, *dictum*, hest, behest, call, beck, nod.

des-, dis-patch; message, direction, injunction, charge, instructions; appointment, fixture.

demand, exaction, imposition, requisition, claim, reclamation, revendication; *ultimatum* etc. (*terms*) 770; request etc. 765; requirement.

dictation; dict-, mand-ate; *caveat*, decree, decree -nisi, – absolute, *senatus consultum*; precept; pre-, re-script; writ, ordination, bull, edict, decretal, dispensation, prescription, brevet, placet, ukase, *firman*, hatti-sheriff, warrant, passport, *mittimus, mandamus*, summons, subpoena, *nisi prius*, interpellation, citation; word, – of command; *mot d'ordre*; bugle –, trumpet- call; beat of drum, tattoo; order of the day; enactment etc. (*law*) 963; *plébiscite* etc. (*choice*) 609.

V. command, order, decree, enact, ordain, dictate, direct, give orders.

prescribe, set, appoint, mark out; set –, prescribe –, impose- a task; set to work, put in requisition etc. 926.

bid, enjoin, charge, call upon, instruct; require, – at the hands of; exact, impose, tax, task; demand; insist on etc. (*compel*) 744.

claim, lay claim to, revendicate, reclaim.

cite, summon; call –, send- for; subpoena; beckon.

issue a command; make –, issue –, promulgate- -a requisition; – a decree, – an order etc. *n.*; give the -word of command, – word, – signal; call to order; give –, lay down- the law; assume the command etc. (*authority*) 737; remand.

be -ordered etc.; receive an order etc. *n.*

Adj. commanding etc. *v.*; authoritative etc. 737; decret-ory, -ive, -al; imperative, jussive, decisive, final.

Adv. in a commanding tone; by a -stroke, – dash- of the pen; by order, at beat of drum, on the first summons; at the word of command.

Phr. the decree is gone forth; *sic volo sic jubeo; le Roi le veut.*

742. Disobedience.—N. disobedience, insubordination, contumacy; infraction, -fringement; violation, non-compliance; non-observance etc. 773.

revolt, rebellion, mutiny, outbreak, rising, uprising, putsch, insurrection, *émeute*; riot, tumult etc. (*disorder*) 59; strike etc. (*resistance*) 719; barring out; defiance etc. 715.

mutinousness etc. *adj.*; mutineering; sedition, treason; high –, petty –, misprison of- treason; *premunire; lèse- majesté*; violation of law etc. 964; defection, secession, revolution, *sabotage*, bolshevism, *Sinn Fein*.

insurgent, mutineer, rebel, revolter, rioter, traitor, *carbonaro, sansculottes,* red republican, communist, Fenian, chartist, *frondeur;* seceder, runagate, brawler, anarchist, demagogue; suffragette; Spartacus, Masaniello, Wat Tyler, Jack Cade; bolshevist, bolshevik, maximalist, ringleader.

V. disobey, violate, infringe; shirk; set at defiance etc. (*defy*) 715; set authority at naught, run riot, fly in the face of, bolt, take the law into one's own hands; kick over the traces.

turn −, run- restive; champ the bit; strike etc. (*resist*) 719; rise, − in arms; secede; mutiny, rebel.

Adj. disobedient; uncompl-ying, -iant; unsubmissive; unruly, ungovernable; insubordinate, impatient of control; rest-iff, -ive; refractory, contumacious; recusant etc. (*refuse*) 764; recalcitrant; resisting etc. 719; lawless, mutinous, seditious, insurgent, riotous, revolutionary.

disobeyed, unobeyed; unbidden.

743. Obedience.—N. obedience; observance etc. 772; compliance; submission etc. 725; subjection etc. 749; non-resistance; passiveness, passivity, resignation.

allegiance, loyalty, fealty, homage, deference, devotion, fidelity, constancy.

submiss-ness, -iveness; ductility etc. (*softness*) 324; obsequiousness etc. (*servility*) 886.

V. be -obedient etc. *adj.*; obey, bear obedience to; submit etc. 725; comply, answer the helm, come at one's call; do -one's bidding, − what one is told − suit and service; attend to orders, serve - devotedly, −, loyally, − faithfully.

follow, − the lead of, − to the world's end; serve etc. 746; play second fiddle.

Adj. obedient; compl-ying, -iant; law-abiding, loyal, faithful, leal, devoted; at one's -call, − command, − orders, − beck and call; under - beck and call, − control.

restrainable; resigned, passive; submissive etc. 725; henpecked; pliant etc. (*soft*) 324.

unrest-ed, -ing.

Adv. obediently etc. *adj.*; in compliance with, in obedience to.

Phr. to hear is to obey; as −, if- you please; at your service.

744. Compulsion.—N. compulsion, coercion, coaction, constraint, eminent domain, duress, enforcement, press, conscription.

force; brute −, main −, physical- force; the sword, *ultima ratio;* club −, mob −, lynch- law; *argumentum baculinum, le droit du plus fort,* martial law.

restraint etc. 751; necessity etc. 601; *force majeure;* Hobson's choice; the spur of necessity.

V. compel, force, make, drive, coerce, constrain, enforce, necessitate, oblige.

force upon, press; cram −, thrust −, force-down the throat; say it must be done, make a point of, insist upon, take no denial; put down, dragoon.

extort, wring from; put −, turn- on the screw; drag into; bind, − over; pin −, tie- down; require, tax, put in force; commandeer; restrain etc. 751.

Adj. compelling etc. *v.*; coercive, coactive, inexorable etc. 739; compuls-ory, -atory; obligatory, stringent, peremptory, binding.

forcible, not to be trifled with; irresistible etc. 601; compelled etc. *v.*; fain to.

Adv. by -force etc. *n.*, − force of arms; on compulsion, perforce; *vi et armis,* under the lash; at the point of the -sword, − bayonet; forcibly; by a strong arm.

under protest, in spite of one's teeth; against one's will etc. 603; *nolens volens* etc. (*of necessity*) 601; by stress of -circumstances, − weather; under press of; *de rigueur.*

745. Master.—N. master, *padrone;* lord, − paramount; command-er, -ant; captain; chief, -tain; *sahib,* sirdar, sachem, sheik, head, senior, governor, *duce,* ruler, dictator; leader etc. (*director*) 694.

lord of the ascendant; cock of the -walk, − roost; grey mare; mistress.

potentate; liege, − lord; suzerain, sovereign, monarch, autocrat, despot, tyrant, oligarch, overlord.

crowned head, emperor, king, anointed king, majesty, *imperator,* protector, president, stadtholder, judge.

caesar, kaiser, czar, sultan, grand Turk, caliph, imaum, shah, padishah, sophi, mogul, great mogul, khan, cham; lama, tycoon, mikado, inca, cazique; domn; vaivode; wai-, way-wode; landamman; seyyid, cacique.

prince, duke etc. (*nobility*) 875; arch-duke, doge, elector; seignior; mar−, land-grave; rajah, emir, nizam, nawab, negus.

empress, queen, sultana, czarina, princess, infanta, duchess, margravine, begum, maharani.

regent, viceroy, exarch, palatine, khedive, hospodar, beglerbeg, three-tailed bashaw, pasha, pashaw, bashaw, bey, beg, dey, scherif, tetrarch, satrap, mandarin, subhadar, nabob, maharajah; burgrave; laird etc. (*proprietor*) 779; High Commissioner.

the -authorities, − powers that be, − government; staff, *état major,* aga, official, man in office, person in authority.

[Naval authorities] admiral, -ty, − of the fleet; rear-, vice-, port-admiral; senior-, naval officer, S.N.O., commodore, captain, commander, lieutenant-commander, lieutenant, sub-lieutenant, midshipman, warrant −, petty- officer, leading seaman; skipper, mate, master.

[Military authorities] marshal, field-marshal, *maréchal;* general, -issimo; commander-in-chief, *seraskier, hetman;* lieutenant-, major-general; commandant; colonel, lieutenant-colonel, major, captain, centurion, skipper, lieutenant, second-lieutenant, officer, staff-officer, *aide de camp,* brigadier, brigade-major, adjutant, *jemidar,* ensign, cornet, cadet, subaltern, warrant officer, quartermaster, noncommissioned officer, N.C.O.; sergeant, -major; top-sergeant, color sergeant; corporal, -major; lance-, acting-corporal; drum major; shavetail.

[Air authorities] air -marshal, − commodore; group captain, squadron leader, wing commander, flight lieutenant, flying −, pilot- officer.

[Civil authorities] judge etc. 967; mayor, -alty; prefect, chancellor, archon, provost, magistrate, syndic; alcalde, alcaid; burgomaster, *corregidor,* seneschal, alderman, warden, constable, portreeve; lord mayor, sheriff; officer etc. (*executive*) 965.

746. Servant.—N. subject, liegeman; servant, retainer, follower, henchman, servitor, domestic, menial, help, lady help, *employé, attaché*; official. retinue, suite, *cortège*, staff, court.

attendant, squire, usher, page, buttons, donzel, footboy; dog robber; train-, cup-bearer; waiter, busboy, tapster, butler, livery servant, lackey, footman, flunkey, valet, *valet de chambre*; boots; scout, gyp; equerry, groom; jockey, hostler, ostler, tiger, orderly, messenger, cad, gillie, caddie; *wallah*; journeyman, herdsman, swineherd.

bailiff, castellan, seneschal, chamberlain, *major-domo*, groom of the chambers.

secretary; under –, assistant- secretary; clerk; clerical staff, stenographer, subsidiary; agent etc. 758; subaltern; under-ling, -strapper; man.

maid, -servant, waitress; handmaid; *confidente*, lady's maid, abigail, *soubrette*; nurse, *bonne, ayah*; nurse-, nursery-, house-, parlor-, waiting-, chamber-, kitchen-, scullery-, between –, laundry –, dairy-maid; *femme* –, *fille- de chambre*; *camarista*; *chef de cuisine, cordon bleu*, cook, scullion, Cinderella; maid –, servant- of all work, tweeny, general servant, girl, slavey; laundress, bed-maker, goodie, char-woman etc. (*worker*) 690.

serf, vassal, slave, negro, helot; bondsman, -woman; bondslave; *âme damnée, odalisque*, ryot, *adscriptus glebae*; vill-ain, -ein; bead-, bede-sman; sizar; pension-er, -ary; client; dependant, -ent; hanger on, stooge, satellite; parasite etc. (*servility*) 886; led captain; *protégé*, ward, hireling, mercenary, puppet, creature.

badge of slavery; bonds etc. 752.

V. serve; minister to, wait –, attend –, dance attendance –, pin oneself- upon; squire, tend, hang on the sleeve of, char, do for; fag; valet.

Adj. in the train of; in one's -pay, – employ; at one's call etc. (*obedient*) 743; in bonds.

747. Scepter. [Insignia of authority.]—N. scepter, regalia, rod of empire, sword of state, mace, *fasces*, wand; staff, – of office; *bâton*, truncheon; flag etc. (*insignia*) 550; ensign –, emblem –, badge –, insignia- of authority, rank marks, brassard, badge, sash; cocked –, brass- hat.

epaulette, aiguilette, crown, star, eagle, bar, double bar, pip, stripe, chevron, curl, ring, anchor, shoulder-strap, tab.

throne, chair, musnud, divan, dais, woolsack. *toga*, pall, mantle, robes of state, ermine, purple.

crown, coronet, diadem, tiara, triple crown, miter, crozier, cardinal's hat etc.; cap of maintenance; decoration; title etc. 877; portfolio.

key, signet, seals, talisman; helm; reins etc. (*means of restraint*) 752.

748. Freedom.—N. freedom, liberty, independence; license etc. (*permission*) 760; facility etc. 705.

scope, range, latitude, play; free –, full- -play, – scope; free stage and no favor; swing, full swing, elbow-room, margin, rope, wide berth; Liberty Hall.

franchise, denization; free –, freed-, liveryman; denizen.

autonomy, self-government, homerule, self-determination, liberalism, free trade; non-interference etc. 706.

immunity, exemption; emancipation etc. (*liberation*) 750; en-, af-franchisement; rights, privileges.

free land, freehold; allodium; frankalmoigne, mortmain.

independent, free-lance, -thinker, -trader.

V. be -free etc. *adj.*; have -scope etc. *n.*, – the run of, – one's own way, – a will of one's own, – one's fling; do what one -likes, – wishes, – pleases, – chooses; go at large, feel at home, paddle one's own canoe; stand on one's -legs, – rights; shift for oneself.

take a liberty; make -free with, – oneself quite at home; use a freedom; take -leave, – French leave.

set free etc. (*liberate*) 750; give the reins to etc. (*permit*) 760; allow –, give- scope etc. *n.* to; give a horse his head.

make free of; give the -freedom of, – franchise; en-, af-franchise.

laisser -faire, – aller; live and let live; leave to oneself; leave –, let- alone; mind one's own business.

Adj. free, – as air; out of harness, independent, at large, loose, scot free; left -alone, – to oneself.

in full swing; uncaught, unconstrained, unbuttoned, unconfined, unrestrained, unchecked, unprevented, unhindered, unobstructed, unbound, uncontrolled, untrammeled.

unsubject, ungoverned, unenslaved, unenthralled, unchained, unshackled, unfettered, unreined, unbridled, uncurbed, unmuzzled, unimpeded.

unrestricted, unlimited, unconditional; absolute; discretionary etc. (*optional*) 600.

unassailed, unforced, uncompelled.

unbiassed, unprejudiced, uninfluenced, spontaneous.

free and easy; at –, at one's- ease; *dégagé*, quite at home; wanton, rampant, irrepressible, unvanquished.

exempt; freed etc. 750; freeborn; autonomous, freehold, allodial; *gratis* etc. 815.

unclaimed, going a begging.

Adv. freely etc. *adj.*; ad libitum etc. (*at will*) 600.

749. Subjection.—N. subjection; depend-ence, -ance, -ency; subordination; thrall, thraldom, enthralment, subjugation, bondage, serfdom; feudal--ism, -ity; vassalage, villenage; slavery, enslavement, involuntary servitude.

service; servi-tude, -torship; tendence, employ, tutelage, clientship; liability etc. 177; constraint etc. 751; oppression etc. (*severity*) 739; yoke etc. (*means of restraint*) 751; submission etc. 725; obedience etc. 743.

V. be -subject etc. *adj.*; be –, lie- at the mercy of; depend –, lean –, hang- upon; fall -a prey to, – under; play second fiddle.

be a -mere machine, – puppet, – football; not dare to say one's soul is his own; drag a chain.

serve etc. 746; obey etc. 743; submit etc. 725.

break in, tame; subject, subjugate; master etc. 731; tread -down, – under foot; weigh down; drag at one's chariot wheels; reduce to -subjection, –

slavery; en-, in-, be-thral; enslave, lead captive; take into custody etc. (*restrain*) 751; rule etc. 737; drive into a corner, hold at the sword's point; keep under; hold in -bondage. − leading strings, − swaddling clothes.

Adj. subject, dependent, subordinate; feud-al, -atory; in subjection to, under control; in -leading strings, − harness; subjected, enslaved etc. *v.*; con-strained etc. 751; subservient, servile, fawning, slavish, obsequious, cringing; down-trodden; over-borne, -whelmed; under the lash, on the hip, led by the nose, henpecked; the -puppet, − sport, − plaything- of; under one's -orders, − command, − thumb; like dirt under one's feet; a slave to; at the mercy of; in the -power, − hands, − clutches- of; at the feet of; at one's beck and call etc. (*obedient*) 743; liable etc. 177; parasitical; stipendiary.

Adv. under.

750. Liberation.—N. liberation, disengagement, release, disenthrallment, enlargement, emancipation; af-, en-franchisement; manumission; discharge, dismissal.

deliverance etc. 672; redemption, extrication, acquittance, absolution; acquittal etc. 970; escape etc. 671.

V. liberate, free; set -free, − clear, − at liberty; render free, emancipate, release; en-, af-franchise; manumit; enlarge; dis-band, -charge, -miss, -enthral; let -go, − loose, − out, − slip; cast −, turn- adrift; deliver etc. 672; absolve etc. (*acquit*) 970; reprieve.

unfetter etc. 751; untie etc. 44; loose etc. (*disjoin*) 44; loosen, relax; un-bolt, -bar, -close, -cork, -clog, -hand, -bind, -latch, -chain, -harness; dis-engage, -entangle; clear, extricate, unloose.

gain −, obtain −, acquire- one's -liberty etc. 748; get -rid, − clear- of; deliver oneself- from; shake off the yoke, slip the collar; break -loose, − prison; tear asunder one's bonds, cast off trammels; escape etc. 671.

Adj. at -liberty, − large, free, liberated etc. *v.*; out of harness etc. 748; adrift.

Int. unhand me! let me go!

751. Restraint.—N. restraint; hindrance etc. 706; coercion etc. (*compulsion*) 744; cohibition, constraint, repression; discipline, control, self-restraint etc. 604.

confinement; durance, duress; im-, prisonment; incarceration, coarctation, entombment, man-cipation, durance vile, thrall, -dom, limbo, cap-tivity; blockade; quarantine; detention.

arrest, -ation; custody, keep, care, charge, ward, restringency.

curb etc. (*means of restraint*) 752; *lettres de cachet.*

limitation, restriction, protection, monopoly; prohibition etc. 761; economic pressure.

prisoner etc. 754.

V. restrain, check; put −, lay- under restraint; en-, in-, be-thral; restrict, debar etc. (*hinder*) 706; constrain; coerce etc. (*compel*) 744; curb, control; hold −, keep- -back, − from, − in, − in check, − within bounds; hold in -leash, − leading strings; withhold.

keep under; repress, suppress; smother; pull in, rein in; hold, − fast; keep a tight hand on; prohibit etc. 761; in-, co-hibit.

enchain; fasten etc. (*join*) 43; fetter, shackle; en-, trammel; bridle, muzzle, gag, pinion, manacle, handcuff, tie one's hands, hobble, bind hand and foot; swathe, swaddle; pin −, peg- down; tether, picket; tie, − up, − down; secure; forge fetters.

confine; shut −, clap −, lock −, box −, mew −, bottle −, cork −, seal −, button- up; shut −, hem −, bolt −, wall −, rail- in; impound, pen, coop; enclose etc. (*circumscribe*) 229; cage; in-, en-cage; close the door upon, cloister; imprison, immure; incarcerate, entomb; clap −, lay- under hatches; put in -irons, − a strait waistcoat; throw −, cast- into prison; put into bilboes.

arrest; take -up, − charge of, − into custody; take −, make- -prisoner, − captive; captivate; lead -captive, − into captivity; send −, commit- to prison; commit; give in -charge, − custody; subjugate etc. 749.

Adj. re-, con-strained; imprisoned etc. *v.*; pent up; jammed in, wedged in; under -restraint, − lock and key, − hatches; serving −, doing- time; in swaddling clothes; on *parole*; in custody etc. (*prisoner*) 754; cohibitive; coactive etc. (*compulsory*) 744.

stiff, restringent, straitlaced, hide-bound.

ice-, wind-, weather-bound; 'cabined, cribbed, confined;' in Lob's pound, laid by the heels.

Adv. in captivity, under arrest, behind the bars, in -prison, − jail, − durance vile.

752. Prison. [Means of restraint.]—**N.** prison, -house; jail, gaol, cage, coop, den, death house, condemned −, cell; stronghold, fortress, keep, donjon, dungeon, *Bastille, oubliette*; bridewell, house of correction, bulks, tool-booth, panopticon, penitentiary, guard-room, clink, can, stir, tronk, jug, lock-up, hold; round −, watch −, station −, sponging-house; station; house of detention, black hole, pen, fold, pound; enclosure etc. 232; penal settlement; chain gang; debtors' prison; reform-atory; federal penitentiary, state prison; criminal lunatic asylum; bilboes, stocks, limbo, quod.

Dartmoor, Newgate, Fleet, Marshalsea; King's (or Queen's) Bench; Sing Sing, Dannemora.

bond; strap, bandage, splint, tourniquet; irons, pinion, gyve, fetter, shackle, trammel, manacle, handcuff, bracelets, darbies, strait waistcoat, strait-jacket.

yoke, collar, halter, harness; muzzle, gag, bit, brake, curb, snaffle, bridle; rein, -s; ribbons, lines, bearing-rein; martingale, leading string; tether, picket, band, guy, chain; cord etc. (*fastening*) 45.

bolt, bar, lock, padlock, rail, wall; paling, palisade; fence; barrier, barricade.

brake, drag etc. (*hindrance*) 706.

753. Keeper.—N. keeper, custodian, *custos*, ranger, warder, jailer, gaoler, turnkey, castellan, guard; watch, -dog, -man; Charley; sen-try, -tinel; watch and ward; *concierge*, coast-guard, *guarda costa*, gamekeeper.

escort, body guard; convoy.

protector, governor, duenna; guardian; gover-ness etc. (*teacher*) 540; nurse, *bonne, ayah, amah.*

754. Prisoner.—N. prisoner, captive, *détenu*, close prisoner.

jail-bird, ticket-of-leave man.

V. stand committed; be -imprisoned etc. 751.

Adj. imprisoned etc. 751; in -prison, – quod, – durance vile, – limbo, – custody, – charge, – chains; under -lock and key, – hatches; on *parole*; detained at his Majesty's pleasure.

755. Commission. [Vicarious authority.]—N. commission, delegation; con-, as-signment; procuration; deputation, legation, mission, embassy; agency, agentship; power of attorney, proxy; clerkship.

errand, charge, *brevet*, diploma, *exequatur*, permit etc. (*permission*) 760.

appointment, nomination, return; charter; ordination; installation, inauguration, investiture; accession, coronation, enthronement.

vicegerency; regency, regentship.

viceroy etc. 745; consignee etc. 758; deputy etc. 759.

V. commission, delegate, depute; consign, assign; charge; in-, en-trust; turn over to; commit, – to the hands of; authorize etc. (*permit*) 760.

put in commission, accredit, engage, hire, bespeak, appoint, name, nominate, return, ordain; install, induct, inaugurate, invest, crown; en-roll, -list.

employ, empower; give power of attorney to; set –, place- over; send out.

be commissioned, be accredited; represent, stand for; stand in the -stead, – place, – shoes- of.

Adj. commissioned etc. v.

Adv. *per procuratione*.

756. Abrogation.—N. abrogation, annulment, nullification; cancelling etc. v.; cancel; revo-cation, -kement; repeal, rescission, defeasance.

dismissal, *congé*, demission; depos-al, -ition; sack, dethronement; disestablish-, disendow-ment; deconsecration.

aboli-tion, -shment; dissolution.

counter-order, -mand; repudiation, retractation; recantation etc. (*tergiversation*) 607.

V. abrogate, annul, cancel; destroy etc. 162; abolish; revoke, repeal, rescind, reverse, retract, recall; over-rule, -ride; set aside; disannul, dissolve, quash, nullify, declare null and void; dis-establish, -endow; deconsecrate.

disclaim etc. (*deny*) 536; ignore, repudiate; recant etc. 607; divest oneself, break off.

counter-mand, -order; do away with; sweep –, brush- away; throw -overboard, – to the dogs; scatter to the winds, cast behind.

dismiss, discard; cast –, turn- off, – out, – adrift, – out of doors, – aside, – away; send -off, – away, – about one's business; discharge, get rid of, fire out, fire etc. (*eject*) 297; jilt.

cashier; break; oust; set down, unseat, -saddle; un-, de-, disen-throne; depose, uncrown; unfrock, strike off the roll; dis-bar, -bench.

be -abrogated etc.; receive its quietus.

Adj. abrogated etc. v.; *functus officio*.

Int. get along with you! begone! go about your business! away with!

757. Resignation.—N. resignation, retirement, abdication, renunciation, abjuration, disclaimer, abandonment, relinquishment.

V. resign; give –, throw- up; lay down, throw up the cards, wash one's hands of, abjure, renounce, forego, disclaim, abandon, relinquish, retract, demit; deny etc. 536.

abrogate etc. 756; desert etc. (*relinquish*) 624; get rid of etc. 782.

abdicate; vacate, – one's seat; accept the stewardship of the Chiltern Hundreds; retire; tender –, send in –, hand in- one's resignation.

Adj. abdicant, renunciatory etc. v.

Phr. 'Othello's occupation's gone.'

758. Consignee.—N. consignee, trustee, nominee, committee.

delegate; commiss-ary, -ioner; emissary, envoy, commissionaire; messenger etc. 534.

diplomatist, diplomat, *corps diplomatique*, embassy; am-, em-bassador; representative, resident, consul, legate, nuncio, internuncio, *chargé d' affaires*, *attaché*.

vicegerent etc. (*deputy*) 759; plenipotentiary.

functionary, placeman, curator; treasurer etc. 801; agent, factor, bailiff, steward, clerk, secretary, attorney, solicitor, proctor, broker, underwriter, commission agent, auctioneer, one's man of business; factotum etc. (*director*) 694; caretaker.

negotiator, go between; middleman; under agent, *employé*; servant etc. 746.

salesman; commercial, – traveler; bagman, *commis-voyageur*, touter.

newspaper –, own –, war –, special-correspondent; reporter.

759. Deputy.—N. deputy, substitute, vice, proxy, *locum tenens*, delegate, representative, next friend, surrogate, secondary.

regent, vicegerent, vizier, minister, vicar; premier etc. (*director*) 694; chancellor, prefect, provost, warden, lieutenant, archon, consul, proconsul; viceroy etc. (*governor*) 745; commissioner etc. 758; plenipotentiary, *alter ego*.

team, eight, eleven; champion.

V. be -deputy etc. n.; stand –, appear –, hold a brief –, answer- for; represent; stand –, walk- in the shoes of; stand in the stead of.

substitute, ablegate, accredit; commission, empower, delegate etc. 755.

Adj. acting; vice, -regal; accredited to.

Adv. in behalf of, by proxy.

760. Permission.—N. permission, leave; allow-, suffer-ance; toler-ance, -ation; liberty, law, license, concession, grace; indulgence etc. (*lenity*) 740; favor, dispensation, exemption, release; connivance; vouchsafement.

authorization, warranty, accordance, admission.

permit, warrant, *brevet*, precept, sanction, authority, *firman*; pass, -port; furlough, license, *carte blanche*, ticket of leave; grant, charter, patent.

V. permit; give -permission etc. n., – power;

let, allow, admit; suffer, bear with, tolerate, recognize; concede etc. 762; accord, vouchsafe, favor, humor, gratify, indulge, stretch a point; wink at, connive at; shut one's eyes to.

grant, empower, charter, enfranchise, privilege, confer a privilege, license, authorize, warrant; sanction; entrust etc. (*commission*) 755.

give *-carte blanche*, − the reins to, − scope to etc. (*freedom*) 748; leave -alone, − it to one, − the door open; open the -door to, − floodgates; give a loose to.

let off; absolve etc. (*acquit*) 970; release, exonerate, dispense with.

ask −, beg −, request- -leave, − permission.

Adj. permitting etc. *v.*; permissive, indulgent; permitted etc. *v.*; patent, chartered, permissible, allowable, lawful, legitimate, legal; legalized etc. (*law*) 963; licit; unforbid, -den; unconditional.

Adv. permissibly; by −, with −, on- -leave etc. *n.*; speciali gratiâ; under favor of; *pace*; *ad libitum* etc. (*freely*) 748, (*at will*) 600; by all means etc. (*willingly*) 602; yes etc. (*assent*) 488.

761. Prohibition.—**N.** pro-, in-hibition; *veto*, disallowance; interdict, -ion; injunction; embargo, ban, *verboten*, taboo, proscription; *index expurgatorius*; restriction etc. (*restraint*) 751; hindrance etc. 706; forbidden fruit.

V. pro-, in-hibit; forbid, put one's *veto* upon, disallow; bar; debar etc. (*hinder*) 706, forefend.

keep -in, − within bounds; restrain etc. 751; cohibit, withhold, limit, circumscribe, clip the wings of, restrict, narrow; interdict, taboo; put −, place- under -an interdiction, − the ban; proscribe, censor; exclude, shut out; shut −, bolt −, show- the door; warn off; dash the cup from one's lips; forbid the banns.

Adj. prohibit-ive, -ory; interdictive; proscriptive; restrictive, exclusive; forbidding etc. *v.*

prohibited etc. *v.*; not -permitted etc. 760; unlicensed, contraband, under the ban of; illegal etc. 964; unauthorized, not to be thought of.

Adv. on no account etc. (*no*) 536.

Int. forbid it heaven! etc. (*deprecation*) 766. hands −, keep- off! hold! stop! avast!

Phr. that will never do.

762. Consent.—**N.** consent; assent etc. 488; acquiescence; approval etc. 931; compliance, agreement, concession; yield-ance, -ingness; accession, acknowledgment, acceptance, agnition.

settlement, ratification, confirmation, adjustment.

permit etc. (*permission*) 760; promise etc. 768.

V. consent; assent etc. 488; yield assent, admit, allow, concede, grant, yield; come -over, − round; give in to, acknowledge, agnize, give consent, comply with, acquiesce, agree to, fall in with, accede, accept, embrace an offer, close with, take at one's word, have no objection.

satisfy, meet one's wishes, settle, come to terms etc. 488; not -refuse etc. 764; turn a willing ear etc. (*willingness*) 602; jump at; deign, vouchsafe; promise etc. 768.

Adj. consenting etc. *v.*; agreeable, compliant; agreed etc. (*assent*) 488; unconditional.

Adv. yes etc. (*assent*) 488; by all means etc. (*willingly*) 602; if −, as- you please; be it so, so be it, well and good, of course.

763. Offer.—**N.** offer, proffer, presentation, tender, bid, overture; propos-al, -ition; motion, invitation; candidature; offering etc. (*gift*) 784.

V. offer, proffer, present, tender; bid; propose, move; make -a motion, − advances; start; invite, hold out, place- at one's disposal, − in one's way, put forward.

hawk about; offer for sale etc. 796; press etc. (*request*) 765; lay at one's feet.

offer −, present- oneself; volunteer, come forward, be a candidate; stand −, bid- for; seek; be at one's service; go a begging; bribe etc. (*give*) 784.

Adj. offer-ing, -ed etc. *v.*; in the market, for sale, to let, disengaged, on hire.

764. Refusal.—**N.** refusal, rejection; non-, in-compliance; denial; declining etc. *v.*; declension; peremptory −, flat −, point blank- refusal; repulse, rebuff; discountenance.

recusancy, renunciation, abnegation, negation, protest, disclaimer; dissent etc. 489; revocation etc. 756.

V. refuse, reject, deny, decline; nill, negative; refuse −, withhold- one's assent; shake the head; close the -hand, − purse; grudge, begrudge, be slow to, hang fire.

be deaf to; turn -a deaf ear to, − one's back upon; set one's face against, discountenance, not hear of, have nothing to do with, wash one's hands of, stand aloof, forswear, set aside, cast behind one; not yield an inch etc. (*obstinacy*) 606.

resist, cross; not -grant etc. 762; repel, repulse; shut −, slam- the door in one's face; rebuff; send back, − to the right about, − away with a flea in the ear; deny oneself, not be at home to; discard etc. (*repudiate*) 610; rescind etc. (*revoke*) 756; disclaim, protest; dissent etc. 489.

Adj. refusing etc. *v.*; rest-ive, -iff; recusant; uncomplying, noncompliant, unconsenting, uncomplaisant, protestant; not willing to hear of, deaf to.

refused etc. *v.*; ungranted, out of the question, not to be thought of, impossible.

Adv. no etc. 536; on no account, not for the world; no thank you.

Phr. *non possumus*; [ironically] your humble servant; *bien obligé*.

765. Request.—**N.** requ-est, -isition; claim etc. (*demand*) 741; petition, suit, prayer; begging letter, round-robin.

motion, overture, application, canvass, address, appeal, apostrophe; imprecation; rogation; proposal, proposition.

orison etc. (*worship*) 990; incantation etc. (*spell*) 993.

mendicancy; asking, panhandling, begging etc. *v.*; postulation, solicitation, invitation, entreaty, importunity, supplication, instance, impetration, imploration, obsecration, obtestation, invocation, interpellation.

V. request, ask; beg, crave, sue, pray, petition, solicit, invite, pop the question, make bold to ask; beg -leave; − a boon; apply to, call to, put to; call -upon, − for; make −, address −, prefer −, put up- a -request, − prayer, − petition; make - application, − a requisition; ask −, trouble- one for; claim etc. (*demand*) 741; offer up prayers etc. (*worship*) 990; whistle for.

beg hard, entreat, beseech, plead, supplicate, implore, apostrophize; conjure, adjure; obtest; cry to, kneel to, appeal to; invoke, evoke; impetrate, imprecate, ply, press, urge, beset, importune, dun, tax, clamor for; cry -aloud, − for help; fall on one's knees; throw oneself at the feet of; come down on one's marrow-bones.

beg from door to door, send the hat round, go a begging; mendicate, mump, cadge, panhandle, beg one's bread.

dance attendance on, besiege, knock at the door.

bespeak, canvass, tout, make interest, court; seek, bid for etc. (*offer*) 763; publish the banns.

Adj. requesting etc. *v.*; precatory; suppli-ant, -cant, -catory; invoc-, imprec-, rog-atory; postulant, mendicant.

importunate, clamorous, urgent; solicitous; cap in hand; on one's -knees, − bended knees, − marrow-bones.

Adv. prithee, do, please, pray; be so good as, be good enough; have the goodness, vouchsafe, will you, I pray thee, if you please.

Int. for -God's, − heaven's, − goodness', − mercy's- sake.

766. Deprecation. [Negative request.]—**N.** deprecation, expostulation; remonstrance; intercession, mediation.

V. deprecate, protest, expostulate, enter a protest, intercede for.

Adj. deprecatory, expostulatory, intercessory, mediatorial.

deprecated, protested.

un-, unbe-sought; unasked etc. (*see* ask etc. 765).

Int. cry you mercy! God forbid! forbid it Heaven! Heaven -forefend, − forbid! far be it from! hands off! etc. (*prohibition*) 761.

767. Petitioner.—**N.** petitioner, solicitor, applicant; suppli-ant, -cant; suitor, candidate, claimant, postulant, aspirant, competitor, bidder; place −, pot- hunter; prizer.

beggar, mendicant, mumper, sturdy beggar, cadger, panhandler.

canvasser, barker, touter etc. 768.

sycophant, parasite etc. 886.

768. Promise.—**N.** promise, undertaking, word, troth, plight, pledge, *parole*, word of honor, vow; oath etc. (*affirmation*) 535; profession, assurance, warranty, guarantee, insurance, obligation; contract etc. 769.

engagement, pre-engagement; affiance; betroth, -al, -ment; marriage -compact, − vow.

V. promise; give a -promise etc. *n.*; undertake, engage; make −, form- an engagement; enter - into, − on- an engagement; bind −, tie −, pledge −, commit −, take upon- oneself; vow; swear etc. (*affirm*) 535; give −, pass −, pledge −, plight- one's -word, − honor, − credit, − troth; betroth, plight faith; take the vows.

assure, warrant, guarantee, vouch for, avouch, covenant etc. 769; attest etc. (*bear witness*) 467.

hold out an expectation; contract an obligation; become -bound to, − sponsor for; answer −, be answerable- for; secure; give security etc. 771; underwrite.

adjure, administer an oath, put to one's oath, swear a witness.

Adj. promising etc. *v.*; promissory; votive; under hand and seal; upon -oath, − affirmation.

promised etc. *v.*; affianced, pledged, bound; committed, compromised; in for it.

Adv. as one's head shall answer for; upon my honor.

Phr. in for a penny, in for a pound.

768a. Release from engagement.—**N.** release etc. (*liberation*) 750.

Adj. absolute; unconditional etc. (*free*) 748.

769. Compact.—**N.** compact, contract, agreement, bargain, deal, transaction; affidation; pact, -ion; bond, covenant, indenture.

stipulation, settlement, convention; compromise, *cartel*.

protocol, treaty, *concordat, Zollverein, Sonderbund*, charter, *Magna Charta*, Pragmatic Sanction.

negotiation etc. (*bargaining*) 794; diplomacy etc. (*mediation*) 724; negotiator etc. (*agent*) 758.

ratification, completion, signature, seal, sigil, signet.

V. contract, covenant, agree for, engage etc. (*promise*) 768.

treat, negotiate, stipulate, make terms; bargain etc. (*barter*) 794.

make −, strike- a bargain; come to -terms, − an understanding; compromise etc. 774; set at rest; close, − with; conclude, complete, settle; confirm, ratify, clench, subscribe, underwrite; en-, in-dorse; put the seal to; sign, seal etc. (*attest*) 467; indent.

take one at one's word, bargain by inch of candle.

Adj. contractual, agreed etc. *v.*; conventional; under hand and seal; signed, sealed and delivered.

Phr. *caveat emptor.*

770. Conditions.—**N.** conditions, terms; articles, − of agreement.

clauses, provisions; proviso etc. (*qualification*) 469; covenant, stipulation, obligation, *ultimatum, sine quâ non; casus foederis.*

V. make −, come to- -terms etc. (*contract*) 769; make it a condition, stipulate, insist upon, make a point of; bind, tie up.

Adj. conditional, provisional, guarded, fenced, hedged in.

Adv. conditionally etc. (*with qualification*) 469; provisionally, *pro re natâ*; on condition; with a reservation.

771. Security.—N. security; guaran-ty, -tee; gage, waranty, bond, tie, pledge, plight, mortgage, debenture, hypothecation, bill of sale, lien, pignus, pawn, pignoration; real security; bottomry; collateral, vadium.

stake, deposit, earnest, handsel, caution.

promissory note; bill, – of exchange; I.O.U.; personal security, covenant, specialty; *parole* etc. (*promise*) 768.

acceptance, indorsement, signature, execution, stamp, seal.

spon-sor, -sion, -sorship; surety, bail; main-pernor, hostage.

recognizance; deed –, covenant- of indemnity.

authentication, verfication, warrant, certificate, voucher, docket, doquet; record etc. 551; probate, attested copy.

receipt; ac-, quittance; discharge, release.

muniment, title-deed, instrument; deed, – poll; assurance, insurance, indenture; charter etc. (*compact*) 769; charter-poll; paper, parchment, settlement, will, testament, last will and testament, codicil.

V. give -security, – bail, – substantial bail; go bail; pawn, impawn, hock, spout, mortgage, hypothecate, impignorate.

guarantee, warrant, assure; accept, indorse, underwrite, insure.

execute, stamp; sign, seal etc. (*evidence*) 467.

let, set; grant –, take –, hold- a lease; hold in pledge; lend on security etc. 787.

Adj. secure, -ed; pledged etc. *v.*; in pawn, on deposit.

772. Observance.—N. observance, performance, compliance; obedience, etc. 743; fulfilment, satisfaction, discharge; acquit-tance, -tal.

adhesion; acknowledgment; fidelity etc. (*probity*) 939; exact etc. 494- observance.

V. observe, comply with, respect, acknowledge, abide by; cling to, adhere to, be faithful to, act up to; meet, fulfil; carry -out, – into execution; execute, perform, keep, satisfy, discharge; do one's office.

perform –, fulfill –, discharge –, acquit oneself of- an obligation; make good; make good –, keep- one's -word, – promise; redeem one's pledge; keep faith with, stand to one's engagement.

Adj. observant, faithful, true, loyal; honorable etc. 939; true as the -dial to the sun, – needle- to the pole; punct-ual, -ilious; meticulous; literal etc. (*exact*) 494; as good as one's word.

Adv. faithfully etc. *adj.*

773. Non-observance.—N. non-observance etc. 772; evasion, inobservance, failure, omission, neglect, laches, laxity, informality.

infringement, infraction; violation, transgression.

retractation, repudiation, nullification; protest; forfeiture.

lawlessness; disobedience etc. 742; bad faith etc. 940.

V. fail, neglect, omit, elude, evade, give the go by to, cut, set aside, ignore; shut –, close- one's eyes to, avoid.

infringe, transgress, pirate, violate, break, trample under foot, do violence to, drive a coach and six through.

discard, protest, repudiate, fling to the winds, set at naught, nullify, declare null and void; cancel etc. (*wipe off*) 552.

retract, go back from, be off, forfeit, go from one's word, palter; stretch –, strain- a point.

Adj. violating etc. *v.*; lawless, transgressive; elusive, evasive; lax, casual; non-observant.

unfulfilled etc. (*see* fulfil etc. 772).

774. Compromise.—N. com-promise, mutation, -position; middle term, *mezzo termine*; compensation etc. 30; adjustment, mutual concession.

V. com-promise, -mute, -pound; take the mean; split the difference, meet one half way, give and take; come to terms etc. (*contract*) 769; submit to –, abide by- arbitration; patch up, bridge over, fix up, arrange; adjust, – differences; agree; make -the best of, – a virtue of necessity; take the will for the deed.

775. Acquisition.—N. acquisition; gaining etc. *v.*; obtainment; procur-ation, -ement; purchase, descent, inheritance; gift etc. 784.

recovery, retrieval, revendication, replevin; redemption, salvage, trover; find, *trouvaille*, foundling.

gain, thrift; money-making, -grubbing; lucre, filthy lucre, loaves and- fishes, the main -chance, pelf; emolument etc. 973; wealth etc. 803.

profit, earnings, winnings, innings, clean-up, pickings, perquisite, net profit; income etc. (*receipt*) 810; pro-ceeds, -duce, -duct; out-come, -put; return, fruit, crop, harvest, tilth; second crop, aftermath; benefit etc. (*good*) 618.

sweepstakes, trick, prize, pool.

[Fraudulent acquisition] subreption; theft, stealing etc. 791.

V. acquire, get, gain, win, earn, obtain, procure, gather, annex; collect etc. 72; pick, – up; glean, take etc. 789.

find; come –, pitch –, light- upon; scrape -up, – together; get in, reap and carry, net, bag, sack, bring home, secure, come across, derive, draw, get in the harvest.

profit; make –, draw- profit; turn to -profit, -. account; make -capital out of, – money by; obtain a return, reap the fruits of; reap –, gain- an advantage; turn -a penny, – an honest penny; make the pot boil, bring grist to the mill; make –, coin –, raise- money; raise -funds, – the wind; fill one's pocket etc. (*wealth*) 803.

treasure up etc. (*store*) 636; realize, clear; produce etc. 161; take etc. 789.

get back, recover, regain, retrieve, revendicate, replevy, redeem, come by one's own.

come -by, – in for; receive etc. 785; inherit; step into, – a fortune, – the shoes of; succeed to.

get -hold of, – between one's finger and thumb, – into one's hand, – at; take –, come into –, enter into- possession.

be -profitable etc. *adj.*; pay, answer.

accrue etc. (*be received*) 785.

Adj. acquir-ing, -ed etc. *v.*; acquisitive; produc tive. profitable, advantageous, gainful, remunerative, paying, lucrative.

776. Loss.—N. loss; de-, perdition; forfeiture, lapse.

privation, bereavement; deprivation etc. (*dispossession*) 789; riddance.

V. lose; incur –, experience –, meet with- a loss; miss; mislay, let slip, allow to slip through the fingers, squander; be without etc. (*exempt*) 777a; forfeit.

get rid of etc. 782; waste etc. 638.

be lost, lapse.

Adj. losing etc. *v.*; not having etc. 777a.

shorn of, deprived of; denuded, bereaved, bereft, *minus*, cut off; dispossessed etc. 789; rid of, quit of; out of pocket.

lost etc. *v.*; long lost; irretrievable etc. (*hopeless*) 859; irredentist; off one's hands.

Int. farewell to! adieu to! good riddance!

777. Possession.—N. possession, seisin; owner ship etc. 780; occupancy; hold, -ing; tenure, tenancy, feodality, dependency; villenage; socage, chivalry, knight service.

exclusive possession, impropriation, monopoly, corner; retention etc. 781; pre-possession, occupancy; nine points of the law.

future possession, heritage, inheritance, heirship, reversion, fee, seigniority, feud, fief.

bird in hand, *uti possidetis, chose* in possession.

V. possess, have, hold, occupy, enjoy; be - possessed of etc. *adj.*; have -in hand etc. *adj.*; own etc. 780; command.

inherit; come -to, – in for.

engross, monopolize, forestall, regrate, im propriate, have all to oneself, corner; have a firm hold of etc. (*retain*) 781; get into one's hand etc. (*acquire*) 775.

belong to, appertain to, pertain to; be -in one's possession etc. *adj.*; vest in.

Adj. possessing etc. *v.*; worth; possessed of, seized of, master of, in possession of; endowed –, blest –, instinct –, fraught –, laden –, charged –, instilled –, with.

possessed etc. *v.*; on hand, by one; in hand, in store, in stock; in one's -hands, – grasp, – possession; at one's -command, – disposal; one's own etc. (*property*) 780.

unsold, unshared.

777a. Exemption.—N. exemption; exception, immunity, privilege, release etc. 927a; absence etc. 187.

V. not -have etc. 777; be -without etc. *adj.*

Adj. exempt from, devoid of, without, un possessed of, unblest with, immune from.

not -having etc. 777; unpossessed; untenanted etc. (*vacant*) 187; without an owner.

unobtained, unacquired.

778. Participation. [Joint possession.]—**N.** participation; co-, joint-tenancy; possession –, tenancy- in common; joint –, common- stock; co-, partnership; communion; community of - possessions, – goods; communalism, communism, socialism, collectivism; co-operation etc. 709; profit sharing.

snacks, co-sportion, picnic, hotchpotch; co heirship, -parceny, -parcenary; gavelkind.

participator, sharer; co-, partner; shareholder; co-, joint-tenant; tenants in common; co-heir, - parcener.

communist, socialist.

V. par-ticipate, -take; share, – in; come in for a share; go -shares, – snacks, – halves; share and share alike.

have –, possess –, be seized- -in common, – as joint tenants etc. *n.*

join in; have a hand in etc. (*co-operate*) 709.

Adj. partaking etc. *v.*; communistic, socialistic, co-operative, profit sharing.

Adv. share and share alike.

779. Possessor.—N. possessor, holder; occup ant, -ier; tenant; person –, man- -in possession etc. 777; renter, lodger, lessee, under-lessee; zemindar, ryot; tenant -on sufferance, – at will, – from year to year, – for years, – for life.

owner; propriet-or; -ress, -ary; impropriator, master, mistress, lord.

land-holder, -owner, -lord, -lady; lord -of the manor, – paramount; heritor, laird, vavasor, landed gentry, mesne lord.

cestui-que-trust, beneficiary, mortgagor.

grantee, feoffee, relessee, devisee; legat-ee, -ary. trustee; holder etc.- of the legal estate; mort gagee.

right –, rightful- owner.

[Future possessor] heir, – apparent; – presumptive; heiress; inherit-or, -ress, -rix; rever sioner, remainder-man.

780. Property.—N. property, possession, *suum cuique, meum et tuum.*

owner-, proprietor, lord-ship; seignority; empire etc. (*dominion*) 737.

interest, stake, estate, right, title, claim, demand, holding; tenure etc. (*possession*) 777; vested –, contingent –, beneficial –, equitable- interest; use, trust, benefit; legal –, equitable- estate; seisin.

absolute interest, paramount estate, freehold; fee, – simple, – tail; estate -in fee, – in tail, – tail; estate in tail -male, – female, – general.

limitation, term, lease, settlement, strict set tlement, particular estate; estate -for life, – for years, – *pur autre vie*; remainder, reversion, ex pectancy, possibility.

dower, dowry, *dot*, jointure, marriage portion, appanage, inheritance, heritage, patrimony, alimony; legacy etc. (*gift*) 784.

assets, belongings, means, resources, circumstances; wealth etc. 803; money etc. 800; what one -is worth, — will cut up for; estate and effects.

landed —, real- -estate, — property; realty; land, -s; subdivision; plot, site; tenements; hereditaments; corporeal —, incorporeal- hereditaments; acres; ground rent. (*earth*) 342; acquest; messuage.

territory, state, kingdom, principality, realm, empire, protectorate, margravate, dependancy, colony, sphere of influence, mandate.

manor, honor, domain, demesne; farm, ranch, plantation, *hacienda*; allodium etc. (*free*) 748; fieff, feoff, feud, zemindary, dependency.

free-, copy-, lease-holds; chattels real; fixtures, plant, heirloom easement; folkland; right of - common, — user.

personal -property, — estate, — effects; personalty, chattels, goods, effects, movables; stock, — in trade; things, traps, rattle-traps, paraphernalia; equipage etc. 633.

parcels, appurtenances.

impedimenta; lug-, bag-gage; bag and baggage; pelf; cargo, lading.

rent-roll; income etc. (*receipts*) 810.

patent, copyright; *chose* in action; credit etc. 805; debt etc. 806.

V. possess etc. 777; be the -possessor etc. 779- of own; have for one's own, — very own; come in for, inherit; enfeoff.

savor of the realty.

be one's own -property etc. *n.*; belong to; ap-, pertain to.

Adj. one's own; landed, predial, manorial, allodial, seignorial; free-, copy-, lease-hold; feu-, feo-dal; hereditary, entailed, personal.

Adv. to one's -credit, — account; to the good.

to one and -his heirs for ever, — the heirs of his body, — his heirs and assigns, — his executors, administrators and assigns.

781. Retention.—**N.** retention; retaining etc. *v.*; keep, detention, custody; tenacity, firm hold, grasp, gripe, grip, iron grip.

fangs, teeth, claws, talons, nail, hook, tentacle, *tenaculum*; bond etc. (*vinculum*) 45.

clutches, tongs, forceps, pincers, nippers, pliers, tweezers, vise.

paw, hand, finger, wrist, fist, neaf, neif.

bird in hand; captive etc. 754.

V. retain, keep; hold, — fast, — tight, — one's own, — one's ground; clinch, clench, clutch, grasp, gripe, hug, have a firm hold of.

secure, withold, detain; hold —, keepback; keep close; husband etc. (*store*) 636; reserve; have —, keep- in stock etc. (*possess*) 777; enfail, tie up, settle.

Adj. retaining etc. *v.*; retentive, tenacious.

unforfeited, undeprived, undisposed, un-communicated.

incommunicable, inalienable; in mortmain; in strict settlement.

Phr. *uti possidetis.*

782. Relinquishment.—**N.** relinquishment, abandonment etc. (*of a course*) 624; renunciation,

expropriation, dereliction; cession, surrender, dispensation; resignation etc. 757; riddance.

derelict etc. *adj.*; jetsam; waif, foundling, orphan.

v. relinquish, give up, surrender, yield, cede; let -go, — slip; spare, drop, resign, forego, renounce, abjure, abandon, expropriate, give away, dispose of, part with; lay -aside, — apart, — down, — on the shelf etc. (*disuse*) 678; set —, put- aside; make away with, cast behind; discard, cast off, dismiss, maroon.

give -notice to quit, — warning; supersede; be —, get- -rid of, — quit of; eject etc. 297.

rid —, disburden —, divest —, dispossess-oneself of; wash one's hands of; divorce, desert; disinherit, cut off.

cast — throw —, pitch —, fling- -away, — aside, — overboard, — to the dogs; cast —, throw —, sweep- to the winds; put —, turn —, sweep-away; jettison.

quit one's hold.

Adj. relinquished etc. *v.*; cast off, derelict; unowned, unappropriated, unculled; left etc. (*residuary*) 40; divorced; disinherited.

Int. away with!

783. Transfer.—**N.** transfer, conveyance, assignment, alienation, abalienation; demise, limitation; conveyancing; transmission etc. (*transference*) 270; enfeoffment, bargain and sale, lease and release; exchange etc. (*interchange*) 148; barter etc. 794; substitution etc. 147.

succession, reversion; shifting -use, — trust; devolution.

V. transfer, convey; alien, -ate; assign; grant etc. (*confer*) 784; consign; make —, hand- over; pass, hand, transmit, negotiate; hand down; exchange etc. (*interchange*) 148.

change -hands, — from one to another; devolve, succeed; come into possession etc. (*acquire*) 775; take over.

abalienate; disinherit; dispossess etc. 789; substitute etc. 147.

Adj. alienable, negotiable, transferable, reversional.

Phr. estate coming into possession.

784. Giving.—**N.** giving etc. *v.*; bestowal, donation; present-ation, -ment; accordance; concession; delivery, consignment, dispensation, communication, endowment; invest-ment, -iture; award.

almsgiving, charity, liberality, generosity; philanthropy etc. 910.

[Thing given] gift, donation, present, *cadeau*; fairing; free gift, boon, favor, benefaction, grant, offering, oblation, sacrifice, immolation.

grace, act of grace, *bonus, bonanza.*

allowance, contribution, subscription, subsidy, tribute, subvention.

bequest, legacy, devise, will, dotation, appanage; dowry; voluntary -settlement, — conveyance etc. 783; amortization.

alms, largess, bounty, dole, sportule, donative, help, oblation, offertory, Peter's pence, *honorarium*, gratuity, Maundy money, Christmas box, Easter offering, vail, tip, *douceur*, drink money, *pourboire, trinkgeld, backsheesh*; fee etc. (*recompense*) 973; consideration.

bribe, bait, ground-bait; peace-offering, handsel.

giver, grantor etc. *v.*; donor, feoffer, settlor; almoner; testator; investor, subscriber, contributor; fairy godmother; Santa Claus, benefactor etc. 816.

V. deliver, hand, pass, put into the hands of; hand –, make –, deliver –, pass –, turn- over.

present, give away, dispense, dispose of; give –, deal –, dole –, mete –, fork –, shell –, squeeze- out.

pay etc. 807; render, impart, communicate.

concede, cede, yield, part with, shed cast; spend etc. 809.

give, bestow, confer, grant, accord, award, assign.

entrust, consign, vest in.

make a present; allow, contribute, subscribe, donate, furnish its quota.

invest, endow, settle upon; bequeath, leave, devise.

furnish, supply, help; ad-, minister to; afford, spare; accommodate –, indulge –, favor- with; shower down upon; lavish, pour on, thrust upon; tip, bribe; tickle –, grease- the palm; offer etc. 763; sacrifice, immolate.

Adj. giving etc. *v.*; given etc. *v.*; allow-ed, -able; concessional; communicable; charitable, eleemosynary, sportulary, tributary; *gratis* etc. 815.

785. Receiving.—N. receiving etc. *v.*; acquisition etc. 775; reception etc. (*introduction*) 296; suscipiency, acceptance, admission.

re-, ac-cipient; assignee, devisee; lega-tee, -tary; grantee, feoffee, donee, relessee, lessee.

sportulary, stipendiary; beneficiary; pension-er, · ary; almsman.

income etc. (*receipt*) 810.

v. receive; take etc. 789; acquire etc. 775; admit.

take in, catch, touch; pocket; put into one's - pocket, – purse; accept; take off one's hands.

be received; come -in, – to hand; pass –, fall- into one's hand; go into one's pocket; fall to one's lot, – share; come –, fall- to one; accrue; have - given etc. 784 to one.

Adj. receiving etc. *v.*; re-, suscipient.

received etc. *v.*; given etc. 784; second-hand.

not given, unbestowed etc. (*see* give, bestow etc. 784).

786. Apportionment.—N. apportion-, allot-, consign-, assign-, appoint-ment; appropriation; dispensation, -tribution; allocation, division, deal; repartition; administration.

dividend, portion, contingent, share, allotment, lot, cut, split, measure, dose; dole, meed, pittance; *quantum*, ration; ratio, proportion, quota, *modicum*, mess, allowance.

V. apportion, divide; cut, split, divvy; distribute, administer, dispense; billet, allot, detail, cast, share, mete; portion –, parcel –, dole- out; deal, carve.

partition, assign, appropriate, appoint.

come in for one's share etc. (*participate*) 778.

Adj. apportioning etc. *v.*; respective.

Adv. respectively, each to each.

787. Lending.—N. lending etc. *v.*; loan, advance, accommodation, feneration; mortgage etc. (*security*) 771; investment.

mont de piété, pawnshop, hock shop, spout, my uncle's.

lender, pawnbroker, money lender, usurer, Jew, Shylock.

V. lend, advance, loan, accommodate with; lend on security; pawn etc. (*security*) 771.

intrust, invest; place –, put- out to interest; sink, risk.

let, demise, lease, set, under-, sub-let.

Adj. lending etc. *v.*; lent etc. *v.*; unborrowed etc. (*see* borrowed etc. 788).

Adv. in advance; on -loan, – security.

788. Borrowing.—N. borrowing, pledging, pawning.

borrowed plumes; plagiarism etc. (*thieving*) 791.

replevin.

V. borrow, desume; pawn.

hire, rent, farm; take a -lease, – demise; take –, hire- by the -hour, – mile, – year etc.

raise –, take up- money; float bonds; raise the wind; fly a kite, borrow of Peter to pay Paul; run into debt etc. (*debt*) 806.

make use of, plagiarize, pirate.

replevy.

789. Taking.—N. taking etc. *v.*; reception etc. (*taking in*) 296; deglutition etc. (*taking food*) 298; appropriation, prehension, prensation; capture, caption; ap-, de-prehension; abreption, seizure; abduction, -lation; subtraction etc. (*subduction*) 38; abstraction, ademption.

dispossession; depriv-ation, -ement; bereavement; divestment; disherison; distraint, distress; sequestration, confiscation, attachment, execution; eviction etc. 297.

rapacity, extortion, vampirism, predacity, blood-sucking; theft etc. 791.

resumption; repris-e, -al; recovery etc. 775.

clutch, swoop, wrench; grip etc. (*retention*) 781; haul, take, catch; scramble.

taker, captor, capturer; vampire; extortioner.

V. take, catch, hook, nab, bag, sack, pocket, put into one's pocket, scrounge; receive; accept.

reap, crop, cull, pluck; gather etc. (*get*) 775; draw.

ap-, im-propriate; assume, possess oneself of; take possession of; commandeer; lay –, clap- one's hands on; help oneself to; make free with, dip one's hands into, lay under contribution; intercept; scramble for; deprive of.

take –, carry –, bear- -away, – off; abstract; hurry off –, run away- with; abduct; steal etc. 791; ravish; seize; pounce –, spring- upon; swoop -to, – down upon; take by -storm, – assault; snatch, reave.

snap up, nip up, whip up, catch up; kidnap, crimp, capture, lay violent hands on.

get –, lay –, take –, catch –, lay fast –, take firm- hold of; lay by the heels, take prisoner; fasten upon, grip, grapple, embrace, gripe, clasp, grab, clutch, collar, throttle, take by the throat, claw, clinch, clench, make sure of.

catch at, jump at, make a grab at, snap at, snatch at; reach, make a long arm, stretch forth one's hand.

take -from, – away from; deduct etc. 38; retrench etc. (*curtail*) 201; dispossess, ease one of, snatch from one's grasp; tear –, tear away –, wrench –, wrest –, wring- from; extort; deprive of, bereave; disinherit, cut off with a shilling.

oust etc. (*eject*) 297; divest, levy, distrain, confiscate; sequest-er, -rate, accroach; usurp; despoil, strip, fleece, shear, displume, impoverish, eat out of house and home; drain, – to the dregs; gut, dry, exhaust, swallow up; absorb etc. (*suck in*) 296; draw off; suck, – like a leech, – the blood of.

retake, resume; recover etc. 775.

Adj. taking etc. *v.*; privative, prehensile; pred-aceous, -al, -atory, -atorial; rap-acious, -torial; ravenous; parasitic; all-devouring, -engulfing.

bereft etc. 776.

Adv. at one fell swoop.

Phr. give an inch and take an ell.

790. Restitution.—N. restitution, return; ren-, red-dition; reinstatement, restoration; reinvestment, recuperation; repatriation; rehabilitation etc. (*reconstruction*) 660; reparation, atonement, indemnity, compensation, recompense.

release, replevin, redemption; recovery etc. (*getting back*) 775; remitter, reversion.

V. return, restore; recondition; give –, carry – bring- back; render, – up; give up; let go, un-clutch; dis-, re-gorge; regurgitate; recoup, reimburse, repay, indemnify, reinvest, remit, rehabilitate; repair etc. (*make good*) 660.

redeem, recover etc. (*get back*) 775; take back again; revest, revert.

Adj. restoring etc. *v.*; recuperative etc. 660; in full restitution, to compensate for.

Phr. *suum cuique*.

791. Stealing.—N. stealing etc. *v.*; theft, thievery, robbery, latrociny, direption; abstraction, appropriation; plagiar-y, -ism; rape, kidnapping, depredation; raid, hold up.

spoliation, plunder, pillage; sack, -age; rapine, *brigandage*, highway robbery, foray, *razzia*; black-mail; piracy, privateering, buccaneering; filibuster-ing, -ism; burglary; house-breaking; cattle-stealing, -rustling, -lifting.

peculation, embezzlement; fraud etc. 545; lar-ceny, petty larceny, pilfering, shop-lifting.

thievishness, rapacity, kleptomania, Alsatia; den of -Cacus, – thieves.

license to plunder, letters of marque.

V. steal, thieve, rob, purloin, pilfer, filch, lift, prig, bag, nim, crib, cabbage, palm; abstract; appropriate, plagiarize.

convey away, carry off, abduct, kidnap, shanghai, impress, crimp; make –, walk –, run-off with; run away with; spirit away; seize etc. (*lay violent hands on*) 789.

plunder, pillage, rifle, sack, loot, ransack, spoil, spoliate, despoil, strip, sweep, gut, forage, levy black-mail, pirate, pickeer, maraud, lift cattle, rustle, poach, smuggle, run.

stick –, hold- up.

swindle, peculate, embezzle; sponge, mulct, rook, bilk, pluck, pigeon, skin, fleece, diddle; defraud etc. 545; obtain under false pretences; live by one's wits.

rob –, borrow of- Peter to Paul; set a thief to catch a thief.

disregard the distinction between *meum* and *tuum*.

Adj. thieving etc. *v.*; thievish, light-fingered; fur-acious, -tive; piratical; pred-aceous, -al, -atory, -atorial; raptorial etc. (*rapacious*) 789.

stolen etc. *v.*

Phr. *sic vos non vobis*.

792. Thief.—N. thief, robber, *homo trium literarum*, pilferer, rifler, filcher, plagiarist.

spoiler, depredator, pillager, marauder; harpy, shark, land-shark, falcon, moss-trooper, bushranger, Bedouin, brigand, freebooter, bandit, thug, dacoit, pirate, corsair, viking, Paul Jones; buccan-eer, -ier; piqu-, pick-eerer; rover, ranger, privateer, filibuster; rapparee, wrecker, picaroon; smuggler, poacher, plunderer; racketeer.

highwayman, Dick Turpin, Claude Duval, Macheath, knight of the road, footpad, sturdy beggar; abductor, kidnapper.

cut-, pick-purse; pick-pocket, light-fingered gen-try; sharper; card-, skittle-sharper; crook; thimble-rigger; rook, Greek, blackleg, leg, welsher, defaulter; Autolycus, Cacus, Barabbas, Jeremy Diddler; Robert Macaire, artful dodger, trickster; swell mob, *chevalier d'industrie*; shop-lifter.

swindler, peculator; forger, coiner, counterfeiter, shoful; fence, receiver of stolen goods, duffer; smasher.

burglar, housebreaker; cracks-, mags-man; Bill Sikes, Jack Sheppard, Jonathan Wild, Raffles, cat burglar.

793. Booty.—N. booty, spoil, plunder, price, loot, graft, swag, pickings, boodle; *spolia opima*, prey; blackmail; stolen goods.

Adj. looting etc. *n.*; manubial, spoliative.

794. Barter.—N. barter, exchange, scorse, truck system; interchange etc. 148.

a Roland for an Oliver; *quid pro quo*; com-mutation, -position.

trade, commerce, mercature, buying and selling, bargain and sale; traffic, business, nundination, custom, shopping; commercial enterprise, speculation, jobbing, stock-jobbing, *agiotage*, brokery, arbitrage.

dealing, transaction, negotiation, bargain.

free trade.

V. barter, exchange, truck, scorse, swop; in-terchange etc. 148; commutate etc. (*substitute*) 147; compound for.

trade, traffic, buy and sell, give and take, nun-dinate; carry on –, ply –, drive- a trade; be in -

business, – the city; keep a shop, deal in, employ one's capital in.

trade –, deal –, have dealings- with; transact –, do- business with; open –, keep- an account with.

bargain; drive –, make- a bargain; negotiate, bid for; dicker, haggle, higgle; chaffer, huckster, cheapen, beat down; stickle, – for; out-, under-bid; ask, charge; strike a bargain etc. (*contract*) 769.

speculate, give a sprat to catch a herring; buy in the cheapest and sell in the dearest market; rig the market.

Adj. commercial, mercantile, trading; inter-changeable, marketable, staple, in the market, for sale.

wholesale, retail.

Adv. across the counter; on 'change.

795. Purchase.—N. purchase, emption; buying, purchasing, shopping; pre-emption, refusal.

coemption, bribery; slave trade.

buyer, purchaser, *emptor*, vendee; patron, employer, client, customer, *clientèle*.

V. buy, purchase, invest in, procure; rent etc. (*hire*) 788; repurchase, buy in.

keep in one's pay, bribe, suborn; pay etc. 807; spend etc. 809.

make –, complete- a purchase; buy over the counter; pay cash for.

shop, market, go a shopping.

Adj. purchased etc. *v.*

Phr. *caveat emptor.*

796. Sale.—N. sale, vent, disposal; auction, roup, Dutch auction; custom etc. (*traffic*) 794.

vendi-bility, -bleness.

seller, salesman; peddler, smous; vender, vendor, consignor; merchant etc. 797; auctioneer.

V. sell, vend, dispose of, effect a sale; sell -over the counter, – by auction etc. *n.*; dispense, retail; deal in etc. 794; sell -off, – out; turn into money; realize; bring -to, – under- the hammer; put up to auction; auction, offer –, put up- for sale; hawk, peddle, bring to market; offer etc. 763; undersell; dump, unload.

let; mortgage etc. (*security*) 771.

Adj. under the hammer, in the market, for sale.

saleable, marketable, vendible, in demand, having a ready sale; unsaleable etc., unpurchased, unbought; on one's hands.

797. Merchant.—N. merchant, trader, dealer, monger, chandler, salesman; changer; regrater; shop-keeper, -man; trades-man, -people, -folk.

retailer; chapman, hawker, huckster, higgler; peddler, smous, pedlar, *colporteur*, cadger, Autolycus; sutler, *vivandière*; coster-man, -monger; market woman; cheap jack; caterer etc. 637; tallyman.

money-broker, -changer, -lender; stock-broker, -jobber; cambist, usurer, moneyer, banker.

jobber; broker etc. (*agent*) 758; buyer etc. 795; seller etc. 796.

concern; firm etc. (*partnership*) 712.

798. Merchandise.—N. merchandise, ware, commodity, effects, goods, article, stock, produce, staple commodity; stock in trade etc. (*store*) 636; cargo etc. (*contents*) 190.

799. Mart.—N. mart; market, -place, *forum*; fair, bazaar, staple; stock –, exchange; 'change, bourse, Wall Street, Rialto, hall, guildhall; toll-booth, custom-house; Tattersalls.

shop, stall, booth; wharf; office, chambers, counting-house, *bureau*; coun-, comp-ter.

ware-house, -room; *dépôt*, interposit, *entrepôt*, *emporium*, establishment; store etc. 636.

open market, market-overt.

800. Money.—N. money -matters, – market; finance; accounts etc. 811; funds, treasure; capital, stock; assets etc. (*property*) 780; wealth etc. 803; supplies, ways and means, wherewithal, sinews of war, almighty dollar, needful, cash.

sum, amount; balance, -sheet; sum total; proceeds etc. (*receipts*) 810.

currency, circulating medium, specie; coin, – of the realm; piece, hard cash, dollar, sterling coin; pounds, shillings and pence; L. s. d.; guineas; pocket, breeches pocket, purse; money in hand; the best, ready, – money; filthy lucre, shekels, roll, jack, rhino, blunt, dust, bawbees, brass, dibs, dough, mopus, tin, salt, chink, oof, spondulics, pile, wads.

precious metals, gold, silver, copper, nickel; bullion, bar, ingot, nugget.

petty cash; pocket-, pin-money; small –, change; small coin, loose cash; doit, stiver, rap, mite, farthing, *sou*, penny, shilling, bob, tanner, tester, groat, guinea, ducat; *rouleau*; *wampum*; good –, round –, lump- sum; power –, mint –, tons- of money; plum, lac of rupees, millions, money-bags, miser's hoard, stocking, mine of wealth etc. 803.

[Science of coins] numismatics, chrysology.

paper-money; money –, postal –, Post Office-order; note, – of hand; bank –, treasury- note; Bradbury; promissory note; I.O.U., bond; bill, – of exchange; draft, check, order, warrant, *coupon*, debenture, exchequer bill, *assignat*, greenback, gold –, silver- certificate.

copper, nickel, dime, quarter, two bits, half a dollar, dollar, buck, simoleon, fiver, tenner, a twenty, a sawbuck, a century, a grand; eagle, double eagle.

gold standard, bimetallism, fiat money; rate of –, exchange; in-, de-flation.

remittance etc. (*payment*) 807; credit etc. 805; liability etc. 806; solvency etc. 803.

draw-er, -ee; oblig-or, -ee; moneyer, coiner, counterfeiter, forger.

false –, bad- money; base –, counterfeit- coin, flash note, slip, kite; Bank of Elegance.

argumentum ad crumenam.

V. amount to, come to, mount up to; touch the pocket; draw, – upon; endorse etc. (*security*) 771; issue, utter, circulate; discount etc. 813.

forge, counterfeit, coin, circulate –, pass- bad money.

Adj. monetary, pecuniary, crumenal, fiscal, financial, sumptuary, numismatical; sterling; solvent etc. 803.

801. Treasurer.—N. treasurer; bursar, -y; purser, purse-bearer; cash-keeper, banker; depositary; questor, receiver, steward, trustee, chartered –, accountant; Accountant-General, almoner, liquidator, paymaster, cashier, teller; cambist; money-changer etc. (*merchant*) 797.

financier, Chancellor of the Exchequer, minister of finance; Secretary of the Treasury, Director of the Budget, Controller of Currency.

802. Treasury.—N. treasury, bank, exchequer, almonry, fisc, hanaper, bursary; safe; strong-box, -hold, -room; coffer; chest etc. (*receptacle*) 191; depository etc. 636; till, -er; cash-box, -register, purse, pocketbook, wallet; money-bag, -belt, -box, *porte-monnaie*.

purse-strings; pocket, breeches pocket.

sinking fund; stocks; government –, public –, parliamentary- -stocks, – funds, – securities, bonds; gild-edged securities; Consols, Liberty bonds, government bonds, *crédit mobilier*.

803. Wealth.—N. wealth, riches, fortune, handsome fortune, opulence, affluence; good –, easy- circumstances; independence; competence etc. (*sufficiency*) 639; solvency, soundness, solidity.

provision, livelihood, maintenance; alimony, dowry; means, resources, substance; property etc. 780; command of money.

income etc. 810; capital, money; round sum etc. (*treasure*) 800; mint of money, mine of wealth. *El Dorado*, Pactolus, Golconda, Potosi, *bonanza*; philosopher's stone.

long –, full –, well lined –, heavy- purse; purse of Fortunatus.

pelf, Mammon, lucre, filthy lucre; loaves and fishes; fleshpots of Egypt.

rich –, moneyed –, warm- man; man of substance; capitalist, millionaire, Nabob, Croesus, Midas, Plutus, Dives, Timon of Athens; Timo-, Pluto-cracy; Danaë.

V. be -rich etc. *adj.*; roll –, wallow- in -wealth. – riches; have money to burn.

afford, well afford; command -money, – a sum; make both ends meet, hold one's head above water.

become -rich etc. *adj.*; fill one's -pocket etc. (*treasury*) 802; feather one's nest, clean up –, make- a fortune; make money etc. (*acquire*) 775.

enrich, imburse.

worship -Mammon, – the golden calf.

Adj. wealthy, rich, affluent, opulent, moneyed, monied, worth -a great deal, – much; well -to do, – off; warm; well –, provided for.

made of money; rich as Croesus; rolling in -riches, – wealth.

flush, – of -cash, – money, – tin; in -funds, – cash, – full feather; solvent, solid, sound, pecunious, out of debt, all straight; able to pay 20s in the L.

Phr. one's ship coming in.

804. Poverty.—N. poverty, indigence, penury, pauperism, destitution, want; need, -iness; lack,

necessity, privation, distress, difficulties, wolf at the door.

bad –, poor –, needy –, embarrassed –, reduced –, straitened- circumstances; slender –, narrow- means; straits; hand to mouth existence, *res angusta domi*, low water, impecuniosity.

beggary; mendi-cancy, -city; broken –, loss of- fortune; insolvency etc. (*non-payment*) 808.

empty -purse, – pocket; light purse; beggarly account of empty boxes.

poor man, pauper, mendicant, mumper, beggar, starveling; *pauvre diable*.

V. be -poor etc. *adj.*; want, lack, starve, live from hand to mouth, have seen better days, go down in the world, be on one's uppers, come upon the parish; go to -the dogs, – wrack and ruin; not have a -penny etc. (*money*) 800, – shot in one's locker; beg one's bread; *tirer le diable par la queue*; run into debt etc. (*debt*) 806.

render -poor etc. *adj.*; impoverish; reduce, – to poverty, pauperize, fleece, ruin, bring to the parish.

Adj. poor, indigent; poverty-striken; badly –, poorly –, ill- off; poor as -a rat, – a church mouse, – Job's turkey, – Job; fortune-, dower-, money-, penni-less; unportioned, unmoneyed; impecunious; broke, flat; out –, short- of -money, – cash; without –, not worth- a rap etc. (*money*) 800; *qui n'a pas le sou*, out of pocket, hard up; out at -elbows, – heels; seedy, bare-footed; beggar-ly, -ed; destitute; fleeced, strapped, stripped; bereft, bereaved; reduced.

in -want etc. *n.*; needy, necessitous, distressed, pinched, straitened; put to one's -shifts, – last shifts; unable to -keep the wolf from the door, – make both ends meet; embarrassed, under hatches; involved etc. (*in debt*) 806; insolvent etc. (*not paying*) 808.

Adv. in formâ pauperis.

Phr. zonam perdidit.

805. Credit.—N. credit, trust, tick, score, tally, account.

letter of credit, circular note; duplicate; mortgage, lien, debenture, paper credit, floating capital; draft; securities.

creditor, lender, lessor, mortgagee; dun; usurer.

V. keep –, run up- an account with; entrust, credit, accredit.

place to one's -credit, – account; give –, take-credit; fly a kite.

Adj. credit-ing, -ed; accredited.

Adv. on -credit etc. *n.*; to the -account, – credit- of.

806. Debt.—N. debt, obligation, liability, indebtment, debit, score.

arrears, deferred payment, deficit, default; insolvency etc. (*non-payment*) 808; bad debt.

interest; usance, usury; premium; floating -debt, – capital.

debtor, debitor; mortgagor; defaulter etc. 808; borrower.

V. be -in debt etc. *adj.*; owe; incur –, contract- a debt etc. *n.*; run up -a bill, – a score, – an account; go on tick, put on the cuff; borrow etc. 788; run –, get- into debt; outrun the constable.

answer –, go bail- for; back one's note.

Adj. indebted; liable, chargeable, answerable for.

in -debt, – embarrassed circumstances, – difficulties; incumbered, involved; involved –, plunged –, deep –, over head and ears- in debt; deeply involved; fast tied up; insolvent etc. (*not paying*) 808; *minus*, out of pocket.

unpaid; unrequieted, unrewarded; owing, due, in arrear, outstanding.

807. Payment.—N. pay-, defray-ment; discharge; ac-, quittance; settlement, clearance, liquidation, satisfaction, reckoning, arrangement.

acknowledgment, release; receipt, – in full, – in full of all demands; voucher.

repayment, reimbursement, retribution; pay etc. (*reward*) 973; money paid etc. (*expenditure*) 809.

ready money etc. (*cash*) 800; stake, remittance, instalment.

payer, liquidator etc. 801.

V. pay, defray, make payment; pay -down, – on the nail, – ready money, – at sight, – in advance; cash, honor a bill, acknowledge; redeem; pay in kind.

pay one's -way, – shot, – footing;' pay -the piper, – sauce for all, – costs; do the needful; come across; shell –, fork- out; come down with, – the dust; tickle –, grease- the palm; expend etc. 809; put –, lay- down.

discharge, settle, quit, acquit oneself of; account –, reckon –, settle –, be even –, be quits- with; strike a balance; settle –, balance –, square- accounts with; quit scores; foot the bill; wipe –, clear- off old scores; satisfy; pay in full; satisfy –, pay in full of- all demands; clear, liquidate; pay -up, – old debts.

disgorge, make repayment; repay, refund, reimburse, retribute; make compensation etc. 30.

Adj. paying etc., paid etc. *v.*; owing nothing, out of debt, all straight, clear of -debt, – encumbrance; unowed, never indebted.

Adv. to the tune of; on the nail; money –, cash- down; cash on delivery.

808. Non-payment.—N. non-payment; default, defalcation; protest, repudiation; application of the sponge; whitewashing.

insolvency, bankruptcy, failure; overdraft, overdrawn account; insufficiency etc. 640; run upon a bank.

waste paper bonds; dishonored – protested- bills; bogus cheque.

bankrupt, insolvent debtor, lame duck, man of straw, welsher, stag, defaulter, absconder, levanter.

V. non -pay etc. 807; fail, break, stop payment; become -insolvent, – bankrupt; be gazetted.

protest, dishonor, repudiate, nullify.

pay under protest; button up one's pockets, draw the purse strings; apply the sponge; pay over the left shoulder, get whitewashed; swindle etc. 791; run up bills, fly kites.

Adj. not paying; in debt etc. 806; behindhand, in arrear; beggared etc. (*poor*) 804; unable to make both ends meet; *minus*; worse than nothing.

insolvent, bankrupt, in the gazette, gazetted, ruined.

unpaid etc. (*outstanding*) 806; *gratis* etc. 815; unremunerated.

809. Expenditure.—N. expenditure, money going out; out-goings, -lay; expenses, disbursement; prime cost etc. (*price*) 812; circulation; run upon a bank.

[Money paid] payment etc. 807; pay etc. (*remuneration*) 973; bribe etc. 973; fee, footing, garnish; subsidy; tribute, Peter's pence; contingent, quota; donation etc. 784.

pay in advance, earnest, handsel, deposit, instalment.

investment; purchase etc. 795.

V. expend, spend; run –, get- through; pay, disburse; open –, loose –, untie- the purse strings; lay –, shell –, fork- out; bleed; make up a sum, invest, sink money.

fee etc. (*reward*) 973; pay one's way etc. (*pay*) 807; subscribe etc. (*give*) 784; subsidize, bribe.

Adj. expend-ing, -ed etc. *v.*; sumptuary, liberal etc. 816; openhanded, lavish etc. 818; extensive etc. 814.

810. Receipt—N. receipt, accountable –, conditional –, binding –, return- receipt; value received, money coming in; income, incomings, innings, revenue, return, proceeds; gross receipts, net profit; earnings etc. (*gain*) 775.

rent, – roll; rent-al, -age; rack-rent.

premium, *bonus*; sweepstakes, tontine, prize, drawing.

pension, annuity; jointure etc. (*property*) 780; alimony, pittance; emolument etc. (*remuneration*) 973.

V. receive etc. 785; take money; draw –, derive- from; get, be in receipt of, acquire etc. 775; take etc. 789.

bring in, yield, afford, pay, return; accrue etc. (*be received from*) 785.

Adj. receiv-ing, -ed etc. *v.*; profitable etc. (*gainful*) 775.

811. Accounts.—N. accounts, accompts; commercial –, monetary- arithmetic; statistics etc. (*numeration*) 85; money matters, finance, budget, bill, score, reckoning, account.

books, account book, ledger; day –, cash –, pass- book; journal; debtor and creditor –, cash –, petty cash –, running- account; account-current; balance, – sheet; *compte rendu*, account settled.

book-keeping, audit; double –, single- entry; reckoning etc. 85.

chartered –, certified public –, accountant; auditor, actuary, bookkeeper; financier etc. 801; accounting party.

V. keep accounts, enter, post, book, credit, debit, carry over; take stock; balance –, make up –, square –, settle –, wind up –, cast up –, add up –, tot up- accounts; make accounts square.

bring to book, audit, tax, surcharge and falsify.

falsify –, garble –, cook –, doctor- an account.

Adj. monetary etc. 800; account-able, -ing; statistical.

812. Price.—N. price, amount, cost, expense, prime cost, charge, figure, demand, damage, fare, hire; wages etc. (*remuneration*) 973.

dues, duty, toll, tax, impost, cess, sess, tallage, levy, capitation-, poll-, income-, sur-, sales-, super-tax; gabel, *gabelle*; gavel, *octroi*, custom, tariff, excise, assessment, taxation, benevolence, tithe, tenths, exactment, ransom, salvage; broker-, wharf-, lighter-, ton-, freight-age.

worth, rate, value, valuation, appraisement, money's worth, par value; penny etc. -worth; price current, market price, quotation; what it will -fetch etc. *v.*

bill etc. (*account*) 811; shot.

V. bear –, set –, fix- a price; appraise, assess, price, charge, demand, ask, require, exact, run up; distrain; run up a bill etc. (*debt*) 806; have one's price; liquidate.

amount to, come to, mount up to; stand one in, fetch, sell for, cost, bring in, yield, afford.

Adj. priced etc. *v.*; to the tune of, *ad valorem*; mercenary, venal.

Phr. no penny, no paternoster; *point d'argent, point de Suisse*, no longer pipe, no longer dance, no song, no supper.

one may have it for.

813. Discount.—N. discount, abatement, concession, reduction, depreciation, allowance, qualification, set off, drawback, poundage, *agio*, percentage; rebate, -ment; backwardation, contango; salvage; tare and tret.

V. discount, bate; a-, re-bate; deduct, reduce, mark down, take off, allow, give, make allowance; tax, depreciate.

Adj. discounting etc. *v.*

Adv. at a discount, below par.

814. Dearness.—N. dearness etc. *adj.*; high –, famine –, fancy- price; overcharge; extravagance; exorbitance, extortion; heavy pull upon the purse; Pyrrhic victory.

V. be -dear etc. *adj.*; cost -much, – a pretty penny; rise in price, look up.

overcharge, bleed, fleece, skin, extort.

pay -too much, – through the nose, –, too dear for one's whistle.

Adj. dear; high, -priced; of great price, expensive, costly, precious, worth a Jew's eye, dear bought; unreasonable, extravagant, exorbitant, extortionate.

at a premium; not to be had, – for love or money; beyond –, above- price; priceless, of, priceless value.

Adv. dear, -ly; at great –, heavy- cost; *à grands frais*.

Phr. prices looking up; *le jeu ne vaut pas la chandelle*.

815. Cheapness.—N. cheapness, low price; depreciation; bargain; good penny etc.- worth, *bon marché*.

[Absence of charge] gratuity; free -quarters, – seats, – admission, – warren; pass, Annie Oakley; 'run of one's teeth; nominal price, peppercorn rent; labor of love.

drug in the market.

V. be -cheap etc. *adj.*; cost little; come down –, fall- in price.

buy for -a mere nothing, – an old song; have one's money's worth; cheapen, beat down.

Adj. cheap; low, – priced; moderate, reasonable; in-, un-expensive; well –, worth the money; *magnifique et pas cher*; good –, cheap- at the price; dirt –, dog- cheap; cheap, -as dirt, – and nasty; catchpenny.

reduced, marked down, half-price, depreciated, unsaleable.

gratuitous, *gratis*, free, for love, – nothing; cost-expense-less; without charge, not charged, un-taxed; scot –, shot –, rent- free; free of -cost, – expense; honorary, unbought, unpaid, complimentary.

Adv. for a mere song; at -cost price, – prime cost, – a reduction, – a bargain; on the cheap.

816. Liberality.—N. liberality, generosity, munificence; bount-y, -eousness, -ifulness; hospitality; charity etc. (*beneficence*) 906.

benefactor, free giver, Lady Bountiful.

V. be -liberal etc. *adj.*; spend –, bleed- freely; shower down upon; open one's purse strings etc. (*disburse*) 809; spare no expense, give -with both hands, – *carte blanche*.

Adj. liberal, free, generous; charitable etc. (*beneficent*) 906; hospitable; bount-iful, -eous; handsome; unsparing, ungrudging; open-, free-, full-handed; open-, large-, free-hearted; munificent, princely, unstinting.

overpaid.

Adv. liberally, ungrudgingly, with open hand.

817. Economy.—N. economy, frugality; thrift, -iness; prudence, care, husbandry, good housewifery, savingness, retrenchment.

savings; prevention of waste, save-all; cheese parings and candle ends; parsimony etc. 819.

V. be -economical etc. *adj.*; economize, save; retrench; cut- down expenses, – one's coat according to one's cloth, make both ends meet, keep within compass, meet one's expenses, pay one's way; keep one's head above water; husband etc. (*lay by*) 636; save –, invest- money; put out to interest; provide –, save- -for, – against- a rainy day; feather one's nest; look after the main chance.

Adj. economical, frugal, careful, thrifty, saving, chary, spare, sparing; parsimonious etc. 819.

underpaid.

Adv. sparingly etc. *adj.*; *ne quid nimis*.

818. Prodigality.—N. prodi-gality, -gence; un-thriftiness, waste, -fulness; profus-ion, -eness; extravagance; squandering etc. *v.*; lavishness; malversation.

prodigal; spend-, waste-thrift; losel, play-boy, spender, squanderer, locust.

V. be -prodigal etc. *adj.*; squander, lavish, sow broadcast; pour forth like water; pay through the nose etc. (*dear*) 814; spill, waste, dissipate, exhaust, drain, eat out of house and home, overdraw, outrun the constable; run -out, – through; misspend; throw -good money after bad, – the helve after the hatchet; burn the candle at both ends; make ducks and drakes of one's money;

squander one's substance, spend money like water; fool –, potter –, muddle –, fritter –, throwaway one's money; pour water into a sieve, kill the goose that lays the golden eggs; *manger son blé en herbe*.

Adj. prodigal, profuse, thriftless, unthrifty, improvident, wasteful, losel, extravagant, lavish, dissipated, over liberal; full-handed etc. (*liberal*) 816.

penny wise and pound foolish.

Adv. with an unsparing hand; money burning one's pocket; recklessly profuse.

Int. hang the expense!

819. Parsimony.—**N.** parsimony, parcity; parsimoniousness, stinginess etc. *adj.*; stint; illiberality, avarice, tenacity, avidity, rapacity, extortion, venality, cupidity; selfishness etc. 943; *auri sacra fames*.

miser, niggard, churl, screw, tightwad, skinflint, crib, codger, muckworm, money-grubber, pinchfist, scrimp, lickpenny, hunks, curmudgeon, *Harpagon*, Silas Marner, harpy, extortioner, Jew, usurer.

V. be -parsimonious etc. *adj.*; grudge, begrudge, stint, skimp, pinch, gripe, screw, dole out, hold back, withhold, starve, famish, live upon nothing, skin a flint.

drive a -bargain, – hard bargain; cheapen, beat down; stop one hole in a sieve; have an itching palm, grasp, grab.

Adj. parsimonious, penurious, stingy, miserly, mean, shabby, peddling, scrubby, pennywise, near, niggardly, frugal to excess; close; fast-, close-, strait-handed; close-, hard-, tight-fisted; tight, sparing; chary; grudging, griping etc. *v.*; illiberal, ungenerous, churlish, hidebound, sordid, mercenary, venal, covetous, usurious, avaricious, greedy, extortionate, rapacious.

Adv. with a sparing hand.

820. Affections.—**N.** affections, character, qualities, disposition, nature, spirit, tone; temper, -ament; *diathesis*, idiosyncrasy; cast –, habit –, frame- of -mind, – soul; predilection, turn; natural –, turn of mind; bent, bias, predisposition, proneness, proclivity; propen-sity, -sedness, -sion, -dency; vein, humor, mood, grain, mettle; sympathy etc. (*love*) 897.

soul, heart, breast, bosom, inner man; heart's -core, – strings, – blood; heart of hearts, *penetralia mentis*; secret and inmost recesses of the –, cockles of one's- heart; inmost -heart, – soul; back-bone.

passion, pervading spirit; ruling –, master-passion; *furore*; fulness of the heart, heyday of the blood, flesh and blood, flow of soul, force of character.

V. have –, possess- -affections etc. *n.*; be of a -character etc. *n.*; be -affected etc. *adj.*; breathe.

Adj. affected, characterized, formed, molded, cast; at-, tempered; framed; pre-, disposed; prone, inclined; having a -bias etc. *n.*; tinctured –, imbued –, penetrated –, eaten up- with.

inborn, inbred, ingrained, in the grain, congenital, inherent, bred in the bone; deep-rooted, ineffaceable, inveterate; pathoscopic.

Adv. in one's -heart etc. *n.*; at heart; heart and soul etc. 821; in the -vein, – mood.

821. Feeling.—**N.** feeling; suffering etc. *v.*; endurance, tolerance, sufferance, supportance, experience, response; sympathy etc. (*love*) 897; impression, inspiration, affection, sensation, emotion, pathos, deep sense.

fire, warmth, glow, unction, *gusto*, vehemence; ferv-or, -ency; heartiness, cordiality; earnestness, eagerness; *empressment*, ardor, zeal, passion, enthusiasm, *verve*, *furore*, fanaticism; excitation of feeling etc. 824; · fulness of the heart etc. (*disposition*) 820; passion etc. (*state of excitability*) 825; ecstasy etc. (*pleasure*) 827.

blush, suffusion, flush; hectic; tingling, thrill, kick, turn, shock; agitation etc. (*irregular motion*) 315; quiver, heaving, flutter, flurry, fluster, twitter, tremor; throb, -bing; pulsation, palpitation, painting; trepid-, perturb-ation; ruffle, hurry of spirits, pother, stew, ferment.

V. feel; receive an -impression etc. *n.*; be -impressed with etc. *adj.*; entertain –, harbor –, cherish- -feeling etc. *n.*

respond; catch the -flame, – infection; enter the spirit of.

bear, suffer, support, sustain, endure, brook, thole, aby; abide etc. (*be composed*) 826; experience etc. (*meet with*) 151; taste, prove; labor –, smart- under; bear the brunt of, brave, stand.

swell, glow, warm, flush, blush, change color, mantle; turn -color, – pale, – red, – black in the face; blench; crimson, whiten, pale, tingle, thrill, heave, pant, throb, palpitate, go pit-a-pat, tremble, quiver, flutter, twitter; stagger, reel; shake etc. 315; be -agitated, – excited etc. 824; look -blue, – black; wince, draw a deep breath.

impress etc. (*excite the feelings*) 824.

Adj. feeling etc. *v.*; sentient; sensuous; sensorial, -y; emo-tive, -tional; of –, with- feeling etc. *n.*

warm, quick, lively, smart, strong, sharp, acute, cutting, piercing, incisive; keen, – as a razor; trenchant, pungent, racy, *piquant*, poignant, caustic.

impressive, deep, profound, indelible; deep-, home-, heart-felt; swelling, soul-stirring, deep-mouthed, heart-expanding, electric, thrilling, rapturous, ecstatic.

earnest, wistful, eager, breathless; fer-vent, -vid; gushing, passionate, warmhearted, hearty, cordial, sincere, zealous, enthusiastic, glowing, ardent, burning, red-hot, fiery, flaming; boiling, – over.

pervading, penetrating, absorbing; rabid, raving, feverish, fanatical, hysterical; impetuous etc. (*excitable*) 825; overmastering.

impressed –, moved –, touched –, affected –, penetrated –, seized –, imbued etc. 820-with; devoured by; wrought up etc. (*excited*) 824; struck all of a heap; rapt; in a -quiver etc. *n.*; enraptured etc. 829.

Adv. heart and soul, from the bottom of one's heart, *ab imo pectore, de profundis*, at heart, *con amore*, heartily, devoutly, over head and ears.

Phr. the heart -big, – full, – swelling, – beating, – pulsating, – throbbing, – thumping, – beating high, – melting, – overflowing, – bursting, – breaking.

822. Sensibility.—**N.** sensi-bility, -bleness, -tiveness; moral sensibility; impress-, affect-ibility; suscepti-bleness, -bility, -vity; mobility; viva-city, -ciousness; tender-, soft-ness; sentiment-al-ity, -ism.

excitability etc. 825; fastidiousness etc. 868; physical sensibility etc. 375.

sore -point, − place; where the shoe pinches.
V. be -sensible etc. *adj.*; have a -tender, −
warm. − sensitive- heart.

take to −, treasure up in the- heart; shrink.
'die of a rose in aromatic pain;' touch to the
quick.

Adj. sensi-ble, -tive; impressi-ble, -onable;
suscepti-ve, -ble; alive to, impassion-able, -ed;
gushing; warm-, tender-, soft-hearted; tender −, as
a chicken; soft, sentimental, romantic; enthusiastic,
highflying, spirited, mettlesome, vivacious, lively,
expressive, mobile, tremblingly alive; excitable etc.
825; over-sensitive, without skin, thin-skinned;
fastidious etc. 868.

Adv. sensibly etc. *adj.*; to the -quick, − inmost
core.

823. Insensibility.—N. insensi-bility, -bleness;
moral insensibility; inertness, *inertia, vis inertiae*;
impassi-bility, -bleness; inappetency, apathy,
phlegm, dulness, hebetude, supineness, lukewarmness, insusceptibility, unimpressibility.

cold -fit, − blood, − heart; cold-, cool-ness;
frigidity, *sang-froid*; stoicism, imperturbation etc.
(*inexcitability*) 826; *nonchalance,* unconcern, dry
eyes; *insouciance* etc. (*indifference*) 866;
recklessness etc. 863; callousness; heart of stone,
stock and stone, marble, deadness.

torp-or, -idity; obstupefaction, lethargy, coma,
trance; sleep etc. 683; suspended animation; stup-
or, -efaction; paralysis, palsy; numbness etc.
(*physical insensibility*) 376.

neutrality; quietism, vegetation.

V. be -insensible etc. *adj.*; have a rhinoceros
hide; show -insensibility etc *n.*; not -mind, − care,
− be affected by; have no desire for etc. 866; have
−, feel −, take- no interest in; *nil admirari*; not care
a -straw etc. (*unimportance*) 643 for; disregard etc.
(*neglect*) 460; set at naught etc. (*make light of*)
483; turn a deaf ear to etc. (*inattention*) 458;
vegetate.

render -insensible, − callous; blunt, obtund,
numb, benumb, paralyze, chloroform, deaden,
hebetate, stun, stupefy; brut-ify, -alize.

inure; harden, − the heart; steel, case-harden,
sear.

Adj. insensible, unconscious; impassi-ve, -ble;
blind to, deaf to, dead to; un-, in-susceptible; unim-
press-ionable, -ible; passion-, spirit-, heart-, soulless; unfeeling, unmoral.

apathetic; leuco-, phlegmatic; dull, frigid; cold, -
blooded, -hearted; unemotional; cold as charity;
flat, obtuse, inert, supine, sluggish, torpid; sleepy
etc. (*inactive*) 683; languid, half-hearted; tame;
numb, -ed; comatose; anesthetic etc. 376;
stupefied, chloroformed, palsy-stricken.

indifferent, lukewarm; Laodicean; careless, mindless, regardless; inattentive etc. 458; neglectful
etc. 460; disregarding.

unconcerned, *nonchalant, pococurante, insouciant, sans souci*; unambitious etc. 866.

un-affected, -ruffled, -impressed, -inspired, -
excited, -moved, -stirred, -touched, -shocked, -
struck; unblushing etc. (*shameless*) 885;
unanimated; vegetative.

callous, thick-skinned, pachydermatous, impervious; hard, -ened; inured, case-hardened;
steeled −, proof- against; imperturbable etc. (*inexcitable*) 826; unfelt.

Adv. insensibly etc. *adj.*; *aequo animo*; without
being -moved, − touched, − impressed; in cold
blood; with -dry eyes, − withers unwrung.

Phr. never mind; it is of no consequence etc.
(*unimportant*) 643; it cannot be helped; nothing
coming amiss; it is all -the same, − one- to.

824. Excitation.—N. excitation of feeling;
mental −, excitement; suscitation, galvanism,
stimulation, piquancy, provocation inspiration,
calling forth, infection; interest, animation,
agitation, perturbation; subjugation, fascination,
intoxication; en−, ravishment; entrancement, high
pressure.

unction, impressiveness etc. *adj.*; emotional appeal; melodrama; psychological moment, crisis;
sensationalism.

trail of temper, *casus belli*; irritation etc. (*anger*)
900; passion etc. (*state of excitability*) 825; thrill
etc. (*feeling*) 821; repression of feeling etc. 826.

V. excite, affect, touch, move, impress, strike, interest, intrigue, animate, inspire, impassion, smite,
infect; stir −, fire −, warm- the blood; set astir; a-,
wake; a-, waken; call forth; e-, pro-voke; raise up,
summon up, call up, wake up, blow up, get up,
light up; raise; get up steam, rouse, arouse, stir, fire,
kindle, enkindle, apply the torch, set on fire, inflame, illuminate.

stimulate; ex-, suscitate; inspirit; spirit up, stir up,
work up; infuse life into, five new life to; bring −,
introduce- new blood; quicken, sharpen, whet;
work upon etc. (*incite*) 615; hurry on, give a fillip,
put on one's mettle.

fan the -fire, − flame; blow the coals, stir the
embers; fan, − into a flame; foster, heat, warm,
foment, raise to a fever heat; keep -up, − the pot
boiling; revive, rekindle; rake up, rip up.

stir −, play on −, come home to- the feelings;
touch -a string, − a chord, − the soul, − the
heart; go to one's heart, penetrate, pierce, go
through one, touch to the quick, open the wound;
possess −, pervade −, penetrate −, imbrue −,
absorb −, affect −, disturb- the soul.

absorb, rivet the attention; sink into the -mind,
− heart; prey on the mind; intoxicate; over-whelm,
-power; *bouleverser*, upset, turn one's head.

fascinate; enrapture etc. (*give pleasure*) 829.

agitate, perturb, ruffle, fluster, flutter, shake,
disturb, faze, startle, shock, stagger; give one a -
shock, − turn; strike -dumb. − all of a heap; stun,
astound, electrify, galvanize, petrify.

irritate, sting; cut, − to the -heart, − quick; try
one's temper; fool to the top of one's bent, pique;
infuriate, madden, make one's blood boil; lash into
fury etc. (*wrath*) 900.

be -excited etc. *adj.*; flash up, flare up; catch the
infection; thrill etc. (*feel*) 821; mantle; work
oneself up; seethe, boil, simmer, foam, fume,
flame, rage, rave; run mad etc. (*passion*) 825.

Adj. excited etc. *v.*; wrought up, on the *qui vive*,
astir, sparkling; in a -quiver etc. 821, − fever, −
ferment, − blaze. − state of excitement; in
hysterics; black in the face, over-wrought; hot, red-
hot, flushed, feverish; all -of a twitter, − of a flutter, − of a dither, − in a pucker; with -quivering
lips, − tears in one's eyes.

flaming; boiling, − over; ebullient, seething;
foaming, − at the mouth; fuming, raging, carried
away by passion, wild, raving, frantic, mad, dis-

tracted, distraught, beside oneself, out of one's wits, amuck, ready to burst, *bouleversé*, demoniacal.

lost, *eperdu*, tempest-tossed; haggard; ready to sink.

stung to the quick, up, on one's high ropes.

exciting etc. *v.*; impressive, warm, glowing, fervid, swelling, imposing, spirit-stirring, thrilling; high-wrought; soul-stirring, -subduing; heart-swelling, -thrilling; agonizing etc. (*painful*) 830; telling, sensational, melodramatic, hysterical; overpowering, -whelming; more than flesh and blood can bear.

piquant etc. (*pungent*) 392; spicy, appetizing, provocative, *provaquant*, tantalizing.

Adv. till one is black in the face.

Phr. the heart -beating high, — going pit-a-pat, — leaping into one's mouth; the blood -being up, — boiling in one's veins; the eye -glistening, — 'in a fine frenzy rolling;' the head turned.

825. Excitability. [Excess of sensitiveness.]—**N.** excitability, impetuosity, vehemence; boisterousness etc. *adj.*; turbulence; impatience, intolerance, non-endurance; irritability etc. (*irascibility*) 901; itching etc. (*desire*) 865; wincing; disquiet, -ude; restlessness; fidge-ts, -tiness; agitation etc. (*irregular motion*) 315.

trepidation, perturbation, ruffle, hurry, -skurry, fuss, flurry; fluster, flutter; pother, stew, ferment; whirl; thrill etc. (*feeling*) 821; state —, fever- of excitement; transport.

passion, excitement, flush, heat; fever, -heat; fire, flame, fume, blood boiling; tumult; effervescence, ebullition; boiling, — over; whiff, gust, storm, tempest; scene, breaking out, burst, fit, paroxysm, explosion; out-break, -burst; agony.

violence 173; fierceness etc. *adj.*; rage, fury, *furor*, *furore*, desperation, madness, distraction, raving, delirium, brain storm; frenzy, hysterics; intoxication; tearing —, raging- passion, towering rage; anger etc. 900.

fascination, infatuation, fanaticism; Quixot-ism, -ry; *tête montée*.

V. be -impatient etc. *adj.*; not be able to -bear etc. 826; bear ill, wince, chafe, champ the bit; be in a -stew etc. *n.*; be out of all patience, fidget, fuss, not have a wink of sleep; toss, — on one's pillow.

lose one's temper etc. 900; break —, burst —, fly-'out; go —, fly- -off, — off the handle, — off at a tangent; explode; flare up, flame up, fire up, burst into a flame, take fire, fire, burn; boil, — over; foam, fume, rage, rave, rant, tear; go —, run- wild, — mad; go into hysterics; run -riot, — amuck; *battre la campagne*, *faire le diable à quatre*, play the deuce; raise -Cain, — the devil.

Adj. excitable, easily excited, in an excitable state; high strung; irritable etc. (*irascible*) 901; impatient, intolerant.

feverish, febrile, hysterical; delirious, mad, moody, maggoty-headed.

unquiet, mercurial, electric, galvanic, hasty, hurried, restless, fidgety, fussy; chafing etc. *v.*

startlish, mettlesome, high mettled, skittish.

vehement, demonstrative, violent, wild, furious, fierce, fiery, hot-headed, mad-cap.

over-zealous, enthusiastic, impassioned, fanatical; rabid etc. (*eager*) 865.

rampant, clamorous, uproarious, turbulent, tempestuous, tumultuary, boisterous.

impulsive, impetuous, passionate; uncontroll-ed, -able; ungovernable, irrepressible, stanchless, inextinguishable, burning, simmering, volcanic, ready to burst forth.

excit-ed, -ing etc. 824.

Int. pish! pshaw!

Phr. *noli me tangere*.

826. Inexcitability. [Absence of excitability, or of excitement.]—**N.** inexcit- imperturb-, inirritability; even temper, tranquil mind, dispassion; tolerance, toleration, patience.

passiveness etc. (*physical inertness*) 172; hebetude, -ation; impassibility etc. (*insensibility*) 823; stupefaction.

coolness, calmness etc. *adj.*; composure, placidity, indisturbance, imperturbation, *sang-froid*, tranquility, serenity; quiet, -ude; peace of mind, mental calmness.

staidness etc. *adj.*; gravity, sobriety, Quakerism; philosophy, equanimity, stoicism, command of temper; self-possession, -control, -command, -restraint; presence of mind.

submission etc. 725; resignation; suffer-, support-, endur-, long-suffer-, forbear-ance; longanimity; fortitude; patience -of Job, — 'on a monument,' — 'sovereign o'er transmuted ill;' moderation; repression —, subjugation- of feeling; restraint etc. 751.

tranquilization etc. (*moderation*) 174.

V. be -composed etc. *adj.*

laisser -faire, — *aller*; take things -easily, — as they come; take it easy, run on, live and let live; take -easily, — cooly, — in good part; *aequam serva e mentem*.

bear —, well, — the brunt; go through, support, endure, brave, disregard.

tolerate, suffer, stand, bide; abide, aby; bear —, put up —, abide- with; acquiesce; submit etc. (*yield*) 725; submit with a good grace; resign —, reconcile- oneself to; brook, digest, eat, swallow, pocket, stomach; make -light of, — the best of, — a virtue of necessity; put a good face on, keep one's countenance; carry -on, — through; check etc. 751- oneself.

compose, appease etc. (*moderate*) 174; propitiate; repress etc. (*restrain*) 751; render insensible etc. 823; overcome —, allay —, repress- one's -excitability etc. 825; master one's feelings.

make -oneself, — one's mind- easy; set one's mind at -ease, — rest.

calm —, cool- down; thaw, grow cool.

be -borne; — endured; go down.

Adj. in-, un-excitable; imperturbable; unsusceptible etc. (*insensible*) 823; un-, dispassionate; cold-blooded, inirritable; enduring etc. *v.*; stoical, Platonic, philosophic, staid, stayed; sober, — minded; grave; sober —, grave- as a judge; sedate, demure, cool-, level-headed, steady.

easy-going, peaceful, placid, calm; quiet, — as a mouse; tranquil, serene; cool, — as -a cucumber, — custard; undemonstrative.

temperate etc. (*moderate*) 174; composed, collected; un-excited, -stirred, -ruffled, -disturbed, -perturbed, -impassioned; unoffended; unresisting.

meek, tolerant; patient, — as Job; submissive etc. 725; tame; content, resigned, chastened, subdued, lamblike; gentle, — as a lamb; *suaviter in modo*; mild, — as mother's milk; soft as peppermint; armed with patience, bearing with, clement, forbearant, long-suffering.

Adv. 'like patience on a monument smiling at grief;' *aequo animo*, in cold blood etc. 823; more in sorrow than in anger.

Int. patience! and shuffle the cards.

827. Pleasure.—N. pleasure, gratification, enjoyment, fruition; ob-, de-lectation; relish, zest; *gusto* etc. (*physical pleasure*) 377; satisfaction etc. (*content*) 831; complacency.

well-being; good etc. 618; snugness, comfort, ease; cushion etc. 215; *sans souci*, mind at ease.

joy, gladness, delight, glee, cheer, sunshine; cheerfulness etc. 836.

treat, refreshment; frolic, fun, lark, gambol, merry-making; amusement etc. 840; luxury etc. 377; hedonism.

mens sana in corpore sano.

happiness, felicity, bliss; beati-tude, -fication; en-chantment, transport, rapture, ravishment, ecstasy; *summum bonum*; paradise, elysium etc. (*heaven*) 981; third —, seventh— heaven; unalloyed - happiness etc.

honeymoon; palmy —, halcyon- days; golden - age, — time; *Saturnia regna*, Eden, Arcadia, happy valley, Agapemone; Cockaigne.

V. be pleased etc. 829; feel —, experience-pleasure etc. *n.*; joy; enjoy —, hug- oneself; be in - clover etc. 377, — elysium etc. 981; tread on enchanted ground; fall —, go- into raptures.

feel at home, breathe freely, bask in the sunshine.

be -pleased etc. 829- with; receive —, derive-pleasure etc. *n.*- from; take -pleasure etc. *n.*- in; delight in, rejoice in, indulge in, luxuriate in; gloat over etc. (*physical pleasure*) 377; enjoy, relish, like; love etc. 897; take -to, — a fancy to; have a liking for; enter into the spirit of.

take in good part.

treat oneself to, solace oneself with.

Adj. pleased etc. 829; not sorry; glad, -some; pleased as Punch.

happy, blest, blessed, blissful, beatified; happy as -a king, — the day is long; thrice happy, *ter quaterque beatus*; enjoying etc. *v.*; joyful etc. (*in spirits*) 836; hedonic.

in -a blissful state, — paradise etc. 981; — raptures, — ecstasies, — a transport of delight.

comfortable etc. (*physical pleasure*) 377; at ease; content etc. 831; *sans souci*, in clover.

overjoyed, entranced, enchanted; enraptured; en-, ravished; transported; fascinated, captivated.

with -a joyful face, — sparkling eyes.

pleasing etc. 829; ecstatic, beat-ic, -ific; painless, unalloyed, without alloy, cloudless.

Adv. happily etc. *adj.*; with pleasure etc. (*willingly*) 60; with -glee etc. *n.*

phr. one's heart leaping with joy.

828. Pain.—N. mental suffering, pain, dolor; suffer-ing, -ance; ache, smart etc. (*physical pain*) 378; passion.

displeasure, dissatisfaction, discomfort, discom-posure, disquiet; *malaise*; inquietude, uneasiness, vexation of spirit; taking; discontent etc. 832.

dejection etc. 837; weariness etc. 841.

annoyance, irritation, worry, infliction, visitation; plague, bore; bother, -ation; stew, vexation, mortification, chagrin, *esclandre*; *mauvais quart d'heure.*

care, anxiety, solicitude, trouble, trial, ordeal, fiery ordeal, shock, blow, cark, dole, fret, burden, load.

concern, grief, sorrow, distress, affliction, woe, bitterness, gloom, heartache; heavy —, aching —, bleeding —, broken- heart; heavy affliction, gnawing grief; unhappiness, infelicity, misery, tribulation, wretchedness, desolation; despair etc. 859; extremity, prostration, depth of misery.

nightmare, *ephialtes*, incubus.

anguish, agony; throe, tor-ture, -ment; crucifixion, martyrdom; pang, twinge, stab; the rack, the stake; purgatory etc. (*hell*) 982.

hell upon earth; iron age, reign of terror; slough of despond etc. (*adversity*) 735; peck —, sea- of troubles; ills that flesh is heir to etc. (*evil*) 619; miseries of human life; unkindest cut of all.

sufferer, victim, prey, martyr, object of com-passion, wretch, shorn lamb.

V. feel —, suffer —, experience —, undergo —, bear —, endure- pain etc. *n.*; smart, ache etc. (*physical pain*) 378; suffer, bleed, ail; be the victim of; bear — take up- the cross.

labor under afflictions; quaff the bitter cup, have a bad time of it; fall on evil days etc. (*adversity*) 735; go hard with, come to grief, fall a sacrifice to, drain the cup of misery to the dregs, sup full of horrors.

sit on thorns, be on pins and needles, wince, fret, chafe, worry oneself, be in a taking, fret and fume, take -on, — to heart.

grieve; mourn etc. (*lament*) 839; yearn, repine, pine, droop, languish, sink; give way; despair etc. 859; break one's heart; weigh upon the heart etc. (*inflict pain*) 830.

Adj. in —, in a state of —, full of- pain etc. *n.*; suffering etc. *v.*; pained, afflicted, worried, displeased etc. 830; aching, griped, sore etc. (*physical pain*) 378; on the rack; in limbo; be-tween hawk and buzzard.

un-comfortable, -easy; ill at ease; in a -taking, — way; disturbed; discontented etc. 832; out of humor etc. 901*a*; weary etc. 841.

heavy laden, stricken, crushed, a prey to, vic-timized, ill-used.

unfortunate etc. (*hapless*) 735; to be pitied; doomed, devoted, accursed, undone, lost, stranded.

unhappy, infelicitous, poor, wretched, miserable, woe-begone; cheerless etc. (*dejected*) 837; careworn.

concerned, sorry; sorrow-ing, -ful; cut up, chagrined, horrified, horror-stricken; in —, plunged in —, a prey to- grief etc. *n.*; in tears etc. (*lamenting*) 839; steeped to the lips in misery; heart-stricken, -broken, -scalded; broken-hearted; in despair etc. 859.

Phr. 'the iron entered into our soul;' *haeret lateri lethalis arundo;'* one's heart bleeding.

829. Pleasurableness. [Capability of giving pleasure; cause or source of pleasure.]—N. pleasurable-, pleasant-, agreeable-ness etc. *adj.*; pleasure giving, jocundity, delectability; amusement etc. 840.

attraction etc. (*motive*) 615; attractiveness, -

ability; invitingness etc. *adj.*; charm, fascination, captivation, enchantment, witchery, seduction, winsomeness, winning ways, amenity, amiability, sweetness.

loveliness etc. (*beauty*) 845; sunny —, brightside; sweets etc. (*sugar*) 396; goodness etc. 648; manna in the wilderness, land flowing with milk and honey.

treat; regale etc. (*physical pleasure*) 377; dainty; tit-, tid-bit; nuts, *sauce piquante*.

V. cause —, produce —, create —, give —, afford —, procure —, offer —, present —, yield- pleasure etc. 827.

please, charm, delight; gladden etc. (*make cheerful*) 836; take, captivate, fascinate; enchant, entrance, enrapture, transport, bewitch; en-, ravish.

bless, beatify; satisfy; gratify —, desire etc. 865; slake, satiate, quench; indulge, humor, flatter, tickle; tickle the palate etc. (*savory*) 394; regale, refresh; enliven; treat; amuse etc. 840; take —, tickle —, hit- one's fancy; meet one's wishes; win —, gladden —, rejoice —, warm the cockles of- the heart; do one's heart good.

attract, allure etc. (*move*) 615; stimulate etc. (*excite*) 824; interest, intrigue.

make things pleasant, popularize, gild the pill, sweeten.

Adj. causing pleasure etc. *v.*; pleasure-giving; pleas-ing, -ant, -urable; agreeable, cushy; grat-eful, -ifying; leef, lief, acceptable; welcome, — as the roses in May; welcomed; favorite; to one's -taste, — mind, — liking, — heart's content; satisfactory etc. (*good*) 648.

refreshing; comfortable; cordial; genial; glad, - some; sweet, delectable, nice, dainty; delic-ate, - ious; dulcet; luscious etc. 396; palatable etc. 394; luxurious, voluptuous; sensual etc. 377.

attractive etc. 615; inviting, prepossessing, engaging, win-ning, -some; taking, fascinating, captivating, killing; seduc-ing, -tive; alluring, enticing; appetizing etc. (*exciting*) 824; cheering etc. 836; bewitching; interesting, absorbing, enchanting, entrancing, enravishing.

charming; delightful, felicitous, exquisite; lovely etc. (*beautiful*) 845; ravishing, rapturous; heartfelt, thrilling, ecstatic; beat-ic, -ific; seraphic; empyrean; elysian etc. (*heavenly*) 981.

palmy, halcyon, Saturnian.

Phr. *decies repetita placebit.*

830. Painfulness. [Capability of giving pain; cause or source of pain.]—**N.** painfulness etc. *adj.* ; trouble, care etc. (*pain*) 828; trial; af-, in-fliction; cross, blow, stroke, burden, load, curse; bitter -pill,' — draught, — cup; waters of bitterness.

annoyance, grievance, nuisance, vexation, mortification, sickener; bore, bother, pother, hot water, sea of troubles, hornet's nest, plague, pest.

cancer, ulcer, sting, thorn; canker etc. (*bane*) 663; scorpion etc. (*evil-doer*) 913; dagger etc. (*arms*) 727; scourge etc. (*instrument of punishment*) 975; carking —, canker worm of- care.

mishap, misfortune etc. (*adversity*) 735; *désagrément, esclandre*, rub.

source of -irritation, — annoyance; wound, sore subject, skeleton in the closet; thorn in -the flesh, — one's side; where the shoe pinches, gall and wormwood.

sorry sight, heavy news, provocation; affront etc. 929; head and front of one's offending.

infestation, molestation; malignity etc. (*malevolence*) 907.

V. cause —, occasion —, give —, bring —, induce —, produce —, create —, inflict- pain etc. 828; pain, hurt, wound.

pinch, prick, gripe etc. (*physical pain*) 378; pierce, lancinate, cut.

hurt —, wound —, grate upon —, jar upon- the feelings; wring —, pierce —, lacerate —, break —, rend- the heart; make the heart bleed; tear —, rend- the heart-strings; draw tears from the eyes.

sadden; make -unhappy etc. 828; plunge into sorrow, grieve, fash, afflict, distress; cut -up, — to the heart.

displease, annoy, incommode, discommode, discompose, trouble, disquiet, disturb, thwart, cross, perplex, molest, tease, rag, tire, irk, vex, mortify, wherret, worry, plague, bother, pester, bore, pother, harass, harry, badger, heckle, bait, beset, infest, persecute, importune, be troublesome.

wring, harrow, torment, torture; put to the -rack, — question; break on the wheel, rack, scarify; cruci-ate, -fy; convulse, agonize; barb the dart; plant a -dagger in the breast, — thron in one's side.

irritate, provoke, sting, nettle, try the patience, pique, fret, rile, tweak the nose, chafe, gall; sting —, wound —, cut- to the quick; aggrieve, affront, enchafe, enrage, ruffle, sour the temper; give offence etc. (*resentment*) 900.

maltreat, bite, snap at, assail, bully; smite etc. (*punish*) 972.

sicken, disgust, revolt, nauseate, disenchant, repel, offend, shock, stink in the nostrils; go against —, turn- the stomach; make one sick, set the teeth on edge; go against the grain, grate on the ear; stick in one's -throat, — gizzard; rankle, gnaw, corrode, horrify, appal, freeze the blood; chill the spine; make the -flesh creep, — hair stand on end; make the blood -curdle, — run cold; make one shudder.

haunt, — the memory; weigh —, prey- on the - heart, — mind, — spirits; bring one's grey hairs with sorrow to the grave; add a nail to one's coffin.

Adj. causing pain, hurting etc. *v.*; hurtful etc. (*bad*) 649; painful; dolor-ific, -ous; unpleasant; un- dis-pleasing; disagreeable, unpalatable, bitter, distasteful; uninviting; unwelcome; undesir-able, - ed; obnoxious; unacceptable, unpopular, thankless.

unsatisfactory, untoward, unlucky, uncomfortable.

distressing; afflict-ing, -ive; joy-, cheer-, comfortless; dismal, disheartening; depress-ing, -ivè; dreary, melancholy, grievous, piteous; woeful, rueful, mournful, deplorable, pitiable, lamentable; sad, affecting, touching, pathetic.

irritating, provoking, stinging, annoying, aggravating, mortifying, galling; unaccommodating, invidious, vexatious; trouble-, tire-, irk-, weari-some; plagu-ing, -y; awkward.

importunate; teas-, pester-, bother-, harass-, worry-, torment-, cark-ing.

in-toler-, -suffer-, -support-able; un-bear-, - endur-able; past bearing; not to be -borne, — endured; more than flesh and blood can bear; enough to -drive one mad, — provoke a saint, — make a parson swear, — try the patience of Job.

shocking, terrific, grim, appalling, crushing; dreadful, fearful, frightful; thrilling, tremendous, dire; heart-breaking, -rending, -wounding, -corroding, -sickening; harrowing, rending.

odious, hateful, execrable, repulsive, repellent, abhorrent; horri-d, -ble, -fic, -fying; offensive; nause-ous, -ating; disgust-, sicken-, revolt-ing; nasty; loath-some, -ful; fulsome; vile etc. (*bad*) 649; hideous etc. 846.

sharp, acute, sore, severe, grave, hard, harsh, cruel, biting, acrimonious, caustic; cutting, corroding, consuming, racking, excruciating, searching, searing, grinding, grating, agonizing; envenomed.

ruinous, disastrous, calamitous, tragical; desolating, withering; burdensome, onerous, oppressive; cumb-rous, -ersome.

Adv. painfully etc. *adj.*; with -pain etc. 828; deuced.

Int. *hinc illae lachrymae!* woe is me!

Phr. *surgit amari aliquid*; the place being too hot to hold one; the iron entering the soul.

· **831. Content.—N.** content, -ment, -edness; complacency, satisfaction, entire satisfaction, ease, heart's ease, peace of mind; serenity etc. 826; cheerfulness etc. 836; ray of comfort; comfort etc. (*well-being*) 827.

re-, conciliation; resignation etc. (*patience*) 826. waiter on Providence.

V. be -content etc. *adj.*; rest -satisfied, – and be thankful; take the good the gods provide, let well alone, feel oneself at home, hug oneself, lay the flattering unction to one's soul.

take -up with, – in good part; assent etc. 488; be reconciled to, make one's peace with; get over it; take -heart, – comfort; put up with etc. (*bear*) 826.

render -content etc. *adj.*; set at ease, comfort; set one's -heart, – mind- at -ease, – rest; speak peace; conciliate, reconcile, win over, propitiate, disarm, beguile; content, satisfy; gratify etc. 829.

be -tolerated etc. 826; go down, – with; do.

Adj. content, -ed; satisfied etc. *v.*; at -ease, – one's ease, – home; with the mind at ease, *sans souci, sine curâ*, easy-going, not particular; conciliatory; unrepining, of good comfort; resigned etc. (*patient*) 826; cheerful etc. 836.

un-afflicted, -vexed, -molested, -plagued; serene etc. 826; at rest; snug, comfortable; in one's element.

satisfactory, satisfying, ample, sufficient, adequate, tolerable.

Adv. to one's heart's content; *à la bonne heure*; all for the best.

Int. amen etc. (*assent*) 488; very well, so much the better, well and good; it –, that- will do; it cannot be helped.

Phr. nothing comes amiss.

832. Discontent.—N. discontent, -ment; dissatisfaction; dissent etc. 489; labor unrest.

disappointment, mortification; cold comfort; regret etc. 833; repining, taking on etc. *v.*; inquietude, vexation of spirit, soreness; heart-burning, -grief; querulousness etc. (*lamentation*) 839; hypercriticism.

malcontent, grumbler, growler, croaker, *laudator temporis acti*; censurer, complainer, faultfinder, murmurer, Adullamite, Diehard, Bitterender.

the Opposition, cave of Adullam, indignation meeting, 'winter of our discontent.'

V. be -discontented etc. *adj.*; quarrel with one's bread and butter; repine; regret etc. 833; wish one at the bottom of the Red Sea; take -on, – to heart; shrug the shoulders; make a wry –, pull a long-face; knit one's brows; look -blue, – black, – black as thunder, – blank, – glum.

take -in bad part, – ill; fret, chafe, make a piece of work; grumble, croak, grouse; lament etc. 839.

cause -discontent etc. *n.*; dissatisfy, disappoint, mortify, put out, disconcert; cut up; dishearten.

Adj. discontented, dissatisfied etc. *v.*; unsatisfied, ungratified; dissident; dissentient etc. 489; malcontent, exigent, exacting, hypercritical.

repining etc. *v.*; regretful etc. 833; down in the mouth etc. (*dejected*) 837.

in -high dudgeon, – a fume, – the sulks, – the dumps, – bad humor; glum, sulky, sour, – as a crab; soured, sore; out of -humor, – temper.

disappointing etc. *v.*; unsatisfactory.

Int. so much the worse!

Phr. that –, it- will never do.

833. Regret.—N. regret, repining; home sickness, nostalgia; *mal –, maladie- du pays*; lamentation etc. 839; contrition, compunction, penitence etc. 950.

bitterness, heart-burning.

laudator temporis acti etc. (*discontent*) 832.

V. regret, deplore; bewail etc. (*lament*) 839; repine, cast a longing lingering look behind; rue, – the day; repent etc. 950, *infandum renovare dolorem*.

prey –, weigh –, have a weight- on the mind; leave an aching void.

Adj. regretting etc. *v.*; regretful; home-sick.

regretted etc. *v.*; much to be regretted, regrettable; lamentable etc. (*bad*) 649.

Int. what a pity! hang it!

Phr. 'tis -pity, – too true.

834. Relief.—N. relief; deliverance; refreshment etc. 689; easement, softening, alleviation, mitigation, palliation etc. 174; soothing, lullaby; cradle song, *berceuse*.

solace, consolation, comfort, encouragement.

lenitive, restorative etc. (*remedy*) 662; poultice etc. *v.*; cushion etc. 215; crumb of comfort, balm in Gilead; aspirin.

V. relieve, ease, alleviate, mitigate, palliate, soothe, adduce; salve; soften, – down; foment, stupe, poultice; assuage, allay.

cheer, comfort, console; encourage, bear up, pat on the back, give comfort, set at ease; enliven, gladden –, cheer- the heart.

remedy; cure etc. (*restore*) 660; refresh; pour · balm into, – oil on.

smoothe the ruffled brow of care, temper the wind to the shorn-lamb, lay the flattering unction to one's soul.

disburden etc. (*free*) 705; take off a load of care.

be relieved; breathe more freely, draw a long breath; take comfort; dry –, wipe- the -tears, – eyes.

Adj. relieving etc. *v.*; consolatory, soothing; assua-ging, -sive; bal-my, -samic; lenitive, palliative; anodyne etc. (*remedial*) 662; curative etc. 660.

835. Aggravation.—N. aggravation, heightening; exacerbation; exasperation; overestimation etc. 482; exaggeration etc. 549.

V. aggravate, render worse, heighten, embitter, sour; ex-, acerbate; exasperate, envenom; tease, provoke, enrage.

add fuel to the -fire, – flame; fan the flame etc. (*excite*) 824; go from bad to worse etc. (*deteriorate*) 659.

Adj. aggravated etc. *v.*; worse, unrelieved; aggravable; aggravating etc. *v.*

Adv. out of the frying pan into the fire, from bad to worse, worse and worse.

Int. so much the worse!

836. Cheerfulness.—N. cheerfulness etc. *adj.*; geniality, gaiety, *l'allegro*, cheer, good humor, spirits; high –, animal –, flow of- spirits; glee, high glee, light heart; sunshine of the -mind, – breast; *gaieté de coeur, bon naturel*.

liveliness etc. *adj.*; life, alacrity, vivacity, animation, *allégresse*; jocundity, joviality, jollity; levity; jocularity etc. (*wit*) 842.

mirth, merriment, hilarity, exhilaration; laughter etc. 838; merry-making etc. (*amusement*) 840; heyday, rejoicing etc. 838; marriage bells.

nepenthe, Euphrosyne.

optimism etc. (*hopefulness*) 858; self-complacency.

V. be -cheerful etc. *adj.*; have the mind at ease, smile, put a good face upon, keep up one's spirits; view -the bright side of the picture, – things *en couleur de rose; ridentem dicere verum*, cheer up, brighten up, light up, bear up; chirp, take heart, cast away care, drive dull care away, perk up.

rejoice etc. 838; carol, chirrup, lilt; frisk, rollick, give a loose to mirth.

cheer, enliven, elate, exhilarate, gladden, in-spirit, animate, raise the spirits, inspire; put in good humor; cheer –, rejoice- the heart; delight etc. (*give pleasure*) 829.

Adj. cheerful; happy etc. 827; cheer-y, -ly; of good cheer, smiling; blithe; in –, in good- spirits; in high -spirits, – feather; happy as -the day is long, – a king; gay, – as a lark; *allegro*; light, -some, -hearted; buoyant, *débonnaire*, bright, free and easy, airy; janty, jaunty, canty; spright-ly, -ful; spry; spirit-ed, -ful; lively; animated, breezy, vivacious; brisk, – as a bee; sparkling; sportive; full of -play, – spirit; all alive.

sunny, palmy; hopeful etc. 858.

merry, – as a -cricket, – grig, – marriage bell; joyful, joyous, jocund, jovial; jolly, – as a thrush, – as a sandboy; blithesome; glee-ful, -some; hilarious, rattling.

winsome, bonny, hearty, buxom.

play-ful, -some; *folâtre*, playful as a kitten, tricksy, frisky, frolicsome; gamesome; jocose, jocular, waggish; mirth-, laughter-loving; mirthful, rollicking.

elate, -d; exulting, jubilant, flushed; rejoicing etc. 838; cock-a-hoop.

cheering, inspiriting, exhilarating; cardiac, -al; pleasing etc. 829; flourishing, halcyon.

Adv. cheerfully etc. *adj.*

Int. never say die! come! cheer up! hurrah! etc. 838; 'hence loathed melancholy!' begone dull care! away with melancholy!

837. Dejection.—N. dejection; dejectedness etc. *adj.*; depression, prosternation; lowness –, depression- of spirits; weight –, oppression –, damp- on the spirits; low –, bad –, drooping –, depressed- spirits; heart sinking; heaviness –, failure- of heart.

heaviness etc. *adj.*; infestivity, gloom; weariness etc. 841; *taedium vitae*, disgust of life; *mal du pays* etc. (*regret*) 833.

melancholy; sadness etc. *adj.*; *il penseroso, melancholia*, dismals, mumps, mopes, lachrymals, dumps, blues, blue devils, doldrums, vapors, megrims, spleen, horrors, hypochondriasis, pessimism; despondency, slough of Despond; disconsolateness etc. *adj.*; hope deferred, blank despondency.

prostration, – of soul; broken heart; despair etc. 859; cave of -despair, – Trophonius.

demureness etc. *adj.*; gravity, solemnity; long – grave- face.

hypochondriac, seek-sorrow, self-tormentor, *heautontimorumenos, malade imaginaire, médecin tant pis*; croaker, pessimist; mope, mopus.

[Cause of dejection] affliction etc. 830; sorry sight; *memento mori*; damper, wet blanket, Job's comforter; death's head, skeleton at the feast.

V. be -dejected etc. *adj.*; grieve; mourn etc. (*lament*) 839; take on, give way, lose heart, despond, droop, sink.

lower, look downcast, frown, pout; hang down the head; pull –, make- a long face; laugh on the wrong side of the mouth; grin a ghastly smile; look -blue, – like a drowned man; lay –, take- to heart.

mope, brood over; fret; sulk; pine, – away; yearn; repine etc. (*regret*) 833; despair etc. 859.

refrain from laughter, keep one's countenance; be –, look- grave etc. *adj.*; repress a smile, keep a straight face.

depress; dis-courage, -hearten; dis-pirit; damp, dull, deject, lower, sink, dash, knock down, un-man, prostrate, break one's heart; frown upon; cast a -gloom, – shade- on; sadden; damp –, dash –, wither- one's hopes; weigh –, lie heavy –, prey-on the -mind, – spirits; damp –, depress- the spirits.

Adj. cheer-, joy-, spirit-less; uncheer-ful, -y; unlively; unhappy etc. 828; melancholy, dismal, somber, dark, gloomy, adust, *triste*, clouded, murky, lowering, frowning, lugubrious, Acheron-tic, funereal, mournful, lamentable, dreadful.

dreary, flat; dull, – as -a beetle, – ditchwater; depressing etc. *v.*

'melancholy as a gib cat;' oppressed with –; a prey to- melancholy; down-cast, -hearted; down -in the mouth, – on one's luck; heavy-hearted; in the -dumps, – suds, – sulks, – doldrums; in doleful dumps, in bad humor; sullen; mumpish, dumpish; mopish, moping; moody, glum; sulky etc. (*discontented*) 832; out of -sorts, – humor, – heart, – spirits; ill at ease, low-spirited, in low spirits, a cup too low; weary etc. 841; dis-couraged, -heartened; desponding; chop-, jaw-, crest-fallen.

sad, pensive, *penseroso*, tristful; dole-some, -ful; woebegone, lachrymose, in tears, melancholic, hypped, hypochondriacal, bilious, jaundiced, atrabilious, saturnine, splenetic; lackadaisical.

serious, sedate, staid, stayed; grave, – as -a judge, – an undertaker, – a mustard pot; sober, solemn, demure; grim; grim-faced, -visaged; rueful, wan, long-faced.

disconsolate; un-, in-consolable; forlorn, comfortless, desolate, *désolé*, sick at heart; soul-, heartsick; *au désepoir*; in despair etc. 859; lost.

overcome; broken-, borne-, bowed-down; heartstricken etc. (*mental suffering*) 828; cut up, dashed, sunk; unnerved, unmanned; down-fallen, -trodden; broken-hearted; care-worn.

Adv. with -a long face, – tears in one's eyes; sadly etc. *adj.*

Phr. the countenance falling; the heart -failing, – sinking within- one.

838. Rejoicing. [Expression of pleasure.]—**N.** rejoicing, exultation, triumph, jubilation, heyday, flush, revelling; merry-making etc. (*amusement*) 840; jubilee etc. (*celebration*) 883; *paean, Te Deum* etc. (*thanksgiving*) 990; congratulation etc. 896; applause etc. 971.

smile, simper, smirk, grin; broad –, sardonic-grin.

laughter, giggle, titter, crow, cheer, chuckle, snicker, snigger, shout; Homeric laughter, horse – hearty- laugh; guffaw; burst –, fit –, shout –, roar –, peal- of laughter; cachinnation.

risibility; derision etc. 856.

Momus; Democritus the Abderite; rollicker; Laughter holding both his sides.

V. rejoice; thank –, bless- one's stars; congratulate –, hug- oneself; rub –, clap- one's hands; smack the lips, fling up one's cap; dance, skip, caleer; sing, carol, chirrup, chirp; hurrah; cry for –, leap with- joy; exult etc. (*boast*) 884; triumph; hold jubilee etc. (*celebrate*) 883; make merry etc. (*sport*) 840; sing a paean of joy.

smile, simper, smirk, grin, – like a Cheshire cat; mock, laugh in one's sleeve; laugh, – outright; giggle, titter, snigger, crow, smicker, chuckle, snicker, cackle; burst -out, – into a fit of laughter; shout, split, roar.

shake –, split –, hold both- one's sides; roar –, die- with laughter.

raise laughter etc. (*amuse*) 840.

Adj. rejoicing etc. *v.*; jubilant, exultant, triumphant; flushed, elated; laughing etc. *v.*; risible; ready to -burst, – split, – die with laughter; convulsed with laughter.

laughable etc. (*ludicrous*) 853.

Int. hip, hip, -hurrah! huzza! aha! hail! tolderolloll! tra-la la! Heaven be praised! *io triumphe! tant mieux!* so much the better.

Phr. the heart leaping with joy.

839. Lamentation. [Expression of pain.]—**N.** lament, -ation; wail, complaint, plaint, murmur, mutter, grumble, groan, moan, whine, whimper, sob, sigh, suspiration, heaving, deep sigh.

cry etc. (*vociferation*) 411; scream, howl; outcry, wail of woe, frown, scowl.

tear; weeping etc. *v.*; flood of tears, fit of crying, lachrymation, melting mood, weeping and gnashing of teeth.

plaintiveness etc. *adj.*; languishment; condolence etc. 915.

mourning, weeds, willow, cypress, crêpe, crape, deep mourning; sackcloth and ashes; knell etc. 363; dump, deathsong, dirge, coronach, keen, *nenia*, requiem, elegy, *epicedium*; threne; mon-, thren-ody; jeremiad; ululation.

mourner, professional mourner, keener; grumbler etc. (*discontent*) 832; Niobe; Heraclitus.

V. lament, mourn, deplore, grieve, weep over; be-wail, -moan; keen; condole with etc. 915; fret etc. (*suffer*) 828; wear –, go into –, put on-mourning; wear -the willow, – sackcloth and ashes; *infandum renovare dolorem* etc. (*regret*) 833; give sorrow words.

sigh; give –, heave – ; fetch- a sigh; 'waft a sigh from Indus to the pole;' sigh 'like furnace;' wail.

cry, weep, sob, greet, blubber, pipe, snivel, bib-ber, whimper, pule; pipe one's eye; drop –, shed- -tears, – a tear; melt –, burst- into tears; *fondre en larmes*; cry -oneself blind, – one's eyes out.

scream etc. (*cry out*) 411; mew etc. (*animal sounds*) 412; groan, moan, whine, yammer; roar; roar –, bellow- like a bull; cry out lustily, rend the air, yell.

frown, scowl, make a wry face, grimace, gnash one's teeth, wring one's hands, tear one's hair, beat one's breast, roll on the ground, burst with grief.

complain, murmur, mutter, grumble, growl, clamor, make a fuss about, croak, grunt, maunder; deprecate etc. (*disapprove*) 932.

cry out before one is hurt, complain without cause.

Adj. lamenting etc. *v.*; in mourning, in sackcloth and ashes; crying, sorrowing, -ful etc. (*unhappy*) 828; mourn-, tear-ful; lachrymose; plaint-ive, -ful, quer-ulous, -imonious; in the melting mood.

in tears, with tears in one's eyes; with -moistened, – watery- eyes; bathed –, dissolved-in tears; 'like Niobe all tears.'

elagiac, epicedial, threnetic.

Adv. *de profundis; les larmes aux yeux.*

Int. heigh-ho! alas! alack! O dear! ah –, woe is-me! lackadaisy! well –, lack –, alack- a day! well-a-way! alas the day! *O tempora! O mores!* what a pity! *miserabile dictu!* O lud lud! too true!

Phr. tears -standing in, – starting from- the eyes; eyes -suffused, – swimming, – ; brimming –, over- flowing- with tears.

840. Amusement.—**N.** amuse-, entertain-ment; diver-sion, -tissement; reaction, relaxation, solace; pastime, *passetemps*, sport; labor of love; pleasure etc. 827.

fun, frolic, merriment, whoopee, jollity, jovial-ity, -ness; heyday; laughter etc. 838; jocos-ity, -eness; droll-, buffoon-, tomfool-ery; mummery, masquing, pleasantry; wit etc. 842; quip, quirk.

play; game, – at romps; gambol, romp, prank, antic, rig, lark, spree, skylarking, vagary, trick, monkey trick, *gambade, fredaine, escapade, échappée*, bout, *espiéglerie*; practical joke etc. (*ridicule*) 856.

dance; round –, square –, solo –, step –, tap –, clog –, skirt –, sand –, folk –, morris-dance, *pas seul*, step, turn, *chassé*, cut, shuffle, double shuffle; hop, reel, rigadoon, saraband, hornpipe, bolero, fandango, pavan, tarantella, minuet, waltz, polka; galop, -ade; Schottische, *pas de quatre*, Boston, one-, two-step, rumba, tango, maxixe, fox-, turkey-trot, shimmy, ragtime, cakewalk, jazz, blues, Charleston; jig, breakdown, fling, strathspey; *allemande*; gavot, -te; mazurka, morisco; quadrille, lancers, country dance, cotillon, polonaise, Sir Roger de Coverley, Swedish dance; *ballet* etc. (*drama*) 599; ball; *bal, -masqué*, - *costumé*; masquerade, fancy dress ball; *thé dansant*; Terpsichore, choreography, Russian ballet, classical dancing; eurythmics; nautch dance, *danse du ventre*, cancan.

festivity, merry-making; party etc. (*social gathering*) 892; *fête*, festival, gala, *ridotto*; revel-s, -ry, -ling; carnival, brawl, saturnalia, high jinks; feast, banquet etc. (*food*) 298; regale, *symposium*, wassail; carous-e, -al; jollification, junket, wake, pic-nic, *fête champêtre*, garden party, gymkhana, regatta, track meet, field day, jamboree, treat.

round of pleasures, dissipation, a short life and a merry one, racketing, holiday making, high jinks.

rejoicing etc. 838; jubilee etc. (*celebration*) 883.

bonfire, fireworks, *feu-de-joie*, rocket, catherine wheel, roman candle etc.

holiday; gala -, red letter -, play- day; high days and holidays; high -, Bank- holiday; May -, Derby- day; Saint -, Easter -, Whit- Monday; King's birthday, Empire Day; *mi-carême*; *Bairam*; wayzgoose, bean feast, beano.

place of amusement, theater etc. 599; concert-, ball-, assembly-room; music-hall, cinema, movies, talkies, vaudeville; hippodrome, circus, rodeo; *casino*, *kursaal*; winter garden; park, pleasance, arbor; garden etc. 371; pleasure-, play-, cricket-, football-, polo-, croquet-, archery-, hunting-ground; golf links, race course, stadium, gridiron, bowl, speedway, racing track, ring; gymnasium, swimming pool; shooting gallery; tennis-, racket-court; bowling-green, -alley; croquet-lawn, rink, skating rink; roller-coaster, roundabout, carousel, merry-go-round; swing; *montagne russe*; switchback, scenic railway etc.

game, - of -chance, - skill; athletic sports, gymnastics; fencing; archery, rifle-shooting; tournament, pugilism etc. (*contention*) 720; sporting etc. 622; horse-racing, the turf; aquatics etc. 267; skating, roller skating; ski-running, -joring, -jumping; bobsleighing, luging, tobogganing, winter sports; sliding; cricket, tennis, lawn -, table -, deck-tennis, rackets, fives, squash, ping pong, trap bat and ball, battledore and shuttlecock, badminton, *la grâce*; pall mall, tip-cat, croquet, golf, curling, hockey, basketball, soccer, football, Rugby, Association, *pallone*, polo; tent-pegging, tilting at the ring, quintain, greasy pole; quoits, *discus*; throwing the hammer, putting the -weight, - shot, tossing the caber; knurr and spell; leap-frog; hop, skip and jump; French and English, tug of war; blind man's buff, hunt the slipper, hide-and-seek, kiss in the ring; snapdragon; cross questions and crooked answers; jig-saw puzzle; rounders, base-ball, *la crosse* etc.; angling; swimming, diving, water-polo.

billiards, pool, pyramids, snooker, bagatelle; bowls, skittles, ninepins, kail, American bowls.

cards; bridge, auction, contract, whist, rubber;

round game, coon-can, loo, cribbage, *bésique*, pinocle, euchre, drole, *écarté*, skat, picquet, all-fours, quadrille, ombre, reverse, Pope Joan, commit; bo-, boa-ston; *vingt-et-un*; *quinze*, thirty-one, put-and-take, speculation, connections, brag, cassino, lottery, commerce, snip-snap-snorem, lift smoke, blind hookey, Polish bank, poker, banker; faro; Earl of Coventry, Napoleon, nap, patience; pairs; old maid, fright, beggar-my-neighbor; *baccarat*, *chemin de fer*, *monté*, *roulette*.

chess, draughts, backgammon, dominoes, checkers, mah jong, merelles, nine men's morris, go-bang, solitaire; game of -, fox and-goose; lotto; etc.

morra; gambling etc. (*chance*) 621.

toy, plaything, bauble; doll etc. (*puppet*) 554; teetotum; knick-knack etc. (*trifle*) 643; magic lantern etc. (*show*) 448; peep-, puppet-, raree-, gallanty-show; marionettes, Punch and Judy; toy-shop; 'quips and cranks and wanton wiles, nods and becks and wreathed smiles.'

sportsman, gamester, gambler etc. 621; reveler, master of the -ceremonies, - revels; *arbiter elegantiarum*.

V. amuse, entertain, divert, enliven; tickle, - the fancy; titillate, raise a smile, put in good humor; cause -, create -, occasion -, raise -, excite -, produce -, convulse with- laughter; set the table in a roar, be the death of one.

· recreate, solace, cheer, rejoice; please etc. 829; interest; treat, regale.

amuse oneself; game; play, - a game, - pranks, - tricks; sport, disport, toy, wanton, revel, junket, feast, carouse, banquet, make merry; drown care; drive dull care away; frolic, gambol, frisk, romp; caper; dance etc. (*leap*) 309; keep up the ball; run a rig, sow one's wild oats, have one's fling, paint the town red, take one's pleasure; see life; *desipere in loco*, play the fool.

make -, keep- holiday; go a Maying.

while away -, beguile- the time; kill time, dally.

Adj. amusing, entertaining, diverting etc. *v.*; recreative, lusory; pleasant etc. (*pleasing*) 829; laughable etc. (*ludicrous*) 853; witty etc. 842; festive, -al; jovial, jolly, jocund, roguish, rompish; sporting; playful - as a kitten; sportive, ludibrious.

amused etc. *v.*; 'pleased with a feather, tickled with a straw.'

Adv. 'on the light fantastic toe,' at play, in sport.

Int. *vive la bagatelle! vogue la galère!*

Phr. *Deus nobis haec otia fecit; dum vivimus vivamus.*

---

841. Weariness.—N. weariness, defatigation, boredom, *ennui*; lassitude etc. (*fatigue*) 688; drowsiness etc. 683.

disgust, nausea, loathing, sickness; satiety etc. 869; *taedium vitae* etc. (*dejection*) 837.

wearisome-, tedious-ness etc. *adj.*; dull work, tedium, monotony, twice told tale.

bore, button-hole, proser, wet blanket; heavy hours, 'the enemy' [time].

V. weary, tire etc. (*fatigue*) 688; bore; bore - weary -, tire- -to death, - out of one's life, - out of all patience; set -, send- to sleep.

pall, sicken, nauseate, disgust.

harp on the same string; drag its -slow, - weary-length along.

never hear the last of; be -tired etc. *adj.* -of, –
with; yawn; died with *ennui*.

Adj. wearying etc. *v.*; wearing; weari-, tire-, irk-
some; uninteresting, stupid, bald, devoid of interest, dry, monotonous, dull, arid, tedious, humdrum, mortal, flat; pros-y, -ing; slow; soporific,
somniferous, dormitive.

disgusting etc. *v.*; unenjoyed.

weary; tired etc. *v.*; drowsy etc. (*sleepy*) 683;
uninterested, flagging, used up, worn out, *blasé*,
life-weary, weary of life; sick of.

Adv. wearily etc. *adj.*; *usque ad nauseam.*

Phr. time hanging heavily on one's hands;
toujours perdrix; *crambe repetita.*

842. Wit.—N. wit, -tiness; attic -wit, – salt; at-
ticism; salt, *esprit*, point, fancy, whim, humor,
drollery, pleasantry.

farce, buffoonery, fooling, tomfoolery;
harlequinade etc. 599; broad -farce, – humor; fun,
espièglerie; *vis comica.*

jocularity; jocos-ity, -eness; facetiousness; wagg-
ery, -ishness; whimsicality, comicality etc. 853.

smartness, ready wit, banter, *badinage*, *persiflage*, retort, repartee, *quid pro quo*; ridicule etc.
856.

facetiae, quips and cranks; jest, joke, capital
joke; standing -jest, – joke; conceit, quip, quirk,
crank, quiddity, *concetto*, *plaisanterie*, brilliant
idea; merry –, bright –, happy- thought; sally;
flash, – of wit, – of merriment; scintillation; *mot*,
– pour rire; witticism, smart saying, *bon mot*,
jeu d'esprit, epigram; jest book; dry joke,
quodlibet, cream of the jest.

word-play, *jeu de mots*; play -of, – upon-
words; pun, -ning; *double entente* etc. (*ambiguity*)
520; quibble, verbal quibble; conundrum etc. (*riddle*) 533; anagram, acrostic, double acrostic, *nugae
canorae*, trifling, idle conceit, *turlupinade.*

old joke, Joe Miller, chestnut, hoary-headed jest.

V. joke, jest, cut jokes; crack a joke; perpetrate a
-joke, – pun; make -fun of, – merry with; set the
table in a roar etc. (*amuse*) 840; scintillate.

retort, flash back; banter etc. (*ridicule*) 856;
ridentem dicere verum; joke at one's expense.

Adj. witty, attic, salty; quick-, nimble-witted;
keen, clever, smart, brilliant, pungent, jocular,
jocose, funny, waggish, facetious, whimsical,
humorous, gilbertian; playful etc. 840; merry and
wise; pleasant, sprightly, *spirituel*, sparkling,
epigrammatic, full of point, *ben trovato*; comic
etc. 853.

Adv. in joke, in jest, in sport, in play.

843. Dullness.—N. dullness, heaviness, flatness; infestivity etc. 837; stupidity etc. 499; want of
originality, dearth of ideas.

prose, matter of fact; heavy book, *conte à dormir debout*; platitude.

V. be -dull etc. *adj.*; prose, platitudinize, take *au
sérieux*, be caught napping.

render -dull etc. *adj.*; damp, depress, throw cold
water on, lay a wet blanket on; fall flat upon the
ear; hang fire.

Adj. dull, – as ditch water; dry, insipid, jejune;
unentertaining, uninteresting, unlively,

unimaginative; heavisome, heavy-gaited; insulse;
dry as dust; pros-y, -ing, -aic; matter of fact, commonplace, banal, pointless; 'weary, flat, stale and
unprofitable.'

stupid, slow, flat, sluggish, ponderous, humdrum, monotonous; melancholic etc. 837; stolid
etc. 499; plodding.

Phr. *Davus sum non Oedipus.*

844. Humorist.—N. humorist, wag, wit, reparteeist, epigrammatist, gag man, punster; *bel
esprit*, life of the party; wit-snapper, -cracker, -
worm; joker, jester, jokesmith, Joe Miller, *drôle de
corps*, *gaillard*, spark, *persifleur*, banterer.

buffoon, *farceur*, merry-andrew, mime, tumbler,
acrobat, mountebank, charlatan, posturemaster,
harlequin, punch, *pulcinella*, scaramouch, clown;
wearer of the -cap and bells, – motley; motley
fool; pantaloon, gipsy; jack -pudding, – in the
green, – a dandy; zany; mad-cap, pickle-herring,
witling, caricaturist, *grimacier.*

845. Beauty.—N. beauty, the beautiful, *le beau
ideal*, loveliness.

[Science of the perception of beauty]
Callaesthetics.

form, elegance, grace, beauty unadorned; symmetry etc. 242; comeliness, fairness etc. *adj.*;
pulchritude, polish, gloss; good -effect, – looks;
belle tournure; bloom, brilliancy, radiance, splendor, gorgeousness, magnificence; sublimi-ty, -
fication.

concinnity, delicacy, refinement; charm, *je ne
sais quoi*, style, *chic*, swank.

Venus, – of Milo; Aphrodite, Hebe, the Graces,
Peri, Houri, Cupid, Apollo, Hyperion, Adonis,
Antinous, Narcissus; Helen of Troy.

peacock, butterfly; flower, flow'ret gay, rose,
lily, asphodel; garden; flower of, pink of; *bijou*;
jewel etc. (*ornament*) 847; work of art.

pleasurableness etc. 829.

beautifying; landscape gardening; decoration etc.
847; calisthenics.

V. be -beautiful etc. *adj.*; shine, beam, bloom;
become one etc. (*accord*) 23; set off, grace, flatter
one.

render -beautiful etc, *adj.*; beautify; polish, burnish; gild etc. (*decorate*) 847; set out.

'snatch a grace beyond the reach of art.'

Adj. beaut-iful, -eous; handsome; pretty; lovely,
graceful, elegant; delicate, dainty, refined,
exquisite; fair, personable, comely, seemly;
bonny; good-looking; well-favored, -made, -formed,
-proportioned; proper, shapely; symmetrical etc.
(*regular*) 242; harmonious etc. (*color*) 428; sightly.

fit to be seen, passable, not amiss.

goodly, dapper, tight, jimp; gimp; janty, jaunty;
natty, quaint, trim, tidy, neat, spruce, smart,
tricksy.

bright, -eyed; rosy-, cherry-cheeked; rosy, ruddy;
blooming, in full bloom.

brilliant, shining; beam-y, -ing; sparkling,
swanky, splendid, resplendent, dazzling, glowing;
glossy, sleek.

showy, specious; rich, gorgeous, superb,
magnificent, grand, fine, sublime, imposing;
majestic 873.

artistic, -al; aesthetic; pict-uresque, -orial; *fait à piendre*, paintable; well-composed, -grouped, -varied; curious.

enchanting etc. (*pleasure-giving*) 829; attractive etc. (*inviting*) 615; becoming etc. (*accordant*) 23; ornamental etc. 847.

undeformed, undefaced, unspotted; spotless etc. (*perfect*) 650.

846. Ugliness.—N. ugliness etc. *adj.*; deformity, inelegance; disfigurement etc. (*blemish*) 848; want of symmetry, inconcinnity; distortion etc. 243; squalor etc. (*uncleanness*) 653.

forbidding countenance, vinegar aspect, hanging look, wry face, '*spretae injuria formae.*'

eyesore, object, figure, sight, fright, specter, scarecrow, hag, harridan, satyr, witch, toad, baboon, monster, Caliban, Aesop, '*monstrum horrendum informe ingens cui lumen ademptum.*'

V. be -ugly etc. *adj.*; look ill, grin horribly a ghastly smile, make faces.

render -ugly etc. *adj.*; deface; dis-, de-figure; deform, spoil, distort etc. 243; blemish etc. (*injure*) 659; soil etc. (*render unclean*) 653.

Adj. ugly, – as -sin, – a toad, – a scarecrow, – a dead monkey; plain, bald etc. 226; homely etc. (*unadorned*) 849; ordinary, unornamental, inartistic; unsightly, unseemly, uncomely, unshapely, unlovely; sightless, seemless; not fit to be seen; unbeaut-eous, -iful; beautiless; shapeless etc. (*amorphous*) 241; course; garish, over-decorated etc. 882.

mis-shapen, -proportioned; monstrous; gaunt etc. (*thin*) 203; dumpy etc. (*short*) 201; curtailed of its fair proportions; ill-made, -shaped, -proportioned; crooked etc. (*distorted*) 243; hard-featured, -visaged; ill-, hard-, evil-favored; ill-looking; unprepossessing.

graceless, inelegant; ungraceful, ungainly, uncouth, stiff, rugged, rough, gross, rude, awkward, clumsy, slouching, rickety, gawky; lump-ing, -ish; lumbering; hulk-y, -ing; unwieldy.

squalid, haggard; grim, -faced, -visaged; grisly, ghastly; ghost-, death-like; cadaverous, gruesome.

frightful, hideous, odious, uncanny, forbidding, repellant, repulsive; horri-d, -ble; shocking etc. (*painful*) 830.

foul etc. (*dirty*) 653; dingy etc. (*colorless*) 429; gaudy etc. (*color*) 428; disfigured etc. *v.*; discolored (*blemished*) etc. 848.

847. Ornament.—N. ornament, -ation, -al art; ornat-ture, -eness; adorn-ment, decoration, embellishment; architecture.

garnish, polish, varnish, French polish, gilding, japanning, lacquer, ormolu, enamel.

cosmetics, rouge, powder, lipstick, lip salve, mascara; manicure, nail polish; permanent – Marcel – , finger-wave.

pattern, diaper, powdering, panelling, graining, pargeting, inlay, detail; texture etc. 329; richness; tracery, molding, beading, reeding, fillet, listel, strapwork, *coquillage*, flourish, *fleur-de-lis*, arabesque, fret, *anthemion*; egg and -tongue, – dart; *astragal*, zigzag, *acanthus*, *cartouche*; pilaster etc. (*projection*) 250; cyma, ogee.

em-, broidery, needlework; knitting, crochet, tatting, brocade, *brocatelle*, beads, bugles; galloon, lace, gimp, *guipure*, fringe, trapping, border, edging, insertion, *motif*, trimming; *passementerie*; drapery, hanging, tapestry, arras; millinery, ermine.

wreath, festoon, garland, lei, chaplet, flower, nosegay, *bouquet*, posy, 'daisies pied and violets blue.'

tassle, knot; shoulder-knot, *épaulette*, epaulet, aigulet, *aiguilette*, frog; star, rosette, bow; feather, plume, *panache, aigrette.*

jewel, -ry, -lery; bijoutry; *bijou, -terie*; diadem, tiara; pendant, trinket, locket, necklace, armilla, bracelet, bangle, armlet, anklet, ear-, nose- ring, carcanet, chain, *châtelaine*, albert, brooch, torque.

gem, precious stone; diamond, brilliant, beryl, aquamarine, alexandrite, cat's eye, emerald, calcedony, chrysoprase, cornelian, jasper, bloodstone, agate, heliotrope; girasol, -e; onyx, plasma; sard, -onyx; garnet, lapis-lazuli, opal, peridot, chrysolite, sapphire, ruby; spinel, -le; balais; oriental –, topaz; turquois, -e; zircon, jacinth, hyacinth, carbuncle, amethyst; moonstone; pearl, coral.

finery, frippery, gewgaw, gimcrack, knick-knack, tinsel, spangle, sequin, *clinquant*, pinch-beck; paste; excess of ornament etc. (*vulgarity*) 851; gaud, pride, ostentation; frills and furbelows.

illustration, illumination, *vignette*; *fleuron*; head-, tail-piece; *cul-de-lampe*; flowers of rhetoric etc. 577; work of art, article of vertu, *bric-à-brac*, curio, *bibelot*.

V. ornament, embellish, enrich, decorate, adorn, beautify, adonize.

smarten, furbish, polish, gild, varnish, whitewash, enamel, japan, lacquer, paint, grain.

garnish, trim, dizen, bedizen, prink, prank; trick –, fig- out; deck, bedeck, dight, bedight, array; dress, – up, preen, spruce up, titivate; spangle, bespangle, powder; embroider, work; chase, tool, emboss, fret; emblazon, blazon, illuminate; illustrate.

become etc. (*accord with*) 23.

Adj. ornamented, beautified etc. *v.*; ornate, rich, gilt, begilt, tesselated, enamelled, inlaid; festooned; topiary.

smart, gay, tricksy, flowery, glittering; new-gilt, -spangled; fine, – as -a Mayday queen, – fivepence, – a carrot fresh scraped; pranked out, bedight, well-groomed.

in full dress etc. (*fashion*) 852; *en grande -tenue*, – *toilette*; in best bib and tucker, in Sunday best, *endimanché*; dressed to advantage.

showy, flashy; gaudy etc. (*vulgar*) 851; garish, gorgeous.

ornamental, decorative; becoming etc. (*accordant*) 23.

848. Blemish.—N. blemish, disfigurement, deformity; defect etc. (*imperfection*) 651; flaw; injury etc. (*deterioration*) 659; spots on the sun; eyesore.

stain, blot, slur; spot, -tiness; speck, -le; blur, freckle, mole, *macula*, patch, blotch, birthmark, blain, maculation, tarnish, smudge, smear; dirt etc. 653; bruise, black eye, scar, wem; pustule; excrescence, pimple etc. (*protuberance*) 250.

V. disfigure etc. (*injure*) 659; speckle; render ugly etc. 846.

Adj. pitted, freckled, discolored, bloodshot, bruised, disfigured; stained etc. *n.*; imperfect etc. 651; injured etc. (*deteriorated*) 659.

849. Simplicity.—N. simplicity; plain-, homeli-ness; undress, nudity, nakedness, beauty unadorned, chastity, chasteness.

V. be -simple etc. *adj.*

render -simple etc. *adj.*; simplify, chasten, strip of ornament.

Adj. simple, plain; home-ly, -spun; ordinary, household.

natural, unaffected; free from -affectation, − ornament; *simplex munditiis*; *sans façon, en déshabillé*, nude, naked.

chaste, inornate, severe.

un-adorned, -ornamented, -decked, -garnished, -arranged, -trimmed, -varnished.

bald, flat, dull, blank.

850. Taste. [Good taste.]—N. taste; good -, refined -, cultivated- taste; delicacy, refinement, fine feeling, gust, *gusto*, tact, *finesse*; nicety etc. (*discrimination*) 465; polish, elegance, grace.

virtu; dilettanteism, virtuosity; fine art; cul-ture, -ivation.

[Science of taste] esthetics.

man of -taste etc.; *connoisseur*, judge, critic, *conoscente*, *virtuoso*, *amateur*, *dilettante*, Aristarchus, Corinthian, *arbiter elegantarum*, stagirite, euphemist.

'caviar to the general.'

V. appreciate, judge, criticize, discriminate etc. 465.

Adj. in good taste; tasteful, tasty; unaffected, pure, chaste, classical, attic; cultivated, refined; dainty; esthetic, artistic; elegant etc. 578; euphemistic.

to one's -taste, − mind; after one's fancy; *comme il faut*; *tiré à quatre épingles*.

Adv. elegantly etc. *adj.*

Phr. *nihil tetigit quod non ornavit.*

851. Vulgarity. [Bad taste.]—N. vulgar-ity, -ism; barbar-, Vandal-, Gothic-ism; *mauvais goût*, bad taste; Babbittry; *gaucherie*, awkwardness, want of tact; ill-breeding etc. (*discourtesy*) 895; ungentlemanly behavior.

coarseness etc. *adj.*; indecorum, misbehavior.

low-, homeli-ness; low life, *mauvais ton*, rusticity; boorishness etc. *adj.*; brutality; rowdy-, ruffian-, blackguard-ism; ribaldry; slang etc. (*neology*) 563.

bad joke, *mauvaise plaisanterie*.

[Excell of ornament] gaudi-, tawdri-ness; false ornament; finery, frippery, trickery, tinsel, gewgaw, *clinquant*.

rough diamond, tomboy, hoyden, cub, unlicked cub; clown etc. (*commonalty*) 876; Hun, Goth, Vandal, Boeotian; vulgarian; snob, cad, bounder, gent; *parvenu* etc. 876; frump, dowdy; slattern etc. 653.

V. be -vulgar etc. *adj.*; misbehave; talk -, smell of the- shop.

Adj. in bad taste, vulgar, unrefined, gutter.

coarse, indecorus, ribald, gross; unseemly, unbeseeming, unpresentable; *contra bonos mores*; ungraceful etc. (*ugly*) 846.

dowdy, slovenly etc. (*dirty*) 653; ungenteel, shabby genteel; low etc. (*plebeian*) 876;uncourtly; uncivil etc. (*discourteous*) 895; ill-bred, -mannered; underbred; ungentleman-ly, -like; unladylike, unfeminine; wild, − as an unbacked colt.

unkempt, uncombed, untamed, unlicked, un-polished, uncouth, plebeian; incondite; heavy, rude, awkward; home-ly, -spun, -bred; provincial, hick, countrified, rustic, uncultivated, freshwater; boorish, clownish, savage, brutish, blackguard; rowdy, snobbish; barbar-ous, -ic; Gothic, unclassical, doggerel, heathenish, tramontane, out-landish; Bohemian.

obsolete etc. (*antiquated*) 124; unfashionable, old-fashioned, out of date; new-fangled etc. (*unfamiliar*) 83; fantastic, odd etc. (*ridiculous*) 853.

particular; affected etc. 855; meretricious; extravagant, monstrous, horrid; shocking etc. (*painful*) 830.

gaudy, tawdry, bedizened, tricked out, gingerbread; obtrusive, flaunting, loud, flashy, garish, showy.

852. Fashion.—N. fashion, style, *ton, bon ton*, society; good -, polite- society; drawing room, civilized life, civilization, town, *beau monde*, high life, court; world; fashionable -, gay- world; Vanity Fair; show etc. (*ostentation*) 822.

manners, breeding etc. (*politeness*) 894; air, demeanor etc. (*appearance*) 448; *savoir faire*; gentlemanliness, gentility, decorum, propriety, *bienséance*; conventions -, dictates- of society; Mrs. Grundy; convention, -ality; punctilio; form, -ality; etiquette, point of etiquette; custom etc. 613; mode, vogue, style, go; rage etc. (*desire*) 865; prevailing taste, *dernier cri*, dress etc. 225.

man -, woman- of -fashion, − the world; height -, pink -, star -, glass -, leader- of fashion; *arbiter elegantiarum* etc. (*taste*) 850; upper ten thousand etc. (*nobility*) 875; *élite* etc. (*distinction*) 873.

V. be -fashionable etc. *adj.*, − the rage etc. *n.*; have a run, pass current.

follow -, conform to -, fall in with- the fashion etc. *n.*; go with the stream etc. (*conform*) 82; *savoir -vivre*, − *faire*; keep up appearances, behave oneself.

set the -, bring into- fashion; give a tone to -, cut a figure in- society, rub shoulders with nobility, keep one's carriage.

Adj. fashionable; in -fashion etc. *n.*; *à la mode, comme il faut*; admitted -, admissible -in -society etc. *n.*; presentable, decorous, punctilious, conventional etc. (*customary*) 613; genteel; well-bred, -mannered, -behaved, -spoken; gentleman-like, -ly; ladylike; civil, polite etc. (*courteous*) 894.

polished, refined, thoroughbred, courtly; *distingué*, aristocratic, unembarrassed, poised, *dégagé*; ja-, jau-nty; dashing, fast, showy, high toned, toney.

modish, stylish, in the latest style, *recherché*; new-fangled etc. (*unfamiliar*) 83.

in -court, − full, − evening- dress; *en grande tenue* etc. (*ornament*) 847.

Adv. fashionably etc. *adj.*; for fashion's sake.

853. Ridiculousness.—N. ridiculousness etc. *adj.*; comical-, odd-ity etc. *adj.*; extravagance, drollery.

farce, comedy; burlesque etc. (*ridicule*) 856; buffoonery etc. (*fun*) 840; frippery; doggerel verses; Irish bull, Hibernianism, Hibernicism; Spoonerism; absurdity etc. 497; bombast etc. (*unmeaning*) 517; anticlimax, bathos; monstrosity etc. (*unconformity*) 83; laughing stock etc. 857.

V. be -ridiculous etc. *adj.*; pass from the sublime to the ridiculous; make one laugh; play the fool, make a fool of oneself, commit an absurdity.

play a joke on, make a -fool of, – sucker of, – monkey of.

Adj. ridiculous, ludicrous; comic, -al; droll, funny, laughable, *pour rire*, grotesque, farcical, odd; whimsical, – as a dancing bear; fanciful, fantastic, queer, rum, quizzical, waggish, quaint, *bizarre*; eccentric etc. (*unconformable*) 83; strange, outlandish, out of the way, *baroque*, *rocaille*, rococo; awkward etc. (*ugly*) 846.

absurd, extravagant, *outré*, monstrous, preposterous, bombastic, inflated, stilted, burlesque, mock heroic.

drollish; serio-, tragic-comic; gimcrack, contemptible etc. (*unimportant*) 643; doggerel; ironical etc. (*derisive*) 856; risible.

Phr. *'risum teneatis amici?' rideret Heraclitus.*

854. Fop.—N. fop, fine gentleman; swell; dand-y, -iprat; exquisite, coxcomb, toff, beau, macaroni, blade, blood, buck, man about town, fast man; fribble, jemmy, spark, popinjay, puppy, prig, *petit maître*; jacka-napes, -dandy; man milliner; Jemmy Jessamy, carpet-knight, masher, Dundreary, Johnnie, dude.

belle, fine lady, *coquette*, flirt.

855. Affectation.—N. affectation; affectedness etc. *adj.*; acting a part etc. *v.*; pretence etc. (*falsehood*) 544; (*ostentation*) 882; boasting etc. 884.

charlatanism, quakery, shallow profundity, humbug, pretension, airs, pedantry, purism, precisianism, euphuism, prunes and prisms; teratology etc. (*altiloquence*) 577.

mannerism, *simagrée*, grimace.

conceit, foppery, dandyism, man millinery, coxcombry, puppyism.

stiffness, formality, buckram; prudery, demureness, coquetry, mock modesty, *minauderie*, sentimentalism; *mauvaise honte*, false shame.

affector, performer, actor; pedant, pedagogue, *doctrinaire*, purist, euphuist, mannerist; shoneen; *grimacier*; lump of affectation, *précieuse ridicule*, *bas bleu*, blue stocking, poetaster; prig, hypocrite; charlatan etc. (*deceiver*) 548; *petit maître* etc. (*fop*) 854; flatterer etc. 935; *coquette*, prude, puritan; precisian, formalist.

V. affect, act a part, put on; give oneself airs etc. (*arrogance*) 885; boast etc. 884; coquet; simper, mince, attitudinize, strike a pose, pose; flirt a fan; over-act, -play, -do.

Adj. affected, full of affectation, pretentious, pedantic, stilted, stagey, theatrical, big-sounding, *ad captandum*, canting, insincere.

not natural, unnatural; self-conscious; *maniéré*; artificial; over-wrought, -done, -acted; euphuistic etc. 577.

stiff, starch, formal, prim, smug, demure, *tiré à. quatre épingles*, quakerish, puritanical, prudish, pragmatical, priggish, conceited, coxcomical, foppish, dandified; fini-cal, -kin, -cky, mincing, simpering, namby-pamby, sentimental, languishing.

856. Ridicule.—N. ridicule, derision; sardonic -smile, – grin; irrision; snigger; scoffing etc. (*disrespect*) 929; mockery, quiz, banter, irony, *persiflage*, raillery, chaff, *badinage*; quizzing etc. *v.*

squib, satire, skit, quip, quib, grin.

parody, burlesque, travesty; farce etc. (*drama*) 599; caricature, take-off.

buffoonery etc. (*fun*) 840; practical joke, horseplay.

V. ridicule, deride; laugh at, grin at, smile at; snigger; laugh in one's sleeve; banter, rally, chaff, joke, twit, quiz, poke fun at, jolly, roast, rag; fleer; play –, play tricks- upon; fool, – to the top of one's bent; show up.

satirize, parody, caricature, burlesque, travesty.

turn into ridicule; make merry with; make -fun, – game, – a fool, – an April fool- of; rally; scoff etc. (*disrespect*) 929.

raise a laugh etc. (*amuse*) 840; play the fool, make a fool of oneself.

be ridiculous etc. 853.

Adj. deris-ory, -ive; mock; sarcastic, ironical, quizzical, burlesque, Hudibrastic; scurrilous etc. (*disrespectful*) 929.

Adv. in -ridicule etc. *n.*

857. Laughing-stock. [Object and cause of ridicule.]—**N.** laughing-, jesting-, gazing-stock; butt, game, fair game; April fool etc. (*dupe*) 547.

original, oddity; queer –, odd- fish; quiz, square toes; old –, fogey *or* fogy..

monkey; buffoon etc. (*jester*) 844; pantomimist etc. (*actor*) 599.

jest etc. (*wit*) 842.

858. Hope.—N. hope, -s; desire etc. 865; fervent hope, sanguine expectation, trust, confidence, reliance; faith etc. (*belief*) 484; affiance, assurance; secur-eness, -ity; reassurance.

good -omen, – auspices; promise; well-grounded hopes; good –, bright- .prospect; clear sky.

as-, pre-sumption; anticipation etc. (*expectation*) 507.

hopefulness, buoyancy, optimism, enthusiasm, heart of grace, aspiration; optimist, utop-ian, -ist; Pollyanna.

castles in the air, *châteaux en Espagne*, hope chest, *le pot au lait*, Utopia, millennium; day –, golden- dream; dream of Alnaschar; airy hopes, fool's paradise; *mirage* etc. (*fallacies of vision*) 443; fond hope.

beam –, ray –, gleam –, glimmer –, dawn –, flash –, star- of hope; cheer; bit of blue sky, silver lining of the cloud, bottom of Pandora's box, balm in Gilead.

anchor, sheet-anchor, main-stay; staff etc. (*support*) 215; heaven etc. 981.

V. hope, trust, confide, rely on, put one's trust in, lean upon; pin one's -hope, – faith- upon etc. (*believe*) 484.

feel –, entertain –, harbor –, indulge –, cherish –, feed –, foster –, nourish –, encourage –, cling to –, live in- hope etc. *n.*; see land; feel –, rest- -assured, – confident etc. *adj*.

presume; promise oneself; expect etc. (*look forward to*) 507.

hope for etc. (*desire*) 865; anticipate.

be -hopeful etc. *adj.*; look on the bright side of, view on the sunny side, make the best of it, hope for the best; put -a good, – a bold, – the best-face upon; keep one's spirits up; take heart, – of grace; be of good -heart, – cheer; flatter oneself, lay the flattering unction to one's soul.

catch at a straw, hope against hope, count one's chickens before they are hatched.

give –, inspire –, raise –, hold out- hope etc. *n.*; raise expectations; encourage, hearten, cheer, assure, reassure, buoy up, embolden; promise, bid fair, augur well, be in a fair way, look up, flatter, tell a flattering tale.

Adj. hoping etc. *v.*; in -hopes etc. *n.*; hopeful, confident; secure etc. (*certain*) 484; sanguine, in good heart, buoyed up, buoyant, elated, flushed, exultant, enthusiastic; utopian.

unsus-pecting, -picious; fearless, free –, exempt from- -fear, – suspicion, – distrust, – despair; undespairing, self-reliant.

probable, on the high road to; within sight of -shore, – land; promising, propitious; of –, full of-promise; of good omen; auspicious, *de bon augure*; reassuring; encouraging, cheering, inspiriting, looking up, bright, roseate, *couleur de rose*, rose-colored.

Adv. hopefully etc. *adj*.

Phr. *nil desperandum*; never say die, *dum spiro spero, latet scintillula forsan*, all is for the best, *spero meliora*; the wish being father to the thought; 'hope told a flattering tale;' *rusticus expectat dum defluat amnis*.

859. Hopelessness. [Absence, want, or loss of hope.]—**N.** hopelessness etc. *adj.*; despair, desperation; despondency etc. (*dejection*) 837; pessimism.

hope deferred, dashed hopes; vain expectation etc. (*disappointment*) 509.

airy hopes etc. 858; forlorn hope; bad -job, – business; *enfant perdu*; gloomy –, black spots in the- horizon; slough of Despond, cave of Despair. Job's comforter; bird of -bad, – ill-omen.

V. despair; lose –, give up –, abandon –, relinquish- -all hope, – the hope of; give -up, – over; yield to despair; falter; despond etc. (*be dejected*) 837; *jeter le manche après la cognée*.

inspire –, drive to- despair etc. *n.*; disconcert; dash –, crush –, shatter –, destroy- one's hopes; hope against hope.

Adj. hopeless, desperate, despairing, in despair, *au désespoir*, forlorn; inconsolable etc. (*dejected*) 837; broken-hearted.

out of the question, not to be thought of; im-practicable etc. 471; past -hope, – cure, – mending, – recall; at one's last gasp etc. (*death*) 360; given -up, – over.

incurable, cureless, immedicable, remediless, beyond remedy; incorrigible; irre-parable, -mediable, -coverable, -versible, -trievable, -claimable, -deemable, -vocable; ruined, undone; immitigable.

unpromising, unpropitious; inauspicious, ill-omened, threatening, clouded over, lowering, ominous.

Phr. *'lasciate ogni speranza voi ch' entrate;'* its days are numbered; the worst come to the worst.

860. Fear.—N. fear, timidity, diffidence, want of confidence; apprehensive-, fearful-ness etc. *adj.*; solicitude, anxiety, care, apprehension, misgiving; mistrust etc. (*doubt*) 485; suspicion, qualm; hesitation etc. (*irresolution*) 605.

nervous-, restless-ness etc. *adj.*; in-, dis-quietude; flutter, trepidation, fear and trembling, perturbation, tremor, quivering, shaking, trembling, throbbing heart, palpitation, ague fit, cold sweat; abject fear etc. (*cowardice*) 862; mortal funk, heart-sinking, despondency; despair etc. 859.

fright; affright, -ment; alarm, pavor, dread, awe, terror, horror, dismay, consternation, panic, scare, stampede [of horses].

intimidation, terrorism, reign of terror.

[Object of fear] bug-bear, -aboo; scarecrow; hobgoblin etc. (*demon*) 980; daymare, nightmare, Gorgon, Medusa, mormo, ogre, Hurlothrumbo, raw head and bloody bones, fee faw fum, *bête noire, enfant terrible*.

alarmist etc. (*coward*) 862.

V. fear, stand in awe of; be -afraid etc. *adj.*; have -qualms etc. *n.*; apprehend, sit upon thorns, eye askance; distrust etc. (*disbelieve*) 485.

hesitate etc. (*be irresolute*) 605; falter, funk, cower, crouch; skulk etc. (*cowardice*) 862; let 'I dare not' wait upon 'I would;' take -fright, – alarm; start, wince, flinch, shy, shrink; fly etc. (*avoid*) 623.

tremble, shake; shiver, – in one's shoes; shudder, flutter; shake –, tremble- -like an aspen leaf, – all over; quake, quaver, quiver, quail; get the wind up.

grow –, turn- pale; blench, stand aghast; not dare to say one's soul is one's own.

inspire –, excite- -fear, – awe; raise apprehensions; give –, raise –, sound- an alarm; alarm, startle, scare, cry 'wolf,' disquiet, dismay; fright, -en; affright, terrify; astound; frighten from one's propriety; frighten out of one's -wits, – senses, – seven senses; awe; strike -all of a heap, – an awe into, – terror; harrow up the soul, appal, unman, petrify, horrify.

make one's -flesh creep, – hair stand on end, -blood run cold, – teeth chatter; chill one's spine; take away –, stop- one's breath; make one -tremble etc.

haunt, obsess, beset; prey –, weigh- on the mind.

put in -fear, – bodily fear; terrorize, intimidate, cow, daunt, over-awe, abash, deter, discourage; browbeat, bully; threaten etc. 909.

Adj. fearing etc. *v.*; frightened etc. *v.*; in -fear, – a fright etc. *n.*; haunted with the -fear etc. *n.*- of.

afraid, fearful; tim-id, -orous; nervous, diffident, coy, faint-hearted, tremulous, shaky, afraid of one's shadow, apprehensive, restless, fidgety; more frightened than hurt.

aghast; awe-, horror-, terror-, panic- -struck, - stricken; frightened to death, white as a sheet; pale, - as -death, - ashes, - a ghost; breathless, in hysterics.

inspiring fear etc. *v.*; alarming; formidable, redoubtable; perilous etc. (*danger*) 665; portentous; fear-ful, -some; dread, -ful; fell; dire, -ful; shocking; terri-ble, -fic; tremendous; horri-d, -ble, - fic; ghastly; awful, awe-inspiring, eerie, weird; revolting etc. (*painful*) 830.

Adv. *in terrorem.*

Int. 'angels and ministers of grace defend us!'

Phr. *ante tubam trepidat; horresco referens,* one's heart failing one, *obstupui steteruntque comae et vox faucibus haesit.*

861. Courage. [Absence of fear.]—**N.** courage, bravery, valor; resolute-, bold-ness etc. *adj.*; spirit, daring, gallantry, intrepidity; contempt -, defiance- of danger; derring-do; audacity; rashness etc. 863; dash; defiance etc. 715; confidence, self-reliance.

man-liness, -hood; nerve, pluck, mettle; game; heart, - of grace; spunk, gameness, grit, face, virtue, hardihood, fortitude; firmness etc. (*stability*) 150; heart of oak; bottom, backbone etc. (*perseverance*) 604a.

resolution etc. (*determination*) 604; tenacity, bull-dog courage.

prowess, heroism, chivalry.

exploit, feat, achievement; heroic -deed, - act; bold stroke.

man, - of mettle; hero, demigod, paladin, heroine, Amazon, Hector, Joan of Arc; lion, tiger, panther, bulldog; game-, fighting-cock; bully, fire-eater etc. 863; dare-devil.

V. be -courageous etc. *adj.*; dare, venture, make bold; face -, front -, affront -, confront -, brave -, defy -, despise -, mock- danger; look in the face; look -full, - boldly, - danger- in the face; face; meet, - in front; brave, beard; defy etc. 715.

take -, muster -, summon up -, pluck up-courage; nerve oneself, take heart; take -, pluck up- heart of grace; hold up one's head, screw one's courage to the sticking place; come -to, - up to- the scratch; stand, - to one's guns, - fire, - against; bear up - against; hold out etc. (*persevere*) 604a.

put a bold face upon; show -, present- a bold front, face the music; envisage; show fight.

bell the cat, take the bull by the horns, beard the lion in his den, march up to the cannon's mouth, go through fire and water, run the gauntlet, go over the top.

give -, infuse -, inspire- courage; reassure, en-courage, embolden, inspirit, cheer, hearten, nerve, put upon one's mettle, rally, raise a rallying cry; pat on the back, make a man of, keep in countenance.

Adj. courageous, brave; val-iant, -orous; gallant, intrepid; spirit-ed, -ful; high-spirited, -mettled; mettlesome; game, plucky; man-ly, -ful; resolute; stout, -hearted; iron-, lion-hearted; heart of oak; Penthesilean.

bold, - spirited; daring, audacious; fear-, daunt-, dread-, awe-less; un-daunted, -appalled, - dismayed, -awed, -blenched, -abashed, -alarmed, - flinching, -shrinking, -blenching; apprehensive; confident, self-reliant; bold as -a lion, - brass.

enterprising, adventurous; ventur-ous, -esome; dashing, chivalrous; soldierly etc. (*warlike*) 722; heroic.

fierce, savage; pugnacious etc. (*bellicose*) 720.

strong-minded, hardy, doughty; firm etc. (*stable*) 150; determined etc. (*resolved*) 604; dogged, in-domitable etc. (*persevering*) 604a.

up to, - the scratch; upon one's mettle; reassured etc. *v.*; unfeared, undreaded.

Phr. one's blood being up.

862. Cowardice. [Excess of fear.]—**N.** cowardice, pusillanimity; cowardliness etc. *adj.*; timidity, effeminacy.

poltroonery, baseness; dastard-ness, -y; abject fear, funk; Dutch courage; fear etc. 860; white feather, faint heart.

coward, poltroon, dastard, sneak, recreant; shy -, dunghill- cock; coistril, milksop, white-liver, nidget, cur, craven, one that cannot say 'Boo' to a goose; Bob Acres, Jerry Sneak.

alarm-, terror-, pessim-ist; runagate etc. (*fugitive*) 623; shirker.

V. quail etc. (*fear*) 860; be -cowardly etc. *adj.*, - a coward etc. *n.*; funk; cower, skulk, sneak; flinch, shy, fight shy, slink, turn tail; run away etc. (*avoid*) 623; show the white feather, have cold feet, show a yellow streak.

Adj. coward, -ly; fearful, shy; tim-id, -orous; skittish; poor-spirited, spirit-less, soft, effeminate.

weak-minded; infirm of purpose etc. 605; weak-, faint-, chicken-, lily-, pigeon-hearted; yellow; white-, lily-, milk-livered; milksop, smock-faced; unable to say 'Boo' to a goose.

dastard, -ly; base, craven, sneaking, dunghill, recreant; unwar-, unsoldier-like.

'in face a lion but in heart a deer.'

unmanned; frightened etc. 860.

Int. *sauve qui peut!* devil take the hindmost!

Adv. in fear and trembling, in fear of one's life, in a blue funk.

Phr. *ante tubam trepidat,* one's courage oozing out.

863. Rashness.—**N.** rashness etc. *adj.*; temerity, want of caution, imprudence, in-discretion; over-confidence, presumption, audacity.

precipit-ancy, -ation; impetuosity; levity; foolhardi-hood, -ness; heed-, thought-lessness etc. (*inattention*) 458; carelessness etc. (*neglect*) 460; desperation; Quixotism, knight-errantry; fire-eating.

gam-ing, -bling; blind bargain, leap in the dark, fool's paradise; too many eggs in one basket.

desperado, rashling, mad-cap, dare-devil, Hot-spur, fire-eater, bully, *bravo,* Hector, scapegrace, *enfant perdu;* Don Quixote, knight-errant, Icarus; adventurer; gam-bler, -ester; dynamitard.

V. be -rash etc. *adj.*; stick at nothing, play a desperate game; run into danger etc. 665; play with -fire, - edge tools.

carry too much sail, sail too near the wind, ride at single anchor, go out of one's depth.

take a leap in the dark, buy a pig in a poke.

donner tête baissée; knock one's head against a wall etc. (*be unskilful*) 699; rush on destruction; kick against the pricks, tempt Providence, go on a forlorn hope.

count one's chickens before they are hatched; reckon without one's host; catch at straws; trust to –, lean on- a broken reed.

Adj. rash, incautious, indiscreet, injudicious; imprudent, improvident, temerarious; uncalculating; heedless; careless etc. (*neglectful*) 460; without ballast, heels over head; giddy etc. (*inattentive*) 458; wanton, reckless, wild, madcap; desperate, devil-may-care.

hot-blooded, -headed, -brained; head-long, -strong; break-neck; fool-hardy; harebrained; precipitate, impulsive.

over-confident, -weening; ventur-esome, -ous; adventurous, Quixotic; fire-eating, cavalier; free-and-easy.

off one's guard etc. (*inexpectant*) 508.

Adv. post haste, *à corps perdu*, hand over head, *tête baissée*, head- foremost; happen what may.

Phr. neck or nothing, the devil being in one.

864. Caution.—N. caution; cautiousness etc. *adj.*; discretion, prudence, cautel, heed, circumspection, calculation, deliberation; safety first.

foresight etc. 510; vigilance etc. 459; warning etc. 668.

coolness etc. *adj.*; self-possession, -command; presence of mind, *sang froid*; well-regulated mind; worldly wisdom, Fabian policy.

V. be -cautious etc. *adj.*; take -care, – heed, – good care; have a care; mind, – what one is about; be on one's guard etc. (*keep watch*) 459; make assurance double sure; ca' canny.

bespeak etc. (*be early*) 132.

think twice, look before one leaps, keep one's weather eye open, count the cost, look to the main chance, cut one's coat according to one's cloth; feel one's -ground, – way; see how the land lies etc. (*foresight*) 510; wait to see how the cat jumps; bridle one's tongue; *reculer pour mieux sauter* etc. (*prepare*) 673; let well alone, let sleeping dogs lie, *ne pas réveiller le chat qui dort*.

keep out of -harm's way; – troubled waters; keep at a respectful distance, stand aloof; keep –, be- on the safe side.

husband one's resources etc. 636.

caution etc. (*warn*) 668.

Adj. cautious, wary, guarded; on one's guard etc. (*watchful*) 459; *cavendo tutus*; *in medio tutissimus*.

care-, heed-ful; cautelous, stealthy, chary, shy of, circumspect, prudent, canny, safe, non-committal, discreet, politic; sure-footed etc. (*skilful*) 698.

unenterprising, unadventurous, cool, steady, self-possessed; over-cautious.

suspicious, leery, vigilant.

Adv. cautiously, gingerly etc. *adj.*

Int. have a care! look out! *cave canem!*

Phr. *timeo Danaos*; *festina lente*.

865. Desire.—N. desire, wish, fancy, fantasy; want, need, exigency.

mind, inclination, leaning, bent, *animus*, partiality, *penchant*, predilection; propensity etc. 820; willingness etc. 602; liking, love, fondness, relish.

longing, hankering; solicitude, anxiety; yearning, coveting; aspiration, ambition, vaulting ambition; eagerness, zeal, ardor, *empressement*, breathless impatience, over-anxiety; solicitude, impetuosity etc. 825.

appet-ite, -ition, -ence, -ency: sharp appetite, keenness, hunger, stomach, twist; thirst, -iness; drouth, mouth-watering; itch, -ing; prurience, *cacoëthes*, cupidity, lust, concupiscence.

edge of -appetite, – hunger; torment of Tantalus; sweet –, lickerish- tooth; itching palm; longing –, wistful –, sheep's-eye.

avidity; greed, -iness; covetous-, ravenous-ness etc. *adj.*; grasping, craving, canine appetite, rapacity; voracity etc. (*gluttony*) 957.

passion, rage, *furore*, mania, *manie*; inextinguishable desire; dips-, klept-, mon-omania.

[Person desiring] desirer, lover, *amateur*, votary, devotee, aspirant, solicitant, candidate; cormorant etc. 957; sycophant.

[Object of desire] *desideratum*; want etc. (*requirement*) 630; 'consumation devoutly to be wished;' attraction, magnet, allurement, fancy, temptation, seduction, lure, fascination, *prestige*, height of one's ambition; whim, -sey; maggot, hobby, -horse.

Fortunatus's cap, wishing cap, love potion.

V. desire; wish, – for; be -desirous etc. *adj.*; have a -longing etc. *n.*; hope etc. 858.

care for, affect, like, list; take to, cling to, take a fancy to; fancy; prefer etc. (*choose*) 609.

have -an eye, – a mind- to; find it in one's heart etc. (*be willing*) 602; have a fancy for, set one's eyes upon; cast a sheep's eye –, look sweet- upon; take into one's head, have a heart, be bent upon; set one's -cap at, – heart upon, – mind upon; covet.

want, miss, need, lack, desiderate, feel the want of; would fain -have, – do; would be glad of.

be -hungry etc. *adj.*; have a good appetite, play a good knife and fork; hunger –, thirst –, crave –, lust –, itch –, hanker –, run mad- after; raven –, die- for; burn to.

desiderate; sigh –, cry –, gape –, gasp –, pine –, pant –, languish –, yearn –, long –, be on thorns –, hope- for; aspire after; catch at, grasp at, jump at.

woo, court, solicit; fish –, spell –, whistle –, put up- for; ogle.

cause –, create –, raise –, excite –, provoke-desire; whet the appetite; appetize, titillate, allure, attract, take one's fancy, tempt; hold out -temptation, – allurement; tantalize, make one's mouth water, *faire venir l'eau à la bouche*.

gratify desire etc. (*give pleasure*) 829.

Adj. desirous; desiring etc. *v.*; orectic, appetitive; inclined etc. (*willing*) 602; partial to; fain, wishful, optative; anxious, wistful, curious; at a loss for, sedulous, solicitous.

craving, hungry, sharp-set, peckish, ravening, with an empty stomach, esurient, lickerish, thirsty, athirst, parched with thirst, pinched with hunger, famished, dry, drouthy; hungry as a -hunter, – hawk, – horse, – church mouse.

greedy, – as a hog; over-eager, voracious; ravenous, – as a wolf; open-mouthed, covetous, rapacious, grasping, extortionate, exacting, sordid, *alieni appetens*; insati-able, -ate; unquenchable, quenchless; omnivorous.

unsatisfied, unsated, unslaked.

eager, avid, keen; burning, fervent, ardent; agog; all agog; breathless; impatient etc. (*impetuous*) 825; bent –, intent –, set- -on, – upon; mad after, *enragé*, rabid, dying for, devoured by desire.

aspiring, ambitious, vaulting, sky-aspiring.

desirable; popular; desired etc. *v.*; in demand; pleasing etc. (*giving pleasure*) 829; appeti-zing. -ble; tantalizing.

Adv. wistfully etc. *adj.*; fain.

Int. would -that, – it were! O for! *esto perpetua!* if only!

Phr. the wish being the father to the thought; *sua cuique voluptas*; *hoc erat in votis*, the mouth watering, the fingers itching; *aut Caesar aut nullus*.

866. Indifference.—N. indifference, neutrality; coldness etc. *adj.*; unconcern, *insouciance*, *nonchalance*; want of -interest, – earnestness; anorexy, inappetency; apathy etc. (*insensibility*) 823; supineness etc. (*inactivity*) 683; disdain etc. 930; recklessness etc. 863; inattention etc. 458.

V. be -indifferent etc. *adj.*; stand neuter; take no interest in etc. (*insensibility*) 823; have no -desire etc. 865, – taste, – relish- for; not care for; care nothing -for, – about; not care a -straw etc. (*unimportance*) 643 -about, – for; not mind.

set at naught etc. (*make light of*) 483; spurn etc. (*disdain*) 930.

Adj. indifferent, cold, frigid, lukewarm; cool, – as a cucumber; unconcerned, *insouciant*, phlegmatic, *pococurante*, easy-going, devil-may-care, careless, listless, lackadaisical, feckless; half-hearted; un-ambitious, -aspiring, -desirous, -solicitous, -attracted.

un-attractive, -alluring, -desired, -desirable, -cared for, -wished, -valued, all one to.

insipid etc. 391; vain.

Adv. for aught one cares.

Int. never mind.

867. Dislike.—N. dis-like, -taste, -relish, -inclination, -placency.

reluctance; backwardness etc. (*unwillingness*) 603.

repugnance, disgust, queasiness, turn, nausea, loathing; avers-eness, -ation, -ion; abomination, antipathy, abhorrence, horror; mortal –, rooted- -antipathy, – horror; hatred, detestation; hate etc. 898; animosity etc. 900; hydrophobia.

sickener; gall and wormwood etc. (*unsavory*) 395; shuddering, cold sweat.

V. dis-, mis-like, -relish; mind, object to; have rather not, not care for; have –, conceive –, entertain –, take- -a dislike, – an aversion- to; have no -taste, – stomach- for.

shun, avoid etc. 623; eschew; withdraw –, shrink –, recoil- from; not be able to -bear, – abide; – endure; shrug the shoulders at, shudder at, turn up the nose at, look askance at; make a -mouth, – wry face, – grimace; make faces.

loathe, nauseate, abominate, detest, abhor; hate etc. 898; take amiss etc. 900; have enough of etc. (*be satiated*) 869.

cause –, excite- dislike; disincline, repel, sicken; make –, render- sick; turn one's stomach, nauseate, wamble, disgust, shock, stink in the nostrils; go against the -grain, – stomach; stick in the throat; make one's blood run cold etc. (*give pain*) 830; pall.

Adj. disliking etc. *v.*; averse to, loth, adverse; shy of, sick of, out of conceit with; disinclined; heart-, dog-sick; queasy.

disliked etc. *v.*; uncared for, unpopular; out of favor; repulsive, repugnant, repellent; abhorrent, insufferable, fulsome, nauseous; loath-some, -ful; offensive; disgusting etc. *v.*; disagreeable etc. (*painful*) 830; unsavory etc. 395.

Adv. *usque ad nauseam*.

Int. faugh! foh! ugh!

868. Fastidiousness.—N. fastidiousness etc. *adj.*; nicety, meticulosity, hypercriticism, difficulty in being pleased, *friandise*, epicurism, *omnia suspendens naso*.

discrimination, discernment, good taste, perspicacity.

epicure, gourmet.

[Excess of delicacy] prudery, prudishness, primness.

V. be -fastidious etc. *adj.*; split hairs, discriminate, have a sweet tooth.

mince the matter; turn up one's nose at etc. (*disdain*) 930; look a gift horse in the mouth, see spots on the sun.

Adj. fastidious, meticulous, exacting, nice, delicate, *délicat*, finical, finicky, difficult, dainty, lickerish, squeamish, thin-skinned; s-, queasy; hard –, difficult- to please; querulous, particular, over-particular, straitlaced, prudish, prim, scrupulous; censorious etc. 932; hypercritical, discriminating, discerning, perspicacious.

Phr. *noli me tangere*.

869. Satiety.—N. satiety, satisfaction, saturation, repletion, glut, surfeit; weariness etc. 841.

spoiled child; *enfant gâté*; too much of a good thing, *toujours perdrix*; *crambe repetita*.

V. sate, satiate, satisfy, saturate; cloy, quench, slake, pall, glut, gorge, surfeit; bore etc. (*weary*) 841; tire etc. (*fatigue*) 688; spoil.

have -enough of, – quite enough of, – one's fill, – too much of; be -satiated etc. *adj.*

Adj. satiated etc. *v.*; overgorged; *blasé*, used up, sick of, heart-sick.

Int. enough! hold! *eheu jam satis!*

870. Wonder.—N. wonder, marvel; astonish-, amaze-, wonder-, bewilder-ment; amazedness etc. *adj.*; admiration, awe; stup-or, -efaction; stound, fascination; sensation; surprise etc. (*inexpectation*) 508; cynosure.

note of admiration; thaumaturgy etc. (*sorcery*) 992.

V. wonder, marvel, admire; be -surprised etc. *adj.*; start; stare; open –, rub –, turn up- one's eyes; gloar; gape, open one's mouth, hold one's breath; look –, stand- -aghast, – agog; look blank etc. (*disappointment*) 509; *tomber des nues*; not believe one's -eyes, – ears, – senses.

not be able to account for etc. (*unintelligible*) 519; not know whether one stands on one's head or one's heels.

surprise, astonish, amaze, astound; dumbfound, -er; startle, dazzle; strike, – with -wonder, – awe; electrify; stun, stupefy, petrify, confound, bewilder, flabbergast; stagger; throw on one's beam ends, fascinate, turn the head, take away one's breath, strike dumb; make one's -hair stand on end, – tongue cleave to the roof of one's mouth; make one stare.

take by surprise etc. (*be unexpected*) 508.

be -wonderful etc. *adj.*; beggar –, baffle-description; stagger belief.

Adj. surprised etc. *v.*; aghast, all agog, breathless, agape; open-mouthed; awe-, thunder-, moon-, planet-struck; spell-bound; lost in -amazement, – wonder, – astonishment; struck all of a heap, unable to believe one's senses, like a duck in thunder.

wonderful, wondrous; surprising etc. *v.*; unexpected etc. 508; unheard of; mysterious etc. (*inexplicable*) 519; miraculous; *foudroyant*.

in-describable, -expressible, -effable; un-utterable, -speakable.

monstrous, prodigious, stupendous, marvelous; in-conceivable, -credible; in-, un-imaginable; strange etc. (*uncommon*) 83; passing strange.

striking etc. *v.*; over-whelming; wonder-working.

Adv. wonderfully etc. *adj.*; fearfully; for a –, in the name of- wonder; strange to say; *mirabile -dictu*, – visu; to one's great surprise.

with -wonder etc. *n.*, – gaping mouth, – open eyes, – upturned eyes; eyes starting out of one's head.

Int. lo, – and behold! O! hey-day! halloo! what! indeed! really! surely! humph! h'm! good -lack, – heavens, – gracious! – lord! by jove! gad so! well a day! dear me! only think! lack-a-daisy! my -stars, – goodness! gracious goodness! goodness gracious! mercy on us! heavens and earth! God bless me! bless -us, – my heart! odzooks! O gemini! ad-zooks! hoity-toity! strong! Heaven save –, bless-the mark! can such things be! zounds! 'sdeath! what -on earth, – in the world! who would have thought it! etc. (*inexpectation*) 508; fancy! did you ever? you don't say so! what do you say to that! how now! where am I? well I'm blowed! etc.

Phr. *vox faucibus haesit*; one's hair standing on end.

871. Expectance. [Absence of wonder.] —**N.** expectan-ce, -cy etc. (*expectation*) 507; calmness, composure, tranquillity, serenity, coolness, imperturbability etc. 826.

nine days' wonder.

V. expect etc. 507; not -be surprised, – wonder etc. 870; *nil admirari*, make nothing of.

Adj. expecting etc. *v.*; unamazed, astonished at nothing; *blasé* etc. (*weary*) 841; unimaginative, calm, serene, imperturbable etc. 826; expected etc. *v.*; foreseen.

common, ordinary etc. (*habitual*) 613.

Int. no wonder; of course; why not?

872. Prodigy.—**N.** prodigy, phenomenon; wonder, -ment; genius, marvel, miracle; freak, monster etc. (*unconformity*) 83; curiosity, lion, infant prodigy, sight, spectacle; *jeu –, coup- de théâtre*; gazing-stock; sign; portent etc. 512.

bursting of a -shell, – bomb; volcanic eruption, peal of thunder; thunder-clap, -bolt.

what no words can paint; wonders of the world; *annus mirabilis*; *dignus vindice nodus*.

873. Repute.—**N.** distinction, mark, name, figure; repute, reputation, character; good –, high-repute; note, notability, notoriety, *éclat*, 'the bubble reputation,' vogue, celebrity; fame, famousness; renown; popularity, *aura popularis*; esteem, approval, approbation etc. 931; credit, *succès d'estime*, prestige, talk of the town; name to conjure with.

glory, honor; luster etc. (*light*) 420; illustriousness etc. *adj.*

account, regard, respect; reputableness etc. *adj.*; respectability etc. (*probity*) 939; good -name, – report; fair name.

dignity; stateliness etc. *adj.*; solemnity, grandeur, splendor, nobility, majesty, sublimity.

rank, standing, brevet rank, precedence, *pas*, station, place, *status*; position, – in society; order, degree, *locus standi*, caste, condition.

greatness etc. *adj.*; eminence; height etc. 206; importance etc. 642; pre-, super-eminence; high mightiness, primacy; top of the -ladder, – tree.

elevation; ascent etc. 305; super-, ex-altation; dignification, aggrandizement.

dedication, consecration, enthronement, canonization, apotheosis, deification, celebration, enshrinement, glorification.

hero, man of mark, great card, celebrity, worthy, lion, *rara avis*, notability, somebody; man of rank etc. (*nobleman*) 875; pillar of the -state, – society, – church.

chief etc. (*master*) 745; first fiddle etc. (*proficient*) 700; scholar etc. 492; cynosure, mirror; flower, pink, pearl; paragon etc. (*perfection*) 650; choice and master spirits of the age; *élite*; star, sun, constellation, galaxy.

ornament, honor, feather in one's cap, halo, aureole, nimbus; halo –, blaze- of glory; blushing honors; laurels etc. (*trophy*) 733.

memory, posthumous fame, niche in the temple of fame; immor-tality, -tal name; *magni nominis umbra*.

V. be conscious of glory; be proud of etc. (*pride*) 878; exult etc. (*boast*) 884; be vain of etc. (*vanity*) 880.

be -distinguished etc. *adj.*; shine etc. (*light*) 420; shine forth, figure; make –, cut- a -figure, – dash, – splash.

rival, surpass; out-shine, -rival, -vie, -jump; emulate, vie with, eclipse; throw –, cast- into the shade; overshadow.

live, flourish, glitter, scintillate, flaunt; gain –, acquire- honor etc. *n.*; play first fiddle etc. (*be of importance*) 642; bear the -palm, – bell; lead the way; take -precedence, – the wall of; gain –, win-laurels, – spurs, – golden opinions etc. (*approbation*) 931; graduate, take one's degree, pass one's examination, win a -scholarship, – fellowship.

make -a, – some- -noise, – noise in the world; leave one's mark, exalt one's horn, star, have a run, be run after; enjoy popularity, come -into vogue, – to the front; raise one's head.

enthrone, signalize, immortalize, deify, exalt to the skies; hand one's name down to posterity.

consecrate; dedicate to, devote to; enshrine, inscribe, blazon, lionize, blow the trumpet, crown with laurel.

confer −, reflect- honor etc. n. on; shed a luster on; redound to one's honor, ennoble.

give −, do −, pay −, render- honor to; honor, accredit, pay regard to, dignify, glorify; sing praises to etc. (approve) 931; look up to; exalt, aggrandize, elevate, nobilitate.

Adj. distinguished, distingué, noted; of -note etc. n.; honored etc. v.; popular; fashionable etc. 852.

in good odor; in −, in high- favor; reput-, respect-, credit-able.

remarkable etc. (important) 642; notable, notorious; celebrated, renowned, in every one's mouth, talked of; fam-ous, -ed; far-famed; conspicuous, to the front; foremost; in the -front rank, − ascendant.

imperishable, deathless, immortal, never fading, aere perennius; time-honored.

illustrious, glorious, splendid, brilliant, radiant; bright etc. 420; full-blown; honorific.

eminent, prominent; high etc. 206; in the zenith; at the -head of, − top of the tree; peerless, of the first water; superior etc. 33; super-, pre-eminent.

great, dignified, proud, noble, honorable, worshipful, lordly, grand, stately, august, princely, imposing, solemn, transcendent, majestic, sacred, sublime, heaven-born, heroic, sans peur et sans reproche; sacrosanct.

Int. hail! all hail! ave! viva! vive! long life to! glory −, honor- be to!

Phr. one's name -being in every mouth, − living for ever; sic itur ad astra, fama volat, aut Caesar aut nullus; not to know him argues oneself unknown; none but himself could be his parallel, palmam qui meruit ferat.

874. Disrepute.—N. disrepute, discredit; ill-, bad- -repute, -name, -odor, -favor; disapprobation etc. 932; in-gloriousness, derogation; a-, debasement; abjectness etc. adj.; degradation, dedecoration; 'a long farewell to all one's greatness;' odium, obloquy, opprobrium, ignominy.

dishonor, disgrace; shame, humiliation; scandal, baseness, vileness, perfidy, turpitude etc. (improbity) 940; infamy.

tarnish, taint, defilement, pollution.

stain, blot, spot, blur, stigma, brand, reproach, imputation, slur.

crying −, burning- shame; scandalum magnatum, badge of infamy, blot in one's escutcheon; bend −, bar- sinister; champain, point champain; by- word of reproach; Ichabod.

argumentum ad verecundiam; sense of shame etc. 879.

V. be -inglorious etc. adj., incur -disgrace etc. n., have −, earn- a bad name; put −, wear- a halter round one's neck; disgrace −, exposeoneself.

play second fiddle, lose caste, pale one's ineffectual fire; recede into the shade; fall from one's high estate; keep in the background etc (modesty) 881, be conscious of disgrace etc. (humility) 879; look -blue, − foolish, − like a fool; cut a -poor.

− sorry- figure; laugh on the wrong side of the mouth; make a sorry face, go away with a flea in one's ear, slink away.

cause -shame etc. n.; shame, disgrace, put to shame, dishonor; throw −, cast −, fling −, reflect- dishonor etc. n. upon; be a -reproach etc. n. to; derogate from.

tarnish, stain, blot, sully, taint; discredit, degrade, debase, defile; beggar; expel etc. (punish) 972.

impute shame to, brand, post, stigmatize, vilify, defame, slur, cast a slur upon, hold up to shame, send to Coventry; tread − trample- under foot; show up, drag through the mire, heap dirt upon; reprehend etc. 932.

bring low, put down, snub; take down a peg, − lower, − or two.

obscure, eclipse, outshine, take the shine out of; throw −, cast- into the shade; overshadow; leave − put- in the background; push into a corner, put one's nose out of joint; put out, − of countenance.

upset, throw off one's center; discompose, disconcert; put to the blush etc. (humble) 879.

Adj. disgraced etc. v.; blown upon; shorn of -its beams, − one' glory; overcome, down-trodden; loaded with -shame etc. n.; in -bad repute etc. n.; out of -repute, − favor, − fashion, − countenance; at a discount; under -a cloud, − an eclipse; unable to show one's face; in the -shade, − background; out at elbows, down in the world, down and out.

inglorious; nameless, renownless, obscure, unknown to fame; un-noticed, -noted, -honored, -glorified.

shameful; dis-graceful, -creditable, -reputable; despicable; questionable; unbecoming, unworthy; derogatory; degrading, humiliating, infra dignitatem, dedecorous; scandalous, infamous, too bad, unmentionable; ribald, opprobrious; arrant, shocking, outrageous, notorious, shady.

ignominious, scrubby, dirty, abject, vile, beggarly, pitiful, low, mean, shabby; base etc. (dishonorable) 940.

Adv. to one's shame be it spoken.

Int. fie! shame! for shame! proh pudor! O tempora! O mores! ough! sic transit gloria mundi!

875. Nobility.—N. nobility, rank, condition, distinction, optimacy, blood, pur sang, birth, high descent, order; quality, gentility; blue blood of Castile; ancien régime.

high life, haut monde; upper -classes, − ten thousand; élite, aristocracy, great folks; fashionable world etc. (fashion) 852; salariat.

peer, -age; house of -lords, − peers; lords, − temporal and spiritual; noblesse; baronage, knightage; noble, -man; lord, -ling; grandee, magnifico, hidalgo; don, -ship; aristocrat, swell, three-tailed bashaw; gentleman, squire, squireen, patrician, laureate.

gentry, gentlefolk; squirarchy, better sort, magnates, primates, optimates.

king etc. (master) 745; prince, crown prince, Dauphin; duke; marquis, -ate, earl, viscount, baron, thane, banneret, baronet, -cy; knight, -hood; count, armiger, laird; sig-, seig-nior, esquire, boyar, margrave, vavasor, sheik, emir, ameer, scherif, pasha, effendi, sahib.

queen etc. 745; princess, begum, duchess, marchioness; countess etc.; lady, dame.

personage –, man- of -distinction, – mark, – rank; nota-bles, -bilities; celebrity, big-wig, magnate, great man, star; *magni nominis umbra*; 'every inch a king;' grand Panjandrum

V. be -noble etc. *adj.*

Adj. noble, exalted; of -rank etc. *n.*; princely, titled, patrician, aristocratic; high-, well-born; of gentle blood; genteel, *comme il faut*, gentlemanlike, courtly etc. (*fashionable*) 852; highly respectable.

Adv. in high quarters.

876. Commonalty.—N. commonalty, democracy; obscruity; low -condition, – life, – society, – company; *bourgeoisie*; mass of -the people, – society; Brown, Jones, and Robinson; Tom, Dick, and Harry; lower –, humbler- classes, – orders; vulgar –, common- herd; rank and file, *hoc genus omne*; the -many, – general, – crowd, – people, – populace, – multitude, – million, – masses, – mobility, – peasantry; king Mob; proletariat, *fruges consumere nati*, great unwashed; man in the street

mob; rabble, – rout; chaff, rout, horde, *canaille*; scum –, *residuum* –, dregs- of -the people, – society; swinish multitude, *faex populi*; *profanum* –, *ignobile- vulgus*; vermin, riff-raff, tag-rag and bobtail; small fry.

commoner, one of the people, democrat, plebeian, republican, proletary, *prolétaire*, *roturier*, Mr. Snooks, *bourgeois*, *épicier*, Philistine, cockney; *grisette, demi-monde*.

peasant, countryman, boor, carle, churl; vill-ain, -ein; serf, kern, tyke, tike, chuff, ryot, fellah; long-shoreman; swain, clown, hind; clod, -hopper; hobnail, yokel, hick, rube, cider squeezer, bog-trotter, bumpkin; ploughman, -boy; rustic, chawbacon, tiller of the soil; hewers of wood and drawers of water, groundling; gaffer, loon, put, cub, Tony Lumpkin, looby, lout, under-ling; *gamin*, guttersnipe, street arab, mudlark; rough, rowdy, ruffian, roughneck; pot-walloper, slubberdegullion; vulgar –, low- fellow; cad, curmudgeon.

upstart, *parvenu*, *nouveau-riche*, skipjack; nobody, – one knows; *hesterni quirites*, *pessoribus orti*; *bourgeois gentilhomme*, *novus homo*, snob, gent, mushroom, no one knows who, adventurer; man of straw.

beggar, panhandler, gaberlunzie, muckworm, mudlark, *sans-culotte*, raff, tatterdemalion, caitiff, ragamuffin, Pariah, outcast of society, tramp, weary Willie, bum, vagabond, *chiffonaier*, rag-picker, Cinderella, cinderwench, scrub, jade; boots, gossoon.

Goth, Vandal, Hottentot, savage, barbarian, Yahoo; unlicked cub, rough diamond.

barbar-ousness, -ism; Boeotia.

V. be -ignoble etc. *adj.*, – nobody etc. *n.*

Adj. ignoble, common, mean, low, base, vile, sorry, scrubby, beggarly, below par; no great shakes etc. (*unimportant*) 643; home-ly, -spun; vulgar, low-minded; snobbish, *parvenu*.

plebeian, proletarian; of -low, – mean- parentage, – origin, extraction; low-, base-, earth-born, low bred; mushroom, dunghill, risen from the ranks; unknown to fame, obscure, untitled.

rustic, uncivilized; lout-, boor-, clown-, churl-, brut-, raff-ish; rude, unlicked, unpolished.

barbar-ous, -ian, -ic, -esque; cockney, born within sound of Bow bells.

underling, menial, servile, subaltern.

Adv. below the salt.

877. Title.—N. title, honor; knighthood etc. (*nobility*) 875.

royal –, serene- highness, excellency, grace; lordship, worship, Rt. Hon., rever-ence, -end; esquire, sir; madam, *madame*; master, mistress, Mr., Mrs., *signor, señor, Mein Herr, mynheer*; your –, his- honor; handle to one's name.

decoration, laurel, palm, wreath, garland, bays, medal, ribbon, riband, blue ribbon, *cordon*, cross, crown, coronet, star, garter; feather, – in one's cap; chevron, epaulet, *épaulette*, colors, cockade; livery; order, arms, armorial bearings, shield, scutcheon, crest, reward etc. 973.

878. Pride.—N. dignity, self-respect, *mens sibi conscia recti*.

pride; haughtiness etc. *adj.*; high notions, *hauteur*; vainglory, crest; arrogance etc. (*assumption*) 885; pomposity etc. 882.

proud man, highflier; fine -gentleman, – lady; *grande dame*.

V. be -proud etc. *adj.*; put a good face on; look one in the face; stalk abroad, perk oneself up; presume, swagger, strut; rear –, lift up –, hold up- one's head; hold one's head high, look big, take the wall, 'bear like the Turk no rival near the throne,' carry with a high hand; ride the –, mount on one's- high horse; set one's back up, bridle, toss the head; give oneself airs etc. (*assume*) 885; boast etc. 884.

– pride oneself on; glory in, take pride in; pique –, plume –, hug- oneself; stand upon, be proud of; put a good face on; not -hide one's light under a bushel, – put one's talent in a napkin; not think small beer of oneself etc. (*vanity*) 880.

Adj. dignified; stately; proud, -crested; lordly, baronial; lofty-minded; high-souled, -minded, - mettled, -handed, -plumed, -flown, -toned.

haughty, paughty, insolent, lofty, high, mighty, swollen, puffed up, flushed, blown; vain-glorious; purse-proud, fine; proud as -a peacock, Lucifer; bloated with pride.

supercilious, disdainful, bumptious, magisterial, imperious; high-handed, – and mighty; overweening, consequential; arrogant etc. 885; unblushing etc. 880.

stiff, -necked; starch; perked –, stuck- up; in buckram, straitlaced; prim etc. (*affected*) 855.

on one's -high horses, – tight ropes, – high ropes; on stilts; *en grand seigneur*.

Adv. with head erect, with one's nose in the air.

Phr. *odi profanum vulgus et arceo.*

879. Humility.—N. hum-ility, -bleness; meek-, low-ness; lowli-ness, -hood; abasement, self-abasement, -effacement; submission etc. 725; resignation.

condescension; affability etc. (*courtesy*) 894.

modesty etc. 881; verecundity, blush, suffusion, confusion; sense of -shame, — disgrace; humiliation, mortification; let —, set- down.

V. be -humble etc. *adj.*; deign, vouchsafe, condescend; humble —, demean- oneself; stoop, — to conquer; carry coals; submit etc. 725; submit with a good grace etc. (*brook*) 826; yield the palm.

lower one's -tone, — note; sing small, draw in one's horns, sober down; hide one's -face, — diminished head; not dare to show one's face, take shame to oneself, not have a word to say for oneself; feel —, be conscious of- -shame, — disgrace; drink the cup of humiliation to the dregs; eat -humble pie, — one's words, — dirt; be humiliated, receive a snub.

blush -for, — up to the eyes; redden, change color; color up; hang one's head, look foolish, feel small.

render humble; humble, humiliate; let —, set —, take —, tread —, frown- down; snub, abash, abase, make one sing small, strike dumb; teach one -his distance, — his place; take down a peg, — lower; throw —, cast- into the shade etc. 874; stare —, put- out of countenance; put to the blush; confuse, ashame, mortify, disgrace, crush; send away with a flea in one's ear.

get a set down.

Adj. humble, lowly, meek; modest etc. 881; humble-, sober-minded; unoffended; submissive etc. 725; servile etc. 886.

condescending; affable etc. (*courteous*) 894.

humbled etc. *v.*; bowed down, resigned; abashed, ashamed, dashed; out of countenance; down in the mouth; down on one's -knees, — marrow-bones; humbled in the dust, brow-beaten; chap-, crest-fallen; dumbfoundered, flabbergasted, struck all of a heap.

shorn of one's glory etc. (*disrepute*) 874.

Adv. with -downcast eyes, — bated breath, — bended knee; on all fours, on one's feet.

under correction, with due deference.

Phr. I am your -obedient, — very humble- servant; my service to you.

880. Vanity.—N. vanity; conceit, -edness; self-conceit, -complacency, -confidence, -sufficiency, -esteem, -love, -approbation, -praise, -glorification, laudation, -gratulation, -applause, -admiration; *amour-propre*; selfishness etc. 943.

airs, pretensions, mannerism; egotism; prigg-ism, -ishness; coxcombery, gaudery, vainglory, elation; pride etc. 878; ostentation etc. 882; assurance etc. 885.

vox et praeterea nihil; *cheval de bataille*.

ego-ist, -tist; peacock, coxcomb etc. 854; Sir Oracle etc. 887.

V. be -vain etc. *adj.*, — vain of; pique oneself etc. (*pride*) 878; lay the flattering unction to one's soul.

have -too high, — an overweening- opinion of -oneself, — one's talents; blind oneself as to one's own merit; not think -small beer, — *vin ordinaire*- of oneself; put oneself forward; fish for compliments; give oneself airs etc. (*assume*) 885; boast etc. 884.

render -vain etc. *adj.*; inspire with -vanity etc. *n.*; inflate, puff up, turn up, turn one's head.

Adj. vain, — as a peacock; conceited, assured, overweening, pert, forward, perky; vain-glorious, high-flown; ostentatious etc. 882; puffed up, inflated, flushed.

self-satisfied, -confident, -sufficient, -flattering, -admiring, -applauding, -glorious, -opinionated; *entêté* etc. (*wrong-headed*) 481; wise in one's own conceit, pragmatical, overwise, pretentious, priggish; egotistic, -al; *soi-disant* etc. (*boastful*) 884; arrogant etc. 885.

un-abashed, -blushing; un-constrained, ceremonious; free and easy.

Adv. vainly etc. *adj.*

Phr. how we apples swim!

881. Modesty.—N. modesty; humility etc. 879; diffidence, timidity; retiring disposition, unobtrusiveness, bashfulness etc. *adj.*; *mauvaise honte*; blush, -ing; verecundity; self-knowledge.

reserve, constraint; demureness etc. *adj.*; blushing honors.

V. be -modest etc. *adj.*; retire, reserve oneself; give way to; draw in one's horns etc. 879; hide one's face.

keep -private, — in the background, — one's distance; pursue the noiseless tenor of one's way, 'do good by stealth and blush to find it fame,' hide one's light under a bushel, cast a sheep's eye.

Adj. modest, diffident; humble etc. 879; timid, timorous, bashful; shy, nervous, skittish, coy, sheepish, shamefaced, blushing, over-modest.

unpreten-ding, -tious; un-obtrusive, -assuming, -ostentatious, -boastful, -aspiring; poor in spirit.

out of countenance etc. (*humbled*) 879.

reserved, constrained, demure.

Adv. humbly etc. *adj.*; quietly, privately; without -ceremony, — beat of the drum; *sans façon*.

882. Ostentation.—N. ostentation, display, show, flourish, parade, *étalage*, pomp, array, state, solemnity; dash, splash, glitter, strut, swank, side, swagger, pomposity; preten-se, -sions; showing off; fuss.

magnificence, splendor; *coup d'oeil*; grand doings.

coup de théâter; stage -effect, — trick; clap-trap; *mise en scène*; *tour de force*; *chic*.

demonstration, flying colors; tomfoolery; flourish of trumpets etc. (*celebration*) 883; pageant, -ry; spectacle, exhibition, procession; turn —, set- out; grand function; *fête*, gala, field-day, review, march past, promenade, insubstantial pageant.

dress; court —, full —, evening —, ball —, fancy- dress; tailoring, millinery, man-millinery, frippery; foppery; equipage.

ceremon-y, -ial; ritual; form, -ality; etiquette; punct-o, -ilio, -ilious-ness; starched-, stateli-ness.

mummery, solemn mockery, -mouth honor.

attitudinarian; fop etc. 854.

V. be -ostentatious etc. *adj.*; come —, put oneself- forward; attract attention, star it.

make —, cut- a -figure, — dash, — splash; strut, blow one's own trumpet; figure, — away; make a show, — display; glitter.

show -off, — one's paces; parade, march past;

display, exhibit, put forward, hold up; trot — hang- out; sport, brandish, blazon forth; dangle, — before the eyes.

cry up etc. (*praise*) 931; prôner, flaunt, emblazon, prink, set off, mount, have framed and glazed.

put a good, — smiling- face upon; clean the outside of the platter etc. (*disguise*) 544.

Adj. ostentatious, showy, dashing, pretentioura-, jau-nty; grand, pompous, palatial; high sounding; turgid etc. (*big-sounding*) 577; garish, gorgeous; gaudy, — as a -peacock, — butterfly, — tulip; flaunting, flashing, flaming, glittering; gay etc. (*ornate*) 847; colorful.

splendid, magnificent, sumptuous.

theatrical, dramatic, spectacular, scenic, ceremonial, ritual, -istic.

solemn, stately, majestic, formal, stiff, ceremonious, punctilious, starch-ed, -y.

en grande tenue, in best bib and tucker, in Sunday best, *endimanché*.

Adv. with -flourish of trumpet, — beat of drum, — flying colors, — a brass band.

ad captandum vulgus.

883. Celebration.—**N.** celebration, solemnization, jubilee, diamond jubilee, commemoration, ovation, paean, triumph, jubilation.

triumphal arch, bonfire, salute; salvo, — of artillery; *feu de joie*, flourish of trumpets, *fanfare*, colors flying, illuminations, fireworks.

inauguration, installation, presentation; *début*, coming out, birthday anniversary, bi-, ter-, centenary; silver —, golden —, diamond- wedding, - day; coronation; Lord Mayor's show; harvest home, red letter day, festival; trophy etc. 733; *Te Deum* etc. (*thanksgiving*) 990; fete etc. 882; holiday etc. 840.

V. celebrate, keep, signalize, do honor to, commemorate, solemnize, hallow, mark with a red letter, hold high festival, maffick.

pledge, drink to, toast, hob and nob.

inaugurate, install, instate, induct, chair.

rejoice etc. 838; kill the fatted calf, hold jubilee, roast an ox, fire a salute.

. Adj. celebrating etc. *v.*; commemorative, celebrated, immortal.

Adv. in -honor, — commemoration, — celebration of.

Int. hail! all hail! *io -paean, — triumphe!* 'see the conquering hero comes!'

884. Boasting.—**N.** boasting etc. *v.*; boast, vaunt, crake; preten-ce, -sions; puff, -ery; flourish, *fanfaronnade*; gasconade; bluff, swank, brag, - gardism; bravado, bunkum, Buncombe; highfalutin; jact-itation, -ancy; bounce, rant, bluster; venditation, vaporing, rodomontade, bombast, fine talking, tall talk, magniloquence, teratology, heroics; jingoism, Chauvinism; exaggeration etc. 549; gas, hot air.

vanity etc. 880; *vox et praeterea nihil*; much cry and little wool, *brutum fulmen*.

exultation; glorification; flourish of trumpets; triumph etc. 883.

boaster; bragg-art, -adocio; hot air merchant;

Gascon, *fanfaron*, pretender, fourflusher, *soi-disant*; windbag, blowhard, bluffer; chauvinist; blusterer etc. 887; charlatan, jack-pudding, trumpeter; puppy etc. (*fop*) 854.

V. boast, make a boast of, brag, vaunt, puff, show off, flourish, crake, crack, trumpet, strut, swagger, vapor, bluff; draw the long bow.

exult, crow over, neigh, chuckle, triumph; glory, gloat, jubilate; throw up one's cap; talk big, *se faire valoir, faire claquer son fouet*, take merit to oneself, make a merit of, sing Io triumphe, holloa before one is out of the wood.

Adj. boasting etc. *v.*; magniloquent, flaming, Thrasonic, stilted, gasconading, braggart, boastful, pretentious, *soi-disant*; vain-glorious etc. (*conceited*) 880.

elate, -d; jubilant, triumphant, exultant; in high feather; flushed, — with victory; cock-a-hoop; on stilts.

vaunted etc. *v.*

Adv. vauntingly etc. *adj.*; with a brass band.

Phr. 'let the galled jade wince.'

885. Insolence. [Undue assumption of superiority.]—**N.** insolence; haughtiness etc. *adj.*; arrogance, airs; overbearance, brashness, bumptiousness, contumely, disdain; domineering etc. *v.*; tyranny etc. 739.

impertinence; cheek, nerve, sauce; sauciness etc. *adj.*; flippancy, dicacity, petulance, procacity, bluster; swagger, -ing etc. *v.*; bounce; terrorism; jingoism, chauvinism.

as-, pre-sumption; beggar on horseback; usurpation.

impudence, assurance, audacity, self-assertion, hardihood, front, face, brass; shamelessness etc. *adj.*; effrontery, hardened front, face of brass.

assumption of infallibility.

malapert, saucebox etc. (*blusterer*) 887.

V. be -insolent etc. *adj.*; bluster, vapor, swagger, swell, give oneself airs; snap one's fingers, kick up a dust; swear etc. (*affirm*) 535; rap out oaths; roister.

arrogate; as-, pre-sume; make -bold, — free; take a liberty, give an inch and take an ell.

domineer, bully, dictate, hector; lord it over, bulldoze; *traiter de haut, regarder de haut en bas*; exact; snub, huff, beard, fly in the face of; put to the blush; bear —, beat- down; browbeat, intimidate; trample —, tread- -down,   under foot; dragoon, ride roughshod over, terrorize.

out-face, -look, -stare, -brazen, -brave; stare out of countenance; brazen out; lay down the law; teach one's grandmother to suck eggs; assume a lofty bearing; talk —, look- big; put on big looks, act the *grand seigneur*; mount —, ride- the high horse; toss the head, carry with a high hand.

tempt Providence, want snuffing.

Adj. insolent, haughty, arrogant, imperious, magisterial, dictatorial, arbitrary; high-handed, high and mighty; contumelious, supercilious, overbearing, intolerant, domineering; overweening, high-flown.

flippant, pert, cavalier, saucy, forward, impertinent, fresh, malapert.

precocious, assuming, would-be, bumptious.

bluff; brazen-, browed-faced, shameless, aweless, unblushing, unabashed; bold-, bare-faced; dead — lost- to shame.

impudent, audacious, presumptuous, free and easy, devil-may-care, rollicking; janty, jaunty; roistering, blustering, hectoring, swaggering, vaporing; thrasonic, fire-eating, 'full of sound and fury.'

Adv. insolently, with a high hand; *ex cathedrâ*.

Phr. one's bark being worse than his bite.

886. Servility.—N. servility; slavery etc. (*subjection*) 749; obsequiousness etc. *adj.*; subserviency; abasement; pros-tration, -ternation; genuflexion etc. (*worship*) 990; fawning etc. *v.*; tuft-hunting, time-serving, flunkeyism; sycophancy etc. (*flattery*) 933; humility etc. 879.

sycophant, parasite, yes-man; toad, -y, -eater; tuft-hunter; snob, flunkey, lap-dog, spaniel, lick-spittle, smell-feast, *Graeculus esuriens*, hanger on, stooge, *cavaliere servente*, led captain, carpet knight; time-server, fortune-hunter, Vicar of Bray, Sir Pertinax Mac Sycophant, pick-thank; flatterer etc. 935; doer of dirty work; *âme damnée*, tool; reptile; slave etc. (*servant*) 746; courtier; sponge, jackal; truckler.

V. cringe, bow, stoop, kneel, bend the knee; fall on one's knees, prostrate oneself; worship etc. 990.

sneak, crawl, crouch, cower, truckle to, grovel, fawn, toady, lick the feet of, kiss the hem of one's garment.

pay court to; feed —, fatten —, batten- on; dance attendance on, pin oneself upon, hang on the sleeve of, *avaler des couleuvres*, keep time to, fetch and carry, do the dirty work of.

go with the stream, follow the crowd, worship the rising sun, hold with the hare and run with the hounds.

Adj. servile, obsequious; supple, — as a glove; soapy, oily, pliant, cringing, fawning, slavish, groveling, sniveling, mealy-mouthed; beggarly, sycophantic, parasitical; abject, prostrate, down on one's marrow-bones; base, mean, sneaking; crouching etc. *v.*

Adv. hat —, cap- in hand.

887. Blusterer.—N. bluster-, swagger-, vapor-, roister-, brawl-er; brazen-face; *fanfaron*; braggart etc. (*boaster*) 884; bully, terrorist, rough, rough-neck; hooligan, hoodlum, larrikin, ruffian; Mohock, -hawk; drawcansir, swashbuckler, Captain Boabdil, Sir Lucius O'Trigger, Thraso, Pistol, Paroles, Bombastes Furioso, Hector, Chrononhot-onthologos; jingo; desperado, dare-devil, fire-eater; fury etc. (*violent person*) 173; rowdy.

puppy etc. (*fop*) 854; prig; Sir Oracle, dogmatist, *doctrinaire*, stump orator, jack-in-office; saucebox, malapert, jackanapes, minx; bantam-cock.

888. Friendship.—N. friendship, amity; friend-liness etc. *adj.*; brotherhood, fraternity, sodality, confraternity, sorosis, sisterhood; harmony etc. (*concord*) 714; peace etc. 721.

firm —, staunch —, intimate —, familiar —, bosom —, cordial —, tried —, devoted —, lasting —, fast —, sincere —, warm —, ardent- friendship. cordiality, fraternization, *entente cordiale*, good

understanding, *rapprochement*, sympathy, fellow-feeling, response, welcomeness; *camaraderie*.

affection etc. (*love*) 897; favoritism; goodwill etc. (*benovolence*) 906; partiality.

acquaintance, familiarity, intimacy, intercourse, fellowship, knowledge of; introduction.

V. be -friendly etc. *adj.*, — friends etc. 890; — acquainted with etc. *adj.*; know; have the ear of; keep- company with etc. (*sociality*) 892; hold communication —, have dealings —, sympathize- with; have a leaning to; bear good will etc. (*benevolence*) 906; love etc. 897; make much of; befriend etc. (*aid*) 707; introduce to.

set one's horses together; hold out —, extend the right hand of -friendship, — fellowship; become -friendly etc. *adj.*; make -friends etc. 890 with; break the ice, be introduced to; make —, pick —, scrape- acquaintance with; get into favor, gain the friendship of.

shake hands with, fraternize, embrace; receive with open arms, throw oneself into the arms of; meet half way, take in good part.

Adj. friendly, amic-able, -al; well affected, unhostile, neighborly, brotherly, fraternal, sisterly, sympathetic, harmonious, hearty, cordial, warm-hearted, devoted.

friends —, well —, at home —, hand in hand-with; on -good, — friendly, — amicable, — cordial, — familiar, — intimate- -terms, — footing; on -speaking, — visiting- terms; in one's good -graces, — books.

acquainted, familiar, intimate, thick, hand and glove, hail fellow well met, free and easy; welcome.

Adv. amicably etc. *adj.*; with open arms; *sans cérémonie*; arm in arm.

889. Enmity.—N. enmity, hostility; un-friendliness etc. *adj.*; discord etc. 713.

alienation, estrangement; dislike etc. 867; hate etc. 898; antagonism.

heartburning; animosity etc. 900; malevolence etc. 907.

V. be -inimical etc. *adj.*; keep —, hold- at arm's length; be at loggerheads; bear malice etc. 907; fall out; take umbrage etc. 900; harden the heart, alienate, estrange.

Adj. inimical, unfriendly, hostile; at -enmity, — variance, — swords points, — daggers drawn, — open war with; up in arms against; in bad odor with.

on bad —, not on speaking- terms; cool; cold, -hearted; estranged, alienated, disaffected, irreconcilable.

890. Friend.—N. friend, — of one's bosom, intimate acquaintance, neighbor, well-wisher; *alter ego*; best —, bosom —, fast- friend; *amicus usque ad aras*; *fidus Achates*; *persona grata*.

favorer, *fautor*, patron, backer, Maecenas; tutelary saint, good genius, advocate, partisan, sympathizer; ally; friend in need etc. (*auxiliary*) 711.

associate, compeer, comrade, mate, companion, *confrère*, *camarade*, *confidante*, colleague; old —, crony; side-kick; chum, buddy, bunkie, roommate, pal; play-fellow, -mate; classmate, schoolfellow; bed-fellow, -mate; maid of honor.

compatriot; fellow -, countryman, - townsman.

shop-, ship-, mess-mate; fellow -, boon -, potcompanion; co-partner.

Arcades ambo, Pylades and Orestes, Castor and Pollux, Nisus and Euryalus, Damon and Pythias, *par nobile fratrum*.

host, Amphitryon, Boniface; guest, visitor, frequenter, *habitué*; *protégé*.

891. Enemy.—N. enemy; antagonist, foeman; open -, bitter- enemy; opponent etc. 710; back friend.

public enemy, enemy to society, traitor, anarchist etc. 743.

Phr. every hand being against one.

892. Sociality.—N. soci-ality, -ability, -ableness etc. *adj.*; social intercourse; consociation; intercourse, -community; consort-, companion-, fellow-, comrade-ship; clubbism; *esprit de corps*.

conviviality; good -fellowship, - company, *camaraderie*; joviality, jollity, *savoir -vivre*, festivity, festive board, merry-making; loving cup; hospitality, heartiness; cheer.

welcome, -ness; greeting; hearty -, warm -, welcome- reception; urbanity etc. (*courtesy*) 894; intimacy, familiarity.

good -, jolly- fellow, good mixer, Rotarian; *bon enfant*.

social -, family- circle; circle of acquaintance, *coterie*, society, company.

social -gathering, - *réunion*; assembly etc. (*assemblage*) 72; party, entertainment, reception, *levée*, at home, *conversazione*, *soirée*, *matinée*, evening -, morning -, afternoon -, garden -, dinner -, tea -, cocktail- party, symposium, singsong; kettle-, drum; *partie carrée*, dish of tea, *ridotto*, rout, housewarming; ball, prom, hop, dance, *thé dansant*; festival etc. (*amusement*) 840; wedding breakfast; 'the feast of reason and the flow of soul.'

visit, -ing; round of visits; call, morning call; interview etc. (*interlocution*) 588; assignation; tryst, -ing place; appointment.

club etc. (*association*) 712.

V. be -sociable etc. *adj.*; know; be -acquainted etc. *adj.*; associate -, sort -, keep company -, walk hand in hand -with; eat off the same trencher, club together, consort, bear one company, join; make acquaintance with etc. (*friendship*) 888; make advances, fraternize, embrace; intercommunicate.

be -, feel -, make oneself- at home with; make free with; crack a bottle with; take pot luck with, receive hospitality, live at free quarters.

visit, pay a visit; interchange -visits, - cards; call -at, - upon; leave a card; drop in, look in; look one up, beat up one's quarters.

entertain; give a -party etc. *n.*; be at home, see one's friends, hang out, keep open house, do the honors; receive, - with open arms; welcome; give a warm reception etc. *n.* to; kill the fatted calf.

Adj. sociable, companionable, clubbable, clubby, conversable, cosy, cosey, chatty, conversational; homiletical.

convivial; fest-ive, -al; jovial, jolly, hospitable. welcome, - as the roses in May; *fêté*, entertained.

free and easy, hail fellow well met, familiar, on visiting terms, acquainted.

social, neighborly; international, cosmopolitan, gregarious.

Adv. *en famille*, in the family circle; *sans -facon*, - *cérémonie*, arm in arm.

893. Seclusion. Exclusion.—N. seclusion, privacy; retirement; concealment; reclusion, recess; snugness etc. *adj.*; delitescence; rustication, *rus in urbe*; solitude; solitariness etc. (*singleness*) 87; isolation; loneliness etc. *adj.*; estrangement from the world, anchoritism, voluntary exile; aloofness.

cell, hermitage; convent etc. 1000; *sanctum sanctorum*; study, library, den; hide-out.

depopulation, desertion, desolation; wilderness etc. (*unproductive*) 169; howling wilderness; rotten borough, Old Sarum.

exclusion, excommunication, banishment, exile, ostracism, proscription; cut, - direct; dead cut.

inhospit-ality, -ableness etc. *adj.*; un-, dissociability; domesticity, Darby and Joan.

recluse, hermit, eremite, cenobite; anchor-et, -ite; Simon Stylites; Troglodyte, Timon of Athens, Santon, *solitaire*, ruralist, disciple of Zimmermann, closet cynic, Diogenes; outcast, Pariah, casta ~~ outsider, pilgarlic; wastrel, foundling, orphan.

V. be -, live- secluded etc. *adj.*; keep -, stand -, hold oneself- -aloof, - in the background; keep snug; shut oneself up; deny -, seclude- oneself; creep into a corner, rusticate, *aller planter ses choux*; retire, - from the world; hermetize, take the veil; abandon etc. 624.

cut, - dead; refuse to -associate with, - acknowledge; look cool -, turn one's back -, shut the door- upon; repel, blackball, excommunicate, exclude, exile, expatriate; banish, outlaw, maroon, ostracize, proscribe, cut off from, send to Coventry, keep at arm's length, draw a cordon round; boycott, blockade, lay an embargo on, isolate.

depopulate; dis-, un-people.

Adj. secluded, sequestered, retired, delitescent, private, bye; out of the -world, -way; in a backwater; 'the world forgetting by the world forgot.'

snug, domestic, stay-at-home.

unsociable; un-, dis-social; inhospitable, cynical, inconversable, unclubbable, *sauvage*, eremetic.

solitary; lone-ly, -some; isolated, single.

excluded, estranged; unfrequented; uninhabitable, -ed; tenantless; un-tenanted, -occupied; abandoned; deserted, - in one's utmost need; unfriended; kith-, friend-, home-less; lorn, forlorn, desolate.

un-visited, -introduced, -invited, -welcome; under a cloud, left to shift for oneself, derelict, outcast, outside the gates.

banished etc. *v.*; under an embargo.

Phr. *noli me tangere*.

894. Courtesy.—N. courtesy; respect etc. 928; good -manners, - behavior, - breeding; manners; politeness etc. *adj.*; *bienséance*, urbanity, comity, gentility; gentle -, breeding; polish, presence, cultivation, culture; civili-ty, -zation; amenity; suavity; good -temper, – humor; amiability, easy temper, complacency, soft tongue, mansuetude; condescension etc. (*humility*) 879; affability, complaisance, *prévenance*, amiability, gallantry, chivalry; pink of -politeness, – courtesy.

compliment; fair –, soft –, sweet- words; honeyed phrases, flattering remarks, ceremonial; salutation, reception, presentation, introduction, *accueil*, greeting, recognition; welcome, *abord*, respects, *devoir*, regards, remembrances; kind -regards, – remembrances; love, best love, duty; deference.

obeisance etc. (*reverence*) 928; bow, courtesy, curtsy, scrape, *salaam*, *kow-tow*, bowing and scraping; kneeling; genuflexion etc. (*worship*) 990; obsequiousness etc. 886; capping, shaking hands etc. *v.*; grip of the hand, embrace, hug, squeeze, *accolade*, loving cup, *vin d'honneur*, pledge; love token etc. (*endearment*) 902; kiss, buss, salute.

mark of recognition, not; 'nods and becks and wreathed smiles;' valediction etc. 293; condolence etc. 915.

V. be -courteous etc. *adj.*; show -courtesy etc. *n.*

mind one's P's and Q's, behave oneself, be all things to all men, conciliate, speak one fair, take in good part; make – , do- the amiable; look as if butter would not melt in one's mouth; mend one's manners.

receive, do the honors, usher, greet, hail, bid welcome; welcome, – with open arms; shake hands; hold out – press – , squeeze- the hand; bid God speed; speed the parting guest; cheer, serenade.

salute; embrace etc. (*endearment*) 902; kiss, – hands; drink to, pledge, hob and nob; move to, nod to; smile upon.

uncover, cap; touch – , take off- the hat; doff the cap; pull the forelock; present arms; make way for; bow; make one's bow; scrape, curtsy, courtesy; bob a -curtsy, – courtesy; kneel; bow – , bend- the knee; salaam, *kowtow*.

visit, wait upon, present oneself, pay one's respects, pay a visit etc. (*sociability*) 892; dance attendance on etc. (*servility*) 886; pay attentions to; do homage to etc. (*respect*) 928.

prostrate oneself etc. (*worship*) 990.

give – , send- one's duty etc. *n.* to.

render -polite etc. *adj.*; polish, civilize, humanize.

Adj. courteous, polite, civil, mannerly, urbane; well-behaved, -mannered, -bred, -brought up, gently bred, of gentle -breeding, – manners, good-mannered, polished, civilized, cultivated; refined etc. (*taste*) 850; gentlemanlike etc. (*fashion*) 852; gallant, chivalrous, on one's good behavior.

fine – , fair – , soft- spoken; honey-mouthed, -tongued; oily, unctuous, bland, suave; obsequious etc. 886.

ingratiating, winning; gentle, mild; good-humored, cordial, gracious, amiable, tactful, addressful, affable, genial, friendly, familiar; neighborly.

Adv. courteously etc. *adj.*; with a good grace; with -open, – outstretched- arms; *à bras ouverts*; *suaviter in modo*, in good humor.

Int. hail! welcome! well met! *ave!* all hail! good -day, – morning etc., – morrow! God speed! *pax vobiscum!* may your shadow never be less! *chin-chin!*

895. Discourtesy.—**N.** discourtesy; ill-breeding; ill – , bad – , ungainly- manners; insuavity; grouchiness; un-courteousness etc. *adj.*, tactlessness; rusticity, inurbanity; illiberality, incivility, displacency.

disrespect etc. 929; procacity, impudence; barbar-ism, -ity; misbehavior, brutality, blackguard--ism, conduct unbecoming a gentleman, *grossièreté*, *brusquerie*; vulgarity etc. 851.

churlishness etc. *adj.*; spinosity, perversity; moroseness etc. (*sullenness*) 901*a*.

bad-, ill-temper; sternness etc. *adj.*; austerity; moodishness, captiousness etc. 901; cynicism; tartness etc. *adj.*; acrimony, acerbity, virulence, asperity.

scowl, black looks, frown; short answer, rebuff; hard words, contumely: unparliamentary language, personality.

bear, bruin, brute, grouch, blackguard, beast; unlicked cub; frump, cross-patch; saucebox etc. 887.

V. be -rude etc. *adj.*; insult etc. 929; treat with discourtesy; take a name in vain; make -bold, – free- with; take a liberty; stare out of countenance, ogle, point at, put to the blush.

cut; turn -one's back upon, – on one's heel; give the cold shoulder; keep at -a distance, – arm's length; look -cool, – coldly, – black- upon; show the door to, send away with a flea in the ear.

lose one's temper etc. (*resentment*) 900; sulk etc. 901*a*; frown, scowl, glower, pout; snap, snarl, growl.

render -rude etc. *adj.*; brut-alize, -ify.

Adj. dis-, un-courteous; uncourtly; ill-bred, -mannered, -behaved, -conditioned, unbred; un-manner-ly, -ed; im-, un-polite; un-polished, -civilized, -genteel; ungentleman-like, -ly; unladylike; blackguard; vulgar etc. 851; dedecorous; foul-mouthed, -spoken; abusive.

un-civil, -gracious, -ceremonious; cool; pert, forward, obtrusive, impudent, rude, saucy, precocious; insolent etc. 885.

repulsive; un-complaisant, -accommodating, -neighborly, -gallant; inaffable; un-gentle, -gainly; rough, rugged, bluff, blunt, gruff; churl-, boor-, bear-ish; brutal, *brusque*; stern, harsh, austere; cavalier.

tart, sour, crabbed, sharp, short, trenchant, sarcastic, crusty, biting, caustic, virulent, bitter, acrimonious, venomous, contumelious; snarling etc., *v.*; surly, – as a bear; perverse; grim, sullen etc. 901*a*; peevish etc. (*irascible*) 901.

Adv. discourteously etc. *adj.*; with -discourtesy etc. *n.*, – a bad grace.

896. Congratulations.—**N.** con-, gratulation; felicitation; salute etc. 894; condolence etc. 915; compliments of the season; good – , best- wishes.

V. con-, gratulate; felicitate, compliment; give – , wish one- joy; tender – , offer- one's congratulations; wish -many happy returns of the day, – a merry Christmas and a happy new year.

congratulate oneself etc. (*rejoice*) 838.

Adj. con-, gratulatory.

897. Love.—N. love; fondness etc. *adj.*; liking; inclination etc. (*desire*) 865; regard, dilection, admiration, fancy.

affection, sympathy, fellow-felling; tenderness etc. *adj.*; heart, brotherly love; benevolence etc. 906; attachment.

yearning, tender passion, *affaire de coeur*, *amour*, gallantry, passion, flame, devotion, fervor, enthusiasm, transport of love, rapture, enchantment, infatuation, adoration, idolatry.

narcissism, Oedipus complex, Electra complex.

Cupid, Venus, Eros; myrtle; true lover's knot; love -token, – suit, – affair, – tale, – story; the old story, plighted love; courtship etc. 902; *amourette*.

maternal love.

attractiveness, charm; popularity; favorite etc. 899.

lover, suitor, follower, admirer, adorer, wooer, amoret, beau, sweetheart, inamorato, swain, young man, flame, love, truelove; leman, Lothario, gallant, paramor, *amoroso*, *cavaliere servente*, captive, *cicisbeo*; *caro sposo*, Don Juan, sheik, ladies' man, squire of dames, Knave of Hearts.

inamorata, lady-love, idol, darling, duck, Dulcinea, angel, goddess, *cura sposa*; mistress.

betrothed, affianced, *fiancée*.

flirt, *coquette*; amorette; pair of turtle doves; abode of love, *agapemone*.

V. love, like, affect, fancy, care for, take an interest in, be partial to, sympathize with; be -in love etc. *adj.*- with; have –, entertain –, harbor –, cherish- a -love etc. *n.* for; regard, revere; take to, bear love to, be wedded to; set one's affections on; make much of, feast one's eyes on; hold dear, prize, treasure; hug, cling to, cherish, pet, caress etc. 902.

burn; adore, idolize, love to distraction, *aimer eperdument*; dote -on, – upon.

take a fancy to, fall for, be stuck on, look sweet upon; become -enamored etc. *adj.*; fall in love with, lose one's heart; desire etc. 865.

excite love; win –, gain –, secure –, engage- the -love, – affections, – heart; take the fancy of; have a place in –, wind round- the heart; attract, attach, endear, charm, fascinate, captivate, bewitch, seduce, enamor, enrapture, turn the head.

get into favor; ingratiate –, insinuate –, worm- oneself; propitiate, curry favor with, pay one's court to, make a date with, *faire l'aimable*, set one's cap at, flirt, coquet.

Adv. loving etc. *v.*; fond of; taken –, struck- with; smitten, bitten; attached to, wedded to; enamored; charmed etc. *v.*; in love; lovesick; over head and ears in love.

affectionate, tender, sweet upon, sympathetic, loving, fond, amorous, amatory; erotic, uxurious, ardent, passionate, rapturous, devoted, motherly.

loved etc. *v.*; beloved; well –, dearly- beloved; dear, precious, darling, pet, little; favorite, popular.

congenial, to –, after- one's -mind, – taste, – fancy, – own heart.

in one's good -graces etc. (*friendly*) 888; dear as the apple of one's eye, nearest to one's heart.

lovable, adorable; lovely, sweet; attractive, seductive, winning; charming, engaging, interesting, enchanting, captivating, fascinating, intriguing, bewitching; amiable, like an angel, angelic, seraphic.

898. Hate.—N. hate, hatred, vials of hate; Hymn of Hate.

dis-affection, -favor; alienation, estrangement, coolness; enmity etc. 889; animosity etc. 900.

umbrage, pique, grudge; dudgeon, spleen; bitterness, – of feeling; ill –, bad- blood; acrimony; malice etc. 907; implacability etc. (*revenge*) 919.

repugnance etc. (*dislike*) 867; odium, unpopularity; loathing, detestation, antipathy; object of -hatred, – execration; abomination, aversion, *bête noire*; enemy etc. 891; bitter pill; source of annoyance etc. 830.

V. hate, detest, abominate, abhor, loathe; recoil –, shudder- at; shrink from, view with horror, hold in abomination, revolt against, execrate; scowl etc. 895; disrelish etc. (*dislike*) 867.

owe a grudge; bear -spleen, – a grudge, – malice etc. (*malevolence*) 907; conceive an aversion to.

excite –, provoke- hatred etc. *n.*; be -hateful etc. *adj.*; stink in the nostrils; estrange, alienate, repel, set against, sow dissension, set by the ears, envenom, incense, irritate, rile, ruffle, vex; horrify etc. 830.

Adj. hating etc. *v.*; abhorrent; averse from etc. (*disliking*) 867; set against.

bitter etc. (*acrimonious*) 895; implacable etc. (*revengeful*) 919.

un-loved, -beloved, -lamented, -deplored, mourned, -cared for, -endured, -valued; disliked etc. 867.

crossed in love, forsaken, rejected, love-lorn, jilted.

obnoxious, hateful, odious, abominable, repulsive, offensive, shocking, disgusting etc. (*disagreeable*) 830.

invidious, spiteful; malicious etc. 907.

insulting, irritating, provoking.

[Mutual hate] at -daggers drawn, – swords points; not on speaking terms etc.. (*enmity*) 889.

Phr. no love lost between.

899. Favorite.—N. favorite, pet, cosset, minion, idol, jewel, spoiled child, *enfant gâté*; led captain; crony; fondling; apple of one's eye, man after one's own heart; *persona grata*.

love, dear, darling, duck, honey, jewel; mopsey, moppet; sweetheart etc. (*love*) 897.

general –, universal- favorite; idol of the people; matinée idol, movie –, radio- star.

900. Resentment.—N. resentment, displeasure, animosity, anger, wrath, indignation; vexation, exasperation, bitter resentment, wrathful indignation.

pique, umbrage, huff, miff, soreness, dudgeon, acerbity, virulence, bitterness, acrimony, asperity, spleen, gall; heart-burning, -swelling; rankling.

ill –, bad- -humor, – temper; irascibility etc. 901; ill blood etc. (*hate*) 898; revenge etc. 919.

excitement, irritation; warmth, bile, choler, ire, fume, pucker, dander, ferment, ebullition; towering -passion, – rage, *acharnement*, angry mood, taking, pet, tiff, passion, fit, tantrums.

burst, explosion, paroxysm, storm, rage, fury, desperation; violence etc. 173; fire and fury; vials of wrath; gnashing of teeth, hot blood, high words.

scowl etc. 895; sulks etc. 901a.

[Cause of umbrage] affront, provocation, offence; indignity etc. (*insult*) 929; grudge, crow to pluck, sore subject; red rag to a bull; *casus belli.*

Furies, Erinys, Eumenides, Alecto, Megaera, Tisiphone.

buffet, slap in the face, box on the ear, rap on the knuckles.

V. resent; take -amiss, – ill, – to heart, – offence, – umbrage, – huff, – exception; take in - ill part, – bad part, – dudgeon; *ne pas entendre raillerie*; breathe revenge, cut up rough.

fly –, fall –, get- into a -rage, – passion; bridle –, oristle –, froth –, fire –, flare- up; open –, pour out- the vials of one's wrath.

pout, knit the brow, frown, scowl, lower, snarl, growl, gnarl, gnash, snap; redden, color; look - black, – black as thunder, – daggers; bite one's thumb; show –, grind- one's teeth; champ the bit.

chafe, mantle, fume, kindle, fly out, take fire; boil, – over; boil with -indignation, – rage; rage, storm, foam; vent one's -rage, – spleen; lose one's temper, stand on one's hind legs, stamp the foot, kick up a row, fly off the handle, cut up rough; stamp –, quiver –, swell –, foam- with rage; burst with anger; raise Cain, breathe fire and fury.

have a fling at; bear malice etc. (*revenge*) 919.

cause –, raise- anger; affront, offend; give - offence, – umbrage; anger; hurt the feelings; insult, discompose, fret, ruffle, nettle, heckle, huff, pique; excite etc. 824; irritate, stir the blood, stir up bile; sting, – to the quick; rile, provoke, chafe, wound, incense, inflame, enrage, aggravate, add fuel to the flame, fan into a flame, widen the breach, envenom, embitter, exasperate, infuriate, kindle wrath; stick in one's gizzard; rankle etc. 919.

put out of humor; put one's -monkey, – back- up; set –, get- one's back up; raise one's -gorge, – dander, – choler; work up into a passion; make - one's blood boil, – the ears tingle; throw into a ferment, madden, drive one mad; lash into -fury, – madness; fool to the top of one's bent; set by the ears.

bring a hornet's nest about one's ears.

Adj. angry, wrath, irate; ire–, wrath-ful; cross etc. (*irascible*) 901; sulky etc. 901a; bitter, virulent; acrimonious etc. (*discourteous*) etc. 895; violent etc. 173.

warm, burning; boiling, – over; fuming, raging; foaming, – at the mouth; convulsed with rage.

offended etc. *v.*; waxy, *acharné*; wrought, worked up; indignant, hurt, sore, peeved; set against.

fierce, wild, rageful, furious, mad with rage, fiery, infuriate, rabid, savage; relentless etc. 919.

flushed with -anger, – rage; in a -huff, – stew, – fume, – pucker, – passion, – rage, – fury; on one's high ropes, up in arms; in high dudgeon.

Adv. angrily etc. *adj.*; in the height of passion; in the heat of -passion, – the moment.

Phr. one's -blood, – back, – monkey- being up; *fervens difficili bile jecur*; the gorge rising, eyes flashing fire; the blood -rising, – boiling; *haeret lateri lethalis arundo.*

901. Irascibility.—N. irascibility, temper; crossness etc. *adj.*; susceptibility, procacity, petulance, irritability, tartness, acerbity, protervity; pugnacity etc. (*contentiousness*) 720.

excitability etc. 825; bad –, fiery –, crooked –, irritable etc. *adj.*- temper; *genus irritabile*; hot blood.

ill humor etc. (*sullenness*) 901a; asperity etc., churlishness etc. (*discourtesy*) 895.

huff etc. (resentment) 900; a word and a blow.

Sir Fretful Plagiary; brabbler, Tartar; shrew, vixen, virago, termagant, dragon, scold, Xanthippe; porcupine; spit-fire; fire-eater etc. (*blusterer*) 887; fury etc. (*violent person*) 173.

V. be -irascible etc. *adj.*; have a -temper etc. *n.*, – devil in one; fire up etc. (*be angry*) 900.

Adj. irascible; bad-, ill-tempered; irritable, susceptible; excitable etc. 825; thin-skinned etc. (*sensitive*) 822; fretful, fidgety; on the fret.

hasty, over-hasty, quick, warm, hot, testy, touchy, techy, tetchy; like -touchwood, – tinder; huffy; pet-tish, -ulant; waspish, snapp-y, -ish, peppery, fiery, passionate, choleric, shrewish, 'sudden and quick in quarrel.'

querulous, captious, mood-y, -ish; quarrelsome, contentious, disputatious; pugnacious etc. (*bellicose*) 720; cantankerous, exceptious, restive etc. (*perverse*) 901a; churlish etc. (*discourteous*) 895.

cross, – as -crabs, – two sticks, – a cat, – a dog, – the tongs; like a bear with a sore head; fractious, peevish, *acariâtre*.

in a bad temper; sulky etc. 901a; angry etc. 900.

resent-ful, -ive; vindictive etc. 919.

Int. pish!

901a. Sullenness.—N. sullenness etc. *adj.*; morosity, spleen; churlishness etc. (*discourtesy*) 895; irascibility etc. 901.

moodiness etc. *adj.*; perversity; obstinacy etc. 606; torvity, spinosity; crabbedness etc. *adj.*

ill –, bad- -temper, – humor; sulks, dudgeon, mumps, doleful dumps, doldrums, fit of the sulks, *bouderie*, black looks, scowl; huff etc. (*resentment*) 900.

V. be -sullen etc. *adj.*; sulk; frown, scowl, lower, glower, grouse, grouch, crab, gloam, pout, have a hang-dog look, glout.

Adj. sullen, sulky; ill-tempered, -humored, - affected, -disposed; in -an ill, – a bad, – a shocking- -temper, – humor; out of -temper, – humor; knaggy, torvous, crusty, crabbed; sore as a boil; surly etc. (*discourteous*) 895.

moody; spleen-ish, -ly; splenetic, cankered.

cross, -grained; perverse, wayward, humorsome; restive; cantankerous, refractory, intractable, exceptious, sinistrous, deaf to reason, unaccommodating, rusty, crust, froward.

dogged etc. (*stubborn*) 606.

grumpy, glum, grim, grum, morose, frumpish; in the -sulks etc. *n.*, out of sorts; scowl-, glower-, growl-ing.

peevish etc. (*irascible*) 901.

902. Endearment. [Expression of affection or love.]—**N.** endearment, caress; blandish-, blandiment; *épanchement*, fondling, billing and cooing, dalliance.

embrace, salute; kiss, buss, smack, osculation,

deosculation; amorous glances; ogle, side glance, sheep's eyes.

courtship, wooing, suit, addresses, the soft impeachment; love-making; an affair; serenading; caterwauling.

flirting etc. v.; flirtation, gallantry; coquetry, spooning.

ture lover's knot, plighted love, engagement, bethrothal; love -tale, – token, – letter; billet-doux, valentine.

honeymoon; Strephon and Chloe, 'Arry and Arriet.

V. caress, fondle, pet, dandle, nurse; pat, – on the -head, – cheek; chuck under the chin, smile upon, coax, wheedle, cosset, coddle, cocker; make -of, – much of, pamper; cherish, foster, kill with kindness.

clasp, hug, cuddle; fold –, strain- in one's arms; nestle, nuzzle, neck, embrace, kiss, buss, smack, blow a kiss; salute etc. (courtesy) 894.

bill and coo, spoon, toy, dally, flirt, coquet; galli-, gala-vant; philander; make love; pay one's - court, – addresses, – attentions- to; serenade; court, woo; set one's cap at; be –, look- sweet upon; ogle, cast sheep's eyes upon; faire les yeux doux.

fall in love with, win the affections etc. (love) 897; die for.

propose; make –, have- an offer; pop the question; plight one's -troth, – faith; become - engaged, – betrothed.

Adj. caressing etc. v.; 'sighing like furnace;' love-sick, spoony.

carressed etc. v.

903. Marriage.—N. marriage, matrimony, wedlock, union, intermarriage, vinculum matrimonii, nuptial tie, knot.

married state, coverture, bed, cohabitation.

match; betrothment etc. (promise) 768; wedding, nuptials, Hymen, bridal; e-, spousals; leading to the altar etc. v.; nuptial benediction, epithalamium.

torch –, temple- of Hymen; hymeneal altar; honeymoon.

bride, bridegroom; brides-maid; -man.

best –, grooms-man, page, usher.

married -man, – woman, – couple; neogamist, Benedick, partner, spouse, mate, yokemate; husband, man, consort, baron; old –, good- man; wife of one's bosom; help-meet, -mate, rib, better half, grey mare, old woman, good wife; feme, - coverte; squaw, lady; matron, -age, -hood; man and wife; wedded pair, Darby and Joan.

affinity, soul-mate.

mono-, bi-, di-, deutero-, tri-, poly-gamy; mormonism; poly-andry; Turk, Bluebeard.

unlawful –, left-handed –, companionate –, morganatic –, ill-assorted- marriage, mésalliance; mariage de convenance; an affair.

match-maker, marriage broker, matrimonial agent.

V. marry, wive, take to oneself -a wife; be - married, – spliced; go –, pair- off; wed, espouse, lead to the hymeneal altar, take 'for better, for worse,' give one's hand to, bestow one's hand on; remarry; intermarry.

marry, join, handfast; couple etc. (unite) 43; tie

the nuptial knot; give -away, – in marriage; affy, affiance; betroth etc. (promise) 768; publish – bid- the banns; be asked in church.

Adj. married etc. v.; one, – bone and one flesh, marriageable, nubile.

engaged, betrothed, affianced.

matrimonial, marital, conjugal, connubial, wedded; nuptial, hymeneal, spousal, bridal.

Phr. the gray mare the better horse.

904. Celibacy.—N. celibacy, singleness, single blessedness; bachelor-hood, -ship; miso-gamy, -gyny.

virginity, pucelage; maiden-hood, -head.

unmarried man, bachelor, agamist, old bachelor; miso-gamist, -gynist; celibate.

unmarried woman, spinster; maid, -en; virgin, feme sole, old maid; bachelor girl; nun etc.

V. live single; keep bachelor hall.

Adj. un-married, -wedded; wife-, spouse-less; single, virgin, celibate.

905. Divorce.—N. divorce, -ment; separation; judicial separation, separate maintenance; separatio a -mensâ et thoro, – vinculo matrimonii.

widowhood, viduage, viduity, weeds.

widow, -er; relict; dowager; divorcée; cuckold.

V. live -separately, – apart; separate, divorce, disespouse, put away; wear the horns.

906. Benevolence.—N. benevolence, Christian charity; God's -love, – grace, good-will; philanthropy etc. 910; unselfishness etc. 942

good -nature, – feeling, – wishes; kind-, kindliness etc. adj.; lovingkindness, benignity, brotherly love, charity, humanity, fellow-feeling, sympathy; goodness –, warmth- of heart; bon-homie; kind-heartedness; amiability, milk of human kindness, tenderness; love etc. 897; friendship etc. 888.

toleration, consideration, generosity; mercy etc. (pity) 914

charitableness etc. adj., bounty, alms-giving; good works, beneficence, the luxury of doing good.

acts of kindness, a good turn; good –, kind- - offices, – treatment.

good Samaritan, sympathizer, well-wisher, philanthropist, bon enfant; altruist.

V. be -benevolent etc. adj., have one's heart in the right place, bear good will; wish -well, – God speed; view – regard- with an eye of favor; take in good part; take –, feel- an interest in; be, – feel-interested- in; sympathize with, feel for; fraternize etc. (be friendly) 888.

enter into the feelings of others, do as you would be done by, meet halfway.

treat well; give comfort, smooth the bed of death; do -good, – a good turn; render a service, be of use; aid etc. 707.

Adj. benevolent; kind, -ly; wellmeaning; amiable; obliging, accommodating, indulgent, considerate, gracious, complacent, good-humored

warm-, soft-, kind-, tender-, large-, broad-hearted; merciful etc. 914; philanthropic etc. 910; charitable, beneficent, humane, benign, benignant; bount-eous, -iful etc. 816.

good-, well-natured; spleenless; sympath-izing, -etic; complaisant etc. (*courteous*) 894; kindly, well-meant, -intentioned.

fatherly, motherly, brotherly, sisterly; pat-, ma*-, frat-ernal; friendly etc. 888.

Adv. with -a good intention, – the best intentions.

Int. God speed! much good may it do!

907. Malevolence.—**N.** malevolence; bad intent, -ion; un-, dis-kindness; ill -nature, – will, – blood; bad blood; enmity etc. 889; hate etc. 898; malignity; malice, – aforethought, – prepense; maliciousness etc. *adj.*; spite, despite; resentment etc. 900.

uncharitableness etc. *adj.*; incompassionateness etc. 914a; gall, venom, rancor, rankling, virulence, mordacity, acerbity; churlishness etc. (*discourtesy*) 895.

hardness of heart, heart of stone, obduracy; cruelty; cruelness etc. *adj.*; brutality, savagery; ferity, -ocity; barbarity, inhumanity, immanity, truculence, ruffianism; evil eye, cloven -foot, – hoof; Inquisition; torture.

ill –, bad- turn; affront etc. (*disrespect*) 929; outrage, atrocity; ill usage; intolerance, bigotry, persecution; tender mercies [ironical]; 'unkindest cut of all.'

V. be -malevolent etc. *adj.*; bear –, harbor- spleen, – a grudge, – malice; betray –, show- the cloven foot.

hurt etc. (*physical pain*) 378; annoy etc. 830; injure, harm, wrong; do -harm, – an ill office- to; outrage; disoblige, malign, plant a thorn in the breast.

molest, worry, harass, haunt, harry, bait, tease, throw stones at; play the devil with; hunt down, dragoon, hound; persecute, oppress, grind; maltreat; ill-treat, -use.

wreak one's malice on, do one's worst, break a butterfly on the wheel; dip –, imbrue- one's hands in blood; have no mercy etc. 914a.

Adj. male-, unbene-volent; unbenign; ill-disposed, -intentioned, -natured, -conditioned, -contrived; evil-minded, -disposed.

malicious; malign, -ant; rancorous; de-, spiteful; mordacious, caustic, bitter, envenomed, acrimonious, virulent; un-amiable, -charitable; maleficent, venomous, grinding, galling.

harsh, disobliging; un-kind, -friendly, -gracious; treacherous; inofficious; invidious; uncandid; churlish etc. (*uncourteous*) 895; surly, sullen etc. 901a.

cold, -blooded, -hearted; hard-, flint-, marble-, stony-hearted; hard of heart, unnatural; ruthless etc. (*unmerciful*) 914a; relentless etc. (*revengeful*) 919.

cruel; brut-al, -ish, savage, – as a -bear, – tiger; ferine, feral, ferocious; inhuman; barbarous, fell, untamed, tameless, truculent, incendiary; blood-thirsty etc. (*murderous*) 361; atrocious.

fiend-ish, -like; demoniacal; diabolic, -al; devilish, infernal, hellish, Satanic.

Adv. malevolently etc. *adj.*; with -bad intent etc. *n.*

908. Malediction.—**N.** malediction, malison, curse, imprecation, denunciation, execration,

anathema, ban, proscription, excommunication, commination, thunders of the Vatican, fulmination, *maranatha*, aspersion, vilification, vituperation, scurrility.

abuse; foul –, bad –, strong –, un-parliamentary- language, Limehouse; Billingsgate, sauce, evil speaking; cursing etc. *v.*; profane swearing, oath.

threat etc. 909; more bark than bite; invective etc. (*disapprobation*) 932.

V. curse, accurse, imprecate, damn, swear at; slang; curse with bell, book and candle; invoke –, call down- curses on the head of; devote to destruction.

execrate, beshrew, scold; anathematize etc. (*censure*) 932; hold up to execration, denounce, proscribe, excommunicate, fulminate, thunder against; threaten etc. 909; curse up hill and down dale.

curse and swear; swear, – like a trooper; fall a cursing, rap out an oath, damn, cuss.

Adj. curs-ing, -ed etc. *v.*; maledictory.

Int. woe to! beshrew! *ruat coelum!* ill –, woe-betide! confusion seize! damn! confound! blast! curse! devil take! hang! out with! a plague –, out-upon! aroynt! *honi soit!*

Phr. *delenda est Carthago.*

909. Threat.—**N.** threat, menace; defiance etc. 715; abuse, minacity, intimidation; fulmination; commination etc. (*curse*) 908; gathering clouds etc. (*warning*) 668.

V. threat, -en; menace; snarl, growl, gnarl, mutter, bark, bully.

defy etc. 715; intimidate etc. 860; keep –, hold up –, hold out- *in terrorem*; shake –, double –, clinch- the fist at; thunder, talk big, fulminate, use big words, bluster, look daggers.

Adj. threatening, menacing; mina-tory, -cious; comminatory, abusive; *in terrorem*; ominous etc. (*predicting*) 511; defiant etc. 715; under the ban.

Int. *vae victis!* at your peril! do your worst!

910. Philanthropy.—**N.** philanthropy; altruism, humanit-y, -arianism; universal benevolence; *deliciae humani generis*; cosmopolitanism, utilitarianism, the greatest happiness of the greatest number, social science, sociology.

common weal, public welfare, socialism, communism.

patriotism, civism, nationality, love of country, *amor patriae*, public spirit.

chivalry, knight errantry; generosity etc. 942.

philanthropist, altruist etc. 906; utilitarian, Benthamite, socialist, communist, cosmopolite, citizen of the world, *amicus humani generis*; knight errant; patriot.

Adj. philanthropic, altruistic, humanitarian, utilitarian, cosmopolitan; public-spirited, patriotic; humane, large-hearted etc. (*benevolent*) 906; chival-ric, -rous, generous etc. 942.

Adv. pro -bono publico, – aris et focis.

Phr. 'humani nihil a me alienum puto.'

911. Misanthropy.—**N.** misanthropy, incivism; egotism etc. (*selfishness*)- 943; moroseness etc. 901a; cynicism; defeatism.

misanthrope, misanthropist, egotist, cynic, man-hater, Timon, Diogenes.

woman-hater, misogynist.

Adj. misanthropic, antisocial, unpatriotic; egotistical etc. (*selfish*) 943; morose etc. 901*a*.

912. Benefactor.—N. benefactor, savior, good genius, tutelary saint, patron, guardian angel, fairy godmother, good Samaritan; *pater patriae*; salt of the earth etc. (*good man*) 948; auxiliary etc. 711.

913. Evil-doer. [*Maleficent being.*]—N. evil-doer, - worker; wrong doer etc. 949; mischief maker, marplot; oppressor, tyrant; firebrand, incendiary, pyromaniac, anarchist, destroyer, Hun, *Boche*, Vandal, iconoclast; communist; terrorist, *apache*, gunman, gangster, racketeer.

savage, brute, ruffian, barbarian, semi-barbarian, caitiff, desperado; Mo-hock, -hawk; bludgeon man, bully, rough, hooligan, larrikin, dangerous classes, ugly customer; thief etc. 792.

cockatrice, scorpion, hornet; viper, adder; snake, - in the grass; serpent, cobra, asp, rattlesnake, anaconda; canker-, wire-worm; locust, Colorado beetle; torpedo; bane etc. 663.

cannibal; Anthropophag-us, -ist; bloodsucker, vampire, ogre, ghoul, gorilla; vulture; gyr-, ger-falcon.

wild beast, tiger, hyaena, butcher, hangman; cut-throat etc. (*killer*) 361; blood-, sleuth-, hell-hound.

hag, hellhag, beldam, Jezebel.

monster; fiend etc. (*demon*) 980; homicidal maniac, devil incarnate, demon in human shape; Frankenstein's monster.

harpy, siren, vampire; Furies, Eumenides etc. 900.

Attila, scourge of the human race.

Phr. *foenum habet in cornu.*

914. Pity.—N. pity, compassion, commiseration; bowels, - of compassion; condolence etc. 915; sympathy, fellow-feeling, tenderness, yearning, forbearance, humanity, mercy, clemency, exorability; leniency etc. (*lenity*) 740; charity, ruth, long-suffering.

melting mood; *argumentum ad misericordiam*; quarter, grace, *locus poenitentiae*.

sympathizer, champion, partisan.

V. pity; have -, show -, take- pity etc. *n.*; commiserate, compassionate; condole etc. 915; sympathize; feel -, be sorry -, yearn- for; weep, melt, thaw, enter into the feelings of.

forbear, relent, relax, give quarter, wipe the tears, *parcere subjectis*, give a *coup de grâce*, put out of one's misery; be cruel to be kind.

raise -, excite- pity etc. *n.*; touch, soften; melt, - the heart; appeal to one's better feelings; propitiate, disarm.

ask for -mercy etc. *n.*; supplicate etc. (*request*) 765; cry for quarter, beg one's life, kneel, deprecate.

Adj. pitying etc. *v.*; pitiful, compassionate, sympathetic, touched.

merciful, clement, ruthful; humane; humanitarian etc. (*philanthropic*) 910; tender, -

hearted, - as a chicken; soft, - hearted; unhard-ened; lenient etc. 740; exorable, forbearing; melting etc. *v.*; weak.

Int. for pity's sake! mercy! have -, cry you-mercy! God help you! poor -thing, - dear, - fellow! woe betide! *quis talia fando temperet a lachrymis!*

Phr. one's heart bleeding for; *haud ignara mali miseris succurrere disco.*

914a. Pitilessness.—N. pitilessness etc. *adj.*; inclemency; inexorability, hardness of heart; in-flexibility; severity etc. 739; malevolence etc. 907.

V. have no - ; shut the gates of- mercy etc. 914; give no quarter.

Adj. piti-, merci-, ruth-, bowel-less; unpitying, unmerciful, inclement; in-, un-compassionate; inexorable, inflexible; harsh etc. 739; cruel etc. 907; unrelenting etc. 919.

915. Condolence.—N. condolence; lamen-tation etc. 839; sympathy, consolation.

V. condole with, console, sympathize etc. 914; share one's misery; feel for; express -, testify- pity; afford -, supply- consolation; lament etc. 839-with; send one's condolences.

916. Gratitude.—N. gratitude, thankfulness, gratefulness, feeling of obligation.

acknowledgement, recognition, thanksgiving, giving thanks.

thanks, praise, benediction; paean; *Te Deum* etc. (*worship*) 990; grace, - before, - after-meat; thank-offering.

requital.

V. be -grateful etc. *adj.*; thank; give -, render -, return -, offer -, tender- thanks etc. *n.*; acknowledge, requite.

feel -, be -, lie- under an obligation; *savoir gré*; not look a gift horse in the mouth; never forget, overflow with gratitude; thank -, bless-one's stars; fall on one's knees.

Adj. grateful, thankful, obliged, beholden, in-debted to, under obligation.

Int. thanks! many thanks! gramercy! much obliged! thank you! thank Heaven! Heaven be praised!

917. Ingratitude.—N. ingratitude, thanklessness, oblivion of benefits; unthankfulness 'benefits forgot;' thankless -task, - office.

V. be -ungrateful etc. *adj.*; forget benefits; look a gift horse in the mouth.

Adj. un-grateful, -mindful, -thankful; thankless, ingrate, wanting in gratitude, insensible of benefits forgotten; un-acknowledged, -thanked, requited, -rewarded; ill-requited

Int. thank you for nothing! '*et tu Brute!*' '

918. Forgiveness.—N. forgiveness, pardon, condonation, grace, remission, absolution, am-nesty, oblivion; indulgence; reprieve.

conciliation; reconciliation etc. (*pacification*) 723; propitiation.

excuse, exoneration; quittance, release, indemnity; bill –, act –, covenant –; deed- of indemnity: exculpation etc. (*acquittal*) 970.

longanimity, placability, forbearance; *amantium irae*; *locus poenitentiae*.

V. forgive, – and forget; pardon, condone, think no more of, let bygones be bygones, shake hands; forget an injury, bury the hatchet; clean the slate.

excuse, pass over, overlook; wink at etc. (*neglect*) 460; bear with; allow –, make allowances- for; let one down easily, not be too hard upon, pocket the affront; blot out one's transgression.

let off, remit, absolve, give absolution, reprieve; acquit etc. 970.

beg –, ask –, implore- pardon etc. *n.*; conciliate, propitiate, placate; make up a quarrel etc. (*pacify*) 723; let the wound heal.

Adj. forgiving, placable, conciliatory.

forgiven etc. *v.*; un-resented, -avenged, revenged.

Adv. cry you mercy.

Phr. *veniam petimusque damusque vicissim;* more in sorrow than in anger.

919. Revenge.—N. revenge, -ment; vengeance; avenge-ment, -ance; sweet revenge, *vendetta*, death-feud, eye for an eye, blood for blood, a Roland for an Oliver; retaliation etc. 718; day of reckoning.

rancor, vindictiveness, implacability; malevolence etc. 907; ruthlessness etc. 914*a*.

avenger, vindicator, Nemesis, Eumenides.

V. re-, a-venge; take –, have one's- revenge; breathe -revenge, – vengeance; wreak one's vengeance, – anger; give no quarter.

have -accounts to settle, – a crow to pluck, – a rod in pickle; pay off old scores.

keep the wound green; harbor -revenge, – vindictive feeling; bear malice; rankle, – in the breast; have at one's mercy.

Adj. revenge-, venge-ful; vindictive, rancorous; pitiless etc. 914*a*; ruthless, rigorous, avenging, retaliative.

unforgiving, unrelenting; inexorable, stony-hearted, implacable; relent-, remorse-less.

aeternum servans sub pectore vulnus; rankling, immitigable.

Phr. *manet -cicatrix,– altâ mente repostum.* revenge is sweet.

920. Jealousy.—N. jealous-y, -ness; jaundiced eye, heartburning; green-eyed monster; yellows; Juno.

V. be -jealous etc. *adj.*; view with -jealousy, – a jealous eye.

Adj. jealous, – as a Barbary pigeon; jaundiced, yellow-eyed, horn-mad.

921. Envy.—N. envy; enviousness etc. *adj.*; rivalry; *jalousie de métier.*

V. envy, covet, lust after, crave, burst with envy, regard with envious eyes.

Adj. envious, invidious, covetous; *alieni appetens.*

922. Right.—N. right; what -ought to, – should- be; fitness etc. *adj.*; *summum jus.*

justice, equity; equitableness etc. *adj.*; propriety; fair play, impartiality, measure for measure, give and take, *lex talionis*, square deal.

Astraea, Nemesis, Themis.

scales of justice, even-handed justice, retributive justice, *suum cuique*; clear stage –, fair field- and no favor; Queensberry rules.

morals etc. (*duty*) 926; law etc. 963; honor etc. (*probity*) 939; virtue etc. 944.

V. be -right etc. *adj.*; stand to reason.

see -justice done, – one righted, – fair play; do justice to; recompense etc. (*reward*) 973; hold the scales even, give and take; serve one right, put the saddle on the right horse; give -every one, – the devil- his due; *audire alteram partem.*

deserve etc. (*be entitled to*) 924.

Adj. right, good; just, reasonable; fit etc. 924; equ-al, -able, -itable; evenhanded, fair, – and square.

legitimate, justifiable, rightful; as it -should, – ought to- be; lawful etc. (*permitted*) 760, (*legal*) 963.

deserved etc. 924.

Adv. rightly etc. *adj.*; in -justice, – equity, – reason.

without -distinction of, – regard to, – respect to- persons; upon even terms.

Int. all right!

923. Wrong.—N. wrong; what -ought not to, – should not- be; *malum in se*; unreasonableness, grievance; shame.

injustice, unfairness etc. *adj.*; iniquity, foul play, partiality, leaning; favor, -itism; nepotism, party spirit, partisanship; undueness etc. 925; unlawfulness etc. 964.

robbing Peter to pay Paul etc. *v.*; the wolf and the lamb; vice etc. 945.

a custom more honored in the breach than the observance.

V. be -wrong etc. *adj.*; cry to heaven for vengeance.

do -wrong etc. *n.*; be -inequitable etc. *adj.*; favor, lean towards; encroach; impose upon; reap where one has not sown; give an inch and take an ell; rob Peter to pay Paul.

Adj. wrong, -ful; bad, too bad; unjust, -fair; in-, un-equitable; unequal, partial, one-sided.

objectionable; un-reasonable, -allowable, warrantable, -justifiable; not cricket, not playing the game; improper, unfit; unjustified etc. 925; illegal etc. 964; iniquitous, criminal; immoral etc. 945; injurious etc. 649.

in the wrong, – box.

Adv. wrongly etc. *adj.*

Phr. it will not do; this is too bad.

924. Dueness.—N. due, -ness; right, privilege, prerogative, prescription, title, claim, pretension, demand, birthright.

immunity, license, liberty, franchise; vested - interest, − right; licitness.

sanction, authority, warranty, charter; warrant etc. (*permission*) 760; constitution etc. (*law*) 963; tenure; bond etc. (*security*) 771.

deserts, merits, dues.

claimant, appellant; plaintiff etc. 938.

V. be -due etc. *adj.* to, − the due etc. *n.* of; have -right, − title, − claim- to; be entitled to; have a claim upon; belong to etc. (*property*) 780.

deserve, merit, be worthy of, richly deserve.

demand, claim; call upon −, come upon −, appeal to- for; re-vendicate, -claim; exact; insist -on, − upon; challenge; take one's stand, make a point of, require, lay claim to, assert, assume, arrogate, make good; substantiate; vindicate a -claim, − right; make out a case.

give −, confer- a right; sanction, entitle; authorize etc. 760; sanctify, legalize, ordain, prescribe, allot.

give every one his due etc. 922; pay one's dues; have one's -due, − rights; stand upon one's rights.

use a right, assert, enforce, put in force, lay under contribution.

Adj. having a right to etc. *v.*; entitled to; claiming; deserving, meriting, worthy of.

privileged, allowed, sanctioned, warranted, authorized; ordained, prescribed, constitutional, chartered, enfranchised.

prescriptive, presumptive; absolute, indefeasible; un-, in-alienable.

imprescriptible, inviolable, unimpeachable, unchallenged; sacrosanct.

due to, merited, deserved, condign, richly deserved, *emeritus.*

allowable etc. (*permitted*) 760; lawful, licit, legitimate, legal; legalized etc. (*law*) 963.

square, unexceptionable, right; equitable etc. 922; due, *en règle*; fit, -ting; correct, proper, meet, befitting, becoming, seemly; decorous; creditable, up to the mark, right as a trivet; just −, quite- the thing; *selon les règles.*

Adv. duly, *ex officio, de jure*; by -right, − divine right; as is -fitting, − proper, − fitting and proper; *jure divino, Dei gratiâ*, in the name of.

Phr. *civis Romanus sum.*

925. Undueness. [Absence of right.] —N. undueness etc. *adj.*; *malum prohibitum*; impropriety; illegality etc. 964.

falseness etc. *adj.*; emptiness −, invalidity- of title; illegitimacy.

loss of right, disfranchisement, forfeiture.

usurpation, assumption, tort, violation, breach, encroachment, presumption, seizure, stretch, exaction, imposition, lion's share.

usurper, pretender, Carlist; imposter.

V. be -undue etc. *adj.*; not be -due etc. 924.

infringe, encroach, trench on, exact; arrogate, − to oneself; give an inch and take an ell; stretch −, strain- a point; usurp, violate, do violence to; sail under false colors.

dis-franchise, -entitle, -qualify; invalidate.

relax etc. (*be lax*) 738; misbehave etc. (*vice*) 945; misbecome.

Adj. undue; unlawful etc. (*illegal*) 964; unconstitutional, *ultra vires*; illicit; un-authorized, - warranted, -allowed, -sanctioned, -justified; un-, dis-entitled, -qualified; un-privileged, -chartered.

illegitimate, bastard, spurious, false; usurped, tortious.

un-deserved, -merited, -earned; unfulfilled.

forfeited, disfranchised.

improper; un-meet, -fit, -befitting, -seemly; un-, mis-becoming; seemless; *contra bonos mores*; not the thing, out of the question, not to be thought of; preposterous, pretentious, would- be.

926. Duty. —N. duty, what ought to be done, moral obligation, accountableness, liability, *onus*, responsibility; bounden −, imperative- duty; call, − of duty.

allegiance, fealty, tie; engagement etc. (*promise*) 768; part; function, calling etc. (*business*) 625.

morality, morals, decalogue; case of conscience; conscientiousness etc. (*probity*) 939; conscience, inward monitor, still small voice within, sense of duty, tender conscience.

dueness etc. 924; propriety, fitness, seemliness, amenableness, decorum; the -thing, − proper thing; the -right, − proper- thing to do.

[Science of morals] eth-ics, -ology; deon-, aretology; moral −, ethical-philosophy; casuistry, polity.

observance, fulfilment, discharge, performance; acquittal, satisfaction, redemption; good behavior.

V. be -the duty of, − incumbent etc. *adj.* on, − responsible etc. *adj.*; behoove, become, befit, beseem; belong −, pertain- to; fall to one's lot; devolve on; lie -upon, − on one's head, − at one's door; rest -with, − on the shoulders of.

take upon oneself etc. (*promise*) 768.

be −, become- -bound to, − sponsor for; be responsible for; incur a -responsibility etc. *n.*; be −, stand −, lie- under an obligation; have to answer for, owe it to oneself.

impose a -duty etc. *n.*; enjoin, require, exact; bind, − over; saddle with, prescribe, assign, call upon, look to, oblige.

enter upon −, perform −, observe −, fulfil −, discharge −, adhere to −, acquit oneself of −, satisfy- -a duty, − an obligation; act one's part, redeem one's pledge, do justice to, be at one's post; do duty; do one's duty etc. (*be virtuous*) 944.

be on one's good behavior, mind one's P's and Q's.

Adj. obligatory, binding; imperative, peremptory; stringent etc. (*severe*) 739; behooving etc. *v.*; incumbent −, chargeable- on; under obligation; obliged −, bound −, tied- by; saddled with.

due −, beholden −, bound −, indebted- to; tied down; compromised etc. (*promised*) 768; in duty bound.

amenable, liable, accountable, responsible, answerable.

right, meet etc. (*due*) 924; moral, ethical, casuistical, conscientious, ethological.

Adv. with a safe conscience, as in duty bound, on one's own responsibility, at one's own risk, *suo periculo*; *in foro conscientiae*; *quamdiu se bene gesserit*; at one's post, on duty.

Phr. *dura lex sed lex.*

927. Dereliction of Duty. —N. dere; liction of duty; fault etc. (*guilt*) 947- sin etc. (*vice*) 945; nonobservance, -performance, -co-operation; neglect, carelessness, laziness, incompetence, eye-service,

relaxation, infraction, violation, transgression, failure, evasion, indolence; dead letter.

slacker, loafer, striker, non-co-operator.

V. violate; break, – through; infringe; set - aside, – at naught; trample -on, – under foot; slight, neglect, evade, renounce, forswear, repudiate; wash one's hands of; escape, transgress, fail.

call to account etc. (*disapprobation*) 932.

927a. Exemption.—N. exemption, freedom, irresponsibility, immunity, liberty, license, release, exoneration, excuse, dispensation, absolution, franchise, renunciation, discharge; exculpation etc. 970; *aegrotat*.

V. be -exempt etc. *adj.*

exempt, release, acquit, discharge, quit-claim, remise, remit; free, set at liberty, let off, pass over, spare, excuse, dispense with, give dispensation, license; stretch a point; absolve etc. (*forgive*) 918; exonerate etc. (*exculpate*) 970; save the necessity.

Adj. exempt, free, immune, at liberty, scot free; released etc. *v.*; unbound, unencumbered; irresponsible, unaccountable, not answerable; excusable.

928. Respect.—N. respect, regard, consideration; courtesy etc. 894; attention, deference, reverence, honor, esteem, estimation, veneration, admiration; approbation etc. 931.

homage, fealty, obeisance, genuflexion, kneeling, prostration; obsequiousness etc. 886; salaam, *kowtow*, bow, presenting arms, salute.

respects, regards, duty, *devoirs*, *égards*.

devotion etc. (*piety*) 987.

V. respect, regard; revere, -nce; hold in reverence, honor, venerate, hallow; esteem etc. (*approve of*) 931; think much of; entertain –, bear- respect for; have a high opinion of; look up to, defer to; pay -attention, – respect etc. *n.*- to; do –, render- honor to; do the honors; hail; show courtesy etc. 894; salute, present arms; do –, pay- homage to; pay tribute to; kneel to, bow to, bend the knee to; fall down before, prostrate oneself, kiss the hem of one's garment; worship etc. 990.

keep one's distance, make room, observe due decorum, stand upon ceremony.

command –, inspire- respect; awe, impose, overawe, dazzle.

Adj. respecting etc. *v.*; respectful, deferential, decorous, reverential, obsequious, ceremonious, bare-headed, cap in hand, on one's knees; prostrate etc. (*servile*) 886.

respected etc. *v.*; in high -esteem, – estimation; time-honored, venerable, *emeritus*.

Adv. in deference to; with -all, – due, – the highest- respect; with submission.

saving your -grace, – presence; *salva sit reverentia*; *pace tanti nominis*.

Int. hail! all hail! *esto perpetua!* may your shadow never be less!

929. Disrespect.—N. dis-respect, -esteem, - estimation, -favor, -repute; low estimation; disparagement etc. (*dispraise*) 932; (*detraction*) 934.

irreverence; slight, neglect; *spretae injuria formae*; superciliousness etc. (*contempt*) 930.

vilipendency, contumely, affront, dishonor, insult, indignity, outrage, discourtesy etc. 895; practical joking; scurrility, scoffing, sibilation; ir-, derision; mockery; irony etc. (*ridicule*) 856; sarcasm.

hiss, hoot, gibe, flout, jeer, scoff, gleek, taunt, sneer, quip, fling, wipe, slap in the face.

V. hold in disrespect etc. (*despise*) 930; misprize, disregard, slight, undervalue, depreciate, trifle with, set at naught, pass by, push aside, overlook, turn one's back upon, laugh in one's sleeve; be -disrespectful etc. *adj.*, – discourteous etc. 895; treat with -disrespect etc. *n.*; set down, browbeat.

dishonor, desecrate; insult, affront, outrage.

speak slightingly of; disparage etc. (*dispraise*) 932; vilipend, call names; throw –, fling- dirt; drag through the mud, point at, indulge in personalities; make -mouths, – faces; bite the thumb; take –, pluck- by the beard; toss in a blanket, tar and feather.

have –, hold- in derision; deride, scoff, sneer, laugh at, snigger, ridicule, gibe, mock, jeer, taunt, twit, niggle, gleek, gird, flout, fleer; roast, turn into ridicule; guy, burlesque etc. 856; laugh to scorn etc. (*contempt*) 930; smoke; fool; make -game, – a fool, – an April fool- of; play a practical joke; rag; lead one a dance, run the rig upon, have a fling at, scout, hiss, hoot, mob.

Adj. disrespectful; aweless, irreverent; disparaging etc. 934; insulting etc. *v.*; supercilious etc. (*scornful*) 930; rude, derisive, contemptuous, sarcastic; scurri-le, -lous; contumelious.

un-respected, -worshipped, -envied, -saluted; un-dis-regarded.

Adv. disrespectfully etc. *adj.*

930. Contempt.—N. contempt, disdain, scorn, sovereign contempt; despi-sal, -ciency; vilipendency, contumely; slight, sneer, spurn, by-word.

contemptuousness etc. *adj.*; scornful eye; smile of contempt; derision etc. (*disrespect*) 929.

[State of being despised] despisedness.

V. despise, contemn, scorn, disdain, feel contempt for, view with a scornful eye, disregard, slight, not mind; pass by etc. (*neglect*) 460.

look down upon; hold -cheap, – in contempt, – in disrespect; think -nothing, – small beer- of; make light of; underestimate etc. 483; esteem - slightly, – of small or no account; take no account of, care nothing for; set no store by; not care a - straw etc. (*unimportance*) 643; set at naught, laugh in one's sleeve, snap one's fingers at, shrug one's shoulders, turn up one's nose at, pooh-pooh, damn with faint praise; sneeze –, whistle –, sneer- at; curl up one's lip, toss the head, *traiter de haut*; laugh at etc. (*be disrespectful*) 929.

point the finger of –, hold up to –, .laugh to- scorn; scout, hoot, flout, hiss, scoff at.

turn -one's back, – a cold shoulder- upon; tread –, trample- upon, – under foot; spurn, kick; fling to the winds etc. (*repudiate*) 610; send away with a flea in the ear.

Adj. contemptuous; disdain-, scorn-ful; withering, contumelious, supercilious, cynical, haughty, bumptious, cavalier; derisive.

contemptible, despicable; pitiable; pitiful etc. (*unimportant*) 643; despised etc. *v.*; downtrodden; unenvied.

Adv. contemptuously etc. *adj.*

Int. a fig for etc. (*unimportant*) 643; bah! never mind! away with! hang it! fiddle-de-dee!

931. Approbation.—N. approbation; approval, -ement; sanction, advocacy; nod of approbation; esteem, estimation, good opinion, golden opinions, admiration; love etc. 897; appreciation, regard, account, popularity, *kudos*, credit; repute etc. 873.

commendation, praise; laud, -ation; good word; meed —, tribute- of praise; encomium; eulog-y, -ium; *éloge*, panegyric; homage, hero worship; benediction, blessing, benison.

applause, plaudit, clap; clapping, — of hands; accl-aim, -amation; cheer; paean, hosannah; shout —, peal —, chorus —, thunders- of -applause etc. Kentish fire; Prytaneum; blurb.

V. approve; think -good, — much of, — well of, — highly of; esteem, value, prize; set great store -by, — on.

do justice to; appreciate; honor, hold in esteem, look up to, admire; like etc. 897; be in favor of, wish God speed; hail, — with satisfaction.

stand —, stick- up for; uphold, hold up, countenance, sanction; clap —, pat- on the back; keep in countenance, endorse, give credit, recommend; mark with a white -mark, — stone.

commend, praise; be-, laud; compliment, pay a tribute, bepraise; clap, — the hands; applaud, cheer, acclaim, acclamate, encore; panegyrize, eulogize, cry up, *prôner*, puff; extol, — to the skies; magnify, glorify, exalt, boost, swell, make much of; flatter etc. 933; bless, give a blessing to; have —, say- a good word for; speak -well, —highly, — in high terms- of; sing —, sound —, chaunt —, resound- the praises of; sing praises to; cheer —, applaud- to the -echo, — very echo.

redound to the -honor, — praise, — credit- of; do credit to; deserve -praise etc. *n.*; recommend itself; pass muster.

be -praised etc.; receive honorable mention; be in -favor, — high favor- with; ring with the praises of, win golden opinions, gain credit, find favor with, stand well in the opinion of; *laudari a laudato viro*.

Adj. approving etc. *v.*; in favor of; lost in admiration.

commendatory, complimentary, benedictory, laudatory, panegyrical, eulogistic, encomiastic, acclamatory, lavish of praise, uncritical.

approved, praised etc. *v.*; un-censured, impeached; popular, in good odor; in high esteem etc. (*respected*) 928; in —, in high- favor.

deserving —, worthy of- praise etc. *n.*; praiseworthy, commendable, of estimation; good etc. 648; meritorious, estimable, creditable, plausible, unimpeachable; beyond all praise.

Adv. commendably, with credit, to admiration; well etc. 681; with three times three.

Int. hear, hear! well done! *brav-o! -a! -i! bravissimo! euge! macte virtute!* so far so good, that's right, quite right; *optime!* one cheer more; may your shadow never be less! *esto perpetua!* long life to! *viva! enviva!* God speed! *valete et plaudite! encore! bis!*

Phr. *probatum est.*

932. Disapprobation.—N. disappro-bation, -val; improbation; dis-esteem, -valuation, -placency; odium; dislike etc. 867; dissent etc. 489.

dis-praise, -commendation; blame, censure, obloquy; detraction etc. 934; disparagement, depreciation; denunciation; condemnation etc. 971; ostracism; boycott; black-list, -ball; *index expurgatorius, — librorum prohibitorum.*

animadversion, reflection, stricture, objection, exception, criticism; sardonic -grin, — laugh; sarcasm, insinuation, innuendo; bad —, poor —, lefthanded- compliment.

satire; sneer etc. (*contempt*) 930; taunt etc. (*disrespect*) 929; cavil, carping, censoriousness; hypercriticism etc. (*fastidiousness*) 868.

reprehension, remonstrance, expostulation, reproof, reprobation, admonition, increpation, reproach; rebuke, reprimand, castigation, jobation, lecture, curtain lecture, blow up, wigging, dressing, — down; rating, scolding, trimming; correction, set down, rap on the knuckles, *coup de bec*, rebuff; slap, — on the face; home thrust; hit; frown, scowl, black look.

diatribe; jeremiad; *tirade*, philippic.

clamor, outcry, hue and cry; hiss, -ing; sibilation, cat-call; execration etc. 908.

chiding, upbraiding etc. *v.*; exprobration, abuse, vituperation, invective, objurgation, contumely, personal remarks; hard —, cutting —, bitterwords.

evil-speaking; bad language etc. 908; personality.

V. disapprove; dislike etc. 867; lament etc. 839; object to, take exception to; be scandalized at, think ill of; view with -disfavor, — dark eyes, — jaundiced eyes; *nil admirari*, disvalue, improbate.

frown upon, look grave; bend —, knit- the brows; shake the head at, shrug the shoulders; turn up the nose etc. (*contempt*) 930; look -askance, — black upon; look with an evil eye; make a wry -face, — mouth- at; set one's face against.

dis-praise, -commend, -parage; deprecate, speak ill of, not speak well of, slate, condemn etc. (*find guilty*) 971.

blame; lay —, cast- blame upon; censure, *fronder*, reproach, pass censure on, reprobate, impugn.

remonstrate, expostulate, recriminate.

reprehend, chide, admonish; bring —, call- -to account, — over the coals, — to order; take to task, reprove, lecture, bring to book; read a -lesson, — lecture- to; rebuke, correct.

reprimand, chastise, castigate, lash, blow up, trounce, trim, *laver la tête*, overhaul; give it one, — finely; gibbet.

accuse etc. 938; impeach, denounce; hold up to -reprobation, — execration; expose, brand, gibbet, stigmatize; show —, pull —, take- up; cry 'shame' upon; be outspoken; raise a hue and cry against.

execrate etc. 908; exprobrate, speak daggers, vituperate; abuse, —, like a pickpocket; scold, rate, objurgate, upbraid, fall foul of; jaw; rail, — at, — in good set terms; bark at; anathematize, call names; call by -hard, — ugly- names; a-, re-vile; vili-fy, -pend; bespatter; backbite; clapperclaw; rave —, thunder —, fulminate- against; load with reproaches; lash with the tongue.

exclaim —, protest —, inveigh —, declaim —, cry out —, raise one's voice- against.

decry; cry —, run —, frown- down; clamor, hiss,

hoot, mob, ostracize; draw up —, sing- a round robin; black-ball, -list.

animadvert —, reflect- upon; glance at; cast -reflection, — reproach, — a slur- upon; insinuate, damn with faint praise; 'hint a fault and hesitate dislike;' not to be able to say much for.

scoff at, point at; twit, taunt etc. (*disrespect*) 929; sneer at etc. (*despise*) 230; satirize, lampoon; defame etc. (*detract*) 934; depreciate, find fault with, criticize, cut up; pull —, pick- to pieces; take exception; cavil; peck —, nibble —, carp- at; be -censorious etc. *adj.*; pick -holes, — a hole, — a hole in one's coat; make a fuss about.

take —, set- down; snub, snap one up, give a rap on the knuckles; throw a stone -at, — in one's garden; have a -fling, — snap- at; have words with, pluck a crow with; give one a -wipe, — lick with the rough side of the tongue.

incur blame, excite disapprobation, scandalize, shock, revolt; get a bad name, forfeit one's good opinion, be under a cloud, come under the ferule, bring a hornet's nest about one's ears.

take blame, stand corrected; have to answer for.

Adj. disapproving etc. *v.*; scandalized.

disparaging, condemnatory, damnatory, denunciatory, reproachful, abusive, objurgatory, clamorous, vituperative; defamatory etc. 934.

satirical, sarcastic, sardonic, cynical, dry, sharp, cutting, biting, severe, virulent, withering, trenchant, hard upon; censorious, critical, captious, carping, hypercritical; fastidious etc. 868; sparing of —, grudging- praise.

disapproved, chid etc. *v.*; in bad odor, blown upon, unapproved; unblest; at a discount, exploded; weighed in the balance and found wanting.

blameworthy, reprehensible etc. (*guilt*) 947; to —, worthy of- blame, answerable; uncommendable, exceptionable, not to be thought of, bad etc. 649; vicious etc. 945.

un-lamented, -bewailed, -pitied.

Adv. with a wry face; reproachfully etc. *adj.*

Int. it is too bad! it -won't, — will never- do! marry come up! Oh! come! 'sdeath!

forbid it Heaven! God —, Heaven- forbid! out —, fie- upon it! away with! tut! *O tempora! O mores!* shame! fie, — for shame! out on you!

tell it not in Gath!

933. Flattery.—N. flattery, adulation, gloze; bland-ishment, -iloquence; cajolery; fawning, wheedling etc. *v.*; captation, coquetry, sycophancy, obsequiousness, flunkeyism, toad-eating, tuft-hunting; snobbishness.

incense, honeyed words, flummery; bun-kum, -combe; blarney, *placebo*, butter; soft -soap, — sawder; rose water.

voice of the charmer, mouth honor; lip-homage; euphemism; unctuousness etc. *adj.*

V. flatter, praise to the skies, puff; wheedle, cajole, glaver, coax; fawn, —, upon; humor, gloze, soothe, pet, coquet, slaver, butter; be-spatter, -slubber, -plaster, -slaver; lay it on thick, overpraise; earwig, cog, collogue; truckle —, pander *or* pandar —, pay court- to; court; creep into the good graces of; curry favor with, hang on the sleeve of; fool to the top of one's bent; lick the dust.

lay the flattering unction to one's soul, gild the pill, make things pleasant.

overestimate etc. 482; exaggerate etc. 549.

Adj. flattering etc. *v.*; adulatory; mealy-, honey-mouthed; honeyed; smooth, — tongued; soapy, oily, unctuous, blandiloquent, specious; fine-, fair-spoken; plausible, servile, sycophantic, fulsome; courtier-ly, -like.

Adv. *ad captandum.*

934. Detraction.—N. detraction, disparagement, depreciation, vilification, obloquy, scurrility, scandal, defamation, aspersion, traducement, slander, calumny, obtrectation, evil-speaking, backbiting, *scandalum magnatum.*

personality, libel, squib, lampoon, skit, pasquinade; *chronique scandaleuse.*

sarcasm, cynicism; criticism (*disapprobation*) 932; invective etc. 932; envenomed tongue; *spretae injuria formae.*

detractor etc. 936.

V. detract, derogate, decry, depreciate, disparage; run —, cry- down; minimize, make light of; belittle, sneer at etc. (*contemn*) 930; criticize, pull to pieces, pick a hole in one's coat, asperse, cast aspersions, blow upon, bespatter, blacken; vilify, -pend; avile; give a dog a bad name, brand, malign, backbite, libel, lampoon, traduce, slander, defame, calumniate, bear false witness against; speak ill of behind one's back.

'damn with faint praise, assent with civil leer; and without sneering, others teach to sneer.'

fling dirt etc. (*disrespect*) 929; anathematize etc. 932; dip the pen in gall, view in a bad light.

Adj. detracting etc. *v.*; defamatory, detractory, derogatory; disparaging, libellous; scurril-e, -ous; abusive; foul-spoken, -tongued, -mouthed; slanderous; calumni-ous, -atory; sar-castic, -donic; satirical, cynical.

935. Flatterer.—N. flatterer, adulator; eulogist, -phemist; optimist, encomiast, *laudator*, whitewasher, booster.

toad-y, -eater; sycophant, courtier, pickthank, Sir Pertinax MacSycophant; *flâneur, prôneur*; puffer, touter, *claqueur*; claw-back, ear-wig, doer of dirty work; parasite, hanger on etc. (*servility*) 886.

936. Detractor.—N. detractor, reprover; censor, -urer; cynic, critic, caviller, carper, word-catcher.

defamer, backbiter, slanderer, knocker, Sir Benjamin Backbite, lampooner, satirist, traducer, libeller, calumniator, dearest foe, dawplucker, Thersites; Zoilus; good-natured —, candid- friend [satirically]; reviler, vituperator, castigator; shrew etc. 901.

disapprover, *laudator temporis acti.*

937. Vindication.—N. vindication, justification, warrant; exoneration, exculpation; acquittal etc. 970; whitewashing.

extenuation; pallia-tion, -tive; softening, mitigation.

reply, defense; recrimination etc. 938.

apology, gloss, varnish; plea etc. 617; salvo; excuse, extenuating circumstances; allowance, – to be made; *locus poenitentiae.*

apologist, vindicator, justifier; defendant etc. 938.

justifiable charge, true bill.

V. justify, warrant; be an -excuse etc. *n.* - for; lend a color, furnish a handle; vindicate; ex-, disculpate; acquit etc. 970; clear, set right, exonerate, whitewash.

extenuate, palliate, excuse, soften, apologize, varnish, slur, gloze; put a -gloss, – good face-upon; mince; gloss over, bolster up, help a lame dog over a stile.

advocate, defend, plead one's cause; stand –, stick –, speak- up for; contend –, speak- for; bear out, keep in countenance, support; plead etc. 617; say in defense; plead ignorance; confess and avoid, propugn, put in a good word for.

take the will for the deed, make allowance for, do justice to; give -one, – the Devil- his due.

make good; prove -the truth of, – one's case; be justified by the event.

Adj. vindicat-ed, -ing etc. *v.*; vindicat-ive, -ory; palliative; exculpatory; apologetic.

excusable, defensible, pardonable; veni-al, -able; specious, plausible, justifiable.

Phr. *'honi soit qui mal y pense.'*

938. Accusation.—**N.** accusation, charge, imputation, slur, inculpation, exprobation, delation; crimination; in-, ac-, re-crimination; *tu quoque* argument; invective etc. 932.

de-nunciation, -nouncement; libel, challenge, citation, arraignment; im-, ap-peachment; indictment, bill of indictment, true bill; lawsuit etc. 969; condemnation etc. 971.

gravamen of a charge, head and front of one's offending, *argumentum ad hominem*; scandal etc. *(detraction)* 934; *scandalum magnatum.*

accuser, prosecutor, plaintiff, complainant, petitioner; relator, informer; appellant.

accused, defendant, prisoner, panel, co-, respondent; litigant.

V. accuse, charge, tax, impute, twit, taunt with, reproach.

brand with reproach; stigmatize, slur; cast a -stone at, – slur on; incriminate; inculpate, implicate; call to account etc. *(censure)* 932; take to blame, – task; put in the black book.

inform against, indict, denounce, arraign; im-, ap-peach; have up, show up, pull up, challenge, cite, lodge a complaint; prosecute, bring an action against etc. 969.

charge –, saddle- with; lay to one's -door, – charge; lay the blame on, bring home to; cast –, throw- in one's teeth; cast the first stone at.

have –, keep- a rod in pickle for; have a crow to pluck with.

trump up a charge.

Adj. accusing etc. *v.*; accusat-ory, -ive; imputative, denunciatory; re-, criminatory.

accused etc. *v.*; suspected; under -suspicion, – a cloud, – *surveillance*; in -custody, – detention; in the -lock up, – watch house, – house of detention.

accusable, imputable; in-defensible, -excusable; un-pardonable, -justifiable; vicious etc. 945.

Int. look at home; *tu quoque* etc. *(retaliation)* 718.

939. Probity.—**N.** probity, integrity, rectitude; uprightness etc. *adj.*, honesty, faith; honor; good faith, *bona fides*; purity, clean hands.

fairness etc. *adj.*; fair play, justice, equity, impartiality, principle; grace.

constancy; faithfulness etc. *adj.*; fidelity, loyalty; incorrupt-ion, -ibility.

trustworthiness etc. *adj.*; truth, candor, singleness of heart; veracity etc. 543; tender con-science etc. *(sense of duty)* 926.

punctil-iousness, -io; delicacy, nicety; scrupul-osity, -ousness etc. *adj.*; scruple; point, – of honor; punctuality.

dignity etc. *(repute)* 873; respectability, -bleness etc. *adj.*; gentleman; man of -honor, – his word; *fidus Achates, preux chevalier; galantuomo*; truepenny, trump, brick; true Briton, white man, sportsman.

court of honor, a fair field and no favor; *argumentum ad verecundiam.*

V. be -honorable etc. *adj.*, deal -honorably, – squarely, – impartially, – fairly; speak the truth etc. *(veracity)* 543; tell the truth and shame the devil, *vitam impendere vero*; show a proper spirit, make a point of; do one's duty etc. 944; play the game.

redeem one's pledge etc. 926; keep –, be as good as- one's -promise, – word; keep faith with, not fail.

give and take, *audire alteram partem*, give the devil his due, put the saddle on the right horse.

redound to one's honor.

Adj. upright; honest, – as daylight; veracious etc. 543; virtuous etc. 944; honorable; fair, right, just, equitable, impartial, even-handed, square; fair –, open- and aboveboard.

constant, – as the northern star; faithful, loyal, staunch; true, – blue, – to one's colors, – to the core, – as the needle to the pole; true-hearted, trust-y, -worthy; as good as one's word, to be depended on, incorruptible.

manly, straightforward etc. *(ingenuous)* 703; frank, candid, open-hearted.

conscientious, tender-conscienced, right-minded; high-principled, -minded; scrupulous, religious, strict, nice, punctilious, correct, punctual; respect-, reput-able; gentlemanlike.

inviol-able, -ate; un-violated, -broken, -betrayed; un-bought, -bribed.

innocent etc. 946; pure; stainless; un-stained, -tarnished, -sullied, -tainted, -perjured; uncorrupt, -ed; unde-filed, -praved, -bauched; *integer vitae scelerisque purus; justus et tenax propositi.*

chivalrous, jealous of honor, *sans peur et sans reproche*; high-spirited.

supra-mundane, unworldly, overscrupulous.

Adv. honorably etc. *adj.*; *bona fide*; on the square, in good faith, honor bright, *foro conscientiae*, with clean hands; by fair means.

940. Improbity.—**N.** improbity; dishon-esty, -our; deviation from rectitude; disgrace etc. *(disrepute)* 874; fraud etc. *(deception)* 545; lying etc. 544; bad –, Punic- faith; *mala –, Punica, fides*; infidelity; faithlessness etc. *adj.*; Judas kiss, betrayal; scrap of paper.

breach of -promise, – trust, – faith; prodition, disloyalty, divided allegiance, treason, high treason; apostacy etc. (*tergiversation*) 607; non-observance etc. 773.

shabbiness etc. *adj.*; villainy; baseness etc. *adj.*; abjection, debasement, turpitude, moral turpitude, laxity, trimming, shuffling.

perfidy; perfidiousness etc. *adj.*; treachery, double-dealing; unfairness etc. *adj.*; knavery, roguery, rascality, foul-play; jobb-ing, -ery; Tammany, graft; venality, nepotism; corruption, job, shuffle, fishy transaction, barratry; sharp practice, heads I win, tails you lose; mouth-honor etc. (*flattery*) 933.

V. be -dishonest etc. *adj.*; play false; break one's -word, − faith, − promise; jilt, betray, forswear; shuffle etc. (*lie*) 544; live by one's wits, sail near the wind; play with marked cards.

disgrace −, dishonor −, demean −, degrade-oneself; derogate, stoop, grovel, sneak, lose caste; sell oneself, go over to the enemy; seal one's infamy.

Adj. dishon-est, -orable; un-conscientious, -scrupulous; fraudulent etc. 545; knavish; disgraceful etc. (*disreputable*) 874; wicked etc. 945.

false-hearted, disingenuous; unfair, one-sided; double, -tongued, -faced; time-serving, crooked, tortuous, insidious, Machiavellian, dark, slippery; questionable; fishy; perfidious, treacherous, perjured.

infamous, arrant, foul, base, vile, low, ignominious, blackguard;

contemptible, abject, mean, shabby, little, paltry, dirty, scurvy, scabby, sneaking, groveling, scrubby, rascally, pettifogging; beneath one; not cricket.

low-minded, -thoughted; base-minded.

undignified, indign; unbe-coming, -seeming, fitting; de-rogatory, -grading; *infra dignitatem*; ungentleman-ly, -like; un-knightly, -chivalric, -manly, -handsome; recreant, inglorious.

corrupt, venal; debased, mongrel.

faithless, of bad faith, false, unfaithful, disloyal; untrustworthy; trust-, troth-less; lost to shame, dead to honor.

Adv. dishonestly etc. *adj.*; *malâ fide*, like a thief in the night, by crooked paths; by foul means.

Int. *O tempora! O mores!*

941. Knave.—N. knave, rogue, villain; Seapin, rascal; Lazarillo de Tormes; bad man etc. 949; blackguard etc. 949.

traitor, betrayer, arch-traitor, conspirator, stool pigeon, Judas, Catiline; reptile, serpent, snake in the grass, wolf in sheep's clothing, sneak, Jerry Sneak, tell-tale, squealer, mischief-maker, trimmer; renegade etc. (*tergiversation*) 607; truant, recreant; sycophant etc. (*servility*) 886.

942. Disinterestedness.—N. disinterestedness etc. *adj.*; generosity; liberal-ity, -ism; altruism; benevolence etc. 906; elevation, loftiness of purpose, exaltation, magnanimity; chival-ry, -rous spirit; heroism, sublimity.

self-denial, -abnegation, -effacement, -sacrifice, -immolation, -control etc. (*resolution*) 604; stoicism, devotion, martyrdom, *suttee*.

labor of love.

V. be -disinterested etc. *adj.*; make a sacrifice, lay one's head on the block; put oneself in the place of others, do as one would be done by, do unto others as we would men should do unto us.

Adj. disinterested; unselfish; self-denying, sacrificing, -devoted; generous.

handsome, liberal, noble; noble-, high-minded; princely, great, high, elevated, lofty, exalted, spirited, stoical, magnanimous; great-, large-hearted, chivalrous, heroic, sublime.

un-bought, -bribed; uncorrupted etc. (*upright*) 939.

943. Selfishness.—N. selfishness etc. *adj.*; self-love, -indulgence, -worship, -interest; ego-tism, -ism; egocentrism, narcissism; *amour propre* etc. (*vanity*) 880; nepotism.

worldliness etc. *adj.*; world wisdom.

illiberality; meanness etc. *adj.*

time-server; tuft-, fortune-hunter; self-seeker; jobber, worldling; egotist, egoist, monopolist, nepotist, profiteer; temporizer, trimmer; dog in the manger, charity that begins at home.

V. be -selfish etc. *adj.*; please −, indulge −, coddle- oneself; consult one's own -wishes, -pleasure; look after one's own interest; feather one's nest; take care of number one, have an eye to the main chance, know on which side one's bread is buttered; give an inch and take an ell; wangle.

Adj. selfish; self-seeking, -indulgent, -interested; wrapt up −, centered- in self; egotistic, -al; egoistical; egocentric.

illiberal, mean, ungenerous, narrowminded; mercenary, venal; covetous etc. 819.

unspiritual; earthly, -minded; mundane; worldly, -minded, -wise; time-serving.

interested; *alieni appetens sui profusus*.

Adv. ungenerously etc. *adj.*; to gain some private ends; from selfish −, interested- motives.

Phr. *après nous le déluge.*

944. Virtue.—N. virtue; virtuousness etc. *adj.*; morality; moral rectitude; integrity etc. (*probity*) 939; nobleness etc. 873.

morals; ethics etc. (*duty*) 926; cardinal virtues.

merit, worth, desert, excellence, credit; self-control etc. (*resolution*) 604; self-denial etc. (*temperance*) 953.

well-doing; good -actions, − behavior; discharge −, fulfilment −, performance- of duty; well spent life; innocence etc. 946.

V. be -virtuous etc. *adj.*; practice -virtue etc. *n.*; do −, fulfil −, perform −, discharge- one's duty; redeem one's pledge etc. 926; act well, − one's part; fight the good fight; acquit oneself well; command −, master- one's passions; keep -straight, − in the right path.

set -an, − a good- example; be on one's -good, − best- behavior.

Adj. virtuous, good; innocent etc. 946; meritorious, deserving, worthy, desertful, correct; dut-iful, -eous; moral; right, -eous, -minded; well-intentioned, creditable, laudable, commendable, praiseworthy; above −, beyond- all praise; excellent, admirable; sterling, pure, noble.

exemplary; match-, peer-less; saint-ly, -like; heaven-born, angelic, seraphic, godlike.

Adv. virtuously etc. *adj.*; *e merito.*

945. Vice.—N. vice; evil-doing. – courses; wrong doing; wickedness, viciousness etc. *adj.*; iniquity, peccability, demerit; sin, Adam; old – offending- Adam.

immorality, impropriety, indecorum, scandal, laxity, looseness of morals; want of -principle, – ballast; obliquity, backsliding, infamy, demoralization, pravity, depravity, pollution; hardness of heart; brutality etc. (*malevolence*) 907; corruption etc. (*debasement*) 659; knavery etc. (*improbity*) 940; profligacy; lust etc. 961; flagrancy, atrocity; cannibalism.

infirmity; weakness etc. *adj.*; weakness of the flesh, frailty, imperfection; error; weak side; foible; fail-ing. -ure; crying –, besetting- sin; defect, deficiency, shortcoming; cloven foot.

lowest dregs of vice, sink of iniquity, Alsatian den; *gusto picaresco*.

fault, crime; criminality etc. (*guilt*) 947.

sinner etc. 949.

V. be -vicious etc. *adj.*; sin, commit sin, do amiss, err, transgress; misdemean –, forget –, misconduct- oneself; mis-do, -behave; fall, lapse, slip, trip, offend, trespass; deviate from the -line of duty, – path of virtue etc. 944; take a wrong course, go astray; hug a -sin. – fault; sow one's wild oats.

render -vicious etc. *adj.*; demoralize, brutalize; corrupt etc. (*degrade*) 659.

Adj.* vicious, sinful; sinning etc. *v.*; wicked, iniquitous, bad, immoral, unrighteous, wrong, criminal; naughty, incorrect; undut-eous, -iful.

unprincipled, lawless, disorderly, *contra bonos mores*, indecorous, unseemly, improper; dissolute, profligate, scampish; unworthy; worth-, desert-less; disgraceful, recreant; reprehensible, blameworthy, uncommendable; dis-creditable, -reputable.

base, sinister, scurvy, foul, gross, vile, black, grave, facinorous, felonious, nefarious, shameful, scandalous; infamous, villainous, of a deep dye, heinous; flag-rant, -itious; atrocious, incarnate, accursed.

Mephistophelian, satanic, diabolic, hellish, infernal, stygian, fiend-ish, -like, hell-born, demoniacal, devilish.

mis-created, -begotten; demoralized, corrupt, depraved.

evil-minded, -disposed; ill-conditioned; malevolent etc. 907; heart-, grace-, shame-, virtueless; abandoned, lost to virtue; unconscionable; sunk –, lost –, deep –, steeped- in iniquity.

incorrigible, irreclaimable, obdurate, reprobate, past praying for; culpable, reprehensible etc. (*guilty*) 947.

unjustifiable; in-defensible, -excusable; inexpiable, unpardonable, irremissible.

weak, frail, lax, infirm, imperfect, indiscreet; demoralizing, degrading.

Adv. wrong; sinfully etc. *adj.*; without excuse.

Int. *O tempora! O mores!*

*Most of these adjectives are applicable both to the act and to the agent.

946. Innocence.—N. innocence; guiltlessness etc. *adj.*; incorruption, impeccability.

clean hands, clear conscience, *mens sibi conscia recti*.

innocent, new born babe, lamb, dove.

V. be -innocent etc. *adj.*; *nil conscire sibi nullâ pallescere culpâ.*

acquit etc. 970; exculpate etc. (*vindicate*) 937.

Adj. innocent, not guilty, unguilty; guilt-, fault-, sin-, stain-, blood-, spot-less; clear, immaculate; *rectus in curiâ*; un-spotted, -blemished, -erring; undefiled etc. 939; unhardened, Saturnian; Arcadian etc. (*artless*) 703.

in-, un-culpable; unblam-ed, -able; blameless, inerrable, above suspicion; irrepr-oachable, -ovable, -ehensible; un-exceptionable, -objectionable, -impeachable; salvable; venial etc. 937.

harmless; in-offensive, -noxious, -nocuous; dove-, lamb-like; pure, harmless as doves; innocent as -a lamb, – the babe unborn; more sinned against than sinning.

virtuous etc. 944; un-reproved, -impeached, -reproached.

Adv. innocently etc. *adj.*; with clean hands; with a -clear, – safe- conscience.

947. Guilt.—N. guilt, -iness; culpability; crimin-ality, -ousness; deviation from rectitude etc. (*improbity*) 940; sinfulness etc. (*vice*) 945; peccability.

mis-conduct, -behavior, -doing, -deed; malpractice, fault, sin, error, transgression; dereliction, delinquency; indiscretion, lapse, slip, trip, *faux pas, peccadillo*; flaw, blot, omission; fail-ing, -ure.

offence, trespass; mis-demeanor, -feasance, -prision, tort; mal-efaction, -feasance, -versation; crime, felony.

enormity, atrocity, outrage; deadly –, mortal –, unpardonable- sin; died without a name.

corpus delicti.

Adj. guilty, to blame, culpable, peccable, in fault, censurable, reprehensible, blameworthy, uncommendable, illaudable; weighed in the balance and found wanting; exceptionable, objectionable.

Adv. *in flagrante delicto*; red-handed, in the very act.

948. Good Man.—N. good man, worthy.

good woman, goddess, *madonna*, virgin.

model, paragon etc. (*perfection*) 650; good example; hero, demigod, seraph, angel; innocent etc. 946; saint etc. (*piety*) 987; benefactor etc. 912; philanthropist etc. 910; Aristides.

brick, trump, rough diamond, ugly duckling.

salt of the earth; one in ten thousand; one of the best.

Phr. *si sic omnes!*

949. Bad Man.—N. bad man, wrongdoer, worker of iniquity; evil-doer etc. 913; sinner; the- wicked etc. 945; bad example.

rascal, scoundrel, villain, miscreant, caitiff; wretch, reptile, viper, serpent, cockatrice, basilisk, urchin; tiger, monster; devil etc. (*demon*) 980; devil incarnate; demon in human shape, Nana Sahib; hell-hound, -cat; rake-hell.

bad woman, jade, Jezebel, adultress, etc. 962.

scamp, scapegrace, rip, runagate, ne'er-do-well, reprobate, *roué*, rake; limb; one who has sold himself to the devil, fallen angel, *âme damnée*, *vaurien*, *mauvais sujet*, loose fish, sad, dog; lost –, black-sheep; castaway, recreant, defaulter; prodigal etc. 818; libertine etc. 962.

rough, rowdy, ugly customer, ruffian, hoodlum, bully; Jonathan Wild; hangman; incendiary; thief etc. 792; murderer etc. 361.

culprit, delinquent, criminal, melefactor, misdemeanant; felon; convict, jail-bird, ticket-of-leave man; outlaw.

blackguard, *polisson*, loafer, sneak; raps-, rascallion; cullion, mean wretch, varlet, kern, *âme-de-boue*, *drôle*; cur, dog, hound, whelp, mongrel; lown, loon, runnion, outcast, vagabond; rogue etc. (*knave*) 941; scum of the earth, riff-raff; *Arcades ambo*.

Int. sirrah!

950. Penitence.—N. penitence, contrition, compunction, repentance, remorse; regret etc. 833.

self-reproach, -reproof, -accusation, -condemnation, -humiliation; stings –, pangs –, qualms –, prickings –, twinge –, twitch –, touch –, voice- of conscience; compunctious visitings of nature.

acknowledgment, confession etc. (*disclosure*) 529; apology etc. 952; recantation etc. 607; penance etc. 952; resipiscence.

awakened conscience, deathbed repentance, *locus poenitentiae*, stool of repentance, cutty stool.

penitent, Magdalen, prodigal son, returned prodigal, a sadder and wiser man.

V. repent, be sorry for; be -penitent etc. *adj.*; rue; regret etc. 833; think better of; recant etc. 607; knock under etc. (*submit*) 725; plead guilty; sing -*miserere*, – *de profundis*; cry *peccavi*; own oneself in the wrong; acknowledge, confess etc. (*disclose*) 529; humble oneself; beg pardon etc. (*apologize*) 952; turn over a new leaf, put on the new man, turn from sin; reclaim; repent in sackcloth and ashes etc. (*do penance*) 952; learn by experience.

Adj. penitent; repenting etc. *v.*; repentant, contrite; conscience-smitten, -stricken; self-accusing, -convicted.

penitenti-al, -ary; chastened, reclaimed; not hardened; un-hardened.

Adv. *meâ culpâ*.

Phr. *peccavi; erubuit; salva res est; vous l'avez voulu, Georges Dandin.*

951. Impenitence.—N. impenitence, irrepentance, recusance.

hardness of heart, seared conscience, induration, obduracy.

V. be -impenitent etc. *adj.*; steel –, harden- the heart; die -game, – and make no sign.

Adj. impenitent uncontrite, obdurate; hard, -ened; seared, recusant; unrepentant; relent-, remorse-, grace-, shrift-less.

lost, incorrigible, irreclaimable.

unre-claimed, -formed; unrepented, unatoned.

952. Atonement.—N. atonement, reparation; compromise, composition; compensation etc. 30; quittance, quits; indemni-ty, -fication; expiation,

redemption, reclamation, conciliation, propitiation.

amends, apology, *amende honorable*, satisfaction; peace –, sin –, burnt- offering; scapegoat, sacrifice.

penance, fasting, maceration, sackcloth and ashes, white sheet, shrift, flagellation, lustration; purga-tion, -tory.

V. atone, – for; expiate; propitiate; make -amends, – good; reclaim, redeem, repair, ransom, absolve, purge, shrive, do penance, stand in a white sheet, repent in sackcloth and ashes.

set one's house in order, wipe off old scores, make matters up; pay the -forfeit, – penalty.

apologize, beg pardon, express regret, *faire amende honorable*, give satisfaction; come – , fall-down on one's -knees, – marrow bones.

Adj. propitiatory, expiatory; sacrific, -ial, -atory; piacul-ar, -ous.

953. Temperance.—N. temperance, moderation, sobriety, soberness.

forbearance, abnegation; self-denial, -restraint, -control etc. (*resolution*) 604.

frugality; vegetarianism, teetotalism, total abstinence, prohibition; abst-inence, -emiousness, asceticism etc. 955; system of -Pythagoras, – Cornaro; Pythagorism, Stoicism.

vegetarian; Pythagorean, gymnosophist; teetotaler etc. 958; abstainer.

V. be -temperate etc. *adj.*; abstain, forbear, refrain, deny oneself, spare; know when one has had enough; take the pledge; look not upon the wine when it is red.

Adj. temperate, moderate, sober, frugal, sparing; abst-emious, -inent; within compass; measured etc. (*sufficient*) 639.

Pythagorean; vegetarian; teetotal, pussy-foot.

954. Intemperance.—N. intemperance; sensuality, animalism, carnality; pleasure; effeminacy, silkiness; luxur-y, -iousness; lap of -pleasure, – luxury.

indulgence; high-, free- living, in-abstinence, self-indulgence; voluptuousness etc. *adj.*; epicurism, -eanism; sybaritism.

dissipation; licentiousness etc. *adj.*; debauchery; crapulence.

revel-s, -ry; debauch, carousal, jollification, drinking bout, wassail, Saturnalia, orgies; excess, too much; intoxication etc. 959.

Circean cup; drug habit etc. 663.

V. be -intemperate etc. *adj.*; indulge, exceed; live -well, – high, – on the fat of the land; give a loose to -indulgence etc. *n.*; dine not wisely but too well; wallow in -voluptuousness etc. *n.*; plunge into dissipation.

revel, rake, live hard, run riot, sow one's wild oats; slake one's -appetite, – thirst; swill; pamper.

Adj. intemperate, inabstinent, intoxicated etc. 958; sensual, self-indulgent; voluptuous, luxurious, licentious, wild, dissolute, rakish, fast, debauched.

brutish, crapulous, swinish, piggish, hoggish, bestial.

Paphian, Epicurean, Sybaritical; bred –, nursed- in the lap of luxury; indulged, pampered, full-fed.

954a. Sensualist.—N. Sybarite, voluptuary, Sardanapalus, man of pleasure, carpet knight; epicure, -an; *gourm-et*, *-and;* gormandizer, gutling, glutton, pig, hog; votary –, swine- of Epicurus; sensualist; Heliogabalus; free –, hard- liver; libertine etc. 962; hedonist.

955. Asceticism.—N. asceticism, puritanism, sabbatarianism; cynicism, austerity; total abstinence.

mortification, maceration, sackcloth and ashes, flagellation; penance etc. 952; fasting etc. 956; martyrdom.

ascetic; anchor-et, -ite; martyr; *Heautontimorumenos;* hermit etc. (*recluse*) 893; puritan, sabbatarian, cynic.

Adj. ascetic, austere, puritanical; cynical; over-religious.

956. Fasting.—N. fasting; exrophagy; famishment, starvation; banting.

fast, *jour maigre;* fast .–, banyan-day; Lent, quadragesima; Rama-dan, -zan; spare –, meager-diet; lenten -diet, – entertainment; *soupe maigre*, short -rations, – commons; Barmecide feast; hunger strike.

V. fast, starve, clem, famish, perish with hunger; dine with Duke Humphrey; make two bites of a cherry.

Adj. lenten, quadragesimal; unfed; starved etc. *v.;* half-starved; fasting etc. *v.;* hungry etc. 865.

957. Gluttony.—N. gluttony; greed; greediness etc. *adj.;* voracity.

epicurism; good –, high- living; edacity, gulosity, crapulence; gutt-, guzz-ling; over-indulgence.

good cheer, blow out; feast etc. (*food*) 298; gastronomy.

epicure, *bon vivant, gourmand;* glutton, cormorant, hog, belly-god, Apicius, gastronome, gormandizer.

V. gormandize, gorge; over-gorge, -eat- oneself; engorge, eat one's fill, cram, stuff, stodge, glut, satiate; gutt-le, guzz-le; bolt, devour, gobble up; gulp etc. (*swallow food*) 298; raven, eat out of house and home.

have the stomach of an ostrich; play a good knife and fork etc. (*appetite*) 865.

Adj. gluttonous, greedy; gormandizing etc. *v.;* edacious, omnivorous, crapulent, swinish, voracious, devouring.

pampered; over-fed, -gorged.

958. Sobriety.—N. sobriety; teetotalism, temperance etc. 953.

water-drinker; teetotal-er, -ist; abstainer, Good Templar, Rechabite, band of hope; prohibitionist, pussyfoot.

V. take the pledge.

Adj. sober, – as a judge; dry, on the water wagon.

959. Drunkenness.—N. drunkenness etc. *adj.;* intemperance; drinking etc. *v.;* inebri-ety, -ation; ebri-ety, -osity; befuddlement; insobriety; intoxication; temulency, bibacity, wine-bibbing; compotation; deep potations, bacchanals, *bacchanalia*, libations.

oino-, dipso-mania; *delirium tremens*, d.t., alcohol, -ism.

drink; alcoholic drinks, alcohol, booze; gin, blue ruin, grog, brandy, port wine; punch, -bowl; cup, rosy wine, flowing bowl; drop, – too much; dram; beer, wine, spirits etc. (*beverage*) 298; cocktail, nip, peg; stirrup cup.

drunkard, sot, toper, tippler, bibber, wine-bibber; hard –, gin –, dram- drinker; soak, soaker, sponge, tun; love-, toss-pot; thirsty soul, reveller, carouser; Bacchanal, -ian; Bacch-al, -ante; devotee to Bacchus, dipsomaniac.

V. get –, be- drunk etc. *adj.;* see double; take a -drop, – glass- too much; drink, tipple, tope, booze, bouse, guzzle, swill, soak, sot, lush, bib, swig, carouse; sacrifice at the shrine of Bacchus; take to drinking; drink -hard, – deep, – like a fish; have one's swill, drain the cup, splice the main brace, take a hair of the dog that bit you.

liquor, – up; wet one's whistle, take a whet; lift one's elbow; crack a –, pass the- bottle; toss of etc. (*drink up*) 298; go to the -ale, – public house.

make one-drunk etc. *adj.;* inebriate, fuddle, fuzzle, get into one's head.

Adj. drunk, tipsy; intoxicated; inebri-ous, -ate, -ated; in one's_cups; in a state of -intoxication etc. *n.;* temulent, -ive; fuddled, mellow, cut, boosy, fou, fresh, merry, elevated, squiffy; plastered, befuddled, sozzled; flush, -ed; flustered, disguised, groggy, beery, topheavy; potvaliant, glorious; potulent; over-come, -taken; whittled, screwed, tight, primed, oiled, corned, raddled, sewed up, lushy, nappy, muddled, muzzy, bosky, obfuscated, maudlin; crapulous, dead –, blind- drunk.

inter pocula; in –, the worse for- liquor, having had a drop too much, half seas over, three sheets in the wind; under the table, blind to the world, one over the eight.

drunk as -a piper, – a fiddler, – a lord, – Chloe, – an owl, – David's sow, – a wheelbarrow.

drunken, bibacious, bibulous, sottish; given –, addicted- to -drink, – the bottle; toping etc. *v.;* wet.

Phr. *nunc est bibendum.*

960. Purity.—N. purity; decency, decorum, delicacy; continence, chastity, honesty, virtue, modesty, shame; pudicity, *pucelage*, virginity.

vestal, virgin, Joseph, Hippolytus; Lucretia, Diana; prude.

Adj. pure, undefiled, modest, delicate, decent, decorous; *virginibus puerisque;* chaste, continent, virtuous, honest, Platonic.

961. Impurity.—N. impurity; uncleanness etc. (*filth*) 653; immodesty; grossness etc. *adj.;* indelicacy, indecency; impudicity; obscenity, ribaldry, smut, bawdry, *double entendre*, *équivoque;* Aretinism; pornography.

concupiscence, lust, carnality, flesh, salacity; pruriency, lechery, lasciviency, lubricity, lewdness.

incontinence, intrigue, *faux pas*; *amour, -ette*; gallantry; dabauchery, libertinism, *libertinage*, fornication; *liaison*; wenching, venery, dissipation.

seduction; defloration, defilement, abuse, violation, rape; incest.

social evil, harlotry, stupration, whoredom, concubinage. cuckoldom, adultery, advoutry, *crim. con.*; free love.

seraglio, harem, zenana; brothel, bagnio, stew, bawdy-house, *lupanar*, house of ill fame, *bordel*, kip.

V. be -impure etc. *adj.*; intrigue; debauch, defile, assault, attack, seduce; prostitute; abuse, violate, deflower; commit -adultery etc. *n.*

Adj. impure; unclean etc. (*dirty*) 653; not to be mentioned to ears polite; immodest, shameless; indecorous, -delicate, -decent; loose, suggestive; *risqué*, coarse, gross, broad, free, equivocal, smutty, fulsome, ribald, obscene, bawdy, pornographic.

concupiscent, prurient, lickerish, rampant, lustful; carnal, -minded; lewd, lascivious, lecherous, libidinous, erotic, ruttish, salacious; Paphian; voluptuous; incestuous.

· unchaste, light, wanton, licentious, adulterous, debauched, dissolute; of -loose character, – easy virtue; frail, gay, riggish, incontinent, meretricious, rakish, gallant, dissipated; no better than she should be; on the -town, – streets, – *pavé*, – loose.

adulterous, incestuous, bestial.

962. Libertine.—N. libertine; voluptuary etc. 954a; rake, debauchee, loose fish, rip, rake-hell, fast man; *intrigant*, gallant, seducer, fornicator, lecher, satyr, goat, whoremonger, *paillard*, adulterer, gay deceiver, Lothario, Don Juan, Bluebeard.

adulteress, advoutress, courtesan, prostitute, strumpet, tart, hustler, chippy, broad, harlot, whore, punk, *fille de joie*; woman, – of the town; street-walker, Cyprian, miss, piece; frail sisterhood, fallen woman; demirep, wench, trollop, trull, baggage, hussy, drab, bitch, jade, skit, rig, quean, mopsy, slut, minx, harridan; woman -of easy virtue etc. (*unchaste*) 961; wanton, fornicatress; Jezebel, Messalina, Delilah, Thaïs, Phryne, Aspasia, Laïs, *lorette, cocotte, petite dame, grisette; demi-monde*; white slave.

concubine, mistress, fancy woman, kept woman, doxy, *chère amie, bona roba*.

pimp; pand-er, -ar; bawd, *conciliatrix*, procuress, mackerel, wittol.

963. Legality.—N. legality; legitima-cy, teness, legitimization.

legislature; law, code, *corpus juris*, constitution, pandect, charter, act, enactment, statute, rule; canon etc. (*precept*) 697; ordinance, institution, regulation; by-, bye-law, rescript; decree etc. (*order*) 741; *ordonnance*; standing order; *plébiscite* etc. (*choice*) 609.

legal process; form, -ula, -ality; rite; arm of the law; *habeas corpus*.

[Science of law] jurisprudence, nomology; legislation, codification.

equity, common law; *lex* –, *lex nonscripta*, unwritten law; law of nations, international law, *jus gentium*; *jus civile*; civil –, criminal –, canon –, statute –, ecclesiastical- law; *lex mercatoria*. constitutional-ism, -ity; justice etc. 922.

V. legalize, legitimize; enact, ordain; decree etc. (*order*) 741; pass a law; legislate; codify, formulate; authorize.

Adj. legal, legitimate; according to law; vested, constitutional, chartered, legalized; lawful etc. (*permitted*) 760: statut-able, -ory; legislat-orial, -ive.

Adv. legally etc. *adj.*; in the eye of the law; *de jure*.

964. Illegality. [Absence or violation of law.]—**N.** lawlessness; breach –, violation- of law; disobedience etc. 742; unconformity etc. 83.

arbitrariness etc. *adj.*, antinomy, violence, brute force, despotism, outlawry.

mob –, lynch –, club –, Lydford –, martial –, drumhead- law; *coup d'état; le droit du plus fort; argumentum baculinum*.

illegality, informality, unlawfulness, illegitimacy, bar sinister.

trover and conversion; smuggling, boot-legging, rum-running, poaching; simony.

speakeasy, speakie, blind pig.

V. offend against –, violate- the law; set the law at defiance, ride rough-shod over, drive a coach and six through a statute; make the law a dead letter, take the law into one's own hands.

smuggle, run, poach.

Adj. illegal; prohibited etc. 761; not allowed, unlawful, illegitimate, illicit, contraband, actionable.

unchartered, unconstitutional; unwarrant-ed, -able; unauthorized; informal, unofficial; in-, extrajudicial.

lawless, arbitrary; despotic, -al; summary, irresponsible; un-answerable, -accountable.

null and void; a dead letter.

Adv. illegally etc. *adj.*; with a high hand, in violation of law.

965. Jurisdiction. [Executive.]—**N.** jurisdiction, judicature, administration of justice, soc; executive, commission of the peace; magistracy etc. (*authority*) 737.

judge etc. 967; tribunal etc. 966; municipality, corporation, bailiwick, shrievalty; lord lieutenant; lord –, mayor, city manager, alderman etc. 745; sheriff, bailie, shrieve, chief –, constable; police, – force; constabulary, bumbledom.

officer; proctor, high –, commissioner; bailiff, tipstaff, bum-bailiff, catchpoll, beadle; police-man, -constable, -sergeant; *sbirro, alguazil, gendarme*; kavass, *lictor*, macebearer, *huissier*, bedel.

press-gang; exciseman, gauger; custom-house officer, *douanier*.

coroner, edile, aedile, portreeve, paritor; *posse comitatus*.

V. judge, sit in judgment.

Adj. executive, administrative, municipal;

inquisitorial, causidical; judic-atory, -iary, -ial; juridical.

Adv. *coram judice.*

966. Tribunal.—**N.** tribunal, court, board, bench, judicatory, curia; court of -justice. – law, – arbitration; inquisition; guild.

justice –, judgment –, mercy- seat; woolsack; bar, – of justice; dock; forum, hustings, *bureau*, drum-head; jury-, witness-box.

senate-house, town-hall, theater; House of - Lords, – Commons.

assize, eyre; ward-, burgh-mote; superior courts of Westminister; court of -record, – oyer and ter- miner, – assize, – appeal – error; High court of -Judicature, – Appeal; Judicial Committee of the Privy Council; Star-Chamber; Court of -Chancery, – King's *or* Queen's Bench, – Exchequer, – Common Pleas, – Probate, – Arches, – Ad- miralty, – Criminal Appeal; Lords Justices' –, Rolls –, Vice Chancellor's –, Stannary –, Divorce –, Palatine –, ecclesiastical –, county –, police- court; sessions; quarter –, petty- sessions; court -leet, – baron, – of pie poudre, – of common council; board of green cloth.

court-martial; drum-head court-martial; *durbar*, divan; Areopagus; *rota.*

Adj. judicial etc. 965; appellate; curial.

967. Judge.—**N.** judge; justi-ce, -ciar, -ciary; chancellor; justice –, judge- of assize; recorder, common serjeant; puisne –, assistant –, county court- judge; conservator –, justice- of the peace, J.P.; court etc. (*tribunal*) 966; grand –, petty –, coroner's- jury; panel, juror, juryman; twelve men in a box; magistrate, police magistrate, stipendiary, the great unpaid, beak; his -worship, – honor, – lordship; deemster, moderator.

Lord -Chancellor, – Justice; Master of the Rolls, Vice-Chancellor; Lord Chief -Justice, – Baron; Mr. Justice; Baron, – of the Exchequer.

jurat, assessor; arbi-ter, -trator; umpire; refer-ee, -endary; revising barrister; domesman; censor etc. (*critic*) 480; official –, receiver.

archon, tribune, praetor, *ephor*, syndic, *podestà*, mullah, ulema, mufti, cadi, kadi; Rhadamanthus. litigant etc. (*accusation*) 938.

V. adjudge etc. (*determine*) 480; try a -case, – prisoner.

Adj. judicial etc. 965.

Phr. 'a Daniel come to judgment.'

968. Lawyer.—**N.** lawyer, jurist, legist, civilian, pundit, publicist, jurisconsult, legal adviser, ad- vocate; barrister, – at law; counsel, -lor; King's *or* Queen's counsel; K.C.; Q.C.; silk gown, leader; junior, – counsel; stuff gown, serjeant-at-law; bencher, tubman; judge etc. 967.

bar, legal profession, gentleman of the long robe; junior –, outer –, inner- bar; Inns of Court; equity draftsman, conveyancer, pleader, special pleader.

solicitor, attorney, proctor; notary, – public; scrivener, cursitor; writer, – to the signet; S.S.C.; limb of the law; pettifogger.

V. practice -at, – within- the bar; plead; call – to called- -to, – within- the bar; take silk.

Adj. learned in the law; at the bar; forensic.

969. Lawsuit.—**N.** lawsuit, suit, action, cause, petition; litigation; dispute etc. 713.

citation, arraignment, prosecution, im- peachment; accusation etc. 938; presentment, true bill, indictment.

apprehension, arrest; committal; imprisonment etc. (*restraint*) 751.

writ, summons, subpoena, *latitat, nisi prius*; *habeas corpus.*

pleadings; declaration, bill, claim; *procès- verbal*, bill of right, information, *corpus delicti*; affidavit, state of facts; answer, replication, plea, demurrer, rebutter, rejoinder; surre-butter, joinder.

suitor, party to a suit; litigant etc. 938; libellant.

hearing, trial; verdict etc. (*judgment*) 480; ap- peal, – motion; writ of error; *certiorari.*

case, decision, precedent, ruling; decided case, reports.

V. go to –, appeal to the- law; bring to -justice, – trial, – the bar; put on trial, pull up; accuse etc. 938; prefer –, file- a claim etc. *n.*; take the law of, inform against.

serve with a writ, cite, apprehend, arraign, sue, prosecute, bring an action against, indict, impeach, attach, distrain, commit; arrest; summon, -s; give in charge etc. (*restrain*) 751.

empanel a jury, implead, join issue; close the pleadings; set down for hearing.

try, hear a cause; sit in judgment; adjudicate etc. 480.

Adj. litigious etc. (*quarrelsome*) 713; *qui tam*; *coram* –, *sub- judice.*

Adv. *pendente lite.*

Phr. *adhuc sub judice lis est.*

970. Acquittal.—**N.** acquit-tal, -ment; clearance, exculpation, exoneration; discharge etc. (*release*) 750; *quietus*, absolution, compurgation, reprieve, respite; pardon etc. (*forgiveness*) 918.

[Exemption from punishment] impunity, im- munity.

V. acquit, exculpate, exonerate, clear; absolve, whitewash, assoil, discharge, release; liberate etc. 750.

reprieve, respite; pardon etc. (*forgive*) 918; let off, – scot free.

Adj. acquitted etc. *v.*: un-condemned, - punished, -chastised; recommended to mercy.

971. Condemnation.—**N.** condemnation, con- viction, proscription, damnation; death warrant; penalty etc. 974.

attain-der, -ture, -tment.

V. condemn, convict, cast, bring home to, find guilty, damn, doom, sign the death warrant, sen- tence, pass sentence on, attaint, confiscate, proscribe, sequestrate; non-suit.

disapprove etc. 932; accuse etc. 938.

stand condemned.

Adj. condem-, dam-natory; condemned etc. *v.*; non-suited etc. (*failure*) 732; self-convicted.

Phr. *mutato nomine de te fabula narratur.*

972. Punishment.—N. punishment, punition; chast-isement, -ening; correction, castigation.

discipline, infliction, trial; judgment; penalty etc. 974; retribution; thunderbolt, Nemesis; requital etc. (*reward*) 973; penology; retributive justice.

lash, scaffold etc. (*instrument of punishment*) 975; imprisonment etc. (*restraint*) 751; chain gang; transportation, banishment, expulsion, deportation, exile, involuntary exile, ostracism; penal servitude, hard labor; galleys etc. 975; beat.ng etc. v.; flagellation, fustigation, gantlet, *strappado, estrapade, bastinado, argumentum baculinum*, stick law, rap on the knuckles, box on the ear; blow etc. (*impulse*) 276; stripe, cuff, kick, buffet, pummel; slap, — in the face; wipe, douse; *coup de grâce*; torture, rack; picket, -ing; *dragonnade*; capital punishment, extreme penalty; execution; hanging etc. v.; de-capitation, -collation; *garrot-te, -to*; electrocution, lethal chamber; crucifixion, impalement; martyrdom, *auto-da-fé*; *noyade*; *hara-kiri*, happy despatch.

V. punish; chast-ise, -en; castigate, correct, inflict punishment, administer correction, deal retributive justice.

visit upon, pay; pay —, serve- out; settle with, get even with, get one's own back; do for; make short work of, give a lesson to, strafe, serve one right, make an example of; have a rod in pickle for; give it one.

strike etc. 276; deal a blow to, administer the lash, smite; slap, — the face; smack, cuff, box the ears, spank, thwack, thump, beat, lay on, swinge, buffet; thresh, thrash, pummel, drub, leather, trounce, baste, belabor; lace, — one's jacket; dress, give a -dressing, — down; trim, warm, wipe, tund, cob, bang, strap, comb, lash, lick, larrup, whallop, whop, flog, scourge, whip, birch, cane, give the stick, switch, flagellate, horsewhip, *bastinado*, towel, rub down with an oaken towel, rib roast, dust one's jacket, fustigate, pitch into, lay about one, beat black and blue; beat to a -mummy, — jelly; give a black eye; hit on the head; sandbag.

tar and feather; pelt, stone, lapidate; mast-head, keelhaul.

execute; bring to the -block, — gallows; behead; de-capitate, -collate; guillotine; hang, turn off, gibbet, bowstring, hang, draw and quarter; shoot; decimate; burn; electrocute; break on the wheel, crucify; em-, im-pale; flay; lynch; put to death.

torture; put -on, — to- the rack; picket.

banish, exile; trans-, de-port; expel, ostracize; rusticate; drum out; dismiss, -bar, -bench; strike off the roll, unfrock; post.

suffer, — for, — punishment; be -flogged, — hanged etc.; come to the gallows, dance upon nothing, die in one's shoes, be rightly served.

Adj. punishing etc. v.; penal; puni-tory, -tive; inflictive, castigatory; punished etc. v.

Int. *à la lanterne!*

973. Reward.—N. reward, recompense, remuneration, prize, meed, guerdon, reguerdon; indemni-ty, -fication; price; quittance; compensation; reparation, *ersatz*, assythment, redress; retribution, reckoning, acknowledgment, requital, amends, sop; atonement; consideration, return, *quid pro quo*; salvage, perquisite; vail etc. (*donation*) 784; *douceur*, bribe, bait, baksheesh,

tip; hush-, smart-money; black-mail; carcelage; *solatium*.

allowance, salary, stipend, wages; pay, -ment; emolument; tribute; batta, shot, scot; premium, fee, *honorarium*; hire.

crown etc. (*decoration of honor*) 877.

V. re-ward, -compense, -pay, -quite; re-, munerate; compensate; fee, tip, bribe; pay one's footing etc. (*pay*) 807; make amends, indemnify, atone; satisfy, acknowledge.

get for one's pains, reap the fruits of.

Adj. remunerat-ive, -ory; munerary, compensatory, retributive, reparatory.

974. Penalty.—N. penalty; retribution etc. (*punishment*) 972; pain, pains and penalties; *peine forte et dure*; penance etc. (*atonement*) 952; the devil to pay.

fine, mulct, amercement; forfeit, -ure; escheat, damages, deodand, sequestration, confiscation, *premunire*.

V. penalize, fine, mulct, amerce, sconce, confiscate; sequest-rate, -er; escheat; estreat, forfeit.

975. Scourge. [Instrument of punishment.]—**N.** scourge, rod, cane, stick; ra-, rat-tan; birch, — rod; rod in pickle; switch, ferule, cudgel, truncheon; rubber hose.

whip, lash, strap, thong, cowhide, knout; cat, — o'-nine-tails, *sjambok*, quirt; rope's end.

pillory, stocks, whipping-post; cuck-, duck-ing stool; brank; triangle, wooden horse, maiden; thumbscrew, boot, rack, wheel, iron heel; treadmill, crank, galleys.

scaffold; block, axe, *guillotine*; stake; cross; gallows, gibbet, Tyburn tree; drop, noose, rope, halter, bowstring; electric chair, lethal chamber.

house of correction etc. (*prison*) 752.

gaol-, jail-er; executioner; hang-, heads-man; Jack Ketch; lyncher.

976. Deity.—N. Deity, Divinity; God-head, -ship; Omnipotence, Providence.

[Quality of being divine] divin-eness, -ity.

God, Lord, Jehovah, *Deus*; The -Almighty, — Supreme Being, — First Cause; *Ens Entium*; Author —, Creator- of all things; Author of our being; The -Infinite, — Eternal; The All-powerfull, -wise, -merciful, -holy; The Omni-potent, -scient.

[Attributes and perfections] infinite -power, — wisdom, — goodness, — justice, — truth, — love, — mercy; omni-potence, -science, -presence; unity, immutability, holiness, glory, majesty, sovereignty, infinity, eternity.

The -Trinity, — Holy Trinity, — Trinity in Unity, — Triune God; Three in One and One in Three.

God the Father; The -Maker, — Creator, — Preserver.

[Functions] creation, preservation, divine government; The-ocracy, -archy; providence; ways —, dealings —, dispensations —, visitations- of Providence.

God the Son, Jesus, Christ; The -Messiah, — Anointed, — Savior, — Redeemer, — Mediator,

– Intercessor, – Advocate, – Judge; The Son of -
God, – Man, – David; The Only Begotten; The
Lamb of God, The Word; Em-, Im-manuel; The -
King of Kings and Lord of Lords, – King of
Glory, – Prince of Peace, – Good Shepherd, –
Way, – Truth, – Life, – Bread of Life, – Light
of the World; The -Lord our, – Sun of-
Righteousness.

The -Incarnation, – Hypostatic Union, –
Word made Flesh.

[Functions] salvation, redemption, atonement,
propitiation, mediation, intercession, judgment.

God the Holy Ghost, The Holy Spirit, Paraclete;
The -Comforter, – Consoler, – Spirit of Truth,
– Dove.

[Functions] inspiration, unction, regeneration,
sanctification, consolation.

eon, aeon, special providence, *Deus ex
machinâ*; *Avatar*.

V. create, uphold, preserve, govern etc.

atone, redeem, save, propitiate, mediate etc.

predestinate, elect, call, ordain, bless, justify,
sanctify, glorify etc.

Adj. almighty, holy, hallowed, sacred, divine,
heavenly, celestial; messianic; sacrosanct; all-
powerful, -wise, -seeing, -knowing; omnipotent,
omniscient; supreme.

super-human, -natural; ghostly, spiritual, hyper-
physical, unearthly; the-istic, -ocratic, deistic;
anointed.

Adv. *jure divino*, by divine right; *Deo volente*,
D.V.

977. Angel. [Beneficent spirits.]—**N.** angel,
archangel; heavenly host, choir invisible, host of
heaven, sons of God; Michael, Gabriel etc.; seraph,
-im; cherub, -im; ministering spirit, morning star;
saint, *Madonna*; Our Lady, the Blessed Virgin, the
Virgin Mary.

Adj. angelic, seraphic, cherubic.

978. Satan. [Maleficent spirits.]—**N.** Satan, the
Devil, Lucifer, Ahrimanes, Belial; Sammael,
Zamiel, Beelzebub, the Prince of the Devils;
Mephistopheles, his satanic majesty.

the tempter; the evil -one, – spirit; the -author
of evil, – wicked one, – old Serpent; the Prince
of -darkness, – this world, – the power of the air;
the -foul, – arch- fiend; the devil incarnate; the -
common enemy, – angel of the bottomless pit;
Abaddon, Apollyon, Mammon.

fallen agnels, unclean spirits, devils; the -rulers,
– powers- of darkness; inhabitants of Pandemonium; demon etc. 980.

diabolism; devil-ism, -ship, -dom, -ry, -worship;
diablerie; satanism, manicheism; the cloven foot;
black magic etc. 992.

Adj. satanic, diabolic, devilish, infernal, hell-
born.

979. Jupiter.—**N.** god, -dess; heathen gods and
goddesses; Pantheon; Jupiter, Jove, Zeus, Apollo,
Mars, Mercury, Neptune, Vulcan, Bacchus. Pluto,
Saturn, Cupid, Eros, Pan; Juno, Ceres, Proserpina,
Dina, Minerva, Pallas, Athenae, Venus, Aphrodite,
Vesta; The Fates etc. 601.

Allah, Brahma, Vishnu, Siva, Shiva, Krishna,
Juggernaut, Buddha; Ra, Isis, Osiris; Belus, Bel,
Baal, Asteroth etc.; Thor, Odin; Mumbo Jumbo;
good –, tutelary- genius; demiurge, familiar, –
spirit; Sibyl; fairy, fay; sylph, -id; Ariel, peri,
nymph, nereid, dryad, oread, sea-maid, Banshee,
Benshie, Ormuzd; Oberon, Titania, Mab,
hamadryad, naiad, mermaid, kelpie, Ondine, nix,
nixie, sprite; denizens of the air; pixy etc. (*bad
spirit*) 980.

mythology; heathen –, fairy- mythology; Lemprière, folklore.

Adj. fairy-, sylph-like; sylphic.

980. Demon.—**N.** demon, -ry, -ism, -ology; evil
genius, fiend, familiar, – spirit, devil; bad –, un-
clean- spirit; cacodemon, incubus, Frankenstein's
monster, succubus and succuba, Titan, Shedim,
Mephistopheles, Asmodeus, Moloch, Belial,
Ahriman, fury, The Furies etc. 900; harpy; Friar
Rush.

vampire, ghoul; af-, ef-freet; afrite; ogre, -ss;
gnome, gin, djinn, imp, deev, *lamia*; bo-gie, -gle;
nis, kobold, flibbertigibbet, fairy, brownie, pixy,
elf, dwarf, urchin, Puck, Robin Goodfellow; lepre-
cluri-chaune; troll, dwerger, sprite, oaf, changeling,
bad fairy, nixe, pigwidgeon, Will-o'-the-wisp; Erl
King.

[Supernatural appearance] ghost, specter, apparition, genie, spirit, shade, shadow, vision, phantom etc. 443; materialization (*spiritualism*) 992;
hob-, goblin; wraith, spook, werwolf, boggart, banshee, *loup-garou, lemures*; evil eye.

nisse, necks; mer-man, -maid, -folk; siren,
Lorelei; satyr, faun.

Adj. supernatural, weird, uncanny, unearthly,
spectral; ghost-ly, -like; elf-in, -like; fiend-ish, -like;
impish, demoniacal; haunted.

981. Heaven.—**N.** heaven; kingdom of -
heaven, – God; heavenly kingdom; throne –,
presence- of God; inheritance of the saints in light.

Paradise, Eden, abode of the blessed; Holy City,
New Jerusalem; celestial bliss, glory.

[Mythological -heaven] Olympus; [–
paradise] Elysium, Elysian fields, Arcadia, bowers
of bliss, garden of the Hesperides, Islands of the
Blessed; happy hunting-ground; third –, seventh-
heaven; Valhalla (Scandinavian); Nirvana (Buddhist).

future state, eternity, eternal life, life after death,
eternal home, resurrection, translation;
resuscitation etc. 660; apotheosis, deification.

Adj. heavenly, celestial, supernal, unearthly,
from on high, paradisiacal, beatific, elysian, Olym-
pian, Arcadian.

982. Hell.—**N.** hell, bottomless pit, place of
torment; habitation of fallen angels; Pandemonium, Abaddon, Domdaniel.

hell fire; everlasting -fire, – torment; lake of fire
and brimstone; fire that is never quenched, worm
that never dies.

purgatory, limbo, gehenna, abyss.

[Mythological hell] Tartarus, Hades, Avernus,
Styx, Stygian creek, pit of Acheron, Cocytus,

Phlegethon, Lethe; infernal regions, *inferno*, shades below, realms of Pluto.

Pluto, Rhadamanthus, Erebus, Charon, Cerberus; Tophet.

Adj. hellish, infernal, stygian.

983. Theology. [Religious Knowledge.]—**N.** Theology (natural and revealed); Theo-gony, -sophy; Divinity; Hagio-logy, -graphy; Caucasian mystery; monotheism; religion; religious - persuasion, -- sect, — denomination; cult; creed etc. (*belief*) 484; articles —, declaration —, profession —, confession- of faith.

theolog-ue, -ian; divine, schoolman, canonist, monotheist.

Adj. theological, religious; canonical; denominational; sectarian etc. 984.

983a. Orthodoxy.—N. orthodoxy; strictness, soundness, religious truth, true faith; truth etc. 494.

Christian-ity, -ism; Catholic-ism, -ity; 'the faith once delivered to the saints;' hyperorthodoxy etc. 984; iconoclasm.

the Holy —, the Orthodox- Church; Catholic —, Universal —, Apostolic —, Established- Church; temple of the Holy Ghost; Church —, body —, members —, disciples —, followers- of Christ; Christian, — community; true believer; canonist etc. (*theologian*) 983; Christendom, collective body of Christians, the Church Militant.

canons etc. (*belief*) 484; thirty-nine articles; Apostles' —, Nicene —, Athanasian- Creed; Church Catechism; textualy.

Adj. orthodox, sound, literal, strict, faithful, catholic, schismless, Christian, evangelical, scriptural, divine, monotheistic; true etc. 494.

984. Heterodoxy. [Sectarianism.]—**N.** heterodoxy; error etc. 495; false doctrine, heresy, schism; schismantic-ism, -alness; recusancy, backsliding, apostasy; atheism etc. (*irreligion*) 989.

bigotry etc. (*obstinacy*) 606; fanaticism, iconoclasm; hyperorthodoxy, precisianism, bibliolatry, hagiolatry, sabbatarianism, puritanism; idolatry etc. 991; superstition etc. (*credulity*) 486; dissent etc. 489.

sectar-ism, -ianism; nonconformity; secularism; syncretism; religious sects; the clash of creeds.

protestant-, advent-, Arian-, Erastian-, Calvin-, quaker-, method-, anabapt-, Pusey-, tractarian-, ritual-, Origen-, Sabellian-, Socinian-, De-, The-, mon-, material-, positiv-, latitudinairan-ism etc.

High —, Low —, Broad —, Free- Church; ultramontanism; monasticism; pap-ism, -istry; papacy; Anglican-, Catholic-, Roman-ism; popery, Scarlet Lady, Church of Rome, Greek Church; Christian Science, The Church of Christ Scientist.

pagan-, heathen-, ethic-ism; mythology; animism; poly-, di-, tri-, pan-theism; dualism; heathendom.

Juda-, Gentil-, Mahometan-, Islam-, Turc-, Brahmin-, Hindoo-, Buddh-, Lama-, Confucian-, Shinto-, Sabian-, Gnostic-. Soofee-, Hylothe-, Mormon-ism.

Theosophy; Spiritualism, Occultism.

heretic, antichrist; pagan, heathen; pai-, pay-nim; *giaour*; gentile; pan-, poly-theist; idolator; misbeliever, apostate, backslider.

bigot etc. (*obstinacy*) 606; fanatic, dervish, abdal, iconoclast.

latitudinarian, limitarian, Deist, Theist, Unitarian; positivist, materialist; agnostic, sceptic etc. 989.

schismatic; sectar-y, -ian, -ist; seceder, separatist, recusant, dissenter; non-conformist, -juror; Huguenot, Protestant; orthodox dissenter, Congregationalist, Independent; Episcopalian, Presbyterian; Lutheran, Calvinist, Quaker, Methodist, Weslayan; Ana-, Baptist; Dunker; Mormon, Latter-day Saint, Irvingite, Sandemanian, Glassite, Erastian; Sub-, Supra-lapsarian; Gentoo, Antinomian, Swedenborgian, Adventist, Plymouth Brother; Theosophist etc.

Catholic, Roman Catholic, Romanist, papist, ultramontane; Old Catholic, tractarian, Anglican, Puseyite, ritualist; Puritan.

Jew, Hebrew, Rabbist; Mahometan, Mohammedan, Mussulman, Moslem, Islamite, Osmanli; Brahm-in, -an; Parsee, Sofi, Soofee; Buddhist; Zoroastrian, Magi, Gymnosophist, fire-worshipper, Sabian, Gnostic, Sadducee, Rosicrucian etc.

Adj. heterodox, heretical; un-orthodox, scriptural, -canonical; antiscriptural, apocryphal; un-, anti-christian; schismatic, recusant, iconoclastic; sectarian; dis-senting, -sident; secular etc. (*lay*) 997.

pagan; heathen, -ish; ethnic, -al; gentile, painim; pan-, poly-theistic; agnostic, sceptic.

Judaical, Mohammedan, Moslem, Brahminical, Buddhist etc. *n.*; Romish, Protestant etc. *n.*

bigoted etc. (*prejudiced*) 481; (*obstinate*) 606; superstitious etc. (*credulous*) 486; fanatical; idolatrous etc. 991; visionary etc. (*imaginative*) 515.

985. Revelation.—N. revelation, inspiration, *afflatus*.

Word, — of God; Scripture; the -Scriptures, — Bible, — Book of Books; Holy -Writ, — Scriptures; inspired writings, Gospel.

Old Testament, Septuagint, Vulgate, Pentateuch; Octateuch; the -Law, — Jewish Law, — Prophets; major —, minor- Prophets; Hagio-grapha, -logy; Hierographa; Apocrypha.

New Testament; Gospels, Evangelists, Acts, Epistles, Apocalypse, Revelations.

Talmud; Mishna, Masorah.

prophet etc. (*seer*) 513; evangelist, apostle, disciple, saint; the —, the Apostolical- fathers; Holy Men of old, inspired -writers, — penmen.

Adj. scriptural, biblical, sacred, prophetic; evangel-ical, -istic; apostolic, -al; inspired, theopneustic, apocalyptic, ecclesiastical, canonical, textuary.

986. Pseudo-Revelation.—N. the -Koran, — Alcoran; Ly-king, Shaster, Vedas, Zendavesta, Vedidad, Purana, Edda; Go-, Gau-tama; Book of Mormon.

[False prophets and religious founders] Buddha, Zoroaster, Zerdhusht, Confucius, Mahomet.

[Idols] golden calf etc. 991; Baal, Moloch, Dagon.

987. Piety.—N. piety, religion, theism, faith; religiousness, holiness etc. *adj.*; saintship; religionism; sanctimony etc. (*assumed piety*) 988; reverence etc. (*respect*) 928; humility, veneration, devotion; prostration etc. (*worship*) 990; grace, unction, edification; sancti-ty, -tude; consecration.

spiritual existence, odor of sanctity, beauty of holiness.

theopathy, beatification, adoption, regeneration, conversion, justification, sanctification, salvation, inspiration, bread of life; Body and Blood of Christ.

believer, convert, theist, Christian, devotee, pietist; the -good, – righteous, – just, – believing, – elect; Saint, *Madonna*.

the children of -God, – the kingdom, – light.

V. be -pious etc. *adj.*; have -faith etc. *n.*; believe, receive Christ; revere etc. 928; worship etc. 950; be -converted etc.

convert, edify, sanctify, hallow, keep holy, beatify, regenerate, inspire, consecrate, enshrine.

Adj. pious, religious, devout, devoted, reverent, godly, heavenly minded, humble; pure, – in heart; holy, spiritual, pietistic; saint-ly, -like; seraphic, sacred, solemn.

believing, faithful, Christian, Catholic.

elected, adopted, justified, sanctified, regenerated, inspired, consecrated, converted, unearthly, not of the earth.

988. Impiety.—N. impiety; sin etc. 945; irreverence; profan-eness etc. *adj.*, -ity, -ation; blasphemy, desecration, sacrilege; scoffing etc. *v.*

[Assumed piety] hypocrisy etc. (*falsehood*) 544; pietism, cant, pious fraud; lip-devotion, -service, – reverence; mis-devotion, formalism, austerity; sanctimon-y, -iousness etc. *adj.*; pharisaism, precisianism; sabbat-ism, -arianism; *odium theologicum*, sacerdotalism; bigotry etc. (*obstinacy*) 606, (*prejudice*) 481.

hardening, backsliding, declension, perversion, reprobation apostasy, recusancy.

sinner etc. 949; scoffer, blasphemer; sacrilegist; worldling; hypocrite etc. (*dissembler*) 548; Scribes and Pharisees; Tartufe, Maw-worm.

bigot; saint [ironically]; Pharisee, sabbatarian, formalist, methodist, puritan, pietist, precisian; religionist, devotee, ranter, fanatic, wowser.

the -wicked, – evil, – unjust, – reprobate, son of -men, – Belial, – the wicked one; children of darkness.

V. be -impious etc. *adj.*; profane, desecrate, blaspheme, revile, scoff, swear etc. (*malediction*) 908; commit sacrilege.

snuffle; turn up the whites of the eyes; idolize.

Adj. impious; irreligious etc. 989; desecrating etc. *v.*; profane, irreverent, sacrilegious, blasphemous.

un-hallowed, -sanctified, -regenerate; hardened, perverted, reprobate

hypocritical etc. (*false*) 544; canting, pietistical, sanctimonious, unctuous, pharisaical, overrighteous, righteous over much

bigoted, fanatical etc. 481 and 606; priestridden.

Adv. under the -mask, – cloak, – pretence, – form, – guise- of religion.

989. Irreligion.—N. irreligion, indevotion; ungodliness etc. *adj.*; laxity, quietism, apathy, indifference, passivity.

scepticism, doubt; un-, dis-belief; incredul-ity, -ousness etc. *adj.*; want of -faith, – belief; pyrrhonism; doubt etc. 485; agnosticism.

atheism, deism; hylotheism; materialism; positivism; nihilism.

infidelity, freethinking, antichristianity, rationalism.

atheist, anti-christian, sceptic, unbeliever, deist, infidel, pyrrhonist; *giaour*, heathen, alien, gentile, Nazarene; *esprit fort*, freethinker, latitudinarian, rationalist; materialist, positivist, nihilist, agnostic.

V. be -irreligious etc. *adj.*; disbelieve, lack faith; doubt, question etc. 485.

dechristianize; serve Mammon, love darkness better than light.

Adj. irreligious; in-, un-devout; devout-, god-, grace-less; un-godly, -holy, -sanctified, -hallowed; atheistic, without God.

sceptical, free-thinking, un-believing, -converted; incredulous, faithless, lacking faith; deistical; un-, anti-christian.

worldly, mundane, earthly, carnal, unspiritual; worldly etc.- minded.

Adv. irreligiously etc. *adj.*

990. Worship.—N. worship, adoration, devotion, aspiration, latria, homage, service, humiliation; kneeling, genuflexion, prostration.

prayer, invocation, supplication, rogation, intercession, orison, holy breathing; petition etc. (*request*) 765; collect, litany, Lord's prayer, paternoster, *Ave Maria*, rosary; bead-roll; latria, dulia, hyperdulia, vigils; revival; cult.

thanksgiving; giving –, returning- thanks; grace, praise, glorification, benediction, doxology, hosanna; h-, allelujah; *Te Deum, non nobis Domine, nunc dimittis*; paean.

psalm, -ody; hymn, plainsong, chant, chaunt, response, anthem, motet; antiphon, -y.

oblation, sacrifice, incense, libation; burnt – votive –, thank-offering; offertory, collection.

discipline; self-discipline, -examination, -denial; fasting.

divine service, office, duty; morning prayer; mass, matins, evensong, vespers, compline; holy day etc. (*rites*) 998.

worshipper, congregation, communicant, celebrant.

V. worship, lift up the heart, aspire; revere etc. 928; adore, do service, pay homage; humble oneself, kneel; bow –, bend- the knee; fall -down, – on one's knees, prostrate oneself, bow down and worship, recite the rosary.

pray, invoke, supplicate; put –, offer- up – prayers, – petitions; beseech etc. (*ask*) 765; say one's prayers, tell one's beads.

return –, give- thanks; say grace, bless, praise, laud, glorify, magnify, sing praises; give benediction, lead the choir, intone, chant, sing.

propitiate, offer sacrifice, fast, deny oneself; vow, offer vows, give alms.

work out one's salvation, go to church; attend -service, – mass; communicate etc. (*rite*) 998.

Adj. worshipping etc. *v.*; devout, devotional, reverent, pure, solemn, fervid etc (*heartfelt*) 821.

Int. h-, allelujah! hosanna! glory be to God! O Lord! pray God that! God -grant, – bless, – save, – forbid! *sursum corda.*

991. Idolatry.—N. idol-atry, -ism; demon-ism, -olatry; idol –, demon –, devil –, fire- worship; zoolatry, fetishism, Mari-, Bibli-, ecclesi-, heli-olatry.

deification, apotheosis, canonization; hero worship.

sacrifices, hecatomb, holocaust; human sacrifices, immolation, mactation, infanticide, self-immolation, *suttee.*

idol, golden calf, graven image, fetish, *avatar,* Juggernaut, joss, *lares et penates;* Baal etc. 986. idolator etc. *n.*

V. worship -idols, – pictures, – relics; put on a pedestal, bow down to, prostrate oneself before, make sacrifice to; deify, canonize, idolize.

Adj. idolatrous.

992. Sorcery.—N. sorcery; superstition; occult -art, – sciences; black –, magic; the black art, necromancy, theurgy, thaumaturgy; demon-ology, -omy, -ship; *diablerie,* bedevilment; witch-craft, -ery; glamor; fetis-hism, -ism; ghost dance; hoodoo, voodoo; Shamanism [Esquimaux], vampirism; conjuration; bewitchery, exorcism, enchantment, incantation, obsession, possession, mysticism, second sight, mesmerism, animal magnetism; od –, odylic- force; electro-biology, *clairvoyance;* spiritualism, spirit-rapping, table-turning; thought reading, telepathy, thought transference, automatic writing, *planchette,* ouija board; crystal gazing; spirit manifestation, materialization, astral body, ectoplasm etc.

divination etc. (*prediction*) 511; sortilege, ordeal, *sortes Virgiliance;* hocus-pocus etc. (*deception*) 545; oracle etc. 513.

V. practice -sorcery etc. *n.;* cast a -horoscope, – nativity; conjure, exorcise, charm, enchant; bewitch, -devil; overlook, look on with the evil eye; entrance, mesmerize, magnetize; fascinate etc. (*influence*) 615; taboo; wave a wand; rub the -ring, – lamp; cast a spell; call up spirits, – from the vasty deep; raise spirits from the dead; raise –, lay-ghosts; command genii.

Adj. magic, -al; mystic, weird, cabalistic, talismanic, phylacteric, incantatory; charmed etc. *v.*

993. Spell.—N. spell, charm, incantation, exorcism, weird, cabala, exsufflation, cantrap, runes, abracadabra, hocus-pocus, open *sesame,* counter-charm, Ephesian letters, bell, book and candle, Mumbo-jumbo, evil-eye, fee-faw-fum.

talisman, amulet, periapt, telesm, phylactery, philter, wish-bone, merry-thought, mascot, scarab, swastika; fetish; *agnus Dei.*

wand, caduceus, rod, divining rod, lamp of Aladdin, magic carpet, seven-league boots; magic ring; wishing –, Fortunatus's- cap.

994. Sorcerer.—N. sorcerer, magician; thaumat-, the-urgist; conjuror, necromancer, seer, wizard, witch; fairy etc. 980; *lamia,* hag, warlock, charmer, exorcist, voodoo, mage, diviner, dowser; cunning –, , medicine- man, witch doctor; Shaman, figure-flinger, ecstatica, medium, *clairvoyant,* mesmerist, hypnotist; *deus ex machinâ;* astrologer; soothsayer etc. 513.

Katerfelto, Cagliostro, Merlin, Comus, Mesmer, Rosicrucian; Hecate, Circe, Lilith, siren, weird sisters; witch of Endor.

995. Churchdom.—N. church, -dom; ministry, apostleship, priesthood, prelacy, hierarchy, church government, christendom, pale of the church.

clerical-, sacerdotal-, episcopalian-, ultramontan-ism; Theocracy; ecclesiolog-y, -ist; priestcraft, *odium theologicum.*

monach-ism, -y; monasticism, monkhood.

[Ecclesiastical offices and dignities] pontificate; primacy, archbishopric, archiepiscopacy; prelacy; bishop-ric, -dom; episcop-ate, -acy; see, diocese; deanery, stall; canon-ry, -icate; prebend, -aryship; benefice, incumbency, glebe, advowson, living, cure, – of souls; rectorship; vicar-iate, -ship; pastor-ate, -ship; deacon-ry, -ship; -curacy; chaplain, -cy, -ship; cardinal-ate, -ship; abbacy, presbytery.

holy orders, ordination, institution, consecration, induction, reading in, preferment, translation, presentation.

popedom, papacy; the -Vatican, – apostolic see, – see of Rome; religious sects etc. 984.

council etc. 696; conclave, college of cardinals, convocation, synod, consistory, chapter, vestry, presbytery; sanhedrim, *congé d'élire;* ecclesiastical courts, consistorial court, court of Arches.

V. call, ordain, induct, prefer, translate, consecrate, present, elect, bestow.

take -orders, – the veil, – vows.

Adj. ecclesi-astical, -ological; clerical, sacerdotal, priestly, prelatical, pastoral, ministerial, capitular, theocratic; hierarchical, archiepiscopal; episcopal, -ian; canonical; mon-astic, -achal; monkish; abbati-al, -cal; pontifical, papal, apostolic; untramontane, priest-ridden.

996. Clergy.—N. clergy, clericals, ministry, priesthood, presbytery, the cloth, the pulpit.

clergyman, divine, ecclesiastic, churchman, priest, presbyter, hierophant, pastor, shepherd, minister, clerk in holy orders; father, – in Christ; *padre, abbé, curé;* patriarch; reverend; black coat; confessor; sky pilot.

dignitaries of the church; ecclesi-, hier-arch; eminence, reverence, elder, primate, metropolitan, archimandrite, archbishop, bishop, prelate, diocesan, suffragan, dean, subdean, archdeacon, prebendary, canon, rural dean, rector, parson, vicar, perpetual curate, residentiary, beneficiary, incumbent, chaplain, curate, – in charge; deacon, -ess; preacher; lay reader, lecturer; capitular; missionary, propagandist, Jesuit, revivalist, field preacher.

churchwarden, sidesman; clerk, precentor, choir; almoner, *suisse,* verger, beadle, sexton, sacristan; acol-yth, -othyst, -yte; thurifer; chorister, choir boy.

[Roman Catholic priesthood] Pope, *Papa,* Holy

Father, pontiff, high priest, cardinal; ancient —,
flamen; confessor, penitentiary; spiritual director.

cenobite, conventual, abbot, prior, monk, friar,
lay brother, beadsman, mendicant, pilgrim,
palmer; canon-regular, -secular; Jesuit, Franciscan,
Friars minor, Minorites; Observant, Capuchin,
Dominican, Carmelite; Augustinian; Gilbertine;
Austin-, Black-, White-, Grey-, Crossed-, Crutch-
ed- Friars; Bonhomme, Carthusian, Benedictine,
Cistercian, Trappist, Cluniac, Premonstratensian,
Maturine; Templar, Hospitaller.

abb-, prior-, canon-ess; mother superior;
religieuse, nun, sister, *beguine*, novice, postulant.

[Under the Jewish dispensation] prophet, priest,
high priest, Levite; Rabbi, -n; scribe.

[Mohammedan etc.] mullah, ulema, imauam,
sheik; so-fi, -phi; mufti, hadji, muezzin, dervish; fakir, -quir; brahmin, gooroo, druid, bonze, santon,
abdal, Lama, talapoin, caloyer etc.

V. take orders etc. 995.

Adj. the —, the very —, the Right- Reverend;
ordained, in orders, called to the ministry.

997. Laity.—N. laity, flock, fold, congregation,
assembly, brethren, people.

temporality, secularization.

layman, civilian; parishioner, catechumen;
secularist.

V. secularize.

Adj. secular, lay, laical, civil, temporal, profane.

998. Rite.—N. rite; ceremon-y, -ial; ordinance,
observance, function, duty; form, -ulary; solemnity,
sacrament; incantation etc. (*spell*) 993; service,
psalmody etc. (*worship*) 990; liturgies.

ministration; preach-ing, -ment; predication, sermon, homily, exhortation, lecture, discourse,
pastoral

baptism, christening, chrism; immersion; bap-
tismal regeneration; font; circumcision.

confirmation; imposition —, laying on- of hands;
churching, purification, ordination etc. (*churchdom*) 995; excommunication.

Eucharist, Lord's supper, communion; the —,
the holy- sacrament; celebration, high celebration;
missa cantata; offertory; introit; consecration; con-
, tran-substantiation; real presence; elements, bread
and wine; mass; high —, low —, dry- mass.

matrimony etc. 903; burial etc. 363; visitation of
the sick.

seven sacraments, impanation, extreme unction,
last rites, *viaticum*, invocation of saints,
canonization, transfiguration, auricular confession;
fasting; maceration, flagellation, sackcloth and
ashes; penance etc. (*atonement*) 952; absolution;
telling of beads, reciting the rosary, processional;
thurification, incense, holy water, aspersion.

relics, rosary, beads, reliquary, host, cross, rood,
crucifix, pax, pix, pyx, *agnus Dei*, censer, thurible,
patera, urceole; chalice, patten, Holy Grail,
sangrail; seven-branch candle stick, monstrance,
sacring bell.

ritual, rubric, canon, ordinal; liturgy, prayer-
book, book of common prayer, pietas, euchology,

litany, lectionary; missal, breviary, mass-book,
bead-roll.

psalter; psalm —. hymn- book; hymn-al, -ology;
psalmody.

ritual-, ceremonial-ism; sabbat-ism, -arianism;
ritualist, sabbatarian.

holyday, feast, fast; Sabbath, Passover, Pentecost;
Advent, Christmas, Noel, Epiphany, Lent, Shrove
Tuesday, Ash Wednesday, Maundy Thursday;
Passion —, Holy- week; Good Friday, Easter,
Ascension Day, Whitsuntide; Trinity Sunday, Cor-
pus Christi; All-Saints' —, — Souls'- Day; Candle-,
Lam-, Martin-, Michael-mas; hogmanay; Rama-
dan, -zan; Bairam etc. etc.

V. perform service, do duty, minister, officiate,
baptize, dip, sprinkle; confirm, lay hands on; give
—, administer —, take —, receive —, attend —,
partake of- the -sacrament, — communion; communicate; celebrate mass; administer —, receive-
extreme unction; anele, shrive, absolve, confess; do
penance; genuflect; cross oneself, make the sign of
the cross.

excommunicate, ban with bell, book and candle.

preach, sermonize, predicate, lecture.

Adj. ritual, -istic; ceremonial, liturgic; bap-
tismal, eucharistical; paschal.

999. Canonicals.—N. canonicals, vestments;
robe, gown, Geneva gown, frock, pallium, surplice,
cassock, dalmatic, scapulary, cope, scarf, tunicle,
chasuble, alb, *alba*, stole; fan-on, -nel; tonsure,
cowl, hood; calo-te, -tte; bands; capouch, amice,
orarium, ephod; apron, lawn sleeves, pontificals,
pall; miter, tiara, triple crown; shovel —, cardinal's- hat; biretta; crosier; pastoral staff; costume
etc. 225.

1000. Temple.—N. place of worship; house of
God, — prayer.

temple, cathedral, minister, church, kirk, chapel,
meeting-house, bethel, tabernacle, conventicle,
basilica, fane, holy place, chantry, oratory.

synagogue, mosque; marabout; pantheon;
pagoda; joss-house; dagobah, tope; kiosk.

parsonage, rectory, vicarage, manse, deanery,
glebe, church house; Vatican; bishop's palace;
Lambeth.

altar, shrine, sanctuary, Holy of Holies, *sanctum
sanctorum*, sacrarium, -isty; communion —, holy
—. Lord's- table; table of the Lord; pyx; baptistery,
font; piscina, stoup; aumbry; sedile; reredos; rood-
loft, — screen; jube.

chancel, quire, choir, nave, aisle, transept, lady
chapel, vestry, crypt, cloisters, porch; triforum,
clerestory, churchyard, *golgotha*, calvary, Easter
sepulcher; stall, pew, sitting; pulpit, ambo, lectern,
reading-desk, confessional, prothesis, credence,
baldachin, *baldacchino*; jesse, apse, belfry; chap-
ter-house; presbytery.

monastery, priory, abbey, friary, convent, nunnery, cloister.

Adj. claustral, cloistered; monast-ic, -erial; conventual.

INDEX

The numbers refer to the headings under which the words or phrases occur. When the same word or phrase may be used in various senses, the several headings under which it, or its synonyms, will be found, according to those meanings, are indicated by the words printed in Italics. These words in Italics are not intended to explain the meaning of the word or phrase to which they are annexed, but only to assist in the required reference.

When the word given in the Index is itself the title or heading of a category, the number of reference is printed in blacker type, thus: **abode 189.**

abundanti cautelā,
ex – 664
abuse deceive 545
  ill-treat 649
  misuse 679
  malediction 908
  threat 909
  upbraid 932
  violate 961
  – of language 563
  – of terms 523
abusive 895, 934
abut near 197 touch
  199, 215
abutment 717
aby remain 141
  endure 821, 826
abysmal deep 208
abyss space 180
  depth 208
  interval 198
  danger 667
  hell 982
A.C. 106
academic
  teaching 537, 542
  theory 514
academical
  style 578
academicals
  225 robes
academician 492
  Royal – 559
academy 542
acanthus 847
a capite ad calcem
  52
acariâtre 901
acarpous 169
acatalectic 597
acaudal 38
accede 488, 725, 762
accelerate
  early 132
  stimulate 173
  velocity 274
  hasten 684
accension 384
accent sound 402
  tone of voice 580
  rhythm 597
accentuate 642
accentuated 580
accept assent 488
  consent 762
  receive 785
  take 789
acceptable 646, 829
acceptance 771
acceptation 522
acception 522
access 286
  easy of – 705
  means of – 627
accessible 470, 705
accession
  adjunct 39
  increase 35
  addition 37
  - to office 737, 755
  consent 762
accessory
  extrinsic 6
  additive 37
  adjunct 39
  accompanying 88
  aid 707
  auxiliary 711

acciaccatura 413
accidence 567
accident event 151
  chance 156
  disaster 619
  misfortune 735
  fatal – 361
accidental
  extrinsic 6
  fortuitous 156
  undesigned 621
accidents,
  trust to the chap-
  ter of – 621
accipient 785
acclamation
  assent 488
  approbation 931
acclimatize 370, 613
acclivity 217
accloy 641
accolade 894
accommodate
  suit 23
  adjust 27
  aid 707
  reconcile 723
  give 784
  lend 787
  – oneself to 82
accommodation
  space 180
accommodating
  kind 906
accompaniment
  adjunct 39
  coexistence 88
  musical 415
accompany
  add 37
  coexist 88
  concur 120
  music 416
accompli, fait – 729
accomplice 711
accomplish
  execute 161
  complete 729
  succeed 731
accomplishment
  490, 698
accompts 811
accord
  uniform 16
  agree 23
  music 413
  assent 488
  concord 714
  grant 760
  give 784
  of one's own – 602
according
  - as qualification
  469
  – to evidence 467
  – to circumstances
  8
  – to law 963
  – to rule
  conformably 82
  – rumor 527
accordingly
  logically 476
accordion 417
accost 586
accoucheur 631, 662
accouchement 161
account list 86

adjudge 480
  description 594
  credit 805
  money - 811
  fame 873
  approbation 931
  call to – 932
  find one's – in
  useful 644
  success 731
  make no – of 483,
  930
  not – for 519
  on – of motive 615
  behalf 707
  on no – 536
  send to one's – 361
  take into – 457,
  469
  small – 643
  to one's – 780
  turn to –
  improve 658
  use 677
  success 731
  gain 775
  – as deem 484
  – book 551
  – for 155, 522
  – with 794, 807
accountable
  liable 177
  debit 811
  duty 926
accountant 301, 811
  certified public –
  811
accounts 811
accouple 43
accoutered
  armed 717
accouterment
  dress 225
  appliance 633
  equipment 673
accoy 174
accredit
  commission 755,
  759
  money 805
  honor 873
accredited 484, 613
  - to 755, 759
accretion 35, 46
accrimination 938
accroach 789
accrue add 37
  result 154
  acquire 775
  be received 785,
  810
accubation 213
accueil 894
accultural 35
accumbent 213
accumulate
  collect 72
  store 636
  redundance 641
accurate 494
  - knowledge 490
accurse 908
accursed
  disastrous 649
  undone 828
  vicious 945
accusation 938
accuse

disapprove 932
  charge 938
  lawsuit 969
accustom 613
ace small 32
  unit 87
  within an – 197
aceldama kill 361
  arena 728
acephalous 59
acerbate 659, 835
acerbity
  acrimony 395
  sourness 397
  rudeness 895
  spleen 900, 901
  malevolence 907
acervate 72
acetous 397
acetylene 388
acharné 900
Achates, fidus –
  890, 939
ache physical 378
  mental 828
Acheron
  pit of – 982
Acherontic
  moribund 360
  gloomy 837
achievable 470
achieve end 67
  produce 161
  do 680
  accomplish 729
achievement 551,
  861
Achilles, heel of –
  vulnerable 665
achromatism 429
acicular 253
acid 397
acid test 463
acknowledge
  answer 462
  assent 488
  disclose 529
  avow 535
  consent 762
  observe 772
  pay 807
  thank 916
  repent 950
  reward 973
acknowledged
  custom 613
acme 210
  - of perfection 650
Acology 662
acolyte 996
acomous 226
aconite 663
acoustic 418
  - organs 418
acoustics 402
acquaint
  - oneself with 539
  - with 527
acquaintance
  knowledge 490
  information 527
  friend 890
  make – with 888
acquiesce
  assent 488
  willing 488
  consent 762
  tolerate 826

acquire
  develop 161
  get 775
  receive 785
  – a habit 613
  – learning 539
acquirement
  knowledge 490
  learning 539
  talent 698
  receipt 810
acquisition
  knowledge 490
  gain 775
acquit
  liberate 750
  exempt 927a
  vindicate 937
  innocent 946
  absolve 970
acquit oneself
  behave 692
  – of a debt 807
  – of a duty 926
  – of an obligation
  772
acquittal 506, 970
acquittance 771
acres space 180
  land 342
  property 780
Acres, Bob 862
acrid 392, 395
acridity 171
acrimony
  physical 171
  caustic 830
  discourtesy 895
  hatred 898
  anger 900
  malevolence 907
acroamatism 490
acrobat
  strength 159
  actor 599
  proficient 700
  mountebank 844
Acropolis 210
across 219, 708
acrostic 533, 561,
  842
act imitate 19
  physical 170
  - of a play 599
  personate 599
  voluntary 680
  statute 697
  in the – 680, 947
  – a part feign 544
  – one's part 625,
  926
  – upon
  physical 170
  mental 615
  take steps 680
  – up to 772
  – well one's part
  944
  – without author-
  ity 738
acting deputy 759
actinic 420
actinometer 445
action physical 170
  voluntary 680
  battle 720
  law 969
  line of – 692

aedile 965
aegis 717
aegrescit medendo 659
aegrotat 927a
aeolian 349
— harp 417
aequam servare mentem 826
aequo animo 823 826
aerate 334, 353
aere perennius 873
aerial 273
elevated 206
flying 267
gas 334
air 338
— navigation 267
— navigator 269
— mail 534
— patrol 726
— perspective 428
— warfare 722
aerie 189
aerify 334
aerodonetics 267
aerodrome 728
aerodynamics 267, 334, 349
aerolite 318
aerology 338
aeromancy 511
aeromechanics 267
aerometer 338
aeronaut 269
aeronautical 273
aeronautics 267, 338
aeroplane 273
aerostat *balloon* 273
aerostatics 267, 334
aerostation 338
aery 317
Aesculapius 662
Aesop 846
aesthetic
sensibility 375
beauty 845
taste 850
aestival 125
aeternum servans sub pectore vulnus 919
afar 196
affable 879, 894
affair *event* 151
topic 454
business 625
battle 720
love 902, 903
— of honour 720
affaires, charge d' – 758
affaire de coeur 897
affect *relate to* 9
tend to 176
qualify 469
feign 544
touch 824
desire 865
love 897
affectation 855
affected with
feeling 821
disease 655

affectibility 822
affecting 830
affection 821, 897
affections 820
affettuoso 415
affiance 768, 858
affianced 897, 903
affiche 531
affidation 769
affidavit
affirmation 535
record 551
lawsuit 969
affiliation
relation 9
kindred 11
attribution 155
affine 11
affinitive 9
affinity 9, 17
mate 905
affirmation 535, 488
affix *add* 37
sequel 39
fasten 43
letter 561
afflation 349
afflatus 349, 597, 985
afflict 830
— with illness 655
affliction *pain* 828
infliction 830
adversity 735
affluence
sufficiency 639
prosperity 734
wealth 803
affluent *river* 348
afflux 286
afford *supply* 784
wealth 803
yield 810
sell for 812
— *aid &c.* 707
afforestation 371
affranchise
make free of 748
liberate 750
affray 720
affreet 980
affriction 331
affright 860
affront *molest* 830
provocation 900
insult 929
— *danger* 861
affuse 337
afield 186
afire 382
afloat *extant* 1
unstable 149
going on 151
ship 273
navigation 267
ocean 341
news 532
preparing 673
keep oneself – 734
set – *publish* 531
afoot *on hand* 625
preparing 673
astir 682
afore 116
aforementioned 116
aforesaid
preceding 62
repeated 104

prior 116
aforethought 611
aforetime 116
afraid 860
be – *irresolute* 605
– to say *uncertain* 475
afresh 104, 123
Afric heat 382
Afrikander 57
afrite 980
aft 235
after *in order* 63
in time 117
too late 135
rear 235
pursuit 622
be – *intention* 620
pursuit 622
go – *follow* 281
– all *for all that* 30
qualification 469
on the whole 476
– *time* 133
after acceptation 516
after-age 124
after-clap 509
after-crop 65, 168
after-dinner 117
after-glow 40, 65, 420
after-growth 65
after-life 152
aftermath
sequel 65
fertile 168
profit 775
aftermost 235
afternoon 126
– *farmer* 683
after-part 65, 235
after-piece 599
after-taste 65, 390
after-thought
thought 451
memory 505
change of mind 607
after-time 121
afterwards 117
age 745
agacerie 615
again 90, 104
– and again 136
come – *periodic* 138
fall off – 661
live – 660
against
counteraction 179
anteposition 237
provision 673
voluntary opposition 708
chances – 473
declaim – 932
false witness – 934
go – 708
set – *actively* 898
set one's face 764, 932
stand up – *resist* 719
raise &c. one's voice – 489
– one's will 744
– one's expectation 508

– the grain *difficult* 704
painful 830
dislike 867
– the stream 704
– the time when 510
– or e's will 744
– one's wishes 603
agamist 904
agape *open* 260
curious 455
expectant 507
wonder 870
Agapemone 827, 897
agate 847
age *time* 106
period 108
long time 110
era 114
present time 118
oldness 124
advanced life 128
of – 131
from age to – 112
age quod agis! 682
agency
physical 170
instrumentality 631
means 632
employment 677
voluntary action 680
direction 693
commission 755
agenda 625, 626
agent *physical* 153
intermediary 228
voluntary 690
consignee 759
– *provocateur* 615
agentship 755
ages: for – 110
– *ago* 122
agglomerate 46, 72
agglutinate 46
aggrandize
in degree 35
in bulk 194
honor 873
aggravate
increase 35
vehemence 173
exaggerate 549
render worse 659
distress 835
exasperate 900
aggravating 830
aggravation 835
aggregate 50, 72, 84
aggregation 46
aggression 716
aggressor 726
aggrieve 649, 830
aggroup 72
aghast
disappointed 509
fear 860
wonder 870
agile 274, 682
agio 813
agiotage 794
agitate *move* 315
inquire 461
activity 682
excite the feelings

824
– a question 476
agitation [see agitate]
changeableness 149
energy 171
motion 315
in – *preparing* 673
agitator *leader* 694
aglet 554
agley, gang – 732
aglow 382, 420
agnate 11
agnition 762
agnomen 564
agnostic 487
agnosticism 984, 989
agnus Dei 993, 998
ago 122
not long – 123
agog *expectant* 507
desire 865
wonder 870
agoing 682
set – 707
agonism 720
agonizing 824, 830
agony 378, 828
– of death 360
– of excitement 825
agrarian 371
agree *accord* 23
concur 178
assent 488
concord 714
consent 762
compact 769
compromise 774
– in opinion 488
– with *salubrity* 656
agreeable
comfortable 82
physically 377
mentally 829
agreeably to 82
agreement 23 [see agree]
compact 769
agrestic 371
agriculture 371
agronomy 371
aground *fixed* 150
in difficulty 704
failure 732
ague-fit 860
aguets, aux –
expectation 507
ambush 530
aguish *cold* 383
ah me! 839
aha! *rejoicing* 838
ahead 234, 280
go – *progression* 282
shoot – *transcursion* 303
activity 682
rock – 665, 667
Ahrimanes 987, 980
aid 707, 906
by · the – of 631, 632
aide-de-camp 711, 745

aidless 160
aigrette 847
aiguille 253
aiguillette 747, 847
aigulet 847
ail 655, 828
aileron 267, 273
ailment 655
aim 278, 620, 675
– a blow at 716
aimable 894
  faire l' – 897
aimer éperdument
  897
aimless *without*
  motive 615a
  chance 621
air *unsubstantial* 4
  broach 66
  lightness 320
  gas 334
  atmospheric **338**
  wind 349
  tune 415
  appearance 448
  refresh 689
  demeanor 692
  fashionable 852
  beat the – 645
  fill the – 404
  fine – *salubrity* 656
  fish in the – 645
  fowls of the – 366
  in the – 527
  rend the – 404
  take – 531
air-balloon 273
air base 728
air-commodore 745
aircraft 273, 726
air-drawn 515
airdrome 273
air-force 726
air-gun 727
airing 266
air-mail 273
airman 269
airmanship 698
air-marshal 745
air-passage 351
air-pipe 351
airport 273, 292,
  728
air-pump 349
air-raid 716
airs *affectation* 855
  pride 878
  vanity 880
  arrogance 885
air-shaft 351
air service 267
airship 273, 726
air-tight 261
airways 267
airworthy 273, 664
airy [see air]
  windy 349
  unimportant 643
  gay 836
  – hopes 858, 859
  give to – nothing
    a local habita-
    tion &c. 515
aisle *passage* 260
  way 627
  in a church 1000
ait 346
ajar *open* 260

discordant 713
ajee 217
ajutage 260, 350
akimbo *angular* 244
  stand – 715
akin *related* 9
  consanguineous 11
  similar 17
al fresco 220
alabaster *white* 430
alack! 839
alacrity *willing* 602
  active 682
  cheerful 836
Aladdin's lamp 993
alar 267
alarm *warning* 668
  notice of danger
    669
  fear 860
  cause for – 665
  give an – *indicate*
    550
alarmist 862
alarum 114, 550, 669
alas! 839
alate 267
alb 999
albeit 30
albert
  chain 847
albification 430
albinescence 430
albinism 430
albino 443
album 593, 596
albumen
  semi-liquid 352
  protein 357
Alcaic 597
alcaid 745
alcalde 745
alcazar 189
alchemy 144
alcohol 995
Alcoran 986
alcove 191, 252
Aldebaran 423
alderman 745
ale 298
alea, jacta est – 601
aleatory 665
Alecto 173
alectromancy 511
alehouse 189
  go to the – 959
alembic
  conversion 144
  vessel 191
  furnace 386
  laboratory 691
alentours 197
alert *watchful* 457,
  459
  active 682
alerte 669
aleuromancy 511
Alexandrine
  ornate style 577
  verse 597
alexandrite 848
alexipharmic 662
alexiteric 662
algebra 85
algid 383
algology 369
algorithm 85
alguazil 965

alias
  otherwise 18
  pseudonym 565
alibi 187
alien *irrelevant* 10
  foreign 57
  transfer 783
  gentile 989
alienable 783
alienate
  transfer 783
  estrange 44, 889
  set against 898
alienation
  mental – 503
alieni appetens
  grasping 865
  envious 921
  selfish 943
alienism 54
align 278
alight *stop* 265
  arrive 292
  descend 306
  on fire 382
alike 17
  share and share –
    778
aliment *food* 298
alimentary 662
  – *canal* 350
alimentation
  aid 707
alimony
  property 780
  provision 803
  income 810
aliquot 51, 84
aliter visum, diis –
  601
alive
  living 359
  intelligent 498
  active 682
  cheerful 836
  be – with 102
  keep – *continue*
    143
  keep the memory
    – 505
  look – 684
  – to *attention* 457
    cognizant 490
    informed 527
    able 698
    sensible 822
alkahest 335
all *whole* 50
  complete 52
  generality 78
  – absorbing 642
  in – ages 112
  – aboard 495
  – agog 865
  – in all 50
  – along 106
  – along of 154
  – but 32
  – colors 440
  – considered 451,
    480
  – day long 110
  – devouring 190
  in – directions 278
  – engrossing 190
  at – events *com-*
    pensation 30
    qualification 469

  true 494
  resolve 604
  – fours *easy* 705
    cards 840
  – in good time 152
  – hail! *welcome* 292
    honor to 873
    celebration 883
    courtesy 894
  – hands *everybody*
    78
  on – hands 488
  – of a dither 824
  – of a heap 72
  – knowing 976
  – manner of *differ-*
    ence 15
  multiform 81
  with – one's might
    686
  – at once 113
  – one 27, 866
  – out 52
  – over *end* 67
    universal 78
    destruction 162
    space 180
  at – points 52
  – in one's power
    686
  – powerful
    mighty 159
    God 976
  in – quarters 180
  with – respect 928
  in – respects 52,
    494
  – right! 922
  – Saints' day 998
  – searching 461
  – seeing 976
  on – sides 227
  – sorts *diverse* 16a
    mixed 41
    multiform 81
  – talk 4
  – things to all
    men 894
  – the time 106
  at – times 136
  – together 50
  – ways 243, 279
  – wise 976
  – the world and
    his wife 78
  of – work
    useful 644
    maid - 746
Allah 979 ٭
allay
  moderate 174
  pacify 723
  relieve 834
  – *excitability* 826
allective 615
allege *evidence* 467
  assert 535
  plea 617
allegiance 743, 926
allegory 464, 521,
  594
allegro *music* 415
  cheerful 836
allelujah 990
allemande 840
all-embracing 76
alleviate 174, 834
alley *court* 189

passage 26
  way 627
alliance *relation* 9
  kindred 11
  physical co-opera-
    tion 178
  voluntary co-oper-
    ation 709
  party 712
  union 714
allied to *like* 17
alligation 43
allign 278
alliteration
  similarity 17
  style in writing
    577
  poetry 597
allocation 60, 786
allocution 586
allodium *free* 748
  property 780
allopathy 662
alloquy 586
allot *arrange* 60
  distribute 786
  due 924
allow *assent* 488
  admit 529
  permit 760
  consent 762
  give 784
  – to have one's
    own way 740
allowable 760, 924
allowance
  qualification 469
  gift 784
  allotment 786
  discount 813
  salary 973
  with grains of –
    485
  make – for *forgive*
    918
  vindicate 937
alloy *mixture* 41
  combination 48
  debase 659
allude *hint* 514
  mean 516
  refer to 521
  latent 526
  inform 527
allure *move* 615
  create desire 865
alluring 829
allusive
  relative 9
alluvial *level* 213
  land 342
  plain 344
alluvium
  deposit 40
  land 342
  soil 653
ally *combine* 48
  auxiliary 711
  friend 891
alma mater 542
almanac
  list 86
  chronometry 114
  record 551
almighty 157
Almighty, the – 976
almoner
  treasurer 801

science 357
comparative – 368
anatriptic 331
ancestral
  bygone 122
  old 124
  aged 128
ancestry 166
anchor
  connection 45
  stop 265
  safeguard 666
  badge 747
  hope 858
  at – *fixed* 150
  stationed 184
  safe 664
  cast – *settle* 184
  arrive 292
  have an – to wind-
    ward 664
  sheet – *means* 632
anchorage
  location 184
  roadstead 189
  refuge 666
anchored 150
anchorite 893, 955
ancien régime 875
ancient *old* 124
  flag 550
  – *times* 122
ancientness 122
ancillary 707
and 37, 88
andante 415
andiron 386
androgynous 83
anecdote 594
anele 998
anemia 160
anemography 349
ἀνεμῶλια βάζειν 497
anemometer
  wind 349
  measure 466
anent 9
aneroid 338
anesthesia 376,
  381, 683
anew *again* 104
  newly 123
anfractuosity 248
angel
  object of love 897
  good person 948
  supernatural
    being 977
  fallen –
    bad man 949
    devil 978
  guardian –
    safely 664
    auxiliary 711
    benefactor 912
  – of Death 362
  – 's visits 137
angelic 944
angels and minis-
  ters of grace de-
  fend us! 860
angelus 550
anger 900
  more in sorrow
    than in – 826,
    918
angiology 329
angle 244

try 463
  at an – 217
Anglicanism 984
angling 622, 840
anguille au genou,
  rompre l' – 158,
  471
anguilliform 205,
  248
anguis in herbâ 667
anguish
  physical 378
  moral 828
angular 244
  – *velocity* 264
angularity 244
angusta domi, res
  – 804
angustation 203
anhelation 688
anhydrate 340
anhydrous 340
aniline dyes 437
anility 128, 499
animadvert
  consider 451
  attend to 457
  reprehend 932
animal 366
  female – 374
  – *cries* 412
  – *economy* 359
  – *gratification* 377
  – *life* 364
  – *physiology* 368
  – *spirits* 836
  – and vegetable
    kingdom 357
animalcule 193, 366
animalism
  sensuality 954
animality 364
animate
  induce 615
  excite 824
  enliven 836
animation
  life 359
  animality 364
  activity 682
  vivacity 836
  suspended – 823
animism 984
animo, ex – 602
  quo – 620
animosity
  dislike 867
  enmity 889
  hatred 898
  anger 900
animus
  willingness 602
  intention 620
  desire 865
ankle 244
  – deep 208, 209
anklet 847
ankylosis 150
annalist 114, 553
annals
  chronology 114
  record 551
  account 594
anneal 673
annex
  addition 37
  adjunct 39
  junction 43

acquire 775
Annie Oakley 815
annihilate 2, 162
anniversary 138
anno 106
Anno Domini
  era 106
  old age 124
annotation 522, 550
annotator 524
  scholar 492
  interpreter 524
  editor 595
annotto 434
announce
  predict 511
  inform 527
  publish 531
  assert 535
announcer 527
annoy
  molest 649, 907
  disquiet 830
annoyance 828
  source of – 830
annual *periodic* 138
  plant 367
  book 593
annuity 810
annul 162, 750
annular 247
annunciate 527
annus magnus 108
anodyne
  lenitive 174
  remedial 662
  relief 834
anoint *coat* 223
  lubricate 332
  oil 355
anointed
  deity 976
  king 745
anomaly 59, 83
  disorder 59
  irregularity 83
anon 132
anonymous 565
anopsia 442
anorexy 866
another
  different 15
  repetition 104
  – *story* 468, 526
  go upon – *tack* 607
  – *time* 119
answer
  to an inquiry 462
  confute 479
  solution 522
  succeed 731
  pecuniary profit
    775
  pleadings 969
  require an – 461
  – for *deputy* 759
  promise 768
  go bail 806
I'll – for it 535
  – the helm 745
  – the purpose 731
  – to *correspond* 9
  – one's turn 644
answerable
  agreement 23
  liable 177
  bail 806
  duty 926

censurable 932
ant 690
Antaeus 159, 192
antagonism
  difference 14
  physical 179
  voluntary 708
  enmity 889
antagonist 710, 891
antagonistic 24
antarctic 237
antecedence 62, 116
antecedent 64
antechamber 191
ante Christum 106
antedate 115
antediluvian 124
antelope 274
antemundane 124
antenna 379
anteposition 62
anterior
  in order 62
  in time 116
  in place 234
  – *to reason* 477
anteroom 191
antevert 706
anthem 990
anthemion 847
anthology
  book 533
  collection 596
  poem 597
anthracite 388
anthropoid 372
anthropology
  zoology 368
  mankind 372
anthropomancy 511
anthropophagi 913
anthroposcopy 511
anthroposophy 372
antic 840
anti-aircraft gun
  564, 727
antichambre,
  faire – 133
antichristian 984,
  989
antichronism 115
anticipate
  anachronism 115
  priority 116
  future 121
  early 132
  expect 507
  foresee 510
  prepare 673
  hope 858
  in – 116
anticlimax
  decrease 36
  bathos 497, 853
anticlinal 217
anticyclone 265
antidote 662
antigropelos 225
antilogarithm 84
antilogy 477
antimony 663
Antinomian 984
antinomy 964
Antinous 845
antiparallel 217
antipathy 867, 898
antiphon *music* 415
  answer 462

worship 990
antiphrasis 563
antipodes
  difference 14
  distance 196
  contraposition
    237
antipoison 660
antiquary
  past times 122
  scholar 492
  historian 553
antiquas vias,
  stare super –
  613, 670
antiquated 128
antique 124
antiquity 122
antiscriptural 984
antiseptic 652, 662
antisocial 911
antistrophe 597
antithesis
  contrast 14
  difference 15
  opposite 237
  style 574, 577
antitoxin 662
antitype 22
antler 253
antonomasia
  metaphor 521
  nomenclature 564
antonym 14
antrum 252
anvil *support* 215
  on the –
    intended 620
    in hand 625
    preparing 673
anxiety *pain* 828
  fear 860
  desire 865
anxious expectation
  507
any *some* 25
  part 51
  no choice 609a
  at – price 604a
  at – rate
    certain 474
    true 494
  at all hazards 604
anybody 78
anyhow 460, 627
anything one
  knows, for – 491
aorist 109, 119
aorta 350
apace *early* 132
  swift 274
apache 913
apart 44, 87
  set – 636
  wide – 196
apartment 191
  –s 189
  –s to let
    imbecile 499
apathetic 275
apathy
  indifference 465
  insensibility 823
  irreligion 989
ape *imitate* 19
Apelles 559
aperçu 596
aperture 260

apex 210
aphasia 583
aphelion 196
aphonic 403
aphony 581
aphorism 496
aphrodite 845, 979
apiary 370
apiculture 370
Apicius 957
apiece 79
apish 19, 499
aplanatic 429
aplomb
  stability 150
  self-possession
  498
  resolution 604
Apocalypse 985
Apocrypha 985
apocryphal
  uncertain 475
  erroneous 495
  heterodox 984
apodictic 478
apodosis 67
apogee 210
apograph 21
Apollo *sun* 318
  music 416
  luminary 423
  beauty 845
  god 979
  magnus – 500, 695
Apollyon 978
apologue
  metaphor 521
  teaching 537
  description 594
apology *excuse* 617
  vindication 937
  penitence 950
  atonement 952
apophthegm 496
apophysis 250
apoplexy 158, 655
aporetic 487
aposiopesis 585
apostasy
  recantation 607
  dishonor 940
  heterodoxy 984
apostate
  convert 144
  turncoat 607
  impiety 988
apostle *teacher* 540
  disciple 541
  inspired 985
  –'s creed 983a
apostolic 985
  – church 983a
  – see 995
apostrophe
  address 586
  soliloquy 589
  appeal 765
apothecary 662
  –'s weight 319
apothegm 496
apotheosis
  resuscitation 163
  canonization 873
  heaven 981
  hero worship 991
apozem 335, 384
appal 830, 860
appanage

property 780
gift 784
apparatus 633
apparel 225
apparent
  visible 446
  appearing 448
  probable 472
  manifest 525
  heir – 779
apparition
  fallacy of vision
  443
  spirit 980
apparitor 534
appeach 938
appeal 586, 765
  court of – 966
  – to arms 722
  – motion 969
  – from Philip
    drunk to Philip
    sober 658
  – to *call to witness*
  467
  – to for (*claim*) 924
appear 446, 525
  – for 759
  – in print 591
appearance 448
  make one's – 292
  to all – 448
  probable 472
appearances
  keep up – 852
appease 174
appellant 924, 938
appellate 966
appellation 564
append *add* 37
  sequence 63
  hang 214
appendage 39
appendectomy 662
appendix
  adjunct 39
  sequel 65
  end 67
  book 593
appertain
  related to 9
  component 56
  belong 777
  property 780
appetite 865
  tickle the –
  savory 394
appetizing 865
  exciting 824
applaud 931
apple – of discord
  713
  golden –
    allurement 615
  – of one's eye *good*
  648
  love 897
  favorite 899
  – off another tree
  15
  how we –s swim!
  880
apple-green 435
apple-pie order 58
appliance *use* 677
  –s *means* 632
  machinery 633
applicable *relevant*

23
  useful 644
  expedient 646
applicability 9
applicant 767
application *study*
  457
  metaphor 521
  use 677
  request 765
apply, *use* 677
  – a match 384
  – the match to a
    train 66
  – the mind 457
  – a remedy 662
appoggiatura 413
appointment
  employment 625
  order 741
  charge 755
  assignment 786
  interview 892
appointments
  gear 633
apportion *arrange*
  60
  disperse 73
  allot 786
apportionment 786
appositeness 9
apposition
  relation 9
  relevancy 23
  closeness 199
  paraphrase 522
appraise 466, 812
appreciate
  realize 450, 451
  measure 466
  judge 480
  know 490
  taste 850
  approve 931
apprehend
  believe 484
  know 490
  fear 860
  seize 789
apprehension
  idea 453
  taking 789
apprentice 541
  – oneself 676
apprenticeship 539,
  673
apprise 527
apprised of 490
approach
  of time 121
  impend 152
  nearness 197
  move 286
  path 627
approaching 9
approbation 931
appropinquation
  286
appropriate *fit* 23
  peculiar 79
  expedient 646
  assign 786
  take 789
  steal 791
approval 488, 931
  on – 609
approximate
  related to 9

resemble 17
in mathematics 85
nearness 197
approach 286
appulse *meeting* 199
  collision 276
  approach 286
  convergence 290
appurtenance
  part 51
  component 56
  belongings 780
  accompaniment
  88
appurtenant 9
après nous le
  déluge 943
apricot *color* 439
April
  – fool 547, 857
  make an – fool of
  545
  – showers 149
apron *extension* 39
  clothing 225
  defence 717
  canonicals 999
à propos [*see* à]
aprotype 591
apse 1000
apt *consonant* 23
  tendency 176, 177
  docile 539
  willing 602
  clever 698
aqua-fortis 335
aquamarine 435
aquarium 370
Aquarius 348, 636
aquatic *water* 337
aquatics 267
aquatinta 558
aqueduct 350
aqueous 337
aquiline 244
A.R. 106
Arab *wanderer* 268
  horse 271
  street – 876
araba 272
arabesque 847
Arabian
  – perfumes 400
  – nights 515
arable 371
arbalest 727
arbiter *critic* 480
  director 694
  adviser 695
  judge 967
  – elegantiarum
    revels 840
  taste 850
  fashion 852
arbitrage 794
arbitrament 480
  judgment 480
  – of the sword 722
arbitrary
  without relation
  10
  irregular 83
  wilful 606
  capricious 608
  authoritative 737
  severe 739
  insolent 885
  lawless 964

– power 739
arbitrate
  adjudicate 480
  mediate 724
arbitration
  court of – 966
  submit to – 774
arbitrium, ad – 600
arbor 215, 312
arbor *abode* 189
  summer-house
  191
  plaisance 840
arborescent
  ramifying 242
  rough 256
  trees 367
arboriculture 371
arc 245
  heat 382
arcade *street* 189
  curve 245
  gateway 260
Arcades ambo
  alike 17
  friends 890
  bad men 949
Arcadia 827, 981
Arcadian 703, 946
arcanum 533
arch *great* 31
  support 215
  curve 245
  convex 250
  concave 252
  clever 498
  cunning 702
  triumphal – 733,
  883
archaic *old* 124
archaism 122, 563
archangel 977
archbishop 996
archbishopric 995
archdeacon 996
archduchy 181
archduke 745
archegenesis 161
archeologist
  pastimes 122
  scholar 492
archeology 122
archer 726
archery 840
Arches, court of –
  966, 995
archetype 22
archetypal 20
Archeus 359
archfiend 978
archiater 695
archiepiscopal 995
archimandrite 996
archipelago 346
architect 164, 690
architectonic 161
architecture
  arrangement 60
  construction 161
  fabric 329
  ornament 847
architrave 210
archive 551
archlute 417
archon *ruler* 745
  deputy 759
  judge 967
archtraitor 941

arctic *northern* 237
  cold 383
arctics 225
arcuation 245
ardent *fiery* 382
  eager 682
  feeling 821
  loving 897
  – *expectation* 507
  – *imagination* 515
ardet, proximus –
  665, 667
ardor *vigor* 574
  activity 821
  feeling 821
  desire 865
arduous 704
area 181, 182
arefaction 340
arena *space* 180
  region 181
  field of view 441
  field of battle 728
arenaceous 330
areola 247
areolar 219
areometer 321
Areopagus 966
arête 253
aretinism 961
aretology 926
Argand lamp 423
argent 430
argillaceous 324
argosy 273
argot 563
argonaut 269
argue *evidence* 467
  reason 476
  indicate 550
  dissectation 595
argument *disagreement* 24
  · *topic* 454
  discussion 476
  meaning 516
  have the best of
  an – 478
argumentum
  – baculinum
  compel 744
  lawless 964
  punish 972
  – ad crumenam
  800
  – ad hominem
  reasoning 476
  accuse 938
  – ad verecundiam
  939
Argus-eyed 441, 459
argute 498
aria 415
arianism 984
arid 340
  unproductive 169
  uninteresting 841
Ariel *courier* 268
  swift 274
  messenger 534
  spirit 979
arietation 276
arietta 415
aright *well* 618
Ariman [*see* Ahrimanes]
ariolation 511
arioso 415

aris et focis, pro –
  defence 717
  philanthropy 910
arise *exist* 1
  begin 66
  happen 151
  mount 305
  appear 446
  – *from* 154
Aristarchus 850
Aristides
  good man 948
aristocracy
  power 737
  fashion 852
  nobility 875
ἄριστον μέτρον 628
Arithmancy 511
arithmetic 85
ark *abode* 189
  asylum 666
arm *part* 51
  power 157
  instrument 633
  provide 637
  prepare 673
  war 722
  weapon 727
  make a long – 200
  – chair 215
  – in arm
  together 88
  friends 888
  sociable 892
  – of the law 963
  – of the sea 343
armada 726
Armageddon 720,
  722
armament 673, 727
armed 717
  – at all points 673
  – force 726
  – guard 664
armet 717
armful 25
armiger 875
armigerent 726
armigerous 722
armilla 247, 847
armillary sphere
  466
armipotent 157
armistice
  cessation 142
  respite 672
  pacification 723
armless 158
armlet *ring* 247
  gulf 343
  ornament 847
armor *cover* 223
  defence 717
  arms 727
  buckle on one's –
  673
  – plated 223
armored
  – car 726
  – cruiser 726
  – train 726
armorial bearings
  550, 877
armory *store* 636
  workshop 691
arm's length
  at – 196
  keep at –

repel 289
  defence 717
  enmity 889
  seclusion 893
  discourtesy 895
arms 727 [*see* arm]
  heraldry 550
  war 722
  honors 877
  clash of – 720
  deeds of – 720
  with folded – 681
  in – *infant* 129
  throw oneself into
  the – of 666, 880
  under – 722
  up in – *active* 682
  discord 713
  résistance 719
  resentment 900
  enmity 889
Armstrong gun 727
army *collection* 72
  multitude 102
  troops 726
aroma 400
around 227
  lie – 220
arouse *move* 615
  excite 824
  – oneself 682
aroynt *begone* 297
  malediction 908
arquebusade 662
arquebuse 727
arraign 938, 969
arrange
  set in order 60
  plan 626
  compromise 774
  – with creditors
  807
  – itself 58
arrange – matters
  pacify 723
  – *music* 413, 416
  – in a series 69
  – under 76
arrangement 23, 60
  [*see* arrange]
  order 58
  temporary – 111
arrant *identical* 31
  manifest 525
  notorious 531
  bad 649
  disreputable 874
  base 940
arras 847
array *order* 58, 60
  series 69
  assemblage 72
  multitude 102
  dress 225
  prepare 673
  adorn 847
  ostentation 882
  battle – 722
arrear, in – 53, 808
arrears *debt* 806
arrectis auribus
  hear 418
  expect 507
arrest *stop* 142
  restrain 751
  in law 969
  – the attention 457
arrière-pensée

after-thought 65
  mental reservation
  528
  motive 615
  set purpose 620
arrival 292
arrive *happen* 151
  reach 292
  complete 729
  – at a conclusion
  480
  – at the truth 480*a*
arrogant *severe* 739
  proud 878
  insolent 885
arrogate 885, 924
  – to oneself
  undue 925
arrondissement 181
arrosion 331
arrow *swift* 274
  missile 284
  arms 727
  broad – 550
arrow-head
  form 253
  writing 590
'Arry and 'Arriet
  902
ars celare artem
  698
arsenal *store* 636
  workshop 661
arsenic 663
arson 384
art *representation*
  554
  business 625
  skill 698
  cunning 702
  fine – 850
  work of – 845, 847
  – gallery 556
artery 350, 627
artes, hae tibi
  erunt – 627
artesian well 343
artful 544, 702
  – dodge 545, 702
article *thing* 3
  part 51
  matter 316
  chapter 593
  review 595
  goods 798
articled clerk 541
articles
  thirty-nine – 983*a*
  – of agreement
  770
  – of faith 484, 983
articulate 366
articulation
  junction 43
  speech 580
articulo, in –
  transient 111
  dying 360
artifice 626, 702
artificer 690
artificial
  fictitious 545
  cunning 702
  affected 855
  – *language* 579
artillery
  explosion 404
  arms 727

artilleryman 726
artisan 690
artist *painter* &c.
  559
  contriver 626
  agent 690
artiste *music* 416
  drama 599
artistic *skilful* 698
  beautiful 845
  taste 850
  – *language* 578
artlessness 703
aruspex 513
aruspicy 511
arundo, haeret
  lateri lethalis –
  828
as *motive* 615
  – broad as long 27
  – can be 52
  – good as 27
  – if *similar* 17
  suppose 514
  – little as may be
  32
  – it may be
  circumstance 8
  event 151
  chance 156
  – much again 90
  – soon as 120
  – they say 496, 532
  – things are 7
  – things go 151,
  613
  – to 9
  – usual 82
  – it were 17, 521
  – you were 141,
  283
  – well as 37
  – the world wags
  151
ascend *be great* 31
  increase 35
  rise 305
  improve 658
ascendancy
  power 157
  influence 175
  success 731
ascendant
  lord of the – 745
  in the –
  influence 175
  important 642
  success 731
  authority 737
  repute 873
  one's star in the –
  prosperity 734
ascension
  [*see* ascend]
  calefaction 384
  – Day 998
ascent
  [*see* ascend]
  gradient 217
  rise 305
  glory 873
ascertain *fix* 150
  determine 480
ascertained 474,
  490
ascertainment 480*a*
asceticism 955
ascititious

intrinsic 6
additional 37
supplementary 52
ascribe 155
aseptic 652
ash 384
 – colored 432
 – blond 430
ashen 429
Ash Wednesday 998
ashamed 879
ashes corpse 362
dirt 653
lay in – 162
pale as – 429, 860
rise from one's – 660
ashore 342
go – arrive 292
ashy 429
Asian mystery 533
aside laterally 236
whisper 405
private 528
say – 589
set &c. – displace 185
neglect 460
negative 536
reject 610
disuse 678
abrogate 756
discard 782
step – 279
asinine ass 271
fool 499
ask inquire 461
request 765
for sale 794
price 812
 – leave 760
askance 217
eye – fear 860
look – vision 441, 443
dissent 489
dislike 867
disapproval 932
askari 726
asked in church 903
askew 217, 243
aslant 217
asleep 683
aslope 217
Asmodeus 980
asomatous 317
asp animal 366
evil-doer 913
Aspasia 962
aspect feature 5
state 7
situation 183
appearance 448
aspen leaf
shake like an –315, 860
asperity
roughness 256
discourtesy 895
anger 900
irascibility 901
asperse 934
aspersion
malediction 908
rite 998
asphalt
smooth 255

resin 356a
material 635
asphodel 845
aspic 352
asphyxia 360
asphyxiate 361
aspirant 767, 865
aspirate 580
aspirator 349
aspire rise 305
hope 858
desire 865
worship 990
aspirin 834
asportation 270
asquint 217
ass beast of burden 271
fool 501
make an – of
delude 545
 – between two
bundles of
hay 605
 –'s bridge 519
 – in lion's skin
cheat 548
bungler 701
assafetida 401
assagai 727
assail 716, 830
assailant 710, 726
assassin, –ate 361
assault 716, 961
take by – 789
assay 463
asseguay 727
assemblage 72
assembly
council 696
society 892
religious 997
assembly hall 588
assembly room 189
assent belief 484
agree 488
willing 602
consent 762
content 831
assert 535, 924
assess measure 466
determine 480
lax 812
assessor
judge 967
assets 780, 800
asseverate 535
assiduity 110
assiduous 682
assign
commission 755
transfer 270, 783
give 784
allot 786
 – as cause 155
 – a duty 926
 – places 60
assignat 800
assignation 892
place of – 74
assignee donee 785
assimilate
uniform 16
resemble 17
imitate 19
agree 23
transmute 144
assist 707

 – at 186
assistant 711
assister be present 186
assize measure 466
tribunal 966
justice of – 967
associate mix 41
unite 43
collect 72
accompany 88
colleague 690
auxiliary 711
friend 890
 – with 892
association
[see associate]
relation 9
combination 48
co-operation 709
partnership 712
 – of ideas
intellect 450
thought 451
intuition 477
hint 514
 – football 840
assoil acquit 970
assonance
music 413
poetry 597
assort arrange 60
assortment 72, 75
assuage 174, 834
assuetude 613
assume believe 484
suppose 514
falsehood 544
take 789
insolent 885
right 924
 – authority 737
 – a character 554
 – command 741
 – a form 144
 – the offensive 716
assumed name 565
assumption
[see assume]
severity 739
hope 858
usurpation 925
assurance
speculation 156
certainty 474
belief 484
assertion 535
promise 768
security 771
hope 858
vanity 880
insolence 885
make – double
sure safe 664
caution 864
assuredly
assent 488
assythment 973
astatic 320
asterisk 550
astern 235
put the engines –275
fall – 283
asteroid 318
Asteroth 979
asthenia 160
astigmatism 443

astir 682
set – 824
astonish 870
astonished
 – at nothing 871
astonishing
great 31
astound excite 824
fear 860
surprise 870
astra, sic itur ad –360, 873
astraddle 215
Astraea 922
astragal 847
astral 318
 – body 717, 992
 – influence 601
 – plane 317
astray 475, 495
go – deviate 279
sin 945
astriction 43
astride 215
astringent 195
astrolabe 466
astrologer 994
astrology 511
astromancy 511
astronomy 318
astute 498, 702
asunder 44, 196
as poles – 237
asylum hospital 663
retreat 666
defence 717
asymptote 290
at, be – 620
up and – them!
716
ataghan 727
atavism 144, 163
ataxia 158
atelier 556, 691
athanasia 112
Athanasian creed 983a
athanor 386
atheism 989
atheist 487
Athenae 979
Athens, owls to –641
athirst 865
athlete strong 159
gladiator 726
athletic strong 159
strenuous 686
 – sports
contest 720
games 840
athwart
oblique 217
crossing 219
opposing 708
Atkins, Tommy 726
Atlantis 515
Atlas arrangement 60
list 86
strength 159
support 215
maps 554
atmosphere
circumambience 227
air 338
painting 556

atmospheric blue 438
atoll 346
atom small 32, 193
atomic energy 157
atomics 316
atomizer 336
atoms
crush to – 162
atomy 193
atonement
restitution 790
expiation 952
amends 973
religious 976
atony 160
atrabilious 837
atramentous 431
atrium 191
atrocity
malevolence 907
vice 945
guilt 947
atrophy
shrinking 195
disease 655
decay 659
atropos 601
attach join 43
love 897
legal 969
 – importance to 642
attaché
employé 746
diplomatic 758
 – case 191
attack ringing 580
disease 655
assault 716
debauch 961
attaghan 727
attain arrive 292
succeed 731
 – majority 131
attainable 470
attainder
taint 651
at law 971
attainment
knowledge 490
learning 539
skill 698
attar 400
attempter 41, 174
attempered 820
attempt 675
vain – 732
 – impossibilities 471
attend
accompany 88
be present 186
follow 281
apply the mind 457
medically 662
aid 707
serve 746
 – to business 625
 – to orders 743
attendance on
dance – 886
attendant
[see attend]
attention 457
care 459
respect 928

attract – 882
call to – 457
call – to 550
give – 418
pay –s to 894
pay one's –s to
902
attenuate
decrease 36
weaken 158
reduce 195
rarefy 322
attenuated 203
attest
bear testimony 467
affirm 535
adjure 768
attested copy 771
attic *simple* 42
garret 191
summit 210
style 578
wit 842
taste 850
Attila 913
attire 225
attitude
circumstance 8
situation 183
posture 240
attitudinarian 882
attitudinize 855
attollent 307
attorney
consignee 758
at law 968
power of – 755
attract
bring towards 288
induce 615
allure 865
excite love 897
– the attention
457
visible 446
attraction
[see attract]
natural power 157
bring towards
288
attractive
[see attract]
pleasing 829
beautiful 845
attrahent 288
attribute
speciality 79
accompaniment
88
power 157
–s of the Deity 976
– to 155
attribution 155
attrite 330
attrition 330, 331
attroupement 72
attune *music* 415
prepare 673
attuned to
habit 613
attunement 23
auburn 433
A.U.C. 106
auction 796, 840
auctioneer 758, 796
auctorial 599
audacity
courage 861

rashness 863
insolence 885
audible 402
become – 418
scarcely – 405
audience
hearing 418
conversation 588
before an – 599
audire alteram
partem
counter-evidence
468
right 922
justice 939
audit
numeration 85
examination 461
accounts 811
auditive 418
auditor
hearer 418
accountant 811
auditorium 189, 588
auditory
sound 402
hearing 418
theater 599
– apparatus 418
au fait 698
au fond 5
auf wiedersehen
293
Augean
– stable 653
– task 704
auger 262
aught 51
for – one cares
unimportant 643
indifferent 866
for – one knows
ignorance 491
conjecture 514
augment
increase 35
thing added 39
expand 194
augur 513
– well 858
augurate 511
augury 512
august 873
Augustinian 996
auk 366
auld lang syne 122
aulic council 696
aumbry 1000
aunt 11
aura *wind* 349
sensation 380
aurea mediocritas
628
aureate 436
aureola 420
aureole 420, 873
aureolin 436
auribus, arrectis –
418
auricular *hearing*
418
clandestine 528
– confession 998
auri sacra fames
819
aurist 662
aurora
dawn 125

light 420, 423
twilight 422
– australes 423
– borealis 423
Auroral 236
ausculation 418
auspice *omen* 512
auspices
influence 175
prediction 511
protection 664
direction 693
aid 707
under the – of 693,
737
auspicious
opportune 134
prosperous 734
hopeful 858
austerity
harsh taste 395
severe 739
discourteous 895
ascetic 955
pietism 988
austral 237
austromancy 511
authentic 467
certain 474
true 494
authentication
evidence 467
security 771
author 164, 593
projector 626
dramatic – 599
– of our being 976
– of evil 978
– 's proof 591
authoritative 474,
741
authority
testimony 467
sage 500
informant 527
power 737
permission 760
right 924
ensign of – 747
person in – 745
do upon one's own
– 600
authorized *due* 924
legalized 963
authorship
production 161
style 569
writing 590
autobiography 594
autocar 272
autochthonous 188
autocracy 737, 739
autocrat 745
autocratic 600, 737
auto-da-fe 384, 972
autograph 550, 590
Autolycus *thief* 792
pedlar 797
automaniac 504
automatic 601, 633
– pistol 727
– writing 992
automaton 554, 601
automobile 272
automobilist 268
automotive 266
autonomasia 521
autonomy 737, 748

autopsy
post-mortem 363
vision 441
autoptical 446, 535
autotype 558
autumn 126
auxiliary 711
additional 34
helpful 707
– forces 726
avail *benefit* 618
useful 644
succeed 731
of no – 645
– oneself of 677
avalanche *fall* 306
snow 383
redundance 641
avaler les couleu-
vres 725, 886
avant-courier 64,
673
avant-propos 64
avarice 819
avast! *stop* 142, 265
desist 624
forbid 761
avatar *change* 140
deity 976
idol 991
avaunt! 297, 449
ave! *honor* 873
courtesy 894
Ave maria 990
avenge 919
avenue
plantation 371
way 627
aver 535
average *mean* 29,
628
médiocre 651
– circumstances
736
take an – 466
Averni, facilis de-
scensus – 217,
665
Avernus 982
averruncate 297,
301
aversion *unwilling-
ness* 603
dislike 867
hate 898
avert 706
– the eyes 442
aviary 370
aviation 267
aviator 269
avidity *avarice* 819
desire 865
airette 273
avile 932, 934
avion 273
aviso 532
avocation 625
avoidance 623
avoidless 474, 601
avoirdupois 319
avolation 623, 671
avouch 535, 768
avow *assent* 488
disclose 529
assert 535
avulsion 44, 301
avuncular 11
await *future* 121

be kept waiting
133
impend 152
expect 507
awake *attentive* 457
careful 459
intelligent 498
active 682
– to life immortal
360
awaken *inform* 527
excite 824
– the attention 457
– the memory 505
award *adjudge* 480
give 784
aware 490
away 187, 196
break – 623
fly – 293
move – 287
take – from 789
get &c. – 671
throw &c. –
eject 297
reject 610
waste 638
relinquish 782
– from *unrelated* 10
– with! 930, 932
do – with undo 681
abrogate 756
awe *fear* 860
wonder 870
respect 928
aweless *fearless* 861
insolent 885
disrespectful 329
awful 31, 860
– silence 403
awhile 111
awkward
inelegant 579
inexpedient 647
unskilful 699
difficult 704
painful 830
ugly 846
vulgar 851
ridiculous 853
– squad 701
awl 262
awn 253
awning 223, 424
awry *oblique* 217
distorted 243
evil 619
axe *edge tool* 253
impulse 276
weapon 727
for beheading 975
have an – to grind
702
Axinomancy 511
axiom 496
axiomatic 474
axis *support* 215
center 222
rotation 312
axle 312
wheel and – 633
axle load 466
axletree 215
ay 488
ayah 746, 753
aye *ever* 112
yes 488
azimuth

all for the –
  good 618
  prosper 734
  content 831
  hope 858
bad is the – 649
do one's –
  care 459
  try 675
  activity 682
  exertion 686
have the – of it 731
make the – of it
  over-estimate 482
  use 677
  submit 725
  compromise 774
  take easily 826
  hope 858
the – 800
to the – of one's
  belief 484
– bib and tucker
  prepared 673
  ornament 847
  ostentation 882
– friends 890
– intentions 906
– man 903
– part 31, 50
– seller 731
make the – of
  one's time 684
bestead 644
bestial 954, 961
bestir oneself
  activity 682
  haste 684
  exertion 686
bestow 784
– one's hand 903
– thought 451
bestraddle 215
bestrew 73
bestride 206, 215
bet 621
betake oneself to
  journey 266
  business 625
  use 677
bête, pas si – 498
bête noire *bane* 663
  fear 860
  hate 898
bethel 1000
bethink 451, 505
bethral 749, 751
betide 151
betimes 132
betoken
  evidence 467
  predict 511
  indicate 550
betray *disclose* 529
  deceive 545
  dishonor 940
– itself *visible* 446
betrayer 941
betrim 673
betroth 768, 903
betrothed 897
better *good* 648
  improve 658
appeal to one's –
  feelings 914
get – *health* 654
  improve 658
  refreshment 689

restoration 660
get the – of, 479,
  702, 731
think – of 655, 950
seen – days
  deteriorate 659
  adversity 735
  poor 804
– half 903
only – than noth-
  ing 651
– sort 875
for – for worse
  choice 609
  marriage 903
between 228
– cup and lip 111
far – 198
lie – 228
– the lines 526
vibrate – two ex-
  tremes 149
– ourselves 528
– two fires 665
– maid 746
betwixt 228
bevel 217
– gearing 653
bever 298
beverage 298
bévue 732
bevy 72, 102
bewail *regret* 833
  lament 839
beware 665, 668
bewilder
  put out 458
  uncertainty 475
  astonish 870
bewitch
  fascinate 615
  please 829
  excite love 897
  exorcise 992
bey 745
beyond *superior* 33
  distance 196
go – 303
– compare 31, 33
– control 471
– one's depth 208,
  519
– expression 31
– one's grasp 471
– hope 731, 534
– the – mark 303,
  641
– measure 641
– possibility 471
– praise
  perfect 650
  approbation 931
  virtue 944
– price 814
– question 474, 494
– reason 471
– remedy 859
– seas 57
bezel 217
bhang 663
bias *influence* 175
  tendency 176
  slope 217
  prepossession 481
  disposition 820
bib *pinafore* 225
  drink 959
bibber *weep* 839

tope 959
bibble-babble 584
bibelot 847
bibendum, nunc
  est – 959
Bible 895
– oath 535
biblioclasm 162
bibliography 593
bibliolatry
  learning 490
  heterodoxy 984
  idolatry 991
bibliomancy 511
bibliomania 490
bibliomaniac 492
bibliophile 492
bibliopole 593
bibliotheca 593
bibulous 298, 959
bicameral 90
bicapital 90
bice 435, 438
bicentenary 98,
  138, 883
bicker *flutter* 315
  quarrel 713
bicolor 440
biconjugate 91
bicuspid 91
bicycle 272
bid *order* 741
  offer 763
– the banns 903
– defiance 715
– fair *tend* 176
  probable 472
  promise 511
  hope 858
– a long farewell
  624
– for *intend* 620
  offer 763
  request 765
  bargain 794
bidder 767
bide *wait* 133
  remain 141
  take coolly 806
– one's time 133
  watch 507
  inactive 681
bidet 271
biennial
  periodic 138
  plant 367
bienséance 852, 894
bier 363
bifacial 90
bifarious 90
bifid 91
bifold 90
biform 90
bifurcate 91, 244
big *in degree* 31
  in size 192
  wide 194
look – *defy* 715
  proud 878
  insolent 885
talk – 885, 909
– sounding
  loud 404
  words 577
  affected 855
– swollen 194
– with ≈1
– with the fate of

511
bigamy 903
biggin 191
bight 343
bigot *positive* 474
  prejudice 481
  obstinate 606
  heterodox 984
  impious 988
bigotry 907
bigwig *scholar* 492
  sage 500
  nobility 875
bijou *goodness* 648
  beauty 845
  ornament 847
bilander 273
bilateral 90, 236
bilbao 727
bilboes 752
put into – 751
bile 900
bilge *base* 211
  convex 250
  yawn 260
– water 653
bilious 837
bilingual 560
bilk
  disappoint 509
  cheat 545
  steal 791
bill *list* 86
  hatchet 253
  placard 531
  ticket 550
  paper 593
  plan 626
  weapon 727
  money order 800
  money account
  811
  charge 812
  in law 969
true – 969
– and coo 902
– of exchange 771
– of fare *food* 298
  plan 626
– of indictment
  938
–s of mortality 360
– of sale 771
billet *locate* 184
  ticket 550
  apportion 786
billet *epistle* 592
  – doux 902
billfold 191
billhook 253
billiard – ball 249
– room 191
– table *flat* 213
billiards 840
Billingsgate 563,
  908
billion 98
billow *sea* 348
  river 341
billy-cock 225
billy-goat 373
bimetallism 800
bin 191
binary 89
bind *connect* 43
  cover 223
  compel 744
  condition 770

obligation 926
– hand and foot
  751
– oneself 768
– over 744
– up wounds 660
binding 681, 744
bine 367
binnacle 693
binocular 445
binomial 89
biogenesis 161
biograph 448
biography 594
biology 357, 359
bioscope 448
biota 357
biparous 89
bipartite 44, 91
biplane 273
biplicity 89
biquadrate 96
birch *flog* 972
– rod 975
bird 366
kill two –s with
  one stone 682
–'s eye view 441,
  448
–s of a feather 17
the – has flown
  187, 671
– in hand 777, 781
– of ill omen
  omen 512
  warning 668
  hopeless 859
– of passage 268
– of prey 739
a little – told me
  527
birdcage 370
birdlime *glue* 45
  trap 545
biretta 999
birth *beginning* 66
  production 161
  paternity 166
  nobility 875
– place 153
– right 924
birthday 138, 883
– suit 226
birthmark 848
bis *repeat* 104
  approval 931
biscuits, s'embar-
  quer sans – 674
bise 349
bisection 68, 91
bishop *punch* 298
  clergy 996
–'s palace 1000
–'s purple 437
bishopric 995
bisque 33
bissextile 138
bister 433
bistoury 253
bisulcate 259
bit
  small quantity 32
  part 51
  interval 106
  curb 752
just a – 26
– by bit
  by degrees 26

by instalments 51
in detail 79
slowly 275
– between the
  teeth 600, 719
bitch *animal* 366
  female 374
  clumsy 699
  fail 732
  impure 962
bite *eat* 298
  physical pain 378
  cold 385
  cheat 545
  dupe 547
  etch 558
  mental pain 830
  – the dust 725
  – in 259
  – the thumb 900,
  929
  – the tongue 392
biter bit 718
biting *pain* 378
  cold 383
  pungent 392
  painful 830
  discourteous 895
  censorious 932
bitten 897
bitter *beer* 298
  cold 383
  taste 392, 395
  painful 830
  acrimonious 895
  hate 898
  angry 900
  malevolent 907
  – end 67
  – ender 606, 710,
  832
  – pill 735
  – words 932
bitterly *greatly* 31
bitterness
  [*see* bitter]
  pain 828
  regret 833
bitumen 356a
bituminous coal
  388
bivouac
  encamp 184
  camp 189
  repose 265
  watch 668
bi-weekly 138
bizarre 83, 853
blab 529
blabber 584
black *color* 431
  crime 945
  look – *feeling* 821
  discontent 832
  angry 900
  – art 992
  – and blue
  beat 972
  – board 590
  – book 938
  – eye 848, 972
  – in the face
  swear 535
  excitement 821,
  824
  – flag 722
  – hole *crowd* 72
  prison 752

– lead 556
– letter *old* 124
  barbarism 563
  print 591
– list 932
– looks
  discourteous 895
  sullen 901a
  disapprove 932
  magic 998
– mail *theft* 791
  booty 793
  bribe 973
– sheep 949
– spots in the hori-
  zon 859
– swan 83
– and white
  chiaroscuro 420
  colorless 429
  record 551
  writing 590
  prove that – is
  white 477
blackamoor 431
  wash a – white 471
blackball 55, 893,
  932
blackcoat 996
blacken [*see* black]
  defame 934
blackguard
  vulgar 851
  rude 895
  base 940
  vagabond 949
blackleg 792
black Maria 727
blackness 431
blacksmith 690
bladder 191
blade *edge tool* 253
  man 373
  instrument 633
  sharp fellow 682
  proficient 700
  sword 727
  fop 854
blague 545
blain 250, 848
blame 155, 932
  lay – on 938
  take – 932
blameless 946
blameworthy
  disapprove 932
  vice 945
  guilt 947
blanc-bec 701
blancmange 298
blanch 429, 430
bland 174, 894
blandiloquence 933
blandishment
  inducement 615
  endearment 902
  flattery 933
blank 2, 4
  empty 187
  simple 849
  look –
  disappointed 509
  discontent 832
  wonder 870
  point – 576
  – cartridge 158
  – verse 597
blanket 223, 384

wet – 174
toss in a – 929
blare 404, 412
blarney 933
blasé 841, 869
blasphemy 988
blast
  destroy 162
  explosion 173
  wind 349
  sound 404
  adversity 735
  curse 908
  – furnace 386
blatant *loud* 404
  cry 412
  silly 499
blather 584
blatter 412
blaze *heat* 382
  light 420
  mark 550
  excitement 824
  – abroad 531
blazer 225
blazing
  luminary 423
blazon *publish* 531
  repute 873
  ornament 847
  ostentation 882
blé: manger son –
  on herbe 818
bleach 429, 430
bleak 383
blear-eyed 443
bleary 422
bloat 412
blob 250
bleed
  physical pain 378
  remedy 662
  spend money 809
  extort money 814
  moral pain 828
  make the heart –
  830
  – freely *liberal* 816
bleeding
  hemorrhage 299
  remedy 662
  – heart 828
blemish
  imperfection 651
  injure 659
  ugly 846
  defect 848
blench *avoid* 623
  whiten 821
  fear 860
blend 41, 48
  – with 714
bless
  give pleasure 829
  approve 931
  divine function
  976
  worship 990
  – my heart 870
  – one's stars 838,
  916
blessed 827
  abode of the – 981
blessedness
  single – 904
blessing *good* 618
  approval 931
blessings 734

blest 827
  – with 177
bletonism 511
blight
  deteriorate 659
  adversity 735
  – hope 509
blighty 189
blimp 273
blind 223
  shade 424
  cecity 442
  inattentive 458
  ignorant 491
  conceal 528
  screen 530
  deception 545
  instinctive 601
  pretext 617
  insensible 823
  drunk 959
  – alley 261
  – bargain
  uncertain 475
  purposeless 62
  rash 863
  – the eyes *hide* 528
  deceive 545
  – hookey 840
  – lead the blind
  538
  – man's buff 840
  – man's holiday
  evening 126
  dark 421, 422
  – to one's own
  merit 880
  – to the world 959
  – of one eye 443
  – reasoning 486
  – side *prejudice*
  481
  credulity 486
  obstinacy 606
blinders 424, 443
blindness 442
blind pig 964
blink *wink* 443
  neglect 460
  falter 605
  avoid 623
  – at *blind to* 442,
  458
blinkard 443
blinker 424, 530
bliss 827
  celestial 981
blister 250
blithe 836
blizzard 349
bloated
  expanded 194
  misshapen 243
  convex 250
  – with pride 878
blob 250
block *mass* 192
  support 215
  dense 321
  hard 323
  fool 501
  engraving 558
  writing 590
  hinder 706
  execution 975
  bring to the – 972
  wood – 558
  – of buildings 189

– out 230, 240, 973
– printing 591
– up 261, 706
blockade
  surround 227
  close 261
  restrain 751
  exclude 893
blockhead 501
blockhouse 717
blockish 499
blond 429, 430
blood
  consanguinity 11
  fluid 333
  kill 361
  fop 854
  nobility 875
  dye with –
  severe 739
  hands in – *cruel*
  907
  in the – 5
  life – 359
  new – 658, 824
  spill – *war* 722
  – for blood 919
  – boil *excite* 824,
  825
  anger 900
  – run cold 830,
  860
  – heat 382
  – horse 271
  – hound 913
  – letting 297, 662
  – poisoning 655
  – red 434
  – stained 361
  – sucker 789, 913
  – thirsty
  murderous 361
  cruel 907
  – up *excited* 824
  angry 900
bloodless 160
  peace 721
  virtue 946
bloody [*see* blood]
  red 434
  unclean 653
  cruel 907
bloom *youth* 127
  flower 367
  blue 438
  health 654
  prosperity 734
bloomer 495
bloomers 225
blooming 654, 845
blossom
  flower 154, 161,
  367
  prosperity 734
blot *blacken* 431
  error 495
  obliterate 552
  dirty 653
  blemish 848
  disgrace 874
  guilt 947
  – out *destroy* 162
  forgive 918
blotch 848
blouse 225
blow *expand* 194
  knock 276
  wind 349

unexpected 508
disappointment 509
evil 619
action 680
get wind 688
failure 732
prosper 734
pain 828, 830
come to -s 720, 722
deal a - at 716
deal a - to 972
death - 300, 361
- for blow 718
- one's brains out 361
- the coals 824
- down 162
- the fire 384
- the gaff 529
- hole 351
- the horn 416
- hot and cold *lie* 544
irresolute 605
tergiversation 607
caprice 608
- a kiss 902
- off *disperse* 73
- out *food* 298
darken 421
gorge 957
- over *past* 122
- pipe 349, 727
- the trumpet 873
- one's own trumpet 882
- up *destroy* 162
eruption 173
inflate 194
wind 349
excite 824
objurgate 932, 934
blower 349
blowhard 884
blown [see blow]
fatigued 688
proud 878
storm - over 664, 721
- upon 874, 932
blow-out 406
blowzy *swollen* 194
red 434
blubber *fat* 356
cry 839
Blucher boot 225
bludgeon 727
- man 726, 913
blue *sky* 338
color 438
learned 490
bit of - hope 858
look -
disappointed 509
feeling 821
discontent 832
disrepute 874
out of the - 508
swear till all's - 535
- true - 543, 939
- book 86, 551
- blood 875
- devils 837
- jacket 269
- light 550, 669

- pencil 174, 596
- moon 110
- Peter 293, 550
- and red 437
- ribbon 733, 877
- ruin 959
- stocking *scholar* 492
affectation 855
- and yellow 435
Bluebeard
marriage 903
libertine 962
blueness 438
blues 837, 840
bluff *violent* 173
high cliff 206
blunt 254
deceive 545
boasting 884
insolent 885
discourteous 895
blunder *error* 495
absurdity 497
awkward 699
failure 732
- upon 156
blunderbuss 727
blunderhead 701
blunderheaded 499
blunt *weaken* 160
inert 172
moderate v. 174
obtuse 254
benumb 376
damp v. 616
plain-spoken 703
cash 800
deaden 823
discourteous 895
- tool 645
- witted 499
bluntness 254
blur
imperfect vision 443
dirt 653
blemish 848
stigma 874
blurb 931
blurred
invisible 447
blurt out 529, 582
blush *flush* 382
redden 434
feel 821
humbled 879
modest 881
at first - *see* 441
appear 448
manifest 525
put to the -
humble 897
browbeat 885
discourtesy 895
blushing honors 873, 881
bluster *violent* 173
defiant 715
boasting 884
insolent 885
threaten 909
blusterer 887
blustering [see bluster]
windy 349
Bo to a goose, not say - 862

boa 225
boanerges 540
boar 366, 373
board *layer* 204
support 215
food 298
hard 323
council 696
attack 716
tribunal 966
festive - 892
go by the - 158, 162
go on - 293
on - 186, 273
preside at the - 693
- of trade 621
- school 542
boarding-house 189
boarder 188
boards 599, 728
boast 884
not much to - of 651
boasting 884
boaston 840
boat 273
in the same - 88
- race 720
boating 267
boatman 269
boatswain 269
bob *depress* 308
leap 309
oscillate 314
agitate 315
money 800
- a curtsy 894
- for *fish* 463
Bobadil, Captain - 887
bobbed
hair 53
bobbin 312
bobbing *fuel* 388
bobbish 654
bobby *police* 664
bobsleigh 272
bobsleighing 840
bobtailed 53
bocage 367
bocca, per amusare la - 304
Boche 913
boddice 225
bode 511
bodega 189
bodily
substantially 3
wholly 50
material 316
- enjoyment 377
- fear 860
- pain 378
bodkin
go between 228
perforator 262
body *substance* 3
whole 50
assemblage 72
frame 215
matter 316
party 712
in a - *together* 88
- and blood of Christ 987
- clothes 225

- color 556
- of doctrine 490
- forth 554
- guard 717, 753
- of knowledge 490
- politic *mankind* 372
authority 737
keep - and soul together 654
- of water 438
Boeotian *rustic* 371
stupid 499
fool 501
vulgar 851
ignoble 876
Boer 371
bog 345, 653
- trotter 876
boggart 980
boggle *hesitate* 605
awkward 699
difficulty 704
bogie 980
truck 272
bogle 980
bogus 545
Bohemian
unconventional 83
nomad 268
ungenteel 851
boil *violence* 173
effervesce 315
bubble 353
heat 382, 384
ulceration 655
excitement 824, 825
anger 900
- down 195
boiler 356
boisterous
violent 173
hasty 684
excitable 825
bold *prominent* 250
unreserved 525
vigorous 574
brave 861
make - with 895
show a - front 715, 861
- faced 885
- push *essay* 675
- relief *visible* 446
- stroke *plan* 626
success 731
bole 50
bolero 840
bollard 45
bolshevik 144, 146
bolshevist 737, 742
bolster *support* 215
repair 658
aid 707
- up *vindicate* 937
bolt *sift* 42
fasten 43
fastening 45
close 261
move rapidly 274
propel 284
run away 623
escape 671
hindrance 706
shaft 727
disobey 742

shackle 752
thunder - 872
- the door 761
- food 298, 957
- in 751
- upright 212
bolthead 191
bolus *mouthful* 298
remedy 662
bomb 404, 727
- proof 664, 717
- vessel 726
bombard 716
bombardier 726
bombardon 417
bombast
unmeaning 517
magniloquence 577
ridiculous 853
boasting 884
exaggeration 549
Bombastes Furioso 887
bomber
aeroplane 726
bombilation 404
bon de - augure 858
- enfant *social* 892
kindly 906
- gré mal gré 601
- marché 815
- mot 842
- naturel 836
- ton 852
- vivant 957
- voyage 293
bona - fides
veracity 543
probity 939
- roba 962
bonanza 641, 784
wealth 803
bonbon 396
bond *relation* 9
tie 45
compact 769
security 771
money 800
right 924
- of union 9, 45
government - 802
Liberty - 802
bondage 749
bonded together 712
bonds [see bond]
fetters 752
funds 802
in - service 746
tear asunder one's - 750
- of harmony 714
bondsman 746
bone *strength* 159
dense 321
hard 323
bred in the - 5
feel it in one's - 510
- of contention 713, 720
one - and one flesh 903
- to pick *difficulty* 704
discord 713

- setter 662
bonehouse 363
boner 495
bones [see bone]
  corpse 362
  music 417
break no – 648
make no – 602, 705
boneyard 363
bonfire 382
  festivity 840
  celebration 883
make a – of 384
bonhomie 703, 906
bonhomme 996
Boniface 890
bonne 746, 753
  – bouche end 67
  pleasant 377
  savory 394
  saving 636
à la – heure 602, 831
de – volonté 602
bonnet 225
bonny 836, 845
bono: cui –
  intention 620
  utility 644
  inutility 645
  pro – publico 644, 910
bonus extra 641
  gift 784
  money 810
bony 323
bonze 996
bonzer 648
booby 501
  – trap 545
boodle 793
book register 86
publication 531
  record 551
  volume 593
  script 599
  enter accounts 811
at one's –s 539
bring to –
  evidence 467
  account 811
  reprove 932
mind one's – 539
school – 542
without –
  by heart 505
  – of Books 985
  – club 593
  – of fate 601
  – learning 490
  – shop 593
book-case 191
booked dying 360
bookish 490
bookkeeper 553
bookkeeping 811
bookless
  unlearned 493
bookmaking 156
bookseller 593
bookworm 492, 593
boom
  support 215
  sail 267
  rush 274
  impulse 276
  sound 404

obstacle 706
  defence 717
boomerang
  recoil 277
  retribution 718
  weapon 727
boon 784
  beg a – 765
  – companion 890
boor clown 876
boorish 851, 895
boost 276, 482, 931
booster 935
boot box 191
  dress 225
  advantage 618
  punishment 975
to – added 37
  – legging 964
booted and spurred 673
booth 189, 799
bootless 645, 732
boots dress 225
  servant 746
  low person 876
  what – it? 643
booty 793
booze 959
bo-peep 441, 528
bordel 961
border edge 231
  limit 233
  flower bed 371
  ornament 847
  – upon 197, 199
bore diameter 202
  hole 260
  tide 348, 667
  fatigue 688
  trouble 828
  plague 830
  weary 841
bored 456
boreal
  Northern 237
  cold 383
Boreas 349
boredom 841
borer 262
born 359
  – so 5
  – under an evil star 735
  – under a lucky star 734
borne 826
  – down failure 732
  defection 837
borné 499
borough 181, 189
  rotten – 893
  – council 696
borrow 19, 788
  – of Peter &c. 147
borrowed plumes
  deception 545
borrower 806
borrowing 788
bosh absurdity 497
  unmeaning 517
  untrue 546
  trifling 643
bosky 959
bosom breast 221
  mind 450
  affections 820
in the – of 229

- of one's family 221
- friend 890
boss 250, 694, 737
  straw – 694
boston 840
botanic garden 369, 371
Botanomancy 511
Botany 367, 369
botch bungle 59
  mend 660
  unskilful 699
  difficulty 704
  fail 732
both 89
listen with – ears 418
burn the candle at – ends 641
butter one's bread on – sides 641
bother
  uncertainty 475
  bustle 682
  difficulty 704
  trouble 828
  harass 830
bothy 189
bottle
  receptacle 191
  preserve 670
bee in a – 407
crack a – 298
pass the – 959
smelling – 400
- green 435
- holder
  auxiliary 177
  mediator 724
- up remember 505
  hide 528
  restrain 751
bottom
  lowest part 211
  support 215
  posterior 235
  combe 252
  ship 273
  pluck 604a
  courage 861
at – 5
at the – of
  cause 153
go to the – 310
probe to the – 461
from the – of one's heart veracity 543
  feeling 821
- upwards 218
- land 180, 207
bottomless 208
  – pit 982
angel of the – pit 978
bottomry 771
botulism 663
bouche:
  bonne – end 67
  savory 394
  saving 636
  pleasant 829
  – à feu 727
bouderie 901a
boudoir 191
bouffe, opera 599
bouge 250

bough part 51
  curve 245
  tree 367
bought flexure 245
bougie 423
boulder 249
boulevards 227
bouleversement
  revolution 146
  destruction 162
  excite 824
bouillabaise 298
bouillon 298
bounce violence 173
  jump 309
  lie 546
  boast 884
  insolence 885
- upon 292, 508
bouncing large 192
bound
  circumscribe 229
  swift 274
  leap 309
  certain 474
I'll be – 535
- back recoil 277
- by 926
- for direction 278
  destination 620
- to promise 768
  responsible 926
boundary 233
bounden duty 926
bounder 851
boundless 105, 180
bounds 230, 233
keep within –
  moderation 174
  shortcoming 304
  restrain 751
  prohibit 761
- of possibility 470
bountiful 816, 906
Lady – 816
bounty gift 784
bouquet
  fragrant 400
  beauty 847
bourgeois
  middle class 29
  type 591
  commoner 876
bourdon 215
bourgeon 194
bourn 233
bourse 621, 799
bouse 959
bout turn 138
  job 680
  fight 720
  prank 840
drinking – 954
bout
au – du compte 476
au – de son latin
  sophistry 477
  ignorance 491
  difficulty 704
boutade 497, 608
boutonnière 400
bovine 366, 499
bow be inferior 34
  fore part 234
  curve 245
  projection 250
  stoop 308

fiddlestick 417
  weapon 727
  ornament 847
  servility 886
  reverence 894
  respect 928
bend the – 686
draw the long – 884
- down worship 990, 991
- out 297
- submission 725
- window 260
Bow bells
born within sound of – 876
Bowdlerize 652
bowed down 837, 879
bowelless 914a
bowels inside 221
- of compassion 914
- of the earth 208
bower 189, 191
-s of bliss 981
bowery 424
bowie knife 727
bowl vessel 191
  rotate 312
  stadium 840
flowing – 959
- along walk 266
  swift 274
bowlder 249
bowline 45
bowler hat 225
bow-legged 243
bowling-green 213, 840
bowls 840
bowman 726
bowshot 197
bowsprit 234
bowstring execution 972, 975
box house 189
  chest 191
  seat 215
  theater 599
  fight 720
horse – 272
musical – 417
wrong – error 495
  unskilful 699
  dilemma 704
- the compass direction 278
  rotation 312
change of mind 607
- the ear 900, 972
- up 751
boxer 726
boy 129
- scout 534
boyar 875
boyhood 127
boycott 55, 297, 893
brabble 713, 720
brabbler 901
brace tie 43
  fasten 45
  two 89
  strengthen 159
  support 214
  music 413

refresh 689
bracelet *circle* 247
  handcuff 752
  ornament 847
bracer 392
braces 45
brachial 633
Brachygraphy 590
bracing 656
bracken 367
bracket *tie* 43, 45
  couple 89
  support 215
brackish 392
brad 45
bradawl 262
Bradbury 800
Bradshaw 266
brae 206
brag *cards* 840
  boast 884
braggart 884
Braggadocio 884
Brahma 979
Brahmin 984, 996
braid *tie* 43
  ligature 45
  net 219
  variegate 440
brain *kill* 361
  intellect 450
  skill 498
  blow one's -s out 361
  coinage of the – 515
  suck one's -s 461
  rack one's -s 451, 515
brainless 499
brainpan 450
brainsick 458
brain-storm 503, 825
brainwork 451
brainy 498
brake *carriage* 272
  copse 367
  hindrance 706
  curb 752
  apply the – 275
brakeman 268
bramble *thorn* 253
  bane 663
bran 330
brancard 272
branch *member* 51
  class 75
  posterity 167
  fork 244
  tree 367
  – off 91, 291
  – out *ramify* 91
  diffuse style 573
branching
  symmetry 242
brand *burn* 384
  fuel 388
  torch 423
  mark 550
  sword 727
  disrepute 874
  censure 932
  stigmatize 934
  – of discord 713
  – new 123
  – with reproach 938

brandish
  oscillate 314
  flourish 315
  display 882
brandy 959
brangle 713
brangler 710
brank 975
bras
  les – croisés 681
  à – ouverts 894
brashness 885
brass *alloy* 41
  money 800
  insolence 885
  bold as – 861
  – band 417, 882
  with a – 884
  – colored 439
  – hat 745
  – farthing 643
brassard 550, 747
brat 129
brattice 224, 228
bravado 884
brave *confront* 234
  healthy 654
  defy 715
  warrior 726
  bear 821, 826
  courage 861
  – a thousand years 110
bravo
  assassin 361
  desperado 863
  applause 931
bravura 415
brawl *cry* 411
  discord 713
  revel 840
brawler
  disputant 710
  rioter 742
  blusterer 887
brawny 159, 192
bray *grind* 330
  cry 412
Bray, Vicar of – 607, 886
braze 43
brazen 525, 885
  – browed 885
  – faced 885
brazier 386
breach *crack* 44
  gap 198
  quarrel 713
  violation 925
  custom honóred in the – 614
  – of faith 940
  – of law 83, 964
  – of the peace 713
bread 298
  beg – 765
  selfish 943
  quarrel with – and butter 699
  – of idleness 683
  – of life *Christ* 976
  piety 987
  – upon the waters 638
  – and wine 998
breadbasket 191

breadth 202
  chiaroscuro 420
break
  fracture 44
  discontinuity 70
  change 140
  gap 198
  carriage 272
  crumble 328
  disclose 529
  cashier 756
  violate 773, 927
  bankrupt 808
  – away 623
  – bread 298
  – bulk 297
  – camp 293
  – of day *morning* 125
  twilight 422
  – down *destroy* 162
  – one's fetters 614
  – forth 295
  – ground 66
  – a habit 614
  – the heart *pain* 828, 830
  dejection 837
  – the ice 888
  – in *ingress* 294
  domesticate 370
  teach 537
  tame 749
  – in upon *derange* 61
  inopportune 135
  hinder 706
  – a lance 716, 722
  – a law 83
  – loose 671, 750
  – one's neck *powerless* 158
  die 360
  – the neck of *task* 676
  success 731
  – the news 529
  – no bones 648
  – of 660
  – off *cease* 142
  relinquish 624
  abrogate 756
  – out *begin* 66
  violent 173
  disease 655
  excited 825
  – the peace 173, 720
  – Priscian's head 568
  – prison 750
  – the ranks 61
  – short 328
  – silence 582
  – the teeth 579
  – the thread 70
  – through the clouds *visible* 446
  disclose 529
  – through a custom 614
  – up *disjoin* 44

decompose 49
  end 67
  revolution 146
  destroy 162
  – up of the system, 360, 665
  – on the wheel
  physical pain 378
  mental pain 830
  punishment 972
  – with 713
  – with the past 146
  – word *deceive* 525
  improbity 940
breaker
  of horses 268
  reef 346
  wave 348
breakers 348, 667
  surrounded by – 704
  – ahead 665
breakfast 298
breakneck
  precipice 217
  rash 863
breakwater
  refuge 666
  obstruction 706
breast *interior* 221
  confront 234
  convex 250
  mind 450
  oppose 708
  soul 820
  at the – 129
  in the – of 620
  •– the current 719
  – high 206
breastplate 717
breastwork 717
breath *instant* 113
  breeze 349
  life 359
  animality 364
  faint sound 405
  with bated – 581
  hold – *quiet* 265
  expect 507
  wonder 870
  not a – of air 265, 382
  out of – 688
  in the same – 120
  shortness of – 688
  take – 265, 689
  take away one's – *unexpected* 508
  fear 860
  wonder 870
breathe *exist* 1
  blow 349
  live 359
  faint sound 405
  evince 467
  mean 516
  inform 527
  disclose 529
  utter 580
  speak 582
  refresh 689
  – freely 827, 834
  – one's last 360
  not – a word 528
breathing time 687, 723
breathless

voiceless 581
  out of breath 688
  feeling 821
  fear 860
  eager 865
  wonder 870
  – attention 457
  – expectation 507
  – impatience 865
  – speed 684
bred in the bone 820
breech 235
  – loader 727
breeches 225
  wear the – 737
  – buoy 666
  – maker 225
  – pocket
  money 800, 802
breed *kind* 75
  multiply 161
  progeny 167
  animals 370
  rear 537
breeding 161, 852, 894
breeze *wind* 349
  discord 713
breezy 836
brethren 997
breve 413
brevet
  warrant 741
  commission 755
  permit 760
  – rank 873
breviary 998
brevier 591
brevity 201, 572
brew 41, 673
brewing
  impending 152
  storm – 665
bribe *equivalent* 30
  tempt 615
  offer 763
  gift 784
  buy 795
  expenditure 809
  reward 973
bric-à-brac 847
brick *hard* 323
  pottery 384
  material 635
  trump 939, 948
  make -s without straw 471
  – color 434
brickbat 727
bricklayer 690
bride 903
bridewell 752
bridge 45, 627
  – over *join* 43
  facilitate 705
  make peace 723
  compromise 774
  cards 840
bridle *restrain* 751
  rein 752
  – road 627
  – one's tongue 585, 864
  – up 900
brief *time* 111
  space 201
  concise 572
  compendium 596

hold a – for 759
– case 191
briefly *anon* 132
brier
  sharp 253
  pipe 390
  bane 663
brig 273
brigade 726
brigadier 745
brigand 792
brigandage 791
brigandine 717
brigantine 273
bright *shine* 420
  color 428
  intelligent 498
  cheery 836
  beauty 845
  glory 873
  – days 734
  – eyed 845
  – prospect 858
  – side 829
look at the – side
  836, 858
  – thought
  sharp 498
  good stroke 626
  wit 842
brighten up
  furbish 658
brigue 712, 720
brilliant
  shining 420
  good 648
  wit 842
  beautiful 845
  gem 847
  glorious 873
  – idea 842
brilliantine 356
brim 231
  – over 641
brimful 52
brimstone 388
brindled 440
brine 341, 392
bring 270
  – about 153, 729
  – back 790
  – back to the
  memory 505
  – to bear upon
  relation 9
  – *action* 170
  – into being 161
  – to a crisis 604
  – forth 161
  – forward
  evidence 467
  manifest 525
  teach 537
  improve 658
  – grey hairs to the
  grave 735, 830
  – grist to the mill
  644
  – home 775
  – home to 155
  – in *receive* 296
  income 810
  price 812
  – to life 359
  – to light 480a
  – low 874
  – to maturity 673,
  729

– to mind 505
– under one's
  notice 457
– off 672
– out
  discover 480a
  manifest 525
  publish 591
– over
  persuade 484
– to perfection
  677
– into play 677
– to a point 74
– in question 461
– up the rear 235
– round
  persuade 615
  restore 660
– to terms 723
– to *convert* 144
  halt 265
– together 72
– in its train 88
– to trial 969
– up *develop* 161
  vomit 297
  educate 537
– in a verdict 480
– word 527
brink 231
on the –
  almost 32
  coming 121
  near 197
– of the grave 360
briny 392
  – ocean 341
brio *music* 415
  active 682
brisk *prompt* 111
  energetic 171
  active 682
  cheery 836
bristle 253
  – up *stick up* 250
  angry 900
  – with 639, 641
  – with arms 722
bristly 256
Britannia metal
  545
Briticism 563
British 188
  – lion 604
Briton, true – 939
work like a – 686
brittleness 328
britzska 272
broach *begin* 66
  found 153
  reamer 262
  tap 297
  publish 531
  assert 535
broad *general* 78
  space 202
  lake 343
  emphatic 535
  indelicate 961,
  962
  – accent 580
  – awake 459, 682
  – daylight 420,
  525
  – farce 842
  – grin 838
  – highway 627

– hint 527
– meaning 516
– minded 498
broadcast
  disperse 73
  spread 78
  publish 531
  sow – 818
broadcloth 219
broadhearted 906
broadsheet 593
broad-shouldered
  159
broadside 236
  publication 531
  cannonade 716
broadsword 727
Brobdingnagian
  192
brocade 847
brochure 593
Brocken, specter of
  the 443
broder 549
brogue *boot* 225
  dialect 563
broidery 847
broil *heat* 382
  fry 384
  fray 713, 720
broke *poor* 804
broken
  discontinuous 70
  weak 160
  – color 428
  – down
  decrepit 659
  failing 732
  dejected 837
  – English 563
  – fortune 735, 804
  – heart 828, 837
  hopeless 859
  – reed 160, 665
  – meat 645
  – voice 581, 583
  – winded
  disease 655
  fatigue 688
broker 758, 797
brokerage *pay* 812
brokery 794
bromidic 613
bronchia 351
bronze *alloy* 41
  brown 433
  sculpture 557
brooch 847
brood 102, 167
  – over 451, 847
brooding
  preparing 673
brook *stream* 348
  bear 821, 826
broom 652
broth 298
brothel 961
brother *kin* 11
  similar 17
  equal 27
brotherhood 712
brotherly
  friendship 888
  love 897
  benevolence 906
brougham 272
brought to bed 161
brouillerie 713

brouillon 626
brow *top* 210
  edge 231
  front 234
browbeat
  intimidate 860
  swagger 885
  disrespect 929
  –en *humbled* 879
brown 433
  – Bess 727
  – study 451, 458
Brown, Jones and
  Robinson 876
brownie 980
browse 298
bruin 895
bruise *powder* 330
  hurt 619
  injure 649
  blemish 848
bruiser 726
bruit
  report 531, 532
brumal 126, 383
brumous 353
Brummagem 545
brunette 433
brunt *beginning* 66
  impulse 276
bear the –
  difficulty 704
  defence 717
  endure 821, 826
brush *rough* 256
  rapid motion 274
  graze 379
  clean 652
  fight 720
  paint – 556
  – away *reject* 297
  abrogate 756
  – up *clean* 652
  furbish 658
  prepare 673
brushwood 367
brusque *violent* 173
  haste 684
  discourtesy 895
brutal *vulgar* 851
  rude 895
  savage 907
brutalize
  [*see* brutal]
  corrupt 659
  deaden 823
  vice 945
brute *animal* 366
  rude 895
  maleficent 913
  – force
  strength 159
  violence 173
  animal 450a
  severe 739
  compulsion 744
  lawless 964
  – matter 316, 358
Brute, et tu 917
brutish [*see* brute]
  vulgar 851
  ignoble 876
  intemperate 954
brutum fulmen
  impotent 158
  failure 732
  lax 738
  boast 884

bubble
  unsubstantial 4
  transient 111
  little 193
  convexity 250
  light 320
  water 348
  air 353
  error 495
  deceit 545
  trifle 643
  – burst
  fall short 304
  disappoint 509
  fail 732
  – reputation 873
  – and squeak 298
  – up *agitation* 315
buccaneer 791, 792
buceataur 273
Bucephalus 271
buck *stag* 366
  male 373
  wash 652
  money 800
  fop 854
  – basket 191
  – jump 309
  – up 684
bucket 191
  kick the – 360
  drop – in empty
  well 645
  like –s in well 314
buckle *tie* 43
  fastening 45
  distort 243
  curl 248
  – on one's armor
  673
  – to 604, 686
  – with *grapple* 720
buckler 717
buckram 855, 878
  men in – 549
bucolic
  pastoral 370
  poem 597
bud 367
  beginning 66
  germ 153
  expand 194
  graft 300
  – from 154
Buddha 979, 986
Buddhism 984
budding *young* 127
buddy 711, 890
budge 264
budget *heap* 72
  bag 191
  store 636
  finance 811
  – of news 532
buff 436
  blind man's – 840
  native – 226
buffer
  hindrance 706
  defence 717
buffet (170)
  strike 276
  agitate 315
  evil 619
  bad 649
  affront 900
  smite 972
  – the waves 704,

bane 663
  painful 830
candelabrum 423
candent 382
candid *white* 430
  sincere 543
  ingenuous 703
  honorable 939
candidate 767, 865
candidature 763
candle 423
  bargain by inch of
    – 769
  burn – at both
    ends 686
  not fit to hold a –
    to 34
  – ends 40, 817
  – holder 711
  – light 126, 422
  – power 466
  – stick 423, 998
  hold – to sun 645
Candlemas 998
candor
  veracity 543
  artlessness 705
  honor 939
candy *dense* 321
  sweet 396
cane *weapon* 727
  punish 972
  scourge 975
canescent 430
Canicula 423
canicular 382
caniculated 259
canine 366
  – *appetite* 865
canister 191
canker *disease* 655
  deterioration 659
  bane 663
  pain 830
canned goods 670
cannel coal 388
cankered
  sullen 901a
cankerworm 663
  evil-doer 913
  care 830
cannibal 913
cannibalism 945
cannon
  collision 276
  loud 404
  arms 727
  – *fodder* 726
  –'s *mouth war* 722
  courage 861
cannonade 716
cannonball 249, 274
cannoneer 726
cannot 271
cannular 260
canny 498, 702
  ca' – 864
canoe 273
  paddle one's own
    – 748
canon *rule* 80
  ravine 198
  music 415
  belief 484
  precept 697
  priest 996
  rite 998
  – *law* 697

canonical
  regular 82
  inspired 985
  ecclesiastical 995
canonicals 999
canonist 983
canonization
  repute 873
  deification 991
  rite 998
canonry 995
canopy 223
  – of heaven 318
canorous 413
cant *oblique* 217
  jerk 276
  hypocrisy 544
  neology 563
  impiety 988
cantabile 415
cantankerous 901,
  901a
cantata 415
  missa – 998
cantatrice 416
canteen 189, 191
canter 266, 274
  win at a – 705
canterbury
  receptacle 191
Canterbury tale
  546
cantharides 171
canticle 415
cantilever 215
canting 855
cantle 51
cantlet 32, 51
canto 597
canton 181, 737
cantonment 184,
  189
cantrap 993
canty 836
canvas *sail* 267
  picture 556
  under press of –
    274
canvass
  investigate 461
  discuss 476
  dissert 595
  solicit 765
canvasser 767
canyon 350
canzonet 415, 597
caoutchouc 325
cap *be superior* 33
  height 206
  summit 210
  cover 223
  hat 225
  retaliate 718
  complete 929
  salute 894
  fling up one's –
    838
  Fortunatus's – 993
  set one's – at 897,
    902
  – and bells 844
  – fits 23
  – in hand
    request 765
    servile 886
    respect 928
  – of maintenance
    747

capability
  endowment 5
  power 157
  skill 698
  facility 705
capacious *space* 180
  – *memory* 505
capacity
  endowment 5
  power 157
  space 180
  size 192
  intellect 450
  wisdom 498
  office 625
  talent 698
cap-à-pie
  complete 52
  armed –
    prepared 673
    defence 717
    war 722
caparison 225
cape *height* 206
  cloak 225
  projection 250
capella, alla – 415
caper *leap* 309
  dance 840
capful *quantity* 25
  small 32
  – of wind 349
capillament 205
capillary
  hairlike 205
  thin 203
capital *city* 189
  top 201
  letter 561
  important 642
  excellent 648
  money 800
  wealth 803
  make – out of
    pretext 617
    acquire 775
  print in –s 642
  – *messuage* 189
  – *punishment* 972
  ship 726
capitalist 803
capitation 85
  – *tax* 812
capitol 189, 717
capitular 995, 996
capitulate 725
capnomancy 511
capon 373
caponize 38, 158
capote 225
capouch 999
capper 548
capriccio *music* 415
  whim 608
caprice 608
  out of – 615a
capricious
  irregular 139
  changeable 149
  irresolute 605
  whimsical 608
capriole 309
capsize 218, 731
capsized 732
capstan 307, 633
capstone 210
capsular 252
capsule *vessel* 190

tunicle 223
  medicine 662
captain 269, 745
captandum, ad –
  sophistry 477
  deception 545
  affectation 855
  ostentation 882
  flattery 933
captation 933
captious
  capricious 608
  irascible 901
  censorious 932
caption
  taking 789
  beginning 66
  heading 564
captivate
  induce 615
  restrain 751
  please 829
captivated 827
captivating 829, 897
captive
  prisoner 754
  adorer 897
  lead – 749
  make – 751
  – *balloon* 273
captivity 751
capture 789
Capuchin 996
caput 696
  – *mortuum* 645,
    653
caquet 584
car 272
carabineer 726
carack 273
caracole 309
caracoler 266
carafe 191
caramel 396
carambole 276
carapace 717
cara sposa 897
carat 309
caravan 266, 272
caravansary 189
caravel 273
carbine 727
carbohydrates 298
carbon 388
  – dioxide 663
  – monoxide 663
carbonaro 742
carbonization 384
carboy 191
carbuncle *red* 434
  abscess 655
  jewel 847
carcanet 847
carcass
  structure 329
  corpse 362
  bomb 727
carcelage 973
carcinoma 655
card *unravel* 60
  ticket 550
  plan 626
  address – 550
  by the – 82
  great – 873
  house of –s 328
  leave a – 892
  on the –s 152, 177,

470
  play one's – 692
  play one's best –
    686
  play one's –s well
    698
  playing –s 840
  shuffle the –s
    begin again 66
    change 140
    chance 621
    prepare 673
  speak by the –
    care 459
    veracity 543
    phrase 566
  throw up the –s
    757
  ticklish – 704
  trump – 626
  – index 60, 86, 551
  –s to play 632
cardcase 191
cardiac 836
cardigan 225
cardinal *intrinsic* 5
  dress 225
  red 434
  important 642
  excellent 648
  priest 995, 996
  –'s *hat* 747
  – points 278
  – virtues 944
cardioid 245
card-sharper 792
card-sharping 545
care *attention* **459**
  business 625
  adversity 735
  custody 751
  economy 817
  pain 828
  fear 860
  for aught one –s
    643, 866
  begone dull – 836
  drive – away 840
  have the – of 693
  take – 665, 864
  take – of 459
  – for *important*
    642
  desire 865
  love 897
careen *slope* 217
  repair 660
career 625, 692
careless
  inattentive 458
  neglectful 460,
    927
  feeble 575
  insensible 823
  indifferent 866
caress 897, 902
caret *incomplete* 53
  want 640
careworn 828, 837
cargo 270
  large quantity 31
  contents 190
  property 780
  goods 798
  – *boat* 273
caricature
  likeness 19
  copy 21

catalogue 60, 86
catalysis 49, 140
catamaran 273, 726
catemenial 138, 299
cataphonics 402
cataplasm 662
catapult 284, 726, 727
cataract
  waterfall 348
  blindness 442, 443
catarrh 299
catastrophe
  disaster 619
  finish 729
  misfortune 735
  end 67
catch *imitate* 19
  fastening 45
  song 415
  detect 480a
  joke 497
  gather the meaning 518
  cheat 545
  receive 785
  take 789
  by –es 70
  no great – 651
  – at *willing* 602
  desire 865
  – the attention 457
  – one's death 360
  – a disease 655
  – the ear 418
  – the eye 446
  – fire 384
  – a glimpse of 441
  – an idea 498
  – the infection
  excitation 824
  – a likeness 554
  – a sound 418
  – at straws
  overrate 482
  credulous 486
  unskilful 699
  rash 863
  – by surprise 508
  – a Tartar *dupe* 547
  retaliate 718
  – in a trap 545
  – tripping 480a
  – up 789
catching
  infectious 657
catchpenny
  deceiving 545
  trumpery 643
  cheap 815
catchpoll 965
catchword 550
catechism 461, 484
  church – 983a
catechize 461
catechumen 541, 997
categorical
  positive 474
  demonstrative 478
  affirmative 535
categorically true 494
category 7, 75
  in the same – 9

catena 69
catenary 245
catenation 69
cater 298, 637
caterpillar tractor 271
caterwaul
  cat-cry 412
  discord 414
  courting 902
cates 298
catgut 417
  – *scraper* 416
cathartic 652
cathedrâ, ex –
  affirm 535
  school 542
  authority 737
  audacity 885
cathedral 1000
Catherine wheel 840
catholic
  universal 78
  religious 987
  – *church* 983a
  Roman – 984
catholicon 662
Catiline 941
catopsis 441
catoptrics 420
catoptromancy 511
cattle 271, 366
  – *truck* 272.
catwalk 273, 627
Caucasian mystery 983
caucus 696
caudal 67, 235
caudate 214
caudex 215
Caudine forks 162
cauf 370
caught tripping 491
caulk 660
cause *source* 153
  law-suit 969
  final – 620
  take up the – of 707
  tell the – of 522
  –d by 154
causeless
  casual 156
  aimless 621
causerie 588
causeway 627
causidical 965
caustic
  energetic 171
  feeling 821
  painful 830
  gruff 895
  malevolent 907
  – *curve* 245
cautel 864
cautelâ, ex abundanti – 664
cautery 384
caution *warn* 668
  prudence 864
  security 771
  want of – 863
cavalcade 69, 266
cavalier
  horseman 268
  rash 863
  insolent 885

discourteous 895
contemptuous 930
cavaliere servente
  servile 886
  lover 897
cavalry 726
cavatina 415
cave *dwelling* 189
  cell 191
  cavity 252
  – *canem* 864
  – of Adullam 624, 832
  – in *hollow* 252
  submit 725
caveat
  warning 668
  command 741
  – *emptor* 769
cavendo tutus 664, 864
cavern [see cave]
cavernous 252
caviar 392, 393
  – to the general 850
cavil *sophistry* 477
  dissent 489
  censure 932
caviler 936
cavity 252
caw 412
cayak 273
cayenne 392, 393
cazique 745
cease 142
  – to breathe 360
  – to exist 2
ceaseless 112
cecal 261
cecity 442
cecum 261
cede *submit* 725
  relinquish 782
  give 784
ceiling 206, 210, 223
celare artem, ars – 698
cela va sans dire
  conformity 82
  consequence 154
celebrant 990
celebration 883, 998
celebrity 873, 875
celerity 274
celeste 417
celestial
  physical 318
  religious 976
  heaven 981
celibacy 904
cell *abode* 189
  receptacle 191
  cavity 221, 252
  prison 752
  hermitage 893
cellar 191
cellaret 191
cello 417
cellophane 223
cellular 191, 252
cement
  medium 45
  unite 43, 46, 48
  covering 223
  hard 323
  material 635
  – a party 712

cemented
  concord 714
cemetery 363
cenobite 893, 996
cenotaph 363
censer 998
censor
  moderate 174
  critic 480
  ban 761
  detractor 936
censorious 480, 932
censurable 947
censure 932
censurer 936
census 85, 86
  record 551
centaur 83, 366
centenarian 130
centenary
  hundred 98
  period 138
  celebration 883
center 68. 222
  – round 72, 290
centesimal 99
cento 597
centrality 222
centralize
  combine 48
centrifugal 291
centripetal 290
centroidal 222
centuple 98
centurion 745
century
  hundred 98
  period 108
  long time 110
  money 800
ceramic
  bake 384
  – ware 557
cerate 662
Cerberus
  janitor 263
  custodian 664
  hades 932
  sop for – 615
cereal 298
cerebration 451
cerebrum 450
cere-cloth 363
cerement
  covering 223
  wax 356
  burial 363
ceremonious 928
ceremony
  parade 882
  courtesy 894
  rite 998
Ceres 979
cerise 434
cerography 558, 590
Ceromancy 511
ceroplastic 557
certain *special* 79
  indefinite number 100
  sure 474
  belief 484
  true 494
  make – of 480a
  of a – *age* 128
  to a – degree 32
certainly *yes* 488

certainness 474
certainty 474
certes 474, 488
certificate
  evidence 467
  record 551
  security 771
certify 467, 535
certiorari 969
certitude 474
cerulean 438
cess *tax* 812
  sewer 653
cessation 142
cession
  surrender 725
  of property 782
  gift 784
cesspool 653
cestui-que trust 779
cestus 45, 247
chafe
  physical pain 378
  warm 384
  irritate 825
  mental pain 828, 830
  discontent 832
  incense 900
chaff *trash* 643
  ridicule 856
  vulgar 876
  not to be caught with – 698, 702
  winnow – from wheat 609
chaffer 794
chafing-dish 386
chagrin 828
chain *fasten* 43
  vinculum 45
  series 69
  measure 200
  interlinking 219
  measure 466
  gearing 633
  imprison 752
  ornament 847
  drag a – 749
  drag a lengthened – 686
  in –s 754
chain gang 752, 97?
chain-shot 727
chair *support* 215
  vehicle 272
  professorship 54?
  throne 747
  celebration 883
  president 694
  in the – 693
chairman 694
chaise 272
chalcography 558
chalet 189
chalice 191, 998
chalk *earth* 342
  white 430
  mark 550
  drawing 556
  – from cheese 14, 491
  – out *plan* 626
challenge
  question 461
  doubt 485
  claim 924
  defy 715

accuse 938
- comparison 648
cham 745
chamber room 191
council 696
mart 799
sick - 655
chamberlain 746
chambermaid 746
chameleon 149, 440
chamfer 259
chamois 309
champ 298
- the bit disobedi-
ent 742
chafe 825
angry 900
champagne 298
champaign 344
champain 874
Champ de Mars 728
champêtre, fête - 840
champion
best 648
- auxiliary 711
defence 717
combatant 726
representative 759
sympathizer 914
championship 707
chance 156, 621
be one's - 151
game of - 840
great - 472
small - 473
stand a - 177, 470
take one's - 675
-s against one 665
whirligig of - 156
as - would have it 152
chancel 1000
chancellor
president 745
deputy 759
judge 967
- of the exchequer 801
chancery
court of - 966
- suit delay 133
chandelier 214, 423
chandelle, le jeu n'en vaut pas la - 638, 643
dear 814
chandler 797
change
alteration 140
mart 799
small coin 800
inter- 148
radical - 146
sudden - 146
- about 149
- color 821
- for 147
- hands 783
- of mind 607
- of opinion 485
- of place 264
changeableness 149, 605
changeful
fickle 607
changeling

substitute 147
fool 501
changeless 16
changer 797
channel
furrow 259
opening 260
conduit 350
way 627
chant song 415
sing 416
worship 990
chant du cygne 360
chanter 416
chanticleer 366
chantry 1000
chaomancy 511
chaos 59
chap crack 198
jaw 231
fellow 373
- book 593
chapel 1000
chaperon
accompany 88
watch 459
protect 664
chapfallen 878
chaplain 995, 996
chaplet circle 247
garland 550
trophy 733
ornament 847
chapman 797
chapter part 51
topic 454
book 593
council 696
church 995
- of accidents 156, 621
- house 1000
- and verse 467, 494
char burn 384
serve 746
char-à-banc 272
character
nature 5
state 7
class 75
oddity 83
letter 561
drama 599
disposition 820
reputation 873
characteristic
intrinsic 5
special 79
tendency 176
mark 550
characterize 564, 594
characterized 820
charade 533, 599
charcoal fuel 384, 388
black 431
drawing 556
charge fill 52
contents 190
business 625
requisition 630
direction 693
advice 695
precept 697
attack 716
order 741

custody 751
commission 755
bargain for 794
price 812
accusation 938
in - prisoner 754
justifiable - 937
take - of 664
take in - 751
- on attribute 155
- with 155, 777
chargé d'affaires 758
chargeable debt 806
- on duty 926
charger
carrier 271
fighter 726
Charing Cross, pro-claim at - 531
chariot 272
drag at one's - wheels 749
charioteer 268, 694
charity give 784
liberal 816
beneficent 906
pity 914
Christian - 906
cold as - 823
- that begins at home 943
charivari 404, 407
charlatan
ignoramus 493
imposter 548
mountebank 844
boaster 884
charlatanism
ignorance 491
falsehood 544
affectation 855
Charles's wain 318
Charleston 840
Charley 753
charm motive 615
please 829
beauty 845
love 897
conjure 992
spell 993
bear a -ed life 644, 734
charmer 994
voice of the - 933
not listen to voice of - 604
charnel-house 363
Charon 982
chart 527, 554
charter
commission 755
permit 760
compact 769
security 771
privilege 924
chartered
legal 963
- accountant 801, 811
- libertine 962
Chartist 742
charwoman 690, 746
chary
economical 817
stingy 819
cautious 864

Charybdis 312, 665
chase emboss 250
furrow 259
drive away 289
killing 361
forest 367
pursue 622
ornament 847
wild goose - 645
chaser 559
chasm interval 198
opening 260
chassé 840
chassemarée 273
chassepot 727
chasser 297
- balancer 605
chasseur 726
chassis 215
chaste
shapely 242
language 576, 578
simple 849
good taste 850
pure 960
chasten
moderate 174
punish 972
chastened
subdued spirit 826
penitent 950
chastise 932, 972
- with scorpions 739
chasuble 999
chat 588
chat qui dort 667, 668
château 189
- en Espagne 858
chatelaine 847
chatoyant 440
chattels 633, 789
chatter 314, 584
chatterbox 584
chattering of teeth cold 383
chatty 584, 892
chauffeur 268
chaunt 415
song 415
sing 416
worship 990
chaussé 225
Chauvinism 884, 885
chawbacon 876
cheap 643, 815
hold - 930
- jack 797
cheapen haggle 794
begrudge 819
cheapness 815
cheat 545, 548
check
numerical 85
stop 142
moderate 174
counteract 179
slacken 275
plaid 440
experiment 463
measure 466
evidence 468
ticket 550
dissuade 616
hinder 706

misfortune 735
restrain 751
money order 800
- the growth 201
- oneself 826
checkered 149
checkers 440, 840
checkmate
stop 142
success 731
failure 732
check-roll 86
check-string
pull the - 142
cheek side 236
impertinence 885
- by jowl with 88
near 197
cheeks dual 89
cheep 412
cheer repast 298
cry 411
aid 707
pleasure 827
relief 834
mirth 836
rejoicing 838
amusement 840
courage 861
sociality 892
welcome 894
applaud 931
good - hope 858
high living 957
cheerfulness 836
cheerless 830, 837
cheeseparings
remains 40
dirt 653
economy 817
chef de cuisine
proficient 700
servant 746
chef-d'oeuvre 648, 698
cheka 696
chemin
- de fer game 840
- faisant 270
chemise 225
chemist 662
Chemistry 144
organic - 357
cheque 800
chequer 440
- roll 86
cherchez la femme 155
chère amie 962
cherish aid 707
love 897
endearment 902
- a belief 484
- feelings &c. 821
- an idea &c. 451
cherry
- red 434
two bites of a - overrate 482
roundabout 629
clumsy 699
cherry-cheeked 845
cherry-colored 434
cheroot 392
cherub 977
Cheshire cat 838

circumfluent
  lie round 227
  move round 311
circumforaneous
  traveling 266
  circuition 311
circumfuse 73
circumgyration 312
circumjacence 227
circumlocution 573
circumnavigate
  navigation 267
  circuition 311
circumrotation 312
circumscribe
  surround 229
  limit 233, 761
circumscription **229**
circumspection
  attention 457
  care 459
  caution 459
circumstance
  phase 8
  event 151
circumstances
  property 780
  bad – 804
  depend on – 475
  good – 803
  under the – 8
circumstantial 8
  – *account* 594
  – *evidence* 467
  probability 472
circumstantiality
  459
circumstantiate 467
circumvallation
  enclosure 229,
  232
  defence 717
  line of – 233
circumvent
  environ 227
  move round 311
  cheat 545
  cunning 702
  hinder 706
  defeat 731
circumvest 225
circumvolution
  winding 248
  rotation 312
circus
  buildings 189
  drama 599
  arena 728
  amusement 840
cirrus 353
cistern
  receptacle 191
  store 636
Cistercian 996
cit 188
citadel 717
citation 467, 733
cite
  quote as example
  82
  as evidence 467
  summon 741
  accuse 938
  arraign 969
cithern 417
citizen 188
  – *of the world* 910
citriculture 371

citrine 436
city 189
  in the – 794
city manager 965
civet 400
civic 372
civil *courteous* 894
  laity 997
  – *authorities* 745
  – *crown* 733
  – *law* 963
  – *war* 722
civilian *lawyer* 968
  layman 997
civilization
  improvement 658
  fashion 852
  courtesy 894
civilized life 852
civism 910
clack *clatter* 407
  animal cry 412
  talkative 584
clad 225
claim *requisition*
  630
  demand 741
  property 780
  right 924
  lawsuit 969
  – *the attention*
  457
claimant
  petitioner 767
  right 924
clair-obscur 420
clairvoyance 992
clairvoyant 513, **994**
clamant 411
clamber 305
clammy 352
clamor *cry* 411
  wail 839
  – *against* 932
  – *for* 765
clamorous
  [*see* clamor]
  loud 404
  excitable 825
clamp *fasten* 43
  fastening 45
clan *race* 11
  class 166
  family 166
  party 712
clandestine 528
clangor 404
clank 410
clannishness 481
clanship 709
clap *explosion* 406
  applaud 931
  thunder –
  prodigy 872
  – *the hands*
  rejoice 838
  – *on* 31
  – *on the shoulder*
  615
  – *together* 43
  – *up imprison* 751
clapperclaw
  contention 720
  censure 932
claptrap
  pretence 546
  display 882
claquer 935

faire – son fouet
  884
clarence 272
claret color 434
clarify 652
clarinet 417
clarion *music* 417
  war 722
clarity 518
clash *disagree* 24
  cross 179
  concussion 276
  sound 406
  oppose 708
  discord 713
  – *of arms* 720
clasp *fasten* 43
  fastening 45
  stick 46
  come close 197
  belt 230
  embrace 902
class *arrange* 60
  category 75
  learners 541
  party 712
  – *prejudice* 481
  – *room* 542
classic *old* 124
  symmetry 242
classical
  elegant writing
  578
  taste 850
  – *art* 556
  – *dancing* 840
  – *education* 537
  – *music* 415
classicist 492
classics 560
classify 60
classmate 890
clatter 404, 407
claudication
  slowness 275
  failure 732
clause *part* 51
  passage 593
  condition 770
clausis, januis –
  528
claustral 110
clavate 250
clavichord 417
clavier 417
claw *hook* 781
  grasp 789
  – *back* 935
clay *soft* 324
  earth 342
  corpse 362
  material 635
  – *pipe* 392
clay-cold 383
claymore 727
clean
  entirely 52
  perfect 650
  unstained 652
  – *bill of health* 654
  – *breast*
  disclose 529
  – *forgotten* 506
  – *hand*
  proficient 700
  with – *hands*
  honesty 939
  innocence 946

– *out empty* 297
– *shaven* 226
– *sweep*
  revolution 146
  destruction 162
clean-up 775
clear *simple* 42
  sound 413
  light 420
  transparent 425
  visible 446
  certain 474
  intelligible 518
  manifest 525
  easy 705
  liberate 750
  profit 775
  vindicate 937
  innocent 946
  acquit 975
  all – 664, 705
  coast – 664
  get – *off* 671
  keep – *of* 623
  make – 529
  – *for action*
  prepare 673
  – *articulation* 580
  – *conscience* 946
  – *the course* 302
  – *cut* 518
  – *the ground*
  facilitate 705
  – *of distant* 196
  – *off pay* 807
  – *out empty* 297
  clean 652
  – *sighted*
  vision 441
  shrewd 498
  – *sky hope* 858
  – *stage*
  occasion 134
  easy 705
  right 922
  – *thinking* 498
  – *the throat* 297
  – *up light* 420
  intelligible 518
  interpret 522
clearheaded 498
clear-obscure 420
cleat 45
cleavage
  cutting 44
  structure 329
cleave *sunder* 44
  adhere 46
  bisect 91
cleaver 253
cledge 342
clef 413
cleft *divided* 44
  bisected 91
  chink 198
in a – *stick*
  difficulty 704
clem 956
clement
  lenient 740
  long-suffering
  826
  compassionate
  914
clench *compact* 769
  retain 781
  take 789
clepe 564

clepsydra 114
clerestory 191, 1000
clergy 996
clerical 995, **996**
  – *error* 495
  – *staff* 746
clerk *scholar* 492
  recorder 553
  writer 590
  helper 711
  servant 746
  agent 758
  clergy 996
  articled – 541
  – *in holy orders*
  995
  – *of works* 694
clerkship
  commission 755
cleromancy 511
clever
  intelligent 498
  skilful 698
  smart 842
  too – *by half* 702
clew *ball* 249
  interpretation 522
  indication 550
  seek a – 461
click 406
client
  dependant 746
  customer 795
clientship
  subjection 749
cliff *height* 206
  vertical 212
  steep 217
  land 342
climacteric 128
climate *region* 181
  weather 338
  fine – 656
climatology 338
climax
  supremacy 33
  summit 210
  culmination 729
climb 305
  – *on the band-*
  wagon 731
clime 181
clinal 217
clinch *fasten* 43
  close 261
  certify 474
  pun 563
  complete 729
  clutch 781
  snatch 789
  – *an argument* 47
  – *the fist at* 909
clincher 479
cling *adhere* 46
  – *to near* 197
  willing 602
  persevere 604a
  habit 613
  observe 772
  desire 865
  love 897
  – *to hope* 858
  – *to one another*
  709
clinic 662
clink
  resonance 408
  stridor 410

prison 752
clinker brick 384
  dirt 653
clinometer
  oblique 217
  angle 244
clinquant
  ornament 847
  vulgar 851
Clio 594
clip shorten 201
  – the wings
  powerless 158
  speed 264
  slow 275
  useless 645
  hinder 706
  prohibit 761
  – one's words 583
clipper 273
clipping
  small piece 51
clique conclave 696
  party 712
cloaca conduit 350
  foul 653
Cloacina 653
cloak dress 225
  conceal 528
  disguise 530
cloaked 223
cloche 371
clock 114
clockwork 633
  by – uniform 16
  order 58
  regular 80
clod lump 192
  earth 342
  fool 501
  bungler 701
clodhopper 876
clodpated
  stupid 499
clog shoe 225
  hinder 706
  – dance 840
cloison 228
cloisonné 557
cloister arcade 189
  way 627
  restraint 751
  convent 1000
close similar 17
  tight 43
  end 67
  field 181
  court 189
  near 197
  narrow 203
  shut 261
  dense 321
  warm 382
  hidden 528
  concise 572
  taciturn 585
  complete 729
  stingy 819
  examine –ly 457
  keep – hide 528
  retain 781
  tread – upon 281
  – the door upon
  restrain 751
  – the ears 419
  – the eyes
  die 360
  not see 442

– one's eyes to
  not attend 458
  set at naught 773
– at hand
  to-morrow 121
  imminent 152
  near 197
– the hand
  refuse 764
– in upon 290
– inquiry 461
–ly packed 72
– prisoner 754
– quarters 197
  approach 286
  attack 716
  battle 722
– one's ranks 673
– study
  thought 451
  attention 457
– up 197, 290
– with cohere 46
  assent 488
  attack 716
  contend 720
  consent 762
  compact 769
close-mouthed 585
closet
  receptacle 191
  ambush 530
closeted with
  conference 588
  advice 695
close-up 197
closure 142, **261**
clot solidify 321
  earth 342
cloth vocation 625
  napkin 652
  clergy 996
clothes 225
  grave – 363
  – basket 191
clothier 225
Clotho 601
clotpoll 501
clotted 352
cloud
  assemblage 72
  multitude 102
  mist 353
  shade 424
  screen 520
  break through the
    –s 446
  drop from the –s
    508
  in a – 475, 528
  in the –s
  lofty 206
  inattentive 458
  dreaming 515
  under a –
  insane 503
  adversity 735
  disrepute 874
  secluded 893
  censured 932
  accused 938
  – burst 348
  –capt 206
  – of dust 330, 353
  –s gathering
  dark 421
  danger 665
  warning 668

– no bigger than a
    man's hand 668
– of skirmishers
    726
– of smoke 353
– of words 573
clouded
  variegated 440
  dejected 837
  hopeless 859
  – perception 499
cloudiness 571
cloudland 515
cloudless
  light 420
  happy 827
cloudy dim 422,
    426
clough 206
clout 276
cloven 91
cloven foot
  mark 550
  malevolence 907
  vice 945
  Satan 978
  see the – 480a
  show the – 907
clover
  luxury 377
  prosperity 734
  comfort 827
clown
  pantomime 599
  bungler 702
  buffoon 844
  vulgar 851
  rustic 876
cloy 641, 869
club
  place of meeting
    74
  house 189
  association 712
  weapon 727
  sociality 892
  – law
  compulsion 744
  lawless 964
  – together
  co-operate 709
clubby 892
club car 272
clubfooted 243
cluck 412
clue 550
  seek a – 461
clump
  assemblage 72
  projecting mass
    250
  – of trees 367
clumsy
  unfit 647
  awkward 699
  ugly 846
Cluniac 996
clurichaune 980
cluster 72
clutch retain 781
  seize 789
clutches 737
  in the – of 749
clutter 407
coacervation 72
coach
  carriage 272
  teach 537

tutor 540, 673
– painter 540
– road 627
drive a – and six
    through 964
– up 539
coachhouse 191
coachman 268, 694
coaction 744
coadjutant 709
coadjutor 711
coadjuvancy 709
coagency 178, 709
coagmentation 72
coagulate
  cohere 46
  density 321
  semi-liquid 352
coal 388
  call over the –s
    932
  carry –s 879
  – black 431
  carry –s to New-
    castle 641
coalesce
  identity 13
  combine 48
coalheaver
  work like a – 686
coalition 43, 709,
    712
coaming 232
coaptation 23
coarctation
  decrease 36
  contraction 195
  narrow 203
  impede 706
  restraint 751
coarse harsh 410
  dirty 653
  unpolished 674
  garish 846
  vulgar 851
  impure 961
  – grain 329
coast border 231
  slide 266
  navigate 267
  land 342
  – defence 717
  – line 230
coaster 273
coastguard 753
coat layer 204
  paint 223
  habit 225
  cut – according to
  cloth 698
  – of arms 550
  – of mail 717
coating, inner –
    224
coax persuade 615
  endearment 902
  flatter 933
cob horse 271
  punish 972
cobalt 438
cobble mend 660
cobbler 225
cobbles 635
coble 273
cobra 913
cobweb light 320
  fiction 545
  flimsy 643

dirt 653
–s of antiquity
    124
–s of sophistry
    477
cocaine 376, 381,
    663
cochineal 434
cock bird 366
  male 373
  game – 861
  – boat 273
  – and bull story
    546
  – the eye 441
  – of the roost
  best 648
  master 745
  – up vertical 212
  convex 250
cockade badge 550
  title 877
cock-a-hoop
  gay 836
  exulting 884
Cockaigne 827
cockatrice
  monster 83
  piercing eye 548
  evil-doer 913
  miscreant 949
cockcrow 125
cocked hat 225, 745
cocker fold 258
  caress 902
Cocker
  school book 542
  according to – 82
cockle foil 258
  – of one's heart
    820
cockleshell 273
cockloft 191
cockney
  Londoner 188
  plebeian 876
cockpit hold 191
  council 696
  arena 728
cockshut
  morning 125
  evening 126
  dusk 422
cock-sparrow 193
cocksure 484
cockswain 269
cocktail 298, 959
  – party 892
cocoa 298
cocotte 962
coction 384
Cocytus 982
cod shell 223
coddle 902
  – oneself 943
code conceal 528
  precept 697
  law 963
codex 593
codger 819
codicil sequel 65
  testament 771
codify 60, 963
codlin 129
coefficient
  factor 84
  accompany 88

- of 154
- off event 151
disjoin 44
loop-hole 617
escape 671
- on future 121
destiny 152
I defy you 715
attack 716
- to oneself 660
- into operation 170
- out
disclosure 529
publication 531
on the stage 599
- out of effect 154
egress 295
- out with
disclose 529
speak 582
- over
influence 615
consent 762
- to pass state 7
event 151
- to pieces 44
- to the point
speciality 79
attention 457
concise 572
- to the rescue 672
- round
period 138
conversion 144
belief 484
assent 488
change of mind 607
influence 615
restoration 660
be pacified 723
consent 762
- to the same thing 27
- short of
inferior 34
fall short 304
- to one's senses 502
- to a stand 142
- to terms
assent 488
contract 769
it -s to this
concisely 572
- to equal 27
whole 50
arithmetic 85
become 144
effect 154
inherit 777
money 800
price 812
together
assemble 72
converge 290
under 76
upon
unexpected 508
acquire 775
claim 924
- into use 613
- into view 446
into the views of
co-operate 709
- off well 731

- into the world 359
come-down 306, 735
comedy
drama 599
comic 853
comely 845
comestible 298
comet
wanderer 268
star 318
cometary 111
comfit 396
comfort
pleasure 377
delight 827
content 831
relief 834
give - 906
comfortable
pleasing 829
comforter
covering 223
Comforter 976
comfortless
painful 830
dejected 837
comic wit 842
ridiculous 853
- opera 599
- strips 531
coming [see come]
impending 152
- events
prediction 511
- out 883
- time 121
comitia 696
comity 894
comma 142
inverted -s 550
command high 206
requisition 630
authority 737
order 741
possess 777
at one's -
obedient 743
- belief 484
- of language
writing 574
speaking 582
- of money 803
- one's passions 944
- respect 928
- one's temper 826
- a view of 441
commandant 745
commander 269
commandeer 744, 789
commanding
[see command]
important 642
commando 726
commandment 697
comme deux gouttes d'eau 17
comme il faut
taste 850
fashion 852
genteel 875
commemorate 883
commence 66
commencement de

la fin end 67
destruction 162
commend 931
- the poisoned chalice 544
commendable 944
commensurate
accordant 23
numeral 85
adequate 639
comment
reason 476
judgment 480
interpretation 522
criticize 595
commentary 595
commentator 492, 524, 527
commerce
conversation 588
barter 794
cards 840
commercial 811
- arithmetic 811
- traveler 758
commère 599
commination 908, 909
commingle 41
comminute 330
commiserate 914
commissariat 637
commissary
provisions 637
consignee 758
commission
task 625
delegate 755, 759
Royal - 696
- of the peace 965
commissioner 758
commissionaire
doorkeeper 263
messenger 534
consignee 758
commissure 43
commis-voyageur 758
commit do 680
delegate 755
cards 840
arrest 969
- an absurdity 853
- oneself to a course 609
- to the flames 384
- to memory 505
- oneself
clumsy 699
promise 768
- to prison 751
- sin 945
- to writing 551
committee
council 696
consignee 758
(director 694)
commix 41
commode 191
commodious 644
commodity 798
commodore 745
common
general 78
ordinary 82
plain 344
habitual 613

trifling 643
base 876
in - related 9
participate 778
right of - 780
short -s 640
tenant in - 778
make - cause 709
- consent 488
- council 966
- course 613
- herd 876
- law old 124
law 697, 963
- measure 84
- origin 153
- parlance 576
- place 82
- place book
record 551
compendium 596
- saying 496
- sense 498
- sewer 653
- stock 778
- weal
mankind 372
good 681
utility 644
philanthropy 910
Common Pleas
Court of - 966
commonalty 876
commoner 876
commonplace
usual 82
known 490
plain 576
habit 613
unimportant 643
dull 843
commons 298
commonwealth
territory 181
community 372
authority 737
commorant 188
commotion 315
communalism 778
commune
township 181
commune with 588
- oneself 451
communibus annis 29
communicant 990
communicate
join 43
tell 527
correspond 592
give 784
sacrament 998
communication
news 532
of disease 657
oral - 582, 588
communion
discourse 588
society 712
participation 778
sacrament 998
hold - with 888
- table 1000
communiqué 527
communism 737
communist
party 712
rebel 742

participation 778
philanthropy 910
evil doer 913
community
party 712
- at large 372
- of goods 778
commutation
compensation 30
substitution 147
interchange 148
compromise 774
barter 794
commutual 12
compact
joined 43
united 87
receptacle 191
small 193
compressed 195
compendious 201
dense 321
bargain 769
compages
whole 50
structure 329
compagination 43
companion match 17
accompaniment 88
ladder 305
friend 890
companionable 892
companionship 892
companionway 305
company
assembly 72
actors 599
party, partnership 712
troop 726
sociality 892
bear - 88
in - with 88
comparable 9
comparative 464
degree 26
- anatomy 368
comparatively 32
compare 464
- notes 695
comparison 464
compartition 44
compartment
part 51
region 181
place 182
cell 191
carriage 272
compass
degree 26
space 180
surround 227
measure 466
intend 620
guidance 693
achieve 729
box the -
azimuth 278
rotation 312
keep within -
moderation 174
fall short 304
economy 817
points of the - 236
in a small - 193
- about 229

– of thought 498
compassion 914
  object of – 828
compatible
  consentaneous 23
  possible 470
compatriot
  inhabitant 188
  friend 890
compeer *equal* 27
  friend 890
compel 744
compellation 564
compendency 43
compendious 201
compendium 596
  book 593
compensate
  make up for 30
  requite 973
compensation 30
compère 599
competence
  power 157
  sufficiency 639
  skill 698
  wealth 803
competition
  opposition 708
  contention 720
competitor
  opponent 710
  combatant 726
  candidate 767
compilation
  collect 72
  book 593
  compendium 596
compile 54
complacent
  pleased 827
  content 831
  courteous 894
  kind 906
complain 839
complainant 938
complaint
  illness 655
  murmur 839
  lodge a – 938
  – without cause 839
complaisant
  lenient 740
  courteous 894
  kind 906
complement
  adjunct 39
  remainder 40
  part 52
  arithmetic 84
complementary
  correlation 12
  colour 428
complete
  entire 52
  accomplish 729
  compact 769
  – answer 479
  – circle 311
  in a – degree 31
completeness 52
completion 729
complex 59
complexion
  state 7
  color **428**
  appearance 448

compliance
  conformity 82
  obedience 743
  consent 762
  observance 772
complicate
  derange 61
complicated
  disorder 59
  convolution 248
complice 711
complicity 709
compliment
  courtesy 894, 896
  praise 931
  poor – 932
  –s of season 896
complimentary
  free 815
complot 626
comply [see compliance]
compo *coating* 223
  material 635
component 56
componere lites 723, 724
comport
  – oneself 692
  – with 23
compos mentis 502
compose
  make up 54, 56
  produce 161
  moderate 174
  music 416
  write 590
  printing 591
  pacify 723
  assuage 826
composed
  self-possessed 826
composer
  music 413
composite 41
composition 54
  [see compose]
  combination 48
  piece of music 415
  picture 556
  style 569
  writing 590
  building material 635
  compromise 774
  barter 794
  atonement 952
compositor
  printer 591
compost 653
composure 826, 871
compotation 959
compote 298
compound
  mix 41
  combination 48
  limited space 182
  enclosure 232
  compromise 774
  – arithmetic 466
  – for *substitute* 147
  barter 794
comprador 637
comprehend
  compose 54
  include 76
  know 490
  understand 518

comprehension [see comprehend]
  intelligence 498
comprehensive 76
  complete 50
  general 78
  wide 192
  – *argument* 476
compress
  contract 195
  curtail 201
  condense 321
  remedy 662
compressible 322
comprise 76
comprobation
  evidence 467
  demonstration 478
compromise
  dally with 605
  mid-course 628
  taint 659
  danger 665
  pacify 723
  compact 769
  compound **774**
  atone 952
compromised
  promised 768
compter 799
compte rendu
  record 551
  accounts 811
comptroller 694
compulsion 744
compunction 833, 950
compurgation
  evidence 467
  acquittal 970
compute 85
comrade 890
comradeship 892
con *think* 451
  get by heart 505
  learn 539
conation 600
conatu magnas
  nugas, magno –
  waste 638
  unimportance 643
conatus 176
concamerate 245
concatenation
  junction 43
  continuity 69
concavity 252
conceal
  invisible 447
  hide 528
  cunning 702
concealment 528, 893
concede
  assent 488
  admit 529
  permit 760
  consent 762
  give 784
conceit *idea* 453
  folly 499
  supposition 514
  imagination 515
  wit 842
  affectation 855
  vanity 880
conceited
  dogmatic 481

conceivable 470
conceive *begin* 66
  beget 161
  teem 168
  believe 484
  understand 490
  imagine 515
  plan 626
concent 413
concentrate
  assemble 72
  centrality 222
  converge 290
concentric 216, 222
conception
  [see conceive]
  intellect 450
  idea 453
concern
  relation 9
  event 151
  business 625
  importance 642
  firm 797
  grief 828
  – oneself with 625
concert
  agreement 23
  synchronism 120
  music 415
  act in – 709
  in – *musical* 413
  concord 714
  – *measures* 626
concertina 417
concerto 415
concert-room 840
concession
  permission 760
  consent 762
  compromise 774
  giving 784
  discount 813
concesso, ex –
  reasoning 476
  assent 488
concetto 842
conchoid 245
conchology 223
concierge 163, 753
conciliate
  talk over 615
  pacify 723
  satisfy 831
  courtesy 894
  atonement 952
conciliatory [see conciliate]
  concord 714
  forgiving 918
conciliatrix 962
concinnity
  agreement 23
  style 578
  beauty 845
conciseness 572
concision 201
conclave
  assembly 72
  council 696
  church 995
conclude
  end 67
  infer 480
  resolve 604
  complete 729
  compact 769
conclusion

[see conclude]
sequel 65
germination 161
judgment 480
try –s 476
forgone – 611
hasty – 481
conclusive
  [see conclude]
  answer 462
  evidence 467
  certain 474
  proof 478
  – *reasoning* 476
concoct *lie* 544
  write 590
  plan 626
  prepare 673
concomitant
  accompany 88
  same time 120
  concurrent 178
concord *agree* 23
  music **413**
  assent 488
  harmony **714**
concordance 562
  book 593
concordant 173
concordat 769
concordia discors 24, 59
concours 720
concourse
  assemblage 72
  convergence 290
concremation 384
concrete *existent* 3
  mass 46
  definite 79
  density 321
  hardness 323
  materials 635
concubinage 961
concubine 926
concupiscence 865, 961
concur
  co-exist 120
  causation 178
  converge 290
  assent 488
  concert 709
concurrence 178, 216
concussion 276
condemnation 932, 971
condemned cell 752
condense
  compress 195
  dense 321
condensed
  concise 572
condescend 879
condign 924
condiment 393
condisciple 541
condition *state* 7
  modification 469
  supposition 514
  term 770
  repute 873
  rank 875
  in – *plump* 192
  in good – 648
  on – 770
  in perfect – **650**

physical – 316
conditional 8
conditions 770
condolence 914, 915
condone 918
condottiere
  traveller 268
  fighter 726
conduce
  contribute 153
  tend 176
  concur 178
  avail 644
conducive 631
conduct
  transfer 270
  music 416
  procedure 692
  lead 693
  safe –
    passport 631
  safety 664
  – a funeral 363
  – an inquiry 461
  – to 278
conduction 264
conductor 269
  conveyer 271
  director 694
  lightning – 666
conduit 350
conduplicate 89
condyle 250
cone *round* 249
  pointed 253
confabulation 588
confection 396
  confectionary 396
confectioner 637
confederacy
  co-operation 709
  party 712
confederate 711
confer *advise* 695
  give 784
  – benefit 648
  – power 157
  – privilege 760
  – right 924
  – with 588
conference [*see*
  confer]
  council 696
confess *assent* 488
  avow 529
  penitence 950,
  998
  – and avoid 937
confession [*see*
  confess]
  auricular – 998
  – of faith 983
confessional 1000
confessions
  biography 594
confessor 996
confidant 711
confidante
  servant 746
  friend 890
confidence
  trust 484
  hope 858
  courage 861
  in – 528
  – trick 545
confident 535
configuration 240

confine
  region 182
  circumscribe 229
  limit 231, 233
  imprison 751
confined
  narrow judgment
  481
  ill 655
confinement
  childbed 161
confines of
  on the – 197
confirm
  corroborate 467
  assent 488
  consent 762
  compact 769
  rite 998
confirmed 150
  – habit 613
confiscate *take* 789
  condemn 971
  penalty 974
confiture 396
conflagration 382,
  384
conflexure 245
conflict
  opposition 708
  discord 713
  contention 720
conflicting
  contrary 14
  counteracting 179
  – evidence 468
confluence
  junction 43
  convergence 290
  river 348
conflux
  assemblage 72
  convergence 290
conform *assent* 488
  – to rule 494
conformable 23,
  178
conformation 54,
  240
conformity 82, 178
confound
  disorder 61
  destroy 162
  not discriminate
  465a
  perplex 475
  defeat 731
  astonish 870
  curse 908
confounded
  great 31
  bad 649
confraternity
  party 712
  friendship 888
confrère
  colleague 711
  friend 890
confrication 331
confront *face* 234
  compare 464
  oppose 708
  resist 719
  – danger 861
  – witnesses 467
confucianism 984
Confucius 986
confuse *derange* 61

perplex 458
obscure 519
not discriminate
  465a
abash 879
confused *disorder*
  59
  invisible 447
  uncertain 475
  style 571
confusion
  [*see confuse*]
  – seize 908
  – of tongues 560,
  563
  – of vision 443
  – worse-con-
  founded 59
confutation 479
congé 293, 756
  – d'élire 995
congeal *dense* 321
  cold 385
congeneric
  similar 17
  included 76
congenial
  related 9
  agreeing 23
  concord 714
  love 897
congenital 5, 820
congeries 72
congestion 641
conglaciation 385
conglobation 72
conglomerate
  cohere 46
  assemblage 72
  council 696
  dense 321
conglutinate 46
congratulate 896
  – oneself 838
congratulation 896
congregation
  assemblage 72
  worshippers 990
  laity 997
Congregationalist
  984
congress
  assembly 72
  convergence 290
  conference 588
  council 696
Congressional
  Medal 733
Congressional
  Record 551
congreve *fuel* 382
  – rocket 727
congruous
  agreeing 23
  (*expedient* 646)
conical *round* 249
  pointed 253
conjecture 475, 514
conjoin 43
conjoint 48
conjointly 37
conjugal 903
conjugate
  words 562
  grammar 567
  – in all its tenses
  &c. 104
conjugation

junction 43
pair 89
phase 144
grammar 567
conjunction 43
  in – with 37
conjuncture
  contingency 8
  occasion 134
conjure *deceive* 545
  entreat 765
  sorcery 992
  name to – with
  873
  – up *recall* 505
  – up a vision 505
conjuror
  deceiver 548
  sorcerer 994
connaître les des-
  sous des cartes
  490
connate
  intrinsic 5
  kindred 11
  cause 153
connatural
  uniform 16
  similar 17
connect *relate* 9
  link 43
connection
  [*see connect*]
  kin 11
  in – with 9
connections
  cards 840
connective 45
conned, well – 490
connive
  overlook 460
  co-operate 709
  allow 760
connoisseur
  critic 480
  scholar 492
  taste 850
connotate 550
connote 516, 550
  imply 526
connubial 903
connuted 9
conoscente 850
conquer 731
conquered
  (*failure* 732)
conquering hero
  comes 883
conqueror 731
consanguinity 11
consciarecti, mens –
  pride 878
  innocence 946
conscience
  knowledge 490
  moral sense 926
  in all – *great* 31
  affirmation 535
  awakened – 950
  qualms of – 603
  clear – 946
  stricken – 950
  tender – 926
  honor 939
conscientious 926
  scrupulous 939
  – objector 489
conscious

intuitive 450
knowledge 490
– of disgrace 874
– of glory 873
conscript 726
conscription 744
consecrate *use* 677
  dedicate 873
  sanctify 987
  holy orders 995
consecration
  rite 998
consectory 478
  – reasoning 476
consecution 63
consecutive
  following 63
  continuous 69
  – fifth 414
consecutively
  slowly 275
consensus 488
  – of opinion 23
consent *assent* 488
  compliance 762
  with one – 178
consentaneous
  agreeing 23
  (*expedient* 646)
consequence
  event 151
  effect 154
  importance 642
  in – 478
  of no – 643
  take the –s 154
consequent 63
consequential
  deducible 478
  arrogant 878
consequently
  reasoning 476
  effect 154
conservation
  permanence 141
  storage 636
  preservation 670
conservatism 141,
  670
conservative 141,
  712
  – policy 681
conservatoire 542
conservator
  of the peace 967
conservatory
  receptacle 191
  floriculture 371
  furnace 386
  store 636
conserve 396, 636
consider *think* 451
  attend to 457
  examine 461
  adjudge 480
  believe 484
considerable
  in degree 31
  in size 192
  important 642
considerate
  careful 459
  judicious 498
  benevolent 906
consideration
  purchase money
  147
  thought 451

contrition
  abrasion 331
  regret 833
  penitence 950
contrivance 633
contrive
  produce 161
  plan 626
  – to succeed in 731
contriving
  cunning 702
control
  power 157
  influence 175
  regulate 693
  authority 737
  restrain 751
  board of – 696
  under –
  obedience 743
  subjection 749
controller of
  currency 801
controls 273, 693
controversial
  discussion 476
  discordant 713
controversialist
  476, 726
controversy
  disagreement 24
  discussion 476
  debate 588
  contention 720
controvert
  deny 536
controvertible
  uncertain 475
  debatable 476
  untrue 495
contumacy
  obstinacy 606
  disobedience 742
contumely
  arrogance 885
  rudeness 895
  disrespect 929
  scorn 930
  reproach 932
contund 330
contuse 330
conundrum pun
  520
  riddle 533
  wit 842
convalescence 654,
  660
convection 270
convenance
  mariage de – 903
convene 72
conveniences 632
convenient 646, 705
convent 1000
conventicle
  assembly 72
  council 696
  chapel 1000
convention
  agreement 23
  assembly 72
  rule 80
  council 696
  precept 697
  treaty of peace
  723
  compact 769

–s of society 852
conventional 82,
  613
conventual 996,
  1000
convergence 290
convergent 286
conversable
  talk 588
  sociable 892
conversant
  know 490
  skilful 698
conversation 588
conversational
  loquacious 584
  interlocution 588
  sociable 892
conversazione 588,
  892
converse
  reverse 14
  talk 588
conversely 468
conversion 144
  trover and – 964
convert
  change to 140, 144
  opinion 484
  tergiversation 607
  religion 987
  – to use 677
convertible 13, 27
  – terms 522
convexity 250
convey
  transfer 270
  mean 516
  assign 783
  – away 791
  – the knowledge
  of 527
conveyance
  [see convey]
  vehicle 272
conveyancer 968
conveyancing 783
convict
  convince 484
  condemned 949
  condemn 971
convicted, self –
  950
conviction
  confutation 479
  belief 484
  prove guilty 971
convince
  belief 484
  confute 479
  teach 537
convivial 892
convocate 72
convocation
  council 696
  church 995
convoke 72
convolution
  coil 248
  rotation 312
convoy
  accompany 88
  transfer 270
  guard 664
  escort 753
convulse
  derange 61

violent 173
  agitate 315
  bodily pain 378
  mental pain 830
convulsed with
  – laughter 838
  – rage 900
convulsion
  [see convulse]
  disorder 59
  revolution 146
  in –s 325
coo 412
cook heat 384
  falsify 544
  improve 658
  prepare 673
  servant 746
too many –s 699
  – accounts 811
cool moderate 174
  cold 383
  refrigerate 385
  grey 432
  dissuade 616
  cautious 864
  indifferent 866
  unamazed 871
  unfriendly 889
  discourteous 895
look – upon
  unsocial 893
take –ly 826
  – down 826
  – one's heels
  kept waiting 133
  inaction 681
cooler 387
coolheaded
  judicious 498
  unexcitable 826
coolie
  bearer 271
  military 726
coolness
  insensibility 823
  estrangement 898
coon-can 840
coop above 189
  restrain 751
  prison 752
co-operation
  physical 178
  voluntary 709
  participation 778
co-operator 690, 711
co-optation 609
co-ordinate
  equal 27
  arrange 60
  measure 466
cootie 653
cop 664
copal 356a
coparcener 778
copartner
  accompanying 88
  participator 778
  associate 890
copartnership
  co-operation 709
  party 712
cope equal 27
  oppose 708
  contend 720
  canonicals 999
copia verborum

diffuse 573
  loquacious 584
coping stone
  top 210
  completion 729
copious
  diffuse style 573
  abundant 639
coportion 778
copper money 800
  policeman 664
copper-colored
  433, 439
copper-plate
  engraving 558
  writing 590
coppice 367
coprolite 653
copse 367
copula 45
copulation 43
copy
  imitate 19
  facsimile 21
  prototype 22
  news 532
  record 551
  represent 554
  write 590
  for the press 591
  plan 626
  – book 22
copyhold 780
copyist
  imitator 19
  artist 559
  writer 590
copyright 780
coquet lie 544
  change the mind
  607
  affected 855
  endearment 902
  flattery 933
  – with
  irresolute 605
coquette
  affected 854, 855
  flirt 897
coquillage 847
coracle 273
coral 847
  – reef 667
coram judice
  jurisdiction 965
  lawsuit 969
cor Anglais 417
corbeille 191
corbel 215
cord tie 45
  filament 205
cordage 45
cordated 245
cordial
  pleasure 377
  dram 392
  willing 602
  remedy 662
  feeling 821
  grateful 829
  friendly 888
  courteous 894
cordiform 245
cordite 727
cordon
  inclosure 232
  circularity 247

decoration 877
  – bleu 733, 746
  – sanitaire
  safety 664
  preservation 670
corduroy 259
cordwainer
  shoemaker 225
  artificer 690
core gist 5
  source 153
  center 222
  gist 642
true to the – 939
coriaceous 327
Corinthian 850
co-rival
  [see corrival]
cork plug 263
  lightness 320
  – jacket 666
  – up close 261
  restrain 751
corking pin 45
corkscrew
  spiral 248
  perforator 262
  circuition 311
cormorant
  desire 865
  gluttony 957
corn
  projection 250
Cornaro 953
cornea 441
corned 959
cornelian 847
corneous 323
corner place 182
  receptacle 191
  angle 244
  monopoly 777
  – creep into a –
  893
in a dark – 528
  drive into a – 706
  push into a – 874
  rub off –s 82
  – turn a – 311
turn the – 658
  – stone
  support 215
  importance 642
  defence 717
cornet music 417
  officer 745
cornice 210
corniculate 253
cornification 323
Cornish hug 545
corno 417
cornopean 417
cornucopia 639
cornute
  projecting 250
  sharp 253
corollary
  adjunct 39
  deduction 480
corona 247
coronach 839
coronation
  enthronement 755
  celebration 883
coroner 363, 965
  –'s jury 967
coronet hoop 247

insignia 747
title 877
corporal
 corporeal 316
 officer 745
corporate 43
 – body 712
corporation
 bulk 192
 convex 250
 association 712
 jurisdiction 965
corporeal 3, 316, 364
 – hereditaments 780
corporeity 316
corps assemblage 72
 troops 726
à – perdu
 haste 684
 rash 863
 – de reserve 636
corpse 362
corpulence 192
corpus 316
 – Christi 998
 – delicti
 guilt 947
 lawsuit 969
 – juris
 precept 697
 law 963
corpuscle
 small 32
 little 193
corradiation
 focus 74
 convergence 290
corral 232, 370
correct
 orderly 58
 true 494
 inform 527
 disclose 529
 improve 658
 repair 660
 due 924
 censure 932
 honorable 939
 virtuous 944
 punish 972
 – ear 416, 418
 – memory 505
 – reasoning 476
 – style
 grammatical 567
 elegant 578
correction
 [see correct]
 house of – 752
 under – 879
corrective 662
corregidor 745
correlation
 relation 9
 reciprocity 12
correspondence
 correlation 12
 similarity 17
 agreement 23
 writing 592
 – course 537
correspondent
 messenger 534
 journalist 593
 consignee 758
corresponding

similar 17
 agreeing 23
corridor region 181
 place 191
 passage 627
 – train 272
corrigendum 495
corrigible 658
corrival 726
corrivalry 720
corrivation 348
corroborant 662
corroboration
 evidence 467
 assent 488
corrode burn 384
 erode 659
 afflict 830
corrosive
 [see corrode]
 acrid 171
 destructive 649
 – sublimate 663
corrugate
 derange 61
 constrict 195
 roughen 256
 rumple 258
 furrow 259
corruption
 decomposition 49
 neology 563
 foulness 653
 disease 655
 deterioration 659
 improbity 940
 vice 945
corrupting
 noxious 649
corsage 225
corsair 273, 792
corse 362
corselet 225
corset 225
corso 728
cortège
 adjunct 39
 continuity 69
 accompaniment 88
 journey 266
 suite 746
cortes 696
cortex
 cortical 223
coruscate 420
corvette 273, 726
corybantic 503
coryphée 599
Corypheus
 teacher 540
 director 694
coscinomancy 511
cosey 892
cosignificative 522
cosine 217
cosmetic
 remedy 662
 ornament 847
cosmic 318
cosmogony &c. 318
cosmopolitan
 abode 189
 mankind 372
 philanthropic 910
 sociality 892
cosmorama 448
cosmos 60, 318

Cossack 726
cosset
 darling 899
 caress 902
cost 812
 pay –s 807
 to one's –
 evil 619
 badness 649
 – what it may 604
 – price 815
costermonger 797
costless 815
costly 814
costive
 taciturn 585
costume 225
 theatrical – 599
costumé 225
 bal – 840
costumier 225
 theatrical 599
cosy snug 377
 sociable 892
cot abode 189
 bed 215
cote 189
cotenancy 778
coterie class 75
 junto 712
 society 892
coterminous 120
cothurnus 599
cotillon 840
cottage 189
 – piano 417
cottager 188
cotter 188
cotton 205
 – seed oil 356
couch lie 213
 bed 215
 sloop 308
 lurk 528
 – one's lance 720
 – in terms 566
couchant 213
couci-couci 651
cough 349
 churchyard – 655
couleur de rose
 good 648
 prosperity 734
 view en – 836
coulisses 599
coulter 253
council
 senate 696
 church 995
 hold a – 695
 – of education 542
 – school 542
councillor 696
counsel
 advice 695
 lawyer 968
 keep one's own – 528
 take – think 451
 inquire 461
 be advised 695
count clause 51
 item 79
 compute 85
 estimate 480
 lord 875
 – one's chickens before they are

hatched 858, 863
 – the cost 864
 – upon
 believe 484
 expect 507
 to be –ed on one's fingers 103
countenance
 face 234
 appearance 448
 favor 707
 approve 931
 keep in –
 conform 82
 induce 615
 encourage 861
 vindicate 937
 keep one's –
 brook 826
 not laugh 837
 out of –
 abashed 879
 put out of – 874
 stare out of – 885
 – falling
 disappointment 509
 dejection 837
counter contrary 14
 number 84
 table 215
 stern 235
 token 550
 shop-board 799
 over the –
 barter 794
 buy 795
 sell 796
 run – 179
 – to 708
counteract
 compensate 30
 physically 179
 hinder 706
 voluntarily 708
counteraction 14, 179
counterbalance 30
counterblast
 counteract 179
 retaliate 718
countercharge 462
counterchange
 correlation 12
 interchange 148
countercharm 993
countercheck
 mark 550
 hindrance 706
counterclaim 30
counter-evidence 468
counterfeit
 imitate 19
 copy 21
 simulate 544
 sham 545
 coinage 792
counterfoil 550
countermand 756
countermarch 266, 283
countermark 550
countermine
 plan 626
 oppose 708
countermotion 283

counterorder 756
counterpane 223
counterpart
 match 17
 copy 21
 reverse 237
counterplot
 plan 626
 oppose 708
 retaliate 718
counterpoint 415
counterpoise
 compensate 30
 weight 319
 hinder 706
counter-poison 662
counterpole 14
counter-project 718
counter-protest 468
counter-revolution 146
counterscarp 717
countersign
 evidence 467
 assent 488
 mark 550
counterstroke 718
countervail
 outweigh 28
 compensate 30
 evidence 468
counterwork 708
countess 875
counting-house 799
countless 105
countrified 189
 vulgar 851
country
 region 181
 abode 189
 rural 371
 authority 737
 love of – 910
country-dance 840
countryman
 commonalty 876
 friend 890
county 181
 – seat 189
 – town 189
 – school 542
 – council 696
 – court 966
coup
 instantaneous 113
 action 680
 – de bec
 attack 716
 censure 932
 – d'épée dans l'eau 645
 – d'essai 675
 – d'état
 revolution 146
 plan 626
 action 680
 lawless 964
 – de grâce
 end 67
 death-blow 361
 completion 729
 punishment 972
 – de main
 violence 173
 action 680
 attack 716
 – de maître
 excellent 648

642
best 648
- color
white 430
yellow 436
- of the jest 842
creamy 352
crease 258
create *cause* 153
produce 161
imagine 515
created being 366
creation
[see create]
effect 154
world 318
Creator 976
creator 164
creature *thing* 3
effect 154
animal 366
man 372
parasite 711
slave 746
- comforts
food 298
pleasure 377
crèche 542
credat Judaeus
Apella
unbelief 485
absurdity 497
credence *belief* 484
church 1000
credenda 484
credential 467
credible
possible 470
probable 472
belief 484
credit *belief* 484
influence 737
pecuniary 805
account 811
repute 873
approbation 931
desert 944
to one's -
property 780
crédit mobilier 802
creditable *right* 924
creditor 805
credo quia
impossibile 486
credulity 486
credulous person
dupe 547
creed *belief* 484
theology 983
Apostles' - 983a
creek *interval* 198
water 343
creel 191
creep *crawl* 275
tingle 380
(inactivity 683)
- in 294
- into a corner 893
- into the good
graces of 933
- out 529
- upon one 508
- with
multitude 102
redundance 641
creeper 367
creeping
sensation 380

- thing 366
creese 727
cremation
of corpses 363
burning 384
crematorium 363,
386
crematory 386
creme de la crème
648
Cremona 417
crenate 257
crenele 257
crenelle 257
crenulate 257
creole 57
crêpe 248, 839
crepidam, ultra -
471
crepitation 406
crepuscule
dawn 125
dusk 422
crescendo
increase 35
musical 415
crescent
growing 35
street 189
curve 245
cresset 423, 550
crest *supremacy* 33
summit 210
pointed 253
tuft 256
sign 550
armorial 877
pride 878
on the - 33
crest-fallen
dejected 837
humble 879
crevasse 198, 667
crevice 198
crew *assemblage* 72
inhabitants 188
mariners 269
party 712
crib *bed* 215
key 522
granary 636
steal 791
parsimony 819
cribbage 840
cribbed, confined,
cabined - 751
cribble 260
cribriform 260
Crichton,
Admirable -
scholar 492
perfect 650
proficient 700
crick *pain* 378
cricket *game* 840
not - 940
- ground 213
crier 534
send round the -
531
crim. con. 961
crime 945, 947
criminal 923, 945
culprit 949
- law 963
court of - appeal
966
criminality 947
criminate 938

crimp *crinkle* 248
notch 257
brittle 328
deceiver 548
take 789
steal 791
crimple 258
crimson 434, 821
cringe *submit* 725
subject 749
servility 886
crinite 256
crinkle *angle* 244
convolution 248
roughen 256
fold 258
crinoline 225
cripple *disable* 158
weaken 160
injure 659
crippled
disease 655
crisis
conjuncture 8
present time 118
opportunity 134
event 151
strait 704
excitement 824
bring to a - 604
come to a - 729
crisp *rumpled* 248
rough 256
brittle 328
style 572
Crispin 225
criss-cross 219
cristallomantia 511
criterion *test* 463
evidence 467
indication 550
crithomancy 511
critic *judge* 480
taste 850
detractor 936
critical
contingent 8
opportune 134
discriminating
465
important 642
dangerous 665
difficult 704
censorious 932
criticism
judgment 480
dissertation 595
disapprobation
932
detraction 934
critique
[see criticism]
croak *cry* 412
hoarseness 581
stammer 583
warning 668
discontent 832
lament 839
croaker 832, 837
Croat 726
crochet 847
crock 191
crockery 384
crocodile tears 544
crocus *yellow* 436
Croesus 803
croft 189, 232
Croix de Guerre 733

cromlech 363, 551
crone *veteran* 130
fool 501
crony *friend* 890
favourite 899
crook *curve* 245
deviation 279
thief 792
crooked
sloping 217
distorted 243
angular 244
latent 526
crafty 702
ugly 846
dishonorable 940
- path 704
- temper 901
- ways 279
croon 580
crop
stomach 191
harvest 154
shorten 201
eat 298
vegetable 367
store 636
gather 775
take 789
second - 167, 775
- out *visible* 446
disclose 529
- up *begin* 66
take place 151
reproduction 163
cropper *fall* 306
croquet *game* 840
croquette 298
crosier 747, 999
cross *mix* 41
across 219
pass 302
grave 363
oppose 708
failure 732
disaster 735
refuse 764
pain 830
decoration 877
fretful 901
punishment 975
rites 998
fiery - 722
proclaim at the -
roads 531
red - 662
-ed bayonets 708
- breed 63
- cut 628
- fire *interchange*
148
difficulty 704
opposition 708
attack 716
-ed in love 898
- the mind 451
- the path of 706
- and pile 621
- purposes 14
disorder 59
error 495
misinterpret 523
unskilful 699
difficulty 704 /
opposition 708
discord 713
- oneself 998

- questions
inquiry 461
discord 713
game 840
- road 627
- the Rubicon 609
- sea 348
- swords 722
crossbow 727
cross-examine 461
cross-grained 256
obstinate 606
sulky 901a
crossing 219
- sweeper 652
crosspatch 895
crossroads 8
cross-word puzzle
533
crotch 244
crotchet
eccentric 83
music 413
misjudgment 481
obstinacy 606
caprice 608
crouch *lower* 207
stoop 308
fear 860
servile 886
- before 725
croup 235
croupier 694
crow *cry* 412
black 431
rejoice 838
boast 884
pluck a - with 932
as the - flies 278
-'s foot (*age*) 128
-'s nest 210
- to pluck
discord 713
anger 900
accuse 938
crowbar 633
crowd 72
multitude 102
close 197
redundance 641
party 712
vulgar 876
in the - *mixed* 41
madding - 682
crown *top* 210
circle 247
complete 729
trophy 733
scepter 747
install 755
decoration 877
reward 973
to - all 33, 642
-ed head 745
- with laurel 873
- with success 731
crowning
[see crown]
superior 33
end 67
- point 210
cruche à l'eau &c.
tant va la - 735
crucial
crossing 219
proof 478
- test 463
cruciate

physical pain 378
mental pain 830
crucible
  dish 191
  conversion 144
  furnace 386
  experiment 463
  laboratory 691
  put into the – 163
crucifix 219, 998
crucifixion 828
cruciform 219
crucify
  physical torture 378
  mental agony 830
  execution 972
crucis, experimen-
  tum – 463
crude color 428
  – style 579
  unprepared 674
cruel
  painful 830
  inhuman 907
  – to be kind 914
cruelly much 31
cruet 191
cruise
  vessel 191
  navigation 267
cruiser 726
cruising 267
crumb small 32
  powder 330
  – of comfort 834
crumble
  decrease 36
  weak 160
  destruction 162
  brittle 328
  pulverize 330
  spoil 659
  – into dust
  decompose 49
  – under one's feet
  735
crumbling
  [see crumble]
  dangerous 665
crumenal 800
crump
  distorted 243
  curved 245
crumple
  ruffle 256
  fold 258
  – up destroy 162
  crush 195
crunch
  shatter 44
  chew 298
  pulverize 330
crupper 235
crusade 722
crush crowd 72
  destroy 162
  compress 195
  pulverize 330
  humble 879
  – under an iron
  heel 739
  – one's hopes
  disappoint 509
  hopeless 859
crushed 828
crushing 830
crust 223

crustacean 366
crusty 895, 901a
crutch
  support 215
  angle 244
  –ed Friars 996
crux 219, 704
  – criticorum 533
cry human 411
  animal 412
  publish 531, 532
  call 550
  voice 580
  vogue 613
  weep 839
  far – to 196
  full – loud 404
  raise a – 550
  – aloud
  implore 765
  – out against
  dissuade 616
  censure 932
  – down 932, 934
  – for 865
  – before hurt 839
  – for joy 838
  – you mercy
  deprecate 766
  pity 914
  forgive 918
  – shame 932
  – to beseech 765
  – up 931
  – for vengeance
  923
  – wolf false 544
  alarm 669
  – and little wool
  overrate 482
  boast 884
  disappoint 509
crying [see cry]
  urgent 630
  weary 841
  – evil 619
  – shame 874
  – sin 945
crypt cell 191
  grave 363
  ambush 530
  altar 1000
cryptic 475, 528
cryptography
  hidden 528
  writing 590
crystal hard 323
  transparent 425
  snow – 383
  – gazer 513
  – gazing 511, 992
  – oil 356
  clear as – 519
crystalline
  dense 321
  hard 323
  transparent 425
crystallization 321,
  323
csako 225, 717
cub young 129
  vulgar 851
  clown 876
  unlicked – 241
cubby-hole 191
cube
  three dimensions
  92, 93

form 244
cubicle 191
cubist 556
cubit 200
cucking stool 975
cuckold 905
cuckoldom 961
cuckoo
  imitation 19
  repetition 104
  sound 407
  cry 412
cuddle 196, 902
cudgel beat 276
  weapon 727
  punish 975
  take up the –s
  aid 707
  attack 716
  contention 720
  – one's brains
  think 451
  imagine 515
cue hint 527
  watchword 550
  plea 617
  rôle 625
  take one's – from
  695
  in proper – 698
cuff sleeve 225
  blow 276
  punishment 972
cui bono 644, 645
cuique voluptas
  sui – 865
cuirass 717
cuirassier 726
cuisine 298
  batterie de – 957
culbute
  inversion 218
  fall 306
cul-de-lampe
  engraving 558
  ornament 847
cul-de-sac
  concave 252
  closed 261
  difficulty 704
culinary 298
  – art 673
cull dupe 547
  choose 609
  take 789
cullender 260
cullibility 486
cullion 949
cully deceive 545,
  547
culm 388
culminate
  maximum 33
  height 206
  top 210
  complete 729
culpability vice 945
  guilt 947
culprit 949
cult 983
cultivate till 365,
  371
  sharpen 375
  improve 658
  prepare 673
  aid 707
cultivated
  courteous 894

  – taste 850
cultivator 371
culture
  knowledge 490
  improvement 658
  taste 850
  politeness 894
culverin 727
culvert 350
cum multis aliis 37,
  102
cumber load 319
  obstruct 706
cumbersome
  incommodious
  647
  disagreeable 830
cummerbund 225
cumulative 72
  increasing 35
  assembled 72
  – evidence 467
  – vote 609
cumulus 353
cunctando restituit
  rem 681
cunctation 133
cuneiform 244
  – character 590
cunning
  prepense 611
  sagacious 698
  artful 702
  – fellow 700
  – man 994
cup vessel 191
  hollow 252
  beverage 298
  remedy 662
  trophy 733
  tipple 959
  between – and lip
  111
  in one's –s 959
  – that cheers &c.
  298
  – of humiliation
  879
  dash the – from
  one's lips 509
  – too low 837
cupbearer 746
cupboard 191
cupellation 384
Cupid beauty 845
  love 897
  gods 979
cupidity
  avarice 819
  desire 865
cupola height 206
  roof 223
  dome 250
cup-tossing 621
cur dog 366
  coward 862
  sneak 949
curable 658, 660,
  662
curacy 995
curare 663
curate 996
curative 660
curator 694, 758
curb moderate 174
  slacken 275
  dissuade 616
  restrain 751

  shackle 752
curb exchange 621
curbstone 233
curd density 321
  pulp 354
  (cohere 46)
curdle condense 321
  (cohere 46)
  make the blood –
  830
curdled 352
cure reinstate 660
  remedy 662
  preserve 670
  benefice 995
curé 996
cureless 859
curfew 126
curia 966
curio 847
curiosa felicitas 698
curiosity
  unconformity 83
  inquiring 455
  phenomenon 872
curious
  exceptional 83
  inquisitive 455
  true 494
  beautiful 845
  desirous 865
curiously very 31
curl bend 245
  convolution 248
  hair 256
  cockle up 258
  badge 747
  – up one's lip 930
curling game 840
curmudgeon
  miser 819
  plebeian 876
currency
  publicity 531
  money 800
current existing 1
  usual 78
  present 118
  happening 151
  flow 264
  of water 348
  of air 349
  rife 531, 532
  language 560
  habit 613
  danger 667
  account – 811
  against the – 708
  go with the – 82
  pass –
  believed 484
  fashion 852
  stem the – 708
  – belief 488
  – of events 151
  – of ideas 451
  – of time 109
currente calamo
  590
curricle 272
curriculum 537
curry food 298
  rub 331
  condiment 392,
  393
  – favour with
  love 897
  flatter 933

curry-comb 370
curse bane 663
  adversity 735
  painful 830
  malediction 908
cursed bad 649
cursitor 968
cursive 590
cursory
  transient 111
  inattentive 458
  hasty 684
take a – view of 457
  neglect 460
curst 901a
curt short 201
  concise 572
  taciturn 585
curtail retrench 38
  shorten 201
  -ed of its fair portions
  distorted 243
  ugly 846
curtain 223
  shade 424
  hide 528, 530
  theatre 599
  fortification 717
  behind the –
  invisible 447
  inquiry 461
  knowledge 490
  close the – 528
  raise the – 529
  rising of the – 448
  – lecture 932
  – raiser 66, 599
curtsy
  stoop 308, 314
  submit 725
  polite 894
curule 696
curvature 245
curvet leap 309
  turn 311
  oscillate 314
  agitate 315
curvilinear 245
  – motion 311
cushion pillow 215
  soft 324
  relief 834
cushy 829
cusp angle 244
  sharp 253
cuspidor 191
cuss 908
custard 298
custodes? quis custodiet – 459
custodian 753
custody safe 664
  captive 751
  retention 781
.n – prisoner 754
  accused 938
take into – 751
custom old 124
  habit 613
  barter 794
  sale 796
  tax 812
  fashion 852
  – honored in breach 614
customary

[age custom]
  regular 80
customer 795
custom-house 799
  – officer 965
custos 753
  – rotulorum 553
cut divide 44
  bit 51
  discontinuity 70
  interval 198
  curtail 201
  layer 204
  form 240
  notch 257
  blow 276
  eject 297
  reap 371
  physical pain 378
  cold 385
  neglect 460
  carve 557
  engraving 558
  road 627
  attack 716
  portion 786
  affect 824
  mental pain 830
  dance step 840
  decline acquaintance 893
  discourtesy 895
  tipsy 959
  – short 628
  unkindest – of all
  pain 828
  malevolence 907
  – across 302
  – adrift 44
  – along 274
  have a – at 716
  – away 274
  – a whetstone with a razor
  sophistry 477
  waste 638
  misuse 679
  – both ways 468
  – capers 309
  – according to cloth
  economy 817
  caution 864
  – and come again
  repeat 104
  enough 639
  – dead 893
  – direct 893
  – down destroy 162
  shorten 201
  fell 308
  kill 361
  – down expenses 817
  – and dried
  arranged 60
  prepared 673
  – a figure
  appearance 448
  fashion 852
  repute 873
  display 882
  – the first turf 66
  – the ground from under one
  confute 479
  hinder 706
  – to the heart 824,

830
  – ice with influence 175
  – of one's jib 448
  – jokes 842
  – the knot 705
  – off subduct 38
  disjoin 44
  kill 361
  impede 706
  bereft 776
  secluded 893
  – off with a shilling 789
  – open 260
  – out surpass 33
  stop 142
  substitute 147
  plan 626
  – out for 698
  – out work
  prepare 673
  direct 693
  – to pieces
  destroy 162
  kill 361
  – a poor figure 874
  – to the quick 830
  – up root and branch 162
  – up rough 900
  – and run 274
  depart 293
  escape 623
  – short stop 142
  destroy 162
  shorten 201
  silence 581
  – one's stick
  depart 283
  avoid 623
  – one's own throat 699
  – and thrust 716
  – in two 91
  – up divide 44
  destroy 162
  pained 828
  give pain 830
  discontented 832
  dejected 837
  censure 932
  what one will – up for 780
  – one's way through 302
cutaneous 223
cute 698
cuticle 223
cutlass 727
cutlery 253
cut-purse 792
cutter 273
cut-throat
  killer 361
  evil-doer 913
cutting sharp 253
  cold 383
  path 627
  affecting 821
  painful 830
  reproachful 932
cuttings
  excerpta 596
  selections 609
cutty stool 950
cwt. 98, 319
cyanogen 438

cyanide of potassium poison 663
cycle time 106
  period 138
  circle 247
  ride 266
  vehicle 272
  – car 272
cyclist 268
cycloid 247
cyclometer 200
cyclone
  rotation 312
  wind 349
Cyclopean
  strong 159
  huge 192
cyclopedia
  knowledge 490
  book 593
Cyclops
  monster 83
  mighty 159
  huge 192
  dupe 547
cygne
  chant du – 360
  – noir 650
cylindric 249
cyma 847
cymbal 417
cymbalo 417
cymophanous 440
cynic
  misanthrope 911
  detractor 936
  ascetic 955
  closet – 893
cynical
  contemptuous 930
  censorious 932
  detracting 934
cynicism
  discourtesy 895
  contempt 930
cynosure sign 550
  direction 693
  wonder 870
  repute 873
Cynthia of the minute 149
cypher [see cipher]
cypress
  interment 363
  mourning 839
Cyprian 962
cyst 191
czar 745

D

da capo 104
dab small 32
  paint 223
  slap 276
  clever 700
dabble water 337
  dirty 653
  meddle 682
  fribble 683
dabbled wet 339
dabbler 493
dachshund 366
dacoit 792
dactyl 597
dactylogram 467
dactyliomancy 511

dactylonomy
  numeration 85
  symbol 550
dad 166
daddy 166
dado 211
daedal
  variegated 440
daedalion
  convoluted 248
  artistic 698
daft 503
dagger 727
  look -s anger 900
  threat 909
  air drawn – 515
  plant – in breast
  give pain 830
  speak –s 932
  at –s drawn
  opposed 708
  discord 713
  enmity 889
  hate 898
daggle hang 214
  dirty 653
dagoba 1000
Dagon 986
daguerreotype
  represent 554
  paint 556
dahabeah 273
Dail Eireann 696
daily
  frequent 136
  periodic 138
  – occurrence normal 82
  habitual 613
  – paper 531
dainty food 298
  savory 394
  pleasing 829
  delicate 845
  tasty 850
  fastidious 868
dairy 191, 370
  – maid 946
dais support 215
  throne 747
daisy
  fresh as a – 654
  – pied 847
dale 252
dally delay 133
  irresolute 605
  inactive 683
  amuse 840
  fondle 902
dalmatic 999
Daltonism 443
dam parent 166
  close 261
  pond 343
  obstruct 706
damage evil 619
  injure, spoil 659
  price 812
damages 974
damascene 440
damask 434
dame
  woman 374
  teacher 540
  lady 875
damn
  malediction 908
  condemn 971

- to insensible 823
deafen loud 404
deafness 419
deal much 31
 arrange 60
 bargain 768
 allot 786
- a blow
 injure 659
 attack 716
 punish 972
- board 323
- in 794
- out scatter 73
 give 784
- with
 treat of 595
 handle 692
 barter 794
dealer 797
dealings action 680
have - with
 trade 794
 friendly 888
dean 128, 694, 996
deanery office 995
 house 1000
dear
 high-priced 814
 loved 897
 favorite 899
O - ! lament 839
- at any price 646
- me wonder 870
pay - for whistle 647
dearest foe 936
dearness 814
dearth 640
- of ideas 843
death 360
house of - 363
in at the -
 arrive 292
 kill 361
 persevere 604a
pale as -
 colorless 429
 fear 860
put to - 361, 972
still as - 265
violent - 361
be the - of one
 amuse 480
-'s head 837
- in the pot
 unhealthy 657
 hidden danger 667
deathbed repentance 950
death-blow
 end 67
 killing 361
 failure 732
death-house 752
deathless
 perpetual 112
 fame 873
deathlike
 silent 403
 hideous 846
death-song 839
death-struggle 720
death-warrant 971
death-watch 668
débâcle 145
 destruction 162

downfall 306
 torrent 348
debar hinder 706
 restrain 751
 prohibit 761
debark 292
debase depress 308
 foul 653
 deteriorate 659
 degrade 874
debased
 lowered 207
 dishonored 940
debate reason 476
 talk 588
 hesitate 605
 dispute 720
debatable 475
debauch
 spoil 659
 intemperance 954
 impurity 961
debauchee 962
debenture
 security 771
 money 800
 credit 805
debility 160
debit debt 806
 accounts 811
debtor 806
débonnaire 836
debouch 293, 295
débris
 fragments 51
 crumbled 330
 useless 645
debt 806
 out of - 803
 get out of - 807
- of nature 360
debtor 806
- and creditor 811
debunk 529
début beginning 66
 essay 675
 celebration 883
débutant
 learner 541
 drama 599
decade ten 98
 period 108
decadence 659
decagon 244
decalescence 382
decalogue 926
decamp
 go away 293
 run away 623
decant 270
decanter 191
decapitate kill 361
 punish 972
decay decrease 36
 decompose 49
 shrivel 195
 unclean 653
 disease 655
 spoil 659
 adversity 735
 natural - 360
- of memory 506
decayed
 [see decay]
 old 124
 rotten 160
decease 360
deceit

falsehood 544
 deception 545
 cunning 702
deceived
 in error 495
 duped 547
deceiver 548
 gay - 962
decelerate 275
decennary 108
decennium 108
decent
 mediocre 651
 pure 960
decentralize 49
deceptio visûs 443
deception 545
deceptive reasoning 477
decession 293
dechristianize 989
decide
 turn the scale 153
 judge 480
 choose 609
decided great 31
 ended 67
 certain 474
 resolved 604
take a - step 609
deciduous
 transitory 111
 falling 306
 spoiled 659
decies repetita placebit 829
decimal 84, 98, 99
decimate
 subtract 38
 tenth 99
 few 103
 weaken 160
 kill 361
 play havoc 659
 punish 972
decipher 522
decision
 judgment 480
 resolution 604
 intention 620
 law case 969
decisive
 certain 474
 proof 478
 commanding 741
take a - step 609
deck floor 211
 beautify 847
declaim 531, 582
- against 932
declamatory
 style 577
 speech 582
declaration
 affirmation 535
 law pleadings 969
- of faith
 belief 484
 theology 983
- of war 713
declaratory
 meaning 516
 inform 527
declare
 publish 531
declension
 [see decline]
 grammar 567
 backsliding 988

declensions 5
declination
 [see decline]
 deviation 279
 measurement 466
 rejection 610
decline decrease 36
 old 124
 weaken 160
 descent 306
 grammar 567
 be unwilling 603
 reject 610
 disease 655
 become worse 659
 adversity 735
 refuse 764
- of day 126
- of life 128
declivity slope 217
 descent 306
decoction 335, 384
decode 522
decollate 972
décolleté 226
decoloration 429
decomposition 49
deconsecrate 756
decontrol 158
décor 448, 599
decoration
 insignia 747
 ornament 847
 title 877
decorative 556
decorous
 [see decorum]
 fashionable 862
 proper 924
 respectful 928
decorticate 226
decorum
 fashion 852
 duty 926
 purity 960
décousu
 discontinuous 70
 failure 732
decoy attract 288
 deceive 545
 deceiver 548
 entice 615
decrease 36, 195
decree
 judgment 480
 order 741
 law 963, 969
decrement
 decrease 36
 thing deducted 40a
 contraction 195
decrepit old 128
 weak 158, 160
 disease 655
 decayed 659
decrepitate 406
decrescendo 36
decretal 741
decry underrate 483
 censure 932
 detract 934
decumbent 213
decuple 98
decursive 306
decurtation 201
decussation 219
dedecorous
 disreputable 874

discourteous 895
dedicate use 677
 inscribe 873
deduce deduct 38
 infer 480
deducible
 evidence 467
 proof 478
deduct retrench 38
 deprive 789
 subtract 813
deduction
 [see deduce]
 decrement 40a
 reasoning 476
deed evidence 467
 record 551
 act 680
 security 771
-s of arms 720
- without a name 947
deem 484
deemster 967
deep great 31
 profound 208
 sea 341
 sonorous 404
 cunning 702
plough the - 267
- color 428
- in debt 806
- game 702
- knowledge 490
- mourning 839
- note 408
- potations 959
- reflection 451
- sense 821
- sigh 839
- study 457
in - water 704
deepen 35
deep-dyed
 intense 171
 black 431
 vicious 945
deep-felt 821
deep-laid plan 626
deep-mouthed
 resonant 408
 bark 412
 thrilling 821
deep-musing 458
deep-read 490
deep-rooted
 stable 150
 strong 159
 belief 484
 habit 613
 affections 820
deep-sea 208
deep-seated 208, 221
deer 366
in heart a - 862
deev 980
deface
 destroy form 241
 obliterate 552
 injure 659
 render ugly 846
defalcation
 incomplete 53
 contraction 195
 shortcoming 304
 non-payment 808
defame shame 874

unnerve 158
spoil 659
vicious 945
Demosthenes 582
demotic 590
demulcent
mild 174
soothing 662
demur
disbelieve 485
dissent 489
unwilling 603
hesitate 605
without – 602
demure
grave 826
sad 837
affected 855
modest 881
demurrage 132
demurrer 969
den *abode* 189
study 191, 893
sty 653
prison 752
– of thieves 791
denary 98
denaturalize
corrupt 659
denaturalized
abnormal 83
dendriform 242, 367
dendrology 369
denial
negation 536
refusal 764
self– 953
denigrate 431
denization 748
denizen
inhabitant 188
freeman 748
–s of the air 979
–s of the day 366
Denmark, rotten in
the state of –
526
denomination
class 75
name 564
sect 712
religious – 983
denominational
dissent 489
theological 983
– education 537
denominator 84
denote
specify 79
mean 516
indicate 550
dénouement
end 67
result 154
disclosure 529
completion 729
denounce
curse 908
disapprove 932
accuse 938
dense
crowded 72
ignorant 493
density 321
dent 252, 257
dental 561
denticulated 253,
257

dentifrice 652
dentistry 662
denude 226
denuded *loss* 776
– of
insufficient 640
denunciation
[*see* denounce'
deny *dissent* 489
negative 556
refuse 764
– oneself
avoid 623
seclude 893
temperate 953
ascetic 990
Deo volente 470,
976
deobstruct 705
deodand 974
deodorize 399
clean 652
deontology 926
deoppilation 705
deorganization 61
deosculation 902
depart 293
– from
deviate 15, 279
relinquish 624
– this life 360
departed
non-existent 2
department
class 75
region 181
business 625
departure 293
new – 66
point of – 293
depend *hang* 214
contingent 475
– upon
be the effect of 154
evidence 467
trust 484
– on circumstan-
ces 475
depended on, to
be –
certain 474
reliable 484
honorable 939
dependency 777,
780
dependent
effect 154
liable 177
hanging 214
puppet 711
servant 746
subject 749
deperdition 776
dephlegmation 340
depict 554, 556
describe 594
depilation 226
depilatory 662
depletion 638, 640
deplorable *bad* 649
disastrous 735
painful 830
deplore *regret* 833
complain 839
remorse 950
deploy 194
depone 535
deponent 467

depopulate
eject 297
desert 893
deportation
removal 270
emigration 297
expulsion 972
deportment 692
depose
evidence 467
declare 535
dethrone 738, 756
deposit *place* 184
precipitate 321
store 636
security 771
payment 809
depositary 801
deposition
[*see* 'depose,
deposit]
record 551
depository 636
depôt *terminal* 292
store 636
shop 799
– *ship* 726
deprave *spoil* 659
depraved *bad* 649
vicious 945
deprecation 766
pity 914
disapprove 932
depreciation
decrease 36
underestimate 483
discount 813
cheap 815
disrespect 929
censure 932
detraction 934
accusation 938
depredation 791
depredator 792
deprehension 789
depression
lowness 207
depth 208
concavity 252
lowering 308
dejection 837
dulness 843
depressing
painful 830
deprive *subduct* 38
take 798
– of life 361
– of power 158
– of property 789
– of strength 160
deprived of 776
depth *physical* 208
mental 498
out of one's – 304
310
– bomb 727
– of misery 828
– of thought 451
– of winter 383
depurate *clean* 652
improve 658
depuratory 662
deputation 755
depute 755
deputies, chamber
of – 696
deputy 759
dequantitate 36

derangement 61
mental – 503
Derby-day 720
derelict *land* 342
danger 667
relinquish 782
outcast 893
dereliction
relinquishment
624, 782
guilt 947
– of duty 927
deride
ridicule 856
disrespect 929
contempt 930
derivation
origin 153, 154,
155
verbal 562
derive
attribute 155
deduce 480
acquire 775
income 810
dermal 223
dermatology 223
dernier
– *cri* 850
– *ressort* 601
dérobée, à la – 528
derogate
underrate 483
disparage 934
dishonor 940
– *from* 874
derogatory
shame 874
dishonor 940
derrick 307, 633
derring-do 861
dervish 996
désagrément 830
descant *music* 415
diffuseness 573
loquacity 584
dissert 595
descend *slope* 217
go down 306
– to particulars
special 79
describe 594
descendant 167
descensus Averni,
facilis – 665
descent *lineage* 166
fall 306
inheritance 775
description
kind 75
name 564
narration 594
descriptive music
415
descry 441
desecrate
misuse 679
disrespect 929
profane 988
desert
unproductive 169
empty 187
plain 344
run away 623
relinquish 624,
782
merit 944
waste sweetness

on – *air* 638
deserted
outcast 893
deserter 144, 607,
623
desertless 945
deserts 924
deserve
be entitled to 924
merit 944
– *notice* 642
– *belief* 484
désespoir, au –
dejected 837
hopeless 859
déshabillé, en –
not dressed 226
unprepared 674
homely 849
desiccate 340
desiccator 340
desiderate *need* 630
desire 865
desideratum
inquiry 461
requirement 630
desire 865
design
prototype 22
form 240
delineation 554
painting 556
intention 620
plan 626
designate
specify 79
call 564
designation 75
designed
aforethought 611
designer 164, 559
designing
cunning 702
designless 621
désillusioner 529
desinence *end* 67
discontinuance
142
despience 499
désipere in loco 840
desirable 646
desire 865
will 600
have no – for 866
desist
discontinue 142
relinquish 624
inaction 681
desk *box* 191
support 215
school 542
pulpit 1000
désobligeant 272
désoeuvré 681
desolate *alone* 87
ravage 162
afflicted 828
dejected 837
secluded 893
desolating
painful 830
désorienté 475
despair *grief* 828,
859
despatch *eject* 297
kill 361
news 532
epistle 592

nature 5
state 7
temperament 820
diatonic 413
diatribe 932
dibble
  perforator 262
  till 371
dibs *money* 800
dicacity 885
dice 156, 621
  on the – 470
dicer 621
  false as –'s oaths
  546
dichotomy
  bisect 91
  angle 244
dichroism 440
dichromatic 443
dickens 978
dicker 794
dicky 215, 225
dictaphone 553
dictate
  write 590
  enjoin 615
  advise 695
  authority 737
  command 741
dictator 694, 745
  –'s of society 852
dictatorial
  dogmatic 481
  wilful 600
  insolent 885
dictatorship 737,
  739
diction 569
dictionary
  list 86
  words 562
  book 593
dictum
  judgment 480
  maxim 496
  affirmation 535
  command 741
didactic 537
didder 383
diddie 545, 791
Diddler, Jeremy –
  792
diduction 44
die *mould* 22
  expire 360
  engraving 558
  hazard of the –
  621
  never say – 604a
not willingly let –
  670
  – away
  vanish 4
  decrease 36
  cease 142
  the – is cast 601
  – with ennui 841
  – for *desire* 865
  endearment 902
  – game 951
  – hard
  obstinate 606
  resist 719
  – in harness 143,
  604a
  – in the last ditch
  604a

– with laughter
  838
– from the mem-
  ory 536
– and make no
  sign 951
– out 2, 4
– of a rose in aro-
  matic pain 822
– in one's shoes
  972
– a violent death
  361
– hard 710, 832
dies non *never* 107
  rest 687
diet *food* 298
  council 696
  spare – 956
dietetics 662
differ 15
  discord 713
  agree to – 489
  beg to – 439
  – in opinion 489
  – toto coelo
  contrary 14
  dissimilar 18
  dissent 489
difference 15
  [*see differ*]
  numerical 84
  perception of –
  465
  split the – 774
  – engine 85
different 15
  multiform 81
  – time 119
differentia 15
differential 15, 84
  – calculus 85
differentiate 79, 465
differentiation
  calculation 85
  discrimination
  465
difficult 704
  – to please 868
difficulties
  poverty 804
  in – 806
difficulty 704
  question 461
diffide 485
diffident 860, 881
diffluent 348
diffraction 470
  – grating 445
diffuse *mix* 41
  disperse 73
  publish 531
  style 573
diffuseness 104, 573
dig *deepen* 208
  excavate 252
  till 371
  – out 461
  – the foundations
  673
  – up 455, 480a
digamy 903
digest *arrange* 60
  boil 384
  think 451
  compendium 596
  plan 626
  prepare 673

brook 826
diggings 189
dight *dress* 225
  ornament 847
digit 84
digitate 44
digitated 253
digladiation 720
dignify 873
dignitary
  clergy 996
dignity
  glory 873
  pride 878
  honour 939
dignus vindice
  nodus
  unintelligible 519
  difficulty 704
  prodigy 872
digress
  deviate 279
  style 573
digression
  circuit 629
dihedral 89
  – angle 244
diis alitur visum
  disappointment
  509
  necessity 601
dijudication 480
dike *gap* 198
  fence 232
  furrow 259
  gulf 343
  conduit 350
  defence 717
dilaceration 44
dilapidation 659
dilate
  increase 35
  swell 194
  widen 202
  rarefy 322
  expatiate 573
dilatory
  slow 275
  inactive 683
dilection 89
dilemma
  uncertain 475
  logic 476
  choice 609
  difficulty 704
dilettante 492, 850
dilettantism
  knowledge 490
diligence
  coach 272
diligent
  active 682
  – thought 457
dilly-dally
  irresolution 605
  inactivity 683
dilucidation 522
diluent 335
dilute *weaken* 160
  water 337
diluvian 124
dim *dark* 421
  faint 422
  invisible 447
  unintelligible 519
dime 800
dimension 192
dimidiate 91

diminish
  lessen 36
  contract 195
  – the nu nber 103
diminutive 32, 193
diminuendo
  decreasingly 36
  music 415
dimness 422
dimple 252, 257
dimsightedness 443
  unwise 499
din 404
  – in the ear
  repeat 104
  drum 407
  loquacity 584
dine 298
  – with Duke
  Humphrey 87
ding 408
ding-dong
  repeat 104
  chime 407
dining-car 272
dining-room 191
dingle 252
dingy *bout* 273
  dark 421, 422
  colorless 429
  black 431
  gray 432
dinner 298
  – jacket 225
  – party 892
dint *power* 157
  concavity 252
  blow 276
  by – of
  instrumentality
  631
dio, sub – 220, 338
diocesan 996
diocese 181, 995
Diogenes
  recluse 893
  cynic 911
  lantern of –
  inquiry 461
dioptrics 420
diorama *view* 448
  painting 556
diorism 465
dip *slope* 217
  concavity 252
  ladle 270
  direction 278
  insert 300
  descent 306
  plunge 310
  water 337
  candle 423
  baptize 998
  – one's hands into
  take 789
  – into
  glance at 457
  inquire 461
  learn 539
diphthong 561
diploma
  evidence 467
  commission 755
diplomacy
  artfulness 702
  mediation 724
  negotiation 769
diplomatist

messenger 534
expert 700
consignee 758
dipper 191
dipsomania
  insanity 503
  desire 865
  drunkenness 959
dipsomaniac 504
diptych 86, 551
dire *hateful* 649
  disastrous 735
  grievous 830
  fearful 860
direct
  straight 246
  teach 537
  artless 703
  command 741
  – attention to 457
  – one's course
  motion 278
  pursuit 622
  – the eyes to 441
direction
  [*see direct*]
  tendency 278
  indication 550
  management 693
  precept 697
directly *soon* 132
director
  teacher 540
  theater 599
  manager 694
  master 745
  – of the budge.
  801
directorship 737
directory *list* 86
  council 696
diremption 44
direption 791
dirge
  funeral 363
  song 415
  lament 839
dirigible balloon
  273, 726
dirk 727
dirt 653
  throw –
  defame 874
  disrespect 929
  – cheap 815
  like – under one's
  feet 749
dirty *dim* 222
  opaque 426
  unclean 653
  disreputable 874
  dishonorable 940
  – end of stick 699
  – sky 353
  – weather 349
  do – work
  servile 886
  flatterer 935
diruption 162
disability
  impotence 158
disable 158
  weaken 160
disabuse 527, 529
disaccord 713
disadvantage
  evil 619
  inexpedience 647

at a – 34
lie under a – 651
disadvantageous
647, 649
disaffection
dissent 489
enmity 889
hate 898
disaffirm 536
disagreeable 830,
867
disagreement
difference 15
incongruity **24**
dissent 489
discord 713
disallow 761
disannul 756
disappearance 449
disappointment
balk 609
fail 732
discontent 832
disapprobation 706,
932
disapprover 936
disarm *disable* 158
weaken 160
reconcile 831
propitiate 914
disarrange 61
disarray
disorder 59
undress 226
disaster *evil* 619
failure 732
adversity 735
calamity 830
disastrous *bad* 649
disavow 536
disband
separate 44
disperse 73
liberate 750
disbar
abrogate 756
punish 972
disbarment 55
disbelief 485, 487
religious 989
disbench 756, 972
disbowel 297
disbranch 44
disburden
facilitate 705
– one's mind 529
– oneself of 782
disburse 809
disc 220, 234
discard *eject* 297
relinquish 624
disuse 678
abrogate 756
refuse 764
repudiate 773
surrender 782
– from one's
thoughts 458
discarded 495
disceptation 476
discern *see* 441
know 490
discernible 446
discernment 498,
868
discerption 44
discharge
violence 173

propel 284
emit 297
excrete 299
sound 406
acquit oneself 692
complete 729
liberate 750
abrogate 756
pay 807
exempt 927a
acquit 970
– a duty 926, 944
– a function
business 625
utility 644
– itself *egress* 295
river 348
– from the mem-
ory 506
– from the mind
458
– an obligation
772
discind 44
disciple *pupil* 541
votary 711
Christian 985
disciplinarian
master 540
martinet 739
discipline
order 58
teaching 537
training 673
restraint 751
punishment 972
religious 990
disclaim *deny* 536
repudiate 756
abjure 757
refuse 764
disclosure 480a, **529**
discoid *layer* 204
frontal 220
flat 251
discoloration 429
discolored
shabby 659
ugly 846
blemish 848
discomfit 731
discomfiture 732
discomfort
physical 378
mental 828
discommend 932
discommode
hinder 706
annoy 830
discommodious
645, 647
discompose
derange 61
put out 458
hinder 706
pain 830
disconcert 874
anger 900
discomposure 828
disconcert
derange 61
distract 458
disappoint 509
hinder 706
discontent 832
confuse 879
disconcerted
hopeless 859

disconformity 83
discongruity 24
disconnected
style 575
disconnection
irrelation 19
disjunction 44
discontinuity 70
disconsolate 837
discontent **832**
discontinuance
cessation 142
relinquishment
624
discontinuity **70**
discord
difference 15
disagreement 24
of sound **414**
of color 428
dissension **713**
discount
decrease 36
decrement 40a
money **813**
at a –
disrepute 874
disapproved 932
discountenance
disfavor 706
refuse 764
discourage
dissuade 616
sadden 837
frighten 860
discourse
teach 537
speech 582
talk 588
dissert 595
sermon 998
discourtesy **895**
discous 202
discover
perceive 441
solve 462
find 480a
disclose 529
– itself
be seen 446
discovery 480a
discredit
disbelief 485
dishonor 874
discreditable
vicious 945
discreet *careful* 459
cautious 864
discrepancy 15
discrepant 24, 713
discrete
separate 44, 70
single 87
discretion *will* 600
choice 609
skill 698
caution 864
surrender at – 725
use – 609
years of – 131
discrétion à – 600
discrimination
difference 15
nice perception
465
wisdom 498
taste 850
fastidiousness 868

disculpate 937
discumbency 213
discursion 266
discursive
moving 264
migratory 266
wandering 279
argumentative 476
diffuse style 573
conversable 588
disserting 595
discus 840
discuss *eat* 298
reflect 451
inquire 461
reason 476
dissert 595
discussion
[*see discuss*]
open to – 475
under – 461
disdain
indifference 866
fastidious 868
arrogance 885
pride 878
contempt 930
disease **655**
occupational – 655
–d *mind* 503
disembark 292
disembarrass 705
disembody
decompose 49
disperse 73
spiritualize 317
disembogue
emit 295
eject 297
flow out 348
disembowel 297,
301
disembroil 60
disenable 158
disenchant
discover 480a
dissuade 616
displease 830
disencumber 705
disendow 756
disengage
detach 44
facilitate 705
liberate 750
disengaged
to let 763
disentangle
separate 44
arrange 60
unroll 313
decipher 522
facilitate 705
liberate 750
disenthral 750
disenthrone 756
disentitle 925
disespouse 905
disestablish
displace 185
abrogate 756
disesteem 929, 932
disfavor
oppose 708
hate 898
disrespect 929
view with – 932
disfigure
deface 241

injure 659
deform 846
blemish 848
disfranchise 925
disgorge *emit* 297
flow out 348
restore 790
pay 807
disgrace
shame 874
dishonor 940
sense of – 879
disgraceful
vice 945
disgruntle 509
disguise
unlikeness 18
conceal 528
mask 530
falsify 544
untruth 546
disguised in drink
959
disgust *taste* 395
offensive 830
weary 841
dislike 867
hatred 898
– of life 837
dish *destroy* 162
plate 191
food 298
– of tea 892
dishabille
undress 225
unprepared 674
dishearten
dissuade 616
pain 830
discontent 832
deject 837
dished 252, 732
disherison 789
dishevel
loose 47
untidy 59
disorder 61
disperse 73
intermix 219
dishonest *false* 544
base 940
dishonour
disrepute 874
disrespect 929
baseness 940
– *bills* 808
dish-water 653
disillusion 509
disincline
dissuade 616
dislike 867
disinclined 603
disinfect
purify 652
restore 660
disinfectant 662
disingenuous
false 544
dishonorable 940
disinherit
relinquish 782
transfer 783
deprive 789
disintegrate
separate 44
decompose 49
pulverize 330
disinter *exhume* 363

distrait 458
distraught 824
distress
  distraint 789
  poverty 804
  affliction 828
  cause pain 830
  signal of – 669
distressingly
  excessively 31
distribute
  arrange 60
  disperse 44, 73
  allot 786
district 181
  – council 696
distrust
  disbelief 485
  fear 860
distrustful 487
disturb
  derange 61
  change 140
  agitate 315
  excite 824
  distress 828, 830
disturbance 59
disunion
  discord 24
  separation 44
  disorder 59
  discord 713
disuse
  desuetude 614
  relinquish 624
  unemploy 678
disused
  old 124
disvalue 932
ditch
  inclosure 232
  trench 259
  water 343
  conduit 350
  defence 717
  to the last – 606
ditch-water 653
ditheism 984
dither 315
dithyramb
  music 415
  poetry 597
dithyrambic 503
ditto 13, 104
  say – to 488
ditty 415
  – box 191
diurnal 138
diuturnity 110
diva 416
divagate 279, 629
divan sofa 215
  council 696
  throne 696
  tribunal 966
divaricate differ 15
  bifurcate 91
  diverge 291
dive swim 267
  fly 267
  plunge 306, 310
  – into inquire 461
divellicate 44
diver 208
divergence
  difference 15
  variation 20a
  disagreement 24

deviation 279
separation 291
divers different 15
  multiform 81
  many 102
  – coloured 440
diverse 15
diversify
  very 20a
  change 140
diversion
  change 140
  deviation 279
  pleasure 377
  amusement 840
diversity
  difference 15
  irregular 16a
  dissimilar 18
  multiform 81
  – of opinion 489
divert turn 279
  deceive 545
  amuse 840
  – the mind 452, 458
divertissement
  diversion 377
  drama 599
  amusement 840
Dives 803
divest denude 226
  take 789
  – oneself of
  abrogate 756
  relinquish 782
divestment 226
divide differ 15
  separate 44
  part 51
  arrange 60
  arithmetic 85
  bisect 91
  vote 609
  apportion 786
dividend part 51
  number 84
  portion 786
divina particula
  aurae 450
divination
  prediction 511
  sorcery 992
divine predict 511
  guess 514
  perfect 650
  of God 976, 983, 983a
  clergyman 996
divine afflatus 515
  – right.
  authority 737
  due 924
  – service 990
diving 840
diving-bell 208
divining-rod 550, 993
Divinity God 976
  theology 983
divisible
  number 84
division
  [see divide]
  part 51
  class 75
  arithmetic 85
  discord 713

military 726
divisor 84
divorce
  separation 44
  relinquish 782
  matrimonial 905
Divorce Court 966
divulge 529
divulsion 44
divvy 786
dixi 535
dizen 847
dizzard 501
dizzy
  dimsighted 443
  confused 458
  vertigo 503
  – height 206
  – round 312
djerrid 727
djinn 980
do fare 7
  suit 23
  produce 161
  cheat 545
  act 680
  complete 729
  succeed 731
  I beg 765
  all one can – 686
  plenty to – 682
  thing to – 625
  – away with
  destroy 162
  eject 297
  abrogate 756
  – battle 722
  – one's bidding 743
  – business 625
  – to death 361
  – as done by 906, 942
  – for destroy 162
  kill 361
  conquer 731
  serve 746
  punish 972
  – good 906
  – harm 907
  – honor 873
  – into
  translate 522
  – justice to 595
  – like 19
  – little 683
  – no harm 648
  – nothing 681
  – nothing but 136
  – one's office 772
  – as others do 82
  – over 223
  – as one pleases 748
  – a service
  useful 644
  aid 707
  – up 660
  have to – with 680, 692
  – without 678
  – the work 686
  – wrong 923
docere, pisces na-
  tare – 641
docile domesticated 370
  learning 539

willing 602
docimastic 463
dock diminish 36
  cut off 38
  port 189
  shorten 201
  edge 231
  store 636
  tribunal 966
docked
  incomplete 53
docker 690
docket
  list 86
  evidence 467
  note 550
  record 551
  security 771
dockyard 691
doctor
  learned man 492
  restore 660
  remedy 662
  after death the – 135
  – accounts 811
  when –s disagree 475
doctrinaire
  positive 474
  pedant 492
  affectation 855
  blusterer 887
doctrinal 537
doctrinarian 514
doctrine tenet 484
  knowledge 490
document 551
documentary
  evidence 467
dodder 315
doddering 128
dodecahedron 244
dodge change 140
  shift 264
  deviate 279
  oscillate 314
  pursue 461
  avoid 623
  stratagem 702
dodger, artful – 792
dodo 366
  extinct as the – 122
doe swift 274
  deer 366
  female 374
doer
  originator 164
  agent 690
doff 226
  – the cap 894
dog follow 281
  animal 366
  male 373
  pursue 622
  wretch 949
  cast to the –s
  destroy 162
  reject 610
  disuse 678
  abrogate 756
  relinquish 782
fire – 386
go to the –s
  destruction 162
  fail 732
  adversity 735

poverty 804
sea – 269
watch –
  safety 664
  warning 668
  keeper 753
hair of – that bit you 959
let sleeping –s lie 141
  – in manger 706, 943
  –tired 686
  –s of war 722
dog-cart 272
dog-cheap 815
dog-days 382
doge 745
dogged
  obstinate 606
  valour 861
  sullen 901a
dogger 273
doggerel
  verse 597
  ridiculous 851, 853
dog-hole 189
dog-Latin 563
dogma tenet 484
  theology 983
dogmatic
  certain 474
  positive 481
  assertion 535
  obstinate 606
dogmatist 887
dog's ear 258
dog robber 746
dog-sick 867
dog-star 423
dog-trot 275
dog-weary 688
doily 852
doing
  up and – 682
  what one is – 625
doings
  events 151
  actions 680
  conduct 692
doit trifle 643
  coin 800
dolce far niente 681
doldrums
  dejection 837
  sulks 901a
dole
  small quantity 32
  scant 640
  give 784
  allot 786
  parsimony 819
  grief 828
doleful 837
  – dumps 901a
doll small 193
  image 554
dollar 800
dolman 225
dolmen 363, 551
d'olor
  physical 378
  moral 828
dolorem, infandum
  renovare – 833
dolorous 830
dolphin 341

dolt 501
doltish 499
domain
class 75
region 181
property 780
Domdaniel 982
dome *high* 206
roof 223
curvature 245
convex 250
Domesday book
list 86
record 551
domesman 967
domestic
inhabitant 188
home 189
interior 221
servant 746
secluded 893
- animals 366
domesticate
locate 184
acclimatize 613
- animals 370
domicile 189
domiciled 186
domiciliary 188
- visit 461
dominant 175
note in music 413
domination 737
dominical 998
domineer
tyrannize 739
insolence 885
Domini, anno - 106
Dominican 996
Dominie 540
dominion 181, 737
domino *dress* 225
mask 530
game 840
domn 745
don *put on* 225
scholar 492
teacher 540
noble 875
Don Juan 897
donation 784
done *finished* 729
work - 729
- for *spoilt* 659
failure 732
- up
impotent 158
tired 688
have - with
cease 142
relinquish 624
disuse 678
donee 785
donjon 717, 752
donkey *ass* 271
fool 501
talk a -'s hind leg
off 584
donna 374
Donnybrook Fair
disorder 59
discord 713
donor 784
donzel 746
doodle 501
doom *end* 67
fate 152
destruction 162

death 360
judgment 480
necessity 601
sentence 971
- sealed
death 360
adversity 735
doomed 735, 828
doomsday
end 67
future 121
till - 112
door *entrance* 66
cover 223
brink 231
barrier 232
opening 260
passage 627
at one's - 197
beg from door to -
765
bolt the - 666
close the - upon
751
death's - 360
keep within -s 265
lie at one's - 926
lock the - 666
open a - to
liable 177
open the - to
receive 296
facilitate 705
permit 760
show the   to
eject 297
discourtesy 895
- mat 652
doorkeeper 263
doorway 260
dope 376, 545, 663
doquet
security 771
Dorado, El - 803
Doric mode 413
dormant
inert 172
latent 526
asleep 683
dormer 260
dormeuse 272
dormir debout,
conte à - 843
dormitive 841
dormitory 191
dormouse 683
dorp 189
dorsal 235
dorser 191
dorsum 235, 250
dory 273
dose *quantity* 25
part 51
medicine 662
apportion 786
dosser 191
dossier *bundle* 72
record 551
dossil 223, 263
dot *small* 32
place 182
little 193
variegate 440
mark 550
dowry 780
on the - 113
dotage 128, 499
dotard 130, 501

dotation 784
dottle 40, 645
dote *drivel* 499, 503
- upon 897
douanier 965
double
similar 17
increase 35
duplex 90
substitute 147
fold 258
turn 283
finesse 702
march at the - 274
see -
dim sight 443
drunk 959
- acrostic
letters 561
wit 842
- dutch 518
- entry 811
- the fist 909
- march 684
- meaning 520
- a point 311
in - quick time
274
- reef topsails 664
- sure 474
work - tides 686
- up
render powerless
158
double bar 747
double-bass 417
doublecross 545
double-dealing
lie 544
cunning 940
double-distilled 171
double-dyed 428
double-eagle 893
double-edged 90,
171
double entendre
ambiguity 520
impure 961
double-faced
lie 544
cunning 702, 940
double-headed 90
double-minded 605
double-shotted 171
doublet 225
double-tongued
lie 544
cunning 702, 940
doubt
uncertain 475
disbelieve **485**
sceptic 989
doubtful 475
more than - 473
- meaning
unintelligible 519
doubtless
certain 474
belief 484
assent 488
douceur 784, 973
douche 337
dough 324, 354, 800
doughty 861
dour 739
douse
immerse 310
splash 337

blow 972
Dove
Holy Ghost 976
dove
innocent 946
roar like sucking -
174
dovecote 189
dovetail
agree 23
join 43
intersect 219
intervene 228
angle 244
insert 300
dowager 374, 905
dowdy 653, 851
dower 780, 803, 810
dowerless 804
down
below 207
light 320
bear - upon 716
bed of -
pleasure 377
repose 687
come - 306
get - 306
go -
sink 306
calm 826
keep - 36
money - 807
take -
lower 308
rebuff 874
humble 879
- on one's mar-
row-bones 886
- in the mouth 837
- and out 874
- in price 815
go - like a stone
310
be - upon
attack 716
severe 739
downcast 306, 837
- eyes 879
downfall
destruction 162
fall 306
failure 732
misfortune 735
downhill 217, 306
go -
adversity 735
downpour 348
downright
absolute 31
manifest 525
sincere 703
downs 206, 344
down-trodden
submission 725
vanquished 732
subject 749
dejected 837
disrepute 874
contempt 930
downwards 306
downy
smooth 255
plumose 256
soft 324
dowry 780, 784
dowse 276
dowser 994

doxology 990
doxy 897
doyer 128
doyley 652
doze 683
dozen 98
drab *color* 432
slut 653
hussy 962
drabble 653
drachm 319
Draco 694, 739
draff 653
draft [*see also*
draught]
multitude 102
drawing 554, 556
write 590
abstract 596
plan 626
cheque 800
credit 805
- off *displace* 185
transfer 270
draft-horse 271
drag *carriage* 272
crawl 275
traction 285
impediment 706
put on the - 275
- a chain
tedious 109, 110
exertion 686
subjection 749
- into
implicate 54
compel 744
- through mire
disrepute 874
disrespect 929
- on *tedious* 110
- into open day
531
- towards
attract 288
- slow length
long 200
weary 841
draggle 285, 653
- tail 59
drag-net
all sorts 78
dragoman 524
dragon *monster* 83
violent 173
animal 366
irascible 901
dragonnade
attack 716
punish 972
dragoon
soldier 726
compel 744
insolent 885
worry 907
drain
flow out 295
empty 297
dry 340
conduit 350
waste 638
clean 652
unclean 653
exhaust 789
dissipate 818
- the cup
drink 298
drunken 959

- the cup of
  misery 828
- into 348
- pipe 249
- of resources 640

drake *male* 373
fire – 423
dram *drink* 298
  pungent 392
  stimulus 615
- drinking 959
drama 599
dramatic 599
  ostentation 882
- author 599
- critic 599
- poetry 597
dramatis personæ
  mankind 372
  play 599
  agents 690
  party 712
drapery 225, 847
drast 645
drastic 171
draught
  [*see also* **draft**]
  depth 208
  traction 285
  drink 298
  stream of air 349
  delineation 554,
  556
  plan 626
  physic 662
  troops 726
- off 73
draughts
  game 840
draughtsman
  artist 559
draw *equality* 27
  compose 54
  pull 285
  delineate 554, 556
- aside 279
- off the attention
  458
- back
  deduction 40a
  regret 283
  avoid 623
- breath
  refresh 689
  feeling 821
  relief 834
- a cheque 800
- a curtain 424
- down 153
- forth 677
- from 810
- on futurity 132
- in one's horns
  tergiversation 607
  humility 879
- in 195
- an inference 480
- the line 465
- lots 621
- near *time* 121
  approach 286
- off *eject* 297
  hinder 706
  take 789
- on *time* 121
  event 151
  induce 615
- out

protract 110
late 133
prolong 200
extract 301
discover 480a
exhibit 525
diffuse style 573
- over *induce* 615
- a parallel 9
- the pen through
  552
- a picture 594
- profit 775
- and quarter 972
- the sword
  attack 716
  war 722
- the teeth of 158
- together
  assemble 72
  co-operate 709
- towards 288
- up *order* 58
  stop 265
  write 590
- up a statement
  594
- upon *money* 800
- the veil 528
drawback *evil* 619
  imperfection 651
  hindrance 706
  discount 813
drawbar 45
drawbridge
  way 627
  escape 671
  raise the – 666
drawcansir 887
drawee 800
drawer
  receptacle 191
  artist 559
- of water 690
drawers
  dress 225
drawhead 45
drawing
  delineation 554,
  556
  prize 810
drawing-room
  assembly 72
  room 191
  fashion 852
drawl *prolong* 200
  creep 275
  in speech 583
  sluggish 683
drawn *equated* 27
- battle
- *irresistibly* 601
  pacification 723
  incomplete 730
dray 272
- horse 271
drayman 268
dread 860
dreadful *great* 31
  bad 649
  dire 830
  depressing 837
  fearful 860
dreadless 861
dreadnought
  warship 726
dream
  unsubstantial 4

error 495
fancy 515
sleep 683
golden – 858
- of *think* 451
  intend 620
- on other things
  458
dreamer
  madman 504
  imaginative 515
dreamy
  unsubstantial 4
  inattentive 458
  sleepy 683
dreary
  monotonous 16
  solitary 87
  melancholy 830,
  837
dredge *collect* 72
  extract 301
  raise 307
dregs
  remainder 40
  refuse 645
  dirt 653
- of the people 876
- of vice 945
drench *drink* 298
  water 337
  redundance 641
- with *physic* 662
drencher 248
drenching rain 348
dress
  uniformity 16
  agree 23
  equalize 27
  clothes 225
  prepare 673
  ornament 847
  ostentation 882
  full – 852
- circle 599
- the ground 371
- up *falsehood* 544
  represent 554
- wounds 662
- to advantage
  847
dress-coat 225
dresser
  sideboard 215
  surgeon 662
dressing 932, 972
- room 191, 599
dressing-gown 225
dressmaker 225
dribble 295, 348
driblet 25, 32
drift
  accumulate 72
  distance 196
  motion 264
  flying 267
  float 267
  transfer 270
  direction 278
  deviation 279
  approach 286
  wind 349
  meaning 516
  intention 620
  snow – 383
drifter 273
drifting 605
driftless 621

drill *fabric* 219
  bore 260
  auger 262
  teach 537
  prepare 673
- hall 191
drink
  swallow 296
  liquor 298
  tipple 959
- one's fill
  enough 639
- in *imbibe* 296,
  298
- in learning 539
- to *celebrate* 883
  courtesy 894
drinking-bout 954
drink-money 784
drip 295, 348
dripping *wet* 330
  fat 356
drive *airing* 266
  impel 276
  propel 284
  break in 370
  urge 615
  haste 684
  direct 693
  attack 716
  compel 744
- at *mean* 516
  intend 620
- a bargain
  barter 794
  parsimony 819
- care away 836
- a coach and six
  through 83
- into a corner
  difficult 704
  hinder 706
  defeat 731
  subjection 749
- to despair 859
- matters to an
  extremity 604
- from *repel* 289
- one hard 716
- home 729
- in 300
- to the last 133
- out 297
- trade
  business 625
  barter 794
drivel *slobber* 297
  imbecile 499
  mad 503
  rubbish 517
driveler 501, 584
driver 268
  director 694
driving rain 348
drizzle 348
droil 683
droit du plus fort
  744
drôle *cards* 840
drole 949
- de corps 844
drollery
  amusement 840
  wit 842
  ridiculous 853
dromedary 271
drone *slow* 275
  sound 407, 412,

413
  inactive 683
drool 297
droop
  weak 160
  hang 214
  sink 306
  disease 655
  decline 659
  flag 688
  sorrow 828
  dejection 837
drop *small quantity*
  32
  discontinue 142
  powerless 158
  bring forth 161
  spherule 249
  emerge 295
  fall 306
  trickle 348
  relinquish 624
  discard 782
  gallows 975
  let – 308
  ready to –
  fatigue 688
- asleep 683
- astern 283
- from the couds
  508
- dead 360
- by drop
  by degrees 26
  in parts 51
- in the bucket 32
- in upon 674
- into a good
  thing 734
- into the grave
  360
- a hint 527
- all idea of 624
- in *arrive* 292
  immerse 300
  sociality 892
- the mask 529
- off *decrease* 36
  die 360
  sleep 683
- in the ocean
  trifling 643
- the subject 458
- too much 959
dropping fire 70
drop-scene 599
dropsical 194, 641
droshki 272
dross
  remainder 40
  slag 384
  trash 643, 645
  dirt 653
drought
  dryness 340
  insufficiency 640
drouth *desire* 865
drove
  assemblage 72
  multitude 102
drover 370
drown
  affusion 337
  kill 361
  ruin 731, 732
- care 840
- the voice 581
drowsy *slow* 275

sleepy 683
  weary 841
drub
  defeat 731, 732
  punish 972
drudge *labour* 686
  worker 682, 690
drug
  render insensible
    376
  superfluity 641
  trash 643
  remedy 662
  bane 663
  – *in the market*
    815
drugget
  cover 223
  clean 652
  preserve 670
druggist 662
druid 996
drum
  repeat 104
  cylinder 249
  sound 407
  music 417
  party 892
  beat of –
    signal 550
    alarm 669
    war 722
    command 741
    parade 882
  ear – 418
  muffled –
    funeral 363
    non-resonance
      408a
  – *and fife band* 417
  – *fire* 407
  – *out* 972
drum-head 964,
  966
drum-major 745
drummer 416
drunken 959
  reel like a – man
    315
drunkenness 959
dry *arid* 340
  style 575, 576, 579
  hoarse 581
  scanty 640
  preserve 670
  exhaust 789
  tedious 841
  dull 842
  thirsty 865
  cynical 932
  teetotal 958
  run – 640
  with – eyes 823
  – *dock* 189
  – *joke* 842
  – *land* 342
  – *the tears* 834
  – *up* 340, 638
dryad 979
dry-as-dust
  antiquarian 122
  dull 843
dryness 340
dry-nurse
  teach 537
  teacher 540
  aid 707
dry-point 558

dry-rot
  dirt 653
  decay 659
  bane 663
dualism 984
duality 89
duarchy 737
dub 564
dubious 475
ducat 800
duce 745
duchess 745, 875
duchy 181
duck *stoop* 308
  plunge 310
  water 337
  darling 897, 899
  play –*s and*
    drakes
    recoil 277
    prodigality 818
  –*'s egg*
    zero 101
  – *in thunder* 870
ducking-stool 975
duckling 127
duck-pond 370
duct 350
ductile
  elastic 323
  flexible 324
  trimming 607
  easy 705
  docile 743
dud 158, 727
dude 854
duds 225
dudgeon
  dagger 727
  discontent 832
  churlishness 895
  hate 898
  anger 900
  sullenness 901a
due
  expedient 646
  owing 806
  proper 924, 926
  give his – *to*
    right 922
    vindication 937
    fair 939
  in – *course* 109
    occasion 134
  – *respect* 928
  – *sense of* 498
  – *time*
    soon 132
  – *to*
    cause and effect
      154, 155
  give – weight 465
duel 720
duelist 726
dueness 924
duenna
  teacher 540
  guardian 664
  keeper 753
dues 812
duet 415
duff 298
duffer
  bungler 701
  smuggler 792
dug 250
dug-out
  old man 130

boat 273
  defence 717
duke *ruler* 745
  noble 875
dulce domum 189
dulcet
  sweet 396
  sound 405
  melodious 413
  agreeable 829
dulcify 174, 396
dulcimer 417
Dulcinea 897
dulcorate 396
dulia 990
dull *weak* 160
  inert 172
  moderate 174
  blunt 254
  insensible 376,
    381
  sound 405
  dim 422
  colorless 429
  ignorant 493
  stolid 499
  style 575
  inactive 683
  unapt 699
  callous 823
  dejected 837
  weary 841
  prosing 843
  simple 849
  – *of hearing* 419
  – *sight* 443
dullard 501
dullness 843
duly 924
duma 696
dumb 581
  – *animal* 366
  – *show* 550
  – *waiter* 307
  strike –
    ignorant 493
    astonish 870
    humble 879
dumbfounder
  disappoint 509
  silence 581
  astonish 870
  humble 879
dummy
  substitute 147
  impotent 158
  speechless 581
  inactive 683
dump *music* 415
  store 636
  lament 839
  undersell 796
dumpling 298
dumps
  discontent 832
  dejection 837
  sulk 901a
dumpy *little* 193
  short 201
  thick 202
dun *dim* 422
  colorless 429
  grey 432
  dirt 653
  importune 765
  creditor 805
dunce
  ignoramus 493
  fool 501

dunderhead 501
dune 206
dung 653
dungeon 752
dunghill
  dirt 653
  cowardly 862
  baseborn 876
  – *cock* 366
Dunker 984
dunt 716
duo 415
duodecimal 99
duodecimo
  little 193
  book 593
duodenary 98
duologue
  interlocution 588
  drama 599
dupe
  credulous 486
  deceive 545
  deceived 547
duplex 90, 189
duplicate
  imitate 19
  copy 21
  double 90
  tally 550
  record 551
  redundant 641
  pawn 805
duplication
  imitation 19
  doubling 90
  repetition 104
duplicature
  fold 258
duplicity
  duality 89
  falsehood 544
dura lex sed lex 926
durable
  long time 110
  stable 150
durance 141, 751
  in – 754
duration 106
  contingent – 108a
  infinite – 112
durbar
  conference 588
  council 696
  tribunal 966
duress
  compulsion 744
  restraint 751
during 106
  – *pleasure &c.*
    108a
durity 323
dusk
  evening 126
  half-light 422
dusky
  dark 421
  black 431
dust *levity* 320
  powder 330
  corpse 362
  trash 643
  dirt 653
  money 800
  come to –
    die 360
  come down with
    the – 807

humbled in the –
  879
  kick up a – 885
  level with the –
    162
  lick the –
    submit 725
    fail 732
  make to bite the –
    731
  turn to –
    deorganized 358
    die 360
  – *in the balance*
    643
  throw – in the
    eyes
    blind 442
    deceive 545
    plead 617
  – *one's jacket* 972
duster 652
dust-bin, dust-hole
  191, 645
  fit for the –
    useless 645
    dirty 653
    spoilt 659
dustman
  cleaner 652
dust-storm 330
dusty
  powder 330
  dirt 653
Dutch
  double – 519
  high – 519
  – *auction* 796
  – *courage* 862
Dutchman, flying
  515
dutiful 944
duty
  business 625
  work 686
  tax 812
  courtesy 894
  obligation 926
  respect 928
  worship 990
  rite 998
  do one's –
    virtue 944
  on – 680, 682
duumvirate 737
Duval, Claude –
  792
D.V. 470, 976
dwarf
  lessen 36
  small 193
  elf 980
dwell
  reside 186
  abide 265
  – *upon*
    descant 573
dweller 188
dwelling 184, 189
dwindle *lessen* 36
  shrink 195
dyad 89
dye 428
dying 360
dyke [see **dike**]
dynamic energy
  157
dynamics 276

complete 729
carry into – 692
with crushing –
162
in – 5
take – 731
to that – 516
effective
  capable 157
  useful 644
effectuation 729
expedient 646
effects 780, 798
effectual 731
effectually 52
effectuate 729
effeminate
  weak 160
  womenlike 374
  timorous 862
  sensual 954
effeminize 158
effendi 875
effervesce
  energy 171
  violence 173
  agitate 315
  bubble 353
  excited 825
effervescent 338
effete *old* 128
  weak 160
  useless 645
  spoiled 659
efficacious
  [*see* efficient]
efficient
  power 157
  agency 170
  utility 644
  skill 698
effigy 21, 554
effleurer *skim* 267,
460
efflorescence 330
effluxion of time
109
effluence *egress* 295
  flow 348
effluvium 334, 398
efflux 295
efformation 240
effort 686
effreet 980
effrontery 885
effulgence 420
effuse
  pour out 295, 297
  excrete 299
  speech 582
  loquacity 584
effusion of blood
361
effusive 573
eft 366
eftsoons 117
egad 535
égards 928
egesta 299
egestion 297
egg *beginning* 66
  cause 153
  food 298
  walk among –s
704
  too many –s in
one basket
  unskilful 699

(imprudent 863)
– and dart
  ornament 847
– on 615
egg-shaped 247,
249
ego *intrinsic* 5
  speciality 79
  immaterial 317
  non – 6
egocentrism 943
egotism
  vanity 880
  cynicism 911
  selfishness 943
egregious
  exceptional 83
  absurd 497
  exaggerated 549
  important 642
egregiously 31, 33
egress 295
Egyptian darkness
421
eheul fugaces
labuntur anni
111
eiderdown 223
eidouranion 318
Eiffel tower 206
eight *number* 98
  boat 273
  representative 759
eisteddfod 72, 416
eighty 98
either *choice* 609
  happy with – 605
ejaculate
  propel 284
  utter 580
ejection 185, 297
ejecta 299
ejector 349
eke *also* 37
  – out *complete* 52
  spin out 110
ekka 272
El Dorado 803
elaborate
  improve 658
  prepare 673
  laborious 686
  work out 729
elaine 356
élan 276
elapse 109, 122
elastic fluid 334
elasticity
  power 157
  strength 159
  energy 171
  spring 325
elate *cheer* 836
  rejoice 838
  hope 858
  vain 880
  boast 884
elbow *angle* 244
  projection 250
  push 276
  at one's –
  near 197
  advice 695
  lift one's –
  drink 959
  out at –s
  undress 226
  poor 804

disrepute 874
· one's way
  progress 282
  pursuit 622
  active 682
elbow-chair 215
elbow-grease 331
elbow-room 180,
748
elder *older* 124
  aged 128
  veteran 130
  clergy 996
elect *choose* 609
  good 648
  predestinate 976
  pious 987
  clergy 996
election
  numerical 84
  necessity 601
electioneering 609
elector 745
electorate 737
Electra complex
897
electric
  swift 274
  sensation 821
  excitable 825
  car 272
  – blue 438
  – chair 974
  – light 423
  – piano 417
electrician 599, 690
electricity 157, 388
electrify
  unexpected 508
  excite 824
  astonish 870
electro-biology 992
electrocution 972
electrolier 214, 423
electrolyze 49
electro-magnetism
157
electromobile 272
electron 32
electronics 157
electroplate 223
electrotype 21, 591
electuary 662
eleemosynary 784
elegance
  in style 578
  beauty 845
  taste 859
  Bank of – 800
elegy *interment* 363
  poetry 597
  lament 839
element
  component 56
  beginning 66
  cause 153
  matter 316
  in one's –
  facility 705
  content 831
  devouring – 382
  out of its – 195
elementary 42
  – education 537
  – school 542
elements
  Eucharist 998
elench 477

elephant
  large 192
  carrier 271
  white – *bane* 663
elevated
  tipsy 959
elevation
  height 206
  vertical 212
  raising 307
  plan 554
  – of style 574
  improvement 658
  glory 873
  – of mind 942
  angular – 244
élève 541
eleven 98
  representative 759
eleventh hour
  evening 126
  late 133
  opportune 134
elf *infant* 129
  little 193
  imp 980
elicit *cause* 153
  draw out 301
  discover 480a
  manifest 525
eligible 646
Elijah's mantle 63
eliminant 299
eliminate
  subduct 38
  simplify 42
  exclude 55
  weed 103
  extract 301
  reject 610
elision 44, 201
élite *best* 648
  distinguished 873
  aristocratic 875
elixation 384
elixir 662
  – of life 471
elk 223
ell 200
  take an –
  take 789
  insolence 885
  wrong 923
  undue 925
  selfish 943
ellipse 247
ellipsis *shorten* 201
  style 572
ellipsoid 247, 249
elocation 185, 270
elocution 582
éloge 931
elongation 196, 200
elopement 623, 671
eloquence 572, 582
else 37
elsewhere 187
elucidate 522
elude
  sophistry 477
  avoid 623
  escape 671
  succeed 731
  palter 773
elusive 545
elusory 546
elutriate 652
elysian 829, 981

Elysium 827, 981
elytron 223
Elzevir. edition 193
emaciation 195,
203, 640
emanate 151
  go out of 295
  excrete 299
  – from 544
emanation 398
emancipate
  facilitate 705
  free 748, 750
emasculate
  impotent 158
embalm
  interment 363
  perfume 400
  preserve 670
  – in the memory
505
embankment
  esplanade 189
  refuge 666
  fence 717
embar 229
embargo
  stoppage 265
  prohibition 761
  exclusion 893
embark
  transfer 270
  depart 293
  – in *begin* 66
  engage in 676
embarquer sans
  biscuits, s' – 674
embarras de
  – choix 609
embarrass 641,
704, 706
embarrassed 804,
806
embarrassing 475
embase 659
embassy
  errand 532
  commission 755
  consignee 758
embattled
  arranged 60
  leagued 712
  war array 722
embed
  locate 184
  base 215
  enclose 221
  insert 300
embellish 847
embers 384
embezzle 791
embitter
  deteriorate 659
  aggravate 835
  acerbate 900
emblazon
  color 428
  ornament 847
  display 882
emblem 550, 747
embody
  join 43
  combine 48
  form a whole 50
  compose 54
embolden
  hope 858
  encourage 861

embolism 228, 261, 300
embonpoint 192
embosomed
  lodged 184
  interjacent 228
  circumscribed 229
emboss *convex* 250
  ornament 847
embouchure 260
embowel 297
embrace
  cohere 46
  compose 54
  include 76
  enclose 227
  choose 609
  take 789
  friendship 888
  sociality 892
  courtesy 894
  endearment 902
  – *an offer* 760
embrangle 61
embranglement 713
embrasure 257, 260
embrocation 662
embroider
  variegate 440
  lie 544
  ornament 847
embroidery
  adjunct 39
  exaggeration 549
embroil *derange* 61
  discord 713
embroilment 59
embrown 433
embryo
  beginning 66
  cause 153
  in – destined 152
  preparing 673
embryology 357
embryonic 193, 674
embus 293
embusqué 603
emendation 658
emerald *green* 435
  jewel 847
emerge 295, 446
emergency
  circumstance 8
  event 151
  difficulty 704
emeritus 500, 928
emersion 295, 446
emery
  sharpener 253
  – *paper*
  smooth 255
emetic *remedy* 662
émeute 742
emication 420
emigrant 57, 268
emigrate 266, 295
emigré 268, 295
eminence
  height 206
  fame 873
  church dignitary 996
eminent domain 744
eminently 33
emir 745, 875
emissary
  messenger 534

consignee 758
emission 297
emit *eject* 297
  publish 531
  voice 580
  – *vapour* 336
Emmanuel 976
emmet 193
emollient 662
emolument
  acquisition 775
  receipt 810
  remuneration 973
emotion 821
  –al *appeal* 824
  –al *drama* 599
empale 260, 972
empanel 86, 969
empathy 515
emperor 745
emphasis 580
emphatic 535, 642
emphatically 31
empierce
  perforate 260
  insert 300
empire 737, 789
  – *day* 840
empiric 548
empirical 463, 675
empiricism 463
emplane 293
employ
  business 625
  use 677
  servitude 749
  commission 755
  in one's – 746
  – *one's capital in* 794
  – *oneself* 680
  – *one's time in* 625
employé
  servant 746
  agent 758
employer 795
empoison 659
emporium 799
empower
  power 157
  commission 755
  accredit 759
  permit 760
empress 745
empressement
  activity 682
  emotion 821
  desire 865
emprise 676
emption 795
emptor 795
  caveat – 769
empty *clear* 185
  vacant 187
  deflate 195
  drain 297
  ignorant 491
  waste 638
  deficient 640
  useless 645
  beggarly account of – boxes
  poverty 804
  – *one's glass* 298
  – *purse* 804
  – *sound* 517
  – *stomach* 865

– *title name* 564
  undue 925
  – *words* 546
empty-handed 640
empty-headed 4, 491
empurple 437
empyrean *sky* 318
  blissful 829
empyreuma 41
empyrosis 384
emulate *imitate* 19
  goodness 648
  rival 708
  compete 720
  glory 873
emulsion 352
emunctory 350
en – bloc 50
  – *masse* 50
  – *passant*
  parenthetical 10
  transient 111
  à propos 134
  – *rapport* 9
  – *règle order* 58
  conformity 82
  – *route*
  journey 266
  progress 282
enable 157
enact *drama* 599
  action 680
  conduct 692
  complete 729
  order 741
  law 963
enallage 521
enamel *coating* 223
  painting 556
  ornament 847
enameller 559
encage 751
encamp 184, 189
encampment 184
encaustic 556
enceinte
  with child 161
  region 181
  inclosure 232
enchafe 830
enchain 751
enchant *please* 829
enchanted 827
enchanting 845, 897
enchantment
  sorcery 992
enchase 43, 259
enchiridion 593
enchorial 188
encincture 229
encircle 76, 227, 311
enclave *close* 181
  boundary 233
enclose 227, 229
enclosure
  region 181
  envelope 232
  fence 752
encomiast 935
encomium 931
encompass 227, 233
  –ed *with difficulties* 704
encore 104, 931

encounter
  undergo 151
  clash 276
  meet 292
  withstand 708
  contest 720
  – *danger* 665
  – *risk* 621
encourage
  animate 615
  aid 707
  comfort 834
  hope 858
  embolden 861
encroach
  transcursion 303
  do wrong 923
  infringe 925
encumber 704, 706
encumbrance
  clear of – 807
encyclical 531
encyclopedia 490, 593
  walking – 700
encyclopedical
  general 78
  – *knowledge* 490
encysted 229
end
  termination 67
  effect 154
  object 620
  at an – 142
  come to its – 729
  one's journey's – 292
  on – 212
  put an – to
  destroy 162
  kill 361
  begin at the wrong – 699
  – *one's days* 360
  –s *of the earth* 196
  – *to end space* 180
  touching 199
  length 200
  – *of life* 360
  – *in smoke* 732
  – *of one's tether*
  sophistry 477
  ignorant 491
  insufficient 640
  difficult 704
endamage 649
endanger 665
endear 897
endearment 902
endeavor
  pursue 622
  attempt 675
  use one's best – 686
  – *after* 620
endemic
  special 79
  interior 221
  disease 657
endimanché 847, 882
endless
  multitudinous 102
  infinite 105
  perpetual 112
endlessly 16
endlong 200

endocrine 221
endogenous 367
endorse
  evidence 467
  assent 488
  compact 769
  – *a bill* 800
  approve 931
endorsement 550
endosmose 302
endow
  confer power 157
  endowed with
  possessed of 777
endowment
  intrinsic 5
  power 157
  talent 698
  gift 784
endrogynous 83
endue 157
endure *time* 106
  last 110
  persist 143
  continue 141
  undergo 151
  feel 821
  submit to 826
  unable to – 867
  – *for ever* 112
  – *pain* 828
enduring
  indelible 505
endwise 212
enemy *time* 841
  foe 891
  the common – 978
  thing devised by the – 546
  – *to society* 891
energumen 504
energy *power* 157
  strength 159
  physical 171
  resolution 604
  activity 682
enervate 158, 160
enfant, bon – 906
  – *gate*
  prosperity 734
  satiety 869
  favorite 899
  – *perdu*
  hopeless 859
  reckless 863
  – *terrible*
  curiosity 455
  artless 703
  object of fear 860
enfeeble 160
enfeoff 780, 783
Enfield rifle 727
enfilade
  lengthwise 200
  pierce 260
  pass through 302
enfold 229
enforce *urge* 615
  advise 695
  compel 744
  require 924
enfranchise
  free 748
  liberate 750
  permit 760
enfranchised 924
engage
  bespeak 132

induce 615
undertake 676
do battle 722
commission 755
promise 768
compact 769
I'll –
  affirmation 535
– the attention
  457
– with 720
engaged
  marriage 903
be – 135
– in attention 457
engagement
  business 625
  battle 720
  betrothal 902
engaging
  pleasing 829
  amiable 897
engender 161
engine 153, 633
engine-driver 268
engineer 690, 694,
  726
engineering 633
engird 227
English 188
  broken – 563
  king's – 560
  murder the king's
    – 568
  plain –
    intelligible 518
    interpreted 522
    style 576
  – horn 417
engorge
  swallow 296
  gluttony 957
engorgement
  too much 641
engrail 256
engrave
  furrow 259
  mark 550
  – in the memory
    505
engraver 559
engraving 21, 22,
  558
engross write 590
  possess 777
  – the thoughts
    thought 451
    attention 457
engrossed in
  thought 451
engulf
  destroy 162
  plunge 310
  swallow up 296
enhance
  increase 35
  improve 658
enharmonic 413
enigma
  question 461
  secret 533
enigmatic
  uncertain 475
  unintelligible 517
  obscure 519
enigme, mot d' –
  522
enjoin advise 695

command 741
  prescribe 926
enjoy
  physically 377
  possess 777
  morally 827
  – health 654
  – popularity 873
  – a state 7
enkindle heat 384
  excite 824
enlarge
  increase 35
  swell 194
  in writing 573
  liberate 750
  – the mind 537
enlarged views 498
enlighten
  illumine 420
  inform 527
  teach 537
enlightened
  knowledge 490
enlist engage 615
  war 722
  commission 755
  under the ban-
    ners of 707
  – into the service
    677
enliven
  delight 829
  cheer 836
  amuse 840
enmity 889
ennoble 873
ennui 841
enormity
  crime 947
enormous great 31
  big 192
  – number 102
enough much 31
  no more! 142
  sufficient 639
  moderately 651
  satiety 869
  know when one
    has had – 953
  – in all conscience
    641
  – to drive one
    mad 830
  – and to spare 639
enounce 535, 580
enrage 830, 900
enragé 865
enrapture
  excite 824
  beatify 829
  love 897
enraptured 827
enravish 829
enravished 827
enravishment 824
enrich
  improve 658
  wealth 803
  ornament 847
enrobe 225
enroll list 86
  record 551
  – troops 722
  commission 755
ens essence 1
Ens Entium 976
ensample 22

ensanguined 361
ensconce
  conceal 528
  safety 664
ensconced
  located 184
ensemble 50
enshrine
  circumscribe 229
  repute 873
  sanctify 987
  – in the memory
    505
ensiform 253
ensign
  standard 550
  officer 726
  master 745
  – of authority 747
ensilage 637
enslave 749
ensnare 545
ensue follow °3, 117
  happen 151
ensure 474
entablature 210
entail cause 153
  tie up property
    781
entangle
  interlink 43
  derange 61
  ravel 219
  entrap 545
  embroil 713
entangled
  disorder 59
  – by difficulties
    704
entend, cela s' – 613
entente
  agreement 23
  alliance 714
  friendship 888
enter go in 294
  appear 446
  note 551
  accounts 811
  – into the compo-
    sition of 56
  – into details
    special 79
    describe 594
  – into an engage-
    ment 768
  – into the feelings
    of 914
  – into the ideas of
    understand 518
    concord 714
  – in converge 290
  – the lists
    attack 716
    contention 720
  – the mind 451
  – a profession 625
  – into the spirit of
    feel 821
    delight 827
  – upon 66
  – into one's views
    488
enterprise
  pursuit 622
  undertaking 676
  commercial – 794
enterprising
  active 171, 682

courageous 861
entertain
  bear in mind 457
  support 707
  amuse 840
  sociality 892
  – doubts 485
  – feeling 821
  – an idea 451
  – an opinion 484
entertainment 840
  pleasure 377
  repast 298
entêté 481, 606
enthral
  subjection 749
  restraint 751
enthrone 873
enthronement 755
enthusiasm
  language 574
  willingness 602
  feeling 821
  hope 858
  love 897
enthusiast
  madman 504
  obstinate 606
  active 682
enthusiastic
  imaginative 515
  sensitive 822
  excitable 825
  sanguine 858
enthymeme 476
entice 615
enticing 829
entire whole 50
  complete 52
  continuous 69
  – horse 373
entirely much 31
entitle name 564
  give a right 924
entity 1
entoil 545
entomb inter 363
  imprison 751
Entomology 368
entourage 88, 183,
  227
entozoon 193
entrails 221
entrammel 751
entrance
  beginning 66
  ingress 294
  way 627
  enrapture 827,
    829
  magic 992
  give – to 296
entranced 515
entrancement 824
entrap 545
entrain 293
entre nous 528
entreat 765
entrée
  reception 296
  dish 298
  give the – 296
  have the – 294
  – dish 191
entremet 298
entrepôt 636, 799
entrepreneur 599
entre-sol 191

entrust
  commission 755
  give 784
  credit 805
entry beginning 66
  ingress 294
  record 551
entwine join 43
  intersect 219
  convolve 248
enucleate 522
enumerate 85
  – among 76
enumeration 86
enunciate
  inform 527
  affirm 535
  voice 580
envelop 225
envelope 223, 232
envenom
  deprave 659
  exasperate 835
  hate 898
  anger 900
envenomed
  bad 649
  insalubrious 657
  painful 830
  malevolent 907
  – tongue 934
environ 227
environment 183
environs 197
  in such and such –
    183
envisage 515, 861
envoy
  messenger 534
  consignee 758
envy 921
enwrap 225
enzyme 320
Eolian harp 417
Eolus 349
eon 976
épanchement
  manifest 525
  artless 703
  endearment 902
epact 641
épaulette
  badge 550, 747
  ornament 847
  decoration 877
éperdu 824
épergne 191
ephemeral 111
ephemeris
  calendar 114
  record 551
  book 593
Ephesian letters
  993
ephialtes
  physical pain 378
  hindrance 706
  mental pain 828
ephod 999
ephor 967
epic 594, 597
epicedium 839
epicene 81, 83
épicier 876
epicure
  fastidious 868
  sybarite 954a
  glutton 957

epicurean 954
Epicurus, system
of – 954
epicy-cle, -cloid
247
epidemic
  general 78
  disease 655
  insalubrity 657
epidermis 223
epigenesis 161
epigram 496, 842
epigrammatic 572
epigrammatist 844
epigraph 550
epilepsy 315, 655
epilogue
  sequel 65
  end 67
  drama 599
èpingles, tire a
  quatre – 855
Epiphany 998
episcopal 995
Episcopalian 984
episcopate 995
episode
  adjunct 39
  discontinuity 70
  interjacence 228
episodic
  irrelative 10
  style 573
epistle 592
Epistles 985
epistrophe 104
epistyle 210
epitaph 363
epithalamium 903
epithem 662
epithet 564
epitome
  miniature 193
  short 201
  concise 572
epizoötic 657
epoch *time* 106
  instant 113
  date 114
  present time 118
epode 597
eponym 564
epopœa 597
epos 594
epulation 298
epulotic 662
epuration 652
equable 16, 922
equal *even* 27
  equitable 922
  – *chance* 156
  – *times* 120
  – *to power* 157
equality 13, **27**
equalize 213
equanimity 826
equate 27, 30
equations 85
equator 68, 318
equatorial 68, 236
equerry 746
equestrian 268
equibalanced 27
equidistant 68
equilibration 27
equilibrist 599
equilibrium 27
equine *carrier* 271

horse 366
equinox 125, 126
equip 225, 673
equipage
  vehicle 272
  instruments 633
  display 882
equiparent 27
equipment 633
equipoise &c. 27, 30
equiponderate 30
equitable *wise* 498
  just 922
  due 924
  honorable 939
  – *interest* 780
equitation 266
equity *right* 922
  honor 939
  law 963
  in – 922
  – *draftsman* 968
equivalent
  identical 13
  equal 27
  compensation 30
  substitute 147
  translation 522
equivocalness
  dubious 475
  double meaning
  520
  impure 961
equivocate
  sophistry 477
  palter 520·
  lie 544
equivocation
  [*see* equivocate]
  without – 543
équivoque
  double meaning
  520
  impure 961
era *time* 106, 108
  date 114
eradicate
  destroy 162
  extract 301
erase *destroy* 162
  obliterate 331, 552
Erastian 984
erasure 552
Erato 416
ere 116
  – *long* 132
  – *now* 116
  past 122
Erebus *dark* 421
  hell 982
erect *build* 161
  vertical 212
  raise 307
  with head – 878
  – *the scaffolding*
  673
erewhile 116, 122
ergatocracy 737
ergo 476
ergotism 480
ergotize 485
eriometer 445
Erinys 900
Erl King 980
ermine
  badge of authority
  747
  ornament 847

erode 36, 659
Eros 897, 979
erosion 36
erotic 897, 961
err – *in opinion* 495
  – *morally* 945
errand
  message 532
  business 625
  commission 755
errand-boy 534
errant 279
erratic
  irregular 139
  changeable 149
  wandering 279
  capricious 608
erratum 495
erroneous 495
error *fallacy* **495**
  vice 945
  guilt 947
  court of – 966
  writ of – 969
ersatz 973
erst 122
erubescence 434
erubuit salva res
  est 95
eruct 297
eructate 297
erudition 490, 539
eruption
  upheaval 146
  violence 173
  egress 295, 297
  disease 655
  volcanic – 872
escadrille 726
escalade
  mounting 305
  attack 716
escalator 307
escalop 248
escapade
  absurdity 497
  freak 608
  prank 840
escape
  flight **671**
  liberate 750
  evade 927
  means of – 664,
  666
  – the lips
  disclosure 529
  speech 582
  – the memory 506
  – *notice* &c.
  invisible 447
  inattention 458
  latent 526
escarp 717
escarpment
  stratum 204
  height 206
  oblique 217
escharotic
  caustic 171
  pungent 392
eschatology 67
escheat 144, 974
eschew
  avoid 623
  dislike 867
esclandre 828, 830
escort
  accompany 88

safeguard 664
  keeper 753
escritoire 191
esculent 298
escutcheon 550
esophagus 260
esoteric
  private 79
  concealed 528
Espagne, château
  en – *fancy* 515
  hope 858
espalier 232
especial 79
especially 33
espial 441
espiéglerie
  cunning 702
  fun 840
  wit 842
espionnage 441,
  461
esplanade
  houses 189
  flat 213
espouse
  choose 609
  marriage 903
  – a cause *aid* 707
  co-operate 709
esprit
  shrewdness 498
  wit 842
  bel – 844
  – de corps
  bias 481
  co-operation 709
  sociality 892
  (*party* 712)
  – fort
  thinker 500
  irreligious 989
espy 441
esquire 875, 877
essay
  experiment 463
  dissertation 595
  endeavor **675**
essayist 593, 595
esse 1
essence
  nature 5
  scent 398
essential
  intrinsic 5
  great 31
  required 630
  important 642
essentially
  intrinsically 5
  substantially 3
essential stuff 5
establish
  settle 150
  create 161
  place 184
  evidence 467
  demonstrate 478
  – *equilibrium* 27
established
  permanent 141
  habit 613
  – church 983a
establishment
  party 712
  shop 799
estafette 534
estaminet 189

estate *condition* 7
  property 780
  come to man's –
  131
esteem
  believe 484
  repute 873
  approve 931
  in high – 928
estimable 648
estimate
  measure 466
  adjudge 480
  information 527
  – too highly 482
estimation
  [*see* esteem,
  estimate]
estime
  succès d' – 873
estival 382
esto perpetua!
  perpetuity 112
  permanence 141
  desire 865
estop 706
estrade 213
estrange
  alienate 44, 889
  discord 713
  hate 898
estranged
  secluded 893
estrapade
  attack 716
  punishment 972
estreat 974
estuary 343
estuation 384
esurient 865
et – cetera
  add 37
  include 76
  plural 100
  – hoc genus omne
  similar 17
  include 76
  multiform 81
étalage 882
état major 745
etch *furrow* 259
  engraving 558
eternal 112
  – home 981
Eternal, the – 976
eterne 112
eternify 112
eternity 112
  an – 110
  launch into – 360,
  361
ether
  lightness 320
  rarity 322
  vapor 334
  anesthetic 376
ethereal 4
ethicism 984
ethics 926
Ethiopian 431
  –'s skin 150
Ethiopian's skin
  unchangeable 150
ethnology 372
ethnic 984
ethology 926
ethos 5
etiolate 429, 430

etiology *causes* 155, 359
  knowledge 490
  disease 655
etiquette
  custom 613
  fashion 832
  ceremony 882
étoile, à la belle –
  out of doors 220
  in the air 338
Eton jacket 225
étourderie
  inattention 458
  unskilfulness 699
etymological 560
etymology 562
etymon *origin* 153
  verbal 562
Eucharist 998
euchology 998
euchre 840
eudiometer
  air 338
  salubrity 656
euge! 931
eugenics 658
eulogist 935
eulogize 482
eulogy 931
Eumenides *fury* 900
  evil-doers 913
  revenge 919
eunuch 158
eupepsia 654
euphemism
  metaphor 521
  style 577, 578
  flattery 933
euphemist
  man of taste 850
  flatterer 935
euphony 413, 578
Euphrosyne 836
euphuism
  metaphor 521
  elegant style 577
  affected style 579
  affectation 855
Eurasian 41
eureka! 462, 480a
Euripus 343
Eurus 349
eurythmics 537, 840
eurythmy 242
Euterpe 416
euthanasia 360
euthenics 658
evacuate
  quit 293
  excrete 295
  emit 297
evacuation 299
evade *sophistry* 477
  avoid 623
  not observe 773
  exempt 927
evagation 279
evanescent
  small 32
  transient 111
  little 193
  disappearing 449
evangelical 983a, 985
Evangelists 985

evanid 160
evaporable 334
evaporate
  unsubstantial 4
  transient 111
  vaporize 336
evaporation 340
evasion
  sophistry 477
  concealment 528
  falsehood 544
  untruth 546
  avoidance 623
  escape 671
  cunning 702
  non-observance 773
  dereliction 927
eve 126
  on the – of
  transient 111
  prior 116
  future 121
evection 61
even
  uniform 16
  equal 27
  still more 33
  regular 138
  level 213
  straight 246
  flat 251
  smooth 255
  although 469
  in spite of 708
  – course 628
  – now 118
  – so
  for all that 30
  yes 488
  – temper 826
  – terms 922
  – tenor
  uniform 16
  order 58
  continuity 58
  pursue the –
  tenor
  continue 143
  avoid 623
  business 625
  be – with
  retaliate 718
  pay 807
  get – with 972
even-handed 922, 939
evening 126
  shades of – 422
  – classes 537
  – star 423
evenness 16
evensong 126, 990
event 151
  bout 720
  in the – of
  circumstance 8
  expectation 507
  supposition 514
  justified by the – 937
eventful 151
  remarkable 642
  stirring 682
eventide 126
eventual 121
eventuality 151
eventually

effect 154
ever 16, 112
  did you – ? 870
  – and anon 136
  – changing 149
  – recurring 104
ever so 31
  – little 32
  – long 110
  – many 102
evergreen
  continuous 69
  lasting 110
  always 112
  fresh 123
everlasting 112
  – life 152
  – fire 982
evermore 112
eversion 218
evert 140
every 78
  – hand against one 891
  – day
  conformity 82
  frequent 136
  habit 613
  – description 81
  – inch 50
  in – mouth
  assent 488
  news 532
  repute 873
  – other 138
  in – quarter 180
  in – respect 494
  on – side 227
  at – turn 186
  – whit 52
everybody 78
everyone 78
  – his due 922
  – in his turn 148
everywhere 180, 186
evict 297
evidence **467**
  disclose 529
  ocular – 446
évidence, en – 446
evident
  concrete 3
  visible 446
  certain 474
  manifest 525
evidently 516
evil *harm* **619**
  badness 649
  impious 988
  – day
  prepare for – 673
  adversity 735
  – eye *vision* 441
  malevolence 907
  disapprobation 932
  demon 980
  sorcery 992
  spell 993
  – favored 846
  – fortune 735
  – genius 980
  – hour 135
  – one 978
  – plight 735
  through – report &c. 604a

  – star 649
evil-doer **913**
evil-doing 945
evil-minded 907, 945
evil-speaking
  malediction 908
  censure 932
  detraction 934
evince *show* 467
  prove 478
  disclose 529
eviscerate 297, 301
eviscerated 4
evoke *cause* 153
  call upon 765
  excite 824
evolution
  numerical 85
  production 161
  motion 264
  extraction 301
  circuition 311
  turning out **313**
  organization 357
  training 673
  action 680
  military –*e* 722
evolve
  discover 480a
  evolved from 154
  [*and see* evolution]
evulgate 531
evulsion 301
evviva! 931
ewe 366, 374
  – lamb 366
ewer 191
ex
  – animo 602
  – cathedra 542
  – officio 494, 924
  – parte 467
  – pede Herculem 82
  – post facto 122, 133
  – tempore
  instant 113
  occasion 134
exacerbate
  increase 35
  exasperate 173
  aggravate 659, 835
exact *similar* 17
  special 79
  true 494
  style 572
  require **741**
  tax 812
  insolence 885
  claim 924, 926
  – meaning 516
  – memory 505
  – observance 772
  – truth 494
exacting
  severe 739
  discontented 832
  grasping 865
  fastidious 868
exaction
  [*see* exact]
  undue 925
exactly
  just so 488

exaggeration
  increase 35
  expand 194
  overestimate 482
  magnify **549**
  misrepresent 555
exalt
  increase 35
  elevate 307
  extol 931
  – one's horn 873
exalté 504
  tête –e 503
exalted *high* 206
  repute 873
  noble 875
  magnanimous 942
examination
  [*see* examine]
  evidence 467
  undergo – 461
examine 457, 461
example
  pattern 22
  instance 82
  bad – 949
  good – 948
  make an – of 974
  set a good – 944
exanimate
  dead 360
  supine 360
exarch 745
exasperate
  exacerbate 173
  aggravate 835
  enrage 900
excavate 252
excecation 442
exceed *surpass* 33
  remain 40
  transgress 303
  intemperance 954
excel *surpass* 33
  – in *skilful* 698
excellence 648, 944
excellence, par – 642
excellency 877
excelsior 305
except *subduct* 38
  exclude 55
  reject 610
exception
  unconformity 83
  qualification 469
  exemption 777a
  disapproval 932
  take –
  qualify 469
  resent 900
exceptionable
  bad 649
  guilty 947
exceptional
  original 20
  extraneous 57
  unconformable 83
  in an – degree 31
exceptious 901, 901a
exceptis
  excipiendis 469
excern 297
excerpt 609
excerpta *parts* 51
  compendium 596

expose]
appearance 448
– to weather 338
expound
interpret 522
teach 537
expounder 524
express
rapid 274
squeeze out 301
mean 516
declare 525
inform 527
journal 531
intentional 620
by – haste 684
– train 272
– by words 566
expressed, well –
578
expressible 525
expression [see
express]
musical 416
aspect 448
nomenclature 564
phrase 566
mode of – 569
new fangled – 563
expressive
meaning 516
sensibility 822
exprobation 932,
938
expropriation 782
expugnable 665
expugnation 731
expulsion 55 [see
expel]
expunge 162, 552
expurgate 38, 652
expurgatorious,
index – 761
exquisite
savory 394
excellent 648
pleasurable 829
beautiful 845
fop 854
exquisitely 31
exsiccate 340
exsudation 299
exsufflation 993
exsuscitate 824
extant 1
exstasy [see ecstasy]
extemporaneous
[see extempore]
transient 111
extempore
instant 113
early 132
occasion 134
off-hand 612
unprepared 674
extend
expand 194
prolong 200
– to 196
extended 202
extensibility 324
extensile 324
extension [see
extend] 35, 142,
180
– of time 110
extensive 31, 180
– knowledge 490

extenso, in –
whole 50
diffuse 573
extent 26, 180
extenuate
decrease 36
weaken 160
excuse 937
extenuated 203
extenuating cir-
cumstances
469, 937
extenuatory 469
exteriority 220
exterminate 162
extermination 301
external 57, 220
– evidence 467
– senses 375
extinct
inexistent 2
past 122
destroyed 162
darkness 421
become – 4
extincteur 385
extinction of life
360
extinguish
destroy 162
blow out 385
darken 421
extinguisher 165
put an – upon
hinder 706
defeat 731
extirpate 301
extispicious 511
extol
over-estimate 482
praise 931
extort extract 301
compel 744
despoil 789
extorted
dissent 489
extortion 814, 819
extortionate 739,
865
extra 37, 599, 641
ab – 220
extract
draw off 297
take out 301
quotation 596
remedy 662
extraction 301
paternity 166
– of roots 85
extractor 301
extradition 270, 297
extrajudicial 964
extramundane 317
extramural 220
extraneous
extrinsic 6
not related 10
foreign 57
outside 220
extraneousness 57
extraordinary
great 31
exceptional 83
extraregarding 220
extravagant
inordinate 31
violent 173
absurd 497

foolish 499
fanciful 515
exaggerated 549
excessive 641
high-priced 814
prodigal 818
vulgar 851
ridiculous 853
extravagation 303
extravaganza
fanciful 515
drama 599
extravasate 295,
297
extreme
inordinate 31
end 67
– unction 998
extremis, in –
dying 360
difficulty 704
extremist 710
extremity end 67
adversity 735
tribulation 828
drive matters to
an – 604
at the last – 665
extricate
take out 301
deliver 672
facilitate 705
liberate 750
extrinsicality 6
extrinsic evidence
467
extrusion 297, 299
exuberant
– style 573
redundant 639
exudation 295, 299
exulcerate 659
exult 838, 884
exultant 858
exulting 836
exunge 356
exuviae 653
eye circle 247
opening 260
organ of sight 441
all my – and
Betty Martin
546
appear to one's
– 446
before one's –s
front 234
visible 446
manifest 525
cast the –s on
see 441
cast the –s over
attend to 457
catch the – 457
close the –s
blind 442
death 360
sleep 683
dry –s 823
fix the –s on 457
have an – to
attention 457
intention 620
desire 865
in one's –
visible 446
expectant 507
in the –s of

appearance 448
belief 484
keep an – upon
459
look with one's
own –s 459
make –'s at 441
mind's – 515
with moistened –s
839
open the –s to
480a
with open –s 870
set one's –s upon
865
shut one's –s to
inattention 458
permit 760
to the –s 448
under the –s of
186
up to one's –s
641
have one's –s
about one 459
– askance 860
–s draw straws 683
an – for an – 718,
919
– glistening 824
in the – of the law
963
– of the master
693
– of a needle 260
–s open
attention 457
care 459
intention 620
–s opened
disclosure 529
–s out 442
eye-ball 441
eyebrows 256
eyeglass 445
eyelashes 256
eyeless 442
eyelet 260
eyelid 223
eye-shade 443
eye-sight 441
eyesore 846, 848
eye-teeth
have cut one's –
adolescence 131
skill 698
cunning 702
eye-wash 544
eye-witness
spectator 444
evidence 467
eyot 346
eyre 966
eyry 189

F

Fabian policy
delay 133
inaction 681
caution 864
fable error 495
metaphor 521
fiction 546
description 590
fabric state 7
effect 154

texture 329
fabricate
composition 54
make 161
invent 515
falsify 544
fabrication lie 546
fabula narratur, de
te – retaliate 718
condemn 971
fabulist 594
fabulous
enormous 31
imaginary 515
untrue 546
exaggerated 549
faburden 413
façade 234
face exterior 220
covering 223
front 234
aspect 448
oppose 708
resist 719
brave 861
impudence 885
change the – of
146
fly in the – of
disobey 742
put a good – upon
sham 545
calm 826
cheerful 836
hope 858
pride 878
display 882
vindicate 93
in the – of
presence 186
opposite 708
look in the –
see 441
proud 878
make –s
distort 243
ugly 846
disrespect 929
on the – of
manifest 525
show –
present 186
visible 446
not show –
disreputable 874
bashful 879
to one's – 525
wry – 378
– about 279
set one's – against
708
– of the country
344
on the – of the
earth
space 180
world 318
– to face front 234
contraposition
237
manifest 525
– of the thing
appearance 448
facet 220
facetiae 842
facetious 842
facia 234
facile willing 602

irresolute 605
  easy 705
facile princeps 33
facilis descensus
  Averni
  sloping 217
  danger 665
facilitate 705
facility *skill* 698
  easy 705
facing *covering* 223
facinorous 945
façon de parler 521,
  549
fac-simile 21, 554
fact *existence* 1
  event 151
  certainty 474
  truth 494
  in – 535
faction 712, 713
factious 24
factitious 545, 546
factor
  numerical 84
  director 694
  consignee 758
factory 691
factotum
  agent 690
  manager 694
  employé 758
facts *evidence* 467
  summary of – 594
  at variance with –
    471
facula 420
faculties 450
  in possession of
    one's – 502
faculty
  power 157
  profession 625
  skill 698
facundity 582
fad 481, 608
faddle 683
fade *vanish* 4
  transient 111
  become old 124
  droop 160
  grow dim 422
  lose color 429
  disappear 449
  spoil 659
  – from the
    memory 506
fade 391
fadge 23
faex populi 876
fag *cigarette* 392
  labor 686
  fatigue 688
  drudge 690, 746
  – end
    remainder 40
    end 67
faggot 72, 388
fagots and fagots 15,
  465
faience 557
fail *droop* 160
  shortcoming 304
  be confuted 479
  illness 655
  not succeed 732

not observe 773
not pay 808
dereliction 927
failing [*see* fail]
  incomplete 53
  insufficient 640
  vice 945
  guilt 947
  – heart 837
  – luck 735
  – memory 506
  – sight 443
  – strength 160
failure 732
  heart – 360
fain *willing* 602
  compulsive 744
  wish 865
fainéant 683
faint
  small in degree 32
  impotent 158
  weak 160
  sound 405
  dim 422
  color 429
  swoon 688
  – heart *fear* 860
  cowardice 862
  damn with –
    praise 930, 932,
    934
faintness 405
fair *in degree* 31
  pale 429
  white 430
  wise 498
  important 643
  good 648
  moderate 651
  mart 799
  beautiful 845
  just 922
  honorable 939
  – chance 472
  – copy *copy* 21
  writing 590
  – field
    occasion 134
  – game 857
  by – means 631,
    940
  – name 873
  – play 922, 923
  – question 461
  – sex 374
  in a – way
    tending 176
    probable 472
    convalescent 658
    prosperous 734
    hopeful 858
  – weather 734
  – weather sailor
    701
  – wind 705
  – words 894
fairing 784
fairly
  intrinsically 5
  get on – 736
  – well 643
fair-spoken
  courtesy 894
  flattery 933
fairy *fanciful* 515
  fay 979

imp 980
  – godmother 711,
    784, 912
  – tale 545, 594
fairy-land 515
fait: au –
  knowledge 490
  skilful 698
  – accompli
    certain 474
    complete 729
faith *belief* 484
  hope 858
  honor 939
  piety 987
  declaration of –
    983
  bad – 544
  i' – 535
  keep – with –
    observe 772
  plight –
    promise 768
    love 902
  true –
    orthodox 983a
  want of –
    incredulity 487
    irreligious 989
  – healing 662
faithful [*see* faith]
  like 17
  copy 21
  exact 494
  obedient 743
  – memory 505
  – to 772
faithless *false* 544
  dishonorable 940
  sceptical 989
fake 544, 545
fakir 996
falcate 244, 245
falchion 727
falciform
  [*see* falcate]
falcon 792
falconet 727
faldstool 215
fall *autumn* 126
  happen 151
  perish 162
  slope 217
  regression 283
  descend 306
  die 360
  fail 732
  adversity 73
  vice 945
  let – *lower* 308
    inform 527
  water– 348
  – asleep 683
  – astern 235, 283
  – away 105
  – back *return* 283
  recede 287
  relapse 661
  – back upon 677,
    717
  have to – back
    upon 637
  – a cursing 908
  – of the curtain 67
  – into a custom 82
  – of day 125
  – dead 360

  – into decay 659
  – down 990
  – down before 928
  – upon the ear 418
  – flat on the ear
    843
  – at one's feet 725
  – foul of *blow* 276
    hinder 706
    oppose 708
    discord 713
    attack 716
    contention 720
    censure 932
  – for 897
  – to the ground
    be confuted 479
    fail 732
  – into a habit 613
  – from one's high
    estate
    adversity 735
    disrepute 874
  – in *order* 58
    continuity 69
    event 151
  – into
    conversion 144
    river 348
  – in with *agree* 23
    conform 82
    converge 2
    discover 480a
    concord 714
    consent 762
  – on one's knees
    submit 725
    servile 886
    gratitude 916
    worship 990
  – of the leaf 126
  – from the lips 582
  – in love with 897
  – to one's lot
    event 151
    chance 156
    receive 785
    duty 926
  – under one's
    notice 457
  – into oblivion 506
  – off *decrease* 36
    deteriorate 659
  – off again 661
  – out *happen* 151
    quarrel 713
    enmity 889
  – into a passion
    900
  – to pieces
    disjunction 44
    destruction 162
    brittle 328
  – a prey to 732,
    749
  – in price 815
  – into raptures
    827
  – short *inferior* 32
    contract 195
    shortcoming 304
  – of snow 383
  – through *fail* 734
  – to *eat* 298
    take in hand 676
    do battle 722
  – into a trap 547

  – under
    inclusion 76
    subjection 749
  – upon
    discover 480a
    unexpected 508
    devise 626
    attack 716
    – in the way of 186
    – to work 686
fallacy *sophistry*
  477
  error 495
  show the – of 497
fallen angel 949,
  978
fallible 475, 477
falling-out 24
falling star 318, 423
fallow
  unproductive 169
  yellow 436
  unready 674
  inactive 681
false *imitation* 10
  sophistry 477
  error 495
  untrue 544, 546
  spurious 925
  dishonorable 940
  – alarm 669
  – coloring
    misinterpretation
    523
    falsehood 544
  – construction
    523, 544
  – doctrine 984
  – expectation 509
  – hearted 940
  – impression 495
  – light *vision* 443
  – money 800
  – ornament 851
  – plea *untruth* 546
    plea 617
  – position 704
  – pretences 791
  – prophet
    disappoint 509
    pseudo-revelation
    986
  – reasoning 477
  – scent 495, 538
  – shame 855
  – statement 546
  – step 732
  – teaching 538
  – witness
    deceiver 548
    detraction 934
falsehood 544, 546
falsetto *squeak* 410
  want of voice 581
falsify *error* 495
  falsehood 544,
    546
  – accounts 811
  – one's hope 509
falter *slow* 275
  stammer 583
  hesitate 605
  slip 732
  hopeless 859
  fear 860
faltering accents
  605

fame *greatness* 31
 news 532
 renown 873
familiar
 known 490
 habitual 613
 sociable 892
 affable 894
 – *spirit* 979, 980
 on – *terms* 888
familiarize
 teach 537
 habit 613
famille, en – 892
family
 kin 11
 class 75
 ancestors 166
 posterity 167
 party 712
 in the bosom of
 one's – 221
 happy – 714
 – *circle* 892
 – *jars* 713
 – *likeness* 17
 – *tie* 11
 in the – *way* 161
famine 640
 – *price* 814
famine-stricken
 640
famish
 stingy 819
 fasting 956
famished
 insufficient 640
 hungry 865
famous 873
famously 31
fan *blow* 349
 cool 385
 refresh 689
 stimulate 824
 flirt a – 855
 – the embers 505
 – the flame
 violence 173
 heat 384
 aid 707
 excite 824
 – into a flame
 anger 900
 –shaped 194
fanatic
 madman 504
 imaginative 515
 zealot 682
 religious – 988
fanatical
 misjudging 481
 insane 503
 emotional 821
 excitable 825
 heterodox 984
 over-righteous 988
fanaticism 606
fanciful
 imaginative 515
 capricious 608
 ridiculous 853
fancy *think* 451
 idea 453
 believe 484
 suppose 514
 imagine 515
 caprice 608

choice 609
 pugilism 726
 wit 842
 desire 865
 wonder 870
 love 897
 after one's – 850
 indulge one's –
 609
 take a – to
 delight in 827
 desire 865
 take one's –
 please 829
 – *dog* 366
 – *dress* 840
 – *price* 814
 – *woman* 962
fandango 840
fandi, mollia tem-
 pora – 588
fane 1000
fanfare *loudness*
 404
 celebration 883
fanfaron 887
fanfaronnade 884
fangs *venom* 663
 rule 737
 retention 781
fan-light 260
fan-like 202
fannel 999
fanon 999
fantasia 415
fantastic *odd* 83
 absurd 497
 imaginative 515
 capricious 608
 unfashionable 851
 ridiculous 853
fantasy
 imagination 515
 desire 865
fantoccini 554, 599
faquir 996
far – *away* 196
 – be it from
 unwilling 603
 deprecation 766
 – between
 disjunction 44
 few 103
 interval 198
 – from it
 unlike 18
 shortcoming 304
 no 536
 – from the truth
 546
 – and near 180
 – off 196
 – and wide 31,
 180, 196
farce
 absurdity 497
 untruth 546
 drama 599
 wit 842
 ridiculous 853
 mere –
 unimportant 643
 useless 645
farceur
 actor 599
 humorist 844
fardel

bundle 72
 hindrance 706
fare *state* 7
 food 298
 price 812
 bill of –
 list 86
farewell
 departure 293
 relinquishment
 624
 loss 776
 – to greatness 874
far-famed 873
far-fetched 10
far-flung 73
far-gone
 much 31
 insane 503
 spoiled 654
farinaceous 330
farm *till* 371
 property 780
 rent 788
farmer 188, 342,
 371
 afternoon – 683
farm-house 189
Farmer-Labor 712
faro 840
farrago 59
farrier 370
farrow
 produce 161
 litter 167
 multitude 102
far-sighted 442, 510
farther 196
 [*and see* further]
farthing
 quarter 97
 worthless 643
 coin 800
 – *candle* 422
farthingale 225
fasces 747
fascia 205, 247
fascicle 51
fasciculated 72
fascinate
 influence 615
 excite 824
 please 829
 astonish 870
 love 897
 conjure 992
fascinated
 pleased 827
fascination [*see*
 fascinate]
 infatuation 825
 desire 870
fascine 72
Fascisti 712
fas et nefas, per –
 604*a*, 631
fash 830
fashion
 state 7
 form 240
 custom 613
 method 627
 ton 852
 after a –
 middling 32
 after this – 617
 follow the – 82

be in the – 488
 man of – 852
 set the –
 influence 175
 authority 737
 for –'s sake 852
fast *joined* 43
 steadfast 150
 rapid 274
 fashionable 852
 intemperate 954
 not eat 956
 worship 990
 rile 998
 stick – 704
 – *asleep* 683
 – by 197
 – day 956
 – *friend* 890
 – and loose
 sophistry 477
 falsehood 544
 irresolute 605
 tergiversation 607
 caprice 608
 – *man fop* 854
 libertine 962
fasten *join* 43
 hang 214
 restrain 751
 – on the mind 451
 – a quarrel upon
 713
 – upon 789
fastening 45
fast-handed 819
fastidious
 censorious 932
fastidiousness 868
fasting
 insufficiency 640
 worship 990
 penance 952
 abstinence 956
fastness
 asylum 666
 defence 717
fat *corpulent* 192
 expansion 194
 unctuous 355
 oleaginous 356
 kill the –ted calf
 celebration 883
 sociality 892
 – in the fire
 disorder 59
 violence 173
 – of the land
 pleasure 377
 enough 639
 prosperity 734
 intemperance 95
fata – Morgana
 occasion 134
 ignis fatuus 423
 – *obstant* 601
fatal 361
 – *disease* 655
fatalism 601
fatality 601
fate *end* 67
 necessity 601
 chance 621
 be one's – 156
 sure as – 474
Fates 601, 979
fat-head 501

father *eldest* 128
 paternity 166
 priest 996
 Apostolical –s 985
 gathered to one's
 –s 360
 heavy – 599
 – *upon* 155
 Father, God the –
 976
fatherland 189
fatherless 158
fatherly 906
fathom
 length 200
 investigate 461
 solve 462
 measure 466
 discover 480*a*
 knowledge 490
fathomless 208
fatidical 511
fatigation 688
fatigue 688
fatras 643
fatten
 expand 194
 improve 658
 prosperous 734
 – on *parasite* 886
 – *upon*
 feed 298
fatuity 4, 499
fatuous 517
fat-witted 499
faubourg 227
fauces 231
faucet 252
faugh! 867
fault
 break 70
 error 495
 imperfection 651
 failure 732
 vice 945
 guilt 947
 at –
 uncertain 475
 ignorant 491
 unskilful 699
 find – with 932
faultless 650, 946
faulty 495, 651
faun 980
fauna 366
faut: comme il –
 taste 850
 fashion 852
 il s'en – bien 489
 tant s'en – 536
faute 732
 – de mieux
 substitution 147
 necessity 601
fauteuil 215
fautor 890
faux pas
 error 568
 failure 732
 misconduct 947
 intrigue 961
favor
 resemble 16
 badge 550
 letter 592
 aid 707
 indulgence 740

unimportant 643
  contempt 930
fiddlefaddle
  unmeaning 517
  trifle 643
  dawdle 683
fiddler 416
fiddlestick 417
  – end 643
fidelity
  veracity 543
  obedience 743
  observance 772
  honor 939
fidget *changes* 149
  activity 682
  hurry 684
  excitability 825
fidgety
  irresolute 605
  fearful 860
  irascible 901
fiducial 156
fiduciary 484
fidus Achates
  auxiliary 711
  associate 743
  friend 890
fie *disreputable* 874
  – upon it
  censure 932
fief 777
field *opportunity*
  134
  scope 180
  region 181
  plain 344
  agriculture 371
  business 625
  arena 728
  property 780
  the – *hunting* 622
  beasts of the – 366
  playing –s 728
  the potter's – 361
  take the – 722
  – artillery 726
  the – of blood 361
  – of inquiry
    topic 454
    inquiry 461
  – of view
    vista 441
    idea 453
field-day
  contention 720
  amusement 840
  display 882
field-glass 445
field-marshal 745
field-piece 727
field-preacher 996
field-work 717
fiend 913, 980
fiend-like
  malevolent 907
  wicked 945
  fiend 980
fierce *violent* 173
  passion 825
  daring 861
  angry 900
fiery *violent* 173
  hot 382
  strong feeling 821
  excitable 825
  angry 900
  irascible 901

– cross 550, 722
  – furnace 386
  – imagination 515
  – ordeal 828
fife 417
fifer 416
fifth 98, 99
fifty 98
fig
  unimportance 643
  in the name of the
    prophet –s! 497
  – out 847
fight
  contention 720
  warfare 722
  show –
    defence 717
    courage 861
  – one's battles
    again 594
  – against destiny
    606
  – the good fight
    944
  – it out 722
  – shy *avoid* 603,
    623
  coward 862
  – one's way
    pursue 622
    active 682
    exertion 686
fighter 726
fighting-cock 726,
  861
fighting-man 726
figment 515
figurante 599
figurate number 84
figuration 240
figurative
  metaphorical 521
  representing 554
  – *style* 577
figure
  number 84
  form 240
  appearance 448
  metaphor 521
  indicate 550
  represent 554
  price 812
  ugly 846
  cut a –
    repute 873
    display 882
  poor – 874
  – to oneself 515
  – of speech 521
  – out 522
  exaggeration 549
figure-flinger 994
figure-head 4, 550,
  554, 643
figurine 554
figuriste 559
filaceous 205
filament 205
filamentous 256
filch 791
filcher 762
file *subduct* 38
  arrange 60
  row 69
  assemblage 72
  list 86
  reduce 195

smooth 255
  pulverize 330
  record 551
  store 636
  soldiers 726
  – a claim &c. 969
  – off *march* 266
  diverge 291
file-fire 716
filial 167
filiation
  consanguinity 11
  attribution 155
  posterity 167
filibuster 133, 706,
  792
filibustering 791
filiform 205
filigree 219
filings 330
fill *complete* 52
  occupy 186
  contents 190
  stuff 224
  provision 637
  eat one's – 957
  have one's –
    enough 639
    satiety 869
  – the bill 229
  – an office
    business 625
    government 737
  – out
    expand 194
  –ed to overflow-
    ing 641
  – one's pocket 803
  – time 106
  – up *compensate*
    30
    compose 54
    close 261
    restore 660
  – up the time
    inaction 681
fille
  – de chambre 746
  – de joie 962
filled
  – to overflowing
    641
filler 532
fillet *band* 45
  filament 205
  circle 247
  insignia 550
  ornament 847
fillibeg 225
filling 224
fillip
  impulse 276
  propulsion 284
  stimulus 615
  excite 824
filly 271
film *layer* 204
  opaque 426
  semitransparent
    427
  – over the eyes
    dim sight 443
  cinema 448
  ignorant 491
filmy *texture* 329
filter *percolate* 295
  clean 652
filth 653

–y *lucre* 800
filtrate 652
fimbriated 256
fin 267
final *ending* 67
  conclusive 474
  completing 729
  court of – *appeal*
    474
  – cause 620
  – stroke 729
  – touch 729
finale *end* 67
  completion 729
finality 67, 729
finally
  for good 141
  on the whole 476
finance 800, 811
  minister of – 801
financier 801
finch 366
find
  eventuality 151
  adjudge 480
  discover 480a
  acquire 775
  – one's account in
    644
  – the cause of 522
  – a clue to 480a
  – to one's cost 509
  – credence 484
  – it in one's heart
    602
  – in *provide* 637
  – the key of 522
  – the meaning 522
  – means 632
  – oneself *be* 1
    present 186
  – out 480a
  – vent 671
  – one's way 731
  – one's way into
    294
finding
  judgment 480
fine *small* 32
  large 192
  thin 203
  rare 322
  not raining 340
  exact 494
  good 648
  beautiful 845
  adorned 847
  proud 878
  mulct 974
  in – *end* 67
  after all 476
  – air 656
  – arts 554
  – feather 159, 654
  – feeling 850
  – frenzy 515
  – gentleman
    fop 854
    proud 878
  – grain 329
  – lady 854, 878
  one – morning 106
  some – morning
    119
  – powder 330
  – talking
    overrate 482

boast 884
  – writing 577
  – time of it 734
  – voice 580
fine-draw 660
fine-fingered 698
fine-spoken 894,
  933
fine-spun *thin* 203
  sophistry 477
fine-toned 413
finem, respicere –
  510
finery 847, 851
finesse *tact* 698
  artifice 702
  taste 850
finger *touch* 379
  hold 781
  lay the – on
    point out 457
    discover 480a
  lift a – 680
  not lift a – 681
  point the – at 457
  turn round one's
    little – 737
  –'s breadth 203
  at one's –s' end
    near 197
    know 490
    remember 505
  – on the lips
    aphony 581
    taciturnity 585
  – in the pie
    cause 153
    interfere 228
    act 680
    active 682
    co-operate 709
fingerling 193
finger-post 550
finger-print 467
finger-stall 223
fingle-fangle 643
finical
  trifling 643
  affected 855
  fastidious 868
finicky 855, 868
finikin 643
finis 67
  – coronat opus
    729
finish *lend* 67
  symmetry 242
  complete 729
  skill 698
finished
  absolute 31
  perfect 650
  skilled 698
finishing
  – stroke 361
  – touch 729
finite 32
fiord 343
fire *energy* 171
  heat 382
  make hot 384
  stoke 388
  vigor 574
  discharge 756
  enthusiasm 821
  excite 824, 825
  catch – 384

hell – 982
on – 382
open – *begin* 66
play with – 863
signal – 550
take –
  excitable 825
  angry 900
between two –s
  665
under – 665, 722
– at 716
– the blood 824
– and fury 900
– the first shot 716
– of genius 498
– off 284
– a salute 883
– and sword 162
– up *excite* 825
  anger 900
– a volley 716
go through – and
  water
  resolution 604
  perseverance 604a
  courage 861
fire-alarm 669
fire-annihilator 385
fire-arms 727
fire-ball *fuel* 388
  arms 727
fire-balloon 273
fire-barrel 388
fire-bell 669
fire-boat 726
fire-brand
  fuel 388
  instigator 615
  dangerous man
  667
  incendiary 913
fire-brigade 385
fire-curtain 599
fire-drake 423
fire-eater
  fighter 726
  blusterer 887
fire-eating
  rashness 863
  insolence 885
fire-engine 348
fire-escape 671
fire-extinguisher
  385
fire-fly 423
fireless cooker 386
fire-light 422
firelock 727
fireman *stoker* 268
  extinguisher 385
fire-place 386
fire-proof 385, 644
fireside 189
firewood 388
firework
  fire 382
  luminary 423
  celebration 883
  amusement 840
fire-worship 991
fire-worshipper 984
firing *fuel* 388
  explosion 406
firkin 191
firm
  junction 43

stable 150
hard 323
resolute 604
  partnership 712
  merchant 797
  brave 861
stand – 719
– as a rock 604
– belief 484
– hold 781
firmament 318
firman 741, 760
first 66
– blush
  morning 125
  leading 280
  vision 441
  appearance 448
  manifest 525
– blow 716
– cause 976
– that comes 609a
– fiddle
  importance 642
  proficient 700
  authority 737
– come first
  served 609a
– and foremost 66
– impression 66
– and last 87
– line 234
come back to –
  love 607
– move 66
– opportunity 132
at – sight 448
– stage 66
– stone
  preparation 673
  attack 716
on the – summons
  741
of the – water
  best 648
  repute 873
first-born 124 128
first-fruits 154
first-hand 2u, 467
firstlings 128, 154
first-rate
  important 642
  excellent 648
  man-of-war 726
firth 343
fisc 802
fiscal 800
fish *food* 298
  sport 361, 622
  animal 366
food for –es 362
other – to fry
  ill-timed 135
  busy 682
queer – 857
– in the air 645
– for compliments,
  880
– for *seek* 4
  experiment 463
  desire 865
– hatchery 370
– out *inquire* 461
  discover 480a
– in troubled
  waters
  difficult 704

discord 713
– up *raise* 307
  find 480a
– out of water
  disagree 24
  unconformable 83
  displaced 185
  bungler 701
fisherman 361
fishery 370
fishing *kill* 361
  pursue 622
fishing-boat 273
fishpond 343, 370
fish-trail 267
fishy *transaction*
  940
fisk 266, 274
fissile 328
fission 44
fissure 44
  chink 198
fist
  handwriting 590
  grip 781
shake the –
  defy 515
  threat 909
fisticuffs 720
fistula 260
fit *state* 7
  agreeing 23
  equal 27
  paroxysm 173
  agitation 315
  caprice 608
  expedient 646
  healthy 654
  disease 655
  excitement 825
  anger 900
  right 922
  due 924
  duty 926
in –s 315
think – 600
– of abstraction
  458
– of crying 839
– for 698
– out *dress* 225
  prepare 673
– to be seen 845
by –s and starts
  irregular 59
  discontinuous 70
  agitated 315
  capricious 608
  haste 684
fitful
  irregular 139
  changeable 149
  capricious 608
fittings 633
five 98
division by – 99
– act *play* 599
– and twenty 98
Five Year Plan 626
fiver 800
fives *game* 840
fix *join* 43
  arrange 60
  establish 150
  place 184
  immovable 265
  solidify 321

resolve 604
difficulty 704
– the eyes upon
  441
– the foundations
  673
– the memory 505
– the time 114
– the thoughts
  457
– up 774
– upon *discover*
  480a
  choose 609
fixed *intrinsic* 5
  permanent 141
  stable 150
  quiescent 265
  habitual 613
– idea 481
– opinion 484
– periods 138
fixity 141
fixity of purpose
  141
fixture
  appointment 741
  property 780
fizgig 423
fizz 409
fizzle 353
– out 304
flabelliform 194
flabbergast 870
  879
flabby 324
flabbiness 324
flaccid *weak* 160
  soft 324
  empty 640
flag *weak* 160
  flat stone 204
  floor 211
  smoothness 255
  slow 275
  leaf 367
  sign 550
  path 627
  infirm 655
  inactive 683
  tired 688
  weary 841
lower one's – 725
red – *alarm* 669
yellow –
  warning 668
  alarm 669
– man 668
– ship 726
– of truce 723
flag-bearer 534
flagellation
  penance 952
  asceticism 955
  flogging 972
  rite 998
flagelliform 205
flageolet 417
flagitious 945
flagon 191
flagrant
  great 31
  manifest 525
  notorious 531
  atrocious 945
flagrante
  – *bello* 722

– delicto
  sure enough 474
  act 680
  guilt 947
flagration 384
flagstaff *tall* 206
  signal 550
flail 276
flair 450, 698
flake 204
  snow – 383
  – *white* 430
flam 544
flambé 732
flambeau 423
flamboyant 577
flame *fire* 382
  light 420
  luminary 423
  passion 824, 825
  love 897
catch the –
  emotion 821
consign to the –s
  384
add fuel to the –
  173
in –s 382
– up 825
–colored
  red 434
  orange 439
flame-projector 527
flamen 996
flaming *violent* 173
  feeling 821
  excited 824
  ostentatious 882
  boasting 884
flâneur 935
flange *support* 215
  rim 231
  projection 250
flank *side* 236
  protect 664
flannel 384
flap *adjunct* 39
  hanging 214
  move to and fro
  315
  – the memory 505
flapdoodle 517
flapper *girl* 129
flapping *loose* 47
flare *violent* 173
  glare 420
  light 423
  – up
  excited 824, 825
  angry 900
flaring *color* 428
flash *instant* 113
  violent 173
  fire 382
  light 420
eyes – fire 900
– lamp 550
– light 423
– across the mem-
  ory 505
– on the mind
  thought 451
  disclose 529
  impulse 612
– note 800
– in the pan
  unsubstantial 4
  transientness 111

impotent 158
unproductive 169
failure 732
– tongue 563
– up *excited* 824
– upon
unexpected 508
– of wit 842
flashing
ostentatious 882
flashy
gaudy color 428
style 577
ornament 847
vulgar 851
flask 191
flat *inert* 172
abode 189
story 191
low 207
horizontal 213
vapid 391
low tone 408
musical note 413
positive 535
dupe 547
back-scene 599
shoal 667
bungler 701
poor 804
insensible 823
dejected 837
weary 841
dull 843
simple 849
fall – 732
– contradiction
536
– iron 255
– refusal 764
flatfoot 664
flatness 251
flatter *deceive* 545
cunning 702
please 829
grace 845
encourage 858
approbation 931
adulation 933
– oneself
probable 472
hope 858
– the palate 394
flatterer 935
flattering
– remarks 894
– tale
hope 858
– unction to one's
soul
content 831
vain 880
flattery 933
flattery 544, 933
flatulent
gaseous 334
air 338
wind 349
– *style* 573, 575
flatus 334, 349
flaunt 873, 882
flaunting *vulgar* 85
gaudy 428
unreserved 525
flautist 416
**Flavian amphi-
theater** 728

flavor 390
flavoring 393
flavous 436
flaw *break* 70
crack 198
error 495
imperfection 651
blemish 848
fault 947
– in an argument
477
flaxen 436
flay *divest* 226
punish 972
flea *jumper* 309
dirt 653
– in one's ear
repel 289
eject 297
refuse 764
disrepute 874
abashed 879
discourteous 895
contempt 930
flea-bite 643
flea-bitten 440
fleck 32
flecked 440
flection 279
fled *escaped* 671
fledge 673
fledgling 123
flee *avoid* 623
fleece *tegument* 223
strip 789
rob 791
impoverish 804
surcharge 814
fleet *ridicule* 856
insult 929
fleet *ships* 273
swift 274
navy 726
Fleet *prison* 752
fleeting 4, 111
flesh *bulk* 192
animal 364
mankind 372
carnal 961
gain – 194
ills that – *is heir
to evil* 619
disease 655
in the – 359
one – 903
way of all – 360
weakness of the –
945
– and blood
substance 3
materiality 316
animality 364
affections 820
make the – *creep*
pain 830
fear 860
flesh-color 434
flesh-pots 298
– *of Egypt* 734,
803
fleshly 316
fleur-de-lis 847
fleuron 847
flexible 324, 705
flexion
curvature 245
fold 258

deviation 279
flexuous 248
flexure 245, 258
flibbertigibbet 980
flicker
changing 149
waver 314
flutter 315
light 420
dim 422
flickering 139
flier 621
flies *theatre* 599
flight *flock* 102
volitation 267
swiftness 274
departure 293
avoidance 623
escape 671
– *lieutenant* 745
put to –
propel 284
repel 717
vanquish 731
– of *fancy* 515
– of *stairs* 305,
627
– of *time* 109
flighty *inattentive*
458
mad 503
fanciful 515
flim-flam 544, 608
flimsy *unsubstan-
tial* 4
weak 160
rarity 322
soft 324
sophistical 477
trifling 643
flinch *swerve* 607
avoid 623
fear 860
cowardice 862
fling *propel* 284
jig 840
jeer 929
have one's –
active 682
laxity 738
freedom 748
amusement 840
– aside 782
have a – *at*
attack 716
resent 900
disrespect 929
censure 932
– away *reject* 610
waste 638
relinquish 782
– down 308
– to the winds
destroy 162
not observe 773
flint *hard* 323
flint-hearted 907
flintlock 727
flip *beverage* 298
flippant *fluent* 584,
pert 885
flipper *paddle* 267
flirt *propel* 284
coquet 607, 854
love 897
endearment 902
– a fan 855

flit *elapse* 109
changeable 149
move 264
travel 266
swift 274
depart 293
run away 623
flitter
small part 32
changeable 149
flutter 315
flitting 111
float *establish* 150
navigate 267
boat 273
buoy up 305
lightness 320
before the –s
on the stage 599
– on the air 405
– before the eyes
446
– bonds 788
– in the mind
thought 451
imagination 515
floater 683
floating
[*see* float]
rumoured 532
– *battery* 726
– *capital* 805
– *debt* 806
– *dock* 189
flocculent
woolly 256
soft 324
pulverulent 330
flock
assemblage 72
multitude 102
laity 997
–s *and herds* 366
– *together* 72
floe *ice* 383
flog 972
hasten 684
flood *much* 31
crowd 72
river 348
abundance 639
redundance 641
prosperity 734
stem the – 708
– of *light* 420
– of *tears* 839
flood-gate
limit 233
egress 295
conduit 350
open the –s
eject 297
permit 760
flood-light 423,
599
flood-mark 466
flood-tide
increase 35
complete 52
height 206
advance 282
water 337
floor *level* 204
base 211
horizontal 213
support 215
overthrow 731

ground – 191
flop 315
Flora 369
floral 367
florescence 154
floriculture 371
florid *color* 428
red 434
– *style* 577
health 654
florist 371
floss 256
flotilla 273, 726
flotsam and jetsam
73
flounce
trimming 231
jump 309
agitation 315
flounder
change 149
toss 315
uncertain 475
bungle 699
difficulty 704
fail 732
flour 330
flourish
brandish 314, 315
exaggerate 549
language 577
speech 582
prosper 618
healthy 654
prosperous 734
ornament 847
repute 873
display 882
boast 884
– of *trumpets*
loud 404
cheerfulness 836
publish 531
ostentation 882
celebrate 883
boast 884
flout 929, 936
flow *course* 109
hang 214
motion 264
stream 348
murmur 405
abundance 639
– from
result 154
– of *ideas* 451
– in 294
– into *river* 348
– out 295
– over 641
– of *soul*
conversation 588
affections 820
cheerful 836
social 892
– with the tide
705
– of *time* 109
– of *words* 582,
584
flower *essence* 1
produce 161
vegetable 367
prosper 734
beauty 845
ornament 847
repute 873

foozle 732
fop 854
foppery 882
foppish 855
for *cause* 155
 tendency 176
 reason 476
 motive 615
 intention 620
 preparation 673
 have –
  price 812
 – all that
  notwithstanding
  30
 qualification 469
 – all the world
  like 17
 – aught one
  knows 156
 – better for worse
  78
 –– ever 112
 – example 82
 – form's sake 82
 – good
  complete 52
  diuturnity 110
  permanence 141
 – the most part
  great 31
  general 78
  special 79
 – the nonce 118
 – nothing 815
 – a season 106
 – a time 111
 –– the time being
  106
forage
 fool 298
 provision 637
 steal 791
forage-cap 225
foramen 260
foraminous 260
forasmuch as
 relating to 9
 cause 155
 reason 476
 motive 615
foray *attack* 716
 robbery 791
forbear
 avoid 623
 spare 678
 lenity 740
 sufferance 826
 pity 914
 abstain 953
 forbearance 918
forbid 761
 God –
  dissent 489
  deprecation 766
  censure 932
  prayer 990
forbidden fruit
 seduction 615
 prohibition 761
forbidding
 ugly 846
force *corps* 72
 power 157
 strength 159
 agency 170
 energy 171

violence 173
 cultivate 371, 707
 cascade 348
 – *of style* 574
 urne 615
 exertion 686
 compulsion 744
 armed – 726
 brute – 964
 put in – 924
 – of argument 476
 – of arms 744
 – of character 820
 – down the throat
  severe 739
 compel 744
 – majeure 744
 – open 173
 – one's way
  progression 282
  passage 302
forced *irrelative* 10
 – *style* 579
 be – to 601
 – labor 603
 – march 744
forcefully 601
forceps
 extraction 301
 grip 781
forces 726
forcible [*see* force]
ford 302, 627
fore 234
fore and aft
 complete 52
 lengthwise 200
 – schooner 273
fore part 234
forearm 673
forebears 166
forebode 511
·forecast
 foresight 510
 prediction 511
 plan 626
foreclose 706
foredoom 152, 601
forefathers 166
forefend
 prohibit 761
forefinger 379
forego
 relinquish 624
 renounce 757
 surrender 782
foregoing 62, 116
foregone
 past 122
 – conclusion
  prejudged 481
  predetermined
   611
foreground 234
 in the –
  manifest 525
forehead 234
foreign
 alien 10
 extraneous 57
 – accent 580
 – parts 196
foreigner 57
forejudge
 prejudge 481
 foresight 510
foreknow 510

foreland 206, 254
forelay 545
fore ock
 pull the – 894
 take time by the –
  early 132
  occasion 134
foreman 694
foremost
 superior 33
 beginning 66
 front 234
 in advance 280
 important 642
 reputed 873
forenoon 125
forensic 968
foreordain 152
foreordination 601,
 611
forerun 62, 116, 280
forerunner 64, 512
foresee 507, 510
foreseen 871
foreshadow 152,
 511
foreshorten 201
foreshow 511
foresight 116, 510
 caution 864
forest 367
forestage 599
forestry 371
forestall
 prior 116
 early 132
 possession 777
foretaste 510
foretell 511
forethought 459,
 510
foretoken 511
forewarn 511, 668
foreword 64
forfeit *fail* 773
 lose 776
 penalty 974
 – one's good
  opinion 932
forfeiture
 disfranchisement
  925
forfend 706, 717
forgather 72
forge *imitate* 19
 produce 161
 furnace 386
 trump up 544
 workshop 691
 – fetters 751
forged
 false 546
forger
 maker 690
 thief 792
forgery
 deception 545
forget 506
 hand – cunning
  699
 – benefits 917
 – injury 918
 – oneself 945
forgive 918
forgo
 relinquish 624
 renounce 757

surrender 782
forgotten
 past 122
 ingratitude 917
 not to be – 505
 – by the world
  893
fork *bifid* 91
 pointed 244
 – lightning 423
 – out
  give 784
  pay 807
  expenditure 809
forlorn
 dejected 837
 hopeless 859
 deserted 893
 – hope
  danger 665
  rashness 863
form *state* 7
 likeness 21
 make up 54
 order 58
 arrange 60
 convert 144
 produce 161
 bench 215
 shape 240
 educate 537
 pupils 541
 manner 627
 beauty 845
 fashion 852
 etiquette 882
 law 963
 rite 998
 – letter 592
 – part of 56
 – a party 712
 – a resolution 604
formal [*see* form]
 regular 82
 definitive 535
 – *style* 579
 affected 855
 stately 882
 – speech 582
formalism 739, 988
formalist 82
formality·[*see*
 formal]
 ceremony 852
 affectation 855
 law 963
formation
 composition 54
 production 161
 shape 240
formative 153
formed [*see* form]
 attempered 820
former
 in order 62
 prior in time 116
 past 122
formication 380
formidable 704, 860
formless 241
formula *rule* 80
 arithmetic 84
 maxim 496
 precept 697
 law 963
formulary 998
formulate 590

fornication 961
fornicator 962
foro conscientiæ
 veracity 543
 duty 926
 probity 939
forsake 624
forsaken 898
forsooth 535
forspent 688
forswear *lie* 544
 tergiversation 607
 refuse 764
 transgress 927
 improbity 940
fort 666, 717
fort
 le droit du plus –
  compulsion 744
  illegality 964
 un peu – 641
fortalice 717
forte 415, 698
fortelage 717
forth 282
 come –
  egress 295
  visible 446
 go – *depart* 293
 the decree has
  gone – 741
·forthcoming 152,
 673
f.orthwith 132
forthcation 717
fortify 159
fortiori, a – 467, 476
fortissimo 404
fortiter in re 171
fortitude 826, 861
·ortnightly 138
.ortress 717, 752
fortuitous
 extrinsic 6
 chance 156
 undersigned 621
 – concourse of
  atoms 59
fortunate
 opportune 134
 successful 731
 prosperous 734
Fortunatus's – cap
 wish 865
 spell 993
 – purse 803
fortune *chance* 156
 fate 601
 wealth 803
 be one's – 151
 clean up a – 803
 evil – 621, 735
 good – 734
 make one's –
  succeed 731
  wealth 803
 tempt –
  hazard 621
  essay 675
 trick of·– 509
 try one's – 675
 wheel of – 601, 621
fortune-hunter 886,
 943
fortuneless 804
fortune-teller 513
fortune-telling 511

fortunes of
  narrative 594
forty 98
  - winks 683
forum 799
  school 542
  tribunal 966
forward *early* 132
  transmit 270
  advance 282
  willing 602
  improve 658
  active 682
  help 707
  vain 880
  insolent 885
  uncourteous 895
bend - 234
come -
  in sight 446
  offer 763
  display 882
look - to 507
move - 282
press - *haste* 684
put - *aid* 507
  offer 763
put oneself - 880
set - 676
  - *in knowledge* 490
foss 348
fosse
  inclosure 232
  ditch 259
  defence 717
fossil
  ancient 124
  hard 323
  organic 357
  dry bones 362
foster *aid* 707
  excite 824
  caress 902
  - a belief 484
fou 959
foudroyant 870
foul
  collide 276
  bad 649
  dirty 653
  unhealthy 657
  ugly 846
  base 940
  vicious 945
fall - of
  oppose 708
  quarrel 713
  attack 716
  fight 720
  censure 932
run - of
  impede 706
  - fiend 978
  - means 940
  - language
  malediction 908
  - odor 401
  - play *evil* 619
  cunning 702
  wrong 923
  improbity 940
foul-mouthed 895
foul-spoken 934
found 153, 215
foundation
  beginning 66
  stability 150

  base 211
  support 215
  lay the -s 673
  sandy - 667
  shake to its -s 315
founded
  well - 472
  - on base 211
  evidence 467
founder
  originator 164
  sink 310
  fail 732
  religious -s 986
foundery 691
founding 22
foundling
  trover 775
  derelict 782
  outcast 893
fount *type* 591
fountain
  source 153
  river 348
  store 636
  - head 210
  - pen 590
four 95
on all -s 13, 23
  horizontal 213
  easy 705
  prosperous 734
  humble 879
  - in hand 272
  - score &c. 98
  - square 244
  - times 96
  from the - winds 278
fourflusher 884
fourfold 96
four-oar 273
four-poster 215
fourth 96, 97
  musical 413
  - estate 531
four-wheeler 272
fowl 366
fowling-piece 727
fox *animal* 366
  cunning 702
  - chase 622
fox-trot 840
foxy *color* 433, 434
  cunning 720
foyer 191, 599
fracas
  disorder 59
  noise 404
  discord 713
  contention 720
fraction *part* 51
  numerical 84
  less than one 100a
fractious 901
fracture
  disjunction 44
  discontinuity 70
  fissure 198
fragile 160, 328
fragment
  small 32, 193
  part 51, 100a
fragrance 400
fragrant *weed* 392
frail *weak* 160
  brittle 328

  feeble 575
  irresolute 605
  imperfect 651
  failing 945
  impure 961
  - sisterhood 962
frais, à grands - 481
frame
  condition 7
  make 161
  support 215
  border 231
  form 240
  substance 316
  structure 329
  contrive 626
  cucumber - 371
  have -d and
  glazed 822
  - of mind
  inclination 602
  disposition 820
frame-up 626
framework
  support 215
  structure & 9
franchise
  voting 609
  freedom 748
  right 924
  exemption 927a
Franciscan 996
franc-tireur 726
frangible 160, 328
frank *open* 525
  sincere 543
  artless 703
  honorable 939
frankalmoigne 748
Frankenstein 913, 980
frankincense 400
frantic
  violent 173
  delirious 503
  excited 824
fraternal
  brother 11
  concord 714
  friendly 888
fraternity
  [see fraternal]
  party 712
fraternize
  co-operate 48, 709
  agree 714
  sympathize 888
  associate 892
fratricide 361
Frau 374
fraud
  falsehood 544
  deception 545
  pretender 548
  dishonor 940
  pious - 988
fraught *full* 52
  pregnant 161
  possessing 777
  - with danger 665
fray *rub* 331
  battle 720
in the thick of the - 722
frayed 659
frazzle

beaten to a - 732
freak 608, 872
  - of Nature 83
freckle 848
freckled 440
fredaine 840
free
  detached 44, 47
  unconditional 52
  liberate 67
  unobstructed 705
  at liberty 748, 750
  gratis 815
  liberal 816
  insolent 885
  exempt 927a
  impure 961
  - balloon 273
  - and easy
  cheerful 836
  adventurous 863
  vain 880
  insolent 885
  friendly 888
  sociable 892
  - fight 720
  - from
  simple 42
  never - from 613
  - gift 784
  - from imperfec-
   tion 650
  - lance 726
  - land 748
  - liver 954a
  - love 961
  make - of 748
  - play 170, 748
  - quarters
  cheap 815
  hospitality 892
  - space 180
  - stage 748
  - trade
  commerce 794
  - translation 522
  - will 600
  make - with
  frank 703
  take 789
  sociable 892
  uncourteous 895
freebooter 792
freeborn 748
freedman 748
freedom 748
free-handed 816
freehold 780
freely
  willingly 602
freeman 748
freemasonry
  unintelligible 519
  secret 528
  sign 550
  co-operation 709
  party 712
free-spoken 703
freethinker 989
freeze
  benumb 381
  cold 385
  - the blood 830
freezing 38.
  - mixture 387
freight *lade* 184
  cargo 190

transfer 270
freightage 812
freighter 273
freight train 272
French
  peddler's - 563
  - and English 840
  - horn 417
  - leave *avoid* 623
  freedom 748
  - polish 847
frenetic 503
frenzy
  madness 503
  imagination 515
  excitement 825
frequency 136
frequent
  in number 104
  in time 136
  in space 186
  habitual 613
  visit 892
fresco *cold* 383
  painting 556
a -
  out of doors 220
  in the air 338
fresh *additional* 37
  new 123
  flood 348
  cold 383
  color 428
  remembered 505
  unaccustomed 614
  good 648
  healthy 654
  impertinent 885
  tipsy 959
  - breeze 349
  - color 434
  - news 532
freshen 658, 689
freshet 348
freshman 541
freshwater 851
freshwater sailor 701
fret *suffer* 378
  grieve 828
  gall 830
  discontent 832
  sad 837
  ornament 847
  irritate 900
  - and fume 828
fretful 901
fret-work 219
friable 328, 330
friandise 868
friar 996
  -'s lantern 423
  - Rush 980
  Black -s 996
friary 1000
fribble
  slur over 460
  trifle 643
  dawdle 683
  fop 854
fricassee 298
frication 331
friction *force* 157
  obstacle 179
  rubbing 331
  on - wheels 705
friend 711, 890

- ready 673
- rid of 672
- a sight of 441, 490
- through
end 67
transact 692
complete 729
expend 809
- to
extend to 196
arrive 292
- together 72
- into trouble 732
- the wind up 860
- up produce 161
ascend 305
raise 307
learn 539
fabricate 544
prepare 673
rise early 682
foment 824
- into the way of 613
get-away 671
gewgaw
trifle 643
ornament 847
vulgar 851
geyser 382, 386
ghastly
pale 429
hideous 846
frightful 860
ghaut 203
ghetto 189
ghost shade 36.'
fallacy of vision 443
soul 450
writer 593
apparition 980
give up the - 360
needs no - to tell
us 525
pale as a -
colorless 429
fear 86C
- dance 992
ghost-like
ugly 846
ghostly
intellectual 450
supernatural 976, 980
Ghost, Holy - 976
ghoul 913, 980
ghyll 348
giant
large 192
tall 206
- refreshed
strong 159
refreshed 689
-'s strides
distance 196
swift 294
giaour 984, 989
gibber 583
gibberish 517, 563
gibbet
brand 932
execute 972
gallows 975
gibble-gabble 584
gibbous 249, 250

gib-cat male 373
gibe 929
giblets 298
gibus 225
giddy
inattentive 458
vertiginous 503
irresolute 605
capricious 608
bungling 699
giddy-head 501
giddy-paced 315
gift power 157
talent 698
given 784
- of the gab 582
look a - horse in the mouth
fastidious 868
ungrateful 917
gifted 698
gig 272, 273
gigantic
strong 159
large 192
tall 206
giggle 838
giglamps 445
Gilbertian 842
Gilbertine 996
gild coat 223
color 439
ornament 847
- refined gold 641
- the pill
deceive 545
tempt 615
please 829
flatter 933
Gilead, balm in - 834, 858
Giles's Greek, St. - 563
gill 348
gillie 746
gilt 436, 847
- edged 648
gimbals 312
gimcrack
weak 160
brittle 328
trifling 643
ornament 847
ridiculous 853
gimlet 262
gimp
clean 652
pretty 845
decoration 847
gin trap 545
instrument 633
intoxicating 959
demon 980
gin mill 189
gin palace 189
gingerbread
weak 160
vulgar 851
gingerly 174, 459, 864
gingle 408
gipsy
wanderer 268
vag 844
- lingo 563
giraffe 206
girandole 423

girasol 847
gird bind 43
strengthen 159
surround 227
jeer 929
- up one's loins
brace 159
prepare 673
girder 45, 215
girdle bond 45
encircle 227
circumference 230
circle 247
put a - round the earth 311
girl 129, 374
girlhood 12.
girt 45
girth
bond 45
circumference 230
gisarm 727
gist essence 5
meaning 516
important 642
git, ci - 363
gittern 417
give yield 324
melt 382
bestow 784
discount 813
- away 782, 784
in marriage 903
- back 790
- birth to 161
- with both hands 816
- in charge
restrain 751
- chase 622
- consent 762
- one credit for 484
- in custody 751
- expression to 566
- forth 531
- the go by 623
- a horse his head 748
- in submit 725
- into consent 762
- light 420
- the mind to 457
- notice
inform 527
warn 668
- it one
censure 932
punish 972
- out emit 297
publish 531
bestow 784
- over cease 142
relinquish 624
lose hope 859
- place to
substitute 147
avoid 623
- play to the im-
agination 515
- points to 27
- quarter 740
- rise to 153
- one the slip 671
- security 771
- and take

reciprocate 12
compensation 30
interchange 148
retaliation 718
compromise 774
barter 794
equity 922
honour 939
- tongue 531
- a turn to 140
- one to under-
stand 527
- up
not understand 519
unwilling 603
reject 610
relinquish 624
submit 725
resign 757
surrender 782
restore 790
hopeless 859
- up the ghost 360
- way weak 160
brittle 328
submit 725
pine 828
despond 837
modest 881
given [see give]
circumstances 8
supposition 514
received 785
- over dying 360
- time 134
- to 613
giving 784
gizzard 191
stick in one's -
900
glabrous 225
glacial 383
glaciate 385
glacier 383
glacis 217, 717
glad 827, 829
give the - eye 441
would be - of 865
- tidings 532
gladden 834, 836
glade hollow 252
opening 260
shade 424
gladiator 726
gladiatorial 361, 713, 720
gladsome 827, 829
Gladstone bag 191
glair 352
glaive 727
glamor 992
glance look 441
sign 550
see at a - 498
- at
take notice of 457
allude to 527
censure 932
- off deviate 279
diverge 291
gland 221
glare light 420
stare 441
imperfect vision 443
visible 446

glaring
[see glare]
great 31
color 428
visible 446
manifest 525
glass vessel 191
smooth 255
brittle 328
transparent 425
lens 445
musical -es 47
see through a -
darkly 491
- of fashion 852
live in a - house
brittle 328
visible 446
danger 665
- too much 959
glass-coach 272
glasshouse 191, 371
Glassite 984
glassy [see glass]
shining 420
colorless 429
glaucous 435
glave 727
glaver 933
glaze 255
gleam small 32
light 420
glean 609, 775
gleanings 636
glebe land 342
ecclesiastical 995
church 1000
glee music 415
satisfaction 827
merriment 836
gleek 929
glen 252
glengarry 225
glib voluble 584
facile 705
glide lapse 109
move 264
travel 266
fly 267
- into
conversion 144
glider 273
glimmer
light 420
dim 422
visible 446
slight knowledge 490, 491
glimpse 441, 490
glint 420
glissade 306
glisten 420
glitter
shine 420
appear 446
illustrious 882
glittering
ornament 847
display 882
gloam 901a
gloaming 126, 422
gloar look 441
wonder 970
gloat 884
- on look 441
- over 441
pleasure 377

delight 827
globated 249
globe
　sphere 249
　world 318
　on the face of the
　　– 318
　– *trotter* 268
globule 32, 249
glomeration 72
gloom 421, 827, 837
gloomy horizon 859
glorification 884
glorify
　honor 873
　approve 931
　worship 990
glorious
　illustrious 873
　tipsy 959
glory
　light 420
　honor 873
　heaven 981
　King of – 976
　– in 878, 884
　– be to God 990
gloss *smooth* 255
　sheen 420
　interpretation 522
　falsehood 546
　plea 617
　beauty 845
　– of novelty 123
　– over
　neglect 460
　sophistry 477
　falsehood 544
　vindicate 937
glossary 86, 562
glossographer 492
glossologist 492
glossology 560, 562
glossy [*see* gloss]
glottology 560
glout 901*a*
glove 225
　take up the – 720
　throw down the –
　　715
glow *warm* 382
　shine 420
　appear 446
　color 428
　style 574
　passion 821
glower
　glare 443
　discourteous 895
　sullen 901*a*
glowing
　[*see* glow]
　orange 439
　excited 824
　beautiful 845
　– *terms* 574
glow-worm 423
gloze 933, 937
glucose 396
glue *cement* 45
　cementing 46
　semiliquid 352
glum
　discontented 832
　dejected 837
　sulky 901*a*
glut

redundance 641
　satiety 869
gluttony 957
　glutinous 352
glutton 954*a*, 957
　gluttony 957
glycerine 332, 356
glyphography 558
glyptography 558
glyptotheca 557
gnarl *protuberance*
　250
　anger 900
　threat 909
gnarled 256, 321
gnash one's teeth
　839, 900
gnat *little* 193
　strain at a – &c.
　caprice 608
gnaw *eat* 298
　rub 331
　injure 659
gnawing
　– *grief* 828, 830
　– *pain* 378
gnome 496, 980
gnomic 496
gnomon 114
Gnostic 984
go
　cease to exist 2
　energy 171, 682
　move 264
　recede 287
　depart 293
　fade 429
　disappear 449
　fashion 852
　come and – 314
　as things – 613
　– about
　turn round 311
　published 531
　undertake 676
　– across 302
　– after
　in time 117
　in motion 281
　– ahead
　energetic 171
　precede 280
　advance 282
　active 682
　– against 708
　– astray 495
　– away 293
　– back 283, 624
　– bad 659
　– bail 771
　– before 280
　– between
　interjacent 228
　instrumental 631
　mediate 631, 724
　– beyond 303
　– by the board
　　158
　– about your
　　business
　ejection 297
　dismissal 756
　– by
　conform to 82
　elapse 109
　past 122
　outrun 303

subterfuge 702
　give the – by to
　neglect 460
　deceive 545
　avoid 623
　not observe 773
　– by the name of
　　564
　– deep into 461
　– down *sink* 306
　decline 659
　– down with
　believed 484
　tolerated 826
　content 831
　– farther and fare
　　worse 659
　– forth *depart* 293
　publish 531
　– halves 91
　– hand in hand
　accompany 88
　same time 120
　– hard 704
　– on ill 735
　– in 294
　– in for
　resolution 604
　pursuit 622
　– into
　ingress 294
　inquire 461
　dissert 595
　– all lengths
　complete 52
　resolve 604
　exertion 686
　– mad 503
　– near 286
　– no further
　keep secret 528
　– for nothing
　sophistry 477
　unimportant 643
　– off *explode* 173
　depart 293
　die 360
　wither 659
　marry 903
　– on *time* 106
　continue 143
　advance 282
　– on for ever 112
　– one better 303
　– out
　cease 142
　egress 295
　extinct 385
　– out of one's
　　head 506
　– over
　passage 302
　explore 461
　– *apostate* 607
　faithless 940
　– to pieces 162
　– on record 551
　– round 311
　– shares 778
　– to sleep 683
　– through
　meet with 151
　pass 302
　explore 461
　perform 599
　conduct 692
　complete 729

endure 826
　– to *extend* 196
　travel 266
　direction 278
　remonstrance 695
　– up 305
　– to *war* 722
　– with
　assent 488
　concord 714
　– with the stream
　conform 82
　servile 886
　– from one's word
　　773
goad 615
　hasten 684
goal *end* 67
　reach 292
　object 620
　reach the –
　complete 729
goat *substitute* 147
　jumper 309
　lecher 962
　he – *male* 373
　play the – 499
gob 269
gobang 840
gobbet
　small piece 32
　food 298
gobble *cry* 412
　gormandize 957
　eat 298
gobemouche 501,
　547
go-between 758
goblet 191
goblin 980
go-cart 272
GOD 976
　house of – 1000
　kingdom of – 981
　sons of – 977
　–'s acre 363
　– bless me! 870
　– bless you
　farewell 293
　– forbid 766
　–'s grace 906
　– grant 990
　– knows 491
　–'s love 906
　for –'s sake 765
　–'s will 601
　– willing 470
god 979
　household –s 189
　tutelary – 664
goddess *love* 897
　good woman 948
　heathen 979
Godhead 976
godlike 987
godly 944
godsend *good* 618
　prosperity 734
Godspeed
　farewell 293
　hope 858
　courtesy 894
　benevolence 906
　approbation 93
goer *horse* 271
goes [*see* go]
　as one – 270

here – 676
Gog and Magog 192
goggle 441
　– *eyes* 443
goggles 445
going [*see* go]
　general 78
　rumor 532
　– to *happen* 152
　– on
　incomplete 53,
　　730
　current 151
　transacting 625
goiter 250
Golconda 803
gold *yellow* 436
　orange 439
　money 800
　write in letters
　　of – 642
　worth its weight
　　in – 648
gold certificate 800
golden [*see* gold]
　– *age*
　prosperity 734
　pleasure 827
　– *apple* 615
　– *calf*
　wealth 803
　idol 985
　idolatry 991
　– *dream*
　imagination 515
　hope 858
　– *mean*
　moderation 174
　mid-course 628
　– *opinions* 931
　– *opportunity* 134
　– *rule*
　precept 697
　– *season of life*
　　127
　– *wedding* 883
golf 840
Golgotha 363, 1000
Goliath 159, 192
goloshes 225
gondola 273
gondolier 269
gone [*see* go]
　past 122
　absent 187
　dead 360
　– *bad* 653
　– *by*
　antiquated 124
　– out of one's rec-
　　ollection 506
gonfalon 550
gong 417
goniometer 244,
　466
good
　complete 52
　palatable 394
　assent 488
　benefit 618
　beneficial 648
　right 922
　virtuous 944
　pious 987
　"*as* – *as* 197
　be *so* – *as* 765
　do – 906

for –
  diuturnal 110
  permanent 141
make –
  evidence 467
  provide 637
  restore 660
  complete 729
  substantiate 924
  vindicate 937
  atone for 952
so far so – 931
think – 931
to the – 780
turn to – account 731
what's the – 645
  – actions 944
  – at 698
  – auspices 858
  – behavior
  contingent 108a
  duty 926
  virtue 944
in one's – books 888
  – bye 293
  in – case 192
  – chance 472
  – cheer food 298
  cheerful 826
  – circumstances 803
  – condition 192
  – day
  arrival 292
  departure 293
  courtesy 894
  – effect
  goodness 648
  beauty 845
  – enough
  not perfect 651
  be – enough 765
  put a – face upon
  cheerful 836
  proud 878
  – fellow 892
  – fight war 722
  virtue 944
  – for
  useful 644
  salubrious 656
  – fortune 734
  – Friday 998
  – genius
  friend 890
  benefactor 912
  god 979
in one's – graces 888
  – hand 700
  – humor
  concord 714
  cheerfulness 836
  amuse 840
  courtesy 894
  kindly 906
  – intention 906
  – judgment 498
  – lack! 870
  – living
  food 298
  gluttony 957
  – look-out 459
  – looks 845
  – luck 734

– man man 373
  husband 903
  worthy 948
  – manners 894
  much – may it do 906
  – morrow 292
  – name 873
  – nature 906
  – night 293
  – for nothing
  impotence 158
  useless 645
in – odor
  repute 873
  approbation 931
  – offices
  mediation 724
  kind 906
  – old time 122
  – omen 858
  – opinion 931
take in – part
  pleased 827
  courteous 894
  kind 906
  – pennyworth 815
  – at the price 815
  to – purpose 731
  – repute 873
  – sense 498
  – society 852
  – taste 578, 850
  – temper 894
  – thing 648
  – time early 132
  opportune 134
  prosperous 734
  – turn
  kindness 906
  – understanding 714
  – wife
  woman 374
  spouse 903
  – will
  willingness 602
  benevolence 906
  – word
  approval 931
  vindication 937
  – as one's word
  veracity 543
  observance 772
  probity 939
  – works 906
goodie 652, 746
goodly
  great 31
  large 192
  handsome 845
good mixer 892
goodness
  [see good] 648
  virtue 944
  have the –
  request 765
  – gracious! 870
  – of heart 906
goods effects 270, 780
  merchandise 798
good taste 868
Goodwin sands 667
goody 374
gooroo 996
goose hiss 409

game of – 840
giddy as a – 458
tailor's – 255
kill the – with golden eggs 699, 818
a wild – chase 545
gooseberry
  old – 978
  play – 459
  – eyes 411, 443
goosecap 501
goose egg 101
gooseflesh 383
goosequill 590
goose-skin 383
Gordian knot 59, 704
gore stab 260
  blood 361
gorge ravine 198
  conduit 350
  fill 641
  satiety 869
  gluttony 957
raise one's – 900
  – the hook 602
gorge de pigeon 440
gorgeous
  colour 428
  beauty 845
  ornament 847
  ostentation 882
Gorgon 860
gorilla 913
gormandize 298, 954a, 957
gorse 367
gory red 434
  murderous 361
  unclean 653
gospel
  certainty 474
  truth 494
  take for –484
Gospels 985
gossamer
  filament 205
  light 320
  texture 329
gossip news 532
  babbler 584
  conversation 588
gossoon 876
Gotama 986
Goth 851, 876
Gotham, wise men of – 501
gothic
  amorphous 241
gouache 556
gouge concave 252
  perforator 262
goulash 298
gourd 191
gourmand 954a, 957
gourmet 868, 954a
gout 378
goût, haut – 392
goutte d'eau, il se noyerait dans une – 699
govern 693, 737
governess 540
  [see govern]
  ruling power 745

divine – 976
petticoat – 699
governor
  tutor 540
  director 694
  ruler 745
  keeper 753
gowk 501
gown dress 225
  canonicals 999
gownsman 492
grab take 789
  miser 819
grabble 379
grace style 578
  permission 760
  concession 784
  elegance 845
  polish 850
  title 877
  pity 914
  forgiveness 918
  honor 939
  piety 987
  worship 990
act of – 784
God's – 906
with a bad – 603
with a good –
  willing 602
  courteous 894
in one's good –s 888
heart of – 861
say – 990
submit with a good – 826
  – before meat 916
grâce: coup de – 914
la – 840
graceless
  inelegant 579
  ugly 846
  vicious 945
  impenitent 951
  irreligious 989
Graces 845
gracile 203
gracious
  willing 602
  courteous 894
  kind 906
  good – 870
grade degree 26
  arrange 60
  term 71
  ascent 217
on the down – 658
on the up – 659
gradatim
  gradually 26
  in order 58
  continuous 69
  slow 275
gradation
  degree 26
  order 58
  continuity 69
gradient 217
gradual degree 26
  continuous 69
  slow 275
graduate
  adjust 23
  calibrate 26
  arrange 60
  series 69

measure 466
  scholar 492, 873
graduated scale 466
gradus 86, 562
Graeculus esuriens 886
graft join 43
  locate 184
  insert 300
  trees 371
  teach 537
  booty 794
  corruption 940
Grail
  holy – 998
grain essence 5
  small 32
  tendency 176
  little 193
  rough 256
  weight 319
  texture 329
  powder 330
  paint 428
  temper 820
  ornament 847
against the –
  rough 256
  unwilling 603
  opposing 708
in the – 820
  –s of allowance
  qualification 469
  doubt 485
like –s of sand
  incoherent 47
gram 319
gramercy 916
graminivorous 298
grammar
  beginning 66
  teaching 537
  school 542
  language 567
  bad – 568
  comparative – 560
grammarian 492
gramophone 417, 418, 553
granary 636
grand
  great 31
  style 574
  important 642
  money 800
  handsome 845
  glorious 873
  ostentatious 882
  – climacteric 128
  – doings 882
  – duchy 181
  – jury 967
  en – seigneur
  proud 878
  insolent 885
  en –e tenue
  ornament 847
  show 882
  – piano 417
  – style 556
  – tour 266
  – Turk 745
  – vizier 694
grandam 130
grandchildren 167
grandee 875
grande dame 878
grandeur 873

grandfather 130, 166
grandiloquent 577
grandiose 577
grandmother 166
  simple 501
  teach – 538
grandsire 130, 166
grange 189
granite 323
granivorous 298
grano salis, cum 469, 485
grant *admit* 529
  permit 760
  consent 762
  confer 784
  God – 990
  – a lease 771
granted 488
  take for –
  believe 484
  suppose 514
grantee
  possessor 779
  receiver 785
granular 330
granulate 330
granule 32
grapes, sour –
  unattainable 471
  falsehood 544
  excuse 617
grape-shot
  attack 716
  arms 727
graph 554
graphic
  intelligible 518
  painting 556
  descriptive 594
graphite 332
graphito 556
graphology 590
graphometer 244
graphotype 558
grapnel 666
grapple
  fasten 43
  clutch 789
  – with
  - *a question* 461
  - *difficulties* 704
  oppose 708
  resist 719
  contention 720
grappling-iron
  fastening 45
  safety 666
grasp
  comprehend 518
  power 737
  retain 781
  seize 789
  in one's – 737
  possess 777
  tight – *severe* 739
  - at 865
  - of intellect 498
grasping
  miserly 819
  covetous 865
grass 344, 367
  let the – grow
    under one's feet
  neglect 460
  inactive 683

not let the – &c.
  active 682
grasshopper 309
grass-plat 371
grate *rub* 330
  physical pain 378
  stove 386
  - on the ear
  harsh sound 410
  - on the feelings 830
grated
  barred 219
grateful
  physically pleasant 377
  agreeable 829
  thankful 916
grater 260, 330
gratification
  animal – 377
  moral – 827
gratify 829
  permit 760
  please 829
grating [see grate]
  lattice 219
  harsh 713
gratis 815
gratitude 916
gratuitous
  inconsequent 477
  supposititious 514
  voluntary 602
  payless 815
gratuity
  gift 784
  gratis 815
gratulate 896
gravamen 642
grave *great* 31
  engrave 259, 558
  tomb 363
  important 642
  composed 826
  distressing 830
  sad 837
  heinous 945
  beyond the – 360
  look –
  disapprove 932
  rise from the – 660
  silent as the – 403
  sink into the – 360
  on this side of the
    – 359
  - in the memory 505
  - note 408
  - trap 599
gravel
  earth 342
  material 635
  puzzle 704
graveolent 398
graven image 991
graver 558
graving dock 189
gravitate
  descend 306
  weigh 319
  - towards 176
gravity *force* 157
  weight 319
  vigor 574

importance 642
sedateness 826
seriousness 827
  center of – 222
  specific –
  weight 319
  density 321
gravy 333
  - boat 191
gray 432 [and *see* grey]
graze *touch* 199
  browse 298
  rub 331
  brush 379
grazier 370
gré, savoir – 916
grease
  lubricate 332
  oil 356
  - the palm
  tempt 615
  give 784
  pay 807
greasy 355
great *much* 31
  big 192
  glorious 873
  magnanimous 942
  (*important* 642)
  - bear 318
  - circle sailing 628
  - coat 225
  - doings
  importance 642
  bustle 682
  - folks 875
  - gun 626
  - hearted 942
  - Mogul 745
  - number 102
  - primer 591
  - quantity 31
greater 33
  - number 102
  - part 31
  nearly all 50
greatest 33
greatness 31
greave 225
greed
  desire 865
  gluttony 957
greedy
  avaricious 819
green
  new 123
  young 127
  lawn 344
  grass 367
  unripe 397
  color 435
  credulous 486
  novice 491
  unused 614
  healthy 654
  immature 674
  unskilled 699
  board of – cloth 966
  - memory 505
  - old age 128
greenback 800
green-eyed monster 920
greenhorn

novice 493
dupe 547
bungler 701
greenhouse
  receptacle 191
  horticulture 371
greenness 435
green-room 599
greensward 344
Greenwich time 114
greenwood 367
Greek
  unintelligible 519
  sharper 792
  St. Giles's – 563
  - Church 984
  - Kalends 107
greet *weep* 839
  hail 894
greeting
  sociality 892
  –'s! 292
gregarious 892
grenade 727
grenadier
  tall 206
  soldier 726
grey 432
  - beard 130
  - friar 996
  - hairs 128
  bring – hairs to
    the grave
  adversity 735
  harass 830
  - mare
  ruler 737
  master 745
  wife 903
  - matter
  brain 498
  -hound
  swift 274
  animal 366
  ocean –hound 273
gridelin 437
gridiron
  flatness 213
  crossing 219
  stove 386
  stage 599
  stadium 840
grief 828
  come to – 735
grievance
  evil 619
  painful 830
  wrong 923
grieve *mourn* 828
  pain 830
  dejected 837
  complain 839
grievous 649, 830
grievously 31
griffin 83, 366, 493
griffo 41
griffonage 590
grig *merry* 836
grill 382, 384, 461
  - room 189
grille 219
grim
  resolved 604
  painful 830
  doleful 837
  ugly 846

discourteous 895
sullen 901a
–visaged war 722
grimace 243, 839, 855
grimacier
  actor 599
  humorist 844
  affected 855
grimalkin 366
grimy 652
grin *laugh* 838
  ridicule 856
  - and abide 725
  – a ghastly smile
  dejected 837
  ugly 846
grind
  reduce 195
  sharpen 253
  pulverize 330
  pain 378
  learn 539
  oppress 907
  - the organ 416
  - one's teeth 900
grinder
  teacher 330
  noise 404
grinding 739, 830
grindstone 253, 330
grip
  indication 550
  power 737
  retention 781
  clutch 789
  - of the hand 894
gripe [see grip]
  pain 378
  parsimony 819
grisaille
  grey 432
  painting 556
grisette
  woman 374
  commonalty 876
  libertine 962
grisly 846
grist
  materials 635
  provision 637
  - to the mill
  useful 644
  acquire 775
gristle 321, 327
grit
  strength 159
  powder 330
  stamina 604a
  courage 861
  - in the oil
  hindrance 706
gritty 323
grizzled
  grey 432
  variegated 440
groan 411, 839
groat 800
grocer 637
grocery 396
grog 298, 959
groin 244
groom 370, 746
  - well
  - of the chambers 746
  –'s man 903

groove
furrow 259
habit 613
in a – 16
move in a – 82
put in a – for 673

grope
feel 379
experiment 463
try 675
in the dark 442, 704

gross
great 31
whole 50
number 98
ugly 846
vulgar 851
vicious 945
impure 961
– credulity 486
– receipts 810

grosshead 501
grossheaded 499
grossièreté 895
grot [see grotto]

grotesque
odd 83
distorted 243
– style 579
ridiculous 853

grotto
alcove 191
hollow 252

grouch 895, 901a

ground
cause 153
region 181
base 211
lay down 213
support 215
coating 223
land 342
plain 344
evidence 467
teach 537
motive 615
plea 617
above – 359
down to the – 52
dress the – 371
fall to the – 732
get over the – 274
go over the – 302
level with the – 162
maintain one's –
persevere 60₂a
play– 840
prepare the – 673
stand one's –
defend 717
resist 719
– bait 784
– cut from under one 732
– floor
chamber 191
low 207
base 211
– on
attribute 155
– plan 554
– of quarrel 713
– sliding from under one 665
– swell

agitation 315
waves 348
grounded
stranded 732
well– 490
– on basis 211
evidence 467
groundless
unsubstantial 4
illogical 477
erroneous 495
groundling 876
grounds
dregs 653
groundwork
precursor 64
cause 153
basis 211
support 215
preparation 673
group
marshal 60
cluster 72
– captain 745
grouping 60
grouse 852, 901a
grout 45
grove
street 189
glade 252
wood 367
grovel
below 207
move slowly 275
cringe 886
base 940
grow
increase 35
become 144
expand 194
– from
effect 154
– into 144
– less 195
– taller 206
– together 46
– up 194
– upon one 613
grower 164
growl cry 412
complain 839
discourtesy 895
anger 900
threat 909
growler cab 272
discontented 832
sulky 901a
grown up 131
growth [see grow]
development 161
– in size 194
tumor 250
vegetation 367
groyne 706
grub
small animal 193
food 298
– up
eradicate 301
discover 480a
Grub-street writer 593
grudge
unwilling 603
refuse 764
stingy 819
hate 898

anger 900
bear a – 907
owe a – 898
grudging 603
– praise 932
gruel 298
gruesome 846
gruff
harsh sound 410
discourteous 895
grum
harsh sound 410
morose 901a
grumble
cry 411
complain 832, 839
grume 321, 354
grumous 321, 354
grumpy 901a
Grundy, Mrs. 852
grunt 412
complain 839
guano 653
guarantee 768, 771
guard
traveling 268
safety 664
defence 717
soldier 726
sentry 753
advanced – 668
mount –
care 459
safety 664
off one's –
inexpectant 508
throw off one's –
cunning 702
on one's –
careful 459
cautious 864
rear – 668
– against
prepare 673
defence 717
– ship 664, 726
guarda costa 753
guarded
conditions 770
guardian
safety 664
defence 717
keeper 753
– angel
helper 711
benefactor 912
guardless 665
guard-room 752
gubernation 693
gubernatorial 737
gudgeon 547
guerdon 973
guernsey 225
guerre:
nom de – 565
– à outrance &c. 722
guerilla 726
– warfare 720
guess 514
guesswork 514
guest 890
paying – 188
guet:
mot de – 550
–à-pens 545

guffaw 838
guggle
gush 348
bubble 353
resound 408
cry 412
guide
pattern 22
courier 524
teach 537
teacher 540
indicate 550
direct 693
director 694
advise 695
guide-book 527
guided by, be – 82
guideless 665
guide-post 550
guiding star 693
guild 712, 966
guildhall 799
guile
deceit 544, 545
cunning 702
guileless 543, 703
guillotine 972, 975
guilt 947
guiltless 946
guilty:
find – 971
plead – 950
guindé 579
guinea 800
guipure 847
guisard 599
guise
state 7
dress 225
appearance 448
plea 617
mode 627
conduct 692
guiser 599
guitar 417
gulch 198
gules 434
gulf
interval 198
deep 208
lake 343
gull 545, 547
gullible 486
gullet throat 260
rivulet 348
gully gorge 198
hollow 252
opening 260
conduit 350
gulosity 957
gulp swallow 296
take food 298
– down
credulity 486
submit 725
gum fastening 45
fasten 46
resin 356a
– elastic 325
– tree 367
gumbo 298
gummy 352
gumption 498
gun report 406
weapon 727
great – 626
blow great –s 349

sure as a – 474
gunboat 726
gunfire 404
gunman 361
gunner 776
gunnery
warfare 722
cannon 727
gunlayer 284
gunpowder
warfare 722
ammunition 727
not invent – 665
sit on barrel of – 501
gunroom 193
gun-shot 197
gunwale 232
gurge 312, 348
gurgle
flow 348
bubble 353
faint sound 405
resonance 408
gurgoyle 350
gush
flow out 295
flood 348
exaggeration 482
talk 584
gushing
emotional 821
impressible 822
gusset 43
gust wind 349
physical taste 390
passion 825
moral taste 850
gustation 390
gustful 394
gustless 391
gusto [see gust]
physical pleasure 377
emotion 821
gut destroy 162
opening 260
strait 343
eviscerate 297
sack 789
steal 791
gutting 954a
guts inside 221
guttapercha 325
gutter groove 259
conduit 350
vulgarity 851
guttersnipe 876
guttle 957
guttural
letter 561
inarticulate 583
guy
fastening 45, 752
fellow 373
disrespect 929
grotesque 853
guzzle
gluttony 957
drunkenness 959
gybe [see jibe]
gymkhana 720, 840
gymnasium 191
school 542
arena 728, 840
gymnast 159
gymnastics

in action 680
active 682
subjection 749
– up 293
harp
repeat 104
musical instrument 417
weary 841
Harpagon 819
harper 416
harpist 416
harpoon 727
harpsichord 417
harpy
relentless 739
thief 792
miser 819
evil-doer 913
demon 980
harquebuss 727
harridan 846, 962
harrier 366
harrow
agriculture 371
– up the soul 860
harrowing 830
harry *pain* 830
attack 716
persecute 907
Harry, old – 978
harsh
acrid 171
sound 410
style 579
discordant 713
severe 739
disagreeable 830
morose 895
malevolent 907
– *voice* 581
hart 366, 373
hartal 142, 489
harum-scarum 59, 458
haruspice 513
Haruspicy 511
harvest
effect 154
profit 618
store 636
acquisition 775
get in the –
complete 729
succeed 731
– home
celebration 883
– time
autumn 126
exertion 686
has been 122
hash *mix* 41
cut 44
confusion 59
food 298
make a – 699
hashish 863
hasp 43, 45
hassock 215
hastate 253
haste
velocity 274
activity 682
hurry 684
hasten
promote 707
hasty

transient 113
hurried 684
impatient 825
irritable 901
– pudding 298
hat 225
cardinal's – 999
send round the – 765
shovel – 999
– in hand 886
hatch
produce 161
gate 232
opening 260
chickens 370
fabricate 544
shading 556
plan 626
prepare 673
– a plot 626
hatches, under –
restraint 751
prisoner 754
poor 804
hatchet
cutting 253
bury the – 918
dig up the – 722
throw the helve after the – 818
hatchet-faced 203
hatchment
funeral 363
arms 550
record 551
hatchway 260
hate 867, **898**
hateful 649, 830
hath been, the time – 122
hatrack 215
hatter 225
mad as a – 503
hatti-sheriff 741
hatred [*see* hate]
object of – 898
hauberk 717
haud passibus æquis 28, 275
haugh 344
haughty
proud 878
insolent 885
contemptuous 930
haul *drag* 285
catch of fish &c. 789
– down one's flag 725
– in 10
haunch 236
haunt *focus* 74
presence 186
abode 189
alarm 860
persecute 907
– the memory
remember 505
trouble 830
haunted 980
haut
traiter de –
insolence 885
contempt 930
hautboy 417
haut-goût 392

haut-monde 875
hauteur 878
have *confute* 479
ken 49
possess 777
– the advantage 28, 33
– at 716
– no choice 609a
– done! 142
– to do with 9
– no end 112
– other fish to fry 135
– it
discover 480a
believe 484
– one to know 527
– some knowledge of 490
– nothing to do with 10
– for one's own 780
– rather 609
– one's rights 924
– the start 116
– in store 152, 637
– to 620
– up 638
– it your own way
submission 725
haven 292, 666
haversack 191
havoc
destruction 162
cry – *war* 722
play – *spoil* 659
haw 583
hawk *spit* 297
stammer 583
eye of a – 498
– about
publish 531
offer 763
sell 796
– at 716
between – and buzzard 315, 828
know a – from a handsaw 465, 698
hawker 796
hawk-eyed 441
hawking *chase* 622
hawser 45
hay while the sun shines, make – 134
haycock 72
hazard
chance 156, 621
danger 665
at all –s 604
– a conjecture 514
– a proposition 477
haze *mist* 353
uncertainty 475
in a –
hidden 528
hazel 433
hazy *opaque* 426
he 373
head *precedence* 62
beginning 66

class 75
summit 210
coiffure 225
lead 280
froth 353
person 372
intellect 450
topic 454
wisdom 498
picture 556
nomenclature 564
chapter 593
direct 693
director 694
master 745
at the – of
direction 693
authority 737
repute 873
bow the – 308
bring to a – 729
come into one's – 451
come to a – 729
drive into one's – 505
gain – 175
get into one's –
thought 451
learn 505
belief 484
intoxicate 959
give a horse his – 748
hang one's – 879
have in one's – 490
from – to heels 52, 200
hit on the – 912
knock on the – 361
knock one's – against
impulse 276
unskilful 699
fail 732
lie on one's – 926
lift up one's – 878
make – against
oppose 708
resistance 719
success 731
never entered into one's – 458
have no – 506
on one's – 218
off one's – 503
can't get out of one's – 505
over – and ears
deep 641
debt 806
love 897
put into one's –
supposition 514
information 527
put out of one's – 458
run in the – 505
not know whether one stands on – or heels
uncertain 475
wonder 870
take into one's –
thought 451
caprice 608

intention 620
turn the – 824
trouble one's – about 457
as one's – shall answer for 768
with – erect 878
from – to foot 200
– and front
important 642
– and front of one's offending
provocation 830
charge 938
– over heels
inversion 218
rotation 312
– light 423
– line 591
– and shoulders
irrelevant 10
complete 52
haste 684
make neither – nor tail of 519
hold one's – up 307
– above water
safe 664
prosperous 743
wealth 803
with a – on 353
headache 378
head-dress 225
header 310
head-foremost
violent 173
rash 863
head-gear 225
heading *prefix* 64
beginning 66
indication 550
title 564
headland
height 206
projection 250
headlong
hurry 684
rush 863
rush –
violence 173
headman 694
headmost
front 234
precession 280
head-piece
summit 210
intellect 450
helmet 717
ornament 847
head-quarters
focus 74
abode 189
authority 737
head-race 350
head-stone 363
heads
compendium 596
– or tails 156, 621
lay, – together
advice 695
co-operate 709
– I win tails you lose
unfair 940
headship 737
headsman 975

headstrong
  violent 173
  obstinate 606
  rash 863
headway *space* 180
  navigation 267
  progression 282
headwind 708
headwork 451
heady 606
heal *restore* 660
  remedy 662
  let the wound –
  – *forgive* 918
  – the breach
  pacify 723
healing art 662
health 654
  picture of – 654
healthiness 655
health resort 189
healthy 656
heap *quantity* 31
  collection 72
  store 636
  too many 641
heaps 102
  rubbish – 645
hear
  audition 418
  be informed 527
  not – of (*refuse*)
  764
  – a cause
  adjudge 480
  lawsuit 969
  – hear! 931
  – and obey 743
  - out 457
hearer 418
hearing 418, 696
  [*see* hear]
  gain a – 175
  give a – 418
  hard of – 419
  out of – 196
  within – 197
hearken 457
hearsay 532
  – *evidence* 467
hearse 363
heart
  intrinsicality 5
  interior 221
  centre 222
  mind 450
  willingness 602
  essential 642
  affections 820
  courage 861
  love 897
  man after one's
  own – 899
  with all one's –
  438, 602
  at – 820, 821
  from bottom of –
  543
  beating – 821, 824
  break the – 830
  by –
  memory 505
  go to one's – 824
  in good – 858
  with a heavy –
  603
  know by – 490

lay to – 837
learn by – 539
lift up the – 990
lose – 837
lose one's – 897
nearest to one's –
  897
not find it in one's
  – 603
have a place in
  the – 897
put one's – into
  604
set one's – upon
  604
take –
  content 831
  hope 858
  courage 861
take to –
  sensibility 822
  discontent 832
  dejection 837
  anger 900
warm – 822
wind round the –
  897
– bleeding for 914
to one's –'s con-
  tent
  willing 602
  enough 639
  success 731
  pleasure 829
  –'s core
  mind 450
  affections 820
  – expanding 821
  – failing one 837,
  860
do one's – good
  829
  – of grace 858
  – in hand 602
  – leaping with joy
  827, 838
  – leaping into
  one's mouth 824
  – of oak
  strong 159
  hard 323
  – in right place
  906
  – sinking *fear* 860
  – and soul
  completely 52
  willing 602
  resolute 604
  exertion 686
  feeling 821
  – of stone 823, 907
  – swelling 824
heartache 828
heart-breaking 821,
  830
heart-broken 828
heartburning
  discontent 832
  regret 833
  enmity 889
  anger 900
  jealousy 920
hearten 858, 861
heartfelt 821, 829
hearth
  home 189
  fireplace 386

heartless 823, 945
heart-rending 830
heartsease 831
heart-shaped 245
heart-sick
  dejection 837
  dislike 867
  satiety 869
heart-stricken 828
heart-strings, tear
  the – 830
hearty
  willing 602
  healthy 654
  feeling 821
  cheerful 836
  friendly 888
  social 892
  – laugh 838
  – meal 298
  – reception 892
heat *warmth* 382
  make hot 384
  contest 720
  excitement 824,
  825
  dead – 27
  – of passion 900
  – wave 382
heated imagination
  515
heater 386
heath *moor* 344
  plant 367
heathen 984, 989
  – mythology 979
heathenish 851
heather *moor* 344
  plant 367
heaume 717
heautontimoru-
  menos 837, 955
heave *raise* 307
  emotion 821
  – the lead 208,
  466
  – a sigh 839
  – in sight 446
  – to 265
heaven 827, 981
  call – to witness
  535
  in the face of –
  525
  light of – 420
  move – and earth
  686
  will of – 601
  – forfend! 766
  – knows 475, 491
  – be praised 838,
  916
  for –'s sake 765
heaven-born
  wise 498
  repute 873
  virtue 944
heaven-directed
  498
heaven-kissing 206
heavenly
  celestial 318
  rapturous 829
  divine 976
  of heaven 981
  – bodies 318
  – host 977

– kingdom 981
heavenly-minded
  987
heavens 318
  – and earth! 870
Heaviside layer
  338
heavisome 843
heavy *great* 31
  inert 172
  weighty 319
  stupid 499
  actor 599
  sleepy 683
  dull 843
  brutish 851
  – affliction 828
  – artillery 726
  – cost 814
  – dragoon 726
  – father 599
  – gaited 843
  – gun 727
  – hand
  clumsy 699
  severe 739
  – on hand 641
  – heart *loth* 603
  pain 828
  dejection 837
  – hours 841
  – on the mind 837
  – news 830
  – sea
  agitation 515
  waves 348
  – sleep 683
  – type 591
  – wet 298
heavy-laden 706,
  828
hebdomadal 138
Hebe 845
hebetate 823, 826
hebetude
  imbecile 499
  insensible 823
  inexcitable 826
Hebrew
  unintelligible 519
  Jew 984
Hecate 994
hecatomb
  number 98
  sacrifice 991
heckle 830, 900
hectic 382, 821
Hector *brave* 861
  rash 863
  bully 885, 887
hedge
  compensate 30
  inclosure 232
  – in
  circumscribe 229
  hinder 706
  conditions 770
hedgehog 253
hedonism 377, 827
hedonist 954a
heed *attend* 457
  care 459
  beware 668
  caution 864
heedful 457
heedless
  inattentive 458

neglectful 460
oblivious 506
rash 863
heel *support* 215
  lean 217
  deviate 279
  go round 311
  iron – 975
  lay by the –s 162
  turn on one's –
  go back 283
  go round 311
  avoid 623
  – of Achilles 665
heel-piece
  sequel 65
  back 235
  repair 660
heel-tap
  remainder 40
  dress 653
heels *lowness* 207
  at the – of
  near 197
  behind 235
  cool one's – 681
  follow on the – of
  281
  laid by the – 751
  lay by the – 789
  show a light pair
  of – 623
  take to one's –
  623
  tread on the – of
  near 197
  follow 281
  approach 286
  – over head
  inverted 218
  hasty 684
  rash 863
heft *handle* 633
  exertion 686
hegemony
  influence 175
  direction 693
  authority 737
heifer 366
heigho! 839
height *degree* 26
  altitude 206
  summit 210
  at its –
  great 31
  supreme 33
  draw oneself up to
  his full – 307
  – finder 206
heighten
  increase 35
  elevate 307
  exaggerate 549
  aggravate 835
hegira [*see* hejira]
heinous 945
heir *futurity* 121
  posterity 167
  inheritor 779
heirloom 780
heirship 777
hejira 293
Helen of Troy 845
heliacal 318
helical 248
Helicon 597
helicon-horn 417

helicopter 273
Heliogabalus 954a
heliograph
  signal 550
  picture 556
heliography 550
  light 420
  painting 556
Helios 423
heliotrope 847
heliotype 558
helix 248
hell *abyss* 208
  gaming-house 62
  gehenna 982
  – upon earth
  misfortune 735
  pain 828
  – broke loose 59
hell-born 945, 978
hellebore 663
hellish
  malevolent 907
  vicious 945
  hell 982
helluo librorum 492
helm *handle* 633
  scepter 747
  (*authority* 737)
  answer the – 743
  at the – 693
  obey the – 705
  take the – 693
helmet 225, 717
helminthology 368
helmsman 269, 694
helot 746
help *benefit* 618
  utility 644
  remedy 662
  aid 707
  servant 746
  give 784
  it can't be –ed
  submission 725
  never mind 823
  content 831
  God – you 914
  so – me God 535
  – oneself to 789
helper 711
helpless 158, 665
helpmate
  auxiliary 711
  wife 903
helter-skelter 59, 684
helve
  throw the – after
  the hatchet 818
hem *edge* 231
  fold 258
  indeed! 870
  kiss the – of one's
  garment 886
  – in *enclose* 220
  restrain 751
hemi- 91
hemisphere 181
hemispheric 250
hemlock 663
hemorrhage 299
hemp 205
hen 366, 374
  female 374
  – with one chicken

busy 682
henbane 663
hence
  arising from 155
  departure 293
  deduction 476
  – loathed mel-
  ancholy 836
henceforth 121
henchman 746
hencoop 370
hendiadis 91
henna 433
henpecked 743, 749
heptagon 244
heptarchy 98
Heraclitus 839
rideret – 853
herald
  precursor 64
  precession 280
  predict 511
  forerunner 512
  proclaim 531
  messenger 534
heraldry 550
herb 367
herbage 365
herbal 369
herbivorous 298
herborize 369
herculean
  strong 159
  exertion 686
  difficult 704
Herculem, ex pede
  – 550
Hercules 159, 215
  pillars of – 233, 550
herd 72, 102
herdsman 746
here
  situation 183
  presence 186
  arrival 292
  come –! 286
  – below 318
  – goes 676
  – and there
  dispersed 73
  few 103
  place 182, 183
  – there and
  everywhere
  diversity 16a
  space 180
  omnipresence 186
  – to-day and gone
  to-morrow 111
hereabouts 183, 197
hereafter 121, 152
hereby 631
hereditament 780
hereditary
  intrinsic 5
  derivative 154, 167
heredity 167
herein 221
heresy 495, 984
heretic 984
heretofore 122
hereupon 106
herewith 88, 632
heritage

futurity 121
  possession 777
  property 780
heritor 779
hermaphrodite 83
  – brig 273
hermeneutics 522
Hermes 534, 582
hermetically 261
hermit 893, 955
hermitage
  house 189
  cell 191
  seclusion 893
hero *brave* 861
  glory 873
  good man 948
  – *worship* 931, 991
Herod, out-Herod
  – 549
heroic [*see* hero]
  magnanimous 942
  mock – 853
heroics 884
heroin 663
heroine 861
herpetology 368
Herr 373
herring
  pungent 392
  – pond 341
  draw a – across
  the trail 545
  trail of a red –
  615, 706
herring-gutted 203
hesitate
  uncertain 475
  sceptical 485
  stammer 583
  reluctant 603
  irresolute 605
  fearful 860
Hesperian 236
Hesperides, garden
  of the – 981
Hesperus 423
Hessian boot 225
hest 741
hesterni quirites 876
heterarchy 737
heteroclite 83
heterodoxy 489, 984
heterogeneous
  unrelated 10
  different 15
  mixed 41
  multiform 81
  exceptional 83
heterogeneity 15, 16a
heteromorphism 16a
hetman 745
hew *cut* 44
  shorten 201
  fashion 240
  – down 308
hewers of wood
  workers 690
  commonalty 876
hexagon 98, 244
hexahedron 244
hexameter 98, 597

hey! 586
heyday
  exultation 838
  festivity 840
  wonder 870
  – of the blood 820
  – of youth 127
hiation 260
hiatus 198
hibernal 383
hibernate 683
Hibernicism 497, 563
hic:
  – jacet 363
  – labor hoc opus 704
hick 701, 851, 876
hiccup 349
hid under a bushel 460
hidalgo 875
hidden 528
  – meaning 526
hide *skin* 223
  conceal 528
  – diminished head
  inferior 34
  decrease 36
  humility 879
  – one's face
  modesty 881
  – and seek
  deception 545
  avoid 623
  game 840
hide-bound 751, 819
hideous 846
hide-out 893
hiding-place
  abode 189
  ambush 530
  refuge 666
hie 264, 274
  – to 266
hiemal 126
hierarch 996
hierarchy 995
hieratic 590
hieroglyphic
  representation 554
  letter 561
  writing 590
hierographa 985
hieromancy 511
hierophant 996
hieroscopy 511
higgle 794
higgledy piggledy 59
higgler 797
high *much* 31
  lofty 206
  fetid 401
  treble 410
  foul 653
  noted 873
  proud 878
  from on – 981
  on – 206
  think –ly of 931
  – art 556
  – celebration 998
  – color
  color 428

red 434
exaggerate 549
  – commissioner 745
  – days and holi-
  days 840
  in a – degree 31
  – descent 875
  – and dry
  stable 150
  safe 664
  in – esteem 928
  in – feather
  strong 159
  health 654
  cheerful 836
  boasting 884
  – glee 836
  – hand
  violent 173
  resolved 604
  authority 737
  severe 739
  pride 878
  insolence 885
  lawless 964
  – jinks 840
  ride the – horse 878
  – hat 225
  – life *fashion* 852
  rank 875
  – living
  intemperance 954
  gluttony 957
  – mass 998
  – mightiness 873
  – and mighty
  pride 878
  insolence 885
  – note 410
  – notions 878
  – places 210
  – pressure
  energy 171
  excitation of feeling 824
  – price 814
  – priest 996
  in – quarters 875
  – relief 443
  – repute 873
  –ly respectable 875
  on the – road to
  way 627
  hope 858
  on one's – ropes
  excitation 824
  pride 878
  anger 900
  – seas 341
  in – spirits 836
  – tide *wave* 348
  prosperity 734
  – time *late* 133
  occasion 134
  – in tone
  white 430
  – treason
  disobedience 742
  dishonor 940
  – words
  quarrel 713
  anger 900
high-ball 298
high-born 875

holiness *God* 976
  piety 987
holloa 411
  – before one is out
    of the wood 884
hollow
  unsubstantial 4
  completely 52
  incomplete 53
  depth 208
  concavity 252
  channel 350
  – *sound* 408
  specious 477
  false 544
  voiceless 581
  beat – 731
  – truce 723
holm 346
holocaust
  kill 361
  sacrifice 991
    (*destruction* 162)
holograph 590
holster 191
holt 367
holus bolus 684
Holy *of God* 976
  pious 987
  keep – 987
  – breathing 990
  – Church 983a
  – City 981
  – day 998
  – Ghost 976
  temple of the –
    Ghost 983a
  – men of old 985
  – orders 995
  – place 1000
  – Scriptures 985
  – Spirit 976
  – water 998
  – week 998
holystone 652
homage
  submission 725
  fealty 743
  reverence 928
  approbation 931
  worship 990
home *focus* 74
  habitation 189
  near 197
  interior 221
  arrival 292
  refuge 666
  at – *party* 72
  present 186
  within 221
  at ease 705
  social gathering
    892
  be at –
  – *to visitors* 892
  feel at –
    freedom 748
    pleasure 827
    content 831
  look at –
    accusation 938
  make oneself at –
    free 748
    sociable 892
  not be at – 764
  stay at – 265
  at – in

  knowledge 490
    skill 698
  at – with
    friendship 888
  bring – to
    evidence 467
    belief 484
    accuse 938
    condemn 971
  come – 292
  eternal – 98
  from – 187
  get – 292
  go – 283
  go from – 293
  long – 363
  strike –
    energy 171
    attack 716
  – stroke 170
  – thrust
    attack 716
    censure 932
home-bred 851
home-felt 821, 824
home-rule 737, 748
homeless
  unhoused 185
  banished 893
homely
  language 576
  unadorned 849
  common 851, 876
homeopathic
  small 32
  little 193
Homeopathy 662
Homeric
  – *laughter* 838
home-sick 833
home-spun
  texture 329
home-stall 189
homestead 189
homeward bound
  292
homicidal maniac
  913
homicide 361
homiletical 892
homily
  teaching 537
  advice 595
  sermon 998
hominem, argu-
  mentum ad –
  938
homogeneity
  relation 9
  identity 13
  uniformity 16
  simplicity 42
homogenesis 161
homologous 23
homology
  relation 9
  uniformity 16
  equality 27
  concord 714
homonym
  equivocal 520
  vocal sound 580
homophony 413
homunculus 193
Hon. 817
hone 253
honest

  veracious 543
  honorable 939
  pure 960
  – *meaning* 516
  turn an – penny
    775
  – truth 494
honey
  sweet 396
  favorite 899
  milk and – 734
honeycomb
  concave 252
  opening 260
  deterioration 659
honeyed
  – phrases 894
  – words
    allurement 615
    flattery 933
honeymoon
  pleasure 827
  endearment 902
  marriage 903
honey-mouthed
  894, 933
honeysuckle 396
honorarium 784, 973
honorary 815
honor
  demesne 780
  glory 873
  title 877
  respect 928
  approbation 931
  probity 939
  affair of – 720
  do – to 883
  do the – s
    sociality 892
    courtesy 894
    respect 928
  his – *judge* 967
  in – of 883
  man of – 939
  upon my – 535,
    768
  word of – 768
  – be to 873
  – a bill 807
  – in the breach
    923
  – bright
    veracity 543
    probity 939
honte, mauvaise –
  881
hood 225, 999
hooded 223
hoodlum 887
hoodoo 649
hoodwink
  ignore 491
  blind 442
  hide 528
  deceive 545
hoof 211
  cloven – 907
hook *fasten* 43
  fastening 45
  hang 214
  curve 245
  deceive 545
  retain 781
  take 789
  by – or by crook
    631

hookah 392
hooker *ship* 273
hookey, blind – 840
hooks, go off the
  360
hooligan 887, 913
hoop *circle* 247
  cry 411
hoot *cry* 411, 412
  deride 929
  contempt 930
  censure 932
hop *leap* 309
  dance 840, 892
  – off 293
  – skip and jump
    leap 309
    agitation 315
    haste 684
    game 840
  – the twig 360
hope 858
  band of – 958
  beyond – 658, 734
  dash one's –s 837
  excite – 511
  foster – 858
  well-grounded –
    472
  – against hope 859
  – for the best 858
  – deferred
    dejection 837
    lamentation 859
  – for *expect* 507
  desire 865
hope chest 858
hopeful *infant* 129
  probable 472
  hope 858
hopelessness 471,
  859
Hop-o'-my-thumb
  193
hopper 191
horary 108
horde
  assemblage 72
  party 712
  commonalty 876
horizon
  distance 196
  view 441
  expectation 507
  appear on the –
    525
  gloomy – 859
horizontality 213
horn
  receptacle 191
  sharp 253
  music 417
  draw in one's –s
    recant 607
    submit 725
    humility 879
  exalt one's – 873
  wear the –s 905
  –s of a dilemma
    reasoning 476
    difficulty 704
  – in 294
  – mad 920
  – of plenty 639
hornbook 542
hornet
  evil-doer 913

–'s nest
  pitfall 667
  difficulty 704
  adversity 735
  painful 830
  resentment 900
  censure 932
hornpipe 840
hornwork 717
horny 323
Horny, old – 978
horology 114
horoscope 511, 992
horresco referens
  860
horrible *great* 31
  noxious 649
  dire 830
  ugly 846
  fearful 860
horrid [*see* horrible]
  vulgar 851
horrida bella 722
horrific [*see*
  horrible]
horrified 828, 860
horrify 830, 860
horripilation 383
horrisonous 410
horror 860, 867
  view with – 898
horrors 837
  sup full of – 828
horror-stricken 828
hors de combat
  impotent 158
  useless 645
  tired out 688
  put – 731
hors-d'oeuvre 298
horse *hang on* 214
  stand 215
  carrier 271
  animal 366
  male 373
  cavalry 726
  ride the high –
    885
  put the –s to 673
  put up one's –s at
    184
  put up one's –s
    together
    concord 714
    friendship 888
  take – 266
  to – 293
  war – 726
  work like a – 686
  – artillery 726
  – of another color
    15
  – doctor 370
  – and foot 726
  – laugh 838
  – marine 701
  like a – in a mill
    613
  – racing
    pastime 840
    contention 720
  – soldier 726
  – track 627
horseback 266
horse-cloth 225
horseman 268
horsemanship

riding 266
  skill 698
horseplay 856
horse power 466
horse-shoe 245
horse-whip 972
hortation 615, 695
hortative 537
horticulture 371
hortus siccus 369
hosanna 931, 990
hose
  stockings 225
  pipe 348, 350
  extinguisher 385
hosier 225
hospice 189, 662
hospitable 816, 892
hospital 189, 662
  in – 655
hospitality
  [see hospitable]
hospodar 745
host collection 72
  multitude 102
  army 726
  friend 890
  rite 998
reckon without
  one's –
  error 495
  unskilful 699
  rash 863
  – of heaven 977
  – in himself 175
hostage 771
hostel 189
hostelry 189
hostile
  disagreeing 24
  opposed 768
  enmity 889
  in – array 708
  – meeting 720
hostilities 722
hostility 889
hostler 746
hot violent 173
  warm 382
  pungent 392
  red 434
  orange 439
  excited 824
  irascible 901
  make – 384
  – air 482, 884
  – bath 386
  – blood rash 863
  angry 900
  irascible 901
blow – and cold
  inconsistent 477
  falsehood 544
  tergiversation 607
  caprice 608
  in – haste 684
  in – pursuit 622
  – water
  difficulty 704
  quarrel 713
  painful 830
  – water bottle 386
hot air merchant
  884
hot-bed cause 153
  centre 222
  workshop 691

Hotchkiss gun 727
hotchpotch
  mixture 41
  confusion 59
  participation 778
hotel 189
hot-headed 684,
  825
hothouse
  conservatory 371,
  636
  furnace 386
  workshop 691
hot-press 255
Hotspur 863
Hottentot 876
hough 659
hound animal 366
  hunt 622
  persecute 907
  wretch 949
hold with the hare
  but run with the
  –s 607
  – on 615
houppelande 225
hour period 108
  point of time 113
  present time 118
improve the shin-
  ing – 682
one's – is come
  occasion 134
  death 360
  – after hour 110
hour-glass
  chronometer 114
  contraction 195
  narrow 203
Houri 845
hourly time 106
  frequent 136
  periodical 138
house family 166
  locate 184
  abode 189
  theater 599
  make safe 664
  council 696
  firm 712
before the – 454
keep – 184
eat out of – and
  home
  prodigal 818
  gluttony 957
turn out of – and
  home 297
  – of cards 160
  – of correction
  prison 752
  punishment 975
  – of death 363
  – of detention 752
  – divided against
  itself 713
bring the – about
  one's ears 699
  – of Commons
  696, 966
  – of God 1000
  – of Lords 696,
  875, 966
set one's – in
  order 952
  – of peers 696, 875
  – of prayer 1000

– built on sand
  160
turn – out of win-
  dow 713
housebreaker 792
housebreaking 791
house-dog 366
household
  inhabitants 188
  abode 189
  – gods 189,
  – stuff 635
  – troops 726
  – words
  known 490
  language 560
  plain 576, 849
householder 188
housekeeper 637,
  694
housekeeping 692
houseless 185
housemaid 746
house-organ 531
Houses of Parlia-
  ment 191, 696
house-top 210
  proclaim from –
  531
house-room 180
house-warming 892
housewife 682
housewifery 692,
  817
housing
  lodging 189
  covering 223
  horse-cloth 225
hovel 189
hoveller 269
hover high 206
  rove 266
  soar 267
  ascend 305
  irresolute 605
  – about
  move 264
  – over
  near 197
how way 627
  means 632
  – comes it?
  attribution 155
  inquiry 461
  – now 870
howbeit 30
however
  degree 26
  notwithstanding
  30
  except 83
howitzer 727
howker 273
howl
  wind 349
  human cry 411
  animal cry 412
  lamentation 839
howler 495
howling wilderness
  169, 893
hoy 273
hoyden girl 129
  rude 851
hub 222
hubble-bubble 392
hubbub stir 315

noise 404
  discord 713
huckster 794, 797
huddle
  disorder 59
  derange 61
  collect 72
  hug 197
  – on 225
Hudibrastic 856
  – verse 597
hue 428
  – and cry cry 411
  proclaim 531
  pursuit 622
  alarm 669
  raise a – and cry
  932
hueless 429
huff 885, 900
huffy 901
hug cohere 46
  border on 197
  retain 781
  courtesy 894
  love 897
  endearment 902
  – a belief 606
  – oneself
  pleasure 827
  content 831
  rejoicing 838
  pride 878
  – the shore
  navigation 267
  approach 286
  – a sin 945
huge 31, 192
hugger-mugger 528
Huguenot 984
huis clos, à – 528
huissier 965
huke 225
hulk body 50
  ship 273
hulks 752
hulky big 192
  unwieldy 647
  ugly 846
hull 50
hullabaloo 404, 411
hullo! 292
hum
  faint sound 405
  continued sound
  407
  animal sound 412
  sing 416
  deceive 545, 546
  – and haw
  stammer 583
  irresolute 605
  busy – of men 682
human 372
  – race 372
  – sacrifices 991
humane
  benevolent 906
  philanthropic 910
  merciful 914
human.tarian 372,
  910
humanities 560
humanize 894
humano capiti cer-
  vicem jungere
  equinam 24

humation 363
humble meek 879
  modest 881
  pious 987
  –r classes 876
  – oneself
  submit 725
  meek 879
  penitent 950
  worship 990
  eat – pie 725, 879
  your – servant
  dissent 489
  refusal 764
humbug
  falsehood 544
  deception 545
  deceiver 548
  trifle 643
  affectation 855
humdrum 841, 843
humectate 337, 339
humid 339
humiliate 308
humiliation
  adversity 735
  disrepute 874
  sense of shame
  879
  worship 990
  self – 950
humility 879, 987
humming-top 417
hummock 206, 250
humorist 844
humor essence 5
  tendency 176
  liquid 333
  disposition 602
  caprice 608
  aid 707
  indulge 760
  affections 820
  please 829
  wit 842
  flatter 933
  (fun 840)
  in the – 602
  out of – 901a
  peccant –
  unclean 853
  disease 655
humorous 842
humorsome
  capricious 608
  sulky 901a
hump 250
hump-backed 243
humph! 870
Humphrey, dine
  with Duke – 956
Humpty-dumpty
  193
Hun 165, 851, 913
hunch 250, 612
hunch-backed 243
hundred
  number 98
  many 102
  region 181
  the same a – years
  hence 460
hundredth 99
hundredweight 319
hunger 865
hunger-strike 956
hunks 819

ill-defined 447
ill-devised 499, 699
ill-digested 674
ill-disposed 901a,
  907
illegality 964
illegible 519
  render – 552
  – hand 590
illegitimate
  deceitful 545
  undue 925
  illegal 964
ill-fated 735
ill-flavored 395
ill-furnished 640
illiberal
  narrow-minded
  481
  stingy 819
  uncourteous 895
  selfish 943
illicit 925, 964
ill-imagined 499,
  699
illimited 105
ill-intentioned 907
illiterate 491, 498
ill-judged 499, 699
ill-judging 481
ill-made 243, 846
ill-mannered 851,
  895
ill-marked 447
ill-matched 24
ill-mated 24
ill-natured 907
illogical 477, 495
ill-omened 605, 859
ill-proportioned 243
ill-provided 640
ill-qualified 699
ill-requited 917
ill-spent 646
ill-tempered 901
ill-timed 135
ill-treat *bad* 649
  severe 739
  malevolent 907
illuminant 388
illuminate
  enlighten 420
  color 428
  excite 824
  ornament 847
illuminati 492
illumination
  [*see* illuminate]
  book-illustration
  558
  celebration 883
ill-use 907
ill-used 828
illusion
  fallacy of vision
  443
  error 495
illusive, illusory
  sophistical 477
  erroneous 495
  deceitful 545, 546
illustrate
  exemplify 82
  interpret 522
  represent 554
  engravings 558
  ornament 847

illustrious 873
image
  likeness 17
  copy 21
  appearance 448
  idea 453
  metaphor 521
  representation
  554
  graven – *idol* 991
imagery *fancy* 515
  metaphor 521
  representation
  554
imaginable 470
imaginary
  non-existing 2
  fancied 515
  – *quantity* 84
imagination 515
imaum 745, 996
imbecile 158, 499
imbécile 501
imbecility 499
imbed [*see* embed]
imbedded 229
imbibe 296
  – *learning* 539
imbrangle 61
imbricated 223
imbroglio
  disorder 59
  difficulty 704
  discord 713
imbrue
  impregnate 300
  moisten 339
  – one's hands in
  blood
  killing 361
  war 722
  – the soul 824
imbue *mix* 41
  impregnate 300
  moisten 339
  tinge 428
  teach 537
imbued
  affections 820
  – with
  belief 484
  habit 613
  feeling 821
imburse 803
imitation
  copying 19
  copy 21
  representation
  554
immaculate
  perfect 650
  clean 652
  innocent 946
immanent 5, 132
immanity 907
Immanuel 976
immaterial
  unsubstantial 4
immateriality
  spiritual 317
  trifling 643
immature 123, 674
immeasurable 31,
  105
immediate
  continuous 69
immediately 113,

132
immedicabile
  vulnus 619
immedicable 859
immelodious 414
immemorial 124
  from time – 122
  – usage 613
immense *great* 31
  infinite 105
  – *size* 192
immerge}
immerse}
  introduce 300
  dip 337
immersed in 229
immethodical 59
immigrant
  alien 57
  entering 294
immigration 266,
  294
imminent 152, 286
immiscible 47
immission 296
immitigable
  hopeless 859
  revenge 919
immix 41
immobility 150, 265
immoderately 31
immodest 961
immolation
  killing 361
  giving 784
  sacrifice 991
immoral 923, 945
immortal
  perpetual 112
  glorious 873
  celebrated 883
immotile 265
immovable
  stable 150
  quiescent 265
  obstinate 606
immundicity 653
immunity
  health 656
  freedom 748
  right 924
  exemption 777a,
  927a
immure 751
immutable
  stable 150
  deity 976
imo pectore, ab –
  821
imp 980
impact *contact* 43
  impulse 276
  insertion 300
impair 659
impale *transfix* 260
  execute 972
impalpable
  small 193
  powder 330
  intangible 381
impanation 998
impar sibi 608
imparity 28
impart *inform* 527
  give 784
impartial
  judicious 498

  neutral 628
  just 922
  honorable 939
  – *opinion* 484
impassable
  closed 261
  impossible 471
impasse 706
impassible 823
impassion 824
impassionable 822
impassioned
  – *language* 574
  excited 825
impassive 823
impatient 825
  – of control 742
impawn 771
impeach
  censure 932
  accuse 938
  go to law 969
impeachment,
  soft – 902
impeccability 650,
  946
impecunious 804
impede 706
impediment 706
  – in speech 583
impedimenta 633,
  780
impel *push* 276
  induce 615
impend
  future 121
  imminent 132
  destiny 152
  overhang 206
impenetrable
  closed 261
  solid 321
  unintelligible 519
  latent 526
impenitence 951
imperative
  require 630
  command 737,
  741
  severe 739
  duty 926
imperator 745
imperceptible
  small 32
  minute 193
  slow 275
  invisible 447
  latent 526
impercipient 376
imperdible 664
imperfect
  incomplete 53
  failing 651
  vicious 945
imperfection 651
  inferiority 34
  vice 945
imperfectly 32
imperforate 261
imperial
  trunk 191
  beard 256
  authority 737
imperil 665
imperious
  command 737
  proud 878

  arrogant 885
  – *necessity* 601
imperishable 112
  stable 150
  glorious 873
imperium in
  imperio 737
impermanent 111
impermeable
  closed 261
  dense 321
impersonal
  general 78
  neuter 316
impersonate 19,
  554
impersonator 19
imperspicuity 519
impersuasible 606
impertinent
  irrelevant 10
  insolent 885
imperturbable 823,
  826
impervious
  closed 261
  impossible 471
  insensible 823
  – to light 426
  – to reason 606
impetiginous 653
impetrate 765
impetuous
  boisterous 173
  hasty 684
  excitable 825
  rash 863
  eager 865
impetus 276
impi 726
impiety 988
impignorate 787
impinge 276
implacable 848, 919
implant *insert* 300
  teach 537
implanted
  adventitious 6
implausible 473
implead 969
implement 633
impletion 52
implex 41
implicate *involve* 54,
  526
  accuse 938
implicated *related* 9
  component 56
implication
  disorder 59
  meaning 516
  latency 526
implicit 526
  – *belief* 484
implore 765
imply *evidence* 467
  mean 516
  involve 526
impolicy 699
impolite 895
imponderable 4,
  320
imporous 261, 321
import
  put between 228
  ingress 294
  take in 296

insert 300
mean 516
imply 526
be of consequence
642
importance 642
greatness 30
attach – to 642
attach too much
– to 482
of no – 643
importune 765, 830
impose *order* 741
awe 928
– upon
credulity 486
deceive 545
be unjust 923
imposing
important 642
exciting 824
glorious 873
imposition [*see*
impose]
undue 925
– of hands 998
**impossibile, credo
quia** – 486
**impossibilities,
seek after** – 645
impossibility 471
impossible 471
refusal 764
– *quantity*
algebra 84
impost 812
imposthume 655
impostor 548, 925
imposture 545
impotence 158
**impotent conclu-
sion** 732
impound 791
impoverish
weaken 160
waste 638
despoil 789
render poor 804
impracticable
impossible 471
misjudging 481
obstinate 606
difficult 704
imprecation
prayer 765
curse 908
impregnable 159,
664
impregnate *mix* 41
combine 48
fecundate 161,
168
insert 300
teach 537
– with 641
impresario 599
imprescriptible 924
impress *cause*
sensation 375
mark 550
compel 791
excite feeling 824
– upon the mind
memory 505
teach 537
impressed with
belief 484

feeling 821
impressible
motive 615
sensibility 822
impression
sensation 375
idea 453
belief 484
printing 531
mark 550
engraving 558
print 591
emotion 821
make an –
act 171
thought 451
impressionable
375, 822
impressive
language 574
important 642
feeling 821, 824
imprimis 66
imprimit 558
imprint
publisher 531
indication 550
– in the memory
505
imprison
circumscribe 229
restrain 751
punish 972
improbability 473
improbate 932
improbity 940
impromptu 612
– *fait à loisir* 673
improper
incongruous 24
foolish 499
solecism 568
inexpedient 647
wrong 923
unmeet 925
vicious 945
– *time* 135
impropriate 777,
789
impropriator 779
improve
– the occasion 134
– the shining
hour 682
– upon 658
improvement 658
improvident
careless 460
not preparing 674
prodigal 818
rash 863
improvisation
music 415
improvisatore
speech 582
poetry 597
impulse 612
improvise
imagination 515
impulse 612
unprepared 674
improviste, à l' –
508, 612
improvisatrice
612
imprudent 460, 863
impudent 885, 895

impudicity 961
impugn *deny* 536
attack 716
blame 932
impugnation 708
impuissance 158
impulse *push* 276
sudden thought
612
motive 615
blind – 601
creature of – 612
give an – to
propel 284
aid 707
impulsive [*see*
impulse]
intuitive 477
excitable 825
rash 863
impunity *escape* 671
acquittal 970
with – *safely* 664
impurity 653, **961**
imputation
ascribe 155
slur 874
accuse 938
in 221
go – 294
– as much as
relation 9
degree 26
– the circum-
stances 8
– doors 221
– *durancevile* 751
– for
– *force* 1
undertake 676
promise 768
– re 9
– and out 314
–s and outs 182
in: – *articulo* 111
– *extenso whole* 50
diffuse 573
– jail 751
– *limine* 66
– loco 23
– medias res 68
– prison 751
– *propriâ personâ*
79
– toto 52
– transitu
transient 111
transfer 270
– statu pupillari
127
– statu quo 141
– vogue 1
inability 158, 699
inabstinent 954
inaccessible 196,
471
inaccurate 495, 568
inaction 172, **683**
inactivity 683, 172
inadequate
powerless 158
insufficient 640
useless 645
imperfect 651
inadmissible
incongruous 24
excluded 55

extraneous 57
inexpedient 647
inadvertence 458
inadvisable 647
inaffable 895
inalienable
retention 781
right 924
inamorata 897
inane *void* 4
unmeaning 517
unthinking 452
insufficient 640
trivial 643
useless 645
inanimate 360
– matter 358
inanition 158
inanity [*see* inane]
inappetency 823,
866
inapplicable 10, 24
inapposite 10, 24
inappreciable 33,
193
unimportant 643
inapprehensible
stolid 499
unintelligible 519
inappropriate 24,
647
inapt
incongruous 24
impotent 158
useless 645
inexpedient 647
unskilful 699
inarticulate 581,
583
inartificial 703
inartistic 846
inasmuch *whereas* 9
however 26
because 476
inattention 458
inaudible
silence 403
faint sound 405
deaf 419
voiceless 581
inaugural
precursor 64
inaugurate
begin 66
cause 153
install 755
celebrate 883
inauspicious
untimely 135
untoward 649
hopeless 859
inbeing 5
inborn, inbred
intrinsic 5
affections 820
– *proclivity* 601
inca 745
incage 751
incalculable 31, 105
incalescence 382
incandescence 382
incandescent 423
incantation
invocation 765
sorcery 992
spell 993
incantatory 992

incapable 158
incapacious 203
incapacitate 158
incapacity
impotence 158
ignorance 491
stupidity 499
incarcerate 751
incarnadine 434
incarnate
intrinsic 5
bodily 316
fleshly 364
vicious 945
devil –
bad man 949
Satan 978
Incarnation 976
incase 223, 229
incautious 863
incendiary
destroy 162
burn 384
influence 615
malevolent 907
evil-doer 913
bad man 949
incense *fuel* 388
fragrant 400
hate 898
anger 900
flatter 933
worship 990
rite 998
incension
burning 384
incentive 615
inception 66
inceptive 153
inceptor 541
incertitude 475
incessant
repeated 104
ceaseless 112
frequent 136
incest 961
inch *small* 32
length 200
by –es 275
to an – 494
not yield an – 606
give an – and take
an ell 789
– by inch
by degrees 26
in parts 51
slowly 275
not see an – be-
yond one's nose
699
inchoation 66, 673
incide 44
incidence 278
incident 151
incidental
extrinsic 6
circumstance 8
irrelative 10
occurring 151
casual 156
liable 177
chance 621
trivial 643
– *music* 415
incinerate 384
incipience 66
incircumspect 460

incision 44, 259
incisive *energy* 171
  vigor 574
  feeling 821
incisor 253
incite
  exasperate 173
  urge 615
incivility 895
incivism 911
inclasp 229
inclement
  violent 173
  cold 383
  severe 739
  pitiless 914a
inclination
  [*see* incline]
  will 600
  affection 820
  desire 865
  love 897
incline *tendency* 176
  slope 217
  direction 278
  willing 602
  induce 615
  – an ear to 457
  – the head 308
inclined
  disposed 620
  – plane 633
inclose
  surround 227
inclosure **232**
include
  composition 54
  - *in a class* 76
inclusion **76**
inclusive
  additive 37
  component 56
  class 76
incogitancy **452**
incognita, terra –
  491
incognito 528
incognizable 519
incoherence
  physical 47
  mental 503
incombustible 385
income *means* 632
  profit 775
  property 780
  wealth 803
  receipt 810
  – tax 812
incoming
  ingress 294
  receipt 810
incommensurable
  10
  – quantity 84, 85
incommode 706
  hinder 706
incommunicable
  unmeaning 517
  unintelligible 519
  retention 781
incommunicado
  528
incommutable 150
incomparable 33
incompassionate
  914a
incompatible 24

incompatibility 15
incompetence
  inability 158
  incapacity 499
  unskilful 699
  dereliction 927
incompleteness **53**
  non-completion
   730
incompliance 764
incomprehensible
  infinite 105
  unintelligible 519
incomprehension
  491
incompressible 321
inconcealable 525
inconceivable
  unthinkable 452
  impossible 471
  improbable 473
  incredible 485
  unintelligible 519
  wonder 870
inconceptible 519
inconcinnity
  disagreement 24
  ugliness 846
inconclusive 477
inconcoction 674
incondite 851
incongruous
  differing 15
  disagreeing 24
  illogical 477
  ungrammatical
   568
  discordant 713
inconnection 10, 44
inconsequence
  irrelation 10
inconsequential 477
inconsiderable 32,
  643
inconsiderate
  thoughtless 452
  inattentive 458
  neglectful 460
  foolish 699
inconsistent
  contrary 14
  disagreeing 24
  illogical 477
  absurd 497
  foolish 499
  capricious 608
  discord 713
inconsolable 837
inconsonant
  disagreeing 24
  fitful 149
inconspicuous 447
inconstant 149
incontestable 159,
  474, 525
incontiguous 196
incontinent 961
incontinently 132
incontrollable 173
incontrovertible
  150, 474
inconvenience 647
  put to – 706
inconversable 585,
  893
inconvertible 143
inconvincible 487

incorporate 48
  combine 48
  include 76
  materialize 316
incorporation 761
incorporeal 317
  – *hereditaments*
   780
incorrect
  illogical 477
  erroneous 495
  solecism 568
  vicious 945
incorrigible
  obstinate 606
  hopeless 859
  vicious 945
  impenitent 951
incorruption
  probity 939
  innocence 946
incrassate
  increase 194
  density 321
  - *fluids* 352
increase
  - in degree **35**
  - in number 102
  - in size 194
incredible
  great 31
  impossible 471
  improbable 473
  doubtful 485
  wonderful 870
incredulity 487, 989
increment
  increase 35
  addition 37
  adjunct 39
  expansion 194
increpation 932
incriminate 938
incrust 223, 224
incubate 370
incubation 673
incubus
  hindrance 706
  pain 828
  demon 980
inculcate 6, 537
inculpable 946
inculpate 938
inculture 674
incumbency
  business 625
  churchdom 995
incumbent
  inhabitant 188
  high 206
  weight 319
  duty 926
  clergyman 996
incumber 706
incumbered 806
incunabula 66, 127
incur 177
  - blame 932
  - danger 665
  - a debt 806
  - disgrace 874
  - a loss 776
  - the risk 621
incurable
  ingrained 5
  disease 655
  hopeless 859

incuriam, per –
  458, 460
incuriosity **456**
incursion 294, 716
incurvation 245
indagation 461
indebted
  owing 806
  gratitude 916
  duty 926
indecent 961
indeciduous 150
indecipherable 519
indecision 475, 605
indecisive 475
indeclinable 150
indecorous
  vulgar 851
  vicious 945
  impure 961
indeed *existing* 1
  very 31
  assent 488
  truly 494
  assertion 535
  wonder 870
indefatigable
  persevering 604a
  active 682
indefeasible
  stable 150, 474
  due 924
indefectible 650
indefensible
  powerless 158
  submission 725
  accusable 938
  wrong 945
indeficient 650
indefinite
  great 31
  unspecified 78
  infinite 105
  misty 447
  uncertain 475
  inexact 495
  vague 519
indeliberate 612
indelible *stable* 150
  memory 505
  mark 550
  feeling 821
indelicate 961
indemnity
  compensation 30
  restitution 790
  forgiveness 918
  atonement 952
  reward 973
  deed of – 771
indenizen 184
indent *scollop* 248
  list 86
indentation 252,
  257
indenture 769, 771
independence
  irrelation 10
  freedom 748
  wealth 803
Independent 984
indescribable 31,
  870
indesinent 112
indestructible 150
indeterminate
  indefinite 78

  chance 156
  uncertain 475
  irresolute 605
indevotion 989
index
  arrangement 60
  exponent 84
  list 86
  sign 550
  words 62
index expurga-
  torius 761, 932
indexterity 699
Indian:
  – file 69
  – rubber 325
  – summer 126
  – weed 392
indicate
  specify 79
  direct attention to
   457
  mean 516
  mark 550
indication **550**
indicative
  evidence 467
indict *accuse* 938
  arraign 969
indiction 108, 531
indifference
  incuriosity 456
  unwillingness 603
  no choice 609a
  insensibility 823
  unconcern **866**
  irreligion 989
  matter of – 643
indifferent
  [*see* indifference]
  unimportant 643
  bad 649
indigence
  insufficiency 640
  poverty 804
indigenous 5, 186
indigested 674
indigestible 657
indigestion 657
indigitate 457
indign 940
indignation 900
  – meeting 832
indignity 900, 929
indigo 438
indiligence 683
indirect
  oblique 217
  devious 279
  latent 526
  circuitous 629
indiscernible 447
indiscerptible
  whole 50
  unity 87
  dense 321
indiscoverable 526
indiscreet 499, 863,
  945
indiscretion
  guilt 947
indiscriminate
  mixed 41
  unarranged 59
  multiform 81
  casual 621
indiscrimination

ingenuous 703
ingesta 298
ingestion 296
ingle 388
inglorious 874, 940
ingluvies 191
ingot 800
ingraft *add* 37
  join 43
  insert 300
  teach 537
ingrafted
  extrinsic 6
  habit 613
ingrain
  insinuate 228
  color 428
ingrained
  intrinsic 5
  combined 48
  habit 613
  character 820
ingrate 917
ingratiate 897
ingratiating 894
ingratitude 917
ingredient 51, 56
ingress 294
  forcible – 300
ingurgitate 296
ingustible 391
inhabile 699
inhabit 186
inhabitant 188
inhale *receive* 296
  breathe 349
  smell 398
inharmonious
  discord 713
  – *color* 428
  – *sound* 414
inhere 1
inherent 5, 820
inherit 775, 777
inheritance 780
  – *of the saints* 981
inherited
  intrinsic 5
inheritor 779
inhesion 5
inhibit *hinder* 706
  restrain 751
  prohibit 761
inhospitable 893
inhuman 907
inhume 363
inimaginable
  impossible 471
  improbable 473
  wonderful 870
inimical 708, 889
inimitable
  non-imitation 20
  supreme 33
  very good 648
  perfect 650
iniquity 923, 945
  worker of – 949
inirritability 826
initial 66
  – *letter* 558
initiate *begin* 66
  admit 296
  teach 537
initiated *skilful* 698
initiative 66
inject 300, 337

injection 662
injudicial 964
injudicious 499,
  863
injunction
  acquirement 630
  advice 695
  command 741
  prohibition 761
injure *evil* 619
  damage 659
  spite 907
injuria formae,
  spretae – 846,
  930
injury *evil* 619
  badness 649
  damage 659
injustice 923
ink 431
  pen and – 590
  before the – *is dry*
  132
  – *slinging* 720
inkle 45
inkling
  knowledge 490
  supposition 514
  information 527
inkstand 590
inland 221
inlay 440, 847
inlet *beginning* 66
  interval 198
  opening 260
  ingress 294
  – *of the sea* 343
inly 221
inmate 188
inmost 221
  to the – *core* 822
  – *soul* 820
  – *thoughts* 451
inn 189
  – *s of Court* 968
innate 5, 601
innavigable 471
inner 221
  – *coating* 224
  – *man intellect* 450
  affections 820
innermost recesses
  221
innings *land* 342
  acquisition 775
  receipt 810
innkeeper 601
innocence **946**
innocent *fool* 501
  good 648
  healthy 656
  artless 703
  guiltless 946
innocuous *good* 648
  healthy 656
  innocent 946
innominate 565
innovation
  variation 20a
  new 123
  change 140
innoxious
  salubrious 656
  innocent 946
innuendo *hint* 527
  censure 932
innumerable 105

innutritious 657
inobservance 773
inoccupation 681
inoculate
  insert 300
  teach 537
  influence 615
inodorous 399
inoffensive 648, 946
inofficious 907
inoperative
  powerless 158
  unproductive 169
  useless 645
inopportune
  untimely 135
  inexpedient 647
inordinate 31, 641
inorganization **358**
inornate 849
inosculate *join* 43
  intersect 219
  convoluted 248
inquest 461
inquietude
  changeable 149
  uneasy 828
  discontent 832
  apprehension 860
inquinate 659
inquire 461
  – *into* 595
inquirer 461
inquiring *mind* 455
inquiry **461**
inquisition
  inquiry 461
  severity 739
  torture 907
  tribunal 966
inquisitive 455
inquisitorial
  prying 455
  inquiry 461
  severe 739
  jurisdiction 965
inroad *ingress* 294
  devastation 659
  invasion 716
inrolment 551
insalubrity **657**
insanity **503**
insatiable 865
inscribe 590, 873
inscription 551
inscroll 551
inscrutable 519
insculpture 557
insculptured 558
insecable 43, 87
insect *minute* 193
  animal 366
  – *cry* 412
insecure
  uncertain 475
  danger 665
insensate
  foolish 499
  insane 503
insensibility
  slow 275
  physical **376**
  moral **823**
  – *of benefits* 917
  – *to the past* 506
inseparable **43**, 46
insert *locate* 184

interpose 228
  enter 294
  put in 300
  record 551
  – *itself* 300
insertion **300**
  adjunct 39
  ornament 847
inservient 645
inseverable 43, 87
inside 221
  – *out* 218
  turn – *out* 529
insidious
  deceitful 545
  cunning 702
  dishonourable 940
insight 465, 490
insignia 550
  – *of authority* 747
insignificant
  unmeaning 517
  unimportant 643
insincere 544, 855
insinuate
  intervene 228
  ingress 294
  insert 300
  latency 526
  hint 527
  ingratiate **897**
  blame 932
insipid
  style 575
  dull 840
insipidity
  tasteless **391**
  indifferent 866
insist *argue* 476
  command 741
  – *upon affirm* 535
  dwell on 573
  be determined 604
  contend 720
  compel 744
  conditions 770
  due 924
insnare 545
insobriety 959
insolation 382, 384
insolence 878, 885
insoluble *dense* 321
  unintelligible 519
insolvable 519
insolvent
  poverty 804
  debt 806
  non-payment 808
insomnia 682
insouciance
  thoughtlessness
  458
  supineness 823
  indifference 866
inspan 293
inspect 441, 457
inspector 444
  inquisitor 461
  judge 480
  director 694
inspiration
  wisdom 498
  imagination 515
  poetry 577
  impulse 612
  motive 615
  feeling 821

Deity 976
  revelation 985
  religious - 987
inspire *improve* 658
  prompt 615
  animate 824
  cheer 836
  – *courage* 861
  – *hope* 858
  – *respect* 928
inspirit *incite* 615
  animate 824
  encourage 861
inspiriting
  hopeful 858
inspissate 321, 352
instability 149
install *locate* 184
  commission 755
  celebrate 883
instalment
  portion 51
  payment 807, **809**
instance
  example 82
  motive 615
  solicitation 765
instant *moment* 113
  present 118
  destiny 152
  required 630
  importance 642
  active 682
  lose not an – 684
  on the – 132
instantaneity **113**
instanter 113, 132
instar omnium 17,
  82
instate 883
instauration 660
instead 147
instep 245
instigate 615
instil *extrinsic* 6
  mix 41
  insert 300
  teach 537
instinct
  intellect 450
  intuition 477
  impulse 601
  – *with motive* 615
  possession 777
  brute – 450a
instinctive
  inborn 5
institute *begin* 66
  cause 153
  produce 161
  academy 542
  society 712
  – *an inquiry* 461
institution
  academy 542
  society 712
  political - 963
  church 995
institutor 540
instruct *teach* 537
  advise 695
  precept 697
  order 741
instructed 490
instructor 540
instrument
  implement **633**

inebriation 959
intra, ab – 221
intractable
  obstinate 606
  difficult 704
  sullen 901a
intramural 221
intransient 110
intransigeance 604
intransitive 110
intransmutable
  110, 150
intrap 545
intraregarding 221
intrench 717
  – on 303
intrepid 861
intricate
  confused 59
  convoluted 248
  difficult 704
intrigant
  meddlesome 682
  cunning 702
  libertine 962
intrigue *fascinate*
  615, 897
  plot 626
  activity 682
  cunning 702
  excite 824
  interest 829
  licentiousness 961
intrinsic 5
  – *evidence* 467
  – *habit* 613
  – *truth* 494
intrinsicality 5
introception 296
introduce *lead* 62
  interpose 228
  precede 280
  insert 300
  – new blood 140
  – new conditions
    469
  – to 888
introduction
  [*see* introduce]
  preface 64
  reception 296
  drama 599
  friendship 888
  courtesy 894
introductory
  precursor 64
  beginning 66
  priority 116
introgression 294
introit 998
intromission 228
intromit
  discontinue 142
  receive 296
introspection 441,
  457
introspective 451
introvert 218
intrude
  interfere 24
  inopportune 135
  intervene 228
  enter 294
  encroach 303
intruder 57
intrusiveness 682
intrust 755, 787

intuition *mind* 450
  unreasoning 477
  knowledge 490
intumescence 194,
  250
intwine 43, 243
inunction 223
inundate
  effusion 337
  flow 348
  redundance 641
inunderstanding
  452
inurbanity 895
inure 613, 673
inured
  insensible 823
inusitation 614
inutility 645
invade *ingress* 294
  encroach 303
  attack 716
invalid
  powerless 158
  illogical 477
  diseased 655
  undue 925
invalidate
  disable 158
  weaken 160
  confute 479
invaluable 648
invariable
  intrinsic 5
  uniform 16
  conformable 82
  stable 150
invasion
  ingress 294
  attack 716
invective 932
inveigh 932
inveigle 545, 615
invent
  discover 480a
  imagine 515
  lie 544
  devise 626
invented
  untrue 546
invention 480a
inventive
  skilful 698
inventor 164
inventory 86
inverse 14, 218
inversion
  derangement 61
  change 140
  of position 218
  contraposition
    237
  reversion 145
  language 577
invertebrate 158
invest
  empower 157
  clothe 225
  besiege 227, 716
  commission 755
  give 784
  lend 787
  expend 809
  – *in locate* 184
  purchase 795
  – *money* 817
  – *with ascribe* 155

investigate 461
investment 225
  – *trust* 712
  make –s 673
inveterate *old* 124
  established 150
  inborn 820
  – *belief* 484
  – *habit* 613
invidious
  painful 830
  hatred 898
  spite 907
  envy 921
invigorate
  strengthen 159
invigorating
  healthy 656
invincible 159
inviolable
  secret 528
  right 924
  honor 939
inviolate
  permanent 141
  secret 528
  honorable 939
invious *closed* 261
  pathless 704
invisibility 447
invisible *small* 193
  not to be seen 447
  concealed 526
  – ink 528
  become – 4
invitâ Minervâ 603,
  704
invite *induce* 615
  offer 763
  ask 765
  – the attention
    457
inviting
  [*see* invite]
  pleasing 829
invoice 86
invoke *address* 586
  implore 765
  pray 990
  – *curses* 908
  – *saints* 998
involucrum 223
involuntary
  necessary 601
  unwilling 603
  – *servitude* 749
involution [*see*
  involve]
  algebra 85
involve *include* 54
  derange 61
  wrap 225
  evince 467
  mean 516
  latency 526
involved
  disorder 59
  convoluted 248
  obscure style 571
  in debt 806
involvement 704
invulnerable 664
inward *intrinsic* 5
  inside 221
  – *bound* 294
  – *monitor* 926
inweave 219

inwrap 225
inwrought 5
io triumphe! 838,
  883
Ionic 597
iota 32
I. O. U. 771, 800
ipse dixit 474, 535
ipsissima verba 494
ipso facto 1
irae
  amantium – 918
  tantaene animis
    coelestibus – 900
irascibility 901
irate 900
ire 900
iridescent 440
Iris 268, 534
iris 440, 441
Irish Bull 353
Irishism 497
irk 688, 830
irksome
  tiresome 688
  difficult 704
  painful 830
  weary 841
iron *strength* 159
  smooth 255
  hard 323
  resolution 604
rule with a rod of
  – 739
  – *age adversity* 735
  pain 828
  – *cross* 733
  – gray 432
  – grip 159
  – gripe 781
  – heel 739
  – *necessity* 601
  – rule 739
  – entering into the
    soul 828, 830
  – sway 739
  – will 604
iron-bound **coast**
  land 342
  danger 667
iron-clad
  covering 223
  defence 717
  man of war 726
iron-handed 739
iron-hearted 861
iron-mold 434
irons 752
  fire – 386
  put in – 751
  – in the fire
    business 625
  redundance 641
  active 682
  unskilful 699
irony
  figure of speech
    521
  untruth 546
  ridicule 856
irradiate 420
irrational
  number 84
  illogical 477
  silly 499
irreclaimable
  hopeless 859

vicious 945
  impenitent 951
irreconcilable
  unrelated 10
  discordant 24
  unwilling 603
  opponent 710
  enmity 889
irrecoverable
  past 122
  hopeless 859
irredeemable 859
irredentist 776
irreducible
  discordant 24
  out of order 59
  unchangeable 150
irrefragable 478
irrefutable 474, 478
irregular
  diverse 16a
  out of order 59
  multiform 81
  against rule 83
  – *in recurrence*
    139
  distorted 243
  combatant 726
irregularity **139**
irrelation 10
irrelevant
  unrelated 10
  unaccordant 24
  sophistical 477
  unimportant 643
irreligion 989
irremediable
  bad 649
  hopeless 859
  (spoiled 659)
irremissible 945
irremovable 150
irreparable
  hopeless 859
irrepentance 951
irreprehensible 946
irrepressible
  violent 173
  free 748
  excitable 825
irreproachable 946
irreprovable 946
irresistible
  strong 159
  demonstration
    478
  necessary 601
irresoluble 150
irresolution **605**
irresolvable 87
irresolvedly 605
irrespective 10
irresponsible
  irresolute 605
  exempt 927a
  arbitrary 964
irretrievable
  stable 150
  lost 776
  hopeless 859
irrevealable 528
irreverence 929,
  988
irreversible
  stable 150
  hopeless 859
irrevocable

stable 150
necessary 601
resolute 604
hopeless 859
irrigate 337
irriguous 339
irrision 856, 929
irritabile, genus –
901
irritable 825, 901
irritate *violent* 173
excite 824
pain 830
provoke 898
incense 900
irritation
[see irritate]
pain 828
·source of – 830
irritating
[see irritate]
stringent 171
irruption 294, 716
Irvingite 984
Ishmael 83
is: that – 118
– to be 152
Isis 979
Islamism 984
island 181, 346
–s of the blessed
981
islander 188
isle 346
isobar 338
isocheimal 383
isochronal 114
isochronous 27, 120
isolate 44, 893
isolated 10, 87
isomorphism 240
isoperimetrical 27
isothermal 382
– layer 338
isotonic 413
issue *distribute* 73
focus 74
event 151
effect 154
posterity 167
depart 293
egress 295
stream 348, 349
inquiry 461
publication 531
book 593
ulcer 655
dénouement 729·
·*money* 800
at – *discussion* 476
dissent 489
negation 536
opposition 708
discord 713
contention 720
in – 461
join – *lawsuit* 969
– a command 741
issueless 169
isthmus
connection 45
narrow 203
land 342
italics *mark* 550
put in –
importance 642
itch *titillation* 380

desire 865
itching palm 819
item
addition 37, 39
part 51
speciality 79
unit 87
iteration 104
itinerant 266, 268
itinerary 266, 527
itur ad astra, sic –
360
ivory 430
Ixion 312

J

jab 276
jabber
unmeaning 517
stammer 583
chatter 584
jacent 213
jacet, hic – 363
jacinth 847
jack
rotation 312
ensign 550
instrument 633
money 800
Jack – Cade 742
– Ketch 975
– o' lantern 423
– in office
director 694
bully 887
– at a pinch 711
– Pudding
actor 599
humorist 844
boaster 884
before one can say
' – Robinson'
132
– tar 269
– of all trades 700
jack-a-dandy 844,
854
jackal
auxiliary 711
servility 886
jackanapes 854,
887
Jackass 271
jack-boot 225
jackdaw in pea-
cock's feathers
701
jacket 225
cork – 666
Jacobin 710
Jacquerie 716, 719
jacta est alea 601
jactitation
tossing 315
boasting 884
jaculation 284
jade *horse* 271
fatigue 688
low woman 876
scamp 949
drab 962
jag 257
jagged 244
jail 752

– bird
prisoner 754
bad man 949
jailer 753, 975
jakes 653
jalousie de métier
921
jam *squeeze* 43
crowd 72
food 298
pulp 354
sweet 396
scrape 732
– in *interpose* 228
jamb 215
jamboree 840
jammed in 751
jangle
harsh sound 410
quarrel 713
janissary 726
janitor 263
janty *gay* 836
pretty 845
stylish 852
showy 882
insolent 885
January 138
januis clausis 528
Janus *deceiver* 607
tergiversation 607
close the temple
of – 723
Janus-faced 544
japan *coat* 223
resin 356a
ornament 847
jar *clash* 24
vessel 191
agitation 315
stridor 410
discord 713
– upon the feel-
ings 830
jardinière 191
jargon
absurdity 497
no meaning 517
unintelligible 519
neology 563
jarvey 694
jasper 847
jaundiced
yellow 436
prejudiced 481
dejected 837
jealous 920
view with – eyes
disapprove 932
jaunt 266
jaunting car 272
jaunty [see janty]
javelin 727
jaw *chatter* 584
scold 932
jaw-fallen 837
jaws *mouth* 231
eating 298
– of death 360
jay 584
jaywalker 701
jazz 415, 840
– band 417
jealous of honor
939
jealousy 920
suspicion 485

jecur, difficili bile –
900
jeer 929
Jehovah 976
Jehu 268, 694
jejune *insipid* 391
style 575
scanty 640
dull 843
jell 352
jelly 298, 352
beat to a – 972
jemidar 745
jemmy *lever* 633
dandy 854
je ne sais quoi
exceptional 83
what d'ye call 'em
563
beauty 845
jennet 271
jeopardy 665
jerboa 309
jeremiad
lament 839
invective 932
Jericho, send to –
297
jerk *start* 146
throw 284
pull 285
agitate 315
jerkin 225
jerks, by – 70
Jerry Sneak 862,
941
jersey 225
Jerusalem
the new – 981
Jessamy, Jemmy –
854
jesse 1000
jest *trifle* 643
wit 842
jest-book 842
jester 844
jesting-stock 857
Jesuit *deceiver* 548
priest 996
jesuitical 477, 544
Jesus 976
jet *ship* 273
stream 348
– black 431
– propulsion 267
jetsam 73, 782
jettison 782
jetty *protection* 250
harbor 666
jeu
le – n'en vaut pas
la chandelle
waste 638
unimportant 643
dear 814
– d'esprit 842
– de mots 842
– de théâtre 599
jeune
– premier 599
– veuve 599
Jew *cunning* 702
lender 787
rich 803
extortioner 819
heretic 984
worth a –'s eye

648, 814
–'s harp 417
jewel *gem* 648
ornament 847
favorite 899
jewelery, false –
545
Jezebel *wicked* 913
wretch 949
courtesan 962
jib *front* 234
regression 283
cut of one's –
form 240
appearance 448
jibe 140
jiffy 113
jig 840
jig-saw puzzle 840
jilt *disappoint* 509
deceive 545
deceiver 548
cast off 756
dishonor 940
jilted 898
jimp 845
jingal 727
jingle 408
jingo 887
jingoism 884
jinks, high – 840
jinriksha 272
jinx 649, 735
Joan of Arc 861
job *business* 625
action 680
unfair 940
tough – 704
Job:
patience of – 826,
830
poor as – 804
–'s comforter
dejection 837
hopeless 859
jobation 932
jobber
deceiver 548
tactician 700
merchant 797
trickster 943
jobbernowl 501
jobbery 702, 940
jobbing *barter* 794
jockey *rider* 268
deceive 545
deceiver 548
servant 746
jocose 836, 842
jocoseness *fun* 840
ocular 836, 842
jocund 836, 840
jocundity 829
Joe Miller 842, 844
jog *push* 276
shake 315
– the memory 505
– on *continue* 143
trudge 266
slow 275
advance 282
mediocrity 736
joggle 315
jog-trot
trudge 266
slow 275
habit 613

John Doe and
Richard Roe 4
Johnny 894
John's 653
Johnsonian 577
joie, feu de – 883
join *connect* 43
assemble 72
contiguous 199
arrive 292
party 712
sociality 892
marry 903
– battle 722
– in the chorus 488
– forces, hands,
709
– in 778
– issue *discuss* 476
deny 536
quarrel 713
contend 720
lawsuit 969
– the majority 360
– up
enlist 723
– with 709
joint *junction* 43
part 51
accompanying 88
concurrent 178
meat 298
– concern 721
joint-stock 709, 778
joint-tenancy 778
jointure 780
joist 215
joke *absurdity* 497
trifle 643
wit 842
ridicule 856
in – 842
mere – 643
no – *existing* 1
important 642
practical –
deception 545
ridicule 856
disrespect 929
take a – 498
joker 844
jokesmith 844
joking *apart* 535,
604
jole 236
jollification
amusement 840
intemperance 954
jollity 840, 892
jolly *plump* 192
marine 269
gay 836
ridicule 856
– boat 273
– fellow 892
jolt 276, 315
jolthead 501
Jonah 649
Jones
Davy –' locker 360
Paul – 792
jorum 191
Joseph 960
–'s coat 440
joss 991
– house 1000
jostle *rush* 276

jog 315
clash 713
jot 32, 643
jotting 550, 551
jounce 315
journal *annals* 114
newspaper 531
record 551
magazine 593
narrative 594
accounts 811
journalist
messenger 534
recorder 553
author 593
journey 266
journeyman
artisan 690
servant 746
joust 720
Jove 979
by – 870
sub –
out of doors 220
air 338
jovial *gay* 836
amusement 840
social 892
jowl 236
joy 827
give one – 896
joyful 836
joyless *painful* 830
sad 837
joy stick 693
J.P. 967
Juan, Don – 962
jube 1000
jubeo, sic volo sic –
741
jubilant *gay* 836
rejoicing 838
boastful 884
jubilee 138, 883
jubilitate 884
**Judaeus Apella,
credat** –
disbelief 485
absurdity 497
Judaism 984
Judas *deceiver* 548
knave 941
– kiss
hypocrisy 544
base 940
judge *decide* 480
master 745
taste 850
magistrate 967
Judge *deity* 976
Judgment
Day of – 67
judgment
intellect 450
discrimination
465
decision 480
wisdom 498
sentence 972
judgment-seat 966
judicata, res –
certain 574
judgment 480
judication 480
judicatory 965, 966
judicature 965
Judicature, High

Court of – 966
judice: coram –
jurisdiction 965
lawsuit 969
me – 481
sub – *inquiry* 461
lawsuit 969
judicial 965
– Astrology 511
– murder 361
– separation 905
judicious 498
jug 191, 752
juggernaut
kill 361
god 979
idolatry 991
juggle *deceive* 545
cunning 702
juggler 548, 599
jugulate 361
juice 333
juiceless 340
juicy 339
jujitsu 718
jujube 396
julep 396
jumble *mixture* 41
confusion 59
derange 61
indiscriminate
465a
jument 271
jump
sudden change
146
leap 309
neglect 460
at one – 113
– about 315
– at *willing* 602
pursue 622
hasten 684
consent 762
seize 789
desire 865
– to a conclusion
misjudge 481
credulous 486
– over 460
– up 307, 309
jumper 225
junction 43
juncture
circumstance 8
junction 43
period 134
jungle *disorder* 59
vegetation 367
junior 127, 541
– counsel 968
junk 273
junket *dish* 298
merry-making
840
Juno 920, 979
junta 696
junto 712
jupe 225
Jupiter 979
jurare in verba ma-
gistri 481, 486
jurat 967
jure: de – *due* 924
legal 963
– divino *due* 924
God 976

juridical 965
jurisconsult 968
jurisdiction 965
authority 737
Jurisprudence 963
jurist 480, 968
jury 967
empanel a – 969
– box 966
– mast
substitute 147
refuge 666
jus: summum –
922
– civile
– gentium 963
– nocendi 737
– et norma
loquendi 567
jussive 741
just *accurate* 494
right 922
equitable 939
pious 987
– as *similar* 17
same time 120
– do 639
– now 118
– out 123
– reasoning 476
– so 488
– then 113
– the thing
agreement 23
exact 494
– in time 134
juste milieu
middle 68
moderation 174
mid-course 628
justice
right 922
honor 939
magistrate 967
administration of
– 965
bring to – 969
court of – 966
do – to *eat* 298
duty 926
praise 931
vindicate 937
not do – to 483
retributive – 922,
972
– seat 966
justifiable 922, 937
justification
vindication 937
religious 987
justle *push* 276
contend 720
jut out 250
jute 205
jutty 250
juvenile 127
– lead 599
juxtaposition 199
j'y suis j'y reste
141

K

kadi 967
kail 840
kaiser 745

kaleidoscope 149,
445
καλόν, τὸ – 845
kangaroo 309
κατ' ἐξοχήν
greatness 31
superiority 33
importance 642
Katerfelto 994
kavass 965
K.C. 968
keck 297
kedge *navigate* 267
anchor 666
keek 527
keel 211
– upwards 21
keelhaul 972
keen *energetic* 171
sharp 253
sensible 375
cold 383
intelligent 498
poignant 821
lament 839
witty 842
eager 865
– blast 349
keener 839
keen-eyed 441
keep *do often* 136
persist 141
continue 143
food 298
store 636
provision 637
refuge 666
preserve 670
citadel 717
custody 751
prison 752
observe 772
retain 781
celebrate 883
– alive 359, 670
– aloof 196, 623
– accounts 811
– an account with
805
– apart 44
– at it 143
– away 187
– back *late* 133
conceal 528
dissuade 616
not use 678
restrain 751
retain 781
– the ball rolling
143
– one's bed 655
– body and soul
together *life* 359
health 654
– within bounds
304
– close 781
– company 88
– one in counte-
nance
conformity 82
induce 615
aid 707
encourage 861
– one's counte-
nance
unexcitable 826

landscape
  prospect **448**
  – gardening
  agriculture **71**
  beauty **845**
  – painting **556**
  – painter **559**
land-shark **792**
land-slip **306**
landsman **342**
Landsturm **726**
land-surveying **466**
Landwehr **726**
lane **189**, **260**, **627**
langrel **727**
lang-syne **122**
language **560**
  command of – **582**
  strong –
  vigor **574**
  malediction **908**
languid *weak* **160**
  inert **172**
  slow **275**
  - *style* **575**
  inactive **683**
  torpid **823**
languish
  decrease **36**
  ill **655**
  inactive **683**
  repine **828**
  – for **865**
languishing
  weak **160**
  affected **855**
languishment
  lament **839**
languor
  [*see* languid]
lank **200**
lanky **203**, **206**
lantern
  window **260**
  lamp **423**
  magic – **448**
  – of Diogenes **461**
  – jaws **203**
lanterne, à la – **972**
lanuginous **256**
lanyard **45**
Laodicean **822**
lap *abode* **189**
  support **215**
  interior **221**
  wrap **225**
  encompass **227**, **229**
  drink **298**
  – of luxury
  pleasure **377**
  inactivity **683**
  voluptuousness **954**
lap-dog *animal* **366**
  servile **886**
lapel **39**
lapidary **559**
lapidate *kill* **361**
  attack **716**
  punish **972**
lapidescence **323**
lapis lazuli
  blue **438**
  jewel **847**
lappet **39**, **214**
lapse *course* **109**

past **122**
  conversion **144**
  fall **306**
  degeneracy **659**
  relapse **661**
  loss **776**
  vice **945**
  guilt **947**
  – of memory **506**
  – of time **109**
lapsus calami **495**
lapsus linguae
  mistake **495**
  solecism **568**
  stammering **583**
Laputa, college of **538**
larboard **239**
larceny **791**
lard **356**
lardaceous **355**
larder **636**
  contents of the – **298**
lares et penates
  home **189**
  idols **991**
large
  quantity **31**
  size **192**
  at – *diffuse* **573**
  free **748**
  become – **194**
  – number **102**
  – type **642**
large-hearted
  liberal **816**
  benevolent **906**
  disinterested **942**
larger **194**
largest **784**
largest portion **192**
larghetto **275**, **415**
largiloquent **573**
largo **275**, **415**
lariat **45**, **247**
lark *ascent* **305**
  pleasure **827**
  sprec **840**
  with the – **125**
larmes:
  fondre en – **839**
  – aux yeux **839**
larmoyante,
  comédie – **599**
larrikin **887**, **913**
larrup **972**
larum **404**, **669**
larva **129**
larynx **351**
lascar **269**
lasciate ogni speranza **859**
lascivious **961**
lash *tie together* **43**
  violence **173**
  incite **615**
  censure **932**
  punish **972**
  scourge **975**
  under the – *compelled* **744**
  subject **749**
  – into fury **909**
  – with the tongue **931**
  – the waves **645**

lass *girl* **129**
lassitude **680**, **841**
lasso **45**, **247**
last *model* **22**
  - *in order* **67**
  endure **106**
  durable **110**
  - in time **122**
  continue **141**
  at – **133**
  breathe one's – **360**
  game to the – **604a**
  never hear the – of **104**
  - but one &c. **67**
  die in the – ditch **604a**
  – for ever **112**
  at the – extremity **665**
  – finish **729**
  – gasp **360**
  go to one's – home **360**
  on – legs *weak* **160**
  dying **360**
  spoiled **659**
  adversity **735**
  – resort **666**
  – rites **998**
  – shift **601**
  – sleep **360**
  – stage **67**
  – straw **153**
  – stroke **729**
  – touch **729**
  – word
  affirmation **535**
  obstinacy **606**
  - *year* &c. **122**
latch **43**, **45**
latchet **45**
latch-key **631**
late *past* **122**
  new **123**
  tardy **133**
  dead **360**
  too – **135**
lately **122**, **123**
latency **526**
lateness **133**
latent **172**, **526**
  – *organism* **153**
later **117**
laterality **236**
lateritious **434**
latest **118**
latet anguis in herbâ **66**
lath **205**
  thin as a – **203**
lathe
  region **181**
  machine **633**
lather **332**, **353**
Latin
  au bout de son – **704**
  perdre son – **704**
  thieves' – **563**
latitancy **528**
latitat **969**
latitude *extent* **180**
  region **181**
  breadth **202**

measurement **466**
  freedom **748**
  – and longitude
  situation **183**
latitudinarian **984**, **989**
latration **412**
latria **990**
latrines **653**
latrociny **791**
latter *sequence* **63**
  past **122**
Latter-day Saint **984**
latterly **123**
lattice *crossing* **219**
  opening **260**
laud **931**, **990**
laudable **944**
laudanum **174**
laudari a laudato viro **931**
laudator **935**
  - temporis acti
  past **122**
  habit **613**
  discontent **832**
  detractor **936**
laudatory **931**
laugh **838**
  make one – **853**
  raise a – **840**
  – at *ridicule* **856**
  sneer **929**
  (*undervalue* **483**)
  – to scorn *defy* **715**
  despise **930**
  – in one's sleeve
  latent **526**
  ridicule **856**
  disrespect **929**
  contempt **930**
  – on the wrong side of one's mouth
  disappointed **509**
  dejected **837**
  in disrepute **874**
laughable **853**
laughing:
  no – matter **642**
  – gas **376**
laughing-stock **857**
laughter-loving **836**
launch *begin* **66**
  boat **273**
  propel **284**
  – forth **676**
  – into **676**
  – into eternity **360**, **361**
  – out **573**
  – out against **716**
laundress **652**, **746**
laundry room **191**
  heat **386**
  clean **652**
  – maid **746**
  – man **652**
laureate **875**
  poet – **597**
laurel *trophy* **733**
  glory **873**
  decoration **877**
  repose on one's –s **265**
lava *excretion* **299**

semiliquid **352**
lavatory **652**
lave *water* **337**
  clean **652**
lavender *colour* **437**
laver la tête **932**
lavish *profuse* **641**
  give **784**
  squander **818**
  – of praise **931**
law *regularity* **80**
  statue **697**
  permission **760**
  legality **963**
  court of – **966**
  give the – **737**
  go to – **969**
  Jewish – **985**
  lay down the –
  certainty **474**
  affirm **535**
  command **741**
  learned in the – **968**
  set the – at defiance **964**
  take the – into one's own hands **722**, **742**
  – of the Medes and Persians **80**, **148**
  take the – of **969**
law-abiding **743**
lawful
  permitted **760**
  due **924**
  legal **963**
lawgiver **694**
lawless **59**
  irregular **83**
  mutinous **742**
  non-observant **773**
  vicious **945**
  arbitrary **964**
lawn *plain* **344**
  grass **367**
  agriculture **371**
  – sleeves **999**
  – tennis **840**
lawsuit **969**
lawyer **968**
lax *incoherent* **47**
  soft **324**
  error **495**
  - *style* **575**
  remiss **738**
  non-observance **773**
  dishonorable **940**
  licentious **945**
  irreligious **989**
laxity **738**
lay *moderate* **174**
  place **184**
  ley **344**
  music **415**
  poetry **597**
  bet **621**
  secular **997**
  – about one
  active **682**
  exertion **686**
  attack **716**
  contend **720**
  punish **972**
  – one's account for

484
- apart
- *exclude* 55
relinquish 782
- aside
neglect 460
reject 610
disuse 678
give up 782
- on the table 133
- the axe at the
  root of tree 162
- bare 529
- before 527
- brother 996
- by *store* 636
sickness 655
disuse 678
- to one's charge
  938
- claim to 924
- in the dust 162
- eggs 161
- at the door of
  155
- down [see below]
- at one's feet 763
- figure *nonentity* 4
model 22
representation
  554
- one's finger
  upon 480*a*
- the first stone 66
- the flattering
  unction to one's
  soul 831, 834
- the foundations
  153, 673
- ghosts 992
- hands on
use 677
take 789
rite 998
- under hatches
  751
- one's head on
  the block 942
- heads together
  695, 709
- in *eat* 298
store 636
provide 637
- on 972
open *divest* 226
opening 260
show 525
disclose 529
- oneself open to
  177
- out
horizontal 213
corpse 363
plan 626
expend 809
- oneself out for
  673
- over 133
- reader 996
- under restraint
  751
- in ruins 162
- siege to 716
- stress on 642
- to *attribute* 155
rest 265
- it on thick

cover 223
too much 641
flatter 933
- together 43
- *train* 626
- up *store* 636
sickness 655
disuse 678
- waste 162
lay down *locate* 184
horizontal 213
assert 535
renounce 757
relinquish 782
pay 807
- one's arms
pacification 723
submission 725
- the law
certain 474
assert 535
command 741
insolence 885
- one's life 360
- a plan 626
layer 204
layette 225
layman 699, 997
laystall 653
lazaret 662
lazar-house 662
lazy 683, 927
lazzarone 683
lb. 319
lea *land* 342
plain 344
leach 335
lead *superiority* 33
in order 62
pioneer 64
influence 175
tend 176
soundings 208
- in motion 280
heavy 319
rôle 599
induce 615
direct 693
authority 737
heave the - 466
red - 434
take the -
influence 175
importance 642
authority 737
white - 420
- to the altar 903
- astray 495
- captive
subject 749
restraint 751
- a merry chase
  623
- the choir 990
- a dance
run away 623
circuit 629
difficulty 704
disrespect 929
- the dance 280
- one to expect
  511
- a life 692
- on 693
to no end 645
by the nose 737
- off 62

- the way
precedence 62
begin 66
precession 280
importance 642
direction 693
repute 873
leaden *dim* 422
colorless 429
grey 432
inactive 683
leader
precursor 64
dissertation 595
director 694
counsel 968
- writer 593
leading
beginning 66
important 642
- article 595
- lady 599
- note *music* 413
- part 175
- question 461
- seaman 745
- strings
childhood 127
child 129
pupil 541
subject 749
restraint 751, 752
leads 223
leaf *part* 51
layer 204
plant 367
- of a book 593
turn over a new -
  658
- green 435
leafless 226
leaflet 531
leafy 256
league *length* 200
co-operation 709
party 712
- of Nations 696
leak *crack* 198
dribble 295
waste 638
spring a -
injury 659
- out
disclosure 529
leaky *imperfect* 651
leal 743
lean *thin* 203
oblique 217
- on 215
- to *shed* 191
willing 602
- towards 923
- upon *belief* 484
subjection 749
hope 858
leaning
tendency 176
willingness 602
desire 865
friendship 888
favoritism 923
leap
sudden change
  146
ascent 305
jump 309
s and bounds 274

make a - at 622
- in the dark
experiment 463
uncertain 475
chance 621
rash 863
- with joy 838
- year 138
leap-frog 840
learn 490, 539
- by experience
  950
- by heart 505
learned 490
learner 541
learning 490, 539
lease *property* 780
lending 787
grant a - 771
take a new - of
  life 654
- and release 783
leasehold 780
leash *tie* 43
three 92
hold in - 751
least
- in quantity 34
- in size 193
at the - 32
leather *skin* 223
tough 327
beat 972
nothing like - 481
- bottle 191
- or prunello 643
leave *remainder* 40
part company 44
relinquish 624
permission 760
bequeathe 784
French - 623
take - *depart* 293
freedom 748
- alone
inaction 681
freedom 748
permit 760
- the beaten track
  83
- to chance 621
- an inference 526
- a loophole 705
- in the lurch
pass 303
decisive 545
- no trace
be no more 2
disappear 449
obliterate 552
- it to one 76
- to oneself 748
- off *cease* 142
desuetude 614
relinquish 624
disuse 678
- out 55
- out of one's cal-
  culation 460
- a place 293
- ad referendum
  605
give me - to say
  535
- undecided 609*a*
- undone 730
- a void *regret* 833

- word 527
leaven
component 56
cause 153
lighten 320
qualify 469
unclean 653
deterioration 659
bane 663
leavings
remainder 40
useless 645
lecher 962
lechery 961
lectern 1000
lection *special* 79
interpretation 522
lectionary 998
lecture *teach* 537
speak 582
dissertation 595
censure 932
sermon 998
- room 542
lecturer
teacher 540
preacher 996
lectureship 542
led - captain
follower 746
servile 886
favorite 899
- by the nose 749
ledge *height* 206
horizontal 213
shelf 215
projection 250
ledger *list* 86
record 551
accounts 811
lee 236
leech 662, 695
leef 829
leek eat the -
recant 607
submit 725
Lee-Metford
rifle 727
leer *stare* 441
dumb-show 550
leery 702, 864
lees 653
lee-shore 665, 667
leet, court - 936
lee-wall 666
leeward 236
lee-way *space* 180
tardy 133
navigation 267
deviation 279
progression 282
shortcoming 304
left *residuary* 40
sinistral 239
over the - 545
- alone 748
- in the lurch 732
- to shift for one-
  self 893
pay over the -
  shoulder 808
left-handed
clumsy 699
- compliment 932
- marriage 903
leg *support* 215
walker 266

thief 792
best – foremost 686
fast as –s will carry 274
have a – to stand on 470
keep on one's –s 654
last –s *spoiled* 659
fatigue 688
light on one's –s 734
make a – 894
not a – to stand on *illogical* 477
confuted 479
failure 732
off one's –s *propulsion* 284
on one's –s *upright* 212
elevation 307
speaking 582
in health 654
active 682
free 748
set on one's –s 660
– bail 623
legacy 270, 780, 784
legal *permitted* 760
legitimate 924
relating to law 963
– adviser 968
– estate 780
legality 963
legate 534
legatee 779, 785
legation 755
legato 415
legend 551, 594
legendary *imaginary* 515
legerdemain 146, 545
légèreté 605
leggings 225
leghorn hat 225
legible 518
– hand 590
legion *multitude* 102
army 726
legionary 726
legislation 693, 963
legislative assembly 696
legislator 694
legislature 693, 696
legist 968
legitimate *true* 494
permitted 760
right 922
due 924
legal 963
legume 367
lei 847
leisure 685
at one's – *late* 133
leisurely 275
leman 897
lemma 476
lemon *color* 436
Lemprière 979
lemures 980
lend 787

– aid 707
– countenance 707
– a hand 680
– oneself to *assent* 488
co-operate 709
– on security 789
– wings to 707
lender *creditor* 805
lending 787
length 200
go all –s *resolution* 604
activity 682
exertion 686
at – *in time* 133
full – *portrait* 556
go great –s 549
– and breadth of 50
– and breadth of the land *space* 180
publication 531
– of time 110
lengthen 35, 200
– out *diuturnity* 110
late 133
lengthwise 200
lengthy *long* 200
diffuse 573
lenient *moderate* 174
mild 740
compassionate 914
lenify 174
lenitive *moderating* 174
remedy 662
relieving 834
lenity 740
lens 445
Lent 956, 998
lenten 956
lenticular 245, 250
lentor *slowness* 275
spissitude 352
inactivity 683
lentous 352
leonem, ex ungue – 550
leonine **verses** 597
leopard *variegated* 440
–'s spots *unchanging* 150
leprechaune 980
leprosy 655
lerret 273
lèse-majesté 742
less *inferior* 34
subduction 38
– than no time 113
lessee *possessor* 779
receiver 785
lessen
– in quantity or degree 36
– in size 195
– an evil 658
lesson *teaching* 537
warning 668
give a – to

punish 972
read a – to *censure* 932
say one's – *memory* 505
lessor 805
lest 623
let *hindrance* 706
permit 760
lease 771
lend 787
sell 796
apartments to – *fool* 499
to – 763
– alone *besides* 37
permanence 141
quiescence 265
avoid 623
disuse 678
inaction 681
not complete 730
free 748
– be *permanence* 141
continuance 143
inaction 681
– blood 297
– 'I dare not' wait upon 'I would' 605
– down *depress* 308
humble 879
– down easily *forgive* 918
– fall *drop* 308
inform 527
speak 582
– fly *violence* 173
propel 284
– fly at 716
– go *neglect* 460
liberate 750
relinquish 782
restitution 790
– in *interpose* 228
admit 296
trick 545
– into *inform* 490
disclose 529
– one know 527
– off *violent* 173
propel 284
permit 760
forgive 918
exempt 927a
acquit 970
– out *disperse* 73
lengthen 200
eject 297
disclose 529
liberate 750
– out at 716
– pass 460
– slip
miss an opportunity 135
neglect 460
not complete 730
lose 776
relinquish 782
– the matter stand over 133
– things take their course 143
– well alone

content 831
caution 864
lethal 361
– chamber 975
lethalis arundo, haeret lateri – 900
lethargy 683, 823
Lethe 982
waters of – 506
lethiferous 361
letter *mark* 550
character 561
epistle 592
to the – 494
– card 524
– of credit 805
– of the law 494
– writer 592
letter-bag 534
letter-carrier 534
lettered 490
letterpress 591
letters *knowledge* 490
language 560
description 594
in large – 642
man of – 492
– of marque 791
lettres de cachet 751
leucophlegmatic 823
leucorrhea 299
Levant *east* 236
levant *abscond* 623
levanter *wind* 349
defaulter 808
levée *assemblage* 72
sociality 892
– en masse 719
level *uniform* 16
equal 27
destroy 162
horizontal 213
instrument 213, 217
flat 251
smooth 255
lower 308
– at *direct* 278
intend 620
attack 716
– best 686
– headed 826
– off 27
– with the ground 207
lever *cause* 153
instrument 633
– de rideau 599
leverage 175
leviathan 192
levigate 255, 330
levitate 320
Levite 996
levity *lightness* 320
irresolution 605
trifle 643
jocularity 836
rashness 863
levy *muster* 72
military 726
distrain 789
demand 812
lewd 961

Lewis gun 727
lex – mercatoria 963
– scripta 697
– scripta et non-scripta 963
– talionis *retaliation* 718
right 922
lexicography 562
lexicology 562
lexicon 86, 562
ley 344
liability 177
debt 806
duty 926
liaison 961
liar 548
libation *potation* 298
drunkenness 959
worship 990
libel 934, 938
libelant 989
libeller 936
liberal *ample* 639
generous 816
– party 712
disinterested 942
over – 818
– education *knowledge* 490
teaching 537
liberalism *freedom* 748
liberality *giving* 784
generosity 816
liberate 672
liberation 750
liberavi animam meam 703
libertinage 961
libertine 962
libertinism 961
liberty *freedom* 748
permission 760
right 924
exemption 927a
gain one's – 750
set at – *free* 750
exempt 927a
take a – *arrogate* 739
make free 748
insolence 885
discourtesy 895
libidinous 961
libitum, ad – *at will* 600
enough 639
freely 748
librarian 593, 694
library *room* 191, 593
books 593
storehouse 636
librate 314
libretto 593, 599
licence *laxity* 738
permission 760
right 924
exemption 927a
– to plunder 791
licentiate 492
licentious *lax* 738
dissolute 954

debauched 961
lichgate 363
lichen 367
licit 760, 924
lick *lap* 298
  conquer 731
  punish 972
  – the dust 933
  – into shape 240
lickerish
  savory 394
  desirous 865
  fastidious 868
  licentious 961
lickpenny 819
lickspittle 886
lictor 965
lid 223
lie *situation* 183
  presence 186
  recline 213
  falsehood 544
  untruth 546
  give the – to **536**
  white – 617
  – abed 683
  – in ambush 528
  – by 681
  – at one's door
   926
  – down *flat* 213
  rest 687
  – fallow 674
  – hid 528
  – in *be* 1
  give birth 161
  – low 528
  – under a neces-
   sity 601
  – in a nutshell 32
  – on 215
  – over *defer* 133
  destiny 152
  – in one's power
   157
  – at the root of
   153
  – still 265
  – to
  quiescence 265
  inaction 681
  – under 177
  – in wait for
  expect 507
  inaction 681
lief *pleasant* 829
  as – *willing* 602
  choice 609
liege 745
liegeman 746
lien 771, 805
lienteria 653
lieu 182
  in – of 147
lieutenant 745, 759
  lord – 965
life *essence* 5
  events 151
  vitality **359**
  biography 594
  activity 682
  conduct 692
  cheerful 836
  animal – 364
  battle of – 682
  come to – 660
  infuse into

excite 824
put – into 359
recall to – 660
see – 840
support – 359
take away – 361
tenant for – 779
  – to come 152
  – after death 981
  – or death
  need 630
  important 642
  contention 720
  – and spirit 682
Life, the 976
life-blood 5, 359
life-boat 273, 666
life-giving 168
lifeguards 726
lifeless 172, 360
lifelike 17
lifelong 110
life-preserver 666,
  727
life-size 192
lifetime 108
life-weary 841
lift *raise* 307
  aid 707
  steal 791
  – cattle 836
  – up the eyes 441
  – a finger 680
  – hand against
   716
  – one's head 734
  – up the heart 990
  – the mask 529
  – the voice
  shout 411
  speak 582
lift-smoke 840
ligament 45
ligation 43
ligature 45
light *state* 7
  small 32
  window 260
  velocity 274
  arrive 292
  descend 306
  levity 320
  kindle 384
  watch 388
  luminosity **420**
  luminary 423
  – in *colour* 429
  white 430
  aspect 448
  knowledge 490
  interpretation 522
  unimportant 643
  easy 705
  gay 836
  loose 961
  blue – *signal* 550
  bring to –
  discover 480a
  manifest 525
  disclose 529
  children of – 987
  come to – 529
  false – 443
  foot –s 599
  half – 422
  make – of
  underrate 483

easy 705
inexcitable 826
despise 930
in one's own – 699
obstruct the – 426
  side – 490
see the – *life* 359
  publication 531
transmit – 425
throw – upon 522
a – breaks in upon
  one 529
– under a bushel
  hide 528
  not hide 878
  modesty 881
  – comedy 599
  – cruiser 726
  – fantastic toe 309
  – upon one's feet
   664
  – heart 836
  – of heel 274
  – horse 726
  – infantry 726
  – purse 804
  – and shade 420
  – of truth 543
  – up *illumine* 420
  excite 824
  cheer 836
  – upon *chance* 156
  arrive at 292
  discover 480a
  acquire 775
Light of the World
  976
lighten
  make light 320
  illume 420
  facilitate 705
lighter *boat* 273
lighterage 812
lighterman 269
light-fingered 791,
  792
light-footed 274,
  682
light-headed 503
lighthouse 550
lightless 421
light-minded 605
lightning
  velocity 274
  flash 420
  spark 423
  like greased – 113
lightsome
  luminous 420
  irresolute 605
  cheerful 836
ligneous 367
lignite 388
lignography 558
ligulate 205
like *similar* 17
  relish 394
  enjoy 377, 827
  wish 865
  love 897
  do what one –s
   748
  look – 448
  we shall not look
   upon his – again
   33
  – master like man
   19

– a pin in paper 58
likely 472
  think – 507
likeness 21, 554
  bad – 555
likewise 37
liking 865, 897
  have a – for 827
  to one's – 829
lilac *color* 437
Liliputian 193
Lillith 994
lilt 416, 836
lily *white* 430
  beauty 845
  paint the – 641
lily-livered 862
limæ labor
  improve 658
  toil 686
limature 330, 331
limb *member* 51
  instrument 633
  scamp 949
  – of the law 968
limber 272, 324
limbo *prison* 751,
  752
  pain 828
  purgatory 982
lime *entrap* 545
  – light 423, 531,
   599
Limehouse 908
limine, in – 66
limit *complete* 52
  end 67
  circumscribe 229
  boundary **233**
  qualify 469
  restrain 751
  prohibit 761
limitarian 984
limitation [*see*
  limit]
  estate 780, 783
limited
  – in *quantity* 32
  – in *size* 393
  to a – extent
  imperfect 651
limitless 105
limitrophe 197
limn 556
limner 559
limousine 272
limp *weak* 160
  slow 275
  supple 324
  fail 732
limpid 425
lin 343, 348
lincture 662
line *fastening* 45
  continuous 69
  ancestors 166
  descendants 167
  length 200
  no breadth 203
  string 205
  lining 224
  outline 230
  straight 246
  of steamers 273
  direction 278
  music 413
  appearance 448

measure 466
mark 550
writing 590
verse 597
vocation 625
army and navy
  726
boundary – 233
draw the – 465
drop a – to 526
in a –
  continuous 69
  straight 246
in a – with 278
read between the
  –s 522
sounding – 208
straight – 246
troops of the – 726
  – of action 692
  – of battle 69
  – of battle ship
   726
  – engraving 558
  – of march 278
  – of road 627
lineage *kindred* 11
  series 69
  ancestry 166
  posterity 167
lineament
  outline 230
  feature 240
  appearance **448**
  mark 550
linear
  continuity 69
  pedigree 166
  length 200
linen 225
liner 273
lines
  fortification 717
  hard –
  adversity 735
  severity 739
  reins 752
linger *protract* 110
  delay 133
  loiter 275
lingerie 225
lingo 560, 563
lingua franca 563
linguacious 584
lingual 560, 582
linguist 492
linguistics 560
liniment 356, 662
lining **224**
link *relation* 9
  connect 43
  connecting – 45
  part 51
  term 71
  crossing 219
  torch 423
  golf –s 840
  missing – 53, 729
linked together
  party 712
linoleum 223
linotype 591
linseed oil 356
linsey-wolsey 41
linstock 388
lint 223
lintel 215

loin 235, 236
gird up one's -s
strong 159
prepare 673
- cloth 225
loisir, impromptu
fait à - 673
loiter tardy 133
slow 275
inactive 683
loll sprawl 213
recline 215
inactive 683
lollop 682
lollipop 396
Lombard Street to
a China orange
472
lone 87
lonesome 893
long - in time 110
- in space 200
diffuse 573
go to one's - ac-
count 360
- ago 122
make a - arm
exertion 686
seize 789
-boat 273
draw the - bow
549
take a - breath
refreshment 689
relief 834
- clothes 129
- drawn out 573
- duration 110
-expected 507
- face 832, 837
- for 865
-headed wise 498
- life to glory 873
approval 931
-lived 110
- odds chance 156
improbability 473
difficulty 704
- pending 110
- primer 591
- pull and strong
pull 285
-range 196
- robe 968
- run average 29
whole 50
destiny 152
- sea 348
-- and the short
whole 50
concise 572
-sighted
dim-sighted 443
wise 498
foresight 518
- since 122
- spun 573
- standing
diuturnal 110
old 124
-suffering
lenient 740
inexcitable 826
pity 914
- time 110
-winded 573
longanimity

inexcitable 826
forgiving 918
longevity 110, 128
longhead 500
longing 865
- lingering look
behind 833
longinquity 196
longitude
situation 183
length 200
measurement 466
longitudinal 200
longo intervallo
discontinuity 70
diuturnity 110
distance 196
interval 198
longshore-man
waterman 269
plebeian 876
longways 217
loo 840
looby fool 501
bungler 701
clown 876
look small degree 32
see 441
appearance 448
attend to 457
- about 459, 461
- after 459, 693
- ahead 510
- alive 457, 684
- another way 442
- back 122
- beyond 510
- black or blue
feeling 821
discontent 832
dejection 837
- down upon 930
- in the face
sincerity 703
courage 861
pride 878
- foolish 874
- for 461, 507
- forwards 121,
510
- here 457
- into 457, 461
- before one leaps
864
- like 17, 448
- on 186
- out view 448
attention 457
care 459
seek 461
expect 507
intention 620
business 625
danger 665
warning 668
caution 864
- over examine
461
- round seek 461
- sharp 682
- to 459, 926
- through 461
- up prosper 734
high price 814
hope 858
visit 892
- up to repute 873

respect 928
approbation 931
- upon as 480, 484
looker-on 444
looking-glass 445
loom destiny 152
dim 422
dim sight 443
come in sight 446
weave 691
- of the land 342
- up 31
loon fool 501
clown 876
rascal 949
loop 245, 247, 629
- the loop 245
loop-hole
opening 260
vista 441
plea 617
device 626
escape 671
fortification 717
loose detach 44
incoherent 47
pendent 214
desultory 279
illogical 477
vague 519
- style 575
lax 738
free 748
liberate 750
debauched 961
give a - to
- imagination 515
laxity 738
permit 760
indulgence 954
let - 750
on the - 961
screw - 713
- character 961
at a - end 685
- fish 949, 962
- morals 945
- rein 738
- suggestion 514
- thread 495
leave a - 460
take up a - 664
loosen 47, 750
loot 791, 793
lop 201
- and top 371
lopped
incomplete 53
loppet 699
lop-eared 53
lop-sided 28
loquacity 584
loquendi
cacoëthes - 584
jus et norma - 567
usus - 582
lorcha 273
Lord, lord
ruler 745
nobleman 875
God 976
O - worship 990
- Chancellor 967
- of the creation
372
-'s day 687
-s Justices 966,
967

the - knows 491
- lieutenant 965
- of Lords 976
- of the manor
779
- it over 737, 885
-'s prayer 990
-'s supper 998
-'s table 1000
lordling 875
lordly 873, 878
Lord Mayor 745,
965
-'s show 883
lordship
authority 737
property 780
title 877
judge 967
lore 490, 539
Lorelei 980
lorette 962
lorgnette 445
loricated
clothed 223
lorication
armor 717
lorn 893
lorry 272
lose forget 506
unintelligible 519
fail 732
loss 776
no time to - 684
- one's balance
732
- breath 688
- caste 874, 940
-, the clew 475,
519
- color 429
- one's cunning
699
- the day 732
- flesh 195
- ground
slow 275
regression 283
shortcoming 304
- one's head
bewildered 475
- heart 837
- one's heart 897
- hope 859
- interest in 624
- labor 732
- one's life 360
- no time 682, 684
- oneself 475
- an opportunity
135
- one's reason 503
- sight of
blind 442
disappear 449
neglect 460
oblivion 506
not complete 730
- one's temper 900
- time 683
- one's way
wander 279
uncertainty 475
unskilful 699
difficulty 704
losel 818
losing game 732,

735
loss decrement 40a
death 360
evil 619
deterioration 659
privation 776
at a -
uncertain 475
at a - for
desiring 865
- of fortune 804
- of health 655
- of life 360
- of right 925
- of strength 160
lost non-existing 2
absent 187
invisible 449
abstracted 458
uncertain 475
failure 732
loss 776
over-excited 824
pain 828
dejection 837
impenitent 951
- in admiration
931
- in astonishment
870
- in iniquity 945
- labor 645
- to shame
insolent 885
improbity 940
bad man 949
- to sight 449
- in thought 458
- to virtue 945
lot state 7
quantity 25
group 72
multitude 102
necessity 601
chance 621
sufficient 639
allotment 786
be one's - 151
cast -s 621
cast in one's -
with 609, 709
fall to one's - 156
in -s 51
where one's - is
cast 189
loth 603, 867
Lothario 897, 962
lotion liquid 337
clean 652
remedy 662
loto 840
lottery 156, 840
put into a - 621
lotus-eater 683
loud 404, 525
vulgar 851
lough 343
lounge 191, 683
- suit 225
loup
hurler avec les -s
714
-garou 980
louse 653
lout 501, 701, 876
louvre 351
lovable 897

love *desire* 865
  courtesy 894
  affection 897
  favorite 899
  abode of – 897
  labor of –
    willing 602
  inexpensive 815
  amusement 840
  disinterested 942
  God's – 906
  make – 902
  no – lost 713
  – affair 897
  – of country 910
  – lock 256
  not for – or money
    640, 814
love-knot *token* 550
love-lorn 898
lovely 845, 897
love-making 902
love-pot 959
love-potion 865
lover [*see* love]
love-sick 897, 902
love-story 897, 902
love-token 897, 902
loving-cup 892, 894
loving-kindness
  906
low *small* 32
  not high 207
  – *sound* 405
  moo 412
  vulgar 851
  disreputable 874
  common 876
  base 940
  bring – 308
  – condition 876
  – comedy 599
  at a – ebb
    small 32
    inferior 34
    depressed 308
    waste 638
    deteriorated 659
  – fellow 876
  – life 851
  – note 408
  – origin 876
  – price 815
  – spirits 837
  – tide 207
  – tone *black* 431
  mutter 581
  – water *low* 207
  dry 340
  insufficient 640
  poor 804
low-born 876
low-brow 491
low-lands 207
low-minded 876,
  940
lower *inferior* 34
  decrease 36
  overhang 214
  depress 308
  dark 421
  dim 422
  predict 511
  sad 837
  irate 900
  sulky 901a
  – one's flag 725

– one's note 879
– orders 876
lowering 668, 859
lowly 879
lown 501, 949
lowness [*see* low]
  207
  humility 879
loy 272
loyal *obedient* 743
  observant 772
  honourable 939
lozenge 244, 662
L. s. d. 800
lubbard [*see* lubber]
lubber 683, 701
lubberly 192, 699
lubricant 332
lubrication 255, **332**
lubricity
  slippery 255
  unctuous 355
  impure 961
lucent 420
lucid
  luminous 420
  transparent 425
  intelligible 518
  – *style* 570
  – *interval* 502
lucidus ordo 58
lucifer 388
Lucifer 423, 978
lucimeter 445
luck *chance* 156, 621
  prosperity 734
  good – 858
luckless 735
lucky 134, 731
lucrative 775
lucre 775, 803
Lucretia 960
luctation 720
lucubration 451
luculent 420
lucus a non lucendo
  18, 565
lud! O – 839
ludibrious 840
ludicrous 853
luff 267
lug *pull* 285
  ear 418
luge 272
luggage 270, 780
  – van 272
lugger 273
lugubrious 837
lukewarm
  temperate 382
  irresolute 605
  torpid 823
  indifferent 866
lull *cessation* 142
  mitigate 174
  silence 403
  – to sleep 265
lullaby
  moderate 174
  song 415
  verses 597
  inactivity 683
  relief 834
lumbago 378
lumbar 235
lumbar *disorder* 59
  slow 275

store 636
useless 645
hindrance 706
lumbering 647, 846
lumber-room 191
lumbriciform 249
luminary *star* 318
  light **423**
  sage 500
luminescence 420
luminous *light* 420
  intelligible 518
  – *paint* 423
lump *whole* 50
  chief part 51
  amass 72
  mass 192
  projection 250
  weight 319
  density 321
  in the – 50
  – of affectation
    855
  – sum 800
  – together *join* 43
  combine 48
  assemble 72
lumpish [*see* lump]
  inactive 683
  ugly 846
Luna 318
lunacy 503
lunar 318
  – *caustic* 384
lunatic 503, 504
luncheon 298
lune avec les dents,
  prendre la –
  158, 471
lunette 717
lunge 276, 716
lungs *wind* 349
  loudness 404
  shout 411
  voice 580
luniform &c. 245
lupanar 961
lurch *incline* 217
  sink 306
  oscillation 314
  failure 732
  leave in the –
    outstrip 303
  deceive 545
  relinquish 624
  left in the –
    defeated 732
lure *attraction* 288,
  865
  deceive 545
  entice 615
lurid *dark* 421
  dim 422
  red 434
lurk *unseen* 447
  latent 526
  hidden 528
lurking-place 530
luscious 394, 829
lush *vegetation* 365
  drunkenness 959
lushy 959
lusk 683
lusory 840
lust 865, 961
  – after 921
luster

brightness 420
chandelier 423
glory 873
lustily 404, 686
  cry out – 839
lustless 158
lustration 652, 952
lustrum 108
lusty 159, 192
lusus naturæ 80
lute *cement* 45, 46
  guitar 417
luteous 436
Lutheran 984
luxation 44
luxuriant 168, 639
luxuriate in 377,
  827
luxurious
  pleasant 377
  delightful 829
  intemperate 954
luxury
  physical – 377
  redundance 641
  enjoyment 827
  sensuality 954
lycanthropy 503
Lyceum 542
Lydford law 964
Lydian measure
  415
lyddite 727
lying
  decumbent 213
  deceptive 544
  faithless 986
Ly-king 986
lymph *fluid* 333
  water 337
  transparent 425
lymphatic 337
lynch 972
  – law 964
lyncher 975
lynching 361
lynx-eyed 441, 498
lyre 417
lyric 415
  – poetry 597
lyrist 597

M

Mab 979
macadamize 255,
  635
Macaire, Robert –
  792
macaroni 854
macaronic
  absurdity 497
  neology 563
  verses 597
Macchiavel [*see*
  Machiavelism]
mace
  weapon 727
  scepter 747
mace-bearer 965
maceration
  saturation 337
  atonement 952
  asceticism 955
  rite 998

Macheath 792
Machiavelism
  falsehood 544
  cunning 702
  dishonesty 940
machicolation 257,
  717
machination
  trick 545
  plan 626
  cunning 702
  –s of the devil 619
machinator 626
machine 633
  like a – 698
  – gun 407, 727
  be a mere – 749
machinist
  theatrical – 599
  workman 690
macilent 203
mackerel
  mottled 440
  procuress 962
  – sky 349, 353
mackintosh 225
macrobiotic 110
macrocosm 318
macrography 441
macrology 577
mac Sycophant,
  Sir Pertinax –
  886, 935
mactation 991
macte virtute 931
macula 848
maculate
  unclean 653
maculation 440, 848
mad *insane* 503
  excited 824
  drive one – 900
  go – 825
  – after 865
  – with rage 900
madam 374
mad-brained 503
madcap
  violent 173
  lunatic 504
  excitable 825
  buffoon 844
  rash 863
madder *color* 434
made
  – to one's hand
    673
  – man 734
  – to order 673
madefaction 339
madman 504
Madonna
  good 948
  angel 977
  pious 987
madrigal *music* 415
  verses 597
Maecenas 492, 890
Maelstrom
  whirl 312
  water 348
  pitfall 667
maestro 415
maffick 883
magazine
  periodical 53
  record 551

book 593
store 636
- rifle 727
Magdalen 950, 962
mage 994
magenta 434
maggot *little* 193
  fancy 515
  caprice 608
  desire 865
maggoty
  capricious 608
  unclean 653
- headed
  silly 499
  excitable 825
Magi *sage* 500
  sect 984
magic 175, 992
- lantern
  instrument 445
  show 448
magician 548, 994
magilp 356a
magisterial 878, 885
magistery 30
magistracy 737, 965
magistrate 745, 967
magistrature 737
magistri, jurare in
  verba - 481
  nullius - 487
magma 41
Magna Charta 769
magna pars fui,
  quorum - 690
magnanimity 942
magnate 875
magnet *attract* 288
  desire 865
magnetism
  power 157
  influence 175
  attraction 288
  motive 615
  animal - 992
magnetize
  influence 175
  motive 615
  conjure 992
magni nominis
  umbra
  wreck 659
  repute 873
  rank 875
magnificent
  large 192
  fine 845
  grand 882
magnifico 875
magnifier 445
magnifique et pas
  cher 815
magnify
  increase 35
  enlarge 194
  over-rate 482
  exaggerate 549
  approve 931
  praise 990
magniloquent 577, 884
magnitude 25, 31, 192
magno conatu
  magnas nugas

638, 643
Magnus Apollo 500
magpie 584
magsman 792
maharajah 745
maharani 745
mah jong 840
mahl-stick [*see*
  maulstick]
mahogany
  color 433
Mahomet 986
Mahometan 984
maid *girl* 129
  servant 631, 746
  spinster 374, 904
  - of all work 690
  - of honor 890
maiden *first* 66
  girl 129
  punishment 975
  - speech 66
maidenhood 904
maidenly 374
maigre 956
mail *post* 270, 534
  armor 717
  - coach 272, 534
  - steamer 273
  - van 272, 534
maim 158, 659
main *tunnel* 260
  ocean 341
  conduct 350
  principal 642
  coup de - 680
  in the -
  intrinsically 5
  greatly 31
  on the whole 50
  principally 642
  with might and -
    686
  plough the- 267
main-chance 156
  good 618
  important 642
  profit 775
  look to the -
  foresight 510
  skill 698
  economy 817
  caution 864
  selfish 943
main-force
  strength 159
  violence 173
  compulsion 744
mainland 342
main-part 31, 50
mainpernor 771
main-spring 153, 633
mainstay
  support 215
  refuge 666
  hope 858
maintain
  permanence 141
  continue 143
  sustain 170
  support 215
  assert 535
  preserve 670
  - one's course
  persevere 604a
  - the even tenor of

one's way 623
- one's ground 717
maintenance
  [*see* maintain]
  assistance 707
  wealth 803
maintien 692
maison de santé 662
maisonette 189
maitre: coup de -
  goodness 648
  skill 698
  l'oeil e - 459
majesté, lèse- 742
majestic 873, 882
majesty *king* 745
  rank 873
  deity 976
major *greater* **33**
  officer 745
  -domo
  director 694
  retainer 746
  -general 745
  - key 413
  - part *great* 31
  all 50
majority
  superiority 33
  multitude 102
  age 131
  join the - 360
majusculae 561
make
  constitute 54, **56**
  render 144
  produce 161
  form 240
  arrive at 292
  complete 729
  compel 744
  - acquainted with
    527, 539
  - after 622
  - its appearance 446
  - away with 162, 361
  - believe 544, 545, 546
  - the best of 725
  - bold to differ 489
  - a date with 897
  - choice of 609
  - fast 43
  - a fool of 853
  - for 278
  - one's fortune 734
  - fun of 842, 856
  - a fuss 642, 682
  - good
  compensation 30
  complete 52, 729
  establish 150
  evidence 467
  demonstrate 478
  provide 637
  restore 660
  - one's escape 671
  - one's word 772
  - a go of 731
  - haste 684
  - hay while the
    sun shines 134
  - interest 765
  - known 527

- the land 292
- light of 483, 705, 934
- oneself master of 539
- money 775
- a monkey of 853
- much of 549, 642
- no doubt 484
- no secret of 525
- no sign 526, 528
- nothing of
  unintelligible 519
  not wonder 871
- of 902
- off 623, 671
- off with 791
- out *see* 441
  evidence 467
  demonstrate 478
  discover 480a
  know 490
  intelligible 518
  interpret 522
  due 924
- over 658, 783, 784
- peace 723, 724
- a piece of work 832
- things pleasant 702
- a present 784
- public 531
- a push 682
- ready 673
- a requisition 741, 765
- a speech 582
- a sucker of 853
- sure 150, 673
- terms 769
- time 110
- tracks 293
- towards 278
- up [*see below*]
- use of 677
- way 282
- one's way 302, 734
- way for 147, 623
- a wry face 867
make up
  complete 52
  compose 54
  - accounts 811
  - for 30
  - matters 952
  - one's mind
  judgment 480
  belief 484
  resolve 604
  - a quarrel 723
  - a sum 809
  - to approach 286
  address 586
maker *artificer* 690
Maker, the - 976
makeshift 147, 617
make-weight
  inequality 28
  compensation 30
  completeness 52
  making of, be the -
  utility 644
  goodness 648
  aid 707

mal du pays 833
mala fides 940
malachite 435
malacology 368
malade imaginaire 837
maladie du pays 833
maladministration 699
maladroit 699
malady 655
malaise 378, 828
malapert 885, 887
Malaprop, Mrs. - 565
malapropism 495
mal à propos 24, 135
malaria 657, 663
malconformation 243
malcontent 710, 832
male 159, 373
- animal 373
malediction 908
malefaction 947
malefactor 949
malefic 649
maleficent 907
- being 913
malevolence 907
malfeasance 647
malformed 241
malformation 243
malgré 179
- soi 603
malice *hate* 898
  spite 907
  bear - *revenge* 919
- aforethought 907
- prepense 907
malign *bad* 649
  malevolent 907
  detract 934
malignant 649, 907
malignity
  violence 173
malinger 544, 655
malison 908
malkin 653
mall *walk* 189
  club 276
malleable 324
mallet 276
malnutrition 655
mal-odor 401
malpractice 947
malt liquor 298
maltreat
  injure 649
  aggrieve 830
  molest 907
malum
- prohibitum 925
- in se 923
malversation 818, 947
Mameluke 726
mamelon 250
mamma 166
mammal 366
mammiform 250
mammilla 250
Mammon 803, 978

serve - 989
mammoth 192
man *adult* 131
  mankind 372
  male 373
  prepare 673
  workman 690
  servant 746
  courage 861
  husband 903
make a - of 648, 861
Son of - 976
straight - 599
to a - 488
-at-arms 726
one's - of business 758
-'s estate 131
- in office 745
- in the street 876
-of-war 273, 726
-of-war's man 269
- at the wheel 694
- and wife 903
manacle 751, 752
manage 693
- to *succeed* 731
manageable 705
management
  conduct 692
  skill 698
manager
  stage - 599
  director 604
managery 693
manche après la cognée, jeter le - 859
mancible 637
mancipation 751
mandamus 741
mandarin 745
mandate 630, 741
mandible 298
mandolin 417
mandragora 174
mandrel 312
manducation 298
mane 256
man-eater 361
manége 266, 370
manes 362
manet: - altámente repostum 505
- *cicatrix* 919
maneuver 680, 702
manful *strong* 159
  resolute 604
  brave 861
manger 191
manger:
  cela se laisse -.394
  - son blé en herbe 818
mangle
  separate 44
  smooth 255
  injure 659
mangled 53
mangy 655
man-hater 911
manhood 131, 861
mania *insanity* 503
  desire 865
maniac 504
manibus pedibus-

que 686
manic 503
manic-depressive 503
manicure 847
manicheism 978
manichord 417
manie 865
maniéré 855
manifest
  list 86
  visible 446
  obvious 525
  disclose 529
manifestation 525
manifesto 531
manifold 81, 102
manikin *dwarf* 193
  image 554
maniple 103
manipulate
  handle 379
  use 677
  conduct 692
manipulator 621
mankind 372
manly
  adolescent 131
  strong 159
  male 373
  brave 861
  honest 939
manna *food* 396
- in the wilderness
  aid 707
  pleasing 829
manner *kind* 75
  style 569
  way 627
  conduct 692
  in a - 32
  by all - of means 536
  by no - of means 602
  to the - born 5
mannered 579
mannerism
  special 79
  unconformity 83
  affectation 855
  vanity 880
mannerly 894
manners 852, 894
manor 780
  lord of the - 779
  - house 189
manorial 780
Mansard roof 223
manse 1000
mansion 189
manslaughter 361
mansuetude 894
mantelpiece 215
mantilla 225
mantle *spread* 194
  dress 225
  foam 353
  shade 424
  redden 434
  robes 747
  flush 821, 824
  anger 900
mantlet *cloak* 225
  defence 717
Mantology 511
manual *guide* 527

schoolbook 542
  book 593
  advice 695
- labor 686
manubial 793
manufactory 691
manufacture 161, 680
manufacturer 690
manumission 750
manure
  agriculture 371
  dirt 653
  aid 707
manuscript 22, 590
many 102
  the - 876
  for - a day 110
  - irons in the fire 682
  - men many minds 489
  - times *repeated* 104
  frequent 136
many-colored 440
many-sided 81, 236
many-tóngued 532
map 234, 527, 554
  - out 626
mar 659, 706
marabou 83
marabout 1000
maranátha 908
marasmus
  shrinking 195
  atrophy 655
  deterioration 659
maraud 791
marauder 792
marble *ball* 249
  hard 323
  sculpture 557
  tablet 590
  insensible 823
marble 440
marble-hearted 907
march *region* 181
  journey 266
  progression 282
  music 415
  dead - 363
  forced - 684
  on the - 264
  steal a -
  advance 280
  go beyond 303
  deceive 545
  active 682
  cunning 702
  - against 716
  - of events 151
  - of intellect *knowledge* 490
  improvement 658
  - off 293
  - on a point 278
  - past 882
  - of time 109
  - with 199
March, Ides of-601
marches 233
marchioness 875
marcid 203
marconigram 523
marcor 203
mare *horse* 271

female 374
  -'s nest 497, 546
  -'s tail *wind* 349
  cloud 353
marechal 745
margarine 356
margin *space* 180
  edge 231
  redundance 641
  latitude 748
margravate 780
margrave 745, 875
marimba 417
marine *fleet* 273
  sailor 269
  oceanic 341
  soldier 726
  tell it to the -s 489, 497
  - painter 559
  - painting 556
mariner 269
Mariolatry 991
marionnette
  representation 554
  drama 599
  amusement 840
marish 345
marital 903
maritime 267, 341
mark *degree* 26
  term 71
  take cognizance of 450
  attend to 457
  indication 550
  record 551
  writing 590
  object 620
  importance 642
  repute 873
  beyond the - 303
  leave one's - 873
  man of - 873, 875
  near the - 197
  overshoot the - 699
  put a - upon 457
  save the - 870
  up to the -
  enough 639
  good 648
  skill 698
  due 924
  wide of the - 196, 495
  within the - 304
  - down 813
  - off 551
  - out *choose* 609
  plan 626
  command 741
  - of recognition 894
  - with a red letter 883
  - time *chronometry* 114
  halt 265
  wait 507
  - with a white stone 931
marked [see mark]
  great 31
  affirmed 535
  well- 446

in a - degree 31
play with - cards 545
- down 815
marker 550
market *buy* 795
  mart 799
  bring to - 796
  buy in the cheapest &c. - 794
  in the -
  offered 763
  barter 794
  sale 796
  rig the - 794
  - garden 371
  - overt
  manifest 525
  mart 799
  - place *street* 189
  mart 799
  - price 812
  - woman 797
marketable 794, 796
marksman 700
marksmanship 698
marl 342
marmalade 396
marmot 683
maroon
  color 433, 434
  abandon 782, 893
marplot
  bungler 701
  obstacle 706
  malicious 913
marque, letters of - 791
marquee 223
marquetry 440
marquis 875
marriage 903
  companionate - 903
  ill-assorted - 904
  - bells 836
  - portion 780
marriageable 131, 903
marrow *essence* 5
  interior 221
  central 222
  chill to the - 385
marrow-bones, on one's -
  submit 725
  beg 765
  humble 879
  servile 886
  atonement 952
marrowless 158
marry *combine* 48
  assertion 535
  wed 903
- come up *defiance* 715
  anger 900
  censure 932
Mars 722, 979
- orange 439
marsh 345
marshal
  arrange 60
  messenger 534
  auxiliary 711
  officer 745

merged 228
meridian
   region 181
   room 125
   summit 210
   light 420
   – of life 131
merit
   goodness 648
   due 924
   virtue 944
   make a – of 884
   – notice 642
merito, e – 944
meritorious 931
Merlin 994
mermaid 341
   monster 83
   mythology 979,
   980
merman 341
mero motu, ex –
   600
merriment
   cheerful 836
   amusement 840
merry *cheerful* 836
   drunk 959
make – *sport* 840
make – with
   wit 842
   ridicule 856
wish a – Christmas
   &c. 896
– and wise 842
merry-andrew 844
merry-go-round
   312, 840
merry-making 827,
   840, 892
merry-thought 842
mersion 337
meruit ferat, pal-
   mam qui – 873
merveille, à – 731
mesa 344
mésalliance 24, 903
meseems 484
mesh 198, 219
meshes *trap* 545
   difficulty 704
   – of sophistry 477
meshwork 219
mesial
   middle 68
mesmerism 992
mesmerist 994
mesne lord 779
mess *mixture* 41
   disorder 59
   barracks 191
   meal 298
   difficulty 704
   portion 786
make a –
   unskilful 699
   fail 732
message
   intelligence 532
   command 741
Messalina 962
messenger 271
   envoy 534
   servant 746
   – balloon 463
Messiah 976
messianic 976

messmate 890
messuage 189
messy 59
metabolism 140
metacenter 222
metachronism 115
metage 466
metagenesis 140
metagrammatism
   561
metal 635
   Brittania – 545
metallic *sound* 410
metalepsis 521
metallurgy 358
metamorphosis 140
metaphor
   comparison 464
   figure 521
   (*analogy* 17)
metaphrase 522
metaphrast 524
metaphrastic 516
metaphysics 450
metastasis, meta-
   thesis
   change 140
   inversion 218
   displacement 270
mete *measure* 466
   distribute 786
   – out *give* 784
metempsychosis
   140
meteor 318, 423
meteoric 173, 420
meteorology 338
meteoromancy 466
meter 466
meter
   length 200
   poetry 597
metheglin 396
methinks 484
method *order* 58
   way 627
   want of – 59
methodical 60
Methodist 984
methodist
   journalist 988
methodize 60
Methuselah 130
   old as – 12
   since the days of –
   124
meticulous 772
métier 625
métis 83
metonymy 521
metoposcopy
   front 234
   appearance 44
   interpret 522
metrical
   measured 466
   verse 597
metrology 466
   moderation 174
   mid-course 628
metropolis 189
metropolitan
   archbishop 996
mettle *spirit* 820
   courage 861

man of – 861
on one's –
   resolved 604
put on one's –
   excite 824
   encourage 861
mettlesome
   energetic 171
   sensitive 822
   excitable 825
   brave 861
mettre de l'eau
   dans son vin 160
meum et tuum 780
   disregard distinc-
   tion between –
   791
mew *moult* 226
   cry 412
   – up 751
mewed up 229
mewl 412
mews 189
mezzanine floor
   191, 599
mezzo rilievo
   convex 250
   sculpture 557
mezzo termine
   middle 68
   mid-course 628
   compromise 774
Mezzofanti 492
mezzosoprano 416
mezzotint 420, 558
miasm 663
mica 425
micaceous 204
mi-carême 840
Micawber 460
Michael 977
Michaelmas 998
Micomicon 515
microbe 163, 193
microcosm 193
micrography 193,
   441
micrometer 193
micro-organism
   193
microphone 418
microscope 193, 445
microscopic 32, 193
mid 68
Midas 803
mid-course 628
mid-day 125
midden 653
middle - *in degree*
   29
   - *in order* 68
   - *in space* 222,
   228
   - classes 736
   - constriction 203
   - course 29, 628
   - man *director* 694
   agent 758
   - point 29
   - term 68
   compromise 774
middlemost 222
middling 29, 32, 68,
   651
middy 225, 269
midge 193
midget 193

midland 342
midnight *night* 126
   dark 421
   – oil 539, 689
mid-progress 282
midriff 68, 228
midshipman 269,
   745
midships 68
midst - *in order* 68
   central 222
   interjacent 228
in the – of
   mixed with 41
   doing 680
midsummer 125
   – day 138
midway 68
midwife
   instrument 631
   remedy 662
   auxiliary 711
midwifery 161, 662
mien 448, 692
miff 900
might *power* 157
   violence 173
   energy 686
mightily 31
mighty *much* 31
   strong 159
   large 192
   haughty 878
migraine 378
migrate 266, 295
mikado 745
milch cow
   productive 168
   animal 366
   store 636
mild *moderate* 174
   warm 382
   insipid 391
   lenient 740
   calm 826
   courteous 894
mildew 653, 663
mildewed
   spoiled 659
mile 200
milestone 550
   whistle jigs to a –
   645
milieu, juste – 174,
   628
militant 722
   church – 983a
military
   warfare 722
   soldiers 726
   – authorities 745
   – band 417
   – power 737
   – time 132
   – train 726
militate against 708
militia 726
milk *moderate* 174
   semiliquid 352
   cows &c. 370
   white 430
   mild 740
   – a he-goat into a
   sieve 471
flow with – and
   honey *plenty*
   639

   prosperity 734
   pleasant 829
   – of human kind-
   ness 906
   – the ram 645
   – and water
   weak 160
   insipid 391
   unimportant 643
   imperfect 651
milk-livered 862
milksop
   incapable 158
   fool 501
   coward 862
milky [see milk]
   semitransparent
   427
   whiteness 430
   – way 318
mill 330
   notch 257
   machine 633
   workshop 691
   fight 720
like a horse in a –
   312
millennium
   number 98
   period 108
   futurity 121
   utopia 515
   hope 858
millesimal 99
millet seed 193
milliard 98
milliner 225
   man – 854
millinery *dress* 225
   ornament 847
   display 882
   man – 855
million 98
   multitude 102
   people 372
   populace 876
for the –
   intelligible 518
   easy 705
   –s *money* 800
millionaire 803
mill-pond *level* 213
   pond 343
   store 636
mime 19, 599, 844
mimeograph 19
mimeotype 19
mimic 19
mimodrama 599
minacity 909
minaret 206
minatory 668
minauderie 855
mince *cut up* 44
   slow 275
   food 298
   stammer 583
   affected 855
   extenuate 937
   – the matter 868
   not – the matter
   affirm 525
   artless 703
   – the truth 544
mincemeat of
   make – 162
mincing 855

− steps 275
mind *intellect* 450
  attend to 457
  take care 459
  believe 484
  remember 505
  will 600
  willing 602
  purpose 620
  warning 668
  desire 865
  dislike 867
  bear in − 451, 457
  bit of one's − 527
  food for the − 454
  give the − to 457
  have a − 602, 865
  in the −
   thought 451
   topic 454
   willing 602
  make up one's −
   484, 604
  never − *neglect* 460
   unimportant 643
  not − 866
  out of − 506
  set one's − upon
   604
  speak one's − 582,
   703
  to one's − *taste* 850
   love 897
  willing − 602
  − one's book 539
  − one's business
   456, 457
  − at ease 827
  make one's − easy
   826
  −'s eye 515
  − what one is
   about 864
minded 602, 620
mindful 457, 505
mindless
  inattentive 458
  imbecile 499
  forgetful 506
  insensible 823
mine
  sap 162
  hollow 252
  open 260
  snare 545
  store 636
  abundance 639
  damage 659
  attack 716
  defence 717
  explosive 727
  dig a − *plan* 626
  prepare 673
  spring a −
   unexpected 508
  attack 716
  − of information
   700
  -layer 726
  -sweeper 726
  -thrower 727
  − of wealth 803
miner 252
  sapper and − 726
mineral 358
  − oil 356
mineralogy 358

Minerva 979
  − *invita* 603, 709
  − *press* 577, 594
mingle 41
miniature *small* 193
  portrait 556
  − *painter* 559
Minié rifle 727
minikin 193
minim *small* 32
  music 413
minimize 36, 483,
  934
minimum.*small* 32
  inferior 34
minion 899
  type 591
minister *instru-*
  mentality 631
  remedy 662
  director 694
  aid 707
  deputy 759
  give 784
  clergy 996
  rites 998
  − to 746
ministerial
  clerical 995
ministering spirit
  977
ministration
  direction 693
  aid 707
  rite 998
ministry
  direction 693
  aid 707
  church 995
  clergy 996
miniver 223
minnesinger 597
minnow 193
minor *inferior* 34
  infant 129
  − key 413
Minorites 996
minority *few* 103
  youth 127
Minos 694
minotaur 83
minster 1000
minstrel 416, 597
minstrelsy 415
mint *mold* 22
  workshop 691
  wealth 803
  − of money 800
minuend 38
minuet 415, 840
minus *less* 34
  subtracted 38
  absent 187
  deficient 304
  loss 776
  in debt 806
  non-payment 808
minusculae 561
minute
  − *in degree* 32
  − *of time* 108
  instant 113
  − *in size* 193
  record 551
  compendium 596
  to the − 132
  − *account* 594

− attention 457
minuteness
  care 459
minutiae 32, 79, 643
minx 887, 962
mirabile
  − *dictu* &c. 870
mirabilis, annus −
  872
miracle 83, 872
  − play 599
miraculous 870
mirage 443
mire 653
mirror *imitate* 19
  reflector 445
  perfection 650
  glory 873
  hold up the − 525
  hold the − up to
   nature 554
  magic − 443
mirth 836
misacceptation 235
misadventure 735
misadvised 699
misanthropy 911
misapply
  misinterpret 523
  misuse 679
  mismanage 699
misapprehend 495,
  523
misappropriate 679
misarrange 61
misbecome 925
misbegotten 243,
  945
misbehave 851, 945
misbehavior 895,
  947
misbelief 485
misbeliever 487,
  984
miscalculate
  misjudge 481
  err 495
  disappoint 509
miscall 565
miscarry 732
miscegenation 41
miscellany
  mixture 41
  collection 72
  generality 78
  compendium 596
mischance 619, 735
mischief 619
  do − 649
  make − 649
mischief-maker
  913, 941
miscible 41
miscite 544
miscompute 481,
  495
misconceive 495,
  523
misconduct 699,
  947
  − oneself 945
misconjecture 481
misconstrue 523
miscorrect 538
miscount 495
miscreance 485
miscreant 949

miscreated 945
misdate 115
misdeed 947
misdemean 945
misdemeanant 949
misdemeanor 947
misdevotion 988
misdirect 538, 699
misdo 945
misdoing 947
misdoubt 485, 523
mise en scène
  appearance 448
  drama 599
  display 882
misemploy 679
miser 819
  −'s hoard 800
miserabile *dictu* 839
miserable *small* 32
  contemptible 943
  unhappy 828
miserably *very* 31
miserere 215
  sing − 950
misericordiam,
  argumentum ad
  − 914
miseries of human
  life 828
miseris succurrere
  disco 914
miserly 819
misery 828
  put out of one's −
   914
misestimate
  misjudge 481
misfeasance 699,
  947
misfit 24
misfortune
  adversity 735
  unhappiness 830
misgiving 485, 860
misgovern 699
misguide 495, 538
misguided 699
mishap *evil* 619
  failure 732
  misfortune 735
  painful 830
Mishna 985
misinform 538
misinformed 491
misinstruct 538
misintelligence 538
misinterpretation
  523
misjoined 24
misjudgment
  sophistry 477
  misjudge 481
  misinterpretation
  523
mislay *derange* 61
  lose 776
mislead *error* 495
  misteach 538
  deceive 545
mislike 867
mismanage 699
mismatch 15, 24
misname 565
misnomer 565
misogamist 904,
  911

misogyny 904
mispersuasion 538
misplace
  derange 61
misplaced
  intrusive 24
  unconformable 83
  displaced 185
misprint 495
misprision
  concealment 528
  guilt 947
  − of treason 742
misprize 483, 929
mispronounce 583
misproportioned
  243, 846
misquote 544
misreckon 481, 495
misrelish 867
misreport 495, 544
misrepresent
  misinterpret 523
  misteach 538
  lie 544
misrepresentation
  555
  untruth 544, 546
misrule
  misconduct 699
  laxity 738
  Lord of − 701
missa cantata 998
missal 998
missay 563, 583
missend 699
misshapen 243, 846
missile 727
missing
  non-existent 2
  absent 187
  disappear 449
  − link 53, 83, 729
mission 625, 755
missionary 540, 996
missive 592
misspell 523
misspend 818
misstate 495, 544
misstatement 495,
  546
mist 353, 424
  in a − 528
  seen through a −
   519
  −s of error 495
  − before the eyes
   443
mistake *error* 495
  misconstrue 523
  mismanage 699
  failure 732
  never was a

miss *girl* 19
  neglect 460
  error 495
  unintelligible 519
  fail 732
  lose 776
  want 865
  courtesan 962
  − one's aim 732
  − fire 732
  − stays 304
  − one's way
   uncertain 475
   unskilful 699

forth – 509
not a – stirring 265
mouse-colored 432
mousehole 260
mouser 366
mousetrap 545
mousseux 353
moustache 256
mouth *entrance* 66
  receptacle 191
  brink 231
  opening 260
  eat 298
  estuary 343
  enunciate 580
  drawl 583
  deep –ed
    resonant 408
    bark 412
  down in the – 879
  make –s 929
  open one's – 582
  stop one's – 581
  word of – 582
  – honor
    falsehood 544
    show 882
    flattery 933
  pass from – to mouth 531
  – wash 652
  – watering 865
mouthful
  quantity 25
  small 32
  food 298
mouthpiece
  speaker 524
  information 527
  speech 582
mouthy *style* 577
moutonné 250
moutons, revenons à nos – 660
movable 264, 270
movables 780
move *begin* 66
  motion 264
  propose 514
  induce 615
  undertake 676
  act 680
  offer 763
  excite 824
  get a – on 684
  good – 626
  on the – 293
  – forward 282
  – from 287
  – in a groove 82
  – heaven and earth 686
  – off 293
  – on *progress* 282
    activity 682
  – out of 295
  – quickly 274
  – slowly 275
  – to 894
moveless 265
movement
  motion 264
  music 415
  action 680
  activity 682

moved with 821
mover 164
movies 448, 599, 840
movie star 899
moving
  keep – 682
  self – 266
  – pictures 448
mow *shorten* 201
  smooth 255
  agriculture 371
  store 636
  – down
  destroy 162
moza 384
M.P. 696
Mr. 373, 877
Mrs. 374
MS. 22, 590.
much 31
make – of
  importance 642
  friends 888
  love 897
  endearment 902
  approval 931
not say – for 932
think – of 928, 931
  – ado *exertion* 686
  difficulty 704
  – ado about nothing
  over-estimate 482
  exaggerate 549
  unimportant 643
  unskilful 699
  – cry and little wool 884
  – the same
  identity 13
  similarity 17
  equality 27
  – speaking 584
mucid 352, 653
mucilage 352
muck 653
run a – *kill* 361
  attack 716
  excitement 825
muckle 31
muckworm 819, 876
mucor 653
mucosity 352
mucronate 253
muculent 352
mud *marsh* 345
  semiliquid 352
  dirt 653
  clear as – 519
  stick in the – 704
  – guard 666
muddle *disorder* 59
  derange 61
  inattention 458
  absurd 497
  difficulty 704
  failure 732
  – one's brains 475
muddled 959
muddle-headed 499
muddy *moist* 339
  dim 422
  opaque 426
  color 429
  stupid 499

mudlark *dirty* 653
  commonalty 876
muezzin 550, 996
muff *incapable* 158
  dress 225
  bungle 699
  bungler 701
muffettee 225
muffle *wrap* 225
  silent 403
  deaden 408a
  conceal 528
  voiceless 581
  stammer 583
muffled *faint* 405
  latent 526
  – drums
  funeral 363
  non-resonance 408a
muffler 225, 384
mufti *undress* 225
  judge 967
  priest 996
mug *cup* 191
  face 234, 448
  pottery 384
  dupe 547
mug-house 189
muggy *moist* 339
  dim 422
  opaque 426
mugient 412
mugwump 607
mulatto
  mixture 41
  exception 83
mulct *steal* 791
  fine 974
mule *mongrel* 83
  beast of burden 271
  obstinate 606
muleteer 694
muliebrity 374
mull
  prominence 250
  sweeten 396
mullah 967, 996
muller 330
mullion 215
mullioned 219
multifarious
  irrelevant 10
  diverse 16a
multiform 81
multiferous 102
multifid
  divided 51
multifold 81
multiformity 81
multigenerous 81
multilateral 236, 244
multilocular 191
multiloquence 582, 584
multinomial 102
multiparous 168
multipartite 44
multiple 84, 102
multiplex 81
multiplicand 84
multiplicate 81
multiplication
  increase 35
  arithmetic 85

multitude 102
  reproduction 163
  productiveness 168
multiplicator 84
multiplicity 102
multiplier 84
multiply 35
multipotent 157
multisonous 404
multitude 72, 102
  the – 876
multum in parvo 596
multure 330
mum 581, 585
  –'s the word 403
mumble *chew* 298
  mutter 583
Mumbo Jumbo 979, 993
mummer 599
mummery
  absurdity 497
  imposture 545
  masquerade 840
  parade 882
mummify 363
mummy *dry* 340
  corpse 362
  beat to a – 972
mump *mutter* 583
  beg 765
mumper 767, 804
mumpish *sad* 837
mumps 837, 901a
munch 298
Munchausen 549
mundane
  world 318
  selfish 943
  irreligious 989
mundation 652
mundivagant 266
munerary 973
munerate 973
municipal 965
municipality 737
munificent 816
muniment
  evidence 465
  record 551
  defence 717
  security 771
munition
  materials 635
  defence 717
mural 717
murder 361
  – the King's English
  solecism 568
  stammering 583
  the – is out 529
murderer 361
muricated 253
murky *dark* 421
  opaque 426
  black 431
  gloomy 837
murmur *purl* 348
  sound 405
  voice 580
  complain 839
murmurer 832
murrain 655
Murray *travel* 266

Lindley – 542
murrey 434
murrion 717
mus, nascitur ridiculus – 509, 643
muscadine 400
muscle 159
muscular 159
muse 451
  [*and see* musing]
Muse *poetry* 597
  historic – 594
  unlettered – 579
musette 417
Muses, the – 416
museum
  collection 72
  store 636
mush 354
mushroom
  new 123
  fungus 367
  upstart 734
  low-born 876
  spring up like –s 163
  – anchor 666
music 415
  face the – 861
  set to – 416
  – of the spheres
    order 58
    universe 318
musical 413, 415, 416
  – comedy 599
  – ear
    musician 416
    hearing 418
  – instruments 417
  – note 413
  – voice 580
music-hall 599, 840
musician 416
musing 451
  – on other things 458
musk 400
musket 727
  shoulder a – 722
musketeer 726
musketry 727
muslin
  semi-transparent 427
musnud
  support 215
  council 696
  scepter 747
muss 59
Mussulman 984
must *necessity* 601
  mucor 653
  compulsion 744
  it – follow 478
  I – say 535
mustachio 256
mustard 392, 393
  after meat – 135
  – gas 663, 727
mustard-seed 193
muster 72, 85
  pass – 639
  not pass – 651
  – courage 861
muster-roll 86
musty 401, 653

make love 902
break one's – 360
– and crop
completely 52
turn out - 297
– of land 342
– and neck 27
– or nothing
resolute 604
rash 863
neckcloth 225
necklace 247, 847
necks 980
necrology 360, 594
necromancer 548,
994
necromancy 992
necropsy 363
necroscopic 363
necrosis 49
nectar 394, 396
need *necessity* 601
requirement 637
insufficiency 640
indigence 804
desire 865
friend in – 711
in one's utmost –
735
needful
necessary 601
requisite 630
money 800
do the – *pay* 807
needle *sharp* 253
perforator 262
compass 693
as the – to the
pole
veracity 543
observance 772
honour 939
– in a bottle of
hay 475
needle-gun 727
needle-shaped 253
needless 641
needle-witted 498
needlewoman 690
needlework 847
ne'er-do-well 949
nefarious 945
negation **536**, 764
negative
inexisting 2
contrary 14
prototype 22
quantity 84
confute 479
deny 536
photograph 558
refuse 764
prove a – 468
neglect **460**
disuse 678
leave undone 730
omit 773
evade 927
disrespect 929
– of time 115
négligé 225, 674
negligence 460
negotiable 270
negotiate
mediate 724
bargain 769
transfer 783

traffic 794
negotiations
breaking off – 713
negotiator 724, 758
negro 431, 746
negus
drink 298
king 745
neif 781
neigh *cry* 412
boast 884
neighbor 197, 890
neighborhood 183,
197, 227
neighborly
aid 707
friendly 888
social 892
courteous 894
neither 610
– here nor there
irrelevant 10
absent 187
– more nor less
equal 27
true 494
– one thing nor
another 83
nem. con. 488
Nemesis
vengeance 919
justice 922
punishment 972
nemine contra-
dicente 488
nemo me impune
lacessit 715
nenia 839
neogamist 903
neologism 123
neology **563**
neophyte 144, 541
névé 383
neoteric 123
nepenthe 662, 836
nephelogy 353
nephew 11
nepotism
nephew 11
wrong 923
dishonest 940
selfish 943
Neptune 341
Nereid 341, 979
nerve 159, 861, 885
exposed – 378
nerveless 158
nervous *weak* 160
style 574
timid 860
modest 881
nescience 491
nest
multitude 102
cradle 153
lodging 189
– of boxes 204
nest-egg 636
nestle *lodge* 186
safely 664
endearment 902
nestling 129
Nestor *veteran* 130
sage 500
advice 695
net *remainder* 40
receptacle 191
intersection 219

inclosure 232
snare 545
difficulty 704
gain 775
– *profit gain* 775
receipt 810
nether 207
nethermost 211
netting 219
nettle *bane* 663
sting 830
incense 900
network
disorder 59
crossing 219
neuralgia 378
neurasthenia 655
neuritis 378
neurology 329
neurotic 662
neuter *matter* 316
no choice 609a
remain –
irresolute 605
stand –
indifferent 866
neutral *mean* 29
no choice 609a
avoidance 623
– tint
colorless 429
grey 432
peace 721
neutrality
mid-course 628
peace 721
insensibility 823
indifference 866
neutralize
compensate 30
counteract 179
never 107
– say die
persevere 604a
cheerful 836
hope 858
it will – do
inexpedient 647
prohibit 761
discontent 832
disapprobation
932
–dying 112
–ending 112
–fading
perpetual 112
glory 873
– forget 916
– to be forgotten
642
– indebted 807
– hear the last of
841
– mind
neglect 460
unimportant 643
insensible 823
indifferent 866
contempt 930
– more 107
– a one 4
– otherwise 16
– to return 122
– was seen the
like 83
– so 31

– tell me 489
– thought of 621
– tired *active* 682
– tiring
persevering 604a
neverness 107
nevertheless 30
new *different* 18
additional 37
novel 123
unaccustomed 614
– birth 660
– blood *change* 140
improve 658
excite 824
– brooms 614, 682
– comer 57
– conditions 469
– departure 66
– edition
repetition 104
reproduction 163
improvement 658
– ideas 537
turn over a – leaf
change 140
repeat 950
give – life to 707,
824
view in a – light
658
put on the – man
950
New Year's Day
138
newaub 745
new-born 123, 129
Newcastle, carry
coals to – 641
new-fangled
unfamiliar 83
change 140
neology 563
new-fashioned 123
new-fledged 129
Newfoundland dog
366
Newgate 752
new-gilt 847
new-model
convert 144
revolutionize 146
improve 658
newness **123**
news **532**
– sheet 531
newsmonger
curious 455
informant 527
news 532
newspaper 531, 551
– correspondent
758
newspaperman 534
newt 366
next
following 63
later 117
future 121
near 197
– friend 759
– of kin 11
– to nothing 32
– world 152
nexus 45
Niagara 348
niais 501

niaiserie 517
nib *cut* 44
end 67
summit 210
point 253
nibble *eat* 298
– at *censure* 932
– at the bait
dupe 547
willing 602
nice
savory 394
discriminative
465
exact 494
good 648
pleasing 829
fastidious 868
honorable 939
– ear 418
– hand 700
– perception 465
– point 704
nicely
completely 52
Nicene Creed 983a
nicety 466
niche *recess* 182
receptacle 191
angle 244
– in the temple of
fame 873
nicher, se – 184
nick *notch* 257
deceive 545
mark 550
– it 731
– of time 124
Nick, Old – 978
nickel
money 800
nicknack 643
nickname 565
nicotine 392, 663
nictitate 443
nidget 862
nidification 189
nidor 398
nidorous 401
nidus 153, 189
niece 11
niggard 819
nigger 431
– in the woodpile
702
niggle *mock* 929
niggling 643
nigh 197
night 421
labor day and –
686
orb of – 318
– and day 136
– school 542
night-cap 225
nightfall 126
nightingale 416
night-gown 225
nightmare
bodily pain 378
dream 515
incubus 706
mental pain 828
alarm 860
nightshade 663
nigrescent 431
nigrification 431

numeral 84, 85
numeration **85**
numerator 84
numerical 85
numerose
  many 102
numerous 102
numismatics 800
numps 501
numskull 501
nun 996
nunc dimittis 990
nuncio 534, 758
nuncupation
  naming 564
nuncupatory
  informing 527
nunindation 794
nunnery 1000
nuptials 903
nurse *remedy* 662
  preserve 670
  help 707
  servant 746
  custodian 753
  fondle 902
  put to – 537
nurseling 129
nursery *infancy* 127
  nest 153
  room 191
  garden 371
  school 542
  workshop 691
  – rhymes 597
  – tale 546, 594
nursing home 493
nurture *feed* 298
  educate 537
  prepare 673
  aid 707
  – a belief 484
  – an idea 451
nut
  – to crack
  fanatic 504
  riddle 533
  difficulty 704
  – oil 365
nut-brown 433
nutmeg 393
nutmeg-grater 330
nuts 618, 829
nutshell *small* 32
  lie in a – 572
  little 193
  compendium 596
nutation 314
nutriment 298
nutrition 707
nutritious *food* 298
  healthy 656
  remedy 662
nutty 499
nuzzle 902
nyctalopy 443
nymph *girl* 129
  woman 374
  mythology 979
  sea – 341
nystagmus 443

O

O! *wonder* 870
  discontent 932

– for *desire* 865
oaf *fool* 501
  bungler 701
  changeling 980
oak *strong* 159
heart of –
  hard 323
  brave 861
oakum 205
oar *paddle* 267
  oarsman 269
  instrument 633
  laboring – 686
  lie upon one's –s 681
ply the –
  navigate 267
  exert 686
pull an – 680
put in an – 228, 682
rest on one's –
  cease 142
  quiescence 265
  repose 687
  stroke – 693
oarsman 269
oasis *separate* 44
  exceptional 83
  land 342
oast-house **386**
oath
  assertion 535
  bad language 908
  on – 543
  rap out –s **885**
  upon – 768
oatmeal 298
obbligato 88, 415
obduction 223
obdurate
  obstinate 606
  severe 739
  malevolent 907
  graceless 945
  impenitent 951
obedience 743
obeisance *bow* 308
  submission 725
  courtesy 894
  reverence 928
obelisk 206, 551
Oberon 979
obese 194
obesity 192
obey 743
  be subject to 749
  – a call 615
  – the helm 705
  – rules 82
obfuscate 421, 426
obfuscated
  drunk 959
obit 360, 363
  post – 360, 363
obiter dictum
  irrelevant 10
  occasion 134
  interjacent 228
obituary 360, 594
object *thing* 3
  matter 316
  take exception 469
  intention 620
  ugly 846
  disapprove 932
  be an –

important 642
– to *dislike* 867
– lesson 82
objection 706, 932
  no – 762
objectionable
  inexpedient 647
  wrong 923, 947
objective
  extrinsic 6
  material 316
objector
  conscientious – 710
objurgate 932
oblate 201
  – spheroid 249
oblation *gift* 784
  religious – 990
oblectation 827
obligation
  necessity 601
  promise 768
  conditions 770
  debt 806
  confer an – 648
  feeling of – 916
  under an – 916, 926
oblige *benefit* 707
  compel 744
  duty 926
oblige, bien –
  refusal 764
obliged
  necessity 601
  grateful 916
  duty 926
obligee 800
obliging
  helping 707
  courteous 894
  kind 906
obliquation 279
obliquity
  slope **217**
  vice 945
  – of judgment 481
  – of vision 443
obliteration **552**
  – of the past 506
oblivion **506**
  nothingness 2
  pardon 506
  forgiveness 918
  redeem from – 505
  – of benefits 917
  – of time 115
oblivious 506
oblong 200
  – spheroid 249
obloquy
  disrepute 874
  disapprobation 932
  detraction 934
obmutescence 581, 585
obnoxious
  pernicious 649
  unpleasing 830
  hateful 898
  – to *liable* 177
obnubilated 422
oboe 417
obreption 528
obscene 653, 961

obscurantist 421, 519, 710
obscure *dark* 421
  dim 422
  unseen 447
  uncertain 475
  unintelligible 519
  eclipse 874
  ignoble 876
obscurity *style* **571**
obscurum per
  obscurius 519
obsecration 765
obsequies 363
obsequious
  subject 749
  servile 886
  courteous 894
  respectful 928
  flattery 932
observance *rule* 82
  attention 457
  habit 613
  practice 692
  fulfilment **772**
  duty 926
  rite 998
observant
  friar 996
observation
  intellect 450
  idea 453
  attention 457
  assertion 535
  – car 272
observatory 318
observe [see *observance, observation*]
  remark 535
  – a duty 926
  – rules 82
observer 444
obsess 860, 992
obsession 716
obsidional 716
obsolete *old* 124
  words 563
  effete 645
obstacle 179, 706
obstant, Fata – 601
obstetrician 631
obstetrics 161, 662
obstinacy 606
  prejudice 481
obstipation 261
obstreperous 173, 404
obstruct *close* 261
  hinder 706
  – the passage of light 426
  – the view 424
obstructive
  opponent 710
obstruent 706
obstupefaction 823
obstupui steterunt-
  que comæ 860
obtain *exist* 1
  prevail 78
  get 775
  – under false pretences 791
obtainable 470
obtenebration 421
obtestation 765

obtrectation 934
obtrude
  interfere 228
  insert 300
  meddle 682
obtruncate 201
obtrusion 228, **706**
obtrusive
  interfering 228
  vulgar 851
  rude 895
obtund *mitigate* 174
  blunt 254
  deaden 376
  paralyze 823
obturate 261
obturator 263
obtuse *blunt* 253
  insensible 376
  imbecile 499
  dull 823
  – angle 244
obtuseness **456a**
obumbrate 421
obverse 234
obviate 706
obvious *visible* 446
  evident 474
  clear 518
  manifest 525
ocarina 417
occasion
  juncture 8
  opportunity **134**
  cause 153
befit the – 646
have – for 630
on the present – 118
on the spur of – 612
occasional 475
occasionally 136
occidental 236, **560**
occiput 235
occision 361
occlusion 261
  unintelligible **919**
  latent 526
  hidden 528
  – art 992
occultism 984
occultation 449, 528
occupancy 186, 777
occupant 188, 779
occupation
  business 625
  in the – of 188
  – road 627
occupied 682
  – by 188
  – with 457, 625
occupier 188, 779
occupy 186, 777
  – the chair 693
  – oneself with 457, 625
  – the mind 451, 457
  – a post 737
  – time 106
occur 1, 151
  – to the mind 451
  – in a place 186
occurrence 151
  of daily – 613
occursion 276

rejection 610
refusal 764
hopeless 859
undue 925
– reach 196, 471
– one's reckoning
uncertain 475
error 495
inexpectation 508
disappointment
509
– repair 659
– repute 874
– season 135
– shape 243
put – sight
invisible 447
neglect 460
conceal 528
– sorts disorder 59
dejection 837
– the sphere of
196
– spirits 837
– one's teens 131
– time
unmusical 414
imperfect 651
spoiled 659
discord 713
– the way
irrelevant 10
exceptional 83
absent 187
distant 196
ridiculous 853
secluded 893
get – the way 623
go – one's way 629
– one's wits 824
– work 681
– the world
dead 360
secluded 893
outbalance 30, 33
outbid 794
outbrave 885
out-brazen 885
outbreak
beginning 66
violence 173
egress 295
discord 713
attack 716
revolt 742
passion 825
outburst
violence 173
egress 295
revolt 825
outcast
unconformable 83
pariah 876
secluded 893
bad man 949
outcome effect 154
egress 295
produce 775
outcry noise 411
complaint 839
censure 932
outdo superior 33
transcursion 303
activity 682
cunning 702
conquer 731
outdoor 220

outer 220
outermost 220
outface 885
outfit 225, 673
outflank flank 236
defeat 731
outgate 295
outgeneral 731
outgo 303
outgoing 295
outgoings 809
outgrow 194
outgrowth 154
out-Herod 33, 174
outhouse 191
outing 266
outjump
transcursion 303
repute 873
outlander 57
outlandish
foreign 10
extraneous 57
irregular 83
barbarous 851
ridiculous 853
outlast 110
outlaw irregular 83
secluded 893
reprobate 949
outlawry 964
outlay 809
outleap 303
outlet opening 260
egress 295
outline contour 230
form 240
features 448
sketch 554
painting 556
plan 626
outlines
rudiments 66
principles 596
outlive 110, 141
outlook view 448
outstare 885
outlying
remaining 40
exterior 220
outmaneuver
trick 545
defeat 731
outnumber 102
outpost
distant 196
circumjacent 227
front 234
outpouring
egress 295
information 527
abundance 639
output egress 295
produce 775
outrage
violence 173
evil 619
badness 649
injury to 659
malevolence 907
disrespect 929
guilt 947
outrageous
excessive 31
violent 173
scandalous 874
outrance: à –

great 31
complete 52
violent 173
guerre – 722
outrank 33, 62
outré
exceptional 83
exaggerate 549
ridiculous 853
outre mer 196
outreach 545
outreckon 482
outride 303
outrider 64
outrigger
support 215
boat 273
outright 52
outrival
superior 33
surpass 303
fame 873
outrun 303
– the constable
debt 806
prodigal 818
outscourings 653
outset 66, 873
outshine 873, 874
outside
extraneous 57
exterior 220
appearance 448
– the gates 893
mere – 544
– car 272
clean the – of the
platter
ostentation 882
outsider 57, 893
outskirts 196, 227
outspan 292
outspeak 582
outspoken say 582
artless 703
be – censure 932
outspread 202
outstanding
remaining 40
outside 220
– debt 806
– feature 642
outstare 885
outstep 303
outstretched 202
with – arms 894
outstrip 303
outtalk 584
outvie 720, 873
outvote 731
outward 220
– bound 293
outweigh 33, 175
outwit 545, 731
outwork
defence 717
outworn 124
oval 247
ovate 247
ovation 883
oven 386
like an – hot 382
over more 33
remainder 40
end 67
past 122
high 206

too much 641
all – completed 729
all – with
destroyed 162
dead 360
failure 732
adversity 735
danger – 664
get – 660
fight one's battles
– again 594
hand – 783
make – 784
set – 755
turn – 218
– and above
superior 33
added 37
remainder 40
redundance 641
– again 104
– against 237
– the border 196
– head and ears
complete 52
height 206
feeling 821
– the hills and far
away 196
– the mark 33
– one's head 208,
641
– the way 237
overabound 641
overact bustle 682
affect 855
overall 225
over-anxiety 865
overarch 223
overawe sway 737
intimidate 860
respect 928
overbalance
unequal 28
compensation 30
superior 33
overbear 175
overbearing 885
overboard, throw –
eject 297
reject 610
disuse 678
abrogate 756
relinquish 782
overborne 732, 749
overburden
redundant 641
bad 649
fatigue 688
overcast cloudy 353
dark 421
dim 422
over-cautious 864
overcharge
exaggerate 549
style 577
redundance 641
dearness 814
overcoat 225
overcolor 549
overcome
prevail 175
induce 615
conquer 731
sad 837
disgraced 874
tipsy 959

– an obstacle 731
over-confident 486,
863
over-credulous 486
over-curious 455
overdate 115
overdecorated 846
over-distension 194
overdo
redundance 641
bustle 682
affectation 855
overdose 641
overdraft 808
overdraw
exaggerate 549
misrepresent 555
prodigal 818
over-due 115, 133
over-eager 865
overeat oneself 957
over-estimation
482
overfatigued 688
overfed 957
overfeed 641
overflow stream 348
redundance 641
– with gratitude
916
overgo 303
overgorged 869,
957
overgrown much 31
large 192
expanded 194
overhang high 206
overhanging
destiny 152
over-hasty 901
overhaul count 85
attend to 457
inquire 461
censure 932
overhead 206
overhear hear 418
be informed 527
overindulgence 957
overjoyed 827
overjump 303
overlap 225, 303
overlay cover 223
exaggerate 549
excess 641
overdo 682
hinder 706
– with ornament
writing 577
overleap 303
over-liberal 818
overlie 223
overload
redundance 641
hinder 706
overlook slight 458
neglect 460
superintend 693
forgive 918
disparage 929
bewitch 992
overlooked 642
not to be – 642
overlooker 694
overlord 745
overlying 206
overmaster 731
overmastery 821

– down	**paronomasia**	*friendship* 888	**parvenu**	651
shorten 201	neology 563	*love* 897	*new* 123	– under the name
paregoric 662	ornament 577	partially 32, 51	*successful* 734	of 564
parenchyma 316,	**paronymous** 562	partible 44	*vulgar* 851	– off *be past* 122
329	**paroxysm**	particeps criminis	*low-born* 876	egress 295
parent 166	*violence* 173	690, 711	parvitude 193	– off for 544
– ship 726	*agitation* 315	**participate** 709, 778	**pas** *precedence* 62	– on 282
parentage 11, 166	*emotion* 825	– in *be a doer* 680	*term* 71	– an opinion 480
parenthesis	*anger* 900	participation 778	*precession* 280	– to the order of
discontinuity 70	parquetry 440	participator 690	*rank* 873	the day 624
inversion 218	**Parr, Old** – 130	particle 32, 330	– de quatre 840	– out of 295
interjacence 228	parricide 361	parti-colored 440	– seul 840	– over
by way of – 134	parrot	*particular item* 51	**pas si bête** 498	*exclude* 55
parenthetical	*imitation* 19	*event* 151	paschal 998	*cross* 302
irrelative 10	*repetition* 104	*attentive* 457	pasha 875	*give* 784
pargeting 847	*loquacity* 584	*careful* 459	pashalic 737	*forgive* 918
parhelion 423	repeat as a – 505	*exact* 494	pashaw 745	*exemption* 927a
pari passu 27, 120	**parry** *confute* 479	*capricious* 608	pasigraphie 560	– over to 709
Pariah	*avert* 623	*odd* 851	pasigraphy 590	– and repass 302,
outlaw 83	*defend* 717	*fastidious* 868	pasquinade 934	314
commonalty 876	**pars magna fui,**	in – 79	**pass** *conjuncture* 8	– in review 457,
outcast 893	quorum – 690	– account 594	*be superior* 33	461
parian	parse 461, 567	– estate 780	*course* 109	– the Rubicon 609
sculpture 557	**Parsee** 984	particularize	*lapse* 122	– sentence on 971
parietal 236	parsimony 819	*special* 79	*happen* 151	– time *exist* 1
parietes 224	parson 996	*describe* 594	*interval* 198	*time* 106
paring 32	parsonage 1000	particularly 31, 33	*defile* 203	*do nothing* 681
parish 181	**part** *divide* 44	particulars 79, 594	*move* 264	– one's time in
bring to the – 804	*portion* 51	partie carrée 892	*transfer* 270	625
come upon the –	*diverge* 291	parting 44	*move through* 302	– to 144
804	*music* 413	**partisan**	*exceed* 303	– through
– council 696	*book* 593	*auxiliary* 711	*vanish* 449	*event* 151
parishioner 997	*rôle* 599	*weapon* 727	*way* 627	*motion* 302
paritor 965	*function* 625	*friend* 890	*difficulty* 704	– one's word 768
parity 17, 27	*duty* 926	*sympathizer* 914	*thrust* 716	**passable** *small* 32
park *house* 189	act a – *action* 680	**partisanship**	*passport* 760	*unimportant* 643
plain 344	take an active –	*warped judgment*	*gratuity* 815	*imperfect* 651
trees 367	682	481	– *as property* 783,	*pretty* 845
artillery 727	bear – in 709	co-operation 709	784	**passado** 716
pleasure ground	component – 56	*partiality* 923	barely – 651	**passage** [see pass]
840	fractional – 100a	partition *wall* 228	let it – 460	*part* 51
– paling 232	in – *a little* 32	*allot* 786	make a – *at* 716	*conversion* 144
parkway 627	for my – 79	partlet 366	pretty – 704	*street* 189
parlance 582	on the – of 707	partly 51	– away	*corridor* 191
in common – 576	play a – in 175	**partner**	*cease to exist* 2	*opening* 260
parlante 415	principal – 642	*companion* 88	*end* 67	*navigation* 267
parlementaire 534,	take the – of 709	*auxiliary* 711	*transient* 111	*moving through*
723	take – with 709	*sharer* 778	*past* 122	302
parler:	take a – in 680	*friend* 890	*cease* 142	*music* 413
façon de – 521	take no – in 623	*spouse* 903	*die* 360	– in *a book* 593
– a tort et à	– company	sleeping – 683	– by *course* 109	*action* 680
travers	*disjunction* 44	**partnership**	*inattention* 458	cut a – 260
illogical 477	*avoid* 623	*party* 712	*neglect* 460	force a – 302
nonsense 497	*quarrel* 713	join – with 709	*disrespectful* 929	– of arms 720
parley *talk* 588	– and parcel 56	**parts** *intellect* 450	– comprehension	**passant, en** –
conference 695	– by part 51	*skill* 698	519	*transit* 270
mediation 724	– song 415	*wisdom* 498	– current 484	*incidentally* 621
parliament 696	– of speech 567	parturition 161	– an examination	pass-book 811
parliamentary	– with 782, 784	**parturiunt montes**	648, 873	**passe:** mot de –
securities 802	partake 778	482, 509	– the eyes over	550
parlor 191	– of the sacrament	**party** *assemblage* 72	457	**passé**
parlor-maid 746	998	*special* 79	– the fingers over	*antiquated* 124
parlous 665	parte, ex – 481	*person* 372	379	*aged* 128
Parnassus 597	parterre *level* 213	*association* 712	– into one's hand	*spoiled* 659
parochial 181, 189	*cultivation* 371	*sociality* 892	785	passed away 122
prejudiced 48	**Parthis mendacior**	– spirit	– through one's	passementerie 847
parody	544	*warped judgment*	hands 625	passenger 268
imitation 19	**parti pris** 611	481	– into 144	– train 272
copy 21	**partial** *unequal* 28	*cooperation* 709	– judgment 480	**passe-partout**
misinterpret 523	*incomplete* 51	*wrong* 923	– a law 963	*key* 260
misrepresent 555	*special* 79	– to *action* 680	– in the mind 451	*instrument* 631
travesty 865	*misjudging* 481	*agent* 690	– muster	passer by 444
parole *speech* 582	*unjust* 923	co-operate 709	*conform to* 82	passer le temps,
on – *restraint* 751	– shadow 422	– to a suit 969	*sufficient* 639	pour – 681
prisoner 754	**partiality**	– wall 228	*good* 648	passerout pas, il ne
promise 763	*preponderance* 33	**parva componere**	*approbation* 931	717
Parolles 887	*desire* 865	**magnis** 464	barely – muster	passe-temps 840

pedagogic 537
pedagogue
  scholar 492
  teacher 540
  pedantic 855
pedagogy 537
pedal 633
  – note 408
  – point 416
pedant *scholar* 492
pedantic
  half-learned 491
  - *style* 577
  affected 855
pedantry 481
peddle *meddle* 683
  hawk 796
peddler 796, 797
peddling
  trifling 643
  miserly 819
pederero 727
pedestal 215
  place on a – 307, 931
pedestrian 268
pedicel 215
pedicle 215
pedigree 69, 166
pediment 210, 215
pedlar 797
  –'s French 563
pedometer 200
peduncle 215
peek 441
peel *layer* 204
  skin 223
  uncover 226
  – off *separate* 44
peeler 664
peel-house 717
peep 441
  – behind the curtain 461
  – of day 125
  – into the future 510
  – out 446, 529
peep-hole 260
peep-show 448, 840
peer *equal* 27
  pry 441
  inquire 461
  lord 875
  – out 446
peerless *supreme* 33
  first rate 648
  glorious 873
  virtuous 944
peeved 900
peevish 895, 901
peg *grade* 71
  hang 214
  project 250
  drink 298, 959
  come down a – 306
  let down a – 308
  not stir a – 265, 681
  – away 682
  – to hang on 617
  – on *journey* 266
  – out *die* 360
Pegasus 271
pegomancy 511
pegs *legs* 266

peignoir 225
peindre, fait à – 845
peine forte et dure 974
pejorative 483
pelagic 341
pelerine 225
pelf *gain* 775
  property 780
  money 803
pelisse 225
Pelion, Ossa on – 72, 319
pellet 249, 727
  paper – 643
pellicle 204, 223
pell-mell 59
pellucid 425
pelote 249
pelt *skin* 223
  dress 225
  throw 276
  attack 716
  punish 972
peltry 223
pemmican 298
pen *inclosure* 232
  write 590
  writer 593
  restrain 751
  imprison 752
  ready – 569
  slip of – 495, 568
  stroke of the – *write* 590
  authority 737
  command 741
  – in hand 590
  – and ink 590
  – name 565
  draw the – through 552
penal 972
  – servitude 972
  – settlement 752
penalty 974
  extreme – 972
penance 952, 974
  do – 998
penates, lares et – 189, 991
penchant
  willing 602
  desire 865
  love 897
pencil *bundle* 72
  - *of light* 420
  write 590
pencil-drawing 556
pencraft 590
pendant *match* 17
  flag 550
  ornament 847
pendency *time* 106
  hanging 214
pendente lite 106
  uncertain 475
  lawsuit 969
pendule 114
pendulous 214, 314
pendulum 114, 214
  motion of a – 314
Penelope, work of – 645, 730
penetralia 221
  – mentis 450, 820

penetrate
  ingress 294
  passage 302
  sagacity 498
  – the soul 824
penetrated with 484, 821
penetrating
  sagacious 498
  feeling 821
  – glance 441
penfold 232
peninsula 342
penitence 950
penitentiary 752, 996
pen-knife 253
penman 590
  inspired – 985
penmanship 590
pennant 550
pennate 267
penniless 804
pennon 550
penny 800
  not have a – 804
  cost a pretty – 814
  turn a – 775
  no – no paternoster 812
  in for a – in for a pound 768
  – dreadful 594
  – trumpet 410
  – whistle 410
penny-a-liner 534, 593
penny-a-lining 573
pennyweight 319
penny-wise 819
  – and pound foolish *caprice* 608
  waste 638
  prodigal 818
pennyworth 812
penology 972
penscript 590
pensée, arrière – 528
penseroso 837
pensile 214
pension *income* 810
pensioner
  student 541
  servant 746
  receiver 785
pensive 451, 837
penstock 350
pent up 751
  – in one's memory 505
pentagon 98, 244
pentahedron 244
pentameter 98, 597
Pentateuch 98, 985
Pentecost 998
Penthesilean 861
penthouse 189, 191
pentile 223
penultimate 67
penumbra 421
penurious 819
penury 804
peon 726
people
  kinsfolk 11
  multitude 102

inhabit 186
mankind 372
commonally 876
laity 997
pep 171
  – up 171
pepastic 662
pepper *pungent* 392
  condiment 393
  attack 716
  – and salt 432, 440
peppercorn 643
  – rent 815
peppery
  irascible 901
peptic 662
per 631
  – contra *contrariety* 14
  counter-evidence 468
  opposition 708
  – procuratio 755
  – saltum 70, 113
  – se 87
peradventure 470
peragrate 266
perambulate 266
perambulator
  measure of length 200
  vehicle 272
perceivable 446
perceive
  be sensible of 375
  see 441
  know 490
percentage 84, 813
perceptible 446
perception 453, 490
perceptive 375
perch *location* 184
  abide 186
  habitation 189
  length 200
  height 206
  support 215
  – up 307
perchance 156, 470
percipience 450
percolate 295, 348
percolator 191
percursory 458
percussion 276
  center of – 222
percussive 277
perdition
  destruction 162
  ruin 732
  loss 776
perdre son Latin 704
perdrix, toujours – 841
perdu 528
perdurable 110
perdy 535
peregrination 266
peregrinator 268
peremptory
  assertion 535
  firm 604
  authoritative 737
  rigorous 739
  compulsory 744

duty 926
  – denial 536
  – refusal 764
perennial
  continuous 69
  diuturnal 110
  - *plants* 367
perennius, aere – 873
pererration 266
perfect
  great 31
  entire 52
  excellent 650
  complete 729
perfection 650
  bring to – 729
perfervidum ingenium 682
perfidy 874, 940
perflate 349
perforate 260
perforator 262
perforce 601, 744
perform
  produce 161
  do 170
  - *music* 416
  action 680
  achieve 729
  fulfil 772
  – a circuit 629
  – a duty 926
  – the duties of 625
  – a function 644
  – an obligation 772
  – a part 599, 680
  – a service 998
performable 470
performance
  [see perform]
  effect 154
performer
  musician 416
  stage-player 599
  agent 690
  affectation 855
perfume 400
perfunctory 53, 460
pergola 191
perhaps 470, 514
peri 845, 979
periapt 993
pericranium 450
periculous 665
peridot 847
perihelion 197
peril 665
  at your – 909
  take heed at one's – 668
perilepsis 476
perimeter 230
period *end* 67
  point 71
  - *of time* 106, 108
  recurrence 138
  at fixed -s 138
  well rounded -s 577, 578
periodical
  recurring 138
  book 593
periodicity 138
peripatetic 266, 268
periphery 230

color 434
perfection 650
glory 873
pink of *beauty* 845
– fashion 852
– perfection 650
– politeness 894
pinnace 273
pinnacle 210
pinocle 840
pin-prick 180a
pins *legs* 266
– and needles
bodily pain 378
numb 381
mental pain 828
pinscher 366
Pinto, Fernam
Mendez – 548
pioneer
precursor 64
leader 234
teacher 540
prepare 673
pious 987
– *fraud* 546, 988
pip 747
pipe *tube* 260
conduit 350
vent 351
tobacco 392
sound 410
cry 411
music 416, 417
weep 839
no – no dance 812
– one's eye 839
– of peace 721, 723
pipeclay *habit* 613
strictness 739
piper 416
pay the – 707, 807
piping – hot 382
– time 721, 734
pipkin 191
piquant
pungent 392
– *style* 574
impressive 821
piquante, sauce –
393, 829
pique *fly* 267
excite 824
pain 830
hate 898
anger 900
– oneself
pride 878
piqueerer 792
piquet 717, 726
pirate 773, 791, 792
piroque 273
pirouette 218, 312
turn a – 607
Pisa, tower of – 217
pis-aller 147
piscatorial 366
pisces natare
docere 538, 641
pisciculture 370
piscina 350, 1000
pish! *absurd* 497
trifling 643
excitable 825
irascible 901
piste 551

Pistol 887
pistol 727
pistol-shot 197
piston 263
pit *deep* 208
hole 252
opening 260
extract 301
grave 363
theater 599
danger 667
bottomless – 982
– of Acheron 982
– against 708, 713
– against one
another 464
pit-a-pat
agitation 315
rattle 407
feeling 821
excitation 824
pitch *degrees* 26
term 71
location 184
height 206
summit 210
erect 212
throw 284
descent 306
depression 308
reel 314
resin 356a
musical – 413
black 431
absolute – 416
– of one's breath
411
– *dark* 421
– into *attack* 716
contend 720
punish 972
– overboard 782
– one's tent 292
– and toss 621
– upon reach 292
discover 480a
choose 609
get 775
pitched battle 720
pitcher 191
pitchfork 273, 284
rain –s 348
pitch-pipe 417
piteous 830
piteously *much* 31
pitfall 545, 667
pith *gist* 5
strength 159
interior 221
center 222
meaning 516
important part
642
pithless 158
pithy *meaning* 516
concise 572
vigorous 574
pitiable *bad* 649
painful 830
contemptible 930
pitied, to be – 828
pitiful
unimportant 643
bad 649
disrepute 874
pity 914
pitiless 914a

revengeful 919
pittance
quantity 25
dole 640
allotment 786
income 810
pitted 848
pituitous 352
pity 914
express – 915
what a –
regret 833
lament 839
for – 's sake 914
pivot *junction* 43
cause 153
support 215
axis 222, 312
pix *box* 191, 998
assay 463
pixy 980
pizzicato 415
placable 918
placard 531
placate 723, 918
place
circumstances 8
order 58
arrange 60
term 71
situation 182, 183
locate 184
abode 189
office 625
rank 873
give – to 623
have – 1
in – 183
in – of 147
make a – for 184
out of – 185
take – 151
– to one's credit
805
– itself 58
– in order 60
– upon record 551
– under
include 76
placebit, decies re-
petita – 829
placebo 933
place-hunter 767
placeman 758
placet 488, 741
placid 826
placket 260
plagiarism
imitation 19
borrowing 788
theft 791
plagiarist 792
Plagiary, Sir
Fretful – 901
plagiedral 217
plague *disease* 655
pain 828
worry 830
plague-spot 657
plaguy 704, 830
plaid *shawl* 225
variegation 440
plaidoyer 476
plain
horizontal 213
country 344
obvious 446

meaning 518
manifest 525
style 576
artless 703
ugly 846
simple 849
speak –ly 576
tell one –ly 527
– English 576
– dealing 543
– interpretation
522
– question 461
– sailing 705
– sense 498
– speaking 525,
703
– terms
intelligible 518
interpreted 522
language 576
– truth 494
– words 703
plainness 576
plainsong 990
plain-spoken 525,
703
plaint 411, 839
plaintiff 938
plaintive 839
plaisance
[see pleasance]
plaisanterie 842
plaister 223
plait 219, 258
plan *itinerary* 266
information 527
representation
554
scheme 626
according to – 82
planchette 992
plane *horizontal* 213
flat 251
smooth 255
fly 267
aeroplane 273
soar 305
inclined – 633
planet *world* 318
luminary 423
fate 601
planet-struck
adversity 735
wonder 870
planimeter 466
planish 255
plank *board* 204
program 626
path 627
safety 666
plant *place* 184
insert 300
vegetable 367
agriculture 371
trick 545
tools 633
property 780
– a battery 716
– a dagger in the
breast 830
– oneself 184
– a thorn in the
side 830
plantation
location 184
agriculture 371

estate 780
planter 188
planter ses choux,
aller – 893
plaque 204
plash *lake* 343
stream 348
sound 405, 408
plashy 345
plasm 22
plasma 847
plasmic 240
plaster *cement* 45
covering 223
remedy 662
– up repair 660
plastered 959
plastic *alterable* 149
form 240
soft 324
– arts 557
plastron 717
plat *weave* 219
ground 344
plate *dish* 191
layer 204
covering 223
flat 251
food 298
engraving 558
– layer 690
– printing 558,
591
plateau 213, 344
plated 545
platform
horizontal 213
support 215
stage 542
scheme 626
arena 728
– orator 582
platinum-blond 430
platitude 517, 843
Platonic
contemplative 451
inexcitable 826
chaste 960
– bodies 244
Platonism 451
platoon 726
– fire 716
platter 191
layer 204
flat 251
clean the outside
of the – 544
plaudit 931
plausible
probable 472
sophistical 477
false 544
approbation 931
flattery 933
vindication 937
play *operation* 170
influence 175
scope 180
oscillation 314
music 416
drama 599
use 677
action 680
freedom 748
amusement 840
at – 840
bring into – 677

full – 175
full of – 836
in – 842
– along with 709
– one's best card 686, 698
– of colors 440
– at cross purposes 59, 523
– a deep game 702
– the deuce 825
– the devil 907
– one false
  disappoint 509
  falsehood 544
  deception 545
– fast and loose
  falsehood 544
  irresolute 605
  tergiversation 607
  caprice 608
– on the feelings 824
– first fiddle 642, 873
– the fool
  folly 499
  clumsy 699
  amusement 840
  ridiculous 853
  ridicule 856
– for *chance* 621
– a game
  pursue 622
  conduct 692
  pastime 840
– the game 939
– into the hands of 709
– havoc 659
– hide and seek 528, 623
– a joke 853
give – to the imagination 515
– of light 420
– the monkey 499
– off 545
– a part
  false 544
  drama 599
  action 680
– one's part 625, 692
– second fiddle 34, 749
– one a trick 509, 545
– tricks with 699, 702
– truant 623
– upon 545, 856
– with 460
– upon words
  misinterpret 523
  neology 563
  wit 842
play-boy 818
play-day 840
played out
  end 67
  fatigue 688
  completion 729
  failure 732
player
  musician 416
  actor 599

– piano 417
playfellow 890
playful 836
– imagination 515
playground 728, 840
play-house 599
playmate 890
playsome 836
plaything
  trifle 643
  toy 840
make-a – of 749
playwright 599
plea
  defence 462
  argument 476
  excuse 617
  vindication 937
  lawsuit 969
plead *argue* 467
  plea 617
  beg 765
– one's cause 937
– guilty 950
pleader *lawyer* 968
pleading, special – 477
pleadings 969
pleasance 189, 840
pleasant
  agreeable 829
  amusing 840
  witty 842
make things –
  deceive 545
  induce 615
  please 829
  flatter 933
pleasantry 840, 842
please 829
  as you – 743
  do what one –s 748
  if you –
    obedience 743
    consent 762
    request 765
  – oneself 943
pleasurableness 829
pleasure
  physical - 377
  will 600
  moral - 827
  dissipation 954
  at – 600
  at one's – 737
  during – 108a
  give – 829
  man of – 954a
  make a toil of – 682
  take one's – 840
  will and – 600
  with –
    willingly 602
pleasure-giving 829
pleasure-ground
  demesne 189
  amusement 840
pleat 258
plebeian 851, 876
plébiscite 480, 609
plectrum 417
plectuntur Achivi 739

pledge *affirmation* 535
  promise 768
  security 771
  borrow 788
  drink to 883, 894
  hold in – 771
  take the – 771, 958
  – oneself 768
  – one's word 768
pledget 263, 662
Pleiades 72, 318
plenary 31, 52
plenipotent 157
plenipotentiary
  consignee 758
  deputy 759
plentitude 639
  in the – of power 159
plenty
  multitude 102
  sufficient 639
  – to do 682
plenum *substance* 3
  matter 316
pleonasm
  repetition 104
  diffuseness 573
  redundance 641
plerophory 484
plethora 64
plexal 219
plexus 219
pliable 324
pliant *soft* 324
  irresolute 605
  facile 705
  servile 886
plicature 258
pliers 301, 781
plight *state* 7
  promise 768
  security 771
  evil – 735
  – one's faith 902
  – one's troth 768, 902
plighted love 897, 902
Plimsoll mark 466
plinth 211, 215
plod *journey* 266
  slow 275
  persevere 604a
  work 682
  – along 143
plodding 604a, 682
  dull 843
plot - of ground 181
  plain 344
  story 594
  plan 626
  really 780
  the – thickens
  assemblage 72
plough *furrow* 259
  agriculture 371
  – the ground 673
  – in 228
  – the waves 267
  – one's way 266
ploughboy
  commonalty 876
ploughman 371
ploughshare 253
pluck *cheat* 545

resolution 604
  persevere 604a
  reject 610
  take 789
  steal 791
  courage 861
  – up courage 861
  – a crow with 932
  – out 301
plug 261, 263
  – along 143
plum *number* 98
  sweet 396
  money 800
plumage 256
plumb *vertical* 212
  close 261
  measure 466
plumber 690
plumb-line 212
plum-colored 437
plume *feather* 256
  ornament 847
  borrowed –s 788
  – oneself 878
plume
  coup de – 590
  nom de – 565
plumigerous 256
plummet 208, 212
plumose 256
plump
  instantaneous 113
  fat 192
  plunge 310
  unexpected 508
  – down 306
  – upon 292
plumper
  expansion 194
  vote 609
plunder 791, 793
plunderer 792
plunge
  revolution 146
  insert 300
  dive 306, 310
  immerse 337
  hurry 684
  – into difficulties 704
  – into dissipation 954
  – headlong 684
  – into 676
  – in medias res 576, 604
  – into sorrow 830
plunged
  – in debt 806
  – in grief 828
plunger 621
plurality 100
plus 37
plus fours 225
plush 256
Pluto 979, 982
  realms of – 982
Plutocracy 803
plutonic 382
Plutus 803
pluvial 348
ply *layer* 204
  fold 258
  use 677
  exert 686
  request 765

– one's task 680
– one's trade 625
– a trade 794
Plymouth Brother 984
p.m. 114, 126
pneumatics 334, 338
pneumatology 450
pneumatoscopic 317
poach 791, 964
poacher 792
poachy 345
pock 250
pocket *place* 184
  pouch 191
  diminutive 193
  receive 785
  take 789
  money 800
  treasury 802
  brook 826
  button up one's – 808
  out of – 776, 806
  touch the – 800
  – the affront 725, 918
pocket-book 551
pocket-handkerchief 225
pocket-money 800
pocket-pistol
  bottle 191
pococurante 823, 866
pocula, inter – 959
pod 191, 223
podestà 967
podgy 201
poem 597
  book of –s 593
poenitentiae, locus-
  pity 914
  forgive 918
  vindicate 937
  repent 950
poesy 597
poet 597
poetaster 597, 855
poetic *style* 574
poetic frenzy 515
poetry 597
poignancy
  physical energy 171
  pain 378
  pungency 392
  feeling 821
pogrom 361
point *condition* 8
  degree 26
  small 32
  end 67
  term 71
  poignancy 171
  no magnitude 180a
  place 182
  speck 193
  sharp 253
  topic 454
  mark 550
  vigor 574
  intention 620
  wit 842

punctilio 939
at the – of 197
come to the –
  special 79
  attention 457
  reasoning 476
  plain language
  576
culminating – 210
disputed – 713
from all –s 180
full of – 574
give –s to 27
go straight to
  the – 278
in – *relative* 9
  agreeing 23
  conformable 82
knotty – 704
make a – of
  resolution 604
  contention 720
  compulsion 744
  conditions 770
  due 924
  honor 939
nice – 697
on the – of 111,
  121
to the – 572, 642
–an antithesis 578
– at *direction* 278
  direct attention
  457
  intend 620
  discourtesy 895
  disrespect 929
  censure 932
– of attack 716
at the – of the
  bayonet 173
– of the compass
  278
– of convergence
  74
– of death 360
– in dispute 461
– of etiquette 852
in – of fact 1
– the finger of
  scorn 930
– of honor 939
– of land 250
– a moral 537
– out 155, 457,
  527
– to – race 720
at the – of the
  sword
  violence 173
  severity 739
  compulsion 744
– to *attribute* 155
  direction 278
  probable 472
  predict 511
  mean 516
– of view 441, 448
 oint d'appui 215
oint-blank
  direct 278
  plain language
  576
  refusal 764
point-champain 874
pointed
  great 31

sharp 253
  affirmation 535
  marked 550
  concise 572
  language 574
pointedly
  intention 620
pointer *dog* 366
  indicator 550
pointless 843
poise 27, 319, 852
  mental – 498
poison 659, 663
  – gas 722, 727
poisoned 655
  commend the –
  chalice 544
poisonous 657, 665
poke
  pocket 191
  pig in a –
    uncertain 475
    chance 621
    dawdle 683
    rash 863
  – at 276, 716
  – the fire 384
  – fun at 856
  – one's nose in
  682
  – out *project* 250
poker 386
  cards 840
polacca 273
polacre 273
polar 210
  cold 383
  – co-ordinates 466
polarization 420
polariscope 445
polarity
  duality 89
  counteraction 179
  contraposition
  237
pole *measure of*
  length 200
  tall 206
  summit 210
  axis 222
  punt 267
  rotation 312
  greasy – 840
  opposite –s 237
  from – to pole 180
pole-axe 727
polecat 401
pole-star 550, 693
polemic
  discussion 476
  discord 713
  contention 720
  combatant 726
polemoscope 445
police 965
  – court 966
  – magistrate 967
policeman 664, 965
policy 626, 692
polish *smooth* 255
  rub 331
  furbish 658
  beauty 845
  ornament 847
  taste 850
  politeness 894
  – off *finish* 729

Polish bank 840
polished
  – *language* 578
  fashionable 852
  polite 894
polisson 949
polite 894
  offensive to ears –
  579
  – literature 560
  – society 852
politic *wise* 498
  cunning 702
  cautious 864
  body –
    mankind 372
    government 737
political economy
  692
politician
  director 694
  proficient 700
politics 702
polity *conduct* 692
  authority 737
  duty 926
polka 840
poll 85, 609
  – tax 812
pollard 193, 201
  tree 367
Poll-parrot 584
pollute *soil* 653
  corrupt 659
  disgrace 874
pollution
  disease 655
  vice 945
Pollyanna 858
polo 840
polonaise 840
poltroon 862
polyandry 903
polychord 417
polychromatic 428,
  440
polychrome 440,
  556
polygamy 903
polygastric 191
polyglot 522, 560
polygon
  buildings 189
  figure 244
polygraphy 590
polylogy 573
polymorphic 81
polyphonism 580
polypus 250
polyscope 445
polysyllable 561
polytheism 984
pomade 356
pomatum 356
pommel
  support 215
  round 249
  beat 972
Pomona 369
pomp 882
pom-pom 727
pomposity 882
pompous
  language 577
poncho 225
pond 343, 636
  fish – 370

ponder 451
ponderable 316,
  319
ponderation 319,
  480
ponderous 319
  – *style* 574, 579
  dull 843
pondus fumo, dare
  – 481
poniard 727
pons asinorum 519,
  704
pontifical 995
pontificals 999
pontificate 995
pontiff 996
pontoon
  vehicle 272
  boat 273
  way 627
pony 271
poodle 366
pooh, pooh!
  unimportance 643
  contempt 930
pool *lake* 343
  combination 709
  prize 775
  billiards 840
poop 235
poor *weak* 160
  – *reasoning* 477
  – *style* 575
  insufficient 640
  trifling 643
  indigent 804
  unhappy 828
  cut a – figure 874
  – hand 701
  – head 499
  – house 189
  – man 804
  – in spirit 881
  – stick 501
  – thing 914
poorly 160, 655
  – off 804
poor-spirited 862
pop *noise* 406
  unexpected 508
  – at 716
  – in *ingress* 294
  insertion 300
  – off *die* 360
  – a question 461
  – the question
  request 765
  endearment 902
  – upon *arrive* 292
  discover 480a
Pope
  infallibility 474
  priest 996
Popedom 995
Pope Joan 840
Popery 984
pop-gun *trifle* 643
popinjay 854
poplar *tall* 206
poppy *sedative* 174
populace 876
popular
  in demand 865
  celebrated 873
  favorite 897
  approved 931

  – opinion 488
popularis, aura –
  873
popularize
  render intelligible
  518
  facilitate 705
  make pleasant
  829
populate 184
population 188, 372
populi, vox –
  publication 531
  election 609
  authority 737
populous
  crowded 72
  multitude 102
  presence 186
porcelain
  baked 384
  sculpture 557
porch *entrance* 66
  lobby 191
  mouth 231
  opening 260
  church 1000
porcupine 253, 901
pore *opening* 260
  egress 295
  conduit 350
  – over *look* 441
  apply the mind
  457
  learn 539
porism 461, 480
pornographic 961
porous 260
porpoise 192
porridge 298
porringer 191
port *abode* 189
  sinistral 239
  gait 264
  arrival 292
  carriage 448
  harbor 666
  in – 664
  make – 666
  – admiral 745
  – fire 388
  – wine 959
portable *small* 193
  transferable 270
  light 320
portage 270
portal *entrance* 66
  mouth 231
  opening 260
portative 193, 270
portcullis 706, 717
  let down the – 666
porte-monnaie 802
portend 511
portent 512
portentous
  prophetic 511
  fearful 860
porter *janitor* 263
  carrier 271, 690
porterage 270
portfolio *case* 191
  book 593
  magazine 636
  direction 693
  insignia 747
porthole 260

privity 490
privy *hidden* 528
  latrines 653
  – to 490
Privy Council 966
prize *good* 618
  palm 733
  gain 775
  booty 793
  receipt 810
  love 897
  approve 931
  reward 973
  win the – 731
  – open 173
prizer 767
prize-fighter 726
prize-fighting 720
prizeman 700
pro: – and con
  476, 615
  – formâ 82
  – hâc vice
  special 79
  present time 118
  occasion 134
  seldom 137
  – rata 23
  – re natâ
  circumstances 8
  relation 9
  special 79
  occasion 134
  conditions 770
  – tanto 26, 32
  – tempore 111
proa 273
probability 156, 472
probable 858
probate 771
Probate Court 966
probation
  trial 463
  demonstration
  478
probationary 463,
  675
probationer 541
probative 478
probatum est 478,
  931
probe *depth* 208
  perforator 262
  investigate 461
  measure 466
probity 939
problem *topic* 454
  question 461
  enigma 533
problematical 475
proboscis 250
procacity
  insolence 885
  rudeness 895
  irascibility 901
procedure
  method 627
  action 680
  conduct 692
proceed *time* 109
  advance 282
  – from 154
  – with 692
proceeding
  incomplete 53
  event 151
  action 680

  not finished 730
  course of – 692
proceedings 551
proceeds *gain* 775
  money 800
  receipts 810
procerity 206
procès-verbal
  record 551
  law procceding
  969
process
  projection 250
  conduct 692
  legal – 963
  – engraving 558
  – of time 109
  in – of time 117
procession
  continuity 69
  march 266
  ceremony 882
processional
  rite 998
prochronism 115
proclaim 531
proclivity 176, 820
proconsul 759
proconsulship 737
procrastination 133,
  460, 683
procreant 168
procreate 161, 168
procreator 166
procrustean 82
  – law 80
Procrustes:
  stretch on the bed
  of – 27
proctor *teacher* 540
  officer 694, 965
  consignee 758
  lawyer 968
proctorship 693
procumbent 213
procurator 694
procuration 170,
  755
procure *cause* 153
  induce 615
  get 775
  buy 795
procuress 962
procurement 170
prod 276
prodigal 641, 816
prodigality 818
prodigious 31, 870
prodigy 83, 872
  – of learning 700
prodition 940
prodrome 64
produce
  increase 35
  cause 153
  effect 154
  create 161
  prolong 200
  show 525
  stage 599
  fruit 775
  merchandise 798
  – itself 446
producer 164
product
  multiple 85
  effect 154

  harvest 636
  gain 775
  finished – 154
production 54, 161
  [*and see* pro-
  –duce]
productive
  cause 153
  power 157
  inventive 515
  profitable 775
productiveness 168
proem 64
proemial
  preceding in order
  62
  beginning 66
profane
  desecrate 679
  impious 988
  laical 997
  – swearing 908
profanum vulgus
  876
profession
  assertion 535
  pretence 546
  business 625
  promise 768
  enter a – 625
  – of faith 484, 983
professional 700
  – mourner 363,
  839
professor 492, 540,
  700
professorship 542
proffer 763
proficient
  knowledge 490
  skill 698
  adept 700
proficuous 644
profile
  outline 230
  side 236
  appearance 448
  portraiture 556
profit
  increase 35
  advantage 618
  utility 644
  acquisition 775
  – by *use* 677
  – sharing 778
profitable
  useful 644
  good 648
  gainful 775
profitless 646
profligacy 945
profluent
  progressive 282
  stream 348
profound
  great 31
  deep 208
  learned 490
  wise 498
  sagacious 702
  feeling 821
  – attention 457
  – knowledge 490
  – secret 533
profundis, de –
  839, 950
profuse

  diffuse style 573
  redundant 641
  prodigal 818
profusion 102, 639
prog 298
progenerate 161
progenitive 163
progenitor 166
progeny 167
prognosis 510, 511,
  522, 655
prognostic 511, 512
prognosticate 511
prognostication 507
program
  catalogue 86
  publication 531
  plan 626
progress
  growth 144
  motion 264
  advance 282
  in – *incomplete*
  53, 730
  make – 282
  in mid – 270
  – of science 490
  – of time 109
progression
  gradation 58
  series 69
  numerical – 84
  motion 282
progressive
  continuous 69
  course 109
  advancing 282
  improving 658
prohibition 761
  exclusion 55
  stoppage 706
  teetotalism 953,
  958
project *bulge* 250
  impel 284
  intend 620
  plan 626
projectile 727
projection *map* 554
projector
  lantern 423
  film 445
  designer 626
prolation 580, 582
prole, sine – 169
prolegomena 64
prolepsis 64, 115
proletarian 876
prolific 168
prolix 573
prolocutor
  interpreter 524
  teacher 540
  speaker 582
prologue
  precursor 64
  drama 599
prolong
  protract 110
  late 133
  continue 143
  lengthen 200
prolongation 63,
  143
prolusion 64
prom 892
promenade 266

  display 882
  on pier 189
Promethean 359
prominent
  convex 250
  manifest 525
  important 642
  eminent 873
prominently 31, 33
promiscuous
  mixed 41
  irregular 59
  indiscriminate
  465a
  casual 621
promise
  predict 511
  engage 768
  hope 858
  keep one's – 939
  keep – to ear and
  break to hope
  545
  – oneself 507, 858
promissory 768
  – note 771, 800
promontory
  height 206
  projection 250
  land 342
promote 153, 658,
  707
promoter 626
promotion 658
prompt *early* 132
  remind 505
  tell 527
  induce 615
  active 682
  advise 695
  – memory 505
prompter
  drama 599
  motive 615
  adviser 695
promptuary 636
promulgate 531
  – a decree 741
pronation and
  supination 218
prone
  horizontal 213
proneness
  tendency 176
  disposition 820
prôner 882, 931
prôneur 935
prong 91
pronounce
  judge 480
  assert 535
  voice 580
  speak 582
pronounced 525
pronouncement 531
pronunciamento
  531
pronunciation 580
pronunciative 535
proof *hard* 323
  insensible 376
  test 463
  demonstration
  478
  printing 591
  draft 626
ocular – 446

- an inquiry 461
- the tenor of one's way 625, 881

pursuer 622
pursuit 622
pursuivant 534
pursy 194
purulent 653
purvey 637
purview 620
pus 653
Puseyite 984
push *exigency* 8
 impel 276
 progress 282
 propel 284
 essay 675
 activity 682
 haste 684
 come to the – 704
 – aside 460, 929
 – forward 682, 707
 – from 289
 – to the last 133
 – on *haste* 684
 – out *eject* 297
pushing 282, 284, 682
pusillanimity 862
puss 366
 play – in the corner 148
pussy-foot 528, 958
pustule 250, 848
put *place* 184
 fool 501
 cards 840
 clown 876
 neatly – 576
 – across 484
 – about
 turn back 283
 go round 311
 publish 531
 – aside
 exclude 55
 inattention 458
 neglect 460
 disuse 678
 – away
 – *thought* 452
 relinquish 782
 divorce 905
 – back
 turn back 283
 deteriorate 659
 restore 660
 – before 527
 – by 636
 – a case 82, 514
 – in commission 755
 – a construction on 522
 – on the cuff 806
 – down
 destroy 162
 record 551
 conquer 731
 compel 744
 pay 807
 humiliate 874
 – an end to
 end 67
 stop 142
 destroy 162

- *oneself* 361
- in force
 complete 729
 compel 744
 – forth
 expand 194
 suggest 514
 publish 531
 assert 535
 – *a question* 461
 – *strength* 686
 – forward
 suggest 514
 publish 531
 ostentation 882
 – one's hand to 676
 – the horses to 673
 – in [*see below*]
 – to inconvenience 647
 – a mark upon 457
 – one's nose out of joint 33
 – off *late* 133
 divest 226
 depart 293
 plea 617
 – on *clothe* 225
 deceive 544
 hasten 684
 affect 855
 – out [*see below*]
 – on paper 551
 – over 484, 731
 – a question 461
 – right 660
 – the saddle on the right horse 155
 – the seal to 729, 769
 – to [*see below*]
 – together *join* 43
 combine 48
 assemble 161
 – one's trust in 484
 – up [*see below*]
 – upon 545, 649
put in *arrive* 292
 insert 300
 – an affidavit 535
 – hand 676
 – one's head 514
 – mind 505
 – motion 264
 – order 60
 – the place of 147
 – one's pocket 785
 – practice 692
 – remembrance 505
 – shape 60
 – trim 60, 673
 – the way of 470
 – a word 582, 588
put out
 destroy 162
 outside 220
 extinguish 385
 darken 421
 distract the attention 458
 uncertain 475
 difficult 704
 discontent 832

- of countenance 874
oneself – of court
 sophistry 477
 bungling 699
 – of gear 158
 – of one's head 458
 – of joint 61
 – of one's misery 914
 – to nurse 707
 – of order 59
put to *attribute* 155
 request 765
 – the blush 879
 – death 361
 – the door 261
 – it 704
 – one's oath 768
 – press 591
 – the proof 463
 – the question 830
 – the rack 830
 – rights 60
 – sea 293
 – shame 874
 – silence 581
 – the sword 361
 – task 677
 – use 677
 – the vote 609
put up *assemble* 72
 locate 184
 store 636
 – to auction 796
 – for 865
 – a petition ⎫ 765
 – a prayer ⎬ 990
 – for sale 796
 – a shutter 424
 – the sword 723
 – to 615
 – with 147, 826
putative
 attributed 155
 believed 484
 supposed 514
putid 643
putrefy 653
putrescence 49
putrid 653
putsch 742
puttee 225
putter 683
putting the weight 840
putty 45
puzzle *uncertain* 475
 conceal 528
 enigma 533
 – out 522
puzzled 475, 533
puzzle-headed 499
puzzling 519
pyemia 655
pyjamas 225
Pylades and Oréstes 890
pylon 206
pyramid *heap* 72
 height 206
 point 253
pyramids
 billiards 840
pyre 363

pyriform 249
pyrology 282
pyromaniac 384, 504, 913
pyromancy 511
pyrometer 389
pyrotechnics 423
pyrotechny 382
Pyrrhic victory 814
pyrrhonism 487, 989
Pythagorean 953
Pythia *oracle* 513
Python, -ess 513
pyx *vessel* 191, 998
 temple 1000

Q

Q-boat 726
Q.C. 968
Q.E.D. 478
quack *cry* 412
 imposter 548
quackery
 falsehood 544
 want of skill 699
 affectation 855
quacksalver 548
quad 189
quadragesima 956
quadrangle
 four-sided 95
 precinct 182
 house 189
 angular 244
quadrant 244, 247
quadrate with 23
quadratic 95
quadrature
 four 95
 angle 244
quadrennial 95
quadrible 96
quadrifid 97
quadriga 95, 272
quadrilateral
 sides 236
 angles 244
quadrille 840
quadripartition 97
quadrisection 97
quadrivalent 95
quadroon 41
quadruped 366
quadruplet 96
quadruplex 96
quadruplication 96
quaere 461
quaff 298
 – the bitter cup 828
quaggy 345
quagmire
 marsh 345
 dirty 653
 difficult 704
quail 860, 862
quaint *odd* 83
 pretty 845
 ridiculous 853
quake *oscillate* 314
 shake 315
 cold 383
 fear 860

quakerish 826, 855
Quakerism 984
qualification
 [*see qualify*]
 power 157
 modification 469
 skill 698
 discount 813
qualify *change* 140
 modify 469
 deny 536
 teach 537
qualis ab incepto 141
qualities
 character 820
quality *nature* 5
 power 157
 tendency 176
 nobility 875
qualm *disbelief* 485
 unwilling 603
 fear 860
qualms of con-science 950
quamdiu se bene gesserit 108a
quand même
 compensating 30
 opposed 708
quandary 475, 704
quantity 25, 31, 102
quantum *amount* 25
 allotment 786
 – mutatus 140
 – sufficit 639
quaquaversum 278
quarantine 664, 751
quarrel 24, 713
 – with one's bread and butter
 bungling 699
 discontent 832
quarrelsome 901
quarry *object* 620
 mine 636
quart 97
quarter *cut up* 44
 fourth 95
 quadrisection 97
 period 108
 region 181
 locate 184
 abode 189
 side 236
 direction 278
 forbearance 740
 money 800
 mercy 914
 give – 914
 give no –
 kill 361
 severe 739
 pitiless 914a
 revenge 919
 – of a hundred 98
 – upon 184
quarter-day 138
quarter-deck 210
quarterly
 periodical 531
quartermaster 637
quartern 95
quarteron 41
quarters *abode* 189
 take up one's – 184

radically 31
radication 613
radio 532
radio-active 171
316
radio-activity 420
radio-graph 421,
554
radiogram
wireless 532
X-ray 554
radiometer 420, 445
radiomicrometer
389
radiophone 418
radio star 899
radiotelegraph 534
radiotelephone 534
radium 423
radius 200, 202
radix 153
radoter 499
radoteur 501
raff 653, 876
raffle 156
Raffles
thief 792
raft 273
rafter 215
rag 32
lease 830, 856,
929
ragamuffin 876
rage *violence* 173
influence 175
excitement 824,
825
fashion 852
desire 865
wrath 900
the battle -s 722
ragged 226
ragoût 41, 298
rag-picker 876
rags *clothes* 225
useless 645
do to - 384
tear to - 162
worn to - 659
ragtime 415, 473
raid 716, 791
rail *inclosure* 232
prison 752
- at 932
- in
circumscribe 229
restrain 751
railing 232
raillerie, ne pas en-
tendre - 900
raillery 856
railway 627
- speed 274
- station 292
raiment 225
rain *stream* 348
sufficient 639
- or shine 474,
604
rainbow 440
raincoat 225
rainless 340
rains but it pours,
never - 641
rainy day 735
provide against
a - 673, 817

rainy season 348
raise *increase* 35
produce 161
erect 212
elevate 307
excite 824
- alarm 860
- anger 900
- one's banner
722
- a cry 531
- a dust 682
- expectations 858
- the finger 550
- funds 775
- one's head
improve 658
refresh 689
prosperity 734
repute 873
- ghosts 992
- hope 511
- a hue and cry
against 932
- a laugh 840
- the mask 529
- money 788
- a question 461,
485
- a report 531
- a siege 723
- the spirits 836
- spirits from the
dead 992
- a storm 173
- troops 722
- up 212, 824
- the voice 441
- one's voice 535,
932
- the wind 775,
778
raised *convex* 250
raison:
- d'être 620
- de plus 467
raj 737
rajah 745
rajpoot 726
rake *drag* 285
gardening 371
clean 652
profligate 949
intemperance 954
libertine 962
- out 301
- up *collect* 72
extract 301
recall 505
excite 824
- up evidence 467
rake-hell 949, 962
raking-fire 716
rakish
intemperate 954
licentious 961
rallentando 415
rally *arrange* 60
improve 658
restore 660
ridicule 856
encourage 861
- round *order* 58
co-operate 709
rallying: - cry 550,
861
- point 74

ram *impulse* 276
sheep 366
male 373
man-of-war 726
milk the - 645
- down 261, 321
- in 300
Ramadan 956, 993
ramage 367
ramble *stroll* 266
wander 279
folly 499
delirium 503
digress 573
rambler 269
rambling 139
ramification *part* 51
bisection 91
posterity 167
filament 205
symmetry 242
divergence 291
rammer 263, 276
ramose 242
ramp *slope* 217
climb 305
leap 309
rampage 173
rampant
violent 173
prevalent 175
vertical 212
raised 307
free 748
vehement 825
licentious 961
rampart 717
ramrod 263
ramshackle 665
ranch 780
rancid 401, 653
rancor 907, 919
randan 273
random *casual* 156
carriage 272
uncertain 475
aimless 621
talk at -
sophistry 477
exaggerate 549
loquacity 584
- *experiment* 463
chance 621
range *extent* 26
collocate 60
series 69
term 71
class 75
space 180
distance 196
roam 266
direction 278
stove 386
freedom 748
out- 196
long - 196
within - 197
-finder 200
- itself 58
- under, - with 76
ranger
director 694
keeper 753
thief 792
rank *have place* 1
degree 26
thorough 31

collocate 60
row 69
term 71
vegetation 365
fetid 401
estimate 480
bad 649
soldiers 726
glory 873
nobility 875
mar-of - 875
- and file
continuity 69
soldiers 726
commonalty 876
- marks 745
rankle *unclean* 653
corrupt 659
painful 830
animosity 900
malevolence 907
revenge 919
ranks
fill up the - 660
risen from the -
876
ransack *seek* 461
deliver 672
plunder 791
price 812
atonement 952
- one's brains
451, 515
ransom 672
rant
unmeaning 517
exaggeration 549
diffuse style 573
turgescence 577
speech 582
acting 599
excitement 825
boasting 884
ranter *talker* 584
false piety 988
rantipole 458
rap *blow* 276
sound 406
trifle 643
money 800
not worth a - 804
- on the knuckles
angry 900
censure 932
punish 972
- out *affirm* 535
voice 580
speak 582
- out oaths 885,
908
rapacity
taking 789
stealing 791
avarice 819
greed 865
rape 791, 961
- oil 356
rapid 274
- slope 217
- strides
progress 282
velocity 274
- succession 136
rapids 348
rapier 727
rapine 791
rapparee 792

rappel 722
rapping, spirit -
992
rapport 9
rapports, sous tous
les - 494
rapprochement
714, 888
rapscallion 949
rapt *attention* 457
inattention 458
emotion 821
- in thought 451
raptorial 789, 791
rapture 827, 897
rapturous 827
rara avis
exceptional 83
good 648
famous 873
rare *exceptional* 83
few 103
infrequent 137
light 322
excellent 648
raree show 448, 840
rarefaction 194, 322
rari nantes 103
rarity 322
rasa, tabula - 552
rascal 941, 949
rascality 940
rase *obliterate* 552
rash
skin disease 655
reckless 863
rasher 204
rashness 863
rasp 330, 331
rasper *difficult* 704
rasure 552
rat *recant* 607
smell a -
discover 480a
doubt 485
rataplan 407
rat-a-tat 407
ratchet 253
rate *degree* 26
motion 264
measure 466
estimation 480
price, tax 812
abuse 932
at a great - 274
rath *early* 132
fort 717
rather 32, 643
have - 609
- good 651
have - not 867
ratification
confirm 467
affirm 488
consent 762
compact 769
ratio *relation* 9
degree 26
proportion 84
apportionment
786
ratiocination 476
ration *quantity* 25
food 298
provisions 637
allotment 786
short -s 956

interchange 148
assent 488
concord 714
retaliate 718
reciprocity 709
recision 38
recital 415
recitativo 415
recite
enumerate 85
speak 582
narrate 594
reck 459
reckless
careless 460
defiant 715
rash 863
recklessly profuse
818
reckon count 85
– among 76
– upon 484, 507
– with 807
– without one's
host
unskilful 699
fail 732
rash 863
reckoning
numeration 85
measure 466
expectation 507
payment 807
accounts 811
reward 973
day of – 919
out of one's – 704
reclaim restore 660
command 741
due 924
atonement 952
reclaimed
penitent 950
recline lie flat 213
depress 308
repose 687
– on 215
recluse 893
recognition
[see recognize]
courtesy 894
thanks 916
means of – 550
recognizable 446,
518
– by 550
recognizance 771
recognize see 441
attention 457
discover 480a
assent 488
know 490
remember 505
understand 518
permit 760
recognized
influential 175
customary 613
– maxim 496
recoil reaction 179
repercussion 277
reluctance 603
shun 623
from which
reason –s 471
– at hate 898
– from dislike 867

recollect 505
recommence 66
recommend 695,
931
– itself
approbation 931
recompense 790,
973
reconcile agree 23
pacify 723
content 831
forgive 918
– oneself to 826
recondite 519, 528
recondition 660,
790
reconnaissance 441
reconnoitre 441,
461
reconsideration 451
on – 658
reconstitute 660
reconstruct 660
reconvert 660
record 551
break the – 33
court of – 966
gramophone – 551
recorder 553
judge 967
recount 594
recoup 30, 790
recourse 677
recovery
improvement 658
reinstatement 660
getting back 775
restitution 790
– of strength 689
recreant
coward 862
base 940
knave 941
vicious 945
bad man 949
recreation 840
recrement 653
recriminate 932
recrimination 938
recrudescence 661
recruit strength 159
learner 541
provision 637
health 654
repair 658
reinstate 660
refresh 689
aid 707
auxiliary 711
soldier 726
beat up for –s
673, 707
rectangle 244
rectangular 214,
244
rectify
straighten 246
improve 658
re-establish 660
rectilinear 346
rectitude 939, 944
rector 694, 996
rectorship 995
rectory 1000
rectus in curiâ 946
reculer pour mieux
sauter 673, 702

reculons, à – 283
recumbent 213, 217
recuperation 790
recuperative 660
recur
repeat 104
frequent 136
periodic 138
– to the mind 505
– to 677
recure 660
recursion 292
recurvity 245
recusant
dissenting 489
denying 536
disobedient 742
refusing 764
impenitent 951
heterodox 984
red 434
paint the town –
840
turn – feeling 821
– book list 86
– coat 726
– cross 662
– flag 668
– hot great 31
violent 173
hot 382
emotion 821
excited 824
– letter 550, 883
–letter day
important 642
rest 687
amusement 840
celebration 883
– light 669
– rag to a bull 900
– republican 742
– tape 613
– tapist 694
– and yellow 439
redact 590, 658
redan 717
redargue 479
red cap 271
redden color 434
humble 879
angry 900
reddition
interpretation 522
restitution 790
redeem
compensate 30
substitute 147
reinstate 660
deliver 672
regain 775
restore 790
pay 807
atone 952
– from oblivion
505
– one's pledge
772, 926
Redeemer 976
redemption
[see redeem]
liberation 750
duty 926
salvation 976
red-handed
murder 361
in the act 680

guilty 947
redict 905
redingote 225
redintegrate 660
redintegratio
amoris 607
redivivus 660
redness 434
redolence
odor 398
fragrance 400
redouble
increase 35
duplication 90
repeat 104
redoubt 717
redoubtable 860
redound to
conduce 176
– one's honor
glory 873
approbation 931
honor 939
redress restore 660
remedy 662
reward 973
red-tape 694, 739
reduce lessen 36
– in number 103
weaken 160
contract 195
shorten 201
lower 308
subdue 731
discount 813
– to ashes 384
– to demonstra-
tion 478
– to a mean 29
– to order 60
– to poverty 804
– to powder 330
– the speed 275
– in strength 160
– to subjection 749
– to convert 144
– to writing 551
reduced [see reduce]
impoverished 804
– to the last ex-
tremity 665
– to a skeleton 659
– to straits 704
reductio ad absur-
dum 476, 479
reduction
[see reduce]
arithmetical 85
conversion 144
at a – 815
– of temperature
385
redundance
diffuseness 573
too much 641
redundancy 104
reduplication 19, 90
re-echo imitate 19
repeat 104
resonance 408
reechy 653
reed weak 160
pan 590
arrow 727
trust to a broken –
699

– instrument 417
reef slacken 275
shoal 346
danger 667
take in a – 664
double – topsails
664
reefer 269
reek gas 334
vaporize 336
liquid 337
hot 382
fester 653
reeking 339, 653
reel rock 314
agitate 315, 851
dance 840
– back yield 725
re-embody
junction 43
combination 48
re-enter 245
re-entrant angle
244
re-establish 660
re-estate 660
refashion 163
refect
strengthen 159
refection
meal 298
refreshment 689
(restoration 660)
refectory 191
refer to relate 9
include 76
attribute 155
cite 467
allude 521
take advice 695
referable 9, 155
referee
judgment 480
judge 967
reference
[see refer]
referendary 967
referendum 480,
609
ad – 461, 605
referrible 9, 155
refine clean 652
– upon 658
refined color 428
fashionable 852
refinement
discrimination
465
wisdom 498
elegance 578, 845
improvement 658
taste 850
over– 477
refit 660
reflect imitate 19
think 451
– dishonor 874
– light 420
– upon censure 932
reflecting 498
reflection 408, 453
reflector mirror 445
reflex copy 21
recoil 277
regressive 283
reflexion 21, 277
light 420

remainder 40
  corpse 362
  vestige 551
organic − 357
'remand *defer* 133
  order 741
remanet 40
remark *observe* 457
  affirmation 535
  worthy of − 642
remarkable
  great 31
  exceptional 83
  important 642
remarry 903
Rembrandtesque
  160
remediable, reme-
  dial 660, 662
remediless 859
remedy 660, 662
remembrance 505
remembrances 894
rememoration 505
remigration
  regression 283
  arrival 292
  egress 295
remind 505
  that −s me 134
reminiscence 505
remise 927a
remiss
  neglectful 460
  reluctant 603
  idle 683
  lax 738
remission
  cessation 142
  moderation 174
  laxity 738
  forgiveness 918
  exemption 927a
remit
  [*see* remission]
  − one's efforts 681
remittance 807
remittent
  periodic 138
remitter 790
remnant 40
remodel
  convert 144
  revolutionize 146
  improve 658
remonstrance 615,
  766, 932
remora *cohere* 46
  hindrance 706
remorse 950
remorseless 919
remote 10, 196
  − age 122
  − cause 153
  − future 121
remotest idea, not
  have − 491
remotion 270
remount 147
remove *subduct* 38
  term 71
  displace 185
  transfer 270
  recede 287
  depart 293
  dinner 298
  extract 301

school 541
  − the mask 529
removedness
  distance 196
remugient 412
remunerate 973
remunerative 644,
  775
renaissance 660
renascence 660
renascent 163
rencounter
  contact 199
  meeting 292
  fight 720
rend 44
  − the air 404, 411,
  839
  − the heart-strings
  830
render *convert* 144
  interpret 522
  give 784
  restore 790
  − an account
  inform 527
  describe 594
  − *hors de combat* 645
  − a service 644
rendering
  covering 223
rendezvous 72, 74
rendition
  interpretation 522
  restore 790
renegade
  convert 144
  turncoat 607
  fugitive 623
  apostate 941
renew *twice* 90
  repeat 104
  reproduce 163
  recollect 505
  improve 658
  restore 660
  − one's strength
  689
reniform 245
renitence
  counteraction 179
  hardness 323
  elasticity 325
  unwillingness 603
  resistance 719
renitency
  light 420
renounce
  recant 607
  relinquish 624
  resign 757
  abnegate 764
  − *property* 782
  repudiate 927
renovare dolorem,
  infandum − 833
renovate 160, 660
renovated *new* 123
renown 873
renownless 874
rent *tear* 44
  fissure 198
  hire 788
  purchase 795
rental 810
renter 188, 779
rent-free 815

rent-roll 780, 810
rents *houses* 189
renunciation
  [*see* renounce]
  exemption 927a
reorganize
  order 60
  convert 144
  improve 658
  restore 660
repair
  mend 658
  make good 660
  refresh 689
  out of − 659
reparation
  [*see* repair]
  compensation 30
  restitution 790
  atonement 952
  reward 973
repartee 462, 842
reparteeist 844
repartition 786
repass, pass and −
  314
repast 298
repatriation 790
repay 790, 807, 973
repeal 756
repeat *imitate* 19
  duplication 90
  iterate 104
  reproduce 163
  affirm 535
  − by rote 505
repeated 104, 136
repeater
  watch 114
  fire-arm 727
repel *repulse* 289
  deter 616
  defend 717
  resist 719
  refuse 764
  give pain 830
  disincline 867
  banish 893
  excite hate 898
repent 950
repercussion 277
répertoire 399
repertory 636
repetend
  arithmetical 84
  iteration 104
repetition 19, 104
repine
  pain 828
  discontent 832
  regret 833
  sad 837
replace
  substitute 147
  locate 184
  restore 660
replenish 52, 637
repletion
  filling 639
  redundance 641
  satiety 869
replevin
  recovery 775
  borrow 788
  restore 790
replica 21

replication
  answer 462
  law pleadings 969
reply 462, 937
répondre en
  Normand 544
report *noise* 406
  judgment 480
  inform 527
  publish 531
  news 532
  rumor 532
  record 551
  statement 594
  good − 873
  through evil re-
  port and good −
  604a
  − *progress* 527
reporter
  informant 527
  messenger 534
  recorder 553
  journalist 593,
  758
reports *law* 969
repose
  quiescence 265
  leisure 685
  rest 687
  − confidence in
  484
  − *on support* 215
  evidence 467
  − on one's laurels
  142
reposit 184
repository 636
repostum, manet
  alta mente −
  919
repoussé 250
reprehend 932
reprehensible 945,
  947
represent *similar* 17
  imitate 19
  exhibit 525
  intimate 527
  declare 535
  denote 550
  delineate 554
  commission 755
  deputy 759
  − to oneself 515
representation
  [*see* represent]
  copy 21
  portrait 554
  drama 599
representative
  typical 79
  commissioner 758
  deputy 759
  − *government* 737
  − of the people 696
  − of the press
  messenger 534
  writer 593
repress 751
  − one's feelings
  826
  − a smile 837
reprieve
  respite 133, 970
  deliverance 672
  release 750
  pardon 918

reprimand 932
reprint
  copy 21
  repetition 104
  reproduce 183
reprisal
  retaliation 718
  resumption 789
reprise 40a
reproach
  disgrace 874
  blame 932
  accusation 938
reprobate
  disapproved 932
  vicious 945
  bad man 949
  sinner 988
reprobation 932,
  988
reproduce
  imitate 19
  repeat 104
  renovate 163
reproduction [*see*
  reproduce] 21,
  163
reproductive 163
reproof 932
reprover 936
reptile
  animal 366
  servile 886
  knave 941
  miscreant 949
republic
  country 181
  people 372
  government 737
  − of letters 560
republican
  party 712
  government 737
  commonalty 876
republicanism 737
repudiate
  exclude 55
  deny 489
  reject 610
  abrogate 756
  violate 773
  not pay 808
  evade 927
repugn 719
repugnance
  incongruity 24
  resistance 719
  dislike 867
  hate 898
repulse *recoil* 277
  repel 289
  resist 719
  failure 732
  refusal 764
repulsion 157, 289
repulsive
  [*see* repulse]
  unsavory 395
  painful 830
  ugly 846
  disliked 867
  discourteous 895
  hateful 898
repurchase 795
reputable 873, 939
reputation 873
repute 873

request **765**
in - 630
- permission 760
requiem 839
requies, nec mora
nec - 682
requiescat in pace
363, 723
require
need 630
insufficient 640
exact 741
compel 744
price 812
due 924
duty 926
- explanation 519
requirement 630
requisite 630
requisition 741, 765
put in - *use* 677
order 741
requital
retaliation 918
gratitude 916
punishment 972
reward 973
reredos 1000
res ipsa loquitur
525
rescind *cut off* 44
abrogate 756
refuse 746
rescission 44, 756
rescript *answer* 462
transcript 590
letter 592
order 741, 963
rescriptive 761
rescue *preserve* 670
deliver 672
aid 707
research 461
- student 541
reseat 660
resection 44
reseda 435
resemblance 17, 21
resent 900
resentful 901
resentment **900**
reservation
location 184
concealment 528
mental – 477, 528
equivocation 520
untruth 546
with a - 38, 770
reservatory 191,
636
reserve
concealment 528
silence 585
choose 609
store 636
disuse 678
retain 781
shyness 881
in - *destined* 152
prepared 673
- forces 726
- oneself 881
reservoir 636
re-shape 140
resiance 189
resiant 186
reside 1, 186

residence 189
resident
consignee 758
present 186
inhabitant 188
residentiary 186,
188
clergy 996
residue 40
residuum
remainder 40
dregs 653
commonalty 876
resign 757, 782
- one's being 364
- one's breath 360
- oneself 725, 826
resignation [*see*
resign]
submission 725
obedience 743
-abdication 757
renunciation 782
endurance 826
humility 879
resile 277
resilience
regression 283
elasticity 325
resin 356a
resipiscence 950
resist *oppose* 179
withstand 719
disobey 742
refuse 764
resistance 719
résistance, pièce de
- 298
resister
passive – 710
resisting
tenacious 327
resistless 159, 601
resolute 604, 861
resolution
decomposition 49
conversion 144
music 413
topic 454
investigation 461
mental energy **604**
intention 620
scheme 626
courage 861
resolvable into 27,
144
resolve *change* 140
liquefy 335
investigate 461
discover 480a
interpret 522
determine 604
predetermine 611
intend 620
- into elements 49
- into *convert* 144
resonance 402, **408**
resorb 296
resort *assemble* 72
focus 74
dwelling 189
converge 290
last – 601
- to be *present* 186
travel 266
employ 677
resound *loud* 404

ring 408
- *praises* 931
resourceful 698
resources
means 632
property 780
wealth 803
respect *relation* 9
observe 772
fame 873
salutation 894
deference **928**
have – to 9
in no – 536
with – to 9
respectability
mediocrity 736
repute 873
probity 939
respectable
unimportant 643
respectful 928
- *distance* 623,
864
respective 79, 786
respectless 458
respects 894, 928
resperse 73
respicere finem 510
respire *breathe* 349
live 359
refresh 689
respite
intermission 106
defer 133
pause 142
deliver 672
repose 687
reprieve 970
resplendent
luminous 420
splendid 845
respond *accord* 23
answer 462
feel 821
respondent 462
accused 938
response
answer 462, **587**
concord 714
feeling 821
friendship 888
worship 990
responsible 177,
926
responsibility
upon one's own –
600
responsive 375
rest *remainder* 40
pause 141
cessation 142
support 215
quiescence 265
death 360
silence 403
inaction 681
repose 687
at – *repose* 687
content 831
home of – 189
set at –
answer 462
ascertain 474
complete 729
compact 769

set one's mind at –
calm 826
set the question
at – 478, 480
- assured 484, 858
on *support* 215
on one's oars
142, 687
- satisfied 831
- and be thankful
681, 687
- upon
evidence 467
confide 484
- with *duty* 926
restaurant 189
- *car* 272
restaurateur 637
restful 265
resting place
support 215
quiet 265
arrival 292
restitution **790**, 660
restive *averse* 603
obstinate 606
disobedient 742
refusal 764
perverse 901a
restless
changeable 149
moving 264
agitated 315
active 682
excited 825
fearful 860
restoration **660**
restorative
salubrious 656
remedial 662
relieving 834
restore *reinstate*
660
refresh 689
return 790
- equilibrium 27
- harmony 723
- to health 654
restrain 616, 706,
751
restrainable 743
restrained 751
restraint 578, **751**
self – 826, 953
restrict *hinder* 706
restrain 751
prohibit 761
restringency 751
result *remainder* 40
follow 117
effect 154
conclusion 480
completion 729
resultant 48, 154
resume *begin* 66
repeat 104
change 140
restore 660
take 789
résumé 596
resupination 213
resurgence 163, 660
resurrection
reproduction 163
restoration 660
heaven 981

resuscitate
reproduce 163
reinstate 660
retable 215
retail *distribute* **73**
inform 527
barter 794
sell 796
retailer 797
retain *stand* 150
keep 781
- the memory of
505
- one's reason 502
retainer 746
retake 789
retaliation **718**, 919
retard *later* 133
slower 275
hinder 706
retch 297
retection 529
retention **781**
retentive 781
- *memory* 505
reticence 528
reticle 219
reticulation 219,
248
reticule 191
retiform 219
retina 441
retinue *followers* 65
series 69
servants 746
retire *move back* 283
recede 287
resign 757
modest 881
seclusion 893
- into the shade
inferior 34
decrease 36
- from sight
disappear 449
hide 528
retiring
concave 252
- *color* 438
retold 104
retort
receptacle 191
vaporizer 336
boiler 386
answer 462
confutation 479
retaliation 718
wit 842
retouch *restore* 660
retoucher 559
retrace 505
- one's steps **607**
retract
recant 607
annul 756
abjure 757
violate 773
retreat
resort 74
withdraw 187
abode 189
regression **283**
recede 287
ambush 530
refuge 666
escape 671
give way **725**

beat a – 623
retreating
  concave 252
retrench *subduct* 38
  shorten 201
  lose 789
  economize 817
retribution
  retaliation 718
  payment 807
  punishment 972
  reward 973
retrieve *restore* 660
  acquire 775
retriever *dog* 366
retroaction
  counteraction 179
  recoil 277
  regression 283
retroactive
  past 122
retrocession
  regression 283
  recession 287
retrograde
  moving back 283
  deteriorated 659
  relapsing 661
retrogression
  regression 283
  deterioration 659
  relapse 661
retrospection
  past 122
  thought 451
  memory 505
retroussé 245
retroversion 218
retrude 289
return *list* 86
  repeat 104
  periodic 138
  reverse 145
  recoil 277
  regression 283
  arrival 292
  answer 462
  report 551
  relapse 661
  appoint 755
  profit 775
  restore 790
  proceeds 810
  reward 973
  in –
    compensation 30
  – the compliment
    interchange 148
    retaliate 718
  – to the original
    state 660
  –ed *prodigal* 950
  – thanks 916, 990
return game 104
return match 104
reunion *junction* 43
réunion
  assemblage 72
  concord 714
  lieu de – 74
  point de – 74
  social – 892
revamp 140
revanche, en – 718
reveal 529
  – itself 446
reveille 550

réveiller le chat qui
  dort, ne pas –
  668, 864
revel 840, 954
  – in *enjoy* 377
revelation
  disclosure 480a,
  529
  theological 985
  Revelations 985
reveller 840
  drunkard 959
revelling 59, 838
revendicate
  claim 741
  acquisition 775
  due 924
revenge 919
  breathe – 900
revenons à nos
  moutons 283,
  660
revenue 632, 810
reverberate 277,
  408
reverberatory 386
revere *love* 897
  respect 928
  piety 987
reverence *title* 877
  respect 928
  piety 987
  clergy 996
reverenced 500
reverend 877, 996
reverent 987, 990
reverential 928
reverie
  train of thought
  451
  inattention 458
  imagination 515
reversal 218, 607
reverse *contrary* 14
  inversion 218
  – *of a medal* 235
  anteposition 237
  adversity 735
  abrogate 756
  cards 840
  – of the shield 468
reverseless 150
reversible 605
reversion
  [*see reverse*]
  posterity 117
  return 145
  possession 777
  property 780
  succession 783
  remitter 790
reversioner 779
revert *repeat* 104
  return 145
  turn back 283
  revest 790
  – *to* 457
revest 790
revet 223
reviction 660
review *consider* 457
  inquiry 461
  judge 480
  recall 505
  periodical 531
  dissertation 595
  compendium 596

entertainment 599
revise 658
  parade 882
reviewer 480, 595
revile 932, 988
reviler 936
revise *copy* 21
  consider 457
  printing 591
  plan 626
  improve 658
revising barrister
  967
revision, under –
  673
revisit 186
revival
  reproduction 163
  restoration 660
  worship 990
revivalist 996
revive
  reproduce 163
  improve 658
  resuscitate 660
  excite 824
revivify
  reproduce 163
  life 359
  improve 658
  resuscitate 660
revocable 605
revoir, au – 293
revoke 607, 756
revolt *resist* 719
  disobey 742
  shock 830
  disapproval 932
  – against *hate* 898
  – at the idea
  dissent 489
revolting
  painful 830
revolution
  periodicity 138
  change 146
  rotation 312
  disobedience 742
revolutionize 140,
  146
revolve
  [*see revolution*]
  – in the mind 451
revolver 727
revue 599
  intimate – 599
revulsion
  reversion 145
  revolution 146
  inversion 218
  recoil 277
reward 973
reword 104
Reynard
  animal 366
  cunning 702
rez-de-chaussée
  191, 207
rhabdology 85
rhabdomancy 511
Rhadamanthus
  967, 982
rhapsodical
  irregular 139
  imaginary 515
rhapsodist
  fanatic 504

rhapsody
  discontinuity 70
  music 415
  nonsense 497
  fancy 515
  poetry 597
rhetoric *speech* 582
  flowers of – 577
rheum
  excretion 299
  fluidity 333
  water 337
rhino 800
rhinoceros hide
  376, 823
rhomb 244
rhumb 278
rhyme
  similarity 17
  verse 597
  without – or
    reason
    absurd 497
    caprice 608
    motiveless 615a
rhymeless 598
rhymester 597
rhythm
  periodicity 138
  melody 413
  elegance 578
  verse 597
rhythmical
  – *style* 578
rialto 799
rib *support* 215
  ridge 250
  wife 903
ribald *vulgar* 851
  disreputable 874
  impure 961
riband
  [*see ribbon*]
ribbed 259
ribbon *tie* 45
  filament 205
  record 550
  decoration 877
  –s *reins* 152
  handle the – 693
ribroast 972
rich *savory* 394
  color 428
  language 577
  abundant 639
  wealthy 803
  beautiful 845
  ornament 847
  – *man* 803
riches 803
richesses, embarras
  de – 641, 803
richly *much* 31
  – *deserve* 924
rick 72, 846
rickety *weak* 160
  ugly 846
  imperfect 651
rickshaw 272
ricochet 277
ricordo, non mi –
  506
rid *deliver* 672
  get – of *eject* 297
  liberation 750
  loose 776
  relinquish 782

riddance 672, 776,
  782
  good – 776
riddle *arrange* 60
  sieve 260
  secret 533
  clean 652
ride *get above* 206
  move 266
  break in 370
  – at anchor 265
  – full tilt at 622,
    716
  – hard 274
  – one's hobby 622
  – rough shod
    violence 173
    severity 739
    insolence 885
    illegality 964
  – out the storm
    664
  – and tie
    periodicity 138
    journey 266
  – the whirlwind
    604, 737
rideau, lever de –
  599
ridentem dicere
  verum 836, 842
rider *appendix* 39
  equestrian 268
rideret Heraclitus
  853
ridge *narrow* 203
  height 206
  prominence 250
ridicule 856, 929
ridiculous
  absurd 497
  foolish 499
  trifling 643
  grotesque 853
ridiculousness 853
riding *district* 181
  journey 266
ridotto 840, 892
rifacimento 104,
  660
rife *existence* 1
  general 78
  influence 175
riff-raff *dirt* 653
  commonalty 876
  bad folk 949
rifle *musket* 727
  plunder 791
  – *shot* 406
rifled cannon 727
rifleman 726
rifler 792
rifles 726
rifle-shooting 840
rift 44, 198
  – within the lute
    651, 713
rig *dress* 225
  prepare 673
  frolic 840
  strumpet 962
  – the market 794
  run the – *upon* 929
rigadoon 840
rigging *ropes* 45
  gear 225
  instrument 633

riggish 961

right *dextral* 238
  straight 246
  true 494
  property 780
  just 922
  privilege 924
  duty 926
  honor 939
  virtuous 944
  bill of - 969
  by - 924
  have a - to 924
  set - *inform* 527
    disclose 529
  that's - 981
  - about
    [*see below*]
  - ahead 234
  - angle 212
  - ascension 466
  - away 133
  step in the - direc-
    tion 644
  - hand [*see below*]
  - itself 660
  - and left 180,
    227, 236
  - line 246
  - man in the right
    place 23
  in one's - mind
    498, 502
  hit the - nail on
    the head 480*a*,
    698
  - owner 779
  keep the - path
    944
  in the - place 646
  - thing to do 926
  - as a trivet 650
  - word in the
    right place 578
right about: to
  the - 283
  go to the - 311,
    607
  send to the -
    eject 297
    reject 610
    refuse 764
  turn to the - 218,
    279
right hand
  power 157
  dextrality 238
  help 711
  not let the - know
    what the left is
    doing 528
  - of friendship 888
righteous 944
  the - 987
  - overmuch 988
Righteousness:
  Lord our - 976
  Sun of - 976
rightful 922
  - owner 779
rightly served, be
  972
right-minded 939,
  944
rights 748
  put to - 660
  set to - 60

stand on one's -
  748
rigid *regular* 82
  hard 323
  exact 494
  severe 739
rigmarole 517, 573
rigor 383
  - *mortis* 360
rigorous *exact* 494
  severe 739
  revengeful 919
rigor 494, 739
Rigsdag 696
rigueur
  de - 744
rile *annoy* 830
  hate 898
  anger 900
rilievo *convex* 250
  sculpture 557
rill 348
rim 231
rime *chink* 198
  frost 383
rimer 262
rimple 258
rind 223
ring
  fastening 45
  pendency 214
  circle 247
  loud 404
  resonance 408
  test 463
  combination 709
  clique 712
  arena 728, 840
  badge 747
  rub the - 992
  have the true -
    494
  - the changes
    repeat 104
    change 140
    changeable 149
  - in the ear 408
  in a - fence 229,
    232
  - with the praises
    of 931
  - the tocsin 669
  - up 527
ringleader
  director 694
  mutineer 742
ringlet 247, 256
rink 840
rinse 652
rinsings 653
riot *confusion* 59
  derangement 61
  violence 173
  discord 713
  resist 719
  mutiny 742
  run - *activity* 682
    excitement 825
    intemperance 954
  - in *pleasure* 742
rioter 742
riotous 173
rip 949, 962
  - open 260
  - up *tear* 44
  recall the past 505
  excite 824

Rip van Winkle
  130
riparian 342
ripe 673
  - *age old* 128
ripen *perfect* 650
  improve 658
  prepare 673
  complete 729
  - into 144
rippet 713
riposte 462
ripple *ruffle* 256
  shake 315
  water 348
  murmur 405
ripuarian 342
rire, pour - 853
rise *grow* 35
  begin 66
  slope 217
  progress 282
  ascend 305
  stir 682
  revolt 742
  - again 660
  - in arms 722
  - from 154
  - to the occasion
    612
  - in price 814
  - up *elevation* 307
  - in the world 734
risible 838, 853
rising [*see rise*]
  - of the curtain
    66, 448
  - generation 127,
    167
  - ground
    height 206
    slope 217
  worship the - sun
    886
risk *chance* 621
  danger 665
  invest 787
  at any - 604
risqué 961
rissole 298
risum teneatis
  amici? 853
rite 963, 998
  funeral - 363
ritornello 64, 104
ritual
  ostentation 882
  rite 998
ritualism 984
rival
  emulate 648
  oppose 708
  opponent 710
  compete 720
  combatant 726
  outshine 873
rivalry *envy* 921
rive 44
rivel 258
river 348
rivet 43, 45
  - the attention
    457, 824
  - the eyes upon
    441
  - in the memory
    505

- the yoke 739
riveted *firm* 150
rivulet 348
rixation 713
Ro 560
road *street* 189
  direction 278
  way 627
  on the -
    transference 270
    progression 282
    approach 286
  on the high - to
    278
  - to ruin
    destruction 162
    danger, 665
    adversity 735
road-book 266
roads *lake* 343
roadstead 154
  abode 189
  refuge 666
roadster 271
roadway 627
roam 266
roan *horse* 271
  color 433
roar *violence* 173
  wind 349
  sound 404, 407
  bellow 411, 412
  laugh 838
  weep 839
roaring *great* 31
  - *trade* 731, 734
roast *heat* 384
  ridicule 856
  rib - 972
  - and boiled 298
  - an ox 883
rob 354, 791
robber 792
robbery 791
robe 225, 999
robes - of state 747
Robin Goodfellow
  980
Robinson
  say Jack - 132
Robot 554
robust *strong* 159,
  654
roc 83
rocaille 853
rock *firm* 150
  oscillate 314
  hard 323
  land 342
  safety 664
  danger 667
  build on a - 150
  founded on a -
    664
  split upon a - 732
  - ahead 665
  -bound coast 342
  - oil 356
rocket *rapid* 274
  rise 305
  light 423
  ship 273
  signal 550
  arms 727
  fireworks 840
  go up like a - and
    come down like

  the stick 732
rocking-chair 215
rococo 124, 853
rod *support* 215
  measure 466
  scourge 975
  divining 993
  kiss the - 725
  sounding - 208
  - of empire 747
  - in pickle
    prepared 673
    accusation 938
    punishment 972
    scourge 975
rodeo 720, 840
rodomontade
  exaggeration 482
  unmeaning 517
  boast 884
roe 366, 374
Roentgen rays 420
rogation
  request 765
  worship 990
rogue *cheat* 548
  knave 941
  scamp 949
  -'s march 297
roguery 940
roguish
  playful 840
Roi le veut, le -
  741
roister 885
roisterer 887
Roland for an
  Oliver
  retaliation 716
  revenge 719
  barter 794
rôle *drama* 599
  business 625
  plan 626
  conduct 692
roll *list* 86
  fillet 205
  convolution 248
  rotundity 249
  make smooth 255
  move 264
  fly 267
  rotate 312
  rock 314
  flow 384
  sound 407
  record 551
  money 800
  strike off the -
    756, 972
  - along 312
  - in the dust 731
  - on the ground
    839
  - of honour 86
  - in 639, 641
  - on 109
  - into one 43
  - in riches 803
  - up 312
  - up in 225
  - in wealth 803
roll-call 85
roller *fillet* 45
  round 249
  clothing 255
  rotate 312

roller-coaster 840
rollers *billows* 348
rollick 836
rollicker 838
rollicking
　frolicsome 836
　blustering 885
rolling: – pin 249
　– stock 272
　– stone 312
Rolls: Master of
　the –
　recorder 553
　judge 967
　– Court 966
Roman candle 840
Roman Catholic
　984
romance
　music 415
　absurdity 697
　imagination 515
　untruth 546
　fable 594
Romanism 984
romantic
　imaginative 515
　art 556
　sensitive 822
romanticism 515
Romanus sum,
　civis – 924
Romany 563
Rome: Church of
　984
　do at – as the –
　Romans do 82
romp *violent* 173
　game 840
rondeau *music* 415
　poem 597
rondel 597
rondolette 597
rood *area* 180
　cross 998
　– loft 1000
roof 189, 223
roofless 226
rook 791, 792
rookie 726
rookery *nests* 189
　dirt 653
room *occasion* 134
　space 180
　lodge 186
　chamber 191
　plea 617
　assembly – 840
　in the – of 147
　make – for
　opening 260
　respect 928
roommate 890
rooms
　lodgings 189
roomy 180
roost 189
　rule the – 737
rooster 366
root *algebraic* – 84
　cause 153
　place 184
　abide 186
　base 211
　etymon 562
　lie at the – of 642
　pluck up by the

– s 301
strike at the – of
　716
take –
　influence 175
　locate 184
　habit 613
　– and branch 52
　cut up – and
　branch 162
　– out *eject* 297
　extract 301
　discover 480a
rooted
　old 124
　firm 150
　located 184
　habit 613
　deep – 820
　– antipathy 867
　– belief 484
rope *fastening* 45
　cord 205
　freedom 749
　scourge 975
　give – enough 738
　– 's end 975
　– of sand
　incoherence 47
　weakness 160
　impossible 471
　– way 627
rope-dancer 700
rope-dancing 698
ropy 352
roquelaure 225
roric 339
rosa, sub – 528
rosary 990, 998
Roscius 599
rose *pipe* 350
　fragrant 400
　red 434
　beauty 845
　bed of – s 377, 734
　couleur de –
　red 434
　good 648
　prosperity 734
　hope 858
　under the – 528
　welcome as the – s
　in May 829, 892
roseate *red* 434
　hopeful 858
rose-colored
　hope 858
rose-water
　moderation 174
　flattery 933
　not made with –
　704
Rosicrucian
　sect 984
　sorcerer 994
rosin *rub* 331
　resin 356a
Rosinante 271
roster 86
rostrum *beak* 234
　pulpit 542
rosy 434
　– wine 959
rosy-cheeked 845
rot *decompose* 49

absurdity 497
rubbish 517
putrefy 653
disease 655
decay 659
rota 86, 138
Rotarian 892
rotate 138
rotation 312
　periodicity 138
rote, by – 505
　know – 490
　learn – 539
rôti 298
rôtisserie 189
rotogravure 531,
　558
rotten *weak* 160
　bad 649
　foul 653
　decayed 659
　– at the core
　deceptive 545
　diseased 655
　– borough 893
rotulorum, custos –
　553
rotund 249
rotunda 189
rotundity 249
roturier 876
roué 949
rouge 434, 847
rouge-et-noir 621
rough *violent* 173
　shapeless 241
　uneven 256
　pungent 392
　unsavory 395
　sour 397
　sound 410
　unprepared 674
　fighter 726
　ugly 846
　low fellow 876
　bully 887
　churlish 895
　evil-doer 913
　bad man 949
　cut up – 900
　– copy *writing* 590
　unprepared 674
　– diamond
　uncouth 241
　unprepared 674
　artless 703
　vulgar 851
　commonalty 876
　good man 948
　– draft 626
　– guess 514
　– it 686
　– sea 348
　– side of the
　tongue 932
　– and tumble 59
　– weather 173, 349
rough-cast 256
　covering 223
　shape 240
　scheme 626
　unpolished 674
rough-hew 240, 673
roughly
　nearly 197
rough-neck 876,
　887

roughness 256
rough-rider 268
roughshod over,
　ride – 739
roulade 415
rouleau
　assemblage 72
　cylinder 249
　money 800
roulette 621, 840
round *series* 69
　revolution 138
　– of a ladder 215
　curve 245
　circle 247
　rotund 249
　music 415
　fight 720
　all – 227
　bring – 660
　come –
　periodic 138
　recant 607
　persuade 615
　dizzy – 312
　get – 660
　go – 311
　go one's – s 266
　go the –
　publication 531
　make the – of 311
　run the – of 682
　go the same – 104
　turn – *invert* 218
　retreat 283
　revolve 311
　– assertion 535
　– a corner 311
　– dance 840
　– game 840
　– hand 590
　– like a horse in a
　mill 613
　– of the ladder 71
　– number 84, 102
　in – numbers 29,
　197
　– pace 274
　– of pleasures
　377, 840
　– robin
　information 527
　petition 765
　censure 932
　– and round 138,
　312
　– sum 800
　– terms 566
　– trot 274
　– up 370
　– of visits 892
round about
　circumjacent 227
　deviation 279
　circuit 311
　amusement 840
　– phrases 573
　– way 729
rounded periods
　577, 578
roundelay 597
rounders 840
round-house 752
roundlet 247
round-shouldered
　243
roup 796

rouse 615, 824
　– oneself 682
rousing 171
rout *crowd* 72
　agitation 315
　overcome 731
　discomfit 732
　rabble 876
　assembly 892
　put to the – 731
　– out 652
route 627
　en – 270
　en – for 282
routine
　uniform 16
　order 58
　rule 80
　periodic 138
　custom 613
　business 625
rove *travel* 266
　deviate 279
rover *traveller* 268
　pirate 792
roving commission
　475
row *disorder* 59
　series 69
　violence 173
　street 189
　navigate 267
　discord 713
　– in the same
　boat 88
rowdy *vulgar* 851,
　876
　blusterer 887
　bad man 949
rowel 253, 615
rower 269
rowlock 215
royal 737
　– blue 438
　– highness 877
　– road 627, 705
Royal Academician
　559
royalist 737
royaliste que le roi,
　plus 33
royalty 737
Rt. Hon. 877
ruade *impulse* 276
　attack 716
rust *coelum* 908
rub *friction* 331
　touch 379
　difficulty 704
　adversity 735
　painful 830
　– off corners 82
　– down *lessen* 195
　powder 330
　– down with an
　oaken towel 972
　– one's eyes 870
　– one's hands 838
　– up the memory
　505
　– off 552
　– on *slow* 275
　progress 282
　inexcitable 826
　– out 552
　– up 658
　– up the *wrong*

way 713
rubadub 407
rubber 325
  whist 840
rubber boots 225
rubber hose 975
rubber-stamp 82
rubbish
  absurdity 497
  unmeaning 517
  trifling 643
  useless 645
rubble 645
rube 876
rubescence 434
Rubicon *limit* 233
  pass the –
  begin 66
  cross 303
  choose 609
rubicund 434
rubify 434
rubigo 653
rubric 550, 697, 998
rubricate
  redden 434
ruby *red* 434
  gem 648
  ornament 847
ruck 29, 258
  in the – 235
rucksack 191
ructation 297
rudder 273, 693
rudderless 158
ruddle 434
ruddy *red* 434
  beautiful 845
rude *violent* 173
  shapeless 241
  ignorant 491
  inelegant 579
  ugly 846
  vulgar 851
  uncivilized 876
  uncivil 895
  disrespect 929
  – *health* 654
radera 645
radiment 66, 153
rudimental 193,
  674
rudimentary 66
rudiments 490, 542
rudis indigestaque
  moles 59, 241
rue *bitter* 395
  regret 833
  repent 950
rueful 830, 837
ruff 225
ruffian 876
  blusterer 876
  maleficent 913
  scoundrel 949
ruffianism 851, 907
ruffle *disorder* 59
  derange 61
  roughen 259
  fold 258
  feeling 821
  excite 824, 825
  pain 830
  anger 900
rufous 434
rug 215, 223
Rugby

football 840
rugged
  shapeless 241
  rough 256
  difficult 704
  ugly 846
  churlish 895
rugose 256
ruin *destruction* 162
  evil 619
  failure 732
  adversity 735
  poverty 804
ruined
  bankrupt 808
  hopeless 859
ruinous
  painful 830
ruins *remains* 40
rule *mean* 29
  regularity 80
  influence 175
  length 200
  measure 466
  decide 480
  custom 613
  precept 697
  government 737
  law 963
  absence of – 699
  as a – 613
  by – 82
  golden – 697
  obey *a* 82
  – of three 85
  – of thumb
  experiment 463
  unreasoning 477
  essay 675
  unskilled 699
ruler 745
ruling 697, 969
  – *passion* 606, 820
rum *liquor* 298
  queer 853
  – *running* 964
rumba 840
rumble 407
ruminate
  chew 298
  think 451
rummage 461
rummer 191
rumor 531, 532
rump 235
rumple
  disorder 59
  derange 61
  roughen 256
  fold 258
rumpus
  confusion 59
  violence 173
  discord 713
run *generality* 78
  repetition 104
  continuance 106,
  143
  course 109
  eventuality 151
  motion 264
  speed 274
  sequence 281
  liquefy 335
  flow 348
  habit 613
  smuggle 791

contraband 964
  have a – 852, 873
  have – of 748
  near – 197
  ordinary – 29
  race is – 729
  time –s 106
  – abreast 27
  – after 622, 873
  – against 276,
  708, 716
  – at 716
  – away 623
  – away with 789,
  791
  – away with a
  notion
  misjudge 481
  credulous 486
  – back 283
  – a chance
  probable 472
  chance 621
  – counter to 468,
  708
  – its course
  course 109
  complete 729
  past 122
  – into danger 665
  – into debt 806
  – down
  underestimate 483
  pursue 622
  bad 649
  finished 678
  attack 716
  depreciate 932
  detract 934
  – dry 638, 640
  – the eye over
  441, 539
  – the fingers over
  379
  – foul of 276
  – the gauntlet 861
  – on in a groove
  613
  – hard *danger* 665
  difficult 704
  success 731
  – in the head 451,
  505
  – high *great* 31
  violent 173
  – in *introduce* 228
  – into
  conversion 144
  insert 300
  – low 36
  – of luck 156, 734
  – mad 503, 825
  – mad after 865
  – like mad 274
  – of the mill 29
  – amuck
  violent 173
  kill 361
  mad 503
  attack 716
  – on 143
  – out *end* 67
  course 109
  past 122
  antiquated 124
  egress 295
  prodigal 818

  – out on 573
  – over *count* 85
  – in the mind 451
  examine 457
  describe 594
  synopsis 596
  overflow 641
  – in pairs 17
  – parallel 178
  – into port 664
  – a race *speed* 274
  conduct 692
  contend 720
  – in a race
  act 680
  he that –s may
  read 525
  – a rig 840
  – the rig upon 929
  – riot *violent* 173
  exaggerate 549
  redundance 641
  active 682
  disobey 742
  intemperance 954
  – a risk 665
  – rusty 603
  – to seed 128, 659
  – smooth 705, 734
  – a tilt at 716, 720
  – of things 151
  – through
  uniform 16
  influence 175
  be present 186
  kill 361
  expend 809
  prodigal 818
  – up *increase* 35
  build 161
  – up an account
  credit 805
  debt 806
  charge 812
  – up bills 808
  – upon 630
  – upon a bank
  808, 809
  – to waste 638
  – wild 173
run-about 272
runagate
  fugitive 623
  disobey 742
  bad man 949
runaway 623
rundle *circle* 247
  convolution 248
  rotundity 249
rundlet 191
Runes *writing* 590
  poetry 597
  spell 993
rung 215
runnel 348
runner *branch* 51
  courier 268
  messenger 534
running
  continuous 69
  the mind – upon
  451
  the mind – upon
  other things 458
  – account 811
  – commentary 595
  – fight 720

  – hand 590
  – over 641
  – water 348
runnion 949
runt 193
rupture
  disjunction 44
  quarrel 713
rural 189, 371
  – *dean* 893
ruralist 893
rus in urbe 189, 893
ruse 545, 702
Rush, Friar 980
rush *crowd* 72
  violence 173
  velocity 274
  water 348
  plant 367
  trifle 643
  haste 684
  make a – at 716
  – to a conclusion
  481, 486
  – on destruction
  863
  – in medias res
  604
  – into print 591
  – upon 622
rushlight *dim* 422
  candle 423
rusk 298
Russe, montagne –
  480
russet
  brown 433
  red 434
Russian
  – ballet 840
  – bath 386, 652
rust *red* 434
  decay 659
  canker 663
  inaction 683
  moth and – 659
  – of antiquity 122
rustic
  village 189
  agricultural 371
  vulgar 851
  clown 876
rusticate
  punish 972
  seclude 893
rusticity
  impolite 895
rusticus expectat
  dum defluat
  amnis 858
rustle 405, 407, 409
rustling 791
rusty *dirty* 653
  decayed 659
  sluggish 683
  unskilful 699
  sulky 901a
  run – *averse* 603
rut *rule* 80
  furrow 259
  habit 613
  in a – 16
ruth 914
ruthless
  savage 907
  pitiless 914a
  revengeful 919

at – 341
  uncertain 475
  erroneous 495
go to – 293
on the high –s 41
heavy – 315
the seven –s 341
  – of doubt 475
  – of troubles
  difficulty 704
  adversity 735
seaboard 342
seafarer 269
seafaring 267, 273
sea-fight 720
sea-girt 346
sea-going 267, 341
sea-green 435
seal
  matrix 22
  close 261
  evidence 467
  mark 550
  resolve 604
  complete 729
  compact 769
  security 771
  break the – 529
  under – 769
  – the doom of 162
  – one's infamy 940
  – the lips 585
  – of secrecy 528
  – up *restrain* 751
sealed:
  one's fate is – 601
  hermetically – 261
  – book
  ignorance 491
  unintelligible 519
  secret 533
sealing-wax 747
seals *insignia* 747
sealskin 223
seam 43
sea-maid 979
sea-man 269
seamanship 692, 698
sea-mark 550
seamless 50
seamstress 225, 690
seamy side 651
séance 525, 696
sea-piece 556
seaplane 273, 736
sea-port 666
sear *dry* 340
  burn 384
  deaden 823
  – and yellow leaf 128, 659
search *inquire* 461
searching
  severe 739
  painful 830
searchless 519
searchlight 423, 726
seared conscience 951
searing 830
seascape 556
sea-serpent 83
seaside 342
season *mix* 41

time 106
  pungent 392
  accustom 613
  preserve 670
  prepare 673
seasonable 23, 134
seasoning 393
seasons 138
seat *place* 183
  locate 184
  abode 189
  support 215
  posterior 235
  parliament 693
  country – 189
  judgment – 966
  – of government 737
  – of war 728
seated, firmly – 150
seaway 180
seaweed 367
seaworthy 273, 604
sebaceous 355
secant 219
secede *dissent* 489
  relinquish 624
  disobey 742
seceder
  heterodox 984
secern 297
seclusion 893
second
  duplication 90
  – of *time* 108
  instant 113
  – in *music* 413, 415
  abet 707
  play or sing a – 416
  – best 651, 732
  – childhood 128, 499
  – crop 168, 775
  – edition 104
  play – fiddle
  obey 743
  subject 749
  disrepute 874
  – nature 613
  – to none 33
  one's – self 17
  – rate 659
  – sight
  foresight 510
  sorcery 992
  – thoughts
  sequel 65
  thought 451
  improvement 658
  – youth 660
secondary
  inferior 34
  following 63
  imperfect 651
  deputy 759
  – education 537
  – evidence 467
  – school 542
seconder 711
second-hand
  imitation 19
  old 124
  deteriorated 659
  received 785
secondly 90

second-rate 651
secret *key* 522
  latent 526
  hidden 528
  riddle 533
in the – 490
keep a – 585
  – motive 615
  – passage 627, 671
  – place 530
  – writing 590
secrétaire 191
secretary
  recorder 553
  writer 590
  director 694
  auxiliary 711
  servant 746
  consignee 758
  – of state 694
  – of the treasury 801
secrete *excrete* 297
  conceal 528
secretion 299
secretive 528
sect 75
  religious – 983, 984
sectarian
  dissent 489
  ally 711
  heterodox 984
sectary 489
section *division* 44
  part 51
  class 75
  chapter 593
  troops 726
sector *part* 51
  circle 247
secula seculorum,
  in – 112
secular
  centenary 98
  periodic 138
  laity 997
  – education 537
secularism 984
secundum artem 82, 698
secure *fasten* 43
  bespeak 132
  belief 484
  safe 664
  restrain 751
  engage 768
  gain 775
  confident 858
  – an object 731
securities 802–805
security *safely* 664
  pledge 771
  hope 858
  lend on – 787
Sedan
  disaster 162
sedan chair 272
sedate
  thoughtful 451
  calm 826
  grave 837
sedative 174, 662
sedentary 265
sedge 367
sedile 1000
sediment *dregs* 653

sedimentary 40
sedition 742
seduce *entice* 615
  love 897
  debauch 961
seducer 962
seduction 829, 865
sedulous 682, 865
see *view* 441
  look 457
  believe 484
  know 490
  bishopric 995
we shall – 507
  – after 459
  – daylight 480a
  – double 959
  – fit 600, 602
  – at a glance 498
  – justice done 922
  – life 840
  – the light
  born 359
  published 531
  – service 722
  – sights 455
  – through 480a, 498
  – to *attention* 457
  care 459
  direction 693
  – one's way
  foresight 510
  intelligible 518
  skill 698
  easy 705
seed *small* 32
  cause 153
  posterity 167
  grain 330
  run to – *age* 128
  lose health 659
  sow the – 673
seedling 129
seed-plot 168, 371
seed-time of life 127
seedy *weak* 160
  disease 655
  deteriorated 659
  exhausted 688
  needy 804
seeing that 8, 476
seek *inquire* 461
  pursue 622
  offer 763
  request 765
  – safety 664
seek-sorrow 837
seel 217
seem 448
  as it –s good to 600
seeming 488
seemingly 472
seemless 846, 925
seemliness 926
seemly
  expedient 646
  handsome 845
  due 924
seep 295
seer *veteran* 130
  madman 504
  oracle 513
  sorcerer 994
see-saw 12, 314

seethe *wet* 339
  hot 382
  make hot 384
  excitement 824
seething caldron 386
segar 392
segment 44, 51
segnitude 683
s'égosiller 411
segregate
  not related 10
  separate 44
  exclude 55
segregated
  incoherent 47
seigneur, grand –
  pride 878
  insolence 885
seignior 745, 875
seigniority
  authority 737
  possession 777
  property 780
seigniory 737
seine net 232
seisin 777, 780
seismic 314
seismograph 553
seismometer 276, 314
seize 789, 791
  – an opportunity 134
seized with
  disease 655
  feeling 821
seizure 925
sejunction 44
seldom 137
select *choose* 609
  good 648
self 13, 79
  -abasement 879
  -accusing 950
  -admiration 880
  -applause 880
  -appointed task 602
  -assertion 885
  -called 565
  -command 604, 864
  -communing 451
  -complacency 836, 880
  -confidence 880
  -conquest 604
  -conscious 855
  -consultation 451
  -contained 52
  -control 604
  -conviction
  belief 484
  penitent 950
  condemned 971
  -counsel 451
  -deceit *error* 495
  -deception 486
  -defence 717
  -delusion 486
  -denial
  disinterested 942
  temperance 953
  penance 990
  -discipline 990
  -effacement 879,

942
-esteem 880
-evident 474, 525
-examination 990
-existing 1
-government 748
-help 698
-immolation 991
-indulgence
  selfishness 943
  intemperance 954
-interest 943
-knowledge 881
-love 943
-luminous 423
-mastery 604
-opinioned 481
-possession
  sanity 502
  resolution 604
  inexcitability 826
  caution 864
-praise 880
-preservation 717
-reliance
  resolution 604
  hope 858
  courage 861
-reproach 950
-respect 878
-restraint 953
-sacrifice 942
-satisfied 880
-seeking 943
-styled 565
-sufficient 880
-taught 490
-tormentor 837
-will 606
selfishness 943
self-same 13
sell *convince* 484
  absurdity 497
  deception 545
  untruth 546
  sale 796
  - for 812
  - one's life dearly 719, 722
  - off 796
  - oneself 940
  - out 796
seller 796
selon les règles 82
selvedge 231
semaphore 550
semblance
  similarity 17
  imitation 19
  copy 21
  probability 472
  wear the - of
  appearance 448
semeiology 522
semeiotics 550
semester 108
semi- 91
semi-barbarian 913
semibreve 413
semicircle 247
semicircular 245
semicolon 142
semi-diaphanous 427
semi-fluid 352
semi-liquidity 352
semi-lunar 245

seminal 153
seminary 542
semination 673
semi-opaque 427
semi-pellucid 427
semiquaver 413
semitone 413
semi-transparency 427
sempervirent 110
sempiternal 112
sempstress 225, 690
senary 98
senate 696
senate-house 966
senator 695, 696
senatorship 693
senatus consultum 741
send 270, 284
  - adrift 597
  - away
  repel 289
  eject 297
  refuse 764
  - for 741
  - forth 284, 531
  - a letter to 592
  - off 284
  - out *eject* 297
  - packing 289
  commission 755
  - word 527
senescence 128
seneschal
  director 694
  master 745
  servant 746
seneschalship 737
senile 128
senility 158, 659
senior *age* 128
  student 541
  master 745
seniores priores 62, 380
seniority 124, 128
sennight 108
señor 373, 877
señora 374
sensation
  physical sensibility 375
  emotion 821
  wonder 870
sensational 574, 824
sensation drama 599
sensations of touch 380
sense 498, 516
  deep - 821
  horse - 498
  in no - 565
  accept in a particular - 522
  - of duty 926
senseless
  insensible 376
  absurd 497
  foolish 499
  unmeaning 517
senses
  external - 375
  intellect 450
  sanity 502

sensibility 375, 822
sensible
  material 316
  wise 498
sensitive 375, 822
sensorial 821
sensorium 450
sensual 377, 954
sensualist 954a
sensuous
  sensibility 375
  pleasure 377
  feeling 821
sentence
  decision 480
  maxim 496
  affirmation 535
  phrase 566
  condemnation 971
sententious 572, 574
sentient 375, 821
sentiment 453
sentimental
  sensitive 822
  affected 855
sentinel } 263
sentry }
  guardian 664
  watch 668
  keeper 753
separate *disjoin* 44
  exclude 55
  bisect 91
  diverge 291
  divorce 905
  - the chaff from the wheat
  discriminate 465
  select 609
  - into elements 49
  - maintenance 905
separation 49
separatist 489, 984
sepia 433
seposition 44, 55
sepoy 726
sept *kin* 11
  class 75
  clan 166
Septentrional 237
septett 415
septic 655, 657
septicemia 655
septuagenarian 98
Septuagint 985
septum 228
sepulcher 363
  whited - 545
sepulchral
  interment 363
  resonance 408
  stridor 410
  hoarse 581
sepulture 363
sequacious 63
sequacity *soft* 324
  tenacity 327
sequel 65, 117
sequela 65, 154
sequence
  - *in order* 63
  - *in time* 117
  motion 264
  logical - 476
sequent 63
sequester 789, 974

sequestered 893
sequestrate
  seize 789
  condemn 971
  confiscate 974
sequin 847
serac 383
seraglio 961
seraph 948, 977
seraphic
  blissful 829
  virtuous 944
  pious 987
seraphina 417
seraskier 745
sere and yellow leaf 128
serein 339, 348
serenade *music* 415
  compliment 894
  endearment 902
serene
  pellucid 425
  calm 826
  content 831
  imperturbable 871
  - highness 877
serf *slave* 746
  clown 876
serfdom 749
sergeant 745
serial
  continuous 69
  periodic 183
  book 593
seriatim
  in order 58
  continuously 69
  each to each 79
  slowly 275
series 69, 84
sérieux, take au - 843
serio-comic 853
serious *great* 31
  resolved 604
  important 642
  dejected 837
seriously 535
serjeant:
  common - 967
  -at-law 968
sermon *lesson* 537
  speech 582
  dissertation 595
  pastoral 998
  funeral - 363
sermonizer 584
seroon 72
serosity 333, 337
serpent
  tortuous 248
  snake 366
  hiss 409
  wind instrument 417
  wise 498
  deceiver 548
  cunning 702
  evil-doer 913
  knave 941
  demon 949
  the old - 978
  great sea - 515
serpentine 248
serrated 244, 257
serried 72, 321

serum 333, 337
servant *instrumentality* 631
  help 711
  retainer 746
  - of all work 690
serve *benefit* 618
  business 625
  utility 644
  aid 707
  warfare 722
  obey 743
  servant 746
  - an apprenticeship 539
  - faithfully 743
  - loyally 743
  - notice 527
  - out 972
  - one right *retaliation* 718
  right 922
  punish 972
  - as a substitute 147
  - one's turn 644
  - with a writ 969
service *good* 618
  utility 644
  use 677
  warfare 722
  servitude 749
  worship 990
  rite 998
  hold - 363
  at one's - 763
  press into the - 677
  render a - 644, 906
serviceable 644, 648
serviette 652
servile 749, 876, **886**
servitor 746
servitorship 749
servitude 749
  penal - 972
sesame, open - 260
  watchword 550
  spell 993
sesqui- 87
sesquipedalia verba 577
sesquipedalian 200
sess 812
sessile 46
session *council* 696
sessions *law* 966
sestet 597
set
  condition 7
  join 43
  coherence 46
  group 72
  class 75
  firm 150
  tendency 176
  place 184
  form 240
  sharpen 253
  direction 278
  go down 306
  dense 321
  stage 599
  habit 613
  prepare **673**
  gang 712

trill 407
music 416
dissuade 616
injure 659
impress 821
excited 824
fear 860
- one's faith 485
- hands
pacification 723
friendship 888
courtesy 894
forgive 918
- the head
dissent 489
deny 536
refuse 764
disapprove 932
- off 297
- off the yoke 759
- to pieces 162
- one's sides 838
- up 315
shakedown bed 215
shakes, no great –
643, 651
shako 225, 717
shaky weak 160
in danger 665
fearful 860
shallop 273
shallow
not deep 32, 209
ignorant 491
ignoramus 493
foolish 499
trifling 643
- pretext 617
- profundity 855
shallow-brain 501
shallowness 209
shallow-pated 499
shallows
danger 667
sham imitation 19
falsehood 544
deception 545,
546
- fight 720
shaman 994
shamanism 992
shamble 275, 315
shambles 361
shame
disrepute 874
wrong 923
censure 932
chastity 960
cry - upon 932
false – 855
for – 874
sense of – 879
- the devil 939
to one's – be it
spoken 874
shamefaced 881
shameful
disgraceful 874
profligate 945
shameless
bold 525
impudent 885
profligate 945
indecent 961
shampoo 652
shandredhan 272
shanghai 791

shank support 215
instrument 633
Shanks's mare 266
shanty 189
shape 240, 448
- one's course
direction 278
pursuit 622
conduct 692
- out a course 626
shapeless 241, 846
shapely 242, 845
shard 51
share
part 51
participate 778
allotted portion
786
- and share alike
778
shareholder 778
shark 792
sharp
energetic 171
violent 173
acute 253
sensible 375
pungent 392
- sound 410
musical tone 413
intelligent 498
active 682
clever 698
cunning 702
feeling 821
painful 830
rude 895
censorious 932
look – 459, 682
- appetite 865
- contest 720
- ear 418
- eye 441
- fellow 682, 700
- frost 383
- look-out 459,
507
- pain 378
- practice
cunning 702
severity 739
improbity 940
- set 865
sharpen
[see sharp]
excite 824
- one's tools 673
- one's wits 537
sharpener 253
sharper 792
sharpness 253
sharpshooter 726
sharpshooting 716
Shaster 986
shatter disjoin 44
disperse 73
render powerless
158
destroy 162
shatter-brained 503
shattered 160, 688
shave reduce 195
shorten 201
layer 204
smooth 255
grate 330
lie 546

close – 671
shaved 226
shaving small 32
layer 204
filament 205
shave-tail 726, 745
shawl 225
shawm 417
shay 272
she 374
sheaf 72
shear reduce 195
shorten 201
sheep 370
take 789
shears 253
sheath 191, 223
sheathe 225
moderate 174
- the sword 723
sheathing 223
sheave 633
shed scatter 73
building 189
divest 226
emit 297
give 784
- blood 361
- light upon 420
- a luster on 873
- tears 839
Shedim 980
sheen 420
sheep 366
sheep-dog 366
sheep-fold 232
sheepish 881
sheep's eye, cast a –
desire 865
modest 881
endearment 902
sheer simple 42
complete 52
deviate 279
- off avoid 623
sheet layer 204
covering 223
paper 593
come down in –s
rain 348
white – 952
winding – 363
- of fire 382
- of water 343
sheet-anchor
safety 664, 666
hope 858
sheet-lightning 423
sheik ruler 745, 875
lover 897
priest 996
shelf 215, 667
on the –
powerless 158
disused 678
inaction 681
shell cover 223
coffin 363
bombard 716
bomb 727
–burst 404
–shock 655
- out 784, 807,
809
shellac 356a
shellback 269
shell-fish 366

shelter 664, 666
- oneself under
plea of 617
sheltie 271
shelve defer 133
locate 184
slope 217
neglect 460
disuse 678
shelving beach 217
ahend 659
shepherd tender of
sheep 370
director 694
pastor 996
Shepherd, the Good
– 976
shepherd's dog 366
Sheppard, Jack –
792
shere 32
sheriff 745, 965
Shetland pony 271
shew [see show]
shibboleth 550
shield
heraldry 550
safety 664
buckler 666
defend 717
scutcheon 877
look only at one
side of the – 481
reverse of the –
235, 468
under the – of 664
shift change 140
convert 144
substitute 147
changeable 149
chemise 225
move 264
transfer 270
deviate 279
prevaricate 546
plea 617
cunning 702
last – 601
make a – with
147, 677
put to one's –s
704, 804
- one's ground
607
- off defer 133
- for oneself 692,
748
left to – for one-
self 893
- one's quarters
264
- the scene 140
- to and fro 149
shifting [see shift]
transient 111
- sands 149
- trust or use 783
shiftless 674, 699
shillelagh 727
shilling 800
cut off with a –
789
- shocker 594
shilly-shally 605
shimmer 420
shimmy
dance 840

shindy 720
shine light 420
beauty 845
glory 873
take the – out of
874
- in conversation
588
- forth 873
- upon
illumine 420
aid 707
shingle 330
shingled
hair 53
shingles 223
shining [see shine]
- light sage 500
Shintoism 984
shiny 420
ship lade 190
transfer 270
vessel 273
take - 267, 293
one's - coming in
803
- of the line 726
shipboard, on – 273
ship-load 31, 190
shipman 269
shipmate 890
shipment
contents 190
transfer 270
shippen 189
shipping 273
shipshape order 58
conformity 82
skill 698
shipwreck
destruction 162
vanquish 731
failure 732
shire 181
shirk 603, 623, 742
shirker 862
shirt 225
Shiva 979
shive 22, 204
shiver
small piece 32
divide 44
destroy 162
filament 205
shake 315
brittle 328
cold 383
fear 860
go to –s 162
- in one's shoes
860
shivery brittle 328
powdery 330
shoal
assemblage 72
multitude 102
shallow 209
shoals danger 667
surrounded by –
difficulty 704
shoat 366
shock sheaf 72
violence 173
concussion 276
agitation 315
unexpected 508
disease 655

discord 713
affect 821
move 824
pain 828
give pain 830
dislike 867
scandalize 932

shocking bad 649
painful 830
ugly 846
vulgar 851
fearful 860
disreputable 874
hateful 898
in a – temper 901a

shockingly much 31
shod 225
shoddy 645
shoe support 215
dress 225
hindrance 706
stand in the –s of
commission 755
deputy 759
where the –
pinches
badness 649
difficulty 704
opposition 708
sensibility 822
painful 828
shoemaker 225
shofie 272
shoful 792
shog 173
shoneen 855
shoot
offspring 167
expand 194
dart 274
propel 284
kill 361
sprout 365, 367
pain 378
execute 972
teach the young
idea to – 537
– ahead 282
– ahead of 303
– at 716
– out beams 420
– up increase 35
prominent 250
shooting
[see shoot]
chase 622
– pain 378
– star 318, 423
shooting-coat 225
shop 795, 799
keep a – 625, 794
shut up – end 67
cease 142
relinquish 624
rest 687
smell of the – 851
shopkeeper 797
shoplifter 792
shoplifting 791
shopman 797
shopmate 890
shopping 794, 795
shore
support 215
border 231
lawl 342
buttress 717

hug the – 286
on – 342
– up 215, 670
shoreless 180
shorn cut short 21
deprived 776
– of its beams
422, 874
– lamb 828
short
not long 201
brittle 328
concise 572
uncivil 895
come – of, fall – of
inferior 34
shortcoming 304
insufficient 640
in – 572, 596
– allowance 640
– answer 895
– breath 688
– by 201
– of cash 804
– commons
insufficiency 640
fasting 956
– circuit 279, 628
– cut straight 246
mid-course 628
– distance 197
– life and merry
840
– measure 53
at – notice 111,
132
– of small 32
inferior 34
subtraction 38
incomplete 53
shortcoming 304
insufficiency 640
– sea 348
make – work of
destroy 162
active 682
haste 684
complete 729
conquer 731
punish 972
shortage 53
shortcoming
inequality 28
inferiority 34
motion short of
304
non-completion
730
deficiency 945
shorten 201
– sail 275
shorthand 590
short-handed 651
shorthorn 366
short-lived 111
shortly soon 132
shortness 201
for – sake 572
shorts 225
short-sighted
myopic 443
misjudging 481
foolish 499
short-story 594
short-winded 160,
688
short-witted 499

shot missile 284
report 406
variegated 440
guess 514
war material 722,
727
price 812
reward 973
bad – 701
exchange –s 720
good – 700
have a – at 716
like a – 113
off like a – 623
pistol – 406
random – 463, 621
round – 727
– in the locker 632
not have a – in
one's locker 804
– and shell 722
shot-free 815
shot-gun 727
should be:
no better than
she – 961
what – 922
shoulder
support 215
projection 250
shove 276
broad –ed 159
cold – 289
have on one's –s
625
on the –s of
high 206
elevated 307
instrumentality
631
shrug the –s
[see shrug]
rest on the –s of
926
rub –s with no-
bility 852
take upon one's –s
676
– arms 673
– a musket 722
– to shoulder 709,
712
– to the wheel
604, 676
shoulder-knot 847
shoulder-strap 747
shout
loud 404
cry 411
rejoice 838
shove 276
give a – to
aid 707
shovel
receptacle 191
transfer 270
vehicle 272
fire-iron 386
cleanness 652
put to bed with
a – 363
– away 297
shovel-hat 999
show visible 446
appear 448
draw attention
457

evidence 467
demonstrate 478
manifest 525
entertainment 599
parade 882
dumb – 550
make a – 544
mere – 544
peep– 840
– off 525
– one's cards 529
– cause 527
– one's colors,
550
– one's face
presence 186
manifest 525
disclose 529
– fight defy 715
attack 716
defend 717
brave 861
– forth 525
– in front 303
– one's cards 529
– one's hand 529
– a light pair of
heels 623
– itself 446
– of 17, 472
– off 882, 884
– one's teeth 715
– up visible 446
manifest 525
ridicule 856
degrade 874
censure 932
accuse 938
shower
assemblage 72
rain 348
– bath 386
– down
abundance 639
– down upon 784,
816
showman 524
showy color 428
beauty 845
ornament 847
fashion 852
vulgar 851
ostentatious 882
shrapnel 727
shred 32, 205
shredder 260
shrew 901
shrewd
knowing 490
wise 498
cunning 702
shriek 410, 411
shrievalty 965
shrieve 965
shrift
confession 529
absolution 952
shriftless 951
shrill 410, 411
shrimp 193
shrine 363, 1000
receptacle 191
shrink
decrease 36
shrivel 195
go back 283, 287
unwilling 603

avoid 623
sensitive 822
– from fear 860
dislike 867
hate 898
shrive 952, 998
shrivel 195
shrivelled thin 203
shroud cover 225
funeral 363
hide 528
safety 664
defend 717
–ed in mystery
519
shrouds 45
Shrove Tuesday
998
shrub plant 367
plantation 371
shrug sign 550
– the shoulders
dissent 489
submit 725
discontent 832
dislike 867
contempt 930
disapprobation
932
shrunk 193, 195
shudder cold 383
fear 860
make one –
painful 830
– at aversion 867
hate 898
shuffle mix 41
derange 61
change 140
interchange 148
changeable 149
move slowly 275
agitate 315
falsehood 544
untruth 546
irresolute 605
recant 607
dance 840
improbity 940
– the cards
begin again 66
change 140
chance 621
prepare 673
patience and –
the cards 826
– off run away 623
– off this mortal
coil 360
– on 266
shuffler 548
shun 623, 867
shunt 270, 279
shunted
shelved 460
shut 261
– the door 761
– the door in one's
face 764
– the door upon
893
– one's ears 419,
487
– the eyes 442
– one's eyes to
not attend to 458
neglect 460

approve 931
  worship 990
  – in the shrouds 349
  – small 879
singe 382, 384
singer 416
single *unmixed* 42
  unit 87
  secluded 893
  unmarried 904
  ride at – anchor 863
  – combat 720
  – entry
  – file 69
  – out 609
single-handed
  one 87
  easy 705
  unassisted 706
single-minded 703
singleness
  [*see* single]
  – of heart 703, 939
  – of purpose 604a, 703
single-stick 720
singlet 225
Sing Sing 752
sing-song 414, 892
singular *special* 79
  exceptional 83
  one 87
singularly *very* 31
sinister *left* 239
  bad 649
  vicious 945
  bar –
  imperfect 651
  disrepute 874
sinistrality 239
sinistromanual 239
sinistrous
  left-handed 239
  sullen 901a
sink *disappear* 4
  destroy 162
  descend 306
  lower 308
  submerge 310
  neglect 460
  conceal 528
  cloaca 653
  fatigue 688
  vanquish 731
  fail 732
  adversity 735
  invest 787
  pain 828
  depressed 837
  – back 661
  – of corruption 653
  – into the grave 360
  – of iniquity 945
  – in the mind
   thought 451
   memory 505
   excite 824
  – money 809
  – into oblivion 506
  – or swim
   certainty 474
   perseverance 604a
sinking

heart – 837
  – fund 802
sinless 946
sinned against than sinning, more – 946
sinner 949
Sinn Fein 742
sin-offering 952
sinuous 243, 248
sinus 252
sip *small* 32
  drink 298
siphon 350
sippet 298
sir *man* 373
  title 877
  – Oracle 887
sirdar 745
sire 166
siren
  sea-nymph 341
  loud sound 404
  musician 416
  seducing 615
  warning 668
  alarm 669
  evil-doer 913
  demon 980
  sorcerer 994
  song of the –s 615
  – strains 415
sirene *musical instrument* 417
siriasis 503
sirius 423
sirocco *wind* 349
  heat 382
sirrah! 949
sister *kin* 11
  likeness 17
  nurse 662
  nun 996
sisterhood
  party 712
  frail – 962
sisterly 906
sisters:
  weird – 994
  – three 601
sistrum 417
Sisyphus, task of –
  useless 645
  difficult 704
sit 308
  – down *settle* 184
  lie 213
  stoop 308
  – in judgment
   adjudge 480
   jurisdiction 965
   lawsuit 969
  – on 215
  – on thorns
   annoyance 828
   fear 860
site 183, 780
sith 476
sitting [*see* sit]
  incubation 673
  convocation 696
  – up *late* 133
  work 686
sitting-room 191
situ, in – 183, 265
situation
  circumstances 8

place 183
  location 184
  business 625
  out of a – 185
Siva 979
six 98
  – of one and half-a-dozen of the other 27
sixes and sevens, at – 59, 713
sixty 98
sizar 746
size *degree* 26
  magnitude 31
  glue 45
  arrange 60
  dimensions 192
  viscid 352
  – up 480
sizzle 409
sjambok 975
skat 840
skate
  locomotion 266
  vehicle 272
skating 840
skean 727
skedaddle 623
skeel 191
skein 219
  tangled – 59
skeleton
  remains 40
  essential part 30
  thin 203
  support 215
  corpse 362
  plan 626
  reduced to a – 659
  – in the closet 649, 830
  – at the feast 836
skelter 276
skepticism
  doubt 485
  incredulity 487
  irreligion 989
sketch
  form 240
  represent 554
  paint 556
  describe 594
  plan 626
sketcher 559
sketchy
  incomplete 53
  feeble 575
  unfinished 730
skew 217
  –bald 440
skewer 45
ski 266, 272
  –running 840
  –joring 840
  –jumping 840
skiagraphy 421, 554, 556
skid *support* 215
  hindrance 706
skies:
  exalt to the – 873
  praise to the – 933
skiff 273
skill 698
  acquisition of – 539

game of – 840
skillet 191
skilly 293
skim *move* 266
  navigate 267
  rapid 274
  neglect 460
  summarize 596
skimp 460, 819
skimpy 640
skin *outside* 220
  tegument 223
  peel 226
  swindle 791
  fleece 814
  wet to the – 339
  with a whole – 670
  without – 822
  mere – and bone 203
  – a flint 471, 819
  – over 660
skin-deep
  shallow 32, 209
  external 220
skinned: thick– 376
  thin– 375
skinny 203, 223
skip *jump* 309
  neglect 460
  rejoice 838
skipjack
  prosperous 734
  low-born 876
skipper
  sea captain 269
  captain 745
skippingly 70
skips, by – 70
skirmish 720
skirmisher 726
skirt
  appendix 39
  pendent 214
  dress 225
  surrounding 227
  edge 231
  side 236
  – dance 840
skirting 231
skirts of:
  hang upon the –
   sequence 281
  on the –
   near 197
skit *ridicule* 856
  detraction 934
  prostitute 962
skittish
  capricious 608
  excitable 825
  timid 862
  bashful 881
skittle sharper 792
skittles 840
skiver 253
skulk 528, 862
skull 450
skull-cap 225
skunk 401
skurry 684
sky *summit* 210
  world 318
  air 338
  necessity 601
sky-aspiring 865
sky-blue 438

sky-lark 305
sky-larking 840
sky-light 260
sky-line 196
sky-pilot 996
sky-rocket 305
sky-scraper 206, 210
slab *layer* 204
  support 215
  flat 251
  viscous 352
  record 551
slabber *slaver* 297
  unclean 653
slack *loose* 47
  weak 160
  inert 172
  slow 275
  cool 385
  fuel 388
  neglectful 460
  unwilling 603
  insufficient 640
  inactive 683
  lax 738
slacken
  loosen 47
  moderate 174
  repose 687
  hinder 706
  one's pace 275
slacker 460, 603, 623, 927
slag *embers* 384
  inutility 641
  dirt 653
slake *quench* 174
  gratify 829
  satiate 869
  – one's appetite
   intemperance 954
slam 276, 406
  – the door in one's face
   oppose 708
   refuse 764
slammerkin 653
slander 934
slanderer 936
slang 560, 563, 908
slant 217
slap *instantly* 113
  strike 276
  censure 932
  punish 972
  – in the face
   opposition 708
   attack 716
   anger 900
   disrespect 929
   disapprobation 932
  – the forehead 461
slap-dash 684
slash 44, 308
slashing *style* 574
slate
  writing tablet 590
  election 609
  disparage 932
  clean the – 918
  – loose *mad* 503
slate-colored 432
slates *roof* 223
slattern
  disorder 59

dirty 653
bungler 701
vulgar 851
slatternly 699
slaughter 361
slaughter-house 361
slave *instrumentality* 631
toil 686
servant 746
a – to 749
– trade 795
slaver *ship* 273
slobber 297
dirt 653
flatter 933
slavery 686, 749
slavish 749, 886
slay 361
sleave 59
sled 272
sledge 272
sledge-hammer 276
with a – 162, 686
sleek 255, 845
sleep 683
last – 360
rock to – 174
send to – 841
not have a wink of – 825
– with one eye open 459
– at one's post 683
– upon 133, 451
– walker 268
– walking 266
sleeper *support* 215
wake the seven – s 404
sleeping partner 683
sleepless 682
sleepy 683
sleet 383
sleeve *skein* 219
dress 225
hang on the – of 746
wear one's heart upon his – 525, 703
in one's – 528
laugh in one's – 838, 856
sleeveless 499, 608
– errand 645, 699
sleigh 272
sleight *skill* 698
– of hand 545
slender *small* 32
thin 203
trifling 643
– means 804
sleuth 527
– hound 913
slew round 312
slice *cut* 44
piece 51
layer 204
slick 682, 698
slicker 699
slide *elapse* 109
smooth 255
pass 264
locomotion 266

descend 306
– back 661
– in 228
– into 144
sliding 840
sliding-panel 545
sliding-rule 85
slight *small* 32
slender 203
rare 322
neglect 460
disparage 483
feeble 575
trifle 643
dereliction 927
disrespect 929
contempt 930
slight-made 203
slily
surreptitiously 544
craftily 702
slim 203
cunning 702
slime *viscous* 352
dirt 653
sling *hang* 214
project 284
weapon 727
slink *hide* 528
cowardice 862
– away *avoid* 623
disrepute 874
slip *small* 32
elapse 109
child 129
strip 205
petticoat 225
descend 306
error 495
workshop 691
fail 732
false coin 800
vice 945
guilt 947
give one the – 671
let – *liberate* 750
lose 776
relinquish 782
– away 187, 623
– cable 623
– the collar 671, 750
– 'twixt cup and lip 509
let – the dogs of war 722
– in (*or* – into) 294
– the memory 506
– on 225
– out 187
– over *neglect* 460
– of the pen 568
– of the tongue *solecism* 568
stammering 583
– through the fingers *miss an opportunity* 135
escape 671
fail 732
slipper 225
hunt the – 840
slippery
transient 111
smooth 255
greasy 355

uncertain 475
vacillating 607
dangerous 665
facile 705
faithless 940
– ground 667
slipshod 575
slipslop
absurdity 497
solecism 568
weak language 575
slit *divide* 44
chink 198
furrow 259
slither 264
sliver 51
slobber *drivel* 297
slop 337
dirt 653
sloe *black* 431
slog 143
slogan 722
sloop 273
–of-war 726
slop *spill* 297
water 337
dirt 653
slope *oblique* 217
run away 623
sloppy *moist* 339
marsh 345
– *style* 575
slops *clothes* 225
slosh 337, 653
slot 44, 260
sloth 683
slouch *low* 207
oblique 217
move slowly 275
inactive 683
slouching *ugly* 846
slough
quagmire 345
dirt 653
difficulty 704
adversity 735
– of Despond 859
sloven *untidy* 59
bungler 701
slovenly *untidy* 59
careless 460
– *style* 575
dirty 653
awkward 699
vulgar 851
slow *tardy* 133
inert 172
moderate 174
motion 275
inactive 683
wearisome 841
dull 843
by – degrees 26
– movement
music 415
march in – time 275
– as molasses in January 275
be – to
unwilling 603
not finish 730
refuse 764
slow-coach 701
slowness 275
sloyd 537

slubber 653
slubberdegullion 876
sludge 653
slug *slow* 275
inaction 681
inactivity 683
bullet 727
sluggard 275, 683
sluggish 172, 823, 843
sluice *limit* 233
egress 295
river 348
conduit 350
open the –s 297
slum 653
slumber 683
slump 304
slur *blemish* 847
stigma 874
gloss over 937
reproach 938
– over *neglect* 460
slight 483
slush *marsh* 345
semiliquid 352
dirt 653
slut *untidy* 59
female 374
dirty 653
unchaste 962
sly *stealthy* 528
cunning 702
smack
small quantity 32
mixture 41
boat 273
impulse 276
taste 390
thud 406
kiss 902
strike 972
– the lips
pleasure 377
taste 390
savory 394
rejoice 838
– of *resemble* 17
small
– *in degree* 32
– *in size* 193
become – 195
feel – 879
of – account 643
esteem of – account 930
– *arms* 727
– beer 643, 880, 930
– coin 800
– chance 473
– fry 193, 643, 876
– matter 643
– number 103
– part 51
– pica 591
in the – hours 125
on a – scale 32, 193
– talk 588
small-bore 727
small-clothes 225
smaller 34, 195
smallness **32**
smalls 225
smalt 438

smart *pain* 378
active 682
clever 698
feel 821
grief 828
witty 842
pretty 845
ornamental 847
– *pace* 274
– *saying* 842
– *under* 821
smarten 847
smart-money 973
smash 162, 732
smasher 792
smatch 390
smatterer 493
smattering 491
smear *cover* 223
soil 653
blemish 848
smell 398
bad – 401
– of the lamp *ornate style* 577
prepared 673
– powder 722
smell-feast 886
smelling-bottle 400
smelt *heat* 384
prepare 673
smicker 838
smile 836, 838
raise a – 840
– at 856
– of contempt 930
– of fortune **734**
– upon *aid* 707
courtesy 894
endearment 902
smirch 431, 653
smirk 838
smite *maltreat* 649
excite 824
afflict 830
punish 972
smith 690
smithereens 161
smitten *love* 897
– with *moved* 615
smock 225, 258
smock-faced 862
smock-frock 225
smoke
dust 330
vapor 336
heat 382
tobacco 392
discover 480a
suspect 485
unimportant 643
dirt 653
cure 670
disrespect 929
end in –
shortcoming 304
failure 732
– the calumet of peace 723
–ed glasses 424
– screen 424
– stack 260
smoking hot 382
smoking-jacket 225
smoking-room 191
smoky *opaque* 426
dirty 653

smooth *uniform* 16
  calm 174
  flattery 213, 251
  not rough 255
  easy 705
  – the bed of death
  707, 906
  – down 174
  – over 174
  – the ruffled brow
  of care 834
  – sailing 705
  – water *easy* 705
  – the way 705
smooth-bore 727
smoothly, go on –
  prosperous 734
smoothness 255
smooth-tongued
  544, 933
smother
  repress 174
  kill 361
  stifle sound 581
  restrain 751
smoulder *inert* 172
  burn 382
  latent 526
smous 796, 797
smudge 431, 653,
  848
smug *affected* 855
smuggle
  introduce 228
  steal 791
  illegal 964
smuggler 792
smut
  dirt 653
  impurity 961
smutch 431
snack
  small quantity 32
  food 298
snacks, go – 778
snaffle 752
snag *projection* 250
  sharp 253
  danger 667
  hindrance 706
snail *slow* 275
snake *undulation*
  248
  serpent 366
  hissing 406
  miscreant 913
  scotch the – 640
  – in the grass
  hidden 528
  deceiver 548
  bail 649
  source of danger
  667
  evil-doer 913
  knave 941
snake-like
  convoluted 248
snap *break* 44
  eat 298
  brittle 328
  noise 406
  rude 895
  – at *seize* 789
  bite 830
  censure 932
  – of the fingers
  trifle 643

– one's fingers at
  defy 715
  insolence 885
  despise 930
  – the thread 70
  – up *seize* 789
  – one up
  censure 932
  –shot 554
snap-dragon 840
snappish 901
snare *deception* 545
snarl *growl* 412
  rude 895
  angry 900
  threaten 909
snatch
  small quantity 32
  seize 789
  – at *pursue* 622
  seize 789
  – a grace beyond
  the reach of art
  845
  – from one's grasp
  789
  – from the jaws of
  death 662, 672
  – from under
  one's nose 702
  – a verdict 545,
  702
snatches, by – 70
sneak *hide* 528
  coward 862
  servile 886
  base 940
  knave 941
  bad man 949
  – off, – out of 623
sneer *disparage* 929
  contempt 930
  blame 932
sneeze *blow* 349
  snuffle 409
  – at *despise* 930
**sneezed at, not to
  be** – 642
snick 32, 51
snicker 838
sniff *blow* 349
  odor 398
  discovery 480a
sniffle 349
snigger *laugh* 838
  ridicule 856
  disrespect 929
sniggle 545
snip
  small quantity 32
  cut 44
  short 201
  tailor 225
sniping 716
snippet 32
snip-snap 713
snip-snap-snorem
  840
snivel *weep* 839
  sniveling
  servile 886
snob *vulgar* 851
  plebeian 876
  servile 886
snobbishness
  flattery 933
snood

headdress 225
  circle 247
snooker 840
Snooks, Mr. – 876
snooze 683
snozzle 250
snore 411, 683
snort 411, 412
snout 250
snow *ship* 273
  ice 383
  white 430
snow-ball 72
snow-blindness 443
snow-drift 72
snow-shoe 272
snow-storm 383
snub *short* 201.
  hinder 706
  cast a slur 874
  humiliate 879
  bluster 885
  censure 932
snub-nosed 243
snuff *blow* 349
  pungent 392
  odor 398
  up to – 698, 702
  go out like the –
  of a candle 360
  – out 162, 421
  – up 296, 398
snuff-color 433
snuffing, want –
  pert 885
snuffle *blow* 349
  hiss 409
  stammer 583
  hypocrisy 988
snuffy 653
snug *closed* 261
  comfortable 377
  safe 664
  prepared 673
  content 831
  secluded 893
  keep – 528, 893
  make all – 673
snuggery 189
snugness 827
so *similar* 17
  very 31
  therefore 476
  method 627
  – be it 488, 762
  – far so good 618
  – let it be 681
  – much the better
  831, 838
  – much the worse
  832, 835
  – to speak 17, 521
soak *immerse* 300
  water 337
  moist 339
  drunkenness 959
  – up 340
So-and-so, Mr. –
  neology 563
soap *lubricate* 332
  oil 356
  cleanser 652
soapy *unctuous* 355
  servile 886
  flattery 933
soar *great* 31
  height 206

fly 267
  rise 305
sob 839
sober *moderate* 174
  wise 498
  sane 502
  style 576
  grave 837
  temperate 953
  abstinent 958
  – down 174, 502
  humility 879
  in – sadness
  affirmation 535
  – senses 502
  – truth *fact* 494
sober-minded 502
  calm 826
  humble 879
sobriety 958
sobriquet 565
sob sister 534
so-called 545, 565
soc *jurisdiction* 965
socage 777
soccer 840
sociable
  carriage 272
  sociality 892
social *mankind* 372
  sociable 892
  – circle 892
  – evil 961
  – gathering 892
  – science 910
socialism
  government 737
  participation 778
  philanthropy 910
socialist 712
sociality 892
society
  mankind 372
  party 712
  fashion 852
  sociality 892
  position in – 873
Socinianism 984
sociology 712
sock *hosiery* 225
  drama 599
socket 191, 252
socle 215
Socratic method
  461
sod 344
  beneath the – 363
sodality 712, 888
sodden 339, 384
sofa 215
Sofi 984, 996
soft *stop!* 142
  weak 160
  moderate 174
  smooth 255
  not hard 324
  moist 339
  marsh 345
  silence! 403
  – *sound* 405
  dulcet 413
  credulous 486
  silly 499
  lenient 740
  tender 822
  timid 862
  own to the – im-

peachment 529
  – music 415
  – pedal 405
  – sawder 617, 933
  – soap 356, 933
  – tongue, – words
  894
soften [*see* soft]
  moderate 174
  relieve 834
  pity 914
  palliate 937
**softening of the
  brain** 158
softer sex 374
soft-hearted 914
softling 160
softness 324
  persuasibility 615
soft-spoken 894
soggy 339
soho
  attention 457
  parley 586
  hunting 622
soi-disant
  asserting 535
  pretender 548
  misnomer 565
  vain 880
  boastful 884
soil *region* 18
  land 342
  dirt 653
  deface 846
  till the – 371, 673
soirée 892
sojourn 186, 189
sojourner 188
soke 181
solace *relief* 834
  recreation 840
  – oneself with
  pleasure 827
solar 318
  – system 318
  – time 114
solatium 973
sold to the devil 949
soldan [*see* sultan]
solder *join* 43
  cement 45
  cohere 46
soldier 726
soldier-like 722,
  861
sole *alone* 87
  base 211
  support 215
  feme – 904
solecism 568
soleil, coup de –
  hot 384
  mad 503
solemn
  affirmation 535
  important 642
  grave 837
  glorious 873
  ostentatious 882
  religious 987
  worship 990
  – mockery 882
  – silence 403
solemnity *rite* 998
solemnization 883
sol-fa 416

solfeggio 415
solicit *induce* 615
  request 765
  desire 865
  – the attention
    457
solicitor *agent* 758
  petitioner 767
  lawyer 968
solicitous 865
solicitude *care* 459
  pain 828
  anxiety 860
  desire 865
solid *complete* 52
  dense 321
  certain 474
  learned 490
  exact 494
  wise 498
  persevering 604a
  solvent 803
  – angle 244
solidarity
  party 712
solidify 321
soliloquy 589
solitaire *game* 840
  hermit 893
solitary } *alone*
solitude } 87
  secluded 893
solmization 416
solo 87, 415
  – dance 840
Solomon } *wise*
Solon } 498
  sage 500
solstice 125, 126
soluble *fluid* 333
  liquefy 335
solus 87
solution
  liquefaction 335
  answer 462
  explanation 522
  – of continuity 70
solve *liquefy* 335
  discover 480a
  unriddle 522
solvent
  liquefier 335
  monied 803
somatics 316
somber *dark* 421
  black 431
  grey 432
  sad 837
sombrero 225
some *indefinite*
  quantity 25
  small quantity 32
  more than one
    100
–body *person* 372
  important or dis-
    tinguished 642
  in – *degree*
    degree 26
    small 32
  at – *other time* 119
  in – *place* 182
  – ten or a dozen
    102
  – time ago 122
  – time or other
    119

somehow or other
  cause 155
  instrument 631
somersault 218
something *thing* 3
  small degree 32
  matter 316
  – else 15
  – like 17
  – or other 475
sometimes 136
somewhat
  a little 32
  a trifle 643
somewhere 182
  – about 32
somnambulism
  walking 266
  trance 515
somnambulist
  walker 268
  dreamer 515
somniferous
  sleepy 683
  weary 841
somnolence 683
son 167
Son, God the – 976
sonant 402
  letter 561
sonata 415
Sonderbund 769
song *music* 415
  poem 597
  death – 360, 839
  love– 597
  for a mere – 815
  no – no supper 812
  old – 643
songster 416
soniferous 402
sonnet 597
sonneteer 597
sonorous *sound* 402
  loud 404
  language 577
sons of:
  – Belial 988
  – God 977
Soofeeism 984
soon *transient* 111
  future 121
  early 132
  too – for 135
sooner– or later
  another time 119
  future 121
  – said than done
    704
soot 431, 653
sooth 511
  in good – 543
soothe
  allay 174
  relieve 834
  flatter 933
soothing
  faint sound 405
  – syrup 174
soothsay 511
soothsayer 513, 994
soothsaying 511
sop
  small quantity 32
  food 298
  fool 501
  inducement 615

  reward 973
  – to Cerberus 458
  – in the pan 615
soph 492, 541
Sophi 745, 996
sophism 477, 497
sophist *scholar* 492
  dissembler 548
sophister 492
  student 541
sophistical 477
sophisticate *mix* 41
  debase 659
sophisticated
  spurious 545
sophistry 477
  noise 405
  cloaca 653
sophomore 541
soporific 683, 841
soporous 683
soprano 410, 416
sorbet 298
sorcerer 994
sorcery 992
sordes 653
sordet 417
sordid *stingy* 819
  covetous 865
sordine 417
sore
  bodily pain 378
  disease 655
  mental suffering
    828, 830
  discontent 832
  anger 900
  – as a boil 901a
  – place 822
  – subject 830, 900
sorely *very* 31
s'orienter 278
sorites 476
sorority 712
sorrel 433, 434
sorrow 828
  give – words 839
sorry *trifling* 643
  grieved 828
  mean 876
  make a – face 874
  cut a – figure 874
  be – for 750, 914
  in a – plight 732
  – sight 830, 837
sort *degree* 26
  arrange 60
  kind 75
  – with
    sociality 892
sortable }
sortance }
  agreement 23
sortes
  chance 156, 621
  – Virgilianæ
sorcery 992
sortie 716
sortilege
  prediction 511
  sorcery 992
sortilegy 621
sortition 621
sorts, out of –
  ill-health 655
  sulky 901a
S.O.S. 669, 707
so-so *small* 32
  trifling 643

  imperfect 651
sostenuto 415
sot *fool* 501
  drunkard 959
sot à triple étage
  501
sotto voce
  faint sound 405
  conceal 528
  voiceless 581
sou *money* 800
  qui n'a pas le –
    804
soubrette 599, 746
sough *conduit* 350
  noise 405
  cloaca 653
soul *essence* 5
  person 372
  intellect 450
  genius 498
  affections 820
  cure of –s 995
  flow of – 588
  not a – 187
  not dare to say
    one's – is his
    own *subjection*
    749
  fear 860
  – of wit 572
  have one's whole
    – in his work
    686
soulless 683, 823
soul-mate 905
soul-sick 837
soul-stirring 821,
  824
sound *great* 31
  conformable 82
  stable 150
  strong 159
  fathom 208
  bay 343
  noise 402
  investigate 461
  measure 466
  true 494
  wise 498
  sane 502
  good 648
  perfect 650
  healthy 654
  solvent 803
  orthodox 983a
  catch a – 418
  safe and – 654,
    670
  – the alarm
    indication 550
    warning 668
    alarm 669
    fear 860
  – asleep 683
  full of – and fury
    unmeaning 517
    insolent 885
  – the horn 416
  – of limb 654
  – locator 726
  – mind 502
  – the praises of
    931
  – the note of prep-
    aration 673
  – reasoning 476

  – a retreat 283
  – sleep 683
  – a trumpet
    publish 531
    alarm 669
  – of wind 654
sounding: big –
  577
  – brass 517
sounding-board 417
soundings 208
soundless
  unfathomable 208
  silent 403
soup 298, 352
soupçon 32, 41
souplé 298
sour *acid* 397
  discontented 832
  embitter 835
  uncivil 895
  sulky 901
  – grapes
    impossible 471
    excuse 617
  – the temper 830
source *beginning* 66
  cause 153
sourdet 417
sourdine 417
  à la – *noiseless* 405
  concealed 528
sourdough 463
soured 832
sourness 397
sous tous les
  rapports 52
souse 310, 337
South *direction* 278
  North and –
    opposite 237
Southern
  antipodes 237
  – Cross 318
souvenir 505
sovereign
  superior 33
  all-powerful 159
  authorities 737
  ruler 745
  – contempt 930
  – remedy 662
Soviet 696, 737
sow *scatter* 73
  pig 366
  agriculture 371
  female 374
  get the wrong –
    by the ear
    misjudgment 481
    error 495
    mismanage 699
    fail 732
  – broadcast 818
  – dissension 713,
    898
  – the sand 645
  – the seed
    prepare 673
  – the seeds of
    cause 153
    teach 537
  – one's wild oats
    improve 658
    amusement 840
    vice 945
    intemperance 954

– a gap 660
– the mouth 479, 581
– payment 808
– press news 532
– short 142, 265
– short of 304
– the sound 408a
– up 261
– the way 706
stopcock 263
stopgap
  substitute 147
  stopper 263
stoppage
  cessation 142
  hindrance 706
stopper 263
stopping place 292
store *store* 184
  stock 636
  shop 799
in – *destiny* 152
  preparing 673
lay in a – 637
set – by 642, 931
set no – 483
– of knowledge 490
– in the memory 505
store-house 636
store-keeper 636
store-ship 273, 726
storied 594
storm *crowd* 72
  convulsion 146
  violence 173
  agitation 315
  wind 349
  danger 667
  attack 716
  passion 825
  anger 900
ride the – 267
take by –
  conquer 731
  seize 789
– brewing 665
– in a teacup
  overrate 482
  exaggerate 549
  unimportance 643
storthing 696
story *rooms* 191
  layer 204
  news 532
  lie 546
  history 594
the old – 897
as the – goes 532
story-teller 548, 594
stot 366
stound 870
stoup *cup* 191
  altar 1000
stour 59
stout *strong* 159
  large 192
  drink 298
stout-hearted 861
stove *fireplace* 386
  – in 252
stow *locate* 184
  pack *close* 195
  store 636
stowage 180, 184

stowaway 528, 673
strabism 443
straddle 266, 607
Stradivarius 417
strafe 972
straggle 266, 279
straggler 268
straggling 44, 59
straight
  vertical 212
  rectilinear 246
  direction 278
all – *rich* 803
  solvent 807
  – *course* 628
  – *descent* 167
  – *face* 837
  – *sailing* 705
straighten 246
  – up 60
straightforward 278
  truthful 543
  artless 703
  honorable 939
straightness 246
straight shot 278
straightway 132
strain *race* 11
  weaken 160
  operation 170
  violence 173
  percolate 295
  transgress 303
  sound 402
  melody 415
  overrate 482
  exaggerate 549
  style 569
  poetry 597
  voice 580
  clean 652
  effort 686
  fatigue 688
– in the arms 902
– one's eyes 441, 507
– at a gnat and swallow a camel 608
– one's invention 515
– the meaning 523
– every nerve 686
– a point
  go beyond 303
  exaggerate 549
  not observe 773
  undue 925
– the throat 411
strait
  interval 198
  water 343
  difficulty 704
straitened
  poor 804
strait-handed 819
strait-jacket 752
strait-laced
  severe 739
  restraint 751
  fastidious 868
  haughty 878
strait-waistcoat 751, 752
strake 205
stramash 720
strand *thread* 205

shore 231, 342
stranded
  stuck fast 150
  in difficulty 704
  failure 732
  pain 828
strange
  unrelated 10
  exceptional 83
  ridiculous 853
  wonderful 870
  – *bedfellows* 713
  – to *say* 870
strangely *much* 31
stranger 57
a – to 491
strangle
  render powerless 158
  contract 195
  kill 361
strap *fasten* 43
  fastening 45
  restraint 752
  punish 972
  instrument of punishment 975
strappado 972
strapping
  mighty 31
  strong 159
  pace 272
  big 192
strapwork 847
stratagem
  deception 545
  plan 626
  artifice 702
strategic plan 626
  artifice 702
strategist
  planner 626
  director 694
  proficient 700
strategy 692, 722
strath 252
strathspey 840
stratification 204, 329
stratocracy 737
stratosphere 338
stratum 204
stratus 353
straw *scatter* 73
  light 320
  unimportant 643
  care not a – 866, 930
catch at –s
  overrate 482
  credulous 486
  misuse 679
  unskilful 699
  hope 858
  rash 863
the eyes drawing –s 683
in the – 161
man of –
  unsubstantial 4
  cheat 525
  insolvent 808
  low person 876
not worth a – 643, 645
– to show the wind 463

straw-colored 436
straw-hat 225
stray *dispersion* 73
  exceptional 83
  random 156
  wanderer 268
  deviate 279
streak *intrinsicality* 5
  long 200
  narrow 203
  furrow 259
  light 420
  stripe 440
  mark 550
streaked 219, 440
stream *assemble* 72
  move 264
  – of *fluid* 347
  – of *water* 348
  – of *air* 349
  – of *light* 420
  abundance 639
against the – 708
with the –
  conformity 82
  progression 282
  assent 488
  facility 705
  concord 714
  fashion 852
  servility 886
  – of *events* 151
  – of *time* 109
streamer *flag* 550
streaming 47, 73
streamlet 348
street 189, 627
man in the – 876
streets:
  in the open – 525
  on the – 961
street-walker 962
strength
  quantity 25
  degree 26
  greatness 31
  vigor 159
  energy 171
  tenacity 327
  animality 364
  put all one's – into 686
  lose – 655
  tower of – 717
  – of mind 604
strengthen 35
strengthless 160
strenuous
  persevering 604a
  active 682
  exertion 686
Strephon and Chloe 902
stress *emphasis* 580
  requirement 630
  importance 642
  strain 686
  difficulty 704
  by – of 601
  lay – on 476
  – of *circumstances*
    compulsion 744
  – of *weather* 349
stretch *expanse* 180
  expand 194
  extend 200

exaggerate 549
exertion 686
encroach 925
at a – 69
mind on the – 451
on the – 686
upon the – 457
– away to 196
– forth one's hand 680, 789
– of the imagination 515, 549
– the meaning 523
– a point 83, 303
  exaggerate 549
  severity 739
  permit 760
  not observe 773
  undue 925
  exempt 927a
  – to *distance* 196
  length 200
stretcher 215, 272
strew 73
stria, *striated* 259, 440
stricken *pain* 828
  terror– 860
  be – by 655
  – in years 128
strict
  in conformity 82
  exact 494
  severe 739
  conscientious 939
  orthodox 983a
  – *inquiry* 461
  – *interpretation* 522
  – *search* 461
  – *settlement* 780
strictly speaking
  literally 19
  exact 494
  interpreted 522
stricture
  constriction 203
  hindrance 706
  censure 932
stride *distance* 196
  motion 264
  walk 266
strident 410
strides: make – 282
  rapid – 274
stridor 410
strife 713, 720
strigil 652
strike *operate* 170
  hit 276
  resist 719
  disobey 742
  impress 824
  beat 972
  – at 716
  – a balance
    equalize 27
    mean 29
    pay 807
  – a bargain 769, 794
  – a blow *act* 680
  – dumb *dumb* 581
    excitement 824
    wonder 870
    humble 879
  – the eye 457

– the first blow 716
– one's flag 725
– hard 171
– all of a heap 824, 860
– home 171
– in with
  imitate 19
  assent 488
  cooperate 709
– the iron while it is hot 134
– a light 384, 420
– the lyre 416
– the mind 457
– out something new 146, 515
– off *exclude* 55
– one 451
– out *exclude* 55
  destroy 162
  invent 515
  obliterate 552
  scheme 626
– off the roll 756, 972
– at the root of 162
– root 150
– sail 275
– tents 293
– terror 860
– up 416
– with wonder 870
striker 927
striking 525
– likeness 554
strikingly
  greatly 31
string *tie* 43
  ligature 45
  continuity 69
  filament 205
  musical note 413
– together 60, 69
stringed instruments 417
stringent
  energetic 171
  authoritative 737
  strict 739
  compulsory 744
strings: *music* 417
  leading – 541
  pull the – 175, 693
  two – to one's bow 632
stringy 205, 327
strip *adjunct* 39
  narrow 203
  filament 205
  divest 226
  take 780
  rob 791
stripe *length* 200
  variegation 440
  mark 550
  badge 747
  blow 972
stripling 129
stripped *poor* 804
strive *endeavour* 675
  exert 686
  contend 720
– against 720

stroke *impulse* 276
  touch 379
  mark 550
  evil 619
  expedient 626
  disease 655
  action 680
  success 731
  painful 830
  at a – 113
  good – 626
– of death 360
– of the pen
  writing 590
  command 741
– of policy 626
– of time 113
– of word 686
– the wrong way 256
stroll 266
strolling player 599
strong *great* 31
  powerful 159
  energetic 171
  tough 327
  taste 390
  pungent 392
  fetid 401
  healthy 654
  feeling 821
  wonderful! 870
  smell – of 398
– accent 580
– argument 476
  by a – arm 744
– box 802
  with a – hand
  resolution 604
  exertion 686
  severity 739
– language 574
– pull 686
– point 476
strong-headed 498
stronghold
  refuge 666
  defence 717
  prison 752
strong-minded 498, 861
strong-scented 398
strong-willed 604
strop 253
strophe 597
strow 73
struck [*see* stricken, strike]
  awe– 860
– down 732
– all of a heap
  emotion 821
  wonder 870
  humbled 879
– with *love* 897
structural *state* 7
structure
  production 161
  form 240
  texture 329
  organization 357
struggle *exert* 686
  difficulty 704
  contend 720
strum 416, 517
strumpet 962
strung

highly – 825
strut *walk* 266
  pride 878
  parade 882
  boast 884
– and fret one's hour upon a stage 359, 599
strychnine 663
stub 40, 550
stubbed 201
stubble *remains* 40
  useless 645
stubborn
  strong 159
  hard 323
  obstinate 606
  resistance 719
stubby 201
stucco 45, 223
stuck [*see* stick]
– fast 150, 704
  be – on 897
stuck-up 878
stud *hanging-peg* 214
  knob 250
  horses 271
studded *many* 102
  spiked 253
  variegated 440
student 541
stud-farm 370
studied
  predetermined 611
studio *room* 191
  painting 556
  workshop 691
studious
  thoughtful 451
  docile 539
  intending 620
study *copy* 21
  room 191
  thought 451
  attention 457
  research 461
  learning 539
  painting 556
  intention 620
  retreat 893
  brown – 515
stuff *substance* 3
  contents 190
  expand 194
  line 224
  matter 316
  texture 329
  absurdity 497
  unmeaning 517
  material 635
  trifle 643
  overeat 957
  such – as dreams are made of 515
– gown 968
– in 300
– the memory with 505
– and nonsense
  unsubstantial 4
  absurdity 497
  unmeaning 517
– up *close* 261
  hoax 545
stuffed

redundancy 641
stuffing *contents* 190
  lining 224
  stopper 263
stuffy 321, 382
stultified 732
stultify oneself 699
stultiloquy 497
stumble *fall* 306
  flounder 315
  error 495
  unskilful 699
  failure 732
– on *chance* 156
  discover 480a
stumbling-block
  difficulty 704
  hindrance 706
stump
  remainder 40
  trunk 51
  walk 266
  drawing 556
  speak 582
  stir your –s
  active 682
  worn to the – 659
– along *slow* 275
stump orator 582, 887
stumpy *short* 201
stun *physically*
  insensible 376
  loud 404
  deafen 419
  unexpected 508
  morally insensible 823
  affect 824
  astonish 870
stung [*see* sting]
– to the quick 824
stunt *shorten* 201
  performance 680
stunted 193, 195
  insufficient 640
stupe 834
stupefaction 826
stupefy
– *physically* 376
– *morally* 823
  astonish 870
stupendous
  great 31
  large 192
  wonderful 870
stupid
  unsubstantial 4
  misjudging 481
  credulous 486
  unintelligent 499
  tiresome 841
  dull 843
stupor
  insensibility 823
  wonder 870
stupration 961
sturdy *strong* 159
  persevering 604a
– *beggar* 767, 792
stutter 583
sty *house* 189
  enclosure 232
  dirt 653
Stygian *dark* 421
  diabolic 945
  infernal 982

cross the – ferry
  die 360
– shore
  death 360
style *state* 7
  time 114
  painting 556
  graver 558
  name 564
  diction 569
  writing 590
  beauty 845
  fashion 852
stylet
  awl 262
  dagger 727
stylist 578
Stylites, Simon – 893
stylographic pen 590
stylography 590
stylus 590
styptic 397
Styx 982
suasible 602
suasion 615
suave mari magno 664
suaviter in modo 826, 894
suavity 894
sub 34
– spe rati 475
subacid 397
subaction 330
subahdar 745
subalpine 206
subaltern
  inferior 34
  soldier 726
  officer 745
  servant 746
  plebeian 876
subaqueous 208
subastral 318
subaudition 527
subcommittee 696
subconscious 317
subcontrary 237
subcutaneous 221
subdean 996
subdichotomy 91
subdititious 147
subdivide 44
subdivision
  part 51
  class 75
  military 726
  realty 780
subdolous 702
subdominant 413
subdual 731
subduction 38
subdue *calm* 174
  succeed 731
subdued
  morally 826
sub-editor 593
subitaneous 113
subito 113
subjacent 207
subject *dominate* 175
  liable 177
  topic 454
  meaning 516

cess 653
sumpter-horse 271
sumptuary 800, 809
sumptuous 882
sum-total 50
sun 318
  luminary 423
  glory 873
  bask in the – 377
  going down of
    the – 126
  farthing candle to
    the – 645
  under the – 180,
    318
  as the – at noon-
    day *bright* 420
  certain 474
  plain 525
  – oneself 384
Sun:
  – of Righteousness
    976
sunbeam 420
  –s from cucumbers
    471
sunburn *heat* 384
sunburnt *brown* 433
Sunday:
  – Monday &c. 138
  –'s best 847, 882
  – school 542
sunder 44
sundial 114
sundown 126
sundry 102
sunk [*see* sink]
  deep 208
  – fence 717
  – in iniquity 945
  – in oblivion 508
sunken rocks 667
sunless 421
sunlight 420
sunny *warm* 382
  luminous 420
  cheerful 836
sunny side 829
  view the – 858
  – of the hedge 734
sun-painting 556
sunrise 125
sunset 126
  at – 133
sunshade 223, 424
sunshine *light* 420
  prosperity 734
  happy 827
  cheerful 836
sunstroke 384, 503
sun-up 125
suo: – periculo 926
  – sibi gladio hunc
    jugulo
  absurdity 479
  retaliation 718
sup *small quantity*
  32
  feed 298
  – full of horrors
    828
super *theatrical* 599
superable 470
superabound 641
superadd 37
superannuated 128
superb 845

supercargo 694
supercherie 545
supercilious
  proud 878
  insolent 885
  disrespectful 929
  scornful 930
superdreadnought
  726
supereminence
  648, 873
supererogation 641,
  645
superexaltation 873
superexcellence
  648
superfetation 37,
  168
superficial
  shallow 209
  outside 220
  misjudging 481
  ignorant 491
  – extent 180
superficies 220
superfine 648
superfluitant 305
superfluity 40, 641
superfluous 645
superhuman 650,
  976
superimpose 233
superimposed 206
superincumbent
  206, 319
superinduce
  change 140
  cause 153
  produce 161
superintend 693
superintendent 694
superior *greater* 33
  - *in size* 194
  important 642
  good 648
  director 694
superiority 33
superjunction 37
superlative 33
superlatively good
  648
superman 33
supernal 206, 210,
  981
supernatant 206,
  305
supernatural 976,
  980
  – aid 707
supernumerary
  adjunct 39
  theatrical 599
  reserve 636
  redundant 641
superpose 37, 223
supersaturate 641
superscription 550,
  590
supersede
  substitute 147
  disuse 678
  relinquish 782
supersensible 317
superstition
  credulity 486
  error 495
  religion 984

superstratum 220
superstructure 729
supertax 812
supertonic 413
supervacaneous
  641
supervene
  extrinsic 6
  be added 37
  succeed 117
  happen 151
supervise 693
supervisor 694
supination 213
supine
  horizontal 213
  inverted 218
  sluggish 683
  mentally torpid
    823
suppeditate 637
supper 298
supplant 147
supple *soft* 324
  servile 886
supplement
  addition 37
  adjunct 39
  completion 52
  publication 531
  book 593
suppletory 37
suppliant 765, 767
supplicate *beg* 765
  pity 914
  worship 990
supplies
  materials 635
  aid 707
  money 800
supply *store* 636
  provide 637
  give 784
  – aid 707
  – deficiencies 52
  – the place of 147
  – and transport
    726
support *perform* 170
  sustain 215
  evidence 467
  preserve 670
  aid 707
  feel 821
  endure 826
  vindicate 937
  – life 359
supporter 711
  –s *heraldic* 550
suppose 514
supposing 469
supposition 514
supposititious 546
suppress
  destroy 162
  conceal 528
  silent 581
  restrain 751
suppression of
  truth 544
suppuration 653
suppute 85
supralapsarian 984
supramundane 939
supremacy 33, 737
supreme 33
  summit 210

authority 737
  in a – degree 31
Supreme Being 976
surbate 659
surbated 688
surcease 142
surcharge 641
  – and falsify 811
surcingle 45
surcoat 225
surd *number* 84
  deaf 419
  silent letter 561
sure *certain* 474
  belief 484
  safe 664
  make – against
    673
  make – of
  inquire 461
  take 789
  you may be – 535
  to be – *assent* 488
  on – ground 664
  security 771
sure-footed
  careful 459
  skilful 698
  cautious 864
surely 489, 602, 870
sureness 474
surety 474, 664
surf 348, 353
surface *outside* 220
  texture 329
  below the – 526
  lie on the – 518,
    525
  skim the – 460
Surface, Joseph –
  548
surfeit 641, 869
surge *swarm* 72
  swell 305
  rotation 312
  wave 348
surgeon 662
surgery 662
surgit amari
  aliquid 651
surly *gruff* 895
  sullen 901a
  unkind 907
surmise 514
surmount *be*
  superior 33
  tower 206
  transcursion 303
  ascent 305
  – a difficulty
  overcome 731
surmountable 470
surname 564
surpass
  be superior 33
  grow 194
  go beyond 303
  outshine 873
surplice 999
surplus 40, 641
surplusage 641
surprint 550
surprise
  non-expectation
    508
  unprepared 674
  wonder 870

surprisingly 31
surrebutter &c.
  answer 462
  pleadings 969
surrender 725, 782
  – one's life 360
surreptitious
  furtive 528
  deceptive 545
  untrue 546
surrogate 759
surround 227, 229
surroundings
  amidst such and
    such – 183
sursum corda 990
surtax 812
surtout *coat* 225
surveillance
  care 459
  direction 693
  under – 938
survene 151
survey 441, 466
surveyor 85, 694
survive *remain* 40
  long time 110
  permanent 141
susceptibility
  power 157
  tendency 176
  liability 177
  sensibility 375
  motive 615
  impressibility 822
  irascibility 901
suscipient 785
suscitate *cause* 153
  produce 161
  stir up 173
  excite 824
suspect *doubt* 485
  suppose 514
suspected 938
suspectless 484
suspend *defer* 133
  discontinue 142
  hang 214
suspended anima-
  tion 823
suspender 45, 214
suspense
  cessation 142
  uncertainty 475
  expectation 507
  irresolution 605
  in – *inert* 172
suspension
  cessation 142
  hanging 214
  music 413
  – of arms 723
suspicion *doubt* 485
  incredulity 487
  knowledge 490
  supposition 514
  fear 860
  under – 938
suspiration 839
sustain
  continue 143
  strength 159
  perform 170
  support 215
  preserve 670
  aid 707
  endure 821

insolent 885
threat 909
- glibly 584
- nonsense 497
- of signify 516
publish 531
intend 620
- to oneself 589
- oneself out of
breath 584
- over
confer 588
persuade 615
- to in private 586
- at random
illogical 477
loquacity 584
- together 588
- against time
time 106
protract 110
inaction 681
- of the town
gossip 588
fame 873
talkative 582, 584
talked of 873
talkies 599, 840
talking, fine -
over-estimation
482
tall 206
- hat 225
- talk 884
tallage 812
tallies 85
tallow 356
- candle 423
tallow-faced 429
tally agree 23
list 85, 86
sign 550
credit 805
- with conform 82
tally-ho 622
tally-man 797
talma 225
Talmud 985
talons
authority 737
claws 781
talus 217
tam-o'-shanter 225
tambourine 417
tame inert 172
moderate 174
domesticate 370
teach 537
feeble 575
subjugate 749
insensible 823
calm 826
tameless
violent 173
malevolent 907
Tammany 940
tamp 261, 276
tamper with
alter 140
seduce 615
injure 659
meddle 682
tan color 433
tandem
at length 200
vehicle 272
tang taste 390

bane 663
tangent 199
angle 217
fly off at a -
deviate 279
diverge 291
excitable 825
tangere ulcus 505
tangible
material 316
touch 379
exact 494
sufficient 639
useful 644
tangle 61, 219
tangled 59, 704
weave a - web 704
tango 840
tank pool 343
reservoir 636
armored vehicle
726
tankard 191
tanker 273
tant: - mieux 838
- s'en faut. 489
- soit peu 32
tantaene animis
coelestibus irae
900
tantalize balk 509
induce 615
desire 865
tantalizing
exciting 824
Tantalus: torment
of - 537, 865
tantamount 27, 516
tantara 407
tantas componere
lites 723
tanti 642
tantivy speed 274
tantrums 900
tap open 260
plug 263
hit 276
let out 295, 297
sound 406
turn on the - 297
tap-dance 840
tape string 205
measure 466
- machine 553
taper contract 195
narrow 203
candle 423
- to a point 253
tapestry 556, 847
tapinois, en - 528
tapis: on the -
event 151
topic 454
intention 620
plan 626
tap-root 153
taps 550
tapster 746
tar cover 223
sailor 269
pitch 356a
- and feather 929,
972
taradiddle 546
tarantass 272
tarantella 840
tarboosh 225

tardiloquence 583
tardy 133, 275
tare 40a
- and tret 813
tares 645
targe 717
target 620
shield 717
tariff 812
tarmac 635
tarn 343
tarnish
discoloration 429
soil 653
deface 848
disgrace 874
tarpaulin 223
tarry remain 110,
265
later 133
continue 141
- for expect 507
tart pastry 298, 396
acid 397
rude 895
irascible 901
harlot 962
tartan 440
tartane 273
Tartar choleric 901
catch a - dupe 547
unskilful 699
retaliation 718
tartar dirt 653
- emetic 663
Tartarus 982
Tartufe
hypocrisy 544
deceiver 548
impiety 988
task lesson 537
business 625
put to use 677
fatigue 688
command 741
hard - 704
set a - 741
take to - 932
- the memory 505
taskmaster 694
tass 191
tassel 847
taste sapidity 390
experience 821
good taste 850
man of - 850
to one's - savory
394
pleasant 829
love 897
tasteful 850
tasteless insipid
391
tasty 394, 850
tâtonner 463
tatter
small quantity 32
tatterdemalion 876
Tattersalls 799
tatters garments
225
tear to - 162
tatting 847
tattle 588
tattler 532, 588
tattoo
drumming 407

mottled 440
summons 741
taught [see teach]
fastened 43
taunt 929, 938
tauromachy 720
taut 43
tautology 104, 573
tavern 189
tawdry 851
tawny 433, 436
tax inquire 461
employ 677
fatigue 688
command 741
compel 744
request 765
accounts 811
impost 812
discount 813
accuse 938
- one's energies
686
- the memory 505
taxi 266
taxi-cab 272
taxi-driver 268
taxidermy 368
taxis 60
taxonomy 60
Te Deum 990
te fabula narratur,
de - retaliate 718
condemn 971
tea 298
teach 537
- one's grand-
mother 641, 885
- one his place 879
teachable 539
teacher 540, 673
teaching 537
false - 538
teacup, storm in a -
overrate 482, 549
exaggerate 549
teagown 225
team assemblage
69, 72
teamster 694
tea-party 892
tea-pot 191
tear separate 44
violence 173
move rapidly 274
excite 825
weeping 839
- away from 789
- oneself away
623
- asunder one's
bonds 750
- one's hair 839
- out 301
- to pieces
separate 44
destroy 162
- up destroy 162
tear-gas 663, 727
tearful 839
tearing passion 839
tears: draw - 830
shed - 839
- in one's eyes
excited 824
sad 837

tease annoy 830
spite 907
teaser difficult 704
teasing 830
teat 250
tea-table talk 588
technic 698
technica, memoria
- 505
technical
conformable 82
workmanlike 698
- college 542
- education 537
- knowledge 698
- school 542
- term 564
technicality
special 79
cant term 563
formulary 697
technique 556, 698
technocracy 698
technology 698
techy 901
tedious 841
while away the -
hours 681
tedium 841
teem
produce 161
productive 168
abound 639
- with multitude
102
teemful 168
teeming crowd 72
teemless 169
'teens 98
in one's - 127, 129
teeter 314
teeth 330, 781
armed to the -
673, 717, 722
between the - 405
cast in one's - 938
chattering of - 383
have cut one's eye
- 698
in the - of 704, 708
grind one's - 900
the run of one's -
815
set one's - 604
show one's - 900
in spite of one's -
708, 744
make one's - chat-
ter 385, 860
set the - on edge
scrape 331
saw 397
stridor 410
pain the feelings
830
tee 66
teetotalism 953,
958
teetotum 312, 840
teg 366
tegument 223
teind 99
teinoscope 445
tekel upharsin 668
telautograph 553
telegram 532
telegraph

life hangs by a – 360
worn to a – 659
– one's way 266, 302
threadbare 226, 659
threadpaper 203
threat 909
threaten
  future 121
  destiny 152
  danger 665
threatening
  warning 668
  unhopeful 859
three 93
  – in one and one in – 976
  sisters – 601
  go through – hundred and sixty degrees 311
  – sheets in the wind 959
  – times three *number* 98
  approbation 931
threefold 93
three-score 98
  – years and ten 128
three-tailed bashaw
  master 745
  nobility 875
threne 938
threnody 839
thrash 972
  – out 461
threshold
  beginning 66
  edge 231
  at the – *near* 197
  – of an inquiry 461
thrice 93
  – happy 827
  –told tale 573
thrid 302
thrift
  prosperity 734
  gain 775
  economy 817
thriftless 818
thrill
  physical pain 378
  touch 380
  feeling 821
  excitation 824
thrilling
  pleasing 829
  painful 830
thrive 734
throat *opening* 260
  pipe 350, 351
  cut the – 361
  force down the – 739
  stick in one's – 581, 585
  take by the – 789
throb 315, 821
throbbing: – heart 860
  – pain 378
throe
  revolution 146
  violence 173

agitation 315
  physical pain 378
  agony 828
birth– 161
throne *abode* 189
  seat 215
  emblem of authority 747
  ascend the – 737
  occupy the – 737
  power behind the – 526
  – of God 981
throng 72
throttle
  render powerless 158
  close 261
  kill 361
  seize 789
  – down 275
through
  owing to 154
  rid 278
  by means of 631
  get – 729
  go – one 824
  wet – 339
  – thick and thin *complete* 52
  violence 173
throughout 50, 52
  – the world 180
throw *impel* 276
  propel 284
  exertion 686
  – oneself into the arms of 664
  – away *reject* 610
  waste 638
  relinquish 782
  – back 144
  – cold water on 616
  – of the dice 156
  – doubt upon 485
  – down 162, 308
  – oneself at the feet of 725
  – good money after bad 818
  – in 228
  – off [*see below*]
  – open 260, 296
  – out [*see below*]
  – over *destroy* 162
  – overboard *exclude* 55
  destroy 162
  eject 297
  abrogate 756
  – on paper 590
  – away the scabbard 722
  – into the shade *superior* 33
  lessen 36
  surpass 303
  important 642
  – a tub to catch a whale 545
  – up [*see below*]
  – a veil over 528
throw off 297
  – all disguise 529
  – one's guard 508

– the mask 529
  – the scent *misdirect* 538
  avoid 623
throw out 284, 297
  eject 297
  – a feeler 379
  – of gear *disjoin* 44
  derange 61
  – a hint 527
  – a suggestion 514
throwing stick 727
thrown out 704
throw up *eject* 297
  resign 757
  – one's cap 884
  – the game 624
thrum 416
thrush 416
thrust *push* 276
  attack 716
  – in *insert* 300
  (*interpose*) 228
  – one's nose in 682
  – out 55
  – down one's throat 744
  – upon 784
thud 406, 408a
thug *murderer* 361
  thief 792
thumb *touch* 379
  bite the – 929
  one's fingers all –s 699
  rule of –
  experiment 463
  unreasoning 477
  essay 675
  twiddle one's – 681
  under one's – *authority* 737
  subjection 749
  – over 539
  – screw 975
Thumb, Tom – 539
thump
  beat 276
  thud 406
  non-resonance 408a
  punish 972
thumping *great* 31
  big 192
thunder
  violence 173
  noise 404
  prodigy 872
  threaten 909
  look black as – 832, 900
  – against 908, 932
  – of applause 931
  – forth 531
  – at the top of one's voice 411
  –s of the Vatican 908
thunderbolt
  weapon 727
  prodigy 872
thunder-clap 508, 872
thundering *great* 31
  big 192

thunderstorm 173
thunderstruck 870
thurible 400, 998
thurifer 996
thuriferous 400
thurification
  fragrance 400
  rite 998
thus *circumstance* 8
  therefore 8
  – far *little* 32
  limit 233
thwack 276, 972
thwart
  across 219
  harm 649
  obstruct 706
  oppose 708
  cross 830
thwarted 732
tiara *insignia* 747
  ornament 847
  canonicals 999
Tib's eve 107
tick *graze* 199, 379
  oscillation 314
  sound 407
  mark 550
  credit 805
  go on – 806
  – off *record* 551
ticker 553
ticket 86, 550, 609
ticket of leave 760
  – man 754, 949
tickle *touch* 380
  please 829
  amuse 840
  – the fancy 829, 840
  – the ivories 416
  – the palate 394
  – the palm 784, 807
ticklish
  uncertain 475
  dangerous 665
  difficult 704
tidal wave 348, 667
tid-bit 648, 829
tide *ocean* 341
  wave 348
  abundance 639
  prosperity 734
  against the – 708
  drift with the – 705
  go with the – 82
  high &c. – 348
  stem the – 708
  swim with the – 734
  turn of the – 210
  – of events 151
  – over *time* 106
  defer 133
  safe 664
  inaction 681
  succeed 731
  – of time 109
tidings 532
tidy *orderly* 58
  arrange 60
  good 648
  clean 652
  pretty 845
  – up 60

tie *relation* 9
  equality 27
  fasten 43
  fastening 45
  neckcloth 225
  security 771
  obligation 926
  nuptial – 903
  ride and – 266
  –s of blood 11
  – down *hinder* 706
  compel 744
  restrain 751
  – the hands 158, 751
  – oneself 768
  – up *restrain* 751
  condition 770
  entail 771
tie-beam 45
tied up
  busy 135
  in debt 806
tier *continuity* 69
  layer 204
tierce 92
  – and carte 716
tiff 713, 900
tiffin 298
tiger *violent* 173
  servant 746
  courage 861
  savage 907
  evil-doer 913
  bad man 949
tight *fast* 43
  closed 261
  smart 845
  drunk 959
  – grasp 739
  – hand 739
  – rope dancing 698
  keep a – hand on 751
  on one's – ropes 878
tighten 43, 195
tight-fisted 819
tights 225
tightwad 819
tigress 374
tike 876
tilbury 272
tile *roof* 223
  hat 225
  – loose *insane* 503
till *up to the time* 106
  coffer 191
  cultivate 371
  treasury 802
  – doomsday 112
  – now 122
  – the soil 673
tiller
  instrument 633
  money-box 802
  – of the soil *agriculture* 371
  clown 876
tilt *slope* 217
  cover 223
  propel 284
  fall 306
  contention 720
  full – *direct* 278

solecism 568
stammering 583
on the tip of
  one's –
  near 197
  forget 506
  latent 526
  speech 582
wag the – 582
– cleave to the
  roof of one's
  mouth 870
have a – in one's
  head 582
– of land 342
– running loose
  584
keep one's – be-
  tween one's
  teeth 585
tongueless 581
tongue-tied 581
tonic
  musical note 413
  healthy 656
  medicine 662
– sol fa 415
tonicity 159
tonnage 192
tonsillectomy 662
tonsils 351
tonsure 999
tonsured 226
tontine 810
tony 501
Tony Lumpkin 876
too
  also 37
  excess 641
– bad
  disreputable 874
  wrong 923
  censure 932
– clever by half
  702
in a – great degree
  31
– far 641
– hot to hold one
  830
– late 133
– late for 135
– little 640
– many 641
– much [*see below*]
– soon 132
– soon for 135
– true 833 839
too much
  redundance 641
  intemperance 954
have – of 869
make – of 482
– for 471
– of a good thing
  869
tool *instrument* 633
  steer 693
  catspaw 711
  ornament 847
  servile 886
edge – 253
mere – 690
toot 406
tooth *fastening* 45
  projection 250
  sharp 253

roughness 256
notch 257
texture 329
taste 390
sweet –
  desire 865
  fastidious 868
– and nail
  violence 173
  exertion 686
  attack 716
– paste &c. 652
toothache 378
toothed 253
toothsome 394
top *supreme* 33
  summit 210
  roof 223
  spin 312
sleep like a – 683
fool to the – of
  one's bent 545
go over the – 861
– to bottom 52
– coat 225
– hat 225
at the – of the
  heap 210
– of the ladder 873
at the – of one's
  speed 274
from – to toe 200
at the – of the
  tree 210, 873
at the – of one's
  voice 404, 411
toparchy 737
topaz 436, 847
top-boot 225
tope *tomb* 363
  trees 367
  drink 959
  temple 1000
topee 225
toper 959
top-full 52
top-gallant mast,
  206, 210
top-heavy
  unbalanced 28
  inverted 218
  dangerous 665
  tipsy 959
Tophet 982
topiary 847
topic 454
– of the day 532
topical 183
top-mast 206
topmost 210
topography 183
topographer 466
topple
  unbalanced 28
  perish 162
  decay 659
– down *fall* 306
– over 28, 306
topsail schooner
  273
topsawyer 642, 700
top sergeant 745
topsy-turvy 14, 218
toque 225
tor 206
torch 388, 423
apply the – 824

light the – of war
  722
– of Hymen 903
Tories 712
torment
  physical 378
  moral 828, 830
place of – 982
Tormes, Lazarillo
  de – 941
torn [*see tear*]
  discord 713
tornado 312, 349
torpedo *bane* 663
  sluggish 683
  weapon 727
  evil-doer 913
– boat 726
– boat destroyer
  726
– plane 276
torpid, torpor
  inert 172
  inactive 683
  insensible 823
torque 847
  torrefy 384
torrent
  violence 173
  rapid 274
  flow 348
rain in –s 348
torrid 382
torsion 248
torso 50
tort 925, 947
tort et à travers, à –
  disagreement 24
  absurdity 497
  resolution 604
tortious 925
tortile 248
tortive 248
tortoise 275
tortoise-shell 440
tortuous
  twisted 248
  dishonorable 940
torture
  physical 378
  moral 828, 830
  cruelty 907
  punishment 972
– a question 476
torvity 901a
toss *derange* 61
  throw 284
  oscillate 314
  agitate 315
– in a blanket 929
– the caber 840
– the head
  pride 878
  insolence 885
  contempt 930
– off *drink* 298
– overboard 610
– on one's pillow
  825
– up 156, 621
tosspot 959
tot *child* 129
tot homines, tot
  sententiæ 15
total 50, 84
sum – 800
– abstinence 953,

955
– eclipse 421
totality 52
totalizator 621
totally 52
totidem verbis 19,
  494
totient 84
toties quoties 136
totis viribus 686
totitive 84
toto: in – 52
– cœlo 52
totter
  changeable 149
  weak 160
  limp 275
  oscillate 314
  agitate 315
  decay 659
  danger 665
– to its fall 162
touch *relate to* 9
  small quantity 32
  mixture 41
  contact 199
  sensation 379,
    380
  music 416
  test 463
  indication 550
  act 680
  receive 785
  excite 824
  pity 914
– and go
  instant 113
  soon 132
  changeable 149
  easy 705
– the guitar 416
– the hat 894
– the heart 824
– on 516
– to the quick 822
– up 658
– upon 595
in – with 9
touched *crazy* 503
  tainted 653
  compassion 914
– in the wind 655
– with *feeling* 821
touching 830
touchstone 463
touchwood
  fuel 388
  irascible 901
touchy 901
tough *coherent* 46
  tenacious 327
  difficult 704
toujours perdrix
  repetition 104
  weary 841
  satiety 869
toupee 256
tour 266
tour de force
  skill 698
  stratagem 702
  display 882
touring car 272
tourist 268
tournament 720
tourniquet 263
tournure 230, 448

belle – 845
tous les rapports,
  sous – 494
tousle 61
tout *solicit* 765
tout: – au contraire
  14
– court 265
– ensemble 50
– le monde 78
touter *agent* 758
  solicitor 767
  eulogist 935
tow 285
take in – *aid* 707
towage 812
towardly 705
towards 278
draw – 288
move – 286
towel *clean* 652
  flog 972
tower
  stability 150
  edifice 161
  abode 189
  height 206
  soar 305
  defence 717
– of strength
  strong 159
  influential 175
  safety 664
towering *great* 31
  furious 173
  large 192
  high 206
– passion 900
– rage 900
town *city* 189
  fashion 852
man about – 854
on the – 961
all over the – 532
talk of the – 873
– council 696
town-hall 189, 966
township 181
townsman 188
fellow – 892
town-talk 532, 588
toxic 657
toxicology 663
toxophilite 284
toy *trifle* 643
  amusement 840
  fondle 902
toy-dog 366
toy-shop 840
trabant 717
tracasserie 713
trace *inquire* 461
  discover 480a
  mark 550
  record 551
  delineate 554
– back 122
– out 480a
– to 155
– up 461
tracery
  lattice 219
  curve 245
  ornament 847
traces *harness* 45
trachea 351
tracing 21

illogical 477
unconquerable
  strong 159
  persevering 604a
  – will 604
unconquered 719
unconscientious 940
unconscionable
  excessive 31
  unprincipled 945
unconscious
  ignorant 491
  insensible 823
unconsenting 603, 764
unconsidered 452
unconsolable 837
unconsolidated 47
unconsonant 24
unconspicuous 447
unconstitutional 925, 964
unconstrained 748, 880
unconsumed 40
uncontested 474
uncontradicted 488
uncontrite 951
uncontrollable
  violent 173
  necessity 601
  emotion 825
uncontrolled
  free 748
  excitability 825
uncontroverted 488
unconventional 83, 614
unconversant 491, 699
unconverted
  dissenting 489
  irreligious 989
unconvinced 489
uncooked 674
uncopied 20
uncork 750
uncorrupted 939
uncounted 475
uncouple 44
uncourteous 895
uncourtly 851, 895
uncouth
  – *style* 579
  ugly 846
  vulgar 851
uncover
  denude 226
  open 260
  disclose 529
  bow 894
uncreated 2
uncritical 931
uncropped 50
uncrown 756
unction
  emotion 821, 824
  divine functions 976
  piety 987
  extreme – 998
  lay the flattering
  – to one's soul 834, 858
unctuous *oily* 355, 894

flattering 933
  hypocritical 988
unctuousness 355
unculled
  unused 678
  relinquished 782
unculpable 946
uncultivated
  vulgar 85
  ignorant 491
  unprepared 674
uncurbed 748
uncurl 246
uncustomary 83
uncut 50
undamaged (648)
undamped 340
undated
  without date 115
  waving 248
undaunted 861
undazzled 498
undebauched 939
undeceive 527, 529
undeceived 490
undecided
  inquiring 461
  uncertain 475
  irresolute 605
  leave – 609a
undecipherable 519
undecked 849
undecomposed 42
undefaced 845
undefended 725
undefiled
  honest 939
  innocent 946
  chaste 960
undefinable
  uncertain 475
  unmeaning 517
  unintelligible 519
undefined
  invisible 447
  uncertain 475
undeformed 845
undemolished 50
undemonstrable 485
undemonstrated 475
undemonstrative 826
undeniable 474, 478
undeplored 898
undepraved 939
undeprived 781
under *less* 34
  below 207
  subject to 749
  range – 76
  – advisement 454
  – age 127
  – agent 758
  – arrest 751
  – breath 405
  – the conditions 8
  – one's control 743
  – cover
  covered 223
  hidden 528
  safe 664
  – the domination of 737
  – one's eyes 446
  – foot [*see below*]

– full strength 651
  – the head of 9
  – lock and key 664
  – the mark 34
  – press of 744
  – protest 489, 744
  – restraint 751
  – the rule of 737
  – seal 467
  – subjection 749
  – the sun 1
  – way 282
underbid 794
underbreath 405
underbred 851
underclothing 225
undercurrent
  cause 153
  stream 348, 349
  latent 526
  opposing 708
underestimation 483
underfed 640
underfoot 207
  tread – 739
undergo 151
  – a change 144
  – pain 828
undergraduate 541
underground
  low 207
  deep 208
  latent 526
  hidden 528
underhand 526, 528
  – dealing 528
underhung 250
underived 20
underlessee 779
underlet 787
underlie 207, 526
underline
  mark 550
  emphatic 642
underling
  servant 746
  clown 876
undermine
  weaken 158
  burrow 252
  damage 659
  stratagem 702
  hinder 706
undermost 211
underneath 207
undernourished 640
underpaid 817
underpin 215
underplot 626
underprop 215
underrate 483
underreckon 483
undersell 796
underset 215
undershot 250
undersign 467
undersized 193
understand
  know 490
  intelligible 518
  latent 526
  be informed 527
  give one to – 572
  – by 516, 522
  – one another

709, 714
understanding
  agreement 23
  intellect 450
  intelligence 498
  come to an – 488
  intelligible 518
  agree 714
  pacification 723
  compact 769
  good – 714, 888
  by a mutual – 526
  with the – 469
understate 489
understood
  meaning 516
  implied 526
  customary 613
understrapper 746
understudy 134
undertake
  endeavor 676
  promise 768
undertaker 363
undertaking 625, 676
undertone 405
undertow 348
undervalue 483
underwood 367
underwrite
  promise 768
  compact 769
  insurance 771
underwriter 758
undescribed 83
undeserved 925
undeserving of belief 485
undesigned 621
undesigning 703
undesirable 647, 830
undesired 830, 866
undesirous 866
undespairing 858
undestroyed
  existing 1
  whole 50
  persisting 141
undetermined
  chance 156
  inquiry 461
  uncertain 475
  unintelligible 519
  irresolute 605
undeveloped 526
undeviating
  uniform 16
  unchanged 150
  straight 246
  direct 278
  persevering 604a
undevout 989
undigested 674
undignified 940
undiminished 31, 35, 50
undirected 279, 621
undiscernible 447, 519
undiscerning
  blind 442
  inattentive 458
undisciplined 608
undisclosed 526, 528

undiscoverable 519
undiscovered 526
undiscriminating 465a
undisguised
  true 494
  manifest 525
  sincere 543
undismayed 861
undisposed of 678, 781
undisputed 474
undissembling 543
undissolved
  entire 50
  dense 321
undistinguishable 465a
undistinguished 465a
undistorted 246, 494
undistracted 457
undisturbed
  quiescent 265
  repose 685
  unexcited 826
undivided 50, 52
undo *untie* 44
  reverse 145
  destroy 162
  neutralize 179
  not do 681
undoing *ruin* 735
undone *failure* 732
  adversity 735
  pained 828
  hopeless 859
undoubted 474
undoubtedly 488
undraped 226
undreaded 861
undreamt of 452
undress *clothes* 225
  nude 226
  simple 849
undressed 226, 674
undried 339
undrilled 674
undrooping 604a
undueness 925
undulate 248, 314
unduly 32
undutiful 945
undying 112, 150
une aile, ne battre que d' – 683
unearned 925
unearth *eject* 297
  disinter 363
  inquire 461
  discover 480a
unearthly
  immaterial 317
  Deity 976
  demon 980
  heavenly 981
  pious 987
uneasy 828
uneatable 395
unedifying 538
uneducated 491, 674
unembarrassed 705, 852
unembodied 317
unemotional 823

unemployed 678,
681
unencumbered 705,
927a
unendeared 898
unending 112
unendowed 158
– with reason
450a
unendurable 830
unenjoyed 841
unenlightened 491,
499
unenslaved 748
unenterprising 864
unentertaining 843
unenthralled 748
unentitled 925
unenvied 929, 930
unequal 28, 139
inequitable 923
– to 640
unequalled 33
unequipped 674
unequitable 923
unequivocal
great 31
sure 474
clear 518
unerring
certain 474
tone 494
innocent 946
unessayed 678
unessential 643
unestablished 185
uneven *diverse* 16a
unequal 28
irregular 139
rough 256
uneventful 643
unexact 495
unexaggerated 494
unexamined 460
unexampled 83
unexceptionable
good 648
legitimate 924
innocent 946
unexcitable 826
unexcited 823, 826
unexciting 174
unexecuted 730
unexempt 177
unexercised 674,
678
unexerted 172
unexhausted 159,
639
unexpanded 195,
203
unexpected
exceptional 83
inexpectation 508
unexpensive 815
unexplained
not known 491
unintelligible 519
latent 626
unexplored
neglected 460
ignorant 491
unseen 526
unexposed 526
unexpressed 536
unexpressive 517
unextended 317

unextinguished
173, 382
unfaded 428
unfading 112
unfailing 141
unfair *false* 544
unjust 923
dishonorable 940
unfaithful 940
unfaltering 604a
unfamiliar 83
unfashionable 83,
851
unfashioned 241,
674
unfasten 44
unfathomable
infinite 105
deep 208
mysterious 519
unfavorable
out of season 135
hindrance 706
obstructive 708
– chance 473
unfeared 861
unfeasible 471
unfed 640, 956
unfeeling 376, 823
unfeigned 543
unfelt 823
unfeminine
manly 373
vulgar 851
unfertile 169
unfetter 750
unfettered 748
unfinished 53, 730
unfit
inappropriate 24
impotence 158
inexpedient 647
unskilful 699
wrong 923
undue 925
unfitted
not prepared 674
unfix 44
unfixed 149
unflagging 604a
unflammable 385
unflattering 494,
703
unfledged
young 127, 129
unprepared 674
unflinching
firm 604
persevering 604a
brave 861
unfold
straighten 246
evolve 313
interpret 522
manifest 525
disclose 529
– a tale 504
unforbidden 760
unforced 602, 748
unforeseen 508
unforfeited 781
unforgettable 505
unforgiving 919
unforgotten 505
unformed 241, 674
unfortified
pure 42

powerless 158
unfortunate
ill-timed 135
failure 732
adversity 735
unhappy 828
– woman 962
unfounded 546
unfrequent 137
unfrequented 893
unfriended
powerless 158
secluded 893
unfriendly
opposed 708
hostile 889
malevolent 907
unfrock 756, 972
unfrozen 382
unfruitful 169
unfulfilled 713, 925
unfurl
unfold 313
– a flag 525, 550
unfurnished 640,
674
ungainly 846, 895
ungallant 895
ungarnished 849
ungathered 678
ungenerous 819,
943
ungenial 657
ungenteel 851, 895
ungentle 173, 895
ungentlemanly
vulgar 851
rude 895
dishonorable 940
ungifted 499
unglorified 874
unglue 47
ungodly 989
ungovernable
violent 173
disobedient 742
passionate 825
ungoverned 748
ungraceful
– language 579
ugly 846
vulgar 851
ungracious 895, 907
ungrammatical 568
ungranted 764
ungrateful 917
ungratified 832
ungrounded
unsubstantial 4
erroneous 495
ungrudging 816
unguarded
neglected 460
spontaneous 612
unprepared 674
in an – moment
unexpectedly 508
unguem, ad – 494,
650
unguent 356
unguibus et rostro
686
unguided
ignorant 491
impulsive 612
unskilled 699
unguilty 946

unhabitable 187
unhabituated 614
unhackneyed 614
unhallowed 988,
989
unhand 750
unhandseled 123
unhandsome 940
unhandy 699
unhappy
adversity 735
pain 828
dejected 837
make – 830
unharbored 185
unhardened
tender 914
innocent 946
penitent 950
unharmonious 24,
414
unharness 750
unhatched 674
unhazarded 664
unhealthy 655, 657
unheard of
exceptional 83
improbable 473
ignorant 491
wonderful 870
unheated 383
unheed, -ed 460
unheeding 458
unhesitating
belief 484
resolved 604
unhewn 241, 674
unhindered 748
unhinge 61, 158
unhinged
impotent 158
insane 503
unhitch 44
unholy 989
unhonored 874
unhook (44)
unhoped 508
unhorsed 732
unhostile 888
unhouse 297
unhoused 185
unhurt 670
unicorn
monster 83
carriage 272
unideal *existing* 1
no thought 452
true 494
unification 48, 87
uniform
homogeneous 16
simple 42
orderly 58
regular 80
dress 225
symmetry 242
livery 550
uniformity 16
unilluminated 421
unimaginable 471,
473
wonderful 870
unimaginative 576,
843, 868
unimagined 1, 494
unimitated 20

unimpaired 670
unimpassioned 826
unimpeachable
certain 474
true 494
due 924
approved 931
innocent 946
unimpeached 931,
946
unimpeded 705, 748
unimportance 643
unimpressed 838
unimpressible 823
unimproved 659
unincreased 36
unincumbered
easy 705
exempt 927a
uninduced 616
uninfected 652
uninfectious 656
uninflammable 385
uninfluenced
obstinate 606
unactuated 616
free 768
uninfluential 172,
175a
uninformed 491
uningenuous 544
uninhabit, -able,
-ed 187, 893
uninitiated 491, 699
uninjured
perfect 650
healthy 654
preserved 670
uninjurious 656
uninquisitive 456
uninspired 823
uninstructed 491
unintellectual 452,
499
unintelligent 499
unintelligibility 519
unintelligible 519
– style 571
render – 538
unintentional
necessary 601
undesigned 621
uninterested 456,
841, 843
unintermitting
unbroken 69
durable 110
continuing 143
persevering 604a
uninterrupted
continuous 69
perpetual 112
unremitting 893
unintroduced 893
uninured 614
uninvented 526
uninvestigated 491
uninvited 893
uninviting 830
union
agreement 23
junction 43
combination 48
concurrence 178
workhouse 189
party 712
concord 714

marriage 903
unionist 712
union-jack 550
union-pipes 417
unique
  dissimilar 18
  original 20
  exceptional 83
  alone 87
unirritating 174
unison
  agreement 23
  melody 413
  concord 714
unit 51, 87
Unitarian 984
unite join 43
  combine 48
  assemble 72
  concur 178
  converge 290
  party 712
  – one's efforts 709
  – in pairs 89
  – with 709
united 46, 714
unity identity 14
  uniformity 16
  whole 50
  complete 52
  single 87
  concord 714
  – of time 120
Unity, Trinity in –
  976
universal 78
  – Church 983a
  – favourite 899
universality 52
universe 318
university 542
  – education 537
  – extension 537
  go to the – 539
unjust wrong 923
  impious 988
unjustifiable
  wrong 923
  inexcusable 938
  wicked 945
unjustified 923
  undue 925
unkempt
  unclean 753
  vulgar 851
unkennel eject 297
  disclose 529
unkind 907
  -est cut of all 828
unknightly 940
unknit (44)
unknowable 519
unknowing 491
unknown
  ignorant 491
  latent 526
  – to fame
  inglorious 874
  low-born 876
  – quantities 491
unlabored
  - style 578
  unprepared 674
unlace (44)
unlade 297
unladylike
  vulgar 851

rude 895
unlamented
  hated 898
  disapproved 932
unlatch 44, 750
unlawful
  undue 925
  illegal 964
unlearn 506
unlearned 491
unleavened 674
unless
  circumstances 8
  except 83
  qualification 469
unlettered 491
  – Muse 579
unlicensed 761
unlicked
  unprepared 674
  vulgar 851
  clownish 876
  – cub
  youngster 129
  shapeless 241
  unmannerly 895
unlike 18
unlikely 473
unlikeness 15
unlimber 323
unlimited
  great 31
  infinite 105
  free 748
  – space 180
unliquefied 321
unlively 837, 843
unload
  displaced 185
  eject 297
  disencumber 705
unlock unfasten 44
  discover 480a
unlooked for 508
unloose
  unfasten 44
  liberate 750
unloved 898
unlovely 846
unlucky
  inopportune 135
  bad 649
  unfortunate 735
  in pain 830
unmade 2
unmaimed 654
unmake 145
unman
  mutilate 38
  render powerless
  158
  madden 837
  frighten 860
unmanly
  effeminate 374
  dishonorable 940
unmanageable
  unwieldy 647
  perverse 704
unmanned
  dejected 837
  cowardly 862
unmannered 895
unmannerly 895
unmarked 460
unmarred 654, 670
unmarried 904

unmask 529
unmatched
  different 15
  dissimilar 18
  unparalleled 20
unmeaningness 517
unmeant 517
unmeasured
  infinite 105
  undistinguished
  465a
  abundant 639
unmeditated 612
unmeet 925
unmellowed 674
unmelodious 414
unmelted 321
unmentionable 874
  –s 225
unmentioned 526
unmerciful 914a
unmerited 925
unmethodical 59
unmindful
  inattentive 458
  neglectful 460
  ungrateful 917
unmingled 42
unmissed 460
unmistakable
  certain 474
  intelligible 518
  manifest 525
unmitigable 173
unmitigated
  great 31
  complete 52
  violent 173
unmixed 42
unmolested 664,
  831
unmoneyed 804
unmoral 823
unmourned 898
unmoved
  quiescent 265
  obstinate 606
  insensible 823
unmusical 424
  – voice 581
unmuzzled 748
unnamed 565
unnatural
  exceptional 83
  affected 855
  spiteful 907
unnecessary
  redundant 641
  useless 645
  inexpedient 647
unneeded 645
unneighborly 895
unnerved
  powerless 158
  weak 160
  dejected 837
unnoted } 460
unnoticed } 874
unnumbered 105
unnurtured 674
uno saltu 113
unobeyed 742
unobjectionable
  good 648
  pretty good 651
  innocent 946
unobnoxious 648

unobscured 420
unobservant 458
unobserved 460
unobstructed 705,
  749
unobtainable 471
unobtained 777a
unobtrusive 881
unoccupied
  vacant 187
  unthinking 452
  doing nothing 681
  inactive 683
  untenanted 893
unoffended
  enduring 826
  humble 879
unofficial 964
unoften 137
unopened 261
unopposed 709
unorganized 674
  – matter 358
unornamental 846
unornamented
  - style 576
  simple 849
unorthodox 984
unostentatious 881
unowed 807
unowned 782
unpacific 713, 722
unpacified 713
unpack
  unfasten 44
  take out 297
unpaid debt 806
  honorary 815
  the great –
  magistracy 967
  – worker 602
unpalatable 395,
  830
unparagoned
  supreme 33
  best 648
  perfect 650
unparalleled
  unimitated 20
  supreme 33
  exceptional 83
unpardonable 938,
  945
unparliamentary
  language 895,
  908
unpassable 261
unpassionate 826
unpatriotic 911
unpeaceful 720, 722
unpeople
  emigration 297
  banishment 893
unperceived
  neglected 460
  unknown 491
unperformed 730
unperjured 543,
  939
unperplexed 498
unpersuadable 606
unpersuaded 616
unperturbed 826
unphilosophical 499
unpierced 261
unpin (44)
unpitied 932

unpitying 914a
unplaced 185
unplagued 831
unpleasant 830
unpleasing 830
unpoetical 598, 703
unpolished
  rough 256
  inelegant 579
  unprepared 674
  vulgar 851, 876
  rude 895
unpolite 895
unpolluted
  good 648
  perfect 650
unpopular 830, 867
unpopularity 898
unportioned 804
unpossessed 777a
unpractical 699
unprecedented 83,
  137
unprejudiced 498,
  748
unpremeditated
  impulsive 612
  undesigned 621
  unprepared 674
unprepared 508,
  674
unprepossessed 498
unprepossessing
  846
unpresentable 851
unpretending 881
unprevented 748
unprincipled 945
unprivileged 925
unprized 483
unproclaimed 526
unproduced 2
unproductive 645
unproductiveness
  169
unproficiency 699
unprofitable
  unproductive 169
  useless 645
  inexpedient 647
  bad 649
unprolific 169
unpromising 859
unprompted 612
unpronounceable
  519
unpronounced 526
unpropitious
  ill-timed 135
  opposed 708
  hopeless 859
unproportioned 24
unprosperous 735
unprotected 665
unproved 477
unprovided
  scanty 640
  unprepared 674
unprovoked (616)
unpublished 526
unpunctual
  tardy 133
  untimely 135
  irregular 139
unpunished 970
unpurchased 796
unpurified 653

unpurposed 621
unpursued 624
unqualified
incomplete 52
impotent 158
certain 474
unprepared 674
inexpert 699
unentitled 925
– *truth* 494
unquelled 173
unquenchable
strong 159
desire 865
unquenched
violence 173
heat 382
unquestionable 474
unquestionably 488
unquestioned 474, 488
unquiet
motion 264
agitation 315
excitable 825
unravel *untie* 44
arrange 60
straighten 246
evolve 313
discover 480a
interpret 522
disembarrass 705
unreached 304
unread 491
unready 674
unreal
not existing 2
erroneous 495
imaginary 515
unreasonable
impossible 471
illogical 477
misjudging 481
foolish 499
exorbitant 814
unjust 923
unreclaimed 951
unrecognizable 146
unreconciled 713
unrecorded 552
unrecounted 55
unreduced 31
unrefined 851
unreflecting 458
unreformed 951
unrefreshed 688
unrefuted 478, 494
unregarded
neglected 460
unrespected 929
unregenerate 988
unregistered 552
unreined 748
unrelated 10
unrelenting 914a, 919
unreliable
uncertain 475
irresolute 605
dangerous 665
unrelieved 835
unremarked 460
unremembered 506
unremitting
continuous 69
continuing 110
unvarying 143

perseverng 604a
unremoved 184
unremunerated 808
unrenewed 141
unrepealed 141
unrepeated 87, 103
unrepentant 951
unrepining 831
unreplenished 640
unrepressed 173
unreproached 946
unreproved 946
unrequited 806, 917
unresented 918
unresenting 826
unreserved
manifest 525
veracious 543
artless 703
unresisted 743
unresisting 725
unresolved 605
unrespected 929
unrest 149, 264
unrestored 688
unrestrained
capricious 608
unencumbered 705
free 748
unrestricted
undiminished 31
free 748
unretracted 535
unrevenged 918
unreversed 143
unrevoked 143
unrewarded 806, 917
unrhymed 598
unriddle 480a, 529
unrig 645
unrighteous 945
unrip 260
unripe
young 127
sour 397
immature 674
unrivalled 33
unroll *evolve* 313
display 525
unromantic 494
unroot 301
unruffled
calm 174
quiet 265
unaffected 823
placid 826
unruly *violent* 173
obstinate 606
disobedient 742
unsaddle 756
unsafe 665
unsaid 526
unsaleable
useless 645
selling 796
cheap 815
unsaluted 929
unsanctified 988, 939
unsanctioned 925
unsated 865
unsatisfactory
inexpedient 647
bad 649
displeasing 830

discontent 832
unsatisfied 832, 865
unsavouriness 395
unsay *recant* 607
unscanned 460
unscathed 654
unschooled 491
unscientific 477
unscoured 653
unscriptural 984
unscrupulous 940
unseal 529
unsearched 460
unseasonable 24, 135
unseasoned 614, 674
unseat 756
unseemly
inexpedient 647
ugly 846
vulgar 851
undue 925
vicious 945
unseen
invisible 447
neglected 460
latent 526
unseldom 136
unselfish 942
unseparated 46
unserviceable 645
unsettle *derange* 61
unsettled
mutable 149
displaced 185
uncertain 475
– *in one's mind* 503
unsevered 50
unsex 146
unshaded 525
unshaken 159
– *belief* 484
unshapely 846
unshapen 241
unshared 777
unsheathe
– *the sword* 722
unsheltered 665
unshielded 665
unshifting 143
unship 185, 297
unshocked 823
unshorn 50
unshortened 200
unshrinking 604, 861
unsifted 460
unsightly 846
unsinged 670
unskilfulness 699
unslaked 865
unsleeping 604a, 682
unsmooth 256
unsociable 893
unsocial 893
unsoiled 652
unsold 777
unsoldierlike 862
unsolicitous 866
unsolved 526
unsophisticated
simple 42
genuine 494
artless 703

unsorted 59
unsought
avoided 623
unrequested 766
unsound
illogical 477
erroneous 495
deceptive 545
imperfect 651
– *mind* 503
unsown 674
unsparing
abundant 639
severe 739
liberal 816
with an – *hand* 818
unspeakable 31, 870
unspecified 78
unspent 678
unspied 526
unspiritual 316, 989
unspoiled 648
unspotted
clean 652
beautiful 845
innocent 946
unstable 218
changeable 149
uncertain 475
irresolute 605
precarious 665
– *equilibrium* 149
unstaid 149
unstained
clean 652
honorable 939
unstatesmanlike 699
unsteadfast 605
unsteady
mutable 149
irresolute 605
in danger 665
unstinted 639
unstinting 816
unstirred 823, 826
unstopped
continuing 143
open 260
unstored 640
unstrained
turbid 653
relaxed 687
– *meaning* 516
unstrengthened 160
unstruck 823
unstrung 160
unstudied 460
unsubject 748
unsubmissive 742
unsubservient
useless 645
inexpedient 647
unsubstantial 4
weak 160
rare 322
erroneous 495
imaginary 515
unsubstantiality 4
unsuccessful 732
unsuccessive 70
unsuitable
incongruous 24
(*inexpedient* 647)
– *time* 135

unsullied *clean* 652
honorable 939
(*guiltless* 946)
unsung 526
unsupplied 640
unsupported
weak 160
(*unassisted* 706)
– *by evidence* 468
unsuppressed 141
unsurmountable 471
unsurpassed 33
unsusceptible 823
unsuspected
belief 484
latent 526
unsuspecting
hopeful 858
unsuspicious
belief 484
artless 703
hope 858
unsustainable 495
unsweet 395
unswept 653
unswerving
straight 246
direct 278
persevering 604a
unsymmetric 83
unsymmetrical 59, 243
unsystematic 59
untainted *pure* 652
healthy 654
honorable 939
untalked of 526
untamed 851, 907
untarnished 939
untasted 391
untaught 491, 674
untaxed 815
unteach 538
unteachable 499, 699
untenable
powerless 158
illogical 477
undefended 725
untenanted 187, 893
unthanked 917
unthankful 917
unthawed 321, 383
unthinkable 471
unthinking
unconsidered 452
involuntary 601
unthought of 452, 460
unthreatened 664
unthrifty
unprepared 674
prodigal 818
unthrone 756
untidy 59, 653
untie 44, 750
– *the knot* 705
until 106
– *now* 118
untilled 674
untimely 135
– *end* 360
untinged 42
untired 689
untiring 604a

remedy 662
Venetian blinds
351
vengeance 919
cry to heaven
for – 923
with a – 31, 173
vengeful 919
veni vidi vici 731
venial 937
veniam petimusque
damusque vicis-
sim 918
venienti occurrere
morbo 673
venison 394
venom 663, 907
venomous bad 649
poisonous 657
rude 895
maleficent 907
vent opening 260
egress 295
air-pipe 351
disclose 529
escape 671
sale 796
find – egress 295
passage 302
publish 531
escape 671
give – to 297, 529
– one's rage 900
– one's spleen 900
venter 191
ventiduct 351
ventilate
begin 66
air 338
wind 349
discuss 595
– a question 461,
476
ventilator 349, 351
ventosity 349
vent-peg
stopper 263
safely 666
escape 671
ventre
– à terre 274
danse du – 840
ventricle 191
ventriloquism 580
venture
chance 621
danger 665
try 675
courage 861
I'll – to say 535
venturesome
undertaking 677
brave 861
rash 863
venue 74, 183
Venus woman 374
planet 423
beauty 845
love 897
goddess 919
veracity 543
verandah 191
verbal 562
– intercourse 582,
588
– quibble 497, 842
verbatim

imitation 19
exact 494
words 562
verbiage
unmeaning 517
words 562
diffuse 573
verbis:
totidem – 494
– ad verbera 720
verbose 582
verborum, copia –
diffuse 573
eloquence 582
loquacious 584
verbosity
words 562
diffuse 573
loquacity 584
verboten 761
verbum sapienti
527
verdant 367, 435
verd-antique 435
verdict
opinion 480
lawsuit 969
snatch a – 545,
702
verdigris 435
verditer 435
verdure 367, 435
verecundiam, argu-
mentum ad –
874, 939
verecundity 879,
881
veredical 543
Verein 712
verge
tendency 176
near 197
edge 231
limit 233
direction 278
verger 996
veriest 31
verification 463,
771
verify 463
evidence 467
demonstrate 478
find out 480a
verily truly 494
verisimilitude 472
veritable 494
veritas, nuda – 494
vérité, palais de –
703
verity 494
verjuice 397
vermicular
convoluted 248
worm 366
vermiform 248
vermilion 434
vermin
animal 366
unclean 653
base 876
vernacular
native 188
internal 221
language 560
habitual 613
vernal 123, 125
vernier
minuteness 193

– scale 466
vero, vitam impen-
dere – 535, 939
verrons, nous – 507
versatile 149
verse division 51
poetry 597
versed in 490
versicolor 440
versify 597
version change 140
special 79
interpretation 522
versus 278, 708
vert 435
vertebral 222
vertebrate 366
vertex 210
verticality 212
verticity 312
vertigo
rotation 312
delirium 503
verve
imagination 515
vigorous language
574
energy 682
feeling 821
very 31
– best 648
– image 554
– many 102
– minute 113
– much 31
– picture 17
– small 32
– thing
identity 13
agreement 23
exact 494
– true 488
– well 831
Véry light 423
vesicle cell 191
covering 223
globe 249
vesicular 191, 260
vespers 126, 990
vespertine 126
vessel
receptacle 191
tube 260
ship 273
vest place 184
dress 225
– in belong to 777
give 784
Vesta 979
vesta match 388
vestal 960
vested fixed 150
legal 963
– in located 184
– interest
given 780
due 924
vestibule 66, 191
vestige 551
vestigia:
veteris – flammæ
505, 613
– nulla retrorsum
282, 604a
vestment 225, 999
vestry council 696
churchdom 995

church 1000
vesture 225
vesuvian
match 388
veteran old 130
adept 700
warrior 726
veterinary art 370
veteris vestigiá
flammae 505,
613
veto 761
vetturino 694
vex 830, 898
vexata quaestio 704,
713
vexation 828, 830
– of spirit 828
discontent 832
resentment 900
vexatious 830
vexed question
704, 713
vi et armis
violence 173
exertion 686
compulsion 744
viâ 278, 627
viable 359
via lactea 318
viaduct 627
vial 191
vials:
– of hate 898
– of wrath 900
viands 298
viaticum
provision 637
rite 998
vibrate 314
– between two
extremes 149
vibrato 415
vibratory 149
vibroscope 314
vicar deputy 759
clergyman 996
– of Bray 607, 886
vicarage 1000
vicariate 995
vicarious 147
vicarship 995
vice deputy 759
holder 781
wickedness **945**
vice versâ
reciprocal 12
contrary 14
interchange 148
vice-admiral 745
Vice-Chancellor
967
–'s Court 966
vicegerency 755
vicegerent 758, 759
vice-president 694
vice-regal 759
viceroy
governor 745
deputy 759
vicesimal 98
vicinage 197
vicinism 145
vicinity 197, 227
vicious 173, 945
render – 659
– reasoning 477

vicissitude 149
Vickers gun 727
victim dupe 547
defeated 732
sufferer 828
victimize kill 361
deceive 545
injure 649
baffle 731
victis, væ – 722, 909
victor 731
victoria
carriage 272
Victoria Cross 733
victory 731
victual provide 637
victuals 298
videlicet 79, 522
viduage 905
viduity 905
vie good 648
– with 720
vielle 417
view
sight 441
appearance 448
attend to 457
opinion 484
landscape paint-
ing 556
intention 620
bring into – 525
come into – 446
commanding – 441
in – visible 446
intended 420
expected 507
keep in – 457
on – 448
present to the –
448
with a – to 620
– as 484
– in a new light
658
viewer 444
viewless 447
view-point 441
vigesimal 98
vigil care 459
vigilance care 459
wisdom 498
activity 682
caution 864
vigils worship 990
vignette 558, 594,
847
vigor strength 159
energy 171
style **574**
resolution 604
health 654
activity 682
viking 792
vile valueless 643
bad 649
painful 830
disgraceful 874
plebeian 876
dishonorable 940
vicious 945
vilify shame 874
malediction 908
censure 932
detract 934
vilipend
disrespect 929

worth – 646
– away time
  inaction 681
  pastime 840
– speaking of 9, 134
whilom 122
whilst 106
whim fad 481
  fancy 515
  caprice 608
  wil 842
  desire 865
whimper 839
whimsey 515, 865
whimsical [see whim] 853
whimwam 608, 643
whin 367
whine 411, 839
whinyard 727
whip collect 72
  coachman 268
  strike 276
  stir up 315
  urge 615
  hasten 684
  director 694
  flog 972
  scourge 975
– and spur 274
– away 293
– hand 731, 737
– in 300
– on 684
– off 293
– up 789
whipcord 205
whipper-in 694
whippersnapper 129
whipping-post 975
whipster 129
whir rotate 312
  sound 407
whirl rotate 312
  flurry 825
whirligig 312
whirlpool rotate 312
  agitation 315
  water 348
  danger 667
whirlwind
  disorder 59
  agitation 315
  wind 349 ·
reap the –
  product 154
  fail 732
ride the –
  resolution 604
  authority 737
whisk rapid 274
  circulation 311
  agitation 315
– off 297
whisker 256
whisket 191
whisky
  vehicle 272
  drink 298
whisper
  faint sound 405
  tell 527
  conceal 528
  stammer 583
stage – 580
– about

disclose 529
publish 531
– in the ear
  voice 580
whist hush 403
  cards 840
whistle wind 349
  hiss 409
  play music 416
  musical instrument 417
clean as a –
  thorough 52
  perfect 650
  neatly 652
pay too dear for one's –
  inexpedient 647
  unskilful 699
  dear 814
police – 669
wet one's –
  drink 298
  tipple 959
– at 930
– for request 765
  desire 865
– jigs to a milestone 645
– for want of thought
  inaction 681
whit small 32
whit-leather 327
Whit-Monday 840
white 430
– of the eye 41
– feather 862
– flag 723
– frost 383
– heat 382
– horses 348
– lie equivocal 520
  concealment 528
  untruth 546
  plea 617
– liver 862
– as a sheet 860
– slave 962
stand in a – sheet 952
mark with a – stone 642, 931
whitechapel
  vehicle 272
Whitefriars 996
whiteness 430
whitewash
  cover 223
  whiten 430
  cleanse 652
  ornament 847
  justify 937
  acquit 970
whitewashed
get – 808
whitewasher 935
white wings 652
whitey-brown 433
whither
  tendency 176
  direction 278
  inquiry 461
whitlow 655
whittle 44, 253
whittled
  drunk 959

Whitsuntide 998
whiz 409
who 461
– goes there? 669
– would have thought? 508, 870
whoa! 265
whole entire 50
  healthy 654
  make – 660
as a – 50
on the – 476, 480
go the – hog 729
the – time 106
– truth
  truth 494
  disclosure 529
  veracity 543
wholesale
  large scale 31
  whole 50
  abundant 639
  trade 794
wholesome 656
wholly 50, 52
whoop 411
war – 715, 722
whop flog 972
whoopee 840
whopper lie 546
whopping huge 192
whore 962
whoredom 961
whoremonger 962
whorl 248
why cause 153
  attribution 155
  inquiry 461
  indeed 535
  motive 615
– not 868
wibble-wabble 314
wick 388, 423
wicked 945
the – bad men 949
  impious 988
the – one 978
wicker 219
wicket 66, 260
wide 202
– apart 15
–awake hat 225
  intelligent 498
– away 196
– berth 748
– of the mark
  distance 196
  deviation 279
  error 495
– of distant 196
– open 194, 260
– of the truth 495
– world 180, 318
in the – world 180
widen 194
– the breach 713, 900
wide-spread
  great 31
  dispersed 73
  space 180
  expanded 194
widow 905
widowhood 905
width 202
wield

brandish 315
  handle 379
  use 677
– authority 737
– the sword 722
wieldy 705
wife 903
wig 225
wigging 932
wiggle 315
wight 373
wigwam 189
wild
  unproductive 169
  violent 173
  plain 344
  inattentive 458
  mad 503
  shy 623
  unskilled 699
  excited 824, 825
  untamed 851
  rash 863
  angry 900
  licentious 954
run – 825
– animals 366
– beast fierce 173
  evil-doer 913
– goose chase
  caprice 608
  useless 645
  unskilful 699
– imagination 515
sow one's – oats
  grow up 131
  improve 658
  amusement 840
  vice 945
  intemperance 954
Wild, Jonathan –
  thief 792
  bad man 949
wilderness
  disorder 59
  unproductive 169
  space 180
  solitude 893
wild-fire 382
spread like –
  violence 173
  influence 175
  expand 194
  publication 531
wile 545, 702
wilful
  voluntary 600
  obstinate 606
will
  volition 600
  resolution 604
  testament 771
  gift 784
at – 600
at one's own sweet – 608
have one's own – 600, 748
make one's – 360
tenant at – 779
– be 152
– for the deed 774, 937
– of Heaven 601
– he nil he 601
– power 600
– and will not 605

– you 765
Will o' the wisp
  luminary 423
  imp 980
willing or unwilling 601
willingness 602
willow 839
willy-nilly 601, 744
wilted 659
wily 702
wimble 262
wimple 225
win 731, 775
– the affections 897
– golden opinions 931
– the heart 829
– laurels 873
– out 33
– over belief 484
  induce 615
  content 831
wince
  bodily pain 378
  emotion 821
  excitement 825
  mental pain 828
  flinch 860
winch 307, 633
wind convolution [see below]
  velocity 274
  blast 349
  life 359
against the – 278, 708
before the – 278, 734
cast to the –s
  repudiate 610
  disuse 678
  not observe 773
  relinquish 782
close to the – 278
fair – 705
to the four –s 180
get – 531
get the – up 860
see how the – blows
  direction 278
  experiment 463
  foresight 510
  fickle 607
in the – 151, 152
lose – 688
sail near the – direction 278
  skill 698
  sharp practice 940
outstrip the – 274
preach to the –s 645
raise the – 775
scatter to the –s 756
see where the – lies 698
short –ed 688
sport of –s and waves 315
sound of – and limb 654
take the – out of one's sails